Getting Started is as EASY as 1, 2, 3 . . . 4!

1. Sign Up

Instructors register with myBusinessCourse.com

2. Setup Your Course

Add your class details and additional materials.

3. Invite Your Stu...

Students register us... your unique course code.

...assignments. It's simple!

Provide Instruction and Practice 24/7

◆ Assign **homework** from your Cambridge Business Publishers textbook and have myBusinessCourse grade it for you automatically.

◆ With our **eLectures**, your students can revisit accounting topics as often as they like or until they master the topic.

◆ **Guided Examples** show students how to solve select problems.

◆ Make homework due before class to ensure students enter your classroom prepared.

◆ Additional practice and **exam preparation** materials are available to help students achieve better grades and content mastery.

STUDENT SELF-STUDY OPTION

Not all instructors choose to incorporate **myBusinessCourse** into their course. In such cases, students can access the Self-Study option for MBC. The Self-Study option provides most of the learning tools available in the Instructor-Led courses, including:

◆ eLectures
◆ Guided Examples
◆ Practice Quizzes

The Self-Study option does not include homework assignments from the textbook. Only the Instructor-Led option includes homework assignments.

Want to learn more about myBusinessCourse?

Contact your sales representative or visit **www.mybusinesscourse.com**.

STUDENTS: Find your access code on the myBusinessCourse insert on the following pages. If you have a used copy of this textbook, you can purchase access online at **www.mybusinesscourse.com**.

Cambridge Business Publishers
Series in Accounting

Computerized Accounting

◆ **QuickBooks Online**, by Williams
◆ **Computerized Accounting with QuickBooks® 2015**, by Williams
◆ **Computerized Accounting with QuickBooks® 2018**, by Williams

Financial Accounting

◆ **Financial Accounting for Undergraduates, 3e** by Wallace, Nelson, Christensen, and Ferris
◆ **Financial Accounting, 5e** by Dyckman, Hanlon, Magee, and Pfeiffer
◆ **Financial Accounting for MBAs, 7e** by Easton, Wild, Halsey, and McAnally
◆ **Financial Accounting for Executives & MBAs, 4e** by Simko, Ferris, and Wallace
◆ **Cases in Financial Reporting, 8e** by Drake, Engel, Hirst, and McAnally

Financial Accounting Using IFRS

◆ **Financial Accounting, 2e** by Wong, Dyckman, Hanlon, Magee, and Pfeiffer

Managerial Accounting

◆ **Managerial Accounting for Undergraduates, 1e** by Christensen, Hobson, and Wallace
◆ **Managerial Accounting, 8e** by Hartgraves & Morse
◆ **Cases in Managerial and Cost Accounting, 1e** by Allen, Brownlee, Haskins, and Lynch

Combined Financial & Managerial Accounting

◆ **Financial & Managerial Accounting for Undergraduates, 1e** by Wallace, Nelson, Christensen, Hobson, and Ferris
◆ **Financial & Managerial Accounting for Decision Makers, 3e** by Dyckman, Hanlon, Magee, Pfeiffer, Hartgraves, and Morse
◆ **Financial & Managerial Accounting for MBAs, 5e** by Easton, Halsey, McAnally, Hartgraves, and Morse

Intermediate Accounting

◆ **Intermediate Accounting, 1e** by Hanlon, Hodder, Nelson, and Roulstone
◆ **Guide to Intermediate Accounting Research, 1e** by Collins
◆ **Cases in Financial Reporting, 8e** by Drake, Engel, Hirst, and McAnally

Cost Accounting

◆ **Cases in Managerial and Cost Accounting, 1e** by Allen, Brownlee, Haskins, and Lynch

Auditing

◆ **Alpine Cupcakes Audit Case** by Dee, Durtschi, and Mindak

Financial Statement Analysis & Valuation

◆ **Financial Statement Analysis & Valuation, 5e** by Easton, McAnally, Sommers, and Zhang
◆ **Corporate Valuation, 2e** by Holthausen & Zmijewski

Advanced Accounting

◆ **Advanced Accounting, 4e** by Hamlen
◆ **Advanced Accounting, 3e** by Halsey & Hopkins

Governmental and Not-For-Profit Accounting

◆ **Accounting for Governmental and Nonprofit Organizations, 1e** by Patton, Patton, and Ives
◆ **Governmental and Not-for-Profit Accounting: An Active Learning Workbook** by Convery

FASB Codification and eIFRS

◆ **Skills for Accounting Research: Text & Cases, 3e** by Collins

my BusinessCourse

FREE WITH NEW COPIES OF THIS TEXTBOOK*

Start using my BusinessCourse **Today**: **www.mybusinesscourse.com**

my BusinessCourse is a web-based learning and assessment program intended to complement your textbook and faculty instruction.

Student Benefits

- **eLectures**: These videos review the key concepts of each Learning Objective in each chapter.
- **Guided examples**: These videos provide step-by-step solutions for select problems in each chapter.
- **Auto-graded assignments**: Provide students with immediate feedback on select assignments. **(with Instructor-Led course ONLY)**.
- **Quiz and Exam preparation**: myBusinessCourse provides students with additional practice and exam preparation materials to help students achieve better grades and content mastery.

You can access my BusinessCourse 24/7 from any web-enabled device, including iPads, smartphones, laptops, and tablets.

Interactive content that runs on any device.

Built for PCs, iPads, Laptops, Tablets, Smartphones

Financial Accounting for MBAs

Seventh Edition

Peter D. Easton

John J. Wild

Robert F. Halsey

Mary Lea McAnally

Cambridge
BUSINESS PUBLISHERS

To my daughters, Joanne and Stacey
—PDE

To my students and my loving family
—JJW

To my wife Ellie and children, Grace and Christian
—RFH

To my husband Brittan and children Loic, Cindy, Maclean, Lacey, Quinn and Kay
—MLM

Editor-in-Chief: George Werthman
Vice President, Brand Management: Marnee Fieldman
Managing Editor: Katie Jones-Aiello
Development Editor: Jocelyn Mousel
Product Developer: Jill Sternard
Digital Marketing Manager: Dana Vinyard
Compositor: T&D Graphics
Designer: Michael Warrell, Design Solutions

Cambridge Business Publishers

FINANCIAL ACCOUNTING FOR MBAs, Seventh Edition, by Peter D. Easton, John J. Wild, Robert F. Halsey, and Mary Lea McAnally.

Student Edition ISBN 978-1-61853-231-2

Bookstores & Faculty: to order this book, call **800-619-6473** or email **customerservice@cambridgepub.com.**

Students: to order this book, please visit the book's website and order directly online.

Printed in the United States of America.
10 9 8 7 6 5 4 3 2

About the Authors

The combined skills and expertise of Easton, Wild, Halsey, and McAnally create the ideal team to author the first new financial accounting textbook for MBAs in more than a generation. Their collective experience in award-winning teaching, consulting, and research in the area of financial accounting and analysis provides a powerful foundation for this innovative textbook.

 **Peter D. Easton** is an expert in accounting and valuation and holds the Notre Dame Alumni Chair in Accountancy in the Mendoza College of Business. Professor Easton's expertise is widely recognized by the academic research community and by the legal community. Professor Easton frequently serves as a consultant on accounting and valuation issues in federal and state courts.

Professor Easton holds undergraduate degrees from the University of Adelaide and the University of South Australia. He holds a graduate degree from the University of New England and a PhD in Business Administration (majoring in accounting and finance) from the University of California, Berkeley.

Professor Easton's research on corporate valuation has been published in the *Journal of Accounting and Economics, Journal of Accounting Research, The Accounting Review, Contemporary Accounting Research, Review of Accounting Studies,* and *Journal of Business Finance and Accounting.* Professor Easton has served as an associate editor for 11 leading accounting journals and he is currently an associate editor for the *Journal of Accounting Research, Journal of Business Finance and Accounting,* and *Journal of Accounting, Auditing, and Finance.* He is an editor of the *Review of Accounting Studies.*

Professor Easton has held appointments at the University of Chicago, the University of California at Berkeley, Ohio State University, Macquarie University, the Australian Graduate School of Management, the University of Melbourne, Tilburg University, National University of Singapore, Seoul National University, and Nyenrode University. He is the recipient of numerous awards for excellence in teaching and in research. Professor Easton regularly teaches accounting analysis and security valuation to MBAs. In addition, Professor Easton has taught managerial accounting at the graduate level.

 **John J. Wild** is a distinguished professor of accounting and business at the University of Wisconsin at Madison. He previously held appointments at Michigan State University and the University of Manchester in England. He received his BBA, MS, and PhD from the University of Wisconsin.

Professor Wild teaches courses in accounting and analysis at both the undergraduate and graduate levels. He has received the Mabel W. Chipman Excellence-in-Teaching Award, the departmental Excellence-in-Teaching Award, and the MBA Teaching Excellence Award (twice) from the EMBA graduation classes at the University of Wisconsin. He also received the Beta Alpha Psi and Salmonson Excellence-in-Teaching Award from Michigan State University. Professor Wild is a past KPMG Peat Marwick National Fellow and is a prior recipient of fellowships from the American Accounting Association and the Ernst & Young Foundation.

Professor Wild is an active member of the American Accounting Association and its sections. He has served on several committees of these organizations, including the Outstanding Accounting Educator Award, Wildman Award, National Program Advisory, Publications, and Research Committees. Professor Wild is author of several best-selling books. His research articles on financial accounting and analysis appear in *The Accounting Review, Journal of Accounting Research, Journal of Accounting and Economics, Contemporary Accounting Research, Journal of Accounting, Auditing & Finance, Journal of Accounting and Public Policy, Journal of Business Finance and Accounting, Auditing: A Journal of Theory and Practice,* and other accounting and business journals. He is past associate editor of *Contemporary Accounting Research* and has served on editorial boards of several respected journals, including *The Accounting Review* and the *Journal of Accounting and Public Policy.*

Robert F. Halsey is Professor of Accounting at Babson College. He received his MBA and PhD from the University of Wisconsin. Prior to obtaining his PhD he worked as the chief financial officer (CFO) of a privately held retailing and manufacturing company and as the vice president and manager of the commercial lending division of a large bank.

Professor Halsey teaches courses in financial and managerial accounting at both the graduate and undergraduate levels, including a popular course in financial statement analysis for second year MBA students. He has also taught numerous executive education courses for large multinational companies through Babson's school of Executive Education as well as for a number of stock brokerage firms in the Boston area. He is regarded as an innovative teacher and has been recognized for outstanding teaching at both the University of Wisconsin and Babson College.

Professor Halsey co-authors *Advanced Accounting* published by Cambridge Business Publishers. Professor Halsey's research interests are in the area of financial reporting, including firm valuation, financial statement analysis, and disclosure issues. He has publications in *Advances in Quantitative Analysis of Finance and Accounting, The Journal of the American Taxation Association, Issues in Accounting Education, The Portable MBA in Finance and Accounting,* the *CPA Journal, AICPA Professor/Practitioner Case Development Program*, and in other accounting and analysis journals.

Professor Halsey is an active member of the American Accounting Association and other accounting, analysis, and business organizations. He is widely recognized as an expert in the areas of financial reporting, financial analysis, and business valuation.

Mary Lea McAnally is the Philip Ljundahl Professor of Accounting at Mays Business School at Texas A&M University. She obtained her Ph.D. from Stanford University and B. Comm. from the University of Alberta. She worked as a Chartered Accountant (in Canada) and is a Certified Internal Auditor. Prior to arriving at Texas A&M in 2002, Professor McAnally held positions at University of Texas at Austin, Canadian National Railways, and Dunwoody and Company.

Professor McAnally teaches financial reporting, analysis, and valuation in the full-time, Professional, and Executive MBA programs. Through the Mays Center for Executive Development, she works with a wide range of corporate clients. She has also taught at the University of Alberta, University of Calgary, IMADEC (in Austria) and at the Indian School of Business at the Hyderabad and Mohali campuses. She has received numerous faculty-determined and student-initiated teaching awards at the MBA and executive levels. Those awards include the Beazley Award, the Trammell Foundation Award, the MBA Teaching Award, the MBA Association Distinguished Faculty Award, the Award for Outstanding and Memorable Faculty Member, and the Distinguished Achievement Award.

Professor McAnally's research interests include accounting and disclosure in regulated environments, executive compensation, and accounting for risk. She has published articles in the leading academic journals including *Journal of Accounting and Economics, Journal of Accounting Research, The Accounting Review, Review of Accounting Studies,* and *Contemporary Accounting Research.* Professor McAnally received the Mays Business School Research Achievement Award in 2005. She was Associate Editor at *Accounting Horizons,* served on the editorial board of *Contemporary Accounting Research,* and was Guest Editor for the MBA-teaching volume of *Issues in Accounting Education.* She is active in the American Accounting Association.

Preface

Welcome to the Seventh Edition of *Financial Accounting for MBAs*. Our main goal in writing this book was to satisfy the needs of today's business manager by providing the most contemporary, relevant, engaging, and user-oriented textbook available. This book is the product of extensive market research including focus groups, market surveys, class tests, manuscript reviews, and interviews with faculty from across the country. We are grateful to students and faculty who used the First through Sixth Editions and whose feedback greatly benefited this Seventh Edition.

Target Audience

Financial Accounting for MBAs is intended for use in full-time, part-time, executive, and working professional MBA programs that include a financial accounting course as part of the curriculum, and one in which managerial decision making and analysis are emphasized. This book easily accommodates mini-courses lasting several days as well as extended courses lasting a full semester.

Innovative Approach

Financial Accounting for MBAs is managerially oriented and focuses on the most salient aspects of accounting. It helps MBA students learn how to read, analyze, and interpret financial accounting data to make informed business decisions. This textbook makes financial accounting **engaging, relevant,** and **contemporary.** To that end, it consistently incorporates **real company data,** both in the body of each module and throughout assignment material.

> *"If you are looking for a book that students will actually read and learn from, look no further."*
> **Andreas Simon**
> Pepperdine University

Flexible Structure

The MBA curricula, instructor preferences, and course lengths vary across colleges. Accordingly and to the extent possible, the 13 modules that make up *Financial Accounting for MBAs* were designed independently of one another. This modular presentation enables each college and instructor to "customize" the book to best fit the needs of their students. Our introduction and discussion of financial statements constitute Modules 1, 2, and 3. Module 4 presents the analysis of financial statements with an emphasis on analysis of operating profitability. Modules 5 through 10 highlight major financial accounting topics including assets, liabilities, equity, and off-balance-sheet financing. Module 11 details the process for preparing and analyzing the statement of cash flow. Module 12 explains forecasting financial statements and Module 13 introduces simple valuation models. At the end of each module, we present an ongoing analysis project that can be used as a guide for an independent project. Like the rest of the book, the project is independent across the various modules. At the end of the book, we include several useful resources. Appendix A contains compound interest tables and formulas. Appendix B is a chart of accounts used in the book. Appendix C is an illustrative case that applies the techniques described in Modules 1 through 13 to an actual company, Harley-Davidson. Appendix C can be used as a guide, in conjunction with the module-end project questions, by students required to prepare a company analysis.

Transaction Analysis and Statement Preparation

Instructors differ in their coverage of accounting mechanics. Some focus on the effects of transactions on financial statements using the balance sheet equation format. Others include coverage of journal entries and T-accounts. We accommodate both teaching styles in this Seventh Edition. Specifically, Module 2 provides an expanded discussion of the effects of transactions using our innovative financial statement effects template. Emphasis is on the analysis of Apple's summary transactions, which concludes with the preparation of its financial statements. Module 3, which is entirely optional, allows an instructor to drill down and focus on accounting mechanics: journal entries and T-accounts. It illustrates accounting for numerous transactions, including those involving accounting adjustments. It concludes with the preparation of the financial statements. This detailed transaction analysis uses the same financial statement effects template, with journal entries and T-accounts highlighted in the margin. These two modules accommodate the spectrum of teaching styles—instructors can elect to use either or both modules to suit their preferences, and their students are not deprived of any information as a result of that selection.

> *"The text does a balanced job of presenting real financial reporting situations without going too far into the debit/credit weeds."*
> **Joshua Neil**
> University of Colorado—Boulder

Flexibility for Courses of Varying Lengths

Many instructors have approached us to ask about suggested class structures based on courses of varying length. To that end, we provide the following table of possible course designs.

	15 Week Semester-Course	10 Week Quarter-Course	6 Week, Mini-Course	1 Week Intensive-Course
Module 1: Financial Accounting for MBAs	Week 1	Week 1	Week 1	Day 1 (Module 1 and either Module 2 or Module 3)
Module 2: Introducing Financial Statements	Week 2	Week 2	Week 2	
Module 3: Transactions, Adjustments, and Financial Statements	Week 2 (optional)	Week 2 (optional)	Week 2 (optional)	
Module 4: Analyzing and Interpreting Financial Statements	Weeks 3 and 4	Week 3	Week 3	Day 2
Module 5: Revenues, Receivables, and Operating Expenses	Week 5	Week 4	Skim	Skim
Module 6: Inventories, Accounts Payable, and Long-Term Assets	Week 6	Week 5	Week 4	Day 3
Module 7: Current and Long-Term Liabilities	Week 7	Week 6	Week 5	Day 4
Module 8: Stock Transactions, Dividends, and EPS	Week 8	Week 7	Week 6	Day 5
Module 9: Intercorporate Investments	Week 9	Optional	Optional	Optional
Module 10: Leases, Pensions, and Income Taxes	Weeks 10 and 11	Week 8	Optional	Optional
Module 11: Cash Flows	Week 12	Week 9 (or Optional)	Optional	Optional
Module 12: Financial Statement Forecasting	Week 13	Week 10	Optional	Optional
Module 13: Using Financial Statements for Valuation	Week 14			

Managerial Emphasis

Tomorrow's MBA graduates must be skilled in using financial statements to make business decisions. These skills often require application of ratio analyses, benchmarking, forecasting, valuation, and other aspects of financial statement analysis for decision making. Further, tomorrow's MBA graduates must have the skills to go beyond basic financial statements and to interpret and apply nonfinancial statement disclosures, such as footnotes and supplementary reports. This book, therefore, emphasizes real company data, including detailed footnote and other management disclosures, and shows how to use this information to make managerial inferences and decisions. This approach makes financial accounting interesting and relevant for all MBA students.

As MBA instructors, we recognize that the core MBA financial accounting course is not directed toward accounting majors. *Financial Accounting for MBAs* embraces this reality. This book highlights **financial reporting, analysis, interpretation,** and **decision making.** We incorporate the following **financial statement effects template** to train MBA students in understanding the economic ramifications of transactions and their impact on all key financial statements. This analytical tool is a great resource for MBA students in learning accounting and applying it to their future courses and careers. Each transaction is identified in the "Transaction" column. Then, the dollar amounts (positive or negative) of the financial statement effects are recorded in the appropriate balance sheet or income statement columns. The template also reflects the statement of cash flow effects (via the cash column) and the statement of stockholders' equity effects (via the contributed capital and earned capital columns). The earned capital account is immediately updated to reflect any income or loss arising from each transaction (denoted by the arrow line from net income to earned capital). This template is instructive as it reveals the financial impacts of transactions, and it provides insights into the effects of accounting choices.

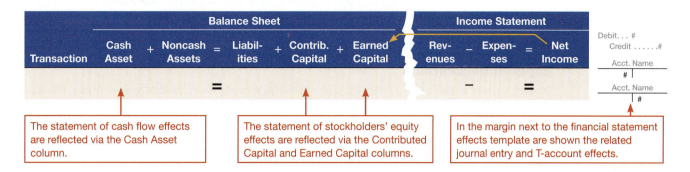

The statement of cash flow effects are reflected via the Cash Asset column.

The statement of stockholders' equity effects are reflected via the Contributed Capital and Earned Capital columns.

In the margin next to the financial statement effects template are shown the related journal entry and T-account effects.

Innovative Pedagogy

Financial Accounting for MBAs includes special features specifically designed for the MBA student.

Focus Companies for Each Module

Each module's content is explained through the accounting and reporting activities of real companies. Each module incorporates a "focus company" for special emphasis and demonstration. The enhanced instructional value of focus companies comes from the way they engage MBA students in real analysis and interpretation. Focus companies were selected based on the industries that MBA students typically enter upon graduation.

MODULE 1	Under Armour	**MODULE 8**	Johnson & Johnson
MODULE 2	Apple	**MODULE 9**	Google
MODULE 3	Apple	**MODULE 10**	Southwest Airlines, FedEx
MODULE 4	Intel	**MODULE 11**	Starbucks
MODULE 5	Pfizer	**MODULE 12**	Procter & Gamble
MODULE 6	Home Depot	**MODULE 13**	Procter & Gamble
MODULE 7	Verizon	**APPENDIX C**	Harley-Davidson

Real Company Data Throughout

Market research and reviewer feedback tell us that one of instructors' greatest frustrations with other MBA textbooks is their lack of real company data. We have gone to great lengths to incorporate real company data throughout each module to reinforce important concepts and engage MBA students. We engage nonaccounting MBA students specializing in finance, taxation, marketing, management, real estate, operations, and so forth, with companies and scenarios that are relevant to them. For representative examples, **SEE PAGES 2-24, 4-23, 5-3, 5-19, 6-23, 7-16, 8-5, 9-20, 10-6, 11-25, and 12-17.**

Footnotes and Other Management Disclosures

Analyzed on their own, financial statements reveal only part of a corporation's economic story. Information essential for a complete analysis of a company's performance and financial position must be gleaned from the footnotes and other disclosures provided by the company. Consequently, we incorporate footnotes and other disclosures generously throughout the text and assignments. For representative examples, **SEE PAGES 7-6, 8-15, 9-7, 9-33, and 10-5.**

Industry-Level Data

We repeatedly emphasize that financial analysis cannot be performed in a vacuum—appropriate benchmarks are critical to a complete understanding of a company's financial performance and position. To this point, we provide graphics that capture industry-level data including many of the ratios we discuss and compute in the modules. For representative examples, **SEE PAGES 4-28, 4-38, 5-23, 6-26, and 7-25.**

Decision Making Orientation

One primary goal of a MBA financial accounting course is to teach students the skills needed to apply their accounting knowledge to solving real business problems and making informed business decisions. With that goal in mind, Managerial Decision boxes in each module encourage students to apply the material presented to solving actual business scenarios. For representative examples, **SEE PAGES 2-14, 4-28, 7-25, 8-11, 9-14, and 10-6.**

Reviews for Each Learning Objective

Financial accounting can be challenging—especially for MBA students lacking business experience or previous exposure to business courses. To reinforce concepts presented in each module and to ensure student comprehension, we include reviews that require students to recall and apply the financial accounting techniques and concepts described in each section. Review questions usually include real financial statement data from a company in the same industry as the module's focus company. For representative examples, **SEE PAGES 4-14, 7-7, 8-12, 9-9, and 10-23.**

Experiential Learning

Students retain information longer if they can apply the lessons learned from the module content. To meet this need for experiential learning, we conclude each module with a hands-on analysis project. A series of questions guides students' inquiry and helps students synthesize the material in the module and integrate material across modules. For representative examples, **SEE PAGES 1-45, 4-63, and 9-53.**

Excellent, Class-Tested Assignment Materials

Excellent assignment material is a must-have component of any successful textbook (and class). We went to great lengths to create the best assignments possible from contemporary financial statements. In keeping with the rest of the book, we used real company data extensively. We also ensured that assignments reflect our belief that MBA students should be trained in analyzing accounting information to make business decisions, as opposed to working on mechanical bookkeeping tasks. There are six categories of assignments: **Questions**, **Mini Exercises**, **Exercises**, **Problems**, **IFRS Applications**, and **Management Applications**. For representative examples, **SEE PAGES 4-43, 5-36, 7-41, 7-45, and 9-52.**

Seventh Edition Changes

Based on classroom use and reviewer feedback, a number of substantive changes have been made in the seventh edition to further enhance the MBA students' experiences.

- Table of Contents is reorganized to facilitate eLearning, with additional in-chapter Reviews and Guided Example videos for all chapters (each Learning Objective has a Review/Guided Example, as well as a corresponding eLecture). Content is also revised to be more streamlined and pointed.

- **New regulations:** This edition covers new standards on Revenue Recognition, Leases, Discontinued Operations, and Marketable Securities.

- **DuPont Model:**
  - Module 4 opens with DuPont Analysis (moved from an appendix) as a simple, yet powerful, analysis framework. For those instructors interested, a disaggregation of ROE that separates operating and nonoperating items is shown later in the module as a natural extension of DuPont analysis.
  - Analysis of financial performance in later modules relies on the DuPont model. However, text boxes include deeper discussion of analyses that gleaned from the operating / nonoperating distinction.

- **Cash flows:** Measures of cash flow are incorporated into the body of the book as new Module 11 (formerly Appendix B). Cash flow computations are simplified, and there is detailed explanation of how to use and analyze cash flow statements, including cash-based ratios and life cycle notions.

- **IFRS:** Global Accounting sections are updated to include new developments.

- **Revenue, Operating Expenses, and Receivables:** Module 5 is reorganized and streamlined to reduce its length and focus its discussion on revenue, operating expenses, and receivables.

- **Receivables and Payables:** Module 5 now includes accounts receivable which are naturally paired with revenues. Accounts payable is moved to Module 6 and presented with inventories. A new section on days to collect receivables, days sales in inventory, days to pay accounts payable, and the cash conversion cycle is added.

- **R&D Costs:** Module 6 now includes R&D facilities along with restructuring as they are part of operations.

- Module 8 includes a complete rewrite of **share-based compensation** with an initial overview of accounting for such compensation that simplifies this complex topic. There is a greater emphasis on restricted stock-type plans that are now more prevalent.

- **Equity Carve-Outs:** Moved to Module 9 because carve-outs can be viewed as a divestiture of a subsidiary investment, and set as a new appendix (to reflect their reduced occurrence).

- **Revised forecasting module:** Module 12 is shortened and rewritten for clarity. It begins with a concrete example of forecasting mechanics (as the opening section for those wishing to cover just the mechanics). Module 12 uses a new **Procter & Gamble** analyst report from **Morgan Stanley** and set as an appendix.

- **Updated financial data and assignments:** Data and financial statements are updated throughout the book to reflect each company's latest available financial statement filings and disclosures.

- **Bond rating:** Explanation of the determination of bond ratings is enhanced with inclusion of Moody's ratings for Verizon.

- **Expanded analysis of allowances accounts:** Added section in Module 6 on accounting for sales allowances, including accounting and analysis of Schedule II allowance disclosures (including effects on sales and adequacy of the allowance account).

- **Pension accounting:** Revised discussion of pension accounting, including a new section on fair valuation of pension obligations, the treatment of pension plans in bankruptcy, and an analysis of pension plans disclosures such as what is operating versus nonoperating (Module 10).

- **Updated Comprehensive Case:** Appendix C (available on the book's website) shows a case analysis using Harley-Davidson financial statements and notes.

- **Foreign currency:** New section on foreign currency effects for revenues, profit, and cash flow.

- **Mechanics:** Transaction analysis revised, streamlined, and covered entirely in Module 3.

- **Derivatives:** Revised derivatives discussion for simpler exposition with new illustrative examples. Added new section on analysis of derivatives to provide MBAs with a tangible take-away.

Fundamentals of Financial Accounting Tutorial

This interactive tutorial is intended for use in programs that either require or would like to offer a pre-term tutorial that creates a baseline of accounting knowledge for students with little to no prior exposure to financial accounting. Initially developed as a pre-term tutorial for first year MBA students, this product can be used as a warm-up for any introductory level financial accounting course. It is designed as an asynchronous, interactive, self-paced experience for students.

Available Learning Modules (You Select)

1. Introducing Financial Accounting (approximate completion time 2 hours)
2. Constructing Financial Statements (approximate completion time 4 hours)
3. Adjusting Entries and Completing the Accounting Cycle (approximate completion time 4 hours)
4. Reporting and Analyzing Cash Flows (approximate completion time 3.5 hours)
5. Analyzing and Interpreting Financial Statements (approximate completion time 3.5 hours)

This is a separate, saleable item. Contact your sales representative to receive more information or email customerservice@cambridgepub.com.

Companion Casebook

Cases in Financial Reporting, 8th edition by Michael Drake (Brigham Young University), Ellen Engel (University of Illinois—Chicago), D. Eric Hirst (University of Texas – Austin), and Mary Lea McAnally (Texas A&M University). This book comprises 27 cases and is a perfect companion book for faculty interested in exposing students to a wide range of real financial statements. The cases are current and cover companies from Japan, Sweden, Austria, the Netherlands, the UK, India, as well as from the U.S. Many of the U.S. companies are major multinationals. Each case deals with a specific financial accounting topic within the context of one (or more) company's financial statements. Each case contains financial statement information and a set of directed questions pertaining to one or two specific financial accounting issues. This is a separate, saleable casebook (**ISBN 978-1-61853-122-3**). Contact your sales representative to receive a desk copy or email customerservice@cambridgepub.com.

Supplement Package

For Instructors

myBusinessCourse: A web-based learning and assessment program intended to complement your textbook and classroom instruction. This easy-to-use course management system grades homework automatically and provides students with with additional help when you are not available. In addition, detailed diagnostic tools assess class and individual performance. myBusinessCourse is ideal for online courses or traditional face-to-face courses for which you want to offer students more resources to succeed. Assignments with the in the margin are available in myBusinessCourse. eLecture videos are available for the chapter Learning Objectives, and Guided Examples for the in-chapter Reviews are available for you to assign students.

Solutions Manual: Created by the authors, the *Solutions Manual* contains complete solutions to all assignments.

PowerPoint: Created by the authors, the PowerPoint slides outline key elements of each module.

Test Bank: Written by the authors, the test bank includes multiple-choice items, matching questions, short essay questions, and problems.

Computerized Test Bank: This computerized version of the test bank enables you to add and edit questions; create up to 99 versions of each test; attach graphic files to questions; import and export ASCII files; and select questions based on type or learning objective. It provides password protection for saved tests and question databases and is able to run on a network.

Website: All instructor materials are accessible via the book's website (password protected) along with other useful links and information. **www.cambridgepub.com**

For Students

eLectures: Each chapter's Learning Objective includes an eLecture video available in our online learning management system, myBusinessCourse (see below for more information).

Guided Examples: Guided Example videos are available for each in-chapter Review, also in myBusinessCourse (see below for more information).

myBusinessCourse is a web-based learning and assessment program intended to complement your textbook and faculty instruction. This easy-to-use program provides you with additional help when your instructor is not available. Guided Example videos are available for all in-chapter Reviews, and eLecture videos are available for each Learning Objective. With Instructor-Led MBC courses, assignments with the in the margin are also available and are automatically graded. Access is free with new copies of this textbook (look for page containing the access code towards the front of the book). If you buy a used copy of the book, you can purchase access at **www.mybusinesscourse.com**.

Student Solutions Manual: Created by the authors, the student solutions manual contains all solutions to the even-numbered assignment materials in the textbook. This is a **restricted** item that is only available to students after their instructor has authorized its purchase. ISBN 978-1-61853-247-3

Website: Useful links are available to students free of charge on the book's website.

Acknowledgments

All seven editions of this book benefited greatly from the valuable feedback of focus group attendees, reviewers, students, and colleagues. We are extremely grateful to them for their help in making this project a success.

Beverley Alleyne, *Belmont University*
Ashiq Ali, *University of Texas—Dallas*
Dan Amiram, *Columbia University*
Walter Austin, *Mercer University*
Steve Baginski, *University of Georgia*
Eli Bartov, *New York University*
Dan Bens, *INSEAD*
Denny Beresford, *University of Georgia*
Richard Bernstein, *The University of Toledo*
James Biagi, *Marywood University*
Mark Bradshaw, *Boston College*
Dennis Bline, *Bryant University*
James Boatsman, *Arizona State University*
John Briginshaw, *Pepperdine University*
Thomas Buchman, *University of Colorado—Boulder*
Edgar Carter, *University of Massachusetts—Lowell*
Mary Ellen Carter, *Boston College*
Judson Caskey, *University of Texas— Austin*
Sandra Cereola, *James Madison University*
Sumantra Chakravarty, *California State University—Fullerton*
Betty Chavis, *California State University—Fullerton*
Agnes Cheng, *Louisiana State University*
Joseph Comprix, *Syracuse University*
Ellen Cook, *University of Louisiana—Lafayette*
Michael Coyne, *Fairfield University*
Araya Debessay, *University of Delaware*

Roger Debreceny, *University of Hawaii—Manoa*
Carol Dee, *University of Colorado—Denver*
Rosemond Desir, *Colorado State University*
Vicki Dickinson, *University of Mississippi*
Jeffrey Doyle, *University of Utah*
Donald Drake, *Georgia State University*
Phil Drake, *Arizona State University*
Joanne Duke, *San Francisco State University*
Cindy Durtschi, *DePaul University*
Thomas Dyckman, *Cornell University*
James Edwards, *University of South Carolina*
John Eichenseher, *University of Wisconsin*
Craig Emby, *Simon Fraser University*
Gerard Engeholm, *Pace University*
Kathryn Epps, *Kennesaw State University*
Bud Fennema, *Florida State University*
Mark Finn, *Northwestern University*
Carol Fischer, *St. Bonaventure University*
Tim Fogarty, *Case Western Reserve University*
Nate Franke, *University of California—Irvine*
Richard Frankel, *Washington University*
Waqar Ghani, *Saint Joseph's University*
Dan Givoly, *Pennsylvania State University*
Andy Garcia, *Bowling Green State University*
Maclean Gaulin, *Rice University*
Julia Grant, *Case Western Reserve University*

Kris Gulick, *University of Iowa*
Karl Hackenbrack, *Vanderbilt University*
Michelle Hanlon, *MIT*
Bob Hartman, *University of Iowa*
David Harvey, *University of Georgia*
Carla Hayn, *University of California— Los Angeles*
Frank Heflin, *Florida State University*
Michele Henney, *University of Oregon*
Elaine Henry, *University of Miami*
Clayton Hock, *Miami University*
Judith Hora, *University of San Diego*
Herbert Hunt, *California State University—Long Beach*
Richard Hurley, *University of Connecticut*
Ross Jennings, *University of Texas—Austin*
Greg Jonas, *Case Western Reserve University*
Sanjay Kallapur, *Indian School of Business*
Greg Kane, *University of Delaware*
Victoria Kaskey, *Ashland University*
Zafar Khan, *Eastern Michigan University*
Saleha Khumawala, *University of Houston*
Marinilka Kimbro, *University of Washington—Tacoma*
Ron King, *Washington University*
Michael Kirschenheiter, *University of Illinois—Chicago*
Phillip J. Korb, *University of Baltimore*
Susan Kulp, *George Washington University*
Krishna Kumar, *George Washington University*
Lisa Kutcher, *University of Oregon*
Brian Leventhal, *University of Illinois—Chicago*
Pierre Liang, *Carnegie Mellon University*
Joshua Livnat, *New York University*
Frank Longo, *Centenary University*
Barbara Lougee, *University of San Diego*
Yvonne Lu, *Lehigh University*
Luann Lynch, *University of Virginia—Darden*
Jason MacGregor, *Baylor University*
Lois Mahoney, *Eastern Michigan University*
Michael Maier, *University of Alberta*
Ron Mano, *Westminster College*
Ronald Marcusson, *DePaul University*
Ariel Markelevich, *Suffolk University*
Jason Matthews, *University of Georgia*
Brian McAllister, *University of Colorado at Colorado Springs*
Bruce McClain, *Cleveland State University*
Karen McDougal, *St. Joseph's University*
James McKinney, *University of Maryland*
Gregory Merrill, *Saint Mary's University*
Greg Miller, *University of Michigan*
Jose Miranda-Lopez, *California State University—Fullerton*
Melanie Mogg, *University of Minnesota*
Steve Monahan, *INSEAD*
John Morris, *Kansas State University*
Philip Morris, *Sam Houston State University*
Dennis Murray, *University of Colorado—Denver*
Sandeep Nabar, *Oklahoma State University*
Suresh Nallareddy, *Columbia University*
Ramesh Narasimhan, *Montclair State University*
Siva Nathan, *Georgia State University*
Joshua Neil, *Colorado University Boulder*
Doron Nissim, *Columbia University*
Gary Olsen, *Carroll University*
Shail Pandit, *University of Illinois—Chicago*
Susan Parker, *Santa Clara University*
William Pasewark, *Texas Tech*
Stephen Penman, *Columbia University*
Mark Penno, *University of Iowa*

Gary Peters, *University of Arkansas*
Kathy Petroni, *Michigan State University*
Christine Petrovits, *New York University*
Kirk Philipich, *University of Michigan—Dearborn*
Morton Pincus, *University of California—Irvine*
Lincoln Pinto, *Concordia University*
Kay Poston, *University of Indianapolis*
Grace Pownall, *Emory University*
David Randolph, *Xavier University*
Laura Rickett, *Kent State University*
Susan Riffe, *Southern Methodist University*
Bruce Samuelson, *Pepperdine University*
Diane Satin, *California State University—East Bay*
Shahrokh Saudagaran, *University of Washington—Tacoma*
Andrew Schmidt, *Columbia University*
Chandra Seethamraju, *Washington University*
Stephen Sefcik, *University of Washington*
Galen Sevcik, *Georgia State University*
Lewis Shaw, *Suffolk University*
Kenneth Shaw, *University of Missouri*
Todd Shawver, *Bloomsburg University*
Evan Shough, *University of North Carolina—Greensboro*
Robin Shuler, *Seattle Pacific University*
Paul Simko, *University of Virginia—Darden*
Andreas Simon, *Pepperdine University*
Kevin Smith, *University of Kansas*
Pam Smith, *Northern Illinois University*
Rod Smith, *California State University—Long Beach*
Hakjoon Song, *The University of Akron*
Xiaofei Song, *Saint Mary's University*
Sri Sridharan, *Northwestern University*
Charles Stanley, *Baylor University*
Jens Stephan, *Eastern Michigan University*
Phillip Stocken, *Dartmouth College*
Jerry Strawser, *Texas A&M University*
Sherre Strickland, *University of Massachusetts—Lowell*
Chandra Subramaniam, *University of Texas—Austin*
K.R. Subramanyam, *University of Southern California*
Ziad Syed, *Texas A&M University*
Gary Taylor, *University of Alabama*
Mark Taylor, *Case Western Reserve University*
Suzanne Traylor, *State University of New York Albany*
Sam Tiras, *Louisiana State University*
Brett Trueman, *University of California—Los Angeles*
Jerry Van Os, *Westminster College*
Mark Vargus, *University of Texas—Dallas*
Lisa Victoravich, *University of Denver*
Robert Vigeland, *Texas Christian University*
Marcia Vorholt, *Xavier University*
James Wallace, *Claremont Graduate School*
Charles Wasley, *University of Rochester*
Greg Waymire, *Emory University*
Andrea Weickgenannt, *Xavier University*
Daniel Weimer, *Wayne State University*
Edward Werner, *Drexel University*
Lourdes White, *University of Baltimore*
Jonathan M. Wild, *Oklahoma State University*
Jeffrey Williams, *University of Michigan*
Peter Wilson, *Babson College*
David Wright, *University of Michigan*
Michelle Yetman, *University of California—Davis*
Tzachi Zack, *Ohio State University*
Xiao-Jun Zhang, *University of California—Berkeley*
Yuan Zhang, *Columbia University*
Yuping Zhao, *University of Houston*

In addition, we are extremely grateful to George Werthman, Lorraine Gleeson, Jill Fischer, Marnee Fieldman, Katie Jones-Aiello, Jocelyn Mousel, Beth Nodus, Dana Vinyard, Debbie McQuade, Terry McQuade, Michael Warrell (Design Solutions), and the entire team at Cambridge Business Publishers for their encouragement, enthusiasm, and guidance. Their market research, editorial development, and promotional efforts have made this book the best-selling MBA text in the market.

Peter   *John*   *Bob*   *Mary Lea*

February 2017

Brief Contents

Contents

Module 1

Financial Accounting for MBAs

Learning Objectives *identify the key learning goals of the module.*

Learning Objectives

LO1 Explain and assess the four main business activities. (p.1-3)

LO2 Identify and discuss the users and suppliers of financial statement information. (p. 1-5)

LO3 Describe and examine the four financial statements, and define the accounting equation. (p. 1-10)

LO4 Explain and apply basic profitability analysis. (p. 1-19)

LO5 Assess business operations within the context of a competitive environment. (p. 1-22)

LO6 Access reports filed with the SEC (Appendix 1A). (p. 1-27)

LO7 Describe the accounting principles and regulations that frame financial statements (Appendix 1B). (p. 1-29)

*A **Focus Company** introduces each module and illustrates the relevance of financial accounting in everyday business.*

UA

Market cap: $16,490 mil
Total assets: $2,869 mil
Revenues: $3,963 mil
Net income: $232 mil

Under Armour Inc. develops, markets, and distributes its branded performance apparel, footwear, and accessories for men, women, and youth. A distinctive element of its marketing and promotion strategy is the direct sales to high-performing athletes and teams at all levels. As a result, Under Armour products have enormous visibility on the Internet and television as well as in magazines and at live sporting events. This exposure helps establish "on-field authenticity" for the brand as consumers see Under Armour products worn by athletes in a wide range of sports.

Over the past three years, Under Armour's revenues have increased by 70% and its profits by 43%. It reported nearly $3 billion in assets, and it financed 58% of its assets with stockholder investment and the other 42% with borrowed money—a conservative financing strategy. Under Armour has used the cash it generates to ramp up inventories; invest in property, plant, and equipment; and acquire other companies that are central to its strategy.

The financial information Under Armour reports is critical to a diverse set of users, including the company's own management team, stockholders, lenders, suppliers, government regulators, and others. Understanding the information contained in these financial statements is central to effective decision-making by these parties.

This module introduces the financial statements that companies such as Under Armour disclose. It also presents basic tools to analyze financial information. We begin with an overview of the information environment companies face, and we discuss the demand for and supply of financial information. We then review financial statements and explain what information they convey. Profitability is described and is used as a focus of much of our application of accounting information. We conclude the module with an introduction to business analysis, which is an important part of drawing inferences from financial statements. The appendix discusses the regulatory environment that defines current financial reporting for companies. [Source: *Under Armour*, 2015 10-K report.]

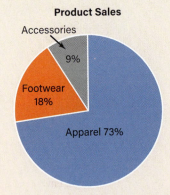

Product Sales

Accessories 9%
Footwear 18%
Apparel 73%

© iStock

Road Map

Road Maps *visually organize the topics, eLecture videos, Guided Example videos, and assignments by Learning Objective.*

LO	Learning Objective | Topics	Page	eLecture	Guided Example	Assignments
1–1	**Explain and assess the four main business activities.** Planning :: Operating :: Investing :: Financing	1-3	e1–1	Review 1-1	1, 21, 59
1–2	**Identify and discuss the users and suppliers of financial statement information.** Information Demand :: Information Supply :: Global Setting	1-5	e1–2	Review 1-2	8, 9, 13, 17,18, 22, 35, 39, 61
1–3	**Describe and examine the four financial statements, and define the accounting equation.** Balance Sheet :: Income Statement :: Statement of Stockholders' Equity :: Statement of Cash Flows	1-10	e1–3	Review 1-3	2, 3, 4, 5, 6, 7, 23, 24, 25, 26, 27, 28, 33, 34, 36, 42, 43, 44, 45, 46, 56, 59, 60
1–4	**Explain and apply basic profitability analysis.** Return on Assets :: Return on Equity :: Relevance of Financial Statements	1-19	e1–4	Review 1-4	19, 20, 31, 37, 38, 40, 41, 42, 43, 44, 47, 48, 49, 50, 51, 55, 57, 58, 60
1–5	**Assess business operations within the context of a competitive environment.** Competitive Environment :: Business Environment :: Competitive Advantage	1-22	e1–5	Review 1-5	10, 11, 30
1–6	**Access reports filed with the SEC (Appendix 1A).** www.SEC.gov :: 10-K :: Interactive Data :: Excel Usage	1-27	e1–6		12, 26, 27, 31
1–7	**Describe the accounting principles and regulations that frame financial statements (Appendix 1B).** Accounting Environment :: Auditing :: Regulatory and Legal	1-29	e1–7		14, 15, 16, 29, 32, 52, 53, 54, 62, 63

Financial Accounting for MBAs

Information Environment	Financial Statements	Profitability Analysis	Broader Business Environment	Regulatory and Legal Environment
■ Reporting on Business Activities ■ Demand for Information ■ Supply of Information	■ Balance Sheet ■ Income Statement ■ Statement of Stockholders' Equity ■ Statement of Cash Flows	■ Measuring Return on Assets ■ Disaggregating Return on Assets ■ Relevance of Accounting	■ Competitive Analysis ■ Business Analysis ■ Analyzing Competitive Advantage	■ Financial Accounting Environment ■ Audits and Governance ■ SEC and the Courts

Reporting on Business Activities

eLectures LO1

MBC Explain and assess the four main business activities.

eLecture icons identify topics for which there are instructional videos in myBusinessCourse (MBC). See the Preface for more information on MBC.

Financial accounting information serves many purposes. To understand this, imagine that we are a specific user of accounting information. For example, imagine we are a:

■ Stock investor—how might we use accounting information to identify a stock to buy?

■ Bond trader—how might we use accounting information to assess a company's ability to repay its debt?

■ Manager—how might we use accounting information to decide whether to acquire another company or divest a current division?

■ Equity and/or credit analyst—how might we use accounting information to prepare an investment appraisal or credit report?

This book explains the concepts, preparation, and application of financial accounting information and, importantly, how decision makers use such information.

■ Managers use financial accounting information for planning purposes and to make operating, investing, and financing decisions.

■ Investors and analysts use financial accounting information to help decide whether to buy or sell stock.

■ Lenders and rating agencies use accounting information to help decide a company's creditworthiness and lending terms.

■ Regulators use accounting information to enact social and economic policies and to monitor compliance with laws.

■ Legal institutions use accounting information to assess fines and reparations in litigation.

■ Other decision makers rely on accounting information for purposes ranging from determining demands in labor union negotiations to levying damages for environmental abuses.

Business Activities To effectively analyze and use accounting information, we must consider the business context in which the information is created—see Exhibit 1.1. All companies engage in four types of activities: they *plan* business activities, *finance* those activities, *invest* in those activities, and then engage in *operating* activities. Companies conduct all these activities while confronting *business forces*, including market constraints and competitive pressures. Prior financial statements provide crucial input for strategic planning. Current financial statements provide information about the relative success of those plans, which can be used to take corrective action or make new operating, investing, and financing decisions.

Exhibit 1.1 depicts the four business activities for a typical company. The outer (purplish) ring is the planning process that reflects the overarching goals and objectives of the company within which strategic decisions are made. Those strategic decisions involve company financing, asset investment and management, and daily operations. **Under Armour**, the focus company for this module, provides the following description of its business strategy in its annual report.

> Our principal business activities are the development, marketing and distribution of branded performance apparel, footwear and accessories for men, women and youth...Our Connected Fitness strategy is focused on connecting with our consumers and increasing awareness and sales of our existing product offerings through our global wholesale and direct to consumer channels. We plan to engage and grow this community by developing innovative applications, services and other digital solutions to impact how athletes and fitness-minded individuals train, perform and live. Our marketing and promotion strategy begins with providing and selling our products to high-performing athletes and teams on the high school, collegiate and professional levels. We execute this strategy through outfitting agreements, professional and collegiate sponsorships, individual athlete agreements and by providing and selling our products directly to team equipment managers and to individual athletes.

Exhibit 1.1 ■ Business Activities

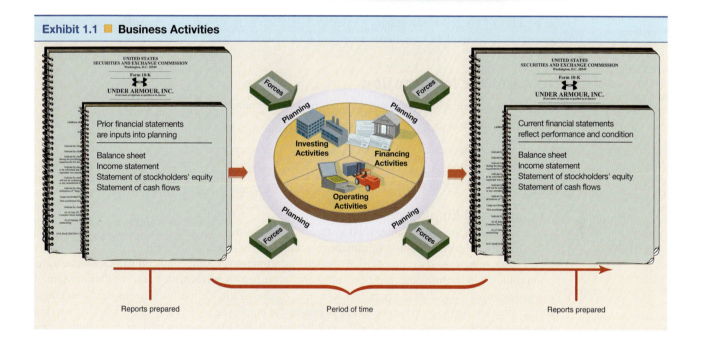

Business Strategy A company's *strategic* (or *business*) *plan* reflects how it plans to achieve its goals and objectives. A plan's success depends on an effective analysis of market demand and supply. Specifically, a company must assess demand for its products and services and assess the supply of its inputs (both labor and capital). The plan must also include competitive analyses, opportunity assessments, and consideration of business threats. We discuss competitive forces later in the module.

Historical financial statements provide insight into the success of a company's strategic plan and are an important input to the planning process. These statements highlight portions of the strategic plan that proved profitable and, thus, warrant additional capital investment. They also reveal areas that are less effective and provide information to help managers develop remedial action.

Once strategic adjustments are planned and implemented, the current period financial statements provide input into the planning process for the next year, and this process begins again. Understanding a company's strategic plan helps focus our analysis of financial statements by placing them in proper context.

Review 1-1 LO1

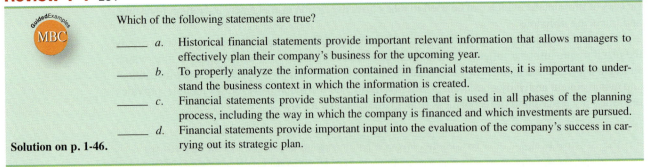

Which of the following statements are true?

_____   *a.*   Historical financial statements provide important relevant information that allows managers to effectively plan their company's business for the upcoming year.

_____   *b.*   To properly analyze the information contained in financial statements, it is important to understand the business context in which the information is created.

_____   *c.*   Financial statements provide substantial information that is used in all phases of the planning process, including the way in which the company is financed and which investments are pursued.

_____   *d.*   Financial statements provide important input into the evaluation of the company's success in carrying out its strategic plan.

Solution on p. 1-46.

Financial Statements: Demand and Supply

LO2 Identify and discuss the users and suppliers of financial statement information.

Learning Objectives are highlighted at the start of the section covering that topic.

Demand for financial statements has existed for centuries as a means to facilitate efficient contracting and risk-sharing. Decision makers and other stakeholders demand information on a company's past and prospective returns and risks. Supply of financial statements is driven by companies' wish to lower financing costs and other costs such as political, contracting, and labor. Managers decide how much financial information to supply by weighing the costs of disclosure against the benefits of disclosure. Regulatory agencies intervene in this process with various disclosure requirements that establish a minimum supply of information.

Demand for Information

The following broad classes of users demand financial accounting information.

- Managers and employees
- Investment analysts and information intermediaries
- Creditors and suppliers
- Stockholders and directors
- Customers and strategic partners
- Regulators and tax agencies
- Voters and their representatives

Managers and Employees

Managers and employees are interested in the company's current and future financial health. This leads to a demand for accounting information on the financial condition, profitability, and prospects of their companies as well as comparative financial information on competing companies and business opportunities. This permits them to benchmark their company's performance and condition. Managers and employees also demand financial accounting information for use in compensation and bonus contracts that are tied to such numbers. The popularity of employee profit sharing and stock ownership plans has further increased demand for financial information. Other sources of demand include union contracts that link wage negotiations to accounting numbers and pension and benefit plans whose solvency depends on company performance. Financial statements provide useful information to company managers to address the following types of questions.

- What product lines, geographic areas, or other segments are performing well compared with our peer companies and our own benchmarks?
- Have we reached the level of profitability necessary to pay bonuses or profit-sharing payments to employees?
- Should we consider expanding or contracting our business?

Investment Analysts and Information Intermediaries

Investment analysts and other information intermediaries, such as financial press writers and business commentators, are interested in predicting companies' future performance. Expectations about future profitability and the ability to generate cash impact stock price and a company's ability to borrow money at favorable terms. Financial reports reflect information about past performance and current resources available to companies. These reports also provide information about claims on those resources, including claims by suppliers, creditors, lenders, and stockholders. This information allows analysts to make informed assessments about future financial performance and condition so they can provide stock recommendations or write commentaries. Financial statements provide useful information to investment analysts to address the following types of questions.

- What are the expected future profit, cash flows, and dividends to use as input into stock-price models?
- Is the company financially solvent and able to meet its financial obligations?
- How do our expectations about the economy, interest rates and the competitive environment affect the company?

Analysts use financial information to prepare research reports similar to the one issued in 2016 by **Morgan Stanley** on Under Armour (below). Analysts use balance sheet numbers, including debt and equity ("eqty") along with income statement numbers, including revenue, earnings per share (EPS), and earnings before interest, tax, depreciation, and amortization (EBITDA) to compute ratios that inform their price target ($64) and their stock rating (underweight). We will discuss analysts and their activities in more depth later. For now, you should know that accounting information is a bedrock for equity analysis.

Excerpts of reports from Morgan Stanley, Moody's, and Deutsche Bank are incorporated to illustrate how accounting information is used by financial services.

Morgan Stanley

Under Armour Inc.| March 3, 2016

MORGAN STANLEY RESEARCH

March 3, 2016

Under Armour Inc.

Priced for Perfection, but We See 5 Concerning Data Points; Reiterate UW

MORGAN STANLEY & CO. LLC
Jay Sole
Jay.Sole@morganstanley.com   +1 212 761-5866
Joseph Wyatt, CFA
Joseph.Wyatt@morganstanley.com   +1 212 761-4206
Edward A Ryan
Eddie.Ryan@morganstanley.com   +1 212 761-4384

Industry View	Stock Rating	Price Target
In-Line	**Underweight**	**$64.00**

UA trades at 65x FY16 EPS and has a PEG of 3x, which compares to a group of high-growth retailers averaging 23x and 1.8x for PEG. Based on our deep-dive work, we see data points suggesting some of UA's growth levers are dissipating and represent risks not priced in.

We've done a deep dive into UA's business: We believe that Under Armour is a terrific company with exceptional management and much growth ahead of it. However, the question is whether UA's growth will justify the stock's 65x P/E. We don't think so. Dissecting UA's business is tricky because of its complex mix of channels, geographies, product categories, and limited disclosure. Our work tries to dig down a level to look at trends in organic store growth, distribution partnerships, and working capital movements and shows growth may be harder to come by in future quarters than many appreciate.

Under Armour Inc. (UA.N, UA US)

Branded Apparel & Footwear / United States of America

Stock Rating	Underweight
Industry View	In-Line
Price target	**$64.00**
Shr price, close (Mar 2, 2016)	$83.93
Mkt cap, curr (mm)	$18,508
52-Week Range	$105.89-63.24

Fiscal Year Ending	12/15	12/16e	12/17e	12/18e
EPS ($)**	1.05	1.29	1.60	2.05
Prior EPS ($)**	-	-	-	-
Consensus EPS ($)§	1.04	1.31	1.68	2.17
P/E, consensus§	77.5	64.1	49.9	38.6
EV/EBITDA**	35.9	31.0	24.8	19.3
Div yld (%)	0.0	0.0	0.0	0.0
Revenue, net ($mm)	3,963	4,965	6,197	7,527
EBIT margin (%)**	10.3	10.1	10.0	10.2
Return on avg eqty (%)**	15.8	16.5	17.1	18.3
Net debt/EBITDA**	0.8	1.2	1.2	1.0

Creditors and Suppliers

Banks and other lenders demand financial accounting information to help determine loan terms, loan amounts, interest rates, and required collateral. Loan agreements often include contractual requirements, called **covenants**, that restrict the borrower's behavior in some fashion. For example, loan covenants might require the loan recipient to maintain minimum levels of working capital, retained earnings, and interest coverage to safeguard lenders. Covenant violations can yield technical default, enabling the creditor to demand early payment or other compensation. Suppliers demand financial information to establish credit terms and to determine their long-term commitment to supply-chain relations. Both creditors and suppliers use financial information to monitor and adjust their contracts and commitments with a company. Financial statements provide useful information to creditors and suppliers to address the following types of questions.

■   Should we extend credit to this company in the form of a loan or line of credit for inventory purchases?

■   What interest rate is reasonable given the company's current debt load and overall risk profile?

■   Is the company in compliance with the existing loan covenants (loan conditions that restrict the borrower's behavior in some fashion, such as minimum levels of working capital, retained earnings, and cash flow, which safeguard lenders)?

Following is Under Armour's disclosure of loan covenants on its credit facility (a line of credit) from a recent annual report.

> **Under Armour Credit Facility**   In May 2014, the Company entered into a new unsecured $650.0 million credit facility. . . . These additional borrowings were used to fund, in part, the acquisition of MFP. . . . The credit agreement contains covenants that, subject to significant exceptions, limit the ability of the Company and its subsidiaries to, among other things, incur additional indebtedness, make restricted payments, pledge their assets as security, make investments, loans, advances, guarantees and acquisitions, undergo fundamental changes and enter into transactions with affiliates. The Company is also required to maintain a ratio of consolidated EBITDA, as defined in the credit agreement, to consolidated interest expense of not less than 3.50 to 1.00 and is not permitted to allow the ratio of consolidated total indebtedness to consolidated EBITDA to be greater than 3.25 to 1.00 ("consolidated leverage ratio"). As of March 31, 2015, the Company was in compliance with these ratios.

Stockholders and Directors

Stockholders and directors and others (such as investment analysts, brokers, and potential investors) demand financial accounting information to assess the profitability and risks of companies and other information useful in their investment decisions. **Fundamental analysis** uses financial information to estimate company value and to form buy-sell stock strategies. Both directors and stockholders use accounting information to evaluate managerial performance. Managers similarly use such information to request an increase in compensation and managerial power from directors. Outside directors are crucial to determining who runs the company, and these directors use accounting information to help make leadership decisions. Financial statements provide useful information to stockholders and directors to address the following questions.

■   Is company management demonstrating good stewardship of the resources that have been entrusted to it?

■   Do we have the information we need to critically evaluate strategic initiatives that management proposes?

Customers and Strategic Partners

Customers (both current and potential) demand accounting information to assess a company's ability to provide products or services and to assess the company's staying power and reliability. Strategic partners wish to estimate the company's profitability to assess the fairness of returns on mutual transactions and strategic alliances. Financial statements provide useful information to customers and strategic partners to address the following questions.

■   Will the company be a reliable supplier?

■   Is the strategic partnership providing reasonable returns to both parties?

Regulators and Tax Agencies

Regulators (such as the Securities and Exchange Commission [SEC], the Federal Trade Commission, and the Federal Reserve Bank) and tax agencies demand accounting information for antitrust assessments, public protection, setting prices, import-export analyses, and setting tax policies. Timely and reliable information is crucial to effective regulatory policy, and accounting information is often central to social and economic policies. For example, governments often grant monopoly rights to electric and gas companies serving specific areas in exchange for regulation over prices charged to consumers. These prices are mainly determined from accounting measures.

Voters and Their Representatives

Voters and their representatives to national, state, and local governments demand accounting information for policy decisions. The decisions can involve economic, social, taxation, and other initiatives. Voters and their representatives also use accounting information to monitor government spending. We have all heard of the $1,000 hammer type stories that government watchdog groups uncovered while sifting through accounting data. Contributors to nonprofit organizations also demand accounting information to assess the impact of their donations.

Supply of Information

In general, the quantity and quality of accounting information that companies supply are determined by managers' assessment of the benefits and costs of disclosure. Managers release information provided the benefits of disclosing that information outweigh the costs of doing so. Both *regulation* and *bargaining power* affect disclosure costs and benefits and thus play roles in determining the supply of accounting information. Most areas of the world regulate the minimum levels of accounting disclosures. In the United States, publicly traded firms must file financial accounting information with the SEC. There are two main compulsory SEC filings.

■ Form **10-K**: the audited annual report that includes the four financial statements, discussed below, with explanatory notes and the management's discussion and analysis (MD&A) of financial results.

■ Form **10-Q**: the unaudited quarterly report that includes summary versions of the four financial statements and limited additional disclosures.

Forms 10-K (which must be filed within 60 [90] days of the year-end for larger [smaller] companies) and 10-Q (which must be filed within 40 [45] days of the quarter-end for larger [smaller] companies, except for the fourth quarter, when it is part of the 10-K) are available electronically from the SEC website (see Appendix 1A). The minimum, regulated level of information is not the standard. Both the quantity and quality of information differ across companies and over time. We need only look at several annual reports to see considerable variance in the amount and type of accounting information supplied. For example, differences abound on disclosures for segment operations, product performance reports, and financing activities. Further, some stakeholders possess ample bargaining power to obtain accounting information for themselves. These typically include private lenders and major suppliers and customers.

Benefits of Disclosure

The benefits of supplying accounting information extend to a company's capital, labor, input, and output markets. Companies must compete in these markets. For example, capital markets provide debt and equity financing; the better a company's prospects, the lower is its cost of capital (as reflected in lower interest rates or higher stock prices). The same holds for a company's recruiting efforts in labor markets and its ability to establish superior supplier-customer relations in the input and output markets.

A company's performance in these markets depends on success with its business activities *and* the market's awareness of that success. Companies reap the benefits of disclosure with good news about their products, processes, management, and so forth. That is, there are real economic incentives for companies to disclose reliable (audited) accounting information, enabling them to better compete in capital, labor, input, and output markets.

What inhibits companies from providing false or misleading good news? There are several constraints. An important constraint imposed by stakeholders is that of audit requirements and legal repercussions associated with inaccurate accounting information. Another relates to reputation effects from disclosures as subsequent events either support or refute earlier news.

Costs of Disclosure

The costs of supplying accounting information include its preparation and dissemination, competitive disadvantages, litigation potential, and political costs. Preparation and dissemination costs can be substantial, but companies have often already incurred those costs because managers need similar information for their own business decisions. The potential for information to yield competitive disadvantages is high. Companies are concerned that disclosures of activities such as product or segment successes, strategic alliances or pursuits, technological or system innovations, and product or process quality improvements will harm their competitive advantages. Also, companies are frequently sued when disclosures create expectations that are not met. Highly visible companies often face political and public pressure, which creates "political costs." These companies often try to appear as though they do not generate excess profits. For example, government defense contractors, large software conglomerates, and oil companies are favorite targets of public scrutiny. Disclosure costs are higher for companies facing political costs.

The SEC adopted Regulation Fair Disclosure (FD), or Reg FD for short, to curb the practice of selective disclosure by public companies (called *issuers* by the SEC) to certain stockholders and financial analysts. In the past, many companies disclosed important information in meetings and conference calls that excluded individual stockholders. The goal of this rule is to level the playing field for all investors. Reg FD reads as follows: "Whenever an issuer discloses any material nonpublic information regarding that issuer, the issuer shall make public disclosure of that information . . . simultaneously, in the case of an intentional disclosure; and . . . promptly, in the case of a non-intentional disclosure." Reg FD increased the cost of voluntary financial disclosure and led some companies to curtail the supply of financial information to all users.

International Accounting Standards

Companies in more than 120 countries, including the European Union, the United Kingdom, Canada, and Japan use International Financial Reporting Standards (IFRS) for their financial reports. Headquartered in London, the International Accounting Standards Board (IASB) oversees the development of IFRS. While the IASB and the Financial Accounting Standards Board (FASB) operate as independent standard-setting bodies, the two boards work together cooperatively, often undertaking joint projects. Consequently, IFRS and U.S. GAAP (generally accepted accounting principles) are generally more alike than different for most transactions.

Currently, there is no formal plan for the U.S. to transition to IFRS or for the IASB and FASB to converge or conform standards. Indeed, there is considerable pushback on complete conformity or convergence from U.S. companies, investors, and the SEC. While conformity is likely not attainable, both boards believe comparable global accounting standards are desirable because comparability would:

- Improve the quality of financial reports.
- Benefit investors, companies, and other market participants who make global investment decisions.
- Reduce costs for both users and preparers of financial statements.
- Make worldwide capital markets more efficient.

Evidence of increasing "comparability" of the two standards includes the following.

- Since 2007, the SEC has permitted foreign companies to file IFRS financial statements without requiring reconciliation to U.S. GAAP. Currently, more than 500 companies with a cumulative market capitalization of trillions of dollars, report to the SEC using IFRS.
- In late 2015, the SEC announced it is considering the possibility of allowing U.S. public companies to provide IFRS-based information as a supplement to U.S. GAAP financial statements.
- The FASB participates actively in the development of IFRS, providing input on IASB projects through the IASB's Accounting Standards Advisory Forum (ASAF).
- Recent joint projects between the two boards relate to leases, financial instruments, revenue recognition, and insurance contracts.

We might ask: are financial statements prepared under IFRS substantially different from those prepared under U.S. GAAP? At a broad level, the answer is no. Both are prepared using accrual accounting and utilize similar conceptual frameworks. Both require the same set of financial statements: a balance sheet, an income statement, a statement of cash flows, a statement of stockholders' equity, and a set of explanatory footnotes. That does not mean that no differences exist. However, the differences are typically technical in nature, and do not differ on broad principles discussed in this book.

At the end of each module, we summarize key differences between U.S. GAAP and IFRS. Also, there are a variety of sources that provide more detailed and technical analysis of similarities and differences between U.S. GAAP and IFRS. The FASB, the IASB, and each of the "Big 4" accounting firms also maintain websites devoted to this issue. Search under IFRS and PwC, KPMG, EY and Deloitte. The two standard-setting bodies also provide useful information. See: FASB (**www.fasb.org/intl/**) and IASB (**www.ifrs.org**).

Review Problems are self-study tools that require the application of the accounting topics covered in each section. To aid learning, solutions are provided at the end of the module.

LO2 Review 1-2

Required

1. Match the users of financial statement information with the types of questions they would typically ask and answer using accounting data.

_____	I.	Managers and employees	a. Is company management demonstrating good stewardship of the resources that have been entrusted to it?
_____	II.	Investment analysts and information intermediaries	b. What product lines have performed well compared with competitors?
_____	III.	Creditors and suppliers	c. What regulated price is appropriate given the company's financial condition?
_____	IV.	Stockholders and directors	d. Is the strategic partnership providing reasonable returns to both parties?
_____	V.	Customers and strategic partners	e. What expectations about the company's future profit and cash flow should we use as input into the pricing of its stock?
_____	VI.	Regulators and tax agencies	f. Is the company in compliance with the contractual terms of its existing loan covenants?

Guided Examples icons denote the availability of a demonstration video in myBusinessCourse (MBC) for each Review Problem—see the Preface for more on MBC.

2. How would having comparable IFRS and U.S. GAAP standards reduce the cost of preparing financial statements for a multinational firm?

Solution on p. 1-46.

Structure of Financial Statements

Companies use four financial statements to periodically report on business activities. These statements are the balance sheet, income statement, statement of stockholders' equity, and statement of cash flows. Exhibit 1.2 shows how these statements are linked across time. A balance sheet reports on a company's financial position at a *point in time*. The income statement, statement of stockholders' equity, and the statement of cash flows report on performance over a *period of time*. The three statements in the middle of Exhibit 1.2 (period-of-time statements) link the balance sheet from the beginning to the end of a period.

A one-year, or annual, reporting period is common and is called the *accounting,* or *fiscal, year*. Of course, firms prepare financial statements more frequently; semiannual, quarterly, and monthly financial statements are common. *Calendar-year* companies have reporting periods beginning on January 1 and ending on December 31. **Under Armour** is a calendar-year company. Some companies choose a fiscal year ending on a date other than December 31, such as when sales and inventory are low. For example, **Target**'s fiscal year ends on the Saturday nearest January 31, after the busy holiday season.

eLectures LO3
MBC Describe and examine the four financial statements, and define the accounting equation.

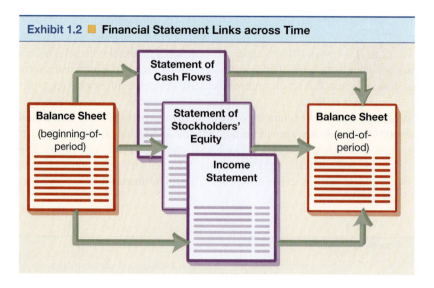

Exhibit 1.2 ■ Financial Statement Links across Time

Balance Sheet

A balance sheet reports a company's financial position at a point in time. The balance sheet reports the company's *resources* (*assets*), namely, what the company owns. The balance sheet also reports the *sources* of asset financing. There are two ways a company can finance its assets. It can raise money from stockholders; this is *owner financing*. It can also raise money from banks or other creditors and suppliers; this is *nonowner financing*. This means both owners and nonowners hold claims on company assets. Owner claims on assets are referred to as *equity,* and nonowner claims are referred to as *liabilities* (or debt). Since all financing must be invested in something, we obtain the following basic relation: *investing equals financing*. This equality is called the **accounting equation**, which follows.

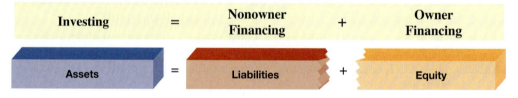

The accounting equation works for all companies at all points in time.

The balance sheet for **Under Armour** is in Exhibit 1.3 (condensed). Refer to this balance sheet to verify the following amounts: assets = $2,868.9 million; liabilities = $1,200.7 million; and equity = $1,668.2 million. Assets equal liabilities plus equity, which reflects the accounting equation: investing equals financing.

Investing Activities

Balance sheets are organized like the accounting equation. Investing activities are represented by the company's assets. These assets are financed by a combination of nonowner financing (liabilities) and owner financing (equity).

For simplicity, UnderArmour's balance sheet in Exhibit 1.3 categorizes assets into short-term and long-term assets (Module 2 explains the composition of assets in more detail). Assets are listed on the balance sheet in order of their nearness to cash, with short-term assets (also called current assets) expected to generate cash within one year from the balance sheet date. For example, the first short-term asset listed is cash, then accounts receivable (amounts owed to Under Armour by its customers that will be collected in cash in the near future), and then inventories (goods available for sale that must first be sold before cash can be collected). Land, buildings, and equipment (often referred to as property, plant, and equipment or just PPE) will generate cash over a long period of time and are, therefore, classified as long-term assets.

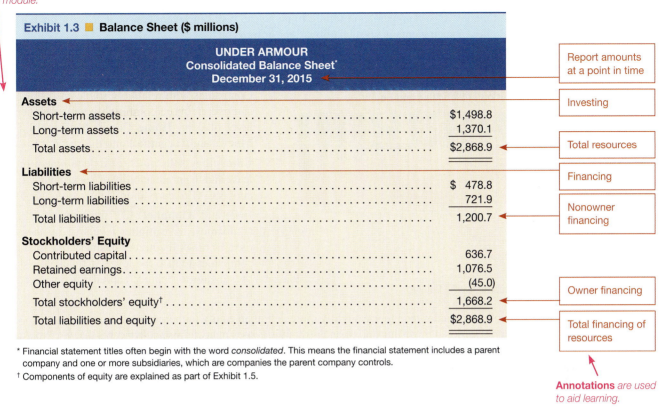

Exhibit 1.3 ■ Balance Sheet ($ millions)

UNDER ARMOUR
Consolidated Balance Sheet*
December 31, 2015

Assets	
Short-term assets	$1,498.8
Long-term assets	1,370.1
Total assets	$2,868.9
Liabilities	
Short-term liabilities	$ 478.8
Long-term liabilities	721.9
Total liabilities	1,200.7
Stockholders' Equity	
Contributed capital	636.7
Retained earnings	1,076.5
Other equity	(45.0)
Total stockholders' equity†	1,668.2
Total liabilities and equity	$2,868.9

Report amounts at a point in time

Investing

Total resources

Financing

Nonowner financing

Owner financing

Total financing of resources

* Financial statement titles often begin with the word *consolidated*. This means the financial statement includes a parent company and one or more subsidiaries, which are companies the parent company controls.

† Components of equity are explained as part of Exhibit 1.5.

Annotations *are used to aid learning.*

The relative proportion of short- and long-term assets is largely determined by a company's industry and business model. This is evident in the graph to the side that depicts the relative proportion of short- and long-term assets for a number of well-known companies.

■ Technology companies like **Cisco Systems** and **Alphabet** (formerly known as Google), often carry large investments in marketable securities that are classified as short-term assets because they can be sold quickly in financial markets.

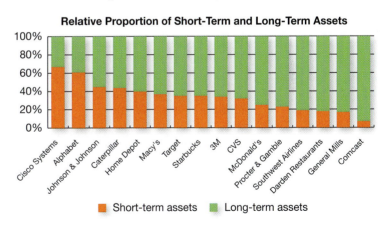

■ Manufacturers and retailers such as **Johnson & Johnson**, **Caterpillar**, **Home Depot**, and **Macy's**, require more investment in property, plant, and equipment in addition to large investments in inventories and accounts receivable from customers. As a result, their balance sheets report a more equal mix of short- and long-term assets.

■ At the other end of the spectrum are transportation companies like **Southwest Airlines** and communications companies like **Comcast** whose business models require large investment in long-term PPE assets.

Although managers can influence the relative amounts and proportion of assets, their flexibility is somewhat limited by the nature of their industries.

Financing Activities

To pay for assets, companies use a combination of owner (or equity) and nonowner financing (liabilities or debt). Owner financing has two components: resources (mostly cash, but sometimes non-cash assets) contributed to the company by its owners, and profits retained by the company. Nonowner financing is borrowed money. We distinguish between these two financing sources for a reason:

borrowed money must be repaid, and failure to do so can result in severe consequences for the borrower. Equity financing entails no such obligation for repayment.

The relative proportion of nonowner and owner financing is largely determined by a company's industry and business model. This is evident in the graph to the side.

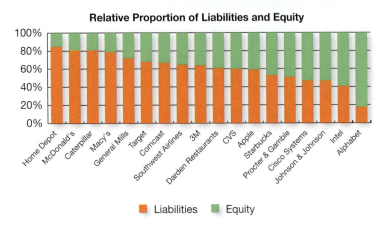

Relative Proportion of Liabilities and Equity

■ Liabilities   ■ Equity

■ Companies with relatively stable cash flows can operate more comfortably with a higher level of debt. **Home Depot**, **McDonald's**, **Macy's** and **Target** fall into this category.

■ **Caterpillar** sells much of its equipment on lease and the predictability of lease payments allows CAT to carry more debt.

■ **Intel** and **Alphabet**, like most technology companies, have higher levels of business risk. To offset the higher business risk, these companies reduce the level of financial risk by substituting equity capital for borrowed funds.

Most public companies tend to use slightly more debt than equity in their capital structures.

Our discussion of investing and financing activities uses many terms and concepts that we explain later in the book. Our desire here is to provide a sneak preview into the interplay among financial statements, manager behavior, and economics. Some questions we might have at this early stage regarding the balance sheet follow.

■ Alphabet reports $73.1 billion of cash on its 2015 balance sheet, nearly half of its total assets. Many high-tech companies carry high levels of cash. Why is that? Is there a cost to holding too much cash? Is it costly to carry too little cash?

■ The relative proportion of short- and long-term assets is largely dictated by companies' business models. Why is this the case? Why is the composition of assets on balance sheets for companies in the same industry similar? By what degree can a company's asset composition safely deviate from industry norms?

■ What are the trade-offs in financing a company by owner versus nonowner financing? If nonowner financing is less costly, why don't we see companies financed entirely with borrowed money?

■ How do stockholders influence the strategic direction of a company? How can long-term creditors influence strategic direction?

■ Most assets and liabilities are reported on the balance sheet at their acquisition price, called *historical cost*. Would reporting assets and liabilities at fair values be more informative? What problems might fair-value reporting cause?

IFRS Insights examine issues related to similarities and differences in accounting practices of the U.S. and other countries.

Review the Under Armour balance sheet summarized in Exhibit 1.3, and think about these questions. We provide answers for each of these questions as we progress through the book.

IFRS Insight   ■   Balance Sheet Presentation and IFRS

Balance sheets prepared under IFRS often classify accounts in reverse order of liquidity (lack of nearness to cash), which is the opposite of what U.S. companies do. For example, intangible assets are typically listed first, and cash is listed last among assets. Also, equity is often listed before liabilities, where liabilities are again listed in order of decreasing liquidity. These choices reflect convention and *not* IFRS requirements.

Income Statement

An **income statement** reports on a company's performance over a period of time and lists amounts for its *top line* revenues (also called sales) and its expenses. Revenues less expenses equals the *bottom-line* net income amount (also called *profit* or *earnings*). Under Armour, as is typical of companies that sell products, reports two basic kinds of operating expenses.

- **Cost of goods sold** (COGS, also called cost of sales). While revenues represent the retail selling price of the goods sold to customers, cost of goods sold is the amount Under Armour paid to purchase or manufacture the goods (inventories) that it sold. Manufacturing and merchandising companies typically include a subtotal called *gross profit*, which is revenues less cost of goods sold. For example, if it costs a company $7 to purchase or manufacture an item of inventory and the item sells for $10, the income statement reports revenues of $10, cost of goods sold of $7, and a gross profit of $3. We use the term gross to mean the profit available to cover all other expenses.
- **Selling, general, and administrative expenses (SG&A).** This is Under Armour's overhead and includes salaries, marketing costs, occupancy costs, HR and IT costs, and all the other operating expenses the company incurs other than the cost of purchasing or manufacturing inventory (which is included in cost of goods sold).

Under Armour's income statement is in Exhibit 1.4. Refer to the income statement to verify the following: revenues of $3,963.3 million, cost of goods sold of $2,057.8 million, and SG&A expenses of $1,497.0 million. After interest expense and income taxes, the company reports net income of $232.6 million. Net income reflects the profit (or earnings) to the company's shareholders for the period.

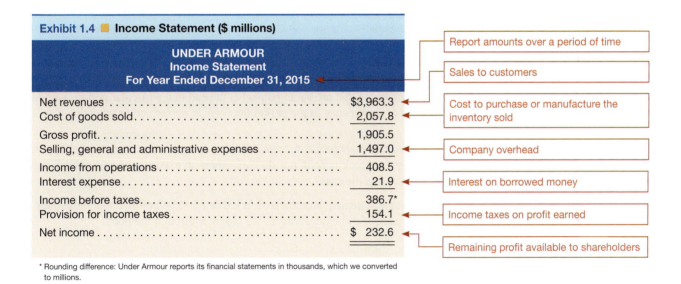

Exhibit 1.4 ▪ Income Statement ($ millions)

UNDER ARMOUR Income Statement For Year Ended December 31, 2015		
Net revenues	$3,963.3	◄── Report amounts over a period of time / Sales to customers
Cost of goods sold	2,057.8	◄── Cost to purchase or manufacture the inventory sold
Gross profit	1,905.5	
Selling, general and administrative expenses	1,497.0	◄── Company overhead
Income from operations	408.5	
Interest expense	21.9	◄── Interest on borrowed money
Income before taxes	386.7*	
Provision for income taxes	154.1	◄── Income taxes on profit earned
Net income	$ 232.6	◄── Remaining profit available to shareholders

* Rounding difference: Under Armour reports its financial statements in thousands, which we converted to millions.

To generate net income, companies engage in operating activities that use company resources to produce, promote, and sell products and services. These activities extend from input markets involving suppliers of materials and labor to a company's output markets, involving customers of products and services. Input markets generate most *expenses* (or *costs*) such as inventory, salaries, materials, and logistics. Output markets generate *revenues* (or *sales*) to customers. Output markets also generate some expenses such as marketing and distributing products and services to customers. Net income arises when revenues exceed expenses. A net loss occurs when expenses exceed revenues.

Relative profitability (net income as a percent of sales) differs widely across industries and even among companies in the same industry. Although effective managers can increase their company's profitability, business models play a large part in determining profit levels. These differences are illustrated in the graph (below) of net income as a percent of sales for several companies.

- **Apple**, **Johnson & Johnson**, **Alphabet**, and **Intel** are dominant in their industries, with products and intellectual property that are protected by patent laws—it could be argued that they operate like monopolies. Consequently, their profit levels are high.

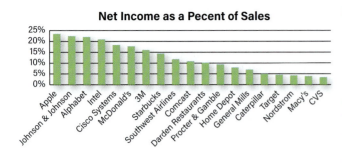

Net Income as a Pecent of Sales

Retailers such as **Target**, **Nordstrom**, **Macy's**, and **CVS** operate in a mature industry and have difficulty differentiating their products. Hence, their net income as a percent of sales is low.

The ability of companies to create barriers to competitive pressure, either by patent protection, effective marketing, or otherwise, is a key factor in determining their level of profitability. Those that compete in highly competitive markets with little product differentiation must concentrate on controlling operating expenses to offset lower gross margins.

As a sneak preview, we might consider the following questions regarding the income statement.

- Assume a company sells a product to a customer who promises to pay in 30 days. Should the seller recognize the sale when it is made or when cash is collected?

- When a company purchases a long-term asset such as a building, its cost is reported on the balance sheet as an asset. Should a company, instead, record the cost of that building as an expense when it is acquired? If not, how should a company report the cost of that asset over the course of its useful life?

- Manufacturers and merchandisers report the cost of a product as an expense when the product sale is recorded. How might we measure the costs of a product that is sold by a merchandiser? By a manufacturer?

- If an asset, such as a building, increases in value, that increase is not reported as income until the building is sold, if ever. What concerns arise if we record increases in asset values as part of income when measurement of that increase is based on appraised values?

- Employees commonly earn wages that are yet to be paid at the end of a particular period. Should their wages be recognized as an expense in the period the work is performed or when the wages are paid?

- Companies are not allowed to report profit on transactions relating to their own stock. That is, they don't report income when stock is sold, nor do they report an expense when dividends are paid to stockholders. Why is this the case?

Review the Under Armour income statement summarized in Exhibit 1.4, and think about these questions. We provide answers for each of these questions as we progress through the book.

Statement of Stockholders' Equity

The **statement of stockholders' equity** reports on year-over-year changes in the equity accounts that are reported on the balance sheet. For each type of equity, the statement reports the beginning balance, a summary of the activity in the account during the year, and the ending balance. **Under Armour**'s statement of stockholders' equity is in Exhibit 1.5. During the recent period, its equity changed due to share issuances and the retention of profit. Under Armour classifies these changes into three categories.

- *Contributed capital*, the stockholders' net contributions to the company.

- *Retained earnings*, net income over the life of the company minus all dividends ever paid.

- *Other equity*, consists of amounts we explain later in the book.

Exhibit 1.5 reconciles the activity in each of the equity accounts from the balance sheet in Exhibit 1.3. We briefly discuss the two larger accounts here and explain the accounts in depth in Module 8.

- **Contributed capital** represents assets the company received from issuing stock to stockholders (also called shareholders). The balance of this account at the beginning of the year was $508.4 million. During the year, Under Armour sold additional shares for $22 million and recorded miscellaneous adjustments of $106.3 million to yield a year-end balance of $636.7 million.

■ **Retained earnings** (also called *earned capital* or *reinvested capital*) represent the cumulative total amount of income the company has earned and that has been retained in the business; that is, not distributed to stockholders in the form of dividends. The change in retained earnings links consecutive balance sheets via the income statement: Ending retained earnings = Beginning retained earnings + Net income for the period − Dividends for the period. Under Armour's retained earnings increased from $856.7 million to $1,076.6 million. This increase is explained by its net income of $232.6 million less other adjustments of $12.7 million. Under Armour paid no dividends in 2015.

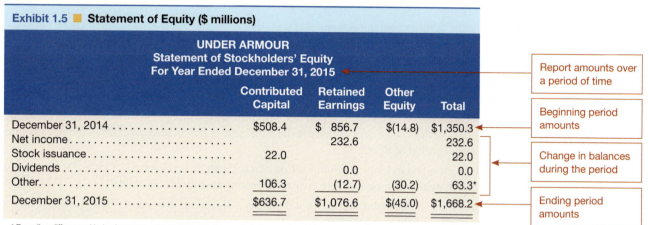

Exhibit 1.5 ■ **Statement of Equity ($ millions)**

UNDER ARMOUR Statement of Stockholders' Equity For Year Ended December 31, 2015	Contributed Capital	Retained Earnings	Other Equity	Total
December 31, 2014	$508.4	$ 856.7	$(14.8)	$1,350.3
Net income		232.6		232.6
Stock issuance	22.0			22.0
Dividends		0.0		0.0
Other	106.3	(12.7)	(30.2)	63.3*
December 31, 2015	$636.7	$1,076.6	$(45.0)	$1,668.2

Report amounts over a period of time

Beginning period amounts

Change in balances during the period

Ending period amounts

* Rounding difference: Under Armour reports its financial statements in thousands, which we converted to millions.

Statement of Cash Flows

The **statement of cash flows** reports the change (either an increase or a decrease) in a company's cash balance over a period of time. The statement reports cash inflows and outflows from operating, investing, and financing activities over a period of time. Under Armour's statement of cash flows is shown in Exhibit 1.6. Its cash balance decreased by $463.3 million in 2015: operating activities used $44.1 million cash, investing activities reduced cash by $847.5 million, and financing activities yielded a cash inflow of $428.3 million.

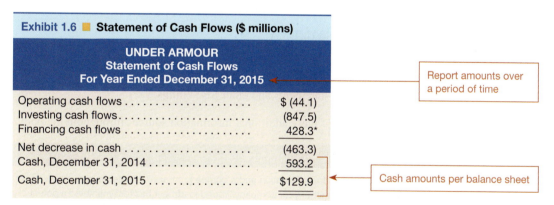

Exhibit 1.6 ■ **Statement of Cash Flows ($ millions)**

UNDER ARMOUR Statement of Cash Flows For Year Ended December 31, 2015	
Operating cash flows	$ (44.1)
Investing cash flows	(847.5)
Financing cash flows	428.3*
Net decrease in cash	(463.3)
Cash, December 31, 2014	593.2
Cash, December 31, 2015	$129.9

Report amounts over a period of time

Cash amounts per balance sheet

* Includes $(11.8) mil. in foreign currency exchange rate changes.

We summarized Under Armour's Statement of Cash Flow in Exhibit 1.6 to simplify the discussion. To give us a feel for the business activity underlying the numbers, during 2015, Under Armour's outflow of cash for operating activities of $44.1 million is primarily the result of building up inventories in advance of expected sales increases. The cash outflow of $847.5 million for investing activities included the purchase of new PPE and the acquisition of **MyFitnessPal Inc.** (a digital nutrition and connected fitness company), to expand the Under Armour Connected Fitness community. These outflows were financed with a combination of existing cash and an increase in borrowed funds.

Under Armour's negative operating cash flow of $44.1 million does not equal its $232.6 million net income. Generally, a company's net cash flow for a period does *not* equal its net income for the period. This is due to timing differences between when revenue and expense items are recognized on the income statement and when cash is received and paid. (We discuss this concept further in subsequent modules.)

Both cash flow and net income numbers are important for business decisions. Each is used in security valuation models, and both help users of accounting reports understand and assess a company's past, present, and future business activities. As a sneak preview, we might consider the following questions regarding the statement of cash flows.

- What is the usefulness of the statement of cash flows? Do the balance sheet and income statement provide sufficient cash flow information?

- What types of information are disclosed in the statement of cash flows and why are they important?

- What kinds of activities are reported in each of the operating, investing, and financing sections of the statement of cash flows? How is this information useful?

- Is it important for a company to report net cash inflows (positive amounts) relating to operating activities over the longer term? What are the implications if operating cash flows are negative for an extended period of time?

- Why is it important to know the composition of a company's investment activities? What kind of information might we look for? Are positive investing cash flows favorable?

- Is it important to know the sources of a company's financing activities? What questions might that information help us answer?

- How might the composition of operating, investing, and financing cash flows change over a company's life cycle?

- Is the bottom-line increase in cash flow the key number? Why or why not?

Review the Under Armour statement of cash flows summarized in Exhibit 1.6, and think about these questions. We provide answers for each of these questions as we progress through the book.

Information Beyond Financial Statements

Important financial information about a company is communicated to various decision makers through means other than the four financial statements. These include the following.

- Management Discussion and Analysis (MD&A)
- Independent auditor report
- Financial statement footnotes
- Regulatory filings, including proxy statements and other SEC filings

We describe and explain the usefulness of these additional information sources throughout the book.

Managerial Decision ■ You Are the Product Manager

There is often friction between investors' need for information and a company's desire to safeguard competitive advantages. Assume you are a key-product manager at your company. Your department has test-marketed a potentially lucrative new product, which it plans to further finance. You are asked for advice on the extent of information to disclose about the new product in the MD&A section of the company's upcoming annual report. What advice do you provide and why? [Answer, p. 1-34]

Managerial Decisions
require you to assume various roles within a business and use your accounting knowledge to address an issue. Solutions are provided at the end of the module.

Managerial Choices in Financial Accounting

Some people mistakenly assume financial accounting is an exact discipline—that is, companies select the one proper accounting method to account for a transaction, and then follow the rules. The reality is that GAAP allows companies choices in preparing financial statements. The choice of methods can yield financial statements that are markedly different from one another in terms of reported income, assets, liabilities, and equity amounts.

People often are surprised that financial statements comprise numerous estimates. For example, companies must estimate the amounts that will eventually be collected from customers, the length of time that buildings and equipment will be productive, the value impairments of assets, the future costs of warranty claims, the eventual payouts on pension plans, and numerous other estimates.

Historically, the FASB has promulgated standards that were quite complicated and replete with guidelines. In recent years, the pendulum has begun to swing away from such rigidity. Now, once financial statements are prepared, company management is required to step back from the details and make a judgment on whether the statements taken as a whole "fairly present" the financial condition of the company as is asserted in the company's audit report (see below).

Moreover, since the enactment of the *Sarbanes-Oxley Act* (SOX), the SEC requires the chief executive officer (CEO) of the company and its chief financial officer (CFO) to personally sign a statement attesting to the accuracy and completeness of the financial statements. This requirement is an important step in maintaining confidence in the integrity of financial accounting. The statements signed by both the CEO and CFO contain the following declarations.

- Both the CEO and CFO have personally reviewed the annual report.

- There are no untrue statements of a material fact that would make the statements misleading.

- Financial statements fairly present in all material respects the financial condition of the company.

- All material facts are disclosed to the company's auditors and board of directors.

- No changes to its system of internal controls are made unless properly communicated.

SOX also imposed fines and potential jail time for executives for untrue statements or omissions of important facts. Presumably, the prospect of personal losses is designed to make these executives more vigilant in monitoring the financial accounting system. More recently, Congress passed the *Wall Street Reform and Consumer Protection Act* of 2010 (or the Dodd-Frank Act). Among the provisions of the act are rules that strengthened SOX by augmenting "claw-back" provisions for executives' ill-gotten gains.

Research Insight ■ Quality of Earnings

A recent study conducted a survey of nearly 400 CFOs on the definition and drivers of earnings quality, with an emphasis on the prevalence and detection of earnings misrepresentation. The CFOs cited the hallmarks of earnings quality as sustainability, absence of one-time items, and backing by actual cash flows. However, they also believe that, in any given period, a remarkable 20% of companies intentionally distort earnings, even while adhering to GAAP. The magnitude of the average misrepresentation is large: 10% of reported earnings.

What are the lessons for us? We can become informed and critical readers of financial reports by first understanding how reports are constructed and the types of assumptions and estimates that are used in their preparation. Much of this information is contained in the footnotes to the financial statements. This textbook will help you acquire the knowledge you need to become an informed and critical reader of financial reports.

Source: Ilia Dichev, John Graham, Campbell R. Harvey, and Shiva Rajgopal. 2016. "The Misrepresentation of Earnings" by *Financial Analyst Journal*, vol. 72, num. 1.

Research Insights *introduce relevant research findings on the topics presented.*

Review 1-3 LO3

The following financial information is from **Nike**, a competitor of Under Armour, for May 31, 2015 ($ millions).

Short-term liabilities	$ 6,334	Cost of goods sold	$16,534
Cash flows from financing	(2,873)	Cash, beginning-year	2,220
Revenues	30,601	Tax expense	932
Stockholders' equity	12,707	Short-term assets	15,976
Cash flows from operations	4,680	Interest income	30
SG&A expenses	9,892	Long-term liabilities	2,559
Long-term assets	5,624	Cash, ending-year	3,852
Cash flows from investing	(175)		

Required

1. Prepare an income statement and statement of cash flows for Nike for the year ended May 31, 2015. Prepare Nike's balance sheet as of May 31, 2015.
2. Compare the balance sheet and income statement of Nike with those of Under Armour in Exhibits 1.3 and 1.4. What differences do we observe?

Solution on p. 1-46.

Analysis of Financial Statements

LO4

Explain and apply basic profitability analysis.

This section previews the analysis framework of this book. This framework is used extensively by market professionals who analyze financial reports to evaluate company management and value the company's debt and equity securities. Analysis of financial performance is crucial in assessing prior strategic decisions and evaluating strategic alternatives.

Return on Assets

Suppose we learn that a company reports a profit of $10 million. Does the $10 million profit indicate the company is performing well? Knowing a company reports a profit is certainly positive as it indicates customers value its goods or services, and its revenues exceed expenses. However, we cannot assess how well it is performing without considering the context. To explain, suppose we learn this company has $500 million in assets. We now assess the $10 million profit as low because, relative to the size of its asset investment, the company earned a paltry 2% return, computed as $10 million divided by $500 million. A 2% return on assets is what a lower-risk investment in government-backed bonds might yield. The important point is that a company's profitability must be assessed with respect to the size of its investment. This is done with a common metric: the *return on assets* (ROA)—defined as net income for that period divided by the average total assets during that period.

Components of Return on Assets

To further isolate components that are driving return on assets, we can separate ROA into two components: profitability and productivity.

- **Profitability relates profit to sales.** This ratio is called the *profit margin* (PM), and it reflects the net income (profit after tax) earned on each sales dollar. Management wants to earn as much profit as possible from sales.

- **Productivity relates sales to assets.** This component, called *asset turnover* (AT), reflects sales generated by each dollar of assets. Management wants to maximize asset productivity to achieve the highest possible sales level for a given level of assets (or to achieve a given level of sales with the smallest level of assets).

Exhibit 1.7 depicts the disaggregation of ROA into these two components. Profitability (PM) and productivity (AT) are multiplied to yield the ROA. Average assets are commonly defined as (beginning-year assets + ending-year assets)/2.

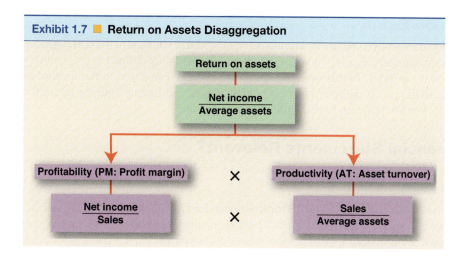

Exhibit 1.7 ■ **Return on Assets Disaggregation**

There are an infinite number of combinations of PM and AT that yield the same ROA. To illustrate, Exhibit 1.8 graphs actual combinations of these two components for companies we highlight in this book (each is identified by its ticker symbol). The graph's green line is the 8% median ROA for the highlighted companies. This is higher than the 5.2% median ROA for all of the Standard & Poor's (S&P) 500 companies in the same year. Companies operating above the median are earning above-average returns on their assets. Technology companies like **Oracle** (ORCL), **Johnson & Johnson** (JNJ), **Apple** (AAPL), and **Intel** (INTC) are characterized by high net profit margins resulting from patent protection that increase barriers to entry and reduce competition. These companies also report substantial assets, typically in the form of marketable securities and intangible assets. Because these investments do not generate "sales," the productivity ratio (AT) is decreased by the inflated assets in the denominator. At the other end of the spectrum, retailers like **Kroger** (KR), **Walmart** (WMT), **TJX Companies** (TJX), and **Target** (TGT) find it difficult to differentiate their products. This open competition keeps prices down, which yields lower profit margins. These retailing companies must focus on increasing AT in order to maintain an acceptable ROA. To do this, they watch inventory and PPE assets carefully and rarely have accounts receivable because most of their trade is cash-and-carry.

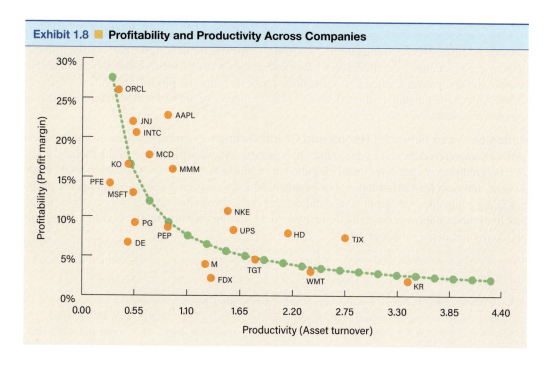

Exhibit 1.8 ■ **Profitability and Productivity Across Companies**

Return on Equity

Another important analysis measure is return on equity (ROE), which is defined as net income divided by average stockholders' equity, where average equity is commonly defined as (beginning-year equity + ending-year equity)/2. In this case, company earnings are compared to the level of stockholder investment. ROE reflects the return to stockholders, which is different from the return for the entire company (ROA). We return to ROE in more detail in Module 4.

Are Financial Statements Relevant?

Accounting, finance, and economic researchers have long investigated the role of financial statement data in capital markets.

Relation between Earnings and Stock Prices Early research focused on whether and how reported earnings are related to stock prices. There is a natural positive relation between expected earnings and stock prices, because stockholders expect dividends, which are paid out of earnings. Early research by Ball and Brown confirmed this expected relation, and the study produced the seminal graph shown here.[1] It shows stock returns trending up during the year for companies that subsequently reported higher earnings (as compared with the prior year) and trending down for companies that subsequently reported lower earnings.

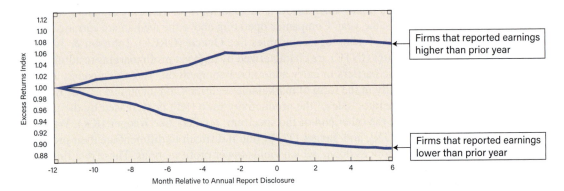

Subsequent research would show that persistent core earnings have the highest predictive ability for future earnings and cash flows. Rigorous financial statement analysis seeks to uncover a company's persistent core operating earnings and cash flows. In a later module, we consider how to forecast future earnings and cash flows using current financial statement information. We also consider financial statement analysis in more depth and conclude that rigorous analysis seeks to uncover the underlying economic and company-specific factors that drive profit margins and productivity ratios we observe. Once we understand the underlying dynamics of the business, we are better able to forecast its future earnings and cash flows.

Relation between Financial Ratios and Credit Ratings Financial markets also use forecasts to price a company's debt and to determine interest rates. As we will discuss in the module on debt financing, credit ratings are determined by a number of financial ratios based on balance sheet, income statement, and cash flow information. For example, Moody's Investors Service, one of the primary credit rating companies for corporate and municipal bonds, uses ratios such as that shown in the table below to evaluate a borrower's ability to repay its debt. Ratings are progressively riskier as we move from left to right in the following table.[2]

---

[1] Ball, R., and P. Brown. 1968. "An empirical evaluation of accounting income numbers." *Journal of Accounting Research* (Autumn): 159–178.

[2] Moody's Investors Service, Rating Methodology: Global Telecommunications Industry.

Moody's Financial Ratios	Aaa	Aa	A	Baa	Ba	B	Caa
Debt/EBITDA	<0.5	0.5–1.0	1.0–2.0	2.0–2.75	2.75–3.75	3.75–6.0	>6.0
FCF/Debt	≥25%	15%–25%	10%–15%	8%–10%	6%–8%	4%–6%	<4%
(EBITDA-CAPEX)/Gross Int. Exp. . .	≥8.0%	6.5–8.0	5.0–6.5	3.5–5.0	2%–3.5%	1.0–2.0	<1

These ratios use debt, EBITDA (earnings before interest, taxes, depreciation and amortization expense), FCF (free cash flow), and CAPEX (capital expenditures, which are purchases of PPE). The table indicates that as the company credit ratings decline (Aaa, Aa, A, Baa, etc.), each ratio becomes progressively "weaker." So, to answer the question: Are financial statements, relevant? Yes. They provide critical input into the pricing of equity and debt securities and, therefore, the creation of shareholder wealth. For that reason, they are also essential in the development and monitoring of corporate strategy.

Managerial Decision ■ **You Are the Chief Financial Officer**

You are reviewing your company's financial performance for the first six months of the year and are unsatisfied with the results. How can you disaggregate ROA to identify areas for improvement? [Answer, p. 1-34]

LO4 **Review 1-4**

Following are selected data from Nike's 2015 10-K.

$ millions	2015
Sales.	$30,601
Net income	3,273
Average assets	20,097
Average stockholders' equity	11,766

Required
a. Compute Nike's ROA. Disaggregate the ROA into its profitability and productivity components.
b. Compute Nike's ROE.

Solution on p. 1-47.

Financial Statements and Business Analysis

Analysis and interpretation of financial statements must consider the broader business context in which a company operates. This section describes how to systematically consider those broader business forces to enhance our analysis and interpretation. This business analysis can sharpen our insights and help us better estimate future performance and company value.

eLectures **LO5**
MBC Assess business operations within the context of a competitive environment.

Analyzing the Competitive Environment

Financial statements are influenced by five important forces that determine competitive intensity: (A) industry competition, (B) buyer power, (C) supplier power, (D) product substitutes, and (E) threat of entry (for further discussion, see Porter, *Competitive Strategy: Techniques for Analyzing Industries and Competitors,* 1980 and 1998).

These five forces are depicted graphically in Exhibit 1.9 and are key determinants of profitability.

Ⓐ **Industry competition** Competition and rivalry raise the cost of doing business as companies must hire and train competitive workers, advertise products, research and develop products, and engage in other related activities.

Exhibit 1.9 ■ **Competitive Forces within the Broader Business Environment**

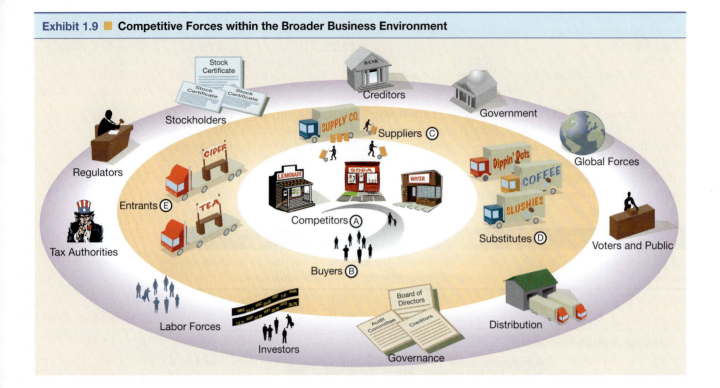

(B) **Bargaining power of buyers** Buyers with strong bargaining power can extract price concessions and demand a higher level of service and delayed payment terms; this force reduces both profits from sales and the operating cash flows to sellers.

(C) **Bargaining power of suppliers** Suppliers with strong bargaining power can demand higher prices and earlier payments, yielding adverse effects on profits and cash flows to buyers.

(D) **Threat of substitution** As the number of product substitutes increases, sellers have less power to raise prices and/or pass on costs to buyers; accordingly, threat of substitution places downward pressure on profits of sellers.

(E) **Threat of entry** New market entrants increase competition; to mitigate that threat, companies expend monies on activities such as new technologies, promotion, and human development to erect *barriers to entry* and to create *economies of scale*.

The relative strength of companies within their industries, and vis-à-vis suppliers and customers, is an important determinant of both their profitability and the structure of their balance sheets. As competition intensifies, profitability likely declines, and the amount of assets companies need to carry on their balance sheet likely increases in an effort to generate more profit. Such changes are revealed in the income statement and the balance sheet.

SWOT Analysis of the Business Environment

As an alternative to Porter-based competitive analysis, some prefer a SWOT analysis of a company. SWOT is an acronym that stands for strengths, weaknesses, opportunities and threats. This analysis can be applied to almost any organization. This approach is universally applicable and easy to apply, and it can be graphically portrayed as follows:

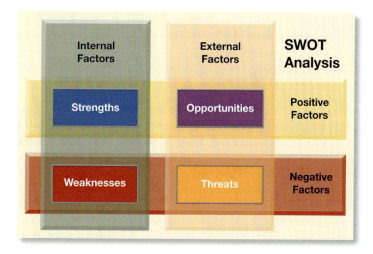

SWOT analysis has two parts.

- Looking internally, we review a company's strengths and weaknesses, while for external purposes, we review the opportunities of and threats to the company. SWOT analysis tries to understand particular strengths and weaknesses that give rise to specific opportunities (to exploit the strengths) and threats (caused by the weaknesses).

- When used as part of an overall strategic analysis, SWOT can provide a good review of strategic options.

However, SWOT is sometimes criticized as too subjective. Two individuals can identify entirely different factors from a SWOT analysis of the same company. This is partly because SWOT is intuitive and allows varying opinions on the relevant factors.

Following is an example of a SWOT analysis on Under Armour.

Competitive Analysis »

Under Armour, Inc. (UA)–Financial and Strategic SWOT Analysis

Strengths	Weaknesses
Brand Line	Product Recalls
Diversified Distribution Channels	
Opportunities	**Threats**
Strong Growth in Footwear Market	Intense Competition
Strategic Acquisition	Rising Counterfeit Goods Market

Analyzing Competitive Advantage

The goal of our analysis is to identify sustainable operating income and cash flow. This is true whether our analysis is focused on valuation of equity securities as a current or prospective investor or on a company's ability to repay its debt as a current or prospective creditor or on trying to grow company value as part of management. This analysis is much deeper than merely eliminating transitory (nonrecurring) items from financial statements. It is an exploration of the following two lines of thought.

1. Does the company have a competitive advantage, and, if so, what factors explain it? Further, is the competitive advantage sustainable?

2. If the company has no competitive advantage, does its management have a plan to develop a sustainable competitive advantage that can be implemented in an acceptable period of time and with a reasonable amount of investment?

Answers to these questions impact forecasts of the company's future performance.

Patents and other protections of intellectual property create **barriers to entry** that allow a company to achieve a competitive advantage and charge higher prices for their products or services and thereby earn excess returns. These legal barriers typically have a finite life, however, and a company must maintain a pipeline of innovations to replace intellectual property that loses patent protection.

Product differentiation also allows companies to earn excess returns. Typically, differentiation is achieved from technological innovation that produces products and services with attributes valued by customers and not easily replicated by competitors. Differentiation along the dimensions of product design, marketing, distribution, and after-sale customer support are examples. Such differentiation has costs such as research and development, advertising, and other marketing expenses.

Another approach to achieve excess returns is to become a **cost leader**. Cost leadership can result from a number of factors, including access to low-cost raw materials or labor (while maintaining quality), manufacturing or service efficiency in the form of cost-efficient processes and manufacturing scale efficiencies, greater bargaining power with suppliers, sophisticated IT systems that permit timely collection of key information, and other avenues.

In the absence of a competitive advantage, our analysis focuses on the likelihood that a company develops such an advantage. Management often discusses strategy with stockholders and equity analysts, which are recorded in conference calls that are readily available or reported in the financial press. In the case of a turnaround situation, our focus is on viability of the plan; that is, can it be achieved at an acceptable cost given the current state of the industry? Moreover, our focus is long term. Companies can often achieve short-term gains at long-term cost, such as by selling profitable segments. Such actions do not create long-term value.

Creating a sustainable competitive advantage that yields excess returns is difficult, and we are wary of forecasted excess returns for an extended period. Through a critical and thorough investigation of financial statements, its footnotes, the MD&A, and all publicly available information, we can identify drivers of a company's competitive advantage. We then test the sustainability and validity of those drivers. This is an important step in assessing competitive advantage.

Review 1-5 LO5

Required

1. Match each of the following statements *a* through *f* with the category to which it relates.

    I. Analyzing the competitive environment

    II. SWOT analysis of the business environment

    III. Analyzing competitive advantage

_____ *a.* Internal factors include a company's strengths and weaknesses.

_____ *b.* Buyers with strong bargaining power can extract price concessions and demand a higher level of service and delayed payment terms; this force reduces both profits and operating cash flows to sellers.

_____ *c.* The goal of our analysis is to identify sustainable operating income and cash flow.

_____ *d.* New market entrants increase competition; to mitigate that threat, companies expend monies on activities such as new technologies, promotion, and human development to erect barriers to entry and to create economies of scale.

_____ *e.* External factors include opportunities and threats.

_____ *f.* If the company has no competitive advantage, does its management have a plan to develop a sustainable competitive advantage that can be implemented in an acceptable period of time and with a reasonable amount of investment?

continued

2. Consider "Industry Competition," one of Porter's Five Forces. Who are Under Armour's three closest competitors? To answer this, use an online investment site such as Yahoo! Finance.
3. Does Under Armour have a competitive advantage? If so, what might explain that advantage?
4. For each competitor, determine total assets, revenue, and net income. Compute 2015 ROA and the two components for PM and AT. Do the ratios support your answer to part 2? (*Hint:* adidas AG has the ticker symbol ADS.DE)

Solution on p. 1-48.

Book Road Map

The book can be broken into four parts—see figure below.

- **Part 1** consists of Modules 1, 2, and 3 and offers an introduction of accounting fundamentals and the business environment.
- **Part 2** consists of Module 4, which introduces analysis of financial statements. Analysis of financial statements is aided by an understanding of how those statements are prepared.
- **Part 3**, which consists of Modules 5 through 11, describes the accounting for assets, liabilities, and equity; this includes accounting for cash flows.
- **Part 4** consists of Modules 12 and 13, which explain the forecasting of financial statements and the valuation of equity. Appendix C is a comprehensive case, which applies many of the analysis tools introduced in this book.

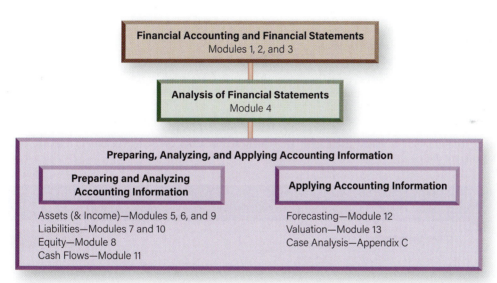

Global Accounting

As we discussed earlier, the United States is among only a few economically developed countries that do not use IFRS. While laws and enforcement mechanisms vary across countries, the demand and supply of accounting information are governed by global economic forces. Thus, it is not surprising that IFRS and U.S. GAAP both prescribe the same set of financial statements. While account titles and note details differ, the underlying principles are the same. That is, U.S. GAAP and IFRS both capture, aggregate, summarize, and report economic activities on an accrual basis.

Given the global economy and liquid transnational capital markets, along with the fact that many non-U.S. companies file IFRS financial statements with the SEC, it is critical that we be

Global Accounting *sections summarize notable difference between IFRS and U.S. GAAP for topics covered in the module.*

conversant with both U.S. GAAP and IFRS. For this purpose, the final section of each module includes a summary of notable differences between these two systems of accounting for topics covered in that module. Also, each module has assignments that examine IFRS companies and their financial statements. By using a wide array of financial information, we will speak the language of accounting in at least two dialects.

Appendix 1A: Accessing SEC Filings

LO6 Access reports filed with the SEC.

As noted in the chapter, all publicly traded companies are required to file various reports with the SEC, two of which are the 10-Q (quarterly financial statements) and the 10-K (annual financial statements). Following is a brief tutorial to access these electronic filings. The SEC's website is **https://www.sec.gov/edgar/searchedgar/ companysearch.html**.

1. In the **Company name** box, type in the name of the company we are looking for. In this case, we are searching for Under Armour. Then click search.

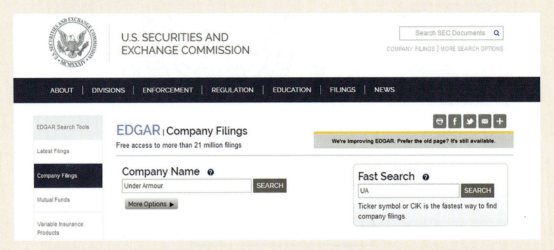

2. Enter the form number under "filing type" we want to access. Click the Search button. In this case, we are looking for the 10-K.

3. Click on the document link for the year we want to access. The filing date listed (2016-02-22 for Under Armour) is about 60 days after the fiscal year end.

4. Exhibits relating to Under Armour's 10-K filing appear; click on the 10-K document.

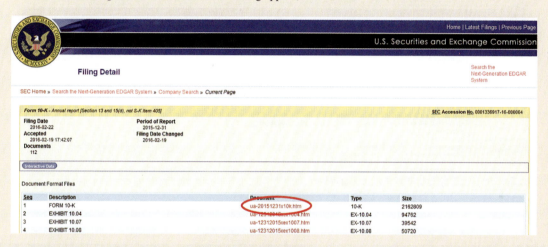

5. The Under Armour 10-K will open; the file is searchable.

6. An alternative is to download an Excel file of the financial statement data. From the Search Results page, click on "Interactive Data."

7. Click on "View Excel Document" to view or download as a spreadsheet. Or, to quickly view the financial statements or notes, use the links in the yellow box on the left.

Appendix 1B: Accounting Principles and Governance

eLectures LO7
MBC Describe the accounting principles and regulations that frame financial statements.

Financial Accounting Environment

Information in financial statements is crucial to valuing a company's debt and equity securities. Financial statement information can affect the price the market is willing to pay for the company's equity securities and interest rates attached to its debt securities.

The importance of financial statements means their reliability is paramount. This includes the crucial role of ethics. To the extent that financial performance and condition are accurately communicated to business decision makers, debt and equity securities are more accurately priced. When securities are mispriced, resources can be inefficiently allocated both within and across economies. Accurate, reliable financial statements are also important for the effective functioning of many other markets, such as labor, input, and output markets.

To illustrate, recall the consequences of a breakdown in the integrity of the financial accounting system at Enron. Once it became clear Enron had not faithfully and accurately reported its financial condition and performance, the market became unwilling to purchase Enron's securities. The value of its debt and equity securities dropped precipitously, and the company was unable to obtain cash needed for operating activities. Within months of the disclosure of its financial accounting irregularities, Enron, with revenues of more than $100 billion and total company value of more than $60 billion, the fifth largest U.S. company, was bankrupt!

Further historical evidence of the importance of financial accounting is provided by the Great Depression of the twentieth century. This depression was caused, in part, by the failure of companies to faithfully report their financial condition and performance.

Oversight of Financial Accounting

The stock market crash of 1929 and the ensuing Great Depression led Congress to pass the 1933 Securities Act. This act had two main objectives: (1) to require disclosure of financial and other information about securities being offered for public sale; and (2) to prohibit deceit, misrepresentations, and other fraud in the sale of securities. This act also required that companies register all securities proposed for public sale and disclose information about the securities being offered, including information about company financial condition and performance. This act became and remains a foundation for contemporary financial reporting.

Congress also passed the 1934 Securities Exchange Act, which created the **Securities and Exchange Commission** (SEC) and gave it broad powers to regulate the issuance and trading of securities. The act also provides that companies with more than $10 million in assets and whose securities are held by more than 500 owners must file annual and other periodic reports, including financial statements that are available for download from the SEC's database (**www.sec.gov**).

The SEC has ultimate authority over U.S. financial reporting, including setting accounting standards for preparing financial statements. Since 1939, however, the SEC has looked primarily to the private sector to set accounting standards. One such private sector organization is the American Institute of Certified Public Accountants (AICPA), whose two committees, the Committee on Accounting Procedure (1939–59) and the Accounting Principles Board (1959–73), authored the initial body of accounting standards.

The **Financial Accounting Standards Board (FASB)** sets U.S. financial accounting standards. The FASB is an independent body overseen by a foundation whose members include public accounting firms, investment managers, academics, and corporate managers. The FASB has published about 200 accounting standards governing the preparation of financial reports. This is in addition to more than 40 standards that were written by predecessor organizations to the FASB, numerous bulletins and interpretations, Emerging Issues Task Force (EITF) statements, AICPA statements of position (SOP), and direct SEC guidance, along with speeches made by high-ranking SEC personnel, all of which form the body of accounting standards governing financial statements. Collectively, these pronouncements, rules, and guidance create what is called **Generally Accepted Accounting Principles (GAAP)**. In 2009, the FASB rolled out the Accounting Standards Codification, a means to simplifying user access to all authoritative U.S. GAAP. The Codification changed the structure of how GAAP are organized, from a standards-based model (with thousands of individual standards) to a topically based model (with roughly 90 topics). The Codification streamlined GAAP research for auditors, analysts, company managers, and students alike.

The standard-setting process is arduous, often lasting up to a decade and involving extensive comment by the public, public officials, accountants, academics, investors, analysts, and corporate preparers of financial reports. The reason for this involved process is that amendments to existing standards or the creation of new standards affect the reported financial performance and condition of companies. Consequently, given the widespread impact of financial accounting, there are considerable economic consequences as a result of accounting changes. To influence the standard-setting process, special interest groups often lobby members of Congress to pressure the SEC and, ultimately, the FASB, on issues about which constituents feel strongly.

Audits and Corporate Governance

Even though key executives must personally attest to the completeness and accuracy of company financial statements, markets demand further assurances from outside parties to achieve the level of confidence necessary to warrant investment, credit, and other business decisions. To that end, companies engage external auditors to provide an opinion about financial statements. Further, companies implement a system of checks and balances that monitor managers' actions, which is called *corporate governance*.

Audit Report

Financial statements for each publicly traded company must be audited by an independent audit firm. There are a number of large auditing firms that are authorized by the SEC to provide auditing services for companies that issue securities to the public: PwC, EY, KPMG, Deloitte, BDO, and RSM, to name a few. These firms provide opinions about financial statements for the large majority of publicly traded U.S. companies. A company's board of directors hires the auditors to review and express an opinion on its financial statements. The audit opinion expressed by PricewaterhouseCoopers, LLP, on the financial statements of Under Armour is reproduced in Exhibit 1.10.

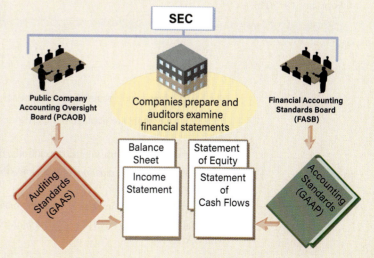

Exhibit 1.10 ▪ **Audit Report for Under Armour**

Report of Independent Registered Public Accounting Firm

To the Board of Directors and Stockholders of Under Armour Inc.

In our opinion, the accompanying consolidated financial statements listed in the index appearing under Item 15(a)(1) present fairly, in all material respects, the financial position of Under Armour Inc. and its subsidiaries at December 31, 2015 and 2014, and the results of their operations and their cash flows for each of the three years in the period ended December 31, 2015, in conformity with accounting principles generally accepted in the United States of America. In addition, in our opinion, the financial statement schedule listed in the index appearing under Item 15(a)(2) presents fairly, in all material respects, the information set forth therein when read in conjunction with the related consolidated financial statements. Also in our opinion, the Company maintained, in all material respects, effective internal control over financial reporting as of December 31, 2015, based on criteria established in *Internal Control—Integrated Framework* issued by the Committee of Sponsoring Organizations of the Treadway Commission (COSO) in 2013. The Company's management is responsible for these financial statements and financial statement schedule, for maintaining effective internal control over financial reporting and for its assessment of the effectiveness of internal control over financial reporting, included in the accompanying Report of Management on Internal Control over Financial Reporting. Our responsibility is to express opinions on these financial statements, on the financial statement schedule, and on the Company's internal control over financial reporting based on our integrated audits. We conducted our audits in accordance with the standards of the Public Company Accounting Oversight Board (United States). Those standards require that we plan and perform the audits to obtain reasonable assurance about whether the financial statements are free of material misstatement and whether effective internal control over financial reporting was maintained in all material respects. Our audits of the financial statements included examining, on a test basis, evidence supporting the amounts and disclosures in the financial statements, assessing the accounting principles used and significant estimates made by management, and evaluating the overall financial statement presentation. Our audit of internal control over financial reporting included obtaining an understanding of internal control over financial reporting, assessing the risk that a material weakness exists, and testing and evaluating the design and operating effectiveness of internal control based on the assessed risk. Our audits also included performing such other procedures as we considered necessary in the circumstances. We believe that our audits provide a reasonable basis for our opinions.

As discussed in Note 2 to the consolidated financial statements, the Company changed the manner in which it accounts for the classification of deferred income tax balances in 2015.

A company's internal control over financial reporting is a process designed to provide reasonable assurance regarding the reliability of financial reporting and the preparation of financial statements for external purposes in accordance with generally accepted accounting principles. A company's internal control over financial reporting includes those policies and procedures that (i) pertain to the maintenance of records that, in reasonable detail, accurately and fairly reflect the transactions and dispositions of the assets of the company; (ii) provide reasonable assurance that transactions are recorded as necessary to permit preparation of financial statements in accordance with generally accepted accounting principles, and that receipts and expenditures of the company are being made only in accordance with authorizations of management and directors of the company; and (iii) provide reasonable assurance regarding prevention or timely detection of unauthorized acquisition, use, or disposition of the company's assets that could have a material effect on the financial statements.

Because of its inherent limitations, internal control over financial reporting may not prevent or detect misstatements. Also, projections of any evaluation of effectiveness to future periods are subject to the risk that controls may become inadequate because of changes in conditions, or that the degree of compliance with the policies or procedures may deteriorate.

/s/ PricewaterhouseCoopers LLP

Baltimore, Maryland
February 19, 2016

The basic "clean" audit report is consistent across companies and includes these assertions.

- Financial statements are management's responsibility. Auditor responsibility is to express an *opinion* on those statements.
- Auditing involves a sampling of transactions, not investigation of each transaction.
- Audit opinion provides *reasonable assurance* the statements are free of *material* misstatements, not a guarantee.
- Auditors review accounting policies used by management and the estimates used in preparing the statements.
- Financial statements *present fairly, in all material respects* a company's financial condition, in conformity with GAAP.

If the auditor cannot make all of these assertions, the auditor cannot issue a clean opinion. Instead, the auditor issues a "qualified" opinion and states the reasons a clean opinion cannot be issued. Financial report readers should scrutinize with care both the qualified audit opinion and the financial statements themselves.

The audit opinion is not based on a test of each transaction. Instead, auditors usually develop statistical samples to make inferences about the larger set of transactions. The audit report is not a guarantee that no misstatements exist. Auditors only provide reasonable assurance that the statements are free of material misstatements. Their use of the word *reasonable* is deliberate, as they do not want to be held to an absolute standard should problems be subsequently uncovered. The word *material* is used in the sense that an item must be of sufficient magnitude to change the perceptions or decisions of the financial statement user (such as a decision to purchase stock or extend credit).

The requirement of auditor independence is the cornerstone of effective auditing and is subject to debate because the company pays the auditor's fees. Regulators have questioned the perceived lack of independence of auditing firms and the degree to which declining independence compromises the ability of auditing firms to challenge a client's dubious accounting.

SOX contains several provisions designed to encourage auditor independence.

1. It established the **Public Company Accounting Oversight Board** (PCAOB) to oversee the development of audit standards and to monitor the effectiveness of auditors.

2. It prohibits auditors from offering certain types of consulting services, and requires audit partners to rotate clients every five years.

3. It requires audit committees to consist of independent members.

Audit Committee

Law requires each publicly traded company to have a board of directors where stockholders elect each director. This board represents the company owners and oversees management. The board also hires the company's executive management and regularly reviews company operations.

The board of directors usually establishes several subcommittees to focus on particular governance tasks, such as compensation, strategic plans, and financial management. Governance committees are commonplace. One of these, the audit committee, oversees the financial accounting system. Exhibit 1.11 illustrates a typical organization of a company's governance structure.

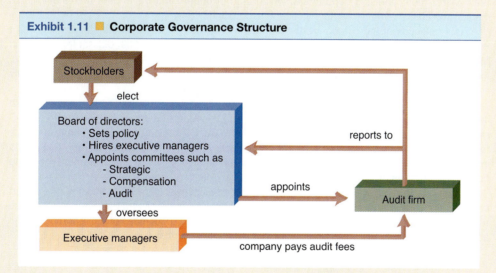

Exhibit 1.11 ◼ Corporate Governance Structure

The audit committee must consist solely of outside directors, and cannot include the CEO. As part of its oversight of the financial accounting system, the audit committee focuses on **internal controls**, which are the policies and procedures used to protect assets, ensure reliable accounting, promote efficient operations, and urge adherence to company policies.

Regulatory and Legal Environment

The regulatory and legal environment provides further assurance financial statements are complete and accurate.

SEC Enforcement Actions

Companies whose securities are issued to the public must file reports with the SEC (see **www.sec.gov**). One of these reports is the 10-K, which includes the annual financial statements (quarterly statements are filed on report 10-Q). The 10-K report provides more information than the company's glossy annual report, which is partly a marketing document (although the basic financial statements are identical). We prefer to use the 10-K because of its additional information.

The SEC critically reviews all the financial reports companies submit. If irregularities are found, the SEC has the authority to bring enforcement actions against companies it believes are misrepresenting their financial condition (remember the phrase in the audit opinion that requires companies to "present fairly, in all material respects, the financial position of . . ."). One such action was brought against **Stein Mart Inc.** and its executives. Following are excerpts from the SEC's press release 2015-200.

SEC Charges Retailer for Improper Valuation and Inadequate Internal Accounting Controls

Washington D.C., Sept. 22, 2015—The Securities and Exchange Commission today charged Stein Mart Inc. for materially misstating its pre-tax income due to improper valuation of inventory subject to price discounts and for having inadequate internal accounting controls.

An SEC investigation found that the Jacksonville, Florida-based retailer often offered its merchandise to customers at retail price reductions referred to as Perm POS markdowns and that merchandise subject to such a markdown never reverted back to its original retail price. Stein Mart reduced the value of inventory subject to these markdowns at the time the item was sold rather than immediately at the time the markdown was applied. As a result, Stein Mart materially misstated its pre-tax income in certain quarterly public filings with the SEC, including an overstatement of almost 30 percent in the first quarter of 2012.

Stein Mart agreed to settle the SEC's charges by paying an $800,000 penalty.

According to the SEC's order instituting a settled administrative proceeding, Stein Mart's internal accounting controls over Perm POS markdowns were inadequate. For example—until at least the middle of 2011–the decision to characterize a markdown as Perm POS resided solely with Stein Mart's merchandising department, which did not understand the impact that Stein Mart's markdowns could have on inventory valuation accounting.

As a reflection of the company's inadequate internal accounting controls surrounding Perm POS markdowns, Stein Mart's chief financial officer, who was hired in 2009, did not learn of Stein Mart's treatment of Perm POS markdowns until the summer of 2011. After consulting with others, the CFO concluded that Stein Mart's Perm POS accounting was acceptable under U.S. generally accepted accounting practices, or GAAP.

In the fall of 2012, Stein Mart raised its accounting treatment of Perm POS markdowns with its external auditor, and the external auditor informed Stein Mart that its accounting for Perm POS markdowns was not acceptable under GAAP. In May 2013, Stein Mart restated its financial results for the first quarter of 2012, all reporting periods in fiscal year 2011, and its annual reporting period in fiscal year 2010. According to the SEC's order, Stein Mart also had inadequate internal accounting controls in the areas of software assets, credit card liabilities, and other inventory-related issues.

In agreeing to settle the charges without admitting or denying the SEC's findings, Stein Mart consented to the SEC's order imposing an $800,000 penalty and requiring the company to cease and desist from committing or causing any violations or any future violations of the reporting, books and records, and internal controls provisions of the federal securities laws.

Courts

Courts provide remedies to individuals and companies that suffer damages as a result of material misstatements in financial statements. Typical court actions involve stockholders who sue the company and its auditors, alleging the company disclosed, and the auditors attested to, false and misleading financial statements. Stockholder lawsuits are chronically in the news, although the number of such suits has declined in recent years. Stanford Law School's Securities Class Action Clearinghouse commented, "Two factors are likely responsible for the decline. First, lawsuits arising from the dramatic boom and bust of U.S. equities in the late 1990s and early 2000s are now largely behind us. Second, improved corporate governance in the wake of the **Enron** and **WorldCom** frauds likely reduced the actual incidence of fraud." Nevertheless, courts continue to wield considerable power.

Business Insight ■ Warren Buffett on Audit Committees

"Audit committees can't audit. Only a company's outside auditor can determine whether the earnings that a management purports to have made are suspect. Reforms that ignore this reality and that instead focus on the structure and charter of the audit committee will accomplish little. As we've discussed, far too many managers have fudged their company's numbers in recent years, using both accounting and operational techniques that are typically legal but that nevertheless materially mislead investors. Frequently, auditors knew about these deceptions. Too often, however, they remained silent. The key job of the audit committee is simply to get the auditors to divulge what they know. To do this job, the committee must make sure that the auditors worry more about misleading its members than about offending management. In recent years auditors have not felt that way. They have instead generally viewed the CEO, rather than the shareholders or directors, as their client. That has been a natural result of day-to-day working relationships and also of the auditors' understanding that, no matter what the book says, the CEO and CFO pay their fees and determine whether they are retained for both auditing and other work. The rules that have been recently instituted won't materially change this reality. What will break this cozy relationship is audit committees unequivocally putting auditors on the spot, making them understand they will become liable for major monetary penalties if they don't come forth with what they know or suspect."

—Warren Buffett, Berkshire Hathaway Annual Report

Business Insights offer recent examples from the business news and popular press.

Guidance Answers

You Are the Product Manager

Pg. 1-17 As a manager, you must balance two conflicting objectives—namely, mandatory disclosure requirements and your company's need to protect its competitive advantages. You must comply with all minimum required disclosure rules. The extent to which you offer additional disclosures depends on the sensitivity of the information; that is, how beneficial it is to your existing and potential competitors. Another consideration is how the information disclosed will impact your existing and potential investors. Disclosures such as these can be beneficial in that they inform investors and others about your company's successful investments. Still, there are many stakeholders impacted by your disclosure decision, and each must be given due consideration.

You Are the Chief Financial Officer

Pg. 1-22 Financial performance is often measured by ROA, which can be disaggregated into the profit margin (profit after tax/sales) and AT (sales/average assets). This disaggregation might lead you to review factors affecting profitability (gross margins and expense control) and to assess how effectively your company is utilizing its assets (the turnover rates). Finding ways to increase profitability for a given level of investment or to reduce the amount of invested capital while not adversely impacting profitability contributes to improved financial performance.

Superscript $^{A(B)}$ denotes assignments based on Appendix 1A (1B).

Questions

Q1-1. Firms engage in four basic types of activities. List the activities. Describe how financial statements can provide useful information for each activity. How can subsequent financial statements be used to evaluate the success of each of the activities?

Q1-2. The accounting equation (Assets = Liabilities + Equity) is a fundamental business concept. Explain what this equation reveals about a company's sources and uses of funds and the claims on company resources.

Q1-3. Companies prepare four primary financial statements. What are those financial statements, and what information is typically conveyed by each?

Q1-4. Does a balance sheet report on a period of time or at a point in time? Explain the information conveyed in the balance sheet.

Q1-5. Does an income statement report on a period of time or at a point in time? Explain the information conveyed in the income statement.

Q1-6. Does a statement of cash flows report on a period of time or at a point in time? Explain the information and activities conveyed in the statement of cash flows.

Q1-7. Explain how a company's four primary financial statements are linked.

Q1-8. Financial statements are used by several interested stakeholders. List three or more potential external users of financial statements. Explain how each constituent on your list might use financial statement information in their decision-making process.

Q1-9. What ethical issues might managers face in dealing with confidential information?

Q1-10 What are the five important forces that confront the company and determine its competitive intensity?

Q1-11 What are the components of a SWOT analysis? For each component, indicate whether it is an internal or external environmental factor.

Procter & Gamble (PG)   **Q1-12.ᴬ** Access the 2015 10-K for **Procter & Gamble** at the SEC's database of financial reports (**www.sec. gov**). Who is P&G's auditor? What specific language does the auditor use in expressing its opinion, and what responsibilities does it assume?

Q1-13. Business decision makers external to the company increasingly demand more financial information from the company. Discuss the reasons why companies have traditionally opposed the efforts of regulatory agencies like the SEC to require more disclosure.

Q1-14.ᴮ What are generally accepted accounting principles, and what organizations presently establish them?

Enron   **Q1-15.ᴮ** Corporate governance has received considerable attention since the collapse of **Enron** and other accounting-related scandals. What is meant by corporate governance? What are the primary means by which sound corporate governance is achieved?

Q1-16.ᴮ What is the primary function of the auditor? In your own words, describe what an audit opinion says.

Q1-17. Describe a decision that requires financial statement information, other than a stock investment decision. How is financial statement information useful in making this decision?

Q1-18. Users of financial statement information are vitally concerned with the company's strategic direction. Despite their understanding of this need for information, companies are reluctant to supply it. Why? In particular, what costs are companies concerned about?

Q1-19. One of Warren Buffett's acquisition criteria is to invest in businesses "earning good return on equity." The ROE formula uses both net income and stockholders' equity. Why is it important to relate net income to stockholders' equity? Why isn't it sufficient to merely concentrate on companies with the highest net income?

Q1-20. One of Buffett's acquisition criteria is to invest in businesses "earning good return on equity while employing little or no debt." Why is Buffett concerned about debt?

Assignments with the ⬤ logo in the margin are available in ᵐʸBusinessCourse.
See the Preface of the book for details.

Mini Exercises

LO1
AT&T (T)

M1-21. **Understanding How the Four Business Activities Are Related**
In its January 2016 press release, **AT&T** revealed that CAPEX for fiscal 2016 (capital expenditures for additional property, plant and equipment) was expected to be in the $22 billion range. How will this planned expenditure affect the other three types of business activities in 2016?

LO2

M1-22. **Understanding What Information Financial Statement Users Demand**
Match each of the financial statement users listed to the question they are most likely to ask.

Financial Statement User	Questions
_____ A. Current shareholders	1. What is the expected net income for next quarter?
_____ B. Company CEO	2. Will the company have enough cash to pay dividends?
_____ C. Banker	3. Has the company paid for inventory purchases promptly in the past?
_____ D. Equity analyst	4. Will there be sufficient profits and cash flow to pay bonuses?
_____ E. Supplier	5. Will the company have enough cash to repay its loans?

M1-23. Relating Financing and Investing Activities

In a recent year, the total assets of **Microsoft Corporation** equal $193,694 million, and its equity is $71,997 million.

LO3
Microsoft (MSFT)

LOs *link assignments to the Learning Objectives of each module.*

Required

a. What is the amount of its liabilities?
b. Does Microsoft receive more financing from its owners or nonowners?
c. What percentage of financing is provided by Microsoft's owners?

M1-24. Relating Financing and Investing Activities

In a recent year, the total assets of **Best Buy** equal $13,519 million, and its liabilities equal $9,141 million.

LO3
Best Buy (BBY)

Required

a. What is the amount of Best Buy's equity?
b. Does Best Buy receive more financing from its owners or nonowners?
c. What percentage of financing is provided by its owners?

M1-25. Applying the Accounting Equation and Computing Financing Proportions

Use the accounting equation to compute the missing financial amounts (a), (b), and (c). Which of these companies is more owner-financed? Which of these companies is more nonowner-financed? Discuss why the proportion of owner financing might differ across these three businesses.

LO3

$ millions	Assets	=	Liabilities	+	Equity
Hewlett-Packard.	$106,882	=	$78,731	+	$ (a)
General Mills	$ 21,712	=	$ (b)	+	$ 5,307
Target	$ (c)	=	$27,305	+	$12,957

Hewlett-Packard (HPQ)
General Mills (GIS)
Target (TGT)

M1-26. Identifying Key Numbers from Financial Statements

Access the September 25, 2015, 10-K for **Starbucks Corporation** at the SEC's database for financial reports (**www.sec.gov**).

LO3, 6
Starbucks (SBUX)

Required

a. What did Starbucks report for total assets, liabilities, and equity at September 25, 2015? Confirm the accounting equation holds.
b. What percent of Starbucks' assets is financed by nonowners?

M1-27. Verifying Linkages Between Financial Statements

Access the 2015 10-K for **DuPont** at the SEC's database of financial reports (**www.sec.gov**). Using its December 31, 2015, consolidated statement of stockholders' equity, prepare a table to reconcile the opening and ending balances of its retained (reinvested) earnings for 2015 by showing the activity in the account during the year.

LO3, 6
E. I. DuPont de Nemours (DD)

M1-28. Identifying Financial Statement Line Items and Accounts

Several line items and account titles are listed below. For each, indicate in which of the following financial statement(s) we would likely find the item or account: income statement (IS), balance sheet (BS), statement of stockholders' equity (SE), or statement of cash flows (SCF).

LO3

a. Cash asset	*d.* Contributed capital	*g.* Cash inflow for stock issued
b. Expenses	*e.* Cash outflow for capital expenditures	*h.* Cash outflow for dividends
c. Noncash assets	*f.* Retained earnings	*i.* Net income

M1-29. Identifying Ethical Issues and Accounting Choices

Assume you are a technology services provider and you must decide on whether to record revenue from the installation of computer software for one of your clients. Your contract calls for acceptance of the software by the client within six months of installation. According to the contract, you will be paid only when the client "accepts" the installation. Although you have not yet received your client's formal acceptance, you are confident it is forthcoming. Failure to record these revenues will cause your company to miss Wall Street's earnings estimates. What stakeholders will be affected by your decision, and how might they be affected?

LO7

LO5   **M1-30.   Assessing the Competitive Environment**

For each of the following companies, briefly explain what type of competitive advantage(s) they have, if any. Select from: barriers to entry, product differentiation, cost leader, or buyer power.

a. Apple	*c.* Pfizer	*e.* American Airlines	*g.* McDonald's
b. Walmart	*d.* Uber	*f.* UPS	

LO4, 6   **M1-31.   Accessing SEC reports and Calculating Ratios**

Pfizer (PFE)

Merck (MRK)

Access the 2015 financial reports at the SEC website for **Pfizer Inc.** and **Merck & Co.**, two close competitors in the pharmaceutical industry.

a. Use data from the companies' balance sheets and income statements to complete the following table.

$ millions	Pfizer	Merck
Total assets..............................	_____	_____
Revenue	_____	_____
Net income..............................	_____	_____

b. Compute the ROA and the components for profit margin and asset turnover for each company. How do the ratios compare?

LO7   **M1-32.   Understanding Internal Controls and Their Importance**

SOX legislation requires companies to report on the effectiveness of their internal controls. The SEC administers SOX, and defines internal controls as follows.

> A process designed by, or under the supervision of, the registrant's principal executive and principal financial officers . . . to provide reasonable assurance regarding the reliability of financial reporting and the preparation of financial statements for external purposes in accordance with generally accepted accounting principles.

Why would Congress believe internal controls are such an important area to monitor and report on?

Exercises

LO3   **E1-33.   Composition of Accounts on the Balance Sheet**

Target (TGT)

Ticker symbols are provided for companies so one can easily obtain additional information.

Answer the following questions about the **Target** balance sheet.

a. Briefly describe the types of assets Target is likely to include in its inventory.
b. What kinds of assets would Target likely include in its property and equipment?
c. Target reports about two-thirds of its total assets as long term. Given Target's business model, why do we see it report a relatively high proportion of long-term assets?

LO3   **E1-34.   Applying the Accounting Equation and Assessing Financial Statement Linkages**

Intel (INTC)

JetBlue (JBLU)

Answer the following questions. (*Hint*: Apply the accounting equation.)

a. **Intel** had assets equal to $103,065 million and liabilities equal to $41,980 million for a recent year-end. What was Intel's total equity at year-end? Why would we expect a company like Intel to report a relatively high proportion of equity vis-à-vis liabilities?
b. At the beginning of a recent year, **JetBlue**'s assets were $7,839 million, and its equity was $2,529 million. During the year, assets increased $821 million, and liabilities increased $140 million. What was JetBlue's equity at the end of the year?
c. What balance sheet account provides the link between the balance sheet and the income statement? Briefly describe how this linkage works.

LO2   **E1-35.   Specifying Financial Information Users and Uses**

Financial statements have a wide audience of interested stakeholders. Identify two or more financial statement users who are external to the company. For each user on your list, specify two questions that could be addressed with financial statement information.

E1-36. Applying Financial Statement Relations to Compute Dividends
Colgate-Palmolive reports the following dollar balances in its retained earnings account.

LO3
Colgate-Palmolive
(CL)

$ millions	2015	2014
Retained earnings	$18,861	$18,832

During 2015, Colgate-Palmolive reported net income of $1,384 million.

Required
a. What amount of dividends, if any, did Colgate-Palmolive pay to its stockholders in 2015?
b. What percent of its net income did Colgate-Palmolive pay out as dividends in 2015?

E1-37. Computing and Interpreting Financial Statement Ratios
Following are selected ratios of Colgate-Palmolive for 2015 and 2014.

LO4
Colgate-Palmolive
(CL)

Return on Assets (ROA) Component	2015	2014
Profitability (Net income/Sales)	8.60%	12.60%
Productivity (Sales/Average assets)	1.36	1.27

a. Was the company profitable in 2015? What evidence do you have of this?
b. Is the change in productivity (asset turnover) a positive development? Explain.
c. Compute the company's ROA for 2015 (show computations).

E1-38. Computing Return on Assets and Applying the Accounting Equation
Nordstrom Inc. reports net income of $600 million for its fiscal year ended January 2016. At the beginning of that fiscal year, Nordstrom had $9,245 million in total assets. By fiscal year ended January 2016, total assets had decreased to $7,698 million. What is Nordstrom's ROA?

LO4
Nordstrom Inc. (JWN)

E1-39. Assessing the Role of Financial Statements in Society
Financial statement information plays an important role in modern society and business.

LO2

a. Identify two or more external stakeholders who are interested in a company's financial statements and what their particular interests are.
b. What are *generally accepted accounting principles*? What organizations have primary responsibility for the formulation of GAAP?
c. What role does financial statement information play in the allocation of society's financial resources?
d. What are three aspects of the accounting environment that can create ethical pressure on management?

E1-40. Computing Return on Equity
Starbucks reports net income for 2015 of $2,757.4 million. Its stockholders' equity is $5,272 million and $5,818 million for 2014 and 2015, respectively.

LO4
Starbucks (SBUX)

a. Compute its return on equity for 2015.
b. Starbucks repurchased over $1.4 billion of its common stock in 2015. How did this repurchase affect Starbucks' ROE?
c. Why do you think a company like Starbucks repurchases its own stock?

Problems

P1-41. Computing Return on Equity and Return on Assets
The following table contains financial statement information for Walmart Stores Inc.

LO4
Wal-Mart Stores Inc.
(WMT)

$ millions	Total Assets	Net Income	Sales	Equity
2015	$199,581	$14,694	$478,614	$80,546
2014	203,490	16,363	482,229	81,394
2013	204,751	16,022	473,076	76,255

Required

a. Compute the return on equity (ROE) for 2014 and 2015. What trend, if any, is evident? How does Walmart's ROE compare with the approximately 18.9% median ROE for companies in the Dow Jones Industrial average for 2015?

b. Compute the return on assets (ROA) for 2014 and 2015. What trends, if any, are evident? How does Walmart's ROA compare with the approximate 7.1% median ROA for companies in the Dow Jones Industrial average for 2015?

c. What factors might allow a company like Walmart to reap above-average returns?

LO3, 4

General Mills Inc. (GIS)

P1-42.   Formulating Financial Statements from Raw Data

Following is selected financial information from **General Mills Inc.** for its fiscal year ended May 29, 2016 ($ millions).

Revenue	$16,563.1	Cost of goods sold	$10,733.6
Cash from operating activities	2,629.8	Cash, ending year	763.7
Cash, beginning year	334.2	Total liabilities	16,405.2
Stockholders' equity	5,307.1	Cash from investing activities	93.4
Noncash assets	20,948.6	Total expenses (other than cost of	
Cash from financing activities*	(2,293.7)	goods sold)	4,092.7

* Cash from financing activities includes the effects of foreign exchange rate fluctuations.

Required

a. Prepare the income statement, the balance sheet, and the statement of cash flows for General Mills for the fiscal year ended May 29, 2016.

b. Does the negative amount for cash from financing activities concern us? Explain.

c. Using the statements prepared for part a, compute the following ratios (for this part only, use the year-end balance instead of the average for assets and stockholders' equity):
   i. Profit margin
   ii. Asset turnover
   iii. Return on assets
   iv. Return on equity

LO3, 4

Abercrombie & Fitch (ANF)

P1-43.   Formulating Financial Statements from Raw Data

Following is selected financial information from **Abercrombie & Fitch** for its fiscal year ended January 30, 2016 ($ thousands).

Noncash assets	$1,844,461	Cash from operating activities	$ 309,941
Cash from investing activities	(122,567)	Cash from financing activities*	(119,504)
Cash, ending year	588,578	Cost of goods sold	1,361,137
Revenue	3,518,680	Cash, beginning year	520,708
Total liabilities	1,137,317	Total expenses (other than cost	
Stockholders' equity	1,295,722	of goods sold)	2,118,984

* Cash from financing activities includes the effects of foreign exchange rate fluctuations.

Required

a. Prepare the income statement, the balance sheet, and the statement of cash flows for Abercrombie & Fitch for the fiscal year ended January 30, 2016.

b. Do the negative amounts for cash from investing activities and cash from financing activities concern us? Explain.

c. Using the statements prepared for part a, compute the following ratios (for this part only, use the year-end balance instead of the average for assets and stockholders' equity):
   i. Profit margin
   ii. Asset turnover
   iii. Return on assets
   iv. Return on equity

P1-44. **Formulating Financial Statements from Raw Data**

Following is selected financial information from **Cisco Systems Inc.** for the year ended July 30, 2016 ($ millions).

Cash, ending year	$ 7,631	Total liabilities	$ 58,067
Cash from operating activities	13,570	Cash from financing activities	(4,699)
Sales	49,247	Noncash assets	114,021
Stockholders' equity	63,585	Cash from investing activities	(8,117)
Cost of goods sold	18,287	Net income	10,739
Total expenses (other than cost of goods sold)	20,221	Cash, beginning year	6,877

Required

a. Prepare the income statement, the balance sheet, and the statement of cash flows for Cisco Systems for the fiscal year ended July 30, 2016.

b. Do the negative amounts for cash from investing activities and cash from financing activities concern us? Explain.

c. Using the statements prepared for part *a*, compute the following ratios (for this part only, use the year-end balance instead of the average for assets and stockholders' equity):

   i. Profit margin

  ii. Asset turnover

 iii. Return on assets

 iv. Return on equity

P1-45. **Formulating a Statement of Stockholders' Equity from Raw Data**

Crocker Corporation began calendar-year 2016 with stockholders' equity of $150,000, consisting of contributed capital of $120,000 and retained earnings of $30,000. During 2016, it issued additional stock for total cash proceeds of $30,000. It also reported $50,000 of net income and paid $25,000 as a cash dividend to stockholders.

Required

Prepare the 2016 statement of stockholders' equity for Crocker Corporation.

P1-46. **Formulating a Statement of Stockholders' Equity from Raw Data**

Winnebago Industries Inc. reports the following selected information in its 2016 Form 10-K ($ thousands).

Contributed capital, August 29, 2015	$ 57,906
Treasury stock, August 29, 2015	(420,610)
Retained earnings, August 29, 2015	585,941
Accumulated other comprehensive income, August 29, 2015	(2,274)

During fiscal year 2016, Winnebago reported the following.

1. Issuance of stock .... $ 699
2. Repurchase of stock 1,157
3. Net income 45,496
4. Cash dividends 10,891
5. Other comprehensive income (loss) 13,249

Required

Use this information to prepare the statement of stockholders' equity for Winnebago's fiscal year ended August 27, 2016.

LO4
Medtronic, plc (MDT)

P1-47. **Computing, Analyzing, and Interpreting Return on Equity and Return on Assets**

Following are summary financial statement data for **Medtronic, plc** for 2014 through 2016.

$ millions	2016	2015	2014
Sales.	$28,833	$ 20,261	$17,005
Net income.	3,538	2,675	3,065
Total assets.	99,782	106,685	37,943
Equity	52,063	53,230	19,443

Required

a. Compute the return on assets and return on equity for 2016 and 2015 (use average assets and average equity), together with the components of ROA (profit margin and asset turnover). What trends do we observe?

b. Which component appears to be driving the change in ROA over this time period?

c. Recompute the ROA and ROE for 2015 using year-end balances instead of averages. Use your results to explain why we typically use averages to compute ratios.

d. Medtronic repurchased a large amount of its common shares in 2016 at a cost of almost $2.83 billion. How did this repurchase affect its return on equity?

LO4
Nordstrom Inc. (JWN)

P1-48. **Computing, Analyzing, and Interpreting Return on Equity and Return on Assets**

Following are summary financial statement data for **Nordstrom Inc.** for fiscal years ended 2014 through 2016.

$ millions	2016	2015	2014
Sales.	$14,095	$13,110	$12,166
Net income.	600	720	734
Total assets.	7,698	9,245	8,574
Equity	871	2,440	2,080

Required

a. Compute return on assets and return on equity for fiscal years ended 2015 and 2016 (use average assets and average equity), together with the components of ROA (profit margin and asset turnover). What trends, if any, do we observe?

b. Which component, if any, appears to be driving the change in ROA over this time period?

LO4
Abercrombie & Fitch (ANF)
TJX Companies (TJX)

P1-49. **Comparing Abercrombie & Fitch and TJX Companies**

Following are selected financial statement data from **Abercrombie & Fitch** (ANF—upscale clothing retailer) and **TJX Companies** (TJX—value-priced clothing retailer, including TJ Maxx).

$ thousands	Company	Total Assets	Net Income	Sales
2015	TJX Companies Inc.	$10,988,750	—	—
2016	TJX Companies Inc.	11,499,482	$2,277,658	$30,944,938
2015	Abercrombie & Fitch	2,505,167	—	—
2016	Abercrombie & Fitch	2,443,039	35,576	3,518,680

Required

a. Compute the return on assets for both companies for the year ended 2016.

b. Disaggregate the ROAs for both companies into the profit margin and asset turnover.

c. What differences are observed? Evaluate these differences in light of the two companies' business models. Which company has better financial performance?

LO4
McDonald's (MCD)

P1-50. **Computing and Interpreting Return on Assets and Its Components**

McDonald's Corporation (MCD) reported the following balance sheet and income statement data for 2013 through 2015.

$ millions	Total Assets	Net Income	Sales
2013	$36,626.3	—	—
2014	34,227.4	$4,757.8	$18,169.3
2015	37,938.7	4,529.3	16,488.3

Required

a. What is MCD's return on assets for 2014 and 2015? Disaggregate MCD's ROA into its net profit margin and its asset turnover.

b. What factor is mainly responsible for the change in MCD's ROA over this period?

P1-51. **Disaggregating Return on Assets over Multiple Periods**

LO4

3M Company (MMM)

Following are selected financial statement data from **3M Company** for 2012 through 2015.

$ millions	Total Assets	Net Income	Sales
2012	$33,876	$4,444	$29,904
2013	33,550	4,659	30,871
2014	31,209	4,956	31,281
2015	32,718	4,833	30,274

Required

a. Compute **3M Company**'s return on assets for 2013 through 2015. Disaggregate the ROA into the profit margin and asset turnover for 2013 through 2015. What trends do we observe?

b. Which ROA component appears to be driving the trend observed in part *a*? Explain.

P1-52.[A] **Reading and Interpreting Audit Opinions**

LO7

Apple (AAPL)

Apple Inc.'s 2016 financial statements include the following audit report from **Ernst & Young LLP**.

> **Report of Ernst & Young LLP, Independent Registered Public Accounting Firm**
>
> The Board of Directors and Shareholders of Apple Inc.:
>
> We have audited the accompanying consolidated balance sheets of Apple Inc. as of September 24, 2016 and September 26, 2015, and the related consolidated statements of operations, comprehensive income, shareholders' equity and cash flows for each of the three years in the period ended September 24, 2016. These financial statements are the responsibility of the Company's management. Our responsibility is to express an opinion on these financial statements based on our audits.
>
> We conducted our audits in accordance with the standards of the Public Company Accounting Oversight Board (United States). Those standards require that we plan and perform the audit to obtain reasonable assurance about whether the financial statements are free of material misstatement. An audit includes examining, on a test basis, evidence supporting the amounts and disclosures in the financial statements. An audit also includes assessing the accounting principles used and significant estimates made by management, as well as evaluating the overall financial statement presentation. We believe that our audits provide a reasonable basis for our opinion.
>
> In our opinion, the financial statements referred to above present fairly, in all material respects, the consolidated financial position of Apple Inc. at September 24, 2016 and September 26, 2015, and the consolidated results of its operations and its cash flows for each of the three years in the period ended September 24, 2016, in conformity with U.S. generally accepted accounting principles.
>
> We also have audited, in accordance with the standards of the Public Company Accounting Oversight Board (United States), Apple Inc.'s internal control over financial reporting as of September 24, 2016, based on criteria established in *Internal Control – Integrated Framework* issued by the Committee of Sponsoring Organizations of the Treadway Commission (2013 framework) and our report dated October 26, 2016 expressed an unqualified opinion thereon.
>
> /s/ Ernst & Young LLP
> San Jose, California
> October 26, 2016

Required

a. To whom is the report addressed? Why?

b. In your own words, briefly describe the audit process. What steps do auditors take to determine whether a company's financial statements are free from material misstatement?

    c. What is the nature of Ernst & Young's opinion? What do you believe the word *fairly* means? Is Ernst & Young providing a guarantee to Apple's financial statement users?

    d. What other opinion is Ernst & Young rendering? Why is this opinion important?

LO7

Apple Inc. (AAPL)

P1-53.   **Reading and Interpreting CEO Certifications**

Following is the CEO certification required by the Sarbanes-Oxley Act and signed by **Apple** CEO Timothy D. Cook. Apple's Chief Financial Officer signed a similar form.

CERTIFICATIONS

I, Timothy D. Cook, certify that:

1. I have reviewed this annual report on Form 10-K of Apple Inc.;

2. Based on my knowledge, this report does not contain any untrue statement of a material fact or omit to state a material fact necessary to make the statements made, in light of the circumstances under which such statements were made, not misleading with respect to the period covered by this report;

3. Based on my knowledge, the financial statements, and other financial information included in this report, fairly present in all material respects the financial condition, results of operations and cash flows of the Registrant as of, and for, the periods presented in this report;

4. The Registrant's other certifying officer(s) and I are responsible for establishing and maintaining disclosure controls and procedures (as defined in Exchange Act Rules 13a-15(e) and 15d-15(e)) and internal control over financial reporting (as defined in Exchange Act Rules 13a-15(f) and 15d-15(f)) for the Registrant and have:

    (a) Designed such disclosure controls and procedures, or caused such disclosure controls and procedures to be designed under our supervision, to ensure that material information relating to the Registrant, including its consolidated subsidiaries, is made known to us by others within those entities, particularly during the period in which this report is being prepared;

    (b) Designed such internal control over financial reporting, or caused such internal control over financial reporting to be designed under our supervision, to provide reasonable assurance regarding the reliability of financial reporting and the preparation of financial statements for external purposes in accordance with generally accepted accounting principles;

    (c) Evaluated the effectiveness of the Registrant's disclosure controls and procedures and presented in this report our conclusions about the effectiveness of the disclosure controls and procedures, as of the end of the period covered by this report based on such evaluation; and

    (d) Disclosed in this report any change in the Registrant's internal control over financial reporting that occurred during the Registrant's most recent fiscal quarter (the Registrant's fourth fiscal quarter in the case of an annual report) that has materially affected, or is reasonably likely to materially affect, the Registrant's internal control over financial reporting; and

5. The Registrant's other certifying officer(s) and I have disclosed, based on our most recent evaluation of internal control over financial reporting, to the Registrant's auditors and the audit committee of the Registrant's board of directors (or persons performing the equivalent functions):

    (a) All significant deficiencies and material weaknesses in the design or operation of internal control over financial reporting which are reasonably likely to adversely affect the Registrant's ability to record, process, summarize, and report financial information; and

    (b) Any fraud, whether or not material, that involves management or other employees who have a significant role in the Registrant's internal control over financial reporting.

Date: October 26, 2016

By: /s/ Timothy D. Cook

       Timothy D. Cook

       Chief Executive Officer

Required

a. Summarize the assertions that Timothy D. Cook made in this certification.

b. Why did Congress feel it important that CEOs and CFOs sign such certifications?

c. What potential liability do you believe the CEO and CFO are assuming by signing such certifications?

P1-54. **Assessing Corporate Governance and Its Effects**

LO7
General Electric (GE)

Review the corporate governance section of General Electric's website (**http://www.ge.com**). Find and click on "investor relations"; then, find and click on "governance," and open the "Governance Principles" PDF.

Required

a. In your words, briefly describe General Electric's governance structure.

b. What is the main purpose of its governance structure?

IFRS Applications

I1-55. **Computing, Analyzing, and Interpreting Return on Equity**

LO4
Canadian Tire
Corporation, Limited

Canadian Tire Corporation, Limited operates retail stores in Canada that sell general merchandise, clothing, and sporting goods. Total stockholders' equity for Canadian Tire (in millions of Canadian dollars) is $4,994.2 in 2015 and $4,855.5 in 2014. In 2015, Canadian Tire reported net income of $659.4 on sales of $12,279.6.

Required

a. What is Canadian Tire's return on equity for 2015?

b. What are total expenses for Canadian Tire for 2015?

c. Canadian Tire used cash to repurchase a large amount of its common stock during the period. What motivations might Canadian Tire have for repurchasing its common stock?

I1-56. **Applying the Accounting Equation and Computing Financing Proportions**

LO3

The following table contains fiscal 2015 information for three companies that use IFRS. Apply the accounting equation to compute the missing financial amounts (a), (b), and (c). Which of these companies is more owner-financed? Which of these companies is more nonowner-financed? Discuss why the proportion of owner financing might differ across these three companies.

In millions	Assets	=	Liabilities	+	Equity	
OMV Group (Austria)	€ 32,664		€18,366		(a)	OMV Group
Ericsson (Sweden).	SEK 284,363		(b)		SEK 147,366	Ericsson
BAE Systems (UK).	(c)		£20,083		£3,002	BAE Systems

I1-57. **Computing Return on Equity and Return on Assets**

LO4
AstraZeneca

The following table contains financial statement information for AstraZeneca, which is a global biopharmaceutical company focused on discovery, development, manufacturing, and commercialization of medicines and is headquartered in London.

$ millions	Total Assets	Net Income	Sales	AstraZeneca Equity
2013	$55,899	$2,571	$25,806	$23,253
2014	58,595	1,235	26,547	19,646
2015	60,124	2,826	24,708	18,509

Required

a. Compute the return on equity (ROE) for 2014 and 2015. What trend, if any, is evident? How does AstraZeneca's ROE compare with the approximately 18.9% median ROE for companies in the Dow Jones Industrial average for 2015?

b. Compute the return on assets (ROA) for 2014 and 2015. What trends, if any, are evident? How does AstraZeneca's ROA compare with the approximate 7.1% median ROA for companies in the Dow Jones Industrial average for 2015?

c. What factors might explain AstraZeneca's below-average returns?

I1-58. **Computing and Interpreting Return on Assets and Its Components**

LO4
Tesco PLC

Tesco PLC, which is one of the world's largest retailers and is headquartered in Cheshunt, U.K., reported the following balance sheet and income statement data for 2014 through 2016.

£ millions	Total Assets	Net Income	Sales
2014	£50,164	£ 974	£63,557
2015	44,214	(5,741)	56,925
2016	43,904	138	54,433

Required

a. What is Tesco's return on assets for 2015 and 2016?

b. Disaggregate Tesco's ROA metrics from part a into profit margin and asset turnover.

c. What factor is mainly responsible for the change in Tesco's ROA over this period?

Management Applications

LO1, 3 **MA1-59. Strategic Financing**

You and your management team are working to develop the strategic direction of your company for the next three years. One issue you are discussing is how to finance the projected increases in operating assets. Your options are to rely more heavily on operating creditors, borrow the funds, or to sell additional stock in your company. Discuss the pros and cons of each source of financing.

LO3, 4 **MA1-60. Statement Analysis**

You are evaluating your company's recent operating performance and are trying to decide on the relative weights you should put on the income statement, the balance sheet, and the statement of cash flows. Discuss the information each of these statements provides and its role in evaluating operating performance.

LO2 **MA1-61. Analyst Relations**

Your investor relations department reports to you that stockholders and financial analysts evaluate the quality of a company's financial reports based on their "transparency," namely, the clarity and completeness of the company's financial disclosures. Discuss the trade-offs of providing more or less transparent financial reports.

LO7 **MA1-62. Ethics and Governance: Management Communications**

Many companies publicly describe their performance using terms such as *EBITDA* or *earnings purged of various expenses* because they believe these terms more effectively reflect their companies' performance than GAAP-defined terms such as *net income*. What ethical issues might arise from the use of such terms, and what challenges does their use present for the governance of a company by stockholders and directors?

LO7 **MA1-63. Ethics and Governance: Auditor Independence**

The SEC has been concerned with the "independence" of external auditing firms. It is especially concerned about how large non-audit (such as consulting) fees might impact how aggressively auditing firms pursue accounting issues they uncover in their audits. Congress passed legislation that prohibits accounting firms from providing both consulting and auditing services to the same client. How might consulting fees affect auditor independence? What other conflicts of interest might exist for auditors? How do these conflicts impact the governance process?

Ongoing Project

An important part of learning is application. To learn accounting, we must practice the skills taught and apply those skills to real world problems. To that end, we have designed a project to reinforce the lessons in each module and apply them to real companies. The goal of this project is to complete a comprehensive analysis of two (or more) companies in the same industry. We will then create a set of forecasted financial statements and a valuation of the companies' equity. This is essentially what financial analysts and many creditors do. We might not aspire to be an analyst or creditor, but by completing a project of this magnitude, we will have mastered financial reporting at a sufficient level to be able to step into any role in an organization. The goal of Module 1's assignment is to obtain and begin to explore the financial reports for two publicly traded companies that compete with each other.

- Select two publicly traded companies that compete with each other. They must be publicly traded, as private company financial statements will not be publicly available. While the two companies do not need to be head-to-head competitors, their main lines of business should broadly overlap.

- Download the annual reports for each company, and peruse them. At this stage, choose companies that are profitable (net income is positive) and that have positive retained earnings and stockholders' equity. Select companies whose financial statements are not overly complicated. (Probably avoid the automotive, banking, insurance, and financial services industries. Automotive companies have large financial services subsidiaries that act like banks for customers, which complicates the analysis. Banking, insurance, and financial services have operations that differ drastically from the usual industrial companies common in practice. While these companies can be analyzed, they present challenges for the beginning analyst.)

- Use the SEC EDGAR Website to locate the recent Form 10-K (or other annual report such as 20-F or 40-F) (**www.sec.gov**). Download a spreadsheet version of financial statements. Use Appendix 1A as a guide.

- Use the annual report and the financial statements, along with any websites, to assess the companies' business environment. Use Porter's Five Forces or a SWOT analysis to briefly analyze the competitive landscape for the two companies. The aim is to understand the competitive position of each company so we can assess their financial statements in a broader business context.

- Explore the financial statements, and familiarize yourself with the company basics. The following give an indication of some questions that guide us as we look for answers.

    ❏ What accounting standards are used, U.S. GAAP, IFRS, or other?

    ❏ What is the date of the most recent fiscal year-end?

    ❏ Determine the relative proportion of short- and long-term assets.

    ❏ Determine the relative proportion of liabilities and equity.

    ❏ Calculate the return on assets (ROA) for the most recent year.

    ❏ Disaggregate ROA into the two component parts as shown in Exhibit 1.7. Compare the numbers/ratios for each company.

    ❏ Find the companies' audit reports. Who are the auditors? Are any concerns raised in the reports?

    ❏ Do the audit reports differ significantly from the one for Under Armour in this module?

Solutions to Review Problems

Review 1-1—Solution

All of the statements a, b, c, and d are true.

Review 1-2—Solution

1. I.   b
   II. e
   III. f
   IV. a
   V.   d
   VI. c

2. The cost of preparing financial statements includes both internal and external costs. Multinational companies that have subsidiaries operating in IFRS jurisdictions must prepare two sets of financial statements and have staff who are familiar with both. This adds labor costs. Auditors bill by the hour, so auditing two sets of financial statements would require more hours and therefore would be costlier for the firm. If the two sets of standards were comparable, both types of costs would decrease.

Review 1-3—Solution

1.

NIKE INC. Income Statement ($ millions) For Year Ended May 31, 2015	
Revenues	$30,601
Cost of goods sold	16,534
Gross profit	14,067
SG&A expenses	9,892
Income from operations	4,175
Interest income	30
Income before taxes	4,205
Provision for income taxes	932
Net income	$ 3,273

NIKE INC. Balance Sheet ($ millions) May 31, 2015			
Short-term assets	$15,976	Short-term liabilities	$ 6,334
Long-term assets	5,624	Long-term liabilities	2,559
		Stockholders' equity	12,707
Total assets	$21,600	Total liabilities and equity	$21,600

NIKE INC. Statement of Cash Flows ($ millions) For Year Ended May 31, 2015	
Cash flows from operations	$4,680
Cash flows from investing	(175)
Cash flows from financing	(2,873)
Net increase (decrease) in cash	1,632
Cash, beginning year	2,220
Cash, ending year	$3,852

2. Nike is a much larger company than Under Armour; with total assets of $21,600 million compared to Under Armour's assets of $2,868.9 million. Nike is about 10 times larger. The income statements of the two companies are markedly different as well. Nike reports nearly eight times as much revenue ($30,601 million compared with $3,963.3 million). The difference in net income is also large. Nike earned $3,273 million whereas Under Armour reported net income of only $232.5 million.

Review 1-4—Solution

a. ROA = Net income/Average assets = $3,273/$20,097 = 16.3%.
   The profitability component is Net income/Sales = $3,273/$30,601 = 10.7%, and the productivity component is Sales/Average assets = $30,601/$20,097 = 1.52. Notice that 10.7% × 1.52 = 16.3%. Thus, the two components, when multiplied, yield ROA.
b. ROE = Net income/Average stockholders' equity = $3,273/$11,766 = 27.8%.

Review 1-5—Solution

1. *a.* II
   b. I
   c. III
   d. I
   e. II
   f. III

2. According to Yahoo! Finance, Under Armour's competitors include Nike, Columbia Sportswear, and adidas AG.

3. Under Armour does have a competitive advantage created by the technical nature of its apparel. The company has patented technology including Coldback and MagZip. The company has immense brand loyalty and a strong reputation for product innovation.

4.

$ millions	Under Armour	Nike	Columbia	adidas
Total assets.	$2,869	$21,600	$1,846	$13,343
Revenue	$3,963	$30,601	$2,326	$16,915
Net income.	$ 233	$ 3,273	$ 174	$ 634
ROA	8.12%	15.15%	9.43%	4.75%
Profit margin (PM).	5.88%	10.70%	7.48%	3.75%
Asset turnover (AT)	1.38	1.42	1.26	1.27

The Under Armour ROA and profit margin are smaller than most of the competitors which is surprising given the company's ability to premium price its products. It might be the case that costs are high for R&D, along with marketing and celebrity promotions.

Module 2

Introducing Financial Statements

Learning Objectives

AAPL

Market cap: $639,939 mil
Total assets: $290,479 mil
Revenues: $233,715 mil
Net income: $53,394 mil

Apple Inc. recently reported sales of over $233 billion and net income exceeding $53 billion. It generated net cash from operating activities of over $81 billion and, at year-end, reported cash and marketable securities on its balance sheet of over $205 billion, which accounts for 70% of its total assets. Its market capitalization was $640 billion, greater than that of several major companies, including Microsoft, Exxon, Facebook, and General Electric.

Driven by the popularity and high profits of its products, including iPads and iPhones, Apple's income statement reported over $71 billion of operating income. This is impressive given that Apple spends over $8 billion each year on research and development and runs expensive advertising campaigns. Yet companies cannot live by profits alone. It is cash that pays bills. Profits and cash flow reflect two different measurement concepts of company performance. Apple's statement of cash flows reported that, while the company generated over $81 billion of cash flow from operations, it also paid out over $11 billion in dividends and issued common stock to executives in its stock option program.

With cash and investments of over $205 billion on its balance sheet, Apple is exceedingly liquid. Liquidity is important for companies like Apple that must react quickly to opportunities and changing market conditions. Like other technology companies, much of Apple's production is subcontracted. Consequently, Apple's property, plant, and equipment make up only 8% of its assets. On the financing side of its balance sheet, about 40% of Apple's resources come from owner financing—from common stock sold to shareholders and from past profits that have been reinvested. Apple's nonowner financing consists of low-cost credit from suppliers (accounts payable), unpaid overhead expenses (accrued liabilities), and fairly low levels of borrowed money.

It is also important to know what is *not* reported in financial statements. Apple's patents, copyrights, and other intellectual property, along with its brand name, create huge barriers to competition that allow the company to earn above-average profits. But while these "intangible assets" create a competitive advantage, few are reported on Apple's balance sheet. As another example, Apple's software engineers write code and create software that generate future profits for Apple. While this is a valuable resource to Apple, it is not reported on its balance sheet because Apple expenses the software engineers' salaries as the code is written. We discuss these and other issues relating to asset recognition and measurement in this module. [Source: *Apple*, 2015 10-K report.]

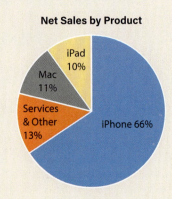

Net Sales by Product

- iPhone 66%
- Services & Other 13%
- Mac 11%
- iPad 10%

© iStock

Road Map

Introducing Financial Statements

Financial Statements	**Articulation of Financial Statements**
▪ Balance Sheet	▪ Retained Earnings Reconciliation
▪ Income Statement	▪ Financial Statement Linkages
▪ Statement of Stockholders' Equity	▪ Additional Information Sources
▪ Statement of Cash Flows	

Balance Sheet

LO1 Examine and interpret a balance sheet.

The balance sheet is divided into three sections: assets, liabilities, and stockholders' equity. It provides information about the resources available to management and the claims against those resources by creditors and stockholders. The balance sheet reports the assets, liabilities, and equity at a *point* in time. Balance sheet accounts are called "permanent accounts" in that they carry over from period to period; that is, the ending balance from one period becomes the beginning balance for the next.

Balance Sheet and the Flow of Costs

Companies incur costs to acquire resources that will be used in operations. Every cost creates either an immediate or a future economic benefit. Determining when the company will realize the benefit from a cost is important.

▪ When a cost creates an *immediate* benefit, such as gasoline used in delivery vehicles, the company records the cost in the income statement as an expense.

▪ When a cost creates a *future* economic benefit, such as inventory to be resold or equipment to be later used for manufacturing, the company capitalizes the cost (i.e., adds it to the balance sheet as an asset). An asset remains on the company's balance sheet until it is used up. When an asset is used up, the company realizes the economic benefit from the asset; that is, there is no future economic benefit left, so there is no asset left. Then, the asset's cost is transferred from the balance sheet to the income statement, where it is recognized as an expense.

Two examples illustrate how asset costs are transferred from the balance sheet to the income statement.

▪ Inventory—when a company purchases or manufactures goods for resale, the cost is recorded on the balance sheet as an asset called *inventories*. When inventories are sold, they no longer have an economic benefit to the company, and their cost is transferred to the income statement in an expense called *cost of goods sold*.

▪ Equipment—when a company acquires equipment, the cost is recorded on the balance sheet in an asset called *equipment* (often included in the general category of property, plant, and equipment, or PPE). As the equipment is used in operations, a portion of the acquisition cost is transferred to the income statement as an expense. To illustrate, if an asset costs $100,000, and 10% is used up during the period in operating activities, then 10% of the asset's cost ($10,000) is transferred from the balance sheet to the income statement. This systematic allocation process is called *depreciation*.

Sometimes, however, companies immediately expense costs that are expected to provide future benefits because their future economic benefits cannot be reliably measured. Advertising and salary costs are examples. We expect, for example, that advertising will produce future benefits in the form of increased sales, but we cannot reliably measure those uncertain benefits. For that reason, we do not recognize an advertising asset; we expense that cost immediately. We immediately expense salaries for the same reason.

The point is that all costs are eventually recognized in the income statement as an expense. Those that create an immediate benefit are recognized as an expense immediately, and those that create a future benefit are added to the balance sheet as an asset (capitalized) and recognized as an expense in the future as the benefit is realized.

Exhibit 2.1 illustrates how costs flow from the balance sheet to the income statement.

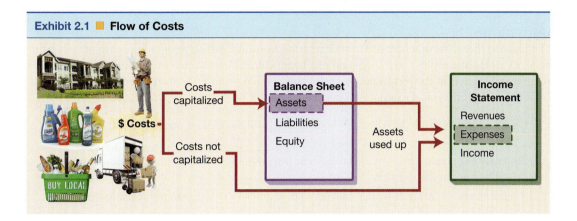

Exhibit 2.1 ■ **Flow of Costs**

Assets

Companies acquire assets to yield a return for their shareholders. Assets are expected to produce economic benefits in the form of revenues, either directly, such as with inventory, or indirectly, such as with a manufacturing plant that produces inventories for sale. To create stockholder value, assets must yield income that is in excess of the cost of the funds used to acquire the assets.

The asset section of the **Apple** balance sheet is shown in Exhibit 2.2. Apple reports $290,479 million in total assets as of September 26, 2015, its year-end. Amounts reported on the balance sheet are at a *point in time*—that is, the close of business on the day of the report. An asset must possess two characteristics to be reported on the balance sheet.

1. It must be owned (or controlled) by the company.

2. It must confer expected future economic benefits that result from a past transaction or event.

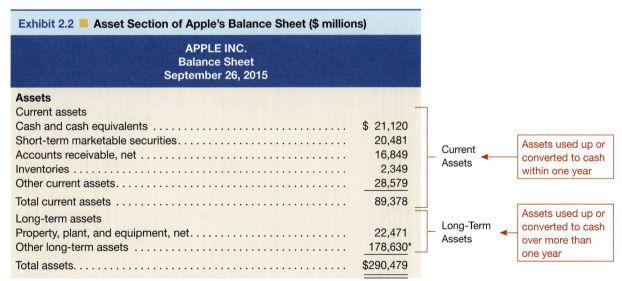

Exhibit 2.2 ■ **Asset Section of Apple's Balance Sheet ($ millions)**

APPLE INC.
Balance Sheet
September 26, 2015

Assets	
Current assets	
Cash and cash equivalents	$ 21,120
Short-term marketable securities	20,481
Accounts receivable, net	16,849
Inventories	2,349
Other current assets	28,579
Total current assets	89,378
Long-term assets	
Property, plant, and equipment, net	22,471
Other long-term assets	178,630*
Total assets	$290,479

Current Assets → Assets used up or converted to cash within one year

Long-Term Assets → Assets used up or converted to cash over more than one year

*Includes $164,065 million of long-term marketable securities

The first requirement, owning or controlling an asset, implies that a company has legal title to the asset, such as the title to property, or has the unrestricted right to use the asset, such as a lease on the property. The second requirement implies that a company expects to realize a benefit from the asset. Benefits can be cash inflows from the sale of an asset or from sales of products produced by the asset. Benefits also can refer to the receipt of other assets, such as an account receivable from a credit sale; or benefits can arise from future services the company will receive, such as prepaying for a year-long insurance policy.

Current Assets

The balance sheet lists assets in order of decreasing **liquidity**, which refers to the ease of converting noncash assets into cash. The most liquid assets are called **current assets**, and they are listed first. A company expects to convert its current assets into cash or use those assets in operations within the coming fiscal year. Typical examples of current assets follow.

> **Cash**—currency, bank deposits, and investments with an original maturity of 90 days or less (called *cash equivalents*).
>
> **Short-term investments**—marketable securities and other investments the company expects to dispose of in the short run.
>
> **Accounts receivable, net**—amounts due to the company from customers arising from the sale of products and services on credit ("net" refers to the subtraction of uncollectible accounts).
>
> **Inventories**—goods purchased or produced for sale to customers.
>
> **Prepaid expenses**—costs paid in advance for rent, insurance, advertising, and other services.

Apple reports current assets of $89,378 million in 2015, which is 31% of its total assets. The amount of current assets is an important measure of liquidity, which relates to a company's ability to make short-term payments. Companies require a degree of liquidity to operate effectively, as they must be able to respond to changing market conditions and take advantage of opportunities. However, current assets such as receivables and inventories are expensive to hold (they must be stored, insured, monitored, financed, and so forth)—and they typically generate relatively low returns. As a result, companies seek to maintain only just enough current assets to cover liquidity needs, but not so much to unnecessarily reduce income.

Long-Term Assets

The second section of the balance sheet reports long-term (noncurrent) assets. Long-term assets include the following.

> **Property, plant, and equipment (PPE), net**—land, factory buildings, warehouses, office buildings, machinery, motor vehicles, office equipment, and other items used in operating activities ("net" refers to the subtraction of accumulated depreciation, the portion of the assets' cost that has been expensed).
>
> **Long-term investments**—investments the company does not intend to sell in the near future.
>
> **Intangible and other assets**—assets without physical substance, including patents, trademarks, franchise rights, goodwill, and other costs the company incurred that provide future benefits.

Long-term assets are not expected to be converted into cash for some time and are, therefore, listed after current assets.

Measuring Assets

Most assets are reported at their original acquisition costs, or **historical costs**, and not at their current market values. When inventories are purchased or manufactured, for example, we know their cost and the expected retail selling price, which is a reasonable estimate of their current market value. But the actual selling price cannot be measured reliably (it is only an expectation). Consequently, we report inventories on the balance sheet at their cost and recognize the gross profit (selling price less cost) when the inventories are sold and the sale price is ultimately determined in a market transaction.[1]

It is important to realize balance sheets only include items that can be reliably measured. If a company cannot value an asset with relative certainty, it does not recognize an asset on the balance sheet. This means that sizable "assets" are *not* reflected on a balance sheet. For example, the well-known apple image is not among the assets listed on Apple's balance sheet. This image is called an "unrecognized intangible asset." While Apple owns the image and expects to realize future benefits from it, its value is not reliably measured. Other intangible assets missing from companies' balance sheets include the Coke bottle silhouette, the iPhone brand name, and the Nike swoosh. Companies only report intangible assets on the balance sheet when the assets are *purchased*. Any *internally created* intangible assets are not reported on a balance sheet.

Excluded intangible assets often relate to *knowledge-based* (intellectual) assets, such as a strong management team, a well-designed supply chain, or superior technology. Although these intangible assets confer a competitive advantage to the company and yield above-normal income (and clear economic benefits to those companies), they cannot be reliably measured. This is one reason why companies in knowledge-based industries are so difficult to analyze and value.

Presumably, however, companies' market values reflect these excluded intangible assets. This can yield a large difference between the market value of a company and the reported amount (book value) of stockholders' equity. This is illustrated in the following ratios of market value to book value (averages from fiscal 2015 year-ends): Apple is 5.4 (computed as $639,939 million/$119,355 million), and Target is 3.4 (computed as $44,150 million /$12,957 million). These market-to-book values (ratios) are greater for companies with large knowledge-based assets that are not reported on the balance sheet but are reflected in company market value (such as with Apple). Companies such as Target have fewer of these assets. Hence, their balance sheets usually reflect a greater portion of company value.

Liabilities and Equity

Liabilities and stockholders' equity (also called shareholders' equity) represent the sources of capital the company uses to finance the acquisition of assets.

- Liabilities represent a company's future economic sacrifices. Liabilities are borrowed funds, such as accounts payable and obligations to lenders. They can be interest-bearing or non-interest-bearing.

- Stockholders' equity represents capital that has been invested by the stockholders, either directly via the purchase of stock, or indirectly in the form of *retained earnings* that reflect earnings that are reinvested in the business and not paid out as dividends.

The liabilities and stockholders' equity sections of the Apple balance sheet are reproduced in Exhibit 2.3. Apple reports $171,124 million of total liabilities and $119,355 million of stockholders' equity as of its 2015 year-end.

Why would Apple obtain capital from both borrowed funds and stockholders? Why not just one or the other? The answer lies in their relative costs and the contractual agreements Apple has with each.

Creditors have the first claim on the assets of the company. As a result, their position is not as risky and, accordingly, their expected return on investment is less than that required by stockholders. Also, interest is tax deductible, whereas dividends are not. This makes debt a less expensive source of capital than equity. So, then, why should a company not finance itself entirely with borrowed funds? The reason is that companies must repay the principal and interest on the debt. If a company cannot make these payments when they come due, creditors can force the company into bankruptcy and potentially put the company out of business. Stockholders, in contrast, cannot require a company to repurchase its stock or even to pay dividends. Thus, companies take on a level of debt they can comfortably repay at reasonable interest costs. The remaining balance required to fund business activities is financed with more costly equity capital.

---

[1] However, one class of assets, marketable securities, is reported on the balance sheet at fair (market) value if the securities are frequently traded in organized markets with sufficient liquidity. Under those conditions, the fair value can be reliably measured. We discuss accounting for marketable securities in a later module.

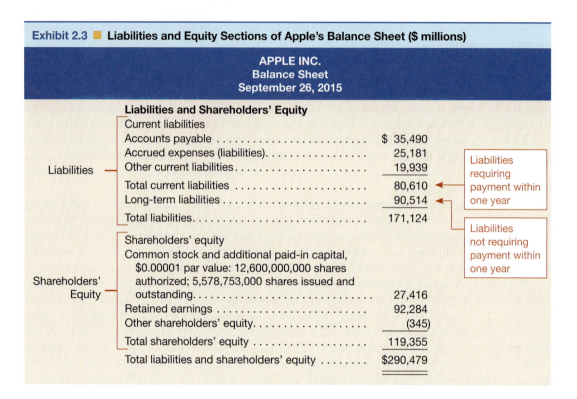

Exhibit 2.3 ■ Liabilities and Equity Sections of Apple's Balance Sheet ($ millions)

APPLE INC.
Balance Sheet
September 26, 2015

Liabilities and Shareholders' Equity

Current liabilities	
Accounts payable	$ 35,490
Accrued expenses (liabilities)................	25,181
Other current liabilities.....................	19,939
Total current liabilities	80,610
Long-term liabilities	90,514
Total liabilities.............................	171,124
Shareholders' equity	
Common stock and additional paid-in capital, $0.00001 par value: 12,600,000,000 shares authorized; 5,578,753,000 shares issued and outstanding..............................	27,416
Retained earnings	92,284
Other shareholders' equity..................	(345)
Total shareholders' equity	119,355
Total liabilities and shareholders' equity	$290,479

Liabilities requiring payment within one year

Liabilities not requiring payment within one year

Current Liabilities

The balance sheet lists liabilities in order of maturity. Obligations that must be settled within one year are called **current liabilities**. Examples of common current liabilities follow.

> **Accounts payable**—amounts owed to suppliers for goods and services purchased on credit.
>
> **Accrued liabilities**—obligations for expenses that have been incurred but not yet paid; examples are accrued wages payable (wages earned by employees but not yet paid), accrued interest payable (interest that is owing but has not been paid), and accrued income taxes (taxes due); also called accrued expenses.
>
> **Unearned revenues**—obligations created when the company accepts payment in advance for goods or services it will deliver in the future; also called advances from customers, customer deposits, or deferred revenues.
>
> **Short-term notes payable**—short-term debt payable to banks or other creditors.
>
> **Current maturities of long-term debt**—principal portion of long-term debt that is due to be paid within one year.

Apple reports current liabilities of $80,610 million on its 2015 balance sheet.

Accounts payable arise when one company purchases goods or services from another company. Typically, sellers offer credit terms when selling to other companies rather than expecting cash on delivery. The seller records an account receivable, and the buyer records an account payable. Apple reports accounts payable of $35,490 million as of the balance sheet date. Accounts payable are relatively uncomplicated liabilities. A transaction (say, an inventory purchase) occurs, a bill is sent, and the amount owed is reported on the balance sheet as a liability.

Apple's accrued liabilities total $25,181 million. Accrued liabilities refer to incomplete transactions. For example, employees work and earn wages but usually are not paid until later, such as several days after the period-end. Wages must be reported as expense in the period employees earn them because those wages payable are obligations of the company, and a liability (wages payable) must be set up on the balance sheet. This is an *accrual*. Other common accruals include the recording of liabilities such as rent and utilities payable, taxes payable, and interest payable on borrowings. All of these accruals involve recognition of expense in the income statement and a liability on the balance sheet.

Net working capital, or simply working capital, reflects the difference between current assets and current liabilities and is defined as follows.

$$\text{Net working capital} = \text{Current assets} - \text{Current liabilities}$$

We usually prefer to see more current assets than current liabilities to ensure that companies are liquid. That is, companies should have sufficient funds to pay their short-term debts as they mature. The net working capital required to conduct business depends on the company's **operating (or cash) cycle**, which is the time between paying cash for goods and receiving cash from customers—see Exhibit 2.4.

Companies, for example, use cash to purchase or manufacture inventories held for resale. Inventories are usually purchased on credit from suppliers (accounts payable). This financing is called **trade credit**. Inventories are sold either for cash or on credit (accounts receivable). When receivables are ultimately collected, a portion of the cash received is used to repay accounts payable, and the remainder goes to the cash account for the next operating cycle.

Exhibit 2.4 ■ Operating Cycle

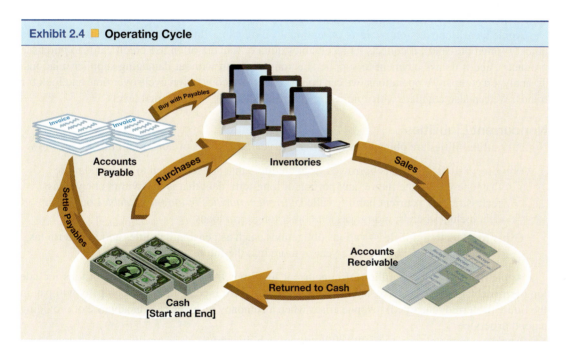

When cash is invested in inventory, the inventory can remain with the company for 30 to 90 days or more. Once inventory is sold, the resulting accounts receivable can remain with the company for another 30 to 90 days. Assets such as inventories and accounts receivable are costly to hold because they tie up cash. As companies complete one operating cycle, sales and gross profit are reported in the income statement, and cash is generated (equal to the sales proceeds less the purchase cost of the inventory sold). A prime objective is to shorten the operating cycle in order to complete as many cycles as possible during the year. Doing so maximizes profit and cash flow. To shorten the operating cycle, managers can undertake any or all of the following actions.

■ Decrease accounts receivable with tighter credit-granting policies and more assertive collection procedures.

■ Reduce inventory levels by improved production systems and management of the depth and breadth of inventory.

■ Increase trade credit to minimize the cash invested in inventories.

Cash Conversion Cycle Analysts often use the "cash conversion cycle" to evaluate company liquidity. The cash conversion cycle is the number of days the company has its cash tied up in receivables and inventories less the number of days of trade credit provided by company suppliers.

Following are the cash conversion cycles for **Apple Inc.** and **3M Company** (a manufacturing company).

Numbers in Days	Apple Inc.	3M Company
Average Days Sales Outstanding.................	26.7 days	50.6 days
+ Average Days Inventory Outstanding..............	5.8 days	85.9 days
− Average Days Payable Outstanding...............	85.2 days	42.2 days
= Average Cash Conversion Cycle	(52.7) days	94.3 days

On average, Apple collects its receivables in 26.7 days, sells its inventories in 5.8 days, and pays its accounts payable in 85.2 days, resulting in a cash conversion cycle of (52.7) days (26.7 + 5.8 − 85.2). The negative cash cycle implies that Apple can invest the cash it receives from sales for 52.7 days before making payment to suppliers, thus realizing the profit and cash flow on the sale as well as investment income. By comparison, 3M, a more typical manufacturing company, collects its receivables in 50.6 days, sells its inventories in 85.9 days, and pays its suppliers in 42.2 days, resulting in a cash conversion cycle of 94.3 days (50.6 + 85.9 − 42.2).

Apple's cash conversion cycle is exceptional on all three dimensions: it sells its inventories quickly (often pre-sold), it collects its receivables quickly (buyers often use credit cards to purchase products), and it delays payment to suppliers as long as it can without damaging supplier relations. To analyze a company's operations, we can compare the cash conversion cycle over time and look for trends. We can also compare with competitor companies to look for abnormal levels.

Noncurrent Liabilities

Noncurrent liabilities are obligations due after one year. Examples of noncurrent liabilities follow.

Long-term debt—amounts borrowed from creditors that are scheduled to be repaid more than one year in the future; any portion of long-term debt that is due within one year is reclassified as a current liability called *current maturities of long-term debt*. Long-term debt includes bonds, mortgages, and other long-term loans.

Other long-term liabilities—various obligations, such as pension liabilities and long-term tax liabilities, that will be settled a year or more into the future.

Apple reports $90,514 million of noncurrent liabilities. Apple's noncurrent liabilities include long-term debt, deferred revenue, and deferred tax liability for income taxes the company will pay in the future. Deferred (unearned) revenue arises when a company receives cash in advance of providing a good or service.

Apple reports total assets of $290,479 million, liabilities of $171,124 million, and shareholders' equity of $119,355 million. This reveals that it finances 59% ($171,124 million/$290,479 million) of its assets with borrowed funds and 41% with shareholder investment. This is in the range of debt levels for large public companies. The S&P 500 companies, for example, report liabilities totaling 64% of assets in 2015. Companies must monitor their financing sources and amounts. Too much borrowing is risky in that borrowed money must be repaid with interest. The level of debt a company can effectively manage is directly related to the stability and reliability of its operating cash flows.

Stockholders' Equity

Stockholders' equity reflects financing provided from company owners. Equity is often referred to as *residual interest*. That is, stockholders have a claim on any assets in excess of what is needed to meet company obligations to creditors. The following are examples of items typically included in equity.

Common stock—par value received from the original sale of common stock to investors.

Additional paid-in capital—amounts received from the original sale of stock to investors in excess of the par value of stock.

Contributed capital

Preferred stock—value received from the original sale of preferred stock to investors; preferred stock has fewer ownership rights than common stock.

Treasury stock—amount the company paid to reacquire its common stock from shareholders.

Retained earnings—accumulated net income (profit) that has not been distributed to stockholders as dividends.

Accumulated other comprehensive income or loss—accumulated changes in asset and liability fair values that are not reported in the income statement.

Earned
capital

The equity section of a balance sheet consists of two basic components: contributed capital and earned capital.

Contributed capital is the net funding a company received from issuing and reacquiring its shares; that is, the funds received from issuing shares less any funds paid to repurchase such. Apple reports $119,355 million in total stockholders' equity. Its contributed capital is $27,416 million. Apple's common stock has a par value of $0.00001 per share (see Exhibit 2.3). This means that, when Apple sells shares of stock, its Common stock account increases by the number of shares sold multiplied by $0.00001, and its Additional paid-in capital account increases by the remainder of the proceeds from the sale (Apple's balance aggregates the common stock and additional paid-in capital accounts, which is acceptable under GAAP). Apple's stockholders (via its board of directors) have authorized the company to issue up to 12.6 billion shares of common stock. As of September 26, 2015, Apple has sold (issued) 5,578,753,000 shares for total proceeds of $27,416 million, or $4.91 per share, on average.

Earned capital is the cumulative net income (loss) that has been retained by the company (not paid out to stockholders as dividends). Apple's earned capital (titled Retained earnings) totals $92,284 million as of its 2015 year-end. Its other equity accounts total $(345) million.

Analysis Insight ▪ Common-Size Balance Sheet

One tool for analyzing a company's balance sheet is the *common size balance sheet*. This is a balance sheet where each item is recast as a percent of total assets. It is called *common size* because each item is scaled by a common denominator. Common sizing the balance sheet enables us to perform the following types of analyses:

- Compare a company's balance sheets across two or more years. Companies provide side-by-side balance sheets for two years, and the 10-K often includes an 11-year history of key balance sheet accounts. If the company has grown or shrunk in size over time, comparing dollars (or other currency) masks shifts in relative size of balance sheet items. Percentages reveal a more accurate picture.

- Compare two or more companies' balance sheets. The common sizing eliminates size differences among companies—we can compare a small firm with a large firm because each asset, liability, and equity account is expressed in percentage terms. The other benefit is that common sizing is unit free, so we can compare companies that report in different currencies.

- Compare balance sheets with an industry average or some other benchmark. The percentages create a common basis for comparison, and this can help assess a particular company's financial position relative to others in the same industry.

Retained Earnings

There is an important relation for retained earnings that reconciles its beginning balance and its ending balance as follows.

> Beginning retained earnings
> + Net income (or − Net loss)
> − Dividends
> ─────────────────────────
> = Ending retained earnings

This is a useful relation to remember. Apple's retained earnings increases (or decreases) each year by the amount of its reported net income (loss) minus its dividends. (There are other items that can impact retained earnings that we discuss in later modules.) After we explain the income statement, we will revisit this relation and show how retained earnings link the balance sheet and income statement.

Business Insight ■ Market Value vs. Book Value

Apple's market value has historically exceeded its book value of equity (see graph). Much of Apple's market value derives from intangible assets, such as brand equity, that are not fully reflected on its balance sheet and from favorable expectations of future financial performance (particularly in recent years). Apple has incurred many costs, such as research and development (R&D), advertising, and promotion, that will yield future economic benefits. However, Apple expensed these costs (did not capitalize them as assets) because their future benefits were uncertain and, therefore, could not be reliably measured. Companies capitalize intangible assets only when those assets are purchased, and not when they are internally developed. Consequently, Apple's balance sheet and the balance sheets of many knowledge-based companies are, arguably, less informative about company value.

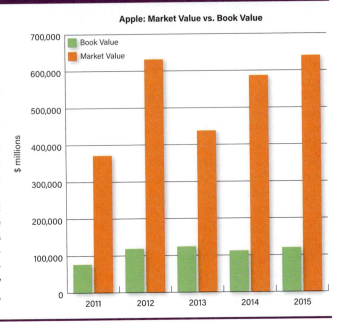

Market Value vs. Book Value Stockholders' equity is the "value" of the company determined by generally accepted accounting principles (GAAP) and is commonly referred to as the company's **book value**. This book value is different from a company's **market value** (market capitalization or *market cap*), which is computed by multiplying the number of outstanding common shares by the company's stock price. We can compute Apple's market cap by multiplying its outstanding shares at September 25, 2015 (5,578,753,000 shares), by its stock price on that date ($114.71), which equals $639,939 million. This is considerably larger than its book value of equity on that date of $119,355 million. Book value and market value can differ for several reasons, mostly related to the following.

■ GAAP generally reports assets and liabilities at historical costs, whereas the market attempts to estimate fair market values.

■ GAAP excludes resources that cannot be reliably measured (due to the absence of a past transaction or event), such as talented management, employee morale, recent innovations, and successful marketing, whereas the market attempts to value these.

■ GAAP does not consider market differences in which companies operate, such as competitive conditions and expected changes, whereas the market attempts to factor in these differences in determining value.

■ GAAP does not usually report expected future performance, whereas the market attempts to predict and value future performance.

Presently, for U.S. companies, median book value is about one-half of market value (yielding a 2.0 market-to-book ratio). This means the market has drawn on information in addition to that provided in the balance sheet and income statement in valuing companies' stock. A major part of this information is in financial statement notes, but not all. It is important to understand that, eventually, all factors determining company market value are reflected in financial statements and book value. Assets are eventually sold, and liabilities are settled. Moreover, talented management, employee morale, technological innovations, and successful marketing are eventually recognized in reported profit. The difference between book value and market value is one of timing.

Research Insight ■ Market-to-Book Ratio

The market-to-book ratio is computed as a company's market value divided by the book value to total equity. It can also be computed as stock price per share divided by book value or equity per share. The market-to-book ratio varies considerably over time, reflecting the variability in the global economy. Specifically, over the past ten years, the median market-to-book ratio for the S&P 500 companies has ranged from a low of 1.6 (during the financial crisis) to a high of 3.2 (immediately preceding the crisis).

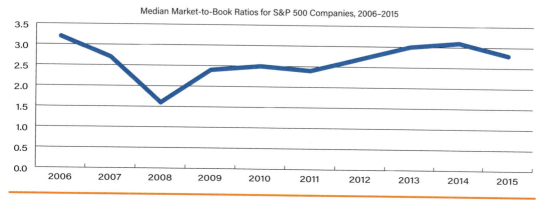

Median Market-to-Book Ratios for S&P 500 Companies, 2006–2015

LO1 **Review 2-1**

Following are account balances ($ millions) for **Microsoft Corporation** as of the fiscal year ended June 30, 2015. Prepare Microsoft's balance sheet as of June 30, 2015.

Total revenue	$ 93,580	Cash flows for financing activities	$ (9,153)
Accounts payable	6,591	Other current assets	7,376
Cash and short-term investments	96,526	Accrued expenses	5,096
Cash flows from operating activities	29,080	Other stockholders' equity	2,522
Other current liabilities	38,171	Accounts receivable	17,908
Inventories	2,902	Long-term liabilities	46,282
Cost of goods sold	33,038	Cash at beginning of year	8,669
Cash flows for investing activities	(23,001)	Other long-term assets	36,780
Retained earnings	9,096	Other expense	9,665
Income tax expense	6,314	Property, plant, and equipment, net	14,731
Operating expenses	32,370	Common stock and paid-in capital	68,465

Solution on p. 2-36.

Income Statement

The income statement reports revenues earned from products sold and services provided during a period, the expenses incurred to produce those revenues, and the resulting net income or loss. The general structure of the income statement follows.

eLectures **LO2**
MBC Examine and interpret an income statement.

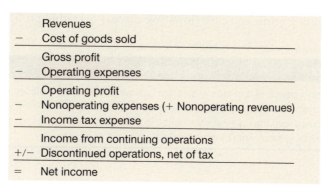

On some income statements we see two lines after the net income line. These lines apportion "consolidated" net income between *net income attributable to noncontrolling interests* and *net income attributable to the parent company shareholders* (also called the controlling interest). Noncontrolling interests arise when a subsidiary company is partially owned by shareholders other than the parent company. We discuss noncontrolling interests in later modules.

See Exhibit 2.5 for **Apple**'s 2015 income statement. Apple reports net income of $53,394 million on sales of $233,715 million. This means about $0.23 of each dollar of sales is brought down to the bottom line ($53,394 million/$233,715 million). Apple's net income margin is higher than that of the average publicly-traded company that reports about $0.06 in profit for each sales dollar. For Apple, the remaining $0.77 ($1.00 − $0.23) is consumed by expenses incurred to generate sales, including costs to manufacture Apple products (cost of sales), as well as wages, advertising, R&D, equipment costs (such as depreciation), and taxes.

Exhibit 2.5 ▬ **Apple's Income Statement ($ millions)**

APPLE INC. Income Statement For Year Ended September 26, 2015	
Net sales.	$233,715
Cost of sales.	140,089
Gross margin	93,626
Operating expenses	
Research and development	8,067
Selling, general, and administrative	14,329
Total operating expenses	22,396
Operating income.	71,230
Other income, net.	1,285
Income before provision for income taxes	72,515
Provision for income taxes.	19,121
Net income.	$ 53,394

Operating expenses are the usual and customary costs a company incurs to support its operating activities. Those include cost of goods sold, selling expenses, depreciation expense, and research and development expense. Not all of these expenses require a cash outlay; for example, depreciation expense is a noncash expense, as are many accrued expenses, such as wages payable, that recognize the expense in advance of cash payment.

Nonoperating expenses relate to the company's financing and investing activities and include interest expense, interest or dividend income, and gains and losses from the sale of securities. We see, for example, that Apple reports $1,285 million of other income. This is nonoperating income. It's important to understand that it is a company's operating activities that create value for shareholders. Granted, investments do earn additional returns, but only at the going market rate, and shareholders could invest at that rate themselves. Apple holding the investments does not create additional shareholder value. It is for this reason our analysis seeks to isolate the core (or sustainable) operating profit and cash flows. We discuss operating profit more thoroughly in a later module.

Alert The FASB has released a preliminary draft of a proposal to restructure financial statements to, among other things, better distinguish operating and nonoperating activities.

Managerial Decision ▬ You Are the Securities Analyst

You are analyzing the performance of a company that hired a new chief executive officer (CEO) during the current year. The current year's income statement includes an expense labeled "asset write-offs." Write-offs represent the accelerated transfer of costs from the balance sheet to the income statement. Are you concerned about the legitimacy of these expenses? Why, or why not? [Answer, p. 2-26]

Recognizing Revenues and Expenses

An important consideration in preparing the income statement is *when* to recognize revenues and expenses. For many revenues and expenses, the decision is easy. When a customer purchases an item, pays with cash, and walks out of the store with the item, we know the sale is made and revenue should be recognized. Or when companies receive and pay an electric bill, they have clearly incurred an expense that should be recognized.

However, should Apple recognize revenue when it sells iPods to a retailer that does not have to pay Apple for 60 days? Should Apple recognize an expense for employees who work this week but will not be paid until the first of next month? The answer to both of these questions is yes.

Two fundamental principles guide recognition of revenues and expenses.

> **Revenue recognition principle**—recognize revenues for goods and services provided to customers at an amount expected to be received.
>
> **Expense recognition (matching) principle**—recognize expenses when *incurred*.

These two principles are the foundation of **accrual accounting**, which is the accounting system used to prepare all GAAP-based financial statements. The general approach is this: first, recognize revenues in the time period when the company satisfies the performance obligations of the sales contract at the amount expected to be received; then, record all expenses *incurred* to generate those revenues during that same time period (this is called matching expenses to revenues). Net income is then correctly reported for that period.

Recognizing revenues does not necessarily imply the receipt of cash. Revenue is *recognized* when the company has done what it is obligated to do under the sales contract, such as, when goods have been transferred or services performed for the customer. This means a sale of goods on credit would qualify for recognition as long as the goods have been transferred to the customer as laid out in the sales contract. The company records revenue but receives no cash; instead, it records an accounts receivable. Likewise, companies recognize an expense when it is *incurred*, even if no cash is paid. For example, companies recognize as expenses the wages earned by employees, even though they will not be paid until the next pay period. The company records an expense but pays no cash; instead, it records an accrued liability for the wages payable.

Accrual accounting requires estimates and assumptions. Examples include estimating how much revenue has been earned on a long-term contract, the amount of accounts receivable that will not be collected, the degree to which equipment has been "used up," and numerous other estimates. All of these estimates and assumptions affect both reported net income and the balance sheet. Judgments affect all financial statements. This is an important by-product of accrual accounting. We discuss these estimates and assumptions, and their effects on financial statements, throughout the book.

Managerial Decision ■ You Are the Operations Manager

You are the operations manager on a new consumer product that was launched this period with very successful sales. The chief financial officer (CFO) asks you to prepare an estimate of warranty costs to charge against those sales. Why does the CFO desire a warranty cost estimate? What issues must you address in arriving at such an estimate? [Answer, p. 2-26]

Reporting of Transitory Items

From time to time, companies will divest a segment of their business as their strategy changes. When they do, we see an additional component of net income located at the bottom of the statement called **discontinued operations**—see Exhibit 2.6. Discontinued operations has two components: (1) the net income (loss) from the segment's business activities prior to sale and (2) any gain or loss on the actual sale of the business. (The income statement must also separately report earnings per share [EPS] from continuing and discontinued operations.)

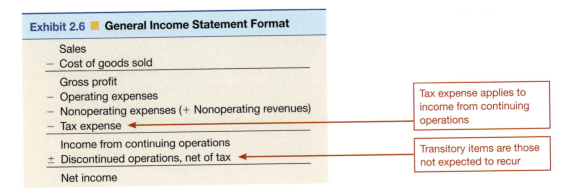

The text associated with the exhibit:

Exhibit 2.6 ■ General Income Statement Format

Sales
− Cost of goods sold

Gross profit
− Operating expenses
− Nonoperating expenses (+ Nonoperating revenues)
− Tax expense ◄——————— Tax expense applies to income from continuing operations

Income from continuing operations
± Discontinued operations, net of tax ◄——————— Transitory items are those not expected to recur

Net income

To be classified as a discontinued operation, the disposal of the business unit must represent a strategic shift that has, or will have, a major effect on the company's financial results. Because these divestitures represent strategic shifts with material financial effects, the reporting of discontinued operations is relatively infrequent.

Discontinued operations are segregated from "Income from continuing operations" because the discontinued operations represent a transitory item; that is, transactions or events that affect the current and prior periods but will not recur. Many financial statement users analyze current-year financial statements to help predict future performance. One good example is a company's stock price, which is heavily influenced by expected future profits and cash flows. Although transitory items help us understand past performance, they are largely irrelevant to predicting future performance. Consequently, investors and other financial statement users focus on income from continuing operations because it represents the profitability that is likely to persist (continue) into the future. Likewise, the financial press tends to focus on income from continuing operations when it discloses corporate earnings (often described as earnings before one-time charges, or street earnings).

In addition to segregating the results of operations of the discontinued operation in the current and previous two years' income statements reported, companies are also required to segregate the discontinued operation's assets and liabilities on its current year's and prior year's balance sheets.

Analyzing the Income Statement

In the prior module, we described an analytical framework to disaggregate return on assets into two important components: (1) profit margin, computed as Net income/Sales, and (2) asset turnover, computed as Sales/Average total assets. To augment the ROA analysis, we look at two additional profitability measures.

■ Gross profit margin (Gross profit/Sales).

■ Margins for operating expenses (Operating expense/Sales).

The **gross profit margin** is influenced by both the selling price of the company's products and the cost to make or buy those products. For example, if we purchase a product for $6 and sell it for $10, our gross profit margin is 40% ([$10 − $6]/$10). We analyze the gross profit margin by comparing the ratio over time and with peer companies' ratios. Typically, a high and/or increasing gross profit margin is a positive sign. A low or declining margin signals more intense competition or a lessening of the desirability of the company's product line or increasing inventory costs.

Analysis of **operating expenses** focuses on each expense category reported by the company as a percentage of sales over time and compared with peer companies. Any deviations from historical trends or significantly higher or lower levels from peer companies should be investigated to uncover causes. A particularly worrisome sign is when margins for operating expenses are declining in the face of falling profits. The concern is that the company has tried to address declining profits by reducing critical expenses such as R&D, marketing, or compensation costs. This generally leads to a short-term improvement at a long-term cost as market share declines and employee morale suffers. We discuss the analysis of the income statement in much more detail in Module 4.

Analysis Insight ■ Common-Size Income Statement

Analysts typically prepare common size income statements as a starting point for their analysis; each income statement item is expressed as a percent of net sales. As with the common size balance sheet, a common size income statement facilitates the same three types of comparisons: one company across years (called time-series analysis), many companies across one year (called cross-sectional analysis), and to a benchmark such as an industry average. Common size analysis is also referred to as "vertical analysis" because the percentages in the column on the income statement add up vertically to 100% of total sales (the top-line number on the income statement). A common size balance sheet adds up vertically to 100% of total assets.

LO2 Review 2-2

Refer to the data in Review 2-1 to answer the requirement.

Required

Prepare Microsoft's income statement for the fiscal year ended June 30, 2015. *Hint:* Refer to Exhibits 2.5 and 2.6 for presentation guidance.

Solution on p. 2-38.

Statement of Stockholders' Equity

The statement of stockholders' equity reconciles the beginning and ending balances of stockholders' equity accounts. The statement of stockholders' equity for **Apple** is shown in Exhibit 2.7.

eLectures **LO3**
MBC Examine and interpret a statement of stockholders' equity.

Exhibit 2.7 ■ Apple's Statement of Stockholders' Equity ($ millions)

APPLE INC. Statement of Shareholders' Equity For Year Ended September 26, 2015				
	Common Stock and Additional Paid-in Capital	Retained Earnings	Accumulated Other Comprehensive Income (Loss)	Total Equity
September 27, 2014...............	$23,313	$87,152	$1,082	$111,547
Stock issuance, net	3,355			3,355
Net income......................		53,394		53,394
Dividends		(11,627)		(11,627)
Other...........................	748	(36,635)	(1,427)	(37,314)
September 26, 2015...............	$27,416	$92,284	$ (345)	$119,355

   Common stock and additional paid-in capital increase by the proceeds from the sale of stock. Retained earnings increase by the net income (or decrease by the net loss) reported in the income statement and decrease by the dividends to shareholders. Accumulated other comprehensive income increases and decreases by changes in asset and liability fair values that are not reported in the income statement (we discuss accumulated other comprehensive income in Module 8).

   In sum, Apple's stockholders' equity begins the year at $111,547 million and ends fiscal 2015 with a balance of $119,355 million for a net increase of $7,808 million, reflecting the issuance of common stock, the recognition of net income, the declaration of dividends to shareholders, and other adjustments.

IFRS Insight ■ Balance Sheet and Income Statement under IFRS

U.S. GAAP and IFRS require a similar set of financial statements with similar formats. Both standards require current and long-term classifications for assets and liabilities, and both recognize revenues when earned and expenses when incurred. Although differences between U.S. GAAP and IFRS do exist at the "detailed level," there are two broader differences worth mention.

■ GAAP makes no formal prescription for the balance sheet and the income statement; however, the SEC requires three years of comparative income statements, whereas IFRS requires only two.

■ GAAP income statements categorize expenses by their function (e.g., cost of sales, selling, or administrative). For IFRS, expenses can be shown either by function or by nature (e.g., materials, labor, or overhead), whichever provides more reliable and relevant information.

Review 2-3 LO3

Use the data in Review 2-1 and the additional data below to prepare Microsoft's statement of stockholders' equity for the fiscal year ended June 30, 2015.

$ millions	Common Stock and APIC	Retained Earnings	Accumulated Other Comprehensive Income
Beginning balance	$68,366	$17,710	$ 3,708

Additional information for fiscal year 2015:
- Stock issuances, net during the year total $99.
- Decrease in accumulated other comprehensive income is $1,186.
- Dividends are $10,063.
- Other decreases in retained earnings total $10,744.

Solution on p. 2-38.

Statement of Cash Flows

LO4

Describe a statement of cash flows.

The balance sheet and income statement are prepared using accrual accounting, in which revenues are recognized when earned and expenses when incurred. This means companies can report income even though no cash is received. Cash shortages—due to unexpected cash outlays or when customers refuse to or cannot pay—can create economic hardships for companies and even cause their demise.

To evaluate company performance, we must assess a company's cash management in addition to its profitability. Obligations to employees, creditors, and others are usually settled with cash. Illiquid companies (those lacking cash) are at risk for failure. Given the importance of cash management, companies must report a statement of cash flows in addition to the balance sheet, income statement, and statement of equity.

The income statement provides information about the economic viability of the company's products and services. It tells us whether the company can sell its products and services at prices that cover its costs and provide a reasonable return to lenders and stockholders. On the other hand, the statement of cash flows provides information about the company's ability to generate cash from those same transactions. It tells us from what sources the company has generated its cash (so we can evaluate whether those sources are persistent or transitory) and what it has done with the cash it generated.

Statement Format and Data Sources

The statement of cash flows is formatted to report cash inflows and cash outflows by the three primary business activities.

- **Cash flows from operating activities** Cash flows from the company's transactions and events that relate to its operations.
- **Cash flows from investing activities** Cash flows from acquisitions and divestitures of investments and long-term assets.
- **Cash flows from financing activities** Cash flows from issuances of and payments toward borrowings and equity.

The combined cash flows from these three sections yield the net change in cash for the period as illustrated by the following cash flow statement for **Apple**.

Exhibit 2.8 ■ Apple's Statement of Cash Flows ($ millions)

APPLE INC. Statement of Cash Flows For Year Ended September 26, 2015	
Cash generated by operating activities	$81,266
Cash used in investing activities	(56,274)
Cash used in financing activities	(17,716)
Net change in cash.	7,276
Cash balance, September 27, 2014.	13,844
Cash balance, September 26, 2015.	$21,120

Apple generated $81,266 million of cash from its operating activities. It used $56,274 million of cash for investing activities, such as the purchase of PPE assets or marketable securities (the parentheses on the numbers in the statement of cash flow imply a "use" or net outflow of cash). Apple used $17,716 million of cash for financing activities, such as paying dividends, repurchasing common stock from the market, or reducing debt. The three types of cash flow together generated $7,276 million of cash during the year, thereby increasing the cash account from $13,844 million at the beginning of fiscal 2015 to $21,120 million at fiscal-year-end. Apple's cash flow picture is healthy: the company generated substantial cash from operating activities and used that cash to invest in PPE infrastructure, reduce debt, and return cash to stockholders in the form of dividends and stock repurchases.

Our analysis of cash flows focuses on the sources and uses of cash.

- Is the company generating cash from operating activities?
- Is the operating cash flow sustainable?
- Is the company investing its cash to grow its infrastructure (PPE) or to enter new markets by acquiring other companies?
- Is the company using its excess cash to build liquidity (purchase of marketable securities)?
- Is the company paying down debt or paying dividends?
- Is the company repurchasing stock?

Ultimately, a company's ending cash balance must be positive. So, if operating cash flow is negative, the company must raise cash from investing activities (the sale of PPE assets or marketable securities) or financing activities (borrowing money, selling stock, or cutting dividends and share repurchases). In the long run, the amount of cash that can be raised from investing and financing activities is finite. Although companies can usually sustain a short-term negative operating cash flow, long-term operating cash outflows are a serious concern. We discuss the statement of cash flows in detail in a later module.

Review 2-4   LO4

Refer to the data in Review 2-1 to answer the requirement.

Required

Solution on p. 2-38.   Prepare Microsoft's statement of cash flows for the fiscal year ended June 30, 2015.

Articulation of Financial Statements

LO5

MBC   Construct
and apply
linkages
among the four
financial statements.

The four financial statements are linked with each other and linked across time. This section demonstrates the linkages (articulation) of financial statements using Apple.

Retained Earnings Reconciliation

One of the most important articulations between financial statements involves the balance sheet and income statement. The two statements are linked via retained earnings. Recall that retained earnings is updated each period as follows.

Beginning retained earnings
± Net income (loss)
− Dividends
= Ending retained earnings

Retained earnings reflect cumulative income that has not yet been distributed to shareholders. Exhibit 2.9 shows Apple's retained earnings reconciliation for 2015.

Exhibit 2.9 ■ **Apple's Retained Earnings Reconciliation ($ millions)**

APPLE INC. Retained Earnings Reconciliation For Year Ended September 26, 2015	
Retained earnings, September 27, 2014	$87,152
Add: Net income	53,394
Less: Dividends	(11,627)
Other adjustments	(36,635)
Retained earnings, September 26, 2015	$92,284

This reconciliation of retained earnings links the balance sheet and the income statement.

In the absence of transactions with stockholders—such as stock issuances and repurchases, and dividend payments—the change in stockholders' equity equals income or loss for the period. The income statement, thus, measures the change in company value as measured by *GAAP*. This is not necessarily company value as measured by the *market*. Of course, all value-relevant items eventually find their way into the income statement. So, from a long-term perspective, the income statement does measure change in company value. This is why stock prices react to reported income and to analysts' expectations about future income.

Financial Statement Linkages

Exhibit 2.10 lays out the linkages among the four financial statements. Apple begins fiscal 2015 with assets of $231,839 million, consisting of cash of $13,844 million and noncash assets of $217,995 million. These investments are financed with $120,292 million from nonowners and $111,547 million

Exhibit 2.10 ■ Articulation of Apple Financial Statements ($ millions)

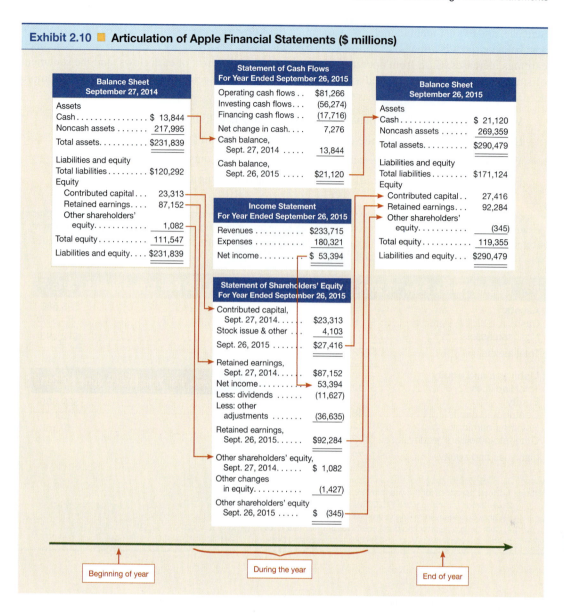

from stockholders. The owner financing consists of contributed capital of $23,313 million, retained earnings of $87,152 million, and other shareholders' equity of $1,082 million.

Exhibit 2.10 shows balance sheets at the beginning and end of Apple's fiscal year on the left and right columns, respectively. The middle column reflects annual operating activities. The statement of cash flows explains how operating, investing, and financing activities increase the cash balance by $7,276 million from $13,844 million at the beginning of the year to $21,120 million at year-end. The ending balance in cash is reported in the year-end balance sheet on the right.

Apple's $53,394 million net income reported on the income statement is linked to the statement of shareholders' equity. Apple's retained earnings increases by net income of $53,394 million and decreases by dividend payments of $11,627 million (other adjustments reduce retained earnings by $36,635 million).

Understanding these linkages gives managers as well as external financial statement users a keener ability to assess the impact transactions have on the financial statements. Every transaction has at least two effects on the financial statements. For example, purchasing new PPE increases non-cash assets and decreases cash on the balance sheet, which in turn affects the statement of cash flows. Many other transactions have more than two effects. For example, consider the cash sale of inventory. This transaction has the following income statement effects: (1) revenue increases, (2) expenses

increase, and (3) net income increases (assuming the sales price exceeded the cost of the inventory). The balance sheet is affected as follows: (1) cash increases, (2) inventory decreases, and (3) retained earnings increases. Cash from operations increases on the statement of cash flows, and the statement of stockholders' equity is affected via retained earnings. With such an understanding, we can more accurately answer questions such as the following.

- What are the financial statement effects of purchasing new PPE versus renting it?
- How is ROA affected when the company discontinues certain operations?
- What are the income statement and balance sheet effects of outsourcing production?
- How will a proposed merger affect profit margin and asset turnover?

Review 2-5 LO5

Assume **Microsoft Corporation** reports the following balances for the prior-year balance sheet and current-year income statement ($ millions). Prepare the articulation of Microsoft's financial statements for fiscal years 2014 and 2015 following the format of Exhibit 2.10.

Balance Sheet, June 30, 2014	
Assets	
Cash	$ 8,669
Noncash assets	163,715
Total assets	$172,384
Liabilities and equity	
Total liabilities	$ 82,600
Equity	
Contributed capital	68,366
Retained earnings	17,710
Other stockholders' equity	3,708
Liabilities and equity	$172,384

Income Statement, For Year Ended June 30, 2015	
Revenues	$93,580
Expenses	81,387
Net income	$12,193

Statement of Cash Flows, For Year Ended June 30, 2015	
Operating cash flows	$29,080
Investing cash flows	(23,001)
Financing cash flows	(9,153)

Notes: 1. Stock issuances for the year are $99.
2. Dividends for the year are $10,063.
3. Other decreases in retained earnings are $10,744.
4. Change in other stockholders' equity for the year is $(1,186).

Solution on p. 2-39.

Additional Information Sources

LO6
Locate and use additional financial information from public sources.

The four financial statements are only a part of the information available to financial statement users. Additional information, from a variety of sources provides useful insight into company operating activities and future prospects. This section highlights additional information sources.

Form 10-K

Companies with publicly traded securities must file with the SEC a detailed annual report and discussion of their business activities in their Form 10-K (quarterly reports are filed on Form 10-Q). Many of the disclosures in the 10-K are mandated by law and include the following general categories:

- **Item 1**, Business
- **Item 1A**, Risk Factors
- **Item 2**, Properties
- **Item 3**, Legal Proceedings
- **Item 4**, Submission of Matters to a Vote of Security Holders
- **Item 5**, Market for Registrant's Common Equity and Related Stockholder Matters

- **Item 6**, Selected Financial Data
- **Item 7**, Management's Discussion and Analysis of Financial Condition and Results of Operations
- **Item 7A**, Quantitative and Qualitative Disclosures About Market Risk
- **Item 8**, Financial Statements and Supplementary Data
- **Item 9**, Changes in and Disagreements with Accountants on Accounting and Financial Disclosure
- **Item 9A**, Controls and Procedures
- **Item 10**, Directors, Executive Officers, and Corporate Governance
- **Item 11**, Executive Compensation
- **Item 12**, Security Ownership of Certain Beneficial Owners and Management and Related Stockholder Matters
- **Item 13**, Certain Relationships and Related Transactions, and Director Independence
- **Item 14**, Principal Accountant Fees and Services

Description of the Business (Item 1)

Companies must provide a general description of their business, including their principal products and services, the source and availability of required raw materials; all patents, trademarks, licenses, and important related agreements; seasonality of the business; any dependence upon a single customer; and competitive conditions, including particular markets in which the company competes, the product offerings in those markets, and the status of its competitive environment. Companies must also provide a description of their overall strategy. **Apple**'s partial disclosure follows.

> The Company is committed to bringing the best user experience to its customers through its innovative hardware, software and services. The Company's business strategy leverages its unique ability to design and develop its own operating systems, hardware, application software and services to provide its customers products and solutions with innovative design, superior ease-of-use and seamless integration. As part of its strategy, the Company continues to expand its platform for the discovery and delivery of digital content and applications through its Internet Services, which allows customers to discover and download digital content, iOS, Mac and Apple Watch applications, and books through either a Mac or Windows-based computer or through iPhone, iPad and iPod touch® devices ("iOS devices") and Apple Watch. The Company also supports a community for the development of third-party software and hardware products and digital content that complement the Company's offerings. The Company believes a high-quality buying experience with knowledgeable salespersons who can convey the value of the Company's products and services greatly enhances its ability to attract and retain customers. Therefore, the Company's strategy also includes building and expanding its own retail and online stores and its third party distribution network to effectively reach more customers and provide them with a high-quality sales and post-sales support experience. The Company believes ongoing investment in research and development ("R&D"), marketing and advertising is critical to the development and sale of innovative products and technologies.

Management's Discussion and Analysis (Item 7)

The management discussion and analysis (MD&A) section of the 10-K contains valuable insight into the company's results of operations. In addition to an executive overview of company status and its recent operating results, the MD&A section includes information relating to critical accounting policies and estimates used in preparing the financial statements, a detailed discussion of sales activity; year-over-year comparisons of operating activities; analysis of gross margin, operating expenses, taxes, and off-balance-sheet and contractual obligations; assessment of factors that affect future results; and financial condition.

Item 7A reports quantitative and qualitative disclosures about market risk. For example, Apple makes the following disclosure relating to its Mac operating system and its iPods, iPhones, iPads, and other products.

The markets for the Company's products and services are highly competitive and the Company is confronted by aggressive competition in all areas of its business. These markets are characterized by frequent product introductions and rapid technological advances that have substantially increased the capabilities and use of mobile communication and media devices, personal computers and other digital electronic devices. The Company's competitors that sell mobile devices and personal computers based on other operating systems have aggressively cut prices and lowered their product margins to gain or maintain market share. The Company's financial condition and operating results can be adversely affected by these and other industry-wide downward pressures on gross margins. Principal competitive factors important to the Company include price, product features (including security features), relative price and performance, product quality and reliability, design innovation, a strong third-party software and accessories ecosystem, marketing and distribution capability, service and support and corporate reputation.

Schedule II—Valuation and Qualifying Accounts

In addition to the 10-K sections described above, the SEC requires companies to report additional information about certain balance sheet accounts. That information explains reserves and allowances the company establishes to reflect expected losses or uncollectible amounts. (We explain these accounts in later modules.) Many companies comply with this requirement by including the required information in notes to financial statements or as additional information at the end of the 10-K. Exhibit 2.11 shows a typical disclosure from Cisco Inc. from its 2015 10-K.

Exhibit 2.11 ◼ **Cisco's Schedule II from 2015 10-K**

SCHEDULE II
VALUATION AND QUALIFYING ACCOUNTS

	Allowances for	
Year Ended July 25, 2015 ($ millions)	**Financing Receivables**	**Accounts Receivable**
Balance at beginning of fiscal year	$349	$265
Provisions.	57	77
Write-offs net of recoveries	(7)	(40)
Foreign exchange and other	(17)	—
Balance at end of fiscal year	$382	$302

Cisco provides information relating to its reserves for anticipated losses on its financing receivables (leases and loans), and on its accounts receivable. Companies often provide similar analysis on estimated sales returns and deferred tax accounts. Our objective in reviewing these accounts is to determine if they are reasonable in amount and, if not, the extent to which our estimate of core operating income differs from that reported in the company's income statement. We discuss this analysis in later modules.

Form 20-F and Form 40-F

Non-U.S. companies that are publicly traded in the United States also file annual reports with the SEC. These foreign companies must furnish, within four months after the fiscal year end, the same audited financial statements required on Form 10-K. The filing, labeled Form 20-F, requires that firms provide financial statements prepared according to U.S. GAAP or IFRS. If the company uses accounting standards other than GAAP or IFRS, Form 20-F must discuss major differences between the accounting principles used and GAAP and provide a table that reconciles net income as reported to U.S. GAAP net income. In addition, each balance sheet item and cash flow measure that differs from U.S. GAAP, must be reconciled. Canadian companies file their annual reports, prepared under IFRS, using Form 40-F.

Form 8-K

Another useful report that is required by the SEC and is publicly available is the Form 8-K. This form must be filed within four business days of any of the following events.

- Quarterly earnings press release
- Entry into or termination of a material definitive agreement (including petition for bankruptcy)
- Exit from a line of business or impairment of assets
- Change in the company's certified public accounting firm
- Change in control of the company
- Departure of the company's executive officers
- Changes in the company's articles of incorporation or bylaws

Outsiders typically use Form 8-K to monitor for material adverse changes in the company.

Analyst Reports

Sell-side analysts provide their clients with objective analyses of company operating activities. Frequently, these reports include a discussion of the competitive environment for each of the company's principal product lines, strengths and weaknesses of the company, and an investment recommendation, including financial analysis and a stock price target. For example, **Oppenheimer** provides the following in its March 18, 2016, report to clients on Apple.

EQUITY RESEARCH

COMPANY UPDATE

March 18, 2016

TECHNOLOGY/EMERGING TECHNOLOGIES AND SERVICES

Stock Rating:

OUTPERFORM

12-18 mo. Price Target	$120.00
AAPL - NASDAQ	$105.80
3-5 Yr. EPS Gr. Rate	20%
52-Wk Range	$134.54-$92.00
Shares Outstanding	5,559.0M
Float	5,559.0M
Market Capitalization	$586,616.9M
Avg. Daily Trading Volume	47,680,756
Dividend/Div Yield	$2.08/1.97%
Book Value	$22.93
Fiscal Year Ends	Sep
2016E ROE	57.3 %
LT Debt	$53,204.0M
Preferred	$0.0M
Common Equity	$128,267M
Convertible Available	No

EPS Diluted	Q1	Q2	Q3	Q4	Year	Mult.
2014A	2.07	1.66	1.28	1.42	6.45	16.4x
2015A	3.06	2.33	1.85	1.96	9.22	11.5x
2016E	3.28A	2.02	1.81	2.15	9.29	11.4x
2017E	--	--	--	--	10.44	10.1x

Revenue ($/mil)	Q1	Q2	Q3	Q4	Year	Mult.
2014A	57.6B	45.6B	37.4B	42.1B	182.8B	3.0x
2015A	74.6B	58.0B	49.6B	51.5B	233.7B	2.3x
2016E	75.9BA	52.7B	48.2B	54.3B	231.1B	2.3x
2017E	--	--	--	--	251.5B	2.2x

Apple Inc.

Looking into Our Crystal Ball

SUMMARY

Next week (3/21) Apple is holding a press event, widely anticipated for new product announcements. While we expect to see several "under the hood" improvements across devices, we are not expecting the same exuberance as last year when Apple shared final details of the Apple Watch. Moreover, we worry investors will find the next several Apple media events underwhelming. In this note, we make predictions of what we expect to see over the next two years as well as provide investors with a history of past events (see appendix). We expect excitement to return as we predict 360 capture to be introduced for the iPhone, an OLED display, deeper Siri integrations, Apple's first IoT device for the home, and a mobile VR headset.

KEY POINTS

- **Capturing Leadership in Smartphone Camera:** the iPhone cameras best embody Apple's ability to elevate off-the-shelf components with superior software engineering skills to differentiate themselves from competition. We believe a series of major overhauls are in line for the upcoming iPhones—we see 360 video and depth sensing as the most likely new features.

- **Siri—The Omnipresent AI Assistant Across All Devices:** We believe Apple will continue to push wider deployment of Siri. This year, we believe Apple will encourage third-party developers to link with Siri in more meaningful ways, as a counterattack to "OK Google" and Amazon Echo.

- **One More Thing—VR:** We believe Apple has been building up to release a mobile VR headset based on potential changes in display technology (OLED), GPU improvement (consistent doubling of performance in recent iterations), and the introduction of more sophisticated sensor fusion, all of which will allow Apple to introduce a VR headset that utilizes current iPhones or iPads.

- **Incremental Improvements:** other non-essential improvements we believe Apple may gradually roll out for its hardware and software are: weather proofing, better battery life, lighter and thinner industrial designs, introduction of new materials, and enhancement and expanding partnerships for HomeKit, HealthKit, CarPlay, and Apple Pay.

- **Bottom Line:** We believe Apple's broadened device line-up and improving user experience will continue to add leverage to its ecosystem, allowing the company to engage and retain users previously untouched. It does this in small steps—and ultimately enables the company to create the next big thing. We don't see this model changing—but we do believe it could frustrate investors.

Credit Services

Several firms, including **Standard & Poor's** (**StandardAndPoors.com**), **Moody's Investors Service** (**Moodys.com**), and **Fitch Ratings** (**FitchRatings.com**), provide credit analysis that assists potential lenders, investors, employees, and other users in evaluating a company's creditworthiness and future financial viability. Credit analysis is a specialized field of analysis, quite different from the equity analysis illustrated here. These firms issue credit ratings on publicly issued bonds as well as on firms' commercial papers.

Data Services

A number of companies supply financial statement data in easy-to-download spreadsheet formats. **Thomson Reuters Corporation** (**ThomsonReuters.com**) provides a wealth of information to its database subscribers, including the widely quoted *First Call* summary of analysts' earnings forecasts. Standard & Poor's provides financial data for all publicly traded companies in its *Compustat* database. This database reports a plethora of individual data items for all publicly traded companies or for any specified subset of companies. These data are useful for performing statistical analysis and making comparisons across companies or within industries. Finally, **Capital IQ** (**CapitalIQ.com**), a division of Standard & Poor's, provides "as presented" financial data that conform to published financial statements, as well as additional statistical data and analysis.

Review 2-6 LO6

Use the SEC website (www.sec.gov/edgar/searchedgar/companysearch.html) to download **Microsoft**'s 2015 10-K, and answer the requirements.

Required
1. On what date did Microsoft file its 2015 10-K with the SEC? Compare this date with the company's fiscal year end. Why do the two dates differ?
2. Item 1 of the 10-K lists the company's executive officers. What are the names of the CEO and CFO?
3. As of June 30, 2015, how many people worked for Microsoft, and where were they located?
4. In the MD&A (10-K Item 7), Microsoft reports some interesting statistics and facts.
   - How many Xbox consoles did the company sell, and what was the growth rate for Xbox Live users?
   - What is Bing's market share?
   - Did the company acquire any other companies during the year? How many, and what was one notable acquisition?

Solution on p. 2-39
5. Who are the company's auditors?

Global Accounting

Both GAAP and IFRS use accrual accounting to prepare financial statements. Although there are vastly more similarities than differences, we highlight below a few of the more notable differences for financial statements.

Balance Sheet The most visible difference is that many IFRS-based balance sheets are presented in reverse order of liquidity. The least liquid asset, usually goodwill, is listed first, and the most liquid asset, cash, is last. The same inverse liquidity order applies to liabilities. There are also several detailed presentation and measurement differences that we explain in other modules. As one example, for GAAP-based balance sheets, bank overdrafts are often netted against cash balances. IFRS does not permit this netting on the balance sheet. However, the IFRS statement of cash flows *does* net the cash balance with any bank overdrafts and, thus, the cash balance on the statement of cash flows might not match the cash amount on the balance sheet.

Income Statement The most visible difference is that GAAP requires three years' of data on the income statement whereas IFRS requires only two. Another difference is that GAAP income statements

classify expenses by *function* and must separately report cost of goods sold, whereas IFRS permits expense classification by *function* (cost of sales, selling and administrative, etc.) or by *type* (raw materials, labor, depreciation, etc.). This means, for example, there is no requirement to report a cost of sales figure under IFRS.

Guidance Answers

You Are the Securities Analyst

Pg. 2-13 Of special concern is the possibility that the new CEO is shifting costs to the current period in lieu of recording them in future periods. Evidence suggests such behavior occurs when a new management team takes control. The reasoning is that the new management can blame poor current period performance on prior management and, at the same time, rid the balance sheet (and the new management team) of costs that would normally be expensed in future periods.

You Are the Operations Manager

Pg. 2-14 The CFO desires a warranty cost estimate that corresponds to the sales generated from the new product. To arrive at such an estimate, you must estimate the expected number and types of deficiencies in your product and the costs to repair each deficiency per the warranty provisions. This is often a difficult task for product engineers because it forces them to focus on product failures and associated costs.

Questions

Q2-1. The balance sheet consists of assets, liabilities, and equity. Define each category, and provide two examples of accounts reported within each category.

Q2-2. Explain how we account for a cost that creates an immediate benefit versus a cost that creates a future benefit.

Q2-3. GAAP is based on the concept of accrual accounting. Define and describe accrual accounting.

Q2-4. Analysts attempt to identify transitory items in an income statement. Define transitory items. What is the purpose of identifying transitory items?

Q2-5. What is the statement of stockholders' equity? What useful information does it contain?

Q2-6. What is the statement of cash flows? What useful information does it contain?

Q2-7. Define and explain the concept of financial statement articulation. What insight comes from understanding articulation?

Q2-8. Describe the flow of costs for the purchase of a machine. At what point do such costs become expenses? Why is it necessary to record the expenses related to the machine in the same period as the revenues it produces?

Q2-9. What are the two essential characteristics of an asset?

Q2-10. What does the concept of liquidity refer to? Explain.

Q2-11. What does the term *current* denote when referring to assets?

Q2-12. Assets are recorded at historical costs even though current market values might, arguably, be more relevant to financial statement readers. Describe the reasoning behind historical cost usage.

Q2-13. Identify three intangible assets that are likely to be *excluded* from the balance sheet because they cannot be reliably measured.

Q2-14. Identify three intangible assets that are recorded on the balance sheet.

Q2-15. What are accrued liabilities? Provide an example.

Q2-16. Define net working capital. Explain how increasing the amount of trade credit can reduce the net working capital for a company.

Q2-17. What is the difference between company *book value* and *market value*? Explain why these two amounts differ.

Q2-18. Describe the linkage between the income statement and the equity section of the balance sheet. Describe the linkage between the statement of cash flows and the equity section of the balance sheet when a company pays dividends.

Assignments with the ⊙ logo in the margin are available in **BusinessCourse**.
See the Preface of the book for details.

Mini Exercises

LO1, 2   **M2-19.** **Identifying and Classifying Financial Statement Items**

Homework

MBC

For each of the following items, indicate whether they would be reported in the balance sheet (B) or income statement (I).

___ *a.* Net income   ___ *d.* Accumulated depreciation ___ *g.* Interest expense
___ *b.* Retained earnings   ___ *e.* Wages expense   ___ *h.* Interest payable
___ *c.* Depreciation expense   ___ *f.* Wages payable   ___ *i.* Sales

LO1, 2   **M2-20.** **Identifying and Classifying Financial Statement Items**

For each of the following items, indicate whether they would be reported in the balance sheet (B) or income statement (I).

Homework

MBC

___ *a.* Machinery   ___ *e.* Common stock   ___ *i.* Taxes expense
___ *b.* Supplies expense   ___ *f.* Factory buildings   ___ *j.* Cost of goods sold
___ *c.* Inventories   ___ *g.* Receivables   ___ *k.* Long-term debt
___ *d.* Sales   ___ *h.* Taxes payable   ___ *l.* Treasury stock

LO6   **M2-21.** **Gather and Use Information from Form 8-K**

Delta Airlines (DAL)

On February 5, 2016, **Delta Airlines** filed a Form 8-K Current Report with the SEC. What important announcement did Delta make that day? *Hint:* Use the SEC website (www.sec.gov/edgar/searchedgar/companysearch.html) to find the Form 8-K.

LO1   **M2-22.** **Assigning Accounts to Sections of the Balance Sheet**

Homework

MBC

Identify each of the following accounts as a component of assets (A), liabilities (L), or equity (E).

___ *a.* Cash and cash equivalents   ___ *e.* Long-term debt
___ *b.* Wages payable   ___ *f.* Retained earnings
___ *c.* Common stock   ___ *g.* Additional paid-in capital
___ *d.* Equipment   ___ *h.* Taxes payable

LO3   **M2-23.** **Determining Missing Information Using the Accounting Equation**

Use knowledge of accounting relations to complete the following table for Boatsman Company.

Homework

MBC

	2016	2017
Beginning retained earnings.	$189,089	$?
Net income (loss)	?	48,192
Dividends	0	15,060
Ending retained earnings	169,634	?

LO3   **M2-24.** **Reconciling Retained Earnings**

Johnson & Johnson (JNJ)

Following is financial information from **Johnson & Johnson** for the year ended January 3, 2016. Prepare the retained earnings reconciliation for Johnson & Johnson for the year ended January 3, 2016 ($ millions).

Retained earnings, Dec. 28, 2014 . .	$97,245	Dividends	$8,173
Net earnings.	15,409	Retained earnings, Jan. 3, 2016.	?
Other retained earnings changes. . .	(602)		

E2-25.   Gather and Use Information from Form 20-F

Stock of **Credit Suisse Group** trades on the New York Stock Exchange as well as in various European stock markets. The company's Form 20-F reported the following.

LO2, 6
Credit Suisse Group
(CS)

> The accompanying consolidated financial statements of Credit Suisse Group AG (the Group) are prepared in accordance with accounting principles generally accepted in the US (US GAAP) and are stated in Swiss francs (CHF). The financial year for the Group ends on December 31.
> On October 21, 2015, the Group announced its new strategy and organization, which included the introduction of a new segment structure. In connection with the strategic review of the Group, restructuring expenses of CHF 355 million were recognized in 2015. Reclassifications have been made to the prior year's consolidated financial statements to conform to the current presentation. The reclassifications had no impact on net income/(loss) or total shareholders' equity.

Required

a. Why would Credit Suisse prepare its financial statements in accordance with U.S. GAAP?

b. Credit Suisse separately reported the CHF 355 million restructuring expense. Explain how this reporting could help analysts who seek to predict future earnings.

E2-26.   Gather and Use Information from Form 20-F

Nippon Telegraph and Telephone Corporation reports the following information in Schedule II of its 2016 Form 20-F. Accounts receivable represents the amount customers owe the company at year-end. The balance in the allowance for doubtful accounts is the company's best estimate of the amount customers will not repay.

LO1, 6
Nippon Telegraph
and Telephone
Corporation (NTT)

VALUATION AND QUALIFYING ACCOUNTS				
For Year Ended March 31 (¥ millions)	Balance at Beginning of Period	Additions Charged to Costs and Expenses	Deductions	Balance at End of Period
Allowance for doubtful accounts, March 31, 2014	¥44,961	¥37,197	¥(35,265)	¥46,893
Allowance for doubtful accounts, March 31, 2015	¥46,893	¥28,504	¥(32,167)	¥43,230
Allowance for doubtful accounts, March 31, 2016	¥43,230	¥32,200	¥(30,194)	¥45,236

Required

The balance in the allowance account increased during 2016 (from ¥ 43,230 million to ¥ 45,236 million) after decreasing during 2015 (from ¥ 46,893 million to ¥ 43,230million). What additional information would an analyst want to use to determine if this variability is of concern?

E2-27.   Constructing Financial Statements from Account Data

Barth Company reports the following year-end account balances at December 31, 2016. Prepare the 2016 income statement and the balance sheet as of December 31, 2016.

LO1, 2

Accounts payable.	$ 16,000	Inventory.	$ 36,000
Accounts receivable.	30,000	Land	80,000
Bonds payable, long-term	200,000	Goodwill	8,000
Buildings.	151,000	Retained earnings.	160,000
Cash.	148,000	Sales revenue	500,000
Common stock.	150,000	Supplies inventory	3,000
Cost of goods sold.	180,000	Supplies expense	6,000
Equipment	70,000	Wages expense	40,000

Homework
MBC

LO1, 2   **E2-28.**   **Constructing Financial Statements from Transaction Data**

Baiman Corporation commences operations at the beginning of January. It provides its services on credit and bills its customers $40,000 for January sales. Its employees also earn January wages of $12,000 that are not paid until the first of February. Complete the following statements for the month-end of January.

Income Statement		
Sales.................	$	
Wages expense		_____
Net income (loss)	$	

Balance Sheet		
Cash..................	$	
Accounts receivable......		_____
Total assets.............	$	
Wages payable..........	$	
Retained earnings		_____
Total liabilities and equity..	$	

LO1, 2, 3, 4, 5   **E2-29.**   **Applying Financial Statement Linkages to Understand Transactions**

Consider the effects of the independent transactions, *a* through *g*, on a company's balance sheet, income statement, and statement of cash flows. Complete the table below to explain the effects and financial statement linkages. Use "+" to indicate the account increases and "−" to indicate the account decreases. Refer to Exhibit 2.10 as a guide for the linkages.

	a.	b.	c.	d.	e.	f.	g.
Balance Sheet							
Cash............................	___	___	___	___	___	___	___
Noncash assets	___	___	___	___	___	___	___
Total liabilities....................	___	___	___	___	___	___	___
Contributed capital.................	___	___	___	___	___	___	___
Retained earnings	___	___	___	___	___	___	___
Other equity	___	___	___	___	___	___	___
Statement of Cash Flows							
Operating cash flow................	___	___	___	___	___	___	___
Investing cash flow.................	___	___	___	___	___	___	___
Financing cash flow	___	___	___	___	___	___	___
Income Statement							
Revenues	___	___	___	___	___	___	___
Expenses	___	___	___	___	___	___	___
Net income.......................	___	___	___	___	___	___	___
Statement of Stockholders' Equity							
Contributed capital.................	___	___	___	___	___	___	___
Retained earnings	___	___	___	___	___	___	___

a. The company issued common stock in exchange for cash and property and equipment.
b. The company paid cash for rent of office furnishings and facilities.
c. The company performed services for clients and immediately received cash earned.
d. The company performed services for clients and sent a bill with payment due within 60 days.
e. The company compensated an office employee with cash as salary.
f. The company received cash as partial payment on the amount owed from clients in transaction *d*.
g. The company paid cash in dividends.

LO1, 2, 3, 4, 5   **E2-30.**   **Applying Financial Statement Linkages to Understand Transactions**

Consider the effects of the independent transactions, *a* through *g*, on a company's balance sheet, income statement, and statement of cash flow. Complete the table below to explain the effects and financial statement linkages. Use "+" to indicate the account increases and "−" to indicate the account decreases. Refer to Exhibit 2-10 as a guide for the linkages.

	a.	b.	c.	d.	e.	f.	g.
Balance Sheet							
Cash....................	___	___	___	___	___	___	___
Noncash assets	___	___	___	___	___	___	___
Total liabilities...........	___	___	___	___	___	___	___
Contributed capital.........	___	___	___	___	___	___	___
Retained earnings	___	___	___	___	___	___	___
Other equity	___	___	___	___	___	___	___
Statement of Cash Flows							
Operating cash flow	___	___	___	___	___	___	___
Investing cash flow.........	___	___	___	___	___	___	___
Financing cash flow	___	___	___	___	___	___	___
Income Statement							
Revenues	___	___	___	___	___	___	___
Expenses	___	___	___	___	___	___	___
Net income..............	___	___	___	___	___	___	___
Statement of Stockholders' Equity							
Contributed capital.........	___	___	___	___	___	___	___
Retained earnings	___	___	___	___	___	___	___

a. Owners invested cash in the company in exchange for shares of common stock.

b. The company received cash from the bank for a loan.

c. The company purchased equipment to manufacture goods for sale and paid with cash.

d. The company manufactured a custom piece of inventory and paid cash for materials and labor. The company sold the inventory for more than cost, and the customer promised to pay for the inventory in 30 days.

e. The company paid monthly rent for a manufacturing space.

f. The company paid $935 cash in dividends to the owners.

g. The company received cash from the customer in transaction d.

E2-31. Identifying and Classifying Balance Sheet and Income Statement Accounts

LO1, 2

Staples Inc. (SPLS)

Following are selected accounts for **Staples Inc.** for the fiscal year ended January 30, 2016..

a. Indicate whether each account appears on the balance sheet (B) or income statement (I).

b. Using the following data, compute total assets and total expenses.

$ millions	Amount	Classification
Sales..	$21,059	___
Accumulated depreciation	4,375	___
Depreciation expense...........................	388	___
Retained earnings	6,900	___
Net income...................................	379	___
Property, plant, and equipment, net	1,586	___
Selling, general, and administrative expense.............	4,600	___
Accounts receivable...........................	1,899	___
Total liabilities...............................	4,788	___
Total stockholders' equity	5,384	___

E2-32. Identifying and Classifying Balance Sheet and Income Statement Accounts

LO1, 2

Target Corporation (TGT)

Following are selected accounts for **Target Corporation**, for the fiscal year ended January 30, 2016..

a. Indicate whether each account appears on the balance sheet (B) or income statement (I).

b. Using the following data, compute total assets and total expenses.

$ millions	Amount	Classification
Total revenues	$73,785	_____
Accrued liabilities	4,236	_____
Depreciation and amortization expense	2,213	_____
Retained earnings	8,188	_____
Net income	3,363	_____
Property, plant, and equipment, net	25,217	_____
Selling, general, and administrative expense	14,665	_____
Inventory	8,601	_____
Total liabilities	27,305	_____
Total stockholders' equity	12,957	_____

LO1, 2

Abercrombie & Fitch (ANF)

TJX Companies (TJX)

E2-33.   Comparing Income Statements and Balance Sheets of Competitors

Following are selected income statement and balance sheet data from two retailers, **Abercrombie & Fitch** (clothing retailer in the high-end market) and **TJX Companies** (clothing retailer in the value-priced market), for the fiscal year ended January 30, 2016.

Income Statement ($ thousands)	ANF	TJX
Sales	$3,518,680	$30,944,938
Cost of goods sold	1,361,137	22,034,523
Gross profit	2,157,543	8,910,415
Total expenses	2,121,967	6,632,757
Net income	$ 35,576	$ 2,277,658

Balance Sheet ($ thousands)	ANF	TJX
Current assets	$1,178,980	$ 6,772,560
Long-term assets	1,254,059	4,726,922
Total assets	$2,433,039	$11,499,482
Current liabilities	$ 534,703	$ 4,402,230
Long-term liabilities	602,614	2,790,177
Total liabilities	1,137,317	7,192,407
Stockholders' equity	1,295,722	4,307,075
Total liabilities and equity	$2,433,039	$11,499,482

a. Express each income statement amount as a percentage of sales. Comment on any differences observed between these two companies, especially as they relate to their respective business models.

b. Express each balance sheet amount as a percentage of total assets. Comment on any differences observed between these two companies, especially as they relate to their respective business models.

c. Which company has a lower proportion of debt? What do the ratios tell us about the relative riskiness of the two companies?

LO1, 2

Apple Inc. (AAPL)

HP Inc. (HPQ)

E2-34.   Comparing Income Statements and Balance Sheets of Competitors

Following are selected income statement and balance sheet data from two computer competitors, **Apple** and **HP Inc.**, for the fiscal years ended September 26, 2015, and October 31, 2015, respectively.

Income Statement ($ millions)	Apple	HP
Sales	$233,715	$103,355
Cost of goods sold	140,089	78,596
Gross profit	93,626	24,759
Total expenses	40,232	20,205
Net income	$ 53,394	$ 4,554

Balance Sheet ($ millions)	Apple	HP
Current assets	$ 89,378	$ 51,787
Long-term assets	201,101	55,095
Total assets	$290,479	106,882
Current liabilities	$ 80,610	$ 42,191
Long-term liabilities	90,514	36,540
Total liabilities	171,124	78,731
Stockholders' equity	119,355	28,151
Total liabilities and equity	$290,479	$106,882

a. Express each income statement amount as a percentage of sales. Comment on any differences observed between the two companies, especially as they relate to their respective business models. (*Hint:* Apple's gross profit as a percentage of sales is considerably higher than HP's. What aspect of Apple's business do we believe is driving its profitability?)

b. Express each balance sheet amount as a percentage of total assets. Comment on any differences observed between the two companies. Apple has chosen to structure itself with a higher proportion of equity (and a lower proportion of debt) than HP. How does this capital structure decision affect our evaluation of the relative riskiness of these two companies?

E2-35. **Comparing Income Statements and Balance Sheets of Competitors**   **LO1, 2**

Following are selected income statement and balance sheet data for two communications companies, **Comcast** and **Verizon**, for the year ended December 31, 2015.

Comcast (CMCSA)
Verizon (VZ)

Income Statement ($ millions)	Comcast	Verizon
Sales	$74,510	$131,620
Operating costs	58,512	98,560
Operating profit	15,998	33,060
Nonoperating expenses	7,585	15,181
Net income	$ 8,413	$ 17,879

Balance Sheet ($ millions)	Comcast	Verizon
Current assets	$ 12,303	$ 22,280
Long-term assets	154,271	222,360
Total assets	$166,574	$244,640
Current liabilities	$ 18,178	$ 35,052
Long-term liabilities	94,418	191,746
Total liabilities	$112,596	226,798
Stockholders' equity*	53,978	17,842
Total liabilities and equity	$166,574	$244,640

*Includes noncontrolling interest

a. Express each income statement amount as a percentage of sales. Comment on any differences observed between the two companies.

b. Express each balance sheet amount as a percentage of total assets. Comment on any differences observed between the two companies, especially as they relate to their respective business models.

c. Both Verizon and Comcast have chosen a capital structure with a higher proportion of liabilities than equity. How does this capital structure decision affect our evaluation of the riskiness of these two companies? Take into consideration the large level of capital expenditures that each must make to remain competitive.

E2-36. **Comparing Financial Information Across Industries**   **LO1, 2**

Use the data and computations required in parts *a* and *b* of exercises E2-33 and E2-34 to compare **TJX Companies** and **Apple Inc.**

TJX Companies (TJX)
Apple Inc. (AAPL)

a. Compare gross profit and net income as a percentage of sales for these two companies. How might differences in their respective business models explain the differences observed?

b. Compare sales versus total assets. What do observed differences indicate about the relative capital intensity of these two industries?

c. Which company has the higher percentage of total liabilities to stockholders' equity? What do these ratios imply about the relative riskiness of these two companies?

LO1, 2, 3, 4, 5   **E2-37.**   **Applying Financial Statement Linkages to Understand Transactions**

Consider the effects of the independent transactions, *a* through *h*, on a company's balance sheet, income statement, and statement of cash flow. Complete the table below to explain the effects and financial statement linkages. Use "+" to indicate the account increases and "−" to indicate the account decreases. Refer to Exhibit 2-10 as a guide for the linkages.

	a.	b.	c.	d.	e.	f.	g.	h.
Balance Sheet								
Cash								
Noncash assets								
Total liabilities								
Contributed capital								
Retained earnings								
Other equity								
Statement of Cash Flows								
Operating cash flow								
Investing cash flow								
Financing cash flow								
Income Statement								
Revenues								
Expenses								
Net income								
Statement of Stockholders' Equity								
Contributed capital								
Retained earnings								

a. Wages are earned by employees but not yet paid.

b. Inventory is purchased on credit.

c. Inventory purchased in transaction *b* is sold on credit (and for more than its cost).

d. Collected cash from transaction *c*.

e. Equipment is acquired for cash.

f. Paid cash for inventory purchased in transaction *b*.

g. Paid cash toward a note payable that came due.

h. Paid cash for interest on borrowings.

Problems

LO1   **P2-38.**   **Constructing and Analyzing Balance Sheet Amounts from Incomplete Data**

3M Company (MMM)

Selected balance sheet amounts for **3M Company**, a manufacturer of consumer and business products, for three recent years follow.

$ millions	Current Assets	Long-Term Assets	Total Assets	Current Liabilities	Long-Term Liabilities	Total Liabilities	Stockholders' Equity*
2013	$12,733	$?	$33,550	$?	$ 8,104	$15,602	$17,948
2014	12,303	18,906	?	5,964	12,103	?	13,142
2015	?	21,732	32,718	7,118	13,853	20,971	?

* Includes noncontrolling interest

Required

a. Compute the missing balance sheet amounts for each of the three years shown.

b. What types of accounts would we expect to be included in current assets? In long-term assets?

P2-39. Use Additional Information from 10-K to Explain Linkages Among Financial Statements   **LO1, 2, 5, 6**

Community Health Systems operates general acute care hospitals in communities across the United States. The company reports the following information in Schedule II of its 2015 10-K.   **Community Health Systems (CYH)**

SCHEDULE II—VALUATION AND QUALIFYING ACCOUNTS					
$ millions	**Balance at Beginning of Year**	**Acquisitions and Dispositions**	**Bad Debt Expense**	**Write-Offs**	**Balance at End of Year**
December 31, 2015, allowance for doubtful accounts ...	$3,504	$ (17)	$3,168	$(2,545)	$4,110
December 31, 2014, allowance for doubtful accounts ...	2,438	960	3,022	(2,916)	3,504
December 31, 2013, allowance for doubtful accounts ...	2,191	—	2,034	(1,787)	2,438

Accounts receivable represents the amount customers owe Community Health Systems for services rendered. The balance in the allowance for doubtful accounts is the company's best estimate of the amount that customers will not repay.

Community Health Systems' balance sheet and income statements reported the following information:

$ millions	**2015**	**2014**	**2013**
Revenue	$22,564	$21,561	$14,853
Operating income before tax	1,337	1,339	917
Total assets.	26,861	27,421	17,117

Required

a. Compute the common-size allowance for doubtful accounts for each year. Compare 2015 to the prior years; what do we observe? What is one conclusion analysts might draw from this analysis?

b. On average, the firms in the S&P 500 report common-size allowance for doubtful accounts between 3% and 5%. Why might Community Health Systems' ratio be so much higher? How could an analyst verify this inference?

c. Compute the common-size bad debt expense for each year. Interpret the ratio for 2015. What trend do we observe?

d. If the company had recorded bad debt expense of $2,668 in 2015 (which is $500 less of bad debt expense), what would the company have reported for operating income before tax? How would retained earnings have been affected? How is cash from operations affected? For this question, ignore tax effects.

P2-40. Gather and Use Additional Information from 10-K   **LO6**

Use the SEC website (www.sec.gov/edgar/searchedgar/companysearch.html) to download the 2015 10-K for **Facebook Inc.**, and answer the following questions.   **Facebook (FB)**

a. On what date did Facebook file its 2015 10-K with the SEC? Compare this date to the company's fiscal year end. Why do the two dates differ?

b. Item 1 of the 10-K reports the company's mission. What is its mission?

c. Who does Facebook see as its main competition? See Item 1 of the 10-K.

d. As of December 31, 2015, how many people worked for Facebook?

e. How many daily active users did Facebook have in December 2015? How does this compare with December 2014.

f. Many companies file Schedule II with the 10-K. One of the components of Schedule II is an estimate of the amount owing from customers that will not be collected (allowance for doubtful accounts). What does Facebook report concerning this schedule? Explain.

g. Who are the company's auditors?

LO1, 2 **P2-41.** **Comparing Operating Characteristics Across Industries**

Following are selected income statement and balance sheet data for companies in different industries.

$ millions	Sales	Cost of Goods Sold	Gross Profit	Net Income	Assets	Liabilities	Stockholders' Equity
Target Corp.	$73,785	$51,997	$21,788	$3,363	$ 40,262	$27,305	$12,957
Nike Inc..	32,376	17,405	14,971	3,760	21,396	9,138	12,258
Harley-Davidson	5,995	3,620	2,375	752	9,991	8,151	1,840
Cisco Systems	49,247	18,287	30,960	10,739	121,652	58,067	63,585

Target Corp. (TGT)
Nike (NKE)
Harley-Davidson (HOG)
Cisco Systems (CSCO)

Required

a. Compute the following ratios for each company.
1. Gross profit/Sales
2. Net income/Sales
3. Net income/Stockholders' equity
4. Liabilities/Stockholders' equity

b. Comment on any differences among the companies' gross profit-to-sales ratios and net income as a percentage of sales. Do differences in the companies' business models explain the differences observed?

c. Which company reports the highest ratio of net income to equity? Suggest one or more reasons for this result.

d. Which company has financed itself with the highest percentage of liabilities to equity? Suggest one or more reasons why this company can take on such debt levels.

LO2, 4 **P2-42.** **Comparing Cash Flows Across Retailers**

Following are selected accounts from the income statement and the statement of cash flows for several retailers, for their fiscal years ended in 2016.

$ millions	Sales	Net Income	Cash Flows from Operating	Cash Flows from Investing	Cash Flows from Financing
Macy's	$ 27,079	$ 1,072	$ 1,984	$ (1,092)	$ (2,029)
Home Depot Inc..	88,519	7,009	9,373	(2,982)	(5,898)
Staples Inc.	21,059	379	978	(374)	(406)
Target Corp.	73,785	3,363	5,844	508	(4,516)
Walmart Stores	478,614	14,694	27,389	(10,675)	(17,144)

Macy's (M)
Home Depot (HD)
Staples (SPLS)
Target (TGT)
Walmart (WMT)

Required

a. Compute the ratio of net income to sales for each company. Rank the companies on the basis of this ratio. Do their respective business models give insight into these differences?

b. Compute net cash flows from operating activities as a percentage of sales. Rank the companies on the basis of this ratio. Does this ranking coincide with the ratio rankings from part *a*? Suggest one or more reasons for any differences observed.

c. Compute net cash flows from investing activities as a percentage of sales. Rank the companies on the basis of this ratio. Does this ranking coincide with the ratio rankings from part *a*? Suggest one or more reasons for any differences observed.

IFRS Applications

LO1, 2 **I2-43.** **Comparing Income Statements and Balance Sheets of Competitors**

Following are selected income statement and balance sheet data from two European grocery chain companies: Tesco PLC (UK) and Ahold (the Netherlands).

Income Statements For Fiscal Year Ended	Tesco February 27, 2016 (£ millions)	Ahold December 30, 2015 (€ millions)
Sales.	£54,433	€38,203
Cost of goods sold.	51,579	27,835
Gross profit.	2,854	10,368
Total expenses	2,716	9,517
Net income.	£ 138	€ 851

Balance Sheet	Tesco February 27, 2016 (£ millions)	Ahold December 30, 2015 (€ millions)
Current assets	£14,828	€ 5,260
Long-term assets	29,076	10,620
Total assets.	£43,904	€15,880
Current liabilities.	£19,714	€ 5,002
Long-term liabilities	15,574	5,257
Total liabilities.	35,288	10,259
Stockholders' equity	8,616	5,621
Total liabilities and equity	£43,904	€15,880

Required

a. Prepare a common-size income statement. To do this, express each income statement amount as a percent of sales. Comment on any differences observed between the two companies. Ahold's gross profit percentage of sales is considerably higher than Tesco's. What might explain this difference?

b. Prepare a common-size balance sheet. To do this, express each balance sheet amount as a percent of total assets. Comment on any differences observed between the two companies.

c. Ahold has chosen to structure itself with a higher proportion of equity (and a lower proportion of debt) than Tesco. How does this capital structure decision affect our assessment of the relative riskiness of these two companies?

Management Applications

MA2-44. Understanding the Company Operating Cycle and Management Strategy   **LO1, 4**

Consider the operating cycle as depicted in Exhibit 2.4 to answer the following questions.

a. Why might a company want to reduce its cash conversion cycle? (*Hint*: Consider the financial statement implications of reducing the cash conversion cycle.)

b. How might a company reduce its cash conversion cycle?

c. Examine and discuss the potential impacts on *customers* and *suppliers* of taking the actions identified in part *b*.

MA2-45. Ethics and Governance: Understanding Revenue Recognition and Expense Recording   **LO2**

Revenue should be recognized when it is earned and expense when incurred. Given some lack of specificity in these terms, companies have some latitude when applying GAAP to determine the timing and amount of revenues and expenses. A few companies use this latitude to manage reported earnings. Some have argued that it is not necessarily bad for companies to manage earnings in that, by doing so, management (1) can better provide investors and creditors with reported earnings that are closer to "core" earnings (i.e., management purges earnings of components deemed irrelevant or distracting so that share prices better reflect company performance) and (2) can present the company in the best light, which benefits both shareholders and employees—a Machiavellian argument that "the end justifies the means."

a. Is it good that GAAP is written as broadly as it is? Explain. What are the pros and cons of defining accounting terms more strictly?

b. Assess (both pro and con) the Machiavellian argument above that defends managing earnings.

Ongoing Project

(This ongoing project began in Module 1 and continues through most of the book; even if previous segments were not completed, the requirements are still applicable to any business analysis.) The goal of this module's project is to perform vertical analysis of the balance sheet and income statement, assess cash flows, and determine market capitalization.

1. *Balance Sheet Analysis.* Prepare a common-size balance sheet. To facilitate this, obtain the balance sheet in spreadsheet form from the SEC website at the the "Interactive Data" link on the search results page. Look for major differences over time. Some questions to consider:
   - What are the company's largest assets? Largest liabilities?
   - What proportion of total assets is financed by owners? (*Hint:* Compare with total equity.)
   - What proportion of total assets is financed by nonowners?

2. *Income Statement Analysis.* Prepare a common size income statement. Express each item on the income statement as a percent of total sales or revenue. Do this for all years on the income statement. Look for major differences over time and between the companies. Do any patterns emerge? Some questions to consider:
   - What are the major expenses?
   - Are there any unusual or discontinued items? Are they large in magnitude?
   - Was the company more or less profitable when compared with the prior year?

3. *Statement of Cash Flows Analysis.* Determine the size and direction (cash source or use) of cash flows from operations, investing, and financing. One goal is to understand the company's pattern of cash flows and to form an opinion about the general strength of its cash flows. Some questions to consider:
   - What were the cash flows from operations? Were they positive?
   - Were operating cash flows smaller or larger than net income?
   - Did the company generate or use cash from investing activities?
   - Did the company generate or use cash from financing activities?

4. *Market Capitalization.* Determine the market capitalization at the most recent year-end. Determine the number of shares outstanding from the balance sheet. Recall that shares outstanding is total shares issued less any treasury shares. Obtain the year-end stock price from an investment website such as Seeking Alpha or Yahoo Finance. Compare market cap with the book value (total equity) of the company.

Solutions to Review Problems

Review 2-1—Solution ($ millions)

MICROSOFT CORPORATION Balance Sheet June 30, 2015			
Cash and short-term investments	$ 96,526	Accounts payable	$ 6,591
Accounts receivable	17,908	Accrued expenses	5,096
Inventories	2,902	Other current liabilities	38,171
Other current assets	7,376	Long-term liabilities	46,282
Property, plant, and equipment, net	14,731	Common stock and paid-in capital	68,465
Other long-term assets	36,780	Retained earnings	9,096
		Other stockholders' equity	2,522
Total assets	$176,223	Total liabilities and equity	$176,223

Review 2-2—Solution ($ millions)

MICROSOFT CORPORATION Income Statement For Year Ended June 30, 2015	
Total revenue	$93,580
Cost of goods sold	33,038
Gross profit	60,542
Operating expenses	32,370
Operating income	28,172
Other expenses	9,665
Income before income tax	18,507
Income tax expense	6,314
Net income	$12,193

Review 2-3—Solution ($ millions)

MICROSOFT CORPORATION Statement of Stockholders' Equity For Year Ended June 31, 2015				
	Common Stock and Paid-in Capital	**Retained Earnings**	**Accumulated Other Comprehensive Income**	**Total Equity**
Beginning balance	$68,366	$17,710	$3,708	$89,784
Stock issuance, net	99			99
Net income		12,193		12,193
Dividends		(10,063)		(10,063)
Other		(10,744)	(1,186)	(11,930)
Ending balance	$68,465	$ 9,096	$2,522	$80,083

Review 2-4—Solution ($ millions)

MICROSOFT CORPORATION Statement of Cash Flows For Year Ended June 30, 2015	
Cash flows from operating activities	$29,080
Cash flows used for investing activities	(23,001)
Cash flows used for financing activities	(9,153)
Net change in cash	(3,074)
Cash balance, beginning of year	8,669
Cash balance, end of year	$ 5,595

Review 2-5—Solution

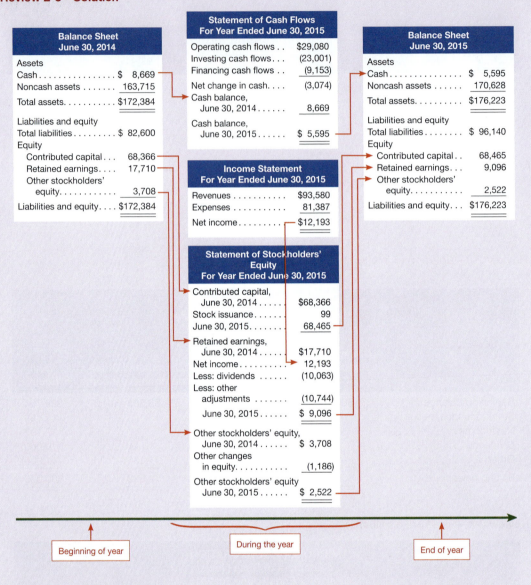

Review 2-6—Solution

1. The 10-K was filed on July 31, 2015, and the company's fiscal year end was June 30, 2015. The SEC filing is a month after year end because the auditors took a month to complete the audit.
2. The company's CEO is Satya Nadella, and the CFO is Amy E. Hood.
3. As of June 30, 2015, Microsoft employed approximately 118,000 people on a full-time basis, roughly 60,000 in the United States and 58,000 internationally.
4. The MD&A reports the following.
   - Xbox console volumes grew to over 12 million, and Xbox Live users increased 22%.
   - Bing exceeded 20% U.S. market share as the company focused its advertising business on search.
   - Microsoft completed 16 acquisitions, including Mojang Synergies, the Swedish video game developer of the Minecraft gaming franchise.
5. The company is audited by Deloitte and Touch out of the Seattle office.

Module 3

Transactions, Adjustments, and Financial Statements

Learning Objectives

LO1 Explain the accounting cycle, and construct the financial statement effects template. (p. 3-3)

LO2 Apply the financial statement effects template to analyze accounting transactions. (p. 3-6)

LO3 Prepare and explain accounting adjustments and their financial statement effects. (p. 3-9)

LO4 Construct financial statements from accounting records. (p. 3-13)

LO5 Explain and apply the closing process. (p. 3-16)

AAPL

Market cap: $639,939 mil
Total assets: $290,479 mil
Revenues: $233,715 mil
Net income: $53,394 mil

Apple Inc. launched the iPhone ten years ago, which is one of the most important products in its history. As of today, Apple has sold over 800 million iPhones, eight times the number of iPads and Mac products combined, as shown in the following.

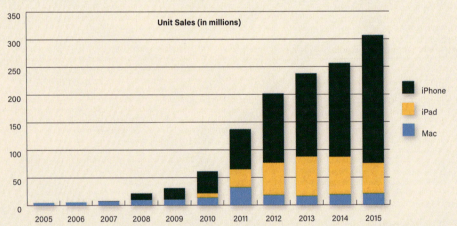

To bring each iPhone to market, Apple must purchase component parts, manufacture them, hire sales personnel, pay advertisers, and distribute finished products. Each of these activities involves a transaction that Apple's accounting system must capture and communicate to its stakeholders.

This module explains how the accounting system captures business transactions, creates financial records, and aggregates the individual records to produce financial reports we read and interpret in company 10-Ks. The resulting financial statements tell the story of Apple's business activities. We analyze those financial statements for insights into company operations and future performance. [Source: *Apple*, 2015 10-K.]

© iStock

Road Map

LO	Learning Objective | Topics	Page	eLecture	Guided Example	Assignments
3-1	**Explain the accounting cycle, and construct the financial statement effects template.** Accounting Cycle :: Template :: T-Account :: Journal Entry	3-3	e3–1	Review 3-1	1, 2, 3, 4, 7, 8
3-2	**Apply the financial statement effects template to analyze accounting transactions.** Transactions :: Applying the Template :: Applying the T-Account and Journal Entry	3-6	e3–2	Review 3-2	5, 6, 9, 10, 12, 13, 14, 15, 16, 17, 21, 24, 28, 29, 30, 36, 37, 39, 40, 42, 44, 45, 46, 47, 48, 49, 50, 56, 57, 58, 59, 60, 62, 63
3-3	**Prepare and explain accounting adjustments and their financial statement effects.** Prepaid Expenses :: Unearned Revenues :: Accrued Expenses :: Accrued Revenues	3-9	e3–3	Review 3-3	5, 6, 16, 17, 18, 20, 26, 27, 29, 30, 31, 32, 33, 34, 35, 45, 46, 47, 48, 49, 50, 51, 52, 53, 54, 55, 57, 58, 60, 64, 65, 66
3-4	**Construct financial statements from accounting records.** Income Statement :: Retained Earnings Statement :: Balance Sheet :: Statement of Equity	3-13	e3–4	Review 3-4	11, 18, 19, 22, 26, 27, 41, 43, 55, 56, 58, 59, 60, 64
3-5	**Explain and apply the closing process.** Revenue Accounts :: Expense Accounts :: Dividend Account	3-16	e3–5	Review 3-5	11, 23, 25, 32, 38, 41, 55, 61

Transactions, Adjustments, and Financial Statements

Accounting for Transactions	Accounting Adjustments	Financial Statement Preparation
■ Accounting Cycle ■ Financial Statement Effects Template ■ T-Account ■ Journal Entry	■ Prepaid Expenses ■ Unearned Revenues ■ Accrued Expenses ■ Accrued Revenues	■ Income Statement ■ Balance Sheet ■ Retained Earnings Statement ■ Statement of Stockholders' Equity ■ Closing Process

Basics of Accounting

eLectures **LO1**
MBC Explain the accounting cycle, and construct the financial statement effects template.

Financial statements report on the financial performance and condition of a business. Those statements are tied to a period or point in time. The period of time is referred to as the accounting cycle, and each cycle consists of four activities.

Four-Step Accounting Cycle

The *accounting cycle* is illustrated in Exhibit 3.1.

■ **Step 1** Record transactions in the accounting records. Each transaction is the result of an external or internal transaction or event, such as a sale to a customer or the payment of wages to employees.

■ **Step 2** Prepare accounting adjustments, which recognize a number of events that have occurred but that have not yet been recorded. These might include the recognition of wage expense and the related wages payable for those employees who have earned wages but have not yet been paid or of depreciation expense for buildings and equipment.

■ **Step 3** Prepare financial statements.

■ **Step 4** Close the books in anticipation of the start of a new accounting cycle.

Exhibit 3.1 ■ Accounting Cycle

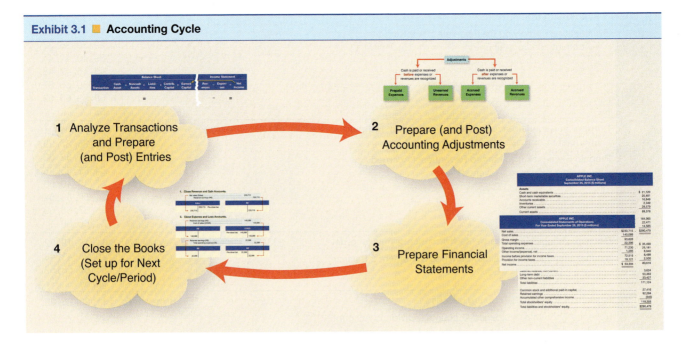

The purpose of this module is to explain the accounting cycle. We use Apple's financials to illustrate the four steps in the accounting cycle. Understanding the financial statement preparation process requires an understanding of the language used to record business transactions in accounting records. The recording and statement preparation processes are readily understood once we learn that language (of financial statement effects) and its mechanics (entries and posting). Even if we never journalize a transaction or prepare a financial statement, understanding the accounting process aids us in analyzing and interpreting accounting reports. Understanding the accounting language also facilitates our communication with business professionals within a company and with members of the business community outside of a company.

Financial Statement Effects Template

As of its 2015 year-end, Apple reports total assets of $290,479 million, total liabilities of $171,124 million, and equity of $119,355 million. The accounting equation for Apple follows ($ millions).

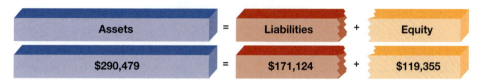

As financial statement users, we often draw on this relation to assess the effects of transactions and events, different accounting methods, and choices that managers make in preparing financial statements. For example, we are interested in knowing the effects of an asset acquisition or sale on the balance sheet, income statement, and cash flow statement. Or, we might want to understand how the failure to recognize a liability would understate liabilities and overstate profits and equity. A useful tool to perform these sorts of analysis is the following **financial statement effects template**.

The template captures the transaction and its effects on the four financial statements: balance sheet, income statement, statement of stockholders' equity, and statement of cash flows. For the balance sheet, we differentiate between cash and noncash assets so as to identify the cash effects of transactions. Likewise, equity is separated into the contributed and earned capital components. Finally, income statement effects are separated into revenues, expenses, and net income (the updating of retained earnings is denoted with an arrow line running from net income to earned capital). This template provides a convenient means to represent relatively complex financial accounting transactions and events in a simple, concise manner for both analysis and interpretation.

In addition to using the template to show the dollar effects of a transaction on the four financial statements, we also include each transaction's *journal entry* and *T-account* representation in the margin. We explain journal entries and T-accounts in the next section; these are part of the bookkeeping aspects of accounting. The margin entries can be ignored without any loss of insight gained from the template.

T-Accounts

The **T-account**, named for its likeness to a "T," is used to reflect increases and decreases to individual accounts. When a transaction occurs, it is recorded (*journalized*); once recorded, the specific accounts affected are updated in the accounting books (*general ledger*) of the company, and the affected accounts are increased or decreased. This process of continuously updating individual account balances is referred to as *posting* transactions to accounts. A T-account provides a simple illustration of the financial effects of each transaction.

Specifically, one side of the T-account is used for increases and the other for decreases. A convenient way to remember which side records increases is to recall the accounting equation: **Assets = Liabilities + Equity**. Assets are on the left side of the equation. So, the left side of an asset T-account records increases in the asset (referred to as the *normal balance* side), and the right side records decreases. Liabilities and equity are on the right side of the accounting equation. So, the right side of a liability and an equity T-account records increases (the *normal balance* side), and the left side records decreases. This relation is represented graphically as follows.

Assets		=	Liabilities		+	Equity	
+	–		–	+		–	+
Increases	Decreases		Decreases	Increases		Decreases	Increases
Normal bal.				Normal bal.			Normal bal.

Journal Entries

Journal entries also capture the effects of transactions. Journal entries reflect increases and decreases to accounts using the language of debits and credits. Debits and credits simply refer to the left or right side of a T-account, respectively.

Account Title	
Debit (Left side)	Credit (Right side)

The left side of the T-account is the debit side, and the right side is the credit side. This holds for all T-accounts. Thus, to record an increase in an asset, we enter an amount on the left, or debit, side of the T-account—that is, we *debit* the account. Decreases in assets are recorded with an entry on the opposite (credit) side. To record an increase in a liability or equity account, we enter an amount on the right, or credit, side of the T-account—we *credit* the account. Decreases in liability or equity accounts are recorded on the left (debit) side.

In the margin of our financial statement effects template, we show the journal entry first, followed by the related T-accounts. In accounting jargon, this sequence relates to *journalizing* the entry and *posting* it to the affected accounts. The T-accounts represent the financial impact of each transaction on the respective asset, liability, or equity accounts.

Review 3-1 LO1

The table below shows account names (in alphabetical order) from the balance sheet and income statement for **Apple Inc.**

Required
Indicate the column where each item best fits. The seven columns correspond to the seven account categories in the financial statement effects template.

	Cash Asset	Noncash Asset	Liabilities	Contributed Capital	Earned Capital	Revenues	Expenses
Accounts payable.....................	___	___	___	___	___	___	___
Accounts receivable, less allowances ...	___	___	___	___	___	___	___
Accrued expenses	___	___	___	___	___	___	___
Acquired intangible assets, net	___	___	___	___	___	___	___
Cash and cash equivalents	___	___	___	___	___	___	___
Common stock and additional paid-in capital	___	___	___	___	___	___	___
Cost of sales........................	___	___	___	___	___	___	___
Current portion of long-term debt	___	___	___	___	___	___	___
Deferred revenue	___	___	___	___	___	___	___
Deferred tax assets	___	___	___	___	___	___	___
Goodwill...........................	___	___	___	___	___	___	___
Inventories	___	___	___	___	___	___	___
Long-term debt	___	___	___	___	___	___	___
Long-term marketable securities	___	___	___	___	___	___	___
Net sales..........................	___	___	___	___	___	___	___
Other current assets.................	___	___	___	___	___	___	___
Other non-current liabilities	___	___	___	___	___	___	___
Property, plant, and equipment, net.....	___	___	___	___	___	___	___

continued

(continued)	Cash Asset	Noncash Asset	Liabilities	Contributed Capital	Earned Capital	Revenues	Expenses
Provision for income taxes............	____	____	____	____	____	____	____
Research and development	____	____	____	____	____	____	____
Retained earnings	____	____	____	____	____	____	____
Selling, general, and administrative	____	____	____	____	____	____	____

Solution on p. 3-35.

Accounting Cycle Step 1—Analyze Transactions and Prepare Entries

This section uses **Apple Inc.**, to illustrate the accounting for selected business transactions. The assumed time frame is one fiscal year. We will begin with the account balances for Apple at the start of the 2015 fiscal year and illustrate the four steps in the accounting cycle. We construct its 2015 financial statements and close its books.

eLectures **LO2**
MBC Apply the financial statement effects template to analyze accounting transactions.

Apple's Transactions

This section provides a comprehensive two-part illustration using the financial statement effects template with a number of transactions underlying Apple's 2015 financial statements.

■ These summary transactions are described in the far left column of Exhibit 3.2, with their financial statement effects shown to the right-hand-side.

■ Detailed explanations for each of the 16 fiscal year transactions are provided in Exhibit 3.3.

Applying the Financial Statement Effects Template

To illustrate Step 1 of the accounting cycle, we consider 16 transactions for Apple. Once details of each transaction are known to Apple's accounting department, entries are made in the company's accounting system. For our learning purposes, we use the financial statement effects template to record these transactions. (Adjusting entries in transactions 17 through 20 are described in the next section.)

In the first two rows of Exhibit 3.2, we present each of Apple's balance sheet accounts and related balances as of September 27, 2014. (The end of its 2014 fiscal year is the beginning of its 2015 fiscal year.) We have aggregated some accounts from the Apple balance sheet to keep the size of the financial statement effects template presentable.

Applying the Journal Entry and T-Account

Although we will not repeatedly refer to journal entries and T-accounts, we will describe them for the first transaction in Exhibit 3.2. Specifically, the $4,103 debit equals the $4,103 credit in the journal entry: assets ($4,103 cash) = liabilities ($0) + equity ($4,103 common stock). This balance in transactions is the basis of *double-entry accounting*. For simplicity, we use acronyms (such as CS for common stock) in journal entries and T-accounts. (A listing of accounts and acronyms is located in Appendix B near the end of the book.) The journal entry for this transaction is

Cash.......................................	4,103	
CS (common stock)....................		4,103

Convention dictates that debits are listed first, followed by credits—the latter are indented.[1] The total debit(s) must always equal the total credit(s) for each transaction. The T-account representation for this transaction follows.

---

[1] There can be more than one debit and one credit for a transaction. To illustrate, assume that Apple raises $300 cash, with $200 from investors and $100 borrowed from a bank. The resulting journal entry is:

Cash...	300	
CS (common stock).....................		200
NP (note payable)		100

Cash		CS	
4,103			4,103

Cash is an asset; thus, a cash increase is recorded on the left or debit side of the T-account. Common stock (CS) is an equity account; thus, a common stock increase is recorded on the right or credit side.

Exhibit 3.2 ■ Financial Statement Effects Template for Apple 2014–2015 ($ millions)

Transaction	Balance Sheet						Income Statement		
	Cash Asset	+ Noncash Assets	= Liabil- ities	+ Contrib. Capital	+ Earned Capital*		Rev- enues	− Expen- ses	= Net Income
September 27, 2014	13,844	217,995	120,292	23,313	88,234				
Step 1—Analyze Transactions, and Prepare Entries									
1. Issue common stock for $4,103 cash	4,103			4,103 Common stock					
2. Purchase $140,327 of inventory on credit		140,327 Inventory	140,327 Accounts payable						
3. Sell inventory costing $140,089 for $225,224 on credit. . .		(140,089) Inventory 225,224 Accounts receivable			85,135		225,224 Sales	140,089 Cost of sales	85,135
4. Receive $225,835 cash on accounts receivable	225,835	(225,835) Accounts receivable							
5. Pay $135,033 cash toward accounts payable	(135,033)		(135,033) Accounts payable						
6. Pay $4,411 cash for operating expenses and taxes	(4,411)				(4,411)			4,411 Operating expenses	(4,411)
7. Pay $11,247 cash for plant assets (PPE)	(11,247)	11,247 PPE							
8. Pay $43,151 cash for short-term and long-term marketable securities	(43,151)	43,151 Marketable securities							
9. Issue short-term debt for $2,191 cash.	2,191		2,191 Short-term debt						
10. Issue long-term debt for $26,976 cash	26,976		26,976 Long-term debt						
11. Pay $514 cash in interest expense.	(514)				(514)			514 Interest expense	(514)
12. Pay $11,627 cash dividends to stockholders	(11,627)				(11,627)				
13. Receive $9,533 cash from customers for products and services to be delivered later	9,533		9,533 Unearned revenue						
14. Receive $1,799 cash in dividends and interest on marketable securities	1,799				1,799			(1,799) Other non- operating income	1,799
15. Pay $19,121 cash for income taxes.	(19,121)				(19,121)			19,121 Income taxes	(19,121)
16. Misc. transactions	(38,057)	8,596	8,601		(38,062)				
Step 2—Prepare Accounting Adjustments									
17. Accrue expenses of $6,728			6,728 Accrued expenses		(6,728)			6,728 Operating expenses	(6,728)
18. Record depreciation expense of $9,400		(9,400) PPE			(9,400)			9,400 Depreciation expense	(9,400)
19. Record amortization expense of $1,857		(1,857) Other assets			(1,857)			1,857 Amortization expense	(1,857)
20. Apple earns previously deferred revenue of $8,491.			(8,491) Unearned revenue		8,491		8,491 Sales		8,491
September 26, 2015	21,120	269,359	171,124	27,416	91,939		233,715	180,321	53,394

* Earned capital includes retained earnings and other equity accounts.

Exhibit 3.3 ■ Details of Transactions for Apple 2014–2015 ($ millions)

Transaction	Description
1. Issue common stock for $4,103 million cash	Cash, common stock, and additional paid-in capital all increase by the proceeds from issuance. (Apple combines common stock and additional paid-in capital on its balance sheet.) The sale of stock is not revenue. It is a financing transaction between the company and its owners (stockholders). Neither the sale or repurchase of stock, nor the payment of dividends to shareholders, affects revenue or expense. Transactions with stockholders never affect net income.
2. Purchase $140,327 million of inventories on account	Inventories are often purchased on account, meaning that suppliers give the company a period of time in which to pay for the purchase. Inventory increases by the purchase price. Because the company has not yet paid for the purchase, accounts payable (a liability) also increases by the purchase price. Note that inventories are not recorded at their expected retail selling price.
3. Sell inventories that cost $140,089 million for $225,224 million on credit	The sale of inventory has two distinct parts: a) **Recognize revenue.** Revenue (net sales) can be recognized because ownership of inventory has transferred to the customer. Because the customer has not yet paid for the inventory, the amount owed to Apple is reported as an account receivable. In order to recognize revenue, Apple has to have performed its part of the sales contract (given possession of the inventory to the customer). The receipt of cash is not required to recognize revenue; an agreement to pay later is sufficient. b) **Record expense.** The cost of inventory is recognized as an expense at the time of sale. An asset remains on the balance sheet until it is used, at which time its cost is transferred to the income statement as an expense. Because Apple has now sold (used) the inventory, its cost is moved from the inventory account on the balance sheet to the income statement as an expense called cost of goods sold.
4. Receive $225,835 million cash on accounts receivable	Cash increases when customers settle their accounts and the accounts receivable balance decreases. Collection of a receivable is not revenue. Instead, revenue is recognized when earned, as in transaction 3.
5. Pay $135,033 million cash toward accounts payable	Cash and accounts payable both decrease by the amount paid to suppliers to settle the account. Note that payment of a payable is not an expense. The expense was recognized when it was incurred, as in transaction 3.
6. Pay $4,411 million cash for operating expenses.	Operating expenses are costs incurred to earn revenue and do business. An example is salaries expense. Cash decreases when employees are paid and salaries expense is recorded in the income statement.
7. Pay $11,247 million cash for property, plant, and equipment (PPE).	Cash decreases and PPE assets increase for the purchase price. The purchase of PPE is not an expense. PPE is reported as an asset on the balance sheet because it creates future (longer-term) economic value. Over time, as PPE is used, its cost is transferred to the income statement as an expense called depreciation expense.
8. Pay $9,248 million and $33,903 million cash to purchase short-term and long-term marketable securities, respectively.	Apple invests its excess cash in marketable securities. This means cash decreases, and marketable securities accounts increase. The company plans to hold some of the investments for a year or less (short-term) and some for longer (long-term), depending on anticipated future cash needs. In the interim, the investments allow the company to earn interest, dividends, and any appreciation in value.
9. Issue commercial paper for $2,191 million cash.	Apple issues commercial paper, a common type of short-term debt. Cash increases by the proceeds of the issuance, and we record an increase in short-term debt on the balance sheet.
10. Issue long-term debt for $26,976 million cash.	Cash increases by the amount of the proceeds, and a long-term liability is recognized for the amount owed. It is classified as long-term because it will not be repaid during the current year. In the year that it matures, the balance to be repaid is moved to the current liability section of the balance sheet as an account called current maturities of long-term debt. As with the sale of stock, neither borrowing of money, nor its repayment, is recognized as revenue or expense. Only the payment of interest on the debt is an expense.
11. Pay $514 million in cash interest expense.	Apple pays interest on its short-term and long-term debts. Cash decreases, and expenses increase by the amount paid. Interest expense is a nonoperating expense—it is not incurred in ordinary operating activities but for financing activities.
12. Pay $11,627 million cash dividends to stockholders.	Cash and retained earnings both decrease from the dividend. The payment of dividends is not an expense. It is a transaction with the company's owners (the stockholders), not with its customers, and no expense is recognized in the income statement. Dividends are paid out of the retained profits of the company, which reduces retained earnings.
13. Receive $9,533 million cash from customers for products and services that are delivered later: $8,940 million within a year and $593 million after a year.	This does not represent revenue because Apple will not deliver the goods and services until later. Apple has not earned the revenue and cannot record the amount on the income statement. Instead, Apple records the amount as a liability, deferred revenue, to reflect the fact that Apple has an obligation to deliver the goods and perform the services. The amount that will be delivered within a year is classified as current liability and the remainder as a long-term liability.
14. Receive $1,799 million cash in dividends and interest on marketable securities.	Cash increases, as does other nonoperating income on the income statement. This nonoperating income includes dividends, interest, and capital gains Apple earns on its short-term and long-term marketable securities. This is not classified as revenue because it is not earned from customers. The financial statement effects template shows the opposite sign of interest expense from transaction 11. We recorded other nonoperating income as a negative expense, which lets us know it is an income item and not an expense.
15. Pay $19,121 million cash for income taxes.	Cash decreases, and tax expense is recognized in the income statement.
16. Record various other transactions.	We aggregate the remaining transactions to Apple's financial statements in this row. These entries affect various balance sheet accounts and transactions we discuss later in the book. None of these transactions affects the income statement.

Review 3-2 LO2

Prestige Inc. experienced the following 12 transactions during the month of January 2017.

1. Issue common stock for $3,000 cash.
2. Purchase inventory for $8,000 on credit.
3. Sell inventory costing $8,000 for $15,000 on credit.
4. Issue long-term debt for $10,000 cash.
5. Pay $15,000 cash for property, plant, and equipment (PPE).
6. Pay $500 cash for salaries.
7. Receive $300 cash in advance from client for future consulting services.
8. Pay $50 cash for interest on long-term debt.
9. Receive $3,000 cash from accounts receivable.
10. Pay $2,500 cash toward accounts payable.
11. Perform consulting services for client who previously paid in transaction 7.
12. Pay $100 cash for dividends.

Required

Record each transaction in the financial statement effects template. The beginning balances for each account are entered into the template. *Note:* The template includes rows for transactions 13 through 16, which are covered in later Reviews in the module.

	Balance Sheet						Income Statement		
	Cash Assets +	Noncash Assets =	Liabil- ities	+ Contrib. Capital +	Earned Capital		Rev- enues −	Expen- ses =	Net Income
Balance January 1, 2017	10,000	41,000	26,000	10,000	15,000		0	0	0
Transactions									
1. Issue common stock for $3,000 cash									
2. Purchase inventory for $8,000 on credit									
3. Sell inventory costing $8,000 for $15,000 on credit.									
4. Issue long-term debt for $10,000 cash									
5. Pay $15,000 cash for PPE									
6. Pay $500 cash for salaries									
7. Receive $300 cash in advance for future consulting services . . .									
8. Pay $50 cash for interest on long-term debt									
9. Receive $3,000 cash from accounts receivable.									
10. Pay $2,500 cash toward accounts payable									
11. Perform consulting services for client who previously paid in 7 . .									
12. Pay $100 cash for dividends									
Accounting Adjustments									
13. Record depreciation of $600									
14. Accrue salaries of $1,000.									
15. Advertising costing $1,300 is aired									
16. Accrue income taxes of $1,200									
Balance January 31, 2017									

Solution on p. 3-36.

Accounting Cycle Step 2—Prepare Accounting Adjustments

LO3

MBC   Prepare and explain accounting adjustments and their financial statement effects.

Recognizing revenue when products and services are delivered at an amount expected to be received (even if not received in cash) *and* recording expenses when incurred (even if not paid in cash) are cornerstones of **accrual accounting**, which is required under GAAP. In addition, understanding accounting adjustments, commonly called *accruals*, is crucial to effectively analyzing and interpreting financial statements.

In this module's Apple illustration, we recorded inventory as a purchase even though no cash was paid, and we recognized the sale as revenue even though no cash was received. Both of these transactions reflect accrual accounting. Some accounting adjustments affect the balance sheet alone (as with purchasing inventory on account in Exhibit 3.2, transaction 2). Other adjustments affect the balance sheet *and* the income statement (as with selling inventory on account in Exhibit 3.2, transaction 3). Accounting adjustments can affect asset, liability, or equity accounts and can either increase or decrease net income.

Companies make adjustments to more accurately report their financial performance and condition. For example, employees might not have been paid for wages earned at the end of an accounting period. Failure to recognize this labor cost would understate the company's total liabilities (because wages payable would be too low) and would overstate net income for the period (because wages expense would be too low). Thus, neither the balance sheet nor the income statement would be accurate without accounting adjustments.

Four Types of Accounting Adjustments Exhibit 3.4 identifies four general types of accounting adjustments, which are briefly described here.

■ **Prepaid expenses** Prepaid expenses reflect advance cash payments that will ultimately become expenses. An example is the payment for radio advertising that will not be aired until sometime in the future.

■ **Unearned revenues** Unearned revenues reflect cash received from customers before any services or goods are provided. An example is cash received from patrons for tickets to an upcoming concert.

■ **Accrued expenses** Accrued expenses are expenses incurred and recognized on the income statement even though they are not yet paid in cash. An example is wages owed to employees who performed work but who have not yet been paid.

■ **Accrued revenues** Accrued revenues are revenues earned and recognized on the income statement even though cash is not yet received. Examples include sales on credit and revenue earned under a long-term contract.

Exhibit 3.4 ■ **Four Types of Accounting Adjustments**

```
                            Adjustments

        Cash is paid or received              Cash is paid or received
        before expenses or                    after expenses or
        revenues are recognized               revenues are recognized

   Prepaid        Unearned          Accrued           Accrued
   Expenses       Revenues          Expenses          Revenues
```

The remainder of this section illustrates how **Apple**'s financial statements would reflect each of these four types of adjustments.

Prepaid Expenses

Assume Apple pays $200 to purchase time on **MTV** for iPod ads. Apple's cash account decreases by $200. Should the $200 advertising cost be recorded as an expense when Apple pays MTV, when MTV airs the ads, or at some other point? Under accrual accounting, Apple must record an expense when it is incurred. That means Apple should expense the cost of the ads when MTV airs them. When Apple pays for the advertisement, it records an asset; Apple "owns" air time that will presumably provide future benefits when the ads air. In the interim, the cost of the ads is an asset on the balance sheet. Apple's financial statement effects template follows for this transaction. There is a decrease in cash and an increase in the advertising asset, called prepaid advertising, when the ad time is paid for. At period-end, $50 of advertisements had aired. At that point, Apple must record an accounting adjustment to reduce the prepaid advertising account by $50 and transfer the cost to the income statement as advertising expense.

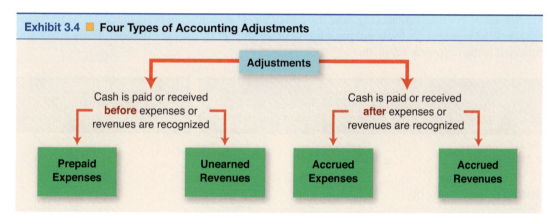

Transaction	Balance Sheet					Income Statement		
	Cash Asset	+ Noncash Assets	= Liabil- ities	+ Contrib. Capital	+ Earned Capital	Rev- enues	− Expen- ses	= Net Income
Pay $200 cash in advance for ad time	−200 Cash	+200 Prepaid Advertising	=				−	=
Record $50 cost of ad air time		−50 Prepaid Advertising	=		−50 Retained Earnings	−	+50 Advertising Expense	= −50

PPDA . 200
  Cash 200

PPDA
200 |
   Cash
       | 200

AE . . . 50
PPDA 50

AE
50 |
   PPDA
       | 50

Unearned Revenues

Assume Apple receives $400 cash from a customer as advance payment on a multi-unit iPod sale to be delivered next month. Apple must record cash received on its balance sheet but cannot recognize revenue from the order until earned, which is generally when iPods are delivered to the customer. Until then, Apple must recognize a liability called unearned, or deferred, revenue that represents Apple's obligation to fulfill the order at some future point. The financial statement effects template for this transaction follows.

```
Cash..400
  UR.......400

    Cash
  400 |
      UR
      |  400
```

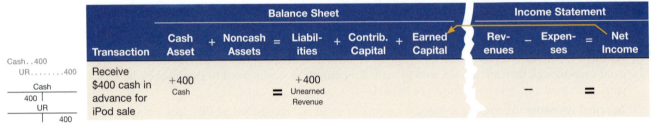

	Balance Sheet					Income Statement		
Transaction	Cash Asset	+ Noncash Assets	= Liabil- ities	+ Contrib. Capital	+ Earned Capital	Rev- enues	− Expen- ses	= Net Income
Receive $400 cash in advance for iPod sale	+400 Cash		= +400 Unearned Revenue				−	=

Assume Apple delivers the iPods a month later (but still within the fiscal quarter). Apple must recognize the $400 as revenue at delivery because it is now earned. Thus, net income increases by $400. The second part of this transaction is to record the cost of the iPods sold. Assuming the cost is $150, Apple reduces iPod inventory by $150 and records cost of goods sold by the same amount. These effects are reflected in the following template.

```
UR ...400
  Sales......400

     UR
  400 |
     Sales
      |  400

COGS..150
  INV .......150

    COGS
  150 |
     INV
      |  150
```

	Balance Sheet					Income Statement		
Transaction	Cash Asset	+ Noncash Assets	= Liabil- ities	+ Contrib. Capital	+ Earned Capital	Rev- enues	− Expen- ses	= Net Income
Deliver $400 of iPods paid in advance			= −400 Unearned Revenues		+400 Retained Earnings	+400 Sales	−	= +400
Record $150 cost of $400 iPod sale		−150 Inventory	=		−150 Retained Earnings		− +150 Cost of Goods Sold	= −150

Accrued Expenses

Assume Apple's sales staff earns $100 of sales commissions this period that will not be paid until next period. The sales staff earned the wages as they made the sales. However, because Apple pays its employees twice a month, the related cash payment will not occur until the next pay period. Should Apple record the wages earned by its employees as an expense even though payment has not yet been made? The answer is yes. The expense recognition principle requires Apple to recognize wages expense when it is *incurred*, even if not paid in cash. It must record wages expense incurred as a liability (wages payable). In the next period, when Apple pays the wages, it reduces both cash and wages payable. Net income is not affected by the cash payment; instead, net income decreased in the previous period when Apple accrued the wage expense.

```
WE ...100
  WP ......100

     WE
  100 |
      WP
      |  100

WP ...100
  Cash ......100

      WP
  100 |
     Cash
      |  100
```

	Balance Sheet					Income Statement		
Transaction	Cash Asset	+ Noncash Assets	= Liabil- ities	+ Contrib. Capital	+ Earned Capital	Rev- enues	− Expen- ses	= Net Income
Current period: Incur $100 of wages not yet paid			= +100 Wages Payable		−100 Retained Earnings		− +100 Wages Expense	= −100
Next period: Pay $100 cash for ac- crued wages	−100 Cash		= −100 Wages Payable				−	=

As another example of accrued expenses, assume Apple rents office space and that it owes $25 in rent at period-end. Apple has incurred rent expense in the current period, and that expense must be recorded this period. Failing to make this adjustment would mean Apple's liabilities (rent payable) would be understated and its income would be overstated. The entry to record the accrual of rent expense for office space follows.

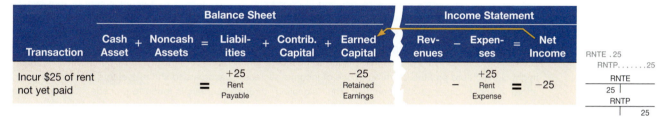

	Balance Sheet						Income Statement				
Transaction	Cash Asset	+	Noncash Assets	=	Liabil- ities	+	Contrib. Capital	+	Earned Capital		Rev- enues	−	Expen- ses	=	Net Income
Incur $25 of rent not yet paid		=			+25 Rent Payable				−25 Retained Earnings			−	+25 Rent Expense	=	−25

```
RNTE .25
   RNTP......25
     RNTE
   25 |
     RNTP
        |   25
```

Accrued Revenues

Assume Apple delivers iPods to a customer in Boston, Massachusetts, who will pay next quarter. The sales price for those units is $500, and the cost is $400. Apple has completed its revenue earning process with this sale and must accrue revenue from the Boston customer even though Apple received no cash. Like all sales transactions, Apple must record two parts, the sales revenue and the cost of sales. The financial effects template for this two-part transaction follows.

	Balance Sheet						Income Statement				
Transaction	Cash Asset	+	Noncash Assets	=	Liabil- ities	+	Contrib. Capital	+	Earned Capital		Rev- enues	−	Expen- ses	=	Net Income
Sell $500 of iPods on credit			+500 Accounts Receivable	=					+500 Retained Earnings		+500 Sales	−		=	+500
Record $400 cost of $500 iPod sale			−400 Inventory	=					−400 Retained Earnings			−	+400 Cost of Goods Sold	=	−400

```
AR ...500
   Sales......500
     AR
   500 |
     Sales
        |   500

COGS 400
   INV .......400
     COGS
   400 |
     INV
        |   400
```

Accounting Adjustments for Apple

Entries 17 through 20 in Exhibit 3.2, which are explained in Exhibit 3.5, reflect the accounting adjustments Apple makes during its fiscal year. These accounting adjustments occur at the end of the accounting period, prior to the preparation of the financial statements. The purpose of accounting adjustments is to adjust balance sheet assets and liabilities so that the financial statements fairly present the company's financial performance and position.

Exhibit 3.5 ◼ **Details of Accounting Adjustments for Apple 2014–2015 ($ millions)**

Adjustment	Description
17. Accrue expenses of $6,728 million	Accrued expenses represent liabilities that have been incurred before the end of the accounting period but have not been recorded. The accrual simultaneously increases liabilities on the balance sheet and expenses in the income statement. Failure to properly accrue expenses would understate liabilities and overstate profit (and retained earnings).
18. Record depreciation expense of $9,400 million	Each period that PPE is used, a portion of the cost of the PPE is transferred to the income statement as *depreciation expense* to reflect the fact that the PPE assets have been used during the period. Failure to record depreciation expense would overstate assets and net income (and retained earnings) for the period.
19. Record amortization expense of $1,857 million	Similar to PPE, certain intangible assets (those that have a limited useful life) are used up over time and amortized. This concept is the same as depreciation, but the word *amortization* is used instead. The accounting adjustment to amortize the intangible assets reduces the balance sheet value of the intangible assets and records an expense. Note that goodwill is not amortized because we assume it has an unlimited useful life. (We discuss intangible assets, including the goodwill asset, in Module 9).
20. Apple earns previously deferred revenue of $8,491 million	When customers pay in advance, Apple records the cash pre-payment as a liability. Once Apple transfers the products or delivers the services to its customers, it can recognize revenue from the sale, typically with an accounting adjustment. The adjustment reduces the unearned revenue liability on the balance sheet and increases revenue in the income statement.

Review 3-3 LO3

Refer to the information in Review 3-2 for Prestige Inc., which is preparing to record its accounting adjustments for month-end January 2017.

Required
Enter the following accounting adjustments in the financial statement effects template, included in Review 3-2.

13. Record depreciation expense of $600.
14. Accrue salaries of $1,000.
15. Advertising costing $1,300 is aired. Prestige had previously paid cash for the advertising and recorded an asset labeled "Prepaid expense."

Solution on p. 3-36.   16. Accrue income taxes of $1,200.

Accounting Cycle Step 3—Prepare Financial Statements

LO4
Construct financial statements from the accounting records.

Once we enter all of the transactions and adjustments into the financial statement effects template, we sum each column to obtain ending balances for the accounts. This is shown on the bottom row of Ex-hibit 3.2, and reflects ending balances of accounts after all of the transactions have been recorded during the accounting period in Step 1 and all of the period-end adjustments have been entered into the ac-counting records in Step 2. With the accounts totaled, we can prepare the financial statements (Step 3).
There is an order to financial statement preparation.

■   First, a company prepares its income statement using the income statement accounts. It then uses the net income number and dividend information to update the retained earnings account.

■   Second, it prepares the balance sheet using the updated retained earnings account along with the remaining balance sheet accounts.

■   Third, it prepares the statement of stockholders' equity.

■   Fourth, it prepares the statement of cash flows using information from the cash account (and other sources).

Income Statement

Our financial statement effects spreadsheet in Exhibit 3.2 summarizes Apple's income statement ac-counts in the last three columns. We use the data from those columns to prepare the income statement in proper form. Apple aggregates its many operating expenses on a line labeled "Total operating expenses." Apple also combines interest expense with other nonoperating income and reports a line labeled "Other income/(expense), net." Apple's income statement for 2015 follows.

APPLE INC. Consolidated Statements of Operations For Year Ended September 26, 2015 ($ millions)	
Net sales.	$233,715
Cost of sales.	140,089
Gross margin	93,626
Total operating expenses	22,396
Operating income.	71,230
Other income/(expense), net	1,285
Income before provision for income taxes.	72,515
Provision for income taxes.	19,121
Net income.	$ 53,394

Apple's income statement includes a subtotal for gross margin, which is a common reporting practice that helps us evaluate company performance and profitability. Apple also reports a subtotal for operating profit. As we will discuss in Module 4, operating profit isolates those activities that create shareholder value and, for that reason, companies frequently report a subtotal for operating profit.

Retained Earnings Statement

Once the income statement is prepared, companies update the retained earnings balance by adding net income and subtracting dividends. We can do likewise using the net income and dividend information from the financial statement effects spreadsheet in Exhibit 3.2. Apple's retained earnings statement for 2015 follows.

APPLE INC. Retained Earnings Statement For Year Ended September 26, 2015 ($ millions)	
Retained earnings, September 27, 2014	$87,152
Add: Net income	53,394
Deduct: Dividends	(11,627)
Miscellaneous adjustments[1]	(36,635)
Retained earnings, September 26, 2015	$92,284

[1] Miscellaneous adjustments include many items explained in later modules. These include the revaluation of financial derivative instruments and the repurchase and retirement of common stock.

Balance Sheet

Once Apple computes the ending balance in retained earnings, it can prepare its balance sheet. Balance sheet accounts are called **permanent accounts** because their respective balances carry over from one period to the next. For example, the cash balance at the end of the current accounting period (ended September 26, 2015) is $21,120 million, which will be the balance at the beginning of the next accounting period (beginning September 27, 2015).

To prepare the balance sheet, we use the ending balances from the last row in the financial statement effects spreadsheet in Exhibit 3.2, along with specific details for accounts within several of the columns. We then apply proper balance sheet format that has subtotals for current assets, current liabilities, total liabilities, and equity to produce Apple's consolidated balance sheet for 2015 as follows.

APPLE INC. Consolidated Balance Sheet September 26, 2015 ($ millions)	
Assets	
Cash and cash equivalents	$ 21,120
Short-term marketable securities.	20,481
Accounts receivable.	16,849
Inventories	2,349
Other current assets.	28,579
Current assets	89,378
Long-term marketable securities	164,065
Property, plant, and equipment, net.	22,471
Other assets.	14,565
Total assets.	$290,479
Liabilities and equity	
Accounts payable.	$ 35,490
Accrued expenses	25,181
Deferred revenue	8,940
Commercial paper	8,499
Current portion of long-term debt	2,500
Current liabilities.	80,610
Deferred revenue, non-current.	3,624
Long-term debt	53,463
Other non-current liabilities	33,427
Total liabilities	171,124
Common stock and additional paid-in capital, ...	27,416
Retained earnings	92,284
Accumulated other comprehensive income.	(345)
Total shareholders' equity	119,355
Total liabilities and shareholders' equity.	$290,479

Statement of Stockholders' Equity

We use the information from the financial statement effects template pertaining to contributed capital and earned capital to prepare the statement of stockholders' equity, as follows. (The final financial statement is the statement of cash flows, which we cover in detail in a later module.)

APPLE INC. Statement of Shareholders' Equity For Year Ended September 26, 2015				
$ millions	Common Stock and Additional Paid-In Capital	Retained Earnings	Accumulated Other Comprehensive Income	Total Shareholders' Equity
Balance, September 27, 2014	$23,313	$87,152	$1,082	$111,547
Stock issuance.	4,103			4,103
Net income.		53,394		53,394
Dividends		(11,627)		(11,627)
Other.		(36,635)	(1,427)	(38,062)
Balance, September 26, 2015	$27,416	$92,284	$ (345)	$119,355

Refer to the information in Reviews 3-2 and 3-3 for Prestige Inc., which is preparing its financial statements for month-end January 2017. In addition, the financial statement effects template included the following (beginning) account balances at January 1, 2017.

Accounts receivable..............	$12,000	Accounts payable................	$ 3,800
Inventory......................	7,200	Unearned revenue	200
Prepaid advertising..............	1,800	Long-term debt	22,000
PPE..........................	20,000	Salaries payable................	0
		Taxes payable..................	0

Required

1. List the 14 accounts, and determine the ending balance for each.
2. Prepare the income statement, statement of retained earnings, and balance sheet at the end of the period. **Solution on p. 3-37.**

Accounting Cycle Step 4—Close the Books

LO5 Explain and apply the closing process.

The **closing process** (or *closing the books*) refers to "zeroing out" the temporary accounts by transferring their ending balances to retained earnings. Income statement accounts—revenues and expenses—and the dividend account are **temporary accounts** because their balances are zero at the start of each accounting period so that only the current period's activities are included. Balance sheet accounts carry over from period to period and are called permanent accounts. The closing process is typically carried out via a series of journal entries that successively zero out each revenue and expense account and the dividend account, transferring those balances to retained earnings. The result is that all income statement accounts and the dividend account begin the next period with zero balances. The balance sheet accounts do not need to be similarly adjusted because their balances carry over from period to period.

Closing with the Template It is important to distinguish our financial statement effects template from companies' accounting systems. The financial statement effects template and T-accounts are pedagogical tools that represent transactions' effects on financial statements. The template is highly stylized, but its simplicity is instructive.

Closing with Journal Entries In practice, managers use journal entries to record transactions and adjustments. The template captures these in summarized fashion. However, in practice, income statement transactions are not automatically transferred to retained earnings, and retained earnings is not continuously updated. Instead, companies have a formal "closing process" at the end of each reporting period—someone or some program must transfer the temporary account balances to retained earnings. Thus, it is important to understand the closing process and why companies "close" the books each period. We describe the mechanical details of the closing process.

Following are the journal entries, along with the T-account entries, **Apple** would make to close out its income statement accounts and dividend account to retained earnings (in millions).

1. Close Revenue and Gain Accounts.

2. Close Expense and Loss Accounts.

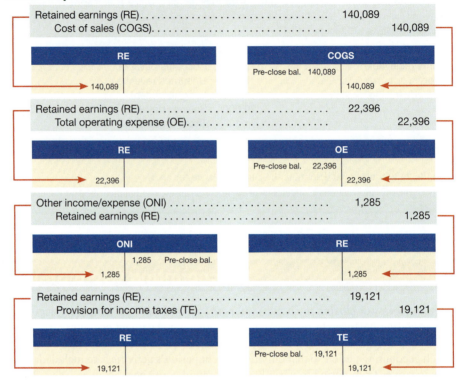

3. Close Dividend Account.

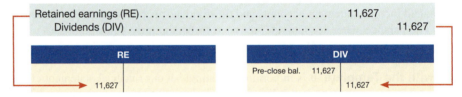

The closing process reduces all of the income statement accounts and the dividend account to zero to begin the next accounting period with a zero balance. This means revenues, expenses, and dividends are accumulated during a period so that the income statement only reflects activities for the period. In contrast, balance sheet accounts carry over from period to period. We can see this from our financial statement effects template for Apple where the bottom row balances as of September 26, 2015, become the top row in the template for the next fiscal year, which begins on September 27, 2015.

Accounting Cycle Summarized

The entire accounting process, from analysis of basic transactions to financial statement preparation to the closing process, is called the **accounting cycle**. As we discuss at the outset of this module and portray graphically in Exhibit 3.1, there are four basic processes in the accounting cycle.

❶ Analyze transactions and prepare (and post) entries.

❷ Prepare (and post) accounting adjustments.

❸ Prepare financial statements.

❹ Perform the closing process.

The analysis and posting of transactions is done regularly during each accounting period. However, the preparation of accounting adjustments and financial statements is only done at the end of an accounting period. At this point, we have explained and illustrated all aspects of the accounting cycle.

Managerial Decision ■ You Are the Chief Financial Officer

Assume that you learn of the leakage of hazardous waste from your company's factory. It is estimated that cleanup could cost $10 million. Part 1: What effect will recording this cost have on your company's balance sheet and its income statement? Part 2: Accounting rules require you to record this cost if it is both probable and can be reliably estimated. Although the cleanup is relatively certain, the cost is a guess at this point. Consequently, you have some discretion whether to record it. Discuss the parties that are likely affected by your decision on whether or not to record the liability and related expense and the ethical issues involved. (Answer, p. 3-19)

LO5 Review 3-5

Refer to the information in Reviews 3-2, 3-3, and 3-4 for Prestige Inc. It has prepared its financial statements and is ready to close its books for month-end January 2017.

Required

Prepare the entries required to close the temporary accounts for Prestige Inc. at the end of January 2017.

Solution on p. 3-38.

Global Accounting

The manner in which accounting data are gathered and recorded does not differ across accounting standards. Thus, the accounting cycle in Exhibit 3.1 applies in countries using IFRS in the same manner as in the United States. The difference is that companies create information systems that conform to the specific accounting rules in that country. For example, the rules for recording research and development (R&D) costs are different in the United States vis-à-vis Germany. Thus, the U.S. company and the German company would each tailor their accounting systems to properly record R&D costs so that each company's financial statements comply with their respective countries' accounting standards. The accounting cycle of each company still involves transactions and adjustments and a closing process. The result is that identical R&D expenditures are classified differently and the resulting financial statements diverge.

Large multinational companies often have subsidiaries in different countries. If a U.S. company has a foreign subsidiary, the foreign laws require a domestic set of financial statements for tax, regulatory, banking, or other purposes. For example, **Apple**'s 2015 Form 10-K reports it has three subsidiaries incorporated in Ireland. The Irish subsidiaries must prepare IFRS financial statements to file with the Irish Revenue Commission (the Irish equivalent of the IRS). During the closing process of the accounting cycle, Apple Inc. (the U.S. parent) must consolidate the subsidiaries, which means all assets and liabilities of the subsidiaries are included on Apple Inc.'s balance sheet. Similarly, all of the revenues and expenses of the subsidiaries are included on Apple Inc.'s income statement. It would not be appropriate for a simple summing of accounts because of differences between IFRS and U.S. GAAP. Instead, Apple Inc. must convert IFRS financial statements to U.S. GAAP equivalent (as well as convert euros to U.S. dollars). To accomplish this, Apple Inc. keeps two sets of accounting records for subsidiaries, one set in GAAP and the other in IFRS. This is not as complicated as it might seem. Companies like Apple use sophisticated computer accounting systems and enterprise resource planning (ERP) systems that are capable of supporting multiple sets of accounting standards.

Appendix 3A: FASB's Financial Statement Presentation Project

Preparers and users of financial statements have long expressed concern that existing accounting standards provide too little guidance on financial statement presentation. Popular opinion is that U.S. GAAP permits too many presentation formats and is silent on specific line items and on the level of detail required in financial statements. This lack of uniformity impairs comparability across companies. For example, some companies disaggregate product costs (such as materials and labor) as well as general and administrative costs (such as rent and utilities) in their income statements, and other entities present highly aggregated product costs and general and administrative expenses. Due to these concerns, there is broad support for a FASB project on financial statement presentation.

Under current accounting standards, the statement of cash flows categorizes a company's cash flows into three categories: operating, investing, and financing. The proposal under consideration at the FASB would require similar classification on the balance sheet and the income statement. The following table illustrates the proposed sections, categories, and subcategories in each financial statement. (Summarized from "Staff Draft of an Exposure Draft JULY 2010" © IFRS Foundation and made available by the FASB [fasb.org/jsp/FASB/FASBContent_C/ProjectUpdatePage&cid=1176164178963].)

Statement of Financial Position (Balance Sheet)	Statement of Comprehensive Income	Statement of Cash Flows
Business section	**Business section**	**Business section**
Operating category	Operating category	Operating category
Operating finance subcategory	Operating finance subcategory	
Investing category	Investing category	Investing category
Financing section	**Financing section**	**Financing section**
Debt category	Debt category	
Equity category		
	Multi-category transaction section	**Multi-category transaction section**
Income tax section	**Income tax section**	**Income tax section**
Discontinued operation section	**Discontinued operation section,** net of tax	**Discontinued operation section**
	Other comprehensive income, net of tax	

The proposed presentation format is consistent with the approach we describe in Module 4—the separation of operating and nonoperating items on the income statement and balance sheet. The Module 4 approach extends the traditional DuPont analysis of return on equity (ROE) by isolating the operating activities of the business in order to evaluate what truly creates shareholder value. While the Module 4 approach sharpens our analysis of ROE, it requires additional effort at present because we must first parse operating from nonoperating components on the financial statements. Under the FASB proposal, financial statements would be formatted along these operating and nonoperating dimensions and standardized across companies. If adopted, the new format will make analysis less effortful.

Guidance Answers

You Are the Chief Financial Officer
Pg. 3-18 Part 1: Liabilities will increase by $10 million for the estimated amount of the cleanup, and an expense in that amount will be recognized in the income statement, thus reducing both income and retained earnings (equity) by $10 million. Part 2: Stakeholders affected by recognition decisions of this type are often much broader than first realized. Management is directly involved in the decision. Recording this cost can affect the market value of the company, its relations with lenders and suppliers, its auditors, and many other stakeholders. Further, if recording this cost is the right accounting decision, failure to do so can foster unethical behavior throughout the company, thus affecting additional company employees.

Questions

Q3-1.   What does the term *fiscal year* mean?

Q3-2.   What is the purpose of a journal?

Q3-3.   Explain the process of posting.

Q3-4.   What four different types of adjustments are frequently necessary before financial statements are prepared at the end of an accounting period? Give at least one example of each type.

Q3-5. On January 1, prepaid insurance was debited for $1,896 related to the cost of a two-year premium, with coverage beginning immediately. How should this account be adjusted on January 31 before financial statements are prepared for the current month?

Q3-6. At the beginning of January, the first month of the accounting year, the supplies account (asset) had a debit balance of $875. During January, purchases of $260 worth of supplies were added (debited) to the account. At the end of January, $630 of supplies were still available. How should this account be adjusted? If no adjustment is made, describe the impact on (a) the income statement for January and (b) the balance sheet prepared at January 31.

Q3-7. The publisher of *Accounting View*, a monthly magazine, received $9,768 cash on January 1 for new subscriptions covering the next 24 months, with service beginning immediately: (*a*) Use the financial statement effects template to record the receipt of the $9,768; and (*b*) use the template to show how the accounts should be adjusted at the end of January before financial statements are prepared for the current month.

Q3-8. Refer to Q3-7. Prepare journal entries for the receipt of cash and the delivery of the magazines.

Q3-9. Trombley Travel Agency pays an employee $950 in wages each Friday for the five-day work week ending on Friday. The last Friday of January falls on January 27. How should Trombley Travel Agency adjust wages expense on January 31, its fiscal year-end?

Q3-10. The Basu Company earns interest amounting to $720 per month on its investments. The company receives the interest revenue every six months, on December 31 and June 30. Monthly financial statements are prepared. Which accounts should Basu adjust on January 31?

Q3-11. What types of accounts are closed at the end of the accounting year? What are the three major steps in the closing process?

Assignments with the logo in the margin are available in BusinessCourse.
See the Preface of the book for details.

Mini Exercises

M3-12. Assessing Financial Statement Effects of Transactions
K. Daniels started Daniels Services, a firm providing art services for advertisers, on June 1. The following accounts are needed to record the transactions for June: Cash, Accounts Receivable, Supplies, Office Equipment, Accounts Payable, Common Stock, Dividends, Service Fees Earned, Rent Expense, Utilities Expense, and Wages Expense. Record the following transactions for June using the financial statement effects template.

LO2

June	1	K. Daniels invested $12,000 cash to begin the business in exchange for common stock.
	2	Paid $950 cash for June rent.
	3	Purchased $6,400 of office equipment on credit.
	6	Purchased $3,800 of art materials and other supplies; the company paid $1,800 cash with the remainder due within 30 days.
	11	Billed clients $4,700 for services rendered.
	17	Collected $3,250 cash from clients on their accounts billed on June 11.
	19	Paid $5,000 cash toward the account for office equipment (see June 3).
	25	Paid $900 cash for dividends.
	30	Paid $350 cash for June utilities.
	30	Paid $2,500 cash for June wages.

M3-13. Preparing Journal Entries and Posting
Refer to the information in M3-12. Prepare a journal entry for each transaction. Create a T-account for each account, and then post the journal entries to the T-accounts (use dates to reference each entry).

LO2

M3-14. Assessing Financial Statement Effects of Transactions
B. Fischer started Fischer Company, a cleaning services firm, on April 1. The company created the following accounts to record the transactions for April: Cash; Accounts Receivable; Supplies; Prepaid Van Lease; Equipment; Notes Payable; Accounts Payable; Common Stock; Dividends; Cleaning Fees Earned; Wages Expense; Advertising Expense; and Van Fuel Expense. Record the following transactions for April using the financial statement effects template.

LO2

April 1   B. Fischer invested $9,000 cash to begin the business in exchange for common stock.
2   Paid $2,850 cash for six months' lease on a van for the business.
3   Borrowed $10,000 cash from a bank and signed a note payable, agreeing to repay it in one year plus 10% interest.
4   Purchased $5,500 in cleaning equipment; the company paid $2,500 cash with the remainder due within 30 days.
5   Paid $4,300 cash for cleaning supplies.
7   Paid $350 cash for advertisements to run in the area newspaper during April.
21   Billed customers $3,500 for services performed.
23   Paid $3,000 cash toward the account for cleaning equipment (see April 4).
28   Collected $2,300 cash from customers on their accounts billed on April 21.
29   Paid $1,000 cash for dividends.
30   Paid $2,750 cash for April wages.
30   Paid $995 cash for gasoline used during April.

LO2 **M3-15. Preparing Journal Entries and Posting**
Refer to the information in M3-14. Prepare a journal entry for each transaction. Create a T-account for each account, and then post the journal entries to the T-accounts (use dates to reference each entry).

LO2, 3 **M3-16. Assessing Financial Statement Effects of Transactions and Adjustments**
Schrand Services offers janitorial services on both a contract basis and an hourly basis. On January 1, Schrand collected $26,100 cash in advance on a six-month contract for work to be performed evenly during the next six months.

a. Prepare the entry on January 1 to reflect the receipt of $26,100 cash for contract work; use the financial statement effects template.
b. Adjust the appropriate accounts on January 31 for the contract work done during January; use the financial statement effects template.
c. At January 31, a total of 30 hours of hourly rate janitor work was performed but unbilled. The billing rate is $19 per hour. Prepare the accounting adjustment needed on January 31 using the financial statement effects template. (The firm uses the fees receivable account to reflect revenue earned but not yet billed.)

LO2, 3 **M3-17. Preparing Accounting Adjustments**
Refer to the information in M3-16. Prepare a journal entry for each of parts *a*, *b*, and *c*.

LO3 **M3-18. Assessing Financial Statement Effects of Transactions and Adjustments**
Selected accounts of Portage Properties, a real estate management firm, are shown below as of January 31, before any accounts have been adjusted.

	Debit	Credit
Prepaid insurance	$3,240	
Supplies	1,540	
Office equipment	6,240	
Unearned rent revenue		$ 5,550
Salaries expense	2,325	
Rent revenue		13,250

Portage Properties prepares monthly financial statements. Using the following information, adjust the accounts as necessary on January 31 using the financial statement effects template.

a. Prepaid insurance represents a two-year premium paid on January 1.
b. Supplies of $710 were still available on January 31.
c. Office equipment is expected to last eight years (or 96 months).
d. Earlier this month, on January 1, Portage collected $5,550 for six months' rent in advance from a tenant renting space for $925 per month.
e. Salaries of $490 have been earned by employees but not yet recorded as of January 31.

LO3 **M3-19. Preparing Accounting Adjustments**
Refer to the information in M3-18. Prepare journal entries for each of parts *a* through *e*.

M3-20. Inferring Transactions from Financial Statements

LO2
Foot Locker Inc. (FL)

Foot Locker Inc., a retailer of athletic footwear and apparel, operates 1,835 stores in the United States, Canada, Europe, Australia, and New Zealand. During its 2015 fiscal year ended in January 2016, Foot Locker purchased merchandise inventory costing $4,942 ($ millions). Assume Foot Locker makes all purchases on credit and its accounts payable is only used for inventory purchases. The following T-accounts reflect information contained in the company's fiscal 2014 and 2015 balance sheets ($ millions).

Inventories			Accounts Payable		
2014 Bal.	1,250			301	2014 Bal.
2015 Bal.	1,285			279	2015 Bal.

a. Use the financial statement effects template to record Foot Locker's 2015 purchases.
b. What amount did Foot Locker pay in cash to its suppliers during fiscal year 2015? Explain.
c. Use the financial statement effects template to record cost of goods sold for its fiscal 2015.

M3-21. Preparing Journal Entries

LO2

Refer to the information in M3-20. Prepare journal entries for each of parts *a, b,* and *c.*

M3-22. Preparing a Statement of Stockholders' Equity

LO4

On December 31, 2016, the accounts of Leuz Architect Services showed credit balances in its common stock and retained earnings accounts of $30,000 and $18,000, respectively. The company's stock issuances for 2017 totaled $6,000, and it paid $9,700 in cash dividends. During 2017, the company had net income of $27,900. Prepare a 2017 statement of stockholders' equity for Leuz Architect Services.

M3-23. Preparing Closing Journal Entries

LO5
General Mills (GIS)

Selected financial information from **General Mills** as of May 29, 2016 follows.

$ millions	Debit	Credit
Net sales.		$16,563.1
Cost of sales.	$10,733.6	
Selling, general, and administrative expense and other	3,073.1	
Interest expense, net	303.8	
Income tax expense.	755.2	
Retained earnings		11,990.8

Assume the company has not yet closed any accounts to retained earnings. Prepare journal entries to close the temporary accounts above. Set up the needed T-accounts, and post the closing entries. After these entries are posted, what is the balance of the retained earnings account?

M3-24. Inferring Transactions from Financial Statements

LO2
Lowe's Companies (LOW)

Lowe's is the second-largest home improvement retailer in the world, with 1,857 stores. During its 2015 fiscal year ended in January 2016, Lowe's purchased merchandise inventory at a cost of $39,051 ($ millions). Assume all purchases were made on account and accounts payable is only used for inventory purchases. The following T-accounts reflect information contained in the company's 2014 and 2015 balance sheets.

Merchandise Inventories			Accounts Payable		
2014 Bal.	8,911			5,124	2014 Bal.
2015 Bal.	9,458			5,633	2015 Bal.

a. Use the financial statement effects template to record Lowe's purchases during fiscal 2015.
b. What amount did Lowe's pay in cash to its suppliers during fiscal-year 2015? Explain.
c. Use the financial statement effects template to record cost of sales for 2015.

M3-25. Closing Process

LO5

As of December 31, Hanlon Consulting's financial records contain the following selected account information.

	Debit	Credit
Service fees earned		$80,300
Rent expense	$20,800	
Salaries expense	48,700	
Supplies expense	5,600	
Depreciation expense	10,200	
Retained earnings		67,000

Prepare entries to close these accounts in journal entry form. Set up T-accounts for each account and post the closing entries to the T-accounts. After these entries are posted, what is the balance of the retained earnings account?

LO3, 4   **M3-26.**   **Computing and Comparing Income and Cash Flow Measures**

Penno Corporation recorded service revenues of $200,000 in 2017, of which $170,000 were on credit and $30,000 were for cash. Moreover, of the $170,000 credit sales for 2017, Penno collected $20,000 cash on those receivables before year-end 2017. The company also paid $25,000 cash for 2017 wages. Its employees also earned another $15,000 in wages for 2017, which were not yet paid at year-end 2017. (*a*) Compute the company's net income for 2017; and (*b*) how much net cash inflow or outflow did the company generate in 2017? Explain why Penno's net income and net cash flow differ.

LO3, 4   **M3-27.**   **Analyzing Transactions to Compute Net Income**

Wasley Corp., a start-up company, provided services that were acceptable to its customers and billed those customers for $350,000 in 2016. However, Wasley collected only $280,000 cash in 2016, and the remaining $70,000 was collected in 2017. Wasley employees earned $225,000 in 2016 wages that were not paid until the first week of 2017. How much net income does Wasley report for 2016? For 2017 (assuming no additional transactions)?

LO2   **M3-28.**   **Analyzing Transactions Using the Financial Statement Effects Template**

Report the effects for each of the following transactions using the financial statement effects template.

a. Issue stock for $1,000 cash.
b. Purchase inventory for $500 cash.
c. Sell inventory in transaction *b* for $3,000 on credit.
d. Receive $2,000 cash toward transaction *c* receivable.

Exercises

LO2, 3   **E3-29.**   **Assessing Financial Statement Effects of Adjustments**

For each of the following separate situations, prepare the necessary accounting adjustments using the financial statement effects template.

a. Unrecorded depreciation on equipment is $720.
b. The supplies account has a balance of $3,870. Supplies still available at the end of the period total $1,100.
c. On the date for preparing financial statements, an estimated utilities expense of $430 has been incurred, but no utility bill has yet been received or paid.
d. On the first day of the current period, rent for four periods was paid and recorded as a $3,200 increase (debit) to prepaid rent and a $3,200 decrease (credit) to cash.
e. Nine months ago, a one-year service policy was sold to a customer, and the seller recorded the cash received by crediting unearned revenue for $1,872. No accounting adjustments have been prepared during the nine-month period. The seller is now preparing annual financial statements.
f. At the end of the period, employee wages of $965 have been incurred but not paid or recorded.
g. At the end of the period, $300 of interest has been earned but not yet received or recorded.

LO2, 3   **E3-30.**   **Preparing Accounting Adjustments**

Refer to the information in E3-29. Prepare journal entries for each accounting adjustment.

E3-31. **Assessing Financial Statement Effects of Adjustments Across Two Periods**
LO3

Oakmont Company closes its accounts on December 31 each year. The company works a five-day work week and pays its employees every two weeks. On December 31, Oakmont accrued $4,700 of salaries payable. On January 9 of the following year, the company paid salaries of $15,000 cash to employees. Prepare entries using the financial statement effects template to (*a*) accrue the salaries payable on December 31, and (*b*) record the salary payment nine days later on January 9.

E3-32. **Preparing Accounting Adjustments**
LO3, 5

Refer to the information in E3-31. Prepare journal entries to accrue the salaries in December, close salaries expense for the year, and pay the salaries in January of the following year. Assume there is no change in the pay rate during the year and no change in the company's work force.

E3-33. **Financial Analysis Using Adjusted Account Data**
LO3

Selected T-account balances for Bloomfield Company are shown below as of January 31, which reflect its accounting adjustments. The firm uses a calendar-year accounting period but prepares *monthly* accounting adjustments.

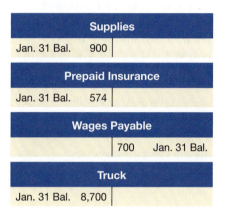

Supplies		Supplies Expense	
Jan. 31 Bal. 900		Jan. 31 Bal. 960	

Prepaid Insurance		Insurance Expense	
Jan. 31 Bal. 574		Jan. 31 Bal. 82	

Wages Payable		Wages Expense	
	700 Jan. 31 Bal.	Jan. 31 Bal. 3,200	

Truck		Accumulated Depreciation—Truck	
Jan. 31 Bal. 8,700			2,610 Jan. 31 Bal.

a. If the amount in supplies expense represents the January 31 adjustment for the supplies used in January, and $620 worth of supplies were purchased during January, what was the January 1 beginning balance of supplies?

b. The amount in the insurance expense account represents the adjustment made at January 31 for January insurance expense. If the original insurance premium was for one year, what was the amount of the premium, and on what date did the insurance policy start?

c. If we assume that no beginning balance existed in either wages payable or wages expense on January 1, how much cash was paid as wages during January?

d. If the truck has a useful life of five years (or 60 months), what is the monthly amount of depreciation expense, and how many months has Bloomfield owned the truck?

E3-34. **Assessing Financial Statement Effects of Adjustments**
LO3

L. Burnett began Burnett Refinishing Service on July 1. Selected accounts are shown below as of July 31, before any accounting adjustments have been made.

	Debit	Credit
Prepaid rent	$6,900	
Prepaid advertising.	630	
Supplies	3,000	
Unearned refinishing fees.		$ 600
Refinishing fees revenue		2,500

Using the following information, prepare the accounting adjustments necessary on July 31 using the financial statement effects template.

a. On July 1, the firm paid one year's rent of $6,900 in cash.

b. On July 1, $630 cash was paid to the local newspaper for an advertisement to run daily for the months of July, August, and September.

    c. Supplies still available at July 31 total $1,100.

    d. At July 31, refinishing services of $800 have been performed but not yet recorded or billed to customers. The firm uses the fees receivable account to reflect amounts due but not yet billed.

    e. In early July, a customer paid $600 in advance for a refinishing project. At July 31, the project is one-half complete.

LO3   **E3-35.** **Preparing Accounting Adjustments and Posting**

Refer to the information in E3-34. Prepare adjusting journal entries for each transaction. Set up T-accounts for each of the ledger accounts, and post the journal entries to them.

LO2   **E3-36.** **Inferring Transactions from Financial Statements**

The Gap Inc. (GPS)

The GAP is a global clothing retailer for men, women, children, and babies. The following information is taken from The Gap's fiscal 2015 annual report.

Selected Balance Sheet Data ($ millions)	2015	2014
Inventories	$1,873	$1,889
Accounts Payable	1,112	1,173

    a. The Gap purchased inventories totaling $10,061 million during fiscal 2015. Use the financial statement effects template to record cost of goods sold for The Gap's fiscal year ended 2015. (Assume accounts payable is used only for recording purchases of inventories and all inventories are purchased on credit.)

    b. What amount did the company pay to suppliers during the year? Record this with the financial statement effects template.

LO2   **E3-37.** **Inferring Transactions and Preparing Journal Entries**

The GAP Inc. (GPS)

Refer to the information in E3-36. Prepare journal entries for each transaction.

LO5   **E3-38.** **Preparing Closing Journal Entries**

The GAP Inc. (GPS)

The GAP Inc.'s fiscal 2015 financial statements provide the balances for the following selected accounts.

$ millions	Debit	Credit
Net sales		$15,797
Cost of goods sold	$10,077	
Operating expenses (other than COGS)	4,196	
Interest expense, net	53	
Income tax expense	551	
Retained earnings (beginning of year)		2,797

Prepare entries to close these accounts in journal entry form. Set up T-accounts for each of the accounts, and post the entries to them. After these entries are posted, what is the balance of the retained earnings account?

LO2   **E3-39.** **Inferring Transactions from Financial Statements**

Costco Wholesale Corporation (COST)

Costco Wholesale Corporation operates membership warehouses selling food, appliances, consumer electronics, apparel, and other household goods at 721 locations across the United States as well as in Canada, the United Kingdom, Japan, Australia, South Korea, Taiwan, Mexico, and Puerto Rico. As of its fiscal year-end 2016, Costco had approximately 86.7 million members. Selected fiscal-year information from the company's balance sheets follows.

Selected Balance Sheet Data ($ millions)	2016	2015
Merchandise inventories	$8,969	$8,908
Deferred membership income (liability)	1,362	1,269

    a. During fiscal 2016, Costco collected $2,739 million cash for membership fees. Use the financial statement effects template to record the cash collected for membership fees.

    b. Costco recorded merchandise costs (i.e., cost of goods sold) of $102,901 million in 2016. Record this transaction in the financial statement effects template.

    c. Determine the value of merchandise Costco purchased during 2016. Use the financial statement effects template to record these merchandise purchases. Assume all of Costco's purchases are on credit.

E3-40. Inferring Transactions and Preparing Journal Entries

Refer to the information in E3-39. Prepare journal entries for transactions in parts *a* through *c*.

LO2
Costco Wholesale
Corporation (COST)

E3-41. Preparing Financial Statements and Closing Process

Beneish Company has the following account balances at December 31, the end of its fiscal year.

LO4, 5

	Debit	Credit
Cash	$ 8,000	
Accounts receivable	6,500	
Equipment	78,000	
Accumulated depreciation		$ 14,000
Notes payable		10,000
Common stock		43,000
Retained earnings		20,600
Dividends	8,000	
Service fees earned		75,000
Rent expense	18,000	
Salaries expense	37,100	
Depreciation expense	7,000	
Totals	$162,600	$162,600

a. Prepare Beneish Corporation's income statement and statement of stockholders' equity for year-end December 31 and its balance sheet as of December 31. The company paid cash dividends of $8,000, and there were no stock issuances or repurchases during the year.

b. Prepare journal entries to close Beneish's temporary accounts.

c. Set up T-accounts for each account and post the closing entries.

E3-42. Analyzing and Reporting Financial Statement Effects of Transactions

M. E. Carter launched Carter Company, a professional services firm on March 1. The firm will prepare financial statements at each month-end. In March (its first month), Carter executed the following transactions. Enter the transactions, *a* through *g*, into the financial statement effects template shown in the module.

LO2

a. Carter (owner) invested in the company $100,000 cash and $20,000 in property and equipment. The company issued common stock to Carter.

b. The company paid $3,200 cash for rent of office furnishings and facilities for March.

c. The company performed services for clients and immediately received $4,000 cash earned.

d. The company performed services for clients and sent a bill for $24,000 with payment due within 60 days.

e. The company compensated an office employee with $4,800 cash as salary for March.

f. The company received $10,000 cash as partial payment on the amount owed from clients in transaction *d*.

g. The company paid $935 cash in dividends to Carter (owner).

E3-43. Analyzing Transactions Using the Financial Statement Effects Template

Refer to transactions *a* through *g* from E3-42. Prepare an income statement for Carter Company for the month of March.

LO4

E3-44. Analyzing Transactions Using the Financial Statement Effects Template

Record the effect of each of the following transactions for Hora Company using the financial statement effects template.

LO2

a. Wages of $500 are earned by employees but not yet paid.

b. $2,000 of inventory is purchased on credit.

c. Inventory purchased in transaction *b* is sold for $4,000 on credit.

d. Collected $3,000 cash from transaction *c*.

e. Equipment is acquired for $5,000 cash.

f. Recorded $1,000 depreciation expense on equipment from transaction *e*.

g. Paid $10,000 cash toward a note payable that came due.

h. Paid $2,000 cash for interest on borrowings.

Problems

LO2, 3   **P3-45.**   **Assessing Financial Statement Effects of Transactions and Adjustments**

The following information relates to December 31 accounting adjustments for Fulton Fast Print Company. The firm's fiscal year ends on December 31.

1. Weekly salaries for a five-day week total $3,600, payable on Fridays. December 31 of the current year is a Tuesday.
2. Fulton Fast Print has $20,000 of notes payable outstanding at December 31. Interest of $200 has accrued on these notes by December 31 but will not be paid until the notes mature next year.
3. During December, Fulton Fast Print provided $900 of printing services to clients who will be billed on January 2. The firm uses the fees receivable account to reflect amounts earned but not yet billed.
4. Starting December 1, all maintenance work on Fulton Fast Print's equipment is handled by Richardson Repair Company under an agreement whereby Fulton Fast Print pays a fixed monthly charge of $400. Fulton Fast Print paid six months' service charge of $2,400 cash in advance on December 1 and increased its Prepaid maintenance account by $2,400.
5. The firm paid $900 cash on December 15 for a series of radio commercials to run during December and January. One-third of the commercials aired by December 31. The $900 payment was recorded in its prepaid advertising account.
6. Starting December 16, Fulton Fast Print rented 800 square feet of storage space from a neighboring business. The monthly rent of $0.80 per square foot is due in advance on the first of each month. Nothing was paid in December, however, because the neighboring business agreed to add the rent for one-half of December to the January 1 payment.
7. Fulton Fast Print invested $5,000 cash in securities on December 1 and earned interest of $38 on these securities by December 31. No interest will be received until January.
8. Annual depreciation on the firm's equipment is $2,175. No depreciation has been recorded during the year.

Required

Prepare Fulton Fast Print Company's accounting adjustments required at December 31 using the financial statement effects template.

LO2, 3   **P3-46.**   **Preparing Accounting Adjustments**

Refer to the information in P3-45. Prepare accounting adjustments required at December 31 using journal entries.

LO2, 3   **P3-47.**   **Assessing Financial Statement Effects of Adjustments Across Two Periods**

Sloan Company has the following account balances at December 31, the end of its fiscal year (all accounts have normal balances).

Prepaid advertising.	$ 1,200	Unearned service fees.	$ 5,400
Wages expense	43,800	Service fees earned.	87,000
Prepaid insurance.	3,420	Rental income	4,900

Required

a. Prepare Sloan Company's accounting adjustments at December 31 using the financial statement effects template and the following additional information.
   1. Prepaid advertising at December 31 is $800.
   2. Unpaid wages earned by employees in December are $2,600.
   3. Prepaid insurance at December 31 is $2,280.
   4. Unearned service fees at December 31 are $3,000.
   5. Rent revenue of $1,000 owed by a tenant is not recorded at December 31.

b. Use the financial statement effects template to record the following transactions on January 4 of the following year:
   1. Payment of $4,800 cash in wages.
   2. Cash receipt from the tenant of the $1,000 rent revenue.

LO2, 3   **P3-48.**   **Preparing Accounting Adjustments**

Refer to the information in P3-47. Prepare journal entries for parts a and b.

P3-49. **Journalizing and Posting Transactions and Adjustments**   LO2, 3

D. Roulstone opened Roulstone Roofing Service on April 1. Transactions for April follow.

Apr. 1   Roulstone contributed $11,500 cash to the business in exchange for common stock.
    2   Paid $6,100 cash for the purchase of a used truck.
    2   Purchased $6,200 of ladders and other equipment; the company paid $1,000 cash, with the balance due in 30 days.
    3   Paid $2,880 cash for a two-year (or 24-month) premium toward liability insurance.
    5   Purchased $1,200 of supplies on credit.
    5   Received an advance of $1,800 cash from a customer for roof repairs to be done during April and May.
   12   Billed customers $5,500 for roofing services performed.
   18   Collected $4,900 cash from customers toward their accounts billed on April 12.
   29   Paid $675 cash for truck fuel used in April.
   30   Paid $100 cash for April newspaper advertising.
   30   Paid $4,500 cash for assistants' wages earned.
   30   Billed customers $4,000 for roofing services performed.

Required

a. Set up T-accounts for the following accounts: cash, accounts receivable, supplies, prepaid insurance, trucks, accumulated depreciation—trucks, equipment, accumulated depreciation—equipment, accounts payable, unearned roofing fees, common stock, roofing fees earned, fuel expense, advertising expense, wages expense, insurance expense, supplies expense, depreciation expense—trucks, and depreciation expense—equipment.

b. Record these transactions for April using journal entries.

c. Post the journal entries from part *b.* to their T-accounts (reference transactions in T-accounts by date).

d. Prepare journal entries to adjust the following accounts: insurance expense, supplies expense, depreciation expense—trucks, depreciation expense—equipment, and roofing fees earned. Supplies still available on April 30 amount to $200. Depreciation for April was $125 on the truck and $35 on equipment. One-fourth of the roofing fee received on April 5 was earned by April 30.

e. Post the adjusting journal entries from part *d.* to their T-accounts.

P3-50. **Assessing Financial Statement Effects of Transactions and Adjustments**   LO2, 3

Refer to the information in P3-49.

Required

a. Use the financial statement effects template to record the transactions for April.

b. Use the financial statement effects template to record the adjustments at the end of April (described in part *d* of P3-49).

P3-51. **Preparing Accounting Adjustments**   LO3

Pownall Photomake Company, a commercial photography studio, completed its first year of operations on December 31. Account balances before year-end adjustments follow; no adjustments have been made to the accounts at any time during the year. Assume that all balances are normal.

Cash............................	$ 4,300	Accounts payable..............	$ 4,060
Accounts receivable.............	3,800	Unearned photography fees......	2,600
Prepaid rent	12,600	Common stock	24,000
Prepaid insurance...............	2,970	Photography fees earned	34,480
Supplies	4,250	Wages expense...............	11,000
Equipment	22,800	Utilities expense	3,420

An analysis of the firm's records discloses the following (business began on January 1).

1. Photography services of $1,850 have been rendered, but customers have not yet paid or been billed. The company uses the fees receivable account to reflect amounts due but not yet billed.
2. Equipment, purchased January 1, has an estimated life of 10 years.
3. Utilities expense for December is estimated to be $400, but the bill will not arrive or be paid until January of next year. (All prior months' utilities bills have been received and paid.)
4. The balance in prepaid rent represents the amount paid on January 1 for a two-year lease on the studio it operates from.

5. In November, customers paid $2,600 cash in advance for photos to be taken for the holiday season. When received, these fees were credited to unearned photography fees. By December 31, all of these fees are earned.
6. A three-year insurance premium paid on January 1 was debited to prepaid insurance.
7. Supplies still available at December 31 are $1,020.
8. At December 31, wages expense of $375 had been incurred but not yet paid or recorded.

Required

Prepare the required adjusting entries using the financial statement effects template.

LO3   **P3-52.**   **Recording Adjustments with Journal Entries and T-Accounts**
Refer to the information in P3-51.

Required

a. Prepare journal entries to record the accounting adjustments.
b. Set up T-accounts for each account, and post the journal entries to them.

LO3   **P3-53.**   **Preparing Accounting Adjustments**
BensEx, a mailing service, has just completed its first year of operations on December 31. Its account balances before year-end adjustments follow; no adjusting entries have been made to the accounts at any time during the year. Assume all balances are normal.

Cash.	$ 1,700	Accounts payable	$ 2,700
Accounts receivable.	5,120	Common stock	9,530
Prepaid advertising.	1,680	Mailing fees earned	86,000
Supplies	6,270	Wages expense	38,800
Equipment	42,240	Rent expense.	6,900
Notes payable	7,500	Utilities expense	3,020

An analysis of the firm's records reveals the following (business began on January 1).

1. The balance in prepaid advertising represents the amount paid for newspaper advertising for one year. The agreement, which calls for the same amount of space each month, covers the period from February 1 of this first year to January 31 of the following year. BensEx did not advertise during its first month of operations.
2. Equipment, purchased January 1, has an estimated life of eight years.
3. Utilities expense does not include expense for December, estimated at $325. The bill will not arrive until January of the following year.
4. At year-end, employees have earned $2,400 in wages that will not be paid until January.
5. Supplies available at year-end amount to $1,520.
6. At year-end, unpaid interest of $450 has accrued on the notes payable.
7. The firm's lease calls for rent of $575 per month payable on the first of each month, plus an amount equal to 0.75% of annual mailing fees earned. The rental percentage is payable within 15 days after the end of the year.

Required

Prepare its adjusting entries using the financial statement effects template.

LO3   **P3-54.**   **Recording Accounting Adjustments with Journal Entries and T-Accounts**
Refer to information in P3-53.

Required

a. Prepare journal entries to record the accounting adjustments.
b. Set up T-accounts for each account, and post the journal entries to them.

LO3, 4, 5   **P3-55.**   **Preparing Accounting Adjustments**
Wysocki Wheels began operations on March 1 to provide automotive wheel alignment and balancing services. On March 31, accounting records revealed the following account balances.

	Debit	Credit
Cash..........................	$ 2,900	
Accounts receivable...............	3,820	
Prepaid rent.....................	4,770	
Supplies.......................	3,700	
Equipment	36,180	
Accounts payable.................		$ 3,510
Unearned service revenue		1,000
Common stock...................		38,400
Service revenue		12,360
Wages expense	3,900	
	$55,270	$55,270

The following information is also available.

1. The balance in prepaid rent was the amount paid on March 1 to cover the first six months' rent.
2. Supplies available on March 31 amounted to $1,360.
3. Equipment has an estimated life of nine years (or 108 months).
4. Unpaid and unrecorded wages at March 31 were $1,560.
5. Utility services used during March were estimated at $390; a bill is expected early in April.
6. The balance in unearned service revenue was the amount received on March 1 from a car dealer to cover alignment and balancing services on cars sold by the dealer in March and April. Wysocki Wheels agreed to provide the services at a fixed fee of $500 each month.

Required
a. Prepare its accounting adjustments at March 31 in journal entry form.
b. Set up T-accounts, and post the accounting adjustments to them.
c. Prepare its income statement for March and its balance sheet at March 31.
d. Prepare entries to close its temporary accounts in journal entry form. Post the closing entries to the T-accounts.

P3-56. **Analyzing Transactions Using the Financial Statement Effects Template** **LO2, 4**
Sefcik Company began operations on the first of October. Following are the transactions for its first month of business.

1. S. Sefcik launched Sefcik Company and invested $50,000 into the business in exchange for common stock. The company also borrowed $100,000 from a local bank.
2. Sefcik Company purchased equipment for $95,000 cash and inventory of $40,000 on credit (the company still owes its suppliers for the inventory at month-end).
3. Sefcik Company sold inventory costing $30,000 for $50,000 cash.
4. Sefcik Company paid $12,000 cash for wages owed employees for October work.
5. Sefcik Company paid interest on the bank loan of $1,000 cash.
6. Sefcik Company recorded $500 of depreciation expense related to its equipment.
7. Sefcik Company paid a dividend of $2,000 cash.

Required
a. Record the effects of each transaction using the financial statement effects template.
b. Prepare the income statement and balance sheet at the end of October.

P3-57. **Analyzing Transactions Using the Financial Statement Effects Template** **LO2, 3**
Following are selected transactions of Mogg Company. Record the effects of each using the financial statement effects template.

1. Shareholders contribute $10,000 cash to the business in exchange for common stock.
2. Employees earn $500 in wages that have not been paid at period-end.
3. Inventory of $3,000 is purchased on credit.
4. The inventory purchased in transaction 3 is sold for $4,500 on credit.
5. The company collected the $4,500 owed to it per transaction 4.
6. Equipment is purchased for $5,000 cash.
7. Depreciation of $1,000 is recorded on the equipment from transaction 6.
8. The supplies account had a $3,800 balance at the beginning of this period; a physical count at period-end shows that $800 of supplies are still available. No supplies were purchased during this period.

Homework
MBC

9. The company paid $12,000 cash toward the principal on a note payable; also, $500 cash is paid to cover this note's interest expense for the period.
10. The company received $8,000 cash in advance for services to be delivered next period.

LO2, 3, 4   **P3-58.**   **Analyzing Transactions Using the Financial Statement Effects Template**

On March 1, S. Penman launched AniFoods Inc., an organic foods retailing company. Following are the transactions for its first month of business.

1. S. Penman contributed $100,000 cash to the company in return for common stock. Penman also lent the company $55,000. This $55,000 note is due one year hence.
2. The company purchased equipment in the amount of $50,000, paying $10,000 cash and signing a note payable to the equipment manufacturer for the remaining balance.
3. The company purchased inventory for $80,000 cash in March.
4. The company had March sales of $100,000, of which $60,000 was for cash and $40,000 on credit. Total cost of goods sold for its March sales was $70,000.
5. The company purchased advertising time from a local radio station for $10,000 cash.
6. During March, $7,500 worth of radio spots purchased in transaction 5 are aired. The remaining spots will be aired in April.
7. Employee wages earned and paid during March total $17,000 cash.
8. Prior to disclosing the financial statements, the company recognized that employees had earned an additional $1,000 in wages that will be paid in the next period.
9. The company recorded $2,000 of depreciation for March relating to its equipment.

Required

a. Record the effect of each transaction using the financial statement effects template.
b. Prepare a March income statement and a balance sheet as of the end of March for AniFoods Inc.

LO2, 4   **P3-59.**   **Analyzing Transactions Using the Financial Statement Effects Template**

Hanlon Advertising Company began the current month with the following balance sheet.

Cash	$ 80,000	Liabilities	$ 70,000
Noncash assets	135,000	Contributed capital	110,000
		Earned capital	35,000
Total assets	$215,000	Total liabilities and equity	$215,000

Following are summary transactions that occurred during the current month.

1. The company purchased supplies for $5,000 cash; none were used this month.
2. Services of $2,500 were performed this month on credit.
3. Services were performed for $10,000 cash this month.
4. The company purchased advertising for $8,000 cash; the ads will run next month.
5. The company received $1,200 cash as partial payment on accounts receivable from transaction 2.
6. The company paid $3,400 cash toward the accounts payable balance reported at the beginning of the month.
7. The company paid $3,500 cash toward this month's wages expenses.
8. The company declared and paid dividends of $500 cash.

Required

a. Record the effects of each transaction using the financial statement effects template.
b. Prepare the income statement for this month and the balance sheet as of month-end.

LO2, 3, 4   **P3-60.**   **Analyzing Transactions Using the Financial Statement Effects Template**

Werner Realty Company began the month with the following balance sheet.

Cash	$ 30,000	Liabilities	$ 90,000
Noncash assets	225,000	Contributed capital	45,000
		Earned capital	120,000
Total assets	$255,000	Total liabilities and equity	$255,000

Following are summary transactions that occurred during the current month.

1. The company purchased $6,000 of supplies on credit.
2. The company received $8,000 cash from a new customer for services to be performed next month.

3. The company paid $6,000 cash to cover office rent for two months (the current month and the next).
4. The company billed clients for $25,000 of work performed.
5. The company paid employees $6,000 cash for work performed.
6. The company collected $25,000 cash from accounts receivable in transaction 4.
7. The company recorded $4,000 depreciation on its equipment.
8. At month-end, $2,000 of supplies purchased in transaction 1 are still available; no supplies were available when the month began.

Required

a. Record the effects of each transaction using the financial statement effects template.
b. Prepare the income statement for this month and the balance sheet as of month-end.

IFRS Applications

I3-61. **Preparing Closing Journal Entries**

LO5
Qantas Airlines

On June 30, 2016, Qantas Airlines reports the following balances:

AUD millions	Debit	Credit
Total passenger and freight revenue		16,200
Manpower and staff related	3,849	
Fuel	3,250	
Aircraft operating variable	3,362	
Depreciation and amortisation	1,224	
Other expenses	2,872	
Finance costs	219	
Income tax expense	395	
Retained earnings (deficit)	1,115	

Assume the company has not yet closed any accounts to retained earnings. Prepare journal entries to close the temporary accounts above. Set up the needed T-accounts, and post the closing entries. After these entries are posted, what is the balance of the retained earnings account?

I3-62. **Inferring Transactions from Financial Statements**

LO2
Rio Tinto

Rio Tinto is a British-Australian multinational metals and mining corporation with headquarters in London, England, and a management office in Melbourne, Australia. Assume the following amounts have not been recorded ($ millions).

Sales revenue..	$34,829
Depreciation and amortization expense....................................	4,645
Income taxes paid	1,792

Use the financial statement effects template to record the following transactions for Rio Tinto for fiscal 2015.

a. Sales revenue. Assume 100% of the company's revenue is credit sales (i.e., sales are on accounts receivable).
b. Depreciation expense.
c. Income taxes paid. Assume this represents the portion of income tax expense paid in cash.

I3-63. **Inferring Transactions and Account Balances from Financial Statements**

LO2
Canadian Tire Corp.

Canadian Tire Corporation is a Canadian firm whose core operation is Canadian Tire, a retail and automotive services operation. Its head office is in Toronto, Ontario. The following T-accounts reflect information in the company's 2014 and 2015 balance sheets (in millions of Canadian dollars).

Inventories	
2014 Balance 1,623.8	
2015 Balance 1,764.5	

Accounts Payable	
	1,961.2 2014 Balance
	1,957.1 2015 Balance

Required

a. Use the financial statement effects template to record Canadian Tire's purchases during fiscal 2015. Assume Canadian Tire incurred cost of goods sold (which the company labels "Cost of producing revenue") of $8,144.3 million during 2015.

b. What amount did Canadian Tire pay in cash to its suppliers during fiscal 2015? Explain. Assume all inventory purchases are made on account and accounts payable reflects only inventory purchases.

c. Use the financial statement effects template to record cost of goods sold for fiscal 2015.

Management Applications

LO3, 4   MA3-64.   Preparing Accounting Adjustments and Financial Statements

Stocken Surf Shop began operations on July 1 with an initial investment of $50,000. During the first three months of operations, the following cash transactions were recorded in the firm's checking account.

Deposits		Checks Drawn	
Initial investment by owner	$ 50,000	Rent	$ 24,000
Collected from customers	81,000	Fixtures and equipment	25,000
Borrowings from bank	10,000	Merchandise inventory	62,000
	$141,000	Salaries	8,000
		Other expenses	13,000
			$132,000

Additional information:

1. Most sales were for cash; however, the store accepted a limited amount of credit sales; at September 30, customers owed the store $9,000.
2. Rent was paid on July 1 for six months.
3. Salaries of $4,000 per month were paid on the first of each month for salaries earned in the month prior.
4. Inventories were purchased for cash; at September 30, inventory of $28,000 was still available.
5. Fixtures and equipment were expected to last five years (or 60 months), with zero salvage value.
6. The bank charges 12% annual interest (1% per month) on the $10,000 bank loan. Stocken took out the loan on July 1.

Required

a. Record all of Stocken's cash transactions, and prepare any necessary adjusting entries at September 30. You may either use the financial statement effects template or journal entries combined with T-accounts.

b. Prepare the income statement for the three months ended September 30 and the balance sheet at September 30.

c. Analyze the statements from part b, and assess the company's performance over its initial three months.

LO3   MA3-65.   Analyzing Transactions, Impacts on Financial Ratios, and Loan Covenants

Kadous Consulting, a firm started three years ago by K. Kadous, offers consulting services for material handling and plant layout. Its balance sheet at the close of the current year follows.

KADOUS CONSULTING Balance Sheet December 31			
Assets		**Liabilities**	
Cash.	$ 3,400	Notes payable	$30,000
Accounts receivable.	20,875	Accounts payable.	4,200
Supplies	13,200	Unearned consulting fees	11,300
Prepaid insurance.	6,500	Wages payable.	400
Equipment, gross	68,500	Total liabilities	45,900
Less: Accumulated		**Equity**	
depreciation	23,975	Common stock.	8,000
Equipment, net.	44,525	Retained earnings	34,600
Total assets.	$88,500	Total liabilities and equity	$88,500

Earlier in the year, Kadous obtained a bank loan of $30,000 cash for the firm. A provision of the loan is that the year-end debt-to-equity ratio (total liabilities to total equity) cannot exceed 1.0. Based on the above balance sheet, the ratio at December 31 of this year is 1.08. Kadous is concerned about being in violation of the loan agreement and requests assistance in reviewing the situation. Kadous believes she might have overlooked some items at year-end. Discussions with Kadous reveal the following.

1. On January 1 of this year, the firm paid a $6,500 insurance premium for two years of coverage; the amount in prepaid insurance has not yet been adjusted.
2. Depreciation on equipment should be 10% of cost per year; the company inadvertently recorded 15% for this year.
3. Interest on the bank loan has been paid through the end of this year.
4. The firm concluded a major consulting engagement in December, doing a plant layout analysis for a new factory. The $8,000 fee has not been billed or recorded in the accounts.
5. On December 1 of this year, the firm received an $11,300 cash advance payment from Dichev Corp. for consulting services to be rendered over a two-month period. This payment was credited to the unearned consulting fees account. One-half of this fee was earned but unrecorded by December 31 of this year.
6. Supplies costing $4,800 were available on December 31; the company has made no adjustment of its Supplies account.

Required

a. What is the correct debt-to-equity ratio at December 31?
b. Is the firm in violation of its loan agreement? Prepare computations to support the correct total liabilities and total equity figures at December 31.

MA3-66. Ethics, Accounting Adjustments, and Auditors   **LO3**

It is the end of the accounting year for Anne Beatty, controller of a medium-sized, publicly held corporation specializing in toxic waste cleanup. Within the corporation, only Beatty and the president know the firm has been negotiating for several months to land a large contract for waste cleanup in Western Europe. The president has hired another firm with excellent contacts in Western Europe to help with negotiations. The outside firm will charge an hourly fee plus expenses but has agreed not to submit a bill until the negotiations are in their final stages (expected to occur in another three to four months). Even if the contract falls through, the outside firm is entitled to receive payment for its services. Based on her discussion with a member of the outside firm, Beatty knows its charge for services provided to date will be $150,000. This is a material amount for the company.

Beatty knows the president wants negotiations to remain as secret as possible so competitors will not learn of the contract the company is pursuing in Europe. In fact, the president recently stated to her, "This is not the time to reveal our actions in Western Europe to other staff members, our auditors, or the readers of our financial statements; securing this contract is crucial to our future growth." No entry has been made in the accounting records for the cost of contract negotiations. Beatty now faces an uncomfortable situation. The company's outside auditor has just asked her if she knows of any year-end adjustments that have not yet been recorded.

Required

a. What are the ethical considerations Beatty faces in answering the auditor's question?
b. How should Beatty respond to the auditor's question?

Solutions to Review Problems

Review 3-1—Solution

	Cash Asset	Noncash Asset	Liabilities	Contributed Capital	Earned Capital	Revenues	Expenses
Accounts payable..........................			X				
Accounts receivable, less allowances		X					
Accrued expenses			X				
Acquired intangible assets, net		X					
Cash and cash equivalents	X						
Common stock and additional paid-in capital ...				X			
Cost of sales.............................							X
Current portion of long-term debt			X				
Deferred revenue			X				
Deferred tax assets		X					
Goodwill................................		X					
Inventories		X					
Long-term debt			X				
Long-term marketable securities		X					
Net sales................................						X	
Other current assets.......................		X					
Other non-current liabilities			X				
Property, plant, and equipment, net...........		X					
Provision for income taxes..................							X
Research and development							X
Retained earnings					X		
Selling, general and administrative							X

Review 3-2—Solution

	Balance Sheet						Income Statement		
	Cash Assets +	Noncash Assets =	Liabil- ities	+	Contrib. Capital +	Earned Capital	Rev- enues −	Expen- ses	= Net Income
Balance January 1, 2017	10,000	41,000	26,000		10,000	15,000	0	0	0
Transactions									
1. Issue common stock for $3,000 cash	3,000				3,000				
2. Purchase inventory for $8,000 on credit		8,000 Inventory	8,000 Accounts payable						
3. Sell inventory costing $8,000 for $15,000 on credit.		(8,000) Inventory 15,000 Accounts receivable				7,000	15,000 Revenue	8,000 Cost of goods sold	7,000
4. Issue long-term debt for $10,000 cash	10,000		10,000 Long-term debt						
5. Pay $15,000 cash for PPE	(15,000)	15,000 PPE							
6. Pay $500 cash for salaries	(500)					(500)		500 Salaries expense	(500)
7. Receive $300 cash in advance for future consulting services . . .	300		300 Unearned revenue						
8. Pay $50 cash for interest on long-term debt	(50)					(50)		50 Interest expense	(50)
9. Receive $3,000 cash from accounts receivable.	3,000	(3,000) Accounts receivable							
10. Pay $2,500 cash toward accounts payable	(2,500)		(2,500) Accounts payable						
11. Perform consulting services for client who previously paid in 7 . .			(300) Unearned revenue			300	300 Revenue		300
12. Pay $100 cash for dividends	(100)					(100)			

Review 3-3—Solution

	Balance Sheet						Income Statement		
	Cash Assets +	Noncash Assets =	Liabil- ities	+	Contrib. Capital +	Earned Capital	Rev- enues −	Expen- ses	= Net Income
Accounting Adjustments									
13. Record depreciation of $600		(600) PPE				(600)		600 Depreciation expense	(600)
14. Accrue salaries of $1,000			1,000 Salaries payable			(1,000)		1,000 Salaries expense	(1,000)
15. Advertising costing $1,300 is aired		(1,300) Prepaid expense				(1,300)		1,300 Advertising expense	(1,300)
16. Accrue income taxes of $1,200			1,200 Taxes payable			(1,200)		1,200 Tax expense	(1,200)
Balance January 31, 2017	8,150	66,100	43,700		13,000	17,550	15,300	12,650	2,650

Review 3-4—Solution

1.

Cash	$ 8,150	Taxes payable	$ 1,200
Accounts receivable	24,000	Unearned revenue	200
Inventory	7,200	Long-term debt	32,000
Prepaid advertising	500	Common stock	13,000
PPE	34,400	Retained earnings	17,550
Accounts payable	9,300	Revenues	15,300
Salaries payable	1,000	Expenses	12,650

2.

PRESTIGE INC. Income Statement For Month Ended January 31, 2017	
Revenues	$15,300
Cost of goods sold	8,000
Gross profit	7,300
Salaries expense	1,500
Depreciation expense	600
Advertising expense	1,300
Operating profit	3,900
Interest expense	50
Profit before tax	3,850
Tax expense	1,200
Net income	$ 2,650

PRESTIGE INC. Statement of Retained Earnings For Month Ended January 31, 2017	
Beginning retained earnings	$15,000
Net income	2,650
Dividends	(100)
Ending retained earnings	$17,550

PRESTIGE INC. Balance Sheet January 31, 2017	
Cash	$ 8,150
Accounts receivable	24,000
Inventories	7,200
Prepaid advertising	500
Current assets	39,850
Property, plant, and equipment	34,400
Total assets	$74,250
Accounts payable	$ 9,300
Wages payable	1,000
Taxes payable	1,200
Unearned revenue	200
Current liabilities	11,700
Long-term debt	32,000
Total liabilities	43,700
Common stock	13,000
Retained earnings	17,550
Total stockholders' equity	30,550
Total liabilities and stockholders' equity	$74,250

Review 3-5—Solution

1. Close revenue account.

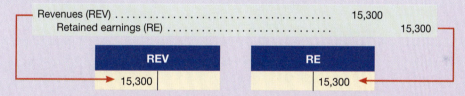

```
Revenues (REV) ........................................  15,300
    Retained earnings (RE) .............................          15,300
```

2. Close expense accounts.

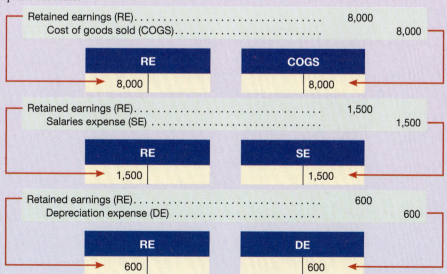

```
Retained earnings (RE) ................................  8,000
    Cost of goods sold (COGS) ..........................          8,000
```

```
Retained earnings (RE) ................................  1,500
    Salaries expense (SE) ..............................          1,500
```

```
Retained earnings (RE) ................................  600
    Depreciation expense (DE) ..........................          600
```

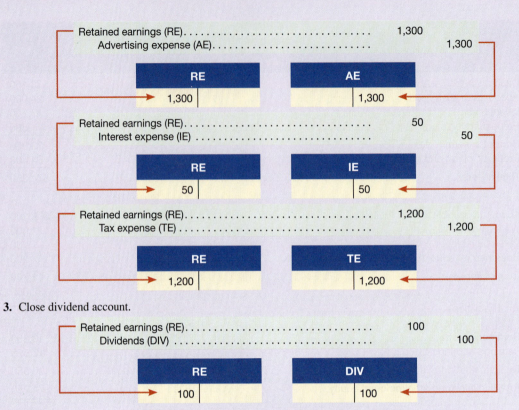

Retained earnings (RE).   1,300
    Advertising expense (AE).   1,300

RE	AE
1,300	1,300

Retained earnings (RE).   50
    Interest expense (IE)   50

RE	IE
50	50

Retained earnings (RE).   1,200
    Tax expense (TE)   1,200

RE	TE
1,200	1,200

3. Close dividend account.

Retained earnings (RE).   100
    Dividends (DIV)   100

RE	DIV
100	100

Module 4

Analyzing and Interpreting Financial Statements

Learning Objectives

LO1 Compute and interpret return on equity (ROE). (p. 4-3)

LO2 Apply DuPont disaggregation of ROE into return on assets (ROA) and financial leverage. (p. 4-4)

LO3 Disaggregate ROA into profitability and productivity and analyze both. (p. 4-6)

LO4 Identify balance sheet operating items and compute net operating assets. (p. 4-14)

LO5 Identify income statement operating items and compute net operating profit after tax. (p. 4-20)

LO6 Compute and interpret return on net operating assets (RNOA). (p. 4-24)

LO7 Disaggregate RNOA into net operating profit margin and net operating asset turnover. (p. 4-26)

LO8 Compute and interpret nonoperating return (Appendix 4A). (p. 4-31)

LO9 Compute and interpret measures of liquidity and solvency (Appendix 4B). (p. 4-36)

INTC

Market cap: $165,530 mil
Total assets: $103,065 mil
Revenues: $55,355 mil
Net income: $11,420 mil

Intel is a leader in the design and manufacturing of advanced integrated digital technology platforms. Its strategy is to offer complete and connected platform computing solutions, consisting of both hardware and software, and to continue to drive "Moore's Law." Through enhanced energy-efficient performance, connectivity, and security, Intel enables platform solutions that span the continuum.

So, how should we measure Intel's financial performance? A company's performance is commonly judged by its profitability. Although the usual focus on profit is important, it is only part of the story. A more meaningful analysis is to compare level of profitability with the amount of capital that has been invested in the business. The most common measure is return on equity (ROE), which is computed as net income divided by average stockholders' equity and focuses on shareholder investment as its measure of invested capital. By focusing on the equity investment, ROE measures return from the perspective of the common shareholder rather than the company overall. Intel's ROE for 2015 was 19.5%, down slightly from 20.5% in the prior year.

Let's consider two other return metrics: return on assets (ROA) and return on net operating assets (RNOA). Return on assets (ROA) measures the profitability of the total assets owned by the company. In 2015, Intel reported an impressive net income of $11 billion. What level of assets was used to generate this $11 billion? Intel's average total assets was $97,483 million during 2015. By dividing net income by average total assets during the year, we see that Intel's ROA, the return on total assets, was 11.7%—for every dollar of assets held by Intel during 2015, the company earned just under 12 cents.

The difference between ROE and ROA shows the effects of the company's use of debt. Intel has borrowed money and invested in assets that create a return. By borrowing at rates that are less than the company's ROA, Intel has substantially increased the shareholders' investment from 11.7% ROA to 19.5% ROE. However, debt can increase the company's risk—where severe consequences can result if debt is not repaid when due.

A potentially more informative metric to use when assessing performance is return on net operating assets (RNOA). RNOA focuses on the returns from the assets that a company uses for operations, net of any operating liabilities. Compared to ROA, RNOA is a more precise measure of the profitability from a company's core operations because RNOA disregards ancillary, or "nonoperating" activities. For Intel, RNOA measures the profitability of the design, manufacturing, and selling of integrated digital technology platforms and excludes the return from investments. In 2015, Intel's RNOA was 22.9%, nearly double its ROA of 11.7%. [Source: *Intel* 2015 10-K.]

© iStock

Road Map

LO	Learning Objective | Topics	Page	eLecture	Guided Example	Assignments
4–1	**Compute and interpret return on equity (ROE).** ROE Definition :: ROE Computation :: ROE Interpretation	4-3	e4–1	Review 4-1	1, 6, 18, 22, 26, 30, 34, 35, 36, 42, 48, 49, 54, 55, 57
4–2	**Apply DuPont disaggregation of ROE into return on assets (ROA) and financial leverage.** ROE Disaggregation :: Return on Assets :: Financial Leverage	4-4	e4–2	Review 4-2	2, 5, 19, 26, 30, 34, 36, 42, 54, 55
4–3	**Disaggregate ROA into profitability and productivity and analyze both.** ROA Disaggregation :: Profitability :: Productivity :: Financial Leverage	4-6	e4–3	Review 4-3	16, 19, 26, 30, 34, 42, 54, 55, 61, 62, 63
4–4	**Identify balance sheet operating items and compute net operating assets.** Operating Focus on Balance Sheet :: RNOA Motivation :: NOA Computation	4-14	e4–4	Review 4-4	9, 20, 24, 41, 45, 48, 50, 51, 59
4–5	**Identify income statement operating items and compute net operating profit after tax.** Operating Focus on Income Statement :: Operating vs Nonoperating :: NOPAT Computation :: Income Tax Expense	4-20	e4–5	Review 4-5	7, 8, 21, 25, 29, 40, 41, 45, 48, 50, 51, 59
4–6	**Compute and interpret return on net operating assets (RNOA).** RNOA Computation :: ROA vs RNOA :: ROA components :: Key Definitions	4-24	e4–6	Review 4-6	6, 22, 23, 27, 31, 32, 33, 35, 36, 41, 45, 48, 50, 51, 56, 57, 59
4–7	**Disaggregate RNOA into net operating profitability and net operating asset turnover.** RNOA Disaggregation :: Net Operating Profit Margin :: Net Operating Asset Turnover :: Trade-Off of Margin and Turnover	4-26	e4–7	Review 4-7	3, 4, 10, 11, 15, 22, 23, 27, 29, 31, 32, 33, 35, 41, 45, 48, 50, 51, 53, 56, 57, 59
4–8	**Compute and interpret nonoperating return (Appendix 4A).** Nonoperating Return Components :: Under Various Conditions	4-31	e4–8	Review 4-8	1, 41, 44, 47, 49, 51, 52, 59
4–9	**Compute and interpret measures of liquidity and solvency (Appendix 4B).** Liquidity Analysis :: Solvency Analysis :: Vertical and Horizontal Analysis :: Limitations of Ratios	4-36	e4–9	Review 4-9	12, 13, 17, 28, 37, 38, 39, 43, 46, 58, 60

Analyzing and Interpreting Financial Statements

Return on Equity (ROE)	Return on Assets (ROA)	Operating Focus	Nonoperating Return	Liquidity and Solvency
■ Measuring ROE ■ Disaggregating ROE with DuPont Analysis ■ Components: Return on Assets and Financial Leverage	■ Measuring ROA ■ Profitability (Profit Margin) ■ Productivity (Asset Turnover) ■ Financial Leverage: Link to ROE	■ Operating Revenues and Expenses ■ Tax on Operating Profit ■ Operating Assets and Liabilities ■ Disaggregating RNOA into Margin and Turnover	■ Measuring Nonoperating Return ■ Leveraging Debt to Increase ROE ■ Risks of Debt Financing ■ Debt Covenants	■ Liquidity: Current Ratio and Quick Ratio ■ Solvency: Liabilities-to-Equity and Times Interest Earned Ratios ■ Limitations of Ratio Analysis

Return on Equity (ROE)

LO1 Compute and interpret return on equity (ROE).

The most common analysis metric used by managers and investors alike, is **return on equity (ROE)**, a powerful summary measure of company performance defined as:[1]

$$ROE = \frac{\text{Net income}}{\text{Average stockholders' equity}}$$

ROE relates net income to the average total stockholders' equity from the balance sheet. ROE measures return from the perspective of the company's stockholders. ROE is an important metric and, in the five years from 2011–2015, return on equity of the S&P 500 firms has ranged from 14% to 15%. Exhibit 4.1 includes Intel's income statement and balance sheet data used to compute its ROE for 2015 of 19.53%.

Exhibit 4.1 ■ Financial Statement Data for Intel Corporation		
$ millions	**Dec. 26, 2015**	**Dec. 27, 2014**
Sales.	$ 55,355	$55,870
Net income.	11,420	11,704
Total assets.	103,065	91,900
Total stockholders' equity	61,085	55,865

$$ROE = \frac{\$11,420}{(\$61,085 + \$55,865)/2} = 19.53\%$$

ROE is a summary return metric that measures the return the company has earned on the book (reported) value of the shareholders' investment. It is one measure of how effective management has been in its role as stewards of the capital invested by shareholders. In our analysis of company performance, we seek to uncover the *drivers* of ROE and how those drivers have trended over time so that we are better able to predict future performance.

---

[1] ROE uses net income, in the numerator, that represents profit earned *during* the year. Therefore, the denominator would ideally reflect equity that the company had *throughout* the year. As an approximation, we use a simple average of the balance sheet values for equity at the start and end of the year to reflect equity during the year.

Following are selected income statement and balance sheet data for **Cisco Systems Inc.**

$ millions	July 25, 2015	July 26, 2014
Sales..........................	$ 49,161	$ 47,142
Net income....................	8,981	7,853
Total assets...................	113,481	105,070
Cisco shareholders' equity........	59,698	56,654

Required

Compute return on equity (ROE) for Cisco Systems for fiscal 2015.

Solution on p. 4-64.

ROE Disaggregation: DuPont Analysis

There are two methods for disaggregating ROE into its components; each provides a different perspective that can inform our analysis.

eLectures **LO2**

MBC Apply DuPont disaggregation of ROE into return on assets (ROA) and financial leverage.

■ The first method is the traditional DuPont analysis that disaggregates return on equity into components of profitability, productivity, and leverage.

■ The second method extends the traditional DuPont analysis by taking an *operating focus* that separates operating and nonoperating activities. Operating activities are the drivers of shareholder value. This method, which focuses on operating or core activities, provides insight into the factors that drive value creation.

Disaggregation of return on equity (ROE) was initially introduced by the **E.I. DuPont de Nemours and Company** to aid its managers in performance evaluation. DuPont realized that management's focus on profit alone was insufficient because profit can be increased simply by the purchase of additional investment in low-yielding, but safe, assets. DuPont wanted managers to think like investors and to manage their portfolio of activities using investment principles that allocate scarce investment capital to competing projects in descending order of return on investment (so-called capital budgeting approach). The DuPont model incorporates this investment perspective into performance measurement by disaggregating ROE into two components.

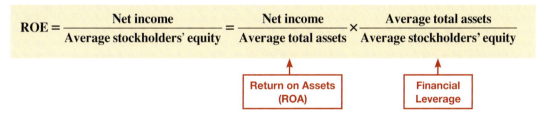

$$ROE = \frac{\text{Net income}}{\text{Average stockholders' equity}} = \frac{\text{Net income}}{\text{Average total assets}} \times \frac{\text{Average total assets}}{\text{Average stockholders' equity}}$$

Return on Assets (ROA) Financial Leverage

Return on equity takes the perspective of company's shareholders and measures rate of return on shareholders' investment—how much net income is earned relative to the equity invested by shareholders. It reflects *both* company performance (as measured by return on assets) *and* how assets are financed (relative use of liabilities and equity). ROE is higher when there is more debt and less equity for a given level of assets (this is because the denominator in ROE, equity, is smaller). There is, however, a tradeoff: while using more debt and less equity results in higher ROE, the greater debt means higher risk for the company.

Return on Assets Component

Return on assets (ROA) measures return from the perspective of the entire company. This return includes both profitability (numerator) and total company assets (denominator). To earn a high return on assets, the company must be profitable *and* manage assets to minimize the assets invested to the level necessary to achieve its profit.

Most operating managers understand the income statement and the focus on profit. However, many of the same managers fail to manage the balance sheet (the denominator in ROA). ROA analysis encourages managers to focus on the profit achieved from the invested capital under their control.

This means that managers seek to increase profits with the same level of assets *and* to decrease assets without decreasing the level of profit. It is this dual focus that makes return on assets a powerful performance measure—focusing managers' attention on *both* the income statement and balance sheet.

Intel's net income is $11,420 million and its total assets are $103,065 million and $91,900 million at fiscal-year-end for 2015 and 2014, respectively (data from Exhibit 4.1). Intel's 11.71% return on assets is computed as follows.

$$\text{ROA} = \frac{\$11,420 \text{ million}}{(\$103,065 \text{ million} + \$91,900 \text{ million})/2} = 11.71\%$$

By comparison, the median return on assets of the S&P 500 companies for the same period was 5.2% and ranged from 5.2% to 6.2% for the 2011–2015 period.

Financial Leverage Component

Financial leverage, the second component of ROE, measures the degree to which the company finances its assets with debt versus equity. Financial leverage is measured in the DuPont analysis as the ratio of average total assets to average stockholders' equity. An increase in this ratio implies an increase in the relative level of debt. This is evident from the accounting equation: assets = liabilities + equity. For example, if assets are financed equally with debt and equity, the accounting equation, expressed in percentage terms is: 100% = 50% + 50%, and financial leverage is 2.0 (100%/50%). If debt increases to 75%, the accounting equation is: 100% = 75% + 25%, and financial leverage is 4.0 (100%/25%).

Measuring financial leverage is important because debt is a contractual obligation and a company's failure to repay principal or interest can result in legal repercussions or even bankruptcy. As financial leverage increases so does the level of debt payments, which all else equal, increases the probability of default and possible bankruptcy. For fiscal 2015, Intel's financial leverage is 1.67, computed as:

$$\text{Financial leverage} = \frac{(\$103,065 \text{ million} + \$91,900 \text{ million})/2}{(\$61,085 \text{ million} + \$55,865 \text{ million})/2} = 1.67$$

By comparison, the median financial leverage of the S&P 500 companies for the same period was 2.74 and ranged from 2.4 to 2.7 for the 2011–2015 period.

Business Insight ▪ Which Accounts Are Used to Compute ROE?

Return on equity has net income in the numerator and stockholders' equity in the denominator. The complexity of company financial statements, however, presents some complications: which net income and stockholders' equity accounts should we use?

- **Preferred Stock.** The ROE formula takes the perspective of the *common* stockholder in that it relates the income available to pay common dividends to the average common stockholder. The presence of preferred stock on the balance sheet requires two adjustments to ROE.

  1. Preferred dividends are subtracted from net income in the numerator.

  2. Preferred stock is subtracted from stockholders' equity in the denominator.

  This modified return on equity is labeled *return on common equity* (ROCE).

$$\text{ROCE} = \frac{\text{Net income} - \text{Preferred dividends}}{\text{Average stockholders' equity} - \text{Average preferred equity}}$$

- **Noncontrolling interests.** Many companies have two sets of stockholders: those that own the common stock of the parent company whose financial statements are under analysis (called *controlling interest*) and those that own shares in one or more of the parent company's subsidiaries (called *noncontrolling interest*). Companies separately identify the stockholders' equity relating to each group and, likewise, net income attributable to each. ROE is computed from the perspective of the controlling (parent company) stockholders and, thus, the numerator is net income attributable to parent company's stockholders and the denominator is equity attributable to parent company's stockholders. We explain controlling and noncontrolling interest in a later module and ROE computations with noncontrolling interests in Appendix 4A.

LO2 **Review 4-2**

Refer to the financial information for **Cisco Systems** reported in Review 4-1.

Required
Compute return on assets (ROA) and financial leverage following DuPont disaggregation of ROE for fiscal 2015. Confirm that ROA × Financial leverage = ROE.

Solution on p. 4-64.

Return on Assets and its Disaggregation

Return on assets (ROA) includes both profitability (in the numerator) and total assets (in the denominator). Managers can increase ROA by increasing profitability for a given level of asset investment or by reducing assets invested to generate a given level of profitability, or both. We gain insight into these two drivers by disaggregating return on assets into two components to isolate its profitability and asset investment levels as:

eLectures LO3
MBC Disaggregate ROA into profitability and productivity and analyze both.

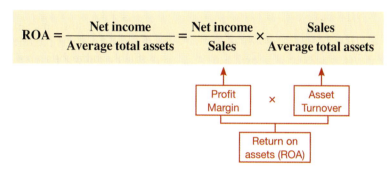

$$ROA = \frac{\text{Net income}}{\text{Average total assets}} = \frac{\text{Net income}}{\text{Sales}} \times \frac{\text{Sales}}{\text{Average total assets}}$$

Return on assets is the product of profit margin and utilization of assets in generating sales (asset turnover). This is the insight that DuPont analysis offers as it focuses managers' attention on both profitability *and* management of the balance sheet. The two drivers of return on assets are:

- **Profit margin (PM).** PM is what the company earns on each sales dollar; a company increases profit margin by increasing its gross profit margin (Gross profit/Sales) and/or reducing its operating expenses as a percent of sales.

- **Asset turnover (AT).** AT is the sales level generated from each dollar invested in assets; a company increases asset turnover (*productivity*) by increasing sales volume with no increase in assets and/or by reducing assets invested without reducing sales.

Business Insight ■ Adjusted ROA

Return on assets is typically under the control of operating managers while the capital structure decision (the relative proportion of debt and equity) is not. Accordingly, a common adjustment is made to the numerator of ROA by adding back the after-tax net interest expense (net of any interest revenue or other nonoperating expense or revenue reported after operating income). The adjusted ROA for **Intel** is as follows ($ in millions).

$$\text{Adjusted ROA} = \frac{\text{Net income} + [\text{Net interest expense} \times (1 - \text{Statutory tax rate})]}{\text{Average total assets}}$$

$$\frac{\$11,420 + [(\$105 - \$315) \times (1 - 37\%)]}{(\$103,065 + \$91,900)/2} = 11.58$$

"Statutory tax rate" in the adjusted ROA formula is the federal statutory tax rate *plus* the state tax rate net of any federal tax benefits; we use the assumed 37% federal and state tax rates as explained in the NOPAT computation later in this module. This adjusted numerator better reflects the company's operating profit as it measures return on assets exclusive of financing costs (independent of the capital structure decision).

The goal is to increase the productivity of the company's assets in generating sales and then to bring as much of each sales dollar to the bottom line (net income). Managers usually understand product pricing, management of production costs, and control of overhead costs. Fewer managers understand the role of the balance sheet. The ROA approach to performance measurement encourages managers to focus on returns achieved from assets under their control, and ROA is maximized with a joint focus on both profitability and productivity.

Analysis of Profitability and Productivity

The complete DuPont return on equity disaggregation follows.

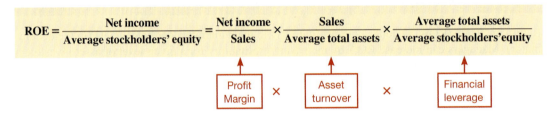

$$ROE = \frac{\text{Net income}}{\text{Average stockholders' equity}} = \frac{\text{Net income}}{\text{Sales}} \times \frac{\text{Sales}}{\text{Average total assets}} \times \frac{\text{Average total assets}}{\text{Average stockholders' equity}}$$

Profit Margin × Asset turnover × Financial leverage

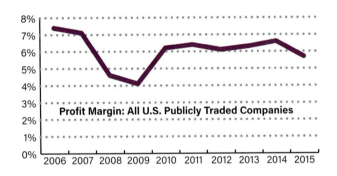

Profit Margin: All U.S. Publicly Traded Companies

Return on equity increases with each of the three components provided the company is profitable and reports a positive stockholders' equity.

In Exhibit 4.2, we compute the disaggregation of Intel's return into profit margin, asset turnover, and financial leverage. The analysis in Exhibit 4.2 represents a *first level* of analysis where we examine ROE over time and in comparison with peers to identify trends and differences from the norm.

Exhibit 4.2 ◼ Disaggregation of Intel's ROE ($ millions)

Profit margin (PM)	$\dfrac{\text{Net income}}{\text{Sales}}$	$\dfrac{\$11,420}{\$55,355}$	= 20.63%
×			×
Asset turnover (AT)	$\dfrac{\text{Sales}}{\text{Average total assets}}$	$\dfrac{\$55,355}{(\$103,065+\$91,900)/2}$	= 0.57
=			=
Return on assets (ROA)	$\dfrac{\text{Net income}}{\text{Average total assets}}$	$\dfrac{\$11,420}{(\$103,065+\$91,900)/2}$	= 11.71%
×			×
Financial leverage (FL)	$\dfrac{\text{Average total assets}}{\text{Average stockholders' equity}}$	$\dfrac{(\$103,065+\$91,900)/2}{(\$61,085+\$55,865)/2}$	= 1.67
=			=
Return on equity (ROE)	$\dfrac{\text{Net income}}{\text{Average stockholders' equity}}$	$\dfrac{\$11,420}{(\$61,085+\$55,865)/2}$	= 19.53%

The *second level* analysis of the components of return on equity seeks to identify factors driving profitability (profit margin) and productivity (asset turnover) and to assess whether financial leverage increases the risk of default and bankruptcy beyond acceptable levels. The framework for second-level analysis is in Exhibit 4.3 and we explain each component in this module.

Exhibit 4.3 ■ DuPont Analysis of Return on Equity

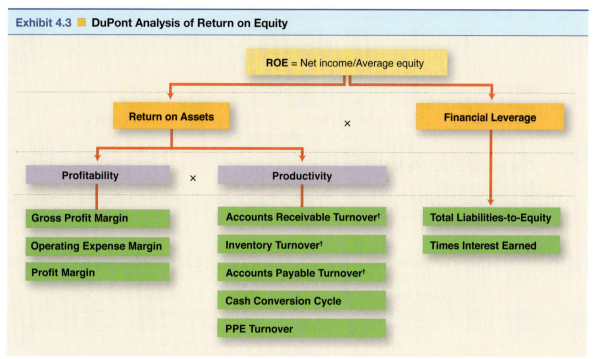

†This metric is also commonly measured "in days"—see discussion below.

Analysis of Profitability

Profit margin (Net income/Sales) reflects the profit in each dollar of sales. For 2015, the median profit margin for all publicly traded companies was 5.7%. During 2006–2015, profit margin ranged from 7.4% (just prior to the recession) to 4.1% (when the recession was at its worst).

Profit margin, while an important measure of profitability, is influenced by *both* gross profit on sales and overhead expenses. Consequently, we gain insight into profitability by separately examining gross profit margin and the SG&A expense margin.

Gross Profit Margin

Gross profit margin (Gross profit/Sales) is influenced by *both* the selling price of a company's products and the cost to make or buy those products. For 2015, the median gross profit margin for all publicly traded companies was 40.5% and it has trended upward over the past 10 years. Gross profit margins differ greatly by industry and depend on a company's specific business model. Consequently, we must be careful in identifying peers for benchmarking to make sure their business models are similar.

We generally prefer gross profit margin to be high and increasing as the opposite usually signals more competition and/or less appeal for the company's product line. When analyzing gross profit margin, it is often helpful to view it on a unit basis, that is, as gross profit for one product unit. If, for example, we purchase a product for $6 and sell it for $10, gross profit margin is 40% ([$10 − $6]/$10). A decline in gross profit margin, then, signals that the spread between the cost to make or buy the product and its selling price has narrowed. This narrowing could be due to several possible reasons, all of which warrant investigation.

■ Perhaps competitive intensity increased and selling prices have dropped to remain competitive.

■ Perhaps the company's product line has lost appeal or its technology is not cutting edge.

■ Perhaps the cost to make or buy products has increased due to increases in material or labor costs and the company cannot pass on that cost increase to customers.

■ Perhaps there is a change in product mix away from high margin products to lower margin products (remember that sales and gross profit includes *all* of the company's products, including both high margin and low margin products).

■ Perhaps the volume of products sold has declined, resulting in an increase in manufacturing cost as factory overhead is spread out over a smaller number of units produced).

It is not enough for our analysis to reveal that a company's gross profit margin has increased or decreased. Instead, we must uncover the *reasons* for the change. It is only with analysis of the underlying cost and pricing structure of a company's products that we are able to predict future levels of gross profit. Many believe that a serious analysis should focus on the *individual product* level and the costs to make or buy those products along with the pricing strategy for the different markets served. That level of granularity is important for effective analysis of gross profit margin.

Operating Expense Margin

The operating expense margin, also referred to as SG&A expense margin (SG&A expense/Sales), measures general operating costs for each sales dollar. These costs include all costs other than those to make or buy the company's products. For 2015, the SG&A expense margin for all publicly traded companies was 21.9% and that margin has remained fairly steady since the economy emerged from recession in 2009.

Analysis of operating expense margin focuses on each expense in whatever detail the company provides in its income statement. We compare the operating expense margin, and the margins for each of its components, over time and against peers (making sure that peers have similar business models). We investigate deviations from historical trends or benchmarks to uncover the cause. We are inclined to judge lower expense levels as favorable, but caution is advised. Perhaps the company has tried to mitigate declining profits by reducing R&D, marketing, or compensation costs. Such activities tend to result in short-term improvements at long-term costs such as reduced market share and damaged employee morale.

Analysis of Productivity

Productivity is reflected in return on assets via turnover of total assets (Sales/Total assets). While a useful measure to gauge overall trend, a more rigorous analysis examines the productivity of each major asset category.

Analysis of Working Capital Components

All turnover ratios have sales (or cost of sales) in the numerator and a balance sheet item in the denominator. The accounts receivable turnover, for example, is Sales/Average accounts receivable (sales is matched with receivables as both are based on selling prices). The inventory turnover is COGS/Average inventories (here we match COGS with inventories as both reflect the cost to make or buy products).

Turnover, while widely reported, has limited usefulness. For example, it is not easy to see how much cash is generated if accounts receivable turnover improves. It is more intuitive to think of the average number of days to collect accounts receivable, the average number of days to sell inventory, or the average number of days to pay accounts payable. Accordingly, a good analysis computes the "days" measures for working capital accounts. Common measures based on days follow.

Ratio	Computation
Days sales outstanding	365 × Average accounts receivable/Sales
+ Days inventory outstanding	365 × Average inventory/COGS
− Days payables outstanding	365 × Average accounts payable/COGS
= Cash conversion cycle	AR days + Inventory days − AP days*

*AP refers to accounts payable, and AR refers to accounts receivable.

Cash Conversion Cycle

The three measures from the table above can be combined to yield the **cash conversion cycle** (Days sales outstanding + Days inventory outstanding – Days payables outstanding). The cash conversion cycle measures the average time (in days) to sell inventories, collect the receivables from the sale, pay the payables incurred for the inventory purchase, and return to cash. This is the same cash conversion cycle we describe in Module 2 (we use the term "operating cycle" in Exhibit 2.4 to describe the same concept). Each time a company completes one cash conversion cycle, it generates profit and cash flow. Managers aim to shorten the cash conversion cycle.

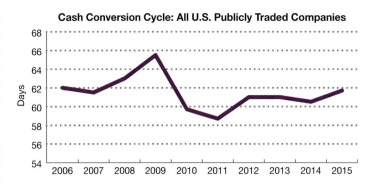

The median cash conversion cycle for all publicly traded companies was 62 days in 2015 and has remained fairly constant since the economy emerged from recession (during recession the average cash conversion cycle rose to 66 days).

Cash conversion cycle depends on the business model of the company, which dictates:

- Credit terms offered to customers.

- Types of inventory carried and depth and breadth of product lines (which influence the time inventories remain unsold).

- Time period in which suppliers are paid for goods and services.

Diversity across business models is evident in the following graphic for medians of the cash conversion cycle for selected industries in 2015.

The variability in the cash conversion cycle across industries reflects fundamental differences in business models. Cash conversion cycle for the healthcare industry, for example, is much longer as a result of the extended period of time to collect receivables from third-party payers such as insurance companies and the government. In contrast, the telecommunications services industry's quick cash conversion results from lower levels of inventory, and rapid collection of receivables from customers who typically pay their phone bill within a month.

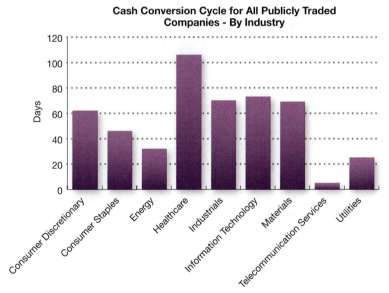

Generally companies prefer a lower cash conversion cycle. This means that the operating cycle is generating profit and cash flow quickly. Our analysis of this measure focuses on trends over time and comparisons to peers (with similar business models).

Sometimes, companies have a *negative* cash conversion cycle. **Apple**'s 2015 cash conversion cycle is one example.

Days sales outstanding	26.7
+ Days inventory outstanding	5.8
− Days payables outstanding	85.2
= Cash conversion cycle	(52.7)

Apple carries little inventory as its products are pre-sold and shipped when manufactured. Consequently, its quick sale of inventory and relatively longer time to pay suppliers results in a negative cash conversion cycle of (52.7) days. The negative number means that Apple is able to invest the cash it receives from the sale of its products for 52.7 days on average before that cash is needed to pay suppliers. This allows Apple to generate both profit from the sale *and* profit from investing cash. A negative cash conversion cycle is generally viewed positively.

A good analysis includes a review of cash conversion cycle over time. **Merck & Co.**, for example, reports improvement in its cash conversion cycle over the 2013–2015 period.

Amounts in Days	2015	2014	2013
Days sales outstanding	60.6	59.7	61.6
+ Days inventory outstanding	125.5	128.4	137.4
− Days payables outstanding	63.0	53.3	43.3
= Cash conversion cycle.	123.1	134.8	155.7

The improvement in Merck's cash conversion cycle reflects improvement in two of the three working capital accounts.

■ It is collecting receivables a bit more slowly (this is not an improvement).

■ It is selling inventories faster (an improvement).

■ It is delaying payment on payables (an improvement).

Two of the three generated additional cash during the period. To compute the amount of cash generated (or used) by changes in each of the measures, multiply the change in the AR measure by sales per day (Sales/365) and the change in the inventory and AP measures by COGS per day (COGS/365), as follows.

$ millions	Amounts in Days			Sales (or COGS) per day		Cash savings
	2015	2014	Change			
Days sales outstanding	60.6	59.7	(0.9) ×	$108.2	=	$ (97.4)
+ Days inventory outstanding	125.5	128.4	2.9 ×	40.9	=	118.6
− Days payables outstanding	63.0	53.3	9.7 ×	40.9	=	396.7
= Cash conversion cycle.	123.1	134.8				$417.9

In 2015, Merck's sales per day were $108.2 million and COGS per day were $40.9 million. Collecting receivables 0.9 days later reduced Merck's cash balance by $97.4 million ($108.2 × 0.9). Larger improvements came from selling inventory more quickly and delaying payment to suppliers. These actions generated $118.6 million and $396.7 million, respectively.

Although these trends for Merck are favorable, we must investigate whether they are *too* favorable. Companies can generate cash by restricting credit policies, by reducing the depth and breadth of their product offerings, and by delaying payment to suppliers ("leaning on the trade"). All of these actions can generate a short-term inflow of cash at a longer-term cost of market position and supplier relations. These questions must be answered by a review of non-financial information in the MD&A section of the 10-K, listening to conference calls with manaagement (on the Investor Relations portion of a company's website), reading the financial press, and reviewing analysts' reports.

Analysis of Plant, Property and Equipment (PPE)

The asset class for which analysis of turnover is most useful is PPE assets (Sales/Average PPE assets). Lower levels of PPE turnover indicate a higher level of capital intensity. PPE asset turnover differs by industry as revealed in the graph for 2015 shown below for publicly traded companies. The energy, telecommunications, and utilities industries require high levels of capital investment and, consequently, report low plant asset turnover.

Because investment in PPE assets is often a large part of the balance sheet, improvement in plant asset turnover can greatly impact the company's return on assets and cash flow. Improvements in PPE turnover are not easy to achieve, however, often requiring:

■ Divestiture of unproductive assets or entire business segments.

■ Joint ventures with other companies to jointly use PPE assets such as distribution networks, information technology, production facilities, and warehouses.

■ Divestiture of production facilities with agreements to purchase finished goods from the facilities' new owners.

■ Sale and leaseback of administrative buildings.

Each of these activities is a strategic and financial event, often requiring integration within the supply chain, new financing, and relationship building. As such, improvements in PPE turnover can be difficult to achieve. If properly structured, however, they can markedly increase asset returns and cash flow.

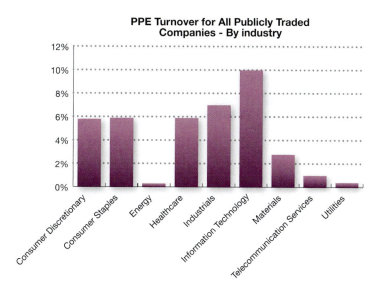

Analysis of Financial Leverage

As companies utilize a larger proportion of borrowed money in their capital structures, they incur obligations for interest payments and the repayment of the amount borrowed (the principal). Those obligations are typically evidenced by a loan agreement (or bond indenture) that contains some or all of the following.

■ Restrictions on certain activities, such as mergers or acquisitions of other companies without approval of lenders.

■ Prohibitions against dividend payments or the repurchase of common stock without approval of lenders.

■ Covenants to maintain required levels of financial ratios, such as a maximum level of financial leverage, minimum levels of the current and quick ratios, minimum level of equity, and minimum level of working capital.

■ Prohibitions against the pledging of assets to secure new borrowings.

■ Remedies to lenders in event of default (failure to make required interest and principal payments when due). These remedies can include seizing company assets or, possibly, forcing the company into bankruptcy and requiring liquidation.

Judicial use of financial leverage is beneficial to stockholders (it is a relatively inexpensive source of capital), but the use of borrowed money adds risk as debt payments are contractual obligations. Analysis typically involves ratios that investigate the *level* of borrowed money relative to equity capital and the level of profitability and *cash flow* relative to required debt payments. Although there are dozens of financial leverage-related ratios in commercial databases, the following two ratios capture the spirit of such analysis.

■ Total liabilities-to-equity ratio (Total liabilities/Stockholders' equity).

■ Times interest earned ratio (Earnings before interest and taxes/Interest expense).

As for all ratios, analysis of financial leverage ratios must consider ratios over time and comparisons with peers. Appropriate financial leverage varies across industries because different business models generate cash flow streams that differ in amount and variability over time. Generally, business models that generate high and stable levels of cash flow can support a higher level of debt.

The median total liabilities-to-equity ratio for all publicly traded companies in 2015 was 0.71, indicating that companies typically borrow money, but have more equity than borrowed money in their capital structures. Financial leverage ratios differ by industry and company size. The median financial leverage ratio for the S&P 500 companies, for example, was 2.74 in 2015 and ranged from 2.4 to 2.7 over the 2011–2015 period.

Exhibit 4.4 shows a summary of ratios used in the DuPont disaggregation of return on equity.

Exhibit 4.4 ■ **Summary of Ratios in DuPont Disaggregation of Return on Equity**

Ratio	Computation	What The Ratio Measures	Positive Indicators Include
Return on equity	Net income ÷ Avg. stockholders' equity, or Return on assets × Financial leverage	ROE measures accounting return to shareholders using net income and the book value of stockholders' equity.	■ Improvement over time and favorable comparison to peers. ■ Greater proportion of ROE from ROA (operations) than financial leverage (risk).
Return on assets	Net income/Avg. total assets or Profit margin × Asset turnover	ROA measures the accounting return on total assets using net income and total assets.	■ Improvement over time in both profit margin and asset turnover. ■ Improvement in gross margins and not solely from expense reduction.
PROFITABILITY			
Gross profit margin	Gross profit / Sales	Gross profit measures the difference between selling price and the cost to make or buy the products sold for the year.	■ Improvement over time due to increases in selling prices and/or reductions in cost to make or buy without compromising product quality. ■ Favorable comparison to peers.
Operating expense margin (or SG&A expense margin)	SG&A expense / Sales	Operating expense margin measures total overhead expense (SG&A) as a percent of sales.	■ Improvement over time. ■ Favorable comparison to peers. ■ No short-term gains at long-term cost (such as unusual reductions in marketing and R&D expenses).
Profit margin (or net profit margin)	Net income / Sales	Profit margin includes effects of both gross profit margin, the operating expense margin, and net nonoperating expenses.	■ Improvement over time. ■ Favorable comparison to peers.
PRODUCTIVITY			
Accounts receivable turnover	Sales / Avg. accounts receivable	AR turnover reflects how effective a company manages the credit issued to customers.	■ Improvement over time. ■ Favorable comparison to peers.
Days sales outstanding (DSO)	365 × (Avg. accounts receivable / Sales)	DSO reflects how well a company's accounts receivables are managed.	■ Maintain sales while reducing days to collect receivables.
Inventory turnover	COGS / Avg. inventory	Inventory turnover reflects the number of times inventory is sold or used during the period.	■ Improvement over time. ■ Favorable comparison to peers.
Days inventory outstanding (DIO)	365 × Avg. inventory/COGS	DIO reflects how many days it takes for a company to sell its inventory.	■ Maintain sales while reducing days to sell inventory.
Accounts payable turnover	COGS ÷ Avg. accounts payable	AP turnover reflects how many times a company pays off its suppliers during the period.	■ Improvement over time. ■ Favorable comparison to peers.
Days payables outstanding (DPO)	365 × (Avg. accounts payable/COGS)	DPO reflects how long it takes a company to pay its invoices from suppliers.	■ Maintain supplier relations while delaying payment to suppliers.
Cash conversion cycle	AR days + Inv days − AP days	Cash conversion (operating) cycle measures the days to convert cash to inventories, receivables to cash, cash to payables.	■ Improvement over time. ■ Favorable comparison to peers.
PPE turnover	Sales / Avg. PPE assets	Plant asset turnover is a productivity measure, comparing the volume of sales generated by plant assets.	■ Improvement over time. ■ Favorable comparison to peers.

continued

Exhibit 4.4 ■ (continued)

Ratio	Computation	What The Ratio Measures	Positive Indicators Include
FINANCIAL LEVERAGE			
Total liabilities-to-equity	Total liabilities ÷ Stockholders' equity	Proportion of liabilities vs. equity in the capital structure.	• Improvement over time. • Favorable comparison to peers. • Relatively lower levels are preferable.
Times interest earned	Earnings before interest and taxes ÷ Interest expense, gross	Pool of operating profit before tax that a company earns relative to its interest expense, gross.	• Improvement over time. • Favorable comparison to peers. • Higher levels are preferable to lower levels.

LO3 **Review 4-3**

Refer to the income statement and balance sheet data for **Cisco Systems Inc.** from Review 4-1 along with the following additional information.

$ millions	Jul. 25, 2015	Jul. 26, 2014
Cost of sales.	$19,480	$19,373
Accounts receivable.	5,344	5,157
Inventories	1,627	1,591
Accounts payable.	1,104	1,032
Liabilities.	53,774	48,409

Required
a. Disaggregate 2015 ROA into components of profitability margin (PM) and asset turnover (AT). Then, prove that their product (multiplication) results in ROA.
b. Compute the gross profit margin.
c. Compute the cash conversion cycle.
d. Compute the total liabilities-to-equity ratio.

Solution on p. 4-64.

Operating Focus on Financial Condition

ROE disaggregation with an *operating focus* recognizes that companies create value mainly through core operations of the business. Operating activities involve the manufacturing and selling of company products and services to customers.

eLectures **LO4**
Identify balance sheet operating items and compute net operating assets.

The balance sheet and income statement include *both* operating and nonoperating items. **Intel**'s balance sheet, for example, includes operating assets and liabilities such as accounts receivable, inventories, plant assets, accounts payable, and accrued liabilities. Intel's balance sheet also includes assets and liabilities that are not related to core operations. These nonoperating items include short-term investments, long-term marketable equity securities, and short-term and long-term debt. Intel's income statement includes revenues and operating expenses such as COGS and SG&A, which relate directly to operations. The income statement also includes nonoperating items such as interest income and expense, dividend income, and gains and losses on sale of securities.

Operating and Nonoperating Returns Return on assets, computed using net income and total assets, reflects a blend of the return on a company's operating assets (its operating profit divided by its operating assets) and its nonoperating return. Accordingly, analysis of a company can be improved if we separately identify the operating and nonoperating components of the business and their separate returns. More specifically:

$$\text{ROE} = \text{Operating return} + \text{Nonoperating return}$$

This shows that ROE consists of two returns: (1) return from the company's operating activities, linked to revenues and expenses from the company's products or services, and (2) return from financing and investing (nonoperating) activities. Companies can use debt to increase their return on equity, but this increases risk because the failure to make required debt payments can yield many legal consequences, including bankruptcy. This is one reason why many top investors such as Warren Buffett focus on acquiring companies whose return on equity is derived primarily from operating activities.

Operating and Nonoperating Liabilities A second, more subtle, issue arises in computing return on equity. In the traditional DuPont analysis, ROE is the product of the return on assets and financial leverage. Financial leverage is the ratio of total assets to stockholders' equity, which increases as the proportion of debt increases relative to equity. The problem is that the "debt" used in this computation includes *all* of the company's debt. However, there is a difference between borrowed money and operating liabilities such as accounts payable and accrued liabilities. Accounts payable and accruals are interest free and are *self-liquidating*, meaning that they are paid when receivables are collected as part of the cash conversion cycle. On the other hand, borrowed money is interest-bearing and often contains severe legal repercussions in the event of non-payment, possibly risking bankruptcy of the company. The operating focus treats these two types of debt differently for ROE analysis, recognizing the interest-free, self-liquidating character of operating liabilities and separately treating borrowed money as a nonoperating activity.

> **ALERT** The FASB released a draft of a proposed new format for financial statements to, among other things, distinguish operating and nonoperating activities.

Return on Net Operating Assets (RNOA)

Operating returns are reflected in the **return on net operating assets (RNOA)**, defined as follows.

$$\text{RNOA} = \frac{\text{Net operating profit after tax (NOPAT)}}{\text{Average net operating assets (NOA)}}$$

To implement this formula, we must first classify the balance sheet and income statement into operating and nonoperating components so that we can assess each separately. We first consider operating activities on the balance sheet and explain how to compute NOA. Second, we consider operating activities on the income statement and explain how to compute NOPAT.

Business Insight ▪ ROE and RNOA

The following graph shows the ROE and RNOA for **Kellogg** and **Walmart**, two companies that report a healthy ROE in the 20%–25% range. The RNOA for each company is markedly different. About 67% of Walmart's ROE comes from operations (14%/21% = 67%) whereas for Kellogg that proportion is only 32% (8%/25% = 32%) and its nonoperating returns make up a much greater proportion of total ROE.

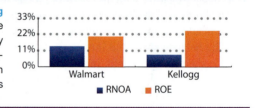

Net Operating Assets (NOA)

RNOA relates net operating profit after tax (NOPAT) to the average net operating assets (NOA) of the company. We compute NOA as follows.

$$\text{Net operating assets} = \text{Operating assets} - \text{Operating liabilities}$$

To compute NOA we must partition the balance sheet into operating and nonoperating items. Exhibit 4.5 shows a typical balance sheet and highlights the operating items, in red boldface.

Exhibit 4.5 ■ Operating and Nonoperating Items in the Balance Sheet

Typical Balance Sheet
Operating Items Highlighted in Red

Current Assets
Cash and cash equivalents
Short-term investments
Accounts receivable
Inventories
Prepaid expenses
Deferred income tax assets
Other current assets
Current assets of discontinued operations
Loans receivable

Long-Term Assets
Long-term investments in securities
Property, plant and equipment, net
Capitalized lease assets
Natural resources
Equity method investments
Goodwill and intangible assets
Deferred income tax assets
Other long-term assets
Long-term assets of discontinued operations
Derivative assets

Current Liabilities
Short-term notes and interest payable
Current maturities of long-term debt
Dividends payable
Accounts payable
Accrued liabilities
Unearned (deferred) revenue
Deferred income tax liabilities
Current liabilities of discontinued operations

Long-Term Liabilities
Bonds and notes payable
Capitalized lease obligations
Pension and other post-employment liabilities
Deferred income tax liabilities
Long-term liabilities of discontinued operations
Derivative liabilities

Stockholders' Equity
All equity accounts
Noncontrolling interest

Operating Assets

Operating assets are those assets directly linked to operating activities, the company's ongoing (continuing) business operations. They typically include receivables; inventories; prepaid expenses; property, plant, and equipment (PPE); and capitalized lease assets. Operating assets are those the company needs to operate normally, and those assets can be purchased outright or leased. Leasing is a way to acquire an asset for use without the upfront cash outlay. If the leased asset is used for operations, then it is an operating asset and we categorize it as such *regardless* of how it was financed.

Operating assets *exclude* short-term and long-term investments in marketable securities. However, companies sometimes purchase equity interests in other companies for strategic purposes. For example, a company might buy the stock of its major supplier or transporter to secure the supply chain. Or a company might take an equity position in another company as a prelude to an acquisition. Such ownership positions usually involve a significant percentage of the outstanding common stock (20% or more). Or a company might enter into a joint venture (JV) or form an alliance with a strategic partner to share resources or risk. Because such investments are strategic and represent part of the ongoing, ordinary operating activities of a company, we categorize them as operating assets.

Intangible assets and goodwill result from mergers with, or acquisitions of, other companies. These deals have the effect of the acquirer buying a collection of operating assets (including operating liabilities). Accordingly, all intangible assets and goodwill are operating assets and we categorize them as such.

Deferred tax assets (and liabilities) are operating items because they most often relate to future tax deductions (or payments) arising from operating activities. We assume that "other" assets and liabilities, and "other" revenues and expenses, are operating unless information suggests otherwise. For example, details in footnotes might reveal that "other" includes nonoperating items. Or the company might explicitly indicate the "other" is nonoperating by reporting the item after a subtotal for income from operations. In these cases, we would consider the "other" as nonoperating.

Operating Liabilities

Operating liabilities are liabilities that arise from operating revenues and expenses. For example, accounts payable and accrued expenses help fund inventories, wages, utilities, and other operating expenses. Unearned revenue is part of operating liabilities because it relates to operating revenue. Similarly, pension and other post-employment obligations relate to long-term obligations for employee retirement and health care, which by definition are operating activities.

Nonoperating Assets

Nonoperating assets include cash and cash equivalents (see Business Insight box on page 4-19) and investments in marketable securities, both short- and long-term. These investments can take many forms. Some companies invest in marketable equity securities to earn a return in the form of dividends and price appreciation. Companies might also purchase bonds or other debt instruments issued by other companies and organizations for interest income and price appreciation. These investments represent nonoperating assets.

We treat all marketable equity and debt investments as nonoperating regardless of whether those non-strategic investments appear on the balance sheet as current or long-term assets.

Sometimes companies make loans to customers, suppliers, or other parties, and we categorize such non-core (receivable) assets as nonoperating. (Note: For financial services companies such as banks and insurance firms, debt and equity securities along with loans and notes to customers, are part of normal operations and are categorized as operating assets; but for non-financial companies such as retailers, manufacturers, and service providers, these items are apart from ordinary operating activities and represent nonoperating assets.)

We categorize assets (and liabilities) from discontinued operations as nonoperating as they represent assets and liabilities that will be sold to another party due to a reorganization or spin-off. Many companies separately disclose discontinued assets (and liabilities) on the balance sheet to distinguish them from continuing net assets. If the discontinued items are not separated on the balance sheet, the footnotes provide details to facilitate a disaggregated analysis. Similarly, assets and liabilities "held for sale" are categorized as nonoperating because the company has formally decided to sell them to another party.

Nonoperating Liabilities

Nonoperating liabilities include all interest-bearing debt, both short- and long-term. This is the case irrespective of whether the debt relates to the purchase of a specific asset, like a mortgage on a building or a loan on equipment. The purpose of the debt does *not* affect its categorization: interest-bearing debt, whether short-term or long-term, whether tied to an operating asset or not, is always categorized as nonoperating.

Lease liabilities are treated as *nonoperating*. Leases are another form of borrowing where a specific asset is acquired for use in exchange for future lease payments. Simply put, leases are like collateralized loans. Accordingly, lease liabilities are categorized exactly as all loans, as *nonoperating*. (Note that lease assets are categorized as operating while lease liabilities are categorized as nonoperating.)

Companies use derivatives (including futures, forward contracts, options, swaps and other financial securities) to hedge (mitigate) risk or to speculate. Derivatives are reported on balance sheets as liabilities or assets, and sometimes both. For analysis purposes, all derivatives are nonoperating items. Admittedly, some derivative positions are operating assets or liabilities; for example, a forward contract on a company's manufacturing raw materials. Other derivatives are clearly nonoperating; for example, an interest rate swap. However, distinguishing between the two is complicated and often impossible for an external analyst. Accordingly, we treat all derivatives as nonoperating, both assets and liabilities.

To summarize, operating assets and liabilities relate to the company's core activities, those required to deliver a company's products or services to its customers. Nonoperating assets and liabilities relate to financing, non-core investing activities, and discontinued operations. (Admittedly, analysts do not all agree on the operating versus nonoperating classification of some assets and liabilities, and we highlight those as we encounter them.)

Exhibit 4.6 shows how a balance sheet can be reorganized into operating and nonoperating items.

Net nonoperating obligations are total nonoperating liabilities less total nonoperating assets. The accounting equation stipulates that Assets = Liabilities + Equity, so we can adjust it to yield the following key identity:

Net operating assets (NOA) = Net nonoperating obligations (NNO) + Stockholders' equity (EQ)

Exhibit 4.6 ■ **Balance Sheet Distinguishing Between Operating and Nonoperating Items**

	Assets	**Liabilities**
Net operating assets (NOA)	**Current operating assets**	**Current operating liabilities**
[Oper. assets – Oper. liabilities]	+ **Long-term operating assets**	+ **Long-term operating liabilities**
	= **Total operating assets**	= **Total operating liabilities**
Net nonoperating obligations (NNO) . . .	Current nonoperating assets	Current nonoperating liabilities
[Nonoper. liabilities − Nonoper. assets]	+ Long-term nonoperating assets	+ Long-term nonoperating liabilities
	= Total nonoperating assets	= Total nonoperating liabilities
		Equity
		Stockholders' equity (EQ)
Equity (NOA − NNO)		
	Total assets	Total liabilities and equity

The following are **Intel**'s balance sheets for 2015 and 2014, with operating assets and operating liabilities in red boldface.

INTEL CORP. Balance Sheets $ millions	Dec. 26, 2015	Dec. 27, 2014
Assets		
Current assets		
Cash and cash equivalents.	$ 15,308	$ 2,561
Short-term investments	2,682	2,430
Trading assets.	7,323	9,063
Accounts receivable, net	**4,787**	**4,427**
Inventories	**5,167**	**4,273**
Deferred tax assets.	**2,036**	**1,958**
Other current assets	**3,053**	**3,018**
Total current assets.	**40,356**	**27,730**
Property, plant and equipment, net	**31,858**	**33,238**
Marketable equity securities	5,960	7,097
Other long-term investments	1,891	2,023
Goodwill	**11,332**	**10,861**
Identified intangible assets, net	**3,933**	**4,446**
Other long-term assets	**7,735**	**6,505**
Total assets.	$103,065	$91,900
Liabilities and stockholders' equity		
Current liabilities		
Short-term debt	$ 2,634	$ 1,596
Accounts payable.	**2,063**	**2,748**
Accrued compensation and benefits	**3,138**	**3,475**
Accrued advertising	**960**	**1,092**
Deferred income	**2,188**	**2,205**
Other accrued liabilities	**4,684**	**4,895**
Total current liabilities	15,667	16,011
Long-term debt*	20,933	12,971
Long-term deferred tax liabilities	**2,539**	**3,775**
Other long-term liabilities	**2,841**	**3,278**
Stockholders' equity		
Common stock and capital in excess of par value	23,411	21,781
Accumulated other comprehensive income.	60	666
Retained earnings	37,614	33,418
Total stockholders' equity.	61,085	55,865
Total liabilities, temporary equity, and stockholders' equity	$103,065	$91,900

* Included in Intel's long-term total debt is $897 million (2015) and $912 million (2014) of convertible debentures that Intel classifies as "temporary equity."

We assume that Intel's "other" assets and liabilities are operating. We can sometimes make a finer distinction if footnotes to financial statements provide additional information. For now, assume that these "other" items reported in balance sheets pertain to operations.

Using Intel's highlighted balance sheet above, we compute net operating assets for 2015 and 2014 as follows (recall that Net operating assets (NOA) = Total operating assets − Total operating liabilities).

Intel's Net Operating Assets ($ millions)	Dec. 26, 2015	Dec. 27, 2014
Operating assets		
Accounts receivable, net	$ 4,787	$ 4,427
Inventories	5,167	4,273
Deferred tax assets	2,036	1,958
Other current assets	3,053	3,018
Property, plant, and equipment, net	31,858	33,238
Goodwill	11,332	10,861
Identified intangible assets, net	3,933	4,446
Other long-term assets	7,735	6,505
Total operating assets	$69,901	$68,726
Operating liabilities		
Accounts payable	$ 2,063	$ 2,748
Accrued compensation and benefits	3,138	3,475
Accrued advertising	960	1,092
Deferred income	2,188	2,205
Other accrued liabilities	4,684	4,895
Long-term deferred tax liabilities	2,539	3,775
Other long-term liabilities	2,841	3,278
Total operating liabilities	$18,413	$ 21,468
Net operating assets (NOA)	$51,488	$ 47,258

Business Insight ■ Why Is Cash a Nonoperating Asset?

Most analysts consider cash as nonoperating because this account consists almost totally of "cash equivalents," which are short-term investments with a scheduled maturity of 90 days or less. Technically, the amount of cash needed to support routine business transactions is considered as operating and the remainder as a nonoperating short-term investment, similar to investments reported as marketable securities. If we know what portion of the cash balance supports operating activities, we would classify that as operating. Unfortunately, companies do not report that information and most analysts feel that it is probably a small portion. As a result, we, like others, treat the entire cash and cash equivalents balance as nonoperating and recognize that we are probably understating net operating assets slightly.

Review 4-4 LO4

Refer to the following balance sheet for **Cisco Systems Inc.** *Hint:* Financing receivables at Cisco Systems are part of ongoing operations and should be classified as operating assets.

$ millions	July 25, 2015	July 26, 2014
Assets		
Cash and cash equivalents	$ 6,877	$ 6,726
Investments	53,539	45,348
Accounts receivable, net	5,344	5,157
Inventories	1,627	1,591
Financing receivables, net	4,491	4,153
Deferred tax assets	2,915	2,808
Other current assets	1,490	1,331
Total current assets	76,283	67,114

continued

$ millions (continued)	July 25, 2015	July 26, 2014
Property and equipment, net	3,332	3,252
Financing receivables, net	3,858	3,918
Goodwill	24,469	24,239
Purchased intangible assets, net	2,376	3,280
Other assets	3,163	3,267
Total assets	$113,481	$105,070
Liabilities		
Short-term debt	$ 3,897	$ 508
Accounts payable	1,104	1,032
Income taxes payable	62	159
Accrued compensation	3,049	3,181
Deferred revenue	9,824	9,478
Other current liabilities	5,687	5,451
Total current liabilities	23,623	19,809
Long-term debt	21,457	20,337
Income taxes payable	1,876	1,851
Deferred revenue	5,359	4,664
Other long-term liabilities	1,459	1,748
Total liabilities	53,774	48,409
Equity		
Common stock and additional paid-in capital	43,592	41,884
Retained earnings	16,045	14,093
Accumulated other comprehensive income	61	677
Total Cisco shareholders' equity	59,698	56,654
Noncontrolling interests	9	7
Total equity	59,707	56,661
Total liabilities and shareholders' equity	$113,481	$105,070

Required

a.   Determine operating assets and operating liabilities for fiscal-year-end 2014 and 2015.

b.   Compute net operating assets (NOA) for fiscal-year-end 2014 and 2015.   **Solution on p. 4-64.**

Operating Focus on Financial Performance

The income statement reports both operating and nonoperating activities. Exhibit 4.7 shows a typical income statement with the operating activities in red boldface.

Operating Line Items   Operating activities are those that relate to bringing a company's products or services to market and any after-sales support. The income statement in Exhibit 4.7 reflects operating activities through revenues, costs of goods sold (COGS), and other expenses. Selling, general, and administrative expense (SG&A) includes wages, advertising, occupancy, insurance, and many other operating expenses the company incurs in the ordinary course of business (some of these are often reported as separate line items in the income statement). Other common operating expenses include depreciation and amortization, restructuring, and research and development expenses. Companies also dispose of operating assets, and can realize gains or losses from their disposal, or write them off partially or completely when they become impaired. These, too, are operating activities. Finally, the reported tax expense on the income statement reflects both operating and nonoperating activities, which explains its mix of "red" and "black" colors. Later in this section we use Intel's income statement to explain how to separately compute tax expense related to operating activities only.

Nonoperating Line Items   Nonoperating activities relate to borrowed money that creates interest expense. Nonoperating activities also relate to investments such as marketable securities and other investments that yield interest or dividend revenue and capital gains or losses from any sales of

eLectures **LO5**
MBC   Identify income statement operating items and compute net operating profit after tax.

nonoperating investments during the period. Often companies report income or loss from subsidiaries or business segments that the board of directors has formally decided to divest. Companies must report these "discontinued operations" on a separate line, below income from continuing operations. The line item includes the net income or loss from discontinued operations along with any gains or losses on the disposal of discontinued net assets. We consider discontinued operations as a nonoperating item on the income statement. For most companies, nonoperating activities yield a net nonoperating *expense*—interest expense usually exceeds interest and other income. When the reverse is true (interest and other income is greater than interest expense), then the net nonoperating item is a *revenue*.

Exhibit 4.7 ■ Operating and Nonoperating Items in the Income Statement

Typical Income Statement
Operating Items Highlighted in Red

Revenues

Cost of sales

Gross profit

Operating expenses

    Selling, general and administrative

    Depreciation and amortization expense

    Restructuring expense

    Research and development

    Asset impairment expense

    Gains and losses on asset disposal

Total operating expenses

Operating income

Interest expense

Interest and dividend revenue

Investment gains and losses

Income from equity method investments

Total nonoperating expenses

Income from continuing operations before taxes

Tax expense

Income from continuing operations

Income (loss) from discontinued operations, net of tax

Consolidated net income

Less: consolidated net income attributable to noncontrolling interest

Consolidated net income attributable to controlling interest (parent company stockholders)

Distinguishing between Operating and Nonoperating Line Items Following are Intel's 2013–2015 income statements with the operating items in red boldface. Intel's operating items include sales, cost of sales, R&D, marketing, general and administrative, restructuring and amortization. Intel's pretax operating income is $14,002 million. Intel's nonoperating activities relate to its borrowed money (interest expense of $337 million) and to its investments (interest and other income of $232 million). The income statement also reports gains on investments of $315 million, which are considered nonoperating. Together, Intel's 2015 pretax nonoperating expense is a "revenue" of $210 ($337 million interest expense − $232 million interest income − $315 million gain). Because Intel's net nonoperating activity is revenue, we consider this as a *negative* net nonoperating expense in our NOPAT calculations.

INTEL CORP. Income Statement			
For 12 Months Ended ($ millions)	Dec. 26, 2015	Dec. 27, 2014	Dec. 28, 2013
Net revenue	$55,355	$55,870	$52,708
Cost of sales	20,676	20,261	21,187
Gross margin	34,679	35,609	31,521
Research and development	12,128	11,537	10,611
Marketing, general and administrative	7,930	8,136	8,088
Restructuring and asset impairment charges	354	295	240
Amortization of acquisition-related intangibles	265	294	291
Operating expenses	20,677	20,262	19,230
Operating income	14,002	15,347	12,291
Interest and other expense (income), net	105	(43)	151
(Gains) on equity investments, net	(315)	(411)	(471)
Income before taxes	14,212	15,801	12,611
Provision for taxes	2,792	4,097	2,991
Net income	$ 11,420	$ 11,704	$ 9,620

Net Operating Profit After Tax (NOPAT)

To compute NOPAT, we start with net operating profit before tax from the income statement and use the following formula:

Net operating profit after tax = Net operating profit before tax − Tax on operating profit

Intel's income statement reports net operating profit before tax of $14,002 million and we need to subtract taxes on operating profit to determine net operating profit after tax.

Tax on Operating Profit The tax expense that companies report on their income statements pertains to both operating *and* nonoperating activities. To compute NOPAT, we need to compute the tax expense relating solely to operating profit as follows:

Tax on operating profit = Tax expense + (Pretax net nonoperating expense × Statutory tax rate)

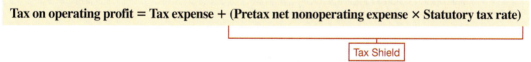

Tax Shield

The amount in parentheses is called the tax shield, which are the taxes that a company saves by having tax-deductible nonoperating expenses (see Tax Shield box below for details). By definition, the taxes saved (by the tax shield) do not relate to operating profits; thus, we must add back the tax shield to total tax expense to compute the tax on operating profit. For companies with nonoperating revenue and gains greater than nonoperating expenses, so called nonoperating revenue, the "pretax net nonoperating expense" is a negative number which yields a negative tax shield. A negative tax shield implies that the company is paying more tax than it would have paid if not for the additional nonoperating income. Tax on operating profit is computed in the same manner as in the equation above, we add the negative tax shield to tax expense.

The statutory federal tax rate for corporations is 35% (per U.S. tax code). Also, most states and some local jurisdictions tax corporate income, and state taxes are deductible for federal tax purposes. The net state tax rate is the statutory rate less the federal tax deduction. The tax rate on operating profit is the sum of the two. On average, the net state tax is about 2%; thus, we use 37% (35% + 2%) as the assumed tax rate on nonoperating expenses and revenues in our examples and assignments at the end of the module.

Business Insight ■ Tax Rates for Computing NOPAT

In our examples and assignments, we assume the statutory tax rate is 37% as this is the approximate average combined federal and state tax rate for public companies. We can, as an alternative, compute a *company-specific* tax rate using the income tax footnote in the 10-K. For example, **Intel** provides the following table in its 10-K for the year ended December 26, 2015.

Fiscal Years Ended	Dec. 26, 2015	Dec. 27, 2014	Dec. 28, 2013
Federal statutory rate effect of:	35.0%	35.0%	35.0%
Non-U.S. income taxed at different rates.	(7.9)	(6.1)	(5.8)
Domestic manufacturing deduction benefit. . .	(2.0)	(2.1)	(2.1)
Research and development tax credits	(1.7)	(1.7)	(3.5)
Other reconciling items	(3.8)	0.8	0.1
Effective rate.	19.6%	25.9%	23.7%

The federal statutory rate is 35.0%, and Intel does pay state taxes but the amount is immaterial and so the company does not separately report the rate (it also reports reductions of 7.9% relating to effects of taxes on income outside the U.S. and several other deductions and credits that total 7.5%). Thus, Intel's effective tax rate (or average) for all of its income is the sum of all its taxes paid less benefits received, or 19.6%. However, the tax shield that we add back in computing NOPAT uses only federal and state tax rates. For Intel, the company-specific tax rate that we could use to compute the tax shield is 35%. It would be incorrect, however, to use Intel's 19.6% company-specific effective tax rate to compute NOPAT, as that rate includes both operating and nonoperating items. We discuss income tax more fully in later modules.

Applying this method to Intel for fiscal 2015, yields a tax shield of $(78) million, that is, a negative tax shield. This is computed as pretax net nonoperating expense of $(210) million times its statutory tax rate of 37% and tax on operating profit is therefore, $2,714 million (computed as $2,792 million + $(78) million). We subtract the tax on operating profit from the net operating profit before tax to obtain NOPAT. Thus, Intel's net operating profit after tax is computed as follows ($ millions).

Net operating profit before tax (NOPBT)		$14,002
Less tax on operating profit		
Tax expense (from income statement)	$2,792	
Plus tax shield $(210) × 37%.	+(78)	(2,714)
Net operating profit after tax (NOPAT)		$11,288

Business Insight ■ Tax Shield

Persons with home mortgages understand well the beneficial effects of the "interest tax shield." To see how the interest tax shield works, consider two individuals, each with income of $50,000 and each with only one expense: a home. Assume that one person pays $10,000 per year in rent; the other pays $10,000 in interest on a home mortgage. Rent is not deductible for tax purposes, whereas mortgage interest (but not principal) is deductible. Assume that each person pays taxes at 25%, the personal tax rate for this income level. Their tax payments are as follows.

	Renter	Homeowner
Income before interest and taxes.	$50,000	$50,000
Less interest deduction	0	(10,000)
Taxable income	$50,000	$40,000
Taxes paid (25% rate).	$12,500	$10,000

The renter reports $50,000 in taxable income and pays $12,500 in taxes. The homeowner deducts $10,000 in interest, which lowers taxable income to $40,000 and reduces taxes to $10,000. By deducting mortgage interest, the homeowner's tax bill is $2,500 lower. The $2,500 is the *interest tax shield*, and we can compute it directly as the $10,000 interest deduction multiplied by the 25% tax rate.

LO5 **Review 4-5**

Refer to the following income statement for Cisco Systems Inc. to answer the requirements.

CISCO SYSTEMS INC.	
Fiscal year ended ($ millions)	**July 25, 2015**
Total revenue	$49,161
Total cost of sales	19,480
Gross margin	29,681
Research and development	6,207
Sales and marketing	9,821
General and administrative	2,040
Amortization of purchased intangible assets	359
Restructuring and other charges	484
Total operating expenses	18,911
Operating income	10,770
Interest income	(769)
Interest expense	566
Other income	(228)
Interest and other income, net	(431)
Income before provision for income taxes	11,201
Provision for income taxes	2,220
Net income	$ 8,981

Required

a. Determine net operating profit before tax (NOPBT) for fiscal 2015.
b. Compute tax on operating profit for fiscal 2015.
c. Compute NOPAT using the formula: NOPBT – Tax on operating profit.

Solution on p. 4-65.

Return on Net Operating Assets (RNOA)

To determine average NOA, we take a simple average of two consecutive years' numbers. Return on net operating assets (RNOA) for Intel for 2015 is computed as follows ($ millions).

LO6
MBC Compute and interpret return on net operating assets (RNOA).

$$\text{RNOA} = \frac{\text{Net operating profit after tax}}{\text{Average net operating assets}} = \frac{\$11,288}{(\$51,488 + \$47,258)/2} = 22.86\%$$

Intel's 2015 RNOA is 22.86%. By comparison, the RNOA for Cisco Systems a competitor to Intel, is 34.78% (this computation is shown in Review 4-6). The average RNOA for publicly traded companies is about 9.2% after the economy emerged from recession in 2010, which is apparent from the Research Insight titled "Ratio Behavior over Time" located before Review 4-6.

RNOA vs ROA A comparison of Intel's RNOA of 22.86% with the ROA of 11.71%, computed earlier, yields insight into the benefits of an operating focus.

$ millions	ROA (DuPont analysis)	RNOA (Operating focus)	Computation
Net income............................	$11,420		
Net operating profit after tax (NOPAT) ...		$11,288	
Average assets......................	$97,483		($103,065 + $91,900)/2
Average net operating assets (NOA)		$49,373	($51,488 + $47,258)/2
ROA	11.71%		$11,420 / $97,483
RNOA..............................		22.86%	$11,288 / $49,373

ROA Components The operating focus to ROE excludes $132 million of net income (relating to investment returns net of interest expense, after tax) and excludes $9,102 million of net nonoperating assets (average investment securities of $28,169 million less average nonoperating liabilities of $19,067 million, computed as [$2,634 +$20,933 +$1,596 +$12,971]/2). The net return on these net nonoperating assets is $1.45\% \left(\frac{\$132\,\text{million}}{\$9,102\,\text{million}} \right)$. The return on assets computed under the traditional DuPont approach is actually a weighted average of the return on operating assets and the return on net nonoperating assets ($ millions).

$$\underset{\substack{\text{From Operating}\\\text{Activities}}}{\left(22.86\% \times \frac{\$49,373}{\$97,483} \right)} + \underset{\substack{\text{From Nonoperating}\\\text{Activities}}}{\left(1.45\% \times \frac{\$9,102}{\$97,483} \right)} = 11.71\%$$

It is clear that both sides of Intel's business create positive returns for shareholders—operations are returning 22.86% and nonoperating activities are returning 1.45%. But the low return on nonoperating activities creates a drag on overall return to the shareholders. This insight is lost with the traditional DuPont analysis. Exhibit 4.8 summarized the key metrics applied in this section. We now extend the operating focus to the second level of analysis for each component of RNOA.

Exhibit 4.8 ■ Key Ratio and Acronym Definitions	
Ratio	**Definition**
ROE: Return on equity................	Net income attributable to controlling interest/Average equity attributable to controlling interest
NOA: Net operating assets	Operating assets less operating liabilities; it excludes nonoperating items such as investments in marketable securities and interest-bearing debt.
NOPAT: Net operating profit after tax......	Operating revenues less operating expenses such as cost of sales, selling, general and administrative expense, and taxes; it excludes nonoperating revenues and expenses such as interest revenue, dividend revenue, interest expense, gains and losses on investments, discontinued operations.
RNOA: Return on net operating assets ...	NOPAT / Average NOA

How do RNOA and ROE behave over time? Following is a graph of average RNOA and ROE for a large set of firms over the past decade. We see there is considerable variability in these ratios over time. The proportion of RNOA to ROE is greater for some periods of time than for others. Yet, in all periods for this large sample of firms, ROE exceeds RNOA. This is evidence of the positive effect of leverage on ROE.

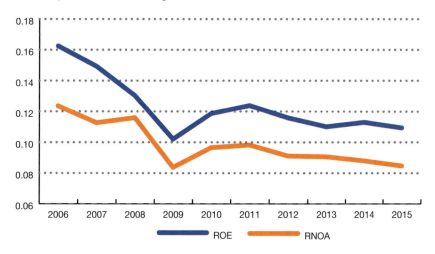

LO6 **Review 4-6**

Refer to Review 4-4 (for NOA) and 4-5 (for NOPAT) for Cisco Systems to complete the following requirement.

Required
Compute and interpret return on net operating assets (RNOA) for fiscal year 2015.

Solution on p. 4-65.

RNOA Disaggregation into Margin and Turnover

Similar to the components of ROA, we can disaggregate RNOA into net operating profit margin and net operating asset turnover to gain further insights into a company's performance. This disaggregation follows.

eLectures **LO7**
MBC Disaggregate RNOA into net operating profitability and net operating asset turnover.

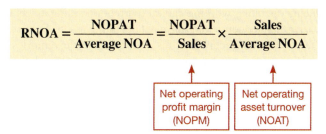

$$\text{RNOA} = \frac{\text{NOPAT}}{\text{Average NOA}} = \frac{\text{NOPAT}}{\text{Sales}} \times \frac{\text{Sales}}{\text{Average NOA}}$$

Net operating profit margin (NOPM)

Net operating asset turnover (NOAT)

Net Operating Profit Margin

Net operating profit margin (NOPM) reveals how much operating profit the company earns from each sales dollar. All things equal, a higher net operating profit margin is preferable. Net operating profit margin is affected by the level of gross profit the company earns on its products (revenue minus cost of goods sold), which depends on product prices and manufacturing or purchase costs. Net operating profit margin is also affected by the level of operating expenses the company requires to support its products or services. This includes overhead costs such as wages, marketing, occupancy, and research and development. Finally, net operating profit margin is affected by the level of competition (which affects product pricing) and the company's willingness and ability to control costs.

Intel's net operating profit margin is computed as follows ($ millions).

$$\text{Net operating profit margin} = \frac{\text{Net operating profit after tax}}{\text{Sales}} = \frac{\$11,288}{\$55,355} = 20.39\%$$

This result means that for each dollar of sales at Intel, the company earns roughly 20.39¢ profit after all operating expenses and taxes. As a reference, the median NOPM for U.S. publicly traded companies with revenues greater than $1 billion in 2015 is about 8¢.

Analysis of net operating profit margin examines the ratio over time and in comparison with peers. As with net profit margin in the DuPont analysis, the net operating profit margin includes effects from the gross profit margin (Gross profit/Sales) and the operating expense margin (Operating expenses/Sales). A second level analysis of net operating profit margin examines these components to uncover underlying trends that drive this ratio.

Net Operating Asset Turnover

Net operating asset turnover (NOAT) measures the productivity of the company's net operating assets. This metric reveals the level of sales the company realizes from each dollar invested in net operating assets. All things equal, a higher NOAT is preferable. Intel's net operating asset turnover ratio follows ($ millions).

$$\text{Net operating asset turnover} = \frac{\text{Sales}}{\text{Average net operating assets}} = \frac{\$55,355}{(\$51,488 + \$47,258)\,/\,2} = 1.12$$

This result means that for each dollar of net operating assets, Intel realizes $1.12 in sales. As a reference, the median for U.S. publicly traded companies with revenues greater than $1 billion in 2015 is about $1.30.

Net operating asset turnover can be increased by either increasing sales for a given level of investment in operating assets, or by reducing the amount of operating assets necessary to generate a dollar of sales, or both. Reducing operating working capital (current operating assets less current operating liabilities) is usually easier than reducing long-term net operating assets. For example, companies can implement strategies to collect their receivables faster, reduce their inventories, and delay payments to their suppliers. All of these actions reduce operating working capital and, thereby, increase NOAT. These strategies must be managed, however, so as not to negatively impact sales or supplier relations. Working capital management is an important part of managing the company effectively.

It is usually more difficult to reduce the level of long-term net operating assets. The level of PPE required by the company is determined more by the nature of the company's business model than by management action. For example, telecommunications companies require more capital investment than do retail stores. Still, there are several actions that managers can take to reduce capital investment. Some companies pursue novel approaches, such as corporate alliances, outsourcing, and use of special purpose entities; we discuss some of these approaches in later modules.

Analysis of net operating asset turnover examines the ratio over time and in comparison with peers. As with asset turnover in the DuPont analysis, the net operating asset turnover includes effects from the turnovers (and corresponding days) of each of the working capital accounts (accounts receivable, inventory, accounts payable) and effects from the long-term operating assets turnover. A second level analysis of net operating profit margin examines these components to uncover underlying trends that drive this ratio.

Managerial Decision ■ You Are the CEO

You are analyzing the performance of your company. Your analysis of RNOA reveals the following (industry benchmarks in parentheses): RNOA is 16% (10%), NOPM is 18% (17%), and NOAT is 0.89 (0.59). What interpretations do you draw that are useful for managing your company? [Answer, p. 4-42]

Trade-Off between Margin and Turnover

Net operating profit margin and turnover of net operating assets are largely affected by a company's business model. This is an important concept. Specifically, an infinite number of combinations of net operating profit margin and net operating asset turnover will yield a given RNOA. This relation is depicted in Exhibit 4.9 (where the curved line reflects the median RNOA for all publicly traded companies during 2015).

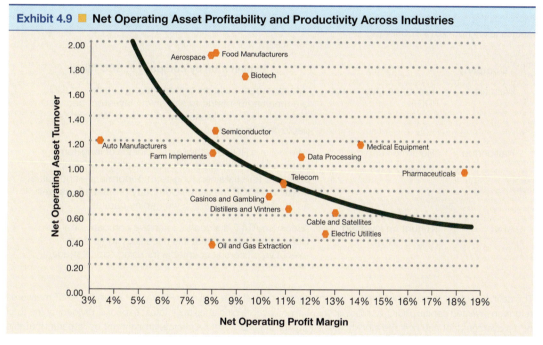

Exhibit 4.9 ■ **Net Operating Asset Profitability and Productivity Across Industries**

This exhibit reveals that some industries, such as oil and gas and utilities, are capital intensive with relatively low net operating asset turnover. Accordingly, for such industries to achieve a required RNOA (to be competitive in the overall market), they must obtain a higher profit margin. On the other hand, companies such as food manufacturers and aerospace companies hold fewer assets and, therefore, can operate on lower net operating profit margins to achieve a sufficient RNOA. This is because their asset turnover is far greater.

This exhibit warns of blindly comparing the performance of companies across different industries. For instance, a higher profit margin in the pharmaceutical industry compared with the food manufacturing is not necessarily the result of better management. Instead, the pharmaceutical companies have higher operating assets (typically intangibles related to intellectual property) and thus, to achieve an equivalent RNOA, pharmaceutical companies must earn a higher profit margin to offset their lower asset turnover. Basic economics suggests that all industries must earn an acceptable return on investment if they are to continue to attract investors and survive.

The trade-off between margin and turnover is relatively straightforward when comparing companies that operate in one industry (*pure-play* firms). Analyzing conglomerates that operate in several industries is more challenging. Conglomerates' margins and turnover rates are a weighted average of the margins and turnover rates for the various industries in which they operate. For example, **Caterpillar Inc.** is a blend of a manufacturing company and a financial institution (**Caterpillar Financial Services Corp.**); thus, the margin and turnover benchmarks for Caterpillar on a consolidated basis are a weighted average of those two industries.

Research Insight ■ NOPM and NOAT Explain Stock Prices

Research shows that stock returns are positively associated with earnings—when companies report higher than expected earnings, stock returns rise. Research also reports that the RNOA components (NOPM and NOAT) are more strongly associated with stock returns and future profitability than earnings (or return on assets) alone. This applies to the short-term market response to earnings announcements and long-term stock price changes. Thus, disaggregating earnings and the balance sheet into operating and nonoperating components is a useful analysis tool.

Source: Soliman, Mark T., "Use of DuPont Analysis by Market Participants," *The Accounting Review*, May 2008, 83(3): 823–853.

Business Insight ■ Other Return Metrics

Many companies report return metrics in their SEC filings (via their proxy statement or their MD&A in the 10-K). Because GAAP does not define return metrics, we see a wide variety in practice. Below are three examples of return metrics taken from 2015 SEC filings.

Company	Ratio	Explanation by company in SEC filing
Walmart	Return on investment (ROI)	"Management believes that return on investment (ROI) is a meaningful metric to share with investors because it helps investors assess how effectively Walmart is deploying its assets."
Halliburton	Return on capital employed (ROCE)	"We believe ROCE is the best indicator of long-term Company performance, while reinforcing the Company's objective for sustained long-term performance and value creation. ROCE measures Company profitability as well as the efficiency by which we deploy capital."
AT&T	Return on invested capital (ROIC)	"Because AT&T is a capital-intensive company, the Committee believes that it is necessary to hold our executive officers accountable for using capital prudently."

The definition of each ratio varies slightly, but the underlying metric is similar to RNOA. For example, AT&T measures return on invested capital (ROIC) as follows: "annual net income plus after-tax interest expense, divided by the total of the average debt and average stockholder equity for the year." At first glance, it might not be apparent but this definition of ROIC is nearly identical to the RNOA we use. Note that NOPAT can be computed as Net income + After-tax nonoperating expenses; if interest is the only nonoperating expense, then the ROIC and RNOA numerators are identical. As for the denominator, AT&T sums average debt and average stockholder equity. Consider the accounting equation: Assets = Liabilities + Stockholders' equity, which can be rewritten as:

$$\frac{\text{Operating}}{\text{assets}} + \frac{\text{Nonoperating}}{\text{assets}} = \frac{\text{Operating}}{\text{liabilities}} + \frac{\text{Nonoperating}}{\text{liabilities}} + \frac{\text{Stockholders'}}{\text{equity}}$$

By rearranging terms we see:

$$\frac{\text{Operating}}{\text{assets}} - \frac{\text{Operating}}{\text{liabilities}} = \frac{\text{Nonoperating}}{\text{liabilities}} - \frac{\text{Nonoperating}}{\text{assets}} + \frac{\text{Stockholders'}}{\text{equity}}$$

On the left is net operating assets (the denominator in RNOA). The right has debt and stockholders' equity (the denominator in ROIC) less any nonoperating assets. Thus, RNOA and ROIC are nearly identical. Because companies generally report metrics that they adapt for their industry, it is important that we understand the exact definition of the metric before comparing metrics across different companies and industries.

LO7 Review 4-7

Use the income statement provided in Review 4-5 for Cisco Systems and the RNOA computed in Review 4-6 to complete the following requirement.

Required
Disaggregate RNOA into components of net operating profit margin and net operating asset turnover for 2015. **Solution on p. 4-65.**

Global Accounting

An important aim of this module is to distinguish between operating and nonoperating items for the balance sheet and income statement. U.S. GAAP and IFRS generally account for items similarly, but there are certain disclosure differences worth noting.

The IFRS balance sheet is similar to its U.S. GAAP counterpart, with the visible exception for the frequent, but not mandatory, reverse ordering of assets and liabilities. However, one notable difference is that IFRS companies routinely report "financial assets" or "financial liabilities" on the balance sheet. We must assess these items. IFRS defines financial assets to include receivables (operating item), loans to affiliates or associates (can be operating or nonoperating depending on the nature of the transactions), securities held as investments (nonoperating), and derivatives (nonoperating). IFRS notes to financial statements, which tend to be more detailed than U.S. GAAP notes, usually detail what financial assets and liabilities consist of. This helps us accurately determine NOA and net non-operating obligations (NNO).

The IFRS income statement usually reports fewer line items than U.S. GAAP income statements and, further, there is no definition of "operating activities" under IFRS. This means we must devote attention to classify operating versus nonoperating income components. Following is a table that shows common U.S. GAAP income statement items and their classification as operating (O) or nonoperating (N). This table also indicates which items are required for IFRS income statements.

Income Statement Line Items	Operating (O) or Nonoperating (N)	Required on IFRS Income Statement
Net sales.	O	YES
Cost of sales.	O	—
Selling, general and administrative (SG&A) expense	O	—
Provisions for doubtful accounts	O	—
Nonoperating income.	N	—
Interest revenue and interest expense	N	YES
Nonoperating expenses	N	—
Income before income taxes	O and N	—
Income tax expense.	O and N	YES
Earnings on equity investments (associates and joint ventures).	O	YES
Income from continuing operations	O	—
Discontinued operations	N	YES
Net income.	O and N	YES
Net income attributable to noncontrolling interest.	N	YES
Net income attributable to controlling interest.	O and N	YES
Earnings per share (Basic EPS and Diluted EPS).	O and N	YES

There is no requirement to report income from operations, yet many IFRS companies do so. However, items that are considered operating such as gains and losses on disposals of operating assets, or income from equity method investments, are often reported below the operating income line. We must examine IFRS income statements and their notes to make an independent assessment of what is operating. IFRS income statements usually report separately the other nonoperating revenues and expenses even though this is not required. We can better assess the nature of these items by reading the accompanying notes.

Appendix 4A: Nonoperating Return Component of ROE

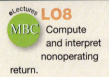
LO8
Compute and interpret nonoperating return.

Nonoperating Return

Recall that ROE can be written as:

$$\text{ROE} = \text{Operating return} + \text{Nonoperating return}$$

In simple form, return on nonoperating activities measures the extent to which a company is using debt to increase its return on equity.

We can infer the nonoperating return indirectly as the difference between ROE and RNOA. We can also compute the nonoperating return directly as follows:

$$\text{Nonoperating return} = \text{Financial Leverage} \times \text{Spread}$$

where Spread is the difference between return on net operating assets and the after-tax cost of debt, net of any after-tax returns on nonoperating assets such as investments in marketable securities.

This means return on equity can be disaggregated as:

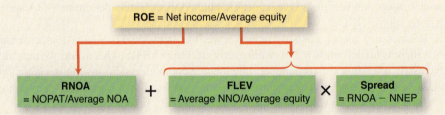

Exhibit 4A.1 provides definitions for each of the terms required in this computation.

Exhibit 4A.1 ■ Nonoperating Return Definitions

NNO:	**Net nonoperating obligations**	Nonoperating liabilities less nonoperating assets
FLEV:	**Financial leverage.**	Average NNO/Average total stockholders' equity
NNE:	**Net nonoperating expense**	NOPAT – Consolidated net income; or Nonoperating expenses × (1 – Statutory tax rate)
NNEP:	**Net nonoperating expense percent** . . .	NNE/Average NNO
Spread:		RNOA – NNEP

In most cases, nonoperating return is positive and it increases ROE. However, there are a number of other situations where the company's nonoperating activities are more complex. And in some situations, the nonoperating return is negative (as for Intel). In this section, we illustrate four specific situations and demonstrate how to directly compute nonoperating return in each case.

Nonoperating Return—with Debt Financing

The following illustration provides the intuition for the simple case when a company has debt (nonoperating obligations) but no nonoperating assets (such as cash).

Assume that a company has $1,000 in average net operating assets during the year and earns net operating profit after tax (NOPAT) of $200; yielding a 20% RNOA (NOPAT/Average NOA = $200/$1,000). (To simplify the example, assume a tax rate of 0%.) The company finances the assets entirely with equity and thus ROE is also 20% (Net income/Average equity = $200/$1,000).

Next assume that the company borrows $500 at 7% and uses the funds to acquire additional operating assets that yield the same RNOA of 20%. Its net operating assets are now $1,500 and its profit is $265, computed as:

Profit from assets financed with equity ($1,000 × 20%)		$200
Profit from assets financed with debt ($500 × 20%)	$100	
Less interest expense from debt ($500 × 7%)	(35)	65
Net income		$265

We see that this company increased its net income by $65 with the addition of debt and ROE is now 26.5% ($265/$1,000). The reason ROE increased is that the company borrowed at 7% and invested in assets that earned 20%.

$$\text{ROE} = \text{Operating return} \quad + \quad \text{Nonoperating return}$$
$$\text{ROE} = \qquad 20\% \qquad + \qquad 6.5\%$$
$$\text{ROE} = \qquad\qquad 26.5\%$$

The company has made good use of debt to increase its ROE for equity holders by 6.5%. We can compute the 6.5% nonoperating return directly as FLEV × Spread, as follows:

$$\text{FLEV} = \frac{\text{Average net nonoperating obligations (NNO)}}{\text{Average stockholders' equity (EQ)}} = \frac{\$500}{\$1,000} = 0.50$$

$$\text{NNEP} = \frac{\text{Net nonoperating expense}}{\text{Average net nonoperating obligations (NNO)}} = \frac{\$35}{\$500} = 7\%$$

$$\text{Spread} = \text{RNOA} - \text{NNEP} = 20\% - 7\% = 13\%$$

$$\text{Nonoperating return} = \text{FLEV} \times \text{Spread} = 0.50 \times 13\% = 6.5\%$$

In this simple example, the company's nonoperating activities relate solely to debt and in that special case, FLEV is identical to the traditional debt-to-equity ratio.

Nonoperating Return—With Debt Financing and Nonoperating Assets

Most companies report both debt and investments on their balance sheets. If that debt markedly exceeds the investment balance, their ROE will look like our first example (with debt only). Instead, if investments predominate, their ROE will look more like Intel's. We compute nonoperating return for McDonald's, a company with both debt and investments.

The table below shows data from McDonald's 2015 financial statements. With these numbers, we can compute NNE as ($638.3 million − $48.5 million) × (1 − 37%) = $371.6 million. McDonald's interest expense on its debt exceeds its nonoperating income and thus, NNE is a positive number. In general NNE can include interest income, dividend income, gains and losses on investments, as well as any income or losses on discontinued operations, all net of tax.

For McDonald's, we compute NOPAT as $4,900.9 million, calculated as net operating profit before tax of $7,145.5 million less taxes on operating profit of $2,244.6 million, computed as [$2,026.4 million + ($589.8 million × 37%)].

Balance Sheet Data ($ millions)	2015	2014
Operating assets	$30,253.2	$32,149.5
Operating liabilities	6,495.6	6,204.6
Net operating assets (NOA)	23,757.6	25,944.9
Nonoperating liabilities	24,355.2	15,169.4
Nonoperating assets	7,685.5	2,077.9
Net nonoperating obligations (NNO)	16,669.7	13,091.5
Equity (EQ)	$ 7,087.9	$12,853.4

continued

continued from previous page

Income Statement Data ($ millions)		
Net operating profit before tax...............		$ 7,145.5
Interest expense........................	$ 638.3	
Nonoperating (income) expense	(48.5)	589.8
Provision for income taxes..................		2,026.4
Net income.............................		$ 4,529.3

We compute McDonald's RNOA as NOPAT/Average NOA = $4,900.9 million/($23,757.6 million + $25,944.9 million/2) = 19.72%. To compute NNEP we use the following definition:

$$\text{Net nonoperating expense percent (NNEP)} = \frac{\text{Net nonoperating expense (NNE)}}{\text{Average net nonoperating obligations (NNO)}}$$

The net nonoperating expense percent (NNEP) measures the average cost of net nonoperating obligations. The denominator uses the average NNO similar to the return calculations (such as ROE and RNOA).

In the case of debt only, from above, net nonoperating expense percent is 7%, computed as $35/$500, which is exactly equal to the interest rate on the loan. With real financial statements, NNEP is more complicated because NNE often includes both interest on borrowed money and nonoperating income, and NNO is the net of nonoperating liabilities less nonoperating assets. Thus NNEP reflects an average return on nonoperating activities. For McDonald's, its 2015 NNEP is 2.50% computed as $371.6 million/[($16,669.7 million + $ 13,091.5 million) /2]. McDonald's RNOA is 19.72%, which means that net operating assets generate more return than the 2.5% cost of net nonoperating obligations. That is, McDonald's earns a Spread of 17.22%, the difference between RNOA (19.72%) and NNEP (2.5%), on each asset financed with borrowed funds. By borrowing funds, McDonald's creates leverage, which can be measured relative to stockholders' equity; that ratio is called financial leverage (FLEV). In sum, total nonoperating return is computed by the following formula:

$$\text{Nonoperating return} = \underbrace{\frac{\text{Average net nonoperating obligations (NNO)}}{\text{Average stockholders' equity (EQ)}}}_{\text{FLEV}} \times \underbrace{(\text{RNOA} - \text{NNEP})}_{\text{Spread}}$$

Two points are immediately clear from this equation. First, ROE increases with the Spread between RNOA and NNEP. The more profitable the return on operating assets, the higher the return to stockholders. Second, the higher the debt relative to equity, the higher the ROE (assuming, of course, a positive Spread).

McDonald's has average NNO of $14,880.6 million [($16,669.7 million + $13,091.5 million)/2] and average equity of $9,970.7 million [($7,087.9 million + $12,853.4 million)/2]. Thus, McDonald's ROE is as follows:

ROE	=	Operating return	+	Nonoperating return
	=	19.72%	+	[$14,880.6/$9,970.7]×[19.72% − 2.50%]
	=	19.72%	+	[1.4924]×[17.22%]
	=		45.42%	

Most companies report both debt and investments on their balance sheets. If that debt markedly exceeds the investment balance, their ROE will look more like our McDonald's example (with net debt). Instead, if investments predominate, their ROE will look more like Intel's (with net investments). It is important to remember that both the average NNO (and FLEV) and NNE can be either positive (debt) or negative (investments), and it is not always the case that ROE exceeds RNOA.

Nonoperating Return—Without Debt Financing, but with Nonoperating Assets

Many tech firms, including Intel, have low levels of debt and maintain large portfolios of marketable securities. They hold these highly liquid assets so that they can respond quickly to new opportunities or react to competitive pressures. With high levels of nonoperating assets and no nonoperating liabilities, the net nonoperating obligations (NNO) has a negative sign (NNO = Nonoperating liabilities − Nonoperating assets). Likewise, FLEV is negative: Average NNO (−)/Average equity (+). Further, net nonoperating expense is negative because investment *income* is a negative nonoperating expense. However, the net nonoperating expense percent (NNEP) is positive because the negative NNE is divided by the negative NNO. We can indirectly determine Intel's nonoperating return as −3.33% by subtracting RNOA from ROE (19.53% − 22.86%). We can also calculate nonoperating return directly.

Intel ($ millions)	2015	2014	Average	Computation
NOA	$51,488	$47,258	$49,373	See page 4-19
NNO	$ (9,597)	$ (8,607)	$ (9,102)	
Equity	$61,085	$55,865	$58,475	From balance sheet on page 4-18
Net income	$11,420	—	—	From income statement on page 4-22
NOPAT	$11,288	—	—	$14,002 − {$2,792 + [$(210) × 37%]}
NNE	$(132)	—	—	$(210) × (1 − 0.37)
FLEV	(0.1557)	—	—	$(9,102)/$58,475
RNOA	22.86%	—	—	$11,288/$49,373
NNEP	1.45%	—	—	$(132)/$(9,102)
Spread	21.41%	—	—	22.86% − 1.45%
ROE	19.53%	—	—	$11,420/$58,475

Intel's NNO is negative because its investment in marketable securities exceeds its debt. Intel's ROE consists of the following components.

$$
\begin{aligned}
ROE &= RNOA + [\quad FLEV \quad \times \quad Spread \ ] \\
&= 22.86\% + [\ -0.1557 \quad \times \quad 21.41\% \ ] \\
&= 22.86\% + \qquad\qquad [-3.33\%] \\
&= 19.53\%
\end{aligned}
$$

Intel's ROE is lower than its RNOA because of its large investment in marketable securities. That is, its excessive liquidity is penalizing its return on equity. The rationale for this seemingly incongruous result is this: Intel's ROE derives from operating and nonoperating assets. Intel's operating assets are providing an outstanding return (22.86%), much higher than the cost of its debt net of the return on its marketable securities (1.45%). Holding liquid assets that are less productive means that Intel's stockholders are funding a sizeable level of liquidity, and sacrificing returns in the process. Why? Many companies in high-tech industries feel the need to maintain excessive liquidity to gain flexibility—the flexibility to take advantage of opportunities and to react quickly to competitor maneuvers. Intel's management, evidently, feels that the investment of costly equity capital in this manner will reap future rewards for its stockholders. Its 19.53% ROE provides some evidence that this strategy is not necessarily misguided.

Nonoperating Return—With Debt Financing, Nonoperating Assets, and Noncontrolling Interest

When a company acquires controlling interest of the outstanding voting stock of another company, the parent company must consolidate the new subsidiary in its balance sheet and income statement. This means that the parent company must include 100% of the subsidiary's assets, liabilities, revenues, and expenses. If the parent acquires less than 100% of the subsidiary's voting stock, the remaining claim of noncontrolling stockholders is reported on the balance sheet as a component of stockholders' equity called noncontrolling interest, and net income is separated into income attributable to company stockholders and that attributable to noncontrolling interests. *The ROE computation, then, should use the net income attributable to company stockholders divided by the average stockholders' equity attributable to controlling interest, which excludes noncontrolling interest.* For firms with noncontrolling interests, we compute RNOA as usual because NOPAT is operating income before any noncontrolling interest on the income statement, and NOA is unaffected by noncontrolling interest on the balance sheet. Similarly, we compute Spread and FLEV as usual. However, we must modify the ROE = RNOA + [FLEV × Spread] formula slightly. Recall that a company's operating and nonoperating activities generate returns to both the controlling interest (labeled CI, which is the parent company's stockholders' equity) and the noncontrolling stockholders (labeled NCI). To account for this, we must multiply the ROE equation, RNOA + [FLEV × Spread], by a ratio that captures the relative income statement and balance sheet effects of the noncontrolling interest. This ratio is called the *noncontrolling interest ratio*, and is computed as follows:

$$\text{Noncontrolling interest ratio} = \left[\frac{\left(\dfrac{\text{Net income attributable to controlling interest (NI}_{CI})}{\text{Net income (NI)}} \right)}{\left(\dfrac{\text{Average equity attributable to controlling interest (CI)}}{\text{Average total equity (EQ)}} \right)} \right]$$

Hence, for companies with a noncontrolling interest (NCI), the disaggregated return on equity is expressed as:

$$\text{ROE} = [\text{RNOA} + (\text{FLEV} \times \text{Spread})] \times \text{NCI ratio}$$

To illustrate the calculation of ROE, FLEV, and Spread in the presence of noncontrolling interest, we consider the balance sheet and income statement items from **Walmart** ($ millions).

Walmart	2015	2014	Average
Balance sheet items			
Net operating assets (NOA)	$124,940	$126,967	$125,954
Net nonoperating obligations (NNO)	$ 41,329	$ 41,030	$ 41,180
Noncontrolling interest (NCI)	3,065	4,543	3,804
Walmart parent stockholders' equity (CI)	80,546	81,394	80,970
Total equity (NCI + CI)	83,611	85,937	84,774
Total net nonoperating obligations and Total equity.	$124,940	$126,967	$125,954
Income statement items			
Net operating profit after tax (NOPAT)	$ 16,634		
Net nonoperating expense (NNE).	1,554		
Net income.	15,080		
Net income attributable to noncontrolling interest (NI$_{NCI}$).	(386)		
Net income attributable to Walmart stockholders (NI$_{CI}$)	$ 14,694		

We compute Walmart's ROE for 2015 using the formula above (computations are in right column).

RNOA = NOPAT/Average NOA	13.21%	$16,634/$125,954
ROE = NI$_{CI}$/Average CI.	18.15%	$14,694/$80,970
FLEV = Average NNO/Average EQ	0.4858	$41,180/$84,774
NNEP = NNE/Average NNO	3.77%	$1,554/$41,180
Spread = RNOA − NNEP	9.44%	13.21% − 3.77%
Noncontrolling interest (NCI) ratio	1.0202	$\left(\dfrac{\$14,694}{\$15,080} \Big/ \dfrac{\$80,970}{\$84,774} \right)$
ROE = [RNOA + (FLEV × Spread)] × NCI ratio . . .	18.16%*	[13.21% + (0.4858 × 9.44%)] × 1.0202

*The 0.01% difference is due to rounding.

Review 4-8 LO8

Refer to **Cisco Systems'** balance sheet from Review 4-4 and its income statement from Review 4-5, along with its ROE and RNOA computations from Reviews 4-1 and 4-6, respectively, to complete the requirements below.

Required
a. Use ROE and RNOA ratios to determine the nonoperating return.
b. Compute net nonoperating obligations (NNO) and FLEV.
c. Compute net nonoperating expense (NNE) and net nonoperating expense as a percentage of NNO (NNEP).
d. Determine Spread using the formula: RNOA – NNEP.
e. Demonstrate that ROE = [RNOA + (FLEV × Spread)] × NCIR.

continued

Note: Cisco's balance sheet (but not its income statement) reports noncontrolling interest. The noncontrolling interest ratio (NCIR) is calculated as follows.

Net income to controlling interest	$ 8,981
Net income......................................	$ 8,981
Numerator of NCI ratio...............................	1.00000
Average equity to controlling interest ($59,698 + $56,654)/2 ...	$58,176
Average total equity ($59,707 + $56,661)/2................	$58,184
Denominator of NCI ratio.............................	0.99986
Noncontrolling interest ratio (NCIR)	1.00014

Solution on p. 4-66.

Appendix 4B: Liquidity and Solvency Analysis

eLectures LO9

MBC Compute and interpret measures of liquidity and solvency.

Companies can effectively use debt to increase return on equity via nonoperating return. We might further ask: if a higher ROE is desirable, why don't companies use the maximum debt possible? The short answer is that lenders such as banks and bondholders, charge successively higher interest rates for increasing levels of debt relative to the amount of equity investment. At some point, the cost of the additional debt exceeds the return on the additional assets acquired from the debt financing. Thereafter, further debt financing does not make economic sense. The market, in essence, places a limit on the level of debt that a company can effectively acquire. In sum, stockholders benefit from increased use of debt provided that the assets financed with the debt earn a return that exceeds the cost of the debt.

Creditors usually require a company to execute a loan agreement that places varying restrictions on the company's operating activities. These restrictions, called *covenants*, help safeguard debtholders in the face of increased risk. Covenants exist because debtholders do not have a voice on the board of directors like stockholders do. These debt covenants impose a "cost" on the company beyond that of the interest rate, and these covenants are more stringent as a company increases its reliance on debt financing.

In this Appendix, we explore how much debt a company can reasonably manage. We examine a number of liquidity and solvency metrics that lenders use to assess the default risk and set interest rates. Credit analysts typically use the same ratios to develop credit ratings, which are key determinants of bond prices and cost of debt financing for public companies.

Liquidity Analysis

Liquidity refers to cash availability: how much cash a company has, and how much it can raise on short notice. Two of the most common ratios used to assess the degree of liquidity are the current ratio and the quick ratio. Both of these ratios link required near-term payments to cash available in the near-term.

Current Ratio

Current assets are assets that a company expects to convert into cash within the next operating cycle, which is typically a year. *Current liabilities* are liabilities that come due within the next year. An excess of current assets over current liabilities (Current assets − Current liabilities), is known as *net working capital* or simply *working capital*.[2] Positive working capital implies that cash generated by "liquidating" current assets would be sufficient to pay current liabilities. The current ratio expresses working capital as a ratio and is computed as follows:

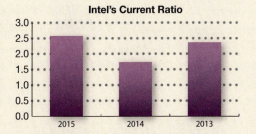

Intel's Current Ratio

---

[2] Both operating assets and operating liabilities can be either current or long-term. "Current" means that the asset is expected to be used, or the liability paid, within the next operating cycle or one year, whichever is longer, which for most companies means a year. Using the current versus long-term nature of operating assets and liabilities we derive two types of net operating assets: net operating working capital (NOWC), and net long-term operating assets. Net operating working capital is defined as:

$$\text{Net operating working capital (NOWC)} = \text{Current operating assets} - \text{Current operating liabilities}$$

For Intel, NOWC is $2,010 million for 2015 ($4,787 million + $5,167 million + $2,036 million + $3,053 million − $2,063 million − $3,138 million − $960 million − $2,188 million − $4,684 million).

$$\text{Current ratio} = \frac{\text{Current assets}}{\text{Current liabilities}}$$

A current ratio greater than 1.0 implies positive working capital. Both working capital and the current ratio consider existing balance sheet data only and ignore cash inflows from future sales or other sources. The current ratio is more commonly used than working capital because ratios allow comparisons across companies of different size. Generally, companies prefer a higher current ratio; however, an excessively high current ratio indicates inefficient asset use. Furthermore, a current ratio less than 1.0 is not always bad for at least two reasons:

1. A cash-and-carry company with comparatively fewer accounts receivable (like Walmart for example) can have potentially few current assets (and a low current ratio), but consistently large operating cash inflows ensure the company will be sufficiently liquid.
2. A company can efficiently manage its working capital by minimizing receivables and inventories and maximizing payables. Walmart, for example, uses its buying power to exact extended credit terms from suppliers. Consequently, because it is essentially a cash-and-carry company, its current ratio is less than 1.0 and is sufficiently liquid.

Intel does not use such a strategy; its accounts receivable and inventory have grown over time whereas accounts payable and accrued expenses have decreased. The aim of current ratio analysis is to discern if a company is having, or is likely to have, difficulty meeting its short-term obligations. Intel's current ratio for 2015 is 2.576 ($40,356 million/$15,667 million). The company's high current ratio derives primarily from its liquid investments.

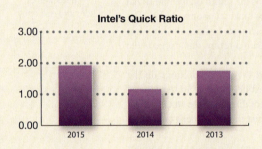

Intel's Quick Ratio

Quick Ratio

The quick ratio is a variant of the current ratio. It focuses on quick assets, which are assets likely to be converted to cash within a relatively short period of time. Specifically, quick assets include cash, marketable securities, and accounts receivable; they exclude inventories, prepaid assets, and other current assets. The quick ratio is defined as follows:

$$\text{Quick ratio} = \frac{\text{Cash} + \text{Marketable securities} + \text{Accounts receivable}}{\text{Current liabilities}}$$

The quick ratio reflects on a company's ability to meet its current liabilities without liquidating inventories. It is a more stringent test of liquidity than the current ratio.

Intel's 2015 quick ratio is 1.92 ($15,308 million + $2,682 million + $7,323 million + $4,787 million)/ $15,667 million. Like the current ratio, Intel's quick ratio has remained fairly constant over the past three years—see margin graph. It is not uncommon for a company's quick ratio to be less than 1.0. Although liquidity is not a major concern for Intel, the decline in the quick ratio is something financial statement users would want to monitor.

Solvency Analysis

Solvency refers to a company's ability to meet its debt obligations, including both periodic interest payments and the repayment of the principal amount borrowed. Solvency is crucial because an insolvent company is a failed company. There are two general approaches to measuring solvency. The first approach uses balance sheet data and assesses the proportion of capital raised from creditors. The second approach uses income statement data and assesses the profit generated relative to debt payment obligations. We discuss each approach in turn.

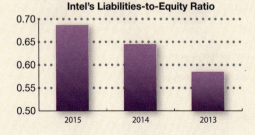

Intel's Liabilities-to-Equity Ratio

Liabilities-to-Equity

The liabilities-to-equity ratio is a useful tool for the first type of solvency analysis. It is defined as follows:

$$\text{Liabilities-to-equity ratio} = \frac{\text{Total liabilities}}{\text{Stockholders' equity}}$$

This ratio conveys how reliant a company is on creditor financing compared with equity financing. A higher ratio indicates less solvency, and more risk. Intel's

2015 liabilities-to-equity ratio is 0.69 ($15,667 million + $20,933 million + $2,539 million + $2,841 million)/$61,085 million. This ratio has increased somewhat from 0.59 to 0.69 over the past three years—but is still significantly lower than 1.5, the median for publicly traded companies. (Because the numerator of this ratio includes the consolidated liabilities of the company, the denominator must use the company's total equity, which includes any noncontrolling interest reported on the balance sheet.)

A variant of this ratio considers a company's long-term debt divided by equity. This approach assumes that current liabilities are repaid from current assets (so-called self-liquidating). Thus, it assumes that creditors and stockholders need only focus on the relative proportion of long-term capital.

In 2015, the median ratio of total liabilities to stockholders' equity, which measures the relative use of debt versus equity in a company's capital structure, is about 1.4 for U.S. publicly traded companies with sales over $1 billion. This means that the average company is financed with about $1.40 of liabilities for each dollar of stockholders' equity. However, the relative use of debt varies considerably across industries as illustrated in Exhibit 4B.1.

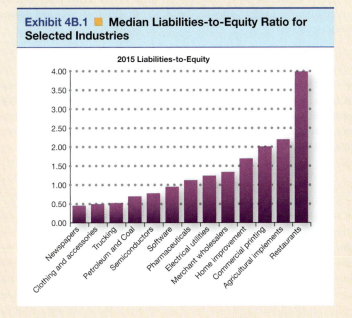

Exhibit 4B.1 ■ **Median Liabilities-to-Equity Ratio for Selected Industries**

Companies in the restaurant, agricultural implement, commercial printing, and home improvement industries have a large proportion of debt. This is typically because companies in these industries have relatively stable cash flows and they can, therefore, support a higher debt level. At the lower end of debt financing are companies, such as newspapers and retail clothing, whose cash flows are less predictable.

Times Interest Earned

The second type of solvency analysis compares profits to liabilities. This approach assesses how much operating profit is available to cover debt obligations. A common measure for this type of solvency analysis is the times interest earned ratio, defined as follows:

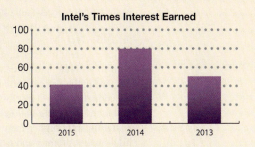

Intel's Times Interest Earned

$$\text{Times interest earned} = \frac{\text{Earnings before interest and taxes}}{\text{Interest expense, gross}}$$

The times interest earned ratio reflects the operating income available to pay interest expense. The underlying assumption is that only interest needs to be paid because the principal will be refinanced. This ratio is sometimes abbreviated as EBIT/I. The numerator is similar to net operating profits after tax (NOPAT), but it is *pretax* instead of after tax. We use earnings before net interest expense, that is, net of any other nonoperating income or expenses. We use gross interest, which does not include interest income or other investment income or expenses.

Management wants this ratio to be sufficiently high so that there is little risk of default. Intel's 2015 times interest earned is a healthy 41.55, computed as ($14,002 million/$337 million) consistently been very high over the past three years, which implies that Intel could suffer a large decline in profitability and still be able to service its interest payments when due. Note that the times interest earned ratio uses gross interest expense in the denominator. Intel's income statement reports $105 million for Interest and other expense (income), net. We can find gross interest expense in footnotes to the financial statements. For Intel in 2015, this amounted to $337 million.

There are many variations of solvency and liquidity analysis and ratios. The basic idea is to construct measures that reflect a company's credit risk exposure. There is not one "best" financial leverage ratio. Instead, as financial statement users, we want to use measures that capture the risk we are most concerned with. It is also important to compute the ratios ourselves to ensure we know what is included and excluded from each ratio.

Vertical and Horizontal Analysis

Companies come in all sizes, which presents difficulties when making comparisons among firms or over time. There are several methods that attempt to overcome this obstacle.

Vertical analysis expresses financial statements in ratio form. Specifically, it is routine to express income statement items as a percent of net sales, and balance sheet items as a percent of total assets. Such *common-size financial statements* facilitate comparisons *across companies* of different sizes and comparisons of accounts within a set of financial statements.

Horizontal analysis is the scrutiny of financial data *across time*. Comparing data across two or more consecutive periods assists in analyzing trends in company performance and in predicting future performance.

Exhibits 4B.2 and 4B.3 present Intel's common-size balance sheets and common-size income statements. We also present data for horizontal analysis by showing three years of common-size statements.

Intel's total assets (in dollars) have increased by 12.2% since 2013 to over $100 billion. The sheer size of Intel can make comparisons with other competitors difficult. A common-size analysis such as shown in Exhibits 4B.2 and 4B.3 allows us to compare companies of different sizes by focusing on the relative proportions of balance sheet and income statement accounts.

Intel's most significant assets are its plant assets and goodwill, which account for 31% and 11% of total assets respectively. The company is capital intensive in its manufacturing operations and the goodwill along with the other intangible assets are a testimony to the company's long-standing strategy of growth by acquisition. During 2015 cash grew sharply and while most of the other nonoperating assets decreased, the year over year change in nonoperating assets was an increase of about 40%. Intel is very liquid and as previously mentioned, the company holds liquid assets for future investment purposes. Operating assets as a percentage of total assets have remained at about the same levels for the three-year period and there is nothing startling on the asset side of the balance sheet.

Intel financed its 40.73% of its total assets with liabilities. In dollar terms, liabilities increased sharply in 2015 to $41,980 million but in common-size terms, this increase was not significant (39% to 41%). The significant increase in liabilities derived almost entirely to the additional debt the company took on in 2015; total debt increased from 15.85% of total assets to 22.87%. At year end, Intel was holding the new borrowed money as cash in anticipation of investment activities in 2016. Operating liabilities declined in both dollar and percentage terms in 2015. A common strategy to improve liquidity is to increase operating liabilities wherever possible (without damaging creditor and supplier relations) so as to improve cash flow. Intel's balance sheet is very liquid and the company does not appear to be engaging in the common strategy.

On the income side, we see that revenue decreased slightly in 2015 after a very significant increase in 2014. We would want to read the MD&A section of the 10-K carefully to understand why sales fell during the year and to determine whether this trend is expected to persist. Despite the decrease in sales, margins are very healthy. Intel's cost of sales decreased fairly significantly in 2014 (by 3.94 percentage points) and then increased slightly in 2015. Over the three-year period, the cost of sales trend is encouraging. For tech companies such as Intel, a major expenditure is research and development. We see that Intel increased its R&D spending during the year both in absolute and percentage terms. R&D costs expensed on the income statement this year may not yield revenue in the current period; revenues may be realized over several future periods. Analysts must carefully read the company's R&D disclosures to assess the long-term potential for dollars spent today. The company held costs down on marketing and general spending. Overall, Intel's relatively high net profit margin is 20.63%, which is significantly higher than what we would see in other more competitive industries. The company produces a high-quality product and is able to command a premium price.

Exhibit 4B.2 ■ Common-Size Balance Sheets

Intel Corporation Common-Size Balance Sheets	Amounts ($ millions)			Percentages		
	Dec. 26, 2015	Dec. 27, 2014	Dec. 28, 2013	Dec. 26, 2015	Dec. 27, 2014	Dec. 28, 2013
Cash and cash equivalents	$ 15,308	$ 2,561	$ 5,674	14.85%	2.79%	6.14%
Short-term investments	2,682	2,430	5,972	2.60%	2.64%	6.47%
Trading assets	7,323	9,063	8,441	7.11%	9.86%	9.14%
Accounts receivable, net	4,787	4,427	3,582	4.64%	4.82%	3.88%
Inventories	5,167	4,273	4,172	5.01%	4.65%	4.52%
Deferred tax assets	2,036	1,958	2,594	1.98%	2.13%	2.81%
Other current assets.	3,053	3,018	1,649	2.96%	3.28%	1.79%
Total current assets	40,356	27,730	32,084	39.16%	30.17%	34.74%
Property, plant and equipment, net	31,858	33,238	31,428	30.91%	36.17%	34.03%
Marketable equity securities	5,960	7,097	6,221	5.78%	7.72%	6.74%
Other long-term investments	1,891	2,023	1,473	1.83%	2.20%	1.59%
Goodwill.	11,332	10,861	10,513	11.00%	11.82%	11.38%
Identified intangible assets, net	3,933	4,446	5,150	3.82%	4.84%	5.58%
Other long-term assets	7,735	6,505	5,489	7.50%	7.08%	5.94%
Total assets.	$103,065	$91,900	$92,358	100.00%	100.00%	100.00%
Short-term debt	$ 2,634	$ 1,596	$ 281	2.56%	1.74%	0.30%
Accounts payable.	2,063	2,748	2,969	2.00%	2.99%	3.21%
Accrued compensation and benefits	3,138	3,475	3,123	3.04%	3.78%	3.38%
Accrued advertising	960	1,092	1,021	0.93%	1.19%	1.11%
Deferred income.	2,188	2,205	2,096	2.12%	2.40%	2.27%
Other accrued liabilities	4,684	4,895	4,078	4.54%	5.33%	4.42%
Total current liabilities.	15,667	16,011	13,568	15.20%	17.42%	14.69%
Long-term debt	20,933	12,971	13,165	20.31%	14.11%	14.25%
Long-term deferred tax liabilities	2,539	3,775	4,397	2.46%	4.11%	4.76%
Other long-term liabilities	2,841	3,278	2,972	2.76%	3.57%	3.22%
Total liabilities	41,980	36,035	34,102	40.73%	39.21%	36.92%
Preferred stock.	—	—	—			
Common stock.	23,411	21,781	21,536	22.71%	23.70%	23.32%
Accumulated other comprehensive income. . .	60	666	1,243	0.06%	0.72%	1.35%
Retained earnings	37,614	33,418	35,477	36.50%	36.36%	38.41%
Total stockholders' equity	61,085	55,865	58,256	59.27%	60.79%	63.08%
Total liabilities and stockholders' equity.	$103,065	$ 91,900	$ 92,358	100.00%	100.00%	100.00%

* Percentages are rounded to two decimals and thus, might not sum to totals and sub-totals.

Exhibit 4B.3 ■ Common-Size Income Statements

Intel Corporation Common-Size Income Statements For year ended	Amounts ($ millions)			Percentages		
	Dec. 26, 2015	Dec. 27, 2014	Dec. 28, 2013	Dec. 26, 2015	Dec. 27, 2014	Dec. 28, 2013
Net revenue	$55,355	$55,870	$52,708	100.00%	100.00%	100.00%
Cost of sales.	20,676	20,261	21,187	37.35%	36.26%	40.20%
Gross margin	34,679	35,609	31,521	62.65%	63.74%	59.80%
Research and development	12,128	11,537	10,611	21.91%	20.65%	20.13%
Marketing, general and administrative	7,930	8,136	8,088	14.33%	14.56%	15.34%
Restructuring and asset impairment charges	354	295	240	0.64%	0.53%	0.46%
Amortization of acquisition-related intangibles . . .	265	294	291	0.48%	0.53%	0.55%
Operating expenses	20,677	20,262	19,230	37.35%	36.27%	36.48%
Operating income.	14,002	15,347	12,291	25.29%	27.47%	23.32%
Interest and other expense (income)	(105)	43	(151)	(0.19)%	0.08%	(0.27)%
Losses (gains) on equity investments, net	(315)	(411)	(471)	(0.57)%	(0.74)%	(0.89)%
Income before taxes.	14,212	15,801	12,611	25.67%	28.28%	23.93%
Provision for taxes	2,792	4,097	2,991	5.04%	7.33%	5.67%
Net income.	$11,420	$11,704	$ 9,620	20.63%	20.95%	18.25%

Limitations of Ratio Analysis

The quality of financial statement analysis depends on the quality of financial information. We ought not blindly analyze numbers; doing so can lead to faulty conclusions and suboptimal decisions. Instead, we need to acknowledge that current accounting rules (GAAP) have limitations, and be fully aware of the company's environment, its competitive pressures, and any structural and strategic changes. This section discusses some of the factors that limit the usefulness of financial accounting information for ratio analysis.

GAAP Limitations Several limitations in GAAP can distort financial ratios. Limitations include:

1. **Measurability**. Financial statements reflect what can be reliably measured. This results in nonrecognition of certain assets, often internally developed assets, the very assets that are most likely to confer a competitive advantage and create value. Examples are brand name, a superior management team, employee skills, and a reliable supply chain.
2. **Non-capitalized costs**. Related to the concept of measurability, is the expensing of costs relating to "assets" that cannot be identified with enough precision to warrant capitalization. Examples are brand equity costs from advertising and other promotional activities, and research and development costs relating to future products.
3. **Historical costs**. Assets and liabilities are usually recorded at original acquisition or issuance costs. Subsequent increases in value are not recorded until realized, and declines in value are only recognized if deemed permanent.

Thus, GAAP balance sheets omit important and valuable assets. Our analysis of ROE and our assessment of liquidity and solvency, must consider that assets can be underreported and that ratios can be distorted. We discuss many of these limitations in more detail in later modules.

Company Changes Many companies regularly undertake mergers, acquire new companies, and divest subsidiaries. Such major operational changes can impair the comparability of company ratios across time. Companies also change strategies, such as product pricing, R&D, and financing. We must understand the effects of such changes on ratios and exercise caution when we compare ratios from one period to the next. Companies also behave differently at different points in their life cycles. For instance, growth companies possess a different profile than do mature companies. Seasonal effects also markedly impact analysis of financial statements at different times of the year. Thus, we must consider life cycle and seasonality when we compare ratios across companies and over time.

Conglomerate Effects Few companies are a pure-play; instead, most companies operate in several businesses or industries. Most publicly traded companies consist of a parent company and multiple subsidiaries, often pursuing different lines of business. Most heavy equipment manufacturers, for example, have finance subsidiaries (**Ford**

Credit Corporation and Caterpillar Financial Services Corporation are subsidiaries of Ford and Caterpillar respectively). Financial statements of such conglomerates are consolidated and include the financial statements of the parent and its subsidiaries. Consequently, such consolidated statements are challenging to analyze. Typically, analysts break the financials apart into their component businesses and separately analyze each component. Fortunately, companies must report financial information (albeit limited) for major business segments in their 10-Ks.

Fuzzy View   Ratios reduce, to a single number, the myriad complexities of a company's operations. No scalar can accurately capture all qualitative aspects of a company. Ratios cannot meaningfully convey a company's marketing and management philosophies, its human resource activities, its financing activities, its strategic initiatives, and its product management. In our analysis we must learn to look through the numbers and ratios to better understand the operational factors that drive financial results. Successful analysis seeks to gain insight into what a company is really about and what the future portends. Our overriding purpose in analysis is to understand the past and present to better predict the future. Computing and examining ratios is one step in that process.

LO9 Review 4-9

Use the income statement and balance sheet for Cisco Systems Inc. from Reviews 4-4 and 4-5.

Required

a. Compute and interpret measures of liquidity for fiscal 2015 and 2014.

b. Compute and interpret liabilities-to-equity ratio for fiscal 2015 and 2014. Compute times interest earned for 2015. (Note: The times interest earned ratio uses interest expense, gross, which is what Cisco Systems reports separately on its income statement.)

Solution on p. 4-66.

Guidance Answers

You Are the CEO

Pg. 4-28 Your company is performing substantially better than its competitors. Namely, your RNOA of 16% is markedly superior to competitors' RNOA of 10%. However, RNOA disaggregation shows that this is mainly attributed to your NOAT of 0.89 versus competitors' NOAT of 0.59. Your NOPM of 18% is essentially identical to competitors' NOPM of 17%. Accordingly, you will want to maintain your NOAT as further improvements are probably difficult to achieve. Importantly, you are likely to achieve the greatest benefit with efforts at improving your NOPM of 18%, which is only marginally better than the industry norm of 17%.

Superscript [A(B)] denotes assignments based on Appendix 4A (4B).

Questions

Q4-1.   Explain in general terms the concept of return on investment. Why is this concept important in the analysis of financial performance?

Q4-2.[A]   (a) Explain how an increase in financial leverage can increase a company's ROE. (b) Given the potentially positive relation between financial leverage and ROE, why don't we see companies with 100% financial leverage (entirely nonowner financed)?

Q4-3.   Gross profit margin (Gross profit/Sales) is an important determinant of NOPAT. Identify two factors that can cause gross profit margin to decline. Is a reduction in the gross profit margin always bad news? Explain.

Q4-4.   When might a reduction in operating expenses as a percentage of sales denote a short-term gain at the cost of long-term performance?

Q4-5.   Describe the concept of asset turnover. What does the concept mean and why is it so important to understanding and interpreting financial performance?

Q4-6.   Explain what it means when a company's ROE exceeds its RNOA. What about when the reverse occurs?

Q4-7.   Discontinued operations are typically viewed as a nonoperating activity in the analysis of the balance sheet and the income statement. What is the rationale for this treatment?

Q4-8. Describe what is meant by the "tax shield."

Q4-9. What is meant by the term "net" in net operating assets (NOA)?

Q4-10. Why is it important to disaggregate RNOA into net operating profit margin (NOPM) and net operating assets turnover (NOAT)?

Q4-11. What insights do we gain from the graphical relation between profit margin and asset turnover?

Q4-12. Explain the concept of liquidity and why it is crucial to company survival.

Q4-13. Identify at least two factors that limit the usefulness of ratio analysis.

Q4-14. Define (1) net nonoperating obligations and (2) net nonoperating expense.

Q4-15. What is the chief difference between the traditional DuPont disaggregation of ROE and the disaggregation based on RNOA?

Q4-16. What is meant by the term cash conversion cycle?

Q4-17. What insights can be gained from a common-sized income statement or balance sheet?

Assignments with the logo in the margin are available in **BusinessCourse**.
See the Preface of the book for details.

Mini Exercises

LO1
Home Depot (HD)

M4-18. Compute ROE

Selected balance sheet and income statement information for **Home Depot** follows. Compute the return on equity for the year ended January 31, 2016.

$ millions	Jan. 31, 2016	Feb. 01, 2015
Operating assets	$40,333	$38,223
Nonoperating assets	2,216	1,723
Total assets	42,549	39,946
Operating liabilities	14,918	13,427
Nonoperating liabilities	21,315	17,197
Total liabilities	36,233	30,624
Total stockholders' equity	6,316	9,322
Sales	88,519	
Net operating profit before tax (NOPBT)	11,774	
Nonoperating expense before tax	753	
Tax expense	4,012	
Net income	7,009	

LO2, 3
Home Depot (HD)

M4-19. Apply DuPont Disaggregation of ROE

Refer to the balance sheet and income statement information for **Home Depot**, from M4-18.

a. Compute ROE and disaggregate the ratio into its DuPont components of ROA and financial leverage.
b. Disaggregate ROA into profitability and productivity components.

LO4
Home Depot (HD)

M4-20. Compute Net Operating Assets (NOA)

Refer to the balance sheet information for **Home Depot**, from M4-18. Compute net operating assets for the years ended January 31, 2016 and February 1, 2015.

LO5
Home Depot (HD)

M4-21. Compute Net Operating Profit after Tax

Refer to the income statement information for **Home Depot**, from M4-18.
Compute net operating profit after tax for the year ended January 31, 2016. Assume a statutory tax rate of 37%.

M4-22. Compute ROE and RNOA with Disaggregation

LO1, 6, 7
Home Depot (HD)

Refer to the balance sheet and income statement information for **Home Depot** from M4-18.

a. Compute return on equity.

b. Compute return on net operating assets (RNOA).

c. Use ROE and RNOA to determine the nonoperating return for the year.

d. Disaggregate RNOA into components of profitability and productivity and show that the product of the two components equals RNOA.

M4-23. Compute RNOA, Net Operating Profit Margin, and NOA Turnover

LO6, 7
Nordstrom Inc.
(JWN)

Selected balance sheet and income statement information for **Nordstrom Inc.**, a department store retailer, follows.

Company ($ millions)	Ticker	2015 Sales	2015 NOPAT	2015 Net Operating Assets	2014 Net Operating Assets
Nordstrom Inc.	JWN	$14,437	$679	$3,081	$4,744

a. Compute its 2015 return on net operating assets (RNOA).

b. Disaggregate RNOA into net operating profit margin (NOPM) and net operating asset turnover (NOAT). Confirm that RNOA = NOPM × NOAT.

M4-24. Identify and Compute Net Operating Assets

LO4
Lowe's Companies Inc. (LOW)

Following is the balance sheet for **Lowe's Companies Inc.** Identify and compute its 2016 net operating assets (NOA).

LOWE'S COMPANIES INC. Consolidated Balance Sheets		
$ millions, except par value	Jan. 29, 2016	Jan. 30, 2015
Current assets		
Cash and cash equivalents	$ 405	$ 466
Short-term investments	307	125
Merchandise inventory—net	9,458	8,911
Other current assets.	391	349
Total current assets	10,561	9,851
Property, less accumulated depreciation.	19,577	20,034
Long-term investments	222	354
Deferred income taxes—net.	241	133
Other assets.	665	1,349
Total assets.	$31,266	$31,721
Current liabilities		
Short-term borrowings.	$ 43	$ —
Current maturities of long-term debt	1,061	552
Accounts payable.	5,633	5,124
Accrued compensation and employee benefits.	820	773
Deferred revenue	1,078	979
Other current liabilities	1,857	1,920
Total current liabilities.	10,492	9,348
Long-term debt, excluding current maturities	11,545	10,806
Deferred revenue—extended protection plans	729	730
Other liabilities	846	869
Total liabilities.	23,612	21,753
Shareholders' equity		
Preferred stock—$5 par value, none issued	—	—
Common stock—$0.50 par value; shares issued and outstanding 910 at January 29, 2016 and 960 at January 30, 2015, respectively.	455	480
Capital in excess of par value	—	—
Retained earnings	7,593	9,591
Accumulated other comprehensive loss	(394)	(103)
Total shareholders' equity	7,654	9,968
Total liabilities and shareholders' equity.	$31,266	$31,721

LO5

Lowe's Companies
Inc. (LOW)

M4-25.   Identify and Compute NOPAT

Following is the income statement for **Lowe's Companies Inc.** Compute its 2016 net operating profit after tax (NOPAT) assuming a 37% total statutory tax rate.

LOWE'S COMPANIES INC. CONSOLIDATED STATEMENTS OF EARNINGS			
Twelve Months Ended (In millions)	Jan. 29, 2016	Jan. 30, 2015	Jan. 31, 2014
Net sales.	$59,074	$56,223	$53,417
Cost of sales.	38,504	36,665	34,941
Gross margin	20,570	19,558	18,476
Expenses:			
Selling, general and administrative	14,115	13,281	12,865
Depreciation.	1,484	1,485	1,462
Interest—net.	552	516	476
Total expenses	16,151	15,282	14,803
Pre-tax earnings.	4,419	4,276	3,673
Income tax provision	1,873	1,578	1,387
Net earnings.	$ 2,546	$ 2,698	$ 2,286

LO1, 2, 3

Macy's Inc. (M)

M4-26.   Compute and Interpret Disaggregation of DuPont Analysis Ratios

Selected balance sheet and income statement information for **Macy's Inc.**, a retailer, follows.

Company ($ millions)	Ticker	2015 Sales	2015 Net Income	2015 Assets	2014 Assets	2015 Stockholders' Equity	2014 Stockholders' Equity
Macy's	M	$27,079	$1,072	$20,576	$21,330	$4,250	$5,378

a. Compute Macy's 2015 return on equity (ROE).
b. Disaggregate ROE into profit margin, asset turnover, and financial leverage. Confirm that ROE = PM × AT × FL.

LO6, 7

Abercrombie & Fitch Co. (ANF)

TJX Companies Inc. (TJX)

M4-27.   Compute RNOA, Net Operating Profit Margin, and NOA Turnover for Competitors

Selected balance sheet and income statement information from **Abercrombie & Fitch Co.** and **TJX Companies Inc.** clothing retailers in the high-end and value-priced segments, respectively, follows.

Company ($ millions)	Ticker	2015 Sales	2015 NOPAT	2015 Net Operating Assets	2014 Net Operating Assets
Abercrombie & Fitch.	ANF	$ 3,519	$ 50	$1,041	$1,213
TJX Companies	TJX	30,945	2,307	3,483	3,112

a. Compute the 2015 return on net operating assets (RNOA) for both companies.
b. Disaggregate RNOA into net operating profit margin (NOPM) and net operating asset turnover (NOAT) for each company. Confirm that RNOA = NOPM × NOAT.
c. Discuss differences observed with respect to NOPM and NOAT and interpret those differences in light of each company's business model.

LO9

Verizon Communications Inc. (VZ)

M4-28.   Compute and Interpret Liquidity and Solvency Ratios

Selected balance sheet and income statement information from **Verizon Communications Inc.** follows.

$ millions	2015	2014
Current assets	$ 22,280	$ 29,499
Current liabilities.	35,052	27,987
Total liabilities.	226,798	218,940
Equity	17,842	13,676
Earnings before interest and taxes.	32,974	21,379
Interest expense, gross	4,920	4,915
Net cash flow from operating activities	38,930	30,631

a. Compute the current ratio for each year and discuss any trend in liquidity. What additional information about the numbers used to calculate this ratio might be useful in helping us assess liquidity? Explain.

b. Compute times interest earned and the liabilities-to-equity for each year and discuss any noticeable change. (The average liabilities-to-equity ratio for the telecommunications industry is 1.7.) Do you have any concerns about Verizon's financial leverage and the company's ability to meet interest obligations? Explain.

c. Verizon's capital expenditures are expected to increase substantially as it seeks to respond to competitive pressures to upgrade the quality of its communication infrastructure. Assess Verizon's liquidity and solvency in light of this strategic direction.

M4-29. Compute NOPAT

Selected income statement information for 2015 is presented below for **Home Depot Inc.** and **Lowe's Companies Inc.**

LO5, 7

Home Depot Inc. (HD)

Lowe's Companies Inc. (LOW)

Company ($ millions)	Ticker	Net Operating Profit Before Tax	Pretax Net Nonoperating Expense	Tax Expense	Statutory Tax Rate	Sales
Home Depot........	HD	$11,774	$753	$4,012	37%	$88,519
Lowe's	LOW	4,971	552	1,873	37%	59,074

a. Compute NOPAT for each company.

b. Compute NOPAT as a percent of sales for each company—referred to as NOPM.

M4-30. Compute and Interpret Measures for DuPont Disaggregation Analysis

Refer to the 2012 fiscal year financial data of **3M Company** from Problem 4-41 to answer the following requirements (perform these computations from the perspective of a 3M shareholder).

LO1, 2, 3

3M Company (MMM)

a. Compute the DuPont model component measures for profit margin, asset turnover, and financial leverage. Then, compute ROA.

b. Compute ROE. Confirm that ROE equals ROE computed using the component measures from part a (ROE = PM × AT × FL).

c. Compute adjusted ROA (assume a statutory tax rate of 37% and pretax net interest expense of $123).

Exercises

E4-31. Compute and Interpret RNOA, Profit Margin, and Asset Turnover of Competitors

Selected balance sheet and income statement information for drug store retailers **CVS Health Corp.** and **Walgreens Boots Alliance** follows.

LO6, 7

CVS Health Corp (CVS)

Walgreens Boots Alliance (WBA)

Company ($ millions)	Ticker	2015 Sales	2015 NOPAT	2015 Net Operating Assets	2014 Net Operating Assets
CVS Health.........	CVS	$153,290	$5,758	$62,159	$48,338
Walgreens Boots Alliance	WBA	103,444	3,642	42,683	22,461

a. Compute the 2015 return on net operating assets (RNOA) for each company.

b. Disaggregate RNOA into net operating profit margin (NOPM) and net operating asset turnover (NOAT) for each company.

c. Discuss any differences in these ratios for each company.

E4-32. Compute, Disaggregate, and Interpret RNOA of Competitors

Selected balance sheet and income statement information for the clothing retailers, **Abercrombie & Fitch Co.** and **The GAP Inc.** follows.

LO6, 7

Abercrombie & Fitch Co. (ANF)

The GAP Inc. (GPS)

Company ($ millions)	Ticker	2015 Sales	2015 NOPAT	2015 Net Operating Assets	2014 Net Operating Assets
Abercrombie & Fitch..	ANF	$ 3,519	$ 50	$1,041	$1,213
The GAP...........	GPS	15,797	953	3,989	3,962

a. Compute the 2015 return on net operating assets (RNOA) for each company.
b. Disaggregate RNOA into net operating profit margin (NOPM) and net operating asset turnover (NOAT) for each company.
c. Discuss any differences in these ratios for each company.

LO6, 7

Nordstrom Inc. (JWN)
L Brands Inc. (LB)

E4-33.   Compute, Disaggregate, and Interpret RNOA of Competitors

Selected balance sheet and income statement information for the clothing retailers **Nordstrom Inc.** and **L Brands Inc.** follows.

Company ($ millions)	Ticker	2015 Sales	2015 NOPAT	2015 Net Operating Assets	2014 Net Operating Assets
Nordstrom	JWN	$14,095	$ 679	$3,081	$4,744
L Brands...........	LTD	12,154	1,416	2,915	3,060

a. Compute the 2015 return on net operating assets (RNOA) for each company.
b. Disaggregate RNOA into net operating profit margin (NOPM) and net operating asset turnover (NOAT) for each company.
c. Discuss any differences in these ratios for each company. Identify the factor(s) that drives the differences in RNOA observed from your analyses in parts a and b.

LO1, 2, 3

Oracle (ORCL)

E4-34.   Disaggregate Traditional DuPont ROE

Selected balance sheet and income statement information for **Oracle Corporation** follows. (Perform the required computations from the perspective of an Oracle shareholder.)

$ millions	May 31, 2015	May 31, 2014
Operating assets	$ 56,535	$51,447
Nonoperating assets	54,368	38,819
Total assets........................	110,903	90,266
Operating liabilities..................	19,847	18,722
Nonoperating liabilities...............	41,958	24,097
Total liabilities	61,805	42,819
Total Oracle stockholders' equity.........	48,663	$46,878
Total revenues	38,226	
Operating income before tax	13,871	
Nonoperating expense before tax	1,037	
Tax expense	2,896	
Net income........................	9,938	

a. Compute return on equity (ROE).
b. Apply the DuPont disaggregation into return on assets (ROA) and financial leverage.
c. Calculate the profitability and productivity components of ROA.
d. Confirm the ROA from part a. above with the full DuPont disaggregation: ROE = PM × AT × FL.

LO1, 6, 7

Macy's Inc. (M)

E4-35.   Compute, Disaggregate and Interpret ROE and RNOA

Selected balance sheet and income statement information from **Macy's Inc.** follows ($ millions). (Perform the required computations from the perspective of Macy's shareholders.)

Company	Ticker	2015 Sales	2015 Net Income	2015 Net Operating Profit After Tax	2015 Net Operating Assets	2014 Net Operating Assets	2015 Stockholders' Equity	2014 Stockholders' Equity
Macy's ...	M	$27,079	$1,072	$1,297	$10,781	$10,441	$4,250	$5,378

a. Compute the 2015 return on equity (ROE) and 2015 return on net operating assets (RNOA).
b. Disaggregate RNOA into net operating profit margin (NOPM) and net operating asset turnover (NOAT). What observations can we make about Macy's NOPM and NOAT?
c. Compute the percentage of RNOA to ROE, and compute Macy's nonoperating return for 2015.

E4-36. Compute and Compare ROE, ROA, and RNOA

LO1, 2, 6
Oracle (ORCL)

Refer to the balance sheet and income statement information for Oracle Corporation in E4-34.

a. Compute return on equity (ROE).
b. Compute return on net assets (ROA).
c. Compute return on net operating assets (RNOA).
d. Compare the three return metrics and explain what each one measures.

E4-37. Compute and Interpret Liquidity and Solvency Ratios

LO9
Comcast Corporation (CMCSA)

Selected balance sheet and income statement information from Comcast Corporation for 2015 and 2014 follows ($ millions).

	Total Current Assets	Total Current Liabilities	Income Before Interest and Taxes	Interest Expense	Total Liabilities*	Stockholders' Equity
2015	$12,303	$18,178	$15,673	$2,702	$112,596	$53,978
2014	13,531	17,410	15,001	2,617	106,118	53,068

*Includes redeemable noncontrolling interests

a. Compute the current ratio for each year and discuss any trend in liquidity. Do you believe the company is sufficiently liquid? Explain. What additional information about the accounting numbers comprising this ratio might be useful in helping you assess liquidity? Explain.
b. Compute times interest earned and the liabilities-to-equity ratio for each year and discuss any noticeable change.
c. What is your overall assessment of the company's liquidity and solvency from the analyses in parts a and b? Explain. *Hint:* Compare the ratios for Comcast to those provided in the module for publicly traded companies.

E4-38. Compute and Interpret Liquidity and Solvency Ratios

LO9
Verizon Communications Inc. (VZ)

Selected balance sheet and income statement information from Verizon Communications Inc. for 2015 and 2014 follows ($ millions).

	Total Current Assets	Total Current Liabilities	Income Before Interest and Taxes	Interest Expense, Gross	Total Liabilities	Stockholders' Equity
2015	$22,280	$35,052	$32,974	$4,920	$226,798	$17,842
2014	29,499	27,987	21,379	4,915	218,940	13,676

a. Compute the current ratio for each year and discuss any trend in liquidity. Do you believe the company is sufficiently liquid? Explain. What additional information about the accounting numbers comprising this ratio might be useful in helping you assess liquidity? Explain.
b. Compute times interest earned and the liabilities-to-equity ratio for each year and discuss any noticeable change.
c. What is your overall assessment of the company's liquidity and solvency from the analyses in parts a and b? Explain.

LO9   **E4-39.   Compute and Interpret Solvency Ratios for Business Segments**

General Electric
Company (GE)

Selected balance sheet and income statement information from General Electric Company and its two principal business segments (Industrial and Financial) for 2015 follows.

$ millions	Pretax Income	Interest Expense	Total Liabilities	Stockholders' Equity
Industrial segment	$3,252	$1,706	$223,910[3]	$ 99,651
Financial segment	(2,739)	2,301	265,411	46,713
Other.........................	7,673[1]	(544)[2]	(96,767)	(46,226)
General Electric Consolidated	$8,186	$3,463	$392,554	$100,138[4]

[1] Includes unallocated corporate operating activities.
[2] Includes intercompany loans and related interest expense; these are deducted (eliminated) in preparing consolidated financial statements.
[3] Includes redeemable noncontrolling interests
[4] Includes noncontrolling interests.

a. Compute times interest earned and the liabilities-to-equity ratio for 2015 for the two business segments (Industrial and Financial) and the company as a whole.
b. What is your overall assessment of the company's solvency? Explain. What differences do you observe between the two business segments? Do these differences correspond to your expectations given each company's business model?
c. Discuss the implications of the analysis of consolidated financial statements and the additional insight that can be gained from a more in-depth analysis of primary business segments.

LO5   **E4-40.   Compute NOPAT Using Tax Rates from Tax Footnote**

TJX Companies (TJX)

The income statement for TJX Companies follows.

TJX COMPANIES Consolidated Statements of Income	
Fiscal Year Ended ($ thousands)	**January 30, 2016**
Net sales......	$30,944,938
Cost of sales, including buying and occupancy costs..................	22,034,523
Selling, general and administrative expenses	5,205,715
Interest expense, net	46,400
Income before provision for income taxes........................	3,658,300
Provision for income taxes......................................	1,380,642
Net income......................................	$ 2,277,658

TJX provides the following footnote disclosure relating to its effective tax rate.

	January 30, 2016
U.S. federal statutory income tax rate	35.0%
Effective state income tax rate.....................................	3.5%
Impact of foreign operations	(0.7)%
All other	(0.1)%
Worldwide effective income tax rate	37.7%

a. Compute TJX's 2015 statutory tax rate using its income tax footnote disclosure.
b. Compute TJX's NOPAT for fiscal year 2015 using its tax rate from part a.

P4-41.   Analysis and Interpretation of Profitability

Balance sheets and income statements for **3M Company** follow.

LO4, 5, 6, 7, 8

3M Company (MMM)

Homework
MBC

3M COMPANY Consolidated Statements of Income			
For Years Ended Dec. 31 ($ millions)	**2015**	**2014**	**2013**
Net sales....................................	$30,274	$31,821	$30,871
Operating expenses			
Cost of sales....................................	15,383	16,447	16,106
Selling, general and administrative expenses	6,182	6,469	6,384
Research, development and related expenses	1,763	1,770	1,715
Total operating expenses	23,328	24,686	24,205
Operating income................................	6,946	7,135	6,666
Interest expense and income			
Interest expense.............................	149	142	145
Interest income................................	(26)	(33)	(41)
Total interest expense—net....................	123	109	104
Income before income taxes	6,823	7,026	6,562
Provision for income taxes......................	1,982	2,028	1,841
Net income including noncontrolling interest..........	4,841	4,998	4,721
Less: Net income attributable to noncontrolling interest	8	42	62
Net income attributable to 3M	$ 4,833	$ 4,956	$ 4,659

3M COMPANY Consolidated Balance Sheets		
At December 31 ($ millions, except per share amount)	**2015**	**2014**
Current assets		
Cash and cash equivalents.............................	$ 1,798	$ 1,897
Marketable securities—current...........................	118	1,439
Accounts receivable—net of allowances of $91 and $94........	4,154	4,238
Inventories:		
Finished goods.....................................	1,655	1,723
Work in process	1,008	1,081
Raw materials and supplies	855	902
Total inventories	3,518	3,706
Other current assets.................................	1,398	1,023
Total current assets................................	10,986	12,303
Marketable securities—noncurrent	9	15
Investments	117	102
Property, plant and equipment..........................	23,098	22,841
Less: Accumulated depreciation	(14,583)	(14,352)
Property, plant and equipment—net	8,515	8,489
Goodwill...	9,249	7,050
Intangible assets—net	2,601	1,435
Prepaid pension benefits	188	46
Other assets..	1,053	1,769
Total assets.......................................	$32,718	$31,209

continued

continued from previous page

At December 31 ($ millions, except per share amount)	2015	2014
Liabilities		
Current liabilities		
Short-term borrowings and current portion of long-term debt....	$ 2,044	$ 106
Accounts payable..	1,694	1,807
Accrued payroll...	644	732
Accrued income taxes	332	435
Other current liabilities	2,404	2,884
Total current liabilities...................................	7,118	5,964
Long-term debt	8,753	6,705
Pension and postretirement benefits......................	3,520	3,843
Other liabilities	1,580	1,555
Total liabilities	$20,971	$18,067
Equity		
3M Company shareholders' equity:		
Common stock, par value $0.01 per share;		
Shares outstanding—2015: 609,330,124;		
Shares outstanding—2014: 635,134,594....................	$ 9	$ 9
Additional paid-in capital.................................	4,791	4,379
Retained earnings	36,575	34,317
Treasury stock	(23,308)	(19,307)
Accumulated other comprehensive income (loss).............	(6,359)	(6,289)
Total 3M Company shareholders' equity	11,708	13,109
Noncontrolling interest...................................	39	33
Total equity..	$11,747	$13,142
Total liabilities and equity	$32,718	$31,209

Required

a. Compute net operating profit after tax (NOPAT) for 2015. Assume that the combined federal and state statutory tax rate is 37%.

b. Compute net operating assets (NOA) for 2015 and 2014. Treat noncurrent investments as a nonoperating item.

c. Compute and disaggregate 3M's RNOA into net operating profit margin (NOPM) and net operating asset turnover (NOAT) for 2015. Demonstrate that RNOA = NOPM × NOAT.

d. Compute net nonoperating obligations (NNO) for 2015 and 2014. Confirm the relation: NOA = NNO + Total equity.

e. Compute return on equity (ROE) for 2015.

f. What is the nonoperating return component of ROE for 2015?

g. Comment on the difference between ROE and RNOA. What inference can we draw from this comparison?

LO1, 2, 3   **P4-42.**   **Compute the DuPont Disaggregation of ROE**

Under Armour Inc. (UA)   Refer to the balance sheets and income statement below for **Under Armour Inc.**

UNDER ARMOUR INC. Consolidated Statements of Income	
For 12 Months Ended ($ in 000s)	**Dec. 31, 2015**
Net revenues	$3,963,313
Cost of goods sold......................................	2,057,766
Gross profit...	1,905,547
Selling, general and administrative expenses	1,497,000
Income from operations.................................	408,547
Interest expense, net	(14,628)
Other expense, net.....................................	(7,234)
Income before income taxes	386,685
Provision for income taxes..............................	154,112
Net income...	$ 232,573

UNDER ARMOUR INC. Consolidated Balance Sheet		
$ in 000s	**Dec. 31, 2015**	**Dec. 31, 2014**
Assets		
Cash and cash equivalents	$ 129,852	$ 593,175
Accounts receivable, net	433,638	279,835
Inventories	783,031	536,714
Prepaid expenses and other current assets.	152,242	87,177
Deferred income taxes.	—	52,498
Total current assets	1,498,763	1,549,399
Property and equipment, net	538,531	305,564
Goodwill	585,181	123,256
Intangible assets, net	75,686	26,230
Deferred income taxes.	92,157	33,570
Other long-term assets	78,582	57,064
Total assets.	$2,868,900	$2,095,083
Liabilities and Stockholders' Equity		
Accounts payable.	$ 200,460	$ 210,432
Accrued expenses	192,935	147,681
Current maturities of long term-debt	42,000	28,951
Other current liabilities	43,415	34,563
Total current liabilities.	478,810	421,627
Long-term debt, net of current maturities	352,000	255,250
Long-term line of credit, noncurrent.	275,000	—
Other long-term liabilities	94,868	67,906
Total liabilities	1,200,678	744,783
Stockholders' equity		
Additional paid-in capital	636,630	508,350
Retained earnings	1,076,533	856,687
Accumulated other comprehensive loss	(45,013)	(14,808)
Total stockholders' equity	1,668,222	1,350,300
Total liabilities and stockholders' equity.	$2,868,900	$2,095,083

Required

a. Compute return on equity (ROE).

b. Apply the DuPont disaggregation into return on assets (ROA) and financial leverage.

c. Calculate the profitability and productivity components of ROA.

d. Confirm the ROA from part a. above with the full DuPont disaggregation: ROE = PM × AT × FL.

P4-43.   Analysis and Interpretation of Liquidity and Solvency   **LO9**

Refer to the financial information of **3M Company** in P4-41 to answer the following requirements.   **3M Company (MMM)**

Required

a. Compute the current ratio and quick ratio for 2015 and 2014. Comment on any observed trends.

b. Compute times interest earned and liabilities-to-equity ratios for 2015 and 2014. Comment on any noticeable changes.

c. Summarize your findings about the company's liquidity and solvency. Do you have any concerns about its ability to meet its debt obligations?

P4-44.   Direct Computation of Nonoperating Return   **LO8**

Refer to the financial information of **3M Company** in P4-41 to answer the following requirements.   **3M Company (MMM)**

Required

a. Compute its financial leverage (FLEV), Spread, and noncontrolling interest (NCI) ratio for 2015. Recall that NNE = NOPAT − Net income.

b. Assume that its return on equity (ROE) for 2015 is 38.95% and its return on net operating assets (RNOA) is 26.58%. Confirm computations to yield the relation: ROE = [RNOA + (FLEV × Spread)] × NCI ratio.

c. What do your computations of the nonoperating return imply about the company's use of borrowed funds?

P4-45.   Analysis and Interpretation of Profitability

Balance sheets and income statements for Costco Wholesale Corporation follow.

COSTCO WHOLESALE CORPORATION Consolidated Statements of Income			
For Fiscal Years Ended ($ millions)	**Aug. 28, 2016**	**Aug. 30, 2015**	**Aug. 31, 2014**
Revenue			
Net sales	$116,073	$113,666	$110,212
Membership fees	2,646	2,533	2,428
Total revenue	118,719	116,199	112,640
Operating expenses			
Merchandise costs	102,901	101,065	98,458
Selling, general and administrative	12,068	11,445	10,899
Preopening expenses	78	65	63
Operating income	3,672	3,624	3,220
Other income (expense)			
Interest expense	(133)	(124)	(113)
Interest income and other, net	80	104	90
Income before taxes	3,619	3,604	3,197
Provision for income taxes	1,243	1,195	1,109
Net income including noncontrolling interests	2,376	2,409	2,088
Net income attributable to noncontrolling interests	(26)	(32)	(30)
Net income attributable to Costco	$ 2,350	$ 2,377	$ 2,058

COSTCO WHOLESALE CORPORATION Consolidated Balance Sheets		
$ millions, except par value and share data	**Aug. 28, 2016**	**Aug. 30, 2015**
Assets		
Current assets		
Cash and cash equivalents	$ 3,379	$ 4,801
Short-term investments	1,350	1,618
Receivables, net	1,252	1,224
Merchandise inventories	8,969	8,908
Other current assets	268	228
Total current assets	15,218	16,779
Property and equipment		
Land	5,395	4,961
Buildings and improvements	13,994	12,618
Equipment and fixtures	6,077	5,274
Construction in progress	701	811
Gross property and equipment	26,167	23,664
Less accumulated depreciation and amortization	(9,124)	(8,263)
Net property and equipment	17,043	15,401
Other assets	902	837
Total assets	$33,163	$33,017

continued

$ millions, except par value and share data	Aug. 28, 2016	Aug. 30, 2015
Liabilities and equity		
Current liabilities		
Accounts payable	$ 7,612	$ 9,011
Current portion long-term debt	1,100	1,283
Accrued salaries and benefits	2,629	2,468
Accrued member rewards	869	813
Deferred membership fees	1,362	1,269
Other current liabilities	2,003	1,695
Total current liabilities	15,575	16,539
Long-term debt, excluding current portion	4,061	4,852
Other liabilities	1,195	783
Total liabilities	20,831	22,174
Equity		
Preferred stock, $0.005 par value:		
100,000,000 shares authorized; no shares issued and outstanding . . .	—	—
Common stock, $0.005 par value:		
900,000,000 shares authorized;		
437,524,000 and 437,952,000 shares issued and outstanding	2	2
Additional paid-in-capital	5,490	5,218
Accumulated other comprehensive loss	(1,099)	(1,121)
Retained earnings	7,686	6,518
Total Costco stockholders' equity	12,079	10,617
Noncontrolling interests	253	226
Total equity	12,332	10,843
Total liabilities and equity	$33,163	$33,017

Required

a. Compute net operating profit after tax (NOPAT) for 2016. Assume that the combined federal and state statutory tax rate is 37%.

b. Compute net operating assets (NOA) for 2016 and 2015.

c. Compute and disaggregate Costco's RNOA into net operating profit margin (NOPM) and net operating asset turnover (NOAT) for 2016; confirm that RNOA = NOPM × NOAT.

d. Compute net nonoperating obligations (NNO) for 2016 and 2015. Confirm the relation: NOA = NNO + Total equity.

e. Compute return on equity (ROE) for 2016.

f. Infer the nonoperating return component of ROE for 2016.

g. Comment on the difference between ROE and RNOA. What does this relation suggest about Costco's use of equity capital?

P4-46. Analysis and Interpretation of Liquidity and Solvency

Refer to the financial information of Costco Wholesale Corporation in P4-45 to answer the following requirements.

Required

a. Compute Costco's current ratio and quick ratio for 2016 and 2015. Comment on any observed trends.

b. Compute Costco's times interest earned and its liabilities-to-equity ratios for 2016 and 2015. Comment on any noticeable change.

c. Summarize your findings about the company's liquidity and solvency. Do you have any concerns about Costco's ability to meet its debt obligations?

P4-47. Direct Computation of Nonoperating Return

Refer to the financial information of Costco Wholesale Corporation in P4-45 to answer the following requirements.

LO9

Costco Wholesale
Corporation (COST)

LO8

Costco Wholesale
Corporation (COST)

Required

a. Compute Costco's financial leverage (FLEV), Spread, and noncontrolling interest (NCI) ratio for 2016; recall, NNE = NOPAT − Net income.

b. Assume that Costco's return on equity (ROE) for 2016 is 20.71% and its return on net operating assets (RNOA) is 20.66%. Confirm computations to yield the relation: ROE = [RNOA + (FLEV × Spread)] × NCI ratio.

c. What do your computations of the nonoperating return in parts *a* and *b* imply about the company's use of borrowed funds?

LO1, 4, 5, 6, 7

Under Armour Inc. (UA)

P4-48. **Analysis and Interpretation of Profitability**

Balance sheets and income statements for **Under Armour Inc.** are found in P4-42. Use these financial statements to answer the requirements.

Required

a. Compute net operating profit after tax (NOPAT) for 2015. Assume that the combined federal and state statutory tax rate is 37%.

b. Compute net operating assets (NOA) for 2015 and 2014.

c. Compute RNOA and disaggregate it into net operating profit margin (NOPM) and net operating asset turnover (NOAT) for 2015. Comment on the drivers of RNOA.

d. Compute return on equity (ROE) for 2015.

e. Comment on the difference between ROE and RNOA. What does this relation suggest about Under Armour's use of debt?

LO1, 8

Under Armour Inc. (UA)

P4-49. **Compute ROE and Nonoperating Return**

Refer to the balance sheets and income statement for **Under Armour Inc.** in P4-42. Use these financials to answer the requirements. For the 2015 fiscal year, Under Armour had a return on net operating assets (RNOA) of 15.17%.

a. Compute ROE.

b. Compute net nonoperating obligations (NNO).

c. Compute FLEV and Spread.

d. Show that ROE = RNOA + (FLEV × Spread).

e. What is the nonoperating return for the year? What does this suggest about Under Armour's use of debt?

LO4, 5, 6, 7, 8

Nordstrom Inc. (JWN)

P4-50. **Analysis and Interpretation of Profitability**

Balance sheets and income statements for **Nordstrom Inc.**, follow. Refer to these financial statements to answer the requirements.

NORDSTROM INC. Consolidated Statements of Earnings			
For Fiscal Years Ended ($ millions)	Jan. 30, 2016	Jan. 31, 2015	Feb. 01, 2014
Net sales.	$14,095	$13,110	$12,166
Credit card revenues	342	396	374
Total revenues	14,437	13,506	12,540
Cost of sales and related buying and occupancy costs	(9,168)	(8,406)	(7,737)
Selling, general and administrative expenses	(4,168)	(3,777)	(3,453)
Earnings before interest and income taxes	1,101	1,323	1,350
Interest expense, net	(125)	(138)	(161)
Earnings before income taxes	976	1,185	1,189
Income tax expense	(376)	(465)	(455)
Net earnings	$ 600	$ 720	$ 734

NORDSTROM INC. Consolidated Balance Sheets		
in millions	Jan. 30, 2016	Jan. 31, 2015
Assets		
Current assets		
Cash and cash equivalents	$ 595	$ 827
Accounts receivable, net	196	2,306
Merchandise inventories	1,945	1,733
Current deferred tax assets, net	—	256
Prepaid expenses and other	278	102
Total current assets	3,014	5,224
Land, buildings and equipment, net	3,735	3,340
Goodwill	435	435
Other assets	514	246
Total assets	$7,698	$9,245
Liabilities and Shareholders' Equity		
Current liabilities		
Accounts payable	$1,324	$1,328
Accrued salaries, wages and related benefits	416	416
Other current liabilities	1,161	1,048
Current portion of long-term debt	10	8
Total current liabilities	2,911	2,800
Long-term debt, net	2,795	3,123
Deferred property incentives, net	540	510
Other liabilities	581	372
Shareholders' equity		
Common stock, no par value: 1,000 shares authorized;		
173.5 and 190.1 shares issued and outstanding	2,539	2,338
Retained earnings	(1,610)	166
Accumulated other comprehensive loss	(58)	(64)
Total shareholders' equity	871	2,440
Total liabilities and shareholders' equity	$7,698	$9,245

Required

a. Compute net operating profit after tax (NOPAT) for 2016. Assume that the combined federal and state statutory tax rate is 37%.

b. Compute net operating assets (NOA) for 2016 and 2015.

c. Compute RNOA and disaggregate it into net operating profit margin (NOPM) and net operating asset turnover (NOAT) for 2016; confirm that RNOA = NOPM × NOAT.

d. Compute net nonoperating obligations (NNO) for 2016 and 2015. Confirm the relation: NOA = NNO + Shareholders' equity.

e. Compute return on equity (ROE) for 2016.

f. Infer the nonoperating return component of ROE for 2016.

g. Comment on the difference between ROE and RNOA. What does this relation suggest about Nordstrom's use of equity capital?

LO4, 5, 6, 7, 8
Mondelēz
International Inc.
(MDLZ)

P4-51. **Analysis and Interpretation of Profitability**

Mondelēz International Inc. is one of the world's largest snacks companies, with a brand portfolio that includes: Nabisco, Oreo, Milka, Cadbury and Trident. The company's balance sheets and income statements follow. Refer to these financial statements to answer the requirements.

MONDELĒZ INTERNATIONAL INC. Consolidated Statement of Earnings			
For the Years Ended December 31 (in millions)	2015	2014	2013
Net revenues	$29,636	$34,244	$35,299
Cost of sales	18,124	21,647	22,189
Gross profit	11,512	12,597	13,110
Selling, general and administrative expenses	7,577	8,457	8,679
Asset impairment and exit costs	901	692	273
Gains on coffee business transactions and divestitures	(6,822)	—	(30)
Loss on deconsolidation of Venezuela	778	—	—
Amortization of intangibles	181	206	217
Operating income	8,897	3,242	3,971
Interest and other expense, net	1,013	688	1,579
Earnings from continuing operations before income taxes	7,884	2,554	2,392
Provision for income taxes	593	353	60
Earnings from continuing operations	7,291	2,201	2,332
Earnings from discontinued operations, net of income taxes	—	—	1,603
Net earnings	7,291	2,201	3,935
Noncontrolling interest	24	17	20
Net earnings attributable to Mondelēz International	$ 7,267	$ 2,184	$ 3,915

MONDELĒZ INTERNATIONAL INC. Consolidated Balance Sheets		
As of December 31 (in millions, expect share data)	2015	2014
Assets		
Cash and cash equivalents	$ 1,870	$ 1,631
Trade receivables (net of allowances of $54 at 2015 and $66 at 2014)	2,634	3,802
Other receivables (net of allowances of $109 at 2015 and $91 at 2014)	1,212	949
Inventories, net	2,609	3,480
Deferred income taxes	—	480
Other current assets	633	1,408
Total current assets	8,958	11,750
Property, plant and equipment, net	8,362	9,827
Goodwill	20,664	23,389
Intangible assets, net	18,768	20,335
Prepaid pension assets	69	53
Equity method investments	5,387	662
Other assets	635	755
Total Assets	$62,843	$66,771

continued

As of December 31 (in millions, expect share data)	2015	2014
Liabilities.		
Short-term borrowings	$ 236	$ 1,305
Current portion of long-term debt	605	1,530
Accounts payable.	4,890	5,299
Accrued marketing.	1,634	2,047
Accrued employment costs	844	946
Other current liabilities	2,713	2,880
Total current liabilities.	10,922	14,007
Long-term debt	14,557	13,821
Deferred income taxes	4,750	5,512
Accrued pension costs.	2,183	2,912
Accrued postretirement health care costs	499	526
Other liabilities	1,832	2,140
Total liabilities	$34,743	$38,918
Equity		
Common stock, no par value (1,996,537,778 shares issued at 2015 and 2014)	—	—
Additional paid-in capital	31,760	31,651
Retained earnings	20,700	14,529
Accumulated other comprehensive losses	(9,986)	(7,318)
Treasury stock, at cost.	(14,462)	(11,112)
Total Mondelēz International shareholders' equity.	28,012	27,750
Noncontrolling interest	88	103
Total equity	28,100	27,853
Total liabilties and equity.	$62,843	$66,771

Required

a. Compute net operating profit after tax (NOPAT) for 2015. Assume that the combined federal and state statutory tax rate is 37%.

b. Compute net operating assets (NOA) for 2015 and 2014.

c. Compute RNOA and disaggregate it into net operating profit margin (NOPM) and net operating asset turnover (NOAT) for 2015; confirm that RNOA = NOPM × NOAT. The median NOPM and NOAT for companies in the packaged food industry is 5% and 2.1, with a median RNOA of 10.5%. Comment on NOPM and NOAT estimates for Mondelēz in comparison to industry medians.

d. Compute net nonoperating obligations (NNO) for 2015 and 2014. Confirm the relation: NOA = NNO + Total equity.

e. Compute return on equity (ROE) for 2015.

f. Infer the nonoperating return component of ROE for 2015.

g. Comment on the difference between ROE and RNOA. What does this relation suggest about Mondelēz's use of debt?

P4-52. **Direct Computation of Nonoperating Return**

Refer to the financial information of **Mondelēz International Inc.** in P4-51 to answer the following requirements.

LO8
Mondelēz International Inc. (MDLZ)

Required

a. Assume that 2015 net nonoperating expenses (NNE) are $638 million and that NOA is $41,628 million and $42,878 million in 2015 and 2014, respectively. Compute financial leverage (FLEV) and Spread for 2015.

b. Compute the 2015 return on equity. The NCI ratio for 2015 is 0.999. Confirm computations to yield the relation: ROE = [RNOA + (FLEV × Spread)] × NCI ratio.

c. What do your computations of the nonoperating return in parts a and b imply about the company's use of borrowed funds?

LO7   **P4-53.**   **Analysis and Interpretation of Profit Margin, Asset Turnover, and RNOA for Several Companies**

Net operating profit margin (NOPM) and net operating asset turnover (NOAT) for several selected companies for the most recent year follow.

Abbott Laboratories (ABT)

FedEx Corp. (FDX)

CVS Health Corp. (CVS)

Mondelēz International Inc. (MDLZ)

Walgreens Boots Alliance (WBA)

Caterpillar Inc. (CAT)

Target Corp. (TGT)

	NOPM	NOAT
Abbott Laboratories............	11.73%	0.95
FedEx Corp.	4.04%	3.50
CVS Health Corp.	3.76%	2.77
Mondelēz International Inc.......	26.76%	0.70
Walgreens Boots Alliance Inc.....	3.52%	3.18
Caterpillar Inc.	5.26%	2.96
Target Corp.	5.02%	5.47

Required

a. Graph NOPM and NOAT for each of these companies. Do you see a pattern that is similar to that shown in this module? Explain. (The graph in the module is based on medians for selected industries; the graph for this problem uses fewer companies than in the module and, thus, will not be as smooth.)

b. Consider the trade-off between profit margin and asset turnover. How can we evaluate companies on the profit margin and asset turnover trade-off? Explain.

LO1, 2, 3   **P4-54.**   **Compute and Analyze Measures for DuPont Disaggregation Analysis**

Costco Wholesale Corporation (COST)

Refer to the fiscal 2016 financial data of **Costco Wholesale Corporation** in P4-45 to answer the following requirements. (Perform the required computations from the perspective of a Costco shareholder.)

Required

a. Compute ROE for fiscal 2016.

b. Confirm that ROE equals ROE computed using the component measures for profit margin, assets turnover, and financial leverage using: ROE = PM × AT × FL.

c. Compute adjusted ROA (assume a statutory tax rate of 37%).

LO1, 2, 3   **P4-55.**   **Compute and Analyze Measures for DuPont Disaggregation Analysis**

Mondelēz International Inc. (MDLZ)

Refer to the fiscal 2015 financial data of **Mondelēz International Inc.** in P4-51 to answer the following requirements. (Perform the required computations from the perspective of a Modelez shareholder.)

Required

a. Compute ROE for fiscal 2015.

b. Confirm that ROE equals ROE computed using the component measures for profit margin, assets turnover, and financial leverage using: ROE = PM × AT × FL.

c. Compute adjusted ROA (assume a statutory tax rate of 37%). Compare the adjusted and unadjusted ROA ratios and explain why they differ.

IFRS Applications

LO6, 7   **I4-56.**   **Compute, Disaggregate, and Interpret RNOA of Competitors**

Shell Oil Company

Royal Dutch Shell

BP Limited

Shell Oil Company is the U.S.-based subsidiary of **Royal Dutch Shell**, a multinational oil company headquartered in The Hague, The Netherlands. **BP Limited** is a multinational oil company headquartered in London U.K. Selected balance sheet and income statement information and assumptions for both Royal Dutch Shell and BP follow.

$ millions	2015 Sales	2015 NOPAT	2015 Net Operating Assets	2014 Net Operating Assets
Royal Dutch Shell..........	$272,156	$3,389	$187,332	$192,604
BP Limited	225,982	(4,135)	122,238	131,457

a. Compute the 2015 return on net operating assets (RNOA) for each company.

b. Disaggregate RNOA into net operating profit margin (NOPM) and net operating asset turnover (NOAT) for each company.

c. Discuss any differences in these ratios for each company. What drives the differences in RNOA observed in parts a and b?

I4-57. **Compute, Disaggregate, and Interpret ROE and RNOA**

LO1, 6, 7
Husky Energy Inc.

Headquartered in Calgary, Alberta, **Husky Energy Inc.** is a publicly traded, integrated energy company, with extensive conventional oil and natural gas assets, substantial heavy oil production and a range of midstream and downstream operations. Operating assets include refineries, upgrading facilities, and pipelines. Selected fiscal year balance sheet and income statement information for Husky Energy follow (Canadian $ millions).

2014 Sales	2014 Net Income	2014 NOPAT	2014 Net Operating Assets	2013 Net Operating Assets	2014 Stockholders' Equity	2013 Stockholders' Equity
$25,052	$1,258	$1,349	$24,300	$20,078	$20,575	$20,078

a. Compute the 2014 return on equity (ROE) and the 2014 return on net operating assets (RNOA).
b. Disaggregate RNOA into net operating profit margin (NOPM) and net operating asset turnover (NOAT).
c. Compute the percentage of RNOA to ROE, and compute Husky's nonoperating return for 2014.

I4-58. **Compute and Interpret Liquidity and Solvency Ratios**

LO9
BHP Billiton

Headquartered in Melbourne, Australia, **BHP Billiton**, is a leading global resources company that operates in diverse commodity and geographic markets. The company is among the world's top producers of iron ore, metallurgical coal, conventional and non-conventional oil and gas, copper, energy coal, aluminum, manganese, uranium, nickel, and silver. BHP Billiton is traded on the Australian Securities Exchange (ASX) and also listed in London, Johannesburg, and New York.

$ millions	Total Current Assets	Total Current Liabilities	Pretax Income	Interest Expense	Total Liabilities	Stockholders' Equity
2014	$22,296	$18,064	$21,735	$995	$66,031	$79,143
2015	16,369	12,853	8,056	702	54,035	64,768

a. Compute the current ratio for each year and discuss any trend in liquidity. Is the company sufficiently liquid? Explain. What additional information about the accounting numbers comprising this ratio might be useful in helping us assess liquidity? Explain.
b. Compute times interest earned and the liabilities-to-equity ratio for each year and discuss any noticeable change.
c. What is the overall assessment of the company's liquidity and solvency from the analyses in parts a and b? Explain.

I4-59. **Analysis and Interpretation of Profitability**

LO4, 5, 6, 7, 8
BT Group plc

BT Group is one of the largest telecommunications services companies in the world, headquartered in London, United Kingdom. Balance sheets and income statements for BT Group follow.

BT GROUP PLC Group Income Statement		
Year Ended March 31 (in millions)	2016	2015
Revenue	£19,042	£17,979
Operating costs	(15,307)	(14,499)
Operating profit (loss)	3,735	3,480
Finance expense	(749)	(876)
Finance income	37	17
Net finance expense	(712)	(859)
Share of post tax profit of associates and joint ventures	6	24
Profit (loss) before taxation	3,029	2,645
Taxation	(441)	(510)
Profit (loss) for the year	£ 2,588	£ 2,135

BT GROUP PLC Group Balance Sheet		
At March 31 (in millions)	**2016**	**2015**
Non-current assets		
Intangible assets	£15,436	£ 3,170
Property, plant and equipment	16,010	13,505
Derivative financial instruments	1,462	1,232
Investments	46	44
Associates and joint ventures	24	26
Trade and other receivables	233	184
Deferred tax assets	1,247	1,559
	34,458	19,720
Current assets		
Programme rights	225	118
Inventories	189	94
Trade and other receivables	4,063	3,140
Current tax receivable	65	65
Derivative financial instruments	177	97
Investments	2,918	3,523
Cash and cash equivalents	497	434
	8,134	7,471
Current liabilities		
Loans and other borrowings	3,237	1,900
Derivative financial instruments	48	168
Trade and other payables	7,289	5,276
Current tax liabilities	271	222
Provisions	171	142
	11,016	7,708
Total assets less current liabilities	£31,576	£19,483
Non-current liabilities		
Loans and other borrowings	£11,032	£ 7,868
Derivative financial instruments	863	927
Retirement benefit obligations	6,382	7,583
Other payables	1,105	927
Deferred tax liabilities	1,262	948
Provisions	552	422
	21,196	18,675
Equity		
Ordinary shares	499	419
Share premium	1,051	1,051
Own shares	(115)	(165)
Merger reserve	8,422	998
Other reserves	690	487
Retained loss	(167)	(1,982)
Total equity	10,380	808
	£31,576	£19,483

Required

a. Compute net operating profit after tax (NOPAT) for 2016. Assume that the tax rate is 20%, which is the statutory rate for the U.K.

b. Compute net operating assets (NOA) for 2016 and 2015.

c. Compute and disaggregate RNOA into net operating profit margin (NOPM) and net operating asset turnover (NOAT) for 2016.

d. Compute net nonoperating obligations (NNO) for 2016 and 2015. Confirm the relation: NOA = NNO + Total equity.

e. Compute return on equity (ROE) for 2016.

f. What is the nonoperating return component of ROE for 2016?

g. Comment on the difference between ROE and RNOA. What inference can we draw from this comparison?

I4-60. **Analysis and Interpretation of Liquidity and Solvency**

LO9
BT Group plc

BT Group is one of the largest telecommunications services companies in the world, headquartered in London, United Kingdom. Refer to the financial information for BT Group in I4-59 to answer the following requirements.

Required

a. Compute the current ratio and quick ratio for 2016 and 2015. Comment on any observed trends.

b. Compute times interest earned and liabilities-to-equity ratios for 2016 and 2015. Comment on any noticeable changes.

c. Summarize the findings about the company's liquidity and solvency. Do we have any concerns about its ability to meet its debt obligations?

Management Applications

MA4-61. **Gross Profit and Strategic Management**

LO3
One way to increase overall profitability is to increase gross profit. This can be accomplished by raising prices and/or by reducing manufacturing costs.

Required

a. Will raising prices and/or reducing manufacturing costs unambiguously increase gross profit? Explain.

b. What strategy might you develop as a manager to (i) increase product prices, or (ii) reduce product manufacturing cost?

MA4-62. **Asset Turnover and Strategic Management**

LO3
Increasing net operating asset turnover requires some combination of increasing sales and/or decreasing net operating assets. For the latter, many companies consider ways to reduce their investment in working capital (current assets less current liabilities). This can be accomplished by reducing the level of accounts receivable and inventories, or by increasing the level of accounts payable.

Required

a. Develop a list of suggested actions that you, as a manager, could undertake to achieve these three objectives.

b. Describe the marketing implications of reducing receivables and inventories, and the supplier implications of delaying payment. How can a company reduce working capital without negatively impacting its performance?

MA4-63. **Ethics and Governance: Earnings Management**

LO3
Companies are aware that analysts focus on profitability in evaluating financial performance. Managers have historically utilized a number of methods to improve reported profitability that are cosmetic in nature and do not affect "real" operating performance. These methods are subsumed under the general heading of "earnings management." Justification for such actions typically includes the following arguments:

- Increasing stock price by managing earnings benefits stockholders; thus, no one is hurt by these actions.

- Earnings management is a temporary fix; such actions will be curtailed once "real" profitability improves, as managers expect.

Required

a. Identify the affected parties in any scheme to manage profits to prop up stock price.

b. Do the ends (of earnings management) justify the means? Explain.

c. To what extent are the objectives of managers different from those of stockholders?

d. What governance structure can you envision that might inhibit earnings management?

Ongoing Project

(This ongoing project began in Module 1 and continues through most of the book; even if previous segments were not completed, the requirements are still applicable to any business analysis.)

Analysis of financial statements commonly includes ROE disaggregation and scrutiny of its components as explained in this module.

1. Compute ROE for all three years reported on the income statement. (*Hint:* Do your companies report noncontrolling interest on the income statement and balance sheet? If so, make certain to use income available to the controlling interest (NICI) in the numerator and equity of the controlling interest (CI) in the denominator. To compute ROE for three years, we must determine average stockholders' equity for three years, which means we need four balance sheet amounts. Because the balance sheets of each company will report only two years, we must collect prior years' financial statements.)

2. Compute RNOA and its two components (NOPM and NOAT) for all three years reported on the income statement. We must use balance sheet numbers for four years to obtain three averages of net operating assets. Examine the income statements and balance sheets to determine the operating and nonoperating items. (*Hint:* Use an online source to understand any line items not described in the textbook. Use cell references in the spreadsheet to compute NOPAT and NOA and the various ratios.)

Compare ROE and RNOA and identify differences over time and between the companies. Evaluate the companies' returns and answer questions such as the following:

- Which company is more profitable?
- How do the operating and nonoperating portions of ROE compare?
- Compare the ROE and RNOA with the graph on page 4-26. If the ratios for the companies under analysis differ from the graph, is there an explanation?
- Is the net operating profit margin similar for the two companies? Given that they are roughly in the same industry, major differences should prompt further exploration.
- Are the companies' net operating asset turnover ratios similar or markedly different? Calculate and compare the cash conversion cycle for each year.

3. Determine FLEV and Spread and the noncontrolling interest ratio (if applicable). Show that:

$$\text{ROE} = [\text{RNOA} + (\text{FLEV} \times \text{Spread})] \times \textbf{Noncontrolling interest ratio}$$

Compare the components of the equation for each company over time and follow up on any differences.

4. Compute the four ratios from Appendix 4B for the recent three years for each company: current ratio, quick ratio, liabilities-to-equity, and times interest earned. Compare the ratios for the companies under analysis and identify differences over time and between companies. Evaluate each company's ability to pay its debts in the short term (liquidity) and the long term (solvency), and in the process address the following:

- Which company is more liquid? More solvent?
- Look at the bar chart in Exhibit 4B.1. If the ratios differ from the industry norm, is there an explanation(s)?
- Do the ratios change over time? If yes, does the change make sense given the economic and competitive factors that affect the industry and the companies?

Solutions to Review Problems

Review 4-1—Solution ($ millions)

$$\text{ROE} = \frac{\$8,981}{(\$59,698 + \$56,654)\,/\,2} = 15.44\%$$

Review 4-2—Solution ($ millions)

ROE = Return on assets (ROA) × Financial leverage

$$\text{ROA} = \frac{\$8,981}{(\$113,481 + \$105,070)\,/\,2} = 8.22\% \qquad \text{Financial leverage} = \frac{(\$113,481 + \$105,070)/2}{(\$59,698 + \$56,654)/2} = 1.878$$

8.22% × 1.878 = 15.44% = ROE

Review 4-3—Solution ($ millions)

a. $$\text{ROA} = \frac{\$8,981}{(\$113,481 + \$105,070)/2} = 8.22\%$$

$$\text{PM} = \frac{\$8,981}{\$49,161} = 18.27\%$$

$$\text{AT} = \frac{\$49,161}{(\$113,481 + \$105,070)/2} = 0.45$$

ROA = Profit Margin (PM) × Asset Turnover (AT)

8.22% = 18.27% × 0.45

b. ($49,161 − $19,480)/$49,161 = 60.38%

c. Days sales outstanding = 365 × [($5,344 + $5,157)/2]/$49,161 = 38.98

Days inventory outstanding = 365 × [($1,627 + $1,591)/2]/$19,480 = 30.15

Days accounts payable outstanding = 365 × [($1,104 + $1,032)/2]/$19,480 = 20.01

Cash conversion cycle = 38.98 + 30.15 − 20.01 = 49.12

d. ($53,774/$59,707) = 0.90

Review 4-4—Solution ($ millions)

a.

$ millions	July 25, 2015	July 26, 2014
Accounts receivable, net	$ 5,344	$ 5,157
Inventories	1,627	1,591
Financing receivables, net	4,491	4,153
Deferred tax assets	2,915	2,808
Other current assets	1,490	1,331
Property and equipment, net	3,332	3,252
Financing receivables, net	3,858	3,918
Goodwill	24,469	24,239
Purchased intangible assets, net	2,376	3,280
Other assets	3,163	3,267
Total operating assets	$53,065	$52,996
Accounts payable	$ 1,104	$ 1,032
Income taxes payable	62	159
Accrued compensation	3,049	3,181
Deferred revenue	9,824	9,478
Other current liabilities	5,687	5,451
Income taxes payable	1,876	1,851
Deferred revenue	5,359	4,664
Other long-term liabilities	1,459	1,748
Total operating liabilities	$28,420	$27,564

b.

$ millions	July 25, 2015	July 26, 2014
Total operating assets	$53,065	$52,996
Total operating liabilities	28,420	27,564
Net operating assets (NOA)	$24,645	$25,432

Review 4-5—Solution ($ millions)

a. NOPBT for fiscal 2015, labeled "Operating income" on the income statement, is $10,770 million.

b. The nonoperating activities at Cisco, labeled "Interest and other income, net" on the income statement totals $(431) which represents nonoperating income (similar to Intel, Cisco has a large amount of investments, nonoperating assets that generate interest income in excess of the company's interest expense).

Interest and other income, net × Statutory tax rate = Tax shield.

$(431) × 37% = $(159)

Provision for income taxes.	$2,220
Add back tax shield	+ (159)
Tax on operating profit	$2,061

c.

Net operating profit before tax (NOPBT)	$10,770
Deduct tax on operating profit	(2,061)
Net operating profit after tax (NOPAT)	$ 8,709

Review 4-6—Solution ($ millions)

$$\text{RNOA} = \frac{\$8,709}{(\$24,645 + \$25,432)/2} = 34.78\%$$

Review 4-7—Solution ($ millions)

$$\text{NOPM} = \frac{\$8,709}{\$49,161} = 17.72\%$$

$$\text{NOAT} = \frac{\$49,161}{(\$24,645 + \$25,432)/2} = 1.963$$

RNOA = Net Operating Profit Margin (NOPM) × Net Operating Asset Turnover (NOAT)

$$34.78\% = 17.72\% \times 1.963$$

Review 4-8—Solution ($ millions)

a. ROE = Operating return (RNOA) + Nonoperating return

15.44% = 34.78% + Nonoperating return

Nonoperating return = 15.44% − 34.78%

Nonoperating return = (19.34)%

b. Net nonoperating obligations = Nonoperating liabilities − Nonoperating assets

	July 25, 2015	July 26, 2014
Short-term debt	$ 3,897	$ 508
Long-term debt	21,457	20,337
Nonoperating liabilities	$ 25,354	$ 20,845
Cash and cash equivalents	$ 6,877	$ 6,726
Investments	53,539	45,348
Nonoperating assets	$ 60,416	$ 52,074
Net nonoperating obligations (NNO)	$(35,062)	$(31,229)

FLEV = Average NNO/Average Total Equity

$$FLEV = \frac{[\$(35,062) + \$(31,229)]/2}{(\$59,707 + \$56,661)/2} = (0.5697)$$

Cisco's FLEV is negative because the company holds significant amounts of nonoperating assets that exceed the company's nonoperating liabilities. That is, NNO is negative which makes FLEV negative.

c.

Nonoperating expense (income)	$(431)
Tax shield at 37%	159
Net nonoperating expense (NNE)	$(272)

$$NNEP = \frac{\$(272)}{[\$(35,062) + \$(31,229)]/2} = 0.82\%$$

d. RNOA − NNEP = 34.78% − 0.82% = 33.96%

e. 15.44% = [34.78% + (−0.5697 × 33.96%)] × 1.00014

RNOA   FLEV   Spread   NCIR

$$NCIR = \frac{\$8,981 / \$8,981}{\$58,176 / \$58,184} = 1.00014$$

Review 4-9—Solution ($ millions)

a. Current ratio 2015: $76,283/$23,623 = 3.23

Current ratio 2014: $67,114/$19,809 = 3.39

Quick ratio 2015: ($6,877 + $53,539 + $5,344)/$23,623 = 2.78

Quick ratio 2014: ($6,726 + $45,348 + $5,157)/$19,809 = 2.89

b. Liabilities-to-equity ratio 2015: $53,774/$59,707 = 0.90

Liabilities-to-equity ratio 2014: $48,409/$56,661 = 0.85

Times interest earned ratio 2015: $10,770/$566 = 19.03

Module 5

Revenues, Receivables, and Operating Expenses

Learning Objectives

LO1 Apply revenue recognition principles and assess results. (p. 5-3)

LO2 Examine and evaluate sales allowances. (p. 5-9)

LO3 Analyze deferred revenue. (p. 5-12)

LO4 Evaluate how foreign currency exchange rates affect revenue. (p. 5-13)

LO5 Analyze accounts receivable and uncollectible amounts. (p. 5-16)

LO6 Evaluate operating expenses and discontinued operations. (p. 5-22)

LO7 Interpret pro forma and non-GAAP disclosures. (p. 5-27)

PFE

Market cap: $210,240 mil

Total assets: $167,460 mil

Revenues: $40,851 mil

Net income: $6,986 mil

Pfizer's business is to discover, develop, manufacture, and market leading prescription medicines. Its operating activities include research and development, manufacturing, advertising, sales, after-sale customer support, and all administrative functions to support operations.

Pfizer reported revenues of $48,851 million in 2015. To recognize revenue, Pfizer makes numerous estimates and choices. Should Pfizer recognize revenue when a customer places an order, when the drug order is shipped, when the customer receives the shipment, or when the customer pays the invoice? What if customers can return unwanted or unused products? What happens if Pfizer discounts prices on large orders or receives payment from its customers in advance of delivery? How do its sales practices affect the timing of revenue recognition? How should Pfizer treat revenue and expenses for transactions made in foreign currencies?

Pfizer's sales are made on credit, and at the end of 2015, Pfizer's receivables for those credit sales totaled $8,176 million, or about 5% of its total assets. By Pfizer granting credit, there is the risk that some customers will fail to pay amounts owed. It is important that Pfizer estimate the portion of accounts receivable that is uncollectible. This results in a more reliable receivables amount on the balance sheet and a better estimate of future cash flows.

This module explains accounting for, and interpretation of, revenues, receivables, and operating expenses, including research and development (R&D). As Pfizer responds to market opportunities, it launches and discontinues certain operations, and we consider the income statement and the balance sheet consequences of such actions. We conclude with a discussion of pro forma and non-GAPP numbers that companies frequently include in Securities and Exchange Commission filings and that analysts commonly cite. [Sources: *Pfizer*, 2015 10-K]

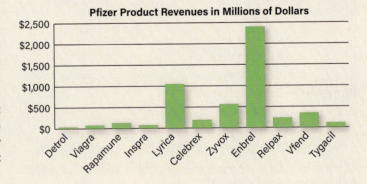

Pfizer Product Revenues in Millions of Dollars

Detrol, Viagra, Rapamune, Inspra, Lyrica, Celebrex, Zyvox, Enbrel, Relpax, Vfend, Tygacil

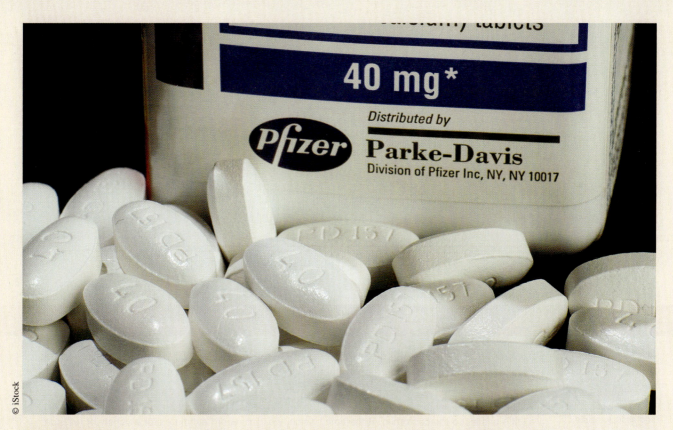

© iStock

Road Map

LO	Learning Objective | Topics	Page	eLecture	Guided Example	Assignments
5-1	**Apply revenue recognition principles and assess results.** Recognition Rules :: Complications :: Long-Term Contracts :: Reporting	5-3	e5–1	Review 5-1	1, 8, 12, 13, 14, 15, 16, 17, 31, 32, 33, 34, 48, 50, 51, 52, 55, 56
5-2	**Examine and evaluate sales allowances.** Accounting :: Reporting & Disclosure :: Analysis	5-9	e5–2	Review 5-2	1, 17, 25, 39, 48, 55, 56
5-3	**Analyze deferred revenue.** Accounting :: Illustrations :: Disclosure and Interpretation	5-12	e5–3	Review 5-3	10, 23, 24, 25, 52
5-4	**Evaluate how foreign currency exchange rates affect revenue.** Economics :: Cash Flows :: Income :: Forecasting	5-13	e5–4	Review 5-4	5, 6, 22, 27, 35, 38, 46, 57, 58
5-5	**Analyze accounts receivable and uncollectible amounts.** Aging :: Accounting :: Magnitude Analysis :: Quality Analysis	5-16	e5–5	Review 5-5	2, 7, 18, 19, 20, 21, 41, 42, 43, 44, 45, 49, 53, 54
5-6	**Evaluate operating expenses and discontinued operations.** Cost of Sales :: SG&A :: R&D :: Discontinued Operations	5-22	e5–6	Review 5-6	4, 11, 28, 30, 36, 37, 40, 51
5-7	**Interpret pro forma and non-GAAP disclosures.** Regulation G :: SEC Warnings :: Market Assessments	5-27	e5–7	Review 5-7	9, 29, 30, 38, 47, 56

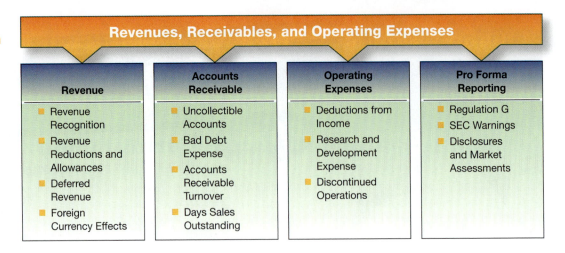

Revenue

LO1

MBC Apply revenue recognition principles and assess results.

Pfizer reported $48,851 million in revenues in 2015, see Exhibit 5.1. The amount Pfizer reports on the income statement is "net" of certain deductions as described in the revenue recognition footnote.

Revenue Recognition We record revenues from product sales when the goods are shipped and title passes to the customer. At the time of sale, we also record estimates for a variety of revenue deductions, such as rebates, chargebacks, sales allowances, and sales returns.

The revenue recognition footnote raises a number of issues related to revenue.

- **Revenue recognition.** Should revenue be recognized when an order is received? When products are shipped? When they are paid for? How should we recognize revenue for long-term contracts spanning more than one year?

Exhibit 5.1 ■ Pfizer's Income Statement

Year Ended December 31 ($ millions)	2015	2014
Revenues	$48,851	$49,605
Costs and expenses:		
Cost of sales	9,648	9,577
Selling, informational, and administrative expenses	14,809	14,097
Research and development expenses	7,690	8,393
Amortization of intangible assets	3,728	4,039
Restructuring charges and certain acquisition-related costs	1,152	250
Other (income)/deductions—net	2,860	1,009
Income from continuing operations before provision for taxes on income	8,965	12,240
Provision for taxes on income	1,990	3,120
Income from continuing operations	6,975	9,119
Discontinued operations:		
Income from discontinued operations—net of tax	17	(6)
Gain/(loss) on disposal of discontinued operations—net of tax	(6)	55
Discontinued operations—net of tax	11	48
Net income before allocation to noncontrolling interests	6,986	9,168
Less: Net income attributable to noncontrolling interests	26	32
Net income attributable to Pfizer Inc.	$ 6,960	$ 9,135

■ **Sales and related allowances.** How should we treat the variety of revenue deductions Pfizer references in its revenue footnote?

■ **Deferred revenue.** How should we treat advance payments made by customers? Should we only recognize revenue when we receive cash?

■ **Foreign currency exchange rates.** How are revenues that are denominated in foreign currencies accounted for? In what way do fluctuations in exchange rates affect Pfizer's income statement?

Revenue (or sales) is the "top line" on the income statement and it includes transactions between the company and its customers during the past year (or, in the case of quarterly reports, during the prior three months). Revenue does not include gains or losses on the sale of assets such as property, plant and equipment (PPE) or investments (or the divestiture of a subsidiary company), nor does it include interest and dividend income on investments or gains or losses on their sale. Those items appear in different sections of the income statement.

Revenue Recognition Rules

The Financial Accounting Standards Board (FASB) has new rules for recognition of revenue that go into effect for financial reporting periods beginning after December 15, 2017, or earlier if companies choose. Although the new rules modify the way in which companies recognize revenue, the core revenue recognition principles remain the same.

■ **Revenue is recognized when the good or service is provided to the customer.**

■ **It is not necessary to receive cash to recognize revenue.**

Every sale involves a contract (express or implied) between the customer and the company whereby the company agrees to transfer a good or service to the customer and the customer agrees to pay for it. All that is necessary for the company to recognize revenue is for the good to be transferred or the service performed. It is at that point the company's *performance obligation* under the contract is satisfied and revenue can be recognized.

Many sales are *on credit* (also said to be *on account*), meaning the customer has agreed to pay the company in the future. The company still recognizes revenue when the good or service is transferred to the customer, and it records an account receivable that it collects at a later date. The recognition of revenue is unaffected by the delayed receipt of cash if the company has fulfilled its performance obligation. (We discuss accounting for accounts receivable later in this module.)

When is the good or service transferred to the customer and the performance obligation satisfied? GAAP provides examples of evidence; a transfer is likely when the customer has:

■ Legal title to the good or has received the service.

■ Physical possession of the good.

■ Assumed the risks and rewards of owning the good or receiving the service.

■ Accepted the good or service and has an obligation to pay the company.

In retail settings, the transfer of the good is straightforward. We take physical possession of groceries or clothes we purchase. In that case, the store has satisfied its obligation, and it recognizes revenue at point of sale.

Revenue recognition can get a bit more complicated, however, if the company sells a bundle of goods for a single price or delivers the goods over a period of time. **Microsoft** provides a typical example in its 2015 10-K.

Revenue recognition for multiple-element arrangements requires judgment to determine if multiple elements exist, whether elements can be accounted for as separate units of accounting, and if so, the fair value for each of the elements. Microsoft enters into arrangements that can include various combinations of software, services, and hardware. Where elements are delivered over different periods of time, and when allowed under U.S. GAAP, revenue is allocated to the respective elements based on their relative selling prices at the inception of the arrangement, and revenue is recognized as each element is delivered.

Complications of Revenue Recognition

The basic revenue recognition principle that applies to a retail store also applies to Microsoft. But Microsoft faces more challenges in administering the principle because, unlike a retail store, Microsoft's sales routinely involve multiple products and services that are sold for one price. The added complication is that Microsoft delivers some products and services at the point of sale and others in the future. In such cases, Microsoft must first separate the sale into distinct goods or services that can each be valued on a stand-alone basis. Then, it recognizes revenue on each *distinct* component. Components are generally viewed as distinct if the:

- Customer can use the good or service on its own.
- Good or service is not highly interrelated with other goods or services sold per the contract.[1]

Once Microsoft separates the sale into distinct product and service components, it apportions the total contract price to each component and then determines the point at which each component is transferred to the customer. Transfers can occur at many points in time, in which case, revenue is recognized over a period of time.

Following are other common types of transactions with complicated revenue recognition. Even though each of these situations is a bit more involved than the sale of groceries, the basic requirement for revenue recognition is the same: recognize revenue when the good or service is transferred to the customer.

- **Nonrefundable up-front fees.** In some industries, companies charge a fee at or near inception of the contract. These fees could be for setup, access, activation, initiation, or membership. In many cases, even though a nonrefundable up-front fee compels the company to undertake an activity at or near contract inception, that activity does not result in the transfer of the goods or service. Instead, the fee is an advance payment for future goods or services and, therefore, would be recognized as revenue when those future goods or services are provided.

- **Bill-and-hold arrangements.** Bill-and-hold arrangements arise when a customer is billed for goods that are ready for delivery, but the company "holds" the goods for shipment later. Revenue is recognized at the later date, when control of the goods transfers to the customer.

- **Consignment sales.** If the seller acts as an *agent* for another company, such as to sell another company's product on its website, it does not recognize the gross amount of the sale as revenue. Instead, it only recognizes its *commission* from the sale. Indicators that the seller is an agent include when the seller:
  - Is not responsible for fulfilling the contract.
  - Does not bear any risk associated with the inventory being sold.
  - Does not have full control over the selling price.
  - Does not bear the risk of loss for uncollectible accounts receivable.
  - Receives commission or another fee from the sale.

- **Licenses.** Software sales can take the form of licensing arrangements of intellectual property (IP). Revenue recognition depends on whether the arrangement confers a right to *use* the IP (arguing for recognition of revenue when the customer can first use the IP) or whether the contract promises to provide *access* to the company's IP (arguing for revenue recognition over a period of time).

- **Franchises.** Franchisors often sell both goods and consulting and other administrative services. The franchisor must separate the sale into separate components for goods and services and recognize the appropriate revenue for each component. The goods component is recognized when the goods are transferred to the buyer. The services component, which might involve the use of a trade name or a license or other service provided over time. In such cases, revenue should be recognized as the services are delivered.

- **Variable consideration.** Portions of the selling price may depend upon future events, such as incentive payments, royalties, and volume discounts. If the good or service has been transferred to

---

[1] For example, under a construction contract, the contractor simultaneously delivers the construction materials and a finished building. Only the finished building is the subject of the contract—the separate materials would not be considered distinct products under the contract.

the customer and the payment is likely and can be reasonably estimated, the seller should estimate the expected amount to be received and recognize that amount in current revenue.

Performance Obligations Satisfied Over Time

Many companies enter into long-term contracts that obligate them to future performance. For example:

- **Turner Construction** enters into a construction contract to build Yankee stadium.
- **Boeing** enters into a contract with domestic and international airlines and the U.S. military to construct planes.
- **Hewlett-Packard Enterprise** enters into long-term contracts with companies to design IT services, implement systems, and provide cloud storage.

For these types of contracts, companies must determine the point at which their performance obligations have been satisfied so that revenue can be recognized. For a multiple-year contract, waiting to recognize revenue until the good is delivered would be problematic because the expense of constructing the product would be recognized as incurred whereas the revenue recorded only at the end of the contract. Although total revenue, expense, and profit would be accurate over the life of the contract, financial statements issued during the interim would report losses with a substantial profit at the end, making evaluation of the company's financial performance difficult during the interim.

Cost-to-Cost Method An accepted practice for many years has been to recognize revenue over the life of a long-term contract in amounts that track the percentage of completion of the contract. Companies typically use the percentage of projected contract costs that have been incurred to estimate the contract's percentage of completion. This method is called the *cost-to-cost method*. (There are other ways to determine percentage of completion, but cost-to-cost is the most common.) For example, if a company incurred 15% of the total expected cost to create the product in the current period, it would recognize revenues equal to 15% of the contract amount. **Raytheon**, a U.S. conglomerate ranked 126 among the Fortune 500, specializes in aerospace, defense, civil government, and cybersecurity. The company describes its revenue recognition practice as follows.

> We generally use the cost-to-cost measure of progress for our long-term contracts unless we believe another method more clearly measures progress towards completion of the contract. Under the cost-to-cost measure of progress, the extent of progress towards completion is measured based on the ratio of costs incurred to date to the total estimated costs at completion of the contract.

To illustrate accounting for long-term contracts using the *cost-to-cost* approach, assume Bayer Construction signs a $10 million contract to construct a building. Bayer estimates construction will take two years and will cost $7,500,000. This means the contract yields an expected gross profit of $2,500,000 over two years. The following table summarizes construction costs incurred each year and the revenue Bayer recognizes.

	Construction Costs Incurred	Percentage Complete	Revenue Recognized
Year 1	$4,500,000	$\frac{\$4,500,000}{\$7,500,000}=60\%$	$10,000,000 × 60% = $6,000,000
Year 2	$3,000,000	$\frac{\$3,000,000}{\$7,500,000}=40\%$	$10,000,000 × 40% = $4,000,000

This table reveals Bayer would report $6 million in revenue and $1.5 million ($6 million − $4.5 million) in gross profit on the construction project in the first year; it would report $4 million in revenue and $1 million ($4 million − $3 million) in gross profit in the second year.

The following template captures the recognition of revenue and expense over this two-year period (M indicates millions).

On the left margin, T-account entries:

```
COGS...4.5M
  Cash.....4.5M
      COGS
  4.5M |
      Cash
        | 4.5M


AR ...6M
  REV.......6M
       AR
   6M |
      REV
        | 6M


COGS 3M
  Cash......3M
      COGS
   3M |
      Cash
        | 3M


AR ...4M
  Rev ......4M
       AR
   4M |
      Rev
        | 4M
```

	Balance Sheet						Income Statement		
Transaction	Cash Asset	+ Noncash Assets	= Liabil- ities	+ Contrib. Capital	+ Earned Capital		Rev- enues	– Expen- ses	= Net Income
Year 1: Record $4.5M construction costs	−4.5M Cash		=		−4.5M Retained Earnings			− +4.5M Cost of Sales	= −4.5M
Year 1: Recognize $6M revenue on partly completed contract		+6M Accounts Receivable	=		+6M Retained Earnings		+6M Revenue	−	= +6M
Year 2: Record $3M construction costs	−3M Cash		=		−3M Retained Earnings			− +3M Cost of Sales	= −3M
Year 2: Recognize $4M revenue for completed contract		+4M Accounts Receivable	=		+4M Retained Earnings		+4M Revenue	−	= +4M

Cost-to-Cost Reporting Bayer's reported revenues and expenses for years 1 and year 2 follow.

At December 31	Year 1	Year 2
Revenues	$6,000,000	$4,000,000
Expenses	4,500,000	3,000,000
Gross profit.	$1,500,000	$1,000,000

Over the two-year period, Bayer recognizes total revenues of $10 million, contract expenses of $7.5 million, and a contract gross profit of $2.5 million.

How Bayer recognizes profit on long-term contracts affects its income statements. In addition, there are often timing differences between when contract costs are paid and when the customer is billed for work performed. These timing differences affect the balance sheet. Raytheon describes the accounting for these timing differences in the following footnote.

> We receive advances, performance-based payments and progress payments from customers that may exceed costs incurred on certain contracts. We classify advance payments and billings in excess of costs incurred as current liabilities. Costs incurred in excess of billings are classified as contracts in process, net.

When Raytheon receives cash in advance of incurring costs under the contract, it records a liability that represents the obligation to deliver the product for which it has been paid. When Raytheon incurs costs to construct the product in excess of the amount it bills the customer, it recognizes that excess as a current asset, contracts in process, as illustrated in the "current assets" section of Raytheon's 2015 balance sheet.

At December 31 ($ millions)	2015	2014
Current assets		
Cash and cash equivalents.	$2,328	$ 3,222
Short-term investments	872	1,497
Contracts in process, net.	**5,564**	**4,985**
Inventories	635	414
Prepaid expenses and other current assets.	413	161
Total current assets.	$9,812	$10,279

The cost-to-cost method of revenue recognition requires an estimate of total costs. This estimate is made at the beginning of the contract and is typically the one used to bid the contract. However, estimates are inherently inaccurate. If the estimate changes during the construction period, the percentage of completion is computed as the total costs incurred to date divided by the *current* estimate of total anticipated costs (costs incurred to date plus total estimated costs to complete).

If total construction costs are underestimated, the percentage of completion is overestimated (the denominator is too low) and revenue and gross profit to date are overstated. The estimation process inherent in this method has the potential for inaccurate or even improper revenue recognition. In addition, estimates of remaining costs to complete projects are difficult for the auditors to verify. This uncertainty adds additional risk to financial statement analysis.

Business Insight ■ Disney's Revenue Recognition

The Walt Disney Company uses a percentage of completion method similar to the cost-to-cost method to determine the amount of production cost to match against film and television revenues. Following is an excerpt from its 10-K.

> Film and television costs include capitalizable production costs, production overhead, interest, development costs, and acquired production costs. . . . Film and television production, participation and residual costs are expensed over the applicable product life cycle based upon the ratio of the current period's revenues to estimated remaining total revenues (Ultimate Revenues) for each production. For film productions, Ultimate Revenues include revenues from all sources that will be earned within ten years from the date of the initial theatrical release. For television series, Ultimate Revenues include revenues that will be earned within ten years from delivery of the first episode, or if still in production, five years from delivery of the most recent episode, if later. For acquired film libraries, remaining revenues include amounts to be earned for up to twenty years from the date of acquisition.

As Disney pays production costs, it records those costs on the balance sheet as inventory. Then, as film and television revenues are recognized, the company matches a portion of production costs (from inventory) against revenues in computing income. Each period, the costs recognized are equal to the proportion of total revenues recognized in the period to the total revenues expected over the life of the film or television show. Thus, estimates of both costs and income depend on the quality of Disney's revenue estimates, which are, likely, imprecise.

Review 5-1 LO1

Part I   Indicate whether revenue should be recognized for each of the following independent situations.

1. A clothing store sells goods to customers who use the store's proprietary (captive) credit card. The store estimates that 2% of the clothes will be returned.
2. A customer purchases a copy machine whose purchase price includes an agreement under which the seller will provide monthly service of the machine for two years at no additional cost.
3. A health club charges an up-front fee to join. Customers are entitled to use the club for one year.
4. A company lists products of other companies on its website and receives a commission equal to a percentage of the selling price when the goods are sold.
5. A franchisor sells franchisees product for sale and provides accounting services on a monthly basis.

Part II   A construction company expends $500,000 for work performed under a contract with a total contract price of $3,000,000 and estimated costs of $2,500,000. It sends a bill to the customer for $400,000 under the terms of the contract.

1. How much revenue and gross profit should the company recognize in the income statement?

Solution on p. 5-51.   2. How is the $400,000 billing reported on the balance sheet?

Sales Allowances

LO2
Examine and evaluate sales allowances.

Many companies offer customers a variety of sales allowances, including rights of return, sales discounts for volume purchases, and retailer promotions (point-of-sale price markdowns and other promotions). All of these costs have the effect of reducing the amount of cash companies receive from sales. **Levi Strauss**, for example, discusses allowances in its 2015 10-K.

> The apparel market is characterized by low barriers to entry for both suppliers and marketers, global sourcing through suppliers located throughout the world, trade liberalization, continuing movement of product sourcing to lower cost countries, and the ongoing emergence of new competitors with widely varying strategies and resources. These factors have contributed, and may continue to contribute, to intense pricing pressure and uncertainty throughout the supply chain. This pressure could have the following effects:
> - result in reduced gross margins across our product lines, and
> - increase retailer demands for allowances, incentives and other forms of economic support.

Levi Strauss's gross profit margin declined from 50.2% in 2014 to 49.4% in 2015, and it explained that this reduction was "due to higher discounted sales across channels, reflecting a promotional marketplace and our efforts to manage our inventory to more appropriate levels."

Accounting for Sales Allowances

GAAP requires companies to report sales revenue at the net amount expected to be received in cash. This means companies are to deduct from gross sales the expected sales returns and other allowances. For example, Levi Strauss reports the following in its revenue recognition footnote.

> We recognize allowances for estimated returns in the period in which the related sale is recorded. We recognize allowances for estimated discounts, retailer promotions and other similar incentives at the later of the period in which the related sale is recorded or the period in which the sales incentive is offered to the customer.

To illustrate, when Levi Strauss recognizes revenue, it increases both sales and accounts receivable, and it also concurrently reduces the gross sales amount by estimated returns and allowances. Assume Levi

Strauss sells jeans costing $80 to a customer for $130 on account. Levi Strauss recognizes the revenue and cost of goods sold (COGS). Because Levi Strauss has offered its customers a right of return, and because prior experience leads the company to expect that returns will occur, Levi Strauss must also set up a reserve for estimated returns. Let's assume Levi Strauss expects returns to amount to 3% of sales. In the same period in which Levi Strauss records the revenue, it also records the estimated returns as follows.

	Balance Sheet						Income Statement		
Transaction	Cash Asset	+ Noncash Assets	= Liabil-ities	+ Contrib. Capital	+ Earned Capital		Rev-enues	− Expen-ses	= Net Income
Establish allowance for sales returns (3% × $130)		−3.90 Allowance for Sales Returns	=		−3.90 Retained Earnings		−3.90 Sales Returns and Allowances	−	= −3.90
Adjust COGS ([$80/$130] × $3.90)		2.40 Inventory Adj. for Estimated Returns	=		2.40 Retained Earnings			− −2.40 COGS Adj. for Estimated Returns	= 2.40

In the first entry, Levi Strauss reduces sales by $3.90 to reflect expected merchandise returns with a corresponding reduction of accounts receivable (similar to the allowance for uncollectible accounts). The second entry reduces COGS by the COGS percentage ($80/$130) and increases inventory for the expected returns. Levi Strauss income statement (through gross profit) follows for the illustration above.

Sales, net ($130 − $3.90)...	$126.10
Cost of goods sold ($80 − $2.40)	77.60
Gross profit..	$ 48.50

Levi Strauss will also report accounts receivable of $126.10, and the estimated product returns of $2.40 will be reported in its inventory account.

Reporting Sales Allowances

Levi Strauss provides a reconciliation of the beginning and ending balances for the past three years for its allowance for sales returns and for its sales discounts and incentives in its 2015 10-K. This is a typical disclosure for companies with sales returns, discounts, and other sales allowances.

Sales Returns ($ thousands)	Balance at Beginning of Period	Additions Charged to Net Sales	Deductions	Balance at End of Period
November 29, 2015	$ 32,191	$152,471	$150,641	$ 34,021
November 30, 2014	$ 32,675	$138,577	$139,061	$ 32,191
November 24, 2013	$ 40,575	$137,613	$145,513	$ 32,675

Sales Discounts and Incentives ($ thousands)	Balance at Beginning of Period	Additions Charged to Net Sales	Deductions	Balance at End of Period
November 29, 2015	$ 98,416	$306,497	$318,639	$ 86,274
November 30, 2014	$110,572	$322,164	$334,320	$ 98,416
November 24, 2013	$102,361	$331,937	$323,726	$110,572

Analysis of Sales Allowances

Two metrics warrant further investigation as we analyze this disclosure.

1. **"Additions charged to net sales" as compared with gross sales for both sales returns and sales discounts and incentives.** This ratio reveals any effects of the pricing pressure on net sales and we would expect the percentage of sales allowances to gross sales to increase (thus reducing net sales) as pricing pressure increases.

2. **Adequacy of the allowance account.** This analysis compares the dollar amount Levi Strauss estimates for future sales returns with the amount actually realized during the year.

For the past three years, Levi Strauss's allowances as a percentage of gross sales have ranged from 8.8% to 9.3% as follows.

Levi's Sales Allowances Analysis ($ thousands)	2015	2014	2013
Net sales.	$4,494,493	$4,753,992	$4,681,691
Allowances:			
Sales returns.	152,471	138,577	137,613
Sales discounts	306,497	322,164	331,937
Gross sales.	$4,953,461	$5,214,733	$5,151,241
Allowances/Gross sales.	9.3%	8.8%	9.1%

The increased pricing pressure Levi Strauss discusses in its analysis of sales above, is evident in the increase in allowances as a percentage of gross sales from 8.8% in 2014 to 9.3% in 2015, which reduced net sales by 50 basis points (½ percentage point). For a company with a net profit margin of 4.7% in 2015, a 50-basis-point reduction in net sales is substantial, and analysts would focus on the allowance percentage in future years to look for further pricing pressure.

To assess the adequacy of the allowance account, we compare annual "deductions" from the allowance account (realized sales returns) with the "additions charged to net sales." The *additions* column is the amount by which the allowance account increased during the year to reflect the company's estimate of future sales returns. Levi Strauss subtracted this amount from gross sales to arrive at net sales reported on the income statement. The deductions column is the actual sales returns from customers along with the cost of realized discounts and other incentives that it gave to its customers to promote sales.

To analyze the adequacy of the allowance account, we look for divergence between the amount charged to sales and the cost actually incurred. If the amount charged to sales is greater than the cost incurred, the company has reduced sales more than is needed and has reduced its profit accordingly. If the amount charged to sales is less than the cost incurred, the company has under-reserved the allowance account, thus increasing profit. Over the three-year period, we see that the two accounts are approximately equal. So, there is not much concern for the adequacy of Levi Strauss's allowance account in 2015.

Review 5-2 LO2

Nordstrom Inc. reports the following on its 2015 income statement.

$ millions	Fiscal 2015	Fiscal 2014	Fiscal 2013
Net sales.	$14,095	$13,110	$12,166
Cost of sales.	9,168	8,406	7,737

The company made the following footnote disclosure.

> We recognize revenue net of estimated returns and excluding sales taxes. Revenue from sales to customers shipped directly from our stores, website and catalog, which includes shipping revenue when applicable, is recognized upon estimated receipt by the customer. We estimate customer merchandise returns based on historical return patterns and reduce sales and cost of sales accordingly. Activity in the allowance for sales returns, net, for the past three fiscal years is as follows:

continued

$ millions	Fiscal 2015	Fiscal 2014	Fiscal 2013
Allowance at beginning of year	$ 160	$ 128	$ 116
Additions	2,720	2,129	1,880
Returns, net	(2,710)	(2,097)	(1,868)
Allowance at end of year	$ 170	$ 160	$ 128

Required

1. The reconciliation includes "Additions" of $2,720 million. What does this item refer to?
2. The reconciliation includes "Returns, net" of $2,710 million. What does this item refer to?
3. Compute the following two metrics for the past three years and comment on the results.
    a. Sales returns/Gross sales.
    b. Adequacy of the allowance account.

Solution on p. 5-51.

Unearned (Deferred) Revenue

eLectures **LO3**

MBC Analyze deferred revenue.

In some industries, it is common to receive cash before recording revenue. Customers might pay in advance for special orders, make deposits for future services, or buy concert tickets, subscriptions, or gift cards. In those cases, companies must record unearned revenues, and only record revenue when those products and services are provided. Specifically, deposits or advance payments are not recorded as revenue until the company performs the services owed or delivers the goods. Until then, the company's balance sheet shows the advance payment as a liability (called unearned revenue or deferred revenue) because the company is obligated to deliver those products and services.

Unearned revenue is particularly common among retailers that:

■ Receive advance payments from customers for products that are not yet delivered.

■ Offer gift cards.

■ Sell extended-protection plan contracts.

Lowe's Companies, the home improvement company, provides several examples of transactions that require revenue to be deferred, as illustrated in the following excerpts from the revenue recognition footnote in its 2015 10-K.

- Revenues from product installation services are recognized when the installation is completed. Deferred revenues associated with amounts received for which customers have not yet taken possession of merchandise or for which installation has not yet been completed were $619 million and $545 million at January 29, 2016, and January 30, 2015, respectively.

- Revenues from stored-value cards, which include gift cards and returned merchandise credits, are deferred and recognized when the cards are redeemed. The liability associated with outstanding stored-value cards was $459 million and $434 million at January 29, 2016, and January 30, 2015, respectively, and these amounts are included in deferred revenue on the consolidated balance sheets. The Company recognizes income from unredeemed stored-value cards at the point at which redemption becomes remote.

- The Company sells separately-priced extended protection plan contracts under a Lowe's-branded program. The Company recognizes revenue from extended protection plan sales on a straight-line basis over the respective contract term.

As we evaluate profitability for companies that report substantial amounts of deferred revenue, we must be aware of changes in deferred revenue liabilities on the balance sheet. Should deferred revenue liabilities decrease, we infer the company's *current* reported revenue was collected from customers in a *prior* accounting period and there have been fewer new prepayments for which revenue will be recognized in future periods. Such a trend could predict future declines in revenue and profit.

Lowe's provides a schedule that allows us to track the deferred revenue liability related to its extended protection plan contracts.

$ millions	2015	2014	2013
Deferred revenue—extended protection plans, beginning of year.	$730	$730	$715
Additions to deferred revenue	350	318	294
Deferred revenue recognized	(351)	(318)	(279)
Deferred revenue—extended protection plans, end of year	$729	$730	$730

In 2015, Lowe's received cash from customers of $350 million for new extended protection plan contracts and recognized revenue of $351 million that related to cash received in prior years. As a result, the balance in the deferred revenue liability account remained at the level Lowe's reported in the prior year (as well as in 2014). From this reconciliation, we would have no reason to predict future revenue declines.

Review 5-3 LO3

AT&T Corporation grants credit to most of its customers. However, a fraction of customers prepay for their wireless services. In addition, the company sells prepaid phone cards and gift certificates.

During 2015, these prepaid product lines generated revenue of $4,662 million, and AT&T reported the following deferred revenue liability on its December 31, 2015, balance sheet.

$ millions	2015	2014
Advanced billings and customer deposits	$4,682	$4,105

Required

1. What economic rationale can we provide to explain why AT&T offers prepaid services?
2. Use the balance sheet information and the total revenue for 2015 to determine the total amount of cash collected from prepaid customers during 2015.
3. If AT&T gift cards have no expiration date, when, if ever, would the company record revenue on the cards? Explain.

Solution on p. 5-52.

Foreign Currency Effects on Revenue

LO4
Evaluate how foreign currency exchange rates affect revenue.

Exhibit 5.1 shows **Pfizer**'s income statement that reports a decrease in revenues from $49,605 million in 2014 to $48,851 million in 2015. Pfizer describes this decrease as follows.

> Revenues in 2015 were $48.9 billion, a decrease of 2% compared to 2014. This reflects an operational increase of $3.0 billion, or 6%, which was more than offset by the unfavorable impact of foreign exchange of $3.8 billion, or 8%.

The reduction of Pfizer's revenues was not the only foreign exchange impact. The strengthening US dollar ($US) also reduced Pfizer's COGS and other operating expenses. Because Pfizer is profitable (revenues > expenses), the foreign currency fluctuations had the net effect of reducing Pfizer's net income for 2015.

Companies routinely conduct business in foreign currencies. Although Pfizer's U.S.-based companies may write purchase and sales contracts that are denominated in foreign currencies, Pfizer's foreign subsidiaries likely transact business almost entirely in foreign currencies. These foreign subsidiaries not only conduct business in foreign currencies, they also maintain their accounting records in currencies other than the $US. Before the financial statements of those subsidiaries can be consolidated with the U.S. parent company, they must first be translated into $US.

As the $US strengthens vis-à-vis other world currencies in which Pfizer conducts its business, each $US buys more of the foreign currency. Conversely, each foreign currency buys less $US. When Pfizer translates a subsidiary's foreign-currency denominated income statement into $US, the income statement shrinks: reported revenues, expenses, and profit are all smaller than before the dollar strengthened. In the consolidation process, Pfizer must also translate the foreign subsidiary's balance sheet and, with a strengthening $US, the foreign currency-denominated balance sheet shrinks as well, reporting lower assets, liabilities, and equity. We examine the income statement effects here, and we defer our discussion of the balance sheet effects to a later module, when we discuss the consolidation process.

Foreign Currency and Cash Flows

Following are three examples of the ways in which foreign currency gains and losses may affect *cash flow*.

1. **When the $US company transacts business denominated in foreign currencies.** A U.S. company might denominate a sales contract in Euros, for example. If the $US strengthens between the date of the sale and the ultimate collection of the Euro-denominated account receivable, the U.S. company suffers a foreign currency transaction loss. Conversely, if the U.S. company purchases goods, the foreign currency denominated account payable would shrink and less $US would be required to settle the obligation, resulting in a foreign currency transaction gain.

2. **When the U.S. parent company borrows money that is denominated in a foreign currency.** If the U.S. parent company borrows in foreign currencies and the $US strengthens, it will take less in $US to repay the foreign currency-denominated liability. If the company planned to repay the loan with $US, the company will realize a gain as it repays the foreign currency-denominated loan.

3. **When the foreign subsidiary's cash is repatriated to the United States.** Most foreign subsidiaries maintain cash in foreign bank accounts (local to the subsidiary) for use in ongoing operations. If the U.S. parent repatriates that cash, however, say, by a cash dividend from the subsidiary to the U.S. parent company, a foreign currency transaction loss can arise if the dollar strengthens before the foreign currency is converted into $US to pay the dividend.

The difference between these three situations and the translation adjustment that arises solely from the consolidation of Pfizer's foreign subsidiaries' profits is that these three transactions describe *realized* losses, whereas the translation losses that Pfizer reports above are *unrealized*.

Regarding contracts denominated in foreign currencies (#1 above) and borrowing in foreign currencies (#2 above), companies frequently hedge their exposures to these potential realized losses by using financial derivative securities. These derivative securities act like an insurance policy to offset the income statement effects of realized gains and losses by transferring some of the risk for foreign currency fluctuations to other parties who are willing to accept that risk for a fee. An effective hedging process reduces the effects of realized gains and losses and greatly reduces the impact on net income. We discuss hedging in more detail in a later module.

Regarding the repatriation of foreign earnings (#3 above), companies usually disclose in the tax footnote the amount of cash they deem as "permanently" reinvested in foreign subsidiaries and which is not subject to tax. Pfizer, for example, discloses, "As of December 31, 2015, we have not made a U.S. tax provision on approximately $80.0 billion of unremitted earnings of our international subsidiaries." These foreign earnings are not likely to be repatriated, but, instead, are likely retained abroad for use in the foreign subsidiary's operations.

Accordingly, the *realized* foreign currency translation effects are likely small, and the foreign currency translation losses (the reduction in revenues, expenses, and profit Pfizer discusses above) are, therefore, likely to be primarily *unrealized* noncash losses.

Foreign Currency and Income

So, how should we treat the foreign currency translation effects on the income statement given that the currency fluctuations reduced Pfizer's revenues, expenses, and profit? One approach would be to back out the revenue and expense effects to yield income statements that are not affected by these foreign currency fluctuations. Pfizer identifies numerous effects on its 2015 income statement in the management discussion and analysis (MD&A) section of its 10-K, including the following.

1. Revenues were reduced by $3.8 billion.
2. COGS was reduced by 10% (approximately $965 million).
3. Foreign currency loss ($806 million) was related to Venezuelan operations.

Backing out these foreign currency translation effects on the 2015 income statement (with similar adjustments to prior year financial statements) would allow us to better isolate Pfizer's operating profit without the distortion of foreign currency exchange rate effects.

Foreign Currency and Future Results

Companies frequently provide guidance for analysts to forecast future income statements. Pfizer's 2015 10-K includes the following guidance to analysts for 2016.

Our Financial Guidance for 2016

The following table provides our financial guidance for full-year 2016:

Reported revenues	$49.0 to $51.0 billion
Adjusted cost of sales as a percentage of reported revenues	21.0% to 22.0%
Adjusted selling, informational and administrative expenses	$13.2 to $14.2 billion
Adjusted research and development expenses	$7.3 to $7.8 billion
Adjusted other (income)/deductions	Approximately ($300 million) of income
Effective tax rate on adjusted income	Approximately 24.0%
Reported diluted Earnings per Share (EPS)	$1.54 to $1.67
Adjusted diluted EPS	$2.20 to $2.30

Pfizer also includes a footnote to its guidance relating to foreign currency effects.

Guidance for 2016 reported revenues also reflects the anticipated negative impact of $2.3 billion as a result of unfavorable changes in foreign exchange rates relative to the U.S. dollar compared to foreign exchange rates from 2015, including $0.8 billion due to the estimated significant negative currency impact related to Venezuela. The anticipated negative impact on reported and adjusted diluted EPS resulting from unfavorable changes in foreign exchange rates compared to foreign exchange rates from 2015 is approximately $0.16, including $0.07 due to the estimated significant negative currency impact related to Venezuela.

Because foreign currency effects are largely noncash items, they should not impact our valuation of the company. Our forecasts of Pfizer's income statement, then, might exclude these effects to better isolate the forecasting of operating cash flow.

Review 5-4 LO4

On January 16, 2015, AT&T closed a $US2.5 billion acquisition of Mexican wireless provider Iusacell from Grupo Salinas. AT&T acquired all of Iusacell's wireless properties, including licenses, network assets, retail stores, and 9.2 million subscribers. In its 2015 annual report, AT&T disclosed these facts ($ millions).

- Following our 2015 acquisitions of wireless businesses in Mexico, we have additional foreign operations that are exposed to fluctuations in the exchange rates used to convert operations, assets and liabilities into U.S. dollars. Since the dates of acquisition, when compared to the U.S. dollar, the . . . Mexican peso exchange rate has depreciated 13.1%.
- Our 2015 international operating revenues were $4,102, with **$1,952 attributable to wireless revenues in Mexico**.
- We are exposed to foreign currency exchange risk through our foreign affiliates and equity investments in foreign companies. We do not hedge foreign currency translation risk in the net assets and income we report from these sources. However, we do hedge a portion of the exchange risk involved in anticipation of highly probable foreign currency-denominated transactions and cash flow streams, such as those related to issuing foreign-denominated debt, receiving dividends from foreign investments, and other receipts and disbursements.

continued

The $US to Mexican peso exchange rates during 2015 were as follows.

	1 $US = pesos		1 $US = pesos
31-Jan	14.975945	31-Jul	18.216009
28-Feb	14.948455	31-Aug	16.734763
31-Mar	15.241323	30-Sep	16.901119
30-Apr	15.388116	31-Oct	16.500190
31-May	15.378000	30-Nov	16.601480
30-Jun	15.695152	31-Dec	17.249549

Required

1. Confirm AT&T's claim concerning the peso devaluation.
2. Using the exchange rates provided, determine what AT&T's revenue attributable to wireless operations in Mexico would have been had the peso not been devalued (i.e., had it remained at the January 31 level of 14.975945). For this question, assume the Mexican operating revenues were realized evenly from February 1 onward.
3. Did the peso devaluation increase or decrease AT&T's net income for 2015 when measured in $US? Explain.
4. Explain why AT&T does not hedge foreign currency translation risk in the net assets and income of its foreign subsidiaries.
5. AT&T states that it does hedge foreign currency-denominated transactions such as debt issuances and dividend payments. Why is that policy different than the "no hedge" policy for the net assets and income of its foreign subsidiaries?

Solution on p. 5-52.

Accounts Receivable

Pfizer reports $8,176 million of trade accounts receivable in the current asset section of its balance sheet.

LO5 Analyze accounts receivable and uncollectible amounts.

As of December 31 ($ millions)	2015	2014
Cash and cash equivalents	$ 3,641	$ 3,343
Short-term investments	19,649	32,779
Trade accounts receivable, less allowance for doubtful accounts: 2015—$384; 2014—$412	**8,176**	**8,401**

Selling goods on account carries the risk that some customers encounter financial difficulty and are unable to pay the amount due. GAAP recognizes this possibility and requires companies to estimate the dollar amount of receivables that are likely to be uncollectible and to report only the net collectible amount on the balance sheet. Pfizer reports net receivables of $8,176 million and estimates that $384 million of its total accounts receivable are uncollectible. From this, we can determine that the gross accounts receivable (the total amount customers owe to Pfizer) is $8,560 million ($8,176 million + $384 million). Pfizer estimates, therefore, that 4.5% ($384 million/$8,560 million) of the total amount of receivables owed, is likely uncollectible.

Aging Analysis of Receivables

Companies frequently employ an **aging analysis** of their accounts receivable to estimate the uncollectible amounts. An aging analysis groups accounts receivable by number of days past due (days the scheduled due date for payment). A common grouping method uses 30-day or 60-day intervals, as shown in the following.

Age of Accounts	Receivable Balance	Estimated Percent Uncollectible	Estimated Uncollectible Accounts
Current	$ 50,000	2%	$1,000
1–60 days past due	30,000	3%	900
61–90 days past due	15,000	4%	600
Over 90 days past due.	5,000	8%	400
Total	$100,000		$2,900

In this example, we assume the seller's credit terms are a typical "2/10, net 30" (customers receive a 2% discount from the amount owed if they make payment within 10 days of the invoice date; or the full amount owed is due 30 days from the invoice date). Accounts listed as 1–60 days past due are those 1 to 60 days past their due date. This would include an account that is 45 days outstanding for a net 30-day invoice. Given this aging schedule, the company draws upon its previous experience of uncollectible accounts of that age. The company has experience that if an account is 1–60 days past due, about 3% of the balance is not collected. Based on that past experience, the company estimates a potential loss of $900 for the $30,000 in the 1–60 days past due group. As expected, the percent uncollectible increases with the age of the account.

The company estimates that $2,900, or 2.9% of its $100,000 of gross accounts receivable, is likely uncollectible. The net amount, $97,100, represents the company's best estimate of what it expects to ultimately collect from its customers.

Accounting for Accounts Receivable

To account for uncollectible amounts, companies use an allowance account similar to the ones discussed above for sales returns and other allowances. The *allowance for uncollectible accounts* (also called the allowance for doubtful accounts) reduces the gross amount of receivables that are reported on the balance sheet.

To illustrate, assume the company sells goods on account for $100,000 and, at the end of the accounting period, performs an aging analysis and establishes the allowance for uncollectible accounts in the amount of $2,900. Our financial statement effects for the sale and the estimate of uncollectible accounts receivable are as follows.

		Balance Sheet						Income Statement		
Transaction	Cash Asset	+ Noncash Assets	= Liabil- ities	+ Contrib. Capital	+ Earned Capital		Rev- enues	– Expen- ses	= Net Income
Sale on account		100,000 Accounts Receivable =			100,000 Retained Earnings		100,000 Sales	–	= 100,000
Establish allowance for uncollectible accounts and record bad debts expense		–2,900 Allowance for Uncollectible = Accounts			–2,900 Retained Earnings			–2,900 – Bad Debts Expense	= –2,900

AR. . . . 100,000
    Rev . . . 100,000

AR	
100,000	

Rev	
	100,000

BDE . . 2,900
    AU. 2,900

BDE	
2,900	

AU	
	2,900

The allowance for uncollectible accounts is subtracted from the gross accounts receivable, and the net amount collectible is reported on the balance sheet.

Accounts receivable (gross amount owed)	$100,000
Less: Allowance for uncollectible accounts.	(2,900)
Accounts receivable, net (reported on balance sheet).	$ 97,100

Companies typically report the allowance for uncollectible accounts along with accounts receivable as follows.

> Accounts receivable, less allowance for uncollectible accounts of $2,900 . . . . $97,100

By setting up the allowance, the company has established a reserve, or a cushion, that it can use to absorb credit losses as they occur. To see how this works, assume a customer who owes $500 files for bankruptcy. If the company determines the receivable is now uncollectible, it must write off the receivable. This is absorbed by the allowance for uncollectible accounts as follows.

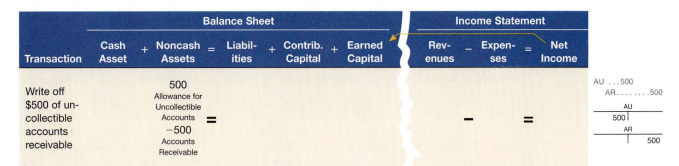

The write off of the uncollectible account receivable results in the following balances at the end of the period.

> | | | |
> |---|---|---|
> | Accounts receivable (gross amount owed) . . . . | $99,500 | ($100,000 − $500) |
> | Less: Allowance for uncollectible accounts . . . . | (2,400) | ($2,900 − $500) |
> | Accounts receivable, net (reported on balance sheet) . . . . | $97,100 | |

We see that the net amount of accounts receivable the company will report at the end of the period is the same $97,100 balance it reported *before* the write-off of the uncollectible account (i.e., because the write-off was completely absorbed by the allowance account established in the previous period.) This leaves the reported amount of net accounts receivable on the balance sheet unchanged. The write-off used up some of the reserve as the allowance decreased from $2,900 to $2,400. Future write-offs will reduce the allowance further. Each period, the company replenishes the allowance account and then draws it down for write-offs.

Analysis of Accounts Receivable–Magnitude

An important analysis tool for accounts receivable is to determine the magnitude and quality of the receivables. The relative magnitude of accounts receivable is usually measured with respect to sales volume using any or all of the following ratios. (Average accounts receivable is a simple average: (Current year balance + Prior year balance)/2.

■ **Accounts receivable turnover**

$$\text{Accounts receivable turnover ratio} = \frac{\text{Sales}}{\text{Average accounts receivable}}$$

■ **Accounts receivable as a percentage of sales**

$$\text{Accounts receivable as a percentage of sales} = \frac{\text{Average accounts receivable}}{\text{Sales}}$$

■ **Days sales outstanding (DSO)**

$$\text{Days sales outstanding} = \frac{365 \times \text{Average accounts receivable}}{\text{Sales}}$$

DSO is, arguably, the most intuitive of the three ratios, and it reveals the number of days, on average, that accounts receivable are outstanding before they are paid. The DSO statistic can be:

- Compared with the company's established credit terms to investigate if the company's customers are conforming to those credit terms.
- Computed over several years for the same company to investigate trends.
- Compared with peer companies.

A lower accounts receivable turnover ratio, a higher percentage of accounts receivable to sales, and a lengthening of the DSO all provide a signal that accounts receivable have grown more quickly than sales. Generally, such a trend is not favorable for two possible reasons.

- **The company is becoming more lenient in granting credit to its customers.** Perhaps this is in response to greater competition, or perhaps the company is finding it difficult to maintain sales volume and is reaching for additional volume by selling to new customers with weaker credit scores.

- **Credit quality is deteriorating.** If existing customers are not paying on time, the level of accounts receivable relative to the level of sales will increase. This will be highlighted in the DSO statistic, which will increase as the percentage of receivables to sales grows. (A third explanation is that the mix of products sold has changed toward markets with longer payment terms.)

What further steps can analysts take to assess an adverse trend in DSO? A first step is to review the MD&A section of the 10-K to learn management's interpretation of the adverse trend. A second step is to review the financial press, analyst reports, and other external reports about the company to glean additional insight.

The ratios we highlight above are often reported in commercial databases that are regularly used by analysts. For example, **Standard & Poors' Capital IQ** reports the following data for **Pfizer**.

Pfizer Inc. (NYSE:PFE) Financial Ratios					
Ratios for Fiscal Period Ending	**2015**	**2014**	**2013**	**2012**	**2011**
Asset turnover					
Total asset turnover	0.3	0.3	0.3	0.3	0.3
Fixed asset turnover.	3.8	4.1	4.0	3.8	3.5
Accounts receivable turnover.	5.9	5.6	5.2	4.6	4.6
Inventory turnover	1.4	1.5	1.5	1.5	1.6
Short-term liquidity					
Current ratio	1.5	2.6	2.4	2.2	2.1
Quick ratio	1.2	2.2	1.9	1.6	1.5
Cash from operations to current liabilities	0.5	0.8	0.8	0.6	0.7
Average days sales outstanding	61.9	65.3	70.9	79.5	79.1
Average days inventory outstanding	254.9	239.0	241.5	244.6	232.2
Average days payable outstanding	110.5	137.9	120.3	134.8	139.5
Average cash conversion cycle	206.4	166.5	192.1	189.2	171.7

We have highlighted the accounts receivable turnover ratio and the days sales outstanding (DSO) ratio. To compute these ratios for 2015, we use Pfizer's 2015 sales of $48,851 million and its accounts receivable, net of $8,176 million and $8,401 million for 2015 and 2014, respectively:

$$2015 \text{ accounts receivable turnover} = \frac{\$48,851}{(\$8,176 + \$8,401)/2} = 5.89 \text{ times}$$

$$\text{Days sales outstanding} = \frac{365 \times (\$8{,}176 + \$8{,}401)/2}{\$48{,}851} = 61.9 \text{ days}$$

A review of the Capital IQ data reveals that Pfizer's accounts receivable turnover ratio has increased over the past five years—a good sign. The downward trend for DSO is another way to measure the positive trend. The metric has declined by 17 days from 79.1 days in 2011 to 61.9 days in 2015.

Collecting receivables more quickly increases operating cash flow. At the current sales volume of $48,851 million, the average sales per day is $133.8 million ($48,851 million/365), and collecting receivables 17 days more quickly generates an additional $2,275 million of cash ($133.8 million/day × 17 days).

Analysis of Accounts Receivable—Quality

To analyze the quality of accounts receivable, we focus on the allowance for uncollectible accounts. Companies are required to report on their balance sheet, the amount of accounts receivable they expect to collect (the gross amount of accounts receivable less the estimated uncollectible accounts). Levi Strauss reports its accounts receivable as follows in its 2015 balance sheet.

$ thousands	Nov. 29, 2015	Nov. 30, 2014
Current assets		
Cash and cash equivalents.	$318,571	$298,255
Trade receivables, net of allowance for doubtful accounts of $11,025 and $12,704	**498,196**	**481,981**

The company also includes Schedule II in its 10-K, where it reports a "roll forward" of the allowance for uncollectible accounts that shows movements in the account.

Allowance for Doubtful Accounts ($ thousands)	Balance at Beginning of Period		Additions Charged to Expenses		Deductions		Balance at End of Period
November 29, 2015	$12,704	+	$1,875	−	$3,554	=	$11,025
November 30, 2014	$18,264	+	$ 662	−	$6,222	=	$12,704
November 24, 2013	$20,738	+	$1,158	−	$3,632	=	$18,264

Reconciling the allowance account from the beginning to the end of the year yields useful insights. The allowance account began 2015 with a balance of $12,704 thousand. Levi Strauss increased the allowance by $1,875 thousand and recognized bad debt expense (included in selling, general and administrative expense) equal to that amount. The allowance was reduced by $3,554 thousand to absorb the write-off of uncollectible accounts receivable during 2015 and ended the year with a balance of $11,025 thousand. The decrease in the account during the year means that Levi Strauss wrote off more than it added to its allowance account. This has been the trend for the past three years—Levi Strauss has written off $13,408 thousand ($3,554 + $6,222 + $3,632) while only increasing the allowance account by $3,695 thousand ($1,875 + $662 + $1,158).

Because Levi Strauss has not replenished the allowance account for the amount of the write-offs for three years, the balance of the allowance account has declined from $20,738 thousand at the beginning of 2013 to $11,025 thousand at the end of 2015. This would not be an issue if gross receivables had declined proportionately, but this is not the case. Instead, the allowance account as a percentage of gross accounts receivable has declined.

$ thousands	2015	2014
Accounts receivable (net)..	$498,196	$481,981
Allowance account..	11,025	12,704
Accounts receivable (gross).....................................	$509,221	$494,685
Allowance account / Accounts receivable (gross)......................	2.2%	2.6%

There are two possible interpretations for this trend.

1. **Credit quality has improved.** If Levi Strauss feels that the collectability of its remaining receivables has improved, it can feel confident in allowing the allowance for uncollectible accounts to decline. An improvement in credit quality might be plausible given that the recession ended during this period and customers are in better financial condition.

2. **Levi Strauss is underestimating the allowance account.** This is the more troubling of the two possibilities. Remember, Levi Strauss reports bad debt expense in its income statement when it *increases* its allowance account. Write-offs have no effect on profit; only the estimation of the loss affects income. So, Levi Strauss might be attempting to increase its profitability by not *adding* to the allowance account, and, thus, avoiding more bad debt expense.

How can we determine which of these two possibilities is more likely? We might compare Levi Strauss with its peer companies to determine if its ratio of allowance account to gross accounts receivable is higher or lower. If Levi Strauss' ratio exceeds industry or peer benchmarks, then the decrease might be reasonable. If Levi Strauss' ratio is lower than industry or peer benchmarks, Levi Strauss may be attempting to inflate its earnings by avoiding the additional drag on profits from bad debt expense (maybe to meet analyst forecasts or to avoid a default in loan covenants). All we know for certain is the allowance account has declined, both in absolute dollar amount and as a percentage of gross accounts receivable. It is difficult to know the reasons unless the company discusses those reasons in its MD&A section of the 10-K or in conference calls with analysts.

Managerial Decision ■ You Are the Receivables Manager

You are analyzing your receivables for the period and you are concerned that the average collection period is lengthening. What specific actions can you take to reduce the average collection period? [Answer, p. 5-32]

Review 5-5 LO5

AT&T Corporation reported the following information on its December 31, 2015, balance sheet.

$ millions	2015	2014
Accounts receivable—net of allowances for doubtful accounts of $704 and $454	$16,532	$14,527

Footnotes to the financial statements reported, "Credit risks are assessed based on historical write-offs, net of recoveries, as well as an analysis of the aged accounts receivable balances with allowances generally increasing as the receivable ages."

Assume the company analyzed and aged its accounts receivable at December 31, 2015, and developed the following table.

$ millions	Accounts Receivable	% Uncollectible
Current.....................................	$12,650	0.5%
1–30 days past due	2,785	5%
31–60 days past due	854	15%
61–90 days past due	589	25%
91–120 days past due	207	55%
Over 120 days past due......................	151	75%

continued

AT&T's allowance for doubtful accounts had a balance of $454 million at January 1, 2015. Assume that during the year, the company wrote off accounts receivable totaling $1,166 million. This exceeded the balance in the account at the start of the year. In its 2015 Form 10-K filing, the company explained that the write-offs were higher than expected due to acquisitions of DIRECTV and wireless properties in Mexico in 2015.

Required
1. As of December 31, 2015, what amount does AT&T expect to collect from its customers?
2. What is the total amount AT&T customers owe the company at December 31, 2015?
3. Use the aging schedule to determine the required balance in the allowance account at December 31, 2015.
4. What amount of bad debt expense will AT&T report on its 2015 income statement?
5. In your opinion, are AT&T's accounts receivable of higher or lower quality in 2015 as compared with 2014?

Solution on p. 5-53.

Expenses and Losses

Pfizer's income statement in Exhibit 5.1 reports a number of expense and loss items.

eLectures **LO6**
MBC Evaluate operating expenses and discontinued operations.

Deductions from Income

The following expense and loss items reported by **Pfizer** are typical of many companies.

■ **Cost of sales.** This is the cost Pfizer incurred to make or buy the products it sold during the year. As goods are manufactured or purchased, the cost is recognized as inventory on the balance sheet. The inventory remains there until the product is sold, at which time the cost is transferred from the balance sheet into the income statement as cost of goods sold. Given that the product is sold, revenue from the sale of the product is also added to the income statement. The difference between revenue and cost of sales is the gross profit on the sale. We discuss this cost together with inventories in Module 6.

■ **Selling, informational and administrative expense.** Usually, this expense category is labelled Selling, general and administrative (SG&A) expense, and it includes a number of general overhead expense categories, such as:

● Salaries and benefits for administrative personnel and executives.

● Rent and utilities for office facilities.

● Marketing and selling expenses.

● IT, legal, and accounting expenses.

● Depreciation for Pfizer's depreciable assets that are used for administrative purposes (we discuss this expense together with property, plant, and equipment in a later module).

■ **Research and development expense.** This is the cost Pfizer incurs to conduct research for new products. We discuss this cost in a separate section below.

■ **Amortization of intangible assets.** When Pfizer acquires an intangible asset, such as a patent, it amortizes that cost over the useful life of the patent (the period of time Pfizer expects the patent to produce cash flow). Amortization expense is a noncash expense, similar to depreciation expense. Often, it is included with the SG&A expense.

■ **Restructuring charges.** This represents the cost Pfizer has incurred and expects to incur to restructure its operations, say, by the elimination of lines of business, consolidation of operations, reduction of the number of employees, and the like. We discuss restructuring charges in a later module.

■ **Provision for taxes on income.** The tax provision shown on the income statement relates to Pfizer's profit. These are taxes that will be paid to federal and state taxing authorities as well as income taxes levied by foreign governments and municipalities. We discuss the income tax expense in a later module. Other types of taxes, such as sales tax or employment taxes are included in SG&A and not with the income tax expense.

- **Discontinued operations.** This represents the operating profit (or loss) plus the gain (or loss) on the sale of businesses Pfizer has decided to divest. We discuss discontinued operations in a separate section below.

- **Income attributable to noncontrolling interest.** Noncontrolling interest arises because Pfizer has one or more subsidiaries where Pfizer does not own 100% of the voting stock. So, while Pfizer owns the controlling interest (> 50% of the voting stock), other shareholders own the balance of the stock (the noncontrolling interest). The income attributable to the noncontrolling interest is their portion of the subsidiary's income (and is added to the noncontrolling interest equity account on Pfizer's balance sheet). The remainder of the subsidiary's net income is credited to Pfizer's shareholders and is added to retained earnings on Pfizer's balance sheet.

Research and Development Expense

Companies in many industries depend heavily on research and development (R&D) for new and improved products and services. For these companies, R&D is critical because failure to offer "cutting edge" technology can lead to loss of market share and even bankruptcy. R&D costs broadly consist of the following.

- Salaries and benefits for researchers and developers.

- Supplies needed to conduct the research.

- Licensing fees for intellectual property or software used in the R&D process.

- Third-party payments to collaborators at other firms and universities.

- Laboratory and other equipment.

- Property and buildings to be used as research facilities. As we discuss in a later module, research facilities are included in PPE and the depreciation on research facilities is included in R&D expense each year.

Accounting for R&D is straightforward: R&D costs are expensed as incurred.

R&D Spending

Exhibit 5.2 shows the median level of R&D spending in 2015 for the S&P 500 firms that report R&D expense on the income statement.

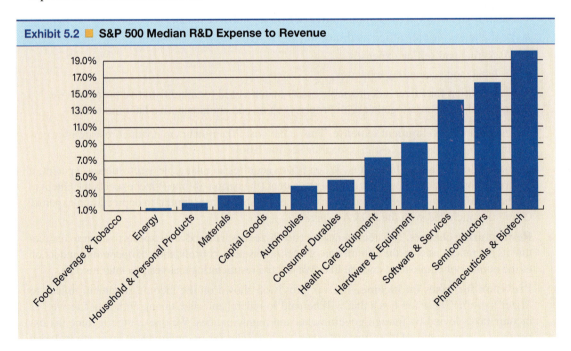

Exhibit 5.2 ■ S&P 500 Median R&D Expense to Revenue

Analysis of R&D

Our analysis of R&D starts with measuring R&D expense in dollars and as a percentage of total revenues. It is important to compare a company's R&D spending to its peers.

R&D is a significant expense for Pfizer as it seeks new compounds and drugs to bring to market. In 2015, Pfizer's R&D expense is $7,690 million or 15.7% of total revenues. As Exhibit 5.3 shows, Pfizer's R&D expense has ranged between 13% and 18% of total revenues over the past 11 years, in line with the 19.5% median for the pharmaceutical and biotech sector. The apparent decline in R&D spending from 2009 through 2013 is attributable to the spike in revenue during those years and not to a decline in R&D spending levels.

Exhibit 5.3 ■ Pfizer R&D Expense

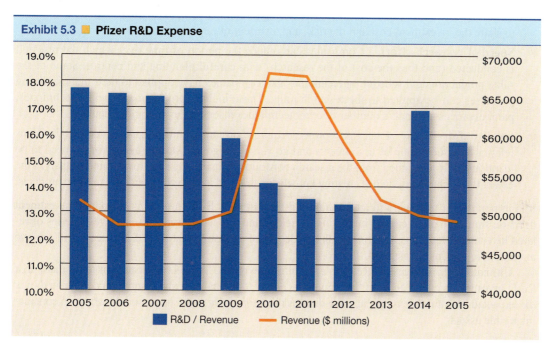

Among Pfizer's peers there are significant differences in the percentage of revenues devoted to R&D expenditures (see Exhibit 5.4). Pfizer's R&D is at the low end of the range among its peers. Our analysis focuses on trends over time and whether other firms are experiencing the same trends. As we saw in Exhibit 5.3, R&D spending might vary in percentage terms due to changes in revenue; our analysis needs to consider both dollar levels and percentages.

Exhibit 5.4 ■ R&D Expenditures to Revenue

	2013	2014	2015
Pfizer	12.9%	16.9%	15.7%
Bristol-Myers Squibb	22.8%	28.6%	35.7%
Merck	17.0%	17.0%	17.0%
Eli Lilly	24.2%	25.2%	26.7%
Abbott Laboratories	7.0%	6.6%	6.9%

Financial analysts usually aim to develop *forward-looking* predictions of a company's income and cash flow. To that end, analysts monitor new products in the pipeline and develop estimates of their ultimate commercial feasibility. For example, analysts following pharmaceutical companies frequently prepare schedules of all drugs in development and monitor closely the success of experimental trials. Analysts also monitor the patent expirations of existing products and estimate the impact on sales after a patent expires.

Company managers have a different reason for analyzing R&D—their aim is to maximize return on R&D investments by selecting projects to fund. Managers have a considerable amount of proprietary information about each R&D project, which they can use to make investment decisions. The goal is to maximize the return on the R&D investment by focusing on the following areas:

- **R&D Costs.** Companies can reduce R&D costs by strategically managing the procurement of raw materials and equipment as they do for other business units, by monitoring closely the investment at each stage of the research process (reducing investment cost in high-risk areas and increasing that investment if and when the risk level falls), by outsourcing portions of the research process as they do for other production and business processes, by identifying failed research ventures early and cutting their losses, by partnering with other companies interested in the research to share the investment cost and the risk, and a variety of other measures.

- **Speed of research effort.** Companies can reduce the period of time over which the research is conducted (and thus the cost of the research) with careful planning and control. Some of the same production and scheduling techniques that companies have applied to their manufacturing processes can be applied to the research units. These include project management techniques, parallel processing, and a number of other techniques discussed in operations courses.

- **Quality of decisions.** Each R&D project requires constant monitoring and numerous decisions relating to a succession of investments and go versus no-go decisions. Failed projects need to be identified early and culled from the research portfolio and managers need to continually analyze the extent to which the research is creating knowledge that will lead to commercially feasible products.

It is important for managers to adopt the mind-set that each R&D project is a separate investment decision similar to other capital-budgeting decisions and one which typically involves a series of related investment decisions. It is only with this degree of discipline that the R&D process will achieve maximum returns on investment.

Ultimately, firms invest in R&D to earn future revenues. There is an argument to be made that R&D investments create an asset that should be added to the balance sheet and then depreciated over the expected life of the new product. We discuss this more fully in the next module when we consider intangible assets.

Discontinued Operations

From time to time, as strategy changes, companies will divest a segment of their business. When this occurs, the company reports the event at the bottom of the income statement by segregating income from continuing versus **discontinued operations**. The line item for discontinued operations has two distinct components.

- Net income (or loss) from the segment's business activities prior to the divestiture or sale.
- Any gain (or loss) on the sale of the business.

In addition to segregating the results of operations of the discontinued operation in the current and previous two years' income statements reported, companies are also required to segregate the discontinued operation's assets and liabilities on the current and prior year's balance sheets.

In 2013, Pfizer sold its animal health business to a newly formed company, Zoetis. Prior to the sale, the animal health business reported a net income of $308 million. Pfizer reported these operating results as "Income from discontinued operations—net of tax" in the 2013 income statement. The sale of the animal health business created a gain on sale of $10,354 million net of tax. That gain represents the difference between the sales proceeds Pfizer received from Zoetis and the amount at which the animal health business was reported on Pfizer's balance sheet on the date of the sale.

Footnotes to Pfizer's 10-K provide data relating to both the income earned by the animal health business through the date of sale along with the gain realized when the business was sold.

Year Ended ($ millions)	December 31, 2013
Revenues	$51,584
Pre-tax income from discontinued operations	408
Provision for taxes on income	100
Income from discontinued operations—net of tax	308
Pre-tax gain on disposal of discontinued operations	10,446
Provision for taxes on income	92
Gain on disposal of discontinued operations—net of tax	10,354
Discontinued operations—net of tax	$10,662

Discontinued operations are segregated in the income statement because they represent a *transitory* item; that is, transactions or events that affect the current period (and in prior periods while the operation was owned by the company) but will not recur. Many readers of financial statements analyze current-year financial statements to gain clues to better predict *future* performance (stock prices, for example, are based on a company's expected profits and cash flows). Although the segregation of transitory items can help us analyze past performance to uncover core operating profit, they are largely irrelevant to predicting future performance. This means investors and other users tend to focus on income from continuing operations because that is the level of profitability that is likely to *persist* (continue) into the future. Likewise, the financial press tends to focus on income from continuing operations when it discloses corporate earnings (often described as "earnings before one-time charges").

Accounting standards relating to discontinued operations have recently changed and have restricted the types of disposals that will be accounted for as discontinued operations. Under the new accounting standard, in order to be classified as a discontinued operation, the disposal of the business unit must represent a *strategic shift* for the company that has or will have a *major effect* on a company's financial results. This represents a substantial hurdle because the company will have to demonstrate that a divestiture represents a strategic shift and creates large financial effects. Consequently, the reporting of discontinued operations is likely to be less frequent in the future.

LO6 Review 5-6

Abbott Laboratories reported the following income statement for fiscal 2015.

ABBOTT LABORATORIES AND SUBSIDIARIES Consolidated Statement of Earnings ($ millions) For Year Ended December 31, 2015	
Net sales	$20,405
Cost of products sold	8,747
Amortization of intangible assets	601
Research and development	1,405
Selling, general, and administrative	6,785
Total operating cost and expenses	17,538
Operating earnings	2,867
Other (income) expense, net	(316)
Earnings from continuing operations before taxes	3,183
Taxes on earnings from continuing operations	577
Earnings from continuing operations	2,606
Earnings from discontinued operations, net of taxes	65
Gain on sale of discontinued operations, net of taxes	1,752
Net earnings from discontinued operations, net of taxes	1,817
Net earnings	$ 4,423

continued

continued from previous page

Abbott's income statements for 2014 and 2013 revealed the following.

$ millions	2014	2013
Net sales.	$20,247	$19,657
Research and development	1,345	1,371

Required

1. Which of the following expenses would **not** be included in selling, general, and administrative expense on the income statement?

   - Salary for the chief executive officer
   - Office supplies
   - Utilities for the research laboratories
   - Depreciation on the company jet
   - Wages for manufacturing employees
   - Shipping costs for products delivered to customers
   - Pharmaceuticals consumed during phase III trials for FDA approvals
   - Depreciation on machines that package and label finished goods

2. Compare R&D expense for 2013 through 2015. (*Hint:* First, determine the common-size expense.) List three types of activities that are included in total R&D expense for Abbott.
3. Explain the item on the income statement labeled, "Earnings from discontinued operations."
4. Explain how the gain on sale of discontinued operations arose.
5. How should analysts treat the net earnings from discontinued operations?
6. Abbott operates dozens of subsidiaries around the world. From the income statement alone, does it appear that Abbott owns 100% of the voting stock of all of its subsidiaries?

Solution on p. 5-53.

Pro Forma Income Reporting

eLectures **LO7**
MBC Interpret pro forma and non-GAAP disclosures.

In its fourth quarter earnings release for 2015, Pfizer described its financial performance as follows.

PFIZER REPORTS FOURTH-QUARTER AND FULL-YEAR 2015 RESULTS PROVIDES 2016 FINANCIAL GUIDANCE

- Fourth-Quarter 2015 Reported Revenues of $14.0 Billion, Reflecting 14% Operational Growth Driven by 22% Operational Growth from the Innovative Products Business
- Full-Year 2015 Reported Revenues of $48.9 Billion, Reflecting 6% Operational Growth Driven by 19% Operational Growth from the Innovative Products Business
- Fourth-Quarter 2015 **Adjusted Diluted EPS** of $0.53 and Reported Diluted EPS of $0.10; Full-Year 2015 Adjusted Diluted EPS of $2.20 and Reported Diluted EPS of $1.24

The company reports revenue growth and specifically highlights "adjusted" diluted EPS (boldface emphasis added). What is this metric, and why does Pfizer report it? To arrive at the adjusted EPS number, Pfizer made a number of deductions and additions to its published GAAP financials because company management believes doing so provides a better measure of Pfizer's financial performance. These adjusted income statements (sometimes referred to as *pro forma* income statements or non-GAAP numbers) are increasingly common.

Regulation G Reconciliation

The Securities and Exchange Commission (SEC), which oversees all publicly traded companies in the United States, requires that companies reconcile such non-GAAP information to GAAP numbers so financial statement readers can have a basis for comparison and can evaluate the excluded items (**Regulation G**). To comply with the regulation, Pfizer provides the following adjusted income statement in the management discussion and analysis (MD&A).

In millions, except per common share data	GAAP Reported	Purchase Accounting Adjustments	Acquisition-Related Costs	Discontinued Operations	Certain Significant Items	Non-GAAP Adjusted
Revenues	$48,851	$ —	$ —	$—	$ —	$48,851
Cost of sales	9,648	(413)	(75)	—	(140)	9,021
Selling, informational and administrative expenses	14,809	—	—	—	(484)	14,324
Research and development expenses	7,690	7	—	—	(44)	7,653
Amortization of intangible assets	3,728	(3,598)	—	—	—	130
Restructuring charges and certain acquisition-related costs	1,152	—	(820)	—	(333)	—
Other (income)/deductions—net	2,075	52	—	—	(2,536)	(409)
Income from continuing operations before provision for taxes on income	9,749	3,953	894	—	3,537	18,133
Provision /(benefit) for taxes on income	1,990	1,110	303	—	949	4,352
Income from continuing operations	7,759	2,843	591	—	2,588	13,781
Discontinued operations—net of tax	11	—	—	(11)	—	—
Net income attributable to noncontrolling interests	26	—	—	—	—	26
Net income attributable to Pfizer Inc.	7,745	2,843	591	(11)	2,588	13,755
Earnings per common share attributable to Pfizer Inc.—diluted	1.24	0.45	0.09	—	0.41	2.20

Table header spanning: **Twelve Months Ended December 31, 2015**

Adjusted income and its components . . . exclude purchase accounting adjustments, acquisition-related costs, discontinued operations and certain significant items . . . As described under Adjusted income in the Management's Discussion and Analysis of Financial Condition and Results of Operations section of Pfizer's Quarterly Report on Form 10-Q for the fiscal quarter ended September 27, 2015, management uses Adjusted income, among other factors, to set performance goals and to measure the performance of the overall company. We believe that investors' understanding of our performance is enhanced by disclosing this measure.

Pfizer's "adjusted" net income is $13,755 million (as compared with GAAP net income of $7,745 million), and excludes costs primarily relating to transitory items, such as costs relating to acquisitions completed during the year, discontinued operations, and other one-time nonrecurring items.[2]

Pfizer's management appears to be thorough in its reporting of "adjusted" income statement items, but other companies may not be. It is important to remember that a company's purpose for making a non-GAAP disclosure is to portray its financial performance the way that management would like us to analyze it. Unscrupulous companies can attempt to lower the bar for analysis by presenting financial results in the best possible light.

SEC Warnings about Pro Forma Numbers

The SEC is very mindful of the potential for abuse in pro forma income statements and cautions investors as follows.[3]

We believe it is appropriate to sound a warning to public companies and other registrants who present to the public their earnings and results of operations on the basis of methodologies other than Generally Accepted Accounting Principles ("GAAP"). This presentation in an earnings release is often referred to as "pro forma" financial information. In this context, that term has no defined

continued

---

[2] "GAAP reported" net income in this 4Q earnings release differs from the 10-K reported net income we present in Exhibit 5.1 because, as Pfizer explains in its earnings release, "Subsidiaries operating outside the U.S. are included for the three and twelve months ended November 30, 2015 and 2014" to facilitate the reporting of the 4Q results.

[3] Excerpted from Securities and Exchange Commission (Release Nos. 33-8039, 34-45124, FR-59) "Cautionary Advice Regarding the Use of 'Pro Forma' Financial Information in Earnings Releases," https://www.sec.gov/rules/other/33-8039.htm.

continued from previous page

meaning and no uniform characteristics. We wish to caution public companies on their use of this "pro forma" financial information and to alert investors to the potential dangers of such information.

"Pro forma" financial information can serve useful purposes. Public companies may quite appropriately wish to focus investors' attention on critical components of quarterly or annual financial results in order to provide a meaningful comparison to results for the same period of prior years or to emphasize the results of core operations. To a large extent, this has been the intended function of disclosures in a company's Management's Discussion and Analysis section of its reports. There is no prohibition preventing public companies from publishing interpretations of their results, or publishing summaries of GAAP financial statements. . .

Nonetheless, we are concerned that "pro forma" financial information, under certain circumstances, can mislead investors if it obscures GAAP results. Because this "pro forma" financial information by its very nature departs from traditional accounting conventions, its use can make it hard for investors to compare an issuer's financial information with other reporting periods and with other companies.

For these reasons . . . we encourage investors to compare any summary or "pro forma" financial presentation with the results reported on GAAP-based financials by the same company. Read before you invest; understand before you commit.

When we read adjusted (pro forma) income statements, it is important to remember they represent management's interpretation of the company's financial performance. We must view those representations as such, not as statements of fact.[4]

Disclosures and Market Assessments

Pro forma income statements must be read and analyzed within the context of the GAAP statements. It is only by a thorough analysis of the GAAP financial statements that we can understand the reasons for, and the implications of, the adjustments management is making with the pro forma statements. We recommend the following steps for a thorough reading of the GAAP financials.

■ Read the reports from the external auditor, and take special note of any deviation from boilerplate language.

■ Peruse the footnote on accounting policies (typically footnote 1), and compare the company's policies with its industry peers. Deviations from the norm can signal opportunism.

■ Examine changes in accounting policies. What would the company have reported absent the change? Did the new policy help it avoid reporting a loss or violating a debt covenant?

■ Compare key ratios over time. Follow up on marked increases or decreases in ratios, read footnotes and the MD&A to see how management explains such changes. Follow up on ratios that do not change when a change is expected. For example, during the tech bubble, **Worldcom Inc.** reported an expense-to-revenue ratio (ER ratio) of 42% quarter after quarter, despite worsening economic conditions. Later, it was discovered that managers had deliberately underreported expenses to maintain the ER ratio. The lesson is that sometimes no change signals managerial intervention.

■ Review ratios of competitors, and consider macroeconomic conditions and how they have shifted over time. Are the ratios reasonable in light of current conditions? Are changes in the income statement aligning with changes on the balance sheet?

■ Identify nonrecurring items, and separately assess their impact on company performance and position.

■ Recast financial statements as necessary to reflect an accounting policy(ies) that is more in line with competitors or one that better reflects economically relevant numbers. We illustrate recasting at several points in future modules. For example, we convert LIFO inventory to FIFO, and we capitalize operating leases.

---

[4] For a good discussion of the issue of accounting *quality*, see Dechow, P., and C. Schrand. "Earnings quality," The Research Foundation of CFA Institute. Charlottesville, VA 2004.

Business Insight ■ Meeting or Beating Analysts' Forecasts

Missing analysts' earnings forecasts can cause stock prices to tumble. Therefore, managers aim to meet or beat Wall Street's expectation, sometimes resorting to earnings management involving accounting accruals, and other times using real actions (such as channel stuffing). Such actions reduce accounting quality. One way analysts and researchers detect potential earnings management is to identify unusual accruals and reversals (negative accruals) and quantify their effect on earnings. Of particular interest are unusual accruals that move earnings per share (EPS) enough to meet or beat analysts' earnings forecasts; such accruals raise suspicion of managerial opportunism. Consider the case of **Green Mountain Coffee**. Its consensus EPS forecast was $0.38 for the second quarter of fiscal 2011, which it beat by $0.10 per share, a 26% margin! The company's stock price shot up nearly 20% to $75.98. But a closer inspection of Green Mountain Coffee's financial statements reveals the company beat earnings forecast not due to stellar performance, but to an accounting anomaly. Its statement of cash flows reveals an unusual (negative) accrual of $22,259 thousand for sales returns for the second quarter of fiscal 2011. GAAP requires that firms report revenues net of anticipated sales returns. When customers return products, the company reduces the allowance for sales returns on the balance sheet. At the end of the quarter, the company estimates sales returns for the current quarter's sales, records the appropriate expense on the income statement, and updates the sales-return allowance. It is atypical for a company to have a negative expense for sales returns. A negative sales-return expense (a reversal) increases revenues and earnings. This is what Green Mountain Coffee reported in 2Q 2011. On an after-tax basis, the reversal increased Green Mountain Coffee's net income by $14,468 thousand, or about $0.10 per share (147,558,595 shares diluted outstanding at March 26, 2011). A skeptical analyst might conclude that the company recorded a negative accrual to beat Wall Street's expectations. Such behavior hinders the quality of reported earnings.

The purported motive for reporting pro forma income is to eliminate transitory (one-time) items to enhance year-to-year comparability. Although this might be justified on the basis that pro forma income has greater predictive ability, important information could be lost in the process. One role for accounting is to report how effective management has been in its stewardship of invested capital. Asset write-downs, liability accruals, and other charges that are eliminated in calculating pro forma income often reflect outcomes of poor management decisions. Our analysis must not blindly eliminate information contained in nonrecurring items by focusing solely on pro forma income. Critics of pro forma income also argue that the items excluded by managers from GAAP income are inconsistent across companies and time. They contend that a major motive for pro forma income is to mislead stakeholders. Legendary investor Warren Buffett puts pro forma in context: "When companies or investment professionals use terms such as 'EBITDA' and 'pro forma,' they want you to unthinkingly accept concepts that are dangerously flawed." (Berkshire Hathaway, Annual Report)

Research Insight ■ Assessing Earnings Quality

It is no secret that corporate executives can and do make choices to deliberately influence reported earnings. GAAP permits choices so that each company can make its financial reports as relevant as possible. But the latitude granted by GAAP opens the door for potential abuse that reduces the quality of financial reports in general and of net earnings in particular. But how prevalent is such deliberate intervention? Can it be detected?

Recently, a team of accounting researchers surveyed and interviewed chief financial officers (CFOs) and other finance executives at 400 firms (169 public and 231 private). The research aimed to uncover CFOs' thinking about earnings quality and reasons for deliberate intervention in the reporting process. According to the CFOs, nearly 20% of public companies and 25% of private companies use allowable discretion in GAAP to misrepresent earnings with average misrepresentations of 12 cents on the dollar. Interestingly, 33% of the misrepresentations *decreased* earnings.

When asked about potential motivations for deliberately misrepresent earnings, CFOs almost unanimously agreed it was "to influence stock price," "to hit earnings benchmarks," and "to influence executive compensation." The researchers compiled a list of 20 red flags that suggest earnings misrepresentation according to the CFOs.

1. GAAP earnings and cash flow from operations move in different direction for 6–8 quarters.
2. Deviations from industry norms on critical metrics, including cash cycle, average profitability, revenue growth, asset impairment, level of disclosure.
3. Consistently meeting or beating earnings targets.
4. Large or frequent one-time items, such as restructuring charges, write-downs, or gains and losses on asset sales.

continued

continued from previous page

5. Large changes in accruals or capitalized costs and insufficient explanation of such changes.
6. Too smooth of an earnings progression (relative to economy, market).
7. Frequent changes in significant accounting policies.
8. Using non-GAAP metrics.
9. High executive and employee turnover, sudden change in top management.
10. Inventory buildup and mismatch between inventory and COGS.
11. Wide swings in earnings, especially without real change in business.
12. Buildups of receivables, deterioration of days sales outstanding.
13. Aggressive use of long-term estimates and lack of explanatory detail on estimates.
14. SEC filings becoming less transparent, uninformative MD&A, complex footnotes.
15. Major jumps or turnarounds or breaks with historical performance.
16. Large incentive compensation payment and management turnover after bonus payments.
17. Repeated restatement of earnings and prior period adjustments.
18. Accruals, assets, and working capital growing faster or slower than revenue.
19. Increased debt and high liabilities.
20. Weak sales growth or declining performance versus the industry.

Source: Dichev, I. D., Graham, J. R., Harvey, C. R. and Rajgopal, S., "Earnings Quality: Evidence from the Field" (2013). Available at SSRN: http://ssrn.com/abstract=2103384 or http://dx.doi.org/10.2139/ssrn.2103384.

Review 5-7 LO7

In its SEC filing for the quarter ended March 31, 2016, **AT&T** provided the proforma disclosures below. Use this information to answer the requirements.

NON-GAAP CONSOLIDATED RECONCILIATION Adjusted EBITDA and Margin		
	Three Months Ended, March 31,	
Unaudited **($ millions)**	**2016**	**2015**
Reported operating income	$ 7,131	$ 5,557
Plus: Depreciation and amortization	6,563	4,578
EBITDA.	13,694	10,135
Adjustments:		
Wireless merger integration costs	42	209
DIRECTV/Mexico merger integration costs	254	89
Employee separation costs	25	217
Gain on transfer of wireless spectrum	(736)	—
Adjusted EBITDA	$13,279	$10,650

Required
1. Why do firms, including AT&T, publicly report non-GAAP information?
2. By deducting the gain on the transfer of wireless spectrum, AT&T reduced its adjusted EBITDA. Why would the company include an adjustment that worsened the reported non-GAAP number?

Solution on p. 5-54.

Global Accounting

Revenue Recognition

The new revenue recognition standard, as discussed in this module, eliminates many prior differences between U.S. GAAP and IFRS. That is, the accounting for revenue is now nearly identical between the two systems. Prior to the new rules (before 2018), companies reporting under IFRS were likely to recognize revenues earlier for the following reasons:

1. U.S. GAAP has specific guidance about what constitutes revenue, how revenue is measured, and the timing of its recognition. Also, U.S. GAAP has extensive, industry-specific revenue recognition guidelines. IFRS is not specific about the timing and measurement of revenue recognition and does not provide industry-specific guidance. With less detailed guidance, the general management preference for reporting income earlier will likely prevail.

2. For multiple-element contracts, both U.S. GAAP and IFRS allocate revenue based on relative fair values of the elements. However, IFRS requires fair-value estimates that are less restrictive.

3. GAAP prohibits percentage of completion method for service transactions whereas IFRS permits that method, with certain exceptions.

For these reasons, IFRS companies are likely to report higher revenues (and net income). This front-loading of revenues is likely more pronounced for high revenue-growth companies and for industries with more multiple-element contracts.

Accounts Receivable

Accounts receivable are accounted for identically with one notable exception. Under IFRS, all receivables are treated as financial assets. This means future cash flows from accounts receivable must be discounted and reported at net present value. This measurement applies to both short- and long-term receivables, assuming the effect of discounting is material. For analysis purposes, we review the notes to determine the discount rate used by the company using IFRS and assess the significance of any discounting. Ratios using accounts receivable (such as turnover ratios and current ratios) can be affected.

Guidance Answers

You Are the Receivables Manager
Pg. 5-21 First, we must realize that extending credit is an important tool in the marketing of your products, often as important as advertising and promotion. Given that receivables are necessary, there are certain ways to speed their collection. (1) We can better screen the customers to whom we extend credit. (2) We can negotiate advance or progress payments from customers. (3) We can use bank letters of credit or other automatic drafting procedures that obviate billing. (4) We can make sure products are sent as ordered, to reduce disputes. (5) We can improve administration of past-due accounts to provide for more timely notices of delinquencies and better collection procedures.

Questions

Q5-1. What is a performance obligation and how is it related to revenue recognition?

Q5-2. Explain how management can shift income from one period into another by using the allowance for uncollectibles account.

Q5-3. Why do companies allow sales returns, and how does this business practice affect reported revenue?

Q5-4. The income statement line item, "Discontinued operations" typically comprises two distinct components. What are they?

Q5-5. What effect, if any, does a weakening $US have on reported sales and net income for companies operating outside the United States?

Q5-6. Explain why analysts might remove foreign exchange gains or losses when analyzing revenue and expenses for the year.

Q5-7. What is meant by "aging" of accounts receivable?

Q5-8. Under what circumstances is it appropriate to use the cost-to-cost method to measure revenue?

Q5-9. What is the concept of pro forma income and why has this income measure been criticized?

Q5-10. What is unearned revenue? Provide three examples of unearned revenue.

Q5-11   What is the current U.S. GAAP accounting treatment for research and development costs?

Q5-12   How would a company recognize revenue on a sale that includes equipment and a multi-year service contract all for one price?

Assignments with the ⬤ logo in the margin are available in ᵐʸBusinessCourse.
See the Preface of the book for details.

Mini Exercises

LO1   **M5-13.   Computing Revenues under Long-Term Contracts**

Camden Corporation agreed to build a warehouse for a client at an agreed contract price of $900,000. Expected (and actual) costs for the warehouse follow: 2016, $202,500; 2017, $337,500; and 2018, $135,000. The company completed the warehouse in 2015. Compute revenues, expenses, and income for each year 2016 through 2018, and for all three years combined, using the cost-to-cost method.

LO1   **M5-14.   Applying the Financial Statement Effects Template.**

Refer to the information for Camden Corporation in M5-13.

a. Use the financial statement effects template to record contract revenues and expenses for each year 2016 through 2018 using the cost-to-cost method.

b. Prepare journal entries and T-accounts to record contract revenues and expenses for each year 2016 through 2018 using the cost-to-cost method.

LO1   **M5-15.   Assessing Revenue Recognition of Companies**

Identify and explain when each of the following companies fulfills the performance obligations implicit in the sales contract.

The GAP (GPS)

Merck & Company (MRK)

Deere & Company (DE)

Bank of America (BAC)

Johnson Controls (JCI)

a. **The GAP**: The GAP is a retailer of clothing items for all ages.

b. **Merck & Company**: Merck engages in developing, manufacturing, and marketing pharmaceutical products. It sells its drugs to retailers such as **CVS** and **Walgreen**.

c. **Deere & Company**: Deere manufactures heavy equipment. It sells equipment to a network of independent distributors, who in turn sell the equipment to customers. Deere provides financing and insurance services both to distributors and customers.

d. **Bank of America**: Bank of America is a banking institution. It lends money to individuals and corporations and invests excess funds in marketable securities.

e. **Johnson Controls**: Johnson Controls manufactures products for the government under long-term contracts.

LO1   **M5-16.   Assessing Risk Exposure to Revenue Recognition**

BannerAD Corporation manages a website that sells products on consignment from sellers. It pays these sellers a portion of the sales price and charges a commission. Identify two potential revenue recognition issues from the perspective of BannerAd Corporation.

LO1, 2   **M5-17.   Estimating Revenue Recognition with Right of Return**

ModCloth Inc.

ModCloth Inc. offers an unconditional return policy. It normally expects 2% of sales at retail selling prices to be returned before the return period expires. Assuming ModCloth records total sales of $10 million for the current period, what amount of *net* sales should it record for this period?

LO5   **M5-18.   Estimating Uncollectible Accounts and Reporting Accounts Receivable**

Mohan Company estimates its uncollectible accounts by aging its accounts receivable and applying percentages to various aged categories of accounts. Mohan computes a total of $2,100 in estimated uncollectible accounts as of its current year-end. Its accounts receivable has a balance of $86,000, and its allowance for uncollectible accounts has an unused balance of $700 before any year-end adjustments.

a. What amount of bad debts expense will Mohan report in its income statement for the current year?

b. Determine the net amount of accounts receivable reported in current assets at year-end.

LO5   **M5-19.   Interpreting the Allowance Method for Accounts Receivable**

At a recent board of directors meeting of Bismark Corp., one of the directors expressed concern over the allowance for uncollectible accounts appearing in the company's balance sheet. "I don't understand this account," he said. "Why don't we just show accounts receivable at the amount owed to us and get rid of that allowance?" Respond to the director's question; include in your response (a) an explanation of why the company has an allowance account, (b) what the balance sheet presentation of accounts receivable is intended to show, and (c) how accrual accounting (as opposed to the cash-basis accounting) affects the presentation of accounts receivable.

M5-20. **Analyzing the Allowance for Uncollectible Accounts**

LO5

Mondelēz International (MDLZ)

Following is the current asset section from the Mondelēz balance sheet.

$ millions	2015	2014
Cash and cash equivalents	$1,870	$ 1,631
Trade receivables (net of allowances of $54 at 2015 and $66 at 2014)	2,634	3,802
Other receivables (net of allowances of $109 at 2015 and $91 at 2014)	1,212	949
Inventories, net	2,609	3,480
Deferred income taxes	—	480
Other current assets	633	1,408
Total current assets	$8,958	$11,750

a. Compute the gross amount of trade receivable for both 2015 and 2014. Compute the percentage of the allowance for uncollectible trade relative to the gross amount of trade receivable for each of those years.

b. Compute the relative size of net trade receivable to total assets; the latter were $62,843 million and $66,771 million for 2015 and 2014, respectively. Interpret the quality of Mondelēz's receivables for 2015 compared with 2014.

M5-21. **Evaluating Accounts Receivable Turnover for Competitors**

LO5

The Procter & Gamble Company (PG)

Colgate-Palmolive Company (CL)

The Procter & Gamble Company and Colgate-Palmolive Company report the following sales and accounts receivable balances ($ millions) for 2015 and 2014.

$ millions	Procter & Gamble		Colgate-Palmolive	
	Sales	Accounts Receivable	Sales	Accounts Receivable
2015	$76,279	$4,861	$16,034	$1,427
2014	80,510	6,386	17,277	1,552

a. Compute the accounts receivable turnover and DSO for both companies for 2015.

b. Identify and discuss a potential explanation for the difference between these competitors' accounts receivable ratios.

M5-22. **Interpreting Foreign Currency Translation Disclosure**

LO4

Procter & Gamble Company (PNG)

Procter & Gamble Company reports the following table in its 10-K report relating to the change in sales from 2015 to 2016.

		Net Sales Change Drivers 2016 vs. 2015			
	Volume	Foreign Exchange	Price	Mix	Net Sales Growth
Beauty	(5)%	(6)%	2%	—	(9)%
Grooming	(2)%	(9)%	5%	(2)%	(8)%
Health care	(2)%	(6)%	2%	1%	(5)%
Fabric & home care	(1)%	(6)%	—	—	(7)%
Baby, feminine & family care	(3)%	(6)%	—	—	(9)%
Total company	(3)%	(6)%	1%	—	(8)%

a. Did total company net sales increase or decrease during the year? By what percentage? How much of this change is attributable to volume versus price changes?

b. What was the effect of foreign exchange rates on sales during the year? From this result, what can we infer about the relative strength of the $US during the period?

c. The Beauty and the Baby, Feminine & Family Care segment sales both decreased by 9%. From this result, can we conclude that the dollar decrease in sales was the same for both segments? Explain.

LO3 **M5-23. Assessing Revenue Recognition for Advance Payments**
Hamilton Company operates a performing arts center. The company sells tickets for its upcoming season of six Broadway musicals and receives $630,000 cash. The performances occur monthly over the next six months.

    a. When should Hamilton record revenue for the Broadway musical series?

    b. Use the financial statement effects template to show the $630,000 cash receipt and recognition of the first month's revenue.

LO3
Target Corporation (TGT)

M5-24. Reporting Unearned Revenue
Target Corporation sells gift cards that can be used at any of the company's Target stores or on Target.com. Target encodes information on the card's magnetic strip about the card's value and the store where it was purchased. Target gift cards do not have expiration dates.

    a. How will Target's balance sheet reflect the gift card? Will the balance sheet amount of these cards be classified as current or noncurrent?

    b. When does Target record revenue from the gift card?

LO2

M5-25. Sales Returns
Which of the following statements is true relating to the allowance for sales returns?

    a. Sales returns is treated as an expense in the income statement and, therefore, reduces profit for the period.

    b. An excess of the amount by which the allowance for sales returns is increased compared with the actual returns for the period indicates the company may have inflated profit for the period.

    c. The amount by which the allowance for sales returns is reduced during the period is recognized as a reduction of sales for the period, thus reducing profit.

    d. Increasing the allowance for sales returns by an amount that is less than the actual returns recognized for the period may indicate either the company is attempting to increase profit for the period or it estimates that less of its products will be returned in the future.

LO3 **M5-26. Deferred Revenue**
True or false: A reduction of the deferred revenue account can be interpreted as a leading indicator of lower future revenues. Explain.

LO4 **M5-27. Foreign Exchange Effects on Sales**
True or false: A multinational company reports that a large amount of its sales is generated in foreign currencies that have strengthened vis-à-vis the $US. Consolidated revenues are likely lower than would have been reported in the absence of such a shift in exchange rates.

LO6 **M5-28. Operating Expenses**
Indicate whether each of the following is true or false.

    a. Amortization expense is a noncash expense similar to depreciation, except it applies to intangible assets.

    b. Income attributable to noncontrolling interests is an expense item that reduces net income.

    c. Discontinued operations relate to any segment of the business a company is selling.

    d. The income (loss) of Discontinued operations and gain (loss) on their sale are reported in the income statement like other revenue and expense items.

LO7
Kellogg Company (K)

M5-29. Pro Forma Numbers
Kellogg's included the following note in its fiscal 2015 10-K report.

> The Company's fiscal year normally ends on the Saturday closest to December 31 and as a result, a 53rd week is added approximately every sixth year. The Company's 2014 fiscal year ended on January 3, 2015, and included a 53rd week. While quarters normally consist of 13-week periods, the fourth quarter of fiscal 2014 included a 14th week.

    a. Why does Kellogg's disclose this issue?

    b. How are year-over-year growth rates affected by the 53rd week?

    c. What pro forma adjustment could Kellogg (or we) make to facilitate the analysis of revenue trends?

LO6, 7
Murphy USA Inc. (MUSA)

M5-30. Discontinued Operations and Pro Forma Disclosures
In its 2015 annual report, Murphy USA stated, "We use EBITDA and Adjusted EBITDA in our operational and financial decision-making, believing that such measures are useful to eliminate certain items in order to focus on what we deem to be a more reliable indicator of ongoing operating performance and our ability to generate cash flow from operations." The following table was included.

$ thousands	2015	2014
EBITDA.......................................	$374,960	$475,738
(Income) loss from discontinued operations, net of taxes	(38,749)	(20,903)
(Gain) loss on sale of assets...............................	4,658	(194)
Accretion of asset retirement obligations....................	1,521	1,200
Other nonoperating income (loss).........................	463	(10,166)
Adjusted EBITDA	$342,853	$445,675

a. What does "EBITDA" stand for, and how does Murphy USA calculate it?

b. To adjust EBITDA, the company subtracted income from discontinued operations. What does the 2015 amount of $38,749 thousand represent?

c. The company subtracted income from discontinued operations of $20,903 thousand in 2014. Can we infer the company discontinued operations in both years?

Exercises

E5-31. **Assessing Revenue Recognition Timing**

LO1

Explain when each of the following businesses fulfills the performance obligations implicit in the sales contract.

a. A clothing retailer like **American Eagle Outfitters Inc.**

b. A contractor like **Boeing Company** that performs work under long-term government contracts.

c. A grocery store like **Supervalu Inc.**

d. A producer of television shows like **MTV** that syndicates its content to television stations.

e. A residential real estate developer that constructs only speculative houses and later sells these houses to buyers.

f. A banking institution like **Bank of America Corp.** that lends money for home mortgages.

g. A manufacturer like **Harley-Davidson Inc.**

h. A publisher of magazines such as **Time-Warner Inc.**

American Eagle
Outfitters Inc. (AEO)

Boeing Co. (BA)

Supervalu Inc. (SVU)

MTV

Bank of America Corp.
(BAC)

Harley-Davidson Inc.
(HOG)

Time-Warner Inc.
(TWX)

E5-32. **Assessing Revenue Recognition Timing and Income Measurement**

LO1

Explain when each of the following businesses fulfills the performance obligations implicit in the sales contract and recognizes revenue. Identify any revenue measurement issues that could arise.

a. RealMoney.Com, a division of **TheStreet Inc.**, provides investment advice to customers for an up-front fee. It provides these customers with password-protected access to its website, where they can download investment reports. RealMoney has an obligation to provide updates on its website.

b. **Oracle Corp.** develops general ledger and other business application software that it sells to its customers. The customer pays an up-front fee for the right to use the software and a monthly fee for support services.

c. **Intuit Inc.** develops tax preparation software that it sells to its customers for a flat fee. No further payment is required, and the software cannot be returned, only exchanged if defective.

d. A developer of computer games sells its software with a 10-day right of return period during which the software can be returned for a full refund. After the 10-day period has expired, the software cannot be returned.

TheStreet Inc. (TST)

Oracle Corp. (ORCL)

Intuit Inc. (INTU)

E5-33. **Constructing and Assessing Income Statements Using Cost-to-Cost Method**

LO1

Assume **General Electric Company** agreed in May 2016 to construct a nuclear generator for NSTAR, a utility company serving the Boston area. The contract price of $750 million is to be paid as follows: $250 million at the time of signing; $250 million on December 31, 2016; and $250 million at completion in May 2017. General Electric incurred the following costs in constructing the generator: $240 million in 2016 and $360 million in 2017.

a. Compute the amount of General Electric's revenue, expense, and income for both 2016 and 2017, and for both years combined, under the cost-to-cost revenue recognition method.

b. Discuss whether or not you believe the cost-to-cost method provides a good measure of General Electric's performance under the contract.

General Electric
Company (GE)

LO1   E5-34.   Constructing and Assessing Income Statements Using Cost-to-Cost Method

On March 15, 2017, Gilbert Construction contracted to build a shopping center at a contract price of $220 million. The schedule of expected (which equals actual) cash collections and contract costs follows.

Year	Cash Collections	Cost Incurred
2017	$ 55 million	$ 36 million
2018	88 million	81 million
2019	77 million	63 million
Total	$220 million	$180 million

a. Calculate the amount of revenue, expense, and net income for each of the three years 2017 through 2019, and for all three years combined, using the cost-to-cost revenue recognition method.

b. Discuss whether or not the cost-to-cost method provides a good measure of this construction company's performance under the contract.

LO4   E5-35.   Foreign Currency Impact

Kellogg Company (K)

Kellogg included the following note in its fiscal 2015 10-K report ($ millions).

Comparable net income attributable to Kellogg	$1,257
Foreign currency impact.	(100)
Currency neutral comparable net income attributable to Kellogg	$1,357

a. Assume the foreign currency impact related entirely to foreign sales. Determine whether the $US strengthened or weakened vis-à-vis the currencies in which Kellogg conducts business.

b. Assume the foreign currency impact related entirely to purchases of goods from foreign vendors. Determine whether the $US strengthened or weakened vis-à-vis the currencies in which Kellogg conducts business.

c. As an analyst, how would we treat this foreign currency impact in our analysis of Kellogg?

LO6   E5-36.   Identifying Operating Income Components

Following is the income statement information from Apollo Medical Devices. Identify the components that we would consider operating.

$ thousands	2016
Net sales.	$4,163,770
Cost of sales before special charges.	1,382,235
Special inventory obsolescence charge.	27,876
Total cost of sales.	1,410,111
Gross profit.	2,753,659
Selling, general and administrative expense	1,570,667
Research and development expense.	531,086
Merger and acquisition costs.	46,914
In-process research and development charges.	12,244
Litigation settlement.	16,500
Operating profit	576,248
Interest expense.	(57,372)
Interest income.	2,076
Gain on disposal of fixed assets	4,929
Impairment of marketable securities	(5,222)
Other income (expense), net	(2,857)
Earnings before income taxes	517,802
Income tax expense.	191,587
Net earnings.	$ 326,215

E5-37. **Identifying Operating Income Components**

Following is the Deere & Company income statement for 2015.

$ millions	2015
Net sales and revenues	
Net sales.	$25,775.2
Finance and interest income	2,381.1
Other income	706.5
Total	28,862.8
Costs and expenses	
Cost of sales.	20,143.2
Research and development expenses.	1,425.1
Selling, administrative and general expenses	2,873.3
Interest expense.	680.0
Other operating expenses	961.1
Total	26,082.7
Income of consolidated group before income taxes	2,780.1
Provision for income taxes.	840.1
Income of consolidated group	1940.0
Equity in income of unconsolidated affiliates.	0.9
Net income.	1940.9
Less: Net income attributable to noncontrolling interests	0.9
Net income attributable to Deere & Company	$ 1,940.0

Notes:
- The income statement includes John Deere commercial and consumer tractor segment, a finance subsidiary that provides loan and lease financing relating to the sales of those tractors, and a health care segment that provides managed health care services for the company and certain outside customers.
- Equity in income of unconsolidated affiliates refers to income John Deere has earned on investments made for strategic purposes.

a. Identify the components in its income statement that you would consider operating.

b. Discuss your treatment of the company's finance and interest income that relates to financing of its John Deere lawn and garden, and commercial tractors.

E5-38. **Analyzing and Interpreting Foreign Currency Translation Effects and Non-GAAP Disclosures**

Kellogg Co. reports the following table and discussion in its 2015 10-K for its reportable segments.

The following table provides an analysis of net sales and operating profit performance for 2015 versus 2014:

$ millions	U.S Morning Foods	U.S. Snacks	U.S. Specialty	North America Other	Europe	Latin America	Asia Pacific	Corporate	Kellogg Consolidated
2015 net sales.	$2,992	$3,234	$1,181	$1,687	$2,497	$1,015	$ 919	$ —	$13,525
2014 net sales.	$3,108	$3,329	$1,198	$1,864	$ 2,869	$1,205	$1,007	$ —	$14,580
As Reported.	(3.7)%	(2.9)%	(1.4)%	(9.5)%	(13.0)%	(15.8)%	(8.8)%	0.0%	(7.2)%
Project K and cost reduction activities.	0.0%	0.0%	0.0%	0.0%	(0.1)%	0.0%	0.0%	0.0%	0.0%
Integration and transaction costs.	0.0%	0.0%	0.0%	0.0%	0.0%	0.0%	(0.1)%	0.0%	0.0%
Acquisitions/divestitures	0.0%	0.0%	(0.8)%	0.0%	2.0%	0.0%	0.0%	0.0%	0.4%
Difference in shipping days	(2.1)%	(1.3)%	(1.3)%	(1.5)%	(1.1)%	0.0%	(0.8)%	0.0%	(1.3)%
Comparable growth	(1.6)%	(1.6)%	0.7%	(8.0)%	(13.8)%	(15.8)%	(7.9)%	0.0%	(6.3)%
Foreign currency impact.	0.0%	0.0%	0.0%	(4.8)%	(13.2)%	(40.4)%	(11.9)%	0.0%	(7.5)%
Currency-Neutral Comparable growth.	(1.6)%	(1.6)%	0.7%	(3.2)%	(0.6)%	24.6%	4.0%	0.0%	1.2%

Foreign exchange risk Our Company is exposed to fluctuations in foreign currency cash flows related to third-party purchases, intercompany transactions, and when applicable, nonfunctional

continued

continued from previous page

currency denominated third-party debt. Our Company is also exposed to fluctuations in the value of foreign currency investments in subsidiaries and cash flows related to repatriation of these investments. Additionally, our Company is exposed to volatility in the translation of foreign currency earnings to U.S. Dollars. Primary exposures include the U.S. Dollar versus the British Pound, Euro, Australian Dollar, Canadian Dollar, and Mexican Peso, and in the case of inter-subsidiary transactions, the British Pound versus the Euro. We assess foreign currency risk based on transactional cash flows and translational volatility and enter into forward contracts, options, and currency swaps to reduce fluctuations in net long or short currency positions. Forward contracts and options are generally less than 18 months duration. Currency swap agreements are established in conjunction with the term of underlying debt issuances.

a. Kellogg reported consolidated sales decreased by 7.2% during 2015. What geographic segment accounted for this overall decrease?

b. Kellogg reports "Comparable growth" that shows various adjustments to reported growth numbers. Explain why Kellogg provides this information in its financial statements. Explain the item labeled "Difference in shipping days."

c. How did foreign currency exchange rates affect sales at each of the geographic segments? What can we infer about the strength of the $US vis-à-vis the currencies in Kellogg's segments?

d. Describe how the accounting for foreign exchange translation affects reported sales and profits.

e. How does Kellogg manage the risk related to its foreign exchange exposure? Describe the financial statement effects of this risk management activity.

LO2

**Barnes & Noble Inc.
(BKS)**

E5-39. Interpreting Revenue Recognition for Gift Cards

Below are the footnotes to **Barnes & Noble Inc.**'s 2016 annual report and membership information obtained from its website.

The Barnes & Noble Member Program offers members greater discounts and other benefits for products and services, as well as exclusive offers and promotions via e-mail or direct mail for an annual fee of $25.00, which is non-refundable after the first 30 days. Revenue is recognized over the twelve-month period based upon historical spending patterns for Barnes & Noble Members. The Barnes & Noble Member Program entitles Members to the following benefits:

- 40% off the list price of the current hardcover Barnes & Noble Store Bestsellers.
- 10% off the marked Barnes & Noble sale price of other eligible items.
- Free Express Shipping.
- Periodic special promotions at Barnes & Noble Stores and at BN.com.

a. Explain in layman's terms how Barnes & Noble accounts for the cash received for its membership program. When does Barnes & Noble record revenue from this program?

b. How does Barnes & Noble's balance sheet reflect those membership fees?

c. Does the 40% discount affect Barnes & Noble's income statement when membership fees are received?

LO6

Target Corp. (TGT)

E5-40. Operating Expenses

Target Corporation's footnote from its 2015 annual report table illustrates the primary items classified in each major expense category: cost of sales (COS), or selling, general and administrative (SG&A). For each expense, indicate whether the item would be included in COS or SG&A.

a. Advertising expenses. . . . . ____

b. Compensation and benefits costs for headquarters employees . . . . ____

c. Compensation and benefits costs for store employees. . . . . ____

d. Compensation and benefits costs for distribution center employees . . . . ____

e. Distribution center costs . . . . ____

f. Freight expenses associated with moving merchandise from our vendors to our distribution centers and our retail stores . . . . ____

g. Freight expenses associated with moving merchandise among our distribution and retail stores. . . . . ____

h. Import costs . . . . ____

continued

i. Inventory shrink and theft. . . . . _____

j. Litigation and defense costs and related insurance recovery . . . . _____

k. Markdowns on slow moving inventory. . . . . _____

l. Occupancy and operating costs for headquarters facilities . . . . _____

m. Occupancy and operating costs of retail locations . . . . _____

n. Outbound shipping and handling expenses associated with sales to our guests. . . . . _____

o. Payment term cash discounts to our vendors . . . . _____

p. Pre-opening costs of stores and other facilities. . . . . _____

q. U.S. credit cards servicing expenses. . . . . _____

r. Vendor reimbursement of specific, incremental, and identifiable advertising costs . . . _____

E5-41. **Estimating Uncollectible Accounts and Reporting Accounts Receivable**

Collins Company analyzes its accounts receivable at December 31 and arrives at the age categories below along with the percentages that are estimated as uncollectible. The balance of the allowance for uncollectible accounts is $1,100 on December 31, before any adjustments.

LO5

Age Group	Accounts Receivable	Estimated Loss %
0–30 days past due	$110,000	1%
31–60 days past due	40,000	2
61–120 days past due	27,000	5
121–180 days past due	14,000	10
Over 180 days past due.	9,000	25
Total accounts receivable.	$200,000	

a. What amount of bad debts expense will Collins report in its income statement for the year?

b. Use the financial statement effects template to record Collins' bad debts expense for the year.

c. What is the balance of accounts receivable on its December 31 balance sheet?

E5-42. **Analyzing and Reporting Receivable Transactions and Uncollectible Accounts Using Percentage-of-Sales Method to Estimate Bad Debt Expense**

At the beginning of the year, Penman Company had the following account balances.

LO5

Accounts receivable.	$356,000
Allowance for uncollectible accounts.	21,400

During the year, Penman's credit sales were $2,008,000, and collections on accounts receivable were $1,963,000. The following additional transactions occurred during the year.

Feb. 17 Wrote off Bava's account, $8,200.

May 28 Wrote off Reed's account, $4,800.

Dec. 15 Wrote off Fischer's account, $2,300.

Dec. 31 Recorded the bad debts expense assuming Penman's policy is to record bad debts expense as 0.9% of credit sales. (*Hint*: The allowance account is increased by 0.9% of credit sales regardless of write-offs.)

Compute the ending balances in accounts receivable and the allowance for uncollectible accounts. Show how Penman's December 31 balance sheet reports the two accounts.

E5-43. **Interpreting the Accounts Receivable Footnote**

Hewlett-Packard Company reports the following in its 2015 10-K report.

LO5

Hewlett-Packard (HPQ)

October 31 ($ millions)	2015	2014
Accounts receivable.	$13,363	$13,832

Footnotes to the company's 10-K provide the following additional information relating to its allowance for doubtful accounts.

For the Fiscal Years Ended October 31 ($ millions)	2015	2014	2013
Allowance for doubtful accounts—accounts receivable			
Balance, beginning of period	$232	$332	$464
Provision for doubtful accounts	46	25	23
Deductions, net of recoveries.	(89)	(125)	(155)
Balance, end of period	$189	$232	$332

a. What is the gross amount of accounts receivables for Hewlett-Packard in fiscal 2015 and 2014?

b. What is the percentage of the allowance for doubtful accounts to gross accounts receivable for 2015 and 2014?

c. What amount of bad debts expense did Hewlett-Packard report each year 2013 through 2015 (ignore increase in allowance from acquisitions)? How does bad debts expense compare with the amounts of its accounts receivable actually written off? (Identify the amounts, and explain.)

d. Explain the changes in the allowance for doubtful accounts from 2013 through 2015. Does it appear that Hewlett-Packard increased or decreased its allowance for doubtful accounts in any particular year beyond what seems reasonable?

LO6   **E5-44.**   **Estimating Bad Debts Expense and Reporting Receivables**

At December 31, Barber Company had a balance of $420,000 in its accounts receivable and an unused balance of $2,600 in its allowance for uncollectible accounts. The company then aged its accounts as follows.

Current	$346,000
1–60 days past due	48,000
61–180 days past due	17,000
Over 180 days past due	9,000
Total accounts receivable.	$420,000

The company has experienced losses as follows: 1% of current balances, 5% of balances 1–60 days past due, 15% of balances 61–180 days past due, and 40% of balances over 180 days past due. The company continues to base its allowance for uncollectible accounts on this aging analysis and percentages.

a. What amount of bad debts expense does Barber report on its income statement for the year?

b. Show how Barber's December 31 balance sheet will report the accounts receivable and the allowance for uncollectible accounts.

LO5   **E5-45.**   **Estimating Uncollectible Accounts and Reporting Receivables over Multiple Periods**

Weiss Company, which has been in business for three years, makes all of its sales on credit and does not offer cash discounts. Its credit sales, customer collections, and write-offs of uncollectible accounts for its first three years follow.

Year	Sales	Collections	Accounts Written Off
2014	$733,000	$716,000	$5,300
2015	857,000	842,000	5,800
2016	945,000	928,000	6,500

a. Weiss recognizes bad debts expense as 1% of sales. (*Hint:* This means the allowance account is increased by 1% of credit sales regardless of any write-offs and unused balances.) What does Weiss' 2013 balance sheet report for accounts receivable and the allowance for uncollectible accounts? What total amount of bad debts expense appears on Weiss' income statement for each of the three years?

b. Comment on the appropriateness of the 1% rate used to provide for bad debts based on your analysis in part *a*.

P5-46. **Foreign Currency Fluctuations and Revenue**

LO4
Boeing Corporation
(BA)

Boeing Corporation has considerable non-U.S. operations. The table below shows Boeing's 2015 revenue by geographic segment along with related exchange rates at the beginning and end of the year. The exchange rates represent the foreign currency equivalent of $1.

Year ended December 31, 2015 ($ millions)	Revenue	USD exchange rate	
		01/01/15	12/31/15
Asia, other than China	$13,433	0.7543	0.7063
Europe	12,248	0.8266	0.9203
China	12,556	6.2025	6.4952
Middle East	10,846	3.6729	3.6729
Oceania	2,601	3.5046	4.3044
Canada	1,870	1.1618	1.3847
Africa	1,398	11.5642	15.5159
Latin America and Caribbean	1,875	14.7414	17.2494
Total non-U.S. revenues	56,827		
United States	39,287		
Total revenues	$96,114		

Required

a. Most of Boeing's contracts are denominated in $US. Assume instead that Boeing wrote contracts for its international customers in their respective domestic currencies. For simplicity, assume the contracts were written on January 2, 2015, and revenue was collected and recognized on December 31, 2015. Use the exchange rate information in the table to calculate the effect on Boeing's 2015 revenue if contracts had been denominated in the various foreign currencies.

b. How would the foreign exchange gain or loss that was computed affect net income?

c. How could Boeing treat such a foreign exchange gain or loss in any non-GAAP disclosures the company might make?

d. How should we, as analysts, treat such a foreign exchange gain or loss?

P5-47. **Non-GAAP Disclosures**

LO7
Kellogg Co. (K)

In its 2015 annual report, Kellogg reported the following non-GAAP reconciliation.

Reconciliation of Certain Non-GAAP Financial Measures				
Consolidated Results ($ millions)	2015	2014	2013	2012
Reported net income	$ 614	$ 632	$1,807	$ 961
Mark-to-market	(298)	(513)	628	(304)
Project K and cost reduction activities	(229)	(218)	(183)	(38)
VIE deconsolidation and other costs impacting comparability	50	(4)	—	
Integration and transaction costs	(22)	(31)	(46)	(34)
Acquisitions/divestitures	5	—	2	—
Shipping day differences	—	25	—	—
Venezuela remeasurement	(149)	—	(11)	—
Comparable net income	1,257	1,373	1,417	1,337
Foreign currency impact	(100)	—	—	
Currency neutral comparable net income	$1,357	$1,373	$1,417	$1,337

• The mark-to-market adjustment pertains largely to unrealized gains and losses on the company's pension plan assets. These assets are held in marketable securities and earn returns that will be used to make retiree pension payments in future years.

- Integration and transaction costs pertain to the cost associated with mergers and acquisitions.

The company makes the following additional statements about the non-GAAP measures.

- Non-GAAP currency-neutral comparable definitions of these metrics are reconciled to the directly comparable measure in accordance with U.S. GAAP within our Management's Discussion and Analysis. We believe the use of such non-GAAP measures provides increased transparency and assists in understanding our underlying operating performance.
- "These non-GAAP measures focus management and investors on the amount of cash available for debt repayment, dividend distribution, acquisition opportunities, and share repurchase."

Required

a. Does Kellogg's reasoning for using and reporting the non-GAAP numbers ring true? Explain.

b. What does Kellogg mean by "currency-neutral" in its reconcilliation?

c. Calculate the year-over-year change (in % terms) in reported net income for the four years presented. Calculate the year-over-year change (in % terms) in the non-GAAP net income. Which trend do we believe more accurately depicts Kellogg's performance over this period?

d. In 2015, did the mark-to-market adjustment increase or decrease GAAP net income? Did the pension assets have additional unrealized gains or losses during fiscal 2015?

e. Explain a potential rationale for the "integration and transaction costs" adjustment. Is there a counter-argument?

LO1, 2   **P5-48.** **Revenue Recognition and Sales Allowances**
Target Corp. (TGT)

Target Corporation reported total sales of $73,785 million in 2015, $72,618 million in 2014, and $71,279 million in 2013. In 2015, cost of sales was $51,997 million.

The revenue recognition footnote from Target's 2015 annual report includes the following.

- Our retail stores generally record revenue at the point of sale.
- Digital channel sales include shipping revenue and are recorded upon delivery to the guest.
- Total revenues do not include sales tax because we are a pass-through conduit for collecting and remitting sales taxes.
- Generally, guests may return national brand merchandise within 90 days of purchase and owned and exclusive brands within one year of purchase. Revenues are recognized net of expected returns, which we estimate using historical return patterns as a percentage of sales.
- Revenue from gift card sales is recognized upon gift card redemption. Our gift cards do not expire. Based on historical redemption rates, a small and relatively stable percentage of gift cards will never be redeemed, referred to as "breakage." Estimated breakage revenue is recognized over time in proportion to actual gift card redemptions and was not material in any period presented.
- Guests receive a 5 percent discount on virtually all purchases and receive free shipping at Target.com when they use their REDcard. These discounts associated with loyalty programs are included as reductions in sales in our Consolidated Statements of Operations and were $1,067 million, $943 million, and $833 million in 2015, 2014, and 2013, respectively.

Required

a. Use the financial statement effects template to record retail sales of $1,000 in a state with a sales-tax rate of 8%. For this question, assume 10% of all merchandise sold is returned within 90 days.

b. Use the financial statement effects template to record the following transaction: On March 4, an internet customer places an order for $2,000 and pays online with a credit card (which is equivalent to cash for accounting purposes). The goods are shipped from the warehouse on March 6, and FedEx confirms delivery on March 7. Ignore shipping costs, sales tax, and returns.

c. Use the financial statement effects template to record the gift card activity during May. Ignore sales tax and returns. Details are as follows.

continued

$ millions	
Gift card balance May 1	$198
New gift cards sold	148
Gift cards redeemed	(172)
Gift card balance May 31	$174

d. Determine the amount of revenue Target collected from customers who used their loyalty card (REDcard™) for 2013 to 2015. What proportion of total revenues come from REDcard™ customers each year? Does the loyalty program seem to be working? Explain.

P5-49. **Research and Development Expense**

International Business Machines Corporation (IBM) reported the following on its 2015 income statement.

LO5
International Business Machines Corporation (IBM)

$ millions	Fiscal 2015	Fiscal 2014	Fiscal 2013
Net sales	$81,741	$92,793	$98,367
Cost of sales	$ 5,247	$ 5,437	$ 5,743
Number of new patents	7,355	7,534	6,809

Required

a. Compare IBM's research and development expense to other publicly traded companies and those in the same industry. Comment on the comparison. (*Hint:* Refer to Exhibit 5.2.)
b. IBM's spending on research and development declined during 2015. Quantify this trend. Is this of potential concern to investors?
c. What other data might analysts and investors collect to form an opinion about the level and effectiveness of IBM's R&D endeavors?

P5-50. **Analyzing and Interpreting Revenue Recognition Policies and Risks**

Amazon.com Inc. provides the following explanation of its revenue recognition policies in its 2015 10-K report.

LO1
Amazon.com Inc. (AMZN)

Sales of our digital devices, including Kindle e-readers, Fire tablets, Fire TVs, and Echo, are considered arrangements with multiple deliverables, consisting of the device, undelivered software upgrades and/or undelivered non-software services such as cloud storage and free trial memberships to other services. The revenue allocated to the device, which is the substantial portion of the total sale price, and related costs are generally recognized upon delivery. Revenue related to undelivered software upgrades and/or undelivered non-software services is deferred and recognized generally on a straight-line basis over the estimated period the software upgrades and non-software services are expected to be provided for each of these devices.

Required

a. What is an arrangement with multiple deliverables? Explain.
b. Explain how companies account for multiple-element contracts in general.
c. Assume Amazon sold a Kindle Paperwhite with wi-fi capabilities for $180 and the company estimated a selling price (ESP) of $20 per unit for future software upgrades. Further assume that a typical customer keeps their Kindle reader about four years. Compute the revenue Amazon would recognize at the point of sale.
d. Use the financial statement effects template to record the initial sale of a Kindle Paperwhite with wi-fi and the accounting adjustment required at the end of the first year.

P5-51. **Analyzing and Interpreting Income Components and Disclosures**
The income statement for **Xerox Corporation** follows.

Years Ended December 31 ($ millions)	2015	2014	2013
Revenues			
Sales.	$ 4,748	$ 5,288	$ 5,582
Outsourcing, maintenance and rentals	12,951	13,865	13,941
Financing	346	387	483
Total Revenues	18,045	19,540	20,006
Costs and Expenses			
Cost of sales.	2,961	3,269	3,550
Cost of outsourcing, maintenance, and rentals	9,691	9,885	9,808
Cost of financing	130	140	163
Research, development and engineering expenses	563	577	603
Selling, administrative and general expenses	3,559	3,788	4,073
Restructuring and asset impairment charges	186	128	115
Amortization of intangible assets	310	315	305
Other expenses, net.	233	232	146
Total costs and expenses	17,633	18,334	18,763
Income before income taxes and equity income	412	1,206	1,243
Income (tax) benefit expense	(23)	215	253
Equity in net income of unconsolidated affiliates.	135	160	169
Income from continuing operations	570	1,151	1,159
(Loss) income from discontinued operations, net of tax	(78)	(115)	20
Net income	492	1,036	1,179
Less: net income attributable to noncontrolling interests . . .	18	23	20
Net income attributable to Xerox	$ 474	$ 1,013	$ 1,159

Required

a. Xerox reports several sources of income. How should revenue be recognized for each of these business activities? Explain.

b. Compute the relative size of sales revenue and of revenue from outsourcing, maintenance, and rentals. (*Hint:* Scale each type of revenue by total revenue.) What observations can be made about the different sources of revenue?

c. Xerox reports $233 million in expenses in 2015 labeled as "Other expenses, net." How can a company use such an account to potentially obscure its actual financial performance?

P5-52. **Analyzing Unearned Revenue Disclosures**
The following disclosures (excerpted) are from the August 28, 2016, annual report of **Costco Wholesale Corporation**.

> **Revenue Recognition** We generally recognize sales, net of estimated returns, at the time the member takes possession of merchandise or receives services. When we collect payment from customers prior to the transfer of ownership of merchandise or the performance of services, the amount received is generally recorded as deferred revenue on the consolidated balance sheets until the sale or service is completed. Membership fee revenue represents annual membership fees paid by our members. We account for membership fee revenue, net of estimated refunds, on a deferred basis, whereby revenue is recognized ratably over the one-year membership period.

Revenue ($ millions)	August 28, 2016	August 30, 2015	August 31, 2014
Net sales.	$116,073	$113,666	$110,212
Membership fees	2,646	2,533	2,428
Total revenue.	$118,719	$116,199	$112,640

continued

Current Liabilities ($ millions)	August 28, 2016	August 30, 2015
Accounts payable.	$ 7,612	$ 9,011
Current portion of long-term debt	1,100	1,283
Accrued salaries and benefits	2,629	2,468
Accrued member rewards	869	813
Deferred membership fees.	1,362	1,269
Other current liabilities	2,003	1,695
Total current liabilities	$15,575	$16,539

Required

a. Explain in layman's terms how Costco accounts for the cash received for membership fees.

b. Use the balance sheet information on Costco's deferred membership fees liability account and its income statement revenues related to membership fees earned during 2016 to compute the cash Costco received during 2016 for membership fees.

c. Use the financial statement effects template to show the effect of the cash Costco received during 2016 for membership fees and the recognition of membership fees revenue for 2016.

P5-53. **Interpreting Accounts Receivable and Related Footnote Disclosure**

LO5

Following is the current asset section from the **W.W. Grainger Inc.** balance sheet.

W.W. Grainger Inc. (GWW)

As of December 31 ($ 000s)	2015	2014	2013
Cash and cash equivalents	$ 290,136	$ 226,644	$ 430,644
Accounts receivable (less allowances for doubtful accounts of $22,288, $22,121 and $20,096, respectively)	1,209,641	1,172,924	1,101,656
Inventories—net	1,414,177	1,356,396	1,305,520
Prepaid expenses and other assets.	85,670	102,669	115,331
Deferred income taxes	0	61,387	75,819
Prepaid income taxes.	49,018	47,529	15,315
Total current assets.	$3,048,642	$2,967,549	$3,044,285

Grainger reports the following footnote relating to its receivables.

Allowance for Doubtful Accounts The following table shows the activity in the allowance for doubtful accounts.

For Years Ended December 31 ($ 000s)	2015	2014	2013
Balance at beginning of period	$22,121	$20,096	$19,449
Provision for uncollectible accounts	10,181	12,945	8,855
Write-off of uncollectible accounts, net of recoveries . .	(10,495)	(9,628)	(7,942)
Business acquisitions, foreign currency and other . . .	481	(1,292)	(266)
Balance at end of period	$22,288	$22,121	$20,096

Required

a. What amount do customers owe Grainger at each of the year-ends 2013 through 2015?

b. What percentage of its total accounts receivable does Grainger deem uncollectible? (*Hint:* percentage of uncollectible accounts = allowance for uncollectible accounts/gross accounts receivable)

c. What amount of bad debts expense did Grainger report in its income statement for each of the years 2013 through 2015?

d. Explain the change in the balance of the allowance for uncollectible accounts since 2013. Specifically, did the allowance increase or decrease as a percentage of gross accounts receivable, and why?

    e. If Grainger had kept its 2015 allowance for uncollectible accounts at the same percentage of gross accounts receivable as it was in 2013, by what amount would its pretax profit have changed? Explain.

    f. Overall, what is your assessment of Grainger's allowance for uncollectible accounts and the related bad debts expense?

LO5

Intuit Inc. (INTU)

P5-54. **Analyzing and Interpreting Receivables and Related Ratios**

Following is the current asset section from Intuit Inc.'s balance sheet. Total revenues were $4,694 million ($1,289 million in product sales and $3,405 million in service revenues and other) in 2016.

July 31 ($ millions)	2016	2015
Current assets:		
Cash and cash equivalents	$638	$ 808
Investments	442	889
Accounts receivable, net of allowance for doubtful accounts of $51 and $45	108	91
Income taxes receivable	20	84
Deferred income taxes	0	231
Prepaid expenses and other current assets	102	94
Current assets of discontinued operations	0	26
Current assets before funds held for customers	1,310	2,223
Funds held for customers	304	337
Total current assets	$1,614	$2,560

Required

    a. What are Intuit's gross accounts receivable at the end of 2015 and 2016?

    b. For both 2016 and 2015, compute the ratio of the allowance for uncollectible accounts to gross receivables. What trend do you observe?

    c. Compute the receivables turnover ratio and the average collection period for 2013 based on gross receivables computed in part a. Does the collection period (days sales in receivables) appear reasonable given Intuit's lines of business (Intuit's products include QuickBooks, TurboTax, and Quicken, which it sells to consumers and small businesses)? Explain.

    d. Is the percentage of Intuit's allowance for uncollectible accounts to gross accounts receivable consistent with what you expect for Intuit's line of business? Explain.

    e. Intuit discloses the following table related to its allowance for uncollectible accounts from its 10-K. Comment on the change in the allowance account during 2015 through 2016.

Allowance for doubtful accounts ($ millions)	Beginning Balance	Additions Charged to Expense	Deductions	Ending Balance
Year ended July 31, 2016	$45	$49	$(43)	$51
Year ended July 31, 2015	$40	$57	$(52)	$45
Year ended July 31, 2014	$38	$50	$(48)	$40

IFRS Applications

LO1, 3

Telstra Corporation Limited

I5-55. **Analyzing Unearned Revenue Transactions and Multiple-Element Arrangements**

Telstra Corporation Limited is an Australian telecommunications and technology company that offers a full range of communications services in all telecommunications markets. In Australia, Telstra provides 17.2 million mobile services, 7.0 million fixed voice services, and 3.4 million retail fixed broadband services. Excerpts from the company's revenue recognition footnote follow.

Revenue Recognition Our categories of sales revenue are recorded after deducting sales returns, trade allowances, discounts, sales incentives, duties and taxes.

Services revenue Revenue from the provision of our telecommunications services includes telephone calls and other services and facilities provided, such as internet and data. We record revenue earned from:

- telephone calls on completion of the call; and
- other services generally at completion, or on a straight line basis over the period of service provided, unless another method better represents the stage of completion.

Installation and connection fee revenues that are not considered to be separate units of accounting are deferred and recognised over the average estimated customer life. Incremental costs directly related to these revenues are also deferred and amortised over the customer contract life. In relation to basic access installation and connection revenue, we apply management judgement to determine the estimated customer contract life. Based on our reviews of historical information and customer trends, we have determined that our average estimated customer life is 5 years.

Sale of goods Our revenue from the sale of goods includes revenue from the sale of customer equipment and similar goods. This revenue is recorded on delivery of the goods sold. Generally we record the full gross amount of sales proceeds as revenue, however if we are acting as an agent under a sales arrangement, we record the revenue on a net basis, being the gross amount billed less the amount paid to the supplier. We review the facts and circumstances of each sales arrangement to determine if we are an agent or principal under the sale arrangement.

Revenue arrangements with multiple deliverables Where two or more revenue-generating activities or deliverables are sold under a single arrangement, each deliverable that is considered to be a separate unit of accounting is accounted for separately. When the deliverables in a multiple deliverable arrangement are not considered to be separate units of accounting, the arrangement is accounted for as a single unit. We allocate the consideration from the revenue arrangement to its separate units based on the relative selling prices of each unit. If neither vendor specific objective evidence nor third party evidence exists for the selling price, then the item is measured based on the best estimate of the selling price (BESP) of that unit. The revenue allocated to each unit is then recognised in accordance with our revenue recognition policies described above.

Required

a. Explain in layman's terms how Telstra records revenue from sales of bundled contracts.

b. Telstra sells a number of prepaid mobile packages for voice, text, and data. Assume a customer pays $100 in cash for a prepaid plan and Telstra activates service immediately. Explain how and when Telstra recognizes the $100 as revenue.

c. Assume that, at the beginning of the fiscal year, a customer makes a volume purchase of 200 iPhones and signs a two-year contract with Telstra for a voice and data package for each phone. The total discounted sales price is $480 per phone, and Telstra pays Apple $640 for each iPhone. Telstra loses money on the handset but makes it up by locking the customer into a long-term service contract. This contract includes free future software upgrades for two years. Because there is no reliable vendor-specific objective evidence, Telstra estimates a BESP of $64 for the future software upgrades. Allocate the consideration received for the 200 units to each respective element in the arrangement, based on its relative selling price (the sale is on account).

d. Use the financial statement effects template to record the original sale in part *c.*, above, and the accounting adjustment at the end of the first fiscal year after the sale.

I5-56. Identifying Operating Income Components

LO1, 2, 7
Mitel (MITL)

Headquartered in Ottawa, Ontario, Canada, **Mitel Networks Corporation** is a high-tech company that provides unified communications solutions for business. The company focuses almost entirely on Voice-over-IP (VoIP) products. Mitel has partners and resellers worldwide and is listed on the NASDAQ; its income statement follows.

MITEL NETWORKS CORPORATION Consolidated Statement of Operations Data	
For Year Ended December 31 (in U.S. dollars, millions)	**2015**
Revenues	$1,157.7
Cost of revenues	543.8
Gross margin	613.9
Expenses:	
Selling, general and administrative	363.0
Research and development	131.4
Special charges and restructuring costs	54.6
Amortization of acquisition-related intangible assets	75.1
	624.1
Operating income (loss)	(10.2)
Interest expense	(32.4)
Debt retirement and other debt costs	(9.6)
Other income (expense), net	20.9
Income tax recovery	10.6
Net income (loss)	$ (20.7)

Required

a. Identify the components considered operating for each year.

b. Identify the nonrecurring items for 2015 and explain how financial analysts would treat each item.

Management Applications

LO4   **MA5-57.   Managing Foreign Currency Risk**

Fluctuations in foreign currency exchange rates can result in increased volatility of revenues, expenses, and profits. Companies generally attempt to reduce this volatility.

a. Identify two possible solutions to reduce the volatility effect of foreign exchange rate fluctuations.

b. What costs would arise if you implemented each of your solutions?

LO1   **MA5-58.   Ethics and Governance: Revenue Recognition**

GAAP revenue recognition standards are based on broad principles rather than bright-line rules. This creates a certain amount of latitude in determining when revenue is earned. Assume a company that normally required acceptance by its customers prior to recording revenue as earned, delivers a product to a customer near the end of the quarter. The company believes customer acceptance is assured but cannot obtain it prior to quarter-end. Recording the revenue would assure "making its numbers" for the quarter. Although formal acceptance is not obtained, the salesperson records the sale, fully intending to obtain written acceptance as soon as possible.

a. What are the revenue recognition requirements in this case?

b. What are the ethical issues relating to this sale?

c. Assume you are on the board of directors of this company. What safeguards can you put in place to ensure the company's revenue recognition policy is followed?

Ongoing Project

(This ongoing project began in Module 1 and continues through most of the book; even if previous segments were not completed, the requirements are still applicable to any business analysis.) Analysis of financial statements commonly includes operating income and its components as explained in this module.

1. *Revenue Recognition*   Revenue is the largest item on the income statement, and we must assess it on a quantitative and qualitative basis.

    - Use horizontal analysis to identify any time trends.
    - Compare the horizontal analyses of the two companies.
    - Consider the current economic environment and the companies' competitive landscape. Given they operate in the same industry, you might expect similar revenue trends.
    - Read the management's discussion and analysis (MD&A) section of the 10-K to learn how the companies' senior managers explain revenue levels and changes.

    Our goal is to determine whether each company's revenue levels and changes seem appropriate and in line with external factors. *Additional analysis*: (a) If the company distinguishes among types of revenue on the income statement, use horizontal and vertical analyses to identify any changes in the product line mix or where sales are growing most quickly. Find the footnote on segment revenues and profits, and identify trends or significant changes. (b) Assess each company's revenue recognition policy by comparing it with the other and with those of some other close competitors. (c) Consider unearned revenue on the balance sheet. How big is it (common size), and is it fluctuating over time? (d) For companies that operate globally, determine the effect of foreign currency fluctuations on revenue. If these are substantial year after year, it might indicate that managers are not effectively hedging, and this would warrant additional investigation.

2. *Accounts Receivable*   The following provides some guidance for analyzing a company's accounts receivable.

    - Are sales primarily on credit, or is a typical sale transacted in cash? Consider the industry and the companies' business model.
    - What is the relative size of accounts receivable? How has this changed over the recent three-year period?
    - Determine the accounts receivable balance relative to gross accounts receivable.
    - What did the company record for bad debt expense? Compute the common size amount.
    - Compute accounts receivable turnover and days sales outstanding for all three years reported on the income statement. One will need to obtain additional balance sheet information to be able to compute average balances for the denominator. Consider the current economic environment and the company's competitive landscape. Would one expect collection to have slowed down or sped up during the year?
    - Does the company have any large customers that increase its credit risk?

    For each point of analysis, compare across companies and over time. The goal is to determine whether each company's accounts receivable (levels and changes) seems appropriate and to gauge the quality of the receivables.

3. *Operating Expenses*   Review and analyze the income statement items.

    - Prepare a common-sized income statement by dividing each item on the income statement by total revenues, net.
    - Compare the common-sized values for the three years presented in the income statement. What changes are there, if any? Are material changes explained in the MD&A? Do the explanations seem reasonable given the current economic environment?
    - Does the company engage in research and development activities? Quantify the amount in dollar terms and common size. Do you observe any patterns? Is the level of R&D expense consistent with peers and industry?
    - Does the company have discontinued operations? If so, how will this impact future operations?

4. *Accounting Quality*   Evaluating accounting quality is more of an art than a science. The point is to form an overall opinion about the reliability of the numbers in the financial statements.

    - Does the company report non-GAAP earnings? What items do they exclude or include? Do the two companies report similar one-time items? Do the items seem reasonable, or do we detect some self-serving disclosures?
    - Consider the list in the Research Insight Box in the module, and use it to assess the quality of the two companies' reported numbers.
    - Use an online investment website to find key ratios for close competitors. Compare to our companies.
    - Find the consensus analysts' EPS forecast for the recent year-end. How did our companies fare? Were there any one-time items or unusual changes in any expenses that might have caused the company to just meet or beat the forecast? This could indicate earnings management.

Solutions to Review Problems

Review 5-1—Solution

Part I

1. Revenue is recognized for the sales price less anticipated returns.

2. The purchase price is apportioned between two components (performance obligations): the value of the copier and the value of the two-year service agreement. Revenue is immediately recognized on the first component. For the second component, revenue is deferred and recognized ratably over two years.

3. Revenue is recognized ratably over the year despite the fact that customers pay up front.

4. Revenue is recognized for the commission only, not the full sales price, because the company is acting as an agent for the other companies.

5. Product sales are recognized as revenue when the product is delivered to the franchisee. Accounting services are recognized as revenue on a monthly basis as the service is provided.

Part II

1. Revenue = $3,000,000 × ($500,000/$2,500,000) = $600,000.

   Gross profit = $600,000 − $500,000 = $100,000.

2. The cost of $500,000 exceeds the billing of $400,000, and the excess of $100,000 is reported as a current asset (such as costs in excess of billings or contracts in progress).

Review 5-2—Solution

1. "Additions" represents the amount of returns allowances recorded during fiscal 2015 for sales during that year.

2. "Returns, net" is the dollar value of actual returns offset by the value of the merchandise returned. The actual returns number is very close to the amount estimated. This indicates that Nordstrom is fairly accurate in its estimation process.

3. *a.* Sales returns/gross sales shows an increasing pattern. The ratio is up from 13.3% two years ago to 16.1% in the most current year. This could indicate that customer satisfaction with products is decreasing. However, Nordstrom's business model focuses on customer satisfaction, and the fact that its margin is very high (35% in 2015) puts the increase in perspective—it is not alarming, but should be monitored.

$ millions	2015	2014	2013
Net sales.	$14,095	$13,110	$12,166
Year-end allowance for sales returns	2,720	2,129	1,880
Gross sales.	$16,815	$15,239	$14,046
% Returned merchandise	16.2%	14.0%	13.4%

   b. Nordstrom's allowance is adequate considering the following ratio of actual to estimate:

$ millions	2015	2014	2013
Actual returns during the year	$2,710	$2,097	$1,868
Estimated returns for the year	$2,720	$2,129	$1,880
Adequacy	99.6%	98.5%	99.4%

Review 5-3—Solution

1. Some customers have very low credit scores and by allowing them to prepay for their wireless services, AT&T increases revenue without the risk of increasing the bad debt expense. Other customers may want a temporary phone while visiting the United States. Still other customers may not want a long-term contract because of uncertainty in their usage. For a variety of reasons, a prepaid wireless service makes economic sense for AT&T. Indeed, the company collected nearly $5 billion in revenue from this product line in 2015.

2. The amount of cash received from the customers is the amount added to the liability.

Advanced Billings and Customer Deposits ($ millions)

Balance at 1/1/2015	$4,105
+ Cash prepayments by customers during the year	??
− Revenue recognized during the year	(4,662)
= Balance at 12/31/2015	$4,682

Cash prepayments by customers during the year = $4,682 + $4,662 − $4,105 = $5,239

---

3. The gift card is booked as a liability when sold, then AT&T would use historical analysis to age the gift cards. For example, the analysis might reveal that by the time a gift card is one year old, there is a 75% chance it will be redeemed, so AT&T would recognize 25% of the value of these cards as revenue (100% − 75%) leaving 75% of the value of the gift card in the liability account. When a gift card is two years old, analysis reveals there is only a 5% chance it will be redeemed, and AT&T would recognize another 70% of the revenue, leaving 5% of the value of the gift card still in the liability account.

Review 5-4—Solution

1. Using the rates provided, we can compute the change in the value of a peso during 2015 as 15.18% [(17.249549/14.975945) − 1 = 15.18%], which is close to the 13.1% AT&T claimed. The difference could be due to the exact date when AT&T measured the rates.

2.

(Revenue in millions)	1 $US = pesos	Monthly Revenue	Revenue in $US at January rate
31-Jan	14.975945		
28-Feb	14.948455	$177.45	$ 177.12
31-Mar	15.241323	177.45	180.59
30-Apr	15.388116	177.45	182.33
31-May	15.378000	177.45	182.21
30-Jun	15.695152	177.45	185.97
31-Jul	18.216009	177.45	215.84
31-Aug	16.734763	177.45	198.29
30-Sep	16.901119	177.45	200.26
31-Oct	16.500190	177.45	195.51
30-Nov	16.601480	177.45	196.71
31-Dec	17.249549	177.45	204.39
		Total	2,119.22
		As reported	1,952.00
		Translation loss	$ 167.22

3. It cannot be determined from the information provided. If the Mexican wireless operations were profitable, then the net income when translated to $US would have been negatively impacted by the peso devaluation, and a translation loss would have reduced AT&T's consolidated net income. However, if the Mexican operations were unprofitable (a net loss for the year), then the weaker peso actually caused the loss to be smaller in $US.

4. AT&T does not hedge these exposures because the gains and losses on net income and foreign net assets are not realized. They are losses created by the accounting rules that require consolidation of all subsidiaries regardless of their location. These gains and losses will fluctuate over time and will only be realized when the foreign profits are repatriated to the United States.

5. These transactions have actual cash consequences to AT&T. The losses are realized when the liabilities are actually repaid in $US or the dividends are actually received by AT&T. Because they have real consequences, AT&T hedges the exposure.

Review 5-5—Solution

1. The company expects to collect $16,532 million, the amount reported on the balance sheet.

2. At December 31, 2015, AT&T's customers owed the company $17,236 million, computed as $16,532 million of accounts receivable, net + $704 of allowance for doubtful accounts. This is the gross accounts receivable.

3. The aging analysis shows that AT&T's allowance account should be $704 million.

$ millions	Accounts Receivable	% uncollectible	Allowance
Current	$12,650	0.50%	$ 63
1–30 days past due	2,785	5%	139
31–60 days past due	854	15%	128
61–90 days past due	589	25%	147
91–120 days past due	207	55%	114
Over 120 days past due	151	75%	113
Total	$17,236		$704

4. Bad debt expense is determined by reconciling the allowance account as follows ($ millions):

Balance January 1, 2015	$ 454
Write-offs during the year.	(1,166)
Allowance available	(712)
Allowance required at December 31, 2015, per aging analysis	704
Bad debt expense	$1,416

5. The quality of AT&T's receivables has declined during the year. The proportion of allowance to gross accounts receivable has increased from 3.03% in 2014 [$454/($14,527 + $454)] to 4.08% in 2015 ($704 million/$17,236 million). Possible causes include the change in customer mix with the increase in sales in Mexico and Latin America and overall decline in credit quality in the United States, or more lax credit granting policies and/or collection processes.

Review 5-6—Solution

1. The following would **not** be included in selling, general and administrative expense.

- Utilities for the research laboratories—this would be included in the research and development expense because it relates to those activities.

- Wages for manufacturing employees—these are costs to manufacture goods and would be included in Cost of products sold.

- Pharmaceuticals consumed during phase III trials for FDA approvals—seeking approvals is part of the research and development process, so these costs would be included on that income statement line item.

- Depreciation on machines that package and label finished goods—this is part of the cost to get the inventory ready for sale and would be included in Cost of products sold.

2.

	2015	2014	2013
R&D expense in $ millions	$1,405	$1,345	$1,371
R&D expense as % of revenue.	6.9%	6.6%	7.0%

Abbott's spending has grown slightly in 2015 compared to prior years. This is evident in both dollar and percentage terms. Abbott engages in basic pharmaceutical research and develops and brings to market successful compounds and drugs. R&D costs include salaries and overhead for R&D employees including scientists, lab workers directly involved with R&D as well as for personnel who indirectly assist and support R&D activities.

3. Abbott sold off or closed some operations during the current fiscal year. From the start of the year until the date of sale or closure, those operations earned a total of $65 million. That amount is reported on the line item labeled "Earnings from discontinued operations."

4. When Abbott discontinued some operations during the current fiscal year, the assets and liabilities were sold. Abbott received proceeds from the sale in excess of the value of the net assets on the balance sheet. That excess was $1,752 after tax.

5. Discontinued operations are segregated in the income statement because they represent a transitory item, which reflect transactions or events that affected the current period but will not recur. One plausible way to treat this is to use the earnings from continuing operations in all ratios and other analysis.

6. When a company does not own 100% of the voting stock of all of its subsidiaries, there are minority shareholders involved—they own the remaining stock. In that case, their proportionate share of the net income of the subsidiaries is shown as a separate line item on the income statement labeled "Noncontrolling interest." Such a line item is not shown on the Abbott Labs income statement, so we might conclude that the company owns 100% of the stock of all of the subsidiaries. Another explanation is the item is immaterial, so Abbott did not call it out specifically.

Review 5-7—Solution

1. Companies, including AT&T, publicly report non-GAAP information to communicate its view of the company's ongoing, persistent earnings. Skeptics of such pro forma numbers suggest companies are simply trying to present their financial results in the best possible light.

2. AT&T management does not seem to be adjusting income up so as to present their financial results in the best possible light. By deliberately reducing the bottom line non-GAAP number, the company seems to be forthcoming. The income statement and/or the footnotes will report the wireless gain, so AT&T might lose credibility if it did not include the item in the non-GAAP reconciliation.

Module 6

Inventories, Accounts Payable, and Long-Term Assets

Learning Objectives

LO1 Apply inventory costing methods. (p. 6-3)

LO2 Examine inventory disclosures in financial statements. (p. 6-8)

LO3 Analyze inventories and the related accounts payable. (p. 6-11)

LO4 Apply capitalization and depreciation of tangible assets. (p. 6-16)

LO5 Evaluate asset sales, impairments, and restructuring activities. (p. 6-20)

LO6 Analyze tangible assets and related activities. (p. 6-25)

HD
Market cap: $167,120 mil
Total assets: $42,549 mil
Revenues: $88,519 mil
Net income: $7,009 mil

Home Depot is the world's largest home improvement retailer, selling an assortment of building materials, home improvement products, and lawn and garden products. Two things stand out when you enter a Home Depot store: its size and its large inventories for sale.

Home Depot stores average 104,000 square feet of enclosed space, with 24,000 additional square feet of outside garden area. The company stocks up to 40,000 different kinds of building materials, home improvement supplies, appliances, and lawn and garden products. Two accounts on its balance sheet, Inventories and Property, Plant and Equipment (PPE), make up 80% of total assets.

Inventories are a major asset for many companies (28% of total assets for Home Depot). Having enough inventories for sale is important, but inventories are costly to hold. Companies typically finance the cost of buying or manufacturing goods. Finished inventories are stored, moved, and insured. Consequently, companies prefer to hold fewer inventories when possible. If companies reduce inventories too much, they risk stock-outs—meaning there is not enough inventory to meet demand. Home Depot says it aims to "reduce our average lead time from supplier to shelf, reduce transportation expenses and improve inventory turns."

Companies often purchase inventories on credit—meaning they do not pay their suppliers when goods are shipped. Instead, the company reports accounts payable, on its balance sheet, reflecting the amount that they will pay to suppliers. Accounts payable are a source of free financing for buyers because accounts payable are usually non-interest bearing. Managing accounts payable is an important task.

Property, plant and equipment (or *tangible assets* or PPE, which we use interchangeably) are often the largest assets on a company's balance sheet—52% of total assets for Home Depot. Its land and buildings are made up of 2,274 stores, of which 90% are owned and the remainder are leased. Most companies need offices, technology and R&D facilities, service centers, manufacturing and distribution facilities, vehicles, land, and a host of other assets. These are large investments and once acquired, property, plant and equipment must be maintained and monitored. Their purchase is a critical decision that usually involves a review of the entire value chain.

Managing inventory and PPE is crucial to creating shareholder value. Those actions affect the balance sheet and the income statement—the latter via cost of goods sold (inventory), depreciation, and gains or losses when PPE assets are sold or impaired. In this module, we explain the measurement and reporting of inventory and PPE. We also describe analysis tools to assess the efficiency and effectiveness of inventory and PPE. [Sources: *Home Depot website and its 2015 10-K*]

© iStock

Road Map

LO	Learning Objective | Topics	Page	eLecture	Guided Example	Assignments
6-1	**Apply inventory costing methods.** Cost Flows :: FIFO :: LIFO :: AC :: Financial Effects	6-3	e6–1	Review 6-1	1, 2, 3, 4, 10, 13, 14, 23, 25, 42
6-2	**Examine inventory disclosures in financial statements.** LCM :: LIFO Liquidation :: LIFO Reserve and Adjustments	6-8	e6–2	Review 6-2	5, 11, 22, 24, 26, 36
6-3	**Analyze inventories and the related accounts payable.** Gross Profit Margin :: Days Inventory Outstanding :: Inventory Turnover :: Days Payable Outstanding :: Cash Conversion Cycle	6-11	e6–3	Review 6-3	6, 15, 19, 20, 32, 35, 36, 40, 42, 43
6-4	**Apply capitalization and depreciation of tangible assets.** Property :: Plant & Equipment :: Depreciation Methods :: R&D Facilities & Equipment	6-16	e6–4	Review 6-4	7, 8, 16, 17, 27, 28, 29, 30, 33
6-5	**Evaluate asset sales, impairments, and restructuring activities.** Asset Sales :: Gains and Losses :: Asset Impairments	6-20	e6–5	Review 6-5	7, 9, 12, 21, 28, 30, 33, 38, 39, 41
6-6	**Analyze tangible assets and related activities.** PPE Turnover :: PPE Useful Life :: PPE Percent Used Up	6-25	e6–6	Review 6-6	18, 31, 32, 34, 35, 37, 38, 41, 42, 43

Inventories and Accounts Payable
■ Inventory Costing Methods
■ Footnote Disclosures
■ Effects of Inventory Costing
■ Inventory Disclosures
■ Inventory Analysis
■ Cash Conversion Cycle

Property, Plant & Equipment
■ Depreciation and Book Value
■ Disposals, Impairments and Restructuring
■ Footnote Disclosures
■ Analysis Tools—Turnover, Useful Life, and Percent Used Up

Inventory—Costing Methods

LO1

Apply inventory costing methods.

For many companies, inventory is among the four largest assets on the balance sheet (along with receivables, property, plant & equipments (PPE), and intangible assets such as goodwill). On the income statement, cost of goods sold (which is directly related to inventory), is the largest expense for many companies and certainly for those in retailing and manufacturing. Companies can choose from among several methods to account for inventory costs and these accounting choices can greatly impact the balance sheet and income statement.

When inventory is purchased or produced, it is "capitalized." That is, it is carried on the balance sheet as an asset until it is sold, at which time its cost is transferred from the balance sheet to the income statement as an expense (cost of goods sold). The process by which costs are removed from the balance sheet when the inventory is sold is important. For example, if higher cost units are transferred from the balance sheet, then cost of goods sold is higher and gross profit (sales less cost of goods sold) is lower. Conversely, if lower cost units are transferred to cost of goods sold, gross profit is higher. The remainder of this section discusses the accounting for inventory including the mechanics, reporting, and analysis of inventory costing.

Capitalization of Inventory Cost

Capitalization means that a cost is recorded on the balance sheet and is not immediately expensed in the income statement. Once costs are capitalized, they remain on the balance sheet as assets until they are used up, at which time they are transferred from the balance sheet to the income statement as expense. If costs are capitalized rather than expensed, then assets, current income, and current equity are all higher.

For purchased inventories (such as merchandise), the amount capitalized is the purchase price. For manufacturers, cost capitalization is more difficult, as **manufacturing costs** consist of three components: cost of direct (raw) materials used in the product, cost of direct labor to manufacture the product, and manufacturing overhead. Direct materials cost is relatively easy to compute. Design specifications list the components of each product, and their purchase costs are readily determined. The direct labor cost per unit of inventory is based on how long each unit takes to construct and the rates for each labor class working on that product. Overhead costs are also capitalized into inventory, and include the costs of depreciation, utilities, supervisory personnel, and other costs that contribute to manufacturing activities—that is, all costs of manufacturing other than direct materials and direct labor.

When inventories are sold, their costs are transferred from the balance sheet to the income statement as cost of goods sold (COGS). COGS is then deducted from sales to yield **gross profit**.

Sales
− Cost of goods sold
= Gross profit

The manner in which inventory costs are transferred from the balance sheet to the income statement affects both the level of inventories reported on the balance sheet and the amount of gross profit (and net income) reported on the income statement.

Inventory Cost Flows

Exhibit 6.1 shows the computation of cost of goods sold.

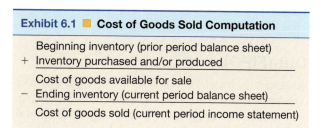

Exhibit 6.1 ■ Cost of Goods Sold Computation

   Beginning inventory (prior period balance sheet)
+ Inventory purchased and/or produced

   Cost of goods available for sale
− Ending inventory (current period balance sheet)

   Cost of goods sold (current period income statement)

The cost of inventory available at the beginning of a period is a carryover from the ending inventory balance of the prior period. Current period inventory purchases (or costs of newly manufactured inventories) are added to the beginning inventory balance, yielding the total cost of goods (inventory) available for sale. Then, the goods available are either sold, and end up in cost of goods sold for the period (reported on the income statement), or the goods available remain unsold and are still in inventory at the end of the period (reported on the balance sheet). Exhibit 6.2 shows this cost flow graphically.

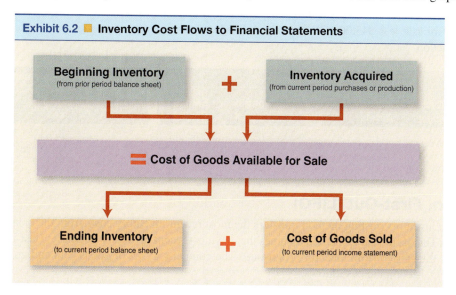

Exhibit 6.2 ■ Inventory Cost Flows to Financial Statements

Beginning Inventory (from prior period balance sheet)

+

Inventory Acquired (from current period purchases or production)

= Cost of Goods Available for Sale

Ending Inventory (to current period balance sheet)

+

Cost of Goods Sold (to current period income statement)

Understanding the flow of inventory costs is important. If all inventory purchased or manufactured during the period is sold, then COGS is equal to the cost of the goods purchased or manufactured. However, when inventory remains at the end of a period, companies must distinguish the cost of the inventories that were sold (cost of goods sold in the income statement) from the cost of the inventories that remain as an asset on the balance sheet.

Exhibit 6.3 illustrates the partial inventory records of a company.

Exhibit 6.3 ■ Summary Inventory Records

Inventory available on January 1, 2017	500 units	@ $100 per unit	$ 50,000
Inventory purchased in 2017	200 units	@ $150 per unit	30,000
Total cost of goods available for sale in 2017 . . .	700 units		$ 80,000
Inventory sold in 2017	450 units	@ $250 per unit	$112,500

This company began the period with 500 units of inventory that were purchased or manufactured for $50,000 ($100 each). During the period the company purchased and/or manufactured an additional 200 units costing $30,000. The total cost of goods available for sale for this period equals $80,000.

The company sold 450 units during 2017 for $250 per unit for total sales of $112,500. Accordingly, the company must remove the cost of the 450 units sold from the inventory account on the balance sheet and match this cost against the revenues generated from the sale. An important question is which costs should management remove from the balance sheet and report as cost of goods sold in the income statement? Three inventory costing methods (FIFO, LIFO and average cost) are common and all are acceptable.

First-In, First-Out (FIFO)

The FIFO inventory costing method transfers costs from inventory in the order that they were initially recorded. That is, FIFO assumes that the first costs recorded in inventory (first-in) are the first costs transferred from inventory (first-out). Applying FIFO to the data in Exhibit 6.3 means that the costs of the 450 units sold comes from *beginning* inventory, which consists of 500 units costing $100 each. The company's cost of goods sold and gross profit, using FIFO, is computed as follows.

Sales..	$112,500
COGS (450 @ $100 each).....................	45,000
Gross profit...................................	$ 67,500

The cost remaining in inventory and reported on the year-end balance sheet is $35,000 ($80,000 goods available for sale less $45,000 COGS). The following financial statement effects template captures the transaction.

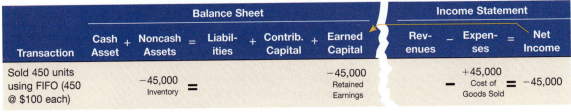

Last-In, First-Out (LIFO)

The LIFO inventory costing method transfers the most recent inventory costs from the balance sheet to COGS. That is, the LIFO method assumes that the most recent inventory purchases (last-in) are the first costs transferred from inventory (first-out). The company's cost of goods sold and gross profit, using LIFO, is computed as follows.

Sales.........................		$112,500
COGS: 200 @ $150 per unit............	$30,000	
250 @ $100 per unit............	25,000	55,000
Gross profit........................		$ 57,500

The cost remaining in inventory and reported on the year-end balance sheet is $25,000 (computed as $80,000 − $55,000). This is reflected in our financial statements effects template as follows.

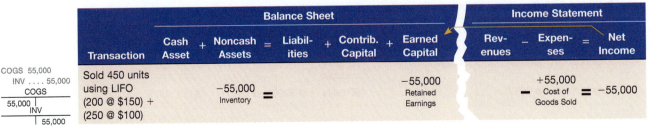

Average Cost (AC)

The average cost method computes the cost of goods sold as an average of the cost to purchase or manufacture all of the inventories that were available for sale during the period. To calculate the average cost of $114.286 per unit the company divides the total cost of goods available for sale by the number of units available for sale ($80,000/700 units). The company's sales, cost of sales, and gross profit follow.

Sales.	$112,500
COGS (450 @ $114.286 per unit).	51,429
Gross profit.	$ 61,071

The cost remaining in inventory and reported on the year-end balance sheet is $28,571 ($80,000 − $51,429). This is reflected in our financial statements effects template as follows.

It is important to understand that the inventory costing method a company chooses to prepare its income statement is independent of the actual flow of inventory. For example, many grocery chains use LIFO inventory but certainly do not sell the freshest products first. (Companies can adopt a new inventory costing method if doing so enhances the quality of the company's financial reports, but changes in inventory costing methods are rare.)

Business Insight ■ Retail Method for Inventory Costing

Retailers such as Home Depot and Lowe's, commonly estimate the cost of ending inventories using the *retail inventory method* (RIM). Retailers know the **cost** of the inventories purchased as well as their **retail** selling price. From this, the retailer computes the **cost-to-retail percentage** and applies that percentage to estimate the cost of the inventory still available at year-end (the ending inventory) as follows.

	Purchase Cost	Retail Selling Price
Beginning inventories.	$100,000	$160,000
+ Purchases during the period	300,000	500,000
= Cost of goods available for sale.	400,000	660,000
(Cost-to-retail percentage: $400,000/$660,000 = 60.6%)		
Sales.		(420,000)
Estimated ending inventory at retail selling prices.		$240,000
Estimated ending inventory at cost (60.6% × $240,000 retail) . . .	(145,440)	
= Cost of goods sold.	$254,560	

This retailer reports inventory of $145,440 on its balance sheet at year-end. The income statement reports sales of $420,000, cost of goods sold of $254,560, and gross profit of $165,440.

This method allows retailers to readily compute ending inventories at retail selling prices (Quantities available × Selling price). The company's inventory system tracks both the purchase cost and the retail selling price of inventories. These are inputs in the cost-to-retail percentage calculation. The cost-to-retail percentage is important and managers review the ratio regularly for reliability. Home Depot describes its inventory costing method as follows.

continued

continued from previous page

> The majority of the Company's Merchandise Inventories are stated at the lower of cost (first-in, first-out) or market, as determined by the retail inventory method . . . Independent physical inventory counts . . . are taken on a regular basis in each store and distribution center to ensure that amounts reflected in the accompanying Consolidated Financial Statements for Merchandise Inventories are properly stated.

Financial Statement Effects of Inventory Costing

This section describes the financial statement effects of different inventory costing methods.

Income Statement Effects

The three inventory costing methods yield differing levels of gross profit as Exhibit 6.4 shows.

Exhibit 6.4 ■ Income Effects from Inventory Costing Methods			
	Sales	Cost of Goods Sold	Gross Profit
FIFO	$112,500	$45,000	$67,500
LIFO	112,500	55,000	57,500
Average cost	112,500	51,429	61,071

Recall that inventory costs *rose* during this period from $100 per unit to $150 per unit. The higher gross profit reported under FIFO arises because FIFO matches older, lower-cost inventory against current selling prices. To generalize: in an inflationary environment, FIFO yields higher gross profit than do LIFO or average cost methods.

In recent years, the gross profit impact from using the FIFO method has been minimal for companies due to lower rates of inflation and increased management focus on reducing inventory quantities through improved manufacturing processes and better inventory controls. The FIFO gross profit effect can still arise, however, with companies subject to high inflation and slow inventory turnover.

Balance Sheet Effects

In our illustration above, the ending inventory using LIFO is less than that reported using FIFO. In periods of rising costs, LIFO inventories are markedly lower than under FIFO. As a result, balance sheets using LIFO do not accurately represent the cost that a company would incur to replace its current investment in inventories.

Caterpillar Inc. (CAT), for example, reports 2015 inventories under LIFO costing $9,700 million. As disclosed in the footnotes to its 10-K, if CAT valued these inventories using FIFO, the reported amount would be $12,298 million, which is $2,498 million greater, a 26% increase (see below). This suggests that CAT's balance sheet omits over $2,498 million in inventories.

> Inventories are stated at the lower of cost or market. Cost is principally determined using the last-in, first-out (LIFO) method. The value of inventories on the LIFO basis represented about 60 percent of total inventories at December 31, 2015 and 2014. If the FIFO (first-in, first-out) method had been in use, inventories would have been $2,498 million and $2,430 million higher than reported at December 31, 2015 and 2014, respectively.

Cash Flow Effects

Unlike most other accounting method choices, inventory costing methods affect taxable income and, thus, taxes paid. When a company adopts LIFO in its tax filings (it must, then, also use LIFO to report to shareholders), in an inflationary economy, pretax profit is lower and so are taxes paid. The tax savings increases operating cash flow (see our 'LIFO Reserve Adjustments to Financial Statements' section that follows). Conversely, in an inflationary economy, using FIFO results in higher taxable income and, consequently, higher taxes payable.

At the beginning of the current period, assume that one of **Home Depot**'s subsidiary companies holds 1,000 units of a certain product with a unit cost of $18. A summary of purchases during the current period follows.

		Units	Unit Cost	Cost
Beginning Inventory		1,000	$18.00	$18,000
Purchases:	#1	1,800	18.25	32,850
	#2	800	18.50	14,800
	#3	1,200	19.00	22,800
Cost of goods available for sale		4,800		$88,450

During the current period, the HD subsidiary sells 2,800 units.

Required

1. Assume that the HD subsidiary uses the first-in, first-out (FIFO) method for this product. Compute the product's cost of goods sold for the current period and the ending inventory balance.
2. Assume that the HD subsidiary uses the last-in, first-out (LIFO) method for this product. Compute the product's cost of goods sold for the current period and the ending inventory balance.
3. Assume that the HD subsidiary uses the average cost (AC) method for this product. Compute the product's cost of goods sold for the current period and the ending inventory balance.
4. As manager, which of these three inventory costing methods would you choose:
   a. To reflect what is probably the physical flow of goods? Explain.
   b. To minimize income taxes for the period? Explain.

Solution on p. 6-42.

Inventory—Reporting

Lower of Cost or Market (LCM)

Footnotes to financial statements describe the inventory accounting method a company uses. To illustrate, **Home Depot** reports $11,809 million in inventory on its 2015 balance sheet as a current asset. Following is an excerpt from Home Depot's footnote.

LO2 Examine inventory disclosures in financial statements.

> **Merchandise Inventories** Our Merchandise Inventories are stated at the lower of cost (first-in, first-out) or market, with approximately 71% valued under the retail inventory method and the remainder under a cost method. Retailers like us, with many different types of merchandise at low unit cost and a large number of transactions, frequently use the retail inventory method. Under the retail inventory method, Merchandise Inventories are stated at cost, which is determined by applying a cost-to-retail ratio to the ending retail value of inventories. As our inventory retail value is adjusted regularly to reflect market conditions, our inventory valued using the retail method approximates the lower of cost or market.

Like many retailers, Home Depot uses FIFO to cost its inventory along with the retail inventory method that we explained above. Then, at the end of each accounting period, Home Depot compares the ending FIFO inventory balance with the market value of the inventory (its replacement cost). If the market value is less than the FIFO amount, Home Depot "writes down" the inventory to its market value. The result is that the inventory is carried on the balance sheet at whichever amount is lower: the cost of the inventory *or* its market value. This process is called reporting inventories at the **lower of cost or market** and creates the following financial statement effects.

- Inventory book value is written down to current market value (replacement cost), reducing inventory and total assets.
- Inventory write-down is reflected as an expense (part of cost of goods sold) on the income statement, reducing current period gross profit, income, and equity.

To illustrate, assume that a company has inventory on its balance sheet at a cost of $27,000. Management learns that the inventory's replacement cost is $23,000 and writes inventories down to a balance of $23,000. The following financial statement effects template shows the adjustment.

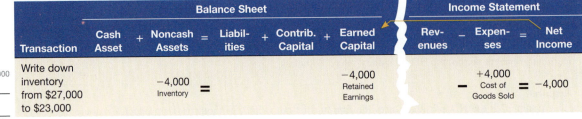

The inventory write-down (a noncash expense) is reflected in cost of goods sold and reduces gross profit by $4,000. Inventory write-downs are included in cost of goods sold. They are *not* reported in selling, general, and administrative expenses, which is common for other asset write-downs. A common occurrence of inventory write-downs is in connection with restructuring activities.

LIFO Reserve Adjustments to Financial Statements

CAT uses LIFO for most of its inventories.[1] Had CAT used FIFO, its 2015 balance sheet would have reported inventories of $12,198 million ($9,700 million + $2,498 million) rather than $9,700 million. This difference, referred to as the **LIFO reserve**, is the amount that must be added to LIFO inventories (from the balance sheet) to adjust them to their FIFO value.

FIFO Inventory = LIFO Inventory + LIFO Reserve

By choosing LIFO, CAT's 2015 balance sheet reported inventories that were $2,498 million lower than had the company used FIFO. Because inventory on the balance sheet affects cost of goods sold (COGS) on the income statement, the LIFO choice had a very important effect on CAT's income statements over the years.[2] CAT's *cumulative* COGS was $2,498 million higher than it would have been had the company used FIFO. (Cumulative here means the aggregate amount over the company's entire history.) This cumulative increase in COGS caused a cumulative decrease in gross profit and pretax profit of the same amount, $2,498 million. Because CAT also uses LIFO for tax purposes, lower pretax profits translated into a lower cumulative tax bill by about $874 million ($2,498 million × 35% assumed corporate tax rate). This had real cash flow consequences: CAT's cumulative operating cash flow was $874 million higher because the company chose LIFO instead of FIFO. The cash savings from lower taxes is often cited as a compelling reason for companies to adopt LIFO.

Disclosures for a LIFO Reserve Because companies can choose among the various inventory costing methods, their financial statements are often not comparable. The problem is most serious when companies hold large amounts of inventory and when prices markedly rise or fall. For example, consider comparing CAT to Kubota, a close competitor that uses the FIFO method to cost its inventory. The table below reports certain financial information for both companies for fiscal 2015.

---

[1] Neither the IRS nor GAAP requires use of a single inventory costing method. That is, companies are allowed to, and frequently do, use different inventory costing methods for different types of inventory (such as spare parts versus finished goods) or inventory in different geographical locations.

[2] Recall: Cost of Goods Sold = Beginning Inventories + Purchases − Ending Inventories. Thus, as ending inventories decrease, cost of goods sold increases.

(Monetary amounts in millions)	CAT LIFO as reported	CAT FIFO as restated	Kubota as reported
Inventory......................................	$ 9,700	$12,198	¥ 338,033
LIFO reserve, 2015............................	$ 2,498	—	—
LIFO reserve, 2014............................	$ 2,430	—	—
Total assets.................................	$78,497	$80,995	¥2,476,820
Inventory as a % of total assets	**12%**	**15%**	**14%**
Cost of goods sold...........................	$33,742	$33,674	¥1,104,761
Revenue (equipment sales)	$44,147	$44,147	¥1,586,937
Cost of goods sold as a % of revenue..............	76.4%	76.3%	69.6%

If we compare the information reported on each company's financial statements ('CAT LIFO as reported' vs. 'Kubota as reported') we would conclude that Caterpillar holds proportionately less inventory than Kubota—12% of total assets for CAT vs. 14% for Kubota. But this is not an apples-to-apples comparison and such a conclusion is erroneous. Fortunately, companies that use LIFO must report their LIFO reserve, and we can use these disclosures to adjust the LIFO numbers to their FIFO equivalents. Once we convert CAT's inventory and its total assets to FIFO (by adding the LIFO reserve, as explained above), we find that the company holds 15% of total assets as inventory, more than Kubota, not less.

Balance Sheet Adjustments for a LIFO Reserve In general, to adjust for LIFO on the balance sheet, we must make three modifications.

- Increase inventories by the LIFO reserve.
- Increase tax liabilities by the tax rate applied to the LIFO reserve.
- Increase retained earnings for the difference.

As an example, to adjust CAT's 2015 balance sheet, we would:

- Increase inventories by $2,498 million.
- Increase tax liabilities by $874 million (the extra cumulative taxes CAT would have had to pay under FIFO, computed as $2,498 million $\times$ 35%).
- Increase retained earnings by the difference of $1,624 million (computed as $2,498 million $-$ $874 million).

Income Statement Adjustments for a LIFO Reserve To compare the income statements of companies that use LIFO, we must adjust cost of goods sold from LIFO to FIFO. To do this, we use the *change* in the LIFO reserve to determine the FIFO cost of goods sold (COGS) as follows.

$$\text{FIFO COGS} = \text{LIFO COGS} - \text{Increase in LIFO Reserve (or + Decrease)}$$

For CAT in 2015, this is: $33,742 million $-$ ($2,498 million $-$ $2,430 million) = $33,674 million.

Had CAT *always used* FIFO, its 2015 COGS would have been $68 million lower (meaning gross profit and pretax income would be $68 million higher), and it would have paid $24 million more in taxes ($68 million $\times$ 35% assumed tax rate). This does not make much difference either in dollar or percentage terms for CAT in 2015 because the LIFO reserve increased only slightly during the year. But for other companies, the impact can be great.

LIFO Liquidations

When companies acquire inventory at different costs, they are required to account for each cost level as a separate inventory pool or layer (for example, there are the $100 and $150 units in our Exhibit 6.3 illustration). When companies reduce inventory levels, older inventory costs flow to the income statement. These older LIFO costs are often markedly different from current replacement costs. Assuming an inflationary environment, sales of older pools often yield a boost to gross profit as older, lower costs are matched against current selling prices on the income statement.

The increase in gross profit resulting from a reduction of inventory quantities in the presence of rising costs is called **LIFO liquidation**. The effect of LIFO liquidation is evident in the following footnote from **Rite Aid**'s 2016 10-K.

> **Inventory** (in $000s) . . . During fiscal 2016, 2015 and 2014, a reduction in inventories related to working capital initiatives resulted in the liquidation of applicable LIFO inventory quantities carried at lower costs in prior years. This LIFO liquidation resulted in a $60,653, $38,867 and $13,894 cost of revenues decrease, with a corresponding reduction to the adjustment to LIFO for fiscal 2016, fiscal 2015 and fiscal 2014, respectively.

Rite Aid reports that reductions in inventory quantities in 2016 led to the sale (at current selling prices) of inventory that had a low balance sheet value—the inventory was valued using costs from prior years when those costs were much lower. As a result of these inventory reductions, COGS was lower, which increased income by $60,653 thousand in 2016. Fiscal years 2015 and 2014 were similarly affected.

IFRS Insight ■ Inventory Measurement under IFRS

Like GAAP, IFRS measures inventories at the lower of cost or market. The cost of inventory generally is determined using the FIFO (first-in, first-out) or average cost method; use of the LIFO (last-in, first-out) method is prohibited under IFRS.

Review 6-2 LO2

Refer to the information in Review 6-1. Consider each of the following as separate situations.

Required
1. Assume HD reports its inventories using the FIFO cost flow assumption as in #1 in Review 6-1 and that the market value (replacement cost) of the inventories on the financial statement date is $30,000. At what amount is inventories reported on the balance sheet?
2. Assume that the HD subsidiary utilizes the LIFO method and delays purchasing lot #3 until the next period. Compute cost of goods sold under this scenario and discuss how the LIFO liquidation affects profit.
3. Assume that the subsidiary uses LIFO for this product. In that case, the company would compute and report a LIFO reserve. What is the amount of LIFO reserve? How would that reserve affect the subsidiary's tax expense for the current period (as compared to FIFO) assuming a marginal tax rate of 35%?

Solution on p. 6-43.

Inventory—Analysis Tools

LO3
Analyze inventories and the related accounts payable.

This section describes several useful tools for analysis of inventory and related accounts.

Gross Profit Analysis

The **gross profit margin (GPM)** is gross profit divided by sales. This important ratio is closely monitored by management, analysts, and other external financial statement users. Exhibit 6.5 shows the gross profit margin on **Home Depot**'s sales for the past three years.

Exhibit 6.5 ■ Gross Profit Margin for Home Depot			
$ millions	**2016**	**2015**	**2014**
Net sales.	$88,519	$83,176	$78,812
Cost of sales.	58,254	54,787	51,897
Gross profit.	$30,265	$28,389	$26,915
Gross profit margin.	34.2%	34.1%	34.2%

The gross profit margin is commonly used instead of the dollar amount of gross profit as the GPM allows for comparisons across companies and over time. A decline in GPM is usually cause for concern since it indicates that the company has less ability to pass on increased product cost to customers or that the company is not effectively managing product costs. Some possible reasons for a GPM decline follow.

■ *Product line is stale.* Perhaps products are out of fashion and the company must resort to mark-downs to reduce overstocked inventories. Or, perhaps the product lines have lost their technological edge, yielding reduced demand.

■ *New competitors enter the market.* Perhaps substitute products are now available from competitors, yielding increased pressure to reduce selling prices.

■ *General decline in economic activity.* Perhaps an economic downturn reduces product demand and places downward pressure on selling prices.

■ *Inventory is overstocked.* Perhaps the company overproduced goods and finds itself in an overstock position. This can require reduced selling prices to move inventory.

■ *Manufacturing costs have increased.* This could be due to poor planning, production glitches, or unfavorable supply chain reconfiguration.

■ *Changes in product mix.* Perhaps the company is selling a higher proportion of low margin goods.

Home Depot's gross profit margin on product sales increased by 0.1 percentage point (34.1% to 34.2%) over the past year. Following is Home Depot's discussion of its gross profit from its 2015 10-K.

> Gross Profit increased 6.6% to $30.3 billion for fiscal 2015 from $28.4 billion for fiscal 2014. Gross Profit as a percent of Net Sales, or gross profit margin, was 34.2% for fiscal 2015 compared to 34.1% for fiscal 2014, an increase of 6 basis points. The increase in gross profit margin for fiscal 2015 reflects benefits from our supply chain driven by lower fuel costs and increased productivity, partially offset by a change in the mix of products sold and the impact of Interline, which has a lower gross profit margin.

Home Depot's gross profit margin increased in 2015 because of lower fuel costs (inbound logistics are included in the cost of inventory) and increased productivity, partially offset by a change in product mix due to a company named **Interline** that Home Depot acquired in 2015. There are a number of factors that can adversely affect gross profit margins: changes in product mix, new products introduced at low prices to gain market share, increases in production costs, sales discounts, inventory obsolescence, warranty costs, and changes in production volume (higher production volume spreads out manufacturing overhead over a greater number of units produced, thus lowering the cost per unit produced).

Competitive pressures mean that companies rarely have the opportunity to completely control gross profit with price increases. Improvements in gross profit on existing product lines typically arise from better management of supply chains, production processes, or distribution networks. Companies that succeed do so because of better performance on basic business processes.

Days Inventory Outstanding and Inventory Turnover

A powerful way to analyze inventory is to compare the income statement activity related to inventory (COGS) to inventory levels on the balance sheet. This helps us assess inventory management and provides insight into the company's efficiency in generating sales. We calculate the number of days required to sell all of the inventory held (on average).

Average days inventory outstanding (DIO), also called *days inventory outstanding*, is computed as follows.

Average Days Inventory Outstanding = 365 × Average Inventory / COGS

Cost of goods sold is in the denominator (instead of sales) because inventory is reported at cost whereas sales includes any gross profit on the inventory. We calculate average inventory as a simple average of the balance at the beginning and the balance at the end of the period.[3]

For Home Depot ($ millions), average days inventory outstanding in 2015 follows.

$$\text{Average Days Inventory Outstanding} = \frac{365 \times (\$11{,}809 + \$11{,}079)/2}{\$58{,}254} = 71.7 \text{ days}$$

The result implies that it takes Home Depot about 72 days, on average, to sell its average inventory. Overall, analysis of days inventory outstanding is important for at least two reasons.

1. *Inventory quality.* Days inventory outstanding can be compared over time and across competitors. Fewer days is viewed favorably, because it implies that products are salable, preferably without undue discounting (we would compare profit margins to assess discounting). Conversely, more days implies that inventory is on the shelves for a longer period of time, perhaps from excessive purchases or production, missed fashion trends or technological advances, increased competition, and so forth. Our conclusions about higher or lower days inventory outstanding must consider alternative explanations including the following.

   - Product mix can include more (or less) higher margin inventories that sell more slowly. This can occur from business acquisitions that consolidate different types of inventory.

   - A company can change its promotion policies. Increased, effective advertising is likely to decrease days inventory outstanding. Advertising expense is in SG&A, not COGS. This means the additional advertising cost is in operating expenses, but the benefit is in gross profit and fewer days. If the promotion campaign is successful, the positive effects in margin and days should more than offset the promotion cost in SG&A.

   - A company can realize improvements in manufacturing efficiency and lower investments in direct materials and work-in-process inventories. Such improvements reduce inventory and, consequently, decrease days inventory outstanding. Although a good sign, it does not yield any information about the desirability of a company's product line.

2. *Asset utilization.* Companies strive to optimize their inventory investment. Carrying too much inventory is expensive, and too little inventory risks stock-outs and lost sales (current and future). Companies can make the following operational changes to optimize inventory.

   - Improved manufacturing processes can eliminate bottlenecks and the consequent buildup of work-in-process inventories.

   - Just-in-time (JIT) deliveries from suppliers, which provide raw materials to the production line when needed, can reduce the level of raw materials and associated holding costs.

   - Demand-pull production, in which raw materials are released into the production process when final goods are demanded by customers instead of producing for estimated demand, can reduce inventory levels. **Harley-Davidson**, for example, does not manufacture a motorcycle until it receives the customer's order; thus, Harley produces for actual, rather than estimated, demand.

Reducing inventories reduces inventory carrying costs, thus improving profitability and increasing cash flows. The reduction in inventory is reflected as an operating cash inflow in the statement of cash flows.

---

[3] This formula uses average inventories. A variant of the ratio considers the number of days to sell the *ending* inventories (365 × Ending inventories/ COGS). For 2016, this ratio is as follows: $\text{Days Inventory Outstanding} = \dfrac{365 \times \$11{,}809}{\$58{,}254} = 74.0$. These two approaches address different issues: the "average days" tells us the number of days it took Home Depot to sell the inventory available for sale during the year. The second approach tells us the number of days it would take Home Depot to sell the current *ending* inventories. It is important that we first identify the issue under investigation and then choose the formula that best addresses that issue.

A similar measure is the **inventory turnover** ratio, which is computed as

Inventory Turnover = Cost of Goods Sold / Average Inventory

For Home Depot ($ millions), the inventory turnover ratio for 2016 is: $\dfrac{\$58{,}254}{(\$11{,}809 + \$11{,}079)/2} = 5.09$. Home Depot is turning its inventories 5.09 times per year.

There is normal tension between the sales side of a company that argues for depth and breadth of inventory, and the finance side that monitors inventory carrying costs and seeks to maximize cash flow. Companies, therefore, seek to *optimize* inventory investment, not minimize it.

Days Payable Outstanding

Most companies purchase inventories on credit, meaning that suppliers allow companies to pay later. The supplier sets credit terms that specify when the invoice must be paid. Sometimes the supplier will offer a discount if the company pays more quickly. A typical invoice might include payment terms of 2/10, net 30, which means that the seller offers a 2% discount if the invoice is paid within 10 days and, if not, requires payment in full to be made in 30 days. Business-to-business (B2B) payables are usually non-interest bearing. This means accounts payable represent a low-cost financing source and companies should defer payment as long as allowed by the vendor. The average length of time that payables are deferred is reflected in the **days payable outstanding (DPO)** ratio, computed as:

$$\text{Days payable outstanding} = \frac{365 \times \text{Average Accounts Payable}}{\text{COGS}}$$

Similar to the days inventory outstanding ratio, COGS is in the denominator because payables relate to the purchase of inventories, which are reported at cost. For Home Depot, days payable outstanding for 2016 is:

$$\text{Days payable outstanding} = \frac{365 \times (\$6,565 + \$5,807)/2}{\$58,254} = 38.8 \text{ days}$$

This means Home Depot pays its suppliers in 38.8 days, on average. This is slightly longer than the typical supplier payment terms of 30 days.

Delaying payment to suppliers allows the purchasing company to increase its available cash (in other words, reduce its necessary level of cash). However, excessive delays (called "leaning on the trade") can damage supplier relationships. Remember, the purchaser's days payable outstanding is the seller's days sales outstanding in accounts receivable—this means as the purchaser gains cash from delaying payment, the seller loses an equal amount. As such, if delays become excessive, sellers might increase product cost or even choose to not sell to the purchaser. In managing the days accounts payable outstanding, companies must take care to maximize available cash while minimizing supply-chain disruption.

Cash Conversion Cycle

The cash conversion cycle is defined as:

Days sales outstanding (accounts receivable)
+ Days inventory outstanding
− Days payable outstanding
= Cash conversion cycle

Each time a company completes one cash conversion cycle, it has purchased and sold inventory (realizing sales and gross profit), and paid accounts payable and collected accounts receivable. The cycle increases cash flow (unless the sales are not-profitable). The aim is to minimize the time to complete a cycle.

Home Depot's cash conversion cycle for the 2012–2016 period follows.

Amounts in days	2016	2015	2014	2013	2012
Days sales outstanding	6.96	6.32	6.47	6.45	6.04
+ Days inventory outstanding	71.70	73.74	76.55	78.49	82.88
− Days payable outstanding	(38.76)	(38.65)	(39.29)	(38.18)	(37.87)
= Cash conversion cycle	39.90	41.41	43.73	46.76	51.05

Since 2012, Home Depot has greatly improved its cash conversion cycle from 51 days in 2012 to about 40 days in 2016. The biggest improvement was for inventory days, which dropped 11 days over the five-year period (82.88 days minus 71.70 days = 11.2 days). Inventory management has been a strategic focus for Home Depot as explained in its 2016 MD&A.

> Our distribution strategy is to provide the optimal flow path for a given product. Rapid Deployment Centers ("RDCs") play a key role in optimizing our network as they allow for aggregation of product needs for multiple stores to a single purchase order and then rapid allocation and deployment of inventory to individual stores upon arrival at the RDC. This results in a simplified ordering process and improved transportation and inventory management. We have 18 mechanized RDCs in the U.S. and two recently opened mechanized RDCs in Canada. Through Project Sync, which is being rolled out gradually to suppliers in several U.S. RDCs, we can significantly reduce our average lead time from supplier to shelf. Project Sync requires deep collaboration among our suppliers, transportation providers, RDCs and stores, as well as rigorous planning and information technology development to create an engineered flow schedule that shortens and stabilizes lead time, resulting in more predictable and consistent freight flow. As we continue to roll out Project Sync throughout our supply chain over the next several years, we plan to create an end-to-end solution that benefits all participants in our supply chain, from our suppliers to our transportation providers to our RDC and store associates to our customers.
>
> Over the past several years, we have centralized our inventory planning and replenishment function and continuously improved our forecasting and replenishment technology. This has helped us improve our product availability and our inventory productivity at the same time. At the end of fiscal 2015, over 95% of our U.S. store products were ordered through central inventory management.

Supply chain optimization is often cited as a key for effective inventory management. Inventories are recognized on the balance sheet when received at the distribution center and the days inventories outstanding clock starts ticking at that moment. Home Depot's challenge, then, is to minimize the time it takes to get the right amount of product from the distribution center to the store shelves. This involves accurate estimates of customer demand for products and an efficient logistics network.

By reducing the average inventory days by 11.2 days, Home Depot increased its cash balance by $1,787.5 million, computed as (Δ refers to 'change in'):

$$\Delta \text{ Cash} = \Delta \text{ Days Inventory Outstanding} \times (\text{COGS}/365)$$

$$= 11.2 \text{ days} \times (\$58,254 \text{ million}/365 \text{ days}) = \$1,787.52 \text{ million}$$

Managerial Decision ■ You Are the Operations Manager

You are analyzing your inventory turnover report for the month and are concerned that the average days inventory outstanding is lengthening. What actions can you take to reduce average days inventory outstanding? [Answer, p. 6-29]

Review 6-3 LO3

Lowe's Companies Inc. is a competitor of Home Depot. It reports the following financial statement data for 2014, 2015 and 2016. Use these data to answer the requirements below.

$ millions	2016	2015	2014
Revenue	$59,074	$56,223	$53,417
Cost of goods sold	38,504	36,665	34,941
Gross profit	20,570	19,558	18,476
Accounts receivable	0	0	0
Inventory	9,458	8,911	9,127
Accounts payable	5,633	5,124	5,008

continued

Required
1. Compute the gross profit margin for 2014, 2015, and 2016.
2. Compute the days inventory outstanding for 2015 and 2016.
3. Compute the days payable outstanding for 2015 and 2016.
4. Compute the cash conversion cycle for 2015 and 2016. By how many days did the cash conversion cycle improve during 2016?
5. Compute the cash savings in 2016 due to the improvement in the cash conversion cycle.

Solution on p. 6-44.

PPE Assets—Capitalization And Depreciation

LO4 Apply capitalization and depreciation of tangible assets.

Property, plant and equipment (PPE or PP&E, also called tangible or fixed assets), is the largest asset for most companies, and depreciation is often second in expenses to cost of goods sold on the income statement. Companies choose the method to compute depreciation, which can markedly impact the income statement and balance sheet. When companies dispose of PPE, a gain or loss often results. Understanding gains and losses on asset sales is important as we assess performance. Also, asset write-downs (and impairments) impact companies' current financial performance *and* future profitability. We must understand these accounting effects when we read and analyze and forecast financial statements.

When PPE is acquired, it is recorded at cost on the balance sheet. This is called *capitalization*, which explains why *expenditures* for PPE are called CAPEX. The amount capitalized on the balance sheet includes all costs to put the assets into service. This includes the cost of the PPE as well as transportation, duties, tax, and necessary costs to install and test the assets.

Instead of purchasing PPE outright, companies often enter into long-term equipment leases to increase operational flexibility or to take advantage of attractive financing terms. If the lease terms convey the "risks and rewards" of ownership, the equipment is capitalized just like other tangible assets. These "capital lease" assets are included in the company's PPE even though the company does not legally own the assets. The rationale is that the company operates the assets as if it did own them. For example, Home Depot includes on its 2015 balance sheet capital lease assets of over $1 billion. (We discuss capital leases in detail in a later module.)

Plant and Equipment

Once capitalized, the cost of plant and equipment is recognized as expense over the period of time that the assets produce revenues (directly or indirectly) in a process called depreciation. Depreciation recognizes *using up* of the asset over its useful life. Only assets that have a useful life are depreciated—**land, for example, does not have a determinable useful life and is therefore *not* depreciated**.

To determine depreciation expense, a company makes three estimates.

1. **Useful life**—period of time over which the asset is expected to generate measurable benefits.

2. **Salvage value**—amount expected for the asset when disposed of at the end of its useful life.

3. **Depreciation method**—estimate of how the asset is used up over its useful life.

With these three estimates, the company can determine a depreciation rate that approximates how the asset is used up over its life. The company uses that rate to systematically decrease the asset's balance sheet value (called the carrying value) such that, at the end of its useful life, the asset's carrying value equals its salvage value. When the asset is sold, the difference between the sales proceeds and its book value is recorded as a gain or loss on sale in the income statement.

Companies can use any reasonable method to depreciate assets. Straight-line depreciation is the most common method in the U.S. and around the world. In its footnotes, Home Depot discloses that it uses straight-line depreciation for all of its property, plant and equipment. The declining-balance method is a distant second. We look at these two methods in more detail.

Straight-Line Method

To illustrate, consider a machine with the following details: $100,000 cost, $10,000 salvage value, and a five-year useful life. Under the straight-line (SL) method, depreciation expense is recognized evenly over the estimated useful life of the asset as follows.

Depreciation Base
Cost − Salvage value
= $100,000 − $10,000
= $90,000

Depreciation Rate
1/Estimated useful life
= 1/5 years
= 20%

Depreciation expense per year for this asset is $18,000, computed as $90,000 × 20%. For the asset's first full year of usage, $18,000 of depreciation expense is reported in the income statement. (If an asset is purchased midyear, it is typically depreciated only for the portion of the year it is used. For example, had the asset in this illustration been purchased on May 31, the company would report $10,500 of depreciation in the first year, computed as 7/12 × $18,000, assuming the company has a December 31 year-end.) This depreciation is reflected in the company's financial statements as follows.

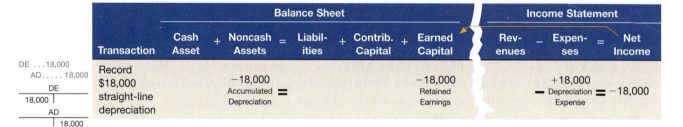

		Balance Sheet					Income Statement		
Transaction	Cash Asset	+ Noncash Assets	= Liabil- ities	+ Contrib. Capital	+ Earned Capital		Rev- enues	− Expen- ses	= Net Income
Record $18,000 straight-line depreciation		−18,000 Accumulated = Depreciation			−18,000 Retained Earnings			+18,000 − Depreciation = Expense	−18,000

DE . . .18,000
　AD. 18,000

DE	
18,000	

AD	
	18,000

The accumulated depreciation (contra asset) account increases by $18,000, thus reducing net PPE by the same amount. Also, $18,000 of the asset cost is transferred from the balance sheet to the income statement as depreciation expense. At the end of the first year the asset is reported on the balance sheet as follows.

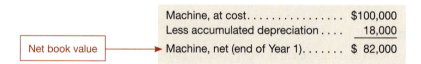

Machine, at cost................	$100,000
Less accumulated depreciation....	18,000
Net book value → Machine, net (end of Year 1).......	$ 82,000

Accumulated depreciation is the sum of all depreciation expense that has been recorded to date. The asset **net book value (NBV)**, or *carrying value*, is cost less accumulated depreciation. Although the word value is used here, it does not refer to market value. Depreciation is a cost allocation concept (transfer of costs from the balance sheet to the income statement), not a valuation concept.

In the second year of usage, another $18,000 of depreciation expense is recorded in the income statement and the net book value of the asset on the balance sheet follows.

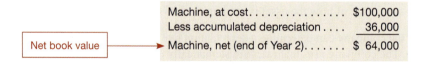

Machine, at cost................	$100,000
Less accumulated depreciation....	36,000
Net book value → Machine, net (end of Year 2).......	$ 64,000

Accumulated depreciation of $36,000 now includes the sum of the first and second years' depreciation, and the net book value of the asset is now reduced to $64,000. After the fifth year, a total of $90,000 of accumulated depreciation will be recorded ($18,000 per year × 5 years), yielding a net book value for the machine of $10,000. The net book value at the end of the machine's useful life is exactly equal to the salvage value that management estimated when the asset was acquired.

Double-Declining-Balance Method

Accelerated methods of depreciation are used by some companies, the most common being the double-declining-balance method. This method records more depreciation in the early years of an asset's useful life (hence the term *accelerated*) and less depreciation in later years. At the end of the asset's useful life, the balance sheet will still report a net book value equal to the asset's salvage value. The difference between straight-line and accelerated depreciation methods is not in the total amount of depreciation, but in the rate at which costs are transferred from the balance sheet to the income statement.

For the double-declining-balance (DDB) method, the depreciation base is net book value, which declines over the life of the asset (this is why the method is called "declining balance"). The depreciation rate is twice the straight-line (SL) rate (which explains the word "double"). The depreciation base and rate for the asset in our illustrative example are computed as follows.

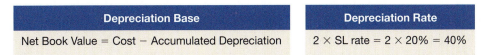

Depreciation Base	Depreciation Rate
Net Book Value = Cost − Accumulated Depreciation	2 × SL rate = 2 × 20% = 40%

The depreciation expense for the first year is $40,000, computed as $100,000 × 40%. This depreciation is reflected in the company's financial statements as follows.

The accumulated depreciation (contra asset) account increases by $40,000 which reduces net PPE (compare this to the $18,000 depreciation under straight-line). This means that $40,000 of the asset cost is transferred from the balance sheet to the income statement as depreciation expense. At the end of the first year, the asset is reported on the balance sheet as follows.

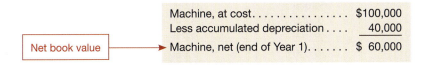

Machine, at cost................	$100,000
Less accumulated depreciation	40,000
Machine, net (end of Year 1).......	$ 60,000

Net book value

In the second year, the net book value of the asset is the new depreciable base, and the company records depreciation of $24,000 ($60,000 × 40%) in the income statement. At the end of the second year, the net book value of the asset on the balance sheet is:

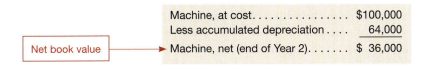

Machine, at cost................	$100,000
Less accumulated depreciation	64,000
Machine, net (end of Year 2).......	$ 36,000

Net book value

Under the double-declining-balance method, a company continues to record depreciation expense in this manner until the salvage value is reached, at which point the depreciation process is discontinued. This leaves a net book value equal to the salvage value, as with the straight-line method. (A variant of DDB allows for a change from DDB to SL at the point when SL depreciation exceeds that for DDB.) The DDB depreciation schedule for the life of this asset is in Exhibit 6.6.

Exhibit 6.6 ■ **Double-Declining-Balance Depreciation Schedule**

Year	Book Value at Beginning of Year	Depreciation Expense	Book Value at End of Year
1	$100,000	$40,000	$60,000
2	60,000	24,000	36,000
3	36,000	14,400	21,600
4	21,600	8,640	12,960
5	12,960	2,960*	10,000

*The formula value of $5,184 ($12,960 × 40%) is *not* reported because it would depreciate the asset below salvage value; only the $2,960 needed to reach salvage value is reported.

Exhibit 6.7 shows the depreciation expense and net book value for both the SL and DDB methods. During the first two years, the DDB method yields a higher depreciation expense compared to the SL method. Beginning in the third year, this pattern reverses and the SL method produces higher depreciation expense. Over the asset's life, the same $90,000 of asset cost is transferred to the income statement as depreciation expense, leaving a salvage value of $10,000 on the balance sheet under both methods.[4]

Companies typically use the SL method for financial reporting purposes and an accelerated depreciation method for tax returns.[5] The reason is that in early years the SL depreciation yields higher income on financial statements, whereas accelerated depreciation yields lower taxable income. Even though this relation reverses in later years, companies prefer to have the tax savings sooner rather than later so that the cash savings can be invested to produce earnings. Further, the reversal may never occur—if depreciable assets are growing at a fast enough rate, the additional first year's depreciation on newly acquired assets more than offsets the lower depreciation expense on older assets, yielding a "permanent" reduction in taxable income and taxes paid.

Exhibit 6.7 ■ **Comparison of Straight-Line and Double-Declining-Balance Depreciation**

Year	Straight-Line		Double-Declining-Balance	
	Depreciation Expense	Book Value at End of Year	Depreciation Expense	Book Value at End of Year
1	$18,000	$82,000	$40,000	$60,000
2	18,000	64,000	24,000	36,000
3	18,000	46,000	14,400	21,600
4	18,000	28,000	8,640	12,960
5	18,000	10,000	2,960	10,000
	$90,000		$90,000	

All depreciation methods yield the same salvage value

Total depreciation expense over asset life is identical for all methods

Research and Development Facilities and Equipment

In a prior module, we introduce R&D expense and explain that it includes costs associated with property and buildings to be used as research facilities. Importantly, ***R&D facilities and equipment*** are not immediately expensed. If they are *general-use* in nature (such as a general research laboratory that can be used for many types of activities), the costs are capitalized on the balance sheet and depreciated over its useful life like other depreciable assets. Only those R&D facilities and equipment

---

[4] A third, common depreciation method is **units-of-production**, which depreciates assets according to use. Specifically, the depreciation base is cost less salvage value, and the depreciation rate is the units produced and sold during the year compared with the total expected units to be produced and sold. For example, if a truck is driven 10,000 miles out of a total expected 100,000 miles, 10% of its nonrecoverable cost is reflected as depreciation expense. This method is common for extractive industries like timber and coal.

[5] The IRS mandates the use of MACRS (Modified Accelerated Cost Recovery System) for tax purposes. This method specifies the useful life for various classes of assets, assumes no salvage value, and generally uses the double-declining-balance method. We discuss MACRS and other income tax issues in a later module.

that are purchased specifically for a single R&D project, and have *no alternative use*, are expensed immediately in the income statement (an unusual situation).

Companies expect R&D efforts ultimately to yield new tangible products and services. This might suggest that *all* R&D costs be capitalized (recognized as assets) on the balance sheet. After all, R&D can create future revenues like other assets including PPE.

However, with the exception of facilities and equipment that have alternative uses, R&D costs are *not* capitalized. Instead, R&D costs are expensed in the income statement as they are incurred. The rationale for this accounting treatment is threefold.

■ Whether any tangible projects or services will be developed is often uncertain while the R&D is ongoing. Indeed, many R&D efforts fail to produce any benefits whatsoever.

■ Even for R&D programs that look promising, the timing of future products and services is uncertain.

■ Salaries for R&D personnel are no different than for other personnel whose salaries and wages are expensed when incurred.

It is generally acknowledged that R&D costs, especially development costs associated with clearly defined products for which a workable prototype has been proven, do create future benefits and have the characteristics of assets. However, the measurement uncertainty argument prevails and R&D costs are not capitalized under GAAP and, with the exception of general-use R&D PPE assets, they are expensed when incurred.

LO4 Review 6-4

On January 2, assume that one of **Home Depot**'s subsidiary companies purchases equipment that fabricates a key-product part. The equipment costs $95,000, and its estimated useful life is five years, after which it is expected to be sold for $10,000.

Required
1. Compute depreciation expense for each year of the equipment's useful life for each of the following depreciation methods:
   a. Straight-line
   b. Double-declining-balance
2. Show how the HD subsidiary reports the equipment on its balance sheet at the end of the third year assuming straight-line depreciation.

Solution on p. 6-44.

PPE Assets—Sales, Impairments, and Restructuring

This section discusses gains and losses from asset sales, restructurings, and the computation and disclosure of asset impairments.

LO5 Evaluate asset sales, impairments, and restructuring activities.

Asset Sales

The gain or loss on the sale (disposition) of a tangible asset is computed as follows.

Gain or Loss on Asset Sale = Proceeds from Sale − Net Book Value of Asset Sold

An asset's net book value is its acquisition cost less accumulated depreciation. When an asset is sold, its acquisition cost and related accumulated depreciation are both removed from the balance sheet and any gain or loss is reported in income from continuing operations.

Gains and losses on asset sales can be large, and analysts must be aware that these gains and losses are usually *transitory operating* income components. Financial statements do not typically report gains and losses from tangible asset sales because, if the gain or loss is small (immaterial), companies include the item in selling, general and administrative expenses. Footnotes can sometimes be informative. To illustrate, **Hilton Worldwide Holdings** provides the following footnote disclosure relating to the sale of the Waldorf Astoria hotel in New York.

> **Waldorf Astoria New York.** In February 2015, we completed the sale of the Waldorf Astoria New York for a purchase price of $1.95 billion. As a result of the sale, we recognized a gain of $143 million included in gain on sales of assets, net in our consolidated statement of operations for the year ended December 31, 2015.

Hilton sold the Waldorf Astoria hotel in New York for $1.95 billion in 2015. If we assume zero tax for simplicity, the hotel was carried on Hilton's balance sheet at a book value of $1.807 billion, where Hilton recognized a gain on sale, net of $143 million ($1.95 billion − $1.807 billion).

Asset Impairments

Tangible assets are reported at their net book values (original cost less accumulated depreciation). This is the case even if the market values of these assets increase subsequent to acquisition. As a result, there can be unrecognized gains hidden within the balance sheet.

On the other hand, if market values of PPE assets subsequently decrease—and the asset value is deemed to be permanently impaired—then, companies must write off the impaired cost and recognize losses on those assets. **Impairment** of PPE assets is determined by comparing the asset's net book value to the sum of the asset's *expected* future (undiscounted) cash flows. If the sum of expected cash flow is greater than net book value, there is no impairment. However, if the sum of the expected cash flow is less than net book value, the asset is deemed impaired and it is written down to its current fair value (generally, the present value of those expected cash flows). Exhibit 6.8 depicts this impairment analysis.

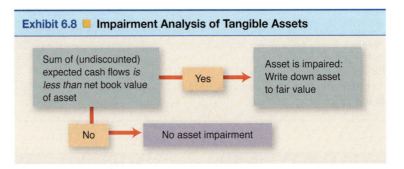

Exhibit 6.8 ■ Impairment Analysis of Tangible Assets

When a company records an impairment charge, assets are reduced by the amount of the write-down and the loss is recognized in the income statement. To illustrate, a footnote to the 2015 10-K of **Chesapeake Energy** reports the following about asset impairments.

> For the year ended December 31, 2015, Chesapeake had a net loss of $14.635 billion, or $22.43 per diluted common share, on total revenues of $12.764 billion. This compares to net income of $2.056 billion, or $1.87 per diluted common share, on total revenues of $23.125 billion for the year ended December 31, 2014. The decrease in net income in 2015 was primarily driven by impairments of our oil and natural gas properties. . . For the year ended December 31, 2015, we reported non-cash impairment charges on our oil and natural gas properties totaling $18.238 billion, primarily resulting from a substantial decrease in the trailing 12-month average first-day-of-the-month oil and natural gas prices throughout 2015, and the impairment of certain undeveloped leasehold interests. The trailing 12-month average first-day-of-the-month prices used to calculate our oil and natural gas reserves decreased from $94.98 per bbl of oil and $4.35 per mcf of natural gas as of December 31, 2014 to $50.28 per bbl of oil and $2.58 per mcf of natural gas as of December 31, 2015.

As oil prices declined in 2015, Chesapeake Energy, like many other oil and gas companies, was forced to write down its oil and gas properties. This led to an impairment charge of $18,238 million. To determine the impairment charge, Chesapeake compared the fair value of certain properties using the 2015 market prices for oil and gas to the properties' carrying value (the net book value on the balance sheet). Because historical prices had dropped drastically during 2015 (from $94.98 to $50.28, for example), the properties' fair value also dropped drastically.

IFRS Insight ■ PPE Valuation under IFRS

Like GAAP, companies reporting under IFRS must periodically assess long-lived assets for possible impairment. Unlike the two-step GAAP approach, IFRS uses a one-step approach: firms compare an asset's net book value to its current fair value (estimated as discounted expected future cash flows) to test for impairment and then reduce net book value to that fair value. Under IFRS, impairment losses can be reversed if the PPE subsequently regains its value. The PPE account is increased to the newly estimated recoverable amount, not to exceed the assets' initial cost adjusted for depreciation. GAAP prohibits such reversals. Another IFRS difference is that PPE can be revalued upwards to fair value each period, if fair value can be measured reliably.

Restructuring Costs

It is not uncommon for a company to face corporate challenges that are so great that the only way forward is to alter its organizational, operational, and financial structures. Such corporate "restructurings" are designed to turn a company around and are frequently initiated in response to poor performance, mounting debt, and shareholder pressure. A restructuring can involve eliminating business segments, selling major assets, downsizing the workforce, and reconfiguring debt. Ultimately, the goal of a restructuring is to positively impact a company's long-term financial performance. But in the short term, restructurings usually have large negative impacts on the company's income statement.

Disclosure of Restructuring Costs

Because of their magnitude, restructurings require enhanced disclosure either as a separate line item in the income statement or as a footnote. Restructuring costs typically include three components:

1. Employee severance or relocation costs.
2. Asset write-downs.
3. Other restructuring costs.

Reporting of employee severance or relocation costs. The first part, **employee severance or relocation costs**, represents accrued (estimated) costs to terminate or relocate employees as part of a restructuring program. To accrue those expenses, the company must:

■ Estimate total costs of terminating or relocating selected employees; these costs might include severance pay (typically a number of weeks of pay based on the employee's tenure with the company), outplacement costs, and relocation or retraining costs for remaining employees.

■ Report *total* estimated costs as an expense (and a liability) in the period the restructuring program is announced. Subsequent payments to employees reduce the restructuring accrual (the liability).

Reporting of asset write-downs. The second part of restructuring costs is **asset write-downs**, also called *write-offs* or *charge-offs*. Restructuring activities usually involve closure or relocation of manufacturing or administrative facilities. This can require the write-down of assets whose fair value is less than book value. For example, restructurings can necessitate the write-down of long-term assets (such as plant assets or goodwill) and of inventories. To determine the amount of the write-down, the company follows the approach in Exhibit 6.8. Remember that write-downs have no cash flow effects unless the write-down has tax consequences.

Reporting of other restructuring costs. The third part of restructuring costs is typically labeled "Other" and includes costs of vacating duplicative facilities, fees to terminate contracts (such as lease agreements and service contracts), and other exit costs (such as legal and asset-appraisal fees). Companies estimate and accrue these costs and reduce the restructuring liability as those costs are paid in cash.

For a company to use the term "restructuring" in the income statement and to accrue restructuring liabilities, the company is required to have a formal restructuring plan that is approved by its board of directors. Also, a company must identify the relevant employees and notify them of its plan. In each subsequent year, the company must disclose in its footnotes the original amount of the Restructuring liability (accrual), how much of that liability is settled in the current period (such as employee payments), how much of the original liability has been reversed because of original cost overestimation, any new accruals for unforeseen costs, and the current balance of the liability. This creates more transparent financial statements, which allow readers to see, in hindsight, if the initial restructuring accrual was overstated (requiring subsequent reversal) or understated (requiring subsequent additions to the restructuring accrual).

Business Insight ■ Pfizer's Restructuring

Pfizer explains its restructuring efforts as follows in its 2015 10-K.

We incur significant costs in connection with acquiring, integrating and restructuring businesses and in connection with our global cost-reduction and productivity initiatives. For example:

- In connection with acquisition activity, we typically incur costs associated with executing the transactions, integrating the acquired operations, and restructuring the combined company; and

- In connection with our cost-reduction and productivity initiatives, we typically incur costs and charges associated with site closings and other facility rationalization actions, workforce reductions and the expansion of shared services, including the development of global systems.

All of our businesses and functions may be impacted by these actions, including sales and marketing, manufacturing and research and development, as well as groups such as information technology, shared services and corporate operations. The following table provides the components of and changes in our restructuring accruals.

$ millions	Employee Termination Costs	Asset Impairment Charges	Exit Costs	Accrual
Balance, January 1, 2014......	$1,685	$ —	$ 94	$1,779
Provision.................	68	45	58	170
Utilization and other..........	(639)	(45)	(100)	(783)
Balance, December 31, 2014...	1,114	—	52	1,166
Provision.................	489	254	68	811
Utilization and other..........	(495)	(254)	(71)	(820)
Balance, December 31, 2015...	$1,109	$ —	$ 48	$1,157

The table reflects Pfizer's restructuring transactions for 2014 and 2015. The right-most "Accrual" column shows totals for the year. Disclosure is required of the beginning-year balance of the restructuring liability accrual ($1,166 million for 2015) together with changes in that liability for the year. During 2015, Pfizer added $811 million to the liability and recorded it as restructuring expense in its income statement. (On the income statement, Pfizer aggregated the $811 million with additional costs relating to its acquisitions of Hospira and Allergan for a total of $1,152 million). It also reduced the liability by $820 million for the payment of employee termination costs, write-offs of impaired assets, and exit costs. The ending balance of $1,157 million is reported on Pfizer's 2015 balance sheet as a liability.

Analysis of Restructuring Costs

Restructuring costs are typically large and, as such, greatly affect reported profits. Our analysis must consider whether these costs are associated with the accounting period in which they are recognized. Following are some guidelines relating to the components of restructuring costs.

Analyzing employee severance or relocation costs and other costs. Companies are allowed to record costs relating to employee separation or relocation that are *incremental* and that do not benefit future periods. Similarly, other accrued costs must be related to the restructuring and not to expenses that would otherwise have been incurred in the future. Thus, accrual of these costs is treated like other liability accruals. We must, however, be aware of over- or understated costs and their effect on current and future profitability. Disclosure rules require a reconciliation of this restructuring accrual in future years (see the preceding Business Insight on Pfizer's restructuring). A reconciliation reveals either overstatements or understatements: overstatements are followed by a reversal of the restructuring liability, and understatements are followed by further accruals. Should a company develop a reputation for recurring reversals or understatements, its management loses credibility.

Research Insight ■ Restructuring Costs and Managerial Incentives

Research has investigated the circumstances and effects of restructuring costs. Some research finds that stock prices increase when a company announces a restructuring as if the market appreciates the company's candor. Research also finds that many companies that reduce income through restructuring costs later reverse a portion of those costs, resulting in a substantial income boost for the period of reversal. These reversals often occur when the company would have otherwise reported an earnings decline. Whether or not the market responds favorably to trimming the fat or simply disregards restructuring costs as transitory and, thus, as uninformative, managers have incentives to characterize such income-decreasing items as "one-time" on the income statement and routinely exclude such charges in non-GAAP, pro forma disclosures. These incentives often derive from contracts such as debt covenants and managerial bonus plans.

Analyzing asset write-downs. Asset write-downs accelerate (or catch up) the depreciation process to reflect asset impairment. Impairment implies the loss of cash-generating capability and, likely, occurs over several years. Thus, prior periods' profits were arguably not as high as reported, and the current period's profit is not as low. This measurement error is difficult to estimate and, thus, many analysts do not adjust balance sheets and income statements for write-downs. At a minimum, however, we must recognize the qualitative implications of restructuring costs for the profitability of recent prior periods and the current period.

Managerial Decision ■ You Are the Financial Analyst

You are analyzing the 10-K of a company that reports a large restructuring expense, involving employee severance and asset write-downs. How do you interpret and treat this cost in your analysis of the company's current and future profitability? [Answer, p. 6-29]

LO5 **Review 6-5**

Part 1. Refer to information in Review 6-4 and to its solution to answer the following requirements.

Required
a. Assume that the HD subsidiary uses straight-line method of depreciation and estimates that, at the end of the third year, the equipment will generate $40,000 in cash flow over its remaining life and that it has a current fair value of $36,000. Is the equipment impaired? If so, what is the effect on the HD subsidiary financial statements?
b. Instead of the facts in part 1, assume that, at the end of the third year, the HD subsidiary sells the equipment for $50,000 cash. What amount of gain or loss does the HD subsidiary report from this sale?

Part 2. The Coca-Cola Company reports the following reconciliation of its restructuring liability for 2015.

$ millions	Severance Pay and Benefits	Outside Services	Other Direct Costs	Total
Accrued balance as of December 31, 2014...	$260	$ 4	$ 21	$285
Costs incurred	$269	$56	$366	$691
Payments.............................	(200)	(47)	(265)	(512)
Noncash and exchange	(185)	(5)	(70)	(260)
Accrued balance as of December 31, 2015...	$144	$ 8	$ 52	$204

Required
a. What amount of expense did Coca-Cola report in its income statement as restructuring expense in 2015?
b. What amount of restructuring liability did Coca-Cola report on its balance sheet for 2015?

Solution on p. 6-44.

PPE Assets—Analysis Tools

eLectures
MBC **LO6** Analyze tangible assets and related activities.

Home Depot reports $22,191 million of property and equipment, net of accumulated depreciation, on its 2015 balance sheet.

$ millions	January 31, 2016	February 1, 2015
Property and Equipment, at cost	$39,266	$38,513
Less Accumulated Depreciation and Amortization	17,075	15,793
Net Property and Equipment	22,191	22,720

Footnotes disclose the company's policies for depreciation and amortization. As for most companies, Home Depot's disclosures are fairly broad.

Depreciation and Amortization The Company's Buildings, Furniture, Fixtures and Equipment are recorded at cost and depreciated using the straight-line method over the estimated useful lives of the assets. Leasehold Improvements are amortized using the straight-line method over the original term of the lease or the useful life of the improvement, whichever is shorter. The Company's Property and Equipment is depreciated using the following estimated useful lives:

Buildings.	5–45 years
Furniture, Fixtures and Equipment.	2–20 years
Leasehold Improvements.	5–45 years

Home Depot also discloses the composition of property and equipment.

Property and Equipment as of January 31, 2016 and February 1, 2015 consisted of the following (amounts in millions).

Property and Equipment, at cost:	January 31, 2016	February 1, 2015
Land	$ 8,149	$ 8,243
Buildings.	17,667	17,759
Furniture, Fixtures and Equipment	10,279	9,602
Leasehold Improvements	1,481	1,419
Construction in Progress	670	585
Capital Leases	1,020	905
	39,266	38,513
Less Accumulated Depreciation and Amortization.	17,075	15,793
Net Property and Equipment.	$22,191	$22,720

We can use these data to compute key ratios to assess the productivity of Home Depot's PPE and the assets' relative age.

PPE Turnover

A crucial issue in analyzing PPE is determining their productivity (utilization). For example, what level of plant assets is necessary to generate a dollar of revenues? How capital intensive are the company and its competitors? To address these and similar questions, we use **PPE turnover**, defined as follows.

> **PPE Turnover (PPET) = Sales / Average PPE, net**

Home Depot's 2015 PPE turnover is 3.9 ($88,519 million/[($22,191 million + $22,720 million)/2]). (We use net PPE in the computation above; arguments for using gross PPE are not as compelling as with receivables because managers have less latitude over accumulated depreciation as compared to the allowance for uncollectibles.)

Higher PPE turnover is preferable to lower. A higher PPE turnover implies a lower capital investment for a given level of sales. Higher turnover, therefore, increases profitability because the company avoids asset carrying costs and because the freed-up assets can generate operating cash flow.

PPE turnover is lower for capital-intensive manufacturing companies than it is for companies in service or knowledge-based industries. To this point, consider the following chart of PPE turnover for selected industries.

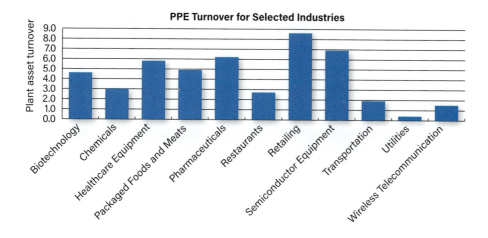

There is wide variability in PPE turnover rate across industries. Capital intensive industries such as utilities, transportation, and wireless telecommunication report relatively low turnover rates, reflecting large levels of capital investment required to compete in those areas.

PPE Useful Life

Home Depot reports that the useful lives of its depreciable assets range from two years for furniture, fixtures and equipment to 45 years for buildings and leasehold improvements. The longer an asset's useful life, the lower the annual depreciation expense reported in the income statement and the higher the income each year. It might be of interest, therefore, to know whether a company's useful life estimates are more conservative or more aggressive than its competitors.

If we assume straight-line (SL) depreciation (which is consistent with the company's policy) and zero salvage value, we can estimate the average useful life for depreciable assets as follows.

> **Average useful life = Depreciable asset cost / Depreciation expense**

The estimated useful life for Home Depot's PPE is 16.3 years ($30,447 million/$1,863 million). We compute depreciable assets of $30,447 million, by excluding two items.

- Land of $8,149 million, which is never depreciated.
- Construction-in-progress of $670 million, which is not depreciated until the assets under construction are completed and placed into service, which is when the company begins to use the assets.

Home Depot, like most companies, does not report depreciation as a separate line item on the income statement. To determine depreciation and amortization expense, we refer to Home Depot's statement of cash flows, that reports "depreciation and amortization" expense of $1,863 million. Amortization expense is like depreciation expense and typically relates to leasehold improvements (a catch-all category for fixtures, lights, flooring, and restrooms that Home Depot installed in its leased buildings) and to intangible assets other than goodwill (which is not amortized). Because Home Depot has no intangible assets other than goodwill, we assume that amortization expense relates to leasehold improvements.

PPE Percent Used Up

We can also estimate the proportion of a company's depreciable assets that have already been transferred to the income statement. This ratio reflects the percent of depreciable assets that are no longer productive and is computed as follows.

$$\text{Percent used up} = \text{Accumulated depreciation} / \text{Depreciable asset cost}$$

Home Depot's assets are 56% used up, computed as $17,075 million/$30,447 million. If a company replaced all of its assets evenly each year, the percent used up ratio would be 50%. Home Depot's depreciable assets are slightly older than this benchmark. Knowing the degree to which a company's assets are used up is of interest in forecasting future cash flows. If, for example, depreciable assets are 80% used up, we might anticipate a higher level of capital expenditures to replace aging assets in the near future. We also expect that older assets are less efficient and will incur higher maintenance costs.

Managerial Decision ■ You Are the Division Manager

You are the manager for a main operating division of your company. You are concerned that a declining PPE turnover is adversely affecting your division's return on net operating assets. What specific actions can you take to increase PPE turnover? [Answer, p. 6-29]

Review 6-6 LO6

Lowe's Companies Inc. reports the following selected financial data for 2016, 2015, and 2014.

$ millions	2016	2015	2014
Revenue	$59,074	$56,223	$53,417
Depreciation expense.	1,484	1,485	1,462
Gross property, plant, and equipment	35,913	35,443	35,074
Accumulated depreciation	(16,336)	(15,409)	(14,240)
Net property, plant and equipment	19,577	20,034	20,834
Footnote data			
Land	7,086	7,040	7,016
Buildings.	17,451	17,247	17,161
Machinery.	10,863	10,426	10,063
Construction-in-progress.	513	730	834

Required
Compute the following measures for 2016 and 2015. (For simplicity, assume that the entire amortization expense relates to property, plant and equipment assets.)
1. PPE turnover.
2. Average useful life.
3. Percent used up.

Solution on p. 6-45.

Global Accounting

Both GAAP and IFRS account similarly for operating assets. Although similarities in accounting dwarf any differences, we highlight some of the more notable differences.

Inventory There are only two notable differences in accounting for inventory.

1. IFRS does not permit use of the LIFO method.
2. IFRS permits companies to reverse inventory write-downs; GAAP does not. This means that if markets recover and inventory previously "impaired" regains some or all of its value, it can be revalued upwards. IFRS notes disclose this revaluation, if material, which permits us to recompute inventory and cost of sales amounts that are comparable to GAAP.

Property, plant, and equipment In accounting for tangible assets, four notable differences deserve mention.

1. GAAP requires the total cost of a tangible asset to be capitalized and depreciated over its useful life. Under IFRS, tangible assets are disaggregated into individual components and then each component is separately depreciated over its useful life. Thus, assets with components with vastly different useful lives, can yield IFRS depreciation expense that is markedly different from that computed using GAAP.
2. Property, plant and equipment can be revalued upward to fair market value under IFRS. The latter will cause IFRS book values of PPE to be higher. Few companies have opted to revalue assets upwards but in some industries, such as real estate, the practice is common.
3. U.S. GAAP applies a two-step approach for determining impairments. Step 1: compare book value to *undiscounted* expected future cash flows; and Step 2: if book value is higher, measure impairment using *discounted* expected future cash flows. IFRS uses *discounted* expected future cash flows for both steps, which means IFRS uses one step. This results in more asset impairments under IFRS.
4. IFRS fair-value impairments for tangible assets can be reversed; that is, written back up after being written down. The notes to PPE articulate such reversals.

Research and Development All R&D costs are expensed under GAAP whereas IFRS allows development costs (but not research costs) to be capitalized as an intangible asset if all of the following six criteria are met.

- It is technically feasible to complete the asset.
- The company intends to complete the asset and use or sell it.
- The company is able to use or sell the asset.
- The company can use the asset to create economic benefits or there is a profitable market for the asset.
- The company has adequate resources to complete the asset.
- Costs related to the asset can be reliably measured.

For some companies and some industries these intangible assets are significant and the IFRS financial statements can be markedly different.

Restructuring There are two differences worth noting.

1. Under IFRS, restructuring expense is recognized when there is a plan for the restructuring and if the affected employees expect the plan to be implemented. Under GAAP, restructuring expense can be recognized earlier because the trigger is board approval of a plan.
2. Consistent with other IFRS accruals, a restructuring provision is recorded at its best estimate. This is usually the expected value or, in the case of a range of possible outcomes that are equally likely, the provision is recorded at the *midpoint* of the range. The GAAP estimate is at the most-likely outcome; and if there is a range of possible outcomes, the provision is recorded as the *minimum* amount of the range.

Guidance Answers

You Are the Operations Manager

Pg. 6-15 Companies need inventories to avoid lost sales opportunities; however, there are several ways to minimize inventory needs. (1) We can reduce product costs by improving product design to eliminate costly features that customers don't value. (2) We can use more cost-efficient suppliers; possibly producing in lower wage-rate parts of the world. (3) We can reduce raw material inventories with just-in-time delivery from suppliers. (4) We can eliminate production bottlenecks that increase work-in-process inventories. (5) We can manufacture for orders rather than for estimated demand to reduce finished goods inventories. (6) We can improve warehousing and distribution to reduce duplicate inventories. (7) We can monitor product sales and adjust product mix as demand changes to reduce finished goods inventories.

You Are the Financial Analyst

Pg. 6-24 Typically, restructuring charges have three components: severance costs, other restructuring-related expenses and asset write-downs (including inventories, PPE, intangible assets, and goodwill). Write-downs occur when an asset's ability to generate cash flow declines and this decline reduces the asset's fair value below its book value (as reported on the balance sheet). Arguably, this decline in cash flow generating ability did not occur solely in the current year. Most likely the decline developed over several periods. It is not uncommon for companies to delay loss recognition, such as write-downs of assets. Thus, prior period income is, arguably, overstated and the current period loss is understated. Turning to severance and other costs, GAAP permits restructuring expense to include only those costs that are *incremental* and will *not* benefit future periods. Like other accruals, restructuring might be over- or understated. In future periods, the company reports actual restructuring expenses, which will provide insight into the adequacy of the accrual in the earlier period.

You Are the Division Manager

Pg. 6-27 PPE is a difficult asset to reduce. Because companies need long-term operating assets, managers usually try to maximize throughput to reduce unit costs. Also, many companies form alliances to share administrative, production, logistics, customer service, IT, and other functions. These alliances take many forms (such as joint ventures) and are designed to spread ownership of assets among many users. The goal is to identify underutilized assets and to increase capacity utilization. Another solution might be to reconfigure the value chain from raw material to end user. Examples include the sharing of IT, or manufacturing facilities, outsourcing of production or administration such as customer service centers, and the use of special purpose entities for asset securitization.

Questions

Q6-1. Why do relatively stable inventory costs across periods reduce the importance of management's choice of an inventory costing method?

Q6-2. Explain why using the FIFO inventory costing method will increase gross profit during periods of rising inventory costs.

Q6-3. If inventory costs are rising, which inventory costing method—first-in, first-out; last-in, first-out; or average cost—yields the (a) lowest ending inventory? (b) lowest net income? (c) largest ending inventory? (d) largest net income? (e) greatest cash flow, assuming the same method is used for tax purposes?

Q6-4. Even though it may not reflect their physical flow of goods, why might companies adopt last-in, first-out inventory costing in periods when costs are consistently rising?

Kaiser Aluminum Corporation (KALU)

Q6-5. In a recent annual report, **Kaiser Aluminum Corporation** made the following statement in reference to its inventories: "The Company recorded pretax charges of approximately $19.4 million because of a reduction in the carrying values of its inventories caused principally by prevailing lower prices for alumina, primary aluminum, and fabricated products." What basic accounting principle caused Kaiser Aluminum to record this $19.4 million pretax charge? Briefly describe the rationale for this principle.

Q6-6. What does the cash conversion cycle measure?

Q6-7. How might a company revise its depreciation expense computation due to a change in an asset's estimated useful life or salvage value?

Q6-8.   What is the benefit of accelerated depreciation for income tax purposes when the total depreciation taken over the asset's life is identical under any method of depreciation?

Q6-9.   What factors determine the gain or loss on the sale of a PPE asset?

Q6-10   What is a LIFO reserve? What information can we learn from the LIFO reserve *and* from the change in the reserve during the year?

Q6-11   Explain the concept of lower of cost or market. What benefit does the LCM rule create for financial statement users?

Q6-12. Identify the three typical categories of restructuring costs and their effects on the balance sheet and the income statement.

Assignments with the ⬤ logo in the margin are available in ᵐʸBusinessCourse.
See the Preface of the book for details.

Mini Exercises

M6-13. **Computing Cost of Goods Sold and Ending Inventory Under FIFO, LIFO, and Average Cost**   **LO1**
Assume that Madden Company reports the following initial balance and subsequent purchase of inventory.

Inventory balance at beginning of year	1,300 units @ $150 each	$195,000
Inventory purchased during the year	1,700 units @ $180 each	306,000
Cost of goods available for sale during the year	3,000 units	$501,000

Assume that 2,000 units are sold during the year. Compute the cost of goods sold for the year and the inventory on the year-end balance sheet under the following inventory costing methods:

a. FIFO
b. LIFO
c. Average Cost

M6-14. **Computing Cost of Goods Sold and Ending Inventory Under FIFO, LIFO, and Average Cost**   **LO1**
Wong Corporation reports the following beginning inventory and inventory purchases.

Inventory balance at beginning of year	400 units @ $12 each	$ 4,800
Inventory purchased during the year	700 units @ $14 each	9,800
Cost of goods available for sale during the year	1,100 units	$14,600

Wong sells 600 of its inventory units during the year. Compute the cost of goods sold for the year and the inventory on the year-end balance sheet under the following inventory costing methods:

a. FIFO
b. LIFO
c. Average Cost

M6-15. **Computing and Evaluating Inventory Turnover for Two Companies**   **LO3**
Abercrombie & Fitch Co. (ANF) and **TJX Companies Inc.** (TJX) report the following information in their respective January 2016 10-K reports relating to their 2012 and 2011 fiscal years.

Abercrombie & Fitch Co. (ANF)

TJX Companies Inc. (TJX)

	Abercrombie & Fitch			TJX Companies		
$ millions	Sales	Cost of Goods Sold	Inventories	Sales	Cost of Goods Sold	Inventories
2015	$3,519	$1,361	$437	$30,945	$22,035	$3,695
2014	3,744	1,430	461	29,078	20,777	3,218

a. Compute the 2015 inventory turnover for each of these two retailers.

b. Discuss any difference you observe in inventory turnover between these two companies. Does the difference confirm your expectations given their respective business models? Explain. (*Hint:* ANF is a higher-end retailer and TJX sells more value-priced clothing.)

c. Describe ways that a retailer can improve its inventory turnover.

LO4   M6-16.   Computing Depreciation Under Straight-Line and Double-Declining-Balance
A delivery van costing $37,000 is expected to have a $2,900 salvage value at the end of its useful life of five years. Assume that the truck was purchased on January 1. Compute the depreciation expense for the first two calendar years under the following depreciation methods.

a. Straight-line
b. Double-declining-balance

LO4   M6-17.   Computing Depreciation Under Straight-Line and Double-Declining-Balance for Partial Years
A company with a calendar year-end, purchases a machine costing $129,000 on July 1, 2016. The machine is expected to be obsolete after five years (60 months) and, thereafter, no longer useful to the company. The estimated salvage value is $6,000. The company's depreciation policy is to record depreciation for the portion of the year that the asset is in service. Compute depreciation expense for both 2016 and 2017 under the following depreciation methods.

a. Straight-line
b. Double-declining-balance

LO6   M6-18.   Computing and Comparing PPE Turnover for Two Companies

Texas Instruments Inc. (TXN)

Intel Corporation (INTC)

Texas Instruments Inc. and **Intel Corporation** report the following information.

$ millions	Intel Corporation		Texas Instruments	
	Sales	**Plant, Property and Equipment, net**	**Sales**	**Plant, Property and Equipment, net**
2015.........	$55,355	$31,858	$13,000	$2,596
2014.........	55,870	33,238	13,045	2,840

a. Compute the 2015 PPE turnover for both companies. Comment on any difference observed.
b. Discuss ways in which high-tech manufacturing companies like these can increase their PPE turnover.

LO3   M6-19.   Computing Cash Conversion Cycle for Two Years

Winnebago Industries (WGO)

Winnebago Industries has the following metrics for 2015 and 2014.

Amounts in days	2015	2014
Days sales outstanding	25.5	19.1
Days inventory outstanding	47.1	48.9
Days payable outstanding	13.9	13.3

Compute the cash conversion cycle for both years. What accounts for the change between the years?

LO3   M6-20.   Using Inventory Analysis Tools

AutoZone (AZO)
O'Reilly (ORLY)

AutoZone and **O'Reilly** are two competitors in the retail automotive parts industry.

$ thousands	AutoZone	O'Reilly
Average 2015 Inventory	$ 3,280,868	$2,592,902
2015 Sales	10,187,340	7,966,674
2015 Cost of goods sold	4,860,309	3,804,031
Average 2014 Inventory	$ 3,000,557	$2,464,918
2014 Sales	9,475,313	7,216,081
2014 Cost of goods sold	4,540,406	3,507,180

a. Use the information above to compute the companies' gross profit margin and days inventory outstanding for both years.

b. Based on these two ratios, which company is more profitable selling its inventory? How has that changed from 2014 to 2015?

c. Based on these two ratios, which company is more efficient with its inventory? How has that changed from 2014 to 2015?

M6-21. Asset Impairment

In 2015, **Winnebago Industries** recorded an impairment loss of $462,000 on its corporate plane. Assume that the plane originally cost the company $2,350,000 and had accumulated depreciation of $1,598,000 at the time of the impairment charge.

a. Why did the company record an impairment loss on the plane?

b. Explain how the company determined the amount of the impairment loss.

c. What was the plane's fair value at the end of 2015?

LO5
Winnebago Industries (WGO)

M6-22. Lower of Cost or Market Adjustment

Marathon Petroleum Corporation disclosed the following in its 2015 annual report. The company reported revenues and cost of revenues of $72,051 million and $55,583 million respectively in 2015.

LO2
Marathon Petroleum Corporation (MPC)

> Inventories are stated at the lower of cost or market. Costs of crude oil, refinery feedstocks and refined products are aggregated on a consolidated basis for purposes of assessing if the LIFO cost basis of these inventories may have to be written down to market values. At December 31, 2015, market values for these inventories, which totaled approximately 4.0 billion gallons, were lower than their LIFO cost basis and, as a result, we recorded an inventory valuation charge of $345 million to cost of revenues to value these inventories at the lower of cost or market.

a. Compute gross profit margin for 2015.

b. What would gross profit margin and the gross profit margin percentage have been if the company had not had to record the lower of cost or market adjustment?

c. At the end of the year, Marathon's LIFO reserve was $684 million. If the company had used FIFO, what would the inventory valuation charge have been?

Exercises

E6-23. Applying and Analyzing Inventory Costing Methods

At the beginning of the current period, Chen carried 1,000 units of its product with a unit cost of $32. A summary of purchases during the current period follows.

LO1

	Units	Unit Cost	Cost
Beginning Inventory	1,000	$32	$32,000
Purchases:#1	1,800	34	61,200
#2	800	38	30,400
#3	1,200	41	49,200

During the current period, Chen sold 2,800 units.

a. Assume that Chen uses the first-in, first-out method. Compute both cost of goods sold for the current period and the ending inventory balance. Use the financial statement effects template to record cost of goods sold for the period.

b. Assume that Chen uses the last-in, first-out method. Compute both cost of goods sold for the current period and the ending inventory balance.

c. Assume that Chen uses the average cost method. Compute both cost of goods sold for the current period and the ending inventory balance.

d. Which of these three inventory costing methods would you choose to:
1. Reflect what is probably the physical flow of goods? Explain.
2. Minimize income taxes for the period? Explain.
3. Report the largest amount of income for the period? Explain.

LO2

General Electric
Company (GE)

E6-24.   Analyzing an Inventory Footnote Disclosure

General Electric Company reports the following footnote in its 10-K report. The company reports its inventories using the LIFO inventory costing method.

December 31 ($ millions)	2015	2014
Raw materials and work in process . . .	$13,415	$ 9,963
Finished goods.	8,199	6,982
Unbilled shipments.	628	755
	22,243	17,701
Less revaluation to LIFO.	206	(62)
	$22,449	$17,639

a. What is the balance in inventories reported on GE's 2015 balance sheet?
b. What would GE's 2015 balance sheet have reported for inventories had the company used FIFO inventory costing?
c. What cumulative effect has GE's choice of LIFO over FIFO had on its pretax income as of year-end 2015? Explain.
d. Assume GE has a 35% income tax rate. As of the 2015 year-end, how much has GE saved in taxes by choosing LIFO over FIFO method for costing inventory? Has the use of LIFO increased or decreased GE's cumulative taxes paid?
e. What effect has the use of LIFO inventory costing had on GE's pretax income and tax expense for 2015 only (assume a 35% income tax rate)?

LO1

E6-25.   Computing Cost of Sales and Ending Inventory

Howell Company has the following financial records for the current period.

	Units	Unit Cost
Beginning inventory	150	$100
Purchases:#1	600	96
#2	500	92
#3	250	90

Ending inventory is 350 units. Compute the ending inventory and the cost of goods sold for the current period using (a) first-in, first-out, (b) average cost, and (c) last-in, first-out.

LO2

Deere & Co. (DE)

E6-26.   Analyzing an Inventory Footnote Disclosure

The inventory footnote from **Deere & Company**'s 2015 10-K follows.

Inventories Most inventories owned by Deere & Company and its U.S. equipment subsidiaries are valued at cost, on the "last-in, first-out" (LIFO) basis. Remaining inventories are generally valued at the lower of cost, on the "first-in, first-out" (FIFO) basis, or market. The value of gross inventories on the LIFO basis represented 66 percent and 65 percent of worldwide gross inventories at FIFO value at October 31, 2015 and 2014, respectively. If all inventories had been valued on a FIFO basis, estimated inventories by major classification at October 31 in millions of dollars would have been as follows:

$ millions	2015	2014
Raw materials and supplies	$1,559	$1,724
Work-in-process.	450	654
Finished goods and parts.	3,234	3,360
Total FIFO value	5,243	5,738
Less adjustment to LIFO value. . . .	1,426	1,528
Inventories	$3,817	$4,210

This footnote reveals that not all of Deere's inventories are reported using the same inventory costing method (companies can use different inventory costing methods for different inventory pools).

a. What amount does Deere report for inventories on its 2015 balance sheet?

b. What would Deere have reported as inventories on its 2015 balance sheet had the company used FIFO inventory costing for all of its inventories?

c. What cumulative effect has the use of LIFO inventory costing had, as of year-end 2015, on Deere's pretax income compared with the pretax income it would have reported had it used FIFO inventory costing for all of its inventories? Explain.

d. Assuming a 35% income tax rate, by what cumulative dollar amount has Deere's tax expense been affected by use of LIFO inventory costing as of year-end 2015? Has the use of LIFO inventory costing increased or decreased Deere's cumulative tax expense?

e. What effect has the use of LIFO inventory costing had on Deere's pretax income and tax expense for 2015 only (assume a 35% income tax rate)?

E6-27. Computing Straight-Line and Double-Declining-Balance Depreciation

LO4

On January 2, Reed Company purchases a laser cutting machine for use in fabrication of a part for one of its key products. The machine cost $75,000, and its estimated useful life is five years, after which the expected salvage value is $5,000. For both parts *a* and *b* below: (1) Compute depreciation expense for *each year* of the machine's five-year useful life under that depreciation method. (2) Use the financial statements effects template to show the effect of depreciation for the first year only for that method. (When equipment is used exclusively in the manufacturing process, the depreciation is more accurately recorded as part of cost of goods sold and not as depreciation expense.)

a. Straight-line

b. Double-declining-balance

E6-28. Computing Depreciation, Net Book Value, and Gain or Loss on Asset Sale

LO4, 5

Zimmer Company owns an executive plane that originally cost $1,280,000. It has recorded straight-line depreciation on the plane for seven full years, calculated assuming an $160,000 expected salvage value at the end of its estimated 10-year useful life. Zimmer disposes of the plane at the end of the seventh year.

a. At the disposal date, what is the (1) cumulative depreciation expense and (2) net book value of the plane?

b. How much gain or loss is reported at disposal if the sales price is:
   1. A cash amount equal to the plane's net book value.
   2. $285,000 cash.
   3. $700,000 cash.

E6-29. Computing Straight-Line and Double-Declining-Balance Depreciation

LO4

On January 2, 2016, Fischer Company purchases a machine that manufactures a part for one of its key products. The machine cost $264,600 and is estimated to have a useful life of six years, with an expected salvage value of $22,500. Compute depreciation expense for 2016 and 2017 for the following depreciation methods.

a. Straight-line.

b. Double-declining-balance.

E6-30. Computing Depreciation, Net Book Value, and Gain or Loss on Asset Sale

Lynch Company owns and operates a delivery van that originally cost $46,400. Lynch has recorded straight-line depreciation on the van for four years, calculated assuming a $5,000 expected salvage value at the end of its estimated six-year useful life. Depreciation was last recorded at the end of the fourth year, at which time Lynch disposes of this van.

a. Compute the net book value of the van on the disposal date.

b. Compute the gain or loss on sale of the van if the disposal proceeds are:
   1. A cash amount equal to the van's net book value.
   2. $21,000 cash.
   3. $17,000 cash.

LO6

Deere & Co. (DE)

E6-31.   Estimating Useful Life and Percent Used Up

The property and equipment footnote from the Deere & Company Equipment and Operations segment follows.

Property and Depreciation   A summary of property and equipment at October 31 follows.

Property and Equipment ($ millions)	Useful Lives* (Years)	2015	2014
Land		$ 114	$ 120
Buildings and building equipment	23	3,016	3,037
Machinery and equipment	11	5,055	5,089
Dies, patterns, tools, etc.	8	1,567	1,552
All other	5	875	889
Construction in progress		345	530
Total at cost		10,972	11,217
Less accumulated depreciation		5,846	5,694
Total		$ 5,126	$5,523

* Weighted averages

Total property and equipment additions in 2015, 2014 and 2013 were $666 million, $1,016 million and $1,158 million, and depreciation was $692 million, $696 million and $637 million, respectively.

a. Compute the estimated useful life of Deere's depreciable assets at year-end 2015. How does this estimate compare with the useful lives reported in Deere's footnote disclosure?

b. Estimate the percent used up of Deere's depreciable assets at year-end 2015. How do you interpret this figure?

LO3, 6

Intel Corp. (INTC)

E6-32.   Computing and Evaluating Inventory and PPE Turnovers

Intel Corporation reports the following financial statement amounts in its 2015 10-K report.

$ millions	Sales	Cost of Goods Sold	Inventories	Plant, property, and equipment, net
2013	$52,708	$21,187	$4,172	$31,428
2014	55,870	20,261	4,273	33,238
2015	55,355	20,676	5,167	31,858

a. Compute the inventory and PPE turnover ratios for both 2014 and 2015.

b. What changes are evident in the turnover rates of Intel for these years? Discuss ways in which a company such as Intel can improve inventory and PPE turnover ratios.

LO4, 5

E6-33.   Computing and Assessing Plant Asset Impairment

On July 1, Arcola Company purchases equipment for $330,000. The equipment has an estimated useful life of 10 years and expected salvage value of $40,000. The company uses straight-line depreciation. Four years later, economic factors cause the fair value of the equipment to decline to $160,000. On this date, Arcola examines the equipment for impairment and estimates $185,000 in undiscounted expected cash inflows from this equipment.

a. Compute the annual depreciation expense relating to this equipment.

b. Compute the equipment's net book value at the end of the fourth year.

c. Apply the test of impairment to this equipment as of the end of the fourth year. Is the equipment impaired? Show supporting computations.

d. If the equipment is impaired at the end of the fourth year, compute the impairment loss.

E6-34. **Computing Asset Related Ratios**

LO6

Dick's Sporting Goods (DKS)

Dick's Sporting Goods included the following information in its year-end 2015 10-K.

Sales.	$7,270,965
PPE, gross	2,665,314
Land	—
Construction in progress	124,400
Accumulated depreciation	1,317,429
PPE, net, at year-end 2014	1,203,382
Depreciation expense.	193,594

Required

a. Compute PPE turnover.

b. Compute the average useful life.

c. Compute the percentage used up of the PPE.

Problems

P6-35. **Evaluating Turnover Ratios Across Industries**

LO3, 6

Nike (NKE)

Best Buy (BBY)

Johnson & Johnson (JNJ)

Boeing (BA)

The table that follows reports balance sheet and income statement information for Nike, Best Buy, Johnson & Johnson, and Boeing from their year-end 2015 SEC filings.

$ millions	Sales	Cost of Goods Sold	Inventory, 2015	Inventory, 2014	PPE, net
Nike	$30,601	$16,534	$ 4,337	$ 3,947	$ 3,011
Best Buy	39,528	30,334	5,051	5,174	2,346
Johnson & Johnson	70,074	21,536	8,053	8,184	15,905
Boeing (product sales)	85,255	73,446	47,257	46,756	12,076

Required

a. Compute the days inventory outstanding for each company for 2015.

b. Compare the days inventory outstanding across the four companies and consider the industries in which they operate. What do we observe?

c. Compute the PPE turnover for each company.

d. Why is the PPE turnover for Best Buy so much higher than that for Boeing?

e. Which metric is likely easier for these companies to improve, inventory days outstanding or PPE turnover? Explain.

P6-36. **Analyzing and Interpreting Inventories and Converting LIFO to FIFO for Ratio Calculation**

LO2, 3

Dow Chemical Co. (DOW)

The current asset section from The Dow Chemical Company's 2015 annual report follows.

December 31 ($ millions)	2015	2014
Cash and cash equivalents	$ 8,577	$ 5,654
Accounts and notes receivable		
Trade (net of allowance for doubtful receivables—2015: $94; 2014: $110)	4,078	4,685
Other.	3,768	4,687
Inventories	6,871	8,101
Deferred income tax assets—current.	827	812
Other current assets.	354	316
Total current assets	$24,475	$24,255

The Dow Chemical inventory footnote follows.

The following table provides a breakdown of inventories.

Inventories at December 31 ($ millions)	2015	2014
Finished goods..........................	$3,850	$4,547
Work in process	1,506	1,905
Raw materials..........................	747	797
Supplies	768	852
Total inventories	$6,871	$8,101

The reserves reducing inventories from a FIFO basis to a LIFO basis amounted to $8 million at December 31, 2015 and $569 million at December 31, 2014. Inventories valued on a LIFO basis, principally hydrocarbon and U.S. chemicals and plastics product inventories, represented 30 percent of the total inventories at December 31, 2015 and 29 percent of total inventories at December 31, 2014.

A reduction of certain inventories resulted in the liquidation of some of the Company's LIFO inventory layers, increasing pretax income $3 million in 2015, decreasing pretax income $23 million in 2014, and increasing pretax income $55 million in 2013.

Required

a. What inventory costing method does Dow Chemical use? As of 2015, what is the effect on cumulative pretax income and cash flow of using this inventory costing method? (Assume a 35% tax rate.) What is the effect on 2015 pretax income and cash flow of using this inventory costing method?

b. Compute inventory turnover and average inventory days outstanding for 2015 (2015 cost of goods sold is $48,778 million). Comment on the level of these two ratios. Is the level what you expected?

c. Determine the FIFO values for inventories for 2014 and 2015, and cost of goods sold for 2015. Recompute inventory turnover and DIO. Compare the ratios to those from part *b*. Which set of ratios would provide more useful analysis?

d. Explain why a reduction of inventory quantities increased income in 2013 through 2015.

LO6

Abbott Laboratories
(ABT)

P6-37.   Estimating Useful Life and Percent Used Up

The property and equipment section of the Abbott Laboratories 2015 balance sheet follows.

		December 31	
Property and equipment, at cost ($ millions)	2015	2014	2013
Land	$ 432	$ 457	$ 502
Buildings.................................	2,769	2,968	2,994
Equipment	8,254	8,480	8,506
Construction in progress	928	727	868
	12,383	12,632	12,870
Less: accumulated depreciation and amortization	6,653	6,697	6,965
Net property and equipment	$ 5,730	$ 5,935	$ 5,905

The company also provides the following disclosure relating to the useful lives of its depreciable assets.

Property and Equipment—Depreciation and amortization are provided on a straight-line basis over the estimated useful lives of the assets. The following table shows estimated useful lives of property and equipment:

Classification	Estimated Useful Lives
Buildings.........	10 to 50 years (average 27 years)
Equipment	3 to 20 years (average 11 years)

During 2015, the company reported $871 million for depreciation expense.

Required

a. Compute the estimated useful life of Abbott Laboratories' depreciable assets. How does this compare with its useful lives footnote disclosure above?

b. Compute the estimated percent used up of Abbott Laboratories' depreciable assets. How do you interpret this figure?

P6-38. **Interpreting and Applying Disclosures on Property and Equipment**

Following are selected disclosures from the 10-K report of Facebook Inc.

Property and Equipment, Net

$ millions	2015	2014
Land	$ 596	$ 153
Buildings.	2,273	1,420
Leasehold equipment.	447	304
Network equipment	3,633	3,020
Computer software, office equipment and other	248	149
Construction in progress	622	738
Total	7,819	5,784
Less: Accumulated depreciation	(2,132)	(1,817)
Property and equipment, net	$5,687	$3,967

Depreciation expense on property and equipment was $1.22 billion, $923 million, and $857 million during 2015, 2014 and 2013, respectively.

Required

a. Compute the PPE turnover for 2015 (Sales in 2015 are $17,928 million).

b. Estimate the useful life, on average, for its depreciable PPE assets.

c. By what percentage are Facebook's assets "used up" at year-end 2015? What implication does the assets used up computation have for forecasting cash flows?

d. Consider the ratios in parts a, b, and c. Interpret them in light of the company's age and business model.

e. The list of PPE assets includes an asset labeled "Construction in progress." What is this asset and what types of costs are included in the $622 million on the balance sheet?

P6-39. **Analyzing and Interpreting Restructuring Costs and Effects**

Hewlett-Packard Inc. reports the following footnote disclosure (excerpted) in its 2015 10-K relating to its 2012 restructuring program.

Fiscal 2015 Restructuring Plan   In connection with the Separation, on September 14, 2015, HP's Board of Directors approved a cost saving and investment proposal which includes a restructuring plan (the "2015 Plan") which will be implemented through fiscal 2018. As part of the 2015 Plan, HP expects up to approximately 33,300 employees to exit the company by the end of 2018. These workforce reductions are primarily associated with the ES segment. The changes to the workforce will vary by country, based on local legal requirements and consultations with employee works councils and other employee representatives, as appropriate. HP estimates that it will incur aggregate pre-tax charges through fiscal 2018 of approximately $2.9 billion in connection with the 2015 Plan, of which the estimated cost for HP Inc. is approximately $280 million. Total estimated charges as a result of workforce reductions are approximately $2.4 billion and total estimated charges for real estate consolidation are approximately $506 million.

Fiscal 2012 Restructuring Plan   On May 23, 2012, HP adopted a multi-year restructuring plan (the "2012 Plan") designed to simplify business processes, accelerate innovation and deliver better results for customers, employees and stockholders. As of October 31, 2015 HP eliminated 55,800 positions in connection with the 2012 Plan, with a portion of those employees exiting the company as part of voluntary enhanced early retirement ("EER") programs in the U.S. and in certain other countries. HP recognized $5.5 billion in total aggregate charges in

continued

continued from previous page

connection with the 2012 Plan, with $4.9 billion related to workforce reductions, including the EER programs, and $589 million related to infrastructure, including data center and real estate consolidation and other items. The severance and infrastructure related cash payments associated with the 2012 Plan are expected to be paid out through fiscal 2021. As of October 31, 2015, the 2012 Plan is considered completed. HP does not expect any additional charges to this plan.

Other Plans   Restructuring plans initiated by HP in fiscal 2008 and 2010 were substantially completed as of October 31, 2015. Severance and infrastructure related cash payments associated with the other plans are expected to be paid out through fiscal 2019.

$ millions	Balance, October 31, 2014	Charges	Cash Payments	Other Adjustments & Non-cash Settlements	Balance, October 31, 2015
Fiscal 2015 Plan					
Severance................	$ —	$390	$ —	$ —	$390
Infrastructure and other	—	1	(1)	—	—
Total 2015 Plan	—	391	(1)	—	390
Fiscal 2012 Plan					
Severance and EER	955	566	(1,101)	(78)	342
Infrastructure and other	98	74	(120)	(4)	48
Total 2012 Plan	1,053	640	(1,221)	(82)	390
Other plans					
Severance................	7	(4)	(1)	(1)	1
Infrastructure..............	54	(10)	(20)	—	24
Total other plans	61	(14)	(21)	(1)	25
Total restructuring plans.......	$1,114	$1,017	$(1,243)	$(83)	$805
Reflected in consolidated balance sheets:					
Accrued restructuring	$ 898				$689
Other liabilities	$ 216				$116

Required

a. Briefly describe the company's 2015 restructuring program. Provide two examples of common noncash charges associated with corporate restructuring activities.

b. Using the financial statement effects template, show the effects on financial statements of the (1) 2015 restructuring charge of $1,017 million, and (2) 2015 cash payment of $1,243 million.

c. Assume that instead of accurately estimating the anticipated restructuring charge in 2015, the company overestimated them by $30 million. How would this overestimation affect financial statements in (1) 2015, and (2) 2016 when severance costs are paid in cash?

d. The company reports that the total charges related to the 2015 restructuring plan will amount to $2.9 billion. What is the effect on the 2015 income statement from this restructuring? Why do investors care to know the total charge if it does not impact current-period earnings?

IFRS Applications

LO3

Volkswagen Group

Daimler AG

I6-40.   **Computing and Evaluating Inventory Turnover for Two Companies**

European car makers, Volkswagen Group (headquartered in Wolfsburg, Germany) and Daimler AG (headquartered in Stuttgart, Germany) report the following information.

| Euros in millions | Volkswagen | | | Daimler | | |
	Sales	Cost of Goods Sold	Inventories	Sales	Cost of Goods Sold	Inventories
2014	€202,458	€165,934	€31,466	€129,872	€101,688	€20,864
2015	213,292	179,382	35,048	149,467	117,670	23,760

Required
a. Compute the 2015 inventory turnover and the 2015 gross profit margin (in %) for each of these two companies.
b. Discuss any difference in inventory turnover and gross profit margin between these two companies. Does the difference confirm expectations given their respective business models? Explain.
c. How could the companies improve inventory turnover?

I6-41.   Estimating Useful Life, Percent Used Up, and Gain or Loss on Disposal

LO5, 6
Husky Energy (HSE)

Husky Energy is one of Canada's largest integrated energy companies. Based in Calgary, Alberta, Husky is publicly traded on the Toronto Stock Exchange. The Company operates in Western and Atlantic Canada, the United States and the Asia Pacific Region with upstream and downstream business segments. The company uses IFRS to prepare its financial statements. During 2015, the company reported depreciation expense of $8,484 million. The property and equipment footnote follows.

Property, Plant and Equipment ($ millions)	Oil and Gas Properties	Processing, Transportation and Storage	Upgrading	Refining	Retail and Other	Total
Cost						
December 31, 2014	$ 47,974	$1,296	$ 2,274	$ 6,561	$ 2,632	$ 60,737
Additions.	2,128	173	46	452	76	2,875
Acquisitions	57	—	—	—	—	57
Transfers from exploration and evaluation. .	97	—	—	—	—	97
Intersegment transfers	6	(6)	—	—	—	—
Changes in asset retirement obligations . .	(107)	—	(7)	(5)	(18)	(137)
Disposals and derecognition	(487)	—	—	(24)	(4)	(515)
Exchange adjustments	720	2	—	1,152	2	1,876
December 31, 2015	$ 50,388	$1,465	$ 2,313	$ 8,136	$ 2,688	$ 64,990
Accumulated depletion, depreciation, amortization and impairment						
December 31, 2014	$(23,687)	$ (527)	$(1,154)	$(1,988)	$(1,394)	$(28,750)
Depletion, depreciation and amortization. .	(7,811)	(48)	(106)	(365)	(154)	(8,484)
Intersegment transfers	(2)	2	—	—	—	—
Disposals and derecognition	370	—	—	18	2	390
Exchange adjustments	(170)	(1)	—	(341)	—	(512)
December 31, 2015	$(31,300)	$ (574)	$(1,260)	$(2,676)	$(1,546)	$(37,356)
Net book value						
December 31, 2014	$24,287	$ 769	$ 1,120	$ 4,573	$ 1,238	$ 31,987
December 31, 2015	19,088	891	1,053	5,460	1,142	27,634

Required
a. Compute the estimated useful life of Husky Energy's depreciable assets at year-end 2015. Assume that land is 10% of "Refining."
b. Estimate the percent used up of Husky Energy's depreciable assets at year-end 2015. How do we interpret this figure?
c. Consider the disposals and derecognition during the year. This refers to assets that were sold and removed from the balance sheet during the year. Calculate the net book value of the total PPE disposed during the year. Assume that Husky Energy received C$72 million cash proceeds for the year. Determine the gain or loss on the disposal.

I6-42. **Analyzing and Interpreting Operating Asset Ratios**

Canadian Tire Corporation, Limited operates retail stores in Canada that sell general merchandise, clothing, and sporting goods. The company offers everyday products and services to Canadians through more than 1,700 retail and gasoline outlets from coast-to-coast. Canadian Tire uses IFRS, and the asset side of the 2015 balance sheet is as follows.

In Millions of CDN Dollars	2015	2014
Cash and cash equivalents	$ 900.6	$ 662.1
Short-term investments	96.1	289.1
Trade and other receivables	915.0	880.2
Loans receivable	4,875.5	4,905.5
Merchandise inventories	1,764.5	1,623.8
Income taxes recoverable	42.2	31.9
Prepaid expenses and deposits	96.1	104.5
Assets classified as held for sale	2.3	13.1
Total current assets	8,692.3	8,510.2
Long-term receivables and other assets	731.2	684.2
Long-term investments	153.4	176.0
Goodwill and intangible assets	1,246.8	1,251.7
Investment property	137.8	148.6
Property and equipment	3,978.2	3,743.1
Deferred income taxes	48.1	39.4
Total assets	$14,987.8	$14,553.2

Required

a. Compute inventory turnover and average inventory days outstanding for 2015 (2015 cost of goods sold is C$8,144.3 million). Comment on the level of these two ratios. Is the level what we expect given Canadian Tire's industry? Explain.

b. GAAP allows for FIFO, LIFO, and average cost inventory costing methods. How does IFRS differ?

c. In periods of rising prices, how will net income be affected under the different inventory costing methods?

d. During 2015, the company recorded revenue of C$12,279.6 and depreciation expense of C$312.8 million. Footnotes reported accumulated depreciation on PPE of C$2,791.6 million, and cost of land and construction in progress of C$874.4 million and C$359.4 million respectively. Compute PPE turnover, average useful life, and percent used up for 2015.

Management Applications

MA6-43. **Managing Operating Asset Reduction**

Return on net operating assets (RNOA = NOPAT/Average NOA, see Module 4) is commonly used to evaluate financial performance. If managers cannot increase NOPAT, they can still increase this return by reducing the amount of net operating assets (NOA). List specific ways that managers could manage the following operating items.

a. Inventories

b. Plant, property and equipment

c. Accounts payable

Ongoing Project

(This ongoing project began in Module 1 and continues through most of the book; even if previous segments were not completed, the requirements are still applicable to any business analysis.)

1. *Inventory* The following provides some guidance for analysis of a company's inventory.

- What is inventory for the company? Does the company manufacture inventory? What proportion of total inventory is raw materials? Work in process? Finished goods?
- Compare the two companies' inventory costing methods. Adjust LIFO inventory and cost of goods sold if necessary. Is the LIFO reserve significant? Estimate the tax savings associated with LIFO costing method. (Use the adjusted COGS and inventory figures for all calculations and ratios.)
- What is the relative size of inventory? How has this changed over the recent three-year period?
- Compute inventory turnover and days inventory outstanding and the cash conversion cycle for all three years reported on the income statement.
- Compute gross profit margin in percentage terms. Consider the current economic environment and the companies' competitive landscape. Can we explain any changes in gross profit levels? Have costs for raw materials and labor increased during the year? Have sales volumes softened? What has happened to unit prices? Read the MD&A to determine senior management's take.
- Does the company face any inventory related risk? What has been done to mitigate this risk? Read the MD&A.

For each point of analysis, compare across companies and over time.

2. *Tangible Assets*   The following provides some guidance to the companies' long-term (tangible) assets.
   - Are tangible assets significant for the companies? What proportion of total assets is held as tangible assets (PPE)? What exactly are the companies' tangible assets? That is, what is their nature?
   - Compare the two companies' depreciation policies. Do they differ markedly?
   - What is the relative size of tangible assets? How has this changed over the three-year period?
   - Did the company increase tangible assets during the year? Was the increase for outright asset purchases or did the company acquire assets via a merger or acquisition?
   - Compute PPE turnover for all three years reported on the income statement.
   - Compute the average age of assets and percentage used up.
   - Are any assets impaired? Is the impairment charge significant? Is the impairment specific to the company or is the industry experiencing a downturn?

For each point of analysis, compare across companies and over time.

3. *Restructuring Activities*   Have the companies restructured operations in the past three years?
   - Determine the amount of the expense on the income statement—look in the footnotes or the MD&A for additional information.
   - Are other close competitors also restructuring during this time period?
   - Read the footnotes and assess the company's restructuring plans. How many years will it take to fully execute the plan? What additional expenditures are required?
   - Find the restructuring liability on the balance sheet (again the notes will help). Does the liability seem reasonable over time? Compare it to total assets and total liabilities each year and look for any patterns.

Solutions to Review Problems

Review 6-1—Solution

Preliminary computation: Units in ending inventory = 4,800 available − 2,800 sold = 2,000

1. First-in, first-out (FIFO)

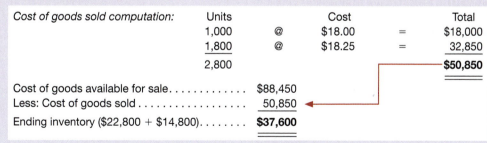

Cost of goods sold computation:	Units		Cost		Total
	1,000	@	$18.00	=	$18,000
	1,800	@	$18.25	=	32,850
	2,800				$50,850

Cost of goods available for sale. $88,450
Less: Cost of goods sold 50,850
Ending inventory ($22,800 + $14,800). **$37,600**

2. Last-in, first-out (LIFO)

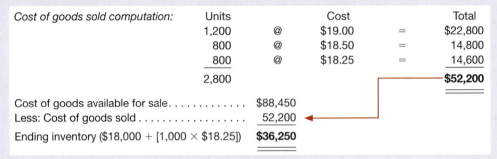

Cost of goods sold computation:	Units		Cost		Total
	1,200	@	$19.00	=	$22,800
	800	@	$18.50	=	14,800
	800	@	$18.25	=	14,600
	2,800				**$52,200**

Cost of goods available for sale. $88,450
Less: Cost of goods sold   52,200
Ending inventory ($18,000 + [1,000 × $18.25])   **$36,250**

3. Average cost (AC)

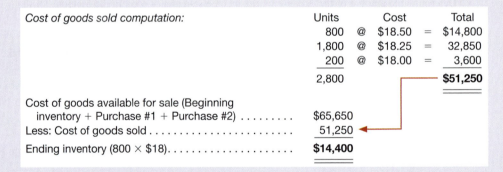

Average unit cost   = $88,450/4,800 units = $18.427
Cost of goods sold = 2,800 × $18.427 = $51,596
Ending inventory   = 2,000 × $18.427 = $36,854

4. *a.*   FIFO is normally the method that most closely reflects physical flow. For example, FIFO would apply to the physical flow of perishable units and to situations where the earlier units acquired are moved out first because of risk of deterioration or obsolescence.

  b.   LIFO results in the highest cost of goods sold during periods of rising costs (as in the HD subsidiary case); and, accordingly, LIFO yields the lowest net income and the lowest income taxes.

Review 6-2—Solution

1. Because the $30,000 market value of the inventories is less than the carrying value of the inventories under FIFO inventory costing, the inventories must be written down to their market value with the write-down reported in the income statement as an increase in COGS. The balance sheet will report the inventory at $30,000.

2. Last-in, first-out with LIFO liquidation

Cost of goods sold computation:	Units		Cost		Total
	800	@	$18.50	=	$14,800
	1,800	@	$18.25	=	32,850
	200	@	$18.00	=	3,600
	2,800				**$51,250**

Cost of goods available for sale (Beginning
  inventory + Purchase #1 + Purchase #2) $65,650
Less: Cost of goods sold   51,250
Ending inventory (800 × $18). **$14,400**

The company's LIFO gross profit has increased by $950 ($52,200 − $51,250) because of the LIFO liquidation. The reduction of inventory quantities matched older (lower) cost layers against current selling prices. The company has, in effect, dipped into lower-cost layers to boost current-period profit—all from a simple delay of inventory purchases.

3. The LIFO reserve is computed as the difference between the inventory cost at LIFO and FIFO. This is $37,600 − $36,250 = $1,350. Using LIFO for inventory costing for the subsidiary resulted in $473 of taxes being deferred in the current period, computed as $1,350 × 35%.

Review 6-3—Solution

$ millions	2016	2015	2014
1. Gross profit margin	$\dfrac{\$20,570}{\$59,074} = 34.8\%$	$\dfrac{\$19,558}{\$56,223} = 34.8\%$	$\dfrac{\$18,476}{\$53,417} = 34.6\%$
2. Days inventory outstanding	$365 \times \dfrac{\dfrac{\$9,458+\$8,911}{2}}{\$38,504} = 87.1$	$365 \times \dfrac{\dfrac{\$8,911+\$9,127}{2}}{\$36,665} = 89.8$	
3. Days payable outstanding	$365 \times \dfrac{\dfrac{\$5,633+\$5,124}{2}}{\$38,504} = 51.0$	$365 \times \dfrac{\dfrac{\$5,124+\$5,008}{2}}{\$36,665} = 50.4$	
4. Cash conversion cycle	$0 + 87.1 - 51.0 = 36.1$	$0 + 89.8 - 50.4 = 39.4$	

Analysis: The cash conversion cycle improved by 3.3 days in 2016, computed as $39.4 - 36.1$.

5. Δ Cash = Δ Cash Conversion Cycle Days $\times$ (COGS/365) = 3.3 days $\times$ ($38,504/365 days) = $348 million

Review 6-4—Solution

1. *a.* Straight-line depreciation expense = ($95,000 − $10,000)/5 years = $17,000 per year
   b. Double-declining-balance rate = 40% (twice straight-line rate = 2 × [100%/5 years] = 40%)

Year	Net Book Value × Rate	Depreciation Expense	Accumulated Depreciation
1	$95,000 × 0.40 =	$38,000	$38,000
2	($95,000 − $38,000) × 0.40 =	22,800	60,800
3	($95,000 − $60,800) × 0.40 =	13,680	74,480
4	($95,000 − $74,480) × 0.40 =	8,208	82,688
5	($95,000 − $82,688) × 0.40 =	2,312*	85,000

*The formula value of $4,925 is not reported for Year 5 because doing so would depreciate the asset below the estimated salvage value; only the $2,312 needed to reach salvage value is depreciated.

2. The HD subsidiary reports the equipment on its balance sheet at its net book value of $44,000.

Equipment, cost..............................	$95,000
Less accumulated depreciation ($17,000 × 3)	51,000
Equipment, net (end of Year 3)....................	$44,000

Review 6-5—Solution

Part 1.

a. The equipment is impaired since the undiscounted expected cash flows of $40,000 are less than the $44,000 net book value of the equipment. The HD subsidiary must write down the equipment to its fair value of $36,000. The effect of this write-down is to reduce the net book value of the equipment by $8,000 ($44,000 − $36,000) and recognize a loss in the income statement.

b. The HD subsidiary must report a gain on this sale of $6,000, computed as proceeds of $50,000 less the net book value of the equipment of $44,000 (see Review 6-4, part 2).

Part 2.

a. Coca-Cola's restructuring expense for 2015 is the increase in the restructuring liability of $691 million.

b. Coca-Cola reports a restructuring liability of $204 million on its 2015 balance sheet.

Review 6-6—Solution

$ millions	2016	2015
PPE turnover	$\dfrac{\$59{,}074}{\dfrac{\$19{,}577 + \$20{,}034}{2}} = 2.98$	$\dfrac{\$56{,}223}{\dfrac{\$20{,}034 + \$20{,}834}{2}} = 2.75$
Average useful life	$\dfrac{\$17{,}451 + \$10{,}863}{\$1{,}484} = 19.1$	$\dfrac{\$17{,}247 + \$10{,}426}{\$1{,}485} = 18.6$
Percent used up	$\dfrac{\$16{,}336}{\$17{,}451 + \$10{,}863} = 57.7\%$	$\dfrac{\$15{,}409}{\$17{,}247 + \$10{,}426} = 55.7\%$

Module 7

Current and Long-Term Liabilities

Learning Objectives

LO1 Explain accounting for accrued liabilities. (p. 7-3)

LO2 Analyze reporting for short-term debt. (p. 7-7)

LO3 Determine the pricing of long-term debt. (p. 7-10)

LO4 Analyze reporting for long-term debt. (p. 7-14)

LO5 Explain how quality of debt is determined. (p. 7-20)

LO6 Apply time value of money concepts (Appendix 7A). (p. 7-26)

VZ

Market cap: $188,300 mil
Total assets: $244,640 mil
Revenues: $131,620 mil
Net income: $18,375 mil

Verizon Communications Inc. is one of the world's leading providers of communication services. It is the largest provider of landline and wireless services in the U.S. with nearly $245 billion in assets.

Verizon recently purchased Vodafone's interest in Verizon Wireless for $130 billion. It raised a large portion of the purchase price by issuing bonds.

During the past four years, Verizon's total liabilities have increased dramatically (to over $225 billion) and its ratio of Verizon's total liabilities to equity increased from 1.6 to 12.7. This increase in financial leverage led Moody's to downgrade Verizon's credit rating. On the positive side, Verizon's return on equity for the recent year was a stunning 124% due in large part to the company's financial leverage.

To remain competitive, Verizon is spending billions to roll out its FiOS phone, data, and video network to give its customers faster Internet service and an alternative to cable. Indeed, over the past three years, Verizon has spent over $51 billion on capital expenditures. The demand for new capital spending is coming at an inopportune time. Verizon is currently saddled with a debt load of over $110 billion as of 2015 (30% of which matures over the next five years) and employee benefit obligations of nearly $30 billion. It is also paying over $8 billion in dividends annually.

This module focuses on liabilities; that is, short-term and long-term obligations. Liabilities represent nonowner financing, one of two financing sources for a company. The other is shareholder (owner) financing. Bonds and notes are a major part of most companies' liabilities. In this module, we show how to price bonds and notes and how the issuance and subsequent payment of the principal and interest affect financial statements. We also discuss the required disclosures that enable us to effectively analyze a company's ability to pay its debts as they come due. [Source: *Verizon*, 2015 10-K.]

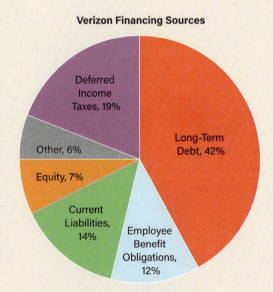

Verizon Financing Sources

- Long-Term Debt, 42%
- Deferred Income Taxes, 19%
- Employee Benefit Obligations, 12%
- Current Liabilities, 14%
- Equity, 7%
- Other, 6%

© iStock

Road Map

LO	Learning Objective | Topics	Page	eLecture	Guided Example	Assignments
7-1	**Explain accounting for accrued liabilities.** Defined :: Contractual Liabilities :: Contingent Liabilities	7-3	e7–1	Review 7-1	1, 2, 7, 9, 13, 21, 27, 28, 29, 30, 48, 51
7-2	**Analyze reporting for short-term debt.** Accounting for ST Debt :: Interest :: Maturities of LT Debt	7-7	e7–2	Review 7-2	8, 17, 45, 54
7-3	**Determine the pricing of long-term debt.** Bond Details :: Par Bonds :: Discount Bonds :: Premium Bonds :: Cost of Debt	7-10	e7–3	Review 7-3	3, 10, 19, 20, 22, 31, 32, 34, 35, 36, 37, 39, 40, 45, 49
7-4	**Analyze reporting for long-term debt.** Debt Disclosures :: Amortization :: Bond Repurchase :: Bond Fair Value	7-14	e7–4	Review 7-4	4, 6, 11, 12, 13, 14, 15, 16, 22, 26, 31, 32, 34, 35, 36, 37, 39, 40, 45, 46, 47, 49, 50, 52
7-5	**Explain how quality of debt is determined.** Credit Ratings Defined :: Determinants of Ratings :: Importance of Ratings	7-20	e7–5	Review 7-5	5, 10, 18, 23, 33, 41, 42, 45, 47, 50
7-6	**Apply time value of money concepts (Appendix 7A).** Present & Future Values :: Single Amounts and Annuities :: Using Excel or Calculator	7-26	e7–6	Review 7-6	19, 20, 22, 24, 25, 38, 43, 44

Current and Long-Term Liabilities

Accruals	Short and Long-term Debt	Credit Quality	Time Value of Money
■ Wages Payable ■ Deferred Revenue ■ Contingent Liabilities	■ Accounting for Debt ■ Pricing Debt ■ Presentation ■ Amortization of Premiums and Discounts ■ Fair Value of Debt	■ Risk Premiums ■ Credit Ratings ■ How Credit Ratings are Determined ■ Why Credit Ratings Matter	■ Lump Sums ■ Annuities ■ Present Value ■ Future Value ■ Bond Pricing

Accrued Liabilities

The current liabilities section of the balance sheet reports liabilities that will normally mature within one year from the balance sheet date. Following is the information that **Verizon** provides in its 2015 annual report and footnotes.

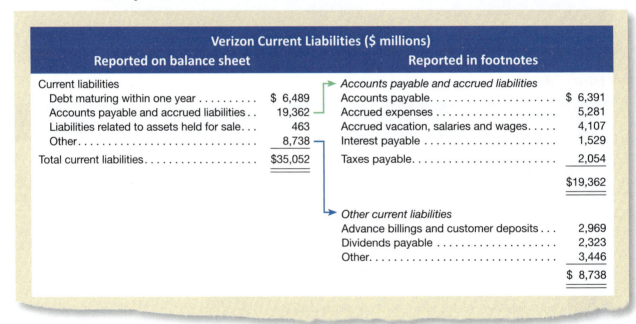

Verizon Current Liabilities ($ millions)			
Reported on balance sheet		**Reported in footnotes**	
Current liabilities		*Accounts payable and accrued liabilities*	
Debt maturing within one year	$ 6,489	Accounts payable.	$ 6,391
Accounts payable and accrued liabilities . .	19,362	Accrued expenses	5,281
Liabilities related to assets held for sale. . .	463	Accrued vacation, salaries and wages.	4,107
Other.	8,738	Interest payable	1,529
Total current liabilities.	$35,052	Taxes payable.	2,054
			$19,362
		Other current liabilities	
		Advance billings and customer deposits . . .	2,969
		Dividends payable	2,323
		Other.	3,446
			$ 8,738

Verizon's current liabilities of $35,052 million includes the following usual categories.

- **Short-term debt and the portion of long-term debt that is scheduled to mature within the next year.** This category typically includes loans from banks, commercial paper borrowings, and scheduled maturities of long-term bonds and notes. These are nonoperating liabilities.

- **Accounts payable.** These are amounts owing to suppliers for the purchase of goods and services on account and are therefore, operating liabilities. We discuss accounts payable with inventory in a prior module because accounts payable are typically related to inventory purchases.

- **Accrued liabilities.** This category typically includes many different accruals. For Verizon, accrued liabilities includes unpaid wages, interest and taxes, advance billings and customer deposits, and dividends payable to shareholders.

eLectures

MBC

LO1 Explain accounting for accrued liabilities.

Accrued Liabilities Defined

Accrued liabilities (or accruals) are adjustments that accountants make to the balance sheet after all transactions have been entered into the accounting records, and prior to the issuance of the financial statements, so that those statements fairly present the financial condition of the company. These adjustments recognize liabilities on the balance sheet (and the related expense on the income statement) that are not the result of external transactions (such as the purchase of goods or services on account that are recognized as accounts payable). Accrued liabilities are incurred in the current period and, therefore, must be recognized in the current period. Accrued liabilities fall into two broad categories.

1. **Accruals for routine contractual liabilities.** These accruals include items such as:
   - Wages that the company is contractually obligated to pay to employees for work performed, but not yet paid for in the current period.
   - Interest that is due in the current period on borrowed money, but has not yet been paid.
   - Income taxes that are owed, but not yet paid, as a result of profit earned during the period.
   - Other operating liabilities that have been incurred but not yet paid for in the current period (like rent, utilities, etc.).

2. **Accruals for contingent liabilities.** Contingent liabilities depend on the occurrence of a future uncertain event in order to determine whether a liability exists and, if so, in what amount. An example is litigation that has been brought against the company whose outcome and amount depends upon adjudication. Another is warranty liabilities for products sold which depend upon the occurrence of product defects to require the company to repair or replace the product purchased.

Accruals for Contractual Liabilities—Wages Payable Example

Many companies pay employees bi-monthly. In the last two weeks of the month, then, employees have worked for the company, have earned wages, but have not yet been paid. If the liability for unpaid wages is not reflected on the month-end balance sheet, liabilities will be understated and wage expense will not be reflected in the income statement, thus overstating profit for the period. To correct for this, accountants make an entry to reflect the unpaid wage liability on the balance sheet and recognize wage expense in the income statement. When the wages are subsequently paid in the following month, cash decreases as does the wage liability.

The accrual entry and subsequent payment are reflected in our financial statement effects template.

	Balance Sheet						Income Statement			
Transaction	Cash Asset	+ Noncash Assets	= Liabil- ities	+ Contrib. Capital	+ Earned Capital		Rev- enues	− Expen- ses	= Net Income
Period 1: Accrued $75 for employee wages earned at period-end			+75 Wages Payable		−75 Retained Earnings			+75 Wages Expense	= −75
Period 2: Paid $75 for wages earned in prior period	−75 Cash		−75 Wages Payable				−	=	

WE . . . 75
  WP 75

WE	
75	

WP	
	75

WP . . . 75
  Cash 75

WP	
75	

Cash	
	75

The following financial statement effects result from this accrual and subsequent payment of employee wages.

- The effect of the accrual in period 1 is to increase wages payable on the balance sheet and to recognize wages expense on the income statement. Failure to recognize this liability and associated expense would understate liabilities on the balance sheet and overstate income in the current period.

- When the company pays employees in the following period, cash and wages payable both decrease. This payment does not result in expense because the expense was recognized in the prior period when the wages were earned by employees and the liability to pay those wages was incurred.

For example, Verizon reports Accrued vacation, salaries and wages of $4,107 million at the 2015 year end. This represents the anticipated vacation pay earned by employees in 2015 for vacations they will take in 2016.

Other contractual accruals of this type are common and they relate to events that are certain. For example, companies can estimate fairly precisely, unpaid rent and utilities, the amount of interest that is due in the current period on borrowed money, and income taxes that are owed as a result of profit earned during the period. All of these are included in accrued liabilities.

Accruals for Contractual Liabilities—Deferred Revenue Example

Deferred (or unearned) revenue represents deposits or other prepayments from customers that the company has not yet earned. Verizon collects prepayments from customers who opt for prepaid phone plans, which are plans that enable customers to obtain wireless services without credit verification by paying for all services in advance. In some cases, Verizon collects deposits from commercial customers in advance of a major installation of communication equipment. Both of these types of prepayments are accrued liabilities until Verizon provides the related services; that is until the prepaid plan is used or the installation is completed. At the end of fiscal 2015, Verizon reports an accrued liability called Advance billings and customer deposits of $2,969 million. (We discuss deferred revenue more fully in a prior module.)

Accruals for Contingent Liabilities Defined

Some accrued liabilities are less certain than others because the ultimate settlement of the liability is contingent on the outcome of some future event(s). Companies must record an accrual (a contingent liability) on the balance sheet, when two conditions are met.

1. It is "probable" that one or more future events will confirm that a liability existed at the financial statement date.

2. The amount required to settle the liability in the future can be reasonably determined at the financial statement date. The amount recorded should be the best estimate of the future expenditure required to settle the obligation. (If the best estimate of the expenditure is a range, and no amount in the range is a better estimate than any other, the company records the minimum amount in the range.)

Common examples of contingent liabilities include:

- Guarantees on the debt of another entity.
- Lawsuits (only for losses, never for lawsuits where the company stands to win).
- Product warranties and recalls.
- Environmental disasters and remediation.

Accruals for Contingent Liabilities—Warranties Example

Warranty liabilities are commitments that manufacturers make to their customers to repair or replace defective products within a specified period of time. If the obligation is *probable* and the amount *estimable* with reasonable certainty, GAAP requires manufacturers to record the expected cost of warranties as a liability and to record the related expected warranty expense in the income statement in the same period that the sales revenue is reported. And, for warranty liabilities, both the probability and the likely amount can be reasonably estimated based on past experience.

To illustrate, assume that a company estimates from past experience that defective units amount to 2% of sales and that each unit will cost $5 to replace. If sales during the period are $10,000, the estimated warranty expense is $1,000 ($10,000 × 2% × $5), and the entries to accrue this liability and to reflect its ultimate payment are shown in the template that follows.

Accruing warranty liabilities has the same effect on financial statements as accruing wages expense. That is, a liability is recorded on the balance sheet and an expense is reported in the income statement. When the defective product is later replaced (or repaired), the liability is reduced together with the cost of the inventory, cash paid for labor to repair the product, parts used in the repair, and any other costs that were necessary to satisfy the claim. (Only a portion of the products estimated to fail does so in the current period; we expect other product failures in future periods. Management monitors this estimate and adjusts it if failure is higher or lower than expected.) As in the accrual of wages, the expense and the liability are reported when incurred and not when paid.

Transaction	Balance Sheet						Income Statement		
	Cash Asset	+ Noncash Assets	= Liabil- ities	+ Contrib. Capital	+ Earned Capital		Rev- enues	− Expen- ses	= Net Income
Accrued $1,000 of ex- pected warranty costs on units sold during the period			= +1,000 Warranty Payable		−1,000 Retained Earnings			− +1,000 Warranty Expense	= −1,000
Delivered $1,000 in replacement products to settle warranty claims		−1,000 Inventory	= −1,000 Warranty Payable					−	=

WRE . . 1,000
WRP . . . 1,000

WRE	
1,000	

WRP	
	1,000

WRP . . 1,000
INV 1,000

WRP	
1,000	

INV	
	1,000

Because the warranty liability and related expense are typically important items for manufacturing companies, information relating to this liability for the current and prior two periods is disclosed in the footnotes to the financial statements. **Harley-Davidson's** warranty footnote in its 2015 annual report is an example.

Product Warranty—Estimated warranty costs are reserved for motorcycles, motorcycle parts and motorcycle accessories at the time of sale. The warranty reserve is based upon historical Company claim data used in combination with other known factors that may affect future warranty claims. The Company updates its warranty estimates quarterly to ensure that the warranty reserves are based on the most current information available . . . The Company maintains reserves for future warranty claims using an estimated cost, which are based primarily on historical Company claim information. Additionally, the Company has from time to time initiated certain voluntary recall campaigns. The Company reserves for all estimated costs associated with recalls in the period that management approves and commits to the recall.

Changes in the Company's warranty and recall liability were as follows (in thousands):

	2015	2014	2013
Balance, beginning of period	$69,250	$64,120	$60,263
Warranties issued during the period	59,259	60,331	59,022
Settlements made during the period	(96,529)	(74,262)	(64,462)
Recalls and changes to pre-existing warranty liabilities . . .	42,237	19,061	9,297
Balance, end of period.	$74,217	$69,250	$64,120

At the beginning of 2015, Harley-Davidson reported a reserve of $69,250 for estimated product warranty and safety recall costs (all $ in thousands for this discussion). During 2015, the company added $59,259 to the reserve relating to warranties on products sold in 2015 and another $42,237 to recognize the estimated liability for product recalls and changes to pre-existing warranty liabilities. This second accrual reflects changes in estimates for costs to repair or replace products sold in prior periods. As a result of these two accruals, Harley-Davidson recognized an expense of $101,496 ($59,259 + $42,237) in its 2015 income statement.

During 2015 the company paid out $96,529 to settle warranty claims. The settlements include cash paid to customers for refunds, wages paid to employees who repair the motorcycles, and the cost of parts used in repairs. It is important to understand that only the *increase* in the liability resulting from additional accruals ($101,496) impacts the income statement, reducing income through additional warranty expense. Payments made to settle warranty claims do not affect current-period income; they merely reduce the pre-existing liability.

GAAP requires that the warranty liability should reflect the estimated cost that the company expects to incur as a result of warranty claims. This is often a difficult estimate to make and is prone to error. There is also the possibility that a company might intentionally underestimate its warranty liability to report higher current income, or overestimate it so as to depress current income and create an additional liability on the balance sheet (*cookie jar reserve*) that can be used to absorb future warranty costs and, thus, to reduce *future* expenses. The overestimation would shift income from the current period to one or more future periods. Warranty liabilities must, therefore, be examined closely and compared with sales levels. Any deviations from the historical relation of the warranty liability to sales, or from levels reported by competitors, should be scrutinized.

IFRS Insight ■ Accruals and Contingencies under IFRS

IFRS requires that a "provision" be recognized as a liability if a present obligation exists, if it is probable that an outflow of resources is required, and if the obligation can be reasonably estimated. These provisions are basically the same as accruals under GAAP such as that for wages. However, unlike GAAP, contingent liabilities are not recorded for IFRS such as an accrual for litigation. Contingencies do not meet the IFRS provisions definition because a present obligation does *not* exist as it may or may not be confirmed by uncertain future events. IFRS requires footnote disclosure of such contingent liabilities unless the eventual payment is remote in which case, no disclosure is required.

Review 7-1 LO1

Consider the balance in the warranty and recall liability at Harley-Davidson for the most recent fiscal year, from the information above. Assume that in the next fiscal year, Harley-Davidson estimates a warranty liability of $70,000 on product sold and incurs a cost of $85,000 during the year to repair or replace defective products. (All $ in thousands for this Review.)

Required

a. What amount of warranty expense will Harley-Davidson report in its income statement next year?
b. What will be the amount of warranty liability that Harley-Davidson reports on next year's balance sheet?
c. Assume that Harley-Davidson mistakenly accrues $90,000 for warranty liability next year (instead of $70,000). What effect will this accrual mistake have on future income statements and balance sheets?

Solution on p. 7-49.

Short-Term Debt

LO2

Analyze reporting for short-term debt.

Companies generally seek to match the maturity of borrowings with the assets they are financing. While PPE assets are appropriately financed with long-term debt and/or equity, seasonal swings in working capital are often financed with a bank line of credit (short-term debt). In this case the bank commits to lend up to a maximum amount with the understanding that the amounts borrowed will be repaid in full sometime during the year. An interest-bearing note evidences any such borrowing.

When the company borrows these short-term funds, it reports the cash received on the balance sheet together with an increase in liabilities (notes payable). The note is reported as a current liability because the company expects to repay it within a year. Although this borrowing has no effect on income or equity, the borrower incurs (and the lender earns) *interest* on the note as time passes. GAAP requires the borrower to accrue the interest liability and the related interest expense each time financial statements are issued.

Accounting for Short-Term Debt

To illustrate, assume that Verizon borrows $1,000 cash on January 1. The note bears interest at a 12% annual rate, and the interest (3% per quarter) is payable on the first day of each subsequent quarter (April 1, July 1, October 1, January 1). Assuming that Verizon issues calendar-quarter financial statements, this borrowing results in the following financial statement effects for January 1 through April 1.

	Balance Sheet						Income Statement			
Transaction	Cash Asset	+ Noncash Assets	= Liabil-ities	+ Contrib. Capital	+ Earned Capital		Rev-enues	− Expen-ses	= Net Income	
Jan 1: Borrow $1,000 cash and issue note payable	+1,000 Cash		= +1,000 Note Payable					−	=	
Mar 31: Accrue quarterly inter-est on 12%, $1,000 note payable			= +30 Interest Payable		−30 Retained Earnings			− +30 Interest Expense	= −30	
Apr 1: Pay $30 cash for interest due	−30 Cash		= −30 Interest Payable					−	=	

Cash..1,000
NP.....1,000

Cash
1,000 |

NP
| 1,000

IE ...30
IP........30

IE
30 |

IP
| 30

IP ...30
Cash......30

IP
30 |

Cash
| 30

The January 1 borrowing increases both cash and notes payable. On March 31, Verizon issues its quarterly financial statements. Although interest is not paid until April 1, the company has incurred three months' interest obligation as of March 31. Failure to recognize this liability and the expense incurred would not fairly present the financial condition of the company. Accordingly, the quarterly accrued interest payable is computed as follows.

Interest Expense = Principal × Annual Rate × Portion of Year Outstanding
$30   = $1,000   ×   12%   ×   3/12

The subsequent interest payment on April 1 reduces both cash and the interest payable that Verizon accrued on March 31. There is no expense reported on April 1, as it was recorded the previous day (March 31) when Verizon prepared its financial statements. (For fixed-maturity borrowings speci-fied in days, such as a 90-day note, we assume a 365-day year for interest accrual computations, see Review 7-2.)

The current liabilities section of the Verizon 2015 balance sheet includes $6,489 million of "debt maturing within one year." Verizon reports details about this amount, in its footnote disclosure to the 2015 annual report, as follows.

At December 31 ($ millions)	2015
Long-term debt maturing within one year	$6,325
Short-term notes payable	158
Commercial paper and other	6
Total debt maturing within one year	$6,489

Included in the $6,489 million are $158 million of "Short-term notes payable" and $6 million of "Commercial paper and other." These common forms of short-term debt allow Verizon to mitigate swings in its working capital.

Current Maturities of Long-Term Debt

Principal payments that must be made during the upcoming 12 months on long-term debt (such as for a mortgage or a maturing bond) are reported as current liabilities called *current maturities of long-term debt*. Some long-term debt, including mortgages, requires a periodic payment that is part principal and part interest. Note that the current maturity is the principal portion only of the payments that will be made in the upcoming year. Consider a 5-year, 4% mortgage of $1 million that requires annual pay-ments of $224,627. We can use a schedule such as the one below, to determine the principal amount owing at each reporting period.

Year	Interest at 4% on Balance Owing	Annual Payment	Principal Reduction	Balance Owing
0				$1,000,000
1	$40,000	$224,627	$184,627	815,373
2	32,615	224,627	192,012	623,361
3	24,934	224,627	199,693	423,668
4	16,947	224,627	207,680	215,988
5	8,640	224,627	215,988	0

In the first year, the amount of interest accrued on the loan is $40,000 ($1 million × 4%). The remainder of the annual payment of $224,627 is a reduction of the principal amount of the loan. On the day the mortgage was taken out, the balance sheet would show a current maturity of $184,627 with the remainder, $815,373 included in long-term debt. Note that as the balance owing on the mortgage decreases, so too does the interest; the current portion increases each year.

Verizon's footnote shown above, includes $6,325 million of "long-term debt maturing within one year." In addition, companies must provide a schedule of the maturities of their long-term debt in the footnotes to the financial statements. Following is the footnote disclosure of debt maturities in Verizon's 2015 annual report.

Maturities of Long-Term Debt

Maturities of long-term debt outstanding at December 31, 2015 are as follows:

Years	(dollars in millions)
2016	$ 6,325
2017	4,195
2018	7,072
2019	5,645
2020	8,860
Thereafter	77,933

The $6,325 million of long-term debt scheduled to mature in 2016 is reported as a current liability in the 2015 balance sheet. The remaining amounts through 2020 are scheduled maturities of long-term debt under the debt contracts. In general, we look for significant amounts maturing in any one year as this raises the question whether the company will have the cash flow to make the required payment. We prefer to see a relatively level debt repayment schedule, like the one above, which allows for an orderly payment or refinancing. To assess whether these amounts are large, consider that Verizon's operating cash flow for 2015 is $38,930 million. So, while the amounts of maturing debt are not insignificant, they should be manageable for Verizon. The size of Verizon's total debt, however, is one reason why the company's credit rating is not high (we discuss credit ratings later in this module).

Review 7-2 LO2

Assume that on January 15, Comcast borrowed $10,000 million on a 90-day, 6% note payable. The bank accrues interest daily based on a 365-day year. Comcast has a December 31 fiscal year end.

Required

Use the financial statement effects template to show the following:
1. The interest accrual Comcast would make on March 31 when it prepares its first-quarter financial statements.
2. Comcast's payment of principal and interest when the note matures on April 14.

Solution on p. 7-49.   3. The reclassification of $9,000 of long-term debt to short-term debt at the end of the fiscal year.

Companies often include long-term nonoperating liabilities in their capital structure to fund long-term assets. Smaller amounts of long-term debt can be readily obtained from banks, private placements with insurance companies, and other credit sources. However, when a large amount of financing is required, the issuance of bonds (and notes) in capital markets is a cost-efficient way to raise funds. The following discussion uses bonds for illustration, but the concepts also apply to long-term notes.

eLectures **LO3**
MBC Determine the pricing of long-term debt.

Bonds are structured like any other borrowing. The borrower receives cash and agrees to pay it back with interest. Generally, the entire **face amount** (principal) of the bond is repaid at maturity (at the end of the bond's life) and interest payments are made in the interim (usually semiannually).

Companies that raise funds in the bond market normally work with an underwriter (like **Goldman Sachs**) to set the terms of the bond issue. The underwriter then sells individual bonds (usually in $1,000 denominations) from this general bond issue to its retail clients and professional portfolio managers (like **The Vanguard Group**), and receives a fee for underwriting the bond issue. These bonds are investments for individual investors, other companies, retirement plans and insurance companies.

After they are issued, the bonds can trade in the secondary market just like stocks. Market prices of bonds fluctuate daily despite the fact that the company's obligation for payment of principal and interest normally remains fixed throughout the life of the bond. Then, why do bond prices change? The answer is that the bond's fixed rate of interest can be higher or lower than the interest rates offered on other securities of similar risk. Because bonds compete with other possible investments, bond prices are set relative to the prices of other investments. In a competitive investment market, a particular bond will become more or less desirable depending on the general level of interest rates offered by competing securities. Just as for any item, competitive pressures will cause bond prices to rise and fall.

Before we discuss the mechanics of long-term debt pricing, we need to define two types of interest rates that we will use to price bonds.

- **Coupon (contract** or **stated) rate** The coupon rate of interest is stated in the bond contract; it is used to compute the dollar amount of interest payments that are paid (in cash) to bondholders during the life of the bond issue.

- **Market (yield** or **effective) rate** This is the interest rate that investors expect to earn on the investment in this debt security; this rate is used to price the bond.

The coupon (contract) rate is used to compute interest payments and the market (yield) rate is used to price the bond. The coupon rate and the market rate are nearly always different. This is because the coupon rate is fixed prior to issuance of the bond and normally remains fixed throughout its life. Market rates of interest, on the other hand, fluctuate continually with the supply and demand for bonds in the marketplace, general macroeconomic conditions, and the borrower's financial condition.

The bond price, both its initial sales price and the price it trades at in the secondary market subsequent to issuance, equals the present value of the expected cash flows to the bondholder. Specifically, bondholders normally expect to receive two different types of cash flows.

1. **Periodic interest payments** (usually semiannual) during the bond's life; these payments are called an *annuity* because they are equal in amount and made at regular intervals.

2. **Single payment** of the face (principal) amount of the bond at maturity; this is called a *lump-sum* because it occurs only once.

The bond price equals the present value of the periodic interest payments plus the present value of the single payment. If the present value of the two cash flows is equal to the bond's face value, the bond is sold at par. If the present value is less than or greater than the bond's face value, the bond sells at a discount or premium, respectively. We next illustrate the issuance of bonds at three different prices: at par, at a discount, and at a premium.

Pricing of Bonds Issued at Par

To illustrate a bond issued (sold) at par, assume that a bond with a face amount of $10 million, has a 6% annual coupon rate payable semiannually (3% semiannual rate), and a maturity of 10 years. Semiannual interest payments are typical for bonds. This means that the issuer pays bondholders two interest payments per year. Each semiannual interest payment is equal to the bond's face value times the annual rate divided by two. Investors purchasing these bonds receive the following cash flows.

Cash Flows	Number of Payments	Dollars per Payment	Total Cash Flows
Semiannual interest payments....	10 years × 2 = 20	$10,000,000 × 3% = $300,000	$ 6,000,000
Principal payment at maturity	1	$10,000,000	10,000,000
			$16,000,000

Specifically, the bond agreement dictates that the borrower must make 20 semiannual payments of $300,000 each, computed as $10,000,000 × (6%/2). At maturity, the borrower must repay the $10,000,000 face amount. To price bonds, investors identify the *number* of interest payments and use that number when computing the present value of *both* the interest payments and the principal (face) payment at maturity.

The bond price is the present value of the periodic interest payments (the annuity) plus the present value of the principal payment (the lump sum). In our example, assuming that investors desire a 3% semiannual market rate (yield), the bond sells for $10,000,000, which is computed as follows.

Present value factors are from Appendix A

Calculator
N = 20
I/Yr = 3
PMT = −300,000
FV = −10,000,000

PV = 10,000,000

	A	B
1	Annual coupon rate	6%
2	Annual market rate	6%
3	Interest payments per year	2
4	Years to maturity	10
5	Face (par) value	10,000,000
6	Issue price	10,000,000
7	= PV(B2/B3,B4*B3,−B5*B1/B3,−B5, 0)	
8	= 10,000,000	

	Payment	Present Value Factor[a]	Present Value
Interest	$ 300,000	14.87747[b]	$ 4,463,200[d]
Principal	$10,000,000	0.55368[c]	5,536,800
			$10,000,000

[a] Mechanics of using tables to compute present values are explained in Appendix 7A; present value factors come from Appendix A near the end of the book.

[b] Present value of an ordinary annuity for 20 periods discounted at 3% per period.

[c] Present value of a single payment in 20 periods discounted at 3% per period.

[d] Rounded.

Because the bond contract pays investors a 3% semiannual rate when investors demand a 3% semiannual market rate, given the borrower's credit rating and the time to maturity, the investors purchase those bonds at the **par (face) value** of $10 million.

Pricing of Bonds Issued at a Discount

As a second illustration, assume investors demand a 4% semiannual return for the 3% semiannual coupon bond, while all other details remain the same. The bond now sells for $8,640,999, computed as follows.

Calculator
N = 20
I/Yr = 4
PMT = −300,000
FV = −10,000,000

PV = 8,640,967*

*rounding difference

	A	B
1	Annual coupon rate	6%
2	Annual market rate	8%
3	Interest payments per year	2
4	Years to maturity	10
5	Face (par) value	10,000,000
6	Issue price	8,640,967
7	= PV(B2/B3,B4*B3,−B5*B1/B3,−B5, 0)	
8	= 8,640,967	

	Payment	Present Value Factor	Present Value
Interest	$ 300,000	13.59033[a]	$4,077,099
Principal	$10,000,000	0.45639[b]	4,563,900
			$8,640,999

[a] Present value of an ordinary annuity for 20 periods discounted at 4% per period.

[b] Present value of a single payment in 20 periods discounted at 4% per period.

Because the bond carries a coupon rate *lower* than what investors demand, the bond is less desirable and sells at a **discount**. More generally, bonds sell at a discount whenever the coupon rate is less than the market rate.

Pricing of Bonds Issued at a Premium

As a third illustration, assume that investors demand a 2% semiannual return for the 3% semiannual coupon bonds, while all other details remain the same. The bond now sells for $11,635,129, computed as follows.

	Payment	Present Value Factor	Present Value
Interest	$ 300,000	16.35143[a]	$ 4,905,429
Principal	$10,000,000	0.67297[b]	6,729,700
			$11,635,129

[a] Present value of an ordinary annuity for 20 periods discounted at 2% per period.
[b] Present value of a single payment in 20 periods discounted at 2% per period.

Because the bond carries a coupon rate *higher* than what investors demand, the bond is more desirable and sells at a **premium**. More generally, bonds sell at a premium whenever the coupon rate is greater than the market rate.[1] Exhibit 7.1 summarizes this relation for bond pricing.

Calculator
N = 20
I/Yr = 2
PMT = −300,000
FV = −10,000,000

PV = 11,635,143*

*rounding difference

	A	B
1	Annual coupon rate	6%
2	Annual market rate	4%
3	Interest payments per year	2
4	Years to maturity	10
5	Face (par) value	10,000,000
6	Issue price	11,635,143
7	= PV(B2/B3,B4*B3,−B5*B1/B3,−B5, 0)
8	= 11,635,143

Exhibit 7.1 ■ **Coupon Rate, Market Rate, and Bond Pricing**

Coupon rate > market rate → Bond sells at a **premium** (above face amount)
Coupon rate = market rate → Bond sells at **par** (at face amount)
Coupon rate < market rate → Bond sells at a **discount** (below face amount)

Effective Cost of Debt

When a bond sells for par, the cost to the issuing company is the cash interest paid. In our first illustration above, the *effective cost* of the bond is the 6% interest paid by the issuer.

When a bond sells at a discount, the issuer must repay more (the face value when the bond matures) than the cash received at issuance (the discounted bond proceeds). This means that the effective cost of a discount bond is greater than if the bond had sold at par. A discount is a cost and, like any other cost, must eventually be transferred from the balance sheet to the income statement as an expense.

When a bond sells at a premium, the borrower received more cash at issuance than it must repay. The difference, the premium, is a benefit that must eventually find its way into the income statement as a *reduction* of interest expense. As a result of the premium, the effective cost of a premium bond is less than if the bond had sold at par.

Bonds are priced to yield the return (market rate) demanded by investors. Consequently, the effective rate of a bond *always* equals the yield (market) rate demanded by investors, regardless of the coupon rate of the bond. This means that companies cannot influence the effective cost of debt by raising or lowering the coupon rate. Doing so will only result in a bond premium or discount. We discuss the factors affecting the yield demanded by investors later in the module.

The effective cost of debt is reflected in the amount of interest expense reported in the issuer's income statement. Because of bond discounts and premiums, interest expense is usually different from the cash interest paid.

Exhibit 7.2 demonstrates the difference between coupon rates and effective rates of interest. On February 23, 2016, **Comcast** issued $2,250 million of debt including 2.75% notes with a face value of $750 million due March 1, 2023. The exhibit shows that the issue price of these notes was 99.847

Calculator
N=14
PMT = −10.3125
FV = 750
PV = −746.2275

I/Yr = 1.4149

---

[1] Bond prices are often stated in percent form. For example, a bond sold at par is said to be sold at 100 (that is, 100% of par). The bond sold at $8,640,999 is said to be sold at 86.41 (86.41% of par, computed as $8,640,999/$10,000,000). The bond sold for a premium is said to be sold at 116.35 (116.35% of the bond's face value).

	A	B
1	Annual coupon rate	2.75%
2	Annual market rate	1.4149%
3	Interest payments per year	2
4	Years to maturity	7
5	Face (par) value	750
6	Issue price	746.2275
7	= RATE(B4*B3, −B5*B1/B3, B6, −B5, 0)	
8	= 1.4149%	

(this is the percent of par value and indicates that the bonds were sold at a discount). Comcast's underwriters took 0.35% in fees ($2.625 million) for underwriting and selling this debt issue and thus, Comcast received proceeds of 99.497% of the face value, or $746,227,500. These notes paid interest semiannually.

If we assume the notes were sold on March 1, 2016 (to simplify the calculations), we can determine that the effective rate on these notes was 1.4149% semiannually or an annual effective rate of 2.8297% (1.4148% × 2).

Exhibit 7.2 ■ Announcement (Tombstone) of Debt Offering to Public

COMCAST

$750,000,000   2.75% Notes due 2023
$1,500,000,000   3.15% Notes due 2026

The Notes due 2023 will bear interest at a rate of 2.75% per year and will mature on March 1, 2023, and the Notes due 2026 will bear interest at a rate of 3.15% per year and will mature on March 1, 2026. We refer to the Notes due 2023, and the Notes due 2026 collectively as the "notes." We will pay interest on the notes on March 1 and September 1 of each year, beginning September 1, 2016. We may redeem any of the notes at any time by paying the applicable Redemption Price described under the heading "Description of the Notes—Optional Redemption."

The notes will be unsecured and will rank equally with all of our and our guarantors' unsecured and unsubordinated indebtedness. The notes will be fully and unconditionally guaranteed by our wholly-owned subsidiaries named in this prospectus supplement and in the accompanying prospectus.

Investing in these securities involves certain risks. See " Item 1A—Risk Factors" beginning on page 25 of Comcast Corporation's ("Comcast") Annual Report on Form 10-K for the year ended December 31, 2015, which is incorporated by reference herein.

	Price to Investors	Underwriters' Discount	Proceeds to Us Before Expenses
Per note due 2023.	99.847%	0.350%	99.497%
Total	$748,852,500	$2,625,000	$746,227,500
Per note due 2026.	99.812%	0.450%	99.362%
Total	$1,497,180,000	$6,750,000	$1,490,430,000

(1) Plus accrued interest, if any, from February 23, 2016, if settlement occurs after that date.

Neither the Securities and Exchange Commission nor any state securities commission has approved or disapproved of these securities or determined if this prospectus supplement or the accompanying prospectus is truthful or complete. Any representation to the contrary is a criminal offense.

The notes will be ready for delivery only through The Depository Trust Company and its participants, including Euroclear SA/NV ("Euroclear") and Clearstream Banking SA ("Clearstream") , in book-entry form on or about February 23, 2016, which is the fifth business day following the date of this prospectus supplement. See "Underwriting."

Joint Book-Running Managers

BofA Merrill Lynch	RBC Capital Markets	Wells Fargo Securities
Barclays		BNP PARIBAS

Co-Managers

Citigroup	Credit Suisse	Deutsche Bank Securities
Goldman, Sachs & Co.	J.P. Morgan	Lloyds Securities
Mizuho Securities	Morgan Stanley	SMBC Nikko
SunTrust Robinson Humphrey	Santander	UBS Investment Bank
US Bancorp	PNC Capital Markets LLC	TD Securities
DNB Markets		

C.L. King & Associates	The Williams Capital Group, L.P.	Lebenthal Capital Markets
Loop Capital Markets	Drexel Hamilton	Ramirez and Co., Inc.
	Mischler Financial Group, Inc.	

Source: https://www.sec.gov/Archives/edgar/data/1166691/000119312516466721/d136987d424b2.htm

On January 1, assume that Comcast issues $300,000 of 15-year, 10% bonds payable for $351,876, yielding an effective semiannual interest rate of 4%. Interest is payable semiannually on June 30 and December 31.

Required
1. Calculate the issue price of this bond.
2. What would the bond issue price be if the semiannual effective interest rate is 6% instead of 4%?

Solution on p. 7-50.

Long-Term Debt—Reporting

This section identifies and describes the financial statement effects of bond transactions.

eLectures **LO4**
MBC Analyze reporting for long-term debt.

Financial Statement Disclosure of Debt Issuance

Companies typically have many debt issues outstanding and disclose the total amount owed as a long-term liability on the balance sheet. The details relating to each of the company's outstanding bonds and notes are provided in a footnote disclosure like the following for Verizon.

Long-Term Debt

Outstanding long-term debt obligations are as follows.

December 31 ($ millions)	Interest Rates %	Maturities	2015	2014
Verizon Communications— notes payable and other . . .	0.30–3.85	2016–2042	$ 26,281	$ 27,617
	4.15–5.50	2018–2055	51,156	40,701
	5.85–6.90	2018–2054	16,420	24,341
	7.35–8.95	2018–2039	2,300	2,264
	Floating	2016–2025	14,100	14,600
Verizon Wireless—notes payable and other	8.88	2018	68	676
Verizon Wireless—Alltel assumed notes	6.80–7.88	2029–2032	686	686
Telephone subsidiaries— debentures	5.13–6.50	2028–2033	575	1,075
	7.38–7.88	2022–2032	1,099	1,099
	8.00–8.75	2019–2031	780	880
Other subsidiaries— debentures and other	6.84–8.75	2018–2028	1,432	1,432
Capital lease obligations (average rate of 3.4% and 4.0% in 2015 and 2014, respectively)			957	516
Unamortized discount, net of premium			(5,824)	(2,954)
Total long-term debt, including current maturities			110,030	112,933
Less long-term debt maturing within one year . .			6,325	2,397
Total long-term debt			$103,705	$110,536

In general, companies report debt net of any discount (or including any premium) and also net of any debt issuance costs (such as the $2.625 million in fees that Comcast's bankers charged for underwriting and selling the $750 million debt issue in Exhibit 7.2).

Balance Sheet Reporting

Verizon's total long-term debt of $110,030 million is reported net of $5,824 million of unamortized discounts and premiums. Of the $110,030 million total, $6,325 million will mature in the next year (reported as a current liability); the balance, $103,705 million, is reported as a long-term liability.

Par Bonds

When a company issues a bond, it receives the cash proceeds and accepts an obligation to make payments per the bond contract. Specifically, cash is increased and a long-term liability (bonds payable) is increased by the same amount. There is no revenue or expense at bond issuance. Using the facts from our $10 million bond illustration above, the issuance of **par bonds** has the following financial statement effects.

Cash. .10,000,000
LTD 10,000,000

Cash
10,000,000 |

LTD
| 10,000,000

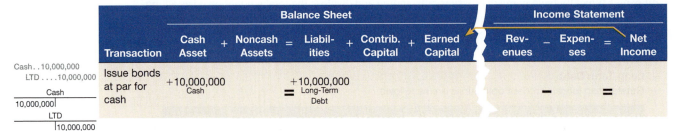

Discount Bonds

When a bond is sold at a discount, the cash proceeds and net bond liability are recorded at the amount of the proceeds received (not the face amount of the bond). Again, using the facts above from our bond discount illustration (where investors demand a 4% semiannual return for the 3% semiannual coupon bond), the issuance of **discount bonds** has the following financial statement effects.

Cash. . .8,640,999
LTD 8,640,999

Cash
8,640,999 |

LTD
| 8,640,999

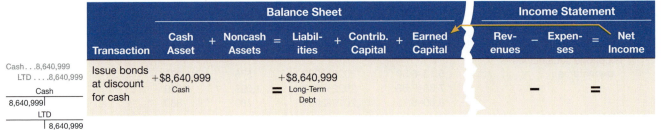

The net bond liability (long-term debt) reported on the balance sheet consists of the following two components.

Bonds payable, face.	$10,000,000
Less bond discount	(1,359,001)
Bonds payable, net	$ 8,640,999

Bonds are reported on the balance sheet net of any discount. When the bond matures, however, the company is obligated to repay the face amount ($10 million). Accordingly, at maturity, the bonds payable account needs to read $10 million, the amount that is owed. This means that between the bond issuance and its maturity, the discount must decline to zero. This reduction of the discount over the life of the bond is called **amortization**. The next section shows how discount amortization results in additional interest expense in the income statement. This amortization causes the effective interest expense to be greater than the periodic cash interest payments.

Premium Bonds

When a bond is sold at a premium, the cash proceeds and net bond liability are recorded at the amount of the proceeds received (not the face amount of the bond). Again, using the facts above from our premium bond illustration (where investors demand a 2% semiannual return for the 3% semiannual coupon bond), the issuance of **premium bonds** has the following financial statement effects.

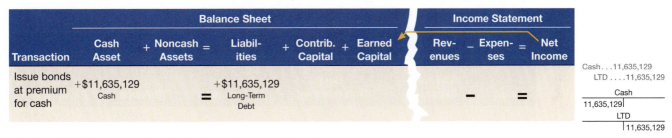

The bond liability reported on the balance sheet consists of two parts.

Bonds payable, face........	$10,000,000
Add bond premium	1,635,129
Bonds payable, net	$11,635,129

The $10 million must be repaid at maturity, and the premium is amortized to zero over the life of the bond. The premium represents a *benefit,* which *reduces* interest expense on the income statement.

Income Statement Reporting

As we saw in Exhibit 7.2, **Comcast** received $746,227,500 when it issued the $750 million notes. The difference of $3,772,500 has two parts: the discount of $1.1475 million (calculated as [100% − 99.847%] × $750 million) and the fees paid to bankers and underwriters to sell the notes (calculated as 0.35% × $750 million or $2.625 million). The total difference of $3,772,500 is an additional borrowing cost for Comcast; a cost over and above the 2.75% interest the company will pay in cash each year. The additional borrowing cost is expensed on the income statement over the life of the notes (from 2016 to 2023) and typically reported together with the 2.75% cash interest that Comcast pays to its lenders. Conversely, if Comcast sold its notes at a premium, it would have received proceeds in excess of the $750 million face amount and that premium would subsequently be reported as a *reduction* of interest expense over the life of the notes.

The process of recognizing additional interest expense in the case of a bond issued at a discount (or reduced interest expense in the case of a bond issued at a premium) is called *amortization*. In both cases, the amount of interest expense that is reported on the income statement each year represents the effective cost of debt, including both the cash interest paid plus a portion of the additional borrowing costs (or less a portion of the benefit of the premium).

Amortization of Discount

Calculator
N = 6
I/Yr = 2
PMT = −9,000
FV = −600,000

PV = 583,195.71

	A	B
1	Annual coupon rate	3%
2	Annual market rate	4%
3	Interest payments per year	2
4	Years to maturity	3
5	Face (par) value	600,000
6	Issue price	583,195.71
7	= PV(B2/B3,B4*B3,−B5*B1/B3,−B5, 0)	
8	= 583,195.71	

Companies amortize discounts and premiums using the effective interest method. To illustrate, assume that **Verizon** issues bonds with a face amount of $600,000, a 3% annual coupon rate payable semi-annually (1.5% semiannual rate), a maturity of three years (six semiannual payment periods), and a market (yield) rate of 4% annual (2% semiannual). These facts yield a bond issue price of $583,195.71, which we round to $583,196 for the bond discount amortization table of Exhibit 7.3.

The interest period is denoted in the left-most column. Period 0 is the point at which the bond is issued, and period 1 and following are successive six-month periods (recall, interest is paid semiannually). Column [A] is interest expense, which is reported in the income statement. Interest expense is computed as the bond's net balance sheet value (the carrying amount of the bond) at the beginning of the period (column [E]) multiplied by the 2% semiannual rate used to compute the bond issue price. Column [B] is cash interest paid, which is a constant $9,000 per the bond contract (face amount × coupon rate). Column [C] is discount amortization, which is the difference between interest expense and cash interest paid. Column [D] is the discount balance, which is the previous balance of the discount less the discount amortization in column [C]. Column [E] is the net bond payable, which is the $600,000 face amount less the unamortized discount from column [D].

Exhibit 7.3 ■ Bond Discount Amortization Table

Period	[A] ([E] × market%) Interest Expense	[B] (Face × coupon%) Cash Interest Paid	[C] ([A] − [B]) Discount Amortization	[D] (Prior bal − [C]) Discount Balance	[E] (Face − [D]) Bond Payable, Net
0				$16,804	$583,196
1	$11,664	$ 9,000	$2,664	14,140	585,860
2	11,717	9,000	2,717	11,423	588,577
3	11,772	9,000	2,772	8,651	591,349
4	11,827	9,000	2,827	5,824	594,176
5	11,884	9,000	2,884	2,940	597,060
6	11,940	9,000	2,940	0	600,000
	$70,804	$54,000	$16,804		

Cash paid plus discount amortization equals interest expense

During the bond life, carrying value is adjusted to par and the discount to zero

The table shows amounts for the six interest payment periods. The amortization process continues until period 6, at which time the discount balance is 0 and the net bond payable is $600,000 (the maturity value). Each semiannual period, interest expense is recorded at 2%, the market rate of interest at the bond's issuance. This rate does not change over the life of the bond, even if the prevailing market interest rates change. An amortization table reveals the financial statement effects of the bond for its duration. Specifically, we see the income statement effects in column [A], the cash effects in column [B], and the balance sheet effects in columns [D] and [E].

Amortization of Premium

Calculator
N = 6
I/Yr = 1
PMT = −9,000
FV = −600,000

PV = 617,386.43

	A	B
1	Annual coupon rate	3%
2	Annual market rate	2%
3	Interest payments per year	2
4	Years to maturity	3
5	Face (par) value	600,000
6	Issue price	617,386.43
7	= PV(B2/B3,B4*B3,−B5*B1/B3,−B5, 0)	
8	= 617,386.43	

To illustrate amortization of a premium bond, we assume that Verizon issues bonds with a $600,000 face value, a 3% annual coupon rate payable semiannually (1.5% semiannual rate), a maturity of three years (six semiannual interest payments), and a 2% annual (1% semiannual) market interest rate. These facts yield a bond issue price of $617,386.43, which we round to $617,386. Exhibit 7.4 shows the premium amortization table for this bond.

Interest expense is computed using the same process that we used for discount bonds. The difference is that the yield rate is 1% semiannual in the premium case. Cash interest paid follows from the bond contract (face amount × coupon rate), and the other columns' computations reflect the premium amortization. After period 6, the premium is fully amortized (equals zero) and the net bond payable balance is $600,000, the amount owed at maturity. Again, an amortization table reveals the financial statement effects of the bond—the income statement effects in column [A], the cash effects in column [B], and the balance sheet effects in columns [D] and [E].

Exhibit 7.4 ■ **Bond Premium Amortization Table**

Period	[A] ([E] × market%) Interest Expense	[B] (Face × coupon%) Cash Interest Paid	[C] ([B] − [A]) Premium Amortization	[D] (Prior bal − [C]) Premium Balance	[E] (Face + [D]) Bond Payable, Net
0				$17,386	$617,386
1	$ 6,174	$ 9,000	$ 2,826	14,560	614,560
2	6,146	9,000	2,854	11,706	611,706
3	6,117	9,000	2,883	8,823	608,823
4	6,088	9,000	2,912	5,911	605,911
5	6,059	9,000	2,941	2,970	602,970
6	6,030	9,000	2,970	0	600,000
	$36,614	$54,000	$17,386		

> During the bond life, carrying value is adjusted to par and the premium to zero

> Cash paid less premium amortization equals interest expense

Financial Statement Effects of Bond Repurchase

Companies report bonds payable at *historical (adjusted) cost*. Specifically, net bonds payable amounts follow from the amortization table, as do the related cash flows and income statement numbers. All financial statement relations are set when the bond is issued; they do not subsequently change.

Once issued, however, bonds trade in secondary markets. The yield rate used to compute bond prices for these subsequent transactions is the market interest rate prevailing at the time. These rates change daily based on the level of interest rates in the economy and the perceived creditworthiness of the bond issuer.

Companies can and sometimes do repurchase (or redeem or *retire*) their bonds prior to maturity. The bond indenture (contract agreement) can include provisions giving the company the right to repurchase its bonds directly from the bond holders. Or, the company can repurchase bonds in the open market. **CVS Health Corporation** reports a "loss on the early extinguishment of debt" of $521 million in fiscal 2014 as described in the financial statement footnotes as follows.

On August 7, 2014, the Company announced tender offers for any and all of the 6.25% Senior Notes due 2027, and up to a maximum amount of the 6.125% Senior Notes due 2039, the 5.75% Senior Notes due 2041 and the 5.75% Senior Notes due 2017, for up to an aggregate principal amount of $1.5 billion. On August 21, 2014, the Company increased the aggregate principal amount of the tender offers to $2.0 billion and completed the repurchase for the maximum amount on September 4, 2014. The Company paid a premium of $490 million in excess of the debt principal in connection with the tender offers, wrote off $26 million of unamortized deferred financing costs and incurred $5 million in fees, for a total loss on the early extinguishment of debt of $521 million.

When a bond repurchase occurs, a gain or loss usually results, and is computed as follows.

Gain or Loss on Bond Repurchase = Net Bonds Payable − Repurchase Payment

The net bonds payable, also referred to as the *book value,* is the net amount reported on the balance sheet. If the issuer pays more to retire the bonds than the amount carried on its balance sheet, it reports a loss on its income statement, usually called *loss on bond retirement*. The issuer reports a *gain on bond retirement* if the repurchase price is less than the net bonds payable.

How should we treat these gains and losses for analysis purposes? That is, do they carry economic effects? The answer is no—the gain or loss on repurchase is exactly offset by the present value of the future cash flow implications of the repurchase. (The Accounting Insight box that follows demonstrates this.) Further, the gain or loss on early retirement is a transitory item and, consequently, will not be repeated in future income statements.

Accounting Insight   ■   Economics of Gains and Losses on Bond Repurchases

CVS repurchased its 6.25% Notes and recorded a loss on the early extinguishment of debt. At the same time, CVS issued $850 million of 2.25% Notes due August 12, 2019. CVS used part of the proceeds to fund the repurchase of the 6.25% Notes. Because interest rates had dropped since the 6.25% Notes were issued, the market value of the 6.25% Notes had increased to $521 million in excess of their carrying amount. To repurchase the Notes, CVS had to pay the market price (and not the face value), which created a large "loss on the early extinguishment of debt."

Although CVS reported the $521 million loss in its income statement, there was no *economic* loss. We use a simple example to explain. Please refer to Exhibit 7.3 relating to a $600,000 bond with a 3% coupon rate that was sold at a discount to yield 4%. At the end of period 2, the bond has a carrying amount on the balance sheet of $588,576.81.

Assume that at the end of period 2, the market rate of interest declines from 4% when the bond was issued, to 2% (1% semiannually). The drop in market rates will affect the market value of the bond. At the end of period 2, there are four interest payments of $9,000 remaining plus the $600,000 face amount of the bond at maturity. The present value of that stream of payments, discounted at the current market rate of 1% semiannual rate, is equal to $611,705.90 (the Excel formula is = PV(1%, 4, −9,000, −600,000)). To repurchase the bond, CVS would have to issue a new bond in the amount of $611,705.90 carrying a 1% coupon rate. Either way, CVS would report a loss on the early extinguishment of debt of $23,129.09 ($611,705.90 − $588,576.81).

Despite reporting an accounting loss on the early extinguishment of debt of $23,129.09, there is no economic loss. Why? Because the present value of the new debt is equal to $611,705.90 (the Excel formula is = PV(1%, 4, −6,117.06, −611,705.90), where 6,117.06 = $611,705.90 × 1%). The present value of the new debt is, therefore, equal to the present value of the remaining payments on the old debt, discounted at the new semiannual market rate of 1%. They are, therefore, equivalent and no economic loss has been sustained.

Fair Value Disclosures

An important analysis issue involves assessing the fair value of bonds and other long-term liabilities. This information is relevant for investors and creditors because it reveals unrealized gains and losses (similar to that reported for marketable securities). GAAP requires companies to provide information about current fair values of their long-term liabilities in footnotes as Verizon does in its 2015 10-K.

Fair Value of Short-term and Long-term Debt

The fair value of our debt is determined using various methods, including quoted prices for identical terms and maturities, which is a Level 1 measurement, as well as quoted prices for similar terms and maturities in inactive markets and future cash flows discounted at current rates, which are Level 2 measurements. The fair value of our short-term and long-term debt, excluding capital leases, was as follows:

At December 31 (dollars in millions)	2015		2014	
	Carrying Amount	Fair Value	Carrying Amount	Fair Value
Short- and long-term debt, excluding capital leases...............	$109,237	$118,216	$112,755	$126,549

The increase in fair value is due to a decline in market rates of interest since the debt was initially issued (or to an increase in the credit rating of the company). These fair values are *not* reported on the balance sheet and changes in these fair values are not reflected in net income. The chief justification for not recognizing fair-value gain and losses is that such amounts can reverse with subsequent fluctuations in market rates of interest and the bonds are repaid at par at maturity.

Assume that on January 1 Comcast issues $300,000 of 15-year, 10% bonds payable for $351,876, yielding an effective semiannual interest rate of 4%. Interest is payable semiannually on June 30 and December 31.

1. Show computations to confirm the issue price of $351,876.
2. Complete Comcast's financial statement effects template for
   a. bond issuance,
   b. semiannual interest payment and premium amortization on June 30 of the first year, and
   c. semiannual interest payment and premium amortization on December 31 of the first year.
3. Prepare an amortization table for the bonds for the first five years (See Exhibit 7.4 for guidance).
4. Assume that at the end of year 5, Comcast repurchases the bonds on the open market. The effective semiannual interest rate has fallen to 2%. What will Comcast have to pay to repurchase these bonds? Determine any gain or loss on the repurchase transaction.

Solution on p. 7-50.

Quality of Debt

Earlier in the module we explained that the effective cost of debt to the issuing company is the market (yield) rate of interest used to price the bond, regardless of the bond coupon rate. The market rate of interest is usually defined as the yield on U.S. Government borrowings such as treasury bills, notes, and bonds, called the *risk-free rate,* plus a *risk premium* (also called a *spread*).

eLectures LO5
MBC Explain how quality of debt is determined.

Yield Rate = Risk-Free Rate + Risk Premium

Both the treasury yield (the so-called risk-free rate) and the corporate yield vary over time as illustrated in the following graphic.

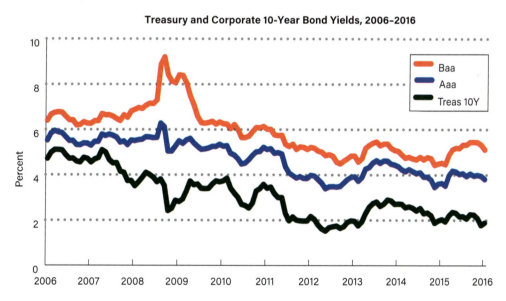

Treasury and Corporate 10-Year Bond Yields, 2006–2016

The rate of interest that investors expect for a particular bond is a function of the risk-free rate and the risk premium, where the latter depends on the creditworthiness of the issuing entity.

The yield increases (shifts upward) as debt quality moves from Treasury securities (generally considered to be risk free), which is the highest-quality debt reflected in the lowest line in the graph, to the Aaa (highest) rated corporates and, finally, to the Baa (lower-rated) corporates shown in this graph. That is, higher credit-rated issuers warrant a lower rate than lower credit-rated issuers. This difference is substantial. For example, in March 2016, the average 10-year treasury bond yield was 1.89%, while the Aaa corporate bond yield was 3.82% and the average Baa (the lowest investment grade corporate bond) yield was 5.13%.

Research indicates that companies that use more conservative accounting policies incur a lower cost of debt. Research also suggests that while accounting conservatism can lead to lower-quality accounting income (because such income does not fully reflect economic reality), creditors are more confident in the numbers and view them as more credible. Evidence also implies that companies can lower the required return demanded by creditors (the risk premium) by issuing high-quality financial reports that include enhanced footnote disclosures and detailed supplemental reports.

What Are Credit Ratings?

A company's credit rating, also referred to as debt rating, credit quality, or creditworthiness, is related to default risk. **Default** refers to the nonpayment of interest and principal and/or the failure to adhere to the various terms and conditions (covenants) of the bond indenture. Companies that want to obtain bond financing from the capital markets, normally first seek a rating on their proposed debt issuance from one of several rating agencies such as **Standard & Poor's**, **Moody's Investors Service**, or **Fitch Ratings**. The aim of rating agencies is to rate debt so that its default risk is more accurately conveyed to, and priced by, the market. Each rating agency uses its own rating system, as Exhibit 7.5 shows. This exhibit includes the general description for each rating class—for example, AAA is assigned to debt of prime maximum safety (highest in creditworthiness). The dotted green line separates investment grade bonds from non-investment grade or speculative bonds. Many investment managers are precluded from purchasing non-investment grade bonds for their client portfolios, thus lessening the liquidity of the bonds.

Exhibit 7.5 ■ Corporate Debt Ratings and Descriptions

Moody's	S&P	Fitch	Description
Aaa	AAA	AAA	Prime Maximum Safety
Aa1	AA+	AA+	High Grade, High Quality
Aa2	AA	AA	
Aa3	AA−	AA−	
A1	A+	A+	Upper-Medium Grade
A2	A	A	
A3	A−	A−	
Baa1	BBB+	BBB+	Lower-Medium Grade
Baa2	BBB	BBB	
Baa3	BBB−	BBB−	
Ba1	BB+	BB+	Non-Investment Grade
Ba2	BB	BB	Speculative
Ba3	BB−	BB−	
B1	B+	B+	Highly Speculative
B2	B	B	
B3	B−	B−	
Caa1	CCC+	CCC	Substantial Risk
Caa2	CCC		In Poor Standing
Caa3	CCC−		
Ca	CC		Extremely Speculative
C	C		May be in Default
		DDD	Default
		DD	
	D	D	

What Determines Credit Ratings?

Verizon bonds are rated Baa1, BBB+, and A− by Moody's, S&P, and Fitch, respectively, as of 2015, a downgrade from the previous ratings of A3, A and A, respectively, as a result of its decision to purchase Vodafone's interest in Verizon Wireless for about $130 billion and the consequent increase in its debt. It is this rating, in conjunction with the maturity of Verizon's bonds, that establishes the market interest rate and the bonds' selling price. There are a number of considerations that affect the rating of a bond. Standard & Poor's lists the following factors, categorized by business risk and financial risk, among its credit rating criteria.

Business Risk	**Financial Risk**
Industry characteristics	Financial characteristics
Competitive position (marketing, technology, efficiency, regulation)	Financial policy
	Profitability
	Capital structure
Management	Cash flow protection
	Financial flexibility

Debt ratings convey information primarily to debt investors who are interested in assessing the probability that the borrower will make interest and principal payments on time. If a company defaults on its debt, debt holders seek legal remedies, including forcing the borrower to liquidate its assets to settle obligations. However, in forced liquidations, debt holders rarely realize the entire amounts owed to them.

Credit Ratings and Financial Ratios

It's important to bear in mind that debt ratings are opinions. Rating agencies use several financial ratios to assess default risk. A partial listing of ratios utilized by Moody's, together with median averages for various ratings, is in Exhibit 7.6. In examining the ratios, recall that debt is increasingly more risky as we move from the first row, Aaa, to the last, C.

Exhibit 7.6 ■ Ratio Values for Different Credit Ratings*

	EBITA/ Avg AT	EBITA Margin	EBITA/ Int Exp	Oper Margin	(FFO + Int Exp)/Int Exp	FFO/ Debt	RCF/Net Debt	Debt/ EBITDA	Debt/ Book Cap	CAPEX/ Dep Exp	Rev Vol
Aaa	16.0%	22.8%	35.7	19.0%	36.0	86.3%	81.5%	0.9	23.7%	1.6	8.6
Aa	14.3%	21.4%	21.1	19.2%	21.1	62.7%	33.8%	1.3	41.1%	1.3	6.5
A	13.6%	19.4%	13.4	16.8%	13.8	46.1%	38.8%	1.6	39.3%	1.3	10.4
Baa	10.3%	15.1%	7.2	14.0%	8.4	31.0%	28.1%	2.5	45.8%	1.2	11.0
Ba	8.6%	12.2%	3.8	10.9%	5.3	22.4%	22.6%	3.4	50.1%	1.2	15.4
B	6.7%	9.7%	1.7	8.1%	3.1	13.6%	13.3%	5.1	67.3%	1.1	17.4
Caa-C	5.6%	5.9%	0.8	5.4%	1.4	3.4%	3.4%	7.7	99.1%	0.9	11.7

* Table reports 2014 median values; from Moody's Financial Metrics™, Key Ratios by Rating and Industry for Global Nonfinancial Corporations: December 2014 (reproduced with permission).

Ratio	Definition
EBITA/Average Assets	EBITA/Average of Current and Previous Year Assets
EBITA Margin	EBITA/Net Revenue
EBITA/Interest Expense	EBITA/Interest Expense
Operating Margin	Operating Profit/Net Revenue
(FFO + Interest Exp)/Interest Exp	(FFO + Interest Expense)/Interest Expense
FFO/Debt	FFO/(Short-Term Debt + Long-Term Debt)
Net Debt	(FFO − Preferred Dividends − Common Dividends − Minority Dividends)/(Short-Term Debt + Long-Term Debt)
Debt/EBITDA	(Short-Term Debt + Long-Term Debt)/EBITDA
Debt/Book Capitalization	(Short-Term Debt + Long-Term Debt)/(Short-Term Debt + Long-Term Debt + Deferred Taxes + Minority Interest + Book Equity)
CAPEX/Depreciation Exp	Capital Expenditures/Depreciation Expense
Revenue Volatility	Standard Deviation of Trailing Five Years of Net Revenue Growth

where: EBITA = Earnings from continuing operations before interest, taxes, and amortization

EBITDA = Earnings from continuing operations before interest, taxes, depreciation, and amortization

FFO = Funds from Operations = Net income from continuing operations plus depreciation, amortization, deferred income taxes, and other noncash items

A review of these ratios indicates that Moody's considers the following factors, grouped by area of emphasis, as relevant in evaluating a company's ability to meet its debt service requirements.

1. Profitability ratios (first four metrics in footnote to Exhibit 7.6)
2. Cash flow ratios (metrics five, six and seven in footnote to Exhibit 7.6)
3. Solvency ratios (metrics eight, nine, ten and eleven in footnote to Exhibit 7.6)

Further, these ratios are variants of many of the ratios we describe elsewhere in the book. Other relevant debt-rating factors include the following.

- **Collateral** Companies can provide security for debt by pledging certain assets against the bond. This is like mortgages on assets. To the extent debt is secured, the debt holder is in a preferred position vis-à-vis other creditors.

- **Covenants** Debt agreements (indentures) can restrict the behavior of the issuing company so as to protect debt holders. For example, covenants commonly prohibit excessive dividend payments, mergers and acquisitions, further borrowing, and commonly prescribe minimum levels for key liquidity and solvency ratios. These covenants provide debt holders an element of control over the issuer's operations because, unlike equity investors, debt holders have no voting rights.

- **Options** Options are sometimes written into debt contracts. Examples are options to convert debt into stock and options allowing the issuing company to repurchase its debt before maturity (usually at a premium).

Research Insight ■ Valuation of Debt Options

Debt instruments can include features such as conversion options, under which the debt can be converted to common stock. Such conversion features are not accounted for separately under GAAP. Instead, convertible debt is accounted for just like debt with no conversion features (unless the conversion option can be separately traded). However, option-pricing models can be used to estimate the value of such debt features even when no market for those features exists. Empirical results suggest that those debt features represent a substantial part of debt value. These findings contribute to the current debate regarding the separation of compound financial instruments into debt and equity portions for financial statement presentation and analysis.

Verizon Credit Rating Example

Moody's cites five general factors (with associated weightings) as determinants of its credit rating of Baa1 for Verizon.

1. **Scale and Business Model, Competitive Environment and Technical Positioning (27%).** Larger scale, which usually goes hand in hand with geographic and business diversity, reduces the risks of a regional weakness or a business downturn. Scale also enhances a company's ability to absorb a temporary disruption, acquisition, or a capital investment mistake. It can also create greater leverage with suppliers of network equipment or handsets, for example. Larger scale enhances access to capital markets and increases financing flexibility. Finally, scale enhances a company's ability to bundle products, increasingly a competitive advantage, and confers a sense of market leadership that can bring superior access to customers.
2. **Operation Environment (16%).** The operating environment exerts external pressures on a company's performance and hence on its credit quality. For telecommunications companies, the operating environment has several different dimensions: regulatory and political framework and market share. Moody's does not disclose how it makes this qualitative assessment of the operating environment.
3. **Financial Policy (5%).** A company's financial policies guide management's appetite for future financial risk and the likely future direction for the company's capital structure. Key issues include leverage, coverage and return targets and liquidity management. Furthermore, dividend and share buyback policies play a significant role in this factor.
4. **Operating Performance (5%).** The level and stability of operating margins is a key consideration in assessing risk to debt holders. The breadth of business models in the telecommunications sector (such as wireline, wireless, regional, national, postpaid, prepaid) makes margin comparisons complex. When considering the scores for this factor, Moody's reviews the EBITDA margin trend, as well as the absolute level. The trend in EBITDA margin measures the direction of earnings (stable, improving or declining), and is a leading indicator of the company's business trajectory.

continued

5. **Financial Strength (47%).** A key component of Moody's analytical process is a review of a company's financial strength, which is essentially its ability to generate cash, service debt, and generate sufficient return to enable continuous access to the capital markets. The strength of the balance sheet is a key indicator of risk because it measures the degree to which a company has borrowed against future cash flow. A strong balance sheet enhances a company's ability to sustain its competitive position and grow in the future. Financial strength can mitigate other risks and provides greater operational flexibility with which to combat competition.

Three-fourths of the ratings weight is accorded to "Scale and Business Model, Competitive Environment and Technical Positioning" (which we introduced in Module 1 in our discussion of the Porter's Five Forces that determine competitive intensity) and "Financial Strength," by far the largest weighting which focuses on historical and forecasted cash flow, liquidity and financial leverage.

Moody's credit rating report on Verizon summarizes the five factors for the current period and for the coming 12 to 18 months. For each factor, Moody's provides a credit rating which corresponds to the ranges shown in Exhibit 7.6.

Rating Factors
Verizon Communications Inc.

Global Telecommunications Industry Grid [1][2]	Current LTM 9/30/2015		[3]Moody's 12-18 Month Forward View	
Factor 1: Scale And Business Model, Competitive Environment And Technical Positioning (27%)	**Measure**	**Score**	**Measure**	**Score**
• Scale (USD Billion)	$130.6	Aaa	$130–$133	Aaa
• Business Model, Competitive Environment and Technical Positioning	Aa	Aa	Aa	Aa
Factor 2: Operation Environment (16%)				
• Regulatory and Political	Baa	Baa	Baa	Baa
• Market Share	Baa	Baa	Baa	Baa
Factor 3: Financial Policy (5%)				
• Financial Policy	A	A	A	A
Factor 4: Operating Performance (5%)				
• EBITDA Margin	36.0%	Baa	36%–37%	Baa
Factor 5: Financial Strength (47%)				
• Debt/EBITDA	2.8	Ba	2.7–2.9	Ba
• (FFO + Interest Expense)/Interest Expense	7.4	A	6.5–7	Baa
• (EBITDA − CAPEX)/Interest Expense	4.6	Baa	5–5.5	A
Rating:				
• Indicated Rating from Grid		A3		Baa1
• Actual Rating Assigned				Baa1

[1] All ratios are based on 'Adjusted' financial data and incorporate Moody's Global Standard Adjustments for Non-Financial Corporations.

[2] As of 9/30/2015(L); Source: Moody's Financial Metrics.

[3] This represents Moody's forward view; not the view of the issuer; and unless noted in the text, does not incorporate significant acquisitions and divestitures.

Source: Moody's Investors Service Credit Opinion: Verizon Communications, Inc. 10 Nov 2015.

We see that the range of values of the ratios indicates an associated range of credit ratings from A to Ba. This is not uncommon as companies will typically exhibit both strengths and weaknesses in various aspects of their financial condition. The final credit rating, then, is a composite of scores on individual dimensions, a weighted agerage.

Moody's, then, summarizes its data to reach the following conclusions.

> **SUMMARY RATING RATIONALE** Verizon's Baa1 long-term debt rating reflects its significant scale of operations, the diversity of its revenue mix and a strong market position across its business segments, particularly wireless. Constraining the rating is the very large amount of debt undertaken to buy out Vodafone's stake in Verizon Wireless, a large common stock dividend, the high levels of capital expenditures required in the industry and our expectation that wireless revenue growth will slow and margin expansion will stall. Consequently, wireless EBITDA growth will be much slower over the next three years than it has been in prior years. The rating assumes that Verizon will use all available cash (outside of typical reinvestment in the business) to deleverage as it strives to reduce the approximately $112 billion of debt (GAAP) on its consolidated balance sheet as of September 30, 2015 (approximately $108 billion of debt at the parent, about $3 billion at the wireline opcos and about $1 billion at VZW).

In our opening vignette, we discuss the increase in financial leverage that accompanied Verizon's acquisition of Verizon Wireless and the significant cash expenditures required to service debt, for capital expenditures (CAPEX) to remain competitive, to make dividend payments to shareholders, and to pay health and retirement benefits to former workers. These are the same considerations that Moody's cites in its credit evaluation for Verizon.

Why Credit Ratings Matter

Moody's ratings methodology focuses primarily on cash flow in relation to financial leverage and seeks to estimate the relative probability that the company will default on its debt obligations (compared with companies in other credit ratings categories). As its credit ratings deteriorate, a company is more likely to be unable to make its debt payments and, consequently, it must pay a higher rate of interest on its borrowings to compensate investors for the risk of default.

So, how good are credit ratings at predicting defaults? Moody's provides the following graphic that illustrates the default rates for each ratings category 7 years into the future.

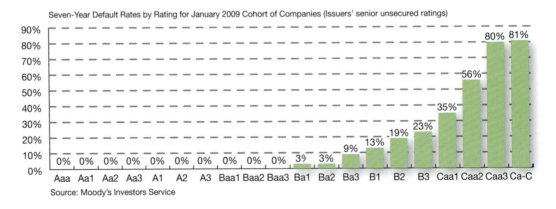

Seven-Year Default Rates by Rating for January 2009 Cohort of Companies (Issuers' senior unsecured ratings)

Source: Moody's Investors Service

In Exhibit 7.5, we identify Baa as the lowest investment grade security, and the graphic above provides corroborating evidence. Below Baa3, the probability of a default begins to increase. On balance, the ratings methodologies used by Moody's, S&P, and Fitch are quite thorough and have a good track record of predicting default rates far into the future.

> **Managerial Decision** ■ **You Are the Vice President of Finance**
>
> Your company is currently rated B1/B+ by the **Moody's** and **S&P** credit rating agencies, respectively. You are considering restructuring to increase your company's credit rating. What types of restructurings might you consider? What benefits will your company receive from those restructurings? What costs will your company incur to implement such restructurings? [Answer, p. 7-32]

LO5 Review 7-5

Assume that Comcast's financial statements for the current period yield the following ratios.

Operating margin	14.2%	FFO/Debt	32.9%
Debt/EBITDA	2.1	EBITA/Interest Expense	3.9

Required
Using the four measures above for Comcast, infer a reasonable credit rating for Comcast.

Solution on p. 7-52.

Global Accounting

IFRS

The FASB and the IASB have worked on a number of joint projects and the differences in accounting for liabilities are limited. We list here some differences that we encounter in studying IFRS financial statements and the implications for comparing GAAP and IFRS companies.

- Under U.S. GAAP, if a contingent liability is probable *and* if it can be reasonably estimated, it must be accrued. Under IFRS, companies can limit disclosure of contingent liabilities if doing so would severely prejudice the entity's competitive or legal position; for example, disclosing the amount of a potential loss on a lawsuit could sway the legal outcome. Accordingly, IFRS likely yields less disclosure of contingencies.

- Accruals sometimes involve a range of estimates. If all amounts within the range are equally probable, U.S. GAAP requires the company to accrue the lowest number in the range whereas IFRS requires the company to accrue the expected amount. Also, contingencies are discounted under IFRS whereas U.S. GAAP records contingencies at their nominal value. For both of these reasons, contingent liabilities are likely smaller under U.S. GAAP.

- IFRS offers more disclosure of liabilities and accruals. For each IFRS provision (the term used for accrued liabilities and expenses), the company must reconcile the opening and closing carrying amounts, describe any additional provision for the period, and explain any reversals for the period. Reconciliation is less prevalent under U.S. GAAP (required for example for allowance for doubtful accounts, warranty accruals, restructuring accruals). Recall that an over-accrual in one period shifts income to a subsequent period when the accrual is reversed. This increased transparency under IFRS might make it easier to spot earnings management.

Appendix 7A: Time Value of Money

This appendix explains the time value of money, which includes the concepts of present and future value. Time value of money concepts are important for pricing long-term bonds and notes, understanding the accounting for debt and other analysis purposes.

eLectures LO6
MBC Apply time value of money concepts.

Present Value Concepts

Would you rather receive a dollar now or a dollar one year from now? Most people would answer, a dollar now. Intuition tells us that a dollar received now is more valuable than the same amount received sometime in the future. Sound reasons exist for choosing the dollar now, the most obvious of which concerns risk. Because the future is uncertain, any number of events can prevent us from receiving the dollar a year from now. To avoid this risk, we choose the earlier date. Another reason is that the dollar received now could be invested. That is, one year from now, we would have the dollar and the interest earned on that dollar.

Present Value of a Single Amount

Risk and interest factors yield the following generalizations: (1) the right to receive an amount of money now, its **present value**, is worth more than the right to receive the same amount later, its **future value**; (2) the longer we must wait to receive an amount, the less attractive the receipt is; (3) the greater the interest rate the greater the amount we will receive in the future. (Putting 2 and 3 together we see that the difference between the present value of an amount and its future value is a function of both interest rate and time, that is, Principal × Interest Rate × Time); and (4) the more risk associated with any situation, the higher the interest rate.

To illustrate, let's compute the amount we would need to receive today (the present value) that would be equivalent to receiving $100 one year from now if money can be invested at 10%. We recognize intuitively that, with a 10% interest rate, the present value (the equivalent amount today) will be less than $100. The $100 received in the future must include 10% interest earned for the year. Thus, the $100 received in one year (the future value) must be 1.10 times the amount received today (the present value). Dividing $100/1.10, we obtain a present value of $90.91 (rounded). This means that we would do as well to accept $90.91 today as to wait one year and receive $100. To confirm the equality of the $90.91 receipt now to a $100 receipt one year later, we calculate the future value of $90.91 at 10% for one year as follows.

$$\$90.91 \times 1.10 \times 1 \text{ year} = \$100 \text{ (rounded)}$$

To generalize, we compute the present value of a future receipt by *discounting* the future receipt back to the present at an appropriate interest rate (also called the *discount rate*). We present this schematically below.

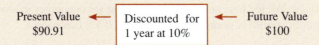

| Present Value $90.91 | ← | Discounted for 1 year at 10% | ← | Future Value $100 |

If either the time period or the interest rate were increased, the resulting present value would decrease. If more than one time period is involved, our future receipts include interest on interest. This is called *compounding*.

Time Value of Money Tables

Appendix A near the end of the book includes time value of money tables. Table 1 is a present value table that we can use to compute the present value of future amounts. A present value table provides present value factors (multipliers) for many combinations of time periods and interest rates that determine the present value of $1.

Present value tables are used as follows. First, determine the number of interest compounding periods involved (three years compounded annually are 3 periods, and three years compounded semiannually are 6 periods). The extreme left-hand column indicates the number of periods. It is important to distinguish between years and compounding periods. The table is for compounding periods (years × number of compounding periods per year).

Next, determine the interest rate per compounding period. Interest rates are usually quoted on a *per year* (annual) basis. The rate per compounding period is the annual rate divided by the number of compounding periods per year. For example, an interest rate of 10% *per year* would be 10% per period if compounded annually, and 5% *per period* if compounded semiannually.

Finally, locate the present value factor, which is at the intersection of the row of the appropriate number of compounding periods and the column of the appropriate interest rate per compounding period. Multiply this factor by the dollars that will be paid or received in the future.

All values in Table 1 are less than 1.0 because the present value of $1 received in the future is always smaller than $1. As the interest rate increases (moving from left to right in the table) or the number of periods increases (moving from top to bottom), the present value factors decline. This illustrates two important facts: (1) present values decline as interest rates increase, and (2) present values decline as the time lengthens. Consider the following three cases.

Case 1. Compute the present value of $100 to be received one year from today, discounted at 10% compounded semiannually.

Calculator
N = 2
I/Yr = 5
PMT = 0
FV = 100

PV = −90.70

	A	B
1	Discount Rate (rate)	5%
2	Number of Periods (nper)	2
3	Annuity (pmt)	0
4	Future value (fv)	100
5	Present value (pv)	(90.70)
6	= PV(B1,B2,B3,B4)	
7	= (90.70)	

Number of periods (one year, semiannually) = 2
Rate per period (10%/2) = 5%
Multiplier = 0.90703
Present value = $100.00 × 0.90703 = $90.70 (rounded)

Case 2. Compute the present value of $100 to be received two years from today, discounted at 10% compounded semiannually.

Calculator
N = 4
I/Yr = 5
PMT = 0
FV = 100

PV = −82.27

	A	B
1	Discount Rate (rate)	5%
2	Number of periods (nper)	4
3	Annuity (pmt)	0
4	Future value (fv)	100
5	Present value (pv)	(82.27)
6	= PV(B1,B2,B3,B4)	
7	= (82.27)	

Number of periods (two years, semiannually) = 4
Rate per period (10%/2) = 5%
Multiplier = 0.82270
Present value = $100 × 0.82270 = $82.27 (rounded)

Case 3. Compute the present value of $100 to be received two years from today, discounted at 12% compounded semiannually.

> Number of periods (two years, semiannually) = 4
> Rate per period (12%/2) = 6%
> Multiplier = 0.79209
> Present value = $100 = 0.79209 = $79.21 (rounded)

Calculator
N = 4
I/Yr = 6
PMT = 0
FV = 100

PV = −79.21

	A	B
1	Discount Rate (rate)	6%
2	Number of Periods (nper)	4
3	Annuity (pmt)	0
4	Future value (fv)	100
5	Present value (pv)	(79.21)
6	= PV(B1,B2,B3,B4)	
7	= (79.21)	

In Case 2, the present value of $82.27 is less than in Case 1 ($90.70) because the time increased from two to four compounding periods—the longer we must wait for money, the lower its value to us today. Then in Case 3, the present value of $79.21 was lower than in Case 2 because, while there were still four compounding periods, the interest rate per year was higher (12% annually instead of 10%)—the higher the interest rate the more interest that could have been earned on the money and therefore the lower the value today.

Present Value of an Annuity

In the examples above, we computed the present value of a single amount (also called a lump sum) made or received in the future. Often, future cash flows involve the same amount being paid or received each period. Examples include semiannual interest payments on bonds, quarterly dividend receipts, or monthly insurance premiums. If the payment or the receipt (the cash flow) is equally spaced over time and each cash flow is the same dollar amount, we have an *annuity*. One way to calculate the present value of the annuity would be to calculate the present value of each future cash flow separately. However, there is a more convenient method.

To illustrate, assume $100 is to be received at the end of each of the next three years as an annuity. When annuity amounts occur at the *end of each period*, the annuity is called an *ordinary annuity*. As shown below, the present value of this ordinary annuity can be computed from Table 1 by computing the present value of each of the three individual receipts and summing them (assume a 5% annual rate).

Future Receipts (ordinary annuity)				
Year 1	Year 2	Year 3	PV Multiplier (Table 1)	Present Value
$100			× 0.95238 =	$ 95.24
	$100		× 0.90703 =	90.70
		$100	× 0.86384 =	86.38
			2.72325	$272.32

Calculator
N = 3
I/Yr = 5
PMT = 100
FV = 0

PV = −272.32

	A	B
1	Discount Rate (rate)	5%
2	Number of Periods (nper)	3
3	Annuity (pmt)	100
4	Future value (fv)	0
5	Present value (pv)	(272.32)
6	= PV(B1,B2,B3,B4)	
7	= (272.32)	

Table 2 in Appendix A provides a single multiplier for computing the present value of an ordinary annuity. Referring to Table 2 in the row for three periods and the column for 5%, we see that the multiplier is 2.72325. When applied to the $100 annuity amount, the multiplier gives a present value of $272.33. As shown above, the same present value (with 1 cent rounding error) is derived by summing the three separate multipliers from Table 1. Considerable computations are avoided by using annuity tables.

Bond Valuation

Recall that a bond agreement specifies a pattern of future cash flows—usually a series of interest payments (cash outflow) and a single payment of the face amount at maturity (cash outflow), and bonds are priced using the prevailing market rate on the day the bond is sold (cash inflow). This is the case for the original bond issuance and for subsequent open-market sales. The market rate on the date of the sale is the rate we use to determine the bond's market value (its price). That rate is the bond's *yield*. The selling price of a bond is determined as follows.

1. Use Table 1 to compute the present value of the future principal payment at the prevailing market rate.
2. Use Table 2 to compute the present value of the future series of interest payments (the annuity) at the prevailing market rate.
3. Add the present values from steps 1 and 2.

We illustrate in Exhibit 7A.1 the price of $100,000, 8%, four-year bonds paying interest semiannually and sold when the prevailing market rate was (1) 8%, (2) 10% or (3) 6%. Note that the price of 8% bonds sold to yield 8% is the face (or par) value of the bonds. A bond issue price of $93,537 (discount bond) yields 10%. A bond issue price of $107,020 (premium bond) yields 6%.

Calculator
N = 8
I/Yr = 4
PMT = −4,000
FV = −100,000

PV = 100,000

	A	B
1	Annual coupon rate	8%
2	Annual market rate	8%
3	Interest payments per year	2
4	Years to maturity	4
5	Face (par) value	100,000
6	Issue price	100,000
7	= PV(B2/B3,B4*B3,−B5*B1/B3,−B5, 0)	
8	= 100,000	

Calculator
N = 8
I/Yr = 5
PMT = −4,000
FV = −100,000

PV = 93,537

	A	B
1	Annual coupon rate	8%
2	Annual market rate	10%
3	Interest payments per year	2
4	Years to maturity	4
5	Face (par) value	100,000
6	Issue price	93,537
7	= PV(B2/B3,B4*B3,−B5*B1/B3,−B5, 0)	
8	= 93,537	

Calculator
N = 8
I/Yr = 3
PMT = −4,000
FV = −100,000

PV = 107,020

	A	B
1	Annual coupon rate	8%
2	Annual market rate	6%
3	Interest payments per year	2
4	Years to maturity	4
5	Face (par) value	100,000
6	Issue price	107,020
7	= PV(B2/B3,B4*B3,−B5*B1/B3,−B5, 0)	
8	= 107,020	

Exhibit 7A.1 ■ Calculation of Bond Price Using Present Value Tables

Future Cash Flows	Multiplier (Table 1)	Multiplier (Table 2)	Present Values at 4% Semiannually
(1) $100,000 of 8%, 4-year bonds with interest payable semiannually priced to yield 8%.			
Principal payment, $100,000 (a single amount received after 8 semiannual periods)	0.73069		$ 73,069
Interest payments, $4,000 at end of each of 8 semiannual periods		6.73274	26,931
Present value (issue price) of bonds			$100,000

Future Cash Flows	Multiplier (Table 1)	Multiplier (Table 2)	Present Values at 5% Semiannually
(2) $100,000 of 8%, 4-year bonds with interest payable semiannually priced to yield 10%.			
Principal payment, $100,000 (a single amount received after 8 semiannual periods)	0.67684		$ 67,684
Interest payments, $4,000 at end of each of 8 semiannual periods		6.46321	25,853
Present value (issue price) of bonds			$ 93,537

Future Cash Flows	Multiplier (Table 1)	Multiplier (Table 2)	Present Values at 3% Semiannually
(3) $100,000 of 8%, 4-year bonds with interest payable semiannually priced to yield 6%.			
Principal repayment, $100,000 (a single amount received after 8 semiannual periods)	0.78941		$ 78,941
Interest payments, $4,000 at end of each of 8 semiannual periods		7.01969	28,079
Present value (issue price) of bonds			$107,020

Time Value of Money Computations Using a Calculator

We can use a financial calculator for time value of money computations. There are five important function keys for these calculations. If we know values for four of those five, the calculator will compute the fifth. Those function keys are:

N	Number of compounding (or discounting) periods
I/Yr	Interest (yield) rate per period—entered in % terms, for example, 12% is entered as 12 and not as 0.12. This key is labeled "interest per year" but it can handle any rate per different compounding periods; for example, if we have semiannual interest payments, our compounding periods are semiannual and the interest rate is the semiannual rate.
FV	Future value of the cash flows, this is a lump sum
PMT	Annuity (coupon) per discount period
PV	Present value of the cash flows, this is a lump sum

Calculator inputs follow for the three examples in Exhibit 7A.1. In these examples, the unknown value is the bond price, which is the present value (PV) of the bond's cash flows. (For additional instruction on entering inputs into a specific calculator, or how to do more complicated computations, review the calculator's user manual or review online calculator tutorials.)

A note about positive and negative signs for variables.   Financial calculators use a convention to capture the direction of cash flows. This can be understood by thinking about the direction of the cash flows from the company's perspective. Consider the examples in Exhibit 7A.1. The unknown value is the bond proceeds, the present value. From the perspective of the company, the interest payment is a cash outflow. We enter this in the calculator as a negative. Again, from the company's perspective, the cash paid to investors when the bond matures is a cash outflow (negative in the calculator). With both PMT and FV entered as negative numbers, the calculator returns a positive number—this can be understood as a cash inflow to the company. As long as we are consistent in the sign of our variables and we understand the calculator convention, we can interpret the result from the calculator. For example, if we enter PMT and FV as positive numbers, the PV returned is a negative number. (This would be considering cash flows from the investor's perspective.) Yet, be careful, if we enter PMT and FV with opposite signs, the result is nonsensical.

Example (1), Exhibit 7A.1: Bond priced to yield 8%.

N   =   8 (4 years $\times$ 2 periods per year = 8 semiannual periods)

I/Yr   =   4 (8% annual yield $\div$ 2 periods per year = 4% semiannually)

FV   =   −100,000 (face value, which is the lump sum that must be repaid in the future, a cash outflow)

PMT =   −4,000 ($100,000 $\times$ 4% semiannual coupon rate, a cash outflow)

PV   = 100,000   (output obtained from calculator)

Example (2), Exhibit 7A.1: Bond priced to yield 10%.

N = 8   I/Yr = 5   FV = −100,000   PMT = −4,000   PV = 93,537

Example (3), Exhibit 7A.1: Bond priced to yield 6%.

N = 8   I/Yr = 3   FV = −100,000   PMT = −4,000   PV = 107,020

Time Value of Money Computations Using Excel

We can use Excel or other spreadsheet software, to perform time value of money calculations. There are a number of functions for time value of money, but all of them involve the same six variables, which are:

rate	Interest (yield) rate per period, entered as either a percent (4%) or as a number 0.04. The variable is labeled rate and should be understood to mean per period; if we have semiannual interest payments, our compounding periods are semiannual and the interest rate is the semiannual rate
nper	Number of compounding or discounting periods
pmt	Annuity per discounting or compounding period; if there is no annuity, enter 0
pv	Present value of the cash flow, this is a lump sum
fv	Future value of the cash flow, this is a lump sum
type	Timing of the annuity payment, this is a 0 or 1 variable; if the annuity is paid at the end of each compounding period (as for interest payments), then type =0; if the annuity is paid at the beginning of each compounding period, then type =1 (type = 0 is the default value in Excel)

The Excel functions for present value and future value are as follows.

= pv(rate,nper,pmt,fv,type)

= fv(rate,nper,pmt,pv,type)

Unlike for a calculator, the variables must be entered in the correct order. Yet, once we open the bracket in the function, Excel prompts us for the variables in order. Similar to the calculator, Excel maintains the convention for positive and negative cash flows.

Example (1), Exhibit 7A.1: Bond priced to yield 8%.

rate	=	4% (8%/2 compounding periods = 4% semiannually)
nper	=	8 (4 years × 2 compounding periods = 8 semiannual periods)
pmt	=	−4,000 ($100,000 × 4% semiannual interest rate); this is a cash outflow so we enter a negative value
fv	=	−100,000 face value, which is the lump sum to be repaid in the future; this is a cash outflow so we enter a negative value
type	=	0 because interest is paid at the end of each semiannual period
	=	PV(rate,nper,pmt,fv,type)
	=	PV(4%, 8, −4000, −100000, 0) = 100,000

Example (2), Exhibit 7A.1: Bond priced to yield 10%.

= PV(5%, 8, −4000, −100000, 0) = 93,537

Example (3), Exhibit 7A.1: Bond priced to yield 6%.

= PV(3%, 8, −4000, −100000, 0) = 107,020

Excel is more powerful than a calculator because we can use cell addresses for the variables. For example, consider the three examples in Exhibit 7A.1 that could be defined as follows.

	A	B
1	Annual coupon rate	8%
2	Annual market rate	8%
3	Interest payments per year	2
4	Years to maturity	4
5	Face (par) value	100,000
6	Annuity type	0
7	Issue price	100,000
8	= PV(B2/B3,B4*B3,−B5*B1/B3,−B5, B6)	
9	= 100,000	

The value in cell B7 is 100,000. By changing cell B2 to 10%, the present value in B7 immediately changes to $93,537 and then when B2 is set to 6%, cell B7 displays $107,020.

Future Value Concepts

Future Value of a Single Amount

The **future value** of a single sum is the amount that a specific investment is worth at a future date if invested at a given rate of compound interest. To illustrate, suppose that we decide to invest $6,000 in a savings account that pays 6% annual interest and we intend to leave the principal and interest in the account for five years. We assume that interest is credited to the account at the end of each year. The balance in the account at the end of five years is determined using Table 3 in Appendix A, which gives the future value of a dollar, as follows.

Calculator
N = 5
I/Yr = 6
PMT = 0
PV = −6,000

FV = 8,029.35

	A	B
1	Discount Rate (rate)	6%
2	Number of Periods (nper)	5
3	Annuity (pmt)	0
4	Present value (pv)	−6,000
5	Future value (fv)	8,029.35
6	= FV(B1,B2,B3,B4)	
7	= 8,029.35	

Principal × Factor = Future Value
$6,000 × 1.33823 = $8,029

The factor 1.33823 is at the intersection of the row for five periods and the column for 6%.

Next, suppose that the interest is credited to the account semiannually rather than annually. In this situation, there are 10 compounding periods, and we use a 3% semiannual rate (one-half the annual rate because there are two compounding periods per year). The future value calculation follows.

$$\text{Principal} \times \text{Factor} = \text{Future Value}$$
$$\$6,000 \quad \times 1.34392 = \quad \$8,064$$

Calculator
N = 10
I/Yr = 3
PMT = 0
PV = −6,000
FV = 8,063.50

X	A	B
1	Discount Rate (rate)	3%
2	Number of Periods (nper)	10
3	Annuity (pmt)	0
4	Present value (pv)	−6,000
5	Future value (fv)	8,063.50
6	= FV(B1,B2,B3,B4)	
7	= 8,063.50	

Future Value of an Annuity

If, instead of investing a single amount, we invest a specified amount *each period,* then we have an annuity. To illustrate, assume that we decide to invest $2,000 at the end of each year for five years at an 8% annual rate of return. To determine the accumulated amount of principal and interest at the end of five years, we refer to Table 4 in Appendix A, which furnishes the future value of a dollar invested at the end of each period. The factor 5.86660 is in the row for five periods and the column for 8%, and the calculation is as follows.

$$\text{Periodic Payment} \times \text{Factor} = \text{Future Value}$$
$$\$2,000 \quad \times 5.86660 = \quad \$11,733$$

Calculator
N = 5
I/Yr = 8
PMT = −2,000
PV = 0
FV = 11,733.20

X	A	B
1	Discount Rate (rate)	8%
2	Number of Periods (nper)	5
3	Annuity (pmt)	−2,000
4	Present value (pv)	0
5	Future value (fv)	11,733.20
6	= FV(B1,B2,B3,B4)	
7	= 11,733.20	

If we decide to invest $1,000 at the end of each six months for five years at an 8% annual rate of return, we would use the factor for 10 periods at 4%, as follows.

$$\text{Periodic Payment} \times \text{Factor} = \text{Future Value}$$
$$\$1,000 \quad \times 12.00611 = \quad \$12,006$$

LO6 Review 7-6

For each of the separate cases *a*, *b*, and *c*, compute the sale price of a $5,000, 5-year bond with a 6% coupon rate (annual rate with interest paid semiannually) sold to yield an annual rate of:

a.   4%
b.   6%
c.   8%

Solution on p. 7-52.

Guidance Answers

You Are the Vice President of Finance

Pg. 7-25 You might consider the types of restructuring that would strengthen financial ratios typically used to assess liquidity and solvency by the rating agencies. Such restructuring includes generating cash by reducing inventory, reallocating cash outflows from investing activities (PPE) to debt reduction, and issuing stock for cash and using the proceeds to reduce debt (an equity for debt recapitalization). These actions increase liquidity or reduce financial leverage and, thus, should improve debt rating. An improved debt rating will attract more investors because your current debt rating is below investment grade and is not a suitable investment for many professionally managed portfolios. An improved debt rating will also lower the interest rate on your debt. Offsetting these benefits are costs such as the following: (1) potential loss of sales from inventory stock-outs; (2) potential future cash flow reductions and loss of market power from reduced PPE investments; and (3) costs of equity issuances (equity costs more than debt because investors demand a higher return to compensate for added risk and, unlike interest payments, dividends are not tax deductible for the company), which can yield a net increase in the total cost of capital. All cost and benefits must be assessed before you pursue any restructuring.

Questions

Q7-1.   What does the term *current liabilities* mean? What assets are usually used to settle current liabilities?

Q7-2.   What is an accrual? How do accruals impact the balance sheet and the income statement?

Q7-3.   What is the difference between a bond's coupon rate and its market interest rate (yield)?

Q7-4. Why do companies report a gain or loss when they repurchase their bonds? Is this a real economic gain or loss?

Q7-5. How do credit (debt) ratings affect the cost of borrowing for a company?

Q7-6. How would you interpret a company's reported gain or loss on the repurchase of its bonds?

Assignments with the ⬤ logo in the margin are available in BusinessCourse.
See the Preface of the book for details.

Mini Exercises

LO1

NCI Building Systems
(NCS)

M7-7. **Interpreting a Contingent Liability Footnote**

NCI Building Systems reports the following footnote to one of its recent 10-Ks related to its manufacturing of metal coil coatings and metal building components.

> We have discovered the existence of trichloroethylene in the ground water at our Southlake, Texas facility. Horizontal delineation concentrations in excess of applicable residential assessment levels have not been fully identified. We have filed an application with the Texas Commission of Environmental Quality ("TCEQ") for entry into the voluntary cleanup program. The cost of required remediation, if any, will vary depending on the nature and extent of the contamination. As of October 28, we have accrued $0.1 million to complete site analysis and testing. At this time, we cannot estimate a loss for any potential remediation costs, but we do not believe there will be a material adverse effect on our Consolidated Financial Statements.

a. How has NCI reported this potential liability on its balance sheet?

b. Does the $0.1 million accrual "to complete site analysis and testing" relate to a contingent liability? Explain.

LO2

M7-8. **Analyzing and Computing Financial Statement Effects of Interest**

Leahy Inc. signed a 90-day, 8% note payable for $13,800 on December 16. Use the financial statement effects template to illustrate the year-end December 31 accounting adjustment Leahy must make.

LO1

M7-9. **Analyzing and Determining Liability Amounts**

For each of the following situations, indicate the liability amount, if any, that is reported on the balance sheet of Bloomington Inc. at December 31, 2016.

a. Bloomington owes $220,000 at year-end 2016 for inventory purchases.

b. Bloomington agreed to purchase a $28,000 drill press in January 2017.

c. During November and December of 2016, Bloomington sold products to a customer and warranted them against product failure for 90 days. Estimated costs of honoring this 90-day warranty during 2017 are $3,100.

d. Bloomington provides a profit-sharing bonus for its executives equal to 5% of reported pretax annual income. The estimated pretax income for 2016 is $800,000. Bonuses are not paid until January of the following year.

LO3, 5

Citigroup Inc.
(C)

M7-10. **Interpreting Relations among Bond Price, Coupon, Yield, and Credit Rating**

The following appeared in Yahoo! Finance (finance.yahoo.com) regarding outstanding bonds issued by **Citigroup Inc.**

Price	Coupon (%)	Maturity	Yield to Maturity (%)	Fitch Ratings
129.87	6.625	2028	3.725	A
114.41	4.950	2043	4.095	A

a. Discuss the relation among the coupon rate, price, and yield for the bond maturing in 2028.

b. Compare the yields on the two bonds. Why are the yields different when the credit ratings are the same?

M7-11. Determining Gain or Loss on Bond Redemption   **LO4**

On April 30, one year before maturity, Middleton Company retired $200,000 of its 9% bonds payable at the current market price of 101 (101% of the bond face amount, or $200,000 × 1.01 = $202,000). The bond book value on April 30 is $196,600, reflecting an unamortized discount of $3,400. Bond interest is currently fully paid and recorded up to the date of retirement. What is the gain or loss on retirement of these bonds? Is this gain or loss a real economic gain or loss? Explain.

M7-12. Interpreting Bond Footnote Disclosures   **LO4**

Bristol-Myers Squibb Co. reports the following long-term debt as part of its MD&A in its 2015 10-K.

Bristol-Myers Squibb Company (BMY)

($ millions) Maturity Date		Obligations Expiring by Period					
	Total	2016	2017	2018	2019	2020	Later Years
Long-term debt ...	$14,972	$1,761	$1,647	$724	$1,081	$506	$9,253

a. What does this information indicate about Bristol-Myers Squibb's future payment obligations for 2016 through 2018?

b. What implications does this payment schedule have for our evaluation of Bristol-Myers Squibb's liquidity and solvency?

M7-13. Classifying Liability-Related Accounts into Balance Sheet or Income Statement   **LO1, 4**

Indicate the proper financial statement classification (balance sheet or income statement) for each of the following liability-related accounts.

Homework
MBC

a. Gain on Bond Retirement   e. Bond Interest Expense
b. Discount on Bonds Payable   f. Bond Interest Payable (due next period)
c. Mortgage Notes Payable   g. Premium on Bonds Payable
d. Bonds Payable   h. Loss on Bond Retirement

M7-14. Interpreting Bond Footnote Disclosures   **LO4**

Comcast Corporation reports the following information from the Management Discussion and Analysis section of its 2012 10-K.

Comcast Corporation (CMCSA)

> We, NBCUniversal and CCCL Parent are subject to the covenants and restrictions set forth in the indentures governing our public debt securities and in the credit agreements governing the Comcast revolving credit facility. The only financial covenant is in this credit facility and pertains to leverage, which is the ratio of debt to operating income before depreciation and amortization, as defined in the credit facility. We test for compliance with the financial covenant for this credit facility on an ongoing basis. As of December 31, 2015, we met this financial covenant by a significant margin. We do not expect to have to reduce debt or improve operating results in order to continue to comply with this financial covenant. In addition, as a result of the acquisition of Universal Studios Japan, we consolidated approximately ¥400 billion (approximately $3.3 billion as of December 31, 2015) in term loans that contain certain financial covenants. As of December 31, 2015, Universal Studios Japan was in compliance with all of these covenants.

a. The financial ratio to which Comcast refers is similar to those discussed in the section on credit ratings and the cost of debt. What effects might these ratios have on the degree of freedom that management has in running Comcast?

b. What pressures might management face if the company's ratios are near covenant limits?

M7-15. Analyzing Financial Statement Effects of Bond Redemption   **LO4**

Weiss Corporation issued $600,000 of 10%, 20-year bonds at 106 on January 1, 2012. Interest is payable semiannually on June 30 and December 31. Through January 1, 2017, Weiss amortized $10,000 of the bond premium. On January 1, 2017, Weiss retired the bonds at 103. Use the financial statement effects template to illustrate the bond retirement at January 1, 2017.

M7-16. Analyzing Financial Statement Effects of Bond Redemption   **LO4**

Camden Inc. issued $450,000 of 8%, 15-year bonds at 96 on July 1, 2012. Interest is payable semiannually on December 31 and June 30. Through June 30, 2014, Camden amortized $6,000 of the bond discount. On July 1, 2017, Camden retired the bonds at 101. Use the financial statement effects template to illustrate the bond retirement.

LO2   **M7-17.   Analyzing and Computing Accrued Interest on Notes**
Compute any interest accrued for each of the following notes payable owed by Penman Inc. as of December 31, 2017 (assume a 365-day year).

Lender	Issuance Date	Principal	Coupon Rate (%)	Term
Nissim.	11/21/2017	$30,000	10%	120 days
Klein	12/13/2017	22,000	8	90 days
Bildersee. . .	12/19/2017	26,000	6	60 days

LO5   **M7-18.   Interpreting Credit Ratings**

Cummins Inc. (CMI)

Cummins Inc. reports the following information in the Management Discussion & Analysis section of its 2015 10-K report.

Credit Ratings   Our ratings and outlook from each of the credit rating agencies as of the date of filing are shown in the table below.

Credit Rating Agency	Senior L-T Debt Rating	Outlook
Standard & Poor's Rating Services	A+	Stable
Fitch Ratings	A+	Stable
Moody's Investors Service Inc.	A2	Stable

Management's Assessment of Liquidity   Our financial condition and liquidity remain strong. Our solid balance sheet and credit ratings enable us to have ready access to credit and the capital markets. We believe our liquidity provides us with the financial flexibility needed to fund working capital, common stock repurchases, capital expenditures, dividend payments, acquisitions of our North American distributors, projected pension obligations, debt service obligations and severance payments. We continue to generate cash from operations in the U.S. and maintain access to $1.7 billion of our revolver as noted above.

a. Cummins has reduced the level of its financial leverage over the past several years. How does the reduction in financial leverage likely affect Cummins' credit ratings?
b. What effect will less financial leverage have on Cummins' borrowing costs? Explain.

LO3, 6   **M7-19.   Computing Bond Issue Price**
Abbington Inc. issues $700,000 of 9% bonds that pay interest semiannually and mature in 10 years. Compute the bond issue price assuming that the prevailing market rate of interest is:

a. 8% per year compounded semiannually.
b. 10% per year compounded semiannually.

LO3, 6   **M7-20.   Computing Issue Price for Zero Coupon Bonds**
Underwood Inc. issues $350,000 of zero coupon bonds that mature in 10 years. Compute the bond issue price assuming that the bonds' market rate is:

a. 8% per year compounded semiannually.
b. 10% per year compounded semiannually.

LO1   **M7-21.   Determining the Financial Statement Effects of Accounts Payable Transactions**
Hobson Company had the following transactions relating to its accounts payable.

a. Purchases $1,260 of inventory on credit.
b. Sells inventory for $1,650 on credit.
c. Records $1,260 cost of sales for transaction b.
d. Receives $1,650 cash toward accounts receivable.
e. Pays $1,260 cash to settle accounts payable.

Use the financial statement effects template to identify the effects (both amounts and accounts) for these transactions.

M7-22. Computing Bond Issue Price and Preparing an Amortization Table in Excel   **LO3, 4, 6**

On January 1, 2017, Springfield Inc. issues $400,000 of 8% bonds that pay interest semiannually and mature in 10 years (December 31, 2026).

a. Using the Excel PRICE function, compute the issue price assuming that the bonds' market rate is 7% per year compounded semiannually. (Use 100 for the redemption value to get a price as a percentage of the face amount, and use 1 for the basis.)

b. Prepare an amortization table in Excel to demonstrate the amortization of the book (carrying) value to the $400,000 maturity value at the end of the 20th semiannual period.

M7-23. Determining Credit Ratings   **LO5**

The chart below shows financial ratios for three companies. Use the data, along with Exhibit 7.6 to determine a bond rating for each of the three companies below.

	EBITA/ Average Assets	Operating Margin	EBITA Margin	EBITA/ Interest Expense	(FFO + Int Exp)/ Int Exp	Debt/ EBITDA	DEBT/ Book Capital- ization	FFO/ Debt	Retained Cash Flow/ Net Debt	CAPEX/ Depre- ciation	Revenue Volatility
Company 1..	12.80%	16.30%	18.82%	15.0	13.4	1.6	38.12%	44.72%	37.64%	1.3	10.1
Company 2..	9.20%	11.40%	13.00%	2.8	5.1	3.3	48.60%	21.73%	21.92%	1.2	16.0
Company 3..	13.87%	18.62%	20.76%	22.2	20.5	1.3	39.87%	60.82%	32.79%	1.3	6.3

M7-24. Applying Time Value of Money Concepts   **LO6**

Complete the missing information in the table below. Assume that all bonds pay interest semiannually.

	Annual Yield	Years to Maturity	Coupon Rate	Face Value	Issue Proceeds
Firm 1	8.00%	15	7.00%	$ 300,000	?
Firm 2	3.00%	10	0.00%	?	$ 556,853
Firm 3	6.50%	?	5.00%	$ 500,000	$ 468,416
Firm 4	?	12	3.50%	$1,000,000	$1,147,822
Firm 5	0.80%	20	2.00%	$ 500,000	?

M7-25. Applying Time Value of Money Concepts   **LO6**

Ozona Minerals issued bonds that mature in 10 years. As is typical for bonds, Ozona Minerals must pay interest only on the $250 million face value. As part of the bond indenture, Ozona Minerals must make annual payments to a sinking fund, which is a pool of money set aside to help repay the bond issue. The sinking fund must be equal to 50% of the face value of the bonds in 10 years (at maturity). If Ozona Minerals can invest at 5%, what amount must the company add to the sinking fund each year to comply with the sinking fund requirement?

M7-26. Calculating Gains and Losses on Early Retirement of Debt   **LO4**

The data below pertain to bonds outstanding at 2016 year end. For each of the following outstanding bonds, determine whether the company would record a gain or a loss if it decided to retire the bonds at the end of fiscal 2016.

	Face Value	Premium (Discount)	Fair Value
Firm 1	$300,000	$45,885	$402,558
Firm 2	750,000	42,550	712,558
Firm 3	500,000	(16,995)	504,770
Firm 4	400,000	(2,250)	385,669

Exercises

LO1   E7-27.   Analyzing and Computing Accrued Warranty Liability and Expense
Canton Company sells a motor that carries a 60-day unconditional warranty against product failure. From prior years' experience, Canton estimates that 3% of units sold each period will require repair at an average cost of $160 per unit. During the current period, Canton sold 100,000 units and repaired 2,400 of those units.

    a. How much warranty expense must Canton report in its current-period income statement?
    b. What warranty liability related to current-period sales will Canton report on its current period-end balance sheet? (*Hint:* Remember that some units were repaired in the current period.)
    c. What analysis issues must we consider with respect to reported warranty liabilities?

LO1   E7-28.   Analyzing Contingent and Other Liabilities
The following independent situations represent various types of liabilities. Analyze each situation and indicate which of the following is the proper accounting treatment for the company: (a) record a liability on the balance sheet, (b) disclose the liability in a financial statement footnote, or (c) neither record nor disclose any liability.

    1. A stockholder has filed a lawsuit against Windsor Corporation. Clinch's attorneys have reviewed the facts of the case. Their review revealed that similar lawsuits have never resulted in a cash award and it is highly unlikely that this lawsuit will either.
    2. Sterling Company signed a 60-day, 10% note when it purchased items from another company.
    3. The Environmental Protection Agency notifies Stark Industries that a state where it has a plant is filing a lawsuit for groundwater pollution against Stark and another company that has a plant adjacent to Stark's plant. Test results have not identified the exact source of the pollution. Stark's manufacturing process often produces by-products that can pollute groundwater.
    4. Franklin Company manufactured and sold products to a retailer that later sold the products to consumers. Franklin Company will replace the product if it is found to be defective within 90 days of the sale to the consumer. Historically, 1.2% of the products are returned for replacement.

LO1   E7-29.   Recording and Analyzing Warranty Accrual and Payment

Harley-Davidson Inc. (HOG)

Refer to the discussion of and excerpt from the **Harley-Davidson Inc.** warranty reserve on page 7-6 to answer the following questions.

    a. Using the financial statement effects template, record separately the 2015 warranty liability transactions relating to the (1) "Warranties issued during the period," (2) "Recalls and changes to preexisting warranty obligations," and (3) "Settlements made during the period."
    b. Does the level of Harley-Davidson's warranty accrual appear to be reasonable?

LO1   E7-30.   Analyzing and Computing Accrued Wages Liability and Expense
Demski Company pays its employees on the 1st and 15th of each month. It is March 31 and Demski is preparing financial statements for this quarter. Its employees have earned $96,000 since the 15th of March and have not yet been paid. How will Demski's balance sheet and income statement reflect the accrual of wages on March 31? What balance sheet and income statement accounts would be incorrectly reported if Demski failed to make this accrual (for each account indicate whether it would be overstated or understated)?

LO3, 4   E7-31.   Analyzing and Reporting Financial Statement Effects of Bond Transactions
On January 1, Remington Corp. issued $500,000 of 15-year, 10% bonds payable for $586,460 yielding an effective interest rate of 8%. Interest is payable semiannually on June 30 and December 31.

    a. Show computations to confirm the issue price of $586,460.
    b. Indicate the financial statement effects using the template for (1) bond issuance, (2) semiannual interest payment and premium amortization on June 30 of the first year, and (3) semiannual interest payment and premium amortization on December 31 of the first year.

LO3, 4   E7-32.   Analyzing and Reporting Financial Statement Effects of Mortgages
On January 1, Patterson Inc. borrowed $1,000,000 on a 10%, 15-year mortgage note payable. The note is to be repaid in equal semiannual installments of $65,051 (payable on June 30 and December 31). Each mortgage payment includes principal and interest. Interest is computed using the effective interest method. Indicate the financial statement effects using the template for (a) issuance of the mortgage note payable, (b) payment of the first installment on June 30, and (c) payment of the second installment on December 31.

E7-33. **Assessing the Effects of Bond Credit Rating Changes**

LO5
Ford Motor Co. (F)

Ford Motor Co. reports the following information from the Risk Factors and the Management Discussion and Analysis sections of its 2015 10-K report.

Credit Ratings Our short-term and long-term debt is rated by four credit rating agencies designated as nationally recognized statistical rating organizations ("NRSROs") by the U.S. Securities and Exchange Commission:

- DBRS Limited ("DBRS");
- Fitch, Inc. ("Fitch");
- Moody's Investors Service, Inc. ("Moody's"); and
- Standard & Poor's Ratings Services, a division of McGraw-Hill Companies ("S&P").

In several markets, locally-recognized rating agencies also rate us. A credit rating reflects an assessment by the rating agency of the credit risk associated with a corporate entity or particular securities issued by that entity. Rating agencies' ratings of us are based on information provided by us and other sources. Credit ratings are not recommendations to buy, sell, or hold securities, and are subject to revision or withdrawal at any time by the assigning rating agency. Each rating agency may have different criteria for evaluating company risk and, therefore, ratings should be evaluated independently for each rating agency.

The following rating actions were taken by these NRSROs since the filing of our Quarterly Report on Form 10-Q for the quarter ended September 30, 2015:

- On November 23, 2015, S&P affirmed its ratings for Ford and Ford Credit, and revised the outlook to positive from stable.

The following chart summarizes certain of the credit ratings and outlook presently assigned by these four NRSROs:

	Ford			Ford Credit			NRSROs
	Issuer Default/ Corporate/ Issuer Rating	Long-Term Senior Unsecured	Outlook/ Trend	Long-Term Senior Unsecured	Short-Term Unsecured	Outlook/ Trend	Minimum Long-Term Investment Grade Rating
DBRS	BBB (low)	BBB (low)	Positive	BBB (low)	R-3	Positive	BBB (low)
Fitch	BBB−	BBB−	Positive	BBB−	F3	Positive	BBB−
Moody's . . .	N/A	Baa3	Stable	Baa3	P-3	Stable	Baa3
S&P *	BBB−	BBB−	Positive	BBB−	A-3	Positive	BBB−

*S&P assigns FCE a long-term senior unsecured credit rating of BBB, a one-notch higher rating than Ford and Ford Credit, with a stable outlook.

a. What financial ratios do credit rating companies such as the four NRSROs listed above, use to evaluate the relative riskiness of borrowers?

b. What economic consequences might there have been for Ford when S&P revised its outlook on the company in November 2015?

c. What type of actions can Ford take to improve its credit ratings?

E7-34. **Analyzing and Reporting Financial Statement Effects of Bond Transactions**

LO3, 4

Winston Inc. reports financial statements each December 31 and issues $400,000 of 9%, 15-year bonds dated May 1, 2017, with interest payments on October 31 and April 30. Assuming the bonds are sold at par on May 1, 2017, complete the financial statement effects template to reflect the following events: (a) bond issuance, (b) the first semiannual interest payment, and (c) retirement of $150,000 of the bonds at 102 on November 1, 2017.

E7-35. **Analyzing and Reporting Financial Statement Effects of Bond Transactions**

LO3, 4

On January 1, 2017, Banek Inc. issued $350,000 of 8%, 9-year bonds for $309,086, which implies a market (yield) rate of 10%. Semiannual interest is payable on June 30 and December 31 of each year.

a. Show computations to confirm the bond issue price.

b. Indicate the financial statement effects using the template for (1) bond issuance, (2) semiannual interest payment and discount amortization on June 30, 2017, and (3) semiannual interest payment and discount amortization on December 31, 2017.

LO3, 4   **E7-36.**   **Analyzing and Reporting Financial Statement Effects of Bond Transactions**
On January 1, 2017, Shields Inc. issued $1,000,000 of 9%, 20-year bonds for $1,098,964, yielding a market (yield) rate of 8%. Semiannual interest is payable on June 30 and December 31 of each year.

a. Show computations to confirm the bond issue price.
b. Indicate the financial statement effects using the template for (1) bond issuance, (2) semiannual interest payment and premium amortization on June 30, 2017, and (3) semiannual interest payment and premium amortization on December 31, 2017.

LO3, 4   **E7-37.**   **Determining Bond Prices, Interest Rates, and Financial Statement Effects**

Deere & Co (DE)

Deere & Company's 2015 10-K reports the following footnote relating to long-term debt for its equipment operations subsidiary. Deere's borrowings include $300 million, 7.125% notes, due in 2031 (highlighted below).

Long-term borrowings at October 31 consisted of the following in millions of dollars:		
Notes and Debentures	**2015**	**2014**
4.375% notes due 2019	$ 750	$ 750
8-1/2% debentures due 2022	105	105
2.60% notes due 2022	1,000	1,000
6.55% debentures due 2028	200	200
5.375% notes due 2029	500	500
8.10% debentures due 2030	250	250
7.125% notes due 2031	**300**	**300**
3.90% notes due 2042	1,250	1,250
Other notes	106	288
Total	$4,461	$4,643

A recent price quote (from **Yahoo! Finance Bond Center**) on Deere's 7.125% notes follows.

Type	Issuer	Price	Coupon (%)	Maturity	YTM (%)	Current Yield (%)	Fitch Rating	Callable
Corp	Deere & CO	142.72	7.125	2031	3.623	4.992	A	No

This price quote indicates that Deere's 7.125% notes have a market price of 142.72 (142.72% of face value), resulting in a yield to maturity of 3.623%.

a. Assuming that these notes were originally issued at par value, what does the market price reveal about interest rate changes since Deere issued its notes? (Assume that Deere's credit rating has remained the same.)
b. Does the change in interest rates since the issuance of these notes affect the amount of interest expense that Deere reports in its income statement? Explain.
c. How much cash would Deere have to pay to repurchase the 7.125% notes at the quoted market price of 142.72%? (Assume no interest is owed when Deere repurchases the notes.) How would the repurchase affect Deere's current income?
d. Assuming that the notes remain outstanding until their maturity, at what market price will the notes sell on their due date in 2031?

LO6   **E7-38.**   **Computing Present Values of Single Amounts and Annuities**

Refer to Tables 1 and 2 in Appendix A near the end of the book to compute the present value for each of the following amounts.

a. $120,000 received 10 years hence if the annual interest rate is:
  1.   10% compounded annually.
  2.   10% compounded semiannually.
b. $2,000 received at the end of each year for the next eight years discounted at 8% compounded annually.

c. $800 received at the end of each six months for the next 15 years if the interest rate is 10% per year compounded semiannually.

d. $250,000 received 10 years hence discounted at 10% per year compounded annually.

E7-39. **Analyzing and Reporting Financial Statement Effects of Bond Transactions**

On January 1, 2017, Arbor Corporation issued $800,000 of 20-year, 11% bonds for $739,815, yielding a market (yield) rate of 12%. Interest is payable semiannually on June 30 and December 31.

a. Confirm the bond issue price.

b. Indicate the financial statement effects using the template for (1) bond issuance, (2) semiannual interest payment and discount amortization on June 30, 2017, and (3) semiannual interest payment and discount amortization on December 31, 2017.

LO3, 4

E7-40. **Analyzing and Reporting Financial Statement Effects of Bond Transactions**

On January 1, 2017, Sparta Company issued $550,000 of 5-year, 12% bonds for $592,470, yielding a market (yield) rate of 10%. Interest is payable semiannually on June 30 and December 31.

a. Confirm the bond issue price.

b. Indicate the financial statement effects using the template for (1) bond issuance, (2) semiannual interest payment and premium amortization on June 30, 2017, and (3) semiannual interest payment and premium amortization on December 31, 2017.

LO3, 4

E7-41. **Calculating Ratios and Estimating Credit Rating**

The following data are from **Under Armour**'s 2015 10-K report ($ thousands).

LO5

Revenue	$3,963,313	Earnings from continuing operations . . .	$ 232,573
Interest expense	14,628	Capital expenditures (CAPEX)	298,928
Tax expense	154,112	Total debt	669,000
Amortization expense . . .	13,840	Average assets	2,481,992
Depreciation expense . . .	87,100		

a. Use the data above to calculate the following ratios: EBITA/Average assets, EBITA Margin, EBITA/Interest expense, Debt/EBITDA, CAPEX/Depreciation Expense. Definitions for these ratios are in Exhibit 7.6.

b. Refer to Exhibit 7.6 and the ratios you calculated in part a. Estimate the credit rating that Moody's might assign to Under Armour.

E7-42. **Calculating Ratios and Estimating Credit Rating**

The following data are from **Kellogg**'s 10-K report dated January 2, 2016 ($ millions).

LO5

Revenue	$13,525	Earnings from continuing operations . . .	$ 614
Interest expense	227	Capital expenditures (CAPEX)	553
Tax expense	159	Total debt	7,759
Amortization expense	8	Average assets	15,209
Depreciation expense	526		

a. Use the data above to calculate the following ratios: EBITA/Average assets, EBITA Margin, EBITA/Interest expense, Debt/EBITDA, CAPEX/Depreciation Expense. Definitions for these ratios are in Exhibit 7.6.

b. Refer to Exhibit 7.6 and the ratios you calculated in part a. Estimate the credit rating that Moody's might assign to Kellogg.

E7-43. **Applying Time Value of Money Concepts**

Fulton Corporation purchases new manufacturing facilities and assumes a 10-year mortgage of $4 million. The annual interest rate on the mortgage is 5.5% and payments are due at the end of each year.

LO6

a. Determine the mortgage payment that Fulton Corporation must make each year.

b. Use Excel to prepare a mortgage amortization schedule for the 10 years.

c. At the end of the first year, what amount will Fulton include as "current maturities of long-term debt" on its balance sheet?

LO6   **E7-44.**   **Applying Time Value of Money Concepts**

Manchester Corporation takes a 20-year mortgage of $15 million. The annual interest rate on the mortgage is 7% and payments are due at the end of each year.

a. Determine the annual mortgage payment.
b. Use the financial statement effects template to record the mortgage proceeds.
c. Use the financial statement effects template to record the first two mortgage payments.

Problems

LO2, 3, 4, 5

PepsiCo Inc.

(PEP)

P7-45.   **Interpreting and Analyzing Debt Footnotes**

PepsiCo Inc. reports $32,322 million of long-term debt outstanding as of December 2015 in the following schedule to its 10-K report.

Debt Obligations and Commitments

$ millions	2015	2014
Short-term debt obligations		
Current maturities of long-term debt	$ 3,109	$ 4,096
Commercial paper (0.3% and 0.1%)	770	746
Other borrowings (10.0% and 17.7%)	192	234
	$ 4,071	$ 5,076
Long-term debt obligations		
Notes due 2015 (1.4%)	$ —	$ 4,093
Notes due 2016 (2.6% and 2.6%)	3,087	3,099
Notes due 2017 (1.2% and 1.6%)	4,392	2,004
Notes due 2018 (3.6% and 4.4%)	4,122	3,410
Notes due 2019 (3.7% and 3.7%)	1,627	1,631
Notes due 2020 (2.4% and 3.8%)	3,830	1,983
Notes due 2021–2046 (3.9% and 4.0%)	15,228	11,657
Other, due 2016–2021 (4.3% and 4.4%)	36	40
	32,322	27,917
Less: current maturities of long-term debt obligations	(3,109)	(4,096)
Total	$29,213	$23,821

Long-Term Contractual Commitments

Payments Due by Period ($ millions)	Total	2016	2017–2018	2019–2020	2021 and beyond
Long-term debt obligations	$32,322	$3,109	$8,396	$5,447	$15,307

Our borrowing costs and access to capital and credit markets may be adversely affected by a downgrade or potential downgrade of our credit ratings.

We expect to maintain Tier 1 commercial paper access, which we believe will facilitate appropriate financial flexibility and ready access to global credit markets at favorable interest rates. Any downgrade of our credit ratings by a credit rating agency, especially any downgrade to below investment grade, whether as a result of our actions or factors which are beyond our control, could increase our future borrowing costs and impair our ability to access capital and credit markets on terms commercially acceptable to us, or at all. Further, any downgrade of our current short-term credit ratings could impair our ability to access the commercial paper market with the same flexibility that we have experienced historically, and therefore require us to rely more heavily on more expensive types of debt financing. Our borrowing costs and access to the commercial paper market could also be adversely affected if a credit rating agency announces that our ratings are under review for a potential downgrade. An increase in our borrowing costs, limitations on our ability to access the global capital and credit markets or a reduction in our liquidity could adversely affect our financial condition and results of operations.

Moody's Investors Service (www.moodys.com) reported the following regarding PepsiCo.

> **Rating Action: Moody's rates Pepsi's $3 billion notes A1; outlook stable**
> New York, October 08, 2015—Moody's today assigned an A1 rating to PepsiCo, Inc.'s new $3 billion senior note offering in 2, 5, and 30 year maturity tranches. PepsiCo will use the proceeds for general corporate purposes. Other ratings were unchanged. The outlook is stable.
> Source: Moody's Investor Service (www.moodys.com)

As of December 2016, the price of its $1 billion 5.0% senior notes maturing in 2018 follows (from **Yahoo! Finance**, reports.finance.yahoo.com):

Type	Issuer	Price	Coupon(%)	Maturity	YTM(%)	Fitch Ratings	Callable
Corp	PEPSICO INC	112.32	5.0	01-Jun-2018	1.374	A	No

Required

a. PepsiCo reports current maturities of long-term debt of $3,109 million as part of short-term debt. Why is this amount reported that way? PepsiCo reports $8,396 million of long-term debt due in 2017–2018. What does this mean? Is this amount important to our analysis of PepsiCo? Explain.

b. The $1 billion 5.0% notes maturing in 2018 are priced at 112.32 (112.32% of face value, or $1.1232 billion) as of December 2016, resulting in a yield to maturity of 1.374%. Assuming that the credit rating of PepsiCo has not changed, what does the pricing of this bond imply about interest rate changes since PepsiCo issued the bond?

c. What does the schedule of long-term contractual commitments reveal that might be useful in analyzing PepsiCo's liquidity?

d. What can investors infer about PepsiCo's creditworthiness given the $3 billion note issuance in 2015? How does this rating action affect the issue proceeds?

e. What type of actions can PepsiCo take to improve its credit ratings?

P7-46.   Interpreting Debt Footnotes on Interest Rates and Interest Expense

CVS Health Corporation discloses the following as part of its long-term debt footnote in its 2015 10-K.

LO4
CVS Health
Corporation (CVS)

BORROWINGS AND CREDIT AGREEMENTS

The following table is a summary of the Company's borrowings as of December 31:

In millions	2015	2014
Commercial paper	$ —	$ 685
3.25% senior notes due 2015	—	550
1.2% senior notes due 2016	750	750
6.125% senior notes due 2016	421	421
5.75% senior notes due 2017	1,080	1,080
1.9% senior notes due 2018	2,250	—
2.25% senior notes due 2018	1,250	1,250
2.25% senior notes due 2019	850	850
6.6% senior notes due 2019	394	394
2.8% senior notes due 2020	2,750	—
4.75% senior notes due 2020	450	450
4.125% senior notes due 2021	550	550
2.75% senior notes due 2022	1,250	1,250
3.5% senior notes due 2022	1,500	—
4.75% senior notes due 2022	400	—
4% senior notes due 2023	1,250	1,250
3.375% senior notes due 2024	650	650
5% senior notes due 2024	300	—
3.875% senior notes due 2025	3,000	—
6.25% senior notes due 2027	453	453
3.25% senior exchange debentures due 2035	5	—

continued

continued from previous page

In millions	2015	2014
4.875% senior notes due 2035	$ 2,000	$ —
6.125% senior notes due 2039	734	734
5.75% senior notes due 2041	493	493
5.3% senior notes due 2043	750	750
5.125% senior notes due 2045	3,500	—
Capital lease obligations	644	391
Other	20	41
Total debt principal	27,694	12,992
Debt premiums	39	—
Debt discounts and deferred financing costs	(269)	(102)
	27,464	12,890
Less:		
Short-term debt (commercial paper)	—	(685)
Current portion of long-term debt	(1,197)	(575)
Long-term debt	$26,267	$11,630

CVS discloses its required principal debt repayments due during each of the next five years and thereafter.

In millions	
2016	$ 1,197
2017	1,113
2018	3,521
2019	1,266
2020	3,224
Thereafter	17,373
Total	$27,694

CVS also discloses the following information.

Interest expense, net—Interest expense, net of capitalized interest, was $859 million, $615 million and $517 million, and interest income was $21 million, $15 million and $8 million in 2015, 2014 and 2013, respectively. Capitalized interest totaled $12 million, $19 million and $25 million in 2015, 2014 and 2013, respectively. Interest paid totaled $629 million, $647 million, and $534 million in 2015, 2014, and 2013 respectively.

The price of the 6.125% senior note due 2039 as of May 2016 follows (from Yahoo! Finance).

Maturity Date	Issuer	Security Type	Coupon	Current Price	Current Yield	Fitch Rating	Callable
2039	CVS Health (NYSE: CVS)	Corporate Debentures	6.125	126.13	4.856	BBB	No

Required

a. What is the average coupon rate (interest paid) on the long-term debt? (*Hint:* Use the interest expense disclosures.)

b. Does your computation of the coupon rate in part *a* seem reasonable given the footnote disclosure relating to specific bond issues? Explain.

c. What is the average effective rate (interest expense) on the long-term debt? Explain how the amount of interest paid can differ from the amount of interest expense recorded in the income statement.

d. On its 2015 balance sheet, CVS reports current maturities of long-term debt of $1,197 million as part of short-term debt. Why is this amount reported that way? Is this amount important to our analysis of CVS? Explain.

e. The $1,500 million 6.125% senior note due in 2039 is priced at 126.13 (126.13% of face value, or $1,891.95 million) as of 2016, resulting in a current yield of 4.856%. Assuming that the credit rating of CVS has not changed, what does the pricing of this 6.125% coupon bond imply about interest rate changes since CVS issued the bond?

P7-47. **Analyzing Debt Terms, Yields, Prices, and Credit Ratings**

Reproduced below is the debt footnote from the 2016 10-K report of Oracle Corporation.

$ millions	May 31, 2016	May 31, 2015
Revolving credit agreements:		
$3,750, LIBOR plus 0.35%, due June 2016.	$ 3,750	$ —
Floating-rate senior notes:		
$1,000, three-month LIBOR plus 0.20%, due July 2017	1,000	1,000
$500, three-month LIBOR plus 0.58%, due January 2019 . . .	500	500
$750, three-month LIBOR plus 0.51%, due October 2019 . . .	750	750
Fixed-rate senior notes:		
$2,000, 5.25%, due January 2016.	—	2,000
$2,500, 1.20%, due October 2017.	2,500	2,500
$2,500, 5.75%, due April 2018.	2,500	2,500
$1,500, 2.375%, due January 2019.	1,500	1,500
$1,750, 5.00%, due July 2019	1,750	1,750
$2,000, 2.25%, due October 2019.	2,000	2,000
$1,000, 3.875%, due July 2020	1,000	1,000
€1,250, 2.25%, due January 2021	1,394	1,352
$1,500, 2.80%, due July 2021	1,500	1,500
$2,500, 2.50%, due May 2022.	2,500	2,500
$2,500, 2.50%, due October 2022.	2,500	2,500
$1,000, 3.625%, due July 2023	1,000	1,000
$2,000, 3.40%, due July 2024	2,000	2,000
$2,500, 2.95%, due May 2025.	2,500	2,500
€750, 3.125%, due July 2025	836	810
$500, 3.25%, due May 2030	500	500
$1,750, 4.30%, due July 2034	1,750	1,750
$1,250, 3.90%, due May 2035.	1,250	1,250
$1,250, 6.50%, due April 2038.	1,250	1,250
$1,250, 6.125%, due July 2039	1,250	1,250
$2,250, 5.375%, due July 2040	2,250	2,250
$1,000, 4.50%, due July 2044	1,000	1,000
$2,000, 4.125%, due May 2045.	2,000	2,000
$1,250, 4.375%, due May 2055.	1,250	1,250
Total senior notes and other borrowings	43,980	42,162
Unamortized discount/issuance costs.	(247)	(278)
Hedge accounting fair value adjustments	122	74
Total notes payable and other borrowings.	43,855	41,958
Notes payable and other borrowings, current	(3,750)	(1,999)
Notes payable, non-current	$40,105	$39,959

Future principal payments (adjusted for the effects of the cross-currency swap agreements associated with the January 2021 Notes) for all of our borrowings at May 31, 2016 were as follows:

$ millions	
Fiscal 2017	$ 3,750
Fiscal 2018	6,000
Fiscal 2019	2,000
Fiscal 2020	4,500
Fiscal 2021	2,655
Thereafter	25,336
Total	$44,241

Reproduced below is a summary of the market values as of December 2016 of select Oracle bonds (from **Morningstar**, www.morningstar.com).

Name	Maturity Date	Amount $	Price	Coupon %	Yield to Maturity %
Oracle 2.95%	5/15/25	2,500	97.9	2.950	3.23
Oracle 4%	7/15/46	3,000	94.3	4.000	4.34
Oracle 4.375%	5/15/55	1,250	93.2	4.375	4.76

Required

a. What is the amount of debt reported on Oracle's May 31, 2016, balance sheet? What are the scheduled maturities for this indebtedness? Why is information relating to a company's scheduled maturities of debt useful in an analysis of its financial condition?

b. Oracle reported $1,467 million in interest expense in the notes to its 2016 income statement. In the note to its statement of cash flows, Oracle indicates that the cash portion of this expense is $1,616 million. What could account for the difference between interest expense and interest paid? Explain.

c. Oracle's long-term debt is rated A1 by Moody's, A+ by S&P, and A+ by Fitch. What factors would be important to consider in attempting to quantify the relative riskiness of Oracle compared with other borrowers? Explain.

d. Oracle's $3,000 million 4% notes traded at 94.3 or 94.3% of par, as of December 2016. What is the market value of these notes on that date? How is the difference between this market value and the $3,000 million face value reflected in Oracle's financial statements? What effect would the repurchase of this entire note issue have on Oracle's financial statements? What does the 94.3 price tell you about the general trend in interest rates since Oracle sold this bond issue? Explain.

e. Examine the yields to maturity of the three bonds in the table above. What relation do we observe between these yields and the maturities of the bonds? Also, explain why this relation applies in general.

IFRS Applications

LO1
**BP p.l.c.
(BP)**

I7-48.   **Interpreting a Contingent Liability Footnote**

BP operates off-shore drilling rigs including rigs in the Gulf of Mexico. On April 20, 2010, explosions and fire on the Deepwater Horizon rig led to the death of 11 crew members and a 200-million-gallon oil spill in the Gulf of Mexico. BP's 2010 annual report (prepared under IFRS) included the following concerning estimates of contingent liabilities (provisions).

> In estimating the amount of the provision, BP has determined a range of possible outcomes for Individual and Business Claims, and State and Local Claims. . . . BP has concluded that a reasonable range of possible outcomes for the amount of the provision as at 31 December 2010 is $6 billion to $13 billion. BP believes that the provision recorded at 31 December 2010 of $9.2 billion represents a reliable best estimate from within this range of possible outcomes.

How did BP record the $9.2 billion estimate in its 2010 financial statements? How would the accounting for this provision differ if BP had prepared its financial statements in accordance with U.S. GAAP?

I7-49. **Interpreting Bond Footnote Disclosures and Computing Effective Interest Rate**

LO3, 4
Foncière des Régions

In October 2012, French real estate company Foncière des Régions issued bonds with a total face value of €500 million. The bond proceeds were €504.087 million. The 2012 annual report has the following note.

Foncière des Régions launched a bond issue as described below:

Issue date.	19/10/2012
Issue amount (€M).	500
Nominal rate.	3.875%
Maturity	16/01/2018

a. Determine the annual interest payments. (*Hint*: Nominal rate of 3.875% is the coupon or face rate of interest.)

b. Assume the bonds are due in 5.25 years (October 2012 till January 2018). Determine the effective interest rate.

c. What amount of interest expense does the company report related to these bonds for the first full year after they are issued?

I7-50. **Analyzing Debt Terms, Yields, Prices, and Credit Ratings**

LO4, 5
Statoil ASA (STO)

Statoil ASA, headquartered in Stavanger, Norway, is a fully integrated petroleum company. The company uses IFRS to prepare its financial statements. Reproduced below is the long-term debt note from its 2015 annual report.

	Carrying amount in NOK billion		Fair value in NOK billion	
At 31 December	**2015**	**2014**	**2015**	**2014**
Total finance debt.	273.6	217.4	289.9	241.6
Less current portion	9.7	12.3	9.7	12.3
Non-current finance debt.	264.0	205.1	280.2	229.3

	Weighted average interest rates in %		Carrying amount in NOK billion at 31 December		Fair value in NOK billion at 31 December	
Unsecured bonds	**2015**	**2014**	**2015**	**2014**	**2015**	**2014**
US dollar (USD)	3.51	3.50	182.9	154.4	190.5	165.0
Euro (EUR)	2.28	3.99	63.4	37.6	66.0	43.8
Great Britain pound (GBP). . .	6.08	6.08	18.0	15.9	23.8	22.3
Norwegian kroner (NOK) . . .	4.18	4.18	3.0	3.0	3.3	3.5
Total			267.3	210.9	283.7	234.7

	At 31 December	
Non-current finance debt maturity profile (in NOK billion)	**2015**	**2014**
Year 2 and 3	54.9	27.3
Year 4 and 5	43.0	44.2
After 5 years	166.1	133.5
Total repayment of non-current finance debt.	264.0	205.1
Weighted average maturity (year).	9	9
Weighted average annual interest rate (%)	3.39	3.78

Reproduced below is a summary of the market values, at December 2016, of the Statoil ASA bonds maturing from 2017 to 2043.

Currency	Maturity Date	Amount Outstanding	Current Price	Coupon	Yield
Statoil Asa USD	08/15/2019	1,500.0	107.4	5.250	2.02
Statoil Asa USD	11/08/2043	750.0	105.7	4.800	4.43
Statoil Asa USD	08/17/2017	1,250.0	101.3	3.125	1.32

Required

a. What is the amount of total finance debt reported on Statoil's 2015 balance sheet? Of the total financial liabilities, what proportion is due within one year?

b. In what currencies has Statoil issued unsecured bonds? Why do companies borrow money in foreign currencies?

c. What are the scheduled maturities for Statoil's indebtedness? Why is information relating to a company's scheduled maturities of debt useful in analyzing financial condition?

d. Statoil's long-term debt is rated A+ by Standard and Poor's and rated Aa3 by Moody's. What factors would be important to consider in quantifying the relative riskiness of Statoil compared to other borrowers? Explain.

e. Statoil's $1,500 million, 5.25% notes traded at 107.4 or 107.4% of par, as of December 2016. What is the market value of these notes on that date? How is the difference between this market value and the $1,500 million face value reflected on Statoil's financial statements? What does the 107.4 price tell you about the general trend in interest rates since Statoil sold this bond issue? Explain.

f. Examine the yields to maturity of the bonds in the previous table. What relation do we observe between these yields and the maturities of the bonds? Explain why this relation applies in general.

LO1

Bombardier Inc.
(BDRBF)

I7-51.   Analyzing Contingent Liabilities: Warranty Reserves

Headquartered in Montreal, Quebec, Canada, **Bombardier Inc.** is a multinational aerospace and transportation company, founded in 1941. The company manufactures regional aircraft, business jets, mass transportation equipment, and recreational equipment and is also a financial services provider. Bombardier is a Fortune Global 500 company and operates two segments: BA (Aerospace) and BT (Transportation). Bombardier's 2015 annual report includes the following details about the company's warranty reserve.

Balance as at December 31, 2014.	$773
Additions.	360
Utilization	(244)
Reversals	(118)
Accretion expense	1
Effect of changes in discount rates	(1)
Effect of foreign currency exchange rate changes.	(46)
Balance as at December 31, 2015.	**$725**
Of which current	$562
Of which non-current	163
	$725

Required

a. In common language, explain what is a warranty reserve. When do companies create such reserves?

b. What amount is included on the 2015 balance sheet for warranty reserve?

c. What amount is included on the 2015 income statement related to warranties?

d. What is meant by "Utilization" in the table? What sort of costs does this entail?

I7-52. **Analyzing Debt Footnotes**

LO4
Valeant (VRX)

Headquartered in Montreal, Canada, Valeant Pharmaceuticals International Inc. is a multinational specialty pharmaceutical company that develops and markets prescription and non-prescription pharmaceuticals, principally in the areas of dermatology and neurology. The company is the largest pharmaceutical company in Canada with a portfolio of more than 500 products and 400 employees involved in R&D activities. The company is listed on both the NYSE and the Toronto Stock Exchange. Its 2015 income statement reported the following line item.

$ millions	2015	2014	2013
Loss of extinguishment on debt.	$20.0	$129.6	$65.0

Required

a. What is a loss on extinguishment of debt? Why does such a loss arise?

b. How does the company calculate the loss on extinguishment of debt?

c. Would we categorize this income statement item as operating or nonoperating?

Management Applications

MA7-53. **Coupon Rate versus Effective Rate**

LO3

Assume that you are the CFO of a company that intends to issue bonds to finance a new manufacturing facility. A subordinate suggests lowering the coupon rate on the bond to lower interest expense and to increase the profitability of your company. Is the rationale for this suggestion a good one? Explain.

MA7-54. **Ethics and Governance: Bond Covenants**

LO2

Because lenders do not have voting rights like shareholders do, they often reduce their risk by invoking various bond covenants that restrict the company's operating, financing and investing activities. For example, debt covenants often restrict the amount of debt that the company can issue (in relation to its equity) and impose operating restrictions (such as the ability to acquire other companies or to pay dividends). Failure to abide by these restrictions can have serious consequences, including forcing the company into bankruptcy and potential liquidation. Assume that you are on the board of directors of a company that issues bonds with such restrictions. What safeguards can you identify to ensure compliance with those restrictions?

Ongoing Project

(This ongoing project began in Module 1 and continues through most of the book; even if previous segments were not completed, the requirements are still applicable to any business analysis.) Review liabilities that arise from operating and financing transactions, including the type and quantity of both categories. The goal is to consider how the companies are financed and whether they can repay their obligations as they come due in the short and longer term.

1. *Accrued liabilities.* Accrued liabilities arise from ordinary operations and provide interest-free financing.

   - Are operating liabilities large for the companies? Compare common-size amounts. What proportion of total liabilities are operating?
   - What are the companies' main operating liabilities?
   - Are there substantial contingencies? What gives rise to these? Read the footnote and determine whether the company has recorded a liability on its balance sheet for these contingencies.

2. *Short and Long-Term Debt.* Examine the debt footnote and consider the following questions.

   - What is the common-size debt and how does that compare to published industry averages?
   - What types of debt does the company have? Is it publicly traded? Are there bank loans? Other types of debt?
   - When does the debt mature? Determine if there is a large proportion due in the next year or two. If so, can the company refinance given its current level of debt?
   - What is the average interest rate on debt? Compare it to the coupon rates reported.

- Read the footnote and the MD&A to see if there are any debt covenants and whether the company is in compliance.
- If the company has publicly traded debt, determine its current price. Sharp drops in bond prices could indicate a deterioration in the company's credit quality.

3. *Credit Ratings.*   Find the companies' credit ratings at two or three ratings agencies' websites.

- What are the credit ratings and how do they compare across the agencies? Are the two companies similarly rated?
- Have the ratings changed during the year? If so, why?
- Are the companies on a credit watch or a downgrade list?
- If possible, find a credit report online and read it to gain a better understanding of the companies' creditworthiness.
- Calculate the ratios in Exhibit 7.6 for your firms. Compare the ratios to those for firms with similar credit ratings. Do the credit ratings for the firms seem reasonable?

Solutions to Review Problems

Review 7-1—Solution (in $000s)

a. $70,000, the amount of the additional warranty liability arising from current-year sales.

b. $74,217 (from the current year end balance) + $70,000 − $85,000 = $59,217

c. Next year's income statement understates profit by the additional mistaken accrual of $20,000. Thus, next year's balance sheet reports a warranty liability that is $20,000 too high. In a subsequent period, assuming that the actual warranty costs incurred are, indeed, $20,000 lower than originally estimated, the company will not need to accrue as much warranty liability. Consequently, future profit will be higher until the reported warranty liability is reduced (by recognition of costs incurred) to an accurate level. Profit has, therefore, been shifted from next year to a future period(s).

Review 7-2—Solution

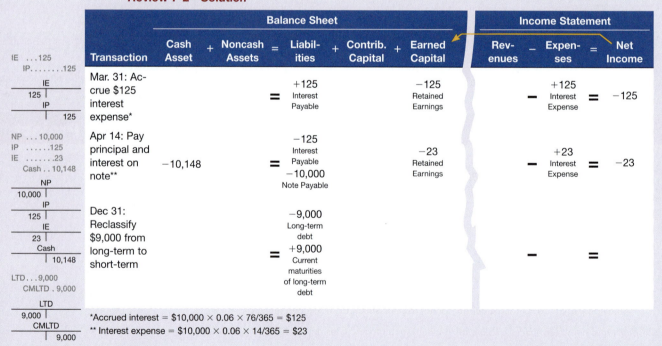

	Balance Sheet						**Income Statement**		
Transaction	**Cash Asset**	**+ Noncash Assets**	**= Liabil- ities**	**+ Contrib. Capital**	**+ Earned Capital**		**Rev- enues**	**− Expen- ses**	**= Net Income**
Mar. 31: Ac- crue $125 interest expense*			= +125 Interest Payable		−125 Retained Earnings			− +125 Interest Expense	= −125
Apr 14: Pay principal and interest on note**	−10,148		= −125 Interest Payable −10,000 Note Payable		−23 Retained Earnings			− +23 Interest Expense	= −23
Dec 31: Reclassify $9,000 from long-term to short-term			= −9,000 Long-term debt +9,000 Current maturities of long-term debt					−	=

IE ...125
IP........125
_____
IE
125
_____
IP
125

NP ...10,000
IP 125
IE 23
Cash .. 10,148
_____
NP
10,000
_____
IP
125
_____
IE
23
_____
Cash
10,148

LTD...9,000
CMLTD . 9,000
_____
LTD
9,000
_____
CMLTD
9,000

*Accrued interest = $10,000 × 0.06 × 76/365 = $125
** Interest expense = $10,000 × 0.06 × 14/365 = $23

Review 7-3—Solution

Issue price for $300,000, 15-year bonds that pay 10% interest discounted at 4% semiannually:

Present value of principal payment ($300,000 × 0.30832) . . . . $ 92,496
Present value of semiannual interest payments ($15,000 × 17.29203). 259,380

Issue price of bonds. $351,876

Calculator
N = 30
I/Yr = 4
PMT = −15,000
FV = −300,000

PV = 351,876

	A	B
1	Annual coupon rate	10%
2	Annual market rate	8%
3	Interest payments per year	2
4	Years to maturity	15
5	Face (par) value	300,000
6	Issue price	351,876
7	= PV(B2/B3,B4*B3,−B5*B1/B3,−B5, 0)	
8	= 351,876	

Issue price for $300,000, 15-year bonds that pay 10% interest, discounted at 6% semiannually:

Present value of principal payment ($300,000 × 0.17411) . . . . $ 52,233
Present value of semiannual interest payments ($15,000 × 13.76483). 206,472

Issue price of bonds. $258,705

Calculator
N = 30
I/Yr = 6
PMT = −15,000
FV = −300,000

PV = 258,706

	A	B
1	Annual coupon rate	10%
2	Annual market rate	12%
3	Interest payments per year	2
4	Years to maturity	15
5	Face (par) value	300,000
6	Issue price	258,706
7	= PV(B2/B3,B4*B3,−B5*B1/B3,−B5, 0)	
8	= 258,706	

Review 7-4—Solution

1.

Issue price for $300,000, 15-year bonds that pay 10% interest, discounted at 4% semiannually:

Present value of principal payment ($300,000 × 0.30832) . . . . $ 92,496
Present value of semiannual interest payments ($15,000 × 17.29203). 259,380

Issue price of bonds. $351,876

Calculator
N = 30
I/Yr = 4
PMT = −15,000
FV = −300,000

PV = 351,876

	A	B
1	Annual coupon rate	10%
2	Annual market rate	8%
3	Interest payments per year	2
4	Years to maturity	15
5	Face (par) value	300,000
6	Issue price	351,876
7	= PV(B2/B3,B4*B3,−B5*B1/B3,−B5, 0)	
8	= 351,876	

2.

	Balance Sheet					Income Statement		
Transaction	Cash Asset +	Noncash Assets =	Liabil- ities +	Contrib. Capital +	Earned Capital	Rev- enues −	Expen- ses =	Net Income
January 1: Issue 10% bonds	+351,876		+351,876 = Long-Term Debt			−	=	
June 30: Pay interest and amor- tize bond premium[1]	−15,000		−925 = Long-Term Debt		−14,075 Retained Earnings	+14,075 Interest − Expense	= −14,075	
December 31: Pay interest and amor- tize bond premium[2]	−15,000		−962 = Long-Term Debt		−14,038 Retained Earnings	+14,038 Interest − Expense	= −14,038	

Cash..351,876
  LTD..351,876

Cash
351,876 |
     LTD
     |351,876

IE ...14,075
LTD...   925
  Cash..15,000

     IE
14,075 |
     LTD
925 |
     Cash
     | 15,000

IE ...14,038
LTD...   962
  Cash..15,000

     IE
14,038 |
     LTD
962 |
     Cash
     | 15,000

[1] $300,000 × 0.10 × 6/12 = $15,000 cash payment; 0.04 × $351,876 = $14,075 interest expense; the difference of $925, is the bond premium amortization, which reduces the net bond carrying amount.

[2] 0.04 × ($351,876 − $925) = $14,038 interest expense. The difference between this amount and the $15,000 cash payment ($962) is the premium amortization, which reduces the net bond carrying amount.

3.

Period	Interest Expense	Cash Interest Paid	Premium Amortization	Premium Balance	Bond Payable, Net
0.........				51,876	351,876
1.........	14,075	15,000	925	50,951	350,951
2.........	14,038	15,000	962	49,989	349,989
3.........	14,000	15,000	1,000	48,989	348,989
4.........	13,960	15,000	1,040	47,949	347,949
5.........	13,918	15,000	1,082	46,867	346,867
6.........	13,875	15,000	1,125	45,742	345,742
7.........	13,830	15,000	1,170	44,572	344,572
8.........	13,783	15,000	1,217	43,355	343,355
9.........	13,734	15,000	1,266	42,089	342,089
10.........	13,684	15,000	1,316	40,773	340,773

4. Comcast would have to pay $447,163 to repurchase the bonds. This would yield a loss on debt repurchase of $106,390 computed as $447,163 − $340,773.

Calculator
N = 20
I/Yr = 2
PMT = −15,000
FV = −300,000
PV = 447,163

X	A	B
1	Annual coupon rate	10%
2	Annual market rate	4%
3	Interest payments per year	2
4	Years to maturity	10
5	Face (par) value	300,000
6	Issue price	447,163
7	= PV(B2/B3,B4*B3,−B5*B1/B3,−B5, 0)	
8	= 447,163	

Review 7-5—Solution

Ratio	Result	Rating
Operating margin	14.2%	Baa
Debt/EBITDA	2.1	Baa
FFO/Debt	32.9%	Baa
EBITA/Interest Expense	3.9	Ba
Overall composite		**Baa**

Review 7-6—Solution

Using the Excel formula PV(rate,nper, pmt,[fv],[type])

a. $5,449.13

b. $5,000.00

c. $4,594.46

Module 8

Stock Transactions, Dividends, and EPS

Learning Objectives

LO1 Examine stock as a financing source and explain its various features. (p. 8-3)

LO2 Analyze stock issuances and repurchases. (p. 8-8)

LO3 Interpret stock-based compensation, including restricted stock and options. (p. 8-12)

LO4 Analyze cash dividends and their financial effects. (p. 8-16)

LO5 Analyze stock splits and stock dividends and their financial effects. (p. 8-19)

LO6 Interpret accumulated other comprehensive income and its components. (p. 8-20)

LO7 Analyze convertible securities and their financial effects. (p. 8-23)

LO8 Interpret earnings per share. (p. 8-24)

JNJ

Market cap: $283,000 mil
Total assets: $133,411 mil
Revenues: $70,074 mil
Net income: $15,409 mil

Johnson & Johnson manufactures and sells over $70 billion of health care products annually. Many of its products are well-known such as Band-Aid bandages, Neutrogena skin care products, Listerine mouth wash, Tylenol headache capsules, Visine eye care, and the Johnson & Johnson line of baby care products.

The company has been very successful and its market capitalization (the market value of its stock, calculated as share price × outstanding common shares) was $283 billion at year-end 2015. Its market capitalization is nearly four times the $71,150 million book value of its stock as reported in the equity section of the balance sheet.

Analysis of owner financing requires us to understand the types of securities that companies issue including common stock, preferred stock, and convertible securities. We should be able to examine the equity section of the balance sheet and know how numbers are computed and what they reflect. We also must understand why we often see a large difference between the price that investors pay for Johnson & Johnson's common stock at the initial public offering and the stock's current value in the market or the stock price when Johnson & Johnson purchases its own shares.

Many companies use stock to compensate employees including the use of restricted stock awards and units, stock options, and employee share purchase plans. It is important for us to understand the implications on owner financing of such compensation. It is also important for us to understand the value and limitations of the earnings per share (EPS) ratio often quoted in the financial press. [Source: *Johnson & Johnson*, 2015 10-K.]

Johnson & Johnson Equity Measures	
Shareholders' equity per share	$ 25.82
Market price per share (year-end close)	102.72
Basic earnings per share of common stock	5.56
Diluted earnings per share of common stock	5.48
Common stock par value per share	1.00
Cash dividends per share	2.95

© Shutterstock

Road Map

LO	Learning Objective | Topics	Page	eLecture	Guided Example	Assignments
8–1	**Examine stock as a financing source and explain its various features.** Equity Terms :: Stockholders' Equity :: Preferred Stock :: Common Stock	8-3	e8–1	Review 8-1	1, 2, 3, 5, 6, 7, 11, 15, 21, 24, 37, 40, 46, 48, 49, 52, 53, 54, 55, 62, 63, 66
8–2	**Analyze stock issuances and repurchases.** Stock Issuance :: Stock Repurchase :: Retirement of Repurchases	8-8	e8–2	Review 8-2	7, 9, 10, 15, 19, 22, 35, 36, 37, 40, 46, 49, 50, 52, 53, 54, 55, 62, 63, 64, 66
8–3	**Interpret stock-based compensation, including restricted stock and options.** Compensation Types :: Compensation Accounting :: Disclosures	8-12	e8–3	Review 8-3	14, 17, 26, 37, 38, 51, 54, 55, 58, 59, 61, 64, 66
8–4	**Analyze cash dividends and their financial effects.** Dividend Payout :: Dividend Yield :: Financial Effects	8-16	e8–4	Review 8-4	4, 12, 13, 15, 25, 28, 29, 31, 39, 41, 42, 43, 44, 54, 62, 65, 66
8–5	**Analyze stock splits and stock dividends and their financial effects.** Stock Splits :: Stock Dividends :: Financial Effects	8-19	e8–5	Review 8-5	8, 23, 27, 29, 32, 45, 65
8–6	**Interpret accumulated other comprehensive income and its components.** AOCI Disclosure and Interpretation :: Other Comprehensive Income	8-20	e8–6	Review 8-6	15, 16, 33, 50, 54, 55, 62, 66
8–7	**Analyze convertible securities and their financial effects.** Disclosures and Interpretation :: Financial Effects	8-23	e8–7	Review 8-7	18, 34, 47, 50, 56, 57, 60
8–8	**Interpret earnings per share.** Basic EPS :: Diluted EPS	8-24	e8–8	Review 8-8	14, 20, 30, 47, 56

Contributed Capital

- Stock Basics
- Book Value
- Market Value
- Statement of Equity
- Preferred Stock
- Common Stock
- Stock Issuance
- Stock Repurchase
- Stock Compensation

Earned Capital

- Cash Dividends
- Stock Dividends
- Stock Splits
- Accumulated Other Comprehensive Income
- Convertible Securities
- Earnings per Share— Basic and Diluted

Stockholders' Equity and Classes of Stock

eLectures
MBC
LO1
Examine stock as a financing source and explain its various features.

Companies raise funds by selling shares of stock to investors in addition to borrowing. But, unlike debtholders and other lenders to the company, shareholders elect a Board of Directors that hires executives to oversee company operations. While interest and principal paid to lenders is fixed by contract, shareholders have no contractual return. There is, however, the potential for shareholders to receive dividends and derive large value from future price appreciation of company stock.

The stockholders' equity section of the balance sheet reports the book value of the stockholders' investment, as determined under accounting rules (GAAP). This measurement of book value differs from the market value of stockholders' investment, which is computed as share price multiplied by the number of shares outstanding. Market value is determined by supply and demand for the company's outstanding shares in the marketplace as shares are actively traded among investors.

We explain the components of stockholders' equity section of the balance sheet, the different classes of stock, how we account for share issuances (sales) and repurchases (Treasury stock), and the reporting for dividends to shareholders, stock splits, and convertible securities. We also describe the concept of other comprehensive income and two measures of earnings per share (EPS) that are regularly discussed in the financial press.

Stockholders' Equity Accounts

Stockholders' equity arises on the balance sheet when the shareholders of the company authorize management to issue (sell) shares of stock. After that, the company's management is free to manage the company, consistent with its policies and under the watchful eye of the Board of Directors (representatives of the shareholders who are elected by them and look out for their interests). Over time, stockholders expect their equity to increase and the stockholders' equity section of the balance sheet represents a score card, in a sense, that records how well management has performed with the capital entrusted to them by the shareholders.

The stockholders' equity section of Johnson & Johnson's (JNJ) balance sheet, shown in Exhibit 8.1, includes the following accounts (see the Business Insight box for definitions).

- **Preferred stock.** Johnson & Johnson is authorized to issue up to 2,000,000 preferred shares, but to date has not issued any—the balance is $0.

- **Common stock.** The balance sheet reveals a number of details about the Johnson & Johnson common stock:

  - **Par value.** The par value of its common stock (as stated in its charter) is $1 per share.

  - **Authorized shares.** It can issue up to 4,320,000,000 shares without further approval from shareholders.

  - **Issued shares.** To date, it has sold (issued) 3,119,843,000 shares at the $1 par value and thus, the common stock account has a balance of $3,120 million. It does not report any additional paid-in capital. We can infer that no shares were sold for more than the $1 par value. (See the Coca-Cola illustration on page 8-9 for an example of additional paid-in capital, which Coca-Cola labels "capital surplus.")

■ **Accumulated Other Comprehensive Income (AOCI).** This account reflects the cumulative total of changes to stockholders' equity other than from transactions with owners and transactions reflected in net income. This account can be a positive or negative amount.

■ **Retained earnings.** Defined as the cumulative sum of net income recorded since its inception less all of the dividends the company has ever paid out to shareholders, which nets to $103,879 million. Retained earnings increased during the year, as its net income exceeded the amount of dividends paid out.

■ **Treasury stock.** The company routinely repurchases its own shares on the open market. On January 3, 2016, the company held 364,681,000 shares for which it paid $22,684 million. Like all balance sheet accounts, the treasury stock balance is a cumulative amount that reflects open-market repurchases and subsequent resale of its shares. The account has increased during the year, which implies that Johnson & Johnson purchased additional shares during the current year, net of any shares sold back to the market or granted to employees.

Exhibit 8.1 ■ Stockholders' Equity Section From Johnson & Johnson's Balance Sheet

Shareholders' equity ($ millions, except par value per share)	Jan. 3, 2016	Dec. 28, 2014
Preferred stock — without par value (authorized and unissued 2,000,000 shares). . . .	$ —	$ —
Common stock — par value $1.00 per share		
(authorized 4,320,000,000 shares; issued 3,119,843,000 shares)	3,120	3,120
Accumulated other comprehensive income.	(13,165)	(10,722)
Retained earnings	103,879	97,245
	93,834	89,643
Less: common stock held in treasury, at cost		
(364,681,000 shares and 336,620,000 shares).	22,684	19,891
Total shareholders' equity	71,150	69,752
Total liabilities and shareholders' equity.	$133,411	$130,358

Book Value per Share A measure commonly used by analysts and the financial press, is *book value per share*. This is the equity (net book value) of the company that is available to common shareholders and is defined as:

$$\frac{\text{Book value}}{\text{per share}} = \left(\frac{\text{Stockholders'}}{\text{equity}} - \frac{\text{Preferred}}{\text{stock}}\right) \Big/ \frac{\text{Number of common}}{\text{shares outstanding}}$$

Johnson & Johnson's book value per share at the end of 2015 follows:

$$\frac{\text{JNJ book value}}{\text{per share}} = \frac{\$71,150}{\text{million}} \Big/ \left(\frac{\$3,119.843}{\text{million shares}} - \frac{364.681}{\text{million shares}}\right) = \$25.82 \text{ per share}$$

Market-to-Book In comparison, JNJ's market price per share was $102.72 on December 31, 2015 (the last trading day before JNJ's fiscal year end). The ratio of market price per share to book value per share is the **market-to-book ratio**. For JNJ, at year-end 2015, market-to-book was 3.98. The median market-to-book for the S&P 500 companies at the end of 2015 was 2.88. So, the market values JNJ higher (relative to the book value of its equity) than the median S&P 500 company.

Business Insight ■ Stockholders' Equity Terms and Phrases

Following are common terms and phrases relating to stockholders' equity that we encounter in the financial press.

- **Board of directors.** Shareholders' elected representatives who hire the CEO and oversee company operations.
- **Preferred stock.** Generally non-voting shares that convey, 1) a dividend preference—preferred stockholders receive dividends on their shares before common stockholders, and 2) a liquidation preference—if a company fails and is liquidated, the assets are sold and liabilities paid, then any remaining cash is paid first to preferred shareholders before payment is made to common shareholders.
- **Common stock.** Shares that allow the holder to elect the company's board of directors and vote on important company issues such as whether to adopt employee benefit plans, acquire other companies, divest current companies, and reorganize or liquidate the company. Common shares receive dividends after preferred shareholders have been paid their required dividends.
- **Dividends.** Company profit that is distributed to shareholders. Profit not distributed as dividends is reinvested in the business and shown on the balance sheet as retained earnings.
- **Declaration date.** The date on which the board of directors authorizes the payment of the dividend (declares the dividend).
- **Date of record.** The date on which the company prepares the list of current stockholders to which the dividend will be paid.
- **Date of payment.** The date on which the dividend is paid to stockholders (who held the stock on the date of record).
- **Residual claim.** When a company fails and is liquidated, all assets are sold and liabilities paid. Each shareholder is entitled to their proportional share of the residual cash, if any. Shareholders are called residual claimants.
- **Authorized shares.** The maximum number of shares that a company can sell (issue) without approval from the shareholders.
- **Issued shares.** The number of shares that have been sold (issued) to date. This is a cumulative number.
- **Initial public offering (IPO).** An initial sale of stock to the public.
- **Par value** and **Additional paid-in capital.** The per share amount (stated in a company's charter) that will be recorded in the common stock account when stock is sold (issued). Par value is unrelated to the stock's market value. The excess of the issue price over the par value is added to the Additional paid-in capital account (also called capital surplus, or capital in excess of par).
- **Paid-in capital.** The *total* amount of cash and other assets paid in to the company by stockholders in exchange for capital stock.
- **Outstanding shares.** The number of shares that are outstanding in the market, determined as the number of issued shares less the number of shares that have been subsequently repurchased by the company.
- **Market price.** The published price at which a share of stock can be purchased ("ask") or sold ("bid").
- **Stock split.** Proportional issuance of shares to stockholders (and a consequent proportional reduction in par value) with no exchange of cash. A stock split does not affect the value of the company. Because the number of outstanding shares increases, while the value of the company remains unchanged, the share price declines proportionally. One goal of a stock split is to reduce the share price to make the stock more marketable.

Statement of Stockholders' Equity

The statement of stockholders' equity reconciles the beginning and ending balances of the stockholders' equity accounts. It highlights the following.

- How net income and dividends impacts retained earnings.
- Cash raised from new shares issued.
- Cash used to repurchase shares in the open market.
- Changes in key balance sheet accounts not recorded in net income or not arising from transactions with shareholders. Each year, these changes are included in an account called **Other Comprehensive Income** (OCI), and the *cumulative* sum of that account is reflected in an equity account called **Accumulated Other Comprehensive Income** (AOCI).

Johnson & Johnson's statement of stockholders' equity, shown in Exhibit 8.2, reveals the following key activities from 2015.

❶ Net income is added to retained earnings, increasing it by $15,409 million.

❷ Cash dividends paid to stockholders reduce retained earnings by $8,173 million.

❸ JNJ's policy is to use treasury shares for employee stock-based compensation plans—see discussion of stock-based compensation later in the module. Treasury stock always has a negative balance because stock buybacks are the opposite of a stock sale. In the statement of stockholders' equity, the positive $2,497 indicates that treasury stock is *reduced* by $2,497 million, which is the *original cost* of the treasury shares used for compensation during the year. The treasury shares issued had a *fair value* of $1,920 million, lower than the cost of the shares. The $577 million difference between fair value of the shares issued ($1,920 million) and the cost ($2,497 million) is deducted from retained earnings.

❹ JNJ purchased additional stock on the open market during the year at a cost of $5,290 million, which is shown as a negative number, increasing the treasury stock account. A portion of the stock repurchase was related to a general share buy-back program. Another portion was to forestall a potential drop in stock price from a dilution related to the stock-based compensation plans.

❺ JNJ reported other comprehensive loss of $(2,443) million—we explain this later in the accumulated other comprehensive income section of this module. Changes in AOCI can be positive or negative.

Exhibit 8.2 ■ Johnson & Johnson's Statement of Stockholders' Equity

$ millions	Total	Retained Earnings	Accumulated Other Comprehensive Income	Common Stock Issued	Treasury Stock
Balance, December 28, 2014..	$69,752	$ 97,245	$(10,722)	$3,120	$(19,891)
❶ Net earnings...............	15,409	15,409			
❷ Cash dividends paid.........	(8,173)	(8,173)			
❸ Employee compensation and stock option plans	1,920	(577)			2,497
❹ Repurchase of common stock	(5,290)				(5,290)
Other.....................	(25)	(25)			
❺ Other comprehensive income (loss), net of tax	(2,443)		(2,443)		
Balance, January 3, 2016.....	$71,150	$103,879	$(13,165)	$3,120	$(22,684)

Preferred Stock

Preferred Stock is a multi-use security with a number of desirable features. In addition to usual dividend and liquidation preferences, preferred stock has two other common features.

■ **Yield.** Preferred stock can be structured to provide investors with a dividend yield that is similar to an interest rate on a bond. Dividends, unlike interest expense, are not deductible for tax purposes. Therefore, the after-tax cost to the company for preferred dividends is higher than the effective interest rate on a bond.

■ **Conversion privileges.** Preferred stock can contain an option that allows investors to convert their preferred shares into common shares at a pre-determined number of common shares per preferred share.

Both of these features are illustrated in the Dow Chemical convertible preferred stock as reported on its balance sheet and related footnote.

At December 31 (In millions, except share amounts)	2015	2014
Stockholders' Equity		
Preferred stock, series A ($1.00 par, $1,000 liquidation preference, 4,000,000 shares)	$4,000	$4,000

> **Cumulative Convertible Perpetual Preferred Stock, Series A.** Equity securities in the form of Cumulative Convertible Perpetual Preferred Stock, Series A were issued on April 1, 2009 to Berkshire Hathaway Inc. in the amount of $3 billion (3 million shares) and the Kuwait Investment Authority in the amount of $1 billion (1 million shares). The Company will pay cumulative dividends on preferred series A at a rate of 8.5 percent per annum in either cash, shares of common stock, or any combination thereof, at the option of the Company . . . Shareholders of preferred series A may convert all or any portion of their shares, at their option, at any time, into shares of the Company's common stock at an initial conversion rate of 24.2010 shares of common stock for each share of preferred series A.

Dow's convertible preferred stock pays a dividend of 8.5% of par value, meaning that it will pay preferred shareholders an annual dividend of $340 million ($4,000 million × 8.5%). The yield to investors is higher than the effective rate on the company's debt securities, and the preferred shares are convertible into common shares at a pre-determined conversion ratio of 24.2010 common shares for each preferred share.

Upon conversion, preferred shareholders will exchange their 8.5% preferred stock for common stock with a dividend of $1.84 per share—this is a 3.5% yield based on a $52 historical stock price. (They also relinquish their liquidation preference—senior position in bankruptcy—although this is only an issue if Dow is in financial difficulty.) In return, they will enjoy any future price appreciation in common stock. The preferred stockholders' conversion decision depends upon their evaluation of Dow's future prospects.

Common Stock

Johnson & Johnson has one class of common stock that has the following attributes (see Exhibit 8.1).

- A par value of $1.00 per share. **Par value** is an arbitrary amount set when the company was formed and has no relation to, or impact on, the stock's market value. Generally, par value is irrelevant from an analysis perspective. It is only used to allocate proceeds from stock issuances between the two contributed capital accounts on the balance sheet: common stock and additional paid-in capital.

- 4,320,000,000 shares of stock have been **authorized** for issuance. The company cannot issue (sell) more shares than have been authorized. If more shares are needed, say for an acquisition, the stockholders must vote to authorize more shares.

- To date, JNJ has **issued** (sold) 3,119,843,000 shares of common. The number of issued shares is a cumulative amount. Year-over-year changes in the number of issued shares represent the number of shares of stock issued in the current year.

- To date, JNJ has repurchased 364,681,000 shares from its stockholders at a cumulative cost of $22,684 million. These shares are currently held in the company's treasury, hence the name **treasury stock**. These shares neither have voting rights nor do they receive dividends.

- Number of **outstanding shares** is equal to the issued shares less treasury shares. There were 2,755,162,000 (3,119,843,000 − 364,681,000) shares outstanding at the end of 2015.

- Number of outstanding common shares multiplied by the market price per share yields the **market capitalization** (or *market cap*) for the company. As of December 31, 2015, JNJ's market capitalization was $283 billion (2,755,162,000 shares outstanding × $102.72 per share).

Many companies report an additional equity account called **noncontrolling interest**. This account arises when the company controls a subsidiary but does not own all of the subsidiary's stock. That is, the company owns > 50% of the stock, but less than 100%. The noncontrolling interest is the portion of the subsidiary's stock NOT owned by the company. The noncontrolling interest account increases with any additional investment made by the noncontrolling shareholders and by their share of the subsidiary's net income whose common stock they own. The account decreases by any dividends paid to the noncontrolling shareholders and by share of any net losses of the subsidiary. For most companies, the dollar amount of noncontrolling interest is small as illustrated in the following excerpt from the equity section of PepsiCo's 2015 balance sheet.

In millions, except per share amounts	2015	2014
PepsiCo Common Shareholders' Equity		
Common stock, par value 1 2/3¢ per share (authorized 3,600 shares, issued, net of repurchased common stock at par value: 1,448 and 1,488 shares, respectively)	$ 24	$ 25
Capital in excess of par value	4,076	4,115
Retained earnings	50,472	49,092
Accumulated other comprehensive loss	(13,319)	(10,669)
Repurchased common stock, in excess of par value (418 and 378 shares, respectively)	(29,185)	(24,985)
Total PepsiCo Common Shareholders' Equity	12,068	17,578
Noncontrolling interests	**107**	**110**
Total Equity	$12,030	$17,548

The $107 million of noncontrolling interest that PepsiCo reports, compared with $12,030 million of total equity, is typical. For comparison, the median noncontrolling interest as a percent of total liabilities and equity for the S&P 500 companies in 2015 was 0.04% (only a dozen companies in the S&P 500 report noncontrolling interest as a percent of total liabilities and equity of greater than 10%). We further explain noncontrolling interest in a later module.

LO1 **Review 8-1**

Stockholders' equity reflects owner financing of an enterprise.

Required
For each of the following, (1) indicate whether the statement is true or false regarding stockholders' equity, and (2) for any identified false statement, indicate how to correct that statement.

___ *a.*   Stockholders' equity represents the market value of the company.
___ *b.*   Stockholders do not manage the company directly, but oversee its operations through its Board of Directors.
___ *c.*   Issued shares represents the number of shares that have been sold to investors.
___ *d.*   Outstanding shares represents the number of shares issued less the number of shares repurchased by the company.
___ *e.*   Preferred stock is entitled to the same per share dividends as common stock.
___ *f.*   Treasury stock represents the cumulative total cost of shares that the company has repurchased, net of any subsequent sales of the treasury shares.

Solution on p. 8-52.

Stock Transactions

Stock Issuance

eLectures **LO2**
MBC   Analyze stock issuances and repurchases.

Companies issue stock to obtain cash and other assets for use in their business. Stock issuances increase assets (cash) by the issue proceeds: the number of shares sold multiplied by the price of the stock on the issue date. Equity increases by the same amount, which is reflected in contributed capital accounts. If the stock has a par value, the common stock account increases by the number of shares sold multiplied by its par value. The additional paid-in capital account increases by the remainder. Stock can also be issued as "no-par" or as "no-par with a stated value." For no-par stock, the common stock account is increased by the entire proceeds of the sale and no amount is assigned to additional paid-in capital. For no-par stock with a stated value, the stated value is treated just like par value, that is, common stock is increased by the number of shares multiplied by the stated value, and the remainder is assigned to the additional paid-in capital account.

Stock Issuance Financial Effects To illustrate, assume that JNJ issues 1,000 shares with a $1.00 par value common stock at a market price of $100 cash per share. This stock issuance has the following financial statement effects.

		Balance Sheet							Income Statement		
Transaction	Cash Asset	+	Noncash Assets	=	Liabil- ities	+	Contrib. Capital	+	Earned Capital	Rev- enues	−	Expen- ses	=	Net Income
Issue 1,000 common shares with $1 par value for $100 cash per share	+100,000		=				+1,000 Common Stock +99,000 Additional Paid-In Capital				−		=	

Cash..100,000
  CS......1,000
  APIC...99,000

Cash
100,000 |
  CS
  | 1,000
  APIC
  | 99,000

Specifically, the stock issuance affects the financial statements as follows.

1. Cash increases by $100,000 (1,000 shares × $100 per share).
2. Common stock increases by the par value of shares sold: 1,000 shares × $1 par value = $1,000.
3. Additional paid-in capital increases by the $99,000 difference between the issue proceeds and par value ($100,000 − $1,000).

Once shares are issued, they are traded in the open market among investors. The proceeds of those sales and their associated gains and losses, as well as fluctuations in the company's stock price subsequent to issuance, do not affect the issuing company and are not recorded in its accounting records.

Stock Disclosures and Interpretation Using our stock issuance illustration above, we can interpret the common stock and additional paid-in capital (capital surplus) disclosures on Coca-Cola's balance sheet.

December 31 (In millions, except par value)	2015	2014
The Coca-Cola Company Shareowners' Equity		
Common stock, $0.25 par value; Authorized—11,200 shares; Issued—7,040 and 7,040 shares, respectively............................	$ 1,760	$ 1,760
Capital surplus...	14,016	13,154
Reinvested earnings..	65,018	63,408
Accumulated other comprehensive income (loss)........................	(10,174)	(5,777)
Treasury stock, at cost — 2,716 and 2,674 shares, respectively..............	(45,066)	(42,225)
Equity attributable to shareowners of the Coca-Cola Company..............	$25,554	$30,320

IFRS Alert
Stock terminology can differ between IFRS and GAAP. Under IFRS, common stock is called *share capital* and additional paid-in capital (APIC) is called *share premium*. Despite different terminology, the accounting is similar.

As of December 31, 2015, Coca-Cola has issued 7,040 million shares of common stock for total proceeds of $15,776 million ($1,760 million + $14,016 million). The $1,760 million in common stock is the total par value for the 7,040 million shares ($0.25 × $7,040 million). The $14,016 million capital surplus account (another title for additional paid-in capital) is the difference between the $15,776 million total issue proceeds and the $1,760 million par value. The average price at which Coke issued the 7,040 million shares is $2.24 ($15,776 million/7,040 million).

Research shows that, historically, companies issuing equity securities experience unusually low stock returns for several years following those offerings. Evidence suggests that this poor performance is partly due to overly optimistic estimates of long-term growth by equity analysts. That optimism causes offering prices to be too high. This over-optimism is most pronounced when the analyst is employed by the brokerage firm that underwrites the stock issue. There is also evidence that companies manage earnings upward prior to an equity offering. This means the observed decrease in returns following an issuance likely reflects the market's negative reaction, on average, to lower earnings, especially if the company fails to meet analysts' forecasts.

Stock Repurchase (Treasury Stock)

JNJ has repurchased 364,681,000 shares of its common stock for a cumulative cost of $22,684 million. One reason a company repurchases shares is because it believes that the market undervalues them. The logic is that the repurchase sends a favorable signal to the market about the company's financial condition, which positively impacts its share price and, thus, allows it to resell those shares for a "gain." Any such gain on resale, however, is *never* reflected in the income statement. Instead, any excess of the resale price over the repurchase price is added to additional paid-in capital. GAAP prohibits companies from reporting gains and losses from stock transactions with their own stockholders.

Another reason companies repurchase shares is to offset the dilutive effects of an employee stock option program. When an employee exercises stock options, the number of shares outstanding increases. Because net income is unchanged, these additional shares reduce earnings per share and are, therefore, *dilutive*. In response, many companies repurchase an equivalent number of shares in the open market to keep outstanding shares constant.

A stock repurchase reduces the size of the company (cash declines and, thus, total assets decline). A repurchase has the opposite financial statement effects from a stock issuance. That is, cash decreases by the price of the shares repurchased (number of shares repurchased multiplied by the purchase price per share), and stockholders' equity decreases by the same amount. The decrease in equity is recorded in a contra equity account called treasury stock. Treasury stock (the contra equity account) has a negative balance, which reduces stockholders' equity. Thus, when the treasury stock contra equity account increases, total stockholders' equity decreases.

When the company subsequently reissues (sells) treasury stock there is no accounting gain or loss. Instead, the difference between the proceeds received and the original purchase price of the treasury stock is reflected as an increase or decrease to additional paid-in capital.

Stock Repurchase Financial Effects To illustrate, assume that 200 common shares of JNJ previously issued for $100 are repurchased for $90 cash per share. This repurchase has the following financial statement effects.

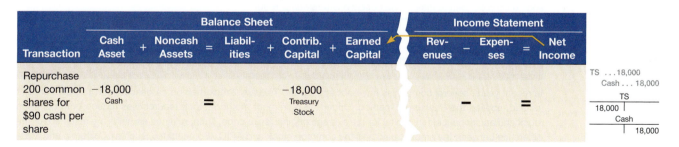

Assets (cash) and stockholders' equity both decrease. Treasury stock (a contra equity account) increases by $18,000, which reduces stockholders' equity by that amount.

Reissuing Treasury Stock Assume that these 200 shares of treasury stock are subsequently resold for $95 cash per share. This resale of treasury stock has the following financial statement effects.

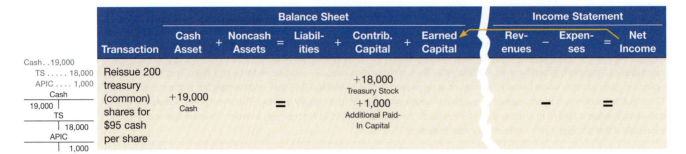

	Balance Sheet								Income Statement				
Transaction	**Cash Asset**	**+**	**Noncash Assets**	**=**	**Liabil- ities**	**+**	**Contrib. Capital**	**+**	**Earned Capital**		**Rev- enues**	**– Expen- ses**	**= Net Income**
Reissue 200 treasury (common) shares for $95 cash per share	+19,000 Cash			=			+18,000 Treasury Stock +1,000 Additional Paid- In Capital					–	=

Cash.. 19,000
  TS 18,000
   APIC 1,000
    Cash
  19,000 |
     TS
            | 18,000
    APIC
            | 1,000

Cash assets increase by $19,000 (200 shares × $95 per share), the treasury stock account is reduced by the $18,000 cost of the treasury shares issued (thus increasing contributed capital), and the $1,000 excess (200 shares × $5 per share) is reported as an increase in additional paid-in capital. (If the reissue price is below the repurchase price, then additional paid-in capital is reduced until it reaches a zero balance, after which retained earnings is reduced.) Again, there is no effect on the income statement as companies are prohibited from reporting gains and losses from repurchases and reissuances of their own stock.

Treasury Stock Disclosures and Interpretation The treasury stock section of JNJ's balance sheet is reproduced below.

In millions, except for share amounts	2015	2014
Common stock held in treasury, at cost (364,681,000 shares and 336,620,000 shares)	$22,684	$19,891

JNJ repurchased a cumulative total of 364,681,000 shares of common stock for $22,684 million, an average repurchase price of $62.20 per share. These shares, while legally owned by JNJ, have no voting rights and receive no dividends. Treasury shares can be reissued should JNJ need to raise capital or acquire another entity. Treasury shares can also be used to compensate employees and executives. Sometimes, companies "retire" treasury stock. In that event, the treasury stock account is reduced by the cost of the treasury shares retired (thus increasing stockholders' equity) and the common stock account is likewise reduced (thus reducing stockholders' equity by the same amount). When treasury shares are retired, total stockholders' equity remains unchanged.

IFRS Alert
Accounting for stock repurchases under IFRS is similar to GAAP except that IFRS provides little guidance on how to allocate the treasury stock to equity accounts. Thus, repurchases can be recorded as an increase to treasury stock, or as a decrease to common stock and APIC (share capital and premium), retained earnings (reserves), or some combination.

Managerial Decision ■ You Are the Chief Financial Officer

As CFO, you believe that your company's stock price is lower than its real value. You are considering various alternatives to increase that price, including the repurchase of company stock in the market. What are some factors you should consider before making your decision? [Answer, p. 8-30]

Business Insight ■ Companies Increasingly Choose Retirement for Treasury Stock

In recent years, several companies have not applied the *Treasury Stock* method as described in this section, but instead, applied the *Retirement* method. Under the retirement method, stock repurchases reduce both common stock and additional paid-in capital for the average original issue price. Then, retained earnings are adjusted for the difference between the amount paid and the common stock and APIC. (Some states, such as California and Massachusetts, now require this method.)

The following stockholders' equity statement from Microsoft demonstrates the retirement method. We see that the repurchase cost of $15,972 million reduces common stock (and APIC) by $3,689 million and retained earnings by $12,283 million. Interestingly, this helps explain why Microsoft reports such a low balance for retained earnings.

continued

Microsoft's Statement of Stockholders' Equity

Year Ended June 30 (In millions)	2016
Common stock and paid-in capital	
Balance, beginning of period	$68,465
Common stock issued	668
Common stock repurchased	(3,689)
Stock-based compensation expense	2,668
Other, net	66
Balance, end of period	68,178
Retained earnings	
Balance, beginning of period	9,096
Net income	16,798
Common stock cash dividends	(11,329)
Common stock repurchased	(12,283)
Balance, end of period	2,282
Accumulated other comprehensive income	
Balance, beginning of period	2,522
Other comprehensive income (loss).	(985)
Balance, end of period	1,537
Total stockholders' equity	$71,997

Following is the equity section of Coca-Cola Company balance sheet for the fiscal quarter ended April 1, 2016.

COCA-COLA COMPANY SHAREOWNERS' EQUITY (In millions, except par value)	Apr. 01, 2016	Dec. 31, 2015
Common stock, $0.25 par value; Authorized—11,200 shares; Issued—7,040 and 7,040 shares, respectively	$ 1,760	$ 1,760
Capital surplus	14,507	14,016
Reinvested earnings.	64,985	65,018
Accumulated other comprehensive income (loss)	(10,789)	(10,174)
Treasury stock, at cost — 2,708 and 2,716 shares, respectively.	(45,549)	(45,066)
Equity attributable to shareowners of the Coca-Cola Company	24,914	25,554
Equity attributable to noncontrolling interests	215	210
Total equity	$25,129	$25,764

Required

a. How much additional common stock did Coca-Cola issue during the first quarter of 2016? Explain.

b. Assume that Coca-Cola issued 400,000 shares during the first quarter at $45 per share. Use the financial statement effects template to record this transaction.

c. Assume that during the first quarter, Coca-Cola purchased approximately 22 million shares on the open market at an average price of $43.45 per share. Use the financial statement effects template to record this transaction. Round numbers to millions.

d. The company sold 30 million shares of treasury stock for $964 million. The treasury shares had an original cost of $15.77 per share. Determine the effect of this transaction on the treasury stock and capital surplus accounts. Round numbers to millions.

Solution on p. 8-53.

Stock-Based Compensation

Common stock has been an important component of executive compensation for decades. The general idea follows: If the company executives own stock they will have an incentive to increase its value. This aligns the executives' interests with those of other stockholders. Although the strength of this alignment is the subject of much debate, its logic compels boards of directors of most American companies to use stock-based compensation.

LO3 Interpret stock-based compensation, including restricted stock and options.

Characteristics of Stock-Based Compensation Plans

Companies use a range of stock-based compensation plans. The Business Insight box below provides details of the types of plans, but they share the following features.

■ **Create incentives for employees to think and act like shareholders.** The amount of the stock award is often tied to corporate performance targets including sales, income, and stock price. Stock-based compensation plans motivate employees to work hard and make decisions that improve company performance.

■ **Encourage employee retention and longevity.** With most plans, employees earn the right to own or purchase shares over time. The period of time over which ownership rights are earned is called the *vesting* period (usually a few years). During this vesting period, employees have greater incentive to stay with the company.

Johnson & Johnson's compensation plans include stock options, restricted stock units (RSUs), and performance share units (these are RSUs that will only be awarded if certain performance targets are met, which creates additional incentives for employees who receive them).

Business Insight ■ Types of Stock-Based Compensation Plans

The following stock-based compensation plans are widely in use today and we often see companies maintain more than one of these plans at the same time.

• **Restricted stock.** Shares are issued to the employee but the employee is *not* free to sell the shares during a restriction period. This creates an incentive for the employee to remain with the company. During the restriction period, the employee has the rights of a shareholder, other than the ability to sell the shares.

• **Restricted stock units (RSUs).** Employee is awarded the right to receive a specified number of shares (or cash equivalent) after a vesting period. Unlike restricted stock, shares are not issued to the employee until after the restriction period, at which time the employee has all of the rights of a shareholder (but not during the vesting period).

• **Stock option plans.** Employees are given the right to purchase shares at a fixed (strike) price for a specified period of time. Similar to restricted stock, there is a waiting period (called a vesting period) before the employee can purchase the shares.

• **Stock appreciation rights (SARs).** Employees are paid in cash or stock for the increase in share price, but do not purchase shares of stock. This is similar to a stock option but with no share purchase required.

• **Employee share purchase plans.** Employees are permitted to purchase shares directly from the company at a discounted price, typically a set percentage (such as 85%) of the prevailing market price.

Most stock-based compensation plans contain forfeiture provisions—if the employee is terminated for cause or, leaves the company before the rights to receive shares are vested, the award is forfeited.

Analysis of Stock-Based Compensation Plans

There are two analysis issues relating to stock-based compensation plans: recognition of the *expense* and potential *dilution*.

Expense Recognition The expense side is straightforward. When shares or options are awarded to employees, companies estimate the fair value of the award and recognize the fair value as compensation expense in the income statement over the period in which the employee provides service.

Potential Dilution Dilution relates to the number of common shares outstanding that have a claim against the company's earnings or net assets. For example, if a company earns $1 million and there are 1,000,000 shares outstanding, the earnings per share (EPS) available to pay dividends is $1. But, if there are 2,000,000 shares outstanding, the EPS available to pay dividends is only $0.50. The drop in EPS due to the increase in the number of outstanding shares is called *dilution* and companies are required to report diluted EPS in their annual reports—we discuss EPS later in this module. In the same way, dilution affects the value of each share of stock. If a company is worth $10 million, the per share price of the company's stock will be half as much if there are 2,000,000 shares outstanding than if there are only 1,000,000.

Mindful of shareholder concerns about the potential dilution of their stock holdings, companies often repurchase shares in an effort to counter the dilutive effects of share issuances under stock-based compensation plans. Johnson & Johnson describes this in its footnotes.

The Company settles employee benefit equity issuances with treasury shares. Treasury shares are replenished throughout the year for the number of shares used to settle employee benefit equity issuances.

To work through the analysis issues relating to employee stock compensation plans, it is important for us to understand:

- How stock-based compensation expense is measured and recorded in the income statement.
- Dilutive effects of stock-based compensation and the cash cost that companies incur to offset that dilution.
- Dilutive effects of stock-based compensation on earnings per share (EPS).

Accounting for Stock-Based Compensation

Regardless of the type of stock-based compensation plan, there are common accounting steps.

- When the award is granted to employees, the company estimates the fair value of the award.
- The fair value of the award is recorded as an expense in the income statement, ratably over the vesting period.
- When the shares are issued, common stock and additional paid-in capital increase in the same manner as for cash-based stock issuances, as described above.

Stock-based compensation expense is included on the income statement but rarely reported as a separate line item. Like other forms of compensation, the expense is included in cost of goods sold (for employees in R&D and manufacturing) or selling general and administrative expense (for employees in selling and administration and executive roles). However, we can determine the amount of the expense from the statement of cash flows. Because stock-based compensation expense is a non-cash expense, companies add back this expense in the statement of cash flow as in the following excerpt from the JNJ statement from 2015.

JOHNSON & JOHNSON AND SUBSIDIARIES			
Consolidated Statements of Cash Flows			
$ millions	**2015**	**2014**	**2013**
Cash flows from operating activities			
Net earnings	$15,409	$16,323	$13,831
Adjustments to reconcile net earnings to cash flows from operating activities:			
Depreciation and amortization of property and intangibles	3,746	3,895	4,104
Stock-based compensation	**874**	**792**	**728**

JNJ adds back the $874 million of stock-based compensation expense, which is included in net income on the income statement, to arrive at cash from operations. (This is similar to the $3,746 million add-back for depreciation expense.)

Interpretation of Stock-Based Compensation The stock-based compensation add-back might lead some to conclude that this form of compensation is cash free. But this is erroneous—a real cash cost occurs when the company buys new treasury shares in the open market to offset the dilution created by the share award to the employees. Consider also that the company used stock-based compensation instead of paying higher salaries or bonuses in cash. The employees bartered for stock. So while companies and analysts often add stock-based compensation expense back when computing and reporting non-GAAP measures such as EBIT and EBITDA, that treatment is not correct. *Stock-based compensation expense* is a real cash cost. To accurately evaluate and forecast operating cash flow, analysts must either include stock-based compensation expense or recognize the related treasury-stock purchase as an operating cash outflow.

In addition to the cash cost that JNJ will incur to offset the potential dilution relating to shares that will be issued to employees, JNJ's earnings per share will be affected. Fortunately, the effect of this potential dilution is a required disclosure in a statistic called diluted earnings per share that is reported on the income statement with details provided in a related footnote disclosure. We discuss diluted earnings per share later in this module.

Footnote Disclosures for Stock-Based Compensation

Footnotes to the 10-K contain extensive descriptions of stock-based compensation plans that describe two facets of a company's stock-based compensation: plan activity and fair value.

Plan Activity Disclosure for plan activity includes:

- Number of shares granted to employees during the year (to illustrate potential dilution to existing shareholders).

- Number of shares issued during the year to satisfy awards that vested.

- Any shares forfeited—when employees leave the company or fail to exercise options within the specified time period.

For example, Johnson & Johnson provides the following information related to activity for its three types of compensation plans.

Shares in thousands	Outstanding Stock Options	Outstanding Restricted Share Units	Outstanding Performance Share Units
Shares at December 28, 2014	115,712	27,693	2,531
Granted	20,484	7,637	931
Issued	(16,683)	(10,164)	(285)
Canceled or forfeited	(2,996)	(1,281)	(99)
Shares at January 3, 2016	116,517	23,885	3,078

Fair Value and Expense Disclosure for fair value and expense includes:

- Fair value of the stock-based compensation awards.

- How fair value is determined. Restricted stock awards are valued using the share price on the date of the award. Stock option plans are valued using option pricing models. The two most common models are the Black-Scholes model and the bilateral model (also called lattice method).

- The expense on the income statement.

- Value of the shares issued to employees over and above the price the employee paid for shares. This difference is called the intrinsic value.

For example, JNJ provides fair value details for its stock option plan in its 2015 10-K. Similar schedules are usually provided for each type of stock-based compensation plan.

	2015	2014	2013
Risk-free rate	1.77%	1.87%	1.01%
Expected volatility	15.48%	14.60%	14.04%
Expected life (in years)	7.0	6.0	6.0
Expected dividend yield	2.90%	3.10%	3.40%

JNJ disclosed the following fair values for stock-based awards during the year.

Stock options	$10.68
Restricted share units	$91.65
Performance share units	$93.54

Interpretation of Fair Values for Different Stock-Based Awards For JNJ, the fair value of RSUs are much higher than the fair value of the options because the two compensation arrangements differ greatly. If stock price drops between the grant date and the time the shares are issued, the employee with the RSU will still receive something of value (the share). The employee with an option could buy the stock at the pre-determined (higher) price. Because it makes no economic sense to pay more for the stock than its market value—the option is worthless and the employee is left empty handed.

The appendix to this module discusses additional accounting and analysis issues for share based compensation.

LO3 Review 8-3

Coca-Cola Company has a number of stock-based compensation plans including stock options, RSUs, and employee stock purchase plans. The company reports the following activity for its stock options.

In millions	Shares
Outstanding on January 1, 2015	305
Granted	13
Exercised	(44)
Forfeited/expired	(8)
Outstanding on December 31, 2015	266

The company also reports the following information in its footnotes.
- Total stock-based compensation expense of $236 million for 2015.
- Fair value of stock options granted during 2015 of $4.38 per share and the options' strike price was $41.89
- Granted 1,857 thousand performance share units during 2015 with a fair value of $37.99 per share.

Required
a. How did Coca-Cola's stock-based compensation expense affect net income for the year?
b. How did the stock-based compensation expense affect cash from operations? Can we infer from this that the expense involves no cash outflow for Coca-Cola?
c. Consider the fair value of the stock options granted during the year. If these options vest over four years, determine the related compensation expense for 2015.
d. Consider the fair value of the performance share units granted during the year. If the average restriction period is two years, determine the related compensation expense for 2015.
e. Explain why the fair value per share of the performance share units is so much larger than the stock option fair value.

Solution on p. 8-53.

Cash Dividends

Let's turn to the *earned capital* portion of stockholders' equity. We discuss the following topics related to earned capital accounts.

LO4 Analyze cash dividends and their financial effects.

- Retained earnings, which represents the cumulative profit that the company has earned since its inception, less the cumulative dividends paid out to shareholders.

- Dividends, which can be paid in cash, in land, in other property, or in additional shares of stock (stock dividends).

- Stock splits, where the company distributes additional shares of stock to existing shareholders.

- Accumulated other comprehensive income (AOCI) that includes a number of items that explain balance sheet changes that are not due to net income or to transactions with shareholders. JNJ reports a negative balance of $(13,165) million in AOCI as of 2015, which is a cumulative other comprehensive *loss*.

Cash Dividend Disclosures

Johnson & Johnson reports retained earnings of $103,879 million, which is higher than the prior year. Many companies, but not all, pay dividends and reasons for dividend payments vary. JNJ reports that it "increased its dividend in 2015 for the 53rd consecutive year," paying $2.95 per share in 2015. Companies typically pay dividends on a quarterly basis.

Outsiders closely monitor dividend payments. It is generally perceived that the level of dividend payments is related to the company's expected long-term recurring income. Accordingly, dividend increases are usually viewed as positive signals about future performance and are accompanied by stock price increases. By that logic, companies rarely reduce their dividends unless absolutely necessary because dividend reductions are often met with substantial stock price declines.

Dividend Payout and Yield

Two common metrics that analysts use to assess a company's dividends are dividend payout and dividend yield. These ratios are computed for common stock dividends and not for preferred stock because, as we explain below, most preferred stock has a stated dividend rate such that a "payout" ratio is not meaningful.

Dividend Payout The dividend payout ratio measures the proportion of the company's earnings that is paid out as dividend—it is defined as:

$$\text{Dividend payout} = \frac{\text{Common stock dividends per share}}{\text{Basic earnings per share (EPS)}}$$

For 2015, JNJ reported dividends per share of $2.95 and basic earnings per share of $5.56. The dividend payout ratio is 53% ($2.95/$5.56). By comparison, the median dividend payout ratio for S&P 500 companies in 2015 is 31%, with 17% of those companies not paying any dividends. More mature, profitable companies, such as JNJ, tend to have a higher payout ratio because they have fewer investment opportunities that require cash.

Dividend Yield Dividend yield is tied to the current market value of the company's stock and is defined as:

$$\text{Dividend yield} = \frac{\text{Common stock dividends per share}}{\text{Current share price}}$$

The ratio measures the cash return to stockholders given the cash investment. Of course, the other way to earn a return is via stock price appreciation, but dividend yield reflects only the one-year cash return. Given JNJ's dividends per share in 2015 of $2.95 and its closing share price on December 31, 2015, of $102.72, the dividend yield is 2.87% ($2.95/$102.72).

Cash Dividends Financial Effects

Cash dividends reduce both cash and retained earnings by the amount of the cash dividends paid. To illustrate, assume that JNJ declares and pays cash dividends in the amount of $10 million. The financial statement effects of this cash dividend payment are as follows.

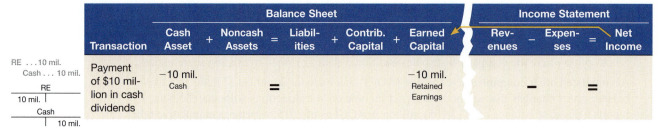

Dividend payments *do not* affect net income. They directly reduce retained earnings and bypass the income statement.

Cumulative Dividends in Arrears Dividends on preferred stock have priority over those on common stock, including unpaid prior years' preferred dividends (called *dividends in arrears*) when preferred stock is cumulative. To illustrate, assume that a company has 15,000 shares of $50 par value, 8% preferred stock outstanding; assume that the preferred stock is cumulative, which means that any unpaid dividends cumulate and must be paid before common dividends. The company also has 50,000 shares of $5 par value common stock outstanding. During its first three years in business, assume that the company declares $20,000 dividends in the first year, $260,000 of dividends in the second year, and $60,000 of dividends in the third year. Cash dividends paid to each class of stock in each of the three years follows.

	Preferred Stock	Common Stock
Year 1—$20,000 cash dividends paid		
Current-year dividend (15,000 shares × $50 par × 8%; but only $20,000 paid, leaving $40,000 in arrears)	$20,000	
Balance to common		$ 0
Year 2—$260,000 cash dividends paid		
Dividends in arrears from Year 1 ([15,000 shares × $50 par × 8%] − $20,000)	40,000	
Current-year dividend (15,000 shares × $50 par × 8%)	60,000	
Balance to common		160,000
Year 3—$60,000 cash dividends paid		
Current-year dividend (15,000 shares × $50 par × 8%)	60,000	
Balance to common		0

LO4 Review 8-4

Wells Fargo (WFC) reports the following information in its 2015 financial statements.

For 12 Months Ended	Dec. 31, 2015	Dec. 31, 2014
Preferred stock: Cash dividends paid ($ millions)	$(1,426)	$(1,235)
Common stock: Cash dividends paid ($ millions)	$(7,400)	$(6,908)
Earnings per common share ($ per share)	$4.180	$4.170
Dividends declared per common share ($ per share).	$1.475	$1.350

Footnotes to Wells Fargo financial statements, disclosed information about preferred stock issuances (excerpted).

	Number of Shares Issued as of Dec. 31, 2015	Par Value per Share in $	Carrying Value (Balance Sheet Net Book Value)—$ millions	Number of Shares Issued as of Dec. 31, 2014
Series L 7.50% Non-Cumulative Perpetual Convertible Class A Preferred Stock	3,968,000	$ 1,000	$3,200	3,968,000
Series U 5.875% Fixed-to-Floating Non-Cumulative Perpetual Class A Preferred Stock.	80,000	$25,000	$2,000	0
Series V 6.000% Non-Cumulative Perpetual Class A Preferred Stock	40,000	$25,000	$1,000	0

Required
a. Use the financial statement effects template to record the preferred and common stock dividends for 2015.
b. If Wells Fargo had paid $100 million more in common stock dividends in 2015, what would have been the after-tax effect on net income for that year?
c. Compute the dividend payout ratio for 2014 and 2015.
d. Compute the dividend yield ratio for 2015.
e. Assume that Wells Fargo issued the Series U and V preferred stock on July 1, 2015. Compute the 2015 total cash dividends for the three preferred stock issuances, shown above.

Solution on p. 8-53.

Stock Splits and Dividends

eLectures
MBC **LO5**
Analyze
stock splits
and stock
dividends and their
financial effects.

Dividends need not be paid in cash. Many companies pay dividends in the form of additional shares of stock. Companies can also distribute additional shares to their shareholders via a stock split. We cover both of these distributions in this section.

Stock Split

A **stock split** happens when a company issues additional common shares to its existing stockholders. Stock splits are usually prompted by the company's desire to reduce its stock price in order to improve marketability of the shares. There seems to be a psychological hurdle for investors when the price of a share exceeds $100. A typical stock split is 2-for-1, which means that the company distributes one additional share for each share owned by shareholders. Because there is no cash flow effect from a stock split, the company's market cap is unaffected by the split. Following the distribution each investor owns twice as many shares that are each worth approximately half as much. So the total market value of their investment is unchanged. Although the split itself has little effect on shareholders, the price per share is reduced, thus increasing the marketability of the shares.

A stock split is not a monetary transaction and, as such, there are no financial statement effects. However, companies must disclose the number of shares outstanding for all periods presented in the financial statements. Additionally, companies must reduce the par value of the stock proportionally (to ½ of the previous par value for a 2:1 stock split) and historical financial statements presented in the current 10-K must be adjusted likewise.

Stock Split in Form of Dividend In November 2015 **Nike** announced that its board of directors approved a 2-for-1 split of both Class A and Class B common shares. The stock split was in the form of a 100 percent stock dividend payable December 23, 2015. After the split, outstanding shares of Class A and Class B common stock doubled to approximately 353 million and 1.36 billion shares respectively, based on the outstanding shares as of November 16, 2015. Nike expected that its common stock would begin trading at the split-adjusted price on December 24, 2015.

Stock Dividend

Companies can also declare a **stock dividend** where shares of stock are distributed to shareholders instead of cash. To account for a stock dividend, the company reduces retained earnings (just as for cash dividends) and increases contributed capital accounts. Cash and the stock's par value per share are both unaffected by a stock dividend. The amount of the dividend in dollar terms depends on the number of shares distributed as a proportion of the total shares outstanding.

Exhibit 8.3 compares the financial statement effects of large stock dividends (where the shares distributed are more than 20–25% of the outstanding shares) with small stock dividends (less than 20–25%) and stock splits. Many companies declare a stock dividend, rather than a stock split, to avoid the reduction of the par value that is required in a stock split. This event is typically described as a *stock split effected in the form of a stock dividend*.

The following disclosure from **Marathon Petroleum Corporation** describes its stock dividend in 2015.

> On April 29, 2015, our board of directors approved a two-for-one stock split in the form of a stock dividend, which was distributed on June 10, 2015 to shareholders of record at the close of business on May 20, 2015. The total number of authorized shares of common stock and common stock par value per share remain unchanged. All historical share and per share data included in this report have been retroactively restated on a post-split basis.

The par value of its stock and the number of authorized shares remained unchanged. Only the number of shares issued changed to reflect the additional shares that Marathon distributed to its shareholders.

Exhibit 8.3 ■ Analysis of Stock Splits and Stock Dividends

Shares Distributed as % of Total Shares Outstanding	Retained Earnings	Par Value per Share	Common Stock at Par	Additional Paid-in Capital
Stock split 100% or greater	No effect	Decreased in inverse proportion to stock split (such as 2-for-1 split, par value is 1/2)	No effect (more shares "issued" but at proportionately lower par value per share)	No effect
Small stock dividend Less than 20–25%	Reduced by market value of shares distributed	No effect	Increased by: Number of shares distributed × Original par value per share	Increased by: Market value of shares distributed – Par value
Large stock dividend More than 20–25%	Reduced by par value of shares distributed	No effect	Increased by: Number of shares distributed × Original par value per share	No effect

LO5 Review 8-5

Assume that the stockholders' equity of Arbitron Inc. at June 30, 2016, follows.

5% preferred stock, $100 par value, 10,000 shares authorized; 4,000 shares issued and outstanding..............................	$ 400,000
Common stock, $5 par value, 200,000 shares authorized; 50,000 shares issued and outstanding.............................	250,000
Paid-in capital in excess of par value-Preferred stock.....................	40,000
Paid-in capital in excess of par value-Common stock.....................	300,000
Retained earnings	656,000
Total stockholders' equity	$1,646,000

Use the financial statement effects template to record each of the following transactions that occurred during July.

July 1 Declared and issued a 100% stock dividend on all outstanding shares of common stock when the market value of the stock was $11 per share.

July 7 Declared and issued a 3% stock dividend on all outstanding shares of common stock when the market value of the stock was $7 per share.

July 31 Declared and paid a cash dividend of $1.20 per share on all outstanding shares.

July 31 Declared a 2:1 stock split of the common stock, effective August 15, 2016.

Solution on p. 8-54.

Accumulated Other Comprehensive Income

LO6 Interpret accumulated other comprehensive income and its components.

Unrealized gains and losses arise when the fair value of an asset or liability on the balance sheet, differs from its cost. For some assets and liabilities (see below), unrealized gains and losses are not reflected in net income nor in retained earnings.

There are selected items recorded on the balance sheet at fair value—see list below. For the accounts listed below, any unrealized gains or losses are captured in the asset or liability section of the balance sheet. However, because unrealized gains or losses are not reported in net income or retained earnings, the balance sheet does not balance. To solve this issue, unrealized gains and losses are added to **accumulated other comprehensive income (AOCI)**, a stockholders' equity account that captures unrealized gains and losses on certain assets and liabilities. Unrealized gains and losses are "held" in AOCI until the related asset is sold (or liability settled) and any gain or loss is realized.

AOCI Components

Following are common items in AOCI—we further describe these items in later modules.

■ **Foreign currency translation adjustments.** Foreign subsidiaries often maintain their financial statements in foreign currencies and these statements are translated into $US before the subsidiaries' financial statements are included in the company's 10-K. The strengthening and weakening of the $US vis-à-vis foreign currencies results in decreases and increases in the $US-value of subsidiaries' assets and liabilities. For subsidiaries with positive equity (the normal case where assets are greater than liabilities), a strengthening of the $US creates an unrealized foreign currency gain. These unrealized gains or losses in the $US value of foreign subsidiaries' assets and liabilities are included in AOCI.

■ **Gains and losses on marketable securities.** Investments in certain types of marketable securities are reported at fair value on the asset side of a company's balance sheet. If the fair value differs from the securities' cost, there are unrealized gains and losses on these securities included in AOCI. (The accounting rules for marketable securities are changing as we explain in another module. Under the new rules, changes in the fair value of marketable securities are reflected in current income and *not* in AOCI).

■ **Employee benefit plans.** Unrealized gains and losses on some pension investments and pension liabilities are reported in AOCI.

■ **Gains and losses on derivatives and hedges.** Unrealized gains and losses on certain financial securities (derivatives) that companies purchase to hedge exposures to interest rate, foreign exchange rate, and commodity price risks are included in AOCI.

AOCI Disclosures and Interpretation

Following is the reconciliation of beginning and ending balances in AOCI for Johnson & Johnson.

$ millions	Foreign Currency Translation	Gain/ (Loss) On Securities	Employee Benefit Plans	Gain/ (Loss) On Derivatives and Hedges	Total Accumulated Other Comprehensive Income (Loss)
December 30, 2012 . . .	$ (296)	$195	$(5,717)	$ 8	$ (5,810)
Net 2013 changes	94	(89)	2,708	237	2,950
December 29, 2013 . . .	(202)	106	(3,009)	245	(2,860)
Net 2014 changes	(4,601)	151	(3,308)	(104)	(7,862)
December 28, 2014 . . .	(4,803)	257	(6,317)	141	(10,722)
Net 2015 changes	(3,632)	347	1,019	(177)	(2,443)
January 3, 2016	$(8,435)	$604	$(5,298)	$ (36)	$(13,165)

JNJ's accumulated other comprehensive income account has become more negative over the past three years mainly as a result of the stronger $US that reduced the value of JNJ's foreign subsidiaries' assets and liabilities when measured in $US. As the $US weakens vis-à-vis foreign currencies, the foreign currency translation account will likely become less negative (or may become positive). Fluctuations in the AOCI account are common. From an analysis perspective, unrealized gains and losses included in AOCI are of limited practical significance unless the underlying transactions are imminent and those gains and losses will be recognized in net income.

Comprehensive Income During the year, market values on the AOCI items inevitably change and so do the unrealized gains and losses in AOCI. Remember, changes in unrealized gains and losses do not flow to the income statement as they are not part of net income. Instead, those changes are aggregated and labeled **other comprehensive income (OCI)**. The following graphic depicts the relation between net income and retained earnings and between comprehensive income and AOCI.

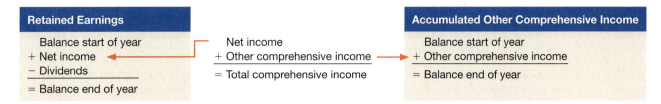

Retained Earnings	Accumulated Other Comprehensive Income
Balance start of year	Balance start of year
+ Net income	+ Other comprehensive income
− Dividends	= Balance end of year
= Balance end of year	

	Net income
	+ Other comprehensive income
	= Total comprehensive income

Following is JNJ's statement of comprehensive income for the year.

Consolidated Statements of Comprehensive Income ($ millions)	12 Months Ended		
	Jan. 3, 2016	Dec. 28, 2014	Dec. 29, 2013
Net earnings..................................	$15,409	$16,323	$13,831
Other comprehensive income (loss), net of tax			
Foreign currency translation.....................	(3,632)	(4,601)	94
Securities	347	151	(89)
Employee benefit plans	1,019	(3,308)	2,708
Derivatives and hedges	(177)	(104)	237
Other comprehensive income (loss)..............	(2,443)	(7,862)	2,950
Total comprehensive income	$12,966	$ 8,461	$16,781

During the year, JNJ reported other comprehensive loss of $2,443 million. This reflects the net change in unrealized gains and losses on AOCI components, which increased the negative balance in AOCI from $(10,722) million to $(13,165) million. See that the components of other comprehensive income are the same components as shown in the "Net 2015 changes" row of Johnson & Johnson's AOCI reconciliation. See also that there is no cash effect from unrealized gains and losses or from any changes in unrealized gains and losses over time.

For analysis purposes, recall that unrealized gains or losses do not affect net income until the assets are sold or the liabilities settled. If the company anticipates selling the assets or settling the liabilities in the short run (say, within the next quarter), those unrealized gains or losses would flow to net income and this could affect our assessment of company profitability and cash flow. But over the long run, unrealized gains and losses might change substantially (as market prices move) and thus, there is no reliable way to include unrealized gains and losses in our analysis.

LO6 Review 8-6

The annual report of The Coca-Cola Company discloses the following related to accumulated other comprehensive income (AOCI).

December 31 ($ millions)	2015	2014
Foreign currency translation adjustment	$ (9,167)	$(5,226)
Accumulated derivative net gains (losses).............................	696	554
Unrealized net gains (losses) on available-for-sale securities	288	972
Adjustments to pension and other benefit liabilities	(1,991)	(2,077)
Accumulated other comprehensive income (loss)......................	$(10,174)	$(5,777)

Required
a. On average, during 2015, did the $US strengthen or weaken vis-à-vis currencies of countries where Coca-Cola has subsidiaries? How do we know?
b. Consider unrealized gains on the available for sale securities of $288 million at year end. Assume that the cost of these securities was $3,000 million. What would have been the effect on net income if Coca-Cola had sold all of these securities on December 31, 2015?
c. Consider unrealized gains on the derivatives of $696 at year end. Is it accurate to conclude that the market value of these derivatives increased during the year? Explain.

Solution on p. 8-55.

Convertible Securities

LO7
Analyze convertible securities and their financial effects.

When common stock is issued, the company receives proceeds equal to the market price of the stock multiplied by the number of shares sold. So, the higher the stock price, the greater the proceeds. Preferred stock and long-term bonds are sold in much the same way, and their market price on the date of sale determines the cash proceeds to the company.

Companies can increase the cash proceeds by including provisions in the preferred stock and bonds agreements that make the securities more desirable. One such provision is a **conversion option** that allows the holder of those securities to convert them into common stock at a pre-set price. While investors own the preferred stock or long-term bond, they receive dividend or interest payments and will have a senior position to common shareholders in the event that the company fails and is liquidated (meaning the preferred stock or bond investors are paid before the common shareholders).

On the other hand, if the company performs well and its prospects are good, the preferred stock or bond investors can exchange their securities for common stock at a pre-agreed exchange ratio. They have the option to become common shareholders. In that case, they can benefit from the company's upside potential and the value of their common shares will increase as the market value of the company increases. This conversion option is valuable to investors and they are willing to pay a higher price for convertible preferred stock or convertible bonds when they are issued. For the company, the issue proceeds are higher.

Convertible Securities Disclosures and Interpretation Earlier in this module we described a **Dow Chemical** convertible preferred stock that carries an 8.5% yield and is convertible (at the shareholder's option) into 24.2010 common shares for each preferred share. This is an attractive feature for investors and it allowed Dow Chemical to realize a higher market price for its preferred stock.

Bonds can have a similar conversion option. Until they are converted, bondholders enjoy interest income and a senior position in liquidation. But, if the company performs well, bondholders can convert their bonds into common stock and enjoy all of the benefits of a common shareholder.

For example, **Xilinx** reported convertible notes (similar to bonds) in its 2015 10-K.

As of March 28, 2015, the Company had $600.0 million principal amount of 2017 Convertible Notes outstanding . . . The 2017 Convertible Notes are convertible into shares of Xilinx common stock at a conversion rate of 33.7391 shares of common stock per $1 thousand principal amount of the 2017 Convertible Notes, representing an effective conversion price of approximately $29.64 per share of common stock . . . One of the conditions allowing holders of the 2017 Convertible Notes to convert during any fiscal quarter is if the last reported sale price of the Company's common stock for at least 20 trading days during a period of 30 consecutive trading days ending on the last trading day of the preceding fiscal quarter is greater than or equal to 130% of the conversion price on each applicable trading day. This condition was met as of March 28, 2015, and as a result, the 2017 Convertible Notes were convertible at the option of the holders. As of March 28, 2015, the 2017 Convertible Notes were classified as a current liability on the Company's consolidated balance sheet.

Because the conversion condition was met as of the statement date, the Notes are convertible at the option of the holder. As such, Xilinx must report the notes as a current liability on its balance sheet. That liability will not be paid in cash. It will be paid by issuing common stock to the note holders.

Convertible Securities Financial Effects To see the effects that conversion would have on Xilinx's financial statements, assume that the bonds are reported at their face amount of $600 million and that all of the bonds are subsequently converted into 20,243,460 shares ([$600 million/$1,000] × 33.7391 shares) of common stock with a par value of $0.01 per share. The financial statement effects of the conversion are as follows (Xilinx reports its balance sheet in $000s).

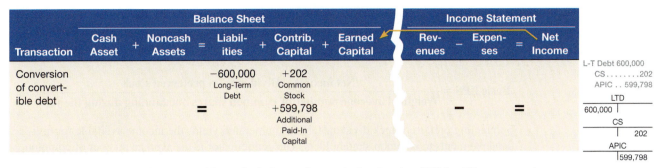

	Balance Sheet						Income Statement				
Transaction	**Cash Asset**	**+ Noncash Assets**	**= Liabil-ities**	**+ Contrib. Capital**	**+ Earned Capital**		**Rev-enues**	**− Expen-ses**	**= Net Income**		
Conversion of convert-ible debt			**−600,000** Long-Term Debt **=**	**+202** Common Stock **+599,798** Additional Paid-In Capital				**−**	**=**		

L-T Debt 600,000
CS 202
APIC . . 599,798

LTD	
600,000	

CS	
	202

APIC	
	599,798

Upon conversion, the debt is removed from the balance sheet at its book value ($600 million assumed in this case) and the common stock is issued for that amount, resulting in an increase in the Common Stock account of $202,435 (assuming 20,243,460 shares issued with a par value of $0.01 per share). Additional paid-in capital is increased for the remaining amount. No gain or loss (or cash inflow or outflow) is recognized as a result of the conversion.

IFRS Insight ■ Convertible Securities under IFRS

Unlike GAAP, convertible securities (called *compound financial instruments* under IFRS) are split into separate debt and equity components. The idea is that the conversion premium is akin to a call option on the company's stock. This embedded option has a value of its own even if it is not legally detachable. Thus, under IFRS, the proceeds from the issuance are allocated between the liability component (at fair value) and an equity component (the residual amount).

IFRS

LO7 Review 8-7

Assume that **Express Scripts Inc.** has issued the following convertible debentures: each $1,000 bond is convertible into 200 shares of $1 par common. Assume that the bonds were sold at a discount, and that each bond has a current unamortized discount equal to $150.

Required
Use the financial statements effect template to record the conversion of one of these convertible debentures.

Guided Examples
MBC

Solution on p. 8-55.

Earnings per Share (EPS)

A common metric reported in the financial press is earnings per share (EPS). EPS is the only ratio defined by GAAP, a testimony to this ratio's perceived importance for users. During the "earnings season"—the time each quarter when public companies release their quarterly earnings reports—EPS disclosures are followed obsessively by Wall Street analysts and investors.

eLectures **LO8** MBC Interpret earnings per share.

We must be careful in using EPS when comparing companies' operating results, as the number of shares outstanding is not necessarily proportional to the income level—that is, a company with twice the level of net income does not necessarily have double the number of common shares outstanding. Management controls the number of common shares outstanding and there is no relation between firm size and number of shares outstanding. For example, consider that JNJ reports Basic EPS of $5.56 for 2015, while in the same year, **Berkshire Hathaway** reports Basic EPS of $14,656! This is because Berkshire Hathaway has so few common shares outstanding, not necessarily because it has stellar profits.

Potential ownership dilution is another concern. As we described earlier, stock options awarded to employees under stock-based compensation plans and convertible securities such as Dow's convertible preferred stock and Xilinx's convertible notes, all have the potential to increase the number of common shares outstanding. Existing shareholders usually take a dim view of this because more common stock outstanding dilutes the ownership of existing shareholders. This is because there are more shareholders laying claim to the available dividends *and* the new shareholders will share equally in the proceeds of liquidation if the company fails. Current shareholders are, therefore, concerned about potential dilution.

To communicate the potential impact of dilution in earnings available for the payment of dividends to shareholders, accounting regulation requires companies to report two EPS statistics.

■ **Basic EPS**. Basic EPS is computed as:

$$\text{Basic EPS} = \frac{\text{Net income} - \text{Dividends on preferred stock}}{\text{Weighted average number of common shares outstanding during the year}}$$

Subtracting preferred stock dividends, in the numerator, yields the income available for dividend payments to common shareholders. The denominator is the average number of common shares outstanding during the year.

■ **Diluted EPS**. Diluted EPS reflects the impact of additional shares that would be issued if all stock options and convertible securities are converted into common shares at the beginning of the year. Diluted EPS never exceeds basic EPS.

Exhibit 8.4 highlights the difference between the two ratios.

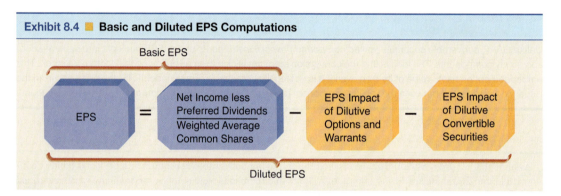

Exhibit 8.4 ■ Basic and Diluted EPS Computations

EPS Disclosures JNJ reports the following table of basic and diluted EPS for 2015.

In millions, except per share amounts	2015
Basic net earnings per share	$5.56
Average shares outstanding—basic.	2,771.8
Potential shares exercisable under stock option plans	141.5
Less: shares repurchased under treasury stock method	(102.6)
Convertible debt shares	2.2
Adjusted average shares outstanding—diluted	2,812.9
Diluted net earnings per share	$5.48

The denominator in diluted earnings per share calculation presumes the most-extreme case: at the beginning of the year, all employees exercise their right to purchase common shares and all convertible debt holders convert their notes to common shares.

JNJ uses the treasury-stock method to determine the dilutive effect of stock options. The method assumes that all options are exercised (141.5 million shares) and that the company uses the proceeds to repurchase shares on the open market at the current stock price (102.6 million shares). The 38.9 million share increase is the net of the shares issued to option holders less the new treasury shares (141.5 million − 102.6 million).

The combined effect is to increase the number of shares in the denominator from 2,771.8 million shares used for the basic EPS calculation to 2,812.9 shares used for the diluted EPS calculation.[1] The

---

[1] The effects of dilutive securities are only included if they actually reduce the EPS number. **Antidilutive** securities *increase* EPS, and are, thus, excluded from the computation. An example of an antidilutive security is employee stock options with an exercise price greater than the stock's current market price. The company could repurchase more shares than would be issued to option holders. This would decrease the number of shares outstanding. These underwater (or out-of-the-money) options are antidilutive and are, therefore, excluded from the EPS computation.

increase in the number of shares in the denominator reduces $5.56 for basic EPS to $5.48 for diluted EPS. Diluted EPS is never greater than basic EPS.

LO8 Review 8-8

Johnson & Johnson reports the following reconciliation of basic net earnings per share to diluted net earnings per share for its fiscal first quarter ended April 3, 2016.

Fiscal First Quarter Ended (in millions)	April 3, 2016
Net earnings, basic.	$4,292
Net earnings, diluted	$4,293
Average shares outstanding — basic.	2,757.2
Potential shares exercisable under stock option plans	144.4
Shares which could be repurchased under treasury stock method.	108.2
Convertible debt shares	2.0

Required
a. Compute basic EPS for the quarter ended April 3, 2016.
b. Determine the total number of shares added to the diluted EPS calculation from stock option plans.
c. Compute diluted EPS for the quarter ended April 3, 2016.
d. Assess whether the results for parts *a*, *b* and *c* suggest a major potential dilution risk for existing common shareholders. Explain.

Solution on p. 8-55.

Global Accounting

Under IFRS, accounting for equity is similar to that under U.S. GAAP. Following are a few terminology differences (seen primarily in European balance sheets).

U.S. GAAP	IFRS
Common stock	Share capital *or* Ordinary shares
Preferred shares	Preference shares
Additional paid-in capital	Share premium
Retained earnings	Reserves
Accumulated other comprehensive income	Other equity *or* Other components of equity
—	Revaluation surplus *or* Revaluation reserve*

* Certain assets including fixed assets and intangible assets may be revalued upwards (and later, revalued downwards) under IFRS. These revaluations do not affect net income or retained earnings but, instead, are reported in a separate equity account. For comparative purposes our analysis might exclude revaluations from both equity and the asset accounts to which they relate.

U.S. GAAP has a more narrow definition of liabilities than IFRS. Therefore, more items are classified as liabilities under IFRS. For example, some preferred shares are deemed liabilities under IFRS and equity under GAAP. (Both systems classify preferred shares that are mandatorily redeemable or redeemable at the option of the shareholder, as liabilities.) For comparative purposes, we look at classification of preferred shares that are not mandatorily redeemable and make the numbers consistent. To do this we add preference shares classified as liabilities under IFRS to equity.

Treasury stock transactions are sometimes difficult to identify under IFRS because companies are not required to report a separate line item for treasury shares on the balance sheet. Instead treasury share transactions reduce share capital and share premium. We must review the statement of shareholders' equity to assess stock repurchases for IFRS companies.

For example, at March 31, 2015, **BT Group plc** reports the following in the equity section of its IFRS balance sheet (in £ millions).

Ordinary shares	£ 419
Share premium	1,051
Own shares	(165)
Other reserves	1,485
Retained (loss) earnings	(1,982)
Total equity	**£ 808**

Its balance sheet reports no treasury stock line item, but footnotes disclose that BT Group's "own shares" of £(165) million changed as follows over the prior year.

£ millions	Treasury Shares
At 1 April 2014	**£(829)**
Net issue of treasury shares	664
At 31 March 2015	**£(165)**

IFRS Insight ■ Preferred Stock Under IFRS

Under IFRS, preferred stock (called *preference shares*) is classified according to its underlying characteristics. Preference shares are classified as equity if they are not redeemable, or redeemable at the option of the issuer. Preference shares are classified as liabilities if the company must redeem the shares (mandatorily redeemable) or if they are redeemable at the option of the shareholder. Under IFRS, the critical feature that distinguishes a liability is if the company must (or can be required to) deliver cash or some other financial instrument to the liability holder. Accounting for payments to preference shareholders follows from the balance sheet classification: cash paid out is recorded as interest expense or dividends, when the shares are classified as liabilities or equity, respectively. Under U.S. GAAP, preferred stock is classified as equity and cash paid out to preferred shareholders is classified as a dividend.

Appendix 8A: Stock-Based Compensation: Reporting and Analyzing

There are four broad types of share-based compensation plans.

1. Employee stock purchase plans
2. Stock awards (unrestricted and restricted)
3. Stock options
4. Stock appreciation rights

Whichever type of plan is used, the accounting objective is the same: *to record the fair value of compensation as expense over the periods in which employees perform services* (the vesting period).

This requires determining the fair value of the compensation and the vesting period. The fair value for each of the types is discussed below along with some important features of each.

Employee Stock Purchase Plans (ESPP)

Compensation expense is the amount of any discount the employee receives when stock is purchased. Common features are:

■ Employees can purchase the company's stock at a discount, commonly ~15%.

■ Employees can purchase stock up to a maximum that can be a flat amount (such as $25,000) or based on the employee's salary (such as 15% of gross salary).

■ Payroll deductions are made monthly and employee can choose when to purchase the stock (such as purchasing when price is low).

Stock Awards

Compensation expense is market price of the stock at the grant date. Common feature is:

■ Employee granted shares with no restrictions. Not a strong incentive because employee can sell stock or leave the company.

Stock Awards—Restricted Stock Awards Compensation expense is the market price of the stock at the grant date. Common features are:

■ Employee granted shares (and legally owns them) but is "restricted" from selling shares until the vesting date (to encourage employee retention).

■ Shares are forfeited if employee quits before vesting date.

■ Often shares are forfeited if performance targets are not met.

■ Employee may or may not receive dividends between the grant date and the vesting date, depending on the plan details. But, restricted stock holds no vote.

Stock Awards—Restricted Stock Units (RSU) Compensation expense is market price of the stock at the grant date. Common features are:

■ Employee receives a stock "unit" but no actual stock, the employee does not legally own any stock. A stock unit is typically equivalent to one share.

■ Employer delivers stock (or cash) to the employee based on a vesting schedule.

■ Employee cannot receive dividends during restriction period as employee does not own any stock.

■ Often RSUs are forfeited if performance targets are not met.

■ Unlike restricted stock, RSUs do not dilute EPS because no shares are issued.

Stock Options

Compensation expense is the estimated fair value of the options at the grant date. Fair value is measured with a model that requires assumptions. Common features are:

■ Employee has right to buy shares in the future, at a price specified at the grant date.

■ The employee cannot buy shares before the vesting date.

■ Options are forfeited if employee quits before vesting period.

■ The employee cannot sell the options.

For stock options, understanding some of the vocabulary is helpful:

■ *Employee stock option:* Security that gives employee the right, but not obligation, to purchase stock at a pre-determined price.

■ *Grant date:* Date the option is awarded to the employee.

■ *Exercise:* Purchase of stock pursuant to an option.

■ *Exercise price:* Pre-determined price at which the stock can be purchased. This is also called the strike price or grant price. In most plans, the exercise price is the stock price on the grant date.

■ *Option term:* Length of time employee can hold the option before it expires. Typically 7–10 years.

■ *Vesting:* Requirement(s) that must be met for employee to have right to exercise the option. Usually options vest with continuation of employment for a specific period of time (such as 4 years) or the meeting of a performance goal (such as revenue growth).

■ *Expiry date:* Date after which the option can no longer be exercised. Once vested, the employee can exercise the option at the grant price at any time over the option term up to the expiration date.

■ *Intrinsic value:* Difference between the current stock price and the exercise price. As the stock price rises so does intrinsic value.

At-the-money option	Intrinsic value = 0	Current stock price = Exercise price
In-the-money option.	Intrinsic value > 0	Current stock price > Exercise price
Out-of-the-money option	Intrinsic value < 0	Current stock price < Exercise price

■ *Option fair value:* Value of the option that considers the intrinsic value and the time value of the option. Determined with a valuation model, most frequently Black-Scholes or lattice model.

Stock Appreciation Rights (SAR)

Compensation expense is the estimated fair value of the SARs at the grant date. Fair value is measured with a model that requires assumptions. Fair value is usually the same as an option with similar terms. Common features are:

- Employee benefits by the amount of any stock price increase but without having to buy shares.
- Settlement date is determined at the grant date (similar to vesting period).
- "Stock appreciation" is the increase in the market price since the grant date; SAR has no value if stock price falls.
- SARs can be settled in stock or cash, depending on plan details.
- Similar to stock option but with no exercise price.

Some plans allow for RSUs and SARs to settle in either stock or cash. If they settle in cash (or if the employee has a cash option), the RSU or SAR is considered a liability. The amount of compensation (and related liability) is estimated each period and adjusted quarterly to reflect changes in the fair value of the RSUs or SARs until the settlement date.

Summary of Share-Based Compensation

The following chart summarizes the accounting for various types of stock based compensation plans.

	Cash	Liability	Common Stock	APIC	Deferred Comp	Treasury Stock	Retained Earnings	Comp Expense
Employee stock purchase plan								
At purchase: Discount compensation expense	↑		↑	↑			↓	↑
Stock grants (awards)								
Grant: Fair value of stock			↑	↑			↓	↑
Restricted stock								
Grant: Fair value of restricted stock				↑	↓			
Vesting: Proportion of restricted stock that vests					↑		↓	↑
Restricted stock units or Stock appreciation rights settled in cash								
Grant: Fair value of restricted stock unit		↑					↓	↑
Settlement: Cash to employee	↓	↓						
Stock options								
Grant: Fair value of options				↑			↓	↑
Exercise: New shares issued	↑		↑	↑				
Exercise: Treasury shares issued	↑					↑		

The chart shows that some plans have cash effects while others do not. Some plans affect common stock and APIC when shares are issued, other plans have no such effect because stock is not issued at all.

Analysis Implications

There are several analysis implications for share-based compensation.

- **Magnitude of Awards**—We consider both the absolute and relative size of compensation expense each period. Large increases or decreases are examined to determine the cause. Footnotes and the MD&A section provide details. For JNJ, stock compensation is increasing in both dollar terms and relative to total sales over the past eight years.

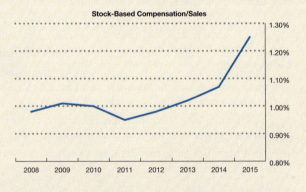

Stock-Based Compensation/Sales

$ millions	2008	2009	2010	2011	2012	2013	2014	2015
Stock-based compensation	$627	$628	$614	$621	$662	$728	$792	$874

The proportion of stock-based compensation to sales varies greatly by industry (see graphic), which highlights the need to evaluate any metric against competitors and industry benchmarks.

- **Dilution potential**–Large compensation plans can create large dilution that is not fully captured in diluted EPS. The dilution calculation for EPS includes all vested shares but none of the unvested shares.

  For example, JNJ's diluted EPS included 38.2 million dilutive shares, net (2,795.4 million − 2,757.2 million). But the footnotes reveal that an additional 486 million shares are yet to be granted and as such, are not included in diluted EPS. One way to quantify this missing dilution is to recompute EPS with a denominator that includes unvested shares. This will be a worst-case scenario

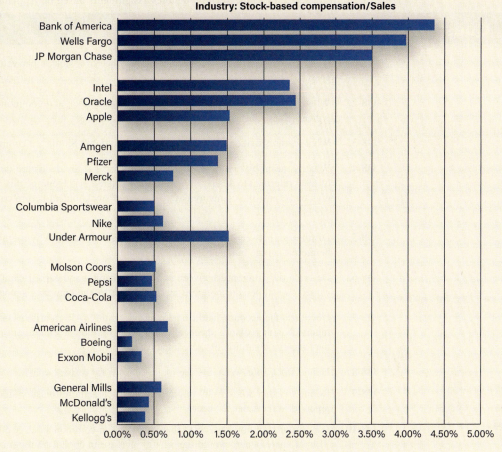

Industry: Stock-based compensation/Sales

because not all unvested shares are ultimately issued, but the adjusted EPS measure could be informative.

- **Tax benefit**–Companies cannot deduct GAAP share-based compensation expense for tax purposes. The tax laws do permit companies to deduct the *intrinsic* value of shares issued. This can be much larger than the GAAP expense and can create large tax savings. To assess this, analysts look at footnotes to determine the size of the tax benefit in the current period as well as the *intrinsic* value of outstanding shares and options. For example, JNJ reports the total intrinsic value of options exercised was $644 million which gave rise to a tax benefit of $253 million. The intrinsic value of outstanding options is $3,065 million, a considerable amount of potential future cash flow. Footnotes to the financial statements include these details.

- **Model assumptions**–Companies select assumptions used in the models that they use to estimate fair value. Analysts examine the assumptions, compare them to prior years and to assumptions used by competitors.

- **Cash flow implications**–When plans allow employees the choice to settle the award in cash instead of in stock, the company must record a liability for the potential cash outflow. This liability must be adjusted each quarter to reflect current stock price. Analysts must consider that for "hot" stocks—this means the liability on the balance sheet might understate the eventual cash outflow.

Guidance Answers

You Are the Chief Financial Officer

Pg. 8-11 Several points must be considered. (1) Buying stock back reduces the number of shares outstanding, which can prop up earnings per share (EPS). However, foregone earnings from the cash used for repurchases can dampen earnings. The net effect is that EPS is likely to increase because of the reduced shares in the denominator. (2) Another motivation is that, if the shares are sufficiently undervalued (in management's opinion), the stock repurchase and subsequent resale can provide a better return than alternative investments. (3) Stock repurchases send a strong signal to the market that management feels its stock is undervalued. This is more credible than merely making that argument with analysts. On the other hand, company cash is diverted from other investments. This is bothersome if such investments are mutually exclusive either now or in the future.

Superscript ᴬ denotes assignments based on Appendix 8A.

Questions

Q8-1. Define *par value stock.* What is the significance of a stock's par value from an accounting and analysis perspective?

Q8-2. What are the basic differences between preferred stock and common stock? That is, what are the typical features of preferred stock?

Q8-3. What features make preferred stock similar to debt? Similar to common stock?

Q8-4. What is meant by preferred dividends in arrears? If dividends are two years in arrears on $500,000 of 6% preferred stock, and dividends are declared at the end of this year, what amount of total dividends must the company pay to preferred stockholders before paying any dividends to common stockholders?

Q8-5. Distinguish between authorized shares and issued shares. Why might the number of shares issued be more than the number of shares outstanding?

Q8-6. Describe the difference between contributed capital and earned capital. Specifically, how can earned capital be considered as an investment by the company's stockholders?

Q8-7. How does the account "additional paid-in capital" (APIC) arise? Does the amount of APIC reported on the balance sheet relative to the common stock amount provide any information about the financial condition of the company?

Q8-8. Define *stock split.* What are the major reasons for a stock split?

Q8-9. Define *treasury stock.* Why might a corporation acquire treasury stock? How is treasury stock reported in the balance sheet?

Q8-10. If a corporation purchases 600 shares of its own common stock at $10 per share and resells them at $14 per share, where would the $2,400 increase in capital be reported in the financial statements? Why is no gain reported?

Q8-11. A corporation has total stockholders' equity of $4,628,000 and one class of $2 par value common stock. The corporation has 500,000 shares authorized; 300,000 shares issued; and 40,000 shares as treasury stock. What is its book value per share?

Q8-12. What is a stock dividend? How does a common stock dividend distributed to common stockholders affect their respective ownership interests?

Q8-13. What is the difference between the accounting for a small stock dividend and the accounting for a large stock dividend?

Q8-14. Employee stock options potentially dilute earnings per share (EPS). What can companies do to offset these dilutive effects and how might this action affect the balance sheet?

Q8-15. What information is reported in a statement of stockholders' equity?

Q8-16. What items are typically reported under the stockholders' equity category of accumulated other comprehensive income (AOCI)?

Q8-17. What are three common forms of stock-based compensation and why do companies use such forms of compensation?

Q8-18. Describe the accounting for a convertible bond. Can the conversion ever result in the recognition of a gain in the income statement?

Mini Exercises

M8-19. **Analyzing and Identifying Financial Statement Effects of Stock Issuances**   LO2

During the current year, Bryant Company, (*a*) issues 8,000 shares of $50 par value preferred stock at $84 cash per share and (*b*) issues 19,000 shares of $1 par value common stock at $10 cash per share. Indicate the financial statement effects of these two issuances using the financial statement effects template.

M8-20. **Understanding EPS Calculations**   LO8

On its Form 10-K for the year ended December 31, 2015, **Bank of America Corp.** reported information related to basic earnings per share. Fill in the missing information.

Bank of America Corp. (BAC)

$ millions, except per share amounts	2015	2014	2013
Net income.	$15,888	$4,833	*d*
Preferred stock dividends	$ 1,483	*b*	$ 1,349
Net income applicable to common shareholders	$14,405	*c*	$10,082
Average common shares outstanding	10,462.282	10,527.818	*e*
Basic earnings per share	*a*	$ 0.36	$ 0.94

M8-21. **Distinguishing Between Common Stock and Additional Paid-in Capital**   LO1

Following is the 2016 stockholders' equity section from the **Cisco Systems Inc.** balance sheet.

Cisco Systems Inc. (CSCO)

Shareholders' Equity (in millions, except par value)	July 2016
Preferred stock, no par value: 5 shares authorized; none issued and outstanding. . .	$ —
Common stock and additional paid-in capital, $0.001 par value: 20,000 shares authorized; 5,029 and 5,085 shares issued and outstanding at July 30, 2016, and July 25, 2015, respectively	44,516
Retained earnings	19,396
Accumulated other comprehensive income.	(326)
Total Cisco shareholders' equity.	63,586
Noncontrolling interests	(1)
Total equity	$63,585

a. For the $44,516 million reported as "common stock and additional paid-in capital," what portion is common stock and what portion is additional paid-in capital?

b. Explain why Cisco does not report the two components described in part *a* separately.

M8-22. **Identifying Financial Statement Effects of Stock Issuance and Repurchase**   LO2

On January 1, Arcola Company issues 7,000 shares of $100 par value preferred stock at $300 cash per share. On March 1, the company repurchases 7,000 shares of previously issued $1 par value common stock at $156 cash per share. Use the financial statement effects template to record these two transactions.

M8-23. **Assessing the Financial Statement Effects of a Stock Split**   LO5

The following is taken from a **Monster Beverage** press release dated October 14, 2016.

Monster Beverage Corp. (MNST)

> Monster Beverage Corporation today announced that its Board of Directors has approved a 3-for-1 split of its common stock which will be effected in the form of a 200% stock dividend. The additional shares will be distributed on November 9, 2016 to stockholders of record at the close of business (Eastern Time) on October 26, 2016. The Company anticipates its common stock to begin trading at the split-adjusted price on November 10, 2016. Upon completion of the stock split, the number of outstanding shares of the Company's common stock will triple to approximately 571 million shares.

The Monster Beverage common stock has a par value of $0.005. What adjustments will Monster Beverage Corporation make to its balance sheet as a result of the stock split?

LO1   **M8-24.   Reconciling Common Stock and Treasury Stock Balances**

Abercrombie & Fitch
Co. (ANF)

Following is the stockholders' equity section from the **Abercrombie & Fitch Co.** balance sheet.

Stockholders' equity ($ thousands, except par value amounts)	January 30, 2016	January 31, 2015
Class A common stock—$0.01 par value: 150,000 shares authorized and 103,300 shares issued at each of January 30, 2016 and January 31, 2015 . . .	$ 1,033	$ 1,033
Paid-in capital	407,029	434,137
Retained earnings	2,530,196	2,550,673
Accumulated other comprehensive loss, net of tax	(114,619)	(83,580)
Treasury stock at average cost: 35,952 and 33,948 shares at January 30, 2016 and January 31, 2015, respectively	(1,532,576)	(1,512,562)
Total Abercrombie & Fitch Co. stockholders' equity	1,295,722	1,389,701
Noncontrolling interests	4,659	0
Total stockholders' equity	$1,291,063	$1,389,701

   a. Show the computation to yield the $1,033 balance reported for common stock.

   b. How many shares are outstanding at 2016 fiscal year-end?

   c. Use the common stock and paid-in capital accounts to determine the average price at which Abercrombie & Fitch issued its common stock.

   d. Use the treasury stock account to determine the average price Abercrombie & Fitch paid when it repurchased its common shares.

LO4   **M8-25.   Identifying and Analyzing Financial Statement Effects of Cash Dividends**

Bank of America
Corp. (BAC)

On its Form 10-K for the year ended December 31, 2015, **Bank of America Corp.** reported the following relating to dividends on its Series 5 Floating Rate Non-Cumulative Preferred stock.

Dividend Payment Date	Dividend Per Share
22-Feb-16	0.25556
23-Nov-15	0.25556
21-Aug-15	0.25556
21-May-15	0.24722
23-Feb-15	0.25556

There were 14,058 million shares of this preferred stock outstanding throughout the year. Determine the total dividends that Bank of America paid during fiscal 2015.

LO3   **M8-26.**[A] **Estimating Stock-Based Compensation Expense**

Rainier Corp. has several types of stock-based compensation plans including a stock purchase plan that allows employees to buy shares at a 15% discount. During 2016, employees purchased 25,000 shares under this plan. Also, the company granted 20,000 stock options with estimated fair value of $10.10 per option. The options vest ratably over three years. Ranier's average stock price during this year was $78.94. Determine Rainier's stock-based compensation expense for 2016.

LO5   **M8-27.   Identifying, Analyzing and Explaining the Effects of a Stock Split**

On September 1, Weiss Company has 300,000 shares of $9 par value ($148 market value) common stock that are issued and outstanding. Its balance sheet on that date shows the following account balances relating to its common stock.

Common stock.	$2,700,000
Paid-in capital in excess of par value.	1,680,000

On September 2, Weiss splits its stock 3-for-2 and reduces the par value to $6 per share.

   a. How many shares of common stock are issued and outstanding immediately after the stock split?

   b. What is the dollar balance of the common stock account immediately after the stock split?

   c. What is the likely reason that Weiss Company split its stock?

M8-28. Determining Cash Dividends to Preferred and Common Shareholders   **LO4**

Hobson Company has outstanding 40,000 shares of $50 par value, 6% cumulative preferred stock and 100,000 shares of $10 par value common stock. The company declares and pays cash dividends amounting to $280,000.

a. If there are no preferred dividends in arrears, how much in total dividends, and in dividends per share, does Hobson pay to each class of stock?

b. If there are one year's dividends in arrears on the preferred stock, how much in total dividends, and in dividends per share, does Hobson pay to each class of stock?

M8-29. Reconciling Retained Earnings   **LO4, 5**

Use the following data to reconcile the 2017 retained earnings for Emerald Company (that is, explain the change in retained earnings during the year).

Total retained earnings, December 31, 2016 ..	$537,000
Stock dividends declared and paid in 2017 ...	46,000
Cash dividends declared and paid in 2017 ...	55,000
Net income for 2017	203,000

M8-30. Calculating and Interpreting EPS Information   **LO8**

Wells Fargo reports the following information in its 2015 Form 10-K.   **Wells Fargo (WFC)**

In millions	2015	2014
Wells Fargo net income	$22,894	$23,057
Preferred stock dividends	$ 1,424	$ 1,236
Common stock dividends	$ 7,400	$ 6,908
Average common shares outstanding	5,136.5	5,237.2
Diluted average common shares outstanding	5,209.8	5,324.4

a. Determine Wells Fargo's basic EPS for fiscal 2015 and for fiscal 2014.

b. Compare the number of common shares outstanding used for the 2015 Basic and Diluted EPS ratios. Provide three examples that explain why the two numbers differ.

M8-31. Calculating and Recording Cash Dividends   **LO4**

On January 27, 2016, **McDonald**'s Board of Directors declared a quarterly cash dividend of $0.89 per   **McDonald's (MCD)** share of common stock payable on March 15, 2016, to shareholders of record at the close of business on March 1, 2016. Assume that there were 906 million shares outstanding during this time period.

Use the financial statement effects template to record the transactions for the following dates:

a. January 27, 2016.

b. March 1, 2016

c. March 15, 2016

M8-32. Determining Effects of Stock Splits   **LO5**

Oracle Corp has had the following stock splits since its inception.   **Oracle Corp. (ORCL)**

Effective Date	Split Amount
October 12, 2000	2 for 1
January 18, 2000	2 for 1
February 26, 1999	3 for 2
August 15, 1997	3 for 2
April 16, 1996	3 for 2
February 22, 1995	3 for 2
November 8, 1993	2 for 1
June 16, 1989	2 for 1
December 21, 1987	2 for 1
March 9, 1987	2 for 1

    a. If the par value of Oracle shares was originally $1, what would Oracle Corp. report as par value per share on its 2015 balance sheet?

    b. On May 10, 2016, Oracle stock traded for about $40. All things equal, if Oracle had never had a stock split, what would a share of Oracle have traded for that same day?

LO6
McDonald's (MCD)

M8-33. Interpreting Comprehensive Income and AOCI

Indicate whether each of the following statements is true or false. If false, indicate how to correct the statement.

    a. The amount reported for accumulated other comprehensive income (AOCI) on the balance sheet must be a positive amount consistent with all other stockholders' equity accounts.

    b. Changes in AOCI are reflected in other comprehensive income, which is different from net income.

    c. Other comprehensive income does not imply a change in cash.

LO7
JetBlue Airways Corporation (JBLU)

M8-34. Analyzing Financial Statement Effects of Convertible Securities

JetBlue Airways Corporation reports the following footnote to its 2015 10-K.

> In June 2009, we completed a public offering for an aggregate principal amount of $115 million of 6.75% Series A convertible debentures due 2039, or the Series A 6.75% Debentures. We simultaneously completed a public offering for an aggregate principal amount of $86 million of 6.75% Series B convertible debentures due 2039, or the Series B 6.75% Debentures. These are collectively known as the 6.75% Debentures. . . The net proceeds were approximately $197 million after deducting underwriting fees and other transaction related expenses. Interest on the 6.75% Debentures is payable semi-annually on April 15 and October 15. Holders of either the Series A or Series B 6.75% Debentures may convert them into shares of our common stock at any time at a conversion rate of 204.6036 shares per $1,000 principal amount of the 6.75% Debentures.

    a. Describe the effects on JetBlue's balance sheet if the convertible bonds are converted.

    b. Would the conversion affect earnings? Explain.

Exercises

LO2

E8-35. Identifying and Analyzing Financial Statement Effects of Stock Transactions

Orson Company reports the following transactions relating to its stock accounts in the current year.

Mar. 2	Issued 10,000 shares of $1 par value common stock at $30 cash per share.
Apr. 14	Issued 15,000 shares of $100 par value, 8% preferred stock at $250 cash per share.
June 30	Purchased 3,000 shares of its own common stock at $22 cash per share.
Sep. 25	Sold 1,500 shares of its treasury stock at $26 cash per share.

Use the financial statement effects template to indicate the effects from each of these transactions.

LO2

E8-36. Identifying and Analyzing Financial Statement Effects of Stock Transactions

Perry Corp. reports the following transactions relating to its stock accounts in the current year.

Feb. 3	Issued 40,000 shares of $5 par value common stock at $27 cash per share.
Feb. 27	Issued 9,000 shares of $50 par value, 8% preferred stock at $88 cash per share.
Mar. 31	Purchased 5,000 shares of its own common stock at $30 cash per share.
June 25	Sold 3,000 shares of its treasury stock at $38 cash per share.
July 15	Sold the remaining 2,000 shares of treasury stock at $29 cash per share.

Use the financial statement effects template to indicate the effects from each of these transactions.

LO1, 2, 3
Campbell Soup Co. (CPB)

E8-37. Analyzing and Computing Average Issue Price and Treasury Stock Cost

Following is the stockholders' equity section from the **Campbell Soup Company** balance sheet. (*Note:* Campbell's uses *shareowners' equity* in lieu of the more common title of stockholders' equity.)

Shareowners' Equity (millions, except per share amounts)	July 31, 2016	August 2, 2015
Preferred stock: authorized 40 shares; none issued	$ —	$ —
Capital stock, $.0375 par value; authorized 560 shares;		
issued 323 shares.	12	12
Additional paid-in capital	354	339
Earnings retained in the business	1,927	1,754
Capital stock in treasury, at cost	(664)	(556)
Accumulated other comprehensive loss	(104)	(168)
Total Campbell Soup Company shareowners' equity	1,525	1,381
Noncontrolling interests	8	(4)
Total equity.	$1,533	$1,377

Campbell Soup Company also reports the following statement of stockholders' equity.

| | Capital Stock | | | | | | | | |
| | Issued | | In Treasury | | Additional Paid-in Capital | Earnings Retained in the Business | Accumulated Other Comprehensive Income (Loss) | Noncontrolling Interests | Total Equity |
(millions, except per share amounts)	Shares	Amount	Shares	Amount					
Balance at August 2, 2015.	323	$12	(13)	$(556)	$339	$1,754	$(168)	$(4)	$1,377
Contribution from noncontrolling interests. . . .									—
Noncontrolling Interests Other Activity.								9	9
Net earnings (loss)						563			563
Other comprehensive income (loss).							64	3	67
Dividends ($1.248 per share)						(390)			(390)
Treasury stock purchased			(3)	(143)					(143)
Treasury stock issued under management incentive and stock option plans			1	35	15				50
Balance at July 31, 2016	323	$12	(15)	$ (664)	$354	$1,927	$(104)	$ 8	$1,533

a. Show the computation, using par value and share numbers, to arrive at the $12 million in the capital (common) stock account.

b. At what average price were the Campbell Soup shares issued?

c. Reconcile the beginning and ending balances of retained earnings.

d. Campbell Soup reports an increase in shareowners' equity relating to the exercise of stock options (titled "Treasury stock issued under management incentive and stock option plans"). This transaction involves the purchase of common stock by employees at a preset price. Describe how this set of transactions affects stockholders' equity.

e. Describe the transaction relating to the "Treasury stock purchased" line in the statement of shareowners' equity.

E8-38.[A]   **Analyzing Stock-Based Compensation**   **LO3**

Howell Company began business on March 1, 2017. At that time, it granted 250,000 options, with a strike price of $5, to computer engineers in lieu of signing bonuses. The fair value of each option was estimated at $1 and the options vest over four years.

a. What benefits did Howell Company create by granting options to the engineers instead of cash signing bonuses?

b. What is the total expense that the company will record associated with the options granted in 2017?

c. What will Howell record in 2017 for stock-option compensation expense?

d. How will the exercise of the options impact the balance sheet, income statement, and statement of cash flows?

LO4   **E8-39.**   **Analyzing Cash Dividends on Preferred and Common Stock**

Everett Company has outstanding 30,000 shares of $50 par value, 6% preferred stock and 70,000 shares of $1 par value common stock. During its first three years in business, it declared and paid no cash dividends in the first year, $310,000 in the second year, and $90,000 in the third year.

a. If the preferred stock is cumulative, determine the total amount of cash dividends paid to each class of stock in each of the three years.

b. If the preferred stock is noncumulative, determine the total amount of cash dividends paid to each class of stock in each of the three years.

LO1, 2   **E8-40.**   **Analyzing and Computing Issue Price, Treasury Stock Cost, and Shares Outstanding**

Altria Group Inc.   Following is the stockholders' equity section from **Altria Group Inc.**'s 2015 balance sheet.
(MO)

December 31 ($ millions, except per share amounts)	2015
Common stock, par value $0.33⅓ per share (2,805,961,317 shares issued).......	$ 935
Additional paid-in capital......................................	5,813
Earnings reinvested in the business.................................	27,257
Accumulated other comprehensive losses	(3,280)
Cost of repurchased stock (845,901,836 shares)......................	(27,845)
Total stockholders' equity attributable to Altria Group Inc.	2,880
Noncontrolling interests......................................	(7)
Total stockholders' equity.......................................	$ 2,873

a. Show the computation to derive the $935 million for common stock.

b. At what average price has Altria issued its common stock?

c. How many shares of Altria common stock are outstanding as of December 31, 2015?

d. At what average cost has Altria repurchased its treasury stock as of December 31, 2015?

e. Why would a company such as Altria want to repurchase $27,845 million of its common stock?

f. What does the Noncontrolling interests account of $(7) million represent?

LO4   **E8-41.**   **Analyzing Cash Dividends on Preferred and Common Stock**

Warren Company began business on June 30, 2015. At that time, it issued 25,000 shares of $40 par value, 8% cumulative preferred stock and 100,000 shares of $5 par value common stock. Through the end of 2017, there has been no change in the number of preferred and common shares outstanding.

a. Assume that Warren declared and paid cash dividends of $103,000 in 2015, $0 in 2016 and $461,000 in 2017. Compute the total cash dividends and the dividends per share paid to each class of stock in 2015, 2016, and 2017.

b. Assume that Warren declared and paid cash dividends of $0 in 2015, $160,000 in 2016, and $278,000 in 2017. Compute the total cash dividends and the dividends per share paid to each class of stock in 2015, 2016, and 2017.

LO4   **E8-42.**   **Identifying and Analyzing Financial Statement Effects of Dividends**

Baez Company has outstanding 25,000 shares of $10 par value common stock. It also has $514,000 of retained earnings. Near the current year-end, the company declares and pays a cash dividend of $1.80 per share and declares and issues a 5% stock dividend. The market price of the stock the day the dividends are declared is $25 per share. Use the financial statement effects template to indicate the effects of these two separate dividend transactions.

LO4   **E8-43.**   **Identifying and Analyzing Financial Statement Effects of Dividends**

The stockholders' equity of Rondon Company at December 31, 2016, appears below.

Common stock, $10 par value, 200,000 shares authorized; 80,000 shares issued and outstanding...................	$800,000
Paid-in capital in excess of par value......................	670,000
Retained earnings	419,000

During 2017, the following transactions occurred.

May 12   Declared and issued a 7% stock dividend; the common stock market value was $23 per share.
Dec. 31   Declared and paid a cash dividend of 95 cents per share.

a. Use the financial statement effects template to indicate the effects of these transactions.
b. Reconcile retained earnings for 2017 assuming that the company reports 2017 net income of $309,000.

E8-44.   Identifying and Analyzing Financial Statement Effects of Dividends   **LO4, 5**
The stockholders' equity of Hammel Company at December 31, 2016, is shown below.

5% preferred stock, $100 par value, 10,000 shares authorized; 6,000 shares issued and outstanding......................	$ 600,000
Common stock, $5 par value, 200,000 shares authorized; 70,000 shares issued and outstanding......................	350,000
Paid-in capital in excess of par value—preferred stock...........	50,000
Paid-in capital in excess of par value—common stock...........	400,000
Retained earnings	747,000
Total stockholders' equity	$2,147,000

The following transactions, among others, occurred during 2017.

Apr. 1   Declared and issued a 100% stock dividend on all outstanding shares of common stock. The market value of the stock was $14 per share.
Dec. 7   Declared and issued a 4% stock dividend on all outstanding shares of common stock. The market value of the stock was $17 per share.
Dec. 20   Declared and paid (1) the annual cash dividend on the preferred stock and (2) a cash dividend of 90 cents per common share.

a. Use the financial statement effects template to indicate the effects of these separate transactions.
b. Compute retained earnings for 2017 assuming that the company reports 2017 net income of $523,000.

E8-45.   Identifying, Analyzing and Explaining the Effects of a Stock Split   **LO5**
On March 1 of the current year, Lackey Company has 500,000 shares of $20 par value common stock that are issued and outstanding. Its balance sheet shows the following account balances relating to common stock.

Common stock.......................	$10,000,000
Paid-in capital in excess of par value......	5,300,000

On March 2, Lackey Company splits its common stock 2-for-1 and reduces the par value to $10 per share.

a. How many shares of common stock are issued and outstanding immediately after the stock split?
b. What is the dollar balance in the common stock account immediately after the stock split?
c. What is the dollar balance in the paid-in capital in excess of par value account immediately after the stock split?

E8-46. **Analyzing and Computing Issue Price, Treasury Stock Cost, and Shares Outstanding**

Following is the stockholders' equity section of the 2015 Caterpillar Inc. balance sheet.

Stockholders' Equity ($ millions)	2015	2014	2013
Common stock of $1.00 par; Authorized shares: 2,000,000,000; Issued shares (2015, 2014, and 2013—814,894,624 shares) at paid-in amount	$ 5,238	$ 5,016	$ 4,709
Treasury stock (2015: 232,572,734; 2014: 208,728,065; and 2013: 177,072,282 shares) at cost	(17,640)	(15,726)	(11,854)
Profit employed in the business	34,208	33,887	31,854
Accumulated other comprehensive income (loss)	(6,997)	(6,431)	(3,898)
Noncontrolling interests	76	80	67
Total stockholders' equity	$14,885	$16,826	$20,878

a. How many shares of Caterpillar common stock are outstanding at year-end 2015?

b. What does the phrase "at paid-in amount" in the common stock account mean?

c. At what average cost has Caterpillar repurchased its stock as of year-end 2015?

d. Why would a company such as Caterpillar want to repurchase its common stock?

e. Explain how CAT's "issued shares" remains constant over the three-year period while the dollar amount of its common stock account increases.

E8-47. **Analyzing Convertible Preferred Stock**

Xerox Corp. reports the following stockholders' equity information in its 10-K report.

Shareholders' Equity (in millions, except par value)	December 31	
	2015	2014
Series A convertible preferred stock	$ 349	$ 349
Common stock, $1 par value	1,013	1,124
Additional paid-in capital	3,017	4,283
Treasury stock, at cost	0	(105)
Retained earnings	9,686	9,535
Accumulated other comprehensive loss	(4,642)	(4,159)
Xerox shareholders' equity	$9,074	$10,678

Preferred Stock As of December 31, 2015, we had one class of preferred stock outstanding. We are authorized to issue approximately 22 million shares of cumulative preferred stock, $1.00 par value per share.

Series A Convertible Preferred Stock: We have issued 300,000 shares of Series A convertible perpetual preferred stock with an aggregate liquidation preference of $300 and an initial fair value of $349. The convertible preferred stock pays quarterly cash dividends at a rate of 8% per year ($24 per year). Each share of convertible preferred stock is convertible at any time, at the option of the holder, into 89.8876 shares of common stock for a total of 26,966 thousand shares (reflecting an initial conversion price of approximately $11.125 per share of common stock), subject to customary anti-dilution adjustments.

Common Stock We have 1.75 billion authorized shares of common stock, $1.00 par value per share. At December 31, 2015, 102 million shares were reserved for issuance under our incentive compensation plans, 48 million shares were reserved for debt to equity exchanges and 27 million shares were reserved for conversion of the Series A convertible preferred stock.

Required

a. At December 31, 2015, Xerox reports $349 million of 8% Series A Convertible Preferred stock. What is the dollar amount of dividends that Xerox must pay on this stock (assume a par value of $100 per share)?

b. Describe the effects that will occur to Xerox's balance sheet and its income statement when the Series A Convertible Preferred stock is converted.

c. What is the benefit, if any, of issuing equity securities with a conversion feature? How are these securities treated in the computation of earnings per share (EPS)?

E8-48. **Analyzing and Computing Issue Price, Treasury Stock Cost, and Shares Outstanding**

Following is the stockholders' equity section of the 2015 Merck & Co. Inc. balance sheet.

LO1

Merck & Co. Inc. (MRK)

Stockholders' Equity ($ millions)	2015
Common stock, $0.50 par value; Authorized—6,500,000,000 shares; Issued—3,577,103,522 shares.	$ 1,788
Other paid-in capital.	40,222
Retained earnings	45,348
Accumulated other comprehensive loss	(4,148)
Stockholders' equity before deduction for treasury stock.	83,210
Less treasury stock, at cost: 795,975,449 shares	38,534
Total Merck & Co. Inc. stockholders' equity.	$44,676

a. Show the computation of the $1,788 million in the common stock account.

b. At what average price were the Merck common shares issued?

c. At what average cost was the Merck treasury stock purchased?

d. How many common shares are outstanding as of December 31, 2015?

Problems

P8-49. **Identifying and Analyzing Financial Statement Effects of Stock Transactions**

The stockholders' equity section of Medina Company at December 31, 2016, follows.

LO1, 2

8% preferred stock, $25 par value, 50,000 shares authorized; 8,400 shares issued and outstanding.	$210,000
Common stock, $10 par value, 200,000 shares authorized; 50,000 shares issued and outstanding.	500,000
Paid-in capital in excess of par value—preferred stock.	85,000
Paid-in capital in excess of par value—common stock.	300,000
Retained earnings	370,000

During 2017, the following transactions occurred.

Jan. 10 Issued 28,000 shares of common stock for $18 cash per share.

Jan. 23 Repurchased 8,000 shares of common stock at $20 cash per share.

Mar. 14 Sold one-half of the treasury shares acquired January 23 for $22 cash per share.

July 15 Issued 2,600 shares of preferred stock for $128,000 cash.

Nov. 15 Sold 1,000 of the treasury shares acquired January 23 for $26 cash per share.

Required

a. Use the financial statement effects template to indicate the effects from each of these transactions.

b. Prepare the December 31, 2017, stockholders' equity section of the balance sheet assuming the company reports 2017 net income of $121,000.

LO2, 6, 7

Under Armour Inc. (UA)

P8-50.   Analyzing Stockholders' Equity Including AOCI and Convertible Securities

Under Armour reported the following stockholders' equity section of the balance sheet for the fiscal year ended December 31, 2015.

Stockholders' Equity ($ 000s)	2015	2014
Class A Common Stock, $0.0003 1/3 par value; 400,000,000 shares authorized as of December 31, 2015 and 2014; 181,646,468 shares issued and outstanding as of December 31, 2015 and 177,295,988 shares issued and outstanding as of December 31, 2014..............	$ 61	$ 59
Class B Convertible Common Stock, $0.0003 1/3 par value; 34,450,000 shares authorized, issued and outstanding as of December 31, 2015 and 36,600,000 shares authorized, issued and outstanding as of December 31, 2014.	11	12
Class C Common Stock, $0.0003 1/3 par value; 400,000,000 shares authorized as of December 31, 2015; 0 shares issued and outstanding as of December 31, 2015.	—	—
Additional paid-in capital	636,630	508,350
Retained earnings	1,076,533	856,687
Accumulated other comprehensive loss	(45,013)	(14,808)
Total stockholders' equity	$1,668,222	$1,350,300

Required

a. Determine the number of Class B Convertible shares that were converted during 2015. *Note*: Class B common shares can be converted into Class A common shares.

b. Explain the effect of the conversion on the Class A Common Stock and Class B Common Stock accounts.

c. During the year, Under Armour issued 1,996,000 Class A Common shares. Assume that it received cash proceeds of $19,136 for this issuance. Explain the effect of this issuance on its stockholders' equity accounts.

d. During the year, foreign currency translation losses increased by $31,816 and unrealized losses on cash flow hedges (derivatives) decreased by $1,611. (i) Use this information to reconcile the accumulated other comprehensive loss account. (ii) What can you conclude about changes in $US against currencies of countries where Under Armour has subsidiaries?

LO3   P8-51.   Identifying and Analyzing Financial Statement Effects of Stock-Based Compensation

The stockholders' equity of Fowler Company at December 31, 2016, follows.

7% Preferred stock, $100 par value, 20,000 shares authorized; 4,000 shares issued and outstanding......................	$ 400,000
Common stock, $15 par value, 300,000 shares authorized; 30,000 shares issued and outstanding......................	450,000
Paid-in capital in excess of par value—preferred stock...........	36,000
Paid-in capital in excess of par value—common stock...........	360,000
Retained earnings	325,000
Total stockholders' equity	$1,571,000

The following transactions, among others, occurred during the following year.

- Employees exercised 12,000 stock options that were granted in 2012 and had a three-year vesting period. These options had an estimated fair value of $2 at the grant date, and an exercise price of $16. There were no other vested or unvested options after this exercise.
- Awarded 1,000 shares of stock to a new executives, when the stock price was $36.
- Sold 10,000 shares to employees under the company-wide stock purchase plan. Under the plan, employees purchased the shares at a 10% discount when the stock price was $33 per share.
- Granted 40,000 new stock options, with a strike price of $34 and an estimated fair value of $6. The options vest over three years.

Required

Prepare the December 31, 2017, statement of stockholders' equity assuming that the company reports 2017 pretax income of $483,000 before the effects of stock-based compensation. Assume the company has a 35% tax rate.

P8-52. **Identifying and Analyzing Financial Statement Effects of Stock Transactions**

The stockholders' equity of Verrecchia Company at December 31, 2016, follows.

LO1, 2

Common stock, $5 par value, 500,000 shares authorized;	
350,000 shares issued and outstanding....................	$1,750,000
Paid-in capital in excess of par value.......................	800,000
Retained earnings	634,000

During 2017, the following transactions occurred.

Jan. 5   Issued 10,000 shares of common stock for $13 cash per share.
Jan. 18   Repurchased 4,000 shares of common stock at $16 cash per share.
Mar. 12   Sold one-fourth of the treasury shares acquired January 18 for $19 cash per share.
July 17   Sold 500 shares of treasury stock for $14 cash per share.
Oct. 1   Issued 5,000 shares of 8%, $25 par value preferred stock for $36 cash per share. This is the first issuance of preferred shares from the 50,000 authorized preferred shares.

Required

a. Use the financial statement effects template to indicate the effects of each transaction.
b. Prepare the December 31, 2017, stockholders' equity section of the balance sheet assuming that the company reports net income of $76,900 for the year.

P8-53. **Identifying and Analyzing Financial Statement Effects of Stock Transactions**

Following is the stockholders' equity of Herrera Corporation at December 31, 2016.

LO1, 2

8% preferred stock, $50 par value, 10,000 shares authorized;	
8,000 shares issued and outstanding......................	$ 400,000
Common stock, $20 par value, 50,000 shares authorized;	
25,000 shares issued and outstanding.....................	500,000
Paid-in capital in excess of par value—preferred stock...........	70,000
Paid-in capital in excess of par value—common stock...........	385,000
Retained earnings	238,000
Total stockholders' equity	$1,593,000

The following transactions, among others, occurred during 2017.

Jan. 15   Issued 1,000 shares of preferred stock for $60 cash per share.
Jan. 20   Issued 4,000 shares of common stock at $34 cash per share.
May 18   Announced a 2-for-1 common stock split, reducing the par value of the common stock to $10 per share. The number of shares authorized was increased to 100,000 shares.
June 1   Issued 2,000 shares of common stock for $56,000 cash.
Sep. 1   Repurchased 2,500 shares of common stock at $16 cash per share.
Oct. 12   Sold 900 treasury shares at $19 cash per share.
Dec. 22   Issued 500 shares of preferred stock for $57 cash per share.

Required

Use the financial statement effects template to indicate the effects of each transaction.

LO1, 2, 3, 4, 6

The Procter & Gamble Company (PG)

P8-54.   Analyzing and Interpreting Equity Accounts and Comprehensive Income
Following is the shareholders' equity section of the 2016 balance sheet for **Procter & Gamble Company** and its statement of shareholders' equity.

June 30 (In millions, expect per share amounts)	2016
Shareholders' Equity	
Convertible Class A preferred stock, stated value $1 per share (600 shares authorized)	$ 1,038
Non-Voting Class B preferred stock, stated value $1 per share (200 shares authorized)	—
Common stock, stated value $1 per share	
(10,000 shares authorized; shares issued: 2016—4,009.2)	4,009
Additional paid-in capital	63,714
Reserve for ESOP debt retirement.	(1,290)
Accumulated other comprehensive income/(loss)	(15,907)
Treasury stock, at cost (shares held: 2016—1,341.2)	(82,176)
Retained earnings	87,953
Noncontrolling interest.	642
Total shareholders' equity	$57,983

Consolidated Statement of Shareholders' Equity

Dollars in millions; Shares in thousands	Common Shares Outstanding	Common Stock	Preferred Stock	Additional Paid-in Capital	Reserve for ESOP Debt Retirement	Accumulated Other Comprehensive Income (Loss)	Treasury Stock	Retained Earnings	Non-controlling Interest	Total
Balance June 30, 2015.	2,714,571	$4,009	$1,077	$63,852	$(1,320)	$(12,780)	$(77,226)	$84,807	$631	$63,050
Net earnings.								10,508	96	10,604
Other comprehensive income						(3,127)				(3,127)
Dividends to shareholders:										
Common.								(7,181)		(7,181)
Preferred, net of tax benefits . . .								(255)		(255)
Treasury purchases	(103,449)						(8,217)			(8,217)
Employee plan issuances.	52,089			(144)			3,234			3,090
Preferred stock conversions.	4,863		(39)	6			33			—
ESOP debt impacts					30			74		104
Noncontrolling interest, net									(85)	(85)
Balance June 30, 2016.	2,668,074	$4,009	$1,038	$63,714	$(1,290)	$(15,907)	$(82,176)	$87,953	$642	$57,983

Required

a. What does the term *convertible* (in reference to the company's Class A preferred stock) mean?

b. How many shares of common stock did Procter & Gamble issue when convertible Class A preferred stock was converted during fiscal 2016?

c. Describe the transactions relating to employee plan issuances. At what average price was the common stock issued for employee stock plans during 2016?

d. What is other comprehensive income? What is the accumulated other comprehensive income account? Explain.

e. What cash dividends did Procter & Gamble pay in 2016 for each class of stock?

P8-55. Analyzing and Interpreting Equity Accounts and Accumulated Other Comprehensive Income
Following is the stockholders' equity section of Beam Inc. balance sheet and its statement of stockholders' equity.

LO1, 2, 3, 6
Beam Inc. (BEAM)

December 31 (In millions, except per share amounts)	2012
Stockholders' equity	
$2.67 Convertible preferred stock	$ —
Common stock, par value $3.125 per share (750.0 shares authorized; 234.9 shares issued; 160.1 shares outstanding in 2012 and 155.9 shares outstanding in 2011)	734.0
Paid-in capital	873.7
Accumulated other comprehensive loss	(186.0)
Retained earnings	6,139.7
Treasury stock, at cost	(2,949.3)
Total equity	$4,612.1

(In millions, except per share amounts)	$2.67 Convertible Preferred Stock	Common Stock	Paid-in Capital	Accumulated Other Comprehensive Income (Loss)	Retained Earnings	Treasury Stock At Cost	Total Equity
Balance at December 31, 2011	$4.7	$734.0	$882.4	$(304.1)	$5,892.6	$(3,109.9)	$4,099.7
Net income	—	—	—	—	382.4	—	382.4
Other comprehensive Income	—	—	—	118.1	—	—	118.1
Dividends	—	—	—	—	(130.1)	—	(130.1)
Stock-based compensation	—	—	13.2	—	(3.2)	126.1	136.1
Tax benefit on exercise of stock options	—	—	12.8	—	—	—	12.8
Conversion of preferred stock	(3.4)	—	(31.2)	—	—	34.5	(0.1)
Redemption of preferred stock	(1.3)	—	(0.4)	—	—	—	(1.7)
Spin-off of Fortune Brands Home & Security Inc.	—	—	(3.1)	—	(2.0)	—	(5.1)
Balance at December 31, 2012	$ —	$734.0	$873.7	$(186.0)	$6,139.7	$(2,949.3)	$4,612.1

Other comprehensive income (in millions)	2012
Foreign currency translation adjustments	
Foreign currency translation gains (losses)	$122.0
Reclassification adjustments included in earnings	—
Tax benefit	2.4
Foreign currency translation adjustments, net	124.4
Derivative instruments	
Derivative instrument losses	(3.4)
Reclassification adjustments included in earnings	3.4
Tax expense	(0.2)
Derivative instruments, net	(0.2)
Pension and other postretirement benefit adjustments	
Current year actuarial loss—pension plans	(28.0)
Current year actuarial loss—other postretirement benefit plans	(0.2)
Reclassification adjustments included in earnings	17.1
Tax benefit	5.0
Pension and other postretirement benefit adjustments, net	(6.1)
Total other comprehensive income	$118.1

Required

a. Explain the "$2.67" component of the convertible preferred stock account title.

b. Show (confirm) the computation that yields the $734.0 million common stock at year-end 2012.

c. At what average price were Beam's common shares issued as of year-end 2012?

d. What is included in Beam's accumulated other comprehensive income for 2012? What other items are typically included in accumulated other comprehensive income?

LO7, 8   **P8-56.**   **Interpreting Footnote Disclosure on Convertible Debentures**

Alloy Inc. (ALOY)   Alloy Inc. reports the following footnote related to its convertible debentures in its 2007 10-K ($ thousands).

> In August 2003, Alloy completed the issuance of $69,300 of 20-Year 5.375% Senior Convertible Debentures due August 1, 2023. If converted, bondholders would currently receive 29.851 shares of Alloy common for each $1,000 face amount bond. Alloy continues to be responsible for repaying the Convertible Debentures in full if they are not converted into shares of Alloy common stock. If not previously converted to common stock, Alloy may redeem the Convertible Debentures after August 1, 2008 at 103% of their face amount from August 1, 2008 through December 31, 2008 and at declining prices to 100% in January 2011 and thereafter, with accrued interest. From August 30, 2006 through December 7, 2006, holders converted approximately $67,903 face amount of their Debentures, in accordance with their terms, into approximately 2,026,000 shares of Alloy common stock. During fiscal 2006, the Company's additional paid-in capital increased by $67,883 as a result of the conversions. At January 31, 2007, the Company had $1,397 in principal amount of outstanding Convertible Debentures. At January 31, 2007, the fair value of the Convertible Debentures was approximately $1,504, which is estimated based on quoted market prices.

Required

a. How did Alloy initially account for the issuance of the 5.375% debentures, assuming that the conversion option cannot be detached and sold separately?

b. Consider the conversion terms reported in the footnote. At what minimum stock price would it make economic sense for debenture holders to convert to Alloy common stock?

c. Use the financial statement effects template to show how Alloy accounted for the conversion of the 5.375% debentures in 2006. The par value of the company's stock is $0.01.

d. Assume that the conversion feature is valued by investors and, therefore, results in a higher initial issuance price for the bonds. What effect will the conversion feature have on the amount of interest expense and net income that Alloy reports?

e. How are the convertible debentures treated in the computation of basic and diluted earnings per share (EPS)?

LO7   **P8-57.**   **Interpreting Disclosure on Convertible Preferred Securities**

Northrop Grumman Corp. (NOC)   The 2008 annual report of Northrop Grumman Corporation includes the following disclosure in its shareholders' equity footnote.

> **Conversion of Preferred Stock**   On February 20, 2008, the company's board of directors approved the redemption of all of the 3.5 million shares of mandatorily redeemable convertible preferred stock on April 4, 2008. Prior to the redemption date, substantially all of the preferred shares were converted into common stock at the election of shareholders. All remaining unconverted preferred shares were redeemed by the company on the redemption date. As a result of the conversion and redemption, the company issued approximately 6.4 million shares of common stock.

Required

a. Explain what is meant by "mandatorily redeemable" and "convertible" preferred stock.

b. The company's balance sheet reports preferred stock of $350 million at December 31, 2007 (and $0 at December 31, 2008). As is typical, Northrop Grumman originally sold these preferred at par. Confirm that the par value of the preferred stock is $100 per share.

c. Northrop's footnotes report that the fair value of the preferred shares was $146 per share at December 31, 2008. What would explain this large increase in its preferred stock's market price?

d. Use the financial statement effects template to record the conversion of the preferred stock on April 4, 2008. Assume that all 3.5 million shares were converted. The par value of the company's common stock is $1 per share.

LO3   **P8-58.**   **Identifying and Analyzing Financial Statement Effects of Share-Based Compensation**

Weaver Industries implements a new share-based compensation plan in 2014. Under the plan, the company's CEO and CFO each will receive non-qualified stock options to purchase 100,000, no par shares. The options vest ratably (1/3 of the options each year) over three years, expire in 10 years, and have an exercise (strike) price of $27 per share. Weaver uses the Black-Scholes model to estimate a fair value per option of $18.

Required

a. Use the financial statement effects template to record the compensation expense related to these options for each year 2014 through 2016.

b. In 2017, the company's stock price is $24. If you were the Weaver Industries CEO, would you exercise your options? Explain.

c. In 2019, the company's stock price is $46 and the CEO exercises all of her options. Use the financial statement effects template to record the exercise.

P8-59. Interpreting Disclosure on Employee Stock Options

LO3

Intel Corporation reported the following in its 2015 10-K report.

Intel Corporation (INTC)

Share-Based Compensation Share-based compensation recognized in 2015 was $1.3 billion ($1.1 billion in 2014 and $1.1 billion in 2013). . . .During 2015, the tax benefit that we realized for the tax deduction from share-based awards totaled $533 million ($555 million in 2014 and $385 million in 2013). . . . We use the Black-Scholes option pricing model to estimate the fair value of options granted under our equity incentive plans and rights to acquire stock granted under the 2006 Plan and rights to acquire shares of common stock under the 2006 Stock Purchase Plan. No options were granted in 2015. We based the weighted average estimated value of employee stock option grants and rights granted under the stock purchase plan, as well as the weighted average assumptions used in calculating the fair value, on estimates at the date of grant, as follows:

	Stock Options			Stock Purchase Plan		
	2015	**2014**	**2013**	**2015**	**2014**	**2013**
Estimated values	n/a	$3.61	$3.11	$6.56	$5.87	$4.52
Expected life (in years) . . .	n/a	5.1	5.2	0.5	0.5	0.5
Risk-free interest rate	n/a	1.7%	0.8%	0.1%	0.1%	0.1%
Volatility	n/a	23%	25%	25%	22%	22%
Dividend yield	n/a	3.6%	3.9%	3.1%	3.2%	4.0%

Additional information with respect to stock option activity is as follows:

In millions	Number of Options	Weighted Average Exercise Price
December 29, 2012	202.8	$20.20
Granted	20.1	$22.99
Exercised	(65.0)	$18.76
Cancelled and forfeited	(3.0)	$22.58
Expired	(1.9)	$22.56
December 28, 2013	153.0	$21.10
Granted	0.6	$25.34
Exercised	(63.7)	$19.87
Cancelled and forfeited	(2.7)	$23.70
Expired	(9.9)	$27.00
December 27, 2014	77.3	$21.30
Granted	—	$ —
Exercised	(21.9)	$20.34
Cancelled and forfeited	(1.1)	$23.23
Expired	(0.1)	$20.87
December 26, 2015	54.2	$21.65
Options exercisable as of:		
December 28, 2013	111.5	$20.25
December 27, 2014	54.7	$20.29
December 26, 2015	43.8	$21.07

Required

a. What did Intel expense for share-based compensation for 2014? How many options did Intel grant in 2014? Compute the fair value of all options granted during 2014. Why do the fair value of the option grants and the expense differ?

b. Intel used the Black-Scholes formula to estimate fair value of the options granted each year. How did the change in volatility from 2013 to 2014 affect share-based compensation in 2014? What about the change in risk-free rate?

c. How many options were exercised during 2015? Estimate the cash that Intel received from its employees when these options were exercised.

d. What was the intrinsic value per share of the options exercised in 2015? If employees who exercised options in 2015 immediately sold them, what "profit" did they make from the shares? (Assume that Intel's stock price was $32.19, on average, during fiscal 2015.)

e. The tax benefit that Intel will receive on the options exercised is computed based on the intrinsic value of the options exercised. Estimate Intel's tax benefit from the 2015 option exercises assuming a tax rate of 37%.

f. What was the average exercise price of the 0.1 million options expired in 2015? Explain what benefit the employees lost by not exercising their options.

LO7

HealthSouth Corporation (HLS)

P8-60. **Analyzing Convertible Preferred Stock Disclosure**

In a press release dated April 22, 2015, HealthSouth provided notice of conversion of their 6.5% Series A Convertible Preferred Stock, as follows.

> HealthSouth Corporation (NYSE: HLS) today announced it is providing notice to the registered holders of the Company's 6.5% Series A Convertible Preferred Stock. Pursuant to Section 5 of the Certificate of Designations for the preferred stock, the Company is exercising its right to cause all of the outstanding shares of the preferred stock to be converted into a number of whole shares of the Company's common stock. On the forced conversion date (April 23, 2015), all 96,245 shares of preferred stock outstanding will be converted. Each share of preferred stock will automatically be converted into 33.9905 shares of common stock.

On April 23, 2015, the carrying value of the Series A Convertible Preferred Stock was $93.2 million and HealthSouth's common stock has a par value of $0.01 per share.

Required

a. How many shares of common stock will HealthSouth issue to preferred stockholders?

b. Use the financial statement effects template to record the forced conversion.

c. Identify and estimate the important benefit to HealthSouth's cash flow from conversion.

d. How will the conversion affect the diluted shares outstanding?

P8-61. **Interpreting Disclosure on Share-Based Compensation**

Intel reported the following information in its 2015 10-K related to its restricted stock plan.

LO3

Intel Corporation (INTC)

Information with respect to outstanding restricted stock unit (RSU) activity is as follows:

In millions	Number of RSUs	Weighted Average Grant-Date Fair Value
December 29, 2012	109.3	$22.03
Granted	53.4	$21.45
Vested	(44.5)	$20.21
Forfeited	(4.9)	$22.06
December 28, 2013	113.3	$22.47
Granted	57.2	$25.40
Vested	(42.5)	$22.33
Forfeited	(8.6)	$22.94
December 27, 2014	119.4	$23.89
Granted	42.4	$31.63
Vested	(46.6)	$23.61
Forfeited	(7.8)	$25.76
December 26, 2015	107.4	$26.93
Expected to vest as of December 26, 2015	102.5	$26.93

The aggregate fair value of awards that vested in 2015 was $1.5 billion ($1.1 billion in 2014 and $1.0 billion in 2013), which represents the market value of our common stock on the date that the RSUs vested. The grant-date fair value of awards that vested in 2015 was $1.1 billion ($949 million in 2014 and $899 million in 2013). The number of RSUs vested includes shares of common stock that we withheld on behalf of employees to satisfy the minimum statutory tax withholding requirements. RSUs that are expected to vest are net of estimated future forfeitures. As of December 26, 2015, there was $1.8 billion in unrecognized compensation costs related to RSUs granted under our equity incentive plans.

Required

a. How do restricted stock and stock options differ? In what respects are they the same?

b. Why do companies impose vesting periods on restricted stock grants?

c. Use the financial statement effects template to record the restricted stock granted to senior executives during 2015. The common stock has a par value of $0.001 per share.

d. Use the financial statement effects template to record the 2015 compensation expense related to Intel's restricted stock awards. (*Hint:* The expense is equal to the grant-date fair value of the RSUs that vested during the year.) Include the tax effects of the compensation expense. Assume a tax rate of 35%.

IFRS Applications

I8-62. **Analyzing and Interpreting Equity Accounts and Comprehensive Income**

Henkel AG & Co. is an international, fast-moving consumer goods (FMCG) company headquartered in Düsseldorf, Germany. Following is its shareholders' equity statement, prepared using IFRS, from its 2015 annual report.

LO1, 2, 4, 6

Henkel AG & Co.

In millions euro	Issued Capital					Other Components					
---	Ordinary Shares	Pre-ferred Shares	Capital Reserve	Treasury Shares	Retained Earnings	Currency Transla-tion	Hedge Reserve per IAS 39	Avail-able-for-Sale Reserve	Shareholders of Henkel AG & Co.	Non-Controlling Interests	Total
At December 31, 2014/ January 1, 2015	€260	€178	€652	€(91)	€11,396	€(723)	€(167)	€3	€11,508	€136	€11,644
Net income	—	—	—	—	1,921	—	—	—	1,921	47	1,968
Other comprehensive income	—	—	—	—	265	582	17	—	830	11	841
Total comprehensive income for the period	—	—	—	—	2,186	582	17	—	2,751	58	2,809
Dividends	—	—	—	—	(564)	—	—	—	(564)	(33)	(597)
Sale of treasury shares	—	—	—	—	—	—	—	—	—	—	—
Changes in ownership interest with no change in control	—	—	—	—	(34)	—	—	—	(34)	(11)	(45)
Other changes in equity	—	—	—	—	—	—	—	—	—	—	—
At December 31, 2015	€260	€178	€652	€(91)	€12,984	€(141)	€(184)	€3	€13,661	€150	€13,811

Required

a. Did Henkel issue any additional ordinary or preferred shares during 2015?

b. How much did Henkel pay in dividends during 2015? To whom were these dividends paid?

c. Did the company repurchase any stock during 2015?

d. Did Henkel sell any treasury shares? If so, what did the company receive in exchange for the sale of treasury stock?

e. Consider the currency translation account. Explain how the change of €582 arose during the year.

f. Henkel reports noncontrolling interest of €150. Why did this account increase during the year?

g. Compute return on equity for 2015. (*Hint:* Use the net income attributable to controlling interest [shareholders of Henkel] and equity attributable to controlling interest.)

LO1, 2   **I8-63.**   **Analyzing and Computing Average Issue Price and Treasury Stock Transactions**

Telefónica, S.A. (TEF)

Telefónica, S.A. is a Spanish broadband and telecommunications provider with operations in Europe, Latin America, North America and Asia. The company's statement of changes in equity reported the following.

In millions €	December 31, 2015	December 31, 2014
Share capital	€ 4,975	€ 4,657
Share premium	3,227	460
Reserves	(9,259)	(5,052)
Treasury shares (141,639,159 and 128,227,971 shares)	(1,656)	(1,586)
Retained earnings	20,604	22,656
Total attributable to equity holders of parent	17,891	21,135
Noncontrolling interests	9,665	9,186
Total equity	**€27,556**	**€30,321**

Required

a. Consider the treasury shares at December 31, 2015. At what average price did the company repurchase these shares?

b. Determine the number of treasury shares, net, the company acquired during 2015. At what average price did the company repurchase shares in 2015?

c. Did the company issue any new shares during the year? If so, what issue proceeds did it receive?

d. Does the company own 100% of the stock of all of its subsidiaries? How do you know?

e. Retained earnings decreased during 2015. Can we conclude that the company reported a net loss for the year?

I8-64. **Interpreting Disclosures on Treasury Stock and Stock-based Compensation** **LO2, 3**

Rio Tinto is listed on stock exchanges in both the UK and Australia. Following is its 2015 statement Rio Tinto (RIO)
of stockholders' equity.

Year ended 31 December 2015 (in $US millions)	Share Capital	Share Premium	Other Reserves	Retained Earnings	Total	Attributable to owners of Rio Tinto Non-Controlling Interests	Total Equity
Opening balance	$4,765	$4,288	$11,122	$26,110	$46,285	$8,309	$54,594
Total comprehensive loss for the year	—	—	(2,020)	(423)	(2,443)	(1,306)	(3,749)
Currency translation arising on Rio Tinto Limited's share capital	(503)	—	—	—	(503)	—	(503)
Dividends	—	—	—	(4,076)	(4,076)	(315)	(4,391)
Share buyback	(88)	—	6	(1,946)	(2,028)	—	(2,028)
Own shares purchased from Rio Tinto shareholders to satisfy share options....	—	—	(25)	(28)	(53)	—	(53)
Treasury shares reissued and other movements.......................	—	12	—	1	13	—	13
Change in equity interest held by Rio Tinto .	—	—	—	20	20	(17)	3
Equity issued to holders of non-controlling interests	—	—	—	—	—	103	103
Companies no longer consolidated	—	—	—	—	—	5	5
Employee share options and other IFRS 2 charges to the income statement.......	—	—	56	78	134	—	134
Closing balance	$4,174	$4,300	$ 9,139	$19,736	$37,349	$6,779	$44,128

a. Consider the share buyback of $2,028 million. Rio Tinto repurchased the shares, cancelled the stock, and removed the related values from the shareholders' equity accounts. Use the financial statement effects template to record this transaction. For purposes here, treat other reserves as an earned capital account.

b. Assume that this company reported in U.S. GAAP and that the share buyback was a typical treasury share transaction. Use the financial statement effects template to record this transaction.

c. Notes to the annual report disclose the following, "Our share ownership policy requires executives to build up and maintain a meaningful shareholding. We have, for our executives, a mandatory conversion of 50 percent of any annual short-term bonus payment into shares, with vesting deferred for three years." What incentives does the mandatory conversion policy create for executives?

I8-65. **Calculating and Recording Cash Dividends** **LO4, 5**

Husky Energy Inc. declared a dividend of CDN $0.30 per share to shareholders of record at the close Husky Energy Inc.
of business on 08/28/15 and payable on 10/01/15. The dividend will be paid in cash; however share- (HSE)
holders can elect to receive stock dividends in the form of common shares of Husky Energy in lieu of
the cash dividend. Use the financial statement effects template to record a $25,000 dividend (on October
1, 2015) to a shareholder who elects to receive the dividend as:

a. Additional common shares—assume Husky's common stock has no par value.

b. Cash.

LO1, 2, 3, 4, 6   **I8-66.**   **Analyzing Stockholders' Equity Accounts and Transactions**
Potash Corporation
(POT)

Potash Corporation—the world's largest potash producer—is a Canadian corporation based in Saska-toon, Saskatchewan. The following is information taken from its financial statements reported in $US but prepared in accordance with IFRS.

Equity Attributable to Common Shareholders (In millions of U.S. dollars)	Share Capital	Contributed Surplus	Accumulated Other Comprehensive Income				Total Accumulated Other Comprehensive Income	Retained Earnings	Total Equity
			Net unrealized gain on available-for-sale investments	Net loss on derivatives designated as cash flow hedges	Net actuarial loss on defined benefit plans	Other			
Balance—December 31, 2014 . . .	$1,632	$234	$623	$(119)	$ —	$(1)	$503	$6,423	$8,792
Net income	—	—	—	—	—	—	—	1,270	1,270
Other comprehensive income (loss)	—	—	(546)	2	36	(9)	(517)	—	(517)
Dividends declared	—	—	—	—	—	—	—	(1,274)	(1,274)
Effect of share-based compensation including issuance of common shares . . .	72	(4)	—	—	—	—	—	—	68
Shares issued for dividend reinvestment plan	43	—	—	—	—	—	—	—	43
Transfer of net actuarial loss on defined benefit plans	—	—	—	—	36	—	(36)	36	—
Balance—December 31, 2015 . . .	$1,747	$230	$ 77	$(117)	$—	$(10)	$(50)	$6,455	$8,382

Authorized   The company is authorized to issue an unlimited number of common shares with-out par value and an unlimited number of first preferred shares. The common shares are not redeemable or convertible. The first preferred shares may be issued in one or more series with rights and conditions to be determined by the Board of Directors. No first preferred shares have been issued.

Issued	Number of Common Shares	Consideration
Balance, December 31, 2014	830,242,574	$1,632
Issued under option plans	4,803,560	72
Issued for dividend reinvestment plan	1,494,017	43
Balance, December 31, 2015	836,540,151	$1,747

a. How many shares are authorized at December 31, 2015?
b. How many shares are issued at December 31, 2015? At what average price were these shares issued as of December 31, 2015?
c. How many shares are issued under option plans at December 31, 2015? At what average price were these shares issued?
d. Does the company have any treasury stock? How do we know?
e. On January 28, 2016, the company's Board of Directors declared a quarterly dividend of $0.25 per share, payable to all shareholders of record on April 12, 2016. Assuming that the number of shares outstanding on April 12, 2016, is the same as on December 31, 2015, what dividends will the com-pany pay?
f. Comprehensive income includes net income plus other comprehensive income. What was the com-pany's comprehensive income for 2015? Why does it differ from net income for 2015?

Ongoing Project

(This ongoing project began in Module 1 and continues through most of the book; even if previous segments were not completed, the requirements are still applicable to any business analysis.) Company analysis should consider how the companies are financed and what transactions were executed with stockholders during the recent year.

1. *Contributed Capital.*   Use the balance sheet and the statement of stockholders' equity to determine how the company has structured its equity.

   - What proportion of assets are financed with equity?
   - What classes of equity does the company have? What transactions occurred during the year?
   - Does the company have treasury stock? Read the MD&A and the footnotes to determine the main reason for holding treasury stock. Assess the treasury stock transactions during the year. How much was spent and/or received? What did the company do with the proceeds? Compare the average price paid for treasury shares to the current stock price.
   - Does the company use share-based compensation? What types of plans are used? What was the magnitude of the compensation? What is the magnitude of the outstanding (unvested) options and/or shares? Compare the level of treasury shares to outstanding (unvested) options and / or shares.
   - Compute the market capitalization of the firms and compare to the book value of equity. Find an online source for the average market-to-book ratio for the industry and see where the firms fit. Follow up on anything unusual.

2. *Earned Capital.*   Recall that the least costly form of financing is internal—that is, plowing earned profits (and cash) into new investments is a low-cost means to grow the company and return even more to stockholders.

   - How profitable were the companies? Compare return on equity for the three-year period and determine causes for major differences over time and between companies.
   - Review accumulated other comprehensive income and determine the main components of that account. How did AOCI change during the year?
   - Did the companies pay cash dividends? Compute the dividend payout and the dividend yield for all three years and compare them.
   - Did the company have any stock splits or pay stock dividends?

3. *Convertible Securities.*   Read the debt footnote to determine if the company has any convertible securities.

   - What types of convertible securities are outstanding?
   - Are these securities substantive? To assess this, consider their common size and their effect on diluted earnings per share.
   - Did the company have any convertible transactions during the year? If yes, determine the effect on the balance sheet and income statement.

Solutions to Review Problems

Review 8-1—Solution

a. **False.** Stockholders' equity is the book value (determined in accordance with GAAP) of the company. It represents the claim that shareholders have against the net assets (assets less liabilities) of the company.

b. **True.** The Board of Directors is the elected representatives of the shareholders who hire the company's CEO and oversee its operations.

c. **True.** Issued shares represents the cumulative number of shares that have been sold (issued) to date.

d. **True.** Outstanding shares is equal to the cumulative number of shares that have been issued less the cumulative number of shares that have been subsequently repurchased by the company.

e. **False.** The amount of annual dividends per share for preferred stock is usually fixed. Common stock receives any remaining dividends after preferred shareholders have been paid and there is no limit to the amount of dividends that common shareholders can receive.

f. **True.** Treasury stock represents the cumulative dollar amount of all share repurchases and subsequent resales on the open market.

Review 8-2—Solution

a. The common stock account did not change during this period, either in the number of shares issued (7,040 million) or in dollars ($1,760 million). Thus, we conclude that the company issued no new stock during the quarter.

b. (in millions)

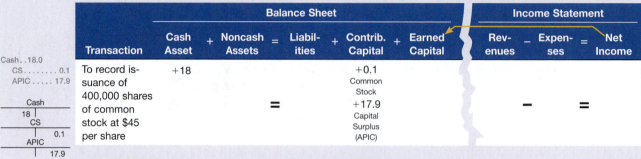

	Balance Sheet					Income Statement		
Transaction	Cash Asset	+ Noncash Assets	= Liabil- ities	+ Contrib. Capital	+ Earned Capital	Rev- enues	− Expen- ses	= Net Income
To record is- suance of 400,000 shares of common stock at $45 per share	+18		=	+0.1 Common Stock +17.9 Capital Surplus (APIC)		−		=

Cash..18.0
  CS........0.1
  APIC.....17.9

Cash	
18	

CS	
	0.1

APIC	
	17.9

c. (in millions)

	Balance Sheet					Income Statement		
Transaction	Cash Asset	+ Noncash Assets	= Liabil- ities	+ Contrib. Capital	+ Earned Capital	Rev- enues	− Expen- ses	= Net Income
To record re- purchase of 22 million shares at $43.45 per share	−956		=	−956 Treasury Stock		−		=

TS ...956
  Cash......956

TS	
956	

Cash	
	956

d. The company will decrease the treasury stock account by $473 million, the original cost of the shares (30 million shares × $15.77 per share). The difference between the market value of the treasury shares ($964 million) and the cost ($473 million) is added to the Capital Surplus account, increasing it by $491 million.

Review 8-3—Solution

a. Coca-Cola's income before tax was reduced by $236 million for the stock-based compensation expense. This was included in "other" line items on the income statement rather than disclosed separately.

b. Stock-based compensation does not affect cash flow, it is a non-cash expense. There is a real cash outflow associated with the compensation—the company buys treasury shares to use for compensation instead of issuing new stock. The cost of the treasury shares is a real cash cost.

c. The fair value of the total stock option grant is $56.94 million computed as $4.38 fair value per share × 13 million shares. With a vesting period of 4 years, the amount of stock option compensation expense on the 2015 income statement is $14.2 million.

d. The fair value of the total RSU grant is $70.5 million computed as $37.99 fair value per share × 1,857 thousand shares. With a restriction period of 2 years, the amount of stock option compensation expense on the 2015 income statement is $35.3 million.

e. There is a chance that the options will not be exercised. If the stock price falls below the option strike price of $41.89 by the time the options expire, the option will have no value to the employee. But even if the stock price falls, the RSU will have value, albeit less than at the grant date. The other issue is that the restriction period for the RSUs is only 2 years whereas the vesting period for the options is 4 years.

Review 8-4—Solution

a. (in millions)

	Balance Sheet					Income Statement		
Transaction	Cash Asset	+ Noncash Assets	= Liabil- ities	+ Contrib. Capital	+ Earned Capital	Rev- enues	− Expen- ses	= Net Income
To record preferred and common stock dividend	−8,826		=		−8,826 Retained Earnings	−		=

RE ...8,826
  Cash 8,826

RE	
8,826	

Cash	
	8,826

b. If Wells Fargo had paid $100 million more in common stock dividends in 2015, net income would not have been affected. Dividends are not included when we determine net income, they are a return of the net income to shareholders.

c.

	Dec. 31, 2015	Dec. 31, 2014
Dividends declared per common share ($ per share).........	$1.475	$1.35
Earnings per common share ($ per share).................	$4.180	$4.17
Dividend payout ratio....................................	35.3%	32.4%

d. The WFC closing stock price on December 31, 2015, was $54.36. (See the Historical Prices link for WFC at http://finance.yahoo.com/) The dividend yield ratio for 2015 is 2.71%, computed as $1.475 / $54.36.

e. Preferred dividends are computed on the stock's face or "par" value and not on book value (carrying value). Cash dividends for the three preferred stock issuances. Note that the Series U and V have a half-year's dividend because they were issued July 1, 2015.

	Number of shares issued as of 12/31/2015	Par value per share	Total par value in $ millions	Dividend rate	Dividend in $ millions
Series L 7.50% Non-Cumulative Perpetual Convertible Class A Preferred Stock..............	3,968,000	$ 1,000	$3,968	7.500%	$297.60
Series U 5.875% Fixed-to-Floating Non-Cumulative Perpetual Class A Preferred Stock	80,000	$25,000	$2,000	5.875%	$ 58.75
Series V 6.000% Non-Cumulative Perpetual Class A Preferred Stock	40,000	$25,000	$1,000	6.000%	$ 30.00

Review 8-5—Solution

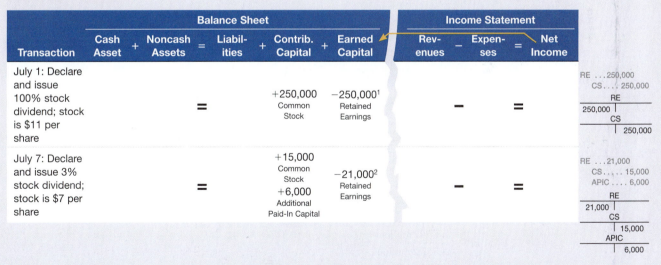

	Balance Sheet								Income Statement				
Transaction	Cash Asset	+	Noncash Assets	=	Liabil- ities	+	Contrib. Capital	+	Earned Capital		Rev- enues	−	Expen- ses	=	Net Income
July 31: Declare and pay cash divi- dend of $1.20 per share	−123,600 Cash			=					−123,600[3] Retained Earnings			−		=
Aug. 15: 2 for 1 stock split	No journal entry													

RE ...123,600
  Cash .. 123,600

RE	
123,600	

Cash	
	123,600

[1] This large stock dividend reduces retained earnings at the par value of shares distributed (50,000 shares × 100% × $5 par value = $250,000). Contributed capital (common stock) increases by the same amount.

[2] This small stock dividend reduces retained earnings at the market value of shares distributed (3% × 100,000 shares × $7 per share = $21,000). Contributed capital increases by the same amount ($15,000 to common stock and $6,000 to paid-in capital). Note that the number of common shares outstanding on December 7 was 100,000—the large stock dividend on April 7 doubled the number of common stock outstanding.

[3] At the time of the cash dividend, there are 103,000 shares outstanding. The cash paid is, therefore, 103,000 shares × $1.20 per share = $123,600.

Review 8-6—Solution

a. The unrealized loss increased during the year. On average, the U.S. dollar strengthened in 2015 vis-à-vis currencies of countries where Coca-Cola has subsidiaries. This means that the assets of foreign subsidiaries, when translated to U.S. dollars, lost value. From this we can conclude that the foreign currency was weaker because foreign assets converted to fewer U.S. dollars.

b. If the securities had been sold, the unrealized gain of $288 would be realized in the income statement as "other income" before tax. If we assume a 35% tax rate on this gain, net income would have been higher by $187.2 million ($288 million × 65%).

c. No. This would only be true if the portfolio of derivatives did not change during 2015. That is unlikely because Coca-Cola frequently engages in hedging transactions. It is possible that Coca-Cola liquidated the entire portfolio during the year, realized the $554 million gain that was unrealized at the end of fiscal 2014, and purchased a completely new set of derivatives.

Review 8-7—Solution

	Balance Sheet								Income Statement				
Transaction	Cash Asset	+	Noncash Assets	=	Liabil- ities	+	Contrib. Capital	+	Earned Capital		Rev- enues	−	Expen- ses	=	Net Income
Convert a bond with $850 book value into 200 common shares with $1 par value				=	−850 Long-Term Debt		+200 Common Stock +650 Additional Paid-In Capital					−		=

LTD ... 850
  CS 200
  APIC 650

LTD	
850	

CS	
	200

APIC	
	650

Review 8-8—Solution

a. $$\text{Basic EPS} = \frac{\$4,292 \text{ million}}{2,757.2 \text{ million}} = \$1.56$$

b.

Potential shares exercisable under stock option plans	144.40
Less: shares which could be repurchased under treasury stock method	(108.20)
Total number of shares added due to the stock option plans	36.2

c. $$\text{Diluted EPS} = \frac{\$4,292 \text{ million}}{(2,757 \text{ million} + 36.2 \text{ million} + 2.0 \text{ million})} = \$1.54$$

d. No. The dilution risk is relatively minor. The difference for EPS is $0.02, which is only a 1.3% dilution, computed as $0.02/$1.56.

Module 9

Intercorporate Investments

Learning Objectives

LO1 Examine and interpret marketable securities reporting. (p. 9-3)

LO2 Analyze and interpret equity method investments. (p. 9-10)

LO3 Explain consolidation and interpret consolidated reports. (p. 9-15)

LO4 Describe and interpret derivative disclosures (Appendix 9A). (p. 9-27)

LO5 Explain equity carve-outs and their financial statement impact (Appendix 9B). (p. 9-32)

GOOG

Market cap: $521,620 mil
Total assets: $147,461 mil
Revenues: $74,989 mil
Net income: $16,348 mil

In its 2015 corporate reorganization, Google created a new company, Alphabet Inc., that owns 100% of Google's stock, effectively making Alphabet the parent of Google. With this new structure, Google will continue to generate cash flow and Alphabet will invest the excess cash in other ventures that provide future growth.

Alphabet's portfolio of companies includes Nest, which invests in the "internet of things" and whose current products include smart thermostats, internet-connected security cameras, and smoke detectors; X, a research lab working on self-driving cars as well as balloon-based internet and drone delivery; Google Fiber, an internet service provider that currently delivers speeds of 1 Gbps in select cities; Calico and Verily, both biotech firms; along with a number of other firms. This holding-company structure is similar to Warren Buffett's Berkshire Hathaway.

Google generates over $20 billion of operating cash flow every year. After funding capital expenditures (which have averaged $9 billion for the past few years), the company invests the excess cash in marketable securities until needed for strategic investments. As of 2015, Google reported cash, cash equivalents, and marketable securities of over $73 billion.

Unlike most other assets that are reported on the balance sheet at historical cost, marketable securities are reported at current market value. As prices fluctuate, Google adjusts the balance sheet value of the marketable securities, which affects reported profits. Google also invests in financial derivative securities that are designed to mitigate two types of risk: (1) the fluctuations in the fair values of Google's assets and liabilities and (2) the risks associated with forecasted purchases of commodities and foreign currencies.

When Alphabet invests strategically in ventures like those referenced above, the financial statement impact depends on Alphabet's level of investment. For example, if Alphabet's ownership position allows it to *control* the venture's activities, Alphabet must consolidate the investee's financial statements with its own. Consolidation raises additional reporting issues, including the accounting for noncontrolling shareholders and foreign subsidiaries. If and when companies like Alphabet dispose of a subsidiary company (by way of an equity carve-out) there are financial statement effects. We discuss these strategic equity investments and divestitures and their financial statement impacts.

Among its investment in marketable securities, Alphabet reports investments in debt securities; that is, in corporate bonds, U.S. government agency bonds, and municipal bonds. These investments are usually reported at cost, not at market value as for equity investments. We discuss the accounting for these investments as well. [Source: *Alphabet*, 2015 10-K]

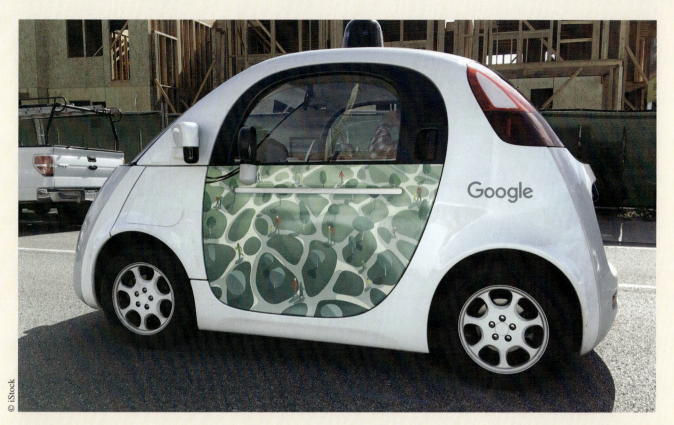

© iStock

Road Map

LO	Learning Objective | Topics	Page	eLecture	Guided Example	Assignments
9–1	**Examine and interpret marketable securities reporting.** Passive Investments :: Fair Value Adjustment :: Non-Marketable Equity Securities :: Debt Securities	9-3	e9–1	Review 9-1	1, 2, 3, 13, 14, 17, 27, 28, 29, 30, 31, 34, 54
9–2	**Analyze and interpret equity method investments.** Significant Influence :: Equity Method Accounting :: Effects of Equity Method	9-10	e9–2	Review 9-2	4, 5, 18, 19, 20, 23, 32, 33, 34, 35, 36, 37, 48, 50, 52, 54
9–3	**Explain consolidation and interpret consolidated reports.** Control :: Consolidation for Investments with Control :: Purchased Goodwill and Intangibles :: Foreign Subsidiaries and AOCI :: Limitations of Consolidated Reporting	9-15	e9–3	Review 9-3	6, 7, 10, 11, 21, 22, 30, 38, 39, 40, 41, 42, 43, 44, 49, 51, 53, 54
9–4	**Describe and interpret derivative disclosures (Appendix 9A).** Fair value Hedging :: Cash flow Hedging :: Analysis of Derivatives	9-27	e9–4	Review 9-4	8, 9, 15, 16, 44, 45, 46, 47
9–5	**Explain equity carve-outs and their financial statement impact (Appendix 9B).** Sell-offs :: Split-offs :: Spin-offs :: Analysis of Equity Carve-outs	9-32	e9–5	Review 9-5	12, 24, 25, 26, 55

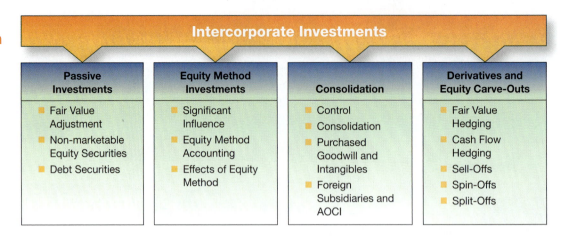

Intercorporate Investments

It is common for one company to purchase the voting stock of another. These purchases, called *intercorporate equity investments*, typically have one or more of the following strategic aims.

■ **Short-term investment of excess cash.** Companies might invest excess cash during slow times of the year (after receivables are collected and before seasonal production begins), or to maintain liquidity in order to counter strategic moves by competitors, or to quickly respond to acquisition opportunities.

■ **Strategic alliances.** Companies use intercorporate investments to gain access to needed resources or expertise such as research and development activities, an established supply chain or distribution market, or production and marketing expertise.

■ **Targeted projects.** Companies might invest in a partnership or joint venture (with equity ownership) to accomplish specific short- to medium-term outcomes such as construction projects or research endeavors. Partnerships and joint ventures can increase the return to the venture partners' investments and reduce risks associated with going it alone.

■ **Market penetration or expansion.** Companies might acquire control of other companies to integrate vertically (by buying a supplier or a customer) or horizontally (by buying a competitor). These investments can help the company expand in existing product or geographic markets or penetrate new markets.

The level of ownership interest the investor (the purchaser) acquires, directly affects the level of influence or control the investor has over the investee company (the company whose securities are purchased), as shown in Exhibit 9.1.

Exhibit 9.1 ■ Accounting for Intercorporate Equity Investments

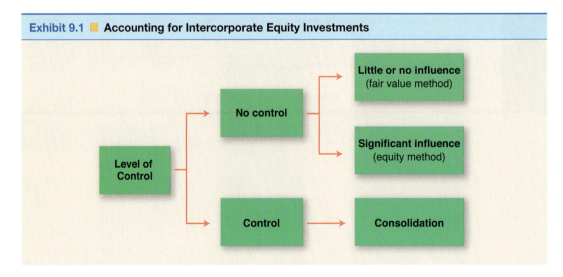

There are three levels of influence or control.

- **Little or no influence (passive investments).** The investor has a relatively small investment and cannot exert influence over the investee. The investor's goal is to realize dividend income and capital gains. Generally, the investor is deemed to have little to no influence if it owns less than 20% of the investee's outstanding voting stock.

- **Significant influence.** The investor can exert "significant influence" over the investee by virtue of the percentage of the outstanding voting stock it owns or owing to legal agreements between the investor and investee, such as a license to use technology. Absent evidence to the contrary, significant influence is presumed when the investor owns between 20% and 50% of the outstanding voting shares.

- **Control.** When a company has control over an investee, it has the ability to elect a majority of the board of directors and, as a result, the ability to affect the investee's strategic direction and the hiring of executive management. Control is generally presumed if the investor company owns more than 50% of the outstanding voting stock of the investee company but can sometimes occur at less than 50% stock ownership by virtue of legal agreements, technology licensing, or other contractual means. The determining factor is the ability to control strategic decisions.

The level of influence/control determines the specific accounting method applied and its financial statement implications as outlined in Exhibit 9.2.

Exhibit 9.2 ■ Investment Type, Accounting Treatment, and Financial Statement Effects

	Accounting	Balance Sheet Effects	Income Statement Effects	Cash Flow Effects
Little or no influence (passive investment)	Fair value method	• Investment account is reported at fair value	• Dividends and capital gains and losses included in income • Interim changes in fair value affect income • Sale of investment yields capital gain or loss	• Dividends and sale proceeds are cash inflows from investing activities • Purchases are cash outflows from investing activities
Significant influence	Equity method	• Investment account equals percent owned of investee company's equity*	• Dividends reduce investment account • Investor reports income equal to percent owned of investee income • Sale of investment yields capital gain or loss	• Dividends and sale proceeds are cash inflows from investing activities • Purchases are cash outflows from investing activities
Control	Consolidation	• Balance sheets of investor and investee are combined	• Income statements of investor and investee are combined • Sale of investee yields capital gain or loss	• Cash flows of investor and investee are combined and retain original classification (operating, investing, or financing) • Sale and purchase of investee are investing cash flows

*Investments are often acquired at purchase prices in excess of book value (the market price of S&P 500 companies was 2.8 times their book value as of July 2016). In this case, the investment account exceeds the proportionate ownership of the investee's equity.

As Exhibit 9.2 shows, there are three basic reporting issues to consider: (1) how investment income and capital gains are recognized in the income statement, (2) at what amount the investment is reported on the balance sheet, and (3) how the cash flow statement classifies cash received and used for the investment. Next we discuss these issues for the three investment types.

Passive Investments in Marketable Securities

Marketable securities are financial instruments that can be bought and sold on a public exchange—this includes marketable equity securities (stocks) and marketable debt securities (bonds). Accounting differs for equity versus debt—first, we discuss equity investments and, in a later section, we discuss debt investments.

Acquisition and Sale

When a company makes a passive investment, it records the shares acquired on the balance sheet at fair value; that is, the purchase price. This is the same as accounting for the acquisition of other assets, such as inventories or PPE. Subsequent to acquisition, passive investments are classified on the balance sheet as current or long-term assets, depending on management's expectations about their ultimate holding period.

When investments are sold, any recognized gain or loss on sale is equal to the difference between the proceeds received and the book (carrying) value of the investment on the balance sheet as follows.

Gain or Loss on Sale = Proceeds from Sale − Book Value of Investment Sold

To illustrate the acquisition and sale of a passive investment, assume **Alphabet** purchases 1,000 shares of **Juniper Networks** for $20 cash per share (this includes transaction costs such as brokerage fees). Alphabet subsequently sells 400 of the 1,000 shares for $23 cash per share. The following financial statement effects template shows how these transactions affect Alphabet.

| Transaction | Balance Sheet | | | | | Income Statement | | |
	Cash Asset	+ Noncash Assets	= Liabil- ities	+ Contrib. Capital	+ Earned Capital	Rev- enues	− Expen- ses	= Net Income
1. Purchase 1,000 shares of Juniper common stock for $20 cash per share	−20,000 Cash	+20,000 Marketable Securities	=				−	=
2. Sell 400 shares of Juniper common stock for $23 cash per share	+9,200 Cash	−8,000 Marketable Securities	=		+1,200 Retained Earnings	+1,200 Gain on Sale	−	= +1,200

Margin notes:

MS ... 20,000
  Cash ... 20,000

MS
20,000 |
  Cash
    | 20,000

Cash .. 9,200
  MS 8,000
  GN 1,200

Cash
9,200 |
  MS
    | 8,000
  GN
    | 1,200

Income statements include the gain or loss on sale of marketable securities as a component of *other income*, which is typically reported separately from operating income and often aggregated with interest and dividend income.

Investments Adjusted to Fair Value

All passive investments in equity securities where there is a readily determinable fair value are reported on the balance sheet at fair value.[1] Changes in the fair value of the investment during the accounting period are reported in earnings. This is a relatively new accounting treatment that is effective in 2018. But because the new rules will apply shortly, most of the financial statements you will read will conform to the new standard. Therefore, our discussion takes the new standard as a given. We discuss the previous accounting standard in a text box below.

For marketable equity securities, fair value is typically the published stock price (as listed on a stock exchange) multiplied by the number of shares owned. But that is not the only way to measure fair value. The accounting rules lay out three specific ways to determine fair value, and all three are acceptable.[2]

Passive investments in marketable securities (including derivative securities, which we discuss in Appendix A) are the only assets that are reported at fair value instead of historical cost. Other assets, including inventory, PPE, and goodwill, are recorded at fair value when it is *lower* than historical cost, but not when fair value *exceeds* historical cost. Why are passive investments recorded at fair value on the balance sheet? The answer is that prices for marketable securities can be easily observed and

---

[1] Recall that passive investments exclude situations where the investor has significant influence (in which case, the equity method of accounting is used) or where the investor has control (and consolidates the investee company). In both these cases, there are no fair value adjustments.

[2] Assets and liabilities recorded at fair value are measured in one of three ways based on the observability of the inputs used to measure fair value (in order of preferred usage):
- Level 1. Quoted market prices if the security is traded in active markets.
- Level 2. Quoted market prices in active markets for *similar* securities and model-based valuation techniques for which all significant inputs are observable in the market or can be derived from observable market data.
- Level 3. Unobservable inputs that are supported by little or no market activities.

reliably measured. The market price of any marketable security results from numerous transactions between willing buyers and sellers on an organized exchange. The market price, therefore, provides an unbiased (objective) estimate of fair value. This reliability is the main reason accounting rules require that passive investments be recorded at fair value on the balance sheet.

Fair Value Adjustments To illustrate the accounting for changes in fair value subsequent to purchase (and before sale), assume Alphabet's investment in Juniper Networks (600 remaining shares purchased for $20 per share) increases in value to $25 per share at year-end. The investment account must be adjusted to fair value to reflect the $3,000 unrealized gain ($5-per-share increase for 600 shares) as follows.

The investment account increases by $3,000 to reflect the increase in the stock's fair value, and the unrealized gain is recorded as income, thus increasing both reported income and retained earnings for the period. (Our illustration uses a portfolio with only one security for simplicity. Portfolios usually consist of multiple securities, and the unrealized gain or loss is computed based on the total cost and total market value of the entire portfolio.)

Accounting Insight ■ Accounting for Equity Investments under Pre-2018 Rules

Before 2018, companies designated passive equity securities as "trading" or as "available-for-sale," and the accounting importance of this distinction follows.

- **Trading securities.** Investments that management intends to actively buy and sell for trading profits. These were reported at fair value with changes in value reflected in earnings (consistent with the new accounting standard).

- **Available-for-sale securities.** Securities that management intends to hold for capital gains and dividend income, although they might be sold if the price is right. These were also reported at fair value on the balance sheet, but changes in fair value were not reported in income. Instead, these unrealized gains and losses were transferred to the equity section of the balance sheet to an account called "accumulated other comprehensive income" (AOCI). When available-for-sale securities were sold, the previously unrealized gain or loss was transferred from AOCI into current earnings.

The previous standard recognized the changes in fair value in earnings, but with a lag, that is, gains and losses on securities classified as available-for-sale were deferred until the securities were sold. Under the new standard, changes in the fair value of *all* marketable equity securities are reflected in current earnings. (As explained below, the prior rules still apply to investments in *debt* securities.)

In the Juniper Networks example above, if Alphabet had classified the investment as available-for-sale, the change in fair value would have been accounted for, under pre-2018 rules, as follows.

	Balance Sheet						Income Statement			
Transaction	Cash Asset	+ Noncash Assets	= Liabil- ities	+ Contrib. Capital	+ Earned Capital		Rev- enues	_ Expen- ses	= Net Income	
If classified as available-for-sale										
$5 increase in fair value of Juniper investment		+3,000 Marketable Securities =			+3,000 AOCI		**–**		**=**	

MS . . . 3,000
AOCI 3,000

MS
3,000 |

AOCI
| 3,000

Non-Marketable Equity Securities

In addition to its marketable equity securities, Alphabet invests in non-marketable equity securities—which refer to the stock of privately held companies with no publicly available stock price. These investments allow Alphabet early access to new technologies or the opportunity to invest prior to an initial public offering.[3] At present, Alphabet carries these investments at cost on the balance sheet. Footnotes report the cost of the non-marketable equity investments as $1.8 billion as of 2015. The 2015 fair value of these investments was approximately $7.5 billion—a clear indication that the investments were a good bet for Alphabet.

Despite these securities being non-marketable, the new accounting standard requires companies to report them on the balance sheet at fair value. This requires companies to obtain necessary cash flow information and other data to support a Level-3 valuation, a time-consuming and imprecise process. Consequently, the new rules give companies the option to measure their non-marketable equity investments at cost, plus or minus changes resulting from observable price changes in orderly transactions for an identical or similar investment of the same issuer.[4] Time will tell us whether companies take this option starting in 2018.

Financial Statement Disclosures

Companies are required to disclose cost and fair values of their investment portfolios in footnotes to financial statements. Alphabet reports the accounting policies for its investments in the following footnote to its 2015 10-K report.

> **Cash, Cash Equivalents, and Marketable Securities**   We invest all excess cash primarily in debt securities including those of the U.S. government and its agencies, corporate debt securities, agency mortgage-backed securities, money market and other funds, municipal securities, time deposits, asset backed securities, and debt instruments issued by foreign governments. We classify all investments that are readily convertible to known amounts of cash and have stated maturities of three months or less from the date of purchase as cash equivalents and those with stated maturities of greater than three months as marketable securities. We carry these securities at fair value, and . . . determine any realized gains or losses on the sale of marketable securities on a specific identification method.

Following is the current asset section of Alphabet's 2015 balance sheet (in millions).

Current Assets	2014	2015
Cash and cash equivalents	$18,347	$16,549
Marketable securities	46,048	56,517
Total cash, cash equivalents, and marketable securities (including securities loaned of $4,058 and $4,531)	64,395	73,066
Accounts receivable, net of allowance of $225 and $296	9,383	11,556
Receivable under reverse repurchase agreements	875	450
Income taxes receivable, net	591	1,903
Prepaid revenue share, expenses and other assets	3,412	3,139
Total current assets	$78,656	$90,114

Alphabet's investments in marketable securities that mature within 90 days of the balance sheet date are recorded together with cash as cash equivalents. The remaining investments are reported as marketable securities. The total of $73,066 million in 2015 is the fair value of the cash and marketable

---

[3] This is the approach Google took with Nest Labs; its original investment was a 12% stake, which was reported as a non-marketable security investment. Then in 2014, once Nest established commercial success, Google bought the remaining Nest stock, making the company a wholly-owned subsidiary.

[4] This valuation approach only applies to passive equity investments with no readily determined fair value. It does not include marketable equity securities or investments accounted for using the equity method, which we explain later.

securities, the value carried on the balance sheet. Footnotes to Alphabet's 2015 10-K provide further information about the composition of its investment portfolio.

As of December 31, 2015 ($ millions)	Adjusted Cost	Gross Unrealized Gains	Gross Unrealized Losses	Fair Value	Cash and Cash Equivalents	Marketable Securities
Cash..................................	$ 7,380	$ 0	$ 0	$ 7,380	$ 7,380	$ 0
Level 1:						
Money market and other funds	5,623	0	0	5,623	5,623	0
U.S. government notes	20,922	27	(48)	20,901	258	20,643
Marketable equity securities	692	155	0	847	0	847
	27,237	182	(48)	27,371	5,881	21,490
Level 2:						
Time deposits.............................	3,223	0	0	3,223	2,012	1,211
Money market and other funds	1,140	0	0	1,140	1,140	0
Fixed-income bond funds	219	0	0	219	0	219
U.S. government agencies.................	1,367	2	(3)	1,366	0	1,366
Foreign government bonds	2,242	14	(23)	2,233	0	2,233
Municipal securities	3,812	47	(4)	3,855	0	3,855
Corporate debt securities.................	13,809	53	(278)	13,584	136	13,448
Agency mortgage-backed securities...........	9,680	48	(57)	9,671	0	9,671
Asset-backed securities.....................	3,032	0	(8)	3,024	0	3,024
	38,524	164	(373)	38,315	3,288	35,027
Total	$73,141	$346	$(421)	$73,066	$16,549	$56,517

This footnote reports the cost of $73,141 million and fair value of $73,066 million of Alphabet's investment portfolio—these are required footnote disclosures. Included in the total, are marketable equity securities at a fair value of $847 million, a relatively small amount in that Alphabet holds mostly debt securities (discussed below). Alphabet's footnote identifies the method used to determine the fair value the securities (Level 1 or Level 2; Alphabet has no securities valued using Level 3 valuation methods).

Investments in Debt Securities

Companies often purchase debt securities, including bonds issued by other companies or by the U.S. government. For example, in the investment footnote shown above, Alphabet reports investments in time deposits, corporate bonds, U.S. government agency bonds, and municipal securities. Companies can choose to classify investments in debt securities as either:

- **Trading securities.** See the Accounting Insight box earlier in this section.
- **Available-for-sale securities.** See the Accounting Insight box earlier in this section.
- **Held-to-maturity securities.** We discuss this method here.

Many debt securities have maturity dates—dates when the security must be repaid by the borrower. If a company buys debt securities, and *management intends to hold the securities to maturity* (as opposed to selling them early), the securities are classified as **held-to-maturity** (HTM).

Held-To-Maturity (HTM) Debt Securities

The cost method applies to held-to-maturity securities. Exhibit 9.4 identifies the reporting of these securities.

Changes in fair value of held-to-maturity securities do not affect either the balance sheet or the income statement. The presumption is that these investments will indeed be held to maturity, at which time their market value will be exactly equal to their face value. Fluctuations in fair value, as a result, are less relevant. Any interest received is recorded in current income. (GAAP gives companies an option to report held-to-maturity investments at fair value; if this fair value option is elected, the accounting for held-to-maturity securities is like that for marketable equity securities, discussed above.)

Exhibit 9.4 ■ Accounting Treatment for Held-to-Maturity Debt Investments

Investment Classification	Reporting of Fair Value Changes	Reporting Interest Received and the Gains and Losses on Sale
Held-to-Maturity (HTM)	Fair value changes are *not* reported in either the balance sheet or income statement (HTM is reported at *amortized cost*)	Interest reported as *other income* in income statement IF sold before maturity (the exception), any gain or loss on sale is reported in income statement

---

Held-To-Maturity (HTM) Debt Securities Reported at Amortized Cost Because the value of debt securities fluctuates with the prevailing rate of interest, the market value of the security will be greater than its face value if current market interest rates are lower than what the security pays for interest. In that case, the acquirer will pay a premium for the security. Conversely, if current market interest rates exceed what the security pays in interest, the acquirer will purchase the security at a discount. (We cover premiums and discounts on debt securities in more detail in the liabilities module.) Either way, the company records the investment at its acquisition cost (like any other asset) and amortizes any discount or premium over the remaining life of the held-to-maturity investment. At any point in time, the acquirer's balance sheet carries the investment at "amortized cost," which is never adjusted for subsequent market value changes.

Review 9-1 LO1

Assume **Yahoo!** had the following four transactions involving investments in marketable securities. Use this information to answer requirement *a*.

1. Purchased 1,000 shares of **Juniper Networks** common stock for $15 cash per share.
2. Received cash dividend of $2.50 per share on Juniper Networks common stock.
3. Year-end market price of Juniper Networks common stock is $17 per share.
4. Sold all 1,000 shares of Juniper Networks common stock for $17,000 cash in the next period.

Yahoo! reports the following table in the footnotes to its 2015 10-K. Use this information to answer requirements *b* through *d*.

As of December 31, 2015 (in $ 000's)	Cost Basis	Gross Unrealized Gains	Gross Unrealized Losses	Estimated Fair Value
Government and agency securities	$ 616,501	$ 24	$ (635)	$ 615,890
Corporate debt securities, commercial paper, time deposits, and CDs	4,589,799	292	(4,908)	4,585,183
Alibaba Group equity securities	2,713,483	28,458,878	—	31,172,361
Hortonworks equity securities	26,246	57,977	—	84,223
Other corporate equity securities.	298	—	(101)	197
Total available-for-sale marketable securities.	$7,946,327	$28,517,171	$(5,644)	$36,457,854

Required

a. Use the financial statement effects template to record the four transactions.
b. What amount does Yahoo! report as investments on its balance sheet? What does this balance represent?
c. What proportion of the portfolio is debt securities versus equity securities?
Solution on p. 9-54.   *d.* Compare the cost and fair value of the portfolio. What accounts for the difference in value?

Equity Investments with Significant Influence

Many companies make equity investments that yield them significant influence over the investee companies. These intercorporate investments are usually made for strategic reasons such as the following.

eLectures **LO2**
MBC Analyze and interpret equity method investments.

- **Prelude to acquisition.** Significant ownership can allow the investor company to gain a seat on the board of directors, from which it can learn much about the investee company, its products, and its industry.

- **Strategic alliance.** Strategic alliances permit the investor to gain trade secrets, technical know-how, or access to restricted markets. For example, a company might buy an equity interest in a company that provides inputs for the investor's production process. This relationship is closer than the usual supplier–buyer relationship and will convey benefits to the investor company.

- **Pursuit of research and development.** Many research activities in the pharmaceutical, software, and oil and gas industries are conducted jointly. The common motivation is to reduce the investor's risk or the amount of capital investment. The investment often carries an option to purchase additional shares, which the investor can exercise if the research activities are fruitful.

The investment can take a number of forms, including marketable securities, as well as other ownership arrangements, such as partnerships, joint ventures, and limited liability companies. A crucial feature in each of these investments is that the investor company has a level of ownership that is sufficient for it to exert *significant influence* over the investee company. GAAP requires that such investments be accounted for using the *equity method*.

Significant influence is the ability of the investor to affect the financing, investing, and operating policies of the investee. Ownership levels of 20% to 50% of the outstanding common stock of the investee typically convey significant influence. Significant influence can also exist when ownership is less than 20%. Evidence of such influence can be that the investor company is able to gain a seat on the board of directors of the investee, or the investor controls technical know-how or patents that are used by the investee, or the investor is able to exert significant influence by virtue of legal contracts with the investee. (There is growing pressure from regulators for determining significant influence by the facts and circumstances of the investment instead of a strict ownership percentage rule.)

Accounting for Investments with Significant Influence

Companies must use the **equity method** when significant influence exists. The equity method reports the investment on the balance sheet at an amount equal to the percentage of the investee's equity owned by the investor; hence, the name equity method. (This assumes acquisition at book value; acquisition at an amount greater than book value is covered later in this section.) Unlike passive investments, whose carrying amounts increase or decrease with the *market value* of the investee's stock, equity method investments increase (decrease) with increases (decreases) in the investee's *stockholders' equity*.

Equity method accounting is summarized as follows.

- Investments are recorded at their purchase cost.

- Dividends received are treated as a recovery of the investment and, thus, reduce the investment balance (dividends are not reported as income).

- The investor reports income equal to its percentage share of the investee's reported net income; the investment account is increased by the percentage share of the investee's income or decreased by the percentage share of any loss.

- Changes in fair value do not affect the investment's carrying value. (GAAP gives companies an option to report equity method investments at fair value unless those investments relate to consolidated subsidiaries; we discuss consolidation later in the module.)

To illustrate the equity method, consider the following scenario: Assume **Google** acquires a 30% interest in Mitel Networks, a company seeking to develop a new technology. This investment is a strategic alliance for Google. At the acquisition date, Mitel's balance sheet reports $1,000 of stockholders' equity, and Google purchases a 30% stake for $300, giving it the ability to exert significant influence over Mitel. At the first year-end, Mitel reports profits of $100 and pays $20 in cash dividends to its shareholders ($6 to Google). Following are the financial statement effects for Google from this investment using the equity method.

		Balance Sheet					Income Statement		
Transaction	Cash Asset	+ Noncash Assets	= Liabilities	+ Contrib. Capital	+ Earned Capital		Revenues	− Expenses	= Net Income
1. Purchase 30% investment in Mitel for $300 cash	−300 Cash	+300 Investment in Mitel =					−		=
2. Mitel reports $100 income; Google's share is $30		+30 Investment in Mitel =			+30 Retained Earnings		+30 Equity Income	−	= +30
3. Mitel pays $20 cash dividends; $6 to Google	+6 Cash	−6 Investment in Mitel =						−	=
Ending balance of Google's investment account		324							

(margin T-accounts)

EMI...300
  Cash......300
  EMI
  300 |
    Cash
        | 300

EMI...30
  EI.........30
  EMI
  30 |
    EI
        | 30

Cash..6
  EMI........6
  Cash
  6 |
    EMI
        | 6

The investment is initially reported on Google's balance sheet at its purchase price of $300, representing a 30% interest in Mitel's total stockholders' equity of $1,000. During the year, Mitel's equity increases to $1,080 ($1,000 plus $100 income and less $20 dividends). Likewise, Google's investment increases by $30 to reflect its 30% share of Mitel's $100 income, and decreases by $6, relating to its share of Mitel's dividends. After these transactions, Google's investment in Mitel is reported on Google's balance sheet at 30% of $1,080, or $324.

Google's investment in Mitel is an asset just like any other asset. As such, it must be tested annually for impairment. If the investment is found to be permanently impaired, Google must reduce the investment amount on the balance sheet and report a loss on the write-down of the investment in its income statement (unlike investments accounted for using the market method, equity method investments are not written up if fair values increase). If and when Google sells Mitel, any gain or loss on the sale is reported in Google's income statement. The gain or loss is computed as the difference between the sales proceeds and the investment's carrying value on the balance sheet. For example, if Google sold Mitel for $500, Google would report a gain on sale of $176 ($500 proceeds − $324 balance sheet value).

Companies often pay more than book value when they make equity investments. For example, if Google paid $400 for its 30% stake in Mitel, Google would initially report its investment at its $400 purchase price. The $400 investment consists of two parts: the $300 equity investment described above and the $100 additional investment. Google is willing to pay the higher purchase price because it believes Mitel's reported equity is below its current market value. Perhaps some of Mitel's assets are reported at costs that are below market values or Mitel has intangible assets such as a patent or internally generated goodwill that are missing from its balance sheet. The $300 portion of the investment is accounted for as described above. Google's management must decide how to allocate the excess of the amount paid over the book value of the investee company's equity and account for the excess accordingly. For example, if management decides the $100 relates to unrecognized depreciable assets, the $100 is depreciated over the assets' estimated useful lives. Or, if it relates to identifiable intangible assets that have a determinable useful life (such as patents), it is amortized over the useful lives of the intangible assets. If it relates to goodwill, however, it is not amortized and remains on the balance sheet at $100 unless and until it is deemed to be impaired. (See Appendix 9A for an expanded illustration.)

Two final points about equity method accounting: First, there can be a substantial difference between the book value of an equity method investment and its fair value. An increase in value is not recognized until the investment is sold. If the fair value of the investment has permanently declined, however, the investment is deemed impaired and written down to that lower fair value. Second, if the investee company reports income, the investor company reports its share. Recognition of equity income by the investor, however, does not mean it has received that income in cash. Cash is only received if the investee pays a dividend. To highlight this, the investor's statement of cash flows will include a reconciling item (a deduction from net income in computing operating cash flow) for its percentage share of the investee's net income. This is typically reported net of any cash dividends received.

Research Insight ■ Equity Income and Stock Prices

Under the equity method of accounting, the investor does not recognize as income any dividends received from the investee, nor any changes in the investee's fair value, until the investment is sold. However, research has found a positive relation between investors' and investees' stock prices at the time of investees' earnings and dividend announcements. This suggests the market includes information regarding investees' earnings and dividends when assessing the stock prices of investor companies and implies the market looks beyond the book value of the investment account in determining stock prices of investor companies.

Equity Method Accounting and ROE Effects

The investor company reports equity method investments on the balance sheet at an amount equal to the percentage owned of the investee company's equity when that investment is acquired at book value. To illustrate, consider the case of the Altria Group Inc.'s equity investment in SABMiller. Altria owns approximately 27% economic and voting interest of SABMiller and provides the following disclosure in its 2015 10-K.

Investment in SABMiller At December 31, 2015, Altria Group Inc. held approximately 27% of the economic and voting interest of SABMiller. Altria Group Inc. accounts for its investment in SABMiller under the equity method of accounting. Pre-tax earnings from Altria Group Inc.'s equity investment in SABMiller were $757 million, $1,006 million and $991 million for the years ended December 31, 2015, 2014 and 2013, respectively. Summary financial data of SABMiller is as follows:

At December 31 ($ millions)	2015	2014
Current assets	$ 4,266	$ 5,878
Long-term assets	38,425	43,812
Current liabilities	6,282	10,051
Long-term liabilities	13,960	14,731
Noncontrolling interests	1,235	1,241

For the Years Ended December 31 ($ millions)	2015	2014	2013
Net revenues	$20,188	$22,380	$22,684
Operating profit	3,690	4,478	4,201
Net earnings	2,838	3,532	3,375

The fair value of Altria Group Inc.'s equity investment in SABMiller is based on unadjusted quoted prices in active markets and is classified in Level 1 of the fair value hierarchy. The fair value of Altria Group Inc.'s equity investment in SABMiller at December 31, 2015 and 2014, was $25.8 billion and $22.5 billion, respectively, as compared with its carrying value of $5.5 billion and $6.2 billion, respectively.

Altria's balance sheet carries the equity investment in SABMiller at $5.5 billion. The stockholders' equity of SABMiller at December 31, 2015, was $21,214 million (calculated from the table above as $4,266 million + $38,425 million − $6,282 million − $13,960 million − $1,235 million). Comparing Altria's $5.5 billion carrying value to SABMiller's total equity, we come close to Altria's 27% investment in SABMiller. (The small difference likely relates to rounding errors when numbers are reported in millions.)

In its income statement, Altria reports equity earnings from SABMiller of $757 million, approximately equal to 27% of SABMiller's reported net earnings of $2,838 million. To reconcile net income to cash from operations on its statement of cash flows, Altria makes two adjustments. First, it subtracts the equity earnings of $757 million—this is a non-cash item included in Altria's net income. Then, it adds the $495 million received in dividends from SABMiller—these were received in cash and, therefore, increase cash from operations. The equity earnings are greater than the cash dividends received; this excess represents undistributed earnings.

Underlying Financial Statement Components It is sometimes helpful to visualize the equity investment in relation to the assets and liabilities to which it relates. Following is a summary of the Altria 2015 balance sheet ($ millions).

Altria	
Cash	$ 2,369
Non-cash assets	24,683
Investment in SABMiller	5,483
Total assets	$32,535

SABMiller	
Total assets	$42,691
Liabilities	$20,242
Noncontrolling interests	1,235
Stockholders' equity	21,214
Liabilities and equity	$42,691

The $5,483 million equity investment on Altria's balance sheet belies a significant (27%) investment in a very large company with assets of nearly $43 billion and liabilities of over $20 billion. Although liabilities are not a serious concern for beer manufacturers, we might want to know more about the investee company if the investment were in a pharmaceutical company with significant potential liabilities or in a venture with highly variable cash flows. The investor company may have no direct legal obligation for the investee's liabilities, but it might need to fund the investee company, via additional investment or advances to maintain the investee's viability, if the company is important to the investor's strategic plan. Further, companies that routinely fund research and development activities through equity investments in other companies, a common practice in the pharmaceutical and software industries, can find themselves supporting underperforming equity-method investments to ensure continued external funding. One cannot always assume, therefore, the investee's liabilities and business fortunes will not adversely affect the investor.

The concern with unreported liabilities becomes particularly problematic when the investee company reports losses that are substantial. In extreme cases, the investee company can become insolvent (when equity is negative) as the growing negative balance in retained earnings more than offsets paid-in capital. Once the equity of the investee company reaches zero, the investor must discontinue accounting for the investment by the equity method. Instead, it accounts for the investment at cost with a zero balance and no further recognition of its proportionate share of investee company losses (until the investee company's equity becomes positive again). In this case, the investor's income statement no longer includes the losses of the investee company and its balance sheet no longer reports the troubled investee company. Unreported liabilities can be especially problematic in this case.

To summarize, under equity method accounting, only the investor's proportion of the investee's equity is reported on the balance sheet (not the underlying assets and liabilities), and only the investor's proportion of the investee's earnings is reported in the income statement (not the underlying sales and expenses). This is illustrated as follows using Google's 30% investment in Mitel. The investee's income statement and balance sheet at the end of the first year is as follows.

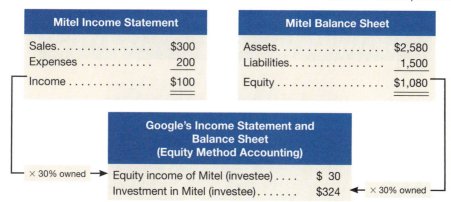

Analysis Implications From an analysis standpoint, because the assets and liabilities are left off the Google balance sheet, and because the sales and expenses are omitted from the Google income statement, the *components* of ROE are markedly affected as follows.

- **Net operating profit margin (NOPM = NOPAT/Sales).** Most analysts include equity income (sales less expenses) in NOPAT because it relates to operating investments. However, investee's sales are not included in the NOPM denominator. The reported NOPM is, thus, overstated.

- **Net operating asset turnover (NOAT = Sales/Average NOA).** Investee's sales are excluded from the NOAT numerator, and net operating assets in excess of the investment balance are excluded from the denominator. This means the impact on NOAT is *indeterminate*.

- **Financial leverage (FLEV = Net nonoperating obligations/Average equity).** Financial leverage is understated due to the absence of investee liabilities in the numerator.

Although ROE components are affected, ROE is unaffected by equity method accounting because the correct amount of investee net income and equity *is* included in the ROE numerator and denominator, respectively. Still, the evaluation of the quality of ROE is affected. Analysis using reported equity method accounting numbers would use an overstated NOPM and an understated FLEV because the numbers are based on net balance sheet and net income statement numbers. As we discuss in a later module, analysts should adjust reported financial statements for these types of items before conducting analysis. One such adjustment might be to consolidate (for analysis purposes) the equity method investee with the investor company.

Managerial Decision ■ You Are the Chief Financial Officer

You are receiving capital expenditure requests for long-term operating asset purchases from various managers. You are concerned that capacity utilization is too low. What potential courses of action can you consider? Explain. [Answer, p. 9-35]

LO2 Review 9-2

Assume **Google** had the following five transactions involving investments in marketable securities accounted for using the equity method. Use this information to answer requirement *a* below.

1. Purchased 5,000 shares of **LookSmart** common stock at $10 cash per share; these shares reflect 30% ownership of LookSmart.
2. Received a $2-per-share cash dividend on LookSmart common stock.
3. Recorded an accounting adjustment to reflect $100,000 income reported by LookSmart.
4. Year-end market price of LookSmart has increased to $12 per common share.
5. Sold all 5,000 shares of LookSmart common stock for $90,000 cash in the next period.

Yahoo! reports a $2,230 million equity investment in **Yahoo! Japan** related to its 35% ownership interest and includes $383.571 million in related earnings on its 2015 income statement. Yahoo!'s footnotes reveal the following financial information about Yahoo! Japan ($ millions). Use this information to answer requirements *b* and *c*.

continued

Twelve Months Ended September 30	2013	2014	2015
Revenues	$4,297	$4,046	$3,769
Gross profit.	3,577	3,262	2,984
Income from operations	2,151	1,896	1,609
Net income	1,355	1,225	1,092

Required

a. Use the financial statement effects template to record the five Google transactions above.

b. Show the computations required to yield the amount Yahoo! reports on its income statement for 2015.

c. Yahoo! discloses the following in its 2015 Form 10-K: "The fair value of the Company's ownership interest in the common stock of Yahoo Japan, based on the quoted stock price, was approximately $8.3 billion as of December 31, 2015." How does this information affect Yahoo!'s balance sheet and income statement for the year?

Solution on p. 9-54.

Equity Investments with Control

eLectures LO3
MBC Explain consolidation, and interpret consolidated reports.

This section discusses accounting for investments where the investor company "controls" the investee company. For example, in its footnote describing its accounting policies, **Alphabet** reports the following.

> **Basis of Consolidation** The consolidated financial statements of Alphabet and Google include the accounts of Alphabet and Google, respectively, and all wholly owned subsidiaries as well as all variable interest entities where we are the primary beneficiary. All intercompany balances and transactions have been eliminated.

This means Alphabet financial statements are an aggregation (an adding up) of those of the parent company, Alphabet, and all its subsidiary companies less any intercompany activities such as intercompany sales or receivables.

Accounting for Investments with Control

Accounting for business combinations (acquiring a controlling interest) goes one step beyond equity method accounting. Under the equity method, the investor's investment balance represents the proportion of the investee's equity owned by the investor, and the investor company's income statement includes its proportionate share of the investee's income. Once control over the investee company is achieved, GAAP requires consolidation for financial statements issued to the public (but not for the internal financial records of the separate companies).

What is control? The big picture is that control is exercised through economic power. Determining economic power can be complicated, but the following items are consistent with economic power.

▪ The investor has the ability to influence the investee's decision making.

▪ The investor can influence the investee's financial results through contractual rights and obligations.

▪ The investor is exposed to variable returns; that is, the investor will absorb any losses as well as benefit from any gains.

▪ The investor has the right to receive residual returns.

If these items are in play, the investment is a **variable interest entity (VIE)** where the investor is the primary beneficiary. All VIEs must be consolidated.

If the VIE test is *not* met, there is a second test: the voting interest test. This test is much more straightforward. If the investor holds more than 50% of the voting stock of the investee, then economic control is in evidence and the investment must be consolidated. We see from Alphabet's footnote above that it consolidates VIEs and all wholly owned entities (as Alphabet owns 100% of the voting stock).

Consolidation accounting includes 100% of the investee's assets and liabilities on the investor's balance sheet and 100% of the investee's sales and expenses on the investor's income statement. Specifically, the consolidated balance sheet includes the gross assets and liabilities of the investee company, and the income statement includes the investee's gross sales and expenses rather than just the investor's share of the investee company's net assets or income. All intercompany sales and expenses, and receivables and payables, are eliminated in the consolidation process to avoid double-counting when, for example, goods are sold from the investee (called a subsidiary) to the investor (called the parent company) for resale to the parent's ultimate customers.

Investments Purchased at Book Value: Subsidiary Wholly-Owned To illustrate, consider the following scenario. Penman Company acquires 100% of the common stock of Nissim Company. The purchase price of $3,000 is equal to the book value of Nissim's stockholders' equity ($2,000 contributed capital plus $1,000 retained earnings). During the next year, Nissim earned $400, bringing its retained earnings to $1,400. On its balance sheet, Penman accounts for the investment in Nissim using the equity method. This is important. Even if the investor (the parent) owns 100% of the investee (the subsidiary), the investor may still record the investment on its (parent-company) balance sheet using the equity method described in the previous section. That is, Penman records an initial balance in the equity investment account in the amount of the purchase price, which is equal to Nissim's stockholders' equity. Thereafter, the equity investment account on Penman's balance sheet will increase and decrease with Nissim's stockholders' equity, reflecting profits earned, losses incurred, and dividends paid.

Because Penman Company owns 100% of the stock of its subsidiary (and, therefore, controls the activities of Nissim), GAAP requires consolidation. That process, shown in Exhibit 9.5, involves summing each balance sheet and income statement account for the two companies *after eliminating any intercompany transactions* (such as the investment Penman has in Nissim Company, together with any intercompany sales/purchases and receivables/payables).

Exhibit 9.5 shows the balance sheets of Penman and Nissim in the first two columns, the consolidating adjustments in the next column, and the consolidated balance sheet in the far right column. The consolidated balance sheet reports total assets of $21,400, total liabilities of $7,000, and equity of $14,400. Because Penman owns 100% of the stock of Nissim and the purchase was made at book value, the equity investment account on Penman's balance sheet equals Nissim's stockholders' equity to which it relates. Both amounts are removed in the consolidation process and each row in the balance sheet is then summed to arrive at the consolidated totals. The result of this process, is to remove both the equity investment account and Nissim's stockholders' equity from the consolidated balance sheet and to replace the equity investment with the assets and liabilities of Nissim to which it relates. *The consolidated stockholders' equity equals the equity of the parent company—this is always the case when the subsidiary is wholly owned.*

The consolidated income statement is shown in Exhibit 9.5. Penman reports equity income in its income statement equal to the net income reported by Nissim Company. The effect of the consolidation process is to remove the equity income account in Penman's income statement and replace it with the sales and expenses of Nissim Company to which it relates. This is accomplished by summing the rows in the income statement and eliminating the equity income account to yield the consolidated income statement. *The consolidated net income equals the net income of the parent company—this is always the case* (because the equity income the parent reports equals the net income of the subsidiary when the subsidiary is wholly owned).

IFRS Alert
Consolidation accounting is generally similar with IFRS; differences exist in technical details, but not with presentation of consolidated financial statements.

Exhibit 9.5 ■ Mechanics of Consolidation Accounting
(Wholly-Owned Subsidiary, Purchased at Book Value)

	Penman Company	Nissim Company	Consolidating Adjustments	Consolidated
Balance Sheet				
Current assets	$ 6,000	$ 1,400		$ 7,400
Investment in Nissim	3,400	0	(3,400)	0
PPE, net	10,000	4,000		14,000
Total assets.	$19,400	$ 5,400		$21,400
Liabilities.	$ 5,000	$ 2,000		$ 7,000
Contributed capital.	10,000	2,000	(2,000)	10,000
Retained earnings	4,400	1,400	(1,400)	4,400
Total liabilities and equity	$19,400	$ 5,400		$21,400
Income statement				
Sales.	$25,000	$10,000		$35,000
Cost of goods sold.	(20,000)	(7,000)		(27,000)
Gross profit.	5,000	3,000		8,000
Operating expenses	(3,600)	(2,600)		(6,200)
Equity income from investment	400	—	(400)	0
Net income.	$ 1,800	$ 400		$ 1,800

Investments Purchased at Book Value: Subsidiary <u>Not</u> Wholly-Owned When a subsidiary is not wholly-owned, we account for the equity interest of noncontrolling shareholders in addition to that of the parent's stockholders. This will affect both the balance sheet and the income statement. To illustrate, assume Penman acquires 80% of Nissim instead of 100%, as in our previous example. Now, the equity investment account on Penman's balance sheet will reflect only 80% of Nissim's equity, and the equity income it reports in its income statement will only reflect 80% of Nissim's net income. The remaining 20% of the net assets of the subsidiary and its net income are owned by noncontrolling shareholders. Their share in the net assets of Nissim is reflected on the consolidated balance sheet in a new account titled **noncontrolling interest**. In addition, we apportion Nissim's net income into the 80%, or $320, attributed to Penman's shareholders and the 20%, or $80, attributed to noncontrolling shareholders.

We demonstrate the accounting for noncontrolling interests in Exhibit 9.6. Again, the balance sheets of Penman and Nissim are shown in the first two columns. The consolidating adjustments are shown in the third column and the consolidated balance sheet and income statement in the last column. The claim of noncontrolling shareholders on Nissim's net assets is recognized in consolidated equity in an account called noncontrolling interest. The $680 noncontrolling interest on the consolidated balance sheet represents the 20% share of the net assets at acquisition ($3,000 × 20% = $600) plus the 20% share of Nissim's net income ($400 × 20% = $80). The $2,720 equity investment account on Penman's balance sheet reflects its 80% interest in Nissim's equity ([$2,000 + $1,400] × 80%). That equity investment account is eliminated in the consolidation process.

Business Insight ■ Accounting for Noncontrolling Interests

When a company acquires less than 100% of a subsidiary, it must account for the interests of the noncontrolling shareholders separately from those of its own shareholders. This has two implications for consolidated financial statements.

1. Consolidated net income is first computed for the company as a whole as revenues less expenses. Then, it is allocated to the portion attributable to the parent's shareholders and the noncontrolling shareholders in proportion to their respective ownership interests.

2. The cumulative balance of the noncontrolling interests is reported on the balance sheet in the stockholders' equity section. It is increased each year by the net income allocated to noncontrolling interests and is decreased by any dividends paid to those noncontrolling shareholders.

The consolidated income statement shows the consolidated revenues, consolidated expenses, and consolidated net income. The $320 equity income account in Penman's income statement reflects 80% of Nissim's net income that it owns ($400 × 80%). This equity income account is eliminated in the consolidation process just like the equity investment account on the balance sheet. When less than 100% of the subsidiary is owned by the parent, the consolidated income statement allocates net income into that portion *attributable to the parent (controlling) shareholders* (80% here) and that portion *attributable to the noncontrolling shareholders* (20% here).

Exhibit 9.6 ■ Mechanics of Consolidation Accounting (Subsidiary Not Wholly-Owned, Purchased at Book Value)

	Penman Company	Nissim Company	Consolidating Adjustments	Consolidated
Balance Sheet				
Current assets	$ 6,000	$1,400		$ 7,400
Investment in Nissim	2,720	0	2,720	0
PPE, net	10,000	4,000		14,000
Total assets.	$18,720	$5,400		$21,400
Liabilities.	$ 5,000	$2,000		$ 7,000
Contributed capital.	9,400	2,000	(2,000)	9,400
Retained earnings	4,320	1,400	(1,400)	4,320
Noncontrolling interest			680	680
Total liabilities and equity	$18,720	$5,400		$21,400
Income statement				
Sales.	$25,000	$10,000		$35,000
Cost of goods sold.	(20,000)	(7,000)		(27,000)
Gross profit.	5,000	3,000		8,000
Operating expenses	(3,600)	(2,600)		(6,200)
Equity income from investment	320	—	(320)	0
Net income.	$ 1,720	$ 400		$ 1,800
Net income attributable to noncontrolling interest . . .				80
Net income attributable to Penman shareholders . . .				$ 1,720

Investments Purchased <u>above</u> Book Value The illustrations above assume the purchase price of the acquisition equals the book value of the investee company. It is more often the case, however, that the purchase price exceeds the book value. This might arise, for example, if an investor company believes it is acquiring something of value that is not reported on the investee's balance sheet—such as tangible assets whose market values have risen above book value or unrecorded intangible assets, such as patents or corporate synergies. When the acquisition price exceeds book value, all net assets acquired (both tangible and intangible) must be recognized on the consolidated balance sheet.

To illustrate, let's return to the example of Exhibit 9.5 in which Penman acquires 100% interest in Nissim. Let's now assume Penman paid a premium to Nissim of $1,000 more than the book value of Nissim's stockholders' equity on the acquisition date (see the increase in Penman's contributed capital to $11,000 reflecting the additional $1,000 of stock issued to Nissim's shareholders). Assume Penman paid the additional $1,000 because Penman expects to realize $1,000 in additional value from corporate synergies, such as increased market presence, ability to consolidate offices, and increased buying power. General synergies such as this are recognized on the balance sheet as an intangible asset with an indefinite useful life, called **goodwill**. The $4,000 investment account now reflects two components: the book value acquired of $3,000 (as before) and an additional $1,000 of newly acquired assets (goodwill asset). Exhibit 9.7 shows the balance sheets of the two companies along with the consolidating adjustments and the consolidated balance sheet, on the date of acquisition. (Note that this example is at the acquisition date and does not include the $400 earned by Nissim during the ensuing year.)

Exhibit 9.7 ■ **Mechanics of Consolidation Accounting (Purchase Price above Book Value)**

	Penman Company	Nissim Company	Consolidating Adjustments	Consolidated
Current assets	$ 6,000	$1,000		$ 7,000
Investment in Nissim	4,000	0	(4,000)	0
PPE, net	10,000	4,000		14,000
Goodwill			1,000	1,000
Total assets.	$20,000	$5,000		$22,000
Liabilities.	$ 5,000	$2,000		$ 7,000
Contributed capital.	11,000	2,000	(2,000)	11,000
Retained earnings	4,000	1,000	(1,000)	4,000
Total liabilities and equity	$20,000	$5,000		$22,000

The consolidated current assets and liabilities are the sum of those accounts on each company's balance sheet. The investment account, however, includes $1,000 of the newly acquired goodwill asset that must now be reported on the consolidated balance sheet. The consolidation process in this case has two steps. First, the $3,000 equity of Nissim Company is eliminated against the equity investment account as before. Then, the remaining $1,000 of the investment account is eliminated and the newly acquired asset ($1,000 of goodwill, which is not reported on Nissim's balance sheet) is added to the consolidated balance sheet. The goodwill asset is now recognized on the consolidated balance sheet as a separate asset and, like all other assets, that goodwill asset must be tested annually for impairment and written down (or written off entirely) if found to be impaired.[5] Goodwill impairments can be large. Calcbench, an online source for financial and accounting data, reported that in 2015, "total impairments stood at $30.78 billion, compared to $12.02 billion in 2014. Average impairment among the S&P 500 jumped from $26.4 million in 2014 to $67.7 million last year. The good news is that only 40 companies in the S&P 500 reported any goodwill impairment at all last year. The bad news: that number is still up 11 percent from 2014, when 36 companies disclosed an impairment charge."[6]

In our example here, we recognized just one intangible asset: goodwill. Often, the excess purchase price is assigned to several intangible assets that have a useful life (such as the value of brands, patents, licensing agreements, and customer relationships; see the text box below for more details). If recognized, the cost of such intangible assets (other than goodwill) are amortized over their useful lives in the same manner we depreciate a tangible asset. Consolidated net income is reduced by the amortization of those intangible assets.

Accounting Insight ■ Accounting for Acquired Intangible Assets

The market value of a company's equity can differ substantially from its book value because of unrecorded assets. These unrecorded assets typically relate to intangible assets such as market position, brand equity, managerial talent, and internally developed technology. When companies are acquired, however, such unrecorded assets are recognized on the acquirer's balance sheet. The purchase price is allocated to the assets acquired and the liabilities assumed. First tangible assets, such as PPE and inventory, are identified and valued. Then, intangible assets are identified and valued. All these assets are recorded on the acquirer's consolidated balance sheet at fair market value just like any other purchased asset. Finally, any excess purchase price is allocated to Goodwill. Common types of intangible assets recognized during acquisitions follow.

- Marketing-related assets such as trademarks and Internet domain names
- Customer-related assets such as customer lists and customer contracts
- Artistic-related assets such as plays, books, and videos

continued

---

[5] In 2015, the FASB proposed a change to the accounting standard to simplify the process involved in determining the impairment, and subsequent write-off, of goodwill. Under the proposal, if the carrying amount of a subsidiary company exceeds its fair value, a goodwill impairment loss would be recognized based on the excess. Current GAAP requires companies to re-estimate goodwill using the current fair value of the subsidiary in the same manner goodwill was determined during the acquisition. The proposed method is less complicated and arguably just as reliable.

[6] http://blog.calcbench.com/post/143549765548/goodwill-impairments-in-2015-not-so-good

- Contract-based assets such as licensing, lease contracts, and franchise and royalty agreements
- Technology-based assets such as patents, in-process research and development, software, databases, and trade secrets

For example, in 2015, when Heinz acquired Kraft for $52,637 million, the purchase price was allocated to the acquired assets and liabilities as follows ($ millions).

Cash.	$ 314
Other current assets.	3,423
Property, plant and equipment.	4,193
Identifiable intangible assets	49,749
Other non-current assets	214
Trade and other payables.	(3,026)
Long-term debt	(9,286)
Net postemployment benefits and other non-current liabilities.	(4,734)
Deferred income tax liabilities	(17,239)
Net assets acquired	23,608
Goodwill on acquisition	29,029
Total consideration	$52,637

Heinz allocated $49,749 million of the purchase price to identifiable intangible assets, which consisted of the following.

	Preliminary Fair Value ($ millions)	Weighted Average Life (in years)
Indefinite-lived trademarks.	$45,082	—
Definite-lived trademarks	1,690	24
Customer relationships	2,977	29
Total identifiable intangible assets . . .	$49,749	

Once recognized, intangible assets with definite useful lives are amortized over their remaining lives. For example, Heinz will amortize the customer relationships over 29 years. Other intangible assets that are considered to be indefinite-lived assets (such as the indefinite-lived trademarks) remain on the balance sheet at their initial value. These assets are tested annually for impairment and written down accordingly, similar to the accounting for all fixed assets and goodwill.

Consolidation of Foreign Subsidiaries (Cumulative Translation Adjustment)

Foreign subsidiaries that are headquartered outside of the U.S. typically conduct business and maintain their accounting records in their own domestic currencies rather than in U.S. dollars. Before the U.S. parent company can consolidate the foreign subsidiary, the foreign currency denominated financial statements must be translated into $US. From day to day, the exchange rate between the $US and the foreign currency changes. So while the value of any of the subsidiary's transactions is known with certainty, its $US equivalent will change depending on the prevailing exchange rate the day the financials are translated.

Consider the example below where a European subsidiary has no changes in its balance sheet during the year (including no net income). Assume the $US strengthens during the year vis-à-vis the euro, moving from 0.800 to 0.909 such that each euro purchases fewer $US ($1.25 dropping to $1.10).

	June 30, 2015		June 30, 2016	
Balance Sheet	€	$	€	$
Assets.	$2,000	$2,500	$2,000	$2,200
Liabilities.	500	625	500	550
Net assets	1,500	**1,875**	1,500	**1,650**
Exchange Rates				
Euro/$US	0.80		0.909	
$US/Euro	1.25		1.100	

The euro-denominated balance sheet does not change year over year, but the translated and consolidated values vary greatly. The upshot is the foreign currency-denominated balance sheet shrinks when the $US strengthens.[7]

At consolidation, the foreign subsidiary's assets and liabilities are reported on the parent's balance sheet at their $US value translated at the rate prevailing on the balance sheet date. Recall that during consolidation, the subsidiaries equity is *not* added to the parent's balance sheet. From the example above, we see that adding the assets and liabilities causes the balance sheet to be out of balance in $US. To balance, we adjust stockholders' equity for the difference. We add the change in net assets arising from the change exchange rate to an account called the **cumulative translation adjustment**. In the example above, the net assets of €1,500 translates to **$1,875** at the start of the year and **$1,650** at the end, a decrease of $225. To balance, we adjust equity downward by $225. Thus, the cumulative translation adjustment account has a negative balance. The parent's consolidated balance sheet will include the following amounts.

June 30, 2016	€	$
Assets.	$2,000	$2,200
Liabilities.	500	550
Cumulative translation adjustment.		(225)

To sum up, when the $US strengthens, the cumulative translation adjustment is negative. Conversely, when the $US weakens, the foreign subsidiary's assets and liabilities increase, as does stockholders' equity, and that increase is evidenced by a positive cumulative translation adjustment on the parent's balance sheet. The cumulative translation adjustment account typically fluctuates between negative and positive values as the $US strengthens and weakens vis-à-vis foreign currencies over time. Most companies aggregate the cumulative translation adjustment with similar adjustments in an account called accumulated other comprehensive income (AOCI), a stockholders' equity account.[8]

Alphabet reports AOCI as part of its stockholders' equity accounts in 2015, as follows.

Stockholders' Equity ($ millions)	2014	2015
Convertible preferred stock, $0.001 par value per share, 100,000 shares authorized; no shares issued and outstanding	$ 0	$ 0
Class A and Class B common stock, and Class C capital stock and additional paid-in capital, $0.001 par value per share: 15,000,000 shares authorized (Class A 9,000,000, Class B 3,000,000, Class C 3,000,000); 680,172 (Class A 286,560, Class B 53,213, Class C 340,399) and par value of $680 (Class A $287, Class B $53, Class C $340) and 687,348 (Class A 292,297, Class B 50,295, Class C 344,756) and par value of $687 (Class A $292, Class B $50, Class C $345) shares issued and outstanding. . . .	28,767	32,982
Accumulated other comprehensive income (loss)	**27**	**(1,874)**
Retained earnings.	75,066	89,223
Total stockholders' equity	$103,860	$120,331

Alphabet's AOCI decreased from $27 million in 2014 to a negative $(1,874) million in 2015. The $1,901 million decrease consists of the following.

$ millions	2015
Change in foreign currency translation adjustment	$(1,067)
Net change in unrealized gains/losses on passive investments	(507)
Net change in derivative securities (cash flow hedges)	(327)
	$(1,901)

---

[7] We discuss this same effect on the income statement in Module 5. In short, when the foreign currency-denominated income statement in translated to $US, a stronger $US means lower sales, expenses, and profit.

[8] Other adjustments that are included in AOCI relate to debt securities and derivative securities, as discussed in this module, and pension adjustments, discussed in a later module. The common feature of all of these adjustments is that they represent unrealized gains and losses on various assets and liabilities. The unrealized gains and losses are recognized in income (realized) *only when* the asset or liability is removed from the balance sheet (sold, settled, or disposed of).

The decrease in AOCI is largely due to the negative translation adjustment caused by the stronger $US vis-à-vis many foreign currencies—the cumulative amount is the aggregation of gains and losses across all the currencies in which Alphabet's subsidiaries transacted during the year.

The year-over-year change in AOCI is formally called **other comprehensive income (or loss)**. We can see from the examples above that Alphabet reported other comprehensive *loss* of $1,901 million in 2015. The financial statements for all companies include a statement of comprehensive income that explains the changes in the AOCI account. The statement of comprehensive income is either presented at the bottom of the income statement or on its own immediately after the income statement. Alphabet, for example, chose the latter. (As explained in more detail in a prior module, Comprehensive income = Net income + Other comprehensive income. For Alphabet in 2015, Comprehensive income = $14,447 million, the sum of Net income ($16,348 million) and Other comprehensive loss ($1,901 million).)

ALPHABET INC. **Consolidated Statements of Comprehensive Income**			
Year Ended December 31 ($ millions)	2013	2014	2015
Net income.	$12,733	$14,136	$16,348
Other comprehensive income (loss):			
Change in foreign currency translation adjustment	89	(996)	(1,067)
Available-for-sale investments:			
Change in net unrealized gains (losses)	(392)	505	(715)
Less: reclassification adjustment for net (gains) losses included in net income.	(162)	(134)	208
Net change (net of tax effect of $212, $60, and $29)	(554)	371	(507)
Cash flow hedges:			
Change in net unrealized gains.	112	651	676
Less: reclassification adjustment for net gains included in net income	(60)	(124)	(1,003)
Net change (net of tax effect of $30, $196, and $115).	52	527	(327)
Other comprehensive loss.	**(413)**	**(98)**	**(1,901)**
Comprehensive income	$12,320	$14,038	$14,447

To conclude, the strengthening or weakening of the $US that causes fluctuations in assets and liabilities, and the cumulative translation adjustment has no effect on cash flow. Changes in the cumulative translation adjustment account are not reflected in net income; the fluctuations are included in AOCI and remain in stockholders' equity as long as the parent owns the foreign subsidiary. If and when a foreign subsidiary is sold, any remaining amount in AOCI that relates to the foreign subsidiary is removed from stockholders' equity and reported in net income.

Consolidation Disclosures To illustrate consolidation mechanics, we consider Caterpillar. The company's Form 10-K reports consolidated financial statements: the parent company financial statements (Machinery and Power Systems) are combined with those of the subsidiary (Financial Products). Exhibit 9.8 (taken from Caterpillar's 10-K) reports the parent and the subsidiary balance sheets separately as well as the adjustments that yield the consolidated financial statements. Following are a few observations relating to Exhibit 9.8.

❶ The parent company (Machinery and Power Systems) reports an investment on its balance sheet called "Investment in Financial Products subsidiaries" with a balance of $3,888 million in 2015. This investment represents the parent's investment in its wholly-owned subsidiaries, and it is accounted for using the equity method. On the parent's books, this investment account represents net assets (total assets less total liabilities) of the Financial Products subsidiaries in the same way Altria's balance sheet represents the percentage it owns of the net assets of SABMiller. The parent maintains its separate parent company financial records for taxation and other internal decision-making purposes. But for external reporting purposes, Caterpillar must present consolidated financial statements. (Caterpillar controls its Financial Products subsidiaries. Altria does not control SABMiller. That is why Caterpillar's must consolidate its Financial Products subsidiaries while Altria reports SABMiller as an equity investment.)

Exhibit 9.8 ■ Caterpillar Consolidated Balance Sheet

At December 31, 2015 ($ millions)	Machinery & Power Systems	Financial Products	Consolidating Adjustments	Consolidated
Balance sheet				
Current assets	$20,306	$15,231	❹$(1,119)	$34,418
Noncurrent assets	24,476	20,500	❹ (897)	44,079
Investment in Financial Products subsidiaries	❶ 3,888		❸ (3,888)	—
Total assets	$48,670	$35,731	$(5,904)	$78,497
Current liabilities	$13,134	$14,300	❹$(1,131)	$26,303
Long-term liabilities	20,651	17,543	❹ (885)	37,309
Stockholders' Equity:				
Common stock	5,238	911	(911)	5,238
Treasury stock	(17,640)	0		(17,640)
Retained earnings	34,208	3,747	(3,747)	34,208
Accumulated other comprehensive income	(6,997)	(896)	896	(6,997)
Noncontrolling interests	76	126	(126)	76
Total stockholders' equity	14,885	❷ 3,888	❸ (3,888)	14,885
Total liabilities and equity	$48,670	$35,731	$(5,904)	$78,497
Income statement				
Revenues	$44,147	$ 3,179	❹$ (315)	$47,011
Operating costs	(41,406)	(2,405)	❹ 56	(43,755)
Operating profit	2,741	774	(259)	3,256
Other income (expense)	(708)	48	259	(401)
Profit before taxes	2,033	822	0	2,855
Provision for income taxes	(512)	(230)	(192)	(742)
Equity in profit of Financial Products subsidiaries	❺ 591		❺ (591)	0
Profit of consolidated companies	2,112	592	(591)	2,113
Less: profit attributable to noncontrolling interests	10	1		11
Profit attributable to Caterpillar shareholders	$ 2,102	$ 591	$ (591)	$ 2,102

❷ The subsidiary balance sheet reports total stockholders' equity in the amount of $3,888 million, the same amount as the equity investment on the parent's balance sheet. That is not a coincidence. As we discuss earlier in this module, if the investment is acquired at book value and the investee company is wholly-owned, the investment account on the parent's balance sheet will always be equal to the stockholders' equity of the subsidiary (investee) company. In this case, Caterpillar formed (not acquired) its financial products subsidiary, which is why the equity investment balance equals the equity of the financial products subsidiary and there are no recorded intangible assets.

❸ The consolidation process eliminates all intercompany investments, including intercompany sales and receivables, which we discuss below. Then, the rows are summed to yield the consolidated totals reported. This first group of eliminations removes the equity investment of $3,888 million from total assets and the subsidiary's stockholders' equity. Notice that the equity investment shows a zero balance (and is, therefore, not reported) on the consolidated balance sheet. Notice also that consolidated stockholders' equity is equal to parent company stockholders' equity (that will always be the case if the equity investment is purchased at book value).

❹ All intercompany transactions are eliminated in both the income statement and the balance sheet to avoid double counting. These include intercompany sales (and offsetting purchases) and intercompany receivables (and offsetting payables).

❺ Finally, because the subsidiaries are wholly-owned, the parent company reports equity income equal to the net income of its subsidiaries ($591 million). This income statement line is eliminated during the consolidation process and replaced by the revenues and expenses to which it relates. Net income remains unchanged, but the consolidated income statement reports the sales and expenses of its Financial Products subsidiaries rather than just the net income.

Following the eliminations of *all intercompany transactions*, the adjusted balance sheets and income statement line items are summed to yield the financial statements reported in Caterpillar's 10-K. In the case that a subsidiary is controlled but not wholly-owned, the consolidated financial statements will also reflect the *noncontrolling interest*, which we discuss above.

Reporting Subsidiary Stock Issuances

After subsidiaries are acquired, they can, and sometimes do, issue stock. If issued to outside investors, the result is an infusion of cash into the subsidiary and a reduction in the parent's percentage ownership. For example, on October 26, 2015, Ferrari N.V., a subsidiary of Fiat Chrysler Automobiles N.V., completed its initial public offering (IPO). Prior to the sale, Fiat Chrysler owned 90% of Ferrari's stock with the remaining 10% owned by the Ferrari family. During the IPO, Ferrari sold 10% of its common shares to the public and received net proceeds of approximately €900 million and Fiat Chrysler reduced its stake to 80 percent of Ferrari's common shares. The €900 million cash received from the sale was accounted for as an increase in Fiat Chrysler's paid-in capital. The sale by a subsidiary (Ferrari) of its stock in an IPO had no effect on the parent's (Fiat Chrysler's) income statement.

Reporting the Sale of Subsidiary Companies

When the parent company sells one of its subsidiaries, it accounts for the subsidiary as a discontinued operation if the sale represents a strategic shift for the company that has, or will have, a major effect on a company's financial results. (We discuss discontinued operations in an earlier module.) In 2015, United Technologies Corporation sold its Sikorsky Aircraft business to Lockheed Martin Corp. for $9,083 million in cash. Once United Technologies decided to sell Sikorsky Aircraft, it accounted for the subsidiary as a discontinued operation with the following financial statement effects.

1. It removed from the consolidated income statement, the revenues and expenses relating to the Sikorsky Aircraft business (for each of the three years presented) and reported a single line on the income statement that represented the operating profit of the Sikorsky Aircraft business unit. This line item is deliberately reported in a separate section below income from continuing operations. This segregation allows investors to focus on income from continuing operations that represent the portion of United Technologies' earnings that are likely to persist and are, therefore, relevant for the pricing of its securities.

2. In 2015, the year of sale, United Technologies reported a $6,042 million pre-tax gain on the sale of the Sikorsky Aircraft business unit (sales proceeds of $9,083 million less the net book value of the Sikorsky Aircraft business unit of $3,041 million on the date of sale).

United Technologies reports the income from operations and gain on sale in its 2015 income statement as follows.

$ millions	2015
Income from continuing operations attributable to common shareowners	$3,996
Discontinued operations	
Income from operations	252
Gain (loss) on disposal	6,042
Income tax expense	(2,684)
Net income from discontinued operations	3,610
Less: Noncontrolling interest in subsidiaries' earnings (loss) from discontinued operations . . .	(2)
Income from discontinued operations attributable to common shareowners	3,612
Net income attributable to common shareowners	$7,608

In its balance sheet, United Technologies segregated the assets and liabilities of the Sikorsky Aircraft business, labelling them as assets (liabilities) "held for sale." Again, designating the assets and liabilities of the discontinued operations as held for sale allows financial statement readers to more easily identify the core operating assets and liabilities of the company that will remain after the sale. Once the discontinued operation is sold, its assets (less liabilities) are converted to cash, a nonoperating asset. It is for this reason that analysts tend to treat discontinued operations as nonoperating in their analysis.

Limitations of Consolidation Reporting

Consolidation of financial statements is meant to present a financial picture of the entire set of companies under the control of the parent. Because investors typically purchase stock in the parent company and not in the subsidiaries, a consolidated view is more relevant than the parent company reporting subsidiaries as equity investments in its balance sheet. Still, we must be aware of certain limitations of consolidation.

1. Consolidated income does not imply the parent company has received any or all of the subsidiaries' net income as cash. The parent can only receive cash from subsidiaries via dividend payments. Conversely, the consolidated cash is not automatically available to the individual subsidiaries. It is quite possible, therefore, for an individual subsidiary to experience cash flow problems even though the consolidated group has strong cash flows. Likewise, unguaranteed debts of a subsidiary are not obligations of the consolidated group. Thus, even if the consolidated balance sheet is strong, creditors of a failing subsidiary are often unable to sue the parent or other subsidiaries to recoup losses.

2. Consolidated balance sheets and income statements are a mix of the various subsidiaries, often from different industries. Comparisons across companies, even if in similar industries, are often complicated by the different mix of subsidiary companies.

3. Consolidated disclosures are highly aggregated, which can preclude effective analysis. Consolidated numbers can mask poorly performing subsidiaries whose losses are offset by the positive performance of others.

Review 9-3 LO3

On January 1, assume **Yahoo! Inc.** purchased all of the common shares of **EarthLink** for $600,000 cash—this is $200,000 more than the book value of EarthLink's stockholders' equity. Balance sheets of the two companies immediately after the acquisition follow.

	Yahoo! (Parent)	EarthLink (Subsidiary)	Consolidating Adjustments	Consolidated
Current assets	$1,000,000	$100,000		
Investment in EarthLink ...	600,000	—		
PPE, net	3,000,000	400,000		_____
Total assets.	$4,600,000	$500,000		_____
Liabilities.	$1,000,000	$100,000		
Contributed capital.	2,000,000	200,000		
Retained earnings	1,600,000	200,000		_____
Total liabilities and equity ..	$4,600,000	$500,000		_____

During purchase negotiations, EarthLink's PPE was appraised at $500,000, and Earthlink had unrecorded patents with a fair value of $25,000. All of EarthLink's remaining assets and liabilities were appraised at values approximating their book values. Also, Yahoo! concluded that payment of an additional $75,000 was warranted because of anticipated corporate synergies. Prepare the consolidating adjustments and the consolidated balance sheet at acquisition.

Solution on p. 9-55.

Global Accounting

Both U.S. GAAP and IFRS account similarly for investments by companies in the debt and equity securities of other companies. However, differences exist, and we highlight the notable ones here.

Passive Investments Under both U.S. GAAP and IFRS, companies classify financial (passive) instruments as trading, available-for-sale, or held-to-maturity.

■ Under IFRS, the definition of financial instrument is much broader, including, for example, accounts receivable and loans to customers or associates. For analysis, such instruments are disclosed in the notes, which will aid our reclassification for comparison purposes.

■ Under both GAAP and IFRS, unlisted securities are valued at fair value. This represents a change in U.S. GAAP effective in 2018.

Equity Method Investment

■ U.S. GAAP permits companies to elect to report equity method investments at fair value with changes in fair value to net income. IFRS only permits this option for mutual funds, insurance companies, and similar entities.

■ For joint ventures, IFRS allows the equity method or proportionate consolidation, whereas GAAP allows proportionate consolidation under very limited circumstances. With proportionate consolidation, the company's share of investee's assets and liabilities (and revenues and expenses) are added line by line on the balance sheet (and income statement). Proportionate consolidation means every line on the IFRS financial statement is "grossed up" as compared with GAAP. The net numbers (equity and income) are identical, but comparisons of individual line items between IFRS and GAAP reports are problematic. This is similar to the effect of equity method accounting versus consolidation.

Consolidation GAAP sets out two ways to determine whether or not consolidation is required—the VIE model and the voting interest model, as discussed above. Under IFRS, consolidation is required when the investor controls the investee; that is, when the investor has power over the investee, is exposed to variable returns from the investee, or can exercise power to affect the amount of return from the investee.

■ Under IFRS, companies can measure noncontrolling interests either at fair value (full goodwill approach) or at the proportionate share of the identifiable net assets acquired (purchased goodwill approach). U.S. GAAP permits fair value only. This IFRS-GAAP difference affects ratios based on operating assets, such as return on net operating assets (RNOA). Because goodwill is not routinely amortized, the difference will have no income statement impact (recall that we exclude noncontrolling interest from our calculation of return on equity).

■ Under U.S. GAAP, parent and subsidiary accounting policies do not need to conform. Under IFRS, parent and subsidiary accounting policies must conform.

■ IFRS fair value impairments for intangible assets, excluding goodwill, can be later reversed (that is, written back up after being written down). Companies must have reliable evidence that the value of the intangible has been restored, and the reversal cannot exceed the original impairment. While the original impairment was reported as a charge on the income statement, subsequent reversals do not affect income but, instead, are added to equity through a "reserve" much like AOCI.

Appendix 9A: Accounting for Derivatives

LO4
Describe and interpret derivative disclosures.

Although there is some speculative use of derivatives by U.S. companies (both industrial and financial), most companies use derivatives to shelter their income statements, balance sheets, and cash flows from fluctuations in the market prices of currencies, commodities, and financial instruments, as well as for market rates of interest. Companies routinely face risk exposures that can markedly affect their balance sheets, profitability, and cash flows. These exposures can be grouped into two general categories.

1. Exposure to changes in the **fair value** of an asset (such as accounts receivable, inventory, marketable securities, or a firm contract to sell an asset) or liability (such as accounts payable, a firm commitment to purchase an asset, or a fixed-rate debt obligation).
2. Exposure to variation in **cash flows** relating to a forecasted transaction (such as *planned* inventory purchases or anticipated foreign revenues) or cash flow exposure relating to a variable-rate debt obligation.

Companies often seek to mitigate these types of risk exposures by purchasing a financial security whose value is negatively correlated with the specific risk the company faces or by entering into a contract that locks in a future value. This transfer of risk is called *hedging*. Some examples include:

- *Forward-exchange contracts* to hedge the foreign currency risk related to an asset or liability denominated in a non-U.S. currency.
- *Futures contracts* to hedge the fair value of commodities held as inventory.
- *Purchased options* to hedge the value of marketable securities.
- *Forward contracts* to hedge a firm commitment to buy or sell inventory.
- *Interest rate swaps* to convert a fixed-rate debt into variable-rate debt or vice versa.
- *Forward, futures,* or *option contracts* to hedge a forecasted sale or purchase of a commodity.

Some of these securities can be purchased in the open market (e.g., options and futures contracts). Other contracts are private agreements between two parties (e.g., forward contracts and swaps). All these types of hedges are called "derivatives" because the value of the hedge (the security or the contract) *derives* from the value of the hedged position—that is, the currency, the commodity, the interest rate that the company seeks to hedge. Regardless of their form, these hedges serve to transfer risk to parties whose core competencies involve managing and pricing risk. Hedging instruments and contracts act like an insurance policy and the cost of the hedge is treated as an ordinary cost of doing business.

For an example of fair value risk, consider a company with a receivable denominated in a foreign currency. If the $US strengthens, the receivable declines in value and the company incurs a foreign-exchange loss. To avoid this situation, the company can hedge the receivable with a foreign-currency derivative. Ideally, when the $US strengthens, the derivative will increase in value by an amount that exactly offsets the decrease in the value of the receivable. As a result, the company's net asset position (receivable less derivative) remains unaffected and no gain or loss arises when the $US weakens or strengthens. For accounting purposes, this is called a **fair value hedge**.

As an example of cash flow risk, consider a company that routinely purchases a food commodity used in its manufacturing process. Any price increases during the coming year will flow to cost of goods sold, and profit will decrease (unless the company can completely pass the price increase along to its customers, which is rarely the case). To avoid this situation, the company can hedge the forecasted inventory purchases with a commodity derivative contract that locks in a price today. When the price of the commodity increases, the derivative contract will shelter the company and, as a result, the company's cost of goods sold remains unaffected. For accounting purposes, this is called a **cash flow hedge**.

Accounting for derivatives essentially boils down to this: all derivatives are reported at fair value on the balance sheet. For fair value hedges, the asset or liability being hedged (the foreign receivable in the example above) is reported on the balance sheet at fair value. If the market value of the hedged asset or liability changes, the value of the derivative changes in the opposite direction if the hedge is effective and, thus, net assets and liabilities are unaffected. Likewise, the related gains and losses are largely offsetting, leaving income unaffected.

For cash flow hedges, there is no hedged asset or liability on the books. In our example above, the anticipated commodity purchases are being hedged. Thus, the company has no inventory yet, and changes in the fair value of the derivative are not met with opposite changes in an asset or liability. For these cash flow hedges, gains or losses from the fair value of the derivative are not reported on the income statement. Instead they are held in AOCI, as part of shareholders' equity. Later, when the hedged item impacts income (say, when the commodity cost is reflected in cost of goods sold), the derivative gain or loss is reclassified from AOCI to income. If the hedge was effective, the gain or loss on the hedged transaction is offset with the loss or gain on the derivative and income is unaffected.

For both fair value and cash flow hedges, income is impacted only to the extent the hedging activities are ineffective. Naturally, if a company uses derivatives to speculate, gains and losses are not offset and directly flow to income. It is this latter activity, in particular, that prompted regulators to formulate newer, tougher accounting standards for derivatives.

Fair Value Hedge Example

To manage a number of risks, Microsoft uses financial derivatives that it designates as fair value hedges.

> Derivative instruments are recognized as either assets or liabilities and are measured at fair value. The accounting for changes in the fair value of a derivative depends on the intended use of the derivative and the resulting designation. For derivative instruments designated as fair value hedges, the gains (losses) are recognized in earnings in the periods of change together with the offsetting losses (gains) on the hedged items attributed to the risk being hedged.

During 2015, Microsoft employed equity contracts to manage the fair value of its marketable securities as well as foreign-exchange contracts to manage foreign currency risk associated with its non-$US-denominated securities. Because Microsoft designated these as fair value hedges, the derivatives and the hedged items (the marketable securities and the $US value of foreign-currency-denominated securities) are all reported at fair value on the balance sheet.

Changes in fair values of the derivatives and the hedged items during the period are reported in current earnings. If the hedges are highly effective, these changes should offset, resulting in little impact on reported profit. Microsoft's footnote disclosure for 2015 shows this offsetting effect.

Fair Value Hedge Gains (Losses)
We recognized in other income (expense), net the following gains (losses) on contracts designated as fair value hedges and their related hedged items:

Year Ended June 30 ($ millions)	2015	2014	2013
Foreign Exchange Contracts			
Derivatives	$ 741	$ (14)	$70
Hedged items	(725)	6	(69)
Total amount of ineffectiveness	$ 16	$ (8)	$ 1
Equity Contracts			
Derivatives	$(107)	$(110)	$ 0
Hedged items	107	110	0
Total amount of ineffectiveness	$ 0	$ 0	$ 0

Had the foreign exchange contracts not been used as hedges, Microsoft's 2015 pre-tax earnings would have been lower by $725 million owing to the loss in value of the hedged items (assets and liabilities) (in $US terms). In contrast, the increase in the fair value of the items hedged with the equity contracts would have increased earnings by $107 million, absent the hedging. So, while hedging reduces negative effects on earnings, companies also give up potential gains. But remember, the objective of hedging is to reduce earnings volatility.

Cash Flow Hedge Example

Southwest Airlines hedges its *expected* jet fuel purchases and accounts for its derivatives as cash flow hedges. These hedges are designed to mitigate fluctuations in fuel costs, especially price hikes that would negatively impact Southwest's income and cash flows. Consistent with the way we deal with fair value hedges, Southwest reports its hedging instruments (derivatives) at fair value on the balance sheet. But, unlike for fair value hedges, changes in the fair value of cash flow hedges are not reflected in current income. Instead, any fair value changes are deferred and recognized as other comprehensive income and carried on the balance sheet as a component of AOCI.

If the price of jet fuel increases, the derivative (the contract that allows Southwest to purchase jet fuel at a lower cost) increases in value, and Southwest reports a deferred gain in AOCI. When Southwest purchases jet fuel, the deferred gain is transferred from AOCI into the fuel expense account in the income statement to (partially) offset the higher fuel costs, thus dampening the negative effect of higher fuel costs.

Of course, if jet fuel costs decline, the fuel derivative contract actually locked in a higher fuel cost. While this seems detrimental to the company, the derivative fair value losses are not included in net income; they are held in AOCI until the lower cost jet fuel is purchased. Then, Southwest transfers the deferred loss from AOCI to the fuel expense account in the income statement, thus dampening the positive effect of lower jet fuel costs.

By hedging its exposure, Southwest is sheltered from significant adverse price movements but also gives up the possibility of profiting from favorable price movements. However, by locking in future fuel costs, the company (and analysts) can better predict earnings and cash flows. In general, hedging transfers the risk of price movements (both increases and decreases) to third parties who are willing to accept that risk and know how to manage and price it.

Footnote disclosures provide information on the derivative fair value gain or loss deferred in AOCI, the portion that has been transferred (reclassified) to the income statement, and the ineffective portion of the hedge. (Derivatives rarely provide a perfectly negative hedge, so it is normal to have a small mismatch between the fair value of the hedging security and the hedged item.) Southwest reports the following in its 2015 10-K.

	Derivatives in Cash Flow Hedging Relationships					
	(Gain) Loss Recognized in AOCI on Derivatives (Effective Portion)		**(Gain) Loss Reclassified from AOCI into Income (Effective Portion)[a]**		**(Gain) Loss Recognized in Income on Derivatives (Ineffective Portion)[b]**	
Year ended December 31 ($ millions)	**2015**	**2014**	**2015**	**2014**	**2015**	**2014**
Fuel derivative contracts . . .	$546*	$749*	$238*	$22*	$ (9)	$7
Interest rate derivatives	4*	6*	13*	14*	(4)	(4)
Total	$550	$755	$251	$36	$(13)	$3

*Net of tax

[a] Amounts related to fuel derivative contracts and interest rate derivatives are included in Fuel and oil and Interest expense, respectively.

[b] Amounts are included in Other (gains) losses, net.

Fuel costs declined significantly in 2015, meaning Southwest (inadvertently) locked in higher fuel costs. This gave rise to a *loss* of $546 million on the fuel derivative contracts, which Southwest deferred and added to AOCI. Also, during 2015, it transferred (reclassified) $238 million of previously accrued deferred losses from AOCI into the fuel expense account in the income statement. Additionally, Southwest recognized a gain of $9 million on the ineffective portion of its fuel hedges—this was included in other (gains) and losses in the 2015 income statement.

As the price of crude oil declined in 2015, jet fuel costs declined as well, leading to higher profits across the airline industry. In 2015, then, hedging wasn't as intense for airlines because the glut in crude oil led to expectations that jet fuel costs would not greatly increase. Consequently, Southwest hedged a smaller proportion of its expected jet fuel usage.

That has not always been the case, however, as the following graph illustrates.

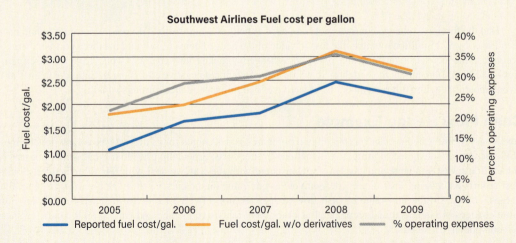

Southwest Airlines Fuel cost per gallon

In 2008, the price of crude oil (and jet fuel) increased markedly, resulting in large losses for the airline industry. As a result of its hedging program, however, Southwest reported jet fuel cost of $2.13/gal. rather than the $2.70/gal. it would have reported had it not hedged its jet fuel costs. Gains on Southwest's hedging portfolio were huge and, in large part, accounted for Southwest's profitability: in 2009, Southwest reported pre-tax gains on its hedging portfolio of over $800 million and reported net income of $99 million.

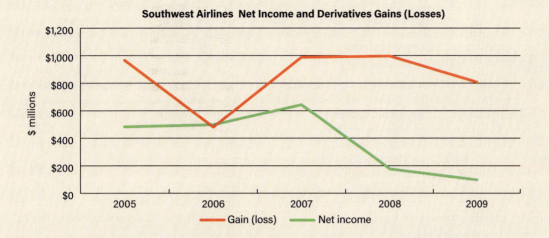

Southwest Airlines Net Income and Derivatives Gains (Losses)

Business Insight ■ Counterparty Risk

The purpose of derivatives is to transfer risk from one company to another. For example, a company might be concerned about the possible decline in the $US value of an account receivable denominated in euros. In order to hedge that risk, the company might execute a forward contract to euros and receive $US. That forward contract only has value, however, if the party on the other side of the transaction (the counterparty) ultimately buys euros from the company when the contract matures. If the counterparty fails to honor its part of the agreement, the forward contract is of no value. The risk that the other party might not live up to its part of the bargain is known as *counterparty risk*. Counterparty risk is very real. Many companies require counterparties to back up their agreement with cash collateral or other acceptable forms of guarantees (e.g., a bank letter of credit). As a result, there is a hidden risk in companies' use of derivatives that is difficult to quantify.

Analysis of Derivatives

The footnote disclosures relating to financial derivatives provide useful information relating to:

- The types of risks the company hedges.
- The amount of exposure hedged (e.g., Southwest reports the number of gallons of jet fuel hedged and total jet fuel consumption for the year).
- The amount of derivative-related gains or losses included in the income statement and where those gains and losses are reflected.
- The amount of deferred profit or loss recognized in AOCI.
- The amount of cash that counterparties have provided to secure receivables or the amount of cash the company has provided to counterparties to collateralize their payables (see, text box on counterparties above).
- The fair value of derivatives and where in the balance sheet they are reported.

We would not have known, for example, the magnitude of the effect of hedging on reported profit for Southwest Airlines were it not for the disclosures in the derivatives footnote. However, disclosures relating to derivatives have also been criticized. In 2013, the **CFA Institute**, a global association of investment professionals, published a report titled "User Perspectives on Financial Instrument Risk Disclosures Under International Financial Reporting Standards Derivatives and Hedging Activities Disclosures (Volume 2)" that compiled feedback from investment managers relating to the quality of derivatives disclosures. The study focused on disclosures mandated by IFRS, but the findings are relevant for U.S. GAAP as well in that the derivative accounting standards are similar under both standards.

The 2013 CFA Institute study reported low user satisfaction with the quality of derivative disclosures. The report summarized its finding as follows.

> Respondents indicated that hedge accounting and disclosure requirements are complex and confusing for users and they do not readily communicate key economic information (e.g. nature of hedging strategies, hedged versus unhedged exposures and hedge effectiveness). The highly complex and arcane nature of hedge accounting rules, along with the partial information regarding hedging activities addressed by hedge accounting disclosures, does not help users to discern the entirety of risk management practices of reporting companies. This explains the ratings of moderate importance of, and low satisfaction with, hedge accounting disclosures.

In sum, footnote disclosures relating to derivatives are very complex, often quite lengthy, and difficult to decipher. While we do obtain some important information about how changes in derivatives' fair values affects reported profit, on balance, the disclosures do not inform us about the company's overall risk exposure and the degree to which management has hedged the company's exposure.

The International Accounting Standards Board, has initiated a project to address these criticisms, and the proposed new model more closely aligns hedge accounting with a company's risk management strategies, and provides improved information about those strategies. FASB chairman Russell Golden recently seemed to be in favor of the IASB's work: "I think that today's hedge accounting in the U.S. is overly proscriptive. I think it prevents companies from actually entering into hedge accounting as something that they think is mitigating their risk, and I think it needs to be improved in the U.S. As we go forward, we will look at what the IASB has finalized to see if it can and should work in the United States, and we will start with that model."

Review 9-4 LO4

PepsiCo Inc. reports the following table in its footnote relating to derivatives.

Pre-tax losses/(gains) on our derivative instruments are categorized as follows:

| | Fair Value/Non-designated Hedges | | Cash Flow Hedges | | | |
	Losses/(Gains) Recognized in Income Statement[a]		Losses/(Gains) Recognized in Accumulated Other Comprehensive Loss		Losses/(Gains) Reclassified from Accumulated Other Comprehensive Loss into Income Statement[b]	
	2015	2014	2015	2014	2015	2014
Foreign exchange......	$ (14)	$ 2	$(112)	$ (70)	$ (97)	$ (16)
Interest rate	17	21	195	135	174	233
Commodity..........	218	170	12	23	20	32
Total	$221	$193	$ 95	$ 88	$ 97	$249

[a] Foreign exchange derivative gains/losses are primarily included in selling, general and administrative expenses. Interest rate derivative gains/losses are primarily from fair value hedges and are included in interest expense. These gains/losses are substantially offset by increases/decreases in the value of the underlying debt, which are also included in interest expense. Commodity derivative gains/losses are included in either cost of sales or selling, general and administrative expenses, depending on the underlying commodity.

[b] Foreign exchange derivative gains/losses are primarily included in cost of sales. Interest rate derivative gains/losses are included in interest expense. Commodity derivative gains/losses are included in either cost of sales or selling, general and administrative expenses, depending on the underlying commodity.

Required

1. What types of risks did PepsiCo hedge with its derivatives in 2015?
2. Did PepsiCo classify these derivatives as fair value or cash flow hedges? How do we know?
3. How did PepsiCo's use of derivatives to hedge, affect its 2015 income?

Solution on p. 9-55.

Appendix 9B: Equity Carve-Outs

Corporate divestitures, or **equity carve-outs**, are increasingly common as companies seek to augment shareholder value through partial or total divestiture of particular subsidiaries or operating units. Generally, equity carve-outs are motivated by the notion that consolidated financial statements obscure the performance of individual business units, thus complicating their evaluation by outsiders. Corporate managers are concerned that this difficulty in assessing the performance of individual business units, limits their ability to reach full valuation. Shareholder value is, therefore, not maximized. In response, conglomerates have divested subsidiaries so the market can individually price them.

LO5
Explain equity carve-outs and their financial statement impact.

Sell-Offs

Equity carve-outs take many forms. The first and simplest form of divestiture is the outright sale of a business unit, called a **sell-off**. In this case, the company sells its equity interest to an unrelated party. The sale is accounted for just like the sale of any other asset. Specifically, any excess (deficit) of cash received over the book value of the business unit sold is recorded as a gain (loss) on the sale. To illustrate, in 2015, **Emerson Electric** sold its mechanical power transmission solutions business as disclosed in the following 10-K excerpt ($ millions, except per share amount).

> In January 2015, the Company completed the sale of its mechanical power transmission solutions business to Regal Beloit Corporation for $1.4 billion, and recognized a pretax gain from the transaction of $939 ($532 after-tax, $0.78 per share). Assets and liabilities sold were as follows: current assets, $182 (accounts receivable, inventories, other current assets); other assets, $374 (property, plant and equipment, goodwill, other noncurrent assets); accrued expenses, $56 (accounts payable, other current liabilities); and other liabilities, $41.

The financial statement effects of this transaction are as follows:

- Emerson Electric received $1.4 billion in cash.
- The mechanical power transmission solutions business was reported on Emerson Electric's balance sheet at $459 million ($182 + $374 − $56 − $41) in January 2015, the month of sale.
- Emerson Electric's gain on sale equaled the proceeds ($1.4 billion) less the carrying amount of the business sold ($459 million), or $939 million ($2 million rounding difference).
- On the statement of cash flows, Emerson Electric subtracts the $939 million non-cash gain on sale from net income in computing net cash flows from operating activities. The cash proceeds of $1.4 billion are reported as a cash inflow in the investing section.

Because selling off the power transmission solutions business did not represent a strategic business shift having a major effect on Emerson Electric's operations and financial results, the company did not report the sell-off as discontinued operations. Instead, they included the transaction in operating income from the industrial automation business, which continues as a business segment for Emerson Electric.

Spin-Offs

A **spin-off** is a second form of divestiture. In this case, the parent company distributes to its stockholders, the shares of the subsidiary company as a dividend. Then, the stockholders own shares in the subsidiary directly rather than through the parent company. In recording this dividend, the parent company reduces retained earnings by the book value of the equity method investment, thereby removing the investment in the subsidiary from the parent's balance sheet.

On July 17, 2015, **eBay Inc.** separated its **PayPal** business via a dividend of PayPal stock to all eBay shareholders, making PayPal an independent company. eBay describes the transaction as follows.

> **Discontinued Operations**   On June 26, 2015, our Board approved the separation of PayPal. . . . To consummate the Distribution, our Board declared a pro rata dividend of PayPal Holdings, Inc. common stock to eBay's stockholders of record as of the close of business on July 8, 2015. . . . Each eBay stockholder received one (1) share of PayPal Holdings, Inc. common stock for every share of eBay common stock held at the close of business on the Record Date. Immediately following the Distribution, PayPal became an independent, publicly traded company and is listed on The NASDAQ Stock Market under the ticker "PYPL." eBay continues to trade on The NASDAQ Stock Market under the ticker "EBAY." We have classified the results of PayPal as discontinued operations in our consolidated statement of income for all periods presented. Additionally, the related assets and liabilities associated with the discontinued operations in the prior year consolidated balance sheet are classified as discontinued operations. In connection with the Distribution, we reviewed our capital allocation strategy to ensure that each of PayPal and eBay would be well capitalized at Distribution. As part of this strategy, we contributed approximately $3.8 billion of cash to PayPal.

eBay treats the distribution of PayPal stock as a dividend equal to the book value of the PayPal subsidiary (think of this as the carrying value of the equity investment), which it reports in the following excerpt from its statement of stockholders' equity

EBAY INC. CONSOLIDATED STATEMENT OF STOCKHOLDERS' EQUITY			
Year Ended December 31 ($ millions)	2015	2014	2013
Retained earnings			
Balance, beginning of year	$18,900	$18,854	$15,998
Net income	1,725	46	2,856
Distribution of PayPal	(12,912)	—	—
Balance, end of year	$ 7,713	$18,900	$18,854

The distribution reduced eBay's assets and equity (retained earnings) by $12,912 million. Because the spin-off was affected as a dividend, there was no effect on net income for 2015.

Split-Offs

The **split-off** is a third form of equity carve-out. In this case, the parent company buys back its own stock using the shares of the subsidiary company instead of cash. After completing this transaction, the subsidiary is an independent, publicly traded company.

The parent treats the split-off like any other purchase of treasury stock. As such, the treasury stock account is increased and the equity method investment account is reduced, reflecting the distribution of that asset. The dollar amount recorded for this treasury stock depends on how the distribution is set up. There are two possibilities.

1. **Pro rata distribution**. Shares are distributed to stockholders on a pro rata basis. Namely, a stockholder owning 10% of the outstanding stock of the parent company receives 10% of the shares of the subsidiary. The treasury stock account is increased by the *book value* of the investment in the subsidiary. The accounting is similar to the purchase of treasury stock for cash, except that shares of the subsidiary are paid to shareholders instead of cash.
2. **Non pro rata distribution**. This case is like a tender offer where individual stockholders can accept or reject the distribution. The treasury stock account is recorded at the *market value* of the shares of the subsidiary distributed. Because the investment account can only be reduced by its book value, a gain or loss on distribution is recorded in the income statement for the difference. (The SEC allows companies to record the difference as an adjustment to additional paid-in capital; the usual practice, as might be expected, is for companies to report any gain as part of income.)

In 2014, **CBS Corporation** split off split-off of its subsidiary, **Outdoor Americas**. The footnotes to CBS Corp's 2015 10-K describe the transaction as follows.

> **DISCONTINUED OPERATIONS**   During 2014, the Company completed the disposition of Outdoor Americas. Outdoor Americas has been presented as a discontinued operation in the Company's consolidated financial statements. In connection with the Company's plan to dispose of Outdoor Americas, in January 2014 Outdoor Americas borrowed $1.60 billion. On April 2, 2014, Outdoor Americas completed an initial public offering ("IPO") through which it sold 23.0 million shares, or approximately 19%, of its common stock for $28.00 per share. Proceeds from the IPO aggregated $615 million, net of underwriting discounts and commissions. The Company received $2.04 billion of the combined IPO and debt proceeds from Outdoor Americas. On July 16, 2014, the Company completed the disposition of its 81% ownership of Outdoor Americas common stock through a tax-free split-off (the "Split-Off") through which the Company accepted 44.7 million shares of CBS Corp. Class B Common Stock from its stockholders in exchange for the 97.0 million shares of Outdoor Americas common stock that it owned. In aggregate, the Company received $4.76 billion from the disposition of Outdoor Americas, including the cash from the IPO and debt proceeds and the fair value of the shares of CBS Corp. Class B Common Stock that were accepted in the Split-Off of $2.72 billion. The Split-Off resulted in a gain of $1.56 billion for the year ended December 31, 2014 which is included in net earnings from discontinued operations and is calculated as follows ($ millions):

continued

Fair value of CBS Corp. Class B Common Stock accepted	
(44,723,131 shares at $60.85 per share on July 16, 2014)...................................	$2,721
Carrying value of Outdoor Americas	(1,162)
Accumulated other comprehensive income...	30
Transaction costs	(32)
Net gain on Split-Off of Outdoor Americas	$1,557

The effect of this transaction was for CBS to exchange its Outdoor Americas stock for CBS stock (its own stock). From an accounting standpoint, the split-off of Outdoor Americas is treated like a stock repurchase using the stock of Outdoor Americas to fund the repurchase instead of cash. As a result of the transaction, the treasury stock account on CBS's balance sheet increased (became more negative) by $2,721 million (the value of CBS Corporation stock "repurchased" during for exchange), which decreased equity by $2,721 million.

	2015		2014		2013	
Year Ended December 31 (In millions)	**Shares**	**Amount**	**Shares**	**Amount**	**Shares**	**Amount**
Treasury Stock, at cost:						
Balance, beginning of year.................	349	$(14,406)	244	$ (8,074)	198	$(5,874)
Class B Common Stock purchased	52	(2,800)	60	(3,612)	46	(2,201)
Outdoor Americas Split-Off................	—	—	45	(2,721)	—	—
Shares paid for tax withholding for stock-based compensation	2	(96)	3	(146)	3	(145)
Issuance of stock for deferred compensation ..	—	1	—	1	—	1
Retirement of treasury stock................	(2)	96	(3)	146	(3)	145
Balance, end of year......................	401	$(17,205)	349	$(14,406)	244	$(8,074)

This decrease to equity was partially offset by the $1,557 million gain on the exchange, which increased retained earnings. This split-off was affected by a tender offer with CBS's shareholders that qualified the transaction as a non pro rata exchange. Consequently, the split-off was valued at market value, which resulted in a gain. CBS's bottom line in 2014 was markedly improved by the split-off.

Analysis of Equity Carve-Outs

Sell-offs, spin-offs, and split-offs all involve the divestiture of an operating segment. Although all three types of carve-outs are one-time occurrences, they can result in substantial gains that can markedly alter the income statement. Consequently, we need to interpret them carefully. This involves learning as many details about the carve-out as possible from the annual report, the Management Discussion and Analysis, and other publicly available information.

Following an equity carve-out, the parent company is rid of the cash flows (positive or negative) of the divested business unit. As such, the divestiture should be treated like any other discontinued operation. Any recognized gain or loss from divestiture is treated as a nonoperating activity. Income (and cash flows) of the divested unit up to the date of sale, however, is part of operations, although discontinued operations are typically segregated.

LO5 Review 9-5

Assume **BearingPoint** announced the split-off of its Canadian subsidiary. BearingPoint reported a gain from the split-off.

Required
1. Describe the accounting for a split-off.
2. Why was BearingPoint able to report a gain on this transaction?

Solution on p. 9-55.

Guidance Answers

You Are the Chief Financial Officer

Pg. 9-14 Capacity utilization is important. If long-term operating assets are used inefficiently, cost per unit produced is too high. Cost per unit does not relate solely to manufacturing products. It also applies to the cost of providing services and many other operating activities. However, if we purchase assets with little productive slack, our costs of production at peak levels can be excessive. Further, the company may be unable to service peak demand and risks losing customers. In response, the company might explore strategic alliances. These take many forms. Some require a simple contract to use another company's manufacturing, service, or administrative capability for a fee (*Note:* These executory contracts are not recorded under GAAP). Another type of alliance is a joint venture to share ownership of manufacturing or IT facilities. In this case, if demand can be coordinated with that of a partner, perhaps operating assets can be more effectively used. As chief financial officer, what thoughts do you have?

Superscript $^{A(B)}$ denotes assignments based on Appendix 9A(9B).

Questions

Q9-1. What is a passive investment? Why do companies have passive investment?

Q9-2. What is an unrealized gain (loss)? Explain.

Q9-3. Where are unrealized gains and losses related to marketable equity securities reported in the financial statements?

Q9-4. What does significant influence imply regarding intercorporate investments? Describe the accounting procedures used for such investments.

Q9-5. On January 1 of the current year, Yetman Company purchases 40% of the common stock of Livnat Company for $500,000 cash. This 40% ownership allows Yetman to exert significant influence over Livnat. During the year, Livnat reports $160,000 of net income and pays $120,000 in cash dividends. At year-end, what amount should appear in Yetman's balance sheet for its investment in Livnat?

Q9-6. What accounting method is used when a stock investment represents more than 50% of the investee company's voting stock and allows the investor company to "control" the investee company? Explain.

Q9-7. What is the underlying objective of consolidated financial statements?

Q9-8.^{A} What is a derivative? How do companies use them to hedge risk?

Q9-9.^{A} For accounting purposes, what are the two types of hedges? How are unrealized derivative gains and losses treated under each accounting method?

Q9-10. What are some limitations of consolidated financial statements?

Q9-11. How does a weakening $US affect the consolidated balance sheet of a company with foreign subsidiaries?

Q9-12.^{B} What is the difference between a spin-off and a split-off? Under what circumstances can either result in the recognition of a gain in the income statement?

Assignments with the ⬤ logo in the margin are available in BusinessCourse.
See the Preface of the book for details.

Mini Exercises

LO1   M9-13. Accounting for Marketable Equity Securities

Assume that Bava Company purchases 23,000 common shares of Jones Company for $12 cash per share. During the year, Bava receives a cash dividend of $1.30 per common share from Jones, and the year-end market price of Jones common stock is $13 per share. How much income does Bava report relating to this investment for the year?

M9-14. Interpreting Disclosures of Investment Securities

LO1
Amgen Inc. (AMGN)

Amgen Inc. reports the following disclosure relating to its December 31, 2015, accumulated other comprehensive income.

$ millions	Foreign Currency Translation	Cash Flow Hedges	Available-for-Sale Securities	Other	AOCI
Balance as of December 31, 2014.........	$(264)	$290	$ (19)	$(15)	$ (8)
Other comprehensive income:					
Foreign currency translation adjustments ...	(257)	—	—	—	(257)
Unrealized (losses) gains	—	150	(299)	8	(141)
Reclassification adjustments to income.....	—	(143)	76	—	(67)
Other.....................	—	—	—	1	1
Income taxes	10	—	(18)	—	(8)
Balance as of December 31, 2015.........	$(511)	$297	$(260)	$ (6)	$(480)

    a. How is Amgen accounting for its investment in marketable equity securities? How do you know? (*Note:* Amgen's 2015 disclosures are consistent with the former accounting rules for marketable equity securities. See the Accounting Insight box on page 9-6 in the module.)

    b. Explain how its 2015 financial statements are impacted by Amgen's unrealized losses on its investment in marketable equity securities.

    c. Explain the reclassification adjustments to income of $76 million.

M9-15. Analyzing Derivatives and Hedging

LO4
Amgen Inc. (AMGN)

Refer to the information for Amgen in M9-14. This information reports activity related to Amgen's cash flow hedges.

    a. Explain how this type of hedging works. Provide an example of how Amgen might use this type of hedging strategy.

    b. How did the hedges affect net income for 2015?

    c. If these same hedges had instead been fair value hedges, what amount would have been added to AOCI for the year?

M9-16. Analyzing Derivatives and Hedging

LO4
Morningstar (MORN)
General Motors (GM)
Emirates Airlines
Apple Inc. (AAPL)
Poole Construction

For each of the following, indicate whether the hedge would be classified as a fair value hedge or a cash flow hedge.

    a. Morningstar locks in a price on a forward contract to buy soybeans over the next 12 months.

    b. General Motors enters into a foreign currency futures contract on Canadian dollars to hedge its C$200 million bond issuance.

    c. Emirates Airlines takes delivery of 10 new Boeing jets. The contract was denominated in $US instead of Emirati Dirams (AED). Emirates will settle the accounts payable in six months. To hedge its exposure, Emirates buys $US futures contracts.

    d. Apple Inc. has foreign currency options to buy Chinese Yuan to hedge payments to FoxConn, the Chinese company that manufactures Apple products.

    e. Poole Construction signs a contract to build a soccer stadium in Mexico. The contract is denominated in Mexican pesos. Poole buys foreign currency options to sell Mexican pesos.

M9-17. Marketable Debt Securities

LO1

In 2017, Jensen Inc. invests excess cash of $4,000,000 in marketable debt securities issued by the U.S. Treasury and several Fortune 100 firms. At the end of the quarter, the fair value of the securities had increased to $4,106,003. Explain how Jensen would report the unrealized gain on these securities if the company classified the investment as either (a) trading, (b) available for sale, or (c) held-to-maturity.

M9-18. Analyzing and Interpreting Equity Method Investments

LO2

Concord Company purchases an investment in Bloomingdale Company at a purchase price of $2 million cash, representing 30% of the book value of Bloomingdale. During the year, Bloomingdale reports net income of $300,000 and pays cash dividends of $90,000. At the end of the year, the market value of Concord's investment is $2.4 million.

  a. What amount does Concord report on its balance sheet for its investment in Bloomingdale?

  b. What amount of income from investments does Concord report? Explain.

  c. Concord's $364,000 unrealized gain in the market value of the Bloomingdale investment (choose one and explain):

   (1) Is not reflected on either its income statement or balance sheet.

   (2) Is reported in its current income.

   (3) Is reported on its balance sheet only.

   (4) Is reported in its accumulated other comprehensive income.

LO2   **M9-19. Computing Income for Equity Method Investments**

Kross Company purchases an equity investment in Penno Company at a purchase price of $2.5 million, representing 40% of the book value of Penno. During the current year, Penno reports net income of $300,000 and pays cash dividends of $100,000. At the end of the year, the fair value of Kross's investment is $2.65 million. What amount of income does Kross report relating to this investment in Penno for the year? Explain.

LO2   **M9-20. Interpreting Disclosures on Investments in Affiliates**

Merck & Co. Inc.
(MRK)

Merck's 10-K report include the following footnote disclosure.

> Investments in affiliates accounted for using the equity method, . . . totaled $702 million at December 31, 2015. These amounts are reported in Other assets.

  a. At what amount are the equity method investments reported on Merck's balance sheet? Does this amount represent Merck's adjusted cost or fair value?

  b. How does Merck account for the dividends received on these investments?

  c. What income does the company report for these investments?

LO3   **M9-21. Computing Consolidating Adjustments and Noncontrolling Interest**

Patterson Company purchases 80% of Kensington Company's common stock for $400,000 cash when Kensington Company has $200,000 of common stock and $300,000 of retained earnings. If a consolidated balance sheet is prepared immediately after the acquisition, what amounts are eliminated when preparing that statement? What amount of noncontrolling interest appears in the consolidated balance sheet?

LO3   **M9-22. Computing Consolidated Net Income**

Bedford Company purchased a 90% interest in Midway Company on January 1 of the current year, and the purchase price reflected 90% of Midway's book value of equity. Bedford Company had $400,000 net income for the current year *before* recognizing its share of Midway Company's net income. If Midway Company had net income of $90,000 for the year, what is the consolidated net income attributable to Bedford shareholders for the year?

LO3   **M9-23. Assigning Purchase Price in Acquisitions**

Jasper Company acquired 80% of Fey Company at the beginning of the current year. Jasper paid $150,000 more than the book value of Fey's stockholders' equity and determined that this excess purchase price related to intangible assets. How does the $150,000 appear on the consolidated Jasper Company balance sheet if the intangible assets acquired related to (*a*) patents or, alternatively, (*b*) goodwill? How would each scenario affect the consolidated income statement?

LO5   **M9-24. Interpreting a Spin-Off Disclosure**

ConAgra Foods (CAG)

On October 11, 2016, Forbes magazine (at forbes.com) reported the following.

> **ConAgra Foods, Inc.,** announced that the separation of its frozen potato portfolio, Lamb Weston Holdings, Inc. (NYSE: "LW"), will be effectuated on November 9, 2016, the distribution date for the transaction. The spin-off will entail a 100% distribution of LW common shares to CAG's shareholders, as of record date November 1, 2016. Shareholders of CAG will receive one share of LW for every three shares of CAG held as of the record date.

  a. Describe the difference between a spin-off and a split-off.

  b. What effects did ConAgra's spin-off of Lamb Weston Holdings have on ConAgra's balance sheet and income statement?

M9-25.   Interpreting a Proposed Split-Off Disclosure

LO5
General Electric (GE)

On October 19, 2015, the following was reported in an article at StreetInsider.com.

> General Electric commenced an offer to exchange GE common stock for common stock of Syn-
> chrony Financial presently owned by GE. This exchange offer is in connection with the previously
> announced separation of Synchrony, the largest provider of private label credit cards in the United
> States, from GE. The exchange offer is expected to conclude the week of November 16, 2015. The
> exchange offer is designed to provide GE shareholders an opportunity to exchange their shares of
> GE common stock for shares of Synchrony common stock at a 7% discount, subject to an upper
> limit of 1.1308 shares of Synchrony common stock per share of GE common stock.

   a. This transaction is a split-off. How do we know?
   b. How will the proposed split-off affect the number of GE shares outstanding?
   c. Given the details revealed in the news article, does the split-off appear to be pro-rata or non pro-rata?
   d. What are the implications to GE if the split-off is non pro-rata?

M9-26.   Interpreting Disclosure Related to Spin-Off

LO5
Johnson Controls
(JCI)

Johnson Controls reports the following in its Form 8-K dated September 9, 2016.

> Johnson Controls' board of directors has approved the previously announced spin-off of its
> global automotive seating and interiors business. The transaction will result in two independent,
> publicly traded companies: Johnson Controls International plc and Adient plc. The spin-off is
> expected to be completed on Oct. 31, 2016. The separation will be effected by the transfer of
> the automotive seating and interiors business from Johnson Controls to Adient plc and the is-
> suance of ordinary shares of Adient directly to holders of Johnson Controls ordinary shares on
> a *pro rata* basis. Each Johnson Controls shareholder will receive one ordinary share of Adient
> for every 10 ordinary shares of Johnson Controls.

   a. Describe the accounting for a spin-off.
   b. What effects did this transaction have on Johnson Controls balance sheet and income statement?

Exercises

E9-27.   Assessing Financial Statement Effects of Marketable Equity Securities

LO1

Use the financial statement effects template to record the following four transactions involving investments in marketable equity securities. Assume that these transactions occur in 2018.

   a. Purchased 18,000 common shares of Baez Inc. for $12 cash per share.
   b. Received a cash dividend of $1.20 per common share from Baez.
   c. Year-end market price of Baez common stock was $11.25 per share.
   d. Sold all 18,000 common shares of Baez for $213,600.

E9-28.   Assessing Financial Statement Effects of Marketable Equity Securities

LO1

Use the financial statement effects template to record the accounts and amounts for the following four
transactions involving investments in marketable equity securities. Assume that these transactions occur
in 2018.

   a. Abney purchases 20,000 common shares of Heller Co. at $16 cash per share.
   b. Abney receives a cash dividend of $1.25 per common share from Heller.
   c. Year-end market price of Heller common stock is $17.50 per share.
   d. Abney sells all 20,000 common shares of Heller for $315,600 cash.

E9-29.   Marketable Debt Securities

LO1

Use the financial statement effects template to record the accounts and amounts for the following four
transactions involving investments in marketable debt securities classified as available-for-sale securities. Assume that these transactions occur in 2016 (before the new rules for securities went into effect).

   a. Loudder Inc. purchases 5,000 bonds with a face value of $1,000 per bond. The bonds are purchased
       at par for cash and pay interest at a semi-annual rate of 4%.
   b. Loudder receives semi-annual cash interest of $200,000.
   c. Year-end fair value of the bonds is $978 per bond.
   d. Shortly after year-end, Loudder sells all 5,000 bonds for $970 per bond.

E9-30.   Interpreting Footnotes on Security Investments

Cisco Systems Inc. reports the following information derived from its 2016 10-K report. (*Note:* Cisco's 2016 disclosures are consistent with the former accounting rules for marketable equity securities. See the Accounting Insight box on page 9-6 in the module.)

$ millions	Shares of Common Stock	Common Stock and Additional Paid-In Capital	Retained Earnings	Accumulated Other Comprehensive Income (Loss)	Total Cisco's Shareholders' Equity	Noncontrolling Interests	Total Equity
Balance at July 25, 2015	5,085	$43,592	$16,045	$ 61	$59,698	$ 9	$59,707
Net income.			10,739		10,739		10,739
Change in:							
Unrealized gains and (losses) on investments, net				103	103	(10)	93
Derivative instruments				(43)	(43)		(43)
Cumulative translation adjustment and other.				(447)	(447)	—	(447)
Other comprehensive income (loss). . .				(387)	(387)	(10)	(397)
Issuance of common stock	113	1,127			1,127		1,127
Repurchase of common stock.	(148)	(1,280)	(2,638)		(3,918)		(3,918)
Repurchase of common stock for tax withholdings on vesting of restricted stock units	(21)	(557)			(557)		(557)
Cash dividends declared			(4,750)		(4,750)		(4,750)
Tax effects from employee stock incentive plans		30			30		30
Share-based compensation.		1,458			1,458		1,458
Purchase acquisitions		146			146		146
Balance at July 30, 2016	5,029	$44,516	$19,396	$(326)	$63,586	$(1)	$63,585

Summary of Available-for-Sale Investments

The following table summarizes the Company's available-for-sale investments (in millions).

July 30, 2016	Amortized Cost	Gross Unrealized Gains	Gross Unrealized Losses	Fair Value
Fixed income securities:				
U.S. government securities	$26,473	$ 73	$(2)	$26,544
U.S. government agency securities	2,809	8	—	2,817
Non-U.S. government and agency securities. . .	1,096	4	—	1,100
Corporate debt securities.	24,044	263	(15)	24,292
U.S. agency mortgage-backed securities	1,846	22	—	1,868
Total fixed income securities.	56,268	370	(17)	56,621
Publicly traded equity securities	1,211	333	(40)	1,504
Total.	$57,479	$703	$(57)	$58,125

a. What is the amount of Cisco's investment portfolio on its balance sheet? Does that amount include any unrealized gains or losses? Explain.

b. What does the number $103 represent in the "Accumulated Other Comprehensive Income" column? Explain.

c. Under the new accounting rules that take effect in 2018, how would Cisco treat the $103?

d. Compute comprehensive income for 2015.

e. During 2015, did the currencies in the countries where Cisco's subsidiaries were headquartered weaken or strengthen?

E9-31. Interpreting Footnote Disclosures for Investments

CNA Financial Corporation provides the following footnote to its 2015 10-K report.

> **Valuation of investments** The company classifies its fixed maturity securities and its equity securities as either available-for-sale or trading, and as which, they are carried at fair value. Changes in fair value of trading securities are reported within Net investment income on the Consolidated Statements of Operations. Changes in fair value related to available-for-sale securities are reported as a component of Other comprehensive income. . .

The following table provides a summary of fixed maturity and equity securities.

December 31, 2015 ($ millions)	Cost or Amortized Cost	Gross Unrealized Gains	Gross Unrealized Losses	Estimated Fair Value
Fixed maturity securities available-for-sale				
Corporate and other bonds	$17,080	$1,019	$342	$17,757
States, municipalities and political subdivisions	11,729	1,453	8	13,174
Asset-backed:				
Residential mortgage-backed	4,935	154	17	5,072
Commercial mortgage-backed	2,154	55	12	2,197
Other asset-backed	923	6	8	921
Total asset-backed	8,012	215	37	8,190
U.S. Treasury and obligations of government sponsored enterprises	62	5	—	67
Foreign government	334	13	1	346
Redeemable preferred stock	33	2	—	35
Total fixed maturity securities available-for-sale	37,250	2,707	388	39,569
Total fixed maturity securities trading	3	—	—	3

 a. At what amount does CNA report its investment in marketable debt securities on its balance sheet? In your answer, identify the portfolio's fair value, cost, and any unrealized gains and losses.
 b. Compute the net unrealized gain or loss on CNA's investment portfolio. How do CNA's balance sheet and income statement reflect this net unrealized gain or loss?
 c. How do CNA's balance sheet and income statement reflect gains and losses realized from the sale of available-for-sale securities?

E9-32. Assessing Financial Statement Effects of Equity Method Securities

Use the financial statement effects template (with amounts and accounts) to record the following transactions involving investments in marketable securities accounted for using the equity method.

 a. Purchased 12,000 common shares of Bakersfield Co. at $9 per share; the shares represent 30% ownership in Bakersfield.
 b. Received a cash dividend of $1.25 per common share from Bakersfield.
 c. Bakersfield reported annual net income of $60,000.
 d. Sold all 12,000 common shares of Bakersfield for $114,500.

E9-33. Assessing Financial Statement Effects of Equity Method Securities

Use the financial statement effects template (with amounts and accounts) to record the following transactions involving investments in marketable securities accounted for using the equity method.

 a. Madison Co. purchases 10,500 common shares of Landau Co. at $8 per share; the shares represent 25% ownership of Landau.
 b. Madison receives a cash dividend of $0.80 per common share from Landau.
 c. Landau reports annual net income of $60,000.
 d. Madison sells all 10,500 common shares of Landau for $93,000.

LO1, 2   **E9-34.**   **Assessing Financial Statement Effects Investments**

On January 1, 2018, Ball Corporation purchased shares of Leftwich Company common stock.

a. Assume that the stock acquired by Ball represents 15% of Leftwich's voting stock and that Ball has no influence over Leftwich's business decisions. Use the financial statement effects template (with amounts and accounts) to record the following transactions.
   1. Ball purchased 5,000 common shares of Leftwich at $15 cash per share.
   2. Leftwich reported annual net income of $40,000.
   3. Ball received a cash dividend of $1.10 per common share from Leftwich.
   4. Year-end market price of Leftwich common stock is $19 per share.

b. Assume that the stock acquired by Ball represents 30% of Leftwich's voting stock and that Ball accounts for this investment using the equity method because it is able to exert significant influence. Use the financial statement effects template (with amounts and accounts) to record the following transactions.
   1. Ball purchased 5,000 common shares of Leftwich at $15 cash per share.
   2. Leftwich reported annual net income of $40,000.
   3. Ball received a cash dividend of $1.10 per common share from Leftwich.
   4. Year-end market price of Leftwich common stock is $19 per share.

LO2   **E9-35.**   **Interpreting Equity Method Investment Footnotes**

Ford Motor Company
(F)

Ford Motor Company includes the following table in its 2015 Form 10-K. The table reports the ownership percentages and carrying value of equity method investments (in millions, except percentages).

Automotive Sector	Ownership Percentage December 31, 2015	Investment Balance	
		December 31, 2015	December 31, 2014
Changan Ford Automobile Corporation, Limited	50.0%	$1,307	$1,301
Jiangling Motors Corporation, Limited.	32.0	636	604
AutoAlliance (Thailand) Co., Ltd.	50.0	429	428
Ford Otomotiv Sanayi Anonim Sirketi	41.0	352	386
Getrag Ford Transmissions GmbH.	50.0	182	232
Changan Ford Mazda Engine Company, Ltd.	25.0	77	69
OEConnection LLC	50.0	36	35
DealerDirect LLC	97.7	30	26
Percepta, LLC	45.0	9	9
Thirdware Solutions Limited.	20.0	9	8
Automotive Fuel Cell Cooperation Corporation	49.9	8	9
U.S. Council for Automotive Research LLC.	33.3	5	5
Chongqing ANTE Trading Co., Ltd.	10.0	4	3
Crash Avoidance Metrics Partnership LLC	50.0	4	2
Blue Diamond Parts, LLC.	25.0	3	3
Nemak, S.A.B. de C.V. (Note 22)	6.8	—	86
Blue Diamond Truck, S. de R.L. de C.V. (Note 22)	25.0	—	8
Ford Malaysia Sdn. Bhd.	49.0	—	2
ZF Transmission Tech, LLC	49.0	—	—
Zebra Imaging, Inc.	0.3	—	—
Total Automotive sector		$3,091	$3,216

a. What does Ford report on its balance sheet at December 31, 2015, for its Automotive Sector investment in equity method affiliates? Does this reflect the adjusted cost or fair value of Ford's interest in these companies?

b. Determine the total stockholders' equity of the Changan Ford Mazda Engine Company at the end of 2015. Explain.

c. Ford owns 97.7% of DealerDirect LLC yet this investment was not consolidated. Speculate on why this might be the case.

d. Assume Jiangling Motors paid no dividends in 2015. Determine Jiangling's net income for the year.

e. Explain why Ford has so many equity-method investments.

E9-36. Analyzing and Interpreting Disclosures on Equity Method Investments

LO2

Cummins Inc. (CMI)

Cummins Inc. reports investments in affiliated companies, consisting mainly of investments in nine manufacturing joint ventures. Cummins reports those investments on its balance sheet at $958 million and provides the following financial information on its investee companies in a footnote to its 10-K report.

Equity Investee Financial Summary $ millions	As of and for the years ended December 31		
	2015	2014	2013
Net sales.	$5,946	$7,426	$7,799
Gross margin	1,265	1,539	1,719
Net income.	521	630	690
Cummins' share of net income	$ 273	$ 330	$ 325
Royalty and interest income.	42	40	36
Total equity, royalty and interest from investees.	$ 315	$ 370	$ 361
Current assets	$2,458	$2,476	
Noncurrent assets	1,539	1,667	
Current liabilities.	(1,796)	(1,875)	
Noncurrent liabilities.	(284)	(420)	
Net assets.	$1,917	$1,848	
Cummins' share of net assets	$ 958	$ 956	

a. What assets and liabilities of unconsolidated affiliates are omitted from Cummins' balance sheet as a result of the equity method of accounting for those investments?

b. Do the liabilities of the unconsolidated affiliates affect Cummins directly? Explain.

c. How does the equity method impact Cummins' ROE and its RNOA components (net operating asset turnover and net operating profit margin)?

E9-37. Interpreting Equity Method Investment Footnotes

LO2

AT&T Inc. (T)

AT&T reports the following footnote to its 2015 10-K report.

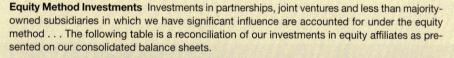

Equity Method Investments Investments in partnerships, joint ventures and less than majority-owned subsidiaries in which we have significant influence are accounted for under the equity method . . . The following table is a reconciliation of our investments in equity affiliates as presented on our consolidated balance sheets.

$ millions	2015	2014
Beginning of year	$ 250	$3,860
Additional investments.	77	226
DIRECTV investments acquired.	1,232	—
Equity in net income of affiliates.	79	175
Dividends and distributions received.	(30)	(148)
Sale of América Móvil shares.	—	(3,817)
Other adjustments	(2)	(46)
End of year.	$1,606	$ 250

Undistributed earnings from equity affiliates were $162 and $88 at December 31, 2015 and 2014.

a. At what amount is the equity investment in affiliates reported on AT&T's balance sheet?

b. Did affiliates pay dividends in 2015? How do you know?

c. How much income did AT&T report in 2015 relating to this investment in affiliates?

d. Interpret the AT&T statement that "undistributed earnings from equity affiliates were $162 and $88 at December 31, 2015 and 2014."

e. How does use of the equity method impact AT&T's ROE and its RNOA components (net operating asset turnover and net operating profit margin)?

f. AT&T accounts for its investment in affiliates under the equity method. Why?

LO3 **E9-38. Constructing the Consolidated Balance Sheet at Acquisition**

On January 1 of the current year, Liu Company purchased all of the common shares of Reed Company for $380,000 cash. Balance sheets of the two firms immediately after the acquisition follow.

	Liu Company	Reed Company	Consolidating Adjustments	Consolidated
Current assets	$ 950,000	$ 70,000		
Investment in Reed.	380,000	—		
PPE, net	1,600,000	305,000		
Goodwill	—	—		_____
Total assets.	$2,930,000	$375,000		
Liabilities.	$ 450,000	$ 55,000		
Contributed capital.	1,850,000	280,000		
Retained earnings	630,000	40,000		_____
Total liabilities and equity	$2,930,000	$375,000		

During purchase negotiations, Reed's PPE was appraised at $332,000, and all of its remaining assets and liabilities were appraised at values approximating their book values. Liu also concluded that an additional $33,000 (for goodwill) demanded by Reed's shareholders was warranted because Reed's earning power was better than the industry average. Prepare the consolidating adjustments and the consolidated balance sheet at acquisition.

LO3 **E9-39. Constructing the Consolidated Balance Sheet at Acquisition**

Winston Company purchased all of Marcus Company's common stock for $600,000 cash on January 1, at which time the separate balance sheets of the two corporations appeared as follows.

	Winston Company	Marcus Company	Consolidating Adjustments	Consolidated
Investment in Marcus.	$ 600,000	$ —		
Other assets	2,300,000	700,000		
Goodwill	—	—		_____
Total assets.	$2,900,000	$700,000		
Liabilities.	$ 900,000	$160,000		
Contributed capital.	1,400,000	300,000		
Retained earnings	600,000	240,000		_____
Total liabilities and equity	$2,900,000	$700,000		

During purchase negotiations, Winston determined the appraised value of Marcus's Other Assets was $720,000, and all of its remaining assets and liabilities were appraised at values approximating their book values. The balance of the purchase price was ascribed to goodwill. Prepare the consolidating adjustments and the consolidated balance sheet at acquisition.

E9-40. **Assessing Financial Statement Effects from a Subsidiary Stock Issuance**

LO3

Sykora Company owns 80% of Walton Company. Information reported by Sykora and Walton as of the current year end follows.

Sykora Company

Shares owned of Walton.	80,000
Book value of investment in Walton	$720,000

Walton Company

Shares outstanding.	100,000
Book value of equity	$900,000
Book value per share	$9

Assume Walton issues 60,000 additional shares of previously authorized but unissued common stock solely to outside investors (none to Sykora) for $14 cash per share. Indicate the financial statement effects of this stock issuance on Sykora using the financial statement effects template.

E9-41. **Estimating Goodwill Impairment**

LO3

On January 1 of the current year, Engel Company purchases 100% of Ball Company for $8.4 million. At the time of acquisition, the fair value of Ball's tangible net assets (excluding goodwill) is $8.1 million. Engel ascribes the excess of $300,000 to goodwill. Assume the fair value of Ball declines to $6.25 million and the fair value of Ball's tangible net assets is estimated at $6.15 million as of December 31.

a. Determine if the goodwill has become impaired and, if so, the amount of the impairment.
b. What impact does the impairment of goodwill have on Engel's financial statements?

E9-42. **Allocating Purchase Price**

LO3

Adobe Systems Inc.
(ADBE)

Adobe Systems Inc. reports the following footnote to its 10-K report.

> **Fotolia** On January 27, 2015, we completed our acquisition of privately held Fotolia, a leading marketplace for royalty-free photos, images, graphics and HD videos. During the first quarter of fiscal 2015, we began integrating Fotolia into our Digital Media reportable segment.
>
> Under the acquisition method of accounting, the total final purchase price was allocated to Fotolia's net tangible and intangible assets based upon their estimated fair values as of January 27, 2015. The total final purchase price for Fotolia was $807.5 million of which $745.1 million was allocated to goodwill that was nondeductible for tax purposes, $204.4 million to identifiable intangible assets and $142.0 million to net liabilities assumed.

a. Of the total assets acquired, what portion is allocated to net intangible assets? What amount was allocated to tangible assets such as inventory and PPE?
b. Are the assets and liabilities of Fotolia reported on the consolidated balance sheet at the book value or at the fair value on the date of the acquisition? Explain.
c. How are the intangible assets accounted for subsequent to the acquisition?
d. Describe the accounting for goodwill. Why is an impairment test difficult to apply?

E9-43. **Constructing the Consolidated Balance Sheet at Acquisition**

LO3

Easton Company acquires 100 percent of the outstanding voting shares of Harris Company. To obtain these shares, Easton pays $420,000 in cash and issues 5,000 of its $10 par value common stock. On this date, Easton's stock has a fair value of $72 per share, and Harris's book value of stockholders' equity is $560,000. Easton is willing to pay $780,000 for a company with a book value for equity of $560,000 because it believes that (1) Harris's buildings are undervalued by $80,000 and (2) Harris has an unrecorded patent that Easton values at $60,000. Easton considers the remaining balance sheet items to be fairly valued (no book-to-market difference). The remaining $80,000 of the purchase price is ascribed to corporate synergies and other general unidentifiable intangible assets (goodwill). The balance sheets at the acquisition date follow.

	Easton Company	Harris Company	Consolidating Adjustments	Consolidated
Cash......................	$ 168,000	$ 80,000		
Receivables	320,000	180,000		
Inventory.................	440,000	260,000		
Investment in Harris	780,000	—		
Land.....................	200,000	120,000		
Buildings, net	800,000	220,000		
Equipment, net............	240,000	100,000		
Total assets..............	$2,948,000	$960,000		
Accounts payable...........	$ 320,000	$ 60,000		
Long-term liabilities	760,000	340,000		
Common stock.............	1,000,000	80,000		
Additional paid-in capital	148,000	—		
Retained earnings	720,000	480,000		
Total liabilities & equity........	$2,948,000	$960,000		

a. Show the breakdown of the investment into the book value acquired, the excess of fair value over book value, and the portion of the investment representing goodwill.

b. Prepare the consolidating adjustments and the consolidated balance sheet on the date of acquisition.

c. How will the excess of the purchase price over book value acquired be treated in years subsequent to the acquisition?

LO3, 4

General Mills Inc. (GIS)

E9-44. **Foreign Translation Adjustment and Derivatives**

General Mills reported the following statement of comprehensive income in its fiscal 2016 Form 10-K.

For 12 Months Ended ($ millions)	29-May-16	31-May-15	25-May-14
Net earnings.................................	$1,736.8	$1,259.4	$1,861.3
Other comprehensive income (loss), net of tax:			
Foreign currency translation....................	(108.7)	(957.9)	(11.3)
Net actuarial income (loss).....................	(325.9)	(358.4)	206.0
Other fair value changes:			
Securities....................................	0.1	0.8	0.3
Hedge derivatives............................	16.0	4.1	5.0
Reclassification to earnings:			
Hedge derivatives............................	(9.5)	4.9	(4.6)
Amortization of losses and prior service costs	128.6	105.1	107.6
Other comprehensive income (loss), net of tax	(299.4)	(1,201.4)	303.0
Total comprehensive income	$1,437.4	$ 58.0	$2,164.3

Required

a. Comprehensive income includes a loss of $108.7 million related to foreign currency translation. Explain what this loss means.

b. On average, did the $US weaken or strengthen vis-à-vis the currencies of the companies' foreign subsidiaries?

c. What was the cash portion of the foreign currency translation loss in 2016?

d. Comprehensive income includes a gain of $16 million related to hedge derivatives. Is this a fair value or a cash flow hedge?

e. Provide four examples of hedging transactions General Mills might engage in.

f. How did the cash flow hedges affect net income during the 2016 fiscal year?

E9-45. Hedging and Use of Derivatives

Intel reports the following in its Form 10-K for fiscal 2015.

LO4

Intel Corporation (INTC)

> **Currency Exchange Rates** In general, we economically hedge currency risks of non-U.S.-dollar-denominated investments in debt instruments and loans receivable with currency forward contracts or currency interest rate swaps. Gains and losses on these non-U.S.-currency investments are generally offset by corresponding gains and losses on the related hedging instruments.
> Substantially all of our revenue is transacted in U.S. dollars. However, a significant portion of our operating expenditures and capital purchases are incurred in or exposed to other currencies, primarily the euro, the Chinese yuan, the Japanese yen, and the Israeli shekel. We have established currency risk management programs to protect against fluctuations in the fair value and the volatility of the functional currency equivalent of future cash flows caused by changes in exchange rates. We generally utilize currency forward contracts in these hedging programs.

Required

a. Consider the first paragraph in Intel's footnote. Explain whether this describes fair value or cash flow hedges.

b. Consider the second paragraph in Intel's footnote. Explain whether this describes fair value or cash flow hedges.

c. Suppose, at year-end, there was an unrealized loss on Intel's currency forward contracts. How would Intel report the derivative on the balance sheet? How would the income statement be affected?

d. What is hedge ineffectiveness and how does it affect Intel's income statement?

E9-46. Hedging and Use of Derivatives

Ford Motor Company reports the following in its Form 10-K for fiscal 2015.

LO4

> Commodity price risk is the possibility that our financial results could be better or worse than planned because of changes in the prices of commodities used in the production of motor vehicles, such as base metals (e.g., steel, copper, and aluminum), precious metals (e.g., palladium), energy (e.g., natural gas and electricity), and plastics/resins (e.g., polypropylene). Accordingly, our normal practice is to use derivative instruments, when available, to hedge the price risk with respect to forecasted purchases of those commodities that we can economically hedge (primarily base metals and precious metals). In our hedging actions, we use derivative instruments commonly used by corporations to reduce commodity price risk (e.g., financially settled forward contracts).

Ford's statement of comprehensive income for 2015 follows.

$ millions	2015	2014
Net income	$7,371	$1,230
Other comprehensive income/(loss), net of tax (Note 17)		
Foreign currency translation	(1,132)	(36)
Marketable securities	(6)	—
Derivative instruments	227	(182)
Pension and other postretirement benefits	(81)	(23)
Total other comprehensive income/(loss), net of tax	(992)	(241)
Comprehensive income	6,379	989
Less: Comprehensive income/(loss) attributable to noncontrolling interests	(2)	—
Comprehensive income attributable to Ford Motor Company	$6,381	$ 989

Required

a. What sort of risks does Ford hedge?

b. Ford describes its hedging strategy. What sort of hedges are these, cash flow or fair value? Explain.

c. The statement of comprehensive income discloses a line item labeled "Derivative instruments." What does this line item represent?

d. The comprehensive income owing to derivatives instruments is $227 million for 2015 and $(182) million for 2014. What can we conclude about the fair value of the derivatives for each of these years?

LO4   E9-47.[A] Reporting and Analyzing Derivatives

Johnson & Johnson
(JNJ)

Johnson & Johnson reports the following information derived from the schedule of Accumulated Other Comprehensive Income and the Consolidated Statements of Comprehensive Income in its 2016 10-K report.

$ millions	Foreign Currency Translation	Gains/ (Losses) on Securities	Employee Benefit Plans	Gains/ (Losses) on Derivatives & Hedges	Total Accumulated Other Comprehensive Income/(Loss)
December 28, 2014	$(4,803)	$257	$(6,317)	$141	$(10,722)
2015 changes.					
Unrealized gain (loss)	—	471	—	(115)	
Net amount reclassed to net earnings . . .	—	(124)	—	(62)	
Net 2015 changes	(3,632)	347	1,019	(177)	(2,443)
January 3, 2016	$(8,435)	$604	$(5,298)	$ (36)	$(13,165)

a. Describe how firms like Johnson & Johnson typically use derivatives.
b. How does Johnson & Johnson report its derivatives designated as cash flow hedges on its balance sheet?
c. By what amount have the unrealized losses of $(115) million on the cash flow hedges affected current income? What are the analysis implications?
d. What does the $(62) million classified as "Net amount reclassed to net earnings" relate to? How has this affected Johnson & Johnson's profit?

Problems

LO2   P9-48.   Analyzing and Interpreting Disclosures on Equity Method Investments

General Mills Inc.
(GIS)

General Mills Inc. invests in a number of joint ventures to manufacture and distribute its food products, as discussed in the following footnote to its fiscal year 2016 10-K report.

> **INVESTMENTS IN UNCONSOLIDATED JOINT VENTURES**
>
> We have a 50 percent equity interest in Cereal Partners Worldwide (CPW), which manufactures and markets ready-to-eat cereal products in more than 130 countries outside the United States and Canada. CPW also markets cereal bars in several European countries and manufactures private label cereals for customers in the United Kingdom. We have guaranteed a portion of CPW's debt and its pension obligation in the United Kingdom.
>
> We also have a 50 percent equity interest in Häagen-Dazs Japan, Inc. (HDJ). This joint venture manufactures and markets Häagen-Dazs ice cream products and frozen novelties.
>
> Results from our CPW and HDJ joint ventures are reported for the 12 months ended March 31.
>
> Joint venture related balance sheet activity follows:
>
> | $ millions | May 29, 2016 | May 31, 2015 |
> |---|---|---|
> | Cumulative investments. . . . . | $518.9 | $530.6 |
> | Goodwill and other intangibles. . . . . | 469.2 | 465.1 |
> | Aggregate advances included in cumulative investments . . | 300.3 | 390.3 |
>
> Joint venture earnings and cash flow activity follows:
>
> | Fiscal Year ($ millions) | 2016 | 2015 | 2014 |
> |---|---|---|---|
> | Sales to joint ventures . . . . | $ 10.5 | $ 11.6 | $12.1 |
> | Net advances (repayments) . . . . | (63.9) | 102.4 | 54.9 |
> | Dividends received. . . . . | 75.1 | 72.6 | 90.5 |

continued

Summary combined financial information for the joint ventures on a 100 percent basis follows:

Fiscal Year ($ millions)	2016	2015	2014
Net sales			
CPW.	$1,674.8	$1,894.5	$2,107.9
HDJ.	369.4	370.2	386.9
Total net sales.	2,044.2	2,264.7	2,494.8
Gross margin	867.6	925.4	1,030.3
Earnings before income taxes	234.8	220.9	219.1
Earnings after income taxes.	186.7	170.7	168.8

$ millions	May 29, 2016	May 31, 2015
Current assets	$ 814.1	$ 800.1
Noncurrent assets	959.9	962.1
Current liabilities.	1,457.3	1,484.8
Noncurrent liabilities.	81.7	118.2

Required

a. How does General Mills account for its investments in joint ventures? How are these investments reflected on General Mills' balance sheet, and how, generally, is income recognized on these investments? Estimate the amount of income that General Mills included in its 2016 income statement as Equity method income.

b. Does the $218.6 million investment reported on General Mills' balance sheet sufficiently reflect the assets and liabilities required to conduct these operations? Explain. *Note:* The $518.9 million disclosed includes cash advances to the joint venture partners of $300.3 million. The net $218.6 million represents the equity method investment.

c. Do you believe the liabilities of these joint venture entities represent actual obligations of General Mills? Explain.

d. What potential problem(s) does equity method accounting present for analysis purposes?

P9-49. **Analyzing and Interpreting Disclosures on Consolidations**

LO3
Snap-on Incorporated (SNA)

Snap-on Incorporated consists of two business units: the manufacturing company (parent corporation) and a wholly-owned finance subsidiary. These two units are consolidated in Snap-on's 10-K report. Following is a supplemental disclosure Snap-on includes in its 10-K report that shows the separate balance sheets of the parent and the subsidiary. This supplemental disclosure is not mandated under GAAP but is voluntarily reported by Snap-on as useful information for investors and creditors. Using this disclosure, answer the following questions.

Required

a. Do the parent and subsidiary companies each maintain their own financial statements? Explain. Why does GAAP require consolidation instead of separate financial statements of individual companies?

b. What is the balance of Investments in Financial Services as of December 31, 2015, on the parent's balance sheet? What is the equity balance of the financial services subsidiary to which this relates as of December 31, 2015? Do you see a relation? Will this relation always exist?

c. Refer to your answer for part a. How does the equity method of accounting for the investment in the subsidiary obscure the actual financial condition of the parent company as compared with the consolidated financial statements?

d. Recall that the parent company uses the equity method of accounting for its investment in the subsidiary and that this account is eliminated in the consolidation process. What is the relation between consolidated net income and the net income of the parent company? Explain.

e. What is the implication for the consolidated balance sheet if the fair value of the financial services subsidiary (subsequent to acquisition) is greater than the book value of its stockholders' equity?

$ millions	Operations*		Financial Services	
	2015	2014	2015	2014
ASSETS				
Current assets				
Cash and cash equivalents.................................	$ 92.7	$ 132.8	$ 0.1	$ 0.1
Intersegment receivables	15.9	16.0	—	—
Trade and other accounts receivable—net................	562.2	550.5	0.3	0.3
Finance receivables—net..................................	–	–	447.3	402.4
Contract receivables—net	8.0	7.6	74.1	66.9
Inventories—net...	497.8	475.5	—	—
Deferred income tax assets	91.0	85.4	18.9	15.6
Prepaid expenses and other assets	111.5	125.5	1.2	0.9
Total current assets.................................	1,379.1	1,393.3	541.9	486.2
Property and equipment—net	412.1	403.4	1.4	1.1
Investment in Financial Services	251.8	218.9	—	—
Deferred income tax assets	105.4	92.9	0.9	0.3
Intersegment long-term notes receivable.................	398.7	232.1	—	—
Long-term finance receivables—net......................	—	—	772.7	650.5
Long-term contract receivables—net.....................	12.1	12.8	254.5	229.2
Goodwill	790.1	810.7	—	—
Other intangibles—net	195.0	203.3	—	—
Other assets	49.9	50.9	1.0	1.0
Total assets...	$3,594.2	$3,418.3	$1,572.4	$1,368.3
LIABILITIES AND EQUITY				
Current liabilities				
Notes payable...	$ 18.4	$ 56.6	$ —	$ —
Accounts payable......................................	148.2	144.7	0.1	0.3
Intersegment payables	—	—	15.9	16.0
Accrued benefits.......................................	52.1	53.8	—	—
Accrued compensation.................................	86.9	95.2	4.1	4.0
Franchisee deposits	64.4	65.8	—	—
Other accrued liabilities	277.7	285.0	25.0	18.2
Total current liabilities	647.7	701.1	45.1	38.5
Long-term debt and intersegment long-term debt..........	—	—	1,260.4	1,094.8
Deferred income tax liabilities...........................	169.6	158.6	0.2	0.6
Retiree health care benefits	37.9	42.5	—	—
Pension liabilities	227.8	217.9	—	—
Other long-term liabilities	80.5	72.9	14.9	15.5
Total liabilities	1,163.5	1,193.0	1,320.6	1,149.4
Total shareholders' equity attributable to Snap-on Inc.	2,412.7	2,207.8	251.8	218.9
Noncontrolling interests	18.0	17.5	—	—
Total equity	2,430.7	2,225.3	251.8	218.9
Total liabilities and equity	$3,594.2	$3,418.3	$1,572.4	$1,368.3

*Snap-on with financial services on the equity method.

IFRS Applications

LO2   **I9-50.**   **Interpreting Equity Method Investment Footnotes**

Carrefour S.A.

Carrefour S.A. is a French multinational retailer headquartered near Paris. The company uses IFRS for its financial reports and reports the following details about its investments in associates, which are accounted for using the equity method.

€ millions	
At December 31, 2013	€ 496
Translation adjustment	5
Share of net income	36
Dividends	(33)
Other.	966
At December 31, 2014	1,471
Translation adjustment	(23)
Share of net income	44
Dividends	(52)
Other.	(7)
At December 31, 2015	€1,433

Required

a. Carrefour holds between 20% and 50% ownership of all its investments in associates. Carrefour uses the equity method to account for these investments. Why?

b. What amount does Carrefour report on its balance sheet for investments in associates at December 31, 2015? What does this amount represent?

c. For the fiscal period ended December 31, 2015, were Carrefour's associates profitable in the aggregate?

d. How do changes in the market value of the associates' stock affect the "Investment in Associates" balance sheet account for Carrefour?

e. How does use of the equity method impact Carrefour's ROE and its RNOA components (net operating asset turnover and net operating profit margin) as compared with the assets and liabilities and the sales and expenses that would be recorded with consolidation?

I9-51. Allocating Purchase Price Including Intangibles

LO3
Deutsche Telekom AG

Deutsche Telekom AG, headquartered in Bonn, Germany, is the largest telecommunications company in Europe. The company uses IFRS to prepare its financial statements. Assume that during 2014, Deutsche Telekom acquired a controlling interest in **Hellenic Telecommunications Organization S.A.** (Hellenic). The table below shows the pre- and post-acquisition values of Hellenic's assets and liabilities.

€ millions	Fair Value at Acquisition Date	Carrying Amounts Immediately Prior to Acquisition
Cash and cash equivalents	€ 1,558	€ 1,558
Non-current assets held for sale	195	158
Other assets	1,716	1,716
Current assets.	3,469	3,432
Intangible assets	5,348	4,734
Goodwill	2,500	3,835
Property, plant, and equipment	6,965	5,581
Other assets	823	782
Non-current assets.	15,636	14,932
Assets.	€19,105	€18,364

Required

a. At the acquisition, which measurement does the company use, fair value or carrying value, to record the acquired tangible and intangible assets on its consolidated balance sheet?

b. At the acquisition date, why is fair value of goodwill less than its carrying value?

c. What are some possible reasons why intangible assets increased in value at the acquisition date?

d. Describe accounting for goodwill. Why is an impairment test difficult to apply?

e. What would Deutsche Telekom record if it determined at the end of fiscal 2014 that the goodwill purchased in the Hellenic acquisition had a reliably measured fair value of €2,000? If the company determined later, in 2017, the fair value of the Hellenic goodwill was €3,000, how would this affect its balance sheet and income statement?

LO2   I9-52.   Interpreting Equity Method Investment Footnotes

BHP Billiton Limited discovers, acquires, develops, and markets natural resources worldwide. Headquartered in Melbourne Australia, the company explores for, develops, produces, and markets oil and gas in the Gulf of Mexico, Western Australia, and Trinidad and Tobago. It also explores for copper, silver, lead, zinc, molybdenum, uranium, gold, iron ore, and metallurgical and thermal coal. The company's 2016 annual report included the following disclosures.

Shareholdings in Associates and Joint Ventures	Country of Incorporation/ Principal Place of Business	Associate or Joint Venture	Principal Activity	Reporting Date	Ownership Interest	
					2016%	2015%
Carbones del Cerrejón LLC (Cerrejón)	Anguilla/ Colombia	Associate	Coal mining in Colombia	31 December	**33.33**	33.33
Compañía Minera Antamina S.A. (Antamina)	Peru	Associate	Copper and zinc mining	31 December	**33.75**	33.75
Samarco Mineração S.A. (Samarco)	Brazil	Joint venture	Iron ore mining	31 December	**50.00**	50.00

The movement for the year in the Group's investments accounted for using the equity method is as follows:

Year ended 30 June 2016 (US$M)	Investment in Associates
At the beginning of the financial year.	$2,668
Share of operating profit of equity accounted investments . . .	140
Investment in equity accounted investments.	58
Dividends received from equity accounted investments	(293)
Other.	2
At the end of the financial year.	$2,575

During the year, the Associates, Cerrejon and Antamina, reported net profit (loss) of $(73) million and $606 million, respectively.

Required

a. The company uses the equity method to account for its investment in associates and joint ventures. Why is this the appropriate method for the three investments disclosed in the footnotes?

b. Billiton reports a total of $140 million as profit from associates accounted for as equity method investments. Use the reported net profit (loss) for the two associates to determine the amount of profit (loss) included in the $140 million.

c. Explain why dividends received of $293 million are shown as a decrease to the equity method investment account.

d. How does the use of the equity method impact Billiton's ROE and its RNOA components (net operating asset turnover and net operating profit margin) as compared to the case of consolidation?

LO3   I9-53.   Interpreting Acquisition Transaction with Goodwill

Loblaw Companies Ltd.

In March 2014, **Loblaw Companies Limited**, Canada's largest food retailer, acquired Canada's largest retail pharmacy chain, **Shoppers Drug Mart**, for $12.3 billion making it the nation's largest retailer. The following information regarding the acquisition is derived from Loblaw Companies' 2015 annual report.

BUSINESS ACQUISITIONS

Acquisition of Shoppers Drug Mart On March 28, 2014, the Company acquired all of the outstanding shares of Shoppers Drug Mart for total consideration of $12,273 million, comprised of approximately $6,600 million of cash and the issuance of approximately 119.5 million common shares of the Company. The Company also issued 10.5 million common shares to Weston for cash that was used in connection with the acquisition of Shoppers Drug Mart . . . The finalized purchase price allocation is summarized as follows:

Net Assets Acquired (millions in Canadian dollars)	
Cash and cash equivalents	$ 27
Accounts receivable	534
Inventories	3,003
Prepaid expenses and other assets	67
Fixed assets	1,792
Investment properties	16
Prescriptions files	5,005
Brands	3,390
Shoppers Optimum loyalty program	490
Other (intangibles)	555
Goodwill	2,360
Deferred income tax assets	68
Other assets	7
Bank indebtedness	(295)
Trade payables and other liabilities	(1,026)
Income taxes payable	(11)
Associate interest	(174)
Provisions	(19)
Long term debt	(1,127)
Deferred income tax liabilities	(2,225)
Other liabilities	(164)
Total net assets acquired	$12,273

Required

a. Identify the tangible and intangible assets the company acquired. What proportion of the total price was for intangible assets?

b. Why is "Prescription files" an intangible asset? How will Loblaw Companies realize value from this asset?

c. Do any of the acquired intangible assets have indefinite lives? Explain.

d. Explain in layman's terms the meaning of goodwill.

e. How will the company account for goodwill in 2016 and beyond?

f. How did Loblaw Companies account for the income of Shoppers Drug Mart in fiscal 2014 (the year Shoppers Drug Mart was acquired)?

Management Applications

MA9-54. **Determining the Reporting of an Investment**   **LO1, 2, 3**

Assume your company acquires 20% of the outstanding common stock of APEX Software as an investment. You also have an option to purchase the remaining 80%. APEX is developing software (its only activity) it hopes to eventually package and sell to customers. You do not intend to exercise your option unless its software product reaches commercial feasibility. APEX has employed your software engineers to assist in the development efforts, and you are integrally involved in its software design. Your ownership interest is significant enough to give you influence over APEX's software design specifications.

Required

a. Describe the financial statement effects of the three possible methods to accounting for this investment (fair value, equity, and consolidation).

b. What method of accounting is appropriate for this investment (fair value, equity, or consolidation)? Explain.

LO5 **MA9-55. Ethics and Governance: Equity Carve-Outs**

Many companies use split-offs as a means to unlock shareholder value. The split-off effectively splits the company into two pieces, each of which can then be valued separately by the stock market. If managers are compensated based on reported profit, how might they strategically structure the split-off? What corporate governance issues does this present?

Ongoing Project

(*This ongoing project began in Module 1 and continues through most of the book; even if previous segments were not completed, the requirements are still applicable to any business analysis.*) Company analysis should include an assessment of the companies' various investments, transactions during the year, the effect on net income, and the balance sheet results at year-end.

1. *Investments in Marketable Securities.* To analyze nonoperating investments in marketable debt and equity securities, consider the following questions that will help us understand both companies' level of excess cash and how they invest it:

   • What is the magnitude of the investments in common-size terms? Has this changed over time? What proportion is short-term versus long-term?

   • What types of investments does the company hold—debt, equity, private-company equity?

   • What explanation do the companies provide for their level of investments? Does the MD&A section of the Form 10-K discuss plans for expansion or other strategic initiatives that would require cash?

2. *Investments with Significant Influence.* Our goal is to assess how the companies structure their operations to better understand their strategies.

   • What types of investments does the company have: associates, joint ventures, or other?

   • Why does the company engage in equity-method investments; what is their intent? Read the MD&A section of the Form 10-K and the financial statement footnotes.

   • What are the main equity-method investments? (IFRS: Does the company have any proportionate consolidation?) How large are these in common-size terms?

   • Have there been changes during the year in terms of new investments or disposals? The MD&A and footnotes will be instructive.

   • Are the equity method investments profitable? Do they provide cash dividends?

3. *Investments with Control (Consolidations).* Most multinational corporations are consolidated entities that structure their operations to meet many goals, including legal requirements, tax planning, and foreign ownership restrictions. Financial statements will not report information to completely comprehend all these intricacies; the goal here is to understand the companies' structure at a very high level.

   • What types of companies does the company control? What are the main subsidiaries?

   • What strategic advantages do these subsidiaries afford? Foreign? Domestic? Supplier or distributors? Read the MD&A section of the Form 10-K and the financial statement footnotes to learn about strategic investment and plans for the future.

   • Have there been new investments during the year? How were these acquisitions financed (debt, equity)? Did these yield intangible assets including goodwill? What proportion of the acquisition price was allocated to intangibles?

   • Were there disposals during the year? Why were these made? Did the transaction cause a gain or loss?

   • Gauge the significance of previously acquired intangibles in common-size terms. Have any been impaired during the year?

   • If the company reports subsidiary-level profit, which are the most profitable? The least?

Solutions to Review Problems

Review 9-1—Solution

a.

Transaction	Cash Asset	+	Noncash Assets	=	Liabil- ities	+	Contrib. Capital	+	Earned Capital		Rev- enues	−	Expen- ses	=	Net Income
Balance Sheet											**Income Statement**				
1. Purchased 1,000 shares of Juniper common stock for $15 cash per share	−15,000 Cash	+	+15,000 Marketable Securities	=								−		=	
2. Received cash dividend of $2.50 per share on Juniper com- mon stock	+2,500 Cash			=						+2,500 Retained Earnings		+2,500 Dividend Income	−		=	+2,500
3. Year-end market price of Juniper common stock is $17 per share			+2,000 Marketable Securities	=						+2,000 Retained Earnings		+2,000 Unrealized Gain	−		=	+2,000
4. Sold 1,000 shares of Juniper common stock for $17,000 cash	+17,000 Cash		−17,000 Marketable Securities	=									−		=	

MS . . . 15,000
  Cash . . . 15,000

MS	
15,000	

Cash	
	15,000

Cash . . 2,500
  DI 2,500

Cash	
2,500	

DI	
	2,500

MS . . . 2,000
  UG 2,000

MS	
2,000	

UG	
	2,000

Cash . . 17,000
  MS 17,000

Cash	
17,000	

MS	
	17,000

b. Yahoo!'s investment portfolio includes both debt and equity securities. The balance sheet reports the investments at fair value totaling $36,457,854 thousand.

c. The portfolio's estimated fair value comprises 14% debt securities, computed as ($615,890 thousand + $4,585,183 thousand)/$36,457,854 thousand, and 86% equity securities.

d. Yahoo!'s investment portfolio has a cost of $7,946,327 thousand and a fair value of $36,457,854 thousand. The difference is mostly attributable to the huge gain in the fair value of Alibaba stock—the original cost was $2.7 billion, and the 2015 fair value is $31.2 billion.

Review 9-2—Solution

a.

Transaction	Cash Asset	+	Noncash Assets	=	Liabil- ities	+	Contrib. Capital	+	Earned Capital		Rev- enues	−	Expen- ses	=	Net Income
Balance Sheet											**Income Statement**				
1. Purchased 5,000 shares of LookSmart common stock at $10 cash per share; these shares reflect 30% ownership	−50,000 Cash	+	+50,000 Investment in LookSmart	=									−		=	
2. Received a $2 per share cash dividend on LookSmart stock	+10,000 Cash		−10,000 Investment in LookSmart	=									−		=	
3. Record 30% share of the $100,000 income reported by LookSmart			+30,000 Investment in LookSmart	=						+30,000 Retained Earnings		+30,000 Equity Income	−		=	+30,000

EMI . . . 50,000
  Cash . . . 50,000

EMI	
50,000	

Cash	
	50,000

Cash . . 10,000
  EMI 10,000

Cash	
10,000	

EMI	
	10,000

EMI . . . 30,000
  EI 30,000

EMI	
30,000	

EI	
	30,000

continued

continued from previous page

	Balance Sheet					Income Statement		
Transaction	**Cash Asset** +	**Noncash Assets** =	**Liabil-ities** +	**Contrib. Capital** +	**Earned Capital**	**Rev-enues** −	**Expen-ses** =	**Net Income**
4. Market value has in-creased to $12 per share			NOTHING RECORDED					
5. Sold all 5,000 shares of LookSmart stock for $90,000	+90,000 Cash	−70,000 Investment in LookSmart			+20,000 Retained Earnings	+20,000 Gain on Sale −	=	+20,000

Cash..90,000
EMI 70,000
GN..... 20,000

CASH
90,000 |

EMI
| 70,000

GN
| 20,000

b. Based on the reported figures, Yahoo!'s proportionate share of the investee's net income would be $382.2 million calculated as $1,092 million × 35%. This is very close to the actual amount included in the income statement for the year.

c. Because the fair value of Yahoo! Japan has increased, Yahoo! has an unrealized gain on their investment. However, because Yahoo! accounts for this investment using the equity method, the unrealized gain does not affect either the balance sheet or the income statement.

Review 9-3—Solution

	Yahoo! (Parent)	EarthLink (Subsidiary)	Consolidating Adjustments	Consolidated
Current assets	$1,000,000	$100,000		$1,100,000
Investment in EarthLink	600,000	—	(600,000)	
PPE, net	3,000,000	400,000	100,000	3,500,000
Intangible assets (patents) ...	—	—	25,000	25,000
Goodwill	—	—	75,000	75,000
Total assets..............	$4,600,000	$500,000		$4,700,000
Liabilities................	$1,000,000	$100,000		$1,100,000
Contributed capital.........	2,000,000	200,000	(200,000)	2,000,000
Retained earnings	1,600,000	200,000	(200,000)	1,600,000
Total liabilities and equity	$4,600,000	$500,000		$4,700,000

Explanation: The $600,000 investment account is eliminated together with the $400,000 book value of Earth-Link's equity to which Yahoo's investment relates. The remaining $200,000 consists of the additional $100,000 in PPE assets, $25,000 in unrecorded intangibles, and $75,000 in goodwill from expected corporate synergies. Following these adjustments, the balance sheet items are summed to yield the consolidated balance sheet.

Review 9-4—Solution

1. PepsiCo used derivatives to hedge foreign currency risk, interest rate risk, and price risk in the commodities it uses to produce its products.

2. PepsiCo employs both fair value and cash flow hedges. Footnote (a) reports that gains/losses from interest rates are primarily related to fair value hedges. The last columns on the table report amounts reclassified from AOCI—the footnotes say these relate to hedges for commodity and foreign-exchange transactions. Because only cash flow hedges have gains and losses in AOCI, we know these are hedges of anticipated transactions, such as sales in foreign currencies and purchases of commodities such as sugar and corn.

3. Fair value hedges reduced current income by $221 million. Cash flow hedges reduced current income by $97 million, the amount reclassified from AOCI into current income.

Review 9-5—Solution

1. A split-off is like a treasury stock transaction, where the subsidiary's shares (owned by the parent) are used instead of cash. If the distribution is non pro rata, the parent can report a gain equal to the difference between the fair value of the subsidiary and its book value on the parent's balance sheet.

2. BearingPoint met the non pro-rata conditions for a split-off as described in part 1, which enabled it to report a gain.

Module 10

Leases, Pensions, and Income Taxes

Learning Objectives

LO1 Analyze and interpret lease disclosures. (p. 10-3)

LO2 Analyze and interpret pension disclosures. (p. 10-11)

LO3 Analyze and interpret income tax reporting. (p. 10-24)

LO4 Use a calculator and present value tables for lease calculations (Appendix 10A). (p. 10-31)

LO5 Examine pension expense in more detail (Appendix 10B). (p. 10-33)

LO6 Examine deferred tax disclosures in more detail (Appendix 10C). (p. 10-35)

LUV

Market cap: $27,886 mil
Total assets: $21,312 mil
Revenues: $19,820 mil
Net income: $2,181 mil

FDX

Market cap: $50,850 mil
Total assets: $37,069 mil
Revenues: $47,453 mil
Net income: $1,050 mil

Southwest Airlines (LUV) and **FedEx (FDX)** are both iconic American brands that share a number of attributes. Both companies are profitable but operate with relatively lean margins. Both have substantial investments in fixed assets, including aircraft and other ground equipment needed to deliver people and packages around the world. Importantly, both have enormous obligations including operating liabilities and debt, topics discussed at length in previous modules. In this module, we consider three additional debt-related topics that pertain to Southwest and FedEx: leases, pension obligations, and deferred taxes.

Southwest Airlines is solvent and profitable, but still must be strategic about its cash flow because the company carries a heavy debt load that includes borrowed money and aircraft leases that reduce available cash flow. The magnitude of obligations arising from aircraft leases often surprises those outside the industry. Specifically, many airlines, including Southwest Airlines, do not typically own the planes they fly. Instead, planes are owned by commercial leasing companies and are leased by the airlines.

Another substantial obligation for many large companies is pensions and long-term health care plans. Companies' balance sheets must report the net pension and health care liabilities (the total liability less related investments that fund the liabilities). For example, in 2015, FedEx Corporation's net pension liability exceeds pension assets by $4 billion. That amount represents 18% of FedEx's total liabilities. We explain the accounting for both pensions and health care obligations and examine footnote disclosures that convey a wealth of information relating to assumptions underlying estimates of those obligations.

Accounting for income taxes and related liabilities and assets also greatly impacts financial statements. Southwest's effective, or average, tax rate in 2015 was 37.4% and its footnotes reveal that it "has been able to utilize accelerated depreciation methods. . . to defer the cash tax payments associated with [its] depreciable assets to future years." We also explain ways in which companies can defer tax payments and other issues relating to the accounting for income taxes. [Sources: *Southwest Airlines*, 2015 10-K and Annual Report; *FedEx*, 2015 10-K and Annual Report]

© iStock

Road Map

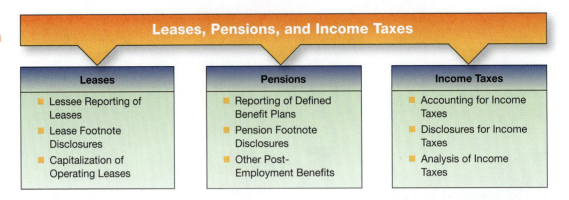

Leases	Pensions	Income Taxes
■ Lessee Reporting of Leases ■ Lease Footnote Disclosures ■ Capitalization of Operating Leases	■ Reporting of Defined Benefit Plans ■ Pension Footnote Disclosures ■ Other Post-Employment Benefits	■ Accounting for Income Taxes ■ Disclosures for Income Taxes ■ Analysis of Income Taxes

Leases

LO1 Analyze and interpret lease disclosures.

A lease is a contract between the owner of an asset (the **lessor**) and the party desiring to use that asset (the **lessee**). Since this is a private contract between two willing parties, it is governed only by applicable commercial law, and can include whatever provisions the parties negotiate.

Leases generally provide for the following terms.

■ The lessor allows the lessee the unrestricted right to use the asset during the lease term.

■ The lessee agrees to make periodic payments to the lessor and to maintain the asset.

■ Title to the asset remains with the lessor, who usually takes physical possession of the asset at lease-end unless the lessee negotiates the right to purchase the asset at its market value or other predetermined price.

From the lessor's standpoint, lease payments are set at an amount that yields an acceptable return on investment, commensurate with the lessee's credit rating. The lessor has an investment in the lease asset, and the lessee gains use of the asset.

The lease serves as a financing vehicle, similar to a secured bank loan. However, there are several advantages to leasing over bank financing.

■ Leases often require less equity investment by the lessee (borrower) compared with bank financing. Leases usually require the first lease payment be made at the inception of the lease. For a 60-month lease, this amounts to a 1/60 (1.7%) investment by the lessee, compared with a bank loan typically requiring 20–30% equity investment by the borrower.

■ Because leases are contracts between two parties, their terms can be structured to meet both parties' needs. For example, a lease can allow variable payments to match the lessee's seasonal cash inflows or have graduated payments for start-up companies.

Lessee Reporting of Leases

The FASB adopted a new lease accounting standard effective for all U.S. companies in 2019. The new rules apply to all years presented in the annual report (both prior and current years), and the standard permits early adoption. Over the next couple of years, we will see financial statements prepared under *both* accounting standards as the transition occurs. This module begins by explaining the accounting for leases under the pre-2019 standards and, then, discusses the changes in the new standard.

Under the pre-2019 standards, GAAP identifies two different approaches for the reporting of leases by the lessee.

■ **Capital lease method**. This method requires that both the lease asset and the lease liability be reported on the balance sheet. The lease asset is depreciated like any other long-term asset. The lease liability is amortized like debt, where lease payments are separated into interest expense and principal repayment.

■ **Operating lease method**. Under this method, neither the lease asset nor the lease liability is reported on the balance sheet. Lease payments are recorded as rent expense by the lessee.

The financial statement effects for the lessee of these methods are summarized in Exhibit 10.1.

Exhibit 10.1 ■ Financial Statement Effects of Lease Type for the Lessee

Lease Type	Assets	Liabilities	Expenses	Cash Flows
Capital	Lease asset reported	Lease liability reported	Depreciation and interest expense	Payments per lease contract
Operating	Lease asset **not** reported	Lease liability **not** reported	Rent expense	Payments per lease contract

Under the **operating method**, lease assets and lease liabilities are *not* recorded on the balance sheet. The company merely discloses key details of the transaction in the lease footnote. The income statement reports the lease payment as rent expense. The cash outflows (payments to lessor) per the lease contract are included in the operating section of the statement of cash flows.

For **capital leases**, both the lease asset and lease liability are reported on the balance sheet.[1] In the income statement, depreciation and interest expense are reported instead of rent expense. Further, although the cash payments to the lessor are identical whether or not the lease is capitalized on the balance sheet, the cash flows are classified differently for capital leases—that is, each payment is part interest (operating cash flow) and part principal (financing cash flow). Operating cash flows are, therefore, greater when a lease is classified as a capital lease.

Classifying leases as "operating" has four financial reporting consequences for the lessee.

1. The lease asset is not reported on the balance sheet. This means that asset turnover is higher because reported assets are lower and revenues are unaffected.

2. The lease liability is not reported on the balance sheet. This means that balance sheet measures of financial leverage (like the total liabilities-to-equity ratio) are improved.

3. Without analytical adjustments (see later section on capitalization of operating leases), the portion of return on equity (ROE) derived from operating activities appears higher, which improves the perceived quality of the company's ROE.

4. During the early years of the lease term, rent expense reported for an operating lease is less than the depreciation and interest expense reported for a capital lease.[2] This means that net income is higher in those early years with an operating lease.[3] Further, if the company is growing and continually adding operating lease assets, the level of profits will continue to remain higher during the growth period.

The benefits of applying the operating method for leases are obvious to managers, thus leading some to avoid lease capitalization. Furthermore, the pre-2019 lease accounting standard includes rigid requirements relating to capitalization. This rigidity has created an unintended negative consequence: managers seeking off-balance-sheet financing can, and routinely do, deliberately structure their leases around GAAP rules so as to report the leases as operating. This motivated the FASB to change the accounting standard.

New Lease Accounting Rules

Analysts and other financial statement users objected to the pre-2019 rules that left operating lease assets and the related liabilities off of the balance sheets. In response, the new accounting standard requires that substantially all lease assets and lease obligations be recognized on the balance sheet at an

---

[1] Under the pre-2019 accounting rules, leases must be capitalized when one or more of the following four criteria are met: (1) The lease automatically transfers ownership of the lease asset from the lessor to the lessee at termination of the lease. (2) The lease provides that the lessee can purchase the lease asset for a nominal amount (a bargain purchase) at termination of the lease. (3) The lease term is at least 75% of the economic useful life of the lease asset. (4) The present value of the lease payments is at least 90% of the fair market value of the lease asset at inception of the lease.

[2] This is true even if the company employs straight-line depreciation for the lease asset since interest expense accrues on the outstanding balance of the lease liability, which is higher in the early years of the lease life. Total expense is the same *over the life of the lease,* regardless of whether the lease is capitalized or not. That is: Total rent expense (from operating lease) = Total depreciation expense (from capital lease) + Total interest expense (from capital lease).

[3] However, net operating profit after tax (NOPAT) is *lower* for an operating lease because rent expense is an operating expense whereas only depreciation expense (and not interest expense) is an operating expense for a capital lease.

amount equal to the present value of the lease payments.[4] The process to capitalize leases is the same as the process to capitalize operating leases for analysis purposes, which we discuss below.

Under the new standard, companies classify all capitalized leases as either a *finance lease* (where the lease transfers control of the lease asset to a lessee and is effectively like purchasing the asset) or an *operating lease* (the lessee controls only the *use* the lease asset, but not the asset itself).

The term "operating lease" in the new standard is different from the use of that term in the current standard. It no longer refers to whether a lease is capitalized or not because, effectively, all leases are capitalized. The classification affects how lease expense is determined and where it appears in the income statement. Lease expense for operating leases is simply the amortization, on a straight-line basis, of the lease asset cost (essentially, the sum of the lease payments). Operating lease expense is included in COGS, R&D expense, or SG&A, depending on the nature of the lease asset.

Lease expense for finance leases has two parts.

■ Amortization of the lease asset (included with other depreciation and amortization expenses).

■ Interest expense on the lease obligation.

Lease expense for finance leases is generally higher in the early years of the lease and lower in later years. Conversely, operating lease expense is generally the same amount each year.

Tests to determine whether a lease is a "finance lease," are similar to those for capital leases under current GAAP, except that the rigid percentages are no longer used (see footnote #1). Instead, lessors assess whether the:

■ Lease term comprises a "major part" of the remaining economic life of the lease asset (vs. a strict 75% under the pre-2019 rules).

■ Present value of the lease payments comprises "substantially all" of the fair value of the lease asset (vs. a strict 90% under the pre-2019 rules).

■ Lease transfers ownership of the underlying asset to the lessee by the end of the lease term.

■ Lease grants the lessee an option to purchase the lease asset that the lessee is reasonably certain to exercise.

These changes are consistent with a general trend in accounting standards to move away from "bright-line" tests and to place more responsibility on the preparers of financial statements to use their professional judgment to assess the substance of the transaction rather than merely appeal to rigid rules or mechanical tests. (*All leases not classified as finance leases are classified as operating leases.* All leases are now reflected on the balance sheet. The lease asset is now commonly called a "right-of-use," or *ROU*, asset.)

IFRS Insight   ■   Lease Accounting under IFRS

U.S. GAAP and IFRS both require that leases be capitalized if the lease asset's risks and rewards are transferred to the lessee. The main difference between the two reporting systems is that IFRS are more principles based and GAAP is more rules based (for example, see the criteria details in this module's footnote 1). Under the new U.S. lease standard, U.S. GAAP is more aligned with IFRS.

Footnote Disclosure of Leases

Under the pre-2019 accounting rules, disclosures of expected payments for leases are required for both operating and capital leases. Southwest Airlines provides a typical disclosure from its 2015 annual report.

Total rental expense for operating leases, both aircraft and other, charged to operations in 2015, 2014, and 2013 was $909 million, $931 million, and $997 million, respectively. The majority of the Company's terminal operations space, as well as 95 aircraft, were under operating leases at December 31, 2015. . . Future minimum lease payments under capital leases and noncancelable operating

continued

---

[4] There are a few exceptions including leases shorter than 1 year (provided that they do not include an option to purchase the underlying asset), as well as leases of intangible assets, rights to explore natural resources, and assets under construction, among other unusual assets.

leases and rentals to be received under subleases with initial or remaining terms in excess of one year at December 31, 2015, were:

$ millions	Capital Leases	Operating Leases	Subleases	LFMP Facility Lease	Operating Leases, Net
2016	$ 46	$ 636	$(103)	$ 24	$ 557
2017	46	624	(103)	24	545
2018	45	551	(102)	25	474
2019	45	479	(97)	25	407
2020	44	359	(78)	26	307
Thereafter	209	961	(66)	634	1,529
Total minimum lease payments	435	$3,610	$(549)	$758	$3,819
Less amount representing interest. . . .	79				
Present value of minimum lease payments	356				
Less current portion	32				
Long-term portion	$324				

The aircraft leases generally can be renewed for one to five years at rates based on fair market value at the end of the lease term. Most aircraft leases have purchase options at or near the end of the lease term at fair market value, generally limited to a stated percentage of the lessor's defined cost of the aircraft.

Lease disclosures provide information concerning current and future payment obligations. These contractual obligations are similar to debt payments and must be factored into our evaluation of the company's financial condition.

Southwest Airlines' footnote disclosure reports minimum (base) contractual lease payment obligations for each of the next five years and the total lease payment obligations that come due in year six and beyond. This is similar to disclosures of future maturities for long-term debt. The company also must provide separate disclosures for operating leases and capital leases (Southwest Airlines has both).

Managerial Decision ■ You Are the Division President

You are the president of an operating division. Your CFO recommends operating lease treatment for asset acquisitions to reduce reported assets and liabilities on your balance sheet. To achieve this classification, you must negotiate leases with shorter base terms and lease renewal options that you feel are not advantageous to your company. What is your response? [Answer, p. 10-37]

Capitalization of Operating Leases

New standards require that all leases be capitalized on the balance sheet. However, before 2019, when the new standards take effect, companies report only capital leases on their balance sheets; information on their operating leases is in footnotes such as that shown above for Southwest.

Analysts commonly capitalize operating leases with a process called "constructive capitalization" in a desire for a more accurate assessment of a company's financial performance and debt loads. Failure to capitalize operating lease assets and lease liabilities for analysis purposes distorts analysis—specifically:

■ **Operating profit margin is understated.** Over the life of the lease, rent expense under operating leases equals depreciation plus interest expense under capital leases; however, only depreciation expense is included in operating profit as interest is a nonoperating expense. Operating expense is, therefore, overstated. While cash payments are the same whether the lease is classified as operating or capital, *operating cash flow* is higher with capital leases since depreciation is an add-back, and the reduction of the capital lease obligation is classified as a *financing* outflow. Operating cash flows are, therefore, lower with operating leases than with capital leases.

- **Asset turnover is overstated** due to nonreporting of lease assets.
- **Financial leverage is understated** by the omitted lease liabilities.

Lease disclosures that are required under the pre-2019 rules allow us to perform a constructive capitalization, that is to capitalize operating leases for analysis purposes. This capitalization process involves three steps (this is the same basic process that managers use to capitalize all leases under the new lease-accounting standard).

❶ Determine the discount rate.

❷ Compute the present value of future lease payments.

❸ Adjust the balance sheet to include the present value from step 2 as both a lease asset and a lease liability. Adjust the income statement to include depreciation and interest in lieu of rent expense.

Step ❶ There are at least two approaches to determine the appropriate discount rate for our analysis.

- If the company discloses capital leases, we can impute (infer) an implicit rate of return: a rate that yields the present value computed by the company given the future capital lease payments (see Business Insight box below).
- Use the rate that corresponds to the company's credit rating or the rate from any recent borrowings involving intermediate-term secured obligations. Companies typically disclose these details in their long-term debt footnote.

To illustrate, we use the Southwest Airlines lease footnote reproduced above. Step 1 estimates the implicit rate for Southwest Airlines' capital leases to be 3.94% (determined by the Business Insight box below on computing the imputed discount rate for leases).

Step ❷ Compute the present value of future operating lease payments using the 3.94% discount rate that we estimated in Step 1, see Exhibit 10.2. Given the widespread use of spreadsheets such as Excel, we use a spreadsheet hereafter (without rounding the numbers). (We demonstrate this computation using both a financial calculator and present value tables in Appendix 10A.)

Exhibit 10.2 ■ Present Value of Operating Lease Payments ($ millions)

	A	B	C	D	E
1	Year	Operating Lease Payment	Discount Factor (*i* = 0.0394)	Present Value	Cell Formula
2	1	$ 557	0.96209	$ 536	=PV(B10,A2,0,−B2)
3	2	545	0.92562	504	=PV(B10,A3,0,−B3)
4	3	474	0.89054	422	=PV(B10,A4,0,−B4)
5	4	407	0.85678	349	=PV(B10,A5,0,−B5)
6	5	307	0.82430	253	=PV(B10,A6,0,−B6)
7	>5	$1,529 ($307 × 4.98 years)	4.44316 × 0.82430	1,124	=PV(B10,B9,−B6,0,0)*PV(B10,A6,0,−1)
8				$3,188	=SUM(D2:D7)
9	Remaining life	$1,529/$307 = 4.98 years			=B7/B6
10	Discount rate	0.0394*			

* See computation of imputed discount rate in Business Insight box that that follows.

Spreadsheet Method The present value of the operating lease payments equals the sum of the present values for each of the lease payments Year 1 through Year 5 and the present value of the lease payments after Year 5. This two-step computation follows:

a. *Present values for Years 1 through 5.*   The present value of lease payment for Years 1 through 5 is computed for each of the first 5 years using the =pv function in Excel. This is shown in rows 2 through 6 in Exhibit 10.2.

b. *Present value for Year 6 and thereafter.*   To compute the present value of the lease payments remaining after Year 5, we make an assumption that the company continues to make lease payments at the Year 5 level for the remainder of the lease term. The remaining lease term is, therefore, estimated as: (Total payments for Year 6 and thereafter)/(Year 5 lease payment) as shown in cell B9 in Exhibit 10.2. This means the remaining payments are an annuity for the remainder of the lease term and we use the Excel present value function for an annuity ("pmt") to determine the present value of the remaining lease payments. This present value is the value of the remaining payments at the beginning of Year 6. What we seek is the present value of those payments at the beginning of Year 1. Thus, we multiply by the present value of a lump sum. See cell E7 in Exhibit 10.2 for the Excel cell definition. The algebraic formula for this is computed as:

$$\$307 \text{ million} \times \frac{1-[1/(1.0394)^{4.98}]}{0.0394} \times \frac{1}{(1.0394)^5}$$

We sum the present values of Year 1 through Year 5 payments and the present value of the payments in Year 6 and beyond to obtain the present value of future operating lease payments; for Southwest, this totals $3,188 million (computed as $536 + $504 + $422 + $349 + $253 + $1,124, as shown in cell D8 in Exhibit 10.2).

Step ❸ Use the computed present value of future operating lease payments to adjust the balance sheet, income statement, and financial ratios as we illustrate below.

Financial Statement Adjustments Failure to capitalize operating leases affects ratio analysis. In Step 2 above, we quantified the assets and liabilities missing from the balance sheet, as $3,188 million. To adjust the balance sheet, we add $3,188 million to both assets and liabilities as illustrated in Exhibit 10.3. Capitalizing the operating leases has a marked impact on Southwest's balance sheet because lease assets (airplanes and real estate) comprise a large portion of the company's net operating assets. All airline companies and many retailers have equally large off-balance-sheet assets and liabilities.

Business Insight ▪ Imputed Discount Rate Computation for Leases

When companies report both operating and capital leases, we can use disclosures in the lease footnote to impute the average interest rate used to discount capital leases. Southwest Airlines reports total undiscounted minimum capital lease payments of $435 million and a discounted value for those lease payments of $356 million. Using Excel, we estimate the discount rate that Southwest used for its capital lease computations with the IRR function, written as "= IRR(values,guess)", as shown in the following spreadsheet. The entries in cells B2 through G2 are taken from Southwest's lease footnote shown earlier in this section. Cells H2 through L2 sum to $209 million, the total lease payments due after 2020 (year 5). We assume that Southwest continues to pay $44 million per year (the same as in 2019) with a final payment of $33 million, until the $209 million is used up. The spreadsheet estimates that Southwest Airlines implicitly used a discount rate of 3.94% to capitalize leases in its 2015 balance sheet.

H14	▼	⋮	×	✓	fx							
	A	B	C	D	E	F	G	H	I	J	K	L	M
1	N	0	1	2	3	4	5	6	7	8	9	10	
2	Amount	−356	46	46	45	45	44	44	44	44	44	33	
3	IRR	3.94%											
4	4									=209			
5		*Formula for cell B3 is IRR(B2:L2,.1)											

Designating leases as operating also affects the income statement. Had the leases been capitalized, Southwest would have recognized depreciation expense relating to the lease assets and interest expense on the lease obligation. By definition, total expense over the life of the lease must equal the total lease payments, regardless of the way in which we account for the lease assets. So, the adjustment to the income statement replaces rent expense with depreciation and interest expense, leaving net income unaffected. Because net income is unaffected, stockholders' equity is also unaffected.

Exhibit 10.3 ◼ **Adjustments from Capitalization of Operating Leases**

$ millions	Reported Amounts	Adjustments	Adjusted Amounts
Total assets.	$21,312	$3,188	$24,500
Total liabilities	13,954	3,188	17,142
Stockholders' equity	7,358	—	7,358
Total revenues	19,820	—	19,820
Net income	2,181	—	2,181

ROE and Disaggregation Effects Adjustments to capitalize operating leases can alter our assessment of ROE components. Using the adjustments we describe in Exhibit 10.3, the impact on the disaggregation of ROE, is summarized in Exhibit 10.4 for **Southwest Airlines**.

Exhibit 10.4 ◼ **Ratio Effects of Adjustments from Capitalization of Operating Leases**

Southwest Airlines ($ millions)	Reported	Adjusted	Computations for Adjusted Numbers
Net profit margin.	11.0%	11.0%	$2,181/$19,820
Asset turnover*.	0.93	0.81	$19,820/$24,500
Return on assets (ROA)*.	10.2%	8.9%	$2,181/$24,500
Financial leverage*	2.90	3.33	$24,500/$7,358
Return on equity (ROE)*	29.6%	29.6%	$2,181/$7,358

* For simplicity, we use year-end values for the denominator in lieu of average values.

Using *year-end* (reported and adjusted) data, the adjusted return on assets (ROA) is 8.9%, lower than the 10.2% computed using the reported financial statements. Since the income statement is unaffected, so is the net profit margin. Adjusted ROA decreases because the adjusted total asset turnover is lower owing to the recognition of the lease assets. After we capitalize Southwest Airlines operating leases, the company is more capital intensive than we would infer by reviewing its unadjusted balance sheet.

Because net income and stockholders' equity are unaffected by the adjustments, Southwest's return on equity (ROE) is unaffected; it is 29.6% either way. The composition of ROE, however, is greatly affected by both ROA and financial leverage. The adjusted figures reveal a much greater capital intensity and financial leverage that is not apparent prior to the constructive capitalization. Specifically, ROA declines due to the recognition of lease assets and financial leverage is 3.33 using adjusted figures versus 2.90 using reported figures. In sum, Southwest's adjusted figures reveal a company with more assets and more financial leverage than was apparent from reported figures.

Financial Analysis Insight ■ Adjustments for Operating vs. Nonoperating Disaggregation of ROE

A powerful way to analyze ROE is to disaggregate it into operating and nonoperating components. Constructive capitalization affects both operating and nonoperating items and requires that we adjust the balance sheet and income statement. To adjust the **balance sheet**, we:

- Add the present value of the operating lease payments from Step 2 to operating assets (PPE).

- Add the present value of the operating lease payments from Step 2 to nonoperating liabilities (long-term debt).

To adjust the **income statement**, we:

- Add depreciation expense from the lease assets to operating expense, computed as $319 million ($3,188 million/9.98 years, where 9.98 years is the 5 years disclosed plus the estimated 4.98 subsequent years).

- Add interest expense from the lease obligation as a nonoperating expense, computed as $126 million ($3,188 million $\times$ 3.94%), where 3.94% is the discount rate used to capitalize the operating leases.

- Remove "rent expense" of $445 million from operating expenses computed as the sum of the depreciation and interest expense ($319 million + $126 million).

Because only depreciation is an operating expense, NOPAT is higher when a lease is classified as a capital lease. The increase in NOPAT, however, is exactly offset by the increase in nonoperating expense, leaving net income unaffected. The following table summarizes these adjustments to Southwest's profitability measures.

ROE Disaggregation ($ millions)	Reported Amounts	Adjustments	Adjusted Amounts
Net operating assets	$ 7,485[a]	$3,188[b]	$10,673
Net nonoperating obligations	127[c]	3,188[b]	3,315
Stockholders' equity	7,358	—	7,358
Total revenues	19,820	—	19,820
Net operating profit after tax (NOPAT)	2,232[d]	79[e]	2,311
Net nonoperating expense	51	79[f]	130
Net income	2,181	—	2,181
Net operating profit margin	11.3%		11.7%
Net operating asset turnover	2.65		1.86
Return on net operating assets (RNOA)	29.8%		21.7%
Return on equity (ROE)	29.6%		29.6%
Nonoperating return	(0.18)%		8.0%
Financial leverage (FLEV)	0.02		0.45

[a] $21,312 − $1,583 − $1,468 − ($7,406 − $637) − $2,490 − $757 − $760 = $7,485. Construction obligation and Other noncurrent liabilities relate to operating activities, as disclosed in 10-K footnotes.

[b] Present value of the operating lease payments from Step 2.

[c] Long-term debt including current portion minus cash and short-term investments: $2,541 + $637 − $1,583 − $1,468 = $127.

[d] ([$4,116 − $556] − [$1,298 + (($121 − $31 − $9} × 0.37)]) = $2,232, where $556 is the net expense relating to the hedging of fuel costs, which is classified as an operating item.

[e] ([$445 rent expense − $319 depreciation expense] × [1 − 0.37]) = $79 million.

[f] ($126 × [1 − 0.37]) = $79, the additional after-tax interest expense on the capitalized lease obligation.

Capitalizing the operating leases decreased RNOA because the increase in net operating profit margin (from 11.3% to 11.7%) was more than offset by a lower net operating asset turnover (from 2.65 to 1.86). The adjusted figures reveal greater financial leverage that is not apparent prior to capitalization. Specifically, financial leverage is 45% of equity using adjusted figures versus 2% of equity using reported figures. By capitalizing the operating leases, we see that financial leverage plays a greater role in ROE. In sum, Southwest's adjusted figures reveal a company with more assets and more financial leverage than was apparent from reported figures.

Review 10-1 LO1

Following is the leasing footnote disclosure from United Parcel Service's (UPS) 2015 10-K report.

We lease certain aircraft, facilities, land, equipment and vehicles under operating leases, which expire at various dates through 2038. Certain of the leases contain escalation clauses and renewal or purchase options. Rent expense related to our operating leases was $669, $676 and $575 million for 2015, 2014 and 2013, respectively.

The following table sets forth the aggregate minimum lease payments under capital and operating leases, the aggregate annual principal payments due under our long-term debt and the aggregate amounts expected to be spent for purchase commitments ($ millions):

Year	Capital Leases	Operating Leases
2016	$ 72	$ 324
2017	73	263
2018	61	197
2019	59	125
2020	53	84
After 2020.	392	266
Total	710	$1,259
Less: imputed interest	(235)	
Present value of minimum capitalized lease payments	$475	
Less: current portion	(46)	
Long-term capitalized lease obligations	$429	

Required

1. Impute the discount rate that UPS uses, on average, to compute the present value of its capital leases.
2. What adjustments would we make to UPS's balance sheet to capitalize the operating leases at the end of 2015? (*Hint:* The implicit rate on its capital leases is approximately 7%; use this approximation to solve parts 2 and 3 if one cannot solve for the implicit rate.) Round the remaining life to 3 decimal places.

Solution on p. 10-64.   3. Assuming the same facts as in part 2, what income statement adjustments might we consider?

Pensions

LO2
MBC Analyze and interpret pension disclosures.

Companies frequently offer post-retirement benefit plans for their employees. There are two general types of plans.

1. **Defined contribution plan**. This plan requires the company to make periodic contributions to an employee's account (usually with a third-party trustee like a bank), and many plans require an employee matching contribution. Following retirement, the employee makes periodic withdrawals from that account. A tax-advantaged 401(k) account is a typical example. Under a 401(k) plan, the employee makes contributions that are exempt from federal taxes until they are withdrawn by the employee after retirement.

2. **Defined benefit plan**. This plan also requires the company make periodic payments to a third party, which then makes payments to an employee after retirement. Payments are usually based on years of service and the employee's salary. The company may *or may not* set aside sufficient funds to cover these obligations (federal law does set minimum funding requirements). As a result, defined benefit plans can be overfunded or underfunded. All pension investments are retained by the third party until paid to the employee. In the event of bankruptcy, employees have the standing of a general creditor, but usually have additional protection in the form of government pension benefit insurance.

The financial statement implications and the accounting for defined contribution plans is similar to a simple accrual of wages payable. When the company becomes liable to make its contribution, it accrues the liability and related expense. Later, when the company makes the payment, its cash and the liability are reduced. The amount of the liability is certain and the company's obligation is fully satisfied once payment has been made.

A defined benefit plan is not so simple. For that type of plan, the company has made a promise to make annual payments to retirees based on a formula that typically includes the employee's final salary level and years of service, both of which are not determined for maybe 30–40 years in the future. Estimating the amount of the liability is difficult and prone to error. While companies typically set aside some cash to fund promised future payments, usually they make only the minimum contribution required by law. This makes it uncertain whether there will be sufficient funds available to make required payments to retirees.

The accounting for defined benefit plans is subjective, amounts are uncertain, and companies frequently revise their estimates. Footnote disclosures are often lengthy and difficult to decipher. Nonetheless, it is possible to use the disclosures to assess how a defined benefit plan impacts company performance and financial condition.

Reporting of Defined Benefit Pension Plans

There are two accounting issues concerning the reporting of defined benefit pension plans.

1. How are pension plans (assets and liabilities) reported in the balance sheet (if at all)?
2. How is the expense relating to pension plans reported in the income statement?

Although companies are increasingly moving away from defined benefit plans and toward 401(k) type plans, over 70% of the S&P 500 companies still report pension plans in 2015, and the cumulative financial effects to U.S. balance sheets and income statements are large. The accounting for defined benefit plans must consider the following.

- Companies estimate pension liability, the present value of the **projected benefit obligations** (or PBO). This involves a number of estimates that include:
  - Number of employees who will reach retirement age while employed with the company.
  - Salary levels at retirement—this requires an estimate of wage inflation.
  - Years of service at retirement.
  - Years over which annual payments will be made—this requires an estimate of life span.

  The company uses these assumptions to estimate the amount that will be paid to employees from retirement until the end of their lives. This amount is discounted (at an assumed rate called the "settlement rate") to yield the present value of the future pension benefits to be paid—the PBO.

- Companies are required by law to set aside funds to make the estimated payments, that is, to "fund" the PBO. Typically, these funds, called **pension plan assets**, are invested in a portfolio of stocks and bonds to earn a return. Each year, a portion of the pension assets is liquidated to make annual payments to retirees. When benefits are paid, pension assets and the pension liability (PBO) are reduced in equal amounts, similar to the payment of cash for wages payable.

- *Balance sheet reporting.* The difference between the fair value of the pension plan assets and the PBO is called the **funded status**. Companies report the funded status on the balance sheet as an asset (if fair value of pension plan assets > PBO) or as a liability (if PBO > fair value of pension plan assets). Companies do not report *both* the pension plan assets and the PBO separately on the balance sheet; only the net amount is reported.

- *Income statement reporting.* Generally, an increase in the funded status (other than from company contributions) decreases pension expense and a decrease in the funded status increases pension expense. Pension expense will increase as the company estimates more benefits to be paid (similar to recording a liability for wages payable), and pension expense will decrease as the pension assets earn investment income.

Balance Sheet Effects

Pension Plan Assets Pension plan assets consist of investments in stocks and bonds. The fair value of the plan assets changes each period from three factors.

Pension Plan Assets
Pension plan assets, beginning balance
+ Actual returns on investments (interest, dividends, gains and losses)
+ Company contributions to pension plan
− Benefits paid to retirees
= Pension plan assets, ending balance

■ **Actual returns**—the value of the assets increases or decreases as a result of interest and dividend income and gains or losses (realized and unrealized) on the stocks and bonds held.

■ **Company contributions**—the pension plan assets increase when the company contributes additional cash to the investment portfolio.

■ **Benefit payments**—the pension plan assets decrease by the amount of benefits paid to retirees during the period.

Pension Plan Liabilities On the liability side, the amount of the projected benefit obligation (PBO) increases and decreases due to four factors.

Projected Benefit Obligation
Projected benefit obligation, beginning balance
+ Service cost
+ Interest cost
+/− Actuarial losses (gains)
− Benefits paid to retirees
= Projected benefit obligation, ending balance

■ **Service cost**—the increase in the PBO resulting from the additional (future) pension benefits earned by employees during the current year. The PBO increases when more employees are hired, wage rates increase, and years of service to the company increase. These items increase the future pension benefits to which employees are entitled.

■ **Interest cost**—the accrual of interest on the outstanding pension liability. The PBO is the present value of the estimated future benefit payments and, each year, the liability increases as more interest is accrued.

■ **Actuarial losses (and gains)**—increases or decreases in the PBO as a result of changes in the estimates used to compute the PBO—these are called *actuarial assumptions*. Examples of actuarial assumptions include changes in estimates of wage inflation (used to estimate final salary levels), termination and mortality rates (used to estimate the anticipated pool of retirees and the pay-out period), and the discount rate (used to compute the present value of future obligations). For example, if a company decreases the discount rate used to compute the present value of future pension plan payments from, say, 4% to 3%, the present value of future benefit payments increases.

■ **Benefits paid to retirees**—both the pension assets and the PBO are reduced by the same amount.

Pension Plan Funded Status The difference between the fair value of the pension assets and the computed PBO at the end of the year is called the funded status and it is reported on the balance sheet as an asset (if pension assets > PBO) or as a liability (if the PBO > pension assets).[5]

Net Pension Asset (or Liability)
Pension plan assets (at market value)
− Projected benefit obligation (PBO)
= Funded status

---

[5] Companies typically maintain many pension plans to cover different classes of employees, located in different jurisdictions. Some are overfunded and others are underfunded. Current GAAP requires companies to separately group all of the overfunded and all of the underfunded plans, and to present a net asset for the overfunded plans or a net liability for the underfunded plans.

In 2015, S&P 500 companies collectively reported a net liability of nearly $400 billion for the funded status. This means that pension obligations were underfunded, on average. Over the 10-year period from 2006-2015, for S&P 500 companies, pension assets have averaged about 81% of pension obligations, indicating that underfunding is common.

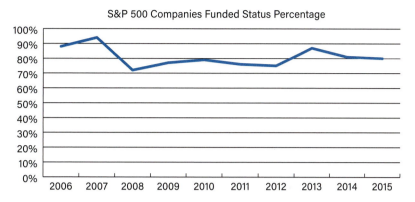

S&P 500 Companies Funded Status Percentage

As **FedEx** discloses in its 2015 10-K, its funding policies are related to IRS and other laws.

> The funding requirements for our U.S. Pension Plans are governed by the Pension Protection Act of 2006, which has aggressive funding requirements in order to avoid benefit payment restrictions that become effective if the funded status determined under IRS rules falls below 80% at the beginning of a plan year. All of our U.S. Pension Plans have funded status levels in excess of 80% and our plans remain adequately funded to provide benefits to our employees as they come due.

In addition, credit rating agencies (such as S&P, Moody's, and Fitch) generally view pension plans as adequately funded at levels above 80%, possibly explaining why companies do not fully fund their pension plans.[6]

IFRS Insight ▪ Reporting of Pension Funded Status under IFRS

Like U.S. GAAP, IFRS requires companies to report the funded status of their defined benefit pension plans on the balance sheet. The IFRS calculation of the unfunded status is slightly different than under GAAP. The IFRS unfunded status is calculated as projected benefit obligation minus the fair value of plan assets; but, unlike GAAP, any actuarial gains are added (losses are subtracted). There are other differences in detailed computations, which means that for pension assets and liabilities it is difficult to reliably compare GAAP and IFRS reports.

Income Statement Effects

Pension expense on the income statement consists of four components.

Net Pension Expense	
	Service cost
+	Interest cost
−	*Expected* return on pension plan assets
±	Amortization of deferred amounts, if any
=	Net pension expense

- ▪ Service cost—described above in the PBO section.
- ▪ Interest cost—described above in the PBO section.
- ▪ **Expected return on pension assets**—the expected interest and dividend income and gains and losses on the portfolio. Expected return increases pension assets and, thereby, *reduces* pension

---

[6] "The 80% Pension Funding Standard Myth," American Academy of Actuaries, July 2012.

expense. This means the pension assets' expected return is deducted to compute net pension expense. (See the text box below for further discussion of the expected return as compared to actual return.)

■ **Amortization of deferred amounts**—differences between the expected and the actual return on pension assets, along with any actuarial gains and losses in the computation of the PBO, are deferred and reported in accumulated other comprehensive income (AOCI). If the deferred amount exceeds certain limits, the excess is amortized, that is, recorded as an expense on the income statement. This amortization is the fourth component of pension expense and can be either a positive (income) or negative (expense) amount. (See the text box below and Appendix 10B.)

It is useful to view these effects on pension expense in the context of the accounting equation. As pension assets increase, so must equity, and as liabilities increase, equity must decrease. These changes in equity reflect increases and decreases in pension expense. A rule of thumb is: as pension assets increase (other than from company contributions), pension expense decreases; and, as the PBO increases, pension expense increases.

Accounting Insight ■ Amortization of Deferred Amounts

Pension expense includes amortization of deferred amounts that arise from two sources: changes in actuarial assumptions *and* unexpected returns on pension assets.

❶ **Changes in actuarial assumptions.** Estimation of the projected benefit obligation (PBO) requires companies to make assumptions about the:

- Proportion of current workers that will ultimately retire from the company and will become eligible for pension payments.

- Expected rate of wage inflation that will, together with length of service, determine employees' benefits.

- Number of years that employees will live (will receive annual pension payments) after retirement.

- Discount rate to use in computing the present value of the estimated payments upon retirement.

Each of these estimates is called an actuarial assumption and companies frequently change these assumptions as the inflation rates and interest rates change and as new information about the employee population becomes available.

A change in any of these actuarial assumptions changes the PBO liability. From the accounting equation (Assets = Liabilities + Equity), we know that if liabilities increase, equity must decrease and if liabilities decrease, equity must increase. The vast majority of companies treat the change in equity arising from a change in estimates as a deferred gain (if equity increases) or a deferred loss (if equity decreases), recognizing the change in equity in other comprehensive income in the current year and, ultimately, in accumulated other comprehensive income (AOCI), a component of equity on the balance sheet. Those deferred gains and losses continue to be recognized in AOCI until they become large, at which point, they are reclassified from AOCI into the current period income statement as either income or expense.[7] As long as the total deferred gains or losses are not excessive, they can remain on the balance sheet in AOCI for a very long time. The deferral of actuarial gains and losses was a concession by the FASB to pave the way for passage of the pension accounting standard.

❷ **Unexpected returns on pension plan assets.** Pension expense includes the *expected* rate of return on pension assets rather than the *actual* rate of return. Pension assets increase with positive returns and decrease with negative returns, and those increases and decreases result in increases and decreases in equity, just like the effects of changes in the PBO. Using *actual* returns on pension assets would make pension expense and net income more volatile. To win approval for the pension standard from corporations, the FASB offered the use of a more stable long-term *expected* rate of return in the computation of pension expense. Actual returns usually differ from expected returns, and that *unexpected* return is included in OCI (and carried in AOCI) just like the deferred actuarial gains and losses relating to the PBO.

AOCI includes both deferred actuarial gains and losses on the PBO and deferred unexpected gains and losses on pension assets. The AOCI balance, therefore, fluctuates over time, becoming positive in some years and negative in others. As long as it doesn't become too large, these deferred gains and losses remain on the balance sheet, not in the income statement.

---

[7] To avoid amortization, the deferred amounts must be less than 10% of the PBO or pension investments, whichever is greater. The excess, if any, is amortized until no further excess remains. When the excess is eliminated (by investment returns or company contributions, for example), the amortization ceases.

Fair Value Accounting for Pensions

The use of expected returns and the deferral and future amortization of actuarial gains and losses serves to smooth reported pension expense and, thereby, dampens earnings volatility. While the majority of companies continue to defer unexpected returns and actuarial gains and losses, recognizing them only if they exceed certain size limits, a number of large public companies have started to recognize those gains and losses in current earnings. **AT&T**, for example, adopted fair-value accounting for pensions in 2010 and now recognizes in current income the actual returns on pension assets (rather than expected returns) and gains (losses) arising from changes in actuarial assumptions. Following is an excerpt from the AT&T 2015 Form 10-K ($ millions).

> We recognize gains and losses on pension and postretirement plan assets and obligations immediately in our operating results. . . Our operating margin was 16.9% in 2015, compared to 9.2% in 2014 and 23.9% in 2013. Contributing $10,021 to the increase in operating income in 2015 was a noncash actuarial gain of $2,152 and an actuarial loss of $7,869 in 2014.

AT&T's actuarial gain arose from a higher discount rate used to compute the PBO, which reduced the PBO and created a gain. The gain was offset by the fact that the actual return on pension assets was less than the expected return. The net actuarial (non-cash) gain increased AT&T's earnings by $2,152 million in 2015, or 10% of pretax earnings. Had AT&T accounted for its pension and other post-retirement plans (OPEB) using the conventional approach, the gains would have flowed through other comprehensive income and earnings would have been unaffected.

AT&T's fair-value approach greatly increases earnings volatility as illustrated in the following graph that shows AT&T's actuarial gains and losses over the past six years.

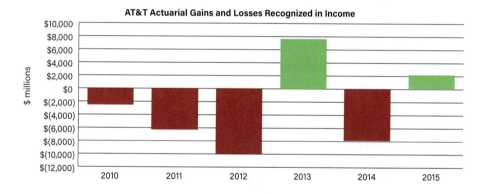

Other companies that have adopted fair value accounting for pensions and OPEB include **Verizon**, **IBM**, **Honeywell**, **FedEx** and **UPS**.

Although U.S. GAAP allows companies to recognize actuarial gains either immediately in current income or deferred in accumulated other comprehensive income (AOCI) and, subsequently amortized to income if they exceed certain limits, International Financial Reporting Standards (IFRS) does not allow an option to recognize actuarial gains and losses in income at all. Instead, IFRS requires actuarial gains and losses be deferred in accumulated other comprehensive income with no subsequent amortization. As a result, these gains are deferred indefinitely.

Business Insight   ■   How Pensions Confound Income Analysis

Overfunded pension plans and boom markets can inflate income. Specifically, when the stock market is booming, pension investments realize large gains that flow to income (via reduced pension expense). Although pension plan assets do not belong to shareholders (as they are the legal entitlement of current and future retirees), the gains and losses from those plan assets are reported in income. The following graph plots the funded status of **General Electric**'s pension plans together with pension expense (revenue) that GE reported from 1998 through 2015.

continued

continued from previous page

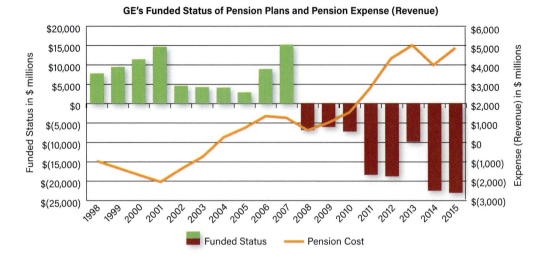

GE's funded status had consistently been positive (indicating an overfunded plan) until the market decline of 2008. The degree of overfunding peaked in 2001 at the height of the stock market, and began to decline during the bear market of the early 2000s. It peaked again in 2007, just prior to the recession and the ensuing bear market. GE reported pension *revenue* (not expense) during 1998–2007. In 2001, GE's reported pension *revenue* was $2,095 million (10.6% of its pretax income). Because of the plan's overfunded status, the expected return and amortization of deferred gains components of pension expense amounted to $5,288 million, far in excess of the service and interest costs of $3,193 million. After 2008, GE recorded pension *expense* (rather than revenue) as the pension plan's overfunding and expected long-term rates of return declined.

Footnote Disclosure—Pension Plan Assets and PBO

GAAP requires extensive footnote disclosures for pensions (and other post-employment benefits which we discuss later). These notes provide details relating to the net pension liability reported in the balance sheet and for the components of pension expense on the income statement.

FedEx Corp.'s pension footnote below indicates that the funded status of its pension plan is $(4,007) million on December 31, 2015. This means FedEx's plan is underfunded. Following are the disclosures FedEx makes in its pension footnote.

Pension Plans ($ millions)	2015	2014
Changes in projected benefit obligation ("PBO") and accumulated postretirement benefit obligation ("APBO")		
PBO/APBO at the beginning of year	$24,578	$22,600
Service cost	653	657
Interest cost	1,096	1,055
Actuarial loss	2,231	1,021
Benefits paid	(815)	(801)
Other	(231)	46
PBO/APBO at the end of year	$27,512	$24,578
Change in plan assets		
Fair value of plan assets at the beginning of year	$21,907	$19,433
Actual return on plan assets	1,718	2,509
Company contributions	746	727
Benefits paid	(815)	(801)
Other	(51)	39
Fair value of plan assets at the end of year	$23,505	$21,907
Funded status of the plans	$ (4,007)	$ (2,671)

During the recent year, FedEx's PBO changed due to the following items.

- **Service cost** ($653 million). Service cost represents the increase in PBO as employees worked for FedEx for another year and earned more benefits.

- **Interest cost** ($1,096 million). Interest cost represents accrual of interest on the PBO liability.

- **Actuarial loss** ($2,231 million). Actuarial losses result from changes in the assumptions used to compute the PBO and unexpected returns on pension assets (that is, the difference between actual and expected returns). In this case, the actuarial loss arose for two reasons, both of which increased the PBO: a reduced discount rate and a change in assumptions about mortality rates reflecting increased life expectancy.

- **Benefits paid** ($815 million). The PBO is reduced by benefits paid to retirees from the pension assets.

FedEx's pension assets changed during the year due to the following identified items.

- **Actual return on pension assets** ($1,718 million). This return includes receipt of dividends and interest as well as changes in the fair value of the plan investments.

- **Company contributions** ($746 million). This represents cash or securities contributed by FedEx to the pension plan assets.

- **Benefits paid** ($815 million). Benefits to retirees are paid out of the pension assets.

FedEx reported $2,146 million of pension expense in 2015. Details of this expense are found in its pension footnote, which follows.

Pension Plans ($ millions)	2015	2014	2013
Service cost	$ 653	$ 657	$ 692
Interest cost	1,096	1,055	968
Expected return on plan assets	(1,678)	(1,495)	(1,383)
Amortization of prior service credit	(115)	(115)	(114)
Actuarial losses (gains) and other	2,190	7	(1,350)
Net periodic benefit cost	$2,146	$ 109	$(1,187)

The service and interest cost components of pension expense, $653 million and $1,096 million respectively, arise from employees working another year for the company and their pension payments being one year closer. These same service and interest costs increase the PBO, as described above. The *expected* return on pension assets ($1,678 million) offsets the service and interest cost. Like AT&T discussed above, FedEx uses the fair value accounting approach in computing pension expense. That approach, like the conventional approach, deducts the expected return on pension assets and, subsequently, includes the difference between the expected return and the actual return in actuarial gains and losses. FedEx's actual return for 2015 of $1,718 million (which increased pension assets, shown above) exceeded the expected return of $1,678 million by $40 million. That $40 million is included with the other actuarial losses ($2,190 million).[8]

Research Insight Valuation Implications of Pension Footnote Disclosures

The FASB requires footnote disclosure of the major components of pension cost presumably because it is useful for investors. Pension-related research has examined whether investors assign different valuation multiples to the components of pension cost when assessing company market value. Research finds that the market does, indeed, attach different interpretation to pension components, reflecting differences in information about perceived permanence in earnings.

---

[8] This amount is not included in the actuarial losses recognized in the computation of the PBO, however, and explains the difference between the $2,190 million recognized in pension expense and the $2,231 million recognized in the PBO computation.

Footnote Disclosure—Future Cash Flows

Companies use their pension plan assets to pay pension benefits to retirees. When markets are booming, pension plan assets can grow rapidly. However, when markets reverse, the value of pension plan assets can decline. The company's annual pension plan contribution is an investment decision that is influenced, in part, by market conditions and minimum required contributions specified by law. Companies' cash contributions come from operating cash flows or borrowed funds.

FedEx paid $815 million in pension benefits to retirees in 2015, and it contributed $746 million to pension assets that year. Cash contributions to the pension plan assets are relevant for an analysis of projected cash flows. Benefits paid in relation to the pension liability balance can provide a clue about the need for *future* cash contributions. Companies are required to disclose the expected benefit payments for five years after the statement date and the remaining obligations thereafter. Following is FedEx's benefit disclosure statement.

Benefit payments, which reflect expected future service, are expected to be paid as follows for the years ending May 31:

$ millions	Pension Plans
2016	$ 913
2017	998
2018	1,047
2019	1,147
2020	1,258
2021–2025	8,107

As of 2015, FedEx pension plan assets account reports a balance of $23,505 million, as discussed above, and during the year, the plan assets generated actual returns of $1,718 million. The pension plan asset account is currently generating investment returns that are more than enough to cover the benefit payments that FedEx expects to pay to retirees as outlined in the schedule above. Should future investment returns decline, however, the company will have to use operating cash flow or borrow money to fund the deficit.

One application of the pension footnote is to assess the likelihood that the company will be required to increase its cash contributions to the pension plan. This estimate is made by examining the funded status of the pension plan and the projected payments to retirees. For severely underfunded plans, the projected payments to retirees might not be covered by existing pension assets and projected investment returns. In this case, the company might need to divert operating cash flow from other prospective projects to cover its pension plan. Alternatively, if operating cash flows are not available, it might need to borrow to fund those payments. This can be especially troublesome as the debt service payments include interest, which increase the required pension contribution. The decline in the financial condition and ultimate bankruptcy of General Motors was due in large part to its inability to meet its pension and health care obligations from pension assets. The company was forced to divert much needed operating cash flow and to borrow funds to meet its cash payment obligations.

Business Insight   ▮   What Happens to Pension Plan When Companies Go Bankrupt?

United Airlines declared bankruptcy in 2002 and petitioned the bankruptcy judge to default on its nearly $10 billion of pension obligations. After approval by the court, the Pension Benefit Guaranty Corporation (PBGC) assumed $6.6 billion of the plan's obligations, with the remaining amount voided by the bankruptcy court. The PBGC is an independent agency of the United States government that was created by the Employee Retirement Income Security Act of 1974 (ERISA). The PBGC pays pension benefits up to the maximum guaranteed benefit set by law to participants who retire at age 65 ($60,136 a year as of 2016). United Airlines emerged from bankruptcy in 2006, free of $35 billion in debt obligations that were wiped out by the bankruptcy court, including its pension obligations. It then proceeded to merge with Continental Airlines.

Footnote Disclosure—Key Assumptions

Recall the following earlier breakdown for pension expense.

Net Pension Expense
Service cost
+ Interest cost
− *Expected* return on pension plan assets
± Amortization of deferred amounts, if any
= Net pension expense

Interest cost is the product of the PBO and the discount rate. This discount rate is set by the company. The expected dollar return on pension assets is the product of the pension plan asset balance and the expected long-run rate of return on the investment portfolio. This rate is also set by the company. Further, PBO is affected by the expected rate of wage inflation, termination and mortality rates, all of which are estimated by the company.

GAAP requires disclosure of several rates used by the company in its estimation of PBO and the related pension expense. FedEx discloses the following in its pension footnote.

	Pension Plans		
Weighted-average actuarial assumptions (Year Ended December 31)*	2015	2014	2013
Discount rate used to determine benefit obligation (BS)	4.42%	4.60%	4.79%
Discount rate used to determine net periodic benefit cost (IS)	4.60	4.79	4.44
Rate of increase in future compensation levels used to determine benefit obligation (BS).	4.62	4.56	4.54
Rate of increase in future compensation levels used to determine net periodic benefit cost (IS).	4.56	4.54	4.62
Expected long-term rate of return on assets (IS)	7.75	7.75	8.00

* We highlight whether the balance sheet (BS) or income statement (IS) is affected.

During 2015, FedEx decreased its discount rate (used to compute the present value of its pension obligations, or PBO) from 4.60% to 4.42%, while leaving unchanged its estimate of the expected return on plan assets. FedEx also increased slightly the anticipated increases in compensation costs used to determine the annual expense.

Changes in these assumptions have the following general effects on pension expense and, thus, profitability. This table summarizes the effects of increases in the various rates. Decreases have the exact opposite effects.

Assumption change	Probable effect on pension expense	Reason for effect
Discount rate ⬆	⬆ or ⬇	While the higher discount rate reduces the PBO, the lower PBO is multiplied by a higher rate when the company computes the interest component of pension expense. The net effect is, therefore, indeterminate.
Investment return ⬆	⬇	The dollar amount of expected return on plan assets is the product of the plan assets balance and the expected long-term rate of return. Increasing the return increases the expected return on plan assets, thus reducing pension expense.
Wage inflation ⬆	⬆	The expected rate of wage inflation affects future wage levels that determine expected pension payments. An increase, thus, increases PBO, which increases both the service and interest cost components of pension expense.

Analysis Implications

There are three important analysis issues relating to pensions.

1. To what extent will the company's pension plans compete with investing and financing needs for the available cash flows?
2. In what ways has the company's choice of estimates affected its profitability?
3. Should pension costs and funded status be treated as operating or nonoperating?

Regarding the first issue, pension plan assets are the source of funds to pay benefits to retirees, and federal law (Employee Retirement Income Security Act) sets minimum standards for pension contributions. Consequently, if investment returns are insufficient, companies must make up the shortfall with additional contributions. Any such additional contributions compete for available operating cash flows with other investing and financing activities. This can be especially severe in a business downturn when operating cash flows are depressed. As pension payments are contractual, companies can be forced to postpone needed capital investment to make the contributions necessary to ensure funding of their pension plans as required by law or labor agreements. Analysts must be aware of funding requirements when projecting future cash flows.

Regarding the second issue, accounting for pensions requires several assumptions, including the expected return on pension investments, the expected rate of wage inflation, the discount rate used to compute the PBO, and other actuarial assumptions that are not reported in footnotes (mortality rates, for example). Each of these assumptions affects reported profit, and analysts must be aware of changes in these assumptions and their effects on profitability. An increase in reported profit that is due to an increase in the expected return on pension investments, for example, is not related to core operating activities and, further, might not be sustainable. Such changes in estimates must be considered in our evaluation of reported profitability.

The third analysis issue relates to the operating vs. nonoperating treatment of pension expense and funded status. Pension expense includes service cost, interest costs, and actuarial cost components (and gains and losses for companies that opt for fair-value accounting). Service cost is, arguably, more related to operating activities than the other components, because service cost arises from the increase in pension benefits earned by employees as they continue to work for the company. Consequently, many analysts argue for operating treatment of service costs. The FASB agrees. In 2016, it proposed a rule change that "would require an employer to report the service cost component in the same line item or items as other compensation costs arising from services rendered by the . . . employees during the period."[9] Under the proposal, the other pension-related costs are reported outside of income from operations, and one could effectively argue for nonoperating treatment of these remaining pension and other postretirement benefit costs.

The operating vs. nonoperating analysis of the funded status on the balance sheet is more difficult. The pension obligation represents a form of compensation and, in that sense, it is operating in nature. However, U.S. GAAP defines the PBO as the "actuarial *present value* . . . of all benefits attributed by the pension benefit formula to employee service rendered before that date" [emphasis ours]. It is the present-value requirement that results in the need to accrue interest expense as a component of pension expense, leading to the argument that a portion of the PBO might be considered as nonoperating. In our view, the GAAP requirement to discount future pension obligations does not change the character of the obligation and, for that reason, we treat the funded status liability as operating. (Very

---

[9] FASB Exposure Draft, "Improving the Presentation of Net Periodic Pension Cost and Net Periodic Postretirement Benefit Cost," January, 2016. Under IFRS, by comparison, there is no requirement to present the various components of pension cost as a net amount. As such, companies have flexibility to present components of net benefit cost within different line items on the income statement.

few companies report a net pension *asset*. But, if they do, we consider the PBO to be equal to zero and treat the excess pension assets as nonoperating as they comprise marketable securities, which we generally treat as nonoperating.)

<table>
<tr><td>Research Insight ■ Why Do Companies Offer Pensions?</td></tr>
</table>

Research examines why companies choose to offer pension benefits. It finds that deferred compensation plans and pensions help align the long-term interests of owners and employees. Research also examines the composition of pension investments. It finds that a large portion of pension fund assets are invested in fixed-income securities, which are of lower risk than other investment securities. This implies that pension assets are less risky than non-pension assets. Pension accounting rules require firms to detail the types of assets held in pension plans. These disclosures presumably help investors better assess the riskiness of pension assets.

Other Post-Employment Benefits (OPEB)

In addition to pension benefits, many companies provide health care and insurance benefits to retired employees. These benefits are referred to as **other post-employment benefits (OPEB)**. These benefits present reporting challenges similar to pension accounting. However, companies most often provide these benefits on a "pay-as-you-go" basis and it is rare for companies to make contributions in advance for OPEB. As a result, this liability, known as the **accumulated post-employment benefit obligation (APBO)**, is largely, if not totally, unfunded. GAAP requires that the unfunded APBO liability, net of any unrecognized amounts, be reported in the balance sheet and the annual service costs and interest costs be accrued as expenses each year. This requirement is controversial for two reasons. First, future health care costs are especially difficult to estimate, so the value of the resulting APBO (the present value of the future benefits) is fraught with error. Second, these benefits are provided at the discretion of the employer and can be altered or terminated at any time. Consequently, employers argue that without a legal obligation to pay these benefits, the liability should not be reported in the balance sheet. (For a more complete discussion of OPEB issues, see: https://www.pwc.com/us/en/corporate-governance/assets/pension-paper.pdf.)

These other post-employment benefits can produce large liabilities. For example, FedEx's footnotes report a funded status for the company's health care obligation of $(929) million in 2015, consisting of an APBO liability of $929 million with no funds set aside for payment of future benefits. Our analysis of cash flows related to pension obligations can be extended to other post-employment benefit obligations. For example, in addition to its pension payments, FedEx discloses that it is obligated to make health care payments to retirees totaling about $40 million per year. Because health care obligations are rarely funded until payment is required (federal minimum funding standards do not apply to OPEB and there is no tax benefit to pre-funding), there are no investment returns to fund the payments. Our analysis of projected cash flows must consider this potential cash outflow in addition to that relating to pension obligations.

<table>
<tr><td>Research Insight ■ Valuation of Nonpension Post-Employment Benefits</td></tr>
</table>

The FASB requires employers to accrue the costs of all nonpension post-employment benefits; known as *accumulated post-employment benefit obligation* (APBO). These benefits consist primarily of health care and insurance. This requirement is controversial due to concerns about the reliability of the liability estimate. Research finds that the APBO (alone) is associated with company value. However, when other pension-related variables are included in the research, the APBO liability is no longer useful in explaining company value. Research concludes that the pension-related variables do a better job at conveying value-relevant information than the APBO number alone, which implies that the APBO number is less reliable.

Review 10-2 LO2

Following is the pension disclosure footnote from American Airlines' 10-K report (in millions).

Pension Benefits	2015	2014
Reconciliation of benefit obligation		
Obligation at January 1	$17,594	$14,899
Service cost	2	3
Interest cost	737	746
Actuarial (gain) loss	(1,159)	2,573
Plan amendments	—	—
Settlements	(3)	(20)
Benefit payments	(776)	(607)
Other	—	—
Obligation at December 31	$16,395	$17,594
Reconciliation of fair value of plan assets		
Fair value of plan assets at January 1	$10,986	$10,057
Actual return on plan assets	(506)	746
Employer contributions	6	810
Settlements	(3)	(20)
Benefit payments	(776)	(607)
Other	—	—
Fair value of plan assets at December 31	$ 9,707	$10,986
Funded status at December 31	$ (6,688)	$ (6,608)

Following is American Airlines' footnote for its pension cost as reported in its income statement (in millions).

Pension Benefits	2015	2014
Defined benefit plans:		
Service cost	$ 2	$ 3
Interest cost	737	746
Expected return on assets	(851)	(786)
Settlements	1	4
Amortization of:		
Prior service cost	28	28
Unrecognized net loss	112	43
Net periodic benefit cost for defined benefit plans	29	38
Defined contribution plans	662	546
	$691	$584

Required

1. What factors impact American Airlines' pension benefit obligation during a period?
2. What factors impact American Airlines' pension plan assets during a period?
3. What amount is reported on the balance sheet relating to American Airlines defined benefit pension plan?
4. How does the expected return on plan assets affect pension expense?
5. How does American Airlines' expected return on plan assets compare with its actual return (in $s) for 2015?
6. How much net pension expense is reflected in American Airlines' 2015 income statement?

Solution on p. 10-65.   7. Assess American Airlines' ability to meet payment obligations to retirees.

Income Taxes

When preparing financial statements for stockholders and other external constituents, companies use GAAP. But when companies prepare their income tax returns, they prepare financial statements using the *Internal Revenue Code (IRC)*. These two different sets of accounting rules recognize revenues and expenses differently in many cases and, as a result, can yield markedly different levels of income. In general, companies desire to report lower income to taxing authorities than they do to their stockholders so that they can reduce their tax liability and increase after-tax cash flow. This practice is acceptable so long as the financial statements are prepared in conformity with GAAP and tax returns are filed in accordance with the IRC.

Timing Differences Create Deferred Tax Assets and Liabilities

As an example, consider the depreciation of long-term assets. For financial reports, companies typically depreciate long-term assets using straight-line depreciation (meaning the same amount of depreciation expense is reported each year over the useful life of the asset). However, for tax returns, companies use an *accelerated* method of depreciation (meaning more depreciation is taken in the early years of the asset's life and less depreciation in later years). When a company depreciates assets at an accelerated rate for tax purposes, the depreciation deduction for tax purposes is higher and taxable income is lower in the early years of the assets' lives. As a result, taxable income and tax payments are reduced and after-tax cash flow is increased. That excess cash can then be reinvested in the business to increase its returns to stockholders.

To illustrate, assume that Southwest Airlines purchases an asset with a five-year life. It depreciates that asset using the straight-line method (equal expense per year) when reporting to stockholders and depreciates the asset at a faster rate (accelerated depreciation) for tax purposes. Annual (full year) depreciation expense under these two methods is depicted in Exhibit 10.5.

During the first 2.5 years in this example, depreciation is higher in the company's tax returns than it is in its GAAP financial statements. In the last 2.5 years, this is reversed, with lower depreciation expense for tax purposes. Taxable income and tax payments are, therefore, higher during the last 2.5 years. The same total amount of depreciation is recognized under both methods over the five-year life of the asset. Only the timing of the recognition of the expense differs.[10]

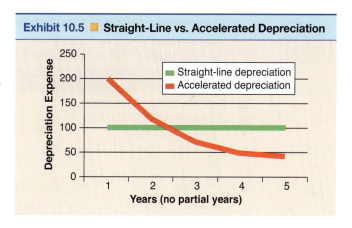

Illustration of Deferred Tax Liabilities We use this timing concept to illustrate the accounting for a **deferred tax liability**. Assume that a company purchases a depreciable asset with a cost of $100 and a two-year useful life. For financial reporting purposes (for GAAP-based reports), it depreciates the asset using the straight-line method, which

yields depreciation expense of $50 per year. For tax reporting (when filing income tax returns), it depreciates the asset on an accelerated basis, which yields depreciation deduction of $75 in the first year and $25 in the second year (the same total amount of depreciation is reported under the two depreciation methods; only the amount of depreciation reported per year differs). Assume that this company reports income before depreciation and taxes of $200 and that its tax rate is 40%. Its income statements, for both financial reporting and tax reporting, for the asset's first year are in Exhibit 10.6A.

---

[10] The Modified Accelerated Cost Recovery System (MACRS) is the current method of accelerated asset depreciation required by the United States income tax code. Under MACRS, all assets are divided into classes that dictate the number of years over which an asset's cost is "recovered" and the percentage of the asset cost that can be depreciated per year is fixed by regulation. For a five-year asset, such as in our example, the MACRS depreciation percentages per year are 20%, 32%, 19.2%, 11.52%, 11.52%, and 5.76%. MACRS assumes that assets are acquired in the middle of the year, hence a half-year depreciation in Year 1 and a half-year depreciation in Year 6. The point after which straight-line depreciation exceeds MACRS depreciation is after about 2.5 years as assumed in the example.

Exhibit 10.6A ■ Year 1 Income Statements: Financial Reporting vs. Tax Reporting

Year 1	Financial Reporting	Tax Reporting
Income before depreciation.	$200	$200
Depreciation.	50	75
Income before tax	150	125
Income tax (40%).	60 [expense]	50 [cash paid]
Net income.	$ 90	$ 75

This company records income tax expense and a related deferred tax liability for the first year as reflected in the following financial statement effects template:

TE . . .60
DTL 10
Cash 50

TE
60
DTL
10
Cash
50

Year 1	Balance Sheet						Income Statement		
Transaction	Cash + Asset	Noncash = Assets	Liabil- ities	+ Contrib. Capital	+ Earned Capital		Rev- enues	− Expen- ses	= Net Income
Record tax expense: expense exceeds cash because of deferral of tax	−50 Cash		+10 = Deferred Tax Liability		−60 Retained Earnings			+60 − Tax = Expense	−60

The reduction in cash reflects the payment of taxes owed to the taxing authority. The increase in deferred tax liability represents an estimate of additional tax that will be payable in the second year (which is the tax liability deferred in the first year). This liability for a future tax payment arises because second-year depreciation expense for tax purposes will be only $25, resulting in taxes payable of $70, which is $10 more than the income tax expense the company reports in its income statement to shareholders in Year 2 as we illustrate in Exhibit 10.6B.

Exhibit 10.6B ■ Year 2 Income Statements: Financial Reporting vs. Tax Reporting

Year 2	Financial Reporting	Tax Reporting
Income before depreciation.	$200	$200
Depreciation.	50	25
Income before tax	150	175
Income tax (40%).	60 [expense]	70 [cash paid]
Net income.	$ 90	$105

At the end of Year 1, the company knows that this additional tax must be paid in Year 2 because the financial reporting and tax reporting depreciation schedules are set when the asset is placed in service. Given these known amounts, the company accrues the deferred tax liability in Year 1 in the same manner as it would accrue any estimated future liability, say for wages payable, by recognizing a liability and the related expense.

At the end of Year 2, the additional income tax is paid and the company's deferred tax liability is now satisfied. Financial statement effects related to the tax payment and expense in Year 2 are reflected in the following template:

TE . . .60
DTL . . .10
Cash 70

TE
60
DTL
10
Cash
70

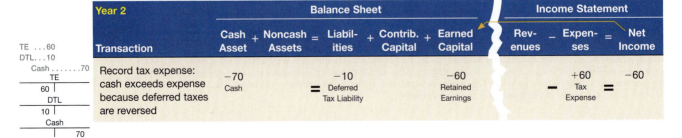

Year 2	Balance Sheet						Income Statement		
Transaction	Cash + Asset	Noncash = Assets	Liabil- ities	+ Contrib. Capital	+ Earned Capital		Rev- enues	− Expen- ses	= Net Income
Record tax expense: cash exceeds expense because deferred taxes are reversed	−70 Cash		−10 = Deferred Tax Liability		−60 Retained Earnings			+60 − Tax = Expense	−60

The income tax expense for financial reporting purposes is $60 each year. However, the cash payment for taxes is $70 in Year 2; the $10 excess reduces the deferred tax liability accrued in Year 1.

Illustration of Deferred Tax Assets Deferred tax assets arise when the tax payment is *greater* than the tax expense for financial reporting purposes (opposite of the illustration above).

For example, restructuring accruals give rise to deferred tax assets. In the year in which a company approves a reorganization plan, it will accrue a restructuring liability for estimated employee severance payments and other costs and it will write down assets to their market values (this reduces the net book value of those assets on the balance sheet). However, for tax purposes, restructuring costs are not deductible until paid in the future, and asset write-downs are not deductible until the loss is realized when the asset is sold. As a result, the restructuring accrual is not a liability for tax reporting until the company makes the payment, and the write-down of assets is not a deductible expense for tax purposes until the assets are sold. Both of these differences (the liability and the assets) give rise to a deferred tax asset. The deferred tax asset will be transferred to the income statement in the future as an expense when the company pays the restructuring costs and sells the impaired assets for a loss.

Another common deferred tax asset relates to **tax loss carryforwards**. Specifically, when a company reports a loss for tax purposes, it can carry back that loss for up to two years to recoup previous taxes paid. Any unused losses can be carried forward for up to twenty years to reduce future taxes. This creates a benefit (an "asset") for tax reporting for which there is no corresponding financial reporting asset. Thus, the company records a deferred tax asset but only if the company is "more likely than not" to be able to use the loss to reduce future taxes. This depends on the company's assessment of whether it will have sufficient profits in the future. (We return to this issue later in the module.)

Valuation Allowance for Deferred Tax Assets

Companies must establish a valuation allowance for deferred tax assets if the future realization of the tax benefits is uncertain. The allowance reduces reported assets, increases tax expense, which reduces equity. (This allowance is similar to accounting for the write-down of any asset.) Once the deferred tax asset valuation allowance is established, it can be reduced (reversed) by one of two events.

■ **The company writes off a deferred tax asset.** In this case, the asset is reduced to zero and the amount written off is subtracted from the deferred tax valuation allowance. There is no effect on income from this write off. (This is similar to the accounting for a write-off of an uncollectible account receivable against the allowance for uncollectible accounts which has no effect on income.) A typical example of a deferred tax asset write-off occurs when net operating loss carryforwards (NOLs) expire before they can be used to offset other profits.

■ **The company determines that the deferred tax assets will be realized.** If the company decides that the realization of the deferred tax assets is more than likely, it can reverse the deferred tax asset valuation allowance. In that case, the deferred tax asset valuation allowance is reduced and tax expense is reduced by the same amount, thus *increasing* net income.

American Airlines provides an example of the reversal of a deferred tax valuation allowance. In 2015, the company determined that its deferred tax assets would likely be realized and reversed the allowance it had previously set up, describing the action as follows in its 2015 10-K.

The Company provides a valuation allowance for its deferred tax assets, which includes the NOLs, when it is more likely than not that some portion, or all, of its deferred tax assets will not be realized. The ultimate realization of deferred tax assets is dependent upon the generation of future taxable income. The Company considers all available positive and negative evidence and makes certain assumptions in evaluating the realizability of its deferred tax assets. As of December 31, 2015, after considering all positive and negative evidence, including the completion of certain critical merger integration milestones as well as the Company's financial performance, the Company concluded that substantially all of its deferred income tax assets were more likely than not to be realized. Accordingly, the Company reversed the valuation allowance, which resulted in a special $3.0 billion non-cash tax benefit recorded in the consolidated statement of operations for 2015.

Following is an excerpt from American Airlines' 2015 income statement, beginning with income before tax.

Year Ended December 31 ($ millions)	2015	2014
Income (loss) before income taxes.	$4,668	$3,268
Income tax provision (benefit).	(3,452)	320
Net income (loss)	$8,120	$2,948

American's net income increased from $2,948 million in 2014 to $8,120 million in 2015, $3 billion of which was due to the reversal of its deferred tax valuation allowance. This change in the valuation allowance increased American Airlines' deferred tax assets, net income, and consequently, retained earnings.

Disclosures for Income Taxes

Excerpts from Southwest Airlines' tax footnote are shown in Exhibit 10.7. Southwest's $1,298 million tax expense reported in its income statement (called the provision) consists of the following two components.

1. **Current tax expense.** Current tax expense is determined from the company's tax returns; it is the amount payable (in cash) to tax authorities (some of these taxes have been paid during the year as the company makes installments).

2. **Deferred tax expense.** Deferred tax expense is the effect on tax expense from changes in deferred tax liabilities and deferred tax assets.

Exhibit 10.7 ■ Income Tax Expense Footnote for Southwest Airlines

$ millions	2015	2014	2013
Current:			
Federal	$1,292	$203	$355
State	114	29	44
Total current	1,406	232	399
Deferred:			
Federal	(97)	421	62
State	(11)	27	(6)
Total deferred	(108)	448	56
Provision for income taxes	$1,298	$680	$455

In financial statement footnotes, companies must disclose the components of deferred tax liabilities and assets. Southwest Airlines' deferred tax footnote (shown in Exhibit 10.8) reports total deferred tax assets of $2,001 million and total deferred tax liabilities of $4,491 million. Southwest's deferred tax liabilities relate to accelerated depreciation, as we illustrate at the start of this section. Its deferred tax assets primarily relate to the recognition of expenses in current income that will be paid in future years (and will become tax deductions then).

Exhibit 10.8 ■ Deferred Taxes Footnote for Southwest Airlines

$ millions	2015	2014
Deferred tax liabilities:		
Accelerated depreciation	$4,429	$4,277
Other	62	51
Total deferred tax liabilities	4,491	4,328
Deferred tax assets:		
Fuel derivative instruments	750	521
Capital and operating leases	81	125
Construction obligation	289	209
Accrued engine maintenance	74	83
Accrued employee benefits	541	334
State taxes	62	65
Business partner income	107	90
Other	97	119
Total deferred tax assets	2,001	1,546
Net deferred tax liability	$2,490	$2,782

Southwest Airlines' 2015 income before tax is $3,479 million. Its tax expense of $1,298 million represents an effective tax rate of 37.3%. The *effective tax rate* is defined as tax expense divided by pretax income ($1,298 million/$3,479 million = 37.3%). By comparison, the federal *statutory tax rate* for corporations (the rate prescribed in current tax regulations) is 35%. Companies must provide a schedule that reconciles the effective tax rate (37.3% for Southwest) with the federal statutory rate of 35%. Following is the schedule that Southwest Airlines reports in its 10-K.

$ millions	2015	2014	2013
Tax at statutory U.S. tax rates	$1,218	$636	$423
Nondeductible items	15	9	10
State income taxes, net of federal benefit	66	37	25
Other, net	(1)	(2)	(3)
Total income tax provision	$1,298	$680	$455

Southwest Airlines presents its tax reconciliation table in dollars. The "Tax at statutory U.S. tax rates" for 2015 of $1,218 million is the 35% U.S. corporate tax rate applied to pretax income of $3,479 million ($3,479 million × 35% = $1,218 million). Its tax expense (provision) is $1,298 million and the difference is due to $15 million of costs that Southwest paid that are not deductible for tax purposes, the state income taxes of $66 million, and the $1 million miscellaneous deduction.

Many companies present the tax reconciliation footnote in percentages. Intel provides an example.

Years Ended ($ millions)	Dec 26, 2015	Dec 27, 2014	Dec 28, 2013
Statutory federal income tax rate	35.0%	35.0%	35.0%
Increase (reduction) in rate resulting from:			
Non-U.S. income taxed at different rates	(7.9)	(6.1)	(5.8)
Settlements, effective settlements, and related remeasurements	(2.9)	—	—
Domestic manufacturing deduction benefit	(2.0)	(2.1)	(2.1)
Research and development tax credits	(1.7)	(1.7)	(3.5)
Other	(0.9)	0.8	0.1
Effective tax rate	19.6%	25.9%	23.7%

Intel's 2015 effective tax rate was a fairly low 19.6% because the income Intel earned outside of the U.S. was taxed at lower rates. This reduced Intel's tax bill by nearly 8 percentage points

The effective tax rate reconciliation table not only provides insight into the company's effective tax rate, it also provides valuable information about transitory items that have affected income taxes and, therefore, net income. In 2015, for example, Intel settled tax disputes that reduced its tax liability by 2.9 percentage points. A tax reduction like that is not likely to recur in the foreseeable future. Accordingly, we might not want to use the 2015 tax rate of 19.6% to forecast future tax rates. Over the past two years, Intel's tax rate has been in the range of 24% to 26%.

Analysis of Income Tax Disclosures

Analysis of deferred taxes can yield useful insights. Some revenue accruals (such as accounts receivable for longer-term contracts) increase deferred tax liabilities as GAAP income exceeds tax income (similar to the effect of using straight-line depreciation for financial reporting purposes and accelerated depreciation for tax returns).

An increase in deferred tax liabilities indicates that a company is reporting higher GAAP income relative to taxable income and can indicate the company is managing earnings upwards. Although an increase in deferred tax liabilities can legitimately result, for example, from an increase in depreciable assets and the use of accelerated depreciation for tax purposes, we must be aware of the possibility that the company might be improperly reporting revenues.

The income tax footnote also reveals any changes in the deferred tax asset valuation account. A decrease in the valuation allowance is often triggered by the write-off of deferred tax assets, typically relating to net operating loss carryforwards (NOLs). These carryforwards allow companies to offset current losses against future income, for up to 20 years (they cannot be used to offset profits across subsidiary companies). If the company does not report sufficient taxable profit within the 20-year period, the NOLs expire unused and the related deferred tax asset must be taken off the balance sheet and charged to the valuation allowance.

As we illustrate with American Airlines above, however, companies can (and do) change their estimate on the recoverability of deferred tax assets. When they do, the valuation allowance is reduced, thereby increasing deferred tax assets and increasing net income dollar-for-dollar by a reduction of income tax expense. The income tax footnote will reveal any such changes in the deferred tax valuation allowance and also the impact on net income.

The reconciliation of statutory and effective tax rates can reveal important transitory items that might impact our forecast of future tax rates. Income tax expense is a large expense item for most companies and the rate we use in our forecasts can greatly affect our expectations of future net income.

Analysis Insight ▉ Deferred Tax Asset Valuation Allowance and Future Earnings

When companies report taxable losses, they are allowed to carryback the loss to offset prior years' taxable income and to carry forward any unused carryback to offset future taxable income, thus reducing future tax liability. This tax loss carryforward creates a deferred tax asset that is only reported on the balance sheet if it is more likely than not that the benefit will be realized. If not, management must establish a valuation allowance to write down the deferred tax asset as explained in this module. Researchers have examined if the establishment of this valuation allowance conveys information about the future profitability of the company. Using a sample of 20,000 annual reports of companies reporting losses, the researchers found that the failure to establish a valuation allowance in the presence of losses is a credible predictor of positive future earnings for up to three years into the future. Further, for publicly traded companies with low analyst coverage, investors do not appear to recognize this valuation-relevant information, suggesting the possibility of a trading strategy to purchase stock in companies reporting losses and having no substantial additions to the valuation allowance account. Time will tell if this trading strategy bears fruit, but the lesson is clear: understanding the income tax footnote is crucial to a thorough analysis of financial statements. Source: Dhaliwal, Dan, Steve Kaplan, Rick Laux, and Eric Weisbrod (2013), "The Information Content of Tax Expense for Firms Reporting Losses," *Journal of Accounting Research*, 51:1, p. 135-164.

Analysis Insight ■ Tax Avoidance: Where in the World is Cash?

Many companies are under scrutiny as governments across the globe seek greater tax revenues. At issue are tax strategies that allow companies to report considerable income to shareholders, but considerably less to the taxing authorities. This is nothing new. Companies have been using tax avoidance strategies for decades. While these strategies comply with tax laws, governments argue that they stretch ethical boundaries. How do these schemes work? One strategy is to establish a subsidiary in a country with lenient tax laws. The Cayman Islands is one such country, as is Ireland. Tax laws define residency (and, thus, the obligation to pay taxes) by considering the management and control of a corporation rather than by where it was formed or incorporated. For Ireland, if the company is not managed and controlled in Ireland, it is not a legal resident of Ireland and, thus, does not pay taxes. Moreover, if the company is not incorporated in the United States, it is not a U.S. tax resident and does not pay taxes there either. To illustrate, assume a foreign company owns the intellectual property (IP) rights (such as software) for an important product sold by a U.S. company. Since most of the value of the product is typically in its IP, the IP owner can charge a large fee to license the IP (to the U.S. company). When the U.S. company sells the product, most of the profit goes to the foreign company by way of the licensing fees. If the foreign company is not a tax resident of any country, most of the profit on the sale is not taxable: the country where the foreign company resides does not use residency for tax purposes and the U.S. only taxes money that is repatriated back to the United States. As long as the cash remains on the foreign company's balance sheet, it is not taxable in the United States. In 2015, for example, Microsoft reported that $94.4 billion of its $96.5 billion reported for cash and cash equivalents was held by its foreign subsidiaries. Companies have long used such strategies to move profits into low (or no) tax countries, fueling ongoing battles with taxing authorities and cries of foul from other taxpayers.

LO3 Review 10-3

Refer to the following information from footnotes to **FedEx**'s 2015 Form 10-K.

The components of the provision for income taxes for the years ended May 31 were as follows ($ millions):

	2015	2014	2013
Current provision (benefit)			
Domestic			
Federal	$ 795	$ 624	$ 512
State and local	102	56	86
Foreign	214	194	170
	1,111	874	768
Deferred provision (benefit)			
Domestic			
Federal	(474)	360	802
State and local	(47)	82	93
Foreign	(13)	18	(41)
	(534)	460	854
Provision for income taxes	$ 577	$1,334	$1,622

A reconciliation of total income tax expense (benefit) and the amount computed by applying the statutory federal income tax rate (35%) to income before taxes for the years ended May 31 is as follows (in millions):

	2015	2014	2013
Taxes computed at federal statutory rate	$569	$1,280	$1,518
Increases (decreases) in income tax from			
State and local income taxes, net of federal benefit	36	90	117
Foreign operations	(43)	(38)	(21)
Other, net	15	2	8
	$577	$1,334	$1,622
Effective Tax Rate	35.5%	36.5%	37.4%

continued

Required
1. What is the total income tax expense that FedEx reports in its 2015 income statement?
2. What amount of its total tax expense did (or will) FedEx pay in cash (that is, what amount is currently payable)?
3. Explain how FedEx calculates its income tax expense.

Solution on p. 10-65.   4. What was the effective tax rate for FedEx for 2015? How does it compare to the 35% federal statutory rate?

Global Accounting

IFRS

We discussed three forms of off-balance-sheet financing. Moreover, there are several differences between U.S. GAAP and IFRS on these items, which we highlight below.

Leases IFRS lease standards currently allow for operating leases, but the standards are such that it is very difficult for a lease agreement to qualify as an operating lease. With the new GAAP standard for leases, which will become effective in 2018, there will be few substantive differences between U.S. GAAP and IFRS for leases. Until then, a complete analysis of lease obligations must include a "pro forma" capitalization of operating leases, to the extent that they are material.

Pensions For pension accounting, there are several disclosure differences and one notable accounting difference. The accounting difference pertains to actuarial gains and losses. As discussed in Appendix 10C, U.S. GAAP permits deferral of actuarial gains and losses and then amortizes them to net income over time. A notable difference is that IFRS companies can recognize all actuarial gains and losses in comprehensive income in the year they occur. These gains and losses are not deferred, and they are *never* reported on the IFRS income statement. Many IFRS companies select this option. Turning to disclosure, one difference is that pension expense is not reported as a single item under IFRS; various components can be aggregated with other expenses. For example, interest cost can be included with other interest expenses and reported as finance expense under IFRS. A second disclosure difference is that IFRS companies do not disclose the full funded status of their pension plan on the balance sheet as U.S. GAAP requires. However, they must do so in the footnotes.

Income Taxes The two accounting standards are largely the same when it comes to accounting for deferred taxes. There are two differences of note.

- Under GAAP, deferred tax assets are recognized in full, and then reduced by a valuation allowance if it is considered more likely than not that some portion of the deferred taxes will not be realized. With IFRS, deferred tax assets are recognized net, that is, if it is more likely than not that future taxable profits will be high enough for the company to use the deferred tax assets. The end result is the same but without the initial recognition of a valuation allowance and any subsequent reversal.

- Presentation differs slightly. Under GAAP, deferred taxes are classified in the same way as the underlying asset or liability (as either current or noncurrent). If there is no underlying asset or liability, deferred taxes are classified based on the anticipated reversal periods. Deferred tax assets and liabilities within an individual tax jurisdiction *may be* offset and then classified as a single amount (either current or non-current). Under IFRS, deferred taxes within an individual tax jurisdiction *must be* presented as non-current on the balance sheet. Footnotes can disclose current versus non-current portion.

Appendix 10A: Lease Capitalization Using a Calculator and Present Value Tables

eLectures **LO4**

MBC Use a calculator and present value tables for lease calculations (Appendix 10A).

This Appendix explains how to compute both the present value of projected operating lease payments and the imputed discount rate using financial calculators and the present value of projected lease payments using present value tables.

Lease Capitalization Using Financial Calculator
We demonstrate keystrokes to compute the present value of the Southwest Airlines projected lease payments for two popular financial calculators: Hewlett-Packard 10bII and Texas Instruments BA II Plus.

Hewlett-Packard 10bII: Present value of projected operating lease payments

Enter #	Key[a]	
1	**P/YR**	Enter the number of periods per year
0	**CF$_j$**	Enter the cash flow in year 0 (current year)
557	**CF$_j$**	Enter the cash flow in year 1
545	**CF$_j$**	Enter the cash flow in year 2
474	**CF$_j$**	Enter the cash flow in year 3
407	**CF$_j$**	Enter the cash flow in year 4
307	**CF$_j$**	Enter the cash flow in year 5 (and assumed thereafter)
5	**N$_j$**	Enter the number of years the year 5 cash flow is paid (including year 5)
301	**CF$_j$**	Enter the cash flow in final partial year [$1,529 − ($307 × 4)]
3.94	**I/YR**	Enter the annual discount rate
	NPV	Press **NPV** button to get present value ($3,188)

[a] To enter a number, type the number and then press the corresponding key; for example, to enter P/YR, type "1" and then press **P/YR**.

Hewlett-Packard 10bII: Imputed discount rate

Enter #	Key	
1	**P/YR**	Enter the number of periods per year
−356[a]	**CF$_j$**	Enter the present value of the capital leases disclosed in the footnote
46	**CF$_j$**	Enter the cash flow in year 1
46	**CF$_j$**	Enter the cash flow in year 2
45	**CF$_j$**	Enter the cash flow in year 3
45	**CF$_j$**	Enter the cash flow in year 4
44	**CF$_j$**	Enter the cash flow in year 5
5	**N$_j$**	Enter the number of years the year 5 cash flow is paid (including year 5)
33	**CF$_j$**	Enter the cash flow in final partial year [$209 − ($44 × 4)]
	IRR	Press **IRR** button to get implicit discount rate (3.940%)

[a] To enter a negative number, type in the absolute value of that number and then press +/− button; for example, to enter the initial cash flow in year 0, enter "356", press +/−, and then press **CF$_j$**.

Texas Instruments BA II Plus: Present value of projected operating lease payments

Key	Enter #[a]	
FORMAT	0	Press the **FORMAT** button and enter decimal places desired
CF	0	Enter the cash flow in year 0 (**CF$_0$**)
↓	557	Enter the cash flow in year 1 (**CO1**)
↓		Frequency (**FO1**) should be pre-set at "1", so nothing need be entered
↓	545	Enter the cash flow in year 2 (**CO2**)
↓		Frequency (**FO2**) should be pre-set at "1"
↓	474	Enter the cash flow in year 3 (**CO3**)
↓		Frequency (**FO3**) should be pre-set at "1"
↓	407	Enter the cash flow in year 4 (**CO4**)
↓		Frequency (**FO4**) should be pre-set at "1"
↓	307	Enter the cash flow in year 5 (**CO5**) and assumed thereafter
↓	5	Enter the number of years the year 5 cash flow is paid (including year 5) (**FO5**)
↓	301	Enter the cash flow in final partial year [$1,529 − ($307 × 4)] (**CO6**)
↓		Frequency (**FO6**) should be pre-set at "1"
NPV	3.94	Press **NPV** button, the pre-set discount rate should say "0"; enter "3.94" the discount rate
↓, CPT	3,188	Press ↓ button and then press **CPT** to get present value

[a] After entering in a number from this column, press **ENTER**.

Texas Instruments BA II Plus: Imputed discount rate

Key	Enter [a]	
FORMAT	0	Press the **FORMAT** button and enter decimal places desired
CF	−356[b]	Enter the cash flow in year 0 (**CF₀**)
↓	46	Enter the cash flow in year 1 (**CO1**)
↓		Frequency (**FO1**) should be pre-set at "1"
↓	46	Enter the cash flow in year 2 (**CO2**)
↓		Frequency (**FO2**) should be pre-set at "1"
↓	45	Enter the cash flow in year 3 (**CO3**)
↓		Frequency (**FO3**) should be pre-set at "1"
↓	45	Enter the cash flow in year 4 (**CO4**)
↓		Frequency (**FO4**) should be pre-set at "1"
↓	44	Enter the cash flow in year 5 and assumed thereafter (**CO5**)
↓	5	Enter the number of years the year 5 cash flow is paid (including year 5) (**FO5**)
	301	Enter cash flow in final partial year [$1,529 − ($307 × 4)] (**CO6**)
IRR		Press **IRR** button, the pre-set IRR should say "0"
↓, CPT		Press ↓ button and then press **CPT** to get implicit discount rate

[a] After typing in a number from this column, press **ENTER**.

[b] To enter a negative number, type in the absolute value of that number and then press **+/−** button; for example, to enter the initial cash flow in year 0, press **CF**, enter "356", press **+/−**, and then press **ENTER**.

Lease Capitalization Using Present Value Tables

Present value tables list the factors for selected interest rates and discount periods (often in whole numbers). To compute the present value of the operating lease payments using those tables (see Appendix A near the end of this book), we must first round the remaining lease term (4.98 for Southwest Airlines) to the nearest whole year (5), and round the discount rate (3.94% for Southwest Airlines) to its nearest whole interest rate (4%). After that, computation of the present value of future operating lease payments is identical to the spreadsheet method and is shown below. We see that the present value of each projected lease payment for Years 1 through 5 is computed using the present value factor for that particular year (taken from tables similar to Appendix A, Table 1, "Present Value of Single Amount") using a discount rate of 4%. To compute the present value of the lease payments remaining after Year 5, we again assume that lease payments continue at the Year 5 amount for the remainder of the lease term. Those payments represent an annuity, $307 for 5 years (4.98 rounded to 5), that is discounted at 4% (taken from tables similar to Appendix A, Table 2, "Present Value of Ordinary Annuity"), which is then discounted back five more years to the present.

Year ($ millions)	Operating Lease Payment	Discount Factor ($i = 0.04$)	Present Value
1	$ 557	0.96154	$ 536
2	545	0.92456	504
3	474	0.88900	421
4	407	0.85480	348
5	307	0.82193	252
>5	1,529 [$307 for 4.98 years]	4.45182 × 0.82193	1,123
			$3,184

Remaining life. . . . . . . $1,529 [$307 for 4.98 years, rounded to 5 years].

Regardless of the method used, the computed amount is the present value of future operating lease payments. That value is $3,188 million using the spreadsheet method, $3,188 million using a calculator, and $3,184 million using present value tables.

Appendix 10B: Amortization Component of Pension Expense

eLectures **LO5**
MBC Examine pension expense in more detail (Appendix 10B).

One of the more difficult aspects of pension accounting relates to the issue of what is recognized on-balance-sheet and what is disclosed in the footnotes off-balance-sheet. This is an important distinction, and the FASB is moving toward more on-balance-sheet recognition and less off-balance-sheet disclosure. The FASB is considering whether to eliminate deferred gains and losses, and to require recognition in the income statement of *all* changes to pension assets and liabilities. (A number of companies have already voluntarily adopted such an approach.)

Until this standard is enacted, **unrecognized gains and losses will only impact reported pension expense via their amortization** (the fourth component of pension expense described earlier in this module).

Sources of Unrecognized Pension Gains and Losses There are three sources of *unrecognized gains and losses*.

1. The difference between actual and expected return on pension investments.
2. Changes in actuarial assumptions such as expected wage inflation, termination and mortality rates, and the discount rate used to compute the present value of the projected benefit obligation.
3. Amendments to the pension plan to provide employees with additional benefits (called **prior service costs**).

Accounting for Unrecognized Pension Gains and Losses Accounting for gains and losses resulting from these three sources is the same; specifically:

- Balance sheets report the net pension asset (overfunded status) or liability (underfunded status) irrespective of the magnitude of deferred gains and losses; that is, based solely on the relative balances of the pension assets and PBO accounts.

- Cumulative unrecognized gains and losses from all sources are recorded in one account, called deferred gains and losses, which is only disclosed in the footnotes, not on-balance-sheet.

- When the balance in the deferred gains and losses account exceeds prescribed levels, companies transfer a portion of the deferred gain or loss onto the balance sheet, with a matching expense on the income statement. This is the amortization process described in the text.

Financial Statement Effects from Unrecognized Pension Gains and Losses Recall that a company reports the *estimated* return on pension investments as a component (reduction) of pension expense. The pension assets, however, increase (decrease) by the *actual* return (loss). The difference between the two returns is referred to as a deferred (unrecognized) gain or loss. To illustrate, assume that the pension plan is underfunded at the beginning of the year by $200, with pension assets of $800, a PBO of $1,000, and no deferred gains or losses. Now, assume that actual returns for the year of $100 exceed the expected return of $70. We can illustrate the accounting for the deferred gain as follows.

Year 1	On Financial Statements				Footnotes	
	Funded Status (Liability)	Retained Earnings	Accumulated Other Comprehensive Income (AOCI)	Income Statement	Pension Assets	PBO
Balance, Jan. 1....	$200		$ 0	$ 0	$800	$1,000
Return..........	(100)	$70	30	70	100	
Balance, Dec. 31 ..	$100	$70	$30	$70	$900	$1,000

The balance sheet at the beginning of the year reports the funded status of the pension plan as a $200 liability, reflecting the underfunded status of the pension plan. Neither the $800 pension asset account, nor the $1,000 PBO appear on-balance-sheet. Instead, their balances are only disclosed in a pension footnote.

During the year, pension assets (off-balance-sheet) increase by the actual return of $100 with no change in the PBO, thus decreasing the pension liability (negative funded status) by $100. The pension expense on the income statement, however, only reflects the expected return of $70, and retained earnings increase by that amount. The remaining $30 is recognized in accumulated other comprehensive income (AOCI), a component of equity on the balance sheet.

These deferred gains and losses do not affect reported profit until they exceed prescribed limits, after which the excess is gradually recognized in income.[11] For example, assume that in the following year, $5 of the $30 deferred gain is amortized (recognized on the income statement as expense, which flows to retained earnings on the balance sheet). This amortization would result in the following effects.

---

[11] The upper (lower) bound on the deferred gains (losses) account is 10% of the PBO or Plan Asset account balance, whichever is greater, at the beginning of the year. Once this limit is exceeded, the excess is amortized until the account balance is below that threshold, irrespective of whether such reduction results from amortization, or changes in the PBO or Pension Asset accounts (from changes in actuarial assumptions, company contributions, or positive investment returns).

Year 2	On Financial Statements				Footnotes	
	Funded Status (Liability)	Retained Earnings	Accumulated Other Comprehensive Income (AOCI)	Income Statement	Pension Assets	PBO
Balance, Jan. 1....	$100	$70	$30	$ 0	$900	$1,000
Amortization......		5	(5)	5		
Balance, Dec. 31 ..	$100	$75	$25	$ 5	$900	$1,000

The deferred gain is reduced by $5 and is now recognized in reported income as a reduction of pension expense. (This amortization is the fourth item in the Net Pension Expense computation table from earlier in this module.) This is the only change, as the pension assets still report a balance of $900 and the PBO reports a balance of $1,000, for a funded status of $(100) that is reported as a liability on the balance sheet.

PBO Assumptions and Unrecognized Pension Gains and Losses In addition to the difference between actual and expected gains (losses) on pension assets, the deferred gains (losses) account includes increases or decreases in the PBO balance that result from changes in assumptions used to compute it, namely, the expected rate of wage inflation, termination and mortality rates for employees, and changes in the discount rate used to compute the present value of the pension obligations. Some of these can be offsetting, and all accumulate in the same deferred gains (losses) account. Justification for off-balance-sheet treatment of these items was the expectation that their offsetting nature would combine to keep the magnitude of deferred gains (losses) small. It is only in relatively extreme circumstances that this account becomes large enough to warrant amortization and, consequently, on-balance-sheet recognition. Further, the amortization portion of reported pension expense is usually small.

Appendix 10C: Expanded Explanation of Deferred Taxes

eLectures **LO6**
MBC Examine deferred tax disclosures in more detail (Appendix 10C).

The module provided an example of how different depreciation methods for tax and financial reporting create a deferred tax liability. That example showed that total depreciation over the life of the asset is the same under both tax and financial reporting, and that the only difference is the timing of the expense or tax deduction. Because depreciation differs each year, the amount at which the equipment is reported will differ as well for book and tax purposes (cost less accumulated depreciation is called *net book value* for financial reporting purposes and *tax basis* for tax purposes). These book vs. tax differences are eliminated at the end of the asset's useful life.

Expanded Example of a Deferred Tax Liability: PPE To understand this concept more completely, we modify the example from the module to include a third year. Assume that the company purchases PPE assets at the start of Year 1 for $120. For financial reporting purposes, the company uses straight-line depreciation and records depreciation of $40 each year (with zero salvage). For tax purposes, assume that the company takes tax depreciation deductions of $60, $50, and $10. Exhibit 10C.1 reports the annual depreciation along with the asset's net book value and its tax basis, for each year-end.

Exhibit 10C.1 ■ Book and Tax Depreciation and Carrying Value					
	Financial Reporting (Net Book Value)	Tax Reporting (Tax Basis)	Book vs. Tax Difference	Deferred Tax Liability (Book vs. Tax Difference × Tax Rate)	Deferred Tax Expense (Increase or Decrease in Deferred Tax Liability)
At purchase: PPE carrying value	$120	$120	$ 0	$ 0	
Year 1: Depreciation...............	(40)	(60)			
End of Year 1: PPE carrying value ...	80	60	$20 ($80 − $60)	$ 8 ($20 × 40%)	$ 8 ($8 − $0)
Year 2: Depreciation...............	(40)	(50)			
End of Year 2: PPE carrying value ...	40	10	$30 ($40 − $10)	$12 ($30 × 40%)	$ 4 ($12 − $8)
Year 3: Depreciation...............	(40)	(10)			
End of Year 3: PPE carrying value ...	0	0	$ 0 ($0 − $0)	$ 0	$(12) ($0 − $12)

The third column in Exhibit 10C.1 shows the "book-tax" difference, which is the difference between GAAP net book value and the tax basis at the end of each year. The fourth column shows the deferred tax liability at the end of each period, computed as the book-tax difference times the tax rate. We see from the fourth column that when the financial reporting net book value is greater than the tax basis, the company has a deferred tax liability on its balance sheet (as in Years 1 and 2). Companies' footnotes provide information about deferred taxes. For example, **Southwest Airlines'** footnote reports a deferred tax liability of $4,429 million for its accelerated depreciation on its property, plant and equipment, which indicates the tax basis for PPE is less than GAAP net book value, on average, for Southwest's PPE.

Accounting standards require a company to first compute the taxes it owes (per its tax return), then to compute any changes in deferred tax liabilities and assets, and finally to compute tax expense reported in the income statement (as a residual amount). Thus, tax expense is not computed as pretax income multiplied by the company's tax rate as we might initially expect. Instead, tax expense is computed as follows.

Tax Expense = Taxes Paid − Increase (or + Decrease) in Deferred Tax Assets + Increase (or − Decrease) in Deferred Liabilities

The far-right column in Exhibit 10C.1 shows the deferred tax expense per year, which is the amount added to, or subtracted from, taxes paid, to arrive at tax expense. If we assume this company had $100 of pre-depreciation income, its taxable income and tax expense (assuming a 40% rate) follows.

	Taxes Paid	Deferred Tax Expense	Total Tax Expense
Year 1	$16 ($100 − $60) × 40%	$ 8	$24
Year 2	$20 ($100 − $50) × 40%	$ 4	$24
Year 3	$36 ($100 − $10) × 40%	$(12)	$24

In this example, the timing difference between the financial reporting and tax reporting derives from PPE and creates a deferred tax liability. Other differences between the two sets of books create other types of deferred tax accounts.

Rules for Deferred Tax Assets and Liabilities from Timing Differences between GAAP and Tax

Exhibit 10C.2 shows the relation between the financial reporting and tax reporting net book values, and the resulting deferred taxes (liability or asset) on the balance sheet.

Exhibit 10C.2 ■ Sources of Deferred Tax Assets and Liabilities

For Assets...

Financial reporting net book value > Tax reporting net book value	→	Deferred tax liability on balance sheet
Financial reporting net book value < Tax reporting net book value	→	Deferred tax asset on balance sheet

For Liabilities...

Financial reporting net book value < Tax reporting net book value	→	Deferred tax liability on balance sheet
Financial reporting net book value > Tax reporting net book value	→	Deferred tax asset on balance sheet

Expanded Example of a Deferred Tax Asset: Restructuring Costs A common deferred tax asset relates to accrued restructuring costs (a liability for financial reporting purposes). Restructuring costs are not deductible for tax purposes until paid in the future and, thus, there is no accrual restructuring liability for tax reporting, which means it has a tax basis of $0. To explain how this timing difference affects tax expense, assume that a company accrues $300 of restructuring costs in Year 1 and settles the liability in Year 2 as follows.

	Financial Reporting (Net Book Value)	Tax Reporting (Tax Basis)	Book vs. Tax Difference	Deferred Tax Asset (Book vs. Tax Difference × Tax Rate)	Deferred Tax Expense (Change in Deferred Tax Asset)
Year 1: Accrue restructuring costs . . .	$(300)	$ 0			
End of Year 1: Liability book value . . .	$ 300	$ 0	$300 ($300 − $0)	$120 ($300 × 40%)	$(120) ($120 − $0)
Year 2: Pay restructuring costs		$(300)			
End of Year 2: Liability book value . . .	$ 0	0	$ 0 ($0 − $0)	$ 0 ($0 × 40%)	$120 ($120 − $0)

Timing differences created by the restructuring liability yield a deferred tax asset in Year 1. Timing differences disappear in Year 2 when the company pays cash for restructuring costs. To see how tax expense is determined, assume that this company has $500 of pre-restructuring income each year; computations follow.

	Taxes Paid	Deferred Tax Expense	Total Tax Expense
Year 1	$200 ($500 − $0) × 40%	$(120)	$ 80
Year 2	$ 80 ($500 − $300) × 40%	$ 120	$200

Deferred tax accounts derive from timing differences between GAAP expenses and tax deductions. This creates differences between the net book value and the tax basis for many assets and liabilities. Southwest Airlines' deferred tax footnote (see Exhibit 10.8) reports several deferred tax assets and liabilities that explain its book-tax difference and the tax basis. As we saw above, Southwest's 2015 deferred tax liability associated with PPE is $4,429 million. This reflects the cumulative tax savings to Southwest from accelerated depreciation for its PPE.

Guidance Answers

You Are the Division President

Pg. 10-6 Lease terms that are not advantageous to your company but are structured merely to achieve off-balance-sheet financing can destroy shareholder value. Long-term shareholder value is created by managing your operation well, including negotiating leases with acceptable terms. Lease footnote disclosures also provide sufficient information for skilled analysts to undo the operating lease treatment. This means that you can end up with de facto capitalization of a lease with lease terms that are not in the best interests of your company and with few benefits from off-balance-sheet financing. There is also the potential for lost credibility with stakeholders.

Superscript $^{A\,(B,\,C)}$ denotes assignments based on Appendix 10A (B, C).

Questions

Q10-1. Under current accounting rules, what are the financial reporting differences between an operating lease and a capital lease? How will this change with the new accounting rules effective in 2019?

Q10-2. Are current footnote disclosures sufficient to overcome nonrecognition on the balance sheet of assets and related liabilities for operating leases? Explain.

Q10-3. Is the expense of a lease over its entire life the same whether or not it is capitalized? Explain.

Q10-4. What are the economic and accounting differences between a defined contribution plan and a defined benefit plan?

Q10-5. Under what circumstances will a company report a net pension asset? A net pension liability?

Q10-6. What are the components of pension expense that are reported in the income statement?

Q10-7. What effect does the use of expected returns on pension investments and the deferral of unexpected gains and losses on those investments have on income?

Q10-8. What are the two components of income tax expense?

Q10-9. Why do deferred taxes arise?

Q10-10. Under what circumstances will deferred taxes likely result in a cash outflow?

Q10-11. What is a valuation allowance for deferred tax assets? Provide two reasons why the valuation allowance would be reversed.

Q10-12.[A] In general, what effect does deferring and later amortizing deferred gains and losses have on a company's income statement?

Q10-13.[C] How do companies compute income tax expense for financial reporting purposes?

Assignments with the ⊙ logo in the margin are available in BusinessCourse.
See the Preface of the book for details.

M10-14. Analyzing and Interpreting Lease Footnote Disclosures

LO1

The GAP Inc. (GPS)

The GAP Inc. discloses the following schedule to its fiscal 2015 (ended January 30, 2016) 10-K report relating to its leasing activities.

The aggregate minimum noncancelable annual lease payments under leases in effect on January 30, 2016, are as follows:

Fiscal Year ($ millions)	
2016	$1,135
2017	1,098
2018	946
2019	821
2020	682
Thereafter	2,118
Total minimum lease commitments	$6,800

a. Compute the present value of GAP's operating leases using a 6% discount rate and round the remaining lease term to the nearest whole year.

b. What types of adjustments might we consider to GAP's balance sheet and income statement for analysis purposes?

M10-15. Analyzing and Capitalizing Operating Lease Payments Disclosed in Footnotes

LO1

Costco Wholesale Corpation (COST)

Costco Wholesale Corporation discloses the following in footnotes to its 10-K report relating to its leasing activities.

At the end of 2016, future minimum payments . . . under noncancelable leases with terms of at least one year were as follows ($ millions):

2017	$ 200
2018	195
2019	184
2020	171
2021	166
Thereafter	2,204
Total	$3,120

Operating leases are not reflected on-balance-sheet. In our analysis of a company, we often capitalize these operating leases, that is, add the present value of the future operating lease payments to both the reported assets and liabilities.

a. Compute the present value of Costco's operating lease payments assuming a 6% discount rate and round the remaining lease term to the nearest whole year.

b. What effect does capitalization of operating leases have on Costco's total liabilities and total assets (it reported total liabilities and total assets of $20,831 million and $33,163 million, respectively)?

LO2

Stanley Black & Decker Inc. (SWK)

M10-16. Analyzing and Interpreting Pension Disclosures—Expenses and Returns

Stanley Black & Decker Inc. discloses the following pension footnote in its 10-K report.

$ millions	2015		
	U.S. Plans	Non-U.S. Plans	Total
Service cost	$ 7.0	$14.4	$ 21.4
Interest cost	54.0	46.8	100.8
Expected return on plan assets	(74.9)	(56.5)	(131.4)
Prior service cost amortization.	1.8	0.9	2.7
Actuarial loss amortization	7.2	7.5	14.7
Settlement/curtailment loss	—	1.5	1.5
Net periodic pension (benefit) expense. . .	$ (4.9)	$14.6	$ 9.7

a. How much pension expense does Stanley Black & Decker report in its 2015 income statement?

b. Explain, in general, how expected return on plan assets affects reported pension expense. How did expected return affect Stanley Black & Decker's 2015 pension expense?

c. Explain use of the word "expected" as it relates to pension plan assets.

LO2

YUM! Brands Inc. (YUM)

M10-17. Analyzing and Interpreting Pension Disclosures—PBO and Funded Status

YUM! Brands Inc. discloses the following pension footnote in its 10-K report.

Pension Benefit Obligation ($ millions)	2015
Change in benefit obligation	
Benefit obligation at beginning of year.	$1,301
Service cost	18
Interest cost	55
Plan amendments.	28
Curtailments	(2)
Special termination benefits	1
Benefits paid.	(50)
Settlements.	(16)
Actuarial (gain) loss.	(196)
Administrative expense.	(5)
Benefit obligation at end of year	$1,134

a. Explain the terms "service cost" and "interest cost."

b. How do actuarial losses arise?

c. The fair value of YUM!'s pension assets is $1,004 million as of 2015. What is the funded status of the plan, and how will this be reflected on YUM!'s balance sheet?

LO2

YUM! Brands Inc. (YUM)

M10-18. Analyzing and Interpreting Pension Disclosures—Plan Assets and Cash Flow

YUM! Brands Inc. discloses the following pension footnote in its 10-K report.

Pension Plan Assets ($ millions)	2015
Fair value of plan assets at beginning of year	$991
Actual return on plan assets.	(10)
Employer contributions.	94
Settlement payments	(16)
Benefits paid.	(50)
Administrative expenses.	(5)
Fair value of plan assets at end of year	$1,004

a. How does the "actual return on plan assets" of $(10) million affect YUM!'s reported profits for 2015?

b. What are the cash flow implications of the pension plan for YUM! in 2015?

c. YUM!'s pension plan paid out $50 million in benefits during 2015. Where else is this payment reflected?

M10-19. Analyzing and Interpreting Retirement Benefit Footnote

Abercrombie & Fitch Co. discloses the following footnote relating to its retirement plans in its 2015 10-K report.

LO2

Abercrombie & Fitch Co. (ANF)

> **Savings And Retirement Plans**   The Company maintains the Abercrombie & Fitch Co. Savings & Retirement Plan, a qualified plan. All U.S. associates are eligible to participate in this plan if they are at least 21 years of age. In addition, the Company maintains the Abercrombie & Fitch Co. Nonqualified Savings and Supplemental Retirement, composed of two sub-plans (Plan I and Plan II). Plan I contains contributions made through December 31, 2004, while Plan II contains contributions made on and after January 1, 2005. Participation in these plans is based on service and compensation. The Company's contributions are based on a percentage of associates' eligible annual compensation. The cost of the Company's contributions to these plans was $15.4 million, $13.8 million and $18.3 million for Fiscal 2015, Fiscal 2014 and Fiscal 2013, respectively.

a. Does Abercrombie have a defined contribution or defined benefit pension plan? Explain.
b. How does Abercrombie account for its contributions to its retirement plan?
c. How does Abercrombie report its obligation for its retirement plan on the balance sheet?

M10-20. Analyzing and Interpreting Lease Disclosure

Dow Chemical Company provided the following footnote in its 2015 10-K report relating to operating leases.

LO1

Dow Chemical Company (DOW)

> **Leased Property**   The Company routinely leases premises for use as sales and administrative offices, warehouses and tanks for product storage, motor vehicles, railcars, computers, office machines, and equipment under operating leases. In addition, the Company leases aircraft in the United States. At the termination of the leases, the Company has the option to purchase certain leased equipment and buildings based on a fair market value determination. Rental expenses under operating leases, net of sublease rental income, were $600 million in 2015, $539 million in 2014 and $490 million in 2013. Future minimum rental payments under operating leases with remaining noncancelable terms in excess of one year are as follows:

Minimum Operating Lease Commitments ($ millions)	December 31, 2015
2016	$ 302
2017	277
2018	249
2019	230
2020	215
2021 and thereafter	1,500
Total	$2,773

Required
a. Dow describes all of its leases as "operating." What is the significance of this designation?
b. How might we treat these operating leases in our analysis of the company?

M10-21. Analyzing and Interpreting Pension Plan Benefit Footnotes

Lockheed Martin Corporation discloses the following funded status for its defined benefit pension plans in its 10-K report.

LO2

Lockheed Martin Corporation (LMT)

Defined Benefit Pension Plans ($ millions)	2015
Unfunded status of the plans	$(11,606)

Lockheed contributed $5 million to its pension plan assets in 2015, down drastically from $2,000 million in the prior year. The company also reports that it is obligated for the following expected payments to retirees in the next five years.

$ millions	Qualified Pension Benefits
2016	$ 2,160
2017	2,240
2018	2,320
2019	2,410
2020	2,500
Years 2021–2025	13,670

a. How is this funded status reported in Lockheed's balance sheet under current GAAP?
b. How should we interpret this funded status in our analysis of the company?
c. What likely effect did the 2015–2016 upturn in the financial markets have on Lockheed's contribution to its pension plans? Explain.

LO3

Apple Inc. (AAPL)

M10-22. Analyzing and Interpreting Income Tax Disclosures

Apple Inc. reports the following footnote disclosure to its 2016 10-K report ($ millions).

The provision for income taxes consisted of the following:

Fiscal Year Ended	September 24, 2016
Federal	
Current	$ 7,652
Deferred	5,043
	12,695
State	
Current	990
Deferred	(138)
	852
Foreign	
Current	2,105
Deferred	33
	2,138
Total	$15,685

a. What amount of income tax expense does Apple report in its income statement for 2016?
b. How much of Apple's income tax expense is current (as opposed to deferred)?
c. Why do deferred tax assets and liabilities arise? How do they impact the tax expense that Apple reports in its 2016 income statement?

M10-23. Analyzing and Interpreting Income Tax Footnote

LO3
Walmart (WMT)

The following is an excerpt from **Walmart**'s 2015 Form 10-K.

A summary of the provision for income taxes is as follows ($ millions):

Current:	
U.S. federal.	$6,165
U.S. state and local	810
International	1,529
Total current tax provision	8,504
Deferred:	
U.S. federal.	(387)
U.S. state and local	(55)
International	(77)
Total deferred tax expense (benefit).	$ (519)

Required

a. What amount of income tax expense does Walmart report in its income statement for 2015?

b. How much of Walmart's income tax expense was determined from the company's tax returns?

c. How did deferred taxes affect Walmart's tax expense for the year?

M10-24. Analyzing Tax Expense

LO6
Walmart (WMT)

Refer to the excerpt from **Walmart**'s 2015 Form 10-K in M10-23. Consider the deferred portion of Walmart's tax provision. Which of the following is plausible? (*Hint*: Consider the tax expense equation in Appendix 10C.)

a. Walmart's deferred tax assets increased during the year.

b. Walmart's deferred tax liabilities decreased during the year.

c. Both *a* and *b* are plausible.

d. Neither *a* nor *b* is plausible.

M10-25. Analyzing Tax Expense

LO6

Crestview Holdings reported the following in its 2015 financial statements.

$ millions	2015	2014
Total deferred tax assets	$ 821	$ 764
Total deferred tax liabilities.	4,089	3,126
Current provision for income taxes	1,372	134

Required

Compute the deferred tax expense for the company for 2015.

M10-26. Using a Financial Calculator to Determine Present Value of Operating Leases

LO4
Coach Inc. (COH)

Coach Inc. reports the following in its 2015 Form 10-K.

The Company leases retail, distribution and office facilities, which expire at various dates through 2036. Future minimum rental payments under non-cancelable operating leases, as of July 2, 2016, are as follows:

Fiscal Year	Amount (millions)
2017.	$ 254.2
2018.	232.4
2019.	209.4
2020.	181.4
2021.	150.4
Subsequent to 2021.	597.4
Total minimum future rental payments.	$1,625.2

Required

Assume that the appropriate discount rate for the operating leases is 5%. Use a financial calculator to determine the present value of the future minimum operating lease payments. Round remaining life to the nearest whole number.

LO4

Coach Inc. (COH)

M10-27. Using Present Value Tables to Determine Present Value of Operating Leases

Refer to the information for Coach Inc. in M10-26.

Required

Assume that the appropriate discount rate for the operating leases is 5%. Use present value tables to determine the present value of the future minimum operating lease payments.

Exercises

LO1

Lowe's Companies
(LOW)

E10-28. Analyzing and Interpreting Leasing Footnote

Lowe's Companies Inc. reports the following footnote relating to its leased facilities in its fiscal 2015 10-K report for the year ended January 29, 2016.

> The Company leases facilities and land for certain facilities under agreements with original terms generally of 20 years. . . . The future minimum rental payments required under operating leases and capitalized lease obligations having initial or remaining noncancelable lease terms in excess of one year are summarized as follows:
>
> | Fiscal Year ($ millions) | Operating Leases | Lease Obligations | Total |
> |---|---|---|---|
> | 2016 . . . . | $ 494 | $ 76 | $ 570 |
> | 2017 . . . . | 489 | 65 | 554 |
> | 2018 . . . . | 470 | 62 | 532 |
> | 2019 . . . . | 440 | 60 | 500 |
> | 2020 . . . . | 415 | 58 | 473 |
> | Later years . . . . | 3,086 | 670 | 3,756 |
> | Total minimum lease payments . . . . | $5,394 | $991 | $6,385 |
> | Less amount representing interest. . . . . | | (465) | |
> | Present value of minimum lease payments . . . . . . | | 526 | |
> | Less current maturities. . . . . | | (34) | |
> | Present value of minimum lease payments, less current maturities . . . . | | $492 | |

a. Confirm that Lowe's capitalized its capital leases using a rate of 8.7%. Lowe's labels its capital leases "Lease Obligations."

b. What effect does the failure to capitalize operating leases have on Lowe's balance sheet? Over the life of the lease, what effect does this classification have on net income?

c. Compute the present value of these operating leases using a discount rate of 8.7% and round the remaining lease term to the nearest whole year. How might we use this information in our analysis of the company?

LO1

Verizon Communications Inc. (VZ)

Homework
MBC

E10-29. Analyzing and Interpreting Footnote on Operating and Capital Leases

Verizon Communications Inc. provides the following footnote relating to leasing activities in its 10-K report.

The aggregate minimum rental commitments under noncancelable leases for the periods shown at December 31, 2015, are as follows:

Years ($ millions)	Capital Leases	Operating Leases
2016	$302	$ 2,744
2017	278	2,486
2018	187	2,211
2019	97	1,939
2020	45	1,536
Thereafter	159	7,297
Total minimum rental commitments	1,068	$18,213
Less interest and executory costs	111	
Present value of minimum lease payments	957	
Less current installments	271	
Long-term obligation at December 31, 2015.	$686	

a. Confirm that Verizon capitalized its capital leases using a rate of 3.85%.

b. What effect does the failure to capitalize operating leases have on Verizon's balance sheet? Over the life of its leases, what effect does this lease classification have on net income?

c. Compute the present value of Verizon's operating leases, assuming a 3.85% discount rate and rounding the remaining lease life to three decimal places. How might we use this additional information in our analysis of the company?

E10-30. Analyzing, Interpreting and Capitalizing Operating Leases

LO1

Staples Inc. reports the following footnote relating to its operating leases in its 10-K report for the 2015 fiscal year ended January 30, 2016 ($ thousands).

Staples Inc. (SPLS)

Future minimum lease commitments due for retail, distribution, fulfillment and support facilities (including restructured facilities) and equipment leases under non-cancelable operating leases are as follows (in millions):

Fiscal Year	Total
2016	$ 685
2017	563
2018	424
2019	317
2020	230
Thereafter	443
	$2,662

a. What dollar adjustment(s) might we consider to Staples' balance sheet and income statement given this information and assuming that Staples intermediate-term borrowing rate is 8% and rounding the remaining lease life to the nearest whole year? Explain.

b. Would the adjustment from part a make a substantial difference to Staples' total liabilities? (Staples reported total assets of nearly $10,172 million and total liabilities of nearly $4,788 million for fiscal 2015.)

E10-31.   Analyzing, Interpreting and Capitalizing Operating Leases

YUM! Brands Inc. reports the following footnote relating to its capital and operating leases in its 2015 10-K report ($ millions).

Future minimum commitments . . . under noncancelable leases are set forth below. At December 26, 2015, the present value of minimum payments under capital leases was $169 million.

Commitments ($ millions)	Capital	Operating
2016	$ 20	$ 672
2017	20	620
2018	20	569
2019	20	516
2020	19	457
Thereafter	188	2,123
	$287	$4,957

a. Confirm that the implicit rate on YUM!'s capital leases is 7.634%. Using a 7.634% discount rate, compute the present value of YUM!'s operating leases and rounding the remaining lease life to three decimal places. Describe the adjustments we might consider to YUM!'s balance sheet and income statement using that information.

b. YUM! reported total liabilities of $7,100 million for 2015. Would the adjustment from part *a* make a substantial difference to YUM!'s total liabilities? Explain.

E10-32.   Analyzing, Interpreting and Capitalizing Operating Leases

TJX Companies Inc. reports the following footnote relating to its capital and operating leases in its 10-K report.

The following is a schedule of future minimum lease payments for continuing operations as of January 30, 2016:

Fiscal Year ($ 000s)	Operating Leases
2017	$1,368,050
2018	1,273,888
2019	1,150,172
2020	1,005,127
2021	845,910
Later years	2,354,674
Total future minimum lease payments	$7,997,821

Required

a. Using a 7% discount rate and rounding the remaining lease life to the nearest whole year, compute the present value of TJX's operating leases. Explain the adjustments we might consider to its balance sheet and income statement using that information.

b. TJX reported total liabilities of $7,192,407 thousand on January 30, 2016. Would the adjustment from part *a* make a substantial difference to the company's total liabilities? Explain.

E10-33. Analyzing and Interpreting Pension Disclosures

General Mills Inc. reports the following pension footnote in its 10-K report.

Defined Benefit Pension Plans ($ millions)	Fiscal Year 2016
Change in Plan Assets	
Fair value at beginning of year	$5,758.5
Actual return on assets	36.3
Employer contributions	23.7
Plan participant contributions	5.7
Benefits payments	(277.5)
Foreign currency	(6.8)
Fair value at end of year	$5,539.9
Change in Projected Benefit Obligation	
Benefit obligation at beginning of year	$6,252.1
Service cost	134.6
Interest cost	267.8
Plan amendment	0.9
Curtailment/other	7.1
Plan participant contributions	5.7
Medicare Part D reimbursements	65.2
Benefits payments	(278.0)
Foreign currency	(6.9)
Projected benefit obligation at end of year	$6,448.5

Estimated benefit payments . . . are expected to be paid from fiscal 2017–2026 as follows:

$ millions	Defined Benefit Pension Plans
2017	$ 277.7
2018	287.9
2019	297.1
2020	306.8
2021	316.4
2022–2026	1,731.5

a. Describe what is meant by *service cost* and *interest cost*.

b. What is the total amount paid to retirees during fiscal 2016? What is the source of funds to make these payments to retirees?

c. Compute the 2016 funded status for the company's pension plan.

d. What are actuarial gains and losses? What are the plan amendment adjustments, and how do they differ from the actuarial gains and losses?

e. General Mills projects payments to retirees of about $300 million per year. How is the company able to contribute only $23.7 million to its pension plan?

f. What effect would a substantial decline in the financial markets have on General Mills' contribution to its pension plans?

E10-34. **Analyzing and Interpreting Pension and Health Care Footnote**

Xerox Corporation reports the following pension and retiree health care ("Other") footnote as part of its 10-K report.

December 31, 2015 ($ millions)	Pension Benefits	Retiree Health
Change in Benefit Obligation		
Benefit obligation, January 1	$11,855	$ 937
Service cost	36	7
Interest cost	295	34
Plan participants' contributions	4	14
Actuarial loss	(332)	(4)
Currency exchange rate changes	(538)	(25)
Plan amendments and curtailments	(17)	(31)
Benefits paid/settlements	(638)	(77)
Benefit obligation, December 31	$10,665	$ 855
Change in Plan Assets		
Fair value of plan assets, January 1	$ 9,214	$ —
Actual return on plan assets	(89)	—
Employer contribution	309	63
Plan participants' contributions	4	14
Currency exchange rate changes	(440)	—
Benefits paid/settlements	(638)	(77)
Other	(4)	—
Fair value of plan assets, December 31	$ 8,356	$ —
Net funded status at December 31	$ 2,309	$(855)

December 31, 2015 ($ millions)	Pension Benefits	Retiree Health
Components of Net Periodic Benefit Cost		
Service cost	$ 36	$ 7
Interest cost	295	34
Expected return on plan assets	(376)	—
Recognized net actuarial loss	96	1
Amortization of prior service credit	2	(18)
Recognized settlement loss	89	—
Recognized curtailment gain	—	(22)
Defined benefit plans	142	2
Defined contribution plans	100	—
Total net periodic cost	$242	$ 2
Other Changes in Plan Assets and Benefit Obligations Recognized in Other Comprehensive Income		
Net actuarial loss	$125	$ (4)
Prior service credit	(16)	(32)
Amortization of net actuarial loss	(185)	(1)
Amortization of net prior service credit	(2)	18
Curtailment gain	—	22
Total recognized in other comprehensive income	$ (78)	$ 3

a. Describe what is meant by *service cost* and *interest cost* (the service and interest costs appear both in the reconciliation of the PBO and in the computation of pension expense).

b. What is the actual return on the pension and the health care ("Other") plan investments in 2015? Was Xerox's profitability impacted by this amount?

c. Provide an example under which an "actuarial loss," such as the $332 million loss in 2015 that Xerox reports, might arise.

d. What is the source of funds to make payments to retirees?

e. How much did Xerox contribute to its pension and health care plans in 2015?

f. How much cash did retirees receive in 2015 from the pension plan and the health care plan? How much cash did Xerox pay these retirees in 2015?

g. Show the computation of the 2015 funded status for the pension and health care plans.

h.[A] The company reports $125 million "Net actuarial loss" in the table relating to other comprehensive income, a credit of $16 million relating to "Prior service credit," a loss of $185 million relating to "Amortization of net actuarial loss," and a credit of $2 million relating to "Amortization of net prior service credit" in the net periodic benefit cost table. Describe the process by which these amounts are transferred from other comprehensive income to pension expense in the income statement.

E10-35. Analyzing and Interpreting Pension and Health Care Disclosures

Verizon Communications Inc. reports the following pension and health care benefits footnote as part of its 10-K report.

LO2
Verizon
Communications Inc.
(VZ)

At December 31, 2015 ($ millions)	Pension	Healthcare
Change in Benefit Obligations		
Beginning of year	$ 25,320	$ 27,097
Service cost	374	324
Interest cost	969	1,117
Plan amendments	—	(45)
Actuarial loss, net	(1,361)	(2,733)
Benefits paid	(971)	(1,370)
Annuity purchase	(2,315)	—
Settlements paid	—	(167)
End of year	$ 22,016	$ 24,223
Change in Plan Assets		
Beginning of year	$ 18,548	$ 2,435
Actual return on plan assets	118	28
Company contributions	744	667
Benefits paid	(971)	(1,370)
Settlements paid	(2,315)	—
End of year	$ 16,124	$ 1,760
Funded Status		
End of year	$ (5,892)	$(22,463)

Years Ended December 31, 2015 ($ millions)	Pension	Healthcare
Service cost	$ 374	$ 324
Amortization of prior service cost (credit)	(5)	(287)
Expected return on plan assets	(1,270)	(101)
Interest cost	969	1,117
Remeasurement (gain) loss, net	(209)	(2,659)
Total	$ (141)	$(1,606)

a. Describe what is meant by *service cost* and *interest cost.*

b. What payments did retirees receive during fiscal 2015 from the pension and health care plans? What is the source of funds to make payments to retirees?

c. Show the computation of Verizon's 2015 funded status for both the pension and health care plans.

d. What expense does Verizon's income statement report for both its pension and health care plans?

LO3

FedEx Corporation
(FDX)

E10-36. Analyzing and Interpreting Income Tax Disclosures

The income tax footnote to the financial statements of **FedEx Corporation** follows.

The components of the provision for income taxes for the years ended May 31 were as follows:

$ millions	2016	2015	2014
Current provision (benefit)			
Domestic			
Federal	$513	$ 795	$ 624
State and local	72	102	56
Foreign	200	214	194
	785	1,111	874
Deferred provision (benefit)			
Domestic			
Federal	155	(474)	360
State and local	(18)	(47)	82
Foreign	(2)	(13)	18
	135	(534)	460
	$920	$ 577	$1,334

a. What is the amount of income tax expense reported in FedEx's 2016, 2015, and 2014 income statements?

b. What percentage of total tax expense is currently payable in each year?

c. One possible reason for the $135 million deferred tax expense in 2016 is that deferred tax liabilities increased during that year. Provide an example that gives rise to an increase in the deferred tax liability.

LO3, 6

Colgate-Palmolive
(CL)

E10-37. Analyzing and Interpreting Income Tax Disclosures

Colgate-Palmolive reports the following income tax footnote disclosure in its 10-K report.

Deferred Tax Balances at December 31 ($ millions)	2015	2014
Deferred tax liabilities		
Goodwill and intangible assets......................	$ (458)	$ (497)
Property, plant and equipment.......................	(380)	(380)
Other..	(150)	(266)
	(988)	(1,143)
Deferred tax assets		
Pension and other retiree benefits	541	638
Tax loss and tax credit carryforwards................	30	33
Accrued liabilities	235	276
Stock-based compensation	123	119
Other..	151	148
	1,080	1,214
Net deferred income taxes	$ 92	$ 71

a. Colgate reports $380 million of deferred tax liabilities in 2015 relating to "Property." Explain how such liabilities arise.

b. Describe how a deferred tax asset can arise from pension and other retiree benefits.

c. Colgate reports $30 million in deferred tax assets for 2015 relating to tax loss and tax credit carryforwards. Describe how tax loss carryforwards arise and under what conditions the resulting deferred tax assets will be realized.

d. Colgate's income statement reports income tax expense of $1,215 million. Assume that cash paid for income tax is $1,259 million and that taxes payable decreased by $23 million. Use the financial statement effects template to record tax expense for 2015. (*Hint:* Show the effects of changes in deferred taxes.)

E10-38. Using a Calculator and Present Value Table to Impute Interest Rate and Determine Present Value of Operating Leases

LO4

AutoZone (AZO)

AutoZone reports the following in its 2015 Form 10-K.

> The Company leases some of its retail stores, distribution centers, facilities, land and equipment, including vehicles. Other than vehicle leases, most of the leases are operating leases. . . . The Company has a fleet of vehicles used for delivery to its commercial customers and stores and travel for members of field management. The majority of these vehicles are held under capital lease.

Future minimum annual rental commitments under non-cancelable operating leases and capital leases were as follows at the end of fiscal 2015:

$ thousands	Operating Leases	Capital Leases
2016	$ 259,175	$ 40,528
2017	250,787	40,562
2018	234,640	28,558
2019	215,692	16,845
2020	192,882	5,077
Thereafter	905,629	—
Total minimum payments required	$2,058,805	131,570
Less: Interest		(3,403)
Present value of minimum capital lease payments		$128,167

Required

a. Use a financial calculator to impute the implicit rate of return (to three decimal places) on the capital leases.

b. Assume that the appropriate discount rate for the operating leases is 1.16%. Use a financial calculator to determine the present value of the future minimum operating lease payments.

c. Assume that the appropriate discount rate for the operating leases is 1%. Use present value tables to determine the present value of the future minimum operating lease payments.

E10-39. Determine Income Statement Effect of Capitalized Leases and Use a Calculator to Determine Present Value of Operating Leases

LO1, 4

Facebook Inc. (FB)

Facebook Inc. reports the following in its 2015 Form 10-K.

> We entered into various capital lease arrangements to obtain property and equipment for our operations. We have also entered into various non-cancelable operating lease agreements for certain of our offices, equipment, land, and data centers with original lease periods expiring between 2016 and 2032. The following is a schedule, by years, of the future minimum lease payments required under non-cancelable capital and operating leases as of December 31, 2015 (in millions):

continued

continued from previous page

	Capital Leases	Operating Leases
2016	$ 16	$ 209
2017	15	230
2018	16	216
2019	16	200
2020	17	159
Thereafter	94	438
Total minimum lease payments	174	$1,452
Less: amount representing interest and taxes	(60)	
Less: current portion of the present value of minimum lease payments.	(7)	
Capital lease obligations, net of current portion . . .	$107	

Required

Assume that Facebook capitalized its leases using a discount rate of 1%.

a. What interest expense will Facebook report on its income statement for fiscal 2016?

b. Assume that the capitalized leases relate to equipment with a remaining useful life of 10 years. What depreciation expense will Facebook report on its income statement for fiscal 2016?

c. Use a financial calculator to determine the present value of the future minimum operating lease payments.

Problems

LO1

The Goldman Sachs Group Inc. (GS)

P10-40.   Analyzing, Interpreting and Capitalizing Operating Leases

Goldman Sachs' 10-K report contains the following lease footnote. This is the only information it discloses relating to its leasing activity.

The firm has contractual obligations under long-term noncancelable lease agreements for office space expiring on various dates through 2069. Rent charged to operating expense was $249 million for 2015. The table below presents future minimum rental payments, net of minimum sublease rentals.

$ in millions	As of December 2015
2016	$ 317
2017	313
2018	301
2019	258
2020	226
2021–thereafter	1,160
Total	$2,575

Required

a. What lease assets and lease liabilities does Goldman Sachs report on its balance sheet? How do we know?

b. What effect does the lease classification have on Goldman Sachs' balance sheet? Over the life of the lease, what effect does this classification have on the company's net income?

c. Using a 6% discount rate and rounding the remaining lease life to the nearest whole year, estimate the assets and liabilities that Goldman Sachs fails to report as a result of its off-balance-sheet lease financing.

d. What adjustments would we consider to Goldman Sachs' income statement corresponding to the adjustments we would make to its balance sheet in part *c*?

e. Indicate the direction (increase or decrease) of the effect that capitalizing these leases would have on the following financial items and ratios for Goldman Sachs: return on equity (ROE), net operating profit after tax (NOPAT), net operating assets (NOA), net operating profit margin (NOPM), net operating asset turnover (NOAT), and measures of financial leverage.

P10-41. Analyzing, Interpreting and Capitalizing Operating Leases

The **Best Buy Co. Inc.** 10-K report has the following footnote related to leasing activities.

LO1

Best Buy Co. Inc. (BBY)

The future minimum lease payments under our capital and operating leases by fiscal year (not including contingent rentals) at January 30, 2016, were as follows:

Fiscal Year ($ millions)	Capital Leases	Operating Leases
2017	$14	$ 813
2018	9	708
2019	6	572
2020	3	439
2021	2	310
Thereafter	12	521
Total minimum lease payments	46	$3,363
Less amount representing interest	(8)	
Present value of minimum lease payments	38	
Less current maturities	(12)	
Present value of minimum lease maturities, less current maturities	$26	

Required

a. What is the balance of the lease liabilities reported on Best Buy's balance sheet?

b. What effect has the operating lease classification had on its balance sheet? Over the life of the lease, what effect does this classification have on the company's net income?

c. Confirm that the implicit discount rate used by Best Buy for its capital leases is 5.55%. Use this discount rate to estimate the assets and liabilities that Best Buy fails to report as a result of its off-balance-sheet lease financing. Round the remaining lease life to two decimals.

d. What adjustments would we make to Best Buy's income statement corresponding to the adjustments we made to its balance sheet in part *c*?

e. Indicate the direction (increase or decrease) of the effect that capitalizing the operating leases would have on the following financial items and ratios for Best Buy: return on equity (ROE), net operating profit after tax (NOPAT), net operating assets (NOA), net operating profit margin (NOPM), net operating asset turnover (NOAT), and measures of financial leverage.

LO1

FedEx Corp. (FDX)

P10-42.   Analyzing, Interpreting and Capitalizing Operating Leases

FedEx Corp. reports total assets of $46,064 and total liabilities of $32,280 for 2016 ($ millions). Its 10-K report has the following footnote related to leasing activities.

A summary of future minimum lease payments under noncancelable operating leases with an initial or remaining term in excess of one year at May 31, 2016, is as follows (in millions):

	Operating Leases		
	Aircraft and Related Equipment	Facilities and Other	Total Operating Leases
2017	$ 454	$ 2,021	$ 2,475
2018	383	1,860	2,243
2019	321	1,632	1,953
2020	240	1,428	1,668
2021	182	1,269	1,451
Thereafter	352	7,671	8,023
Total	$1,932	$15,881	$17,813

Property and equipment recorded under capital leases and future minimum lease payments under capital leases were immaterial at May 31, 2016. Capital lease obligations were reported as part of FedEx's long-term debt to be $63 million at May 31, 2016.

Required

a. What is the balance of lease assets and lease liabilities reported on FedEx's balance sheet? Explain.

b. Assume FedEx uses a rate of 4.8% to discount its capital leases. Use this discount rate and round the remaining lease life to two decimals to estimate the amount of assets and liabilities that FedEx fails to report as a result of its off-balance-sheet lease financing.

c. What adjustments would we make to FedEx's income statement corresponding to the adjustments we make to its balance sheet in part b?

d. Indicate the direction (increase or decrease) of the effect that capitalizing the operating leases would have on the following financial items and ratios for FedEx: return on equity (ROE), net operating profit after tax (NOPAT), net operating assets (NOA), net operating profit margin (NOPM), net operating asset turnover (NOAT), and measures of financial leverage.

e. What portion of total lease liabilities did FedEx report on-balance-sheet and what portion is off-balance-sheet?

f. Based on your analysis, do you believe that FedEx's balance sheet adequately reports its aircraft and facilities assets and related obligations? Explain.

LO2

E. I. du Pont de Nemours and Co. (DD)

P10-43.   Analyzing and Interpreting Pension Disclosures

E. I. du Pont de Nemours and Co.'s 10-K report has the following disclosures related to its retirement plans ($ millions).

Obligations and Funded Status December 31, 2015 ($ millions)	
Change in benefit obligation	
Benefit obligation at beginning of year.	$29,669
Service cost	232
Interest cost	1,084
Plan participants' contributions	19
Actuarial (gain) loss	(1,404)
Benefits paid	(1,761)
Effect of foreign exchange rates	(456)
Net effects of acquisitions/divestitures	(52)
Spin-off of Chemours.	(1,237)
Benefit obligation at end of year	$26,094

continued

Obligations and Funded Status
December 31, 2015 ($ millions)

Change in plan assets

Fair value of plan assets at beginning of year	$20,446
Actual gain on plan assets	88
Employer contributions	308
Plan participants' contributions	19
Benefits paid	(1,761)
Effect of foreign exchange rates	(330)
Net effects of acquisitions/divestitures	(47)
Spin-off of Chemours	(1,226)
Fair value of plan assets at end of year	$17,497

Funded status

U.S. plan with plan assets	$ (6,662)
Non-U.S. plans with plan assets	(748)
All other plans	(1,187)
Total	$ (8,597)

Amounts recognized in the Consolidated Balance
Sheets consist of:

Other assets	$ 11
Other accrued liabilities	(130)
Other liabilities	(8,478)
Net amount recognized	$ (8,597)

Components of net periodic benefit cost and amounts recognized in other comprehensive income
December 31, 2015 ($ millions)

Net periodic benefit cost

Service cost	$ 232
Interest cost	1,084
Expected return on plan assets	(1,554)
Amortization of loss	768
Amortization of prior service (benefit) cost	(9)
Curtailment (gain) loss	(6)
Settlement loss	76
Net periodic benefit cost—Total	591
Less: Discontinued operations	(5)
Net periodic benefit cost—Continuing operations	$ 596

Changes in plan assets and benefit obligations recognized in other comprehensive income

Net loss (gain)	$ 57
Amortization of loss	(768)
Prior service benefit	—
Amortization of prior service benefit (cost)	9
Curtailment gain (loss)	6
Settlement loss	(76)
Effect of foreign exchange rates	(119)
Spin-off of Chemours	(382)
Total (benefit) loss recognized in other comprehensive income, attributable to DuPont	(1,273)
Total recognized in net periodic benefit cost and other comprehensive income	$ (682)

Weighted-average assumptions used to determine net periodic benefit cost for years ended December 31, 2015	
Discount rate	3.93%
Expected return on plan assets	8.10%
Rate of compensation increase	4.01%

The following benefit payments, which reflect future service, as appropriate, are expected to be paid:

$ millions	Pension Benefits
2016	$1,652
2017	1,582
2018	1,585
2019	1,593
2020	1,600
Years 2021–2025	7,992

Required

a. How much pension expense (revenue) does DuPont report in its 2015 income statement?

b. DuPont reports a $1,554 million expected return on pension plan assets as an offset to 2015 pension expense. Approximately, how is this amount computed (estimate from the numbers reported)? What is DuPont's actual gain or loss realized on its 2015 pension plan assets? What is the purpose of using this expected return instead of the actual gain or loss (return)?

c. What main factors (and dollar amounts) affected DuPont's pension liability during 2015? What main factors (and dollar amounts) affected its pension plan assets during 2015?

d. What does the term *funded status* mean? What is the funded status of the 2015 DuPont pension plans?

e. DuPont decreased its discount rate from 4.55% to 3.93% in 2015. What effect(s) does this decrease have on its balance sheet and its income statement?

f. How did DuPont's pension plan affect the company's cash flow in 2015? (Identify any inflows and outflows, including amounts.)

g. Explain how the returns on pension assets affect the amount of cash that DuPont must contribute to fund the pension plan.

LO2, 5

Johnson & Johnson
(JNJ)

P10-44. Analyzing and Interpreting Pension Disclosures

Johnson & Johnson provides the following footnote disclosures in its 10-K report relating to its defined benefit pension plans and its other post-retirement benefits.

December 31, 2015 ($ millions)	Retirement Plans	Other Benefit Plans
Change in Benefit Obligation		
Projected benefit obligation—beginning of year	$26,889	$ 5,081
Service cost	1,037	257
Interest cost	988	186
Plan participant contributions	48	—
Amendments	60	—
Actuarial (gains) losses.	(1,578)	(400)
Divestitures & acquisitions	(5)	—
Curtailments & settlements & restructuring	(20)	(3)
Benefits paid from plan	(773)	(420)
Effect of exchange rates.	(791)	(32)
Projected benefit obligation—end of year	$25,855	$ 4,669

continued

December 31, 2015 ($ millions)	Retirement Plans	Other Benefit Plans
Change in Plan Assets		
Plan assets at fair value—beginning of year	$22,575	$ 79
Actual return (loss) on plan assets	298	1
Company contributions	752	414
Plan participant contributions	48	—
Settlements	(20)	—
Divestitures & acquisitions	(5)	—
Benefits paid from plan assets.	(773)	(420)
Effect of exchange rates.	(621)	—
Plan assets at fair value—end of year	$22,254	$ 74
Funded status—end of year.	$ (3,601)	$(4,595)

December 31, 2015 ($ millions)	Retirement Plans	Other Benefit Plans
Service cost	$1,037	$257
Interest cost	988	186
Expected return on plan assets	(1,809)	(7)
Amortization of prior service cost (credit).	2	(33)
Amortization of net transition obligation	—	—
Recognized actuarial losses.	745	201
Curtailments and settlements	8	—
Net periodic benefit cost	$ 971	$604

	Retirement Plans		Other Benefit Plans	
Worldwide Benefit Plans	2015	2014	2015	2014
Discount rate	3.78%	4.78%	4.31%	5.25%
Expected long-term rate of return on plan assets . . .	8.53	8.46	—	—
Rate of increase in compensation levels	4.05	4.08	4.11	4.29

Required

a. How much pension expense does Johnson & Johnson report in its 2015 income statement?

b.[A] The company reports a $1,809 million expected return on pension plan assets as an offset to 2015 pension expense. Approximately, how is this amount computed? What is the actual gain or loss realized on its 2015 pension plan assets? What is the purpose of using this expected return instead of the actual gain or loss?

c. What factors affected the company's pension liability during 2015? What factors affected the pension plan assets during 2015?

d. What does the term *funded status* mean? What is the funded status of the 2015 pension plans and postretirement benefit plans?

e. The company decreased its discount rate from 4.78% to 3.78% in 2015. What effect(s) does this decrease have on its balance sheet and its income statement?

f. How did Johnson & Johnson's pension plan affect the company's cash flow in 2015?

P10-45. **Analyzing and Interpreting Tax Footnote (Financial Statement Effects Template)**

LO3, 6

Under Armour Inc. reports total tax expense of $154,112 thousand on its income statement for year ended December 31, 2015, and paid cash of $99,708 thousand for taxes. The tax footnote in the company's 10-K filing, reports the following deferred tax assets and liabilities information.

Under Armour Inc. (UA)

December 31 ($ thousands)	2015	2014
Deferred tax assets		
Stock-based compensation.....................	$40,406	$35,161
Allowance for doubtful accounts and other reserves...	33,821	24,774
Accrued expenses	19,999	11,398
Foreign net operating loss carryforward	19,600	16,302
Deferred rent	13,991	11,005
Inventory obsolescence reserves.................	11,956	8,198
Tax basis inventory adjustment	10,019	5,845
U.S. net operating loss carryforward	9,217	4,733
Foreign tax credits	6,151	5,131
State tax credits, net of foreign impact	4,966	4,245
Deferred compensation	2,080	1,858
Other..	6,346	4,592
Total deferred tax assets.....................	178,552	133,242
Less: valuation allowance.....................	(24,043)	(15,550)
Total net deferred tax assets..................	154,509	117,692
Deferred tax liability		
Property, plant and equipment...................	(31,069)	(17,638)
Intangible asset	(22,820)	(7,010)
Prepaid expenses.............................	(8,766)	(6,424)
Other..	(627)	(612)
Total deferred tax liabilities	(63,282)	(31,684)
Total deferred tax assets, net	$91,227	$86,008

Required

  a. Under Armour's deferred tax assets increased during the most recent fiscal year. What explains the change?

  b. Did Under Armour's deferred tax liabilities increase or decrease during the most recent fiscal year? Explain how the change arose.

  c. This company's valuation allowance relates to foreign net operating tax losses. Explain how tax losses give rise to deferred tax assets. Why does the company record a valuation account? What proportion of these losses, at December 31, 2015, does the company believe will likely expire unused?

  d. Explain how the valuation allowance affected 2015 net income.

  e.[A] Use the financial statement effects template to record Under Armour's income tax expense for the fiscal year 2015 along with the changes in both deferred tax assets and liabilities. Assume that income taxes payable increased by $59,623 thousand.

LO3

E. I. du Pont de Nemours and Co. (DD)

P10-46.   Analyzing and Interpreting Income Tax Footnote

Consider the following income tax footnote information for the **E. I. du Pont de Nemours and Company**.

Provision for Income Taxes ($ millions)	2015	2014
Current tax expense on continuing operations		
U.S. federal..	$218	$ 656
U.S. state and local	7	38
International	466	449
Total current tax expense on continuing operations	691	1,143
Deferred tax expense (benefit) on continuing operations		
U.S. federal..	139	91
U.S. state and local	4	(42)
International	(138)	(24)
Total deferred tax expense on continuing operations	5	25
Provision for income taxes on continuing operations	$696	$1,168

continued

The significant components of deferred tax assets and liabilities at December 31, 2015 and 2014, are as follows:

$ millions	2015 Asset	2015 Liability	2014 Asset	2014 Liability
Depreciation	$ —	$ 953	$ —	$1,003
Accrued employee benefits	4,812	374	5,376	746
Other accrued expenses	563	—	555	—
Inventories	125	99	151	137
Unrealized exchange gains/losses.	—	224	—	173
Tax loss/tax credit carryforwards/backs	2,124	—	2,409	—
Investment in subsidiaries and affiliates.	133	154	151	195
Amortization of intangibles.	187	1,331	154	1,353
Other.	215	77	258	110
Valuation allowance	(1,529)	—	(1,704)	—
	$6,630	$3,212	$7,350	$3,717
Net deferred tax asset	$3,418		$3,633	

An analysis of the company's effective income tax rate (EITR) on continuing operations is as follows:

	2015	2014	2013
Statutory U.S. federal income tax rate.	35.0%	35.0%	35.0%
Exchange gains/losses.	8.0	8.1	1.0
Domestic operations	(2.8)	(2.8)	(4.1)
Lower effective tax rates on international operations—net . . .	(11.1)	(11.4)	(14.7)
Tax settlements	(0.7)	(0.6)	(0.3)
Sale of a business	(0.2)	(0.4)	—
U.S. research & development credit.	(1.3)	(0.8)	(2.9)
	26.9%	27.1%	14.0%

Required

a. What is the total amount of income tax expense that DuPont reports in its 2015 income statement? What portion of this expense did DuPont pay during 2015 or expect to pay in 2016?

b. Explain how the deferred tax liability called "depreciation" arises. Under what circumstances will the company settle this liability? Under what circumstances might this liability be deferred indefinitely?

c. Explain how the deferred tax asset called "accrued employee benefits" arises. Why is it recognized as an asset?

d. Explain how the deferred tax asset called "tax loss/tax credit carryforwards/backs" arises. Under what circumstances will DuPont realize the benefits of this asset?

e. DuPont reports a 2015 valuation allowance of $1,529 million. How does this valuation allowance arise? How did the change in valuation allowance for 2015 affect net income? Valuation allowances typically relate to questions about the realizability of tax loss carryforwards. Under what circumstances might DuPont not realize the benefits of its tax loss carryforwards?

f. DuPont's footnote reports the effective income tax rates (EITR) for the three-year period. What explains the difference between the U.S. statutory rate and the company's EITR?

LO3

Pfizer Inc. (PFE)

P10-47. Analyzing and Interpreting Income Tax Disclosures

Pfizer Inc. reports the following footnote disclosure in its 2015 Form 10-K.

$ millions	Dec. 31, 2015	Dec. 31, 2014
Deferred tax assets		
Prepaid/deferred items.	$ 2,247	$ 1,995
Inventories	381	219
Intangibles	1,063	969
Property, plant and equipment.	65	174
Employee benefits	3,302	3,950
Restructurings and other charges	318	114
Legal and product liability reserves	730	1,010
Net operating loss/credit carryforwards	3,808	2,918
State and local tax adjustments.	328	295
All other	310	283
Subtotal	12,552	11,927
Valuation allowance	(2,029)	(1,615)
Total deferred taxes	10,523	10,312
Deferred tax liabilities		
Prepaid/deferred items.	(38)	(53)
Inventories	(190)	(56)
Intangibles	(10,885)	(9,224)
Property, plant and equipment.	(1,096)	(1,242)
Employee benefits	(167)	(154)
Restructurings and other charges	(20)	(28)
Unremitted earnings.	(23,626)	(21,174)
All other	(646)	(783)
Deferred tax liabilities.	(36,668)	(32,714)
Net deferred tax liability	$(26,145)	$(22,402)

Required

a. Describe the terms "deferred tax liabilities" and "deferred tax assets." Provide an example of how these accounts can arise.

b. Intangible assets (other than goodwill) acquired in the purchase of a company are depreciated (amortized) similar to buildings and equipment (see earlier module for a discussion). Describe how the deferred tax liability of $10,885 million relating to intangibles arose.

c. Pfizer has many employee benefit plans, such as a long-term health plan and a pension plan. Some of these are generating deferred tax assets and others are generating deferred tax liabilities. Explain the timing of the recognition of expenses under these plans that would give rise to these different outcomes.

d. Pfizer reports a deferred tax liability labelled "unremitted earnings." This relates to an investment in an affiliated company for which Pfizer is recording income, but has not yet received dividends. Generally, investment income is taxed when received. Explain what information the deferred tax liability for unremitted earnings conveys.

e. Pfizer reports a deferred tax asset relating to net operating loss carryforwards. Explain what loss carryforwards are.

f. Pfizer reports a valuation allowance of $2,029 million in 2015. Explain why Pfizer has established this allowance and its effect on reported profit. Pfizer's valuation allowance was $1,615 million in 2014. Compute the change in its allowance during 2015 and explain how that change affected 2015 tax expense and net income.

IFRS Applications

LO1

Total S.A. (TOT)

I10-48. Analyzing, Interpreting and Capitalizing Operating Leases

Total S.A. is a French multinational oil company and one of the six "supermajor" oil companies in the world. The company is headquartered in Courbevoie, France, and uses IFRS to prepare its financial statements. Total S.A. reports the following footnote relating to its finance and operating leases in its 2015 20-F report (€ millions).

The Group leases real estate, retail stations, ships, and other equipment. The future minimum lease payments on operating and finance leases to which the Group is committed are shown as follows:

For year ended December 31, 2015 (€ millions)	Operating Leases	Finance Leases
2016	€1,430	€ 57
2017	1,049	23
2018	784	23
2019	550	23
2020	442	23
2021 and beyond	1,718	242
Total minimum payments	€5,973	€391

On December 31, 2015, the present value of minimum lease payments under finance leases was €336 million.

a. Confirm that the implicit rate of Total's finance leases is 2.07%.
b. Use 2.07% as the discount rate and round the remaining lease term to three decimals to compute the present value of Total's operating leases.
c. Describe the adjustments we might consider to Total's balance sheet and income statement using the information from part b.
d. Total reported total liabilities of €129,075 million for 2015. Are these finance leases substantial? Would capitalizing the operating leases make a difference to our assessment of Total's liquidity or solvency?

I10-49. **Analyzing, Interpreting and Capitalizing Operating Leases**   **LO1**

LM Ericsson, one of Sweden's largest companies, is a provider of telecommunication and data communication systems. The company reports total assets of SEK 284,363 and total liabilities of SEK 136,997 for 2015 (in millions). Its annual report has the following footnote related to leasing activities.   **LM Ericsson (ERIC)**

As of December 31, 2015, future minimum lease payment obligations for leases were distributed as follows:

In SEK millions	Finance Leases	Operating Leases
2016	73	3,025
2017	72	2,529
2018	72	2,125
2019	72	1,800
2020	551	1,113
2021 and later	6	4,778
Total	846	15,370
Future finance charges	(225)	n/a
Present value of finance lease liabilities	621	n/a

Required
a. What is reported on Ericsson's balance sheet as lease liabilities?
b. Confirm that the implicit rate that Ericsson uses to discount its capital leases is 7.88%. Use this discount rate and round the remaining years to 3 decimals to estimate the amount of assets and liabilities that Ericsson fails to report as a result of its off-balance-sheet lease financing.

c. What adjustments would we make to Ericsson's income statement corresponding to the balance sheet adjustments implied in part *b*?

d. What portion of total lease liabilities did Ericsson report on-balance-sheet and what portion is off-balance-sheet?

e. Indicate the direction (increase or decrease) of the effect that capitalizing the operating leases would have on the following financial items and ratios for Ericsson: return on equity (ROE), net operating profit after tax (NOPAT), net operating assets (NOA), net operating profit margin (NOPM), net operating asset turnover (NOAT), and measures of financial leverage.

f. Based on your analysis, do you believe that Ericsson's balance sheet adequately reports its facilities assets and related obligations? Explain.

LO2
Potash Corporation of Saskatchewan (POT)

I10-50.   Analyzing and Interpreting Pension Disclosures

Potash Corporation of Saskatchewan, the world's largest potash producer, is a Canadian corporation based in Saskatoon, Saskatchewan. The company produces nitrogen and phosphate used to produce fertilizer. At the end of 2015, the company controlled 20% of the world's potash production capacity.

Defined Benefit Plans

The components of total expense recognized in the consolidated statements of income for the company's defined benefit pension were as follows:

December 31, 2015 ($ millions)	
Current service cost for benefits earned during the year	$36
Net interest expense	4
Past service cost, including curtailment gains and settlements	(2)
Foreign exchange rate changes and other	(7)
Components of defined benefit expense recognized in net income	$31

The change in benefit obligations and the change in plan assets for the above defined benefit pension and other post-retirement benefit plans were as follows at December 31, 2015 ($ millions):

Change in benefit obligations	
Balance, beginning of year	$1,403
Current service cost	36
Interest expense	56
Actuarial (gain) loss arising from changes in financial assumptions	(39)
Actuarial (gain) loss arising from changes in demographic assumptions	(15)
Foreign exchange rate changes	(38)
Contributions by plan participants	1
Benefits paid	(48)
Past service costs, including curtailment gains and settlements	(51)
Balance, end of year	$1,305

Change in plan assets	
Fair value, beginning of year	$1,316
Interest included in net income	52
(Loss) return on plan assets (excluding amounts included in net interest)	(55)
Foreign exchange rate changes and other	(31)
Contributions by plan participants	1
Employer contributions	11
Benefits paid	(48)
Settlements	(49)
Fair value, end of year	$1,197
Funded status	$ (108)

Required

a. How much pension expense does Potash Corporation report in its 2015 income statement?

b. What factors affected the company's pension liability during 2015? What factors affected the pension plan assets during 2015?

c. What does the term *funded status* mean? What is the funded status of the 2015 pension plans and post-retirement benefit plans?

d. The company increased its discount rate on the pension obligation from 4% to 4.35% in 2015. What effect(s) does this increase have on the company's balance sheet and income statement?

e. How did Potash Corporation's pension plan affect the company's cash flow in 2015?

I10-51. Analyzing and Interpreting Income Tax Footnote

LO3

Telstra Corporation

(TLS)

Telstra Corporation Limited is an Australian telecommunications and media company that builds and provides land-based and mobile telecom services along with internet and pay television products. The company is Australia's largest enabled mobile network. The footnotes below report income statement and balance sheet data for the company's income taxes (in $US millions).

	As at 30 June	
	2016	2015
Major components of income tax expense		
Current tax expense..	$1,781	$1,722
Deferred tax resulting from the origination and reversal of temporary differences.....................................	16	67
Under/(over) provision of tax in prior years	2	(2)
	$1,799	$1,787
Effective income tax rate	23.5%	29.3%
Reconciliation of notional income tax expense to actual income tax expenses		
Profit before income tax expense from continuing operations	5,600	5,860
Profit before income tax expense from discontinued operations	2,048	232
Profit before income tax expense........................	**$7,648**	**$6,092**
Notional income tax expense calculated at the Australian tax rate of 30%	$2,294	$1,828
Notional income tax expense differs from actual income tax expense due to the tax effect of		
Different tax rates in overseas juristrictions	(28)	14
Non-taxable and non-deductible items	(470)	(39)
Amended assessments	1	(14)
Under/(over) provision of tax in prior years	2	(2)
Income tax expense on profit from continuing and discontinued operations..	**$1,799**	**$1,787**

Deferred Tax (Liability) Asset	2016	2015
Property, plant and equipment............................	$(1,245)	$(1,175)
Intangible assets	(1,011)	(953)
Provision for employee entitlements	364	342
Trade and other payables................................	112	140
Defined benefit (asset) / liability	93	99
Borrowings and derivative financial instruments	(22)	(17)
Revenue received in advance	169	55
Allowance for doubtful debts.............................	34	29
Provision for workers' compensation and other provisions........	17	27
Income tax losses	34	34
Other...	(3)	(9)
Net deferred tax liability	$(1,458)	$(1,428)

Required

a. What income tax expense does Telstra report in its 2016 income statement? How much of this expense was paid during the year or is currently payable?

b. Determine the company's effective tax rate.

c. What is the company's marginal (statutory) tax rate?

d. Telstra reports $1,245 million of deferred tax liabilities in 2016 relating to "Property, plant and equipment." Explain how such liabilities arise.

e. Describe how a $364 million deferred tax asset can arise from "Provision for employee entitlements."

Ongoing Project

(This ongoing project began in Module 1 and continues through most of the book; even if previous segments were not completed, the requirements are still applicable to any business analysis.)   Your project should include a discussion of leases (capital and operating), defined benefit obligations as well as deferred tax assets and liabilities. The objective is to gain a deeper understanding of all of the obligations the company faces and how they affect key performance and leverage ratios.

1. *Capital and Operating Leases.*   Read the debt and lease footnotes to determine whether the company uses leases.

    *   Does the company use leases? What types of assets are leased?

    *   What proportion of leases are capital (finance) versus operating?

    *   Are leases a substantial component of overall financing?

    *   Determine the discount rate implicit in the company's capital leases.

    *   Has the company adopted the new standard for leases? If not, use the rate from above to approximate the amount that would have been included in the balance sheet had the operating leases been capitalized. Is the missing amount economically important?

    *   Quantify the effect that capitalizing the operating leases would have on the following financial items and ratios for each company: return on equity (ROE), net operating profit after tax (NOPAT), net operating assets (NOA), and measures of financial leverage, liquidity, and solvency.

2. *Pensions.*   Read the pension footnote to determine whether the company has defined benefit obligations.

    *   What is the funded status of the pension and other benefits plans? Is the underfunded or overfunded obligation substantial? Compare between the companies.

    *   Are the plans substantial to the company?

    *   How much pension expense does each company report in its income statement? Is this a substantial amount?

    *   Compare the cash paid into the plan assets to the amounts paid to retirees. Assess the cash flow implications of the company's future payment obligations. The point is to determine whether the company will be able to meet its obligations as they come due.

3. *Income Tax Disclosures and Strategies.* Examine the income tax expense and deferred tax assets and liabilities.

    *   Analyze the footnotes and assess the company's effective tax rate. Is it a consistent rate? If not, do the fluctuations seem reasonable?

    *   Do the deferred tax assets and liabilities seem appropriate given the company's industry?

    *   Is there a valuation allowance? If so, how big is it relative to total deferred tax assets? Has the valuation allowance changed markedly during the year? This might indicate income shifting.

Solutions to Review Problems

Review 10-1—Solution

1. The interest rate that **UPS** uses in the computation of its capital lease balance is imputed to be 7.04%; this rate is determined as follows (using a spreadsheet).

	A	B	C	D	E	F	G	H	I	J	K	L	M	N	O	P
D11	▼	:	×	✓	*fx*											
1	N	0	1	2	3	4	5	6	7	8	9	10	11	12	13	
2	Amount	−475	72	73	61	59	53	53	53	53	53	53	53	53	21	
3	IRR	7.04%														
4	4											= 392				
5		*Formula for cell B3 is IRR(B2:O2,.1)														

2. We present the present value computations below for both the actual implicit rate of 7.04% and the rounded 7%.

Year ($ millions)	Operating Lease Payment	Discount Factor ($i = 0.0704$)	Present Value
1	$324	0.93423	$ 303
2	263	0.87279	230
3	197	0.81538	161
4	125	0.76176	95
5	84	0.71165	60
>5	266	2.75324	165**
Remaining life.	3.167*		$1,014

*$266/$84 = 3.167 years
** The annuity factor for 3.167 years at 7.04% is 2.75324.
  $84 × 2.75324 × 0.71165 = $165

Year ($ millions)	Operating Lease Payment	Discount Factor ($i = 0.070$)	Present Value
1	$324	0.93458	$ 303
2	263	0.87344	230
3	197	0.81630	161
4	125	0.76290	95
5	84	0.71299	60
>5	266	2.75534	165*
Remaining life.	3.167		$1,014
Round rate to	7.0%		

*$84 × 2.75534 × 0.71299 = $165

These amounts should be added to the balance sheet for analysis purposes.

3. Income statement adjustments relating to capitalization of operating leases involve two steps:
   a. Remove rent expense of $195 million from operating expense, equal to depreciation and interest on the capitalized leased assets and liabilities in (b).
   b. Add depreciation expense from lease assets to operating expense and also reflect interest expense on the lease obligation as a nonoperating expense. Using the spreadsheet computations above, we assume that the remaining lease term is 8.167 years (five years reported in the lease schedule plus 3.167 years after Year 5). Applying this lease term and zero salvage value, we get an estimated straight-line depreciation for lease assets of $124 million ($1,014 million/8.167 years). Interest expense on the $1,014 million lease liability at the 7.04% capitalization rate is $71 million ($1,014 million × 7.04%). The net adjustment to NOPAT, reflecting the elimination of rent expense and the addition of depreciation expense, is $45 million [($195 million rent expense − $124 million depreciation) × (1 − 0.37)].

Review 10-2—Solution

1. American Airlines' pension benefit obligation increases primarily by service cost, interest cost, and actuarial losses (which are increases in the pension liability as a result of changes in actuarial assumptions). It is decreased by the payment of benefits to retirees and by any actuarial gains.
2. American Airlines' pension assets increase by positive investment returns for the period and cash contributions made by the company. Assets decrease by benefits paid to retirees and by investment losses.
3. American Airlines' funded status is $(6,688) million ($16,395 million PBO − $9,707 million Pension Assets) as of 2015. The negative amount indicates that the plan is underfunded. Consequently, this amount is reflected as a liability on American's balance sheet.
4. Expected return on plan assets acts as an offset to service cost and interest cost in computing net pension cost. As the expected return increases, net pension cost decreases.
5. American Airlines' expected return of $851 million is greater than its actual return of $(506) million in 2015.
6. American Airlines reports a net pension expense of $691 million in its 2015 income statement. Of this, only $29 million pertained to the company's defined benefit plans, and $662 million to defined contribution plans.
7. American Airlines' funded status is negative, indicating an underfunded plan. In 2015, the company contributed only $6 million to the pension plan, down from $810 million in the prior year. The large return on plan assets during the year created the unusual situation that American Airlines was able to conserve cash by cutting pension contributions. American is able to meet its pension obligations at the moment. If markets turn around this might not be as easy for the company.

Review 10-3—Solution

1. Total income tax expense was $577 million for 2015.
2. The current portion of FedEx's tax provision was $1,111 million.
3. Income tax expense is the sum of current taxes (that is, currently payable as determined from the company's federal, state, and foreign tax returns) plus the change in deferred tax assets and liabilities. It is a calculated figure, not a percentage that is applied to pretax income. For 2015, FedEx tax expense was decreased by the deferred provision (an asset) of $534 million.
4. The effective rate for FedEx in 2015 was 35.5% which is close to the federal statutory rate. The additional taxes owing to state and local jurisdictions was offset by the lower taxes due on foreign operations.

Module 11

Cash Flows

Learning Objectives

LO1 Describe the framework for the statement of cash flows. (p. 11-3)

LO2 Determine and analyze net cash flows from operating activities. (p. 11-9)

LO3 Determine and analyze net cash flows from investing activities. (p. 11-16)

LO4 Determine and analyze net cash flows from financing activities. (p. 11-18)

LO5 Examine and interpret cash flow information. (p. 11-21)

LO6 Compute and interpret ratios based on operating cash flows. (p. 11-27)

LO7 Explain and construct a direct method statement of cash flows (Appendix 11A). (p. 11-29)

SBUX

Market Cap: $86,100 mil
Total assets: $12,446 mil
Revenues: $19,163 mil
Net income: $2,759 mil

Starbucks Corporation is the leading retailer, roaster, and brander of specialty coffee. The company has broad geographic reach. At last count, Starbucks operated 8,671 stores in the U.S. and another 3,564 stores in scores of countries around the world. In 2015, the company reported strong operating results: net income of $2,759.3 million on revenue of $19.2 billion.

In 2015, Starbucks reported cash flow from operating activities of $3,749.1 million, 36% greater than its net income. Profit and cash flow are two different concepts, as the graphic below shows.

While profitability is important, it is cash that pays suppliers and employees, and cash pays dividends to shareholders. Thus, we need to understand how cash is generated to effectively analyze the company. In this module, we explore the ways in which cash is generated and used, and we introduce a number of analytical approaches that will help us to better understand the factors that drive cash creation. [Sources: *Starbucks*, 2015 10-K and Annual Report.]

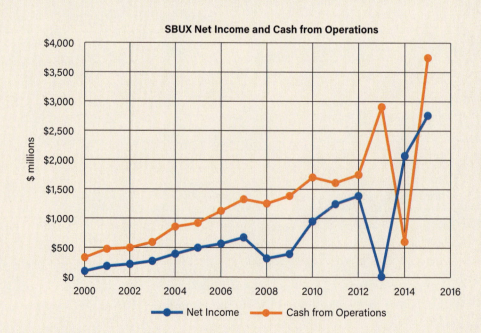

SBUX Net Income and Cash from Operations

© iStock

Road Map

LO	Learning Objective | Topics	Page	eLecture	Guided Example	Assignments
11–1	**Describe the framework for the statement of cash flows.** Relations Among Financial Statements :: Statement of Cash Flows Structure :: Operating Activities Preview :: Investing Activities Preview :: Financing Activities Preview	11-3	e11–1	Review 11-1	1, 2, 3, 4, 22, 23, 24, 30, 49, 50, 51, 56, 57, 58
11–2	**Determine and analyze net cash flows from operating activities.** Steps to Compute Net Cash Flows From Operating Activities	11-9	e11–2	Review 11-2	9, 10, 11, 13, 25, 31, 32, 33, 34, 43, 44, 45, 46, 47, 48, 49, 50, 51
11–3	**Determine and analyze net cash flows from investing activities.** Analyze Remaining Noncash Assets	11-16	e11–3	Review 11-3	10, 32, 36, 38, 43, 44, 45, 46, 47, 48, 49, 50, 52, 53, 54, 55
11–4	**Determine and analyze net cash flows from financing activities.** Analyze Liabilities And Equity :: Balance Sheet Accounts and Cash Flow Effects :: Supplemental Disclosures for Indirect Method	11-18	e11–4	Review 11-4	12, 32, 36, 38, 43, 44, 45, 46, 47, 48, 49, 50, 52, 53, 54, 55
11–5	**Examine and interpret cash flow information.** Cash Flow Components :: Cash Flow Patterns :: Usefulness of Statement Of Cash Flows	11-21	e11–5	Review 11-5	5, 7, 21, 28, 39, 40, 42, 49, 50, 51, 56, 57, 58
11–6	**Compute and interpret ratios based on operating cash flows.** Ratio Analyses of Cash Flows :: Free Cash Flow	11-27	e11–6	Review 11-6	5, 6, 7, 19, 20, 29, 41, 42, 56, 57
11–7	**Explain and construct a direct method statement of cash flows (Appendix 11A).** Cash Flows from Operating Activities :: Cash Flows from Investing and Financing	11-29	e11–7	Review 11-7	8, 14, 15, 16, 17, 18, 26, 27, 35, 36, 37, 52, 53, 54, 55

Module Organization

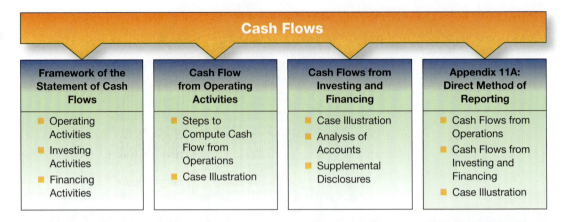

Cash Flows

Framework of the Statement of Cash Flows	Cash Flow from Operating Activities	Cash Flows from Investing and Financing	Appendix 11A: Direct Method of Reporting
▪ Operating Activities ▪ Investing Activities ▪ Financing Activities	▪ Steps to Compute Cash Flow from Operations ▪ Case Illustration	▪ Case Illustration ▪ Analysis of Accounts ▪ Supplemental Disclosures	▪ Cash Flows from Operations ▪ Cash Flows from Investing and Financing ▪ Case Illustration

Framework for the Statement of Cash Flows

LO1 Describe the framework for the statement of cash flows.

The **statement of cash flows** is a financial statement that summarizes information about the flow of cash into and out of a company.[1] Information provided in a statement of cash flows helps managers, investors, and creditors assess the company's ability to generate positive future net cash flows and to meet its debt obligations, its need for external financing, and its ability to pay its dividends. The balance sheet reports the company's financial position at a point in time (the end of each period), whereas the statement of cash flows explains the change in one of its components—cash—from one balance sheet date to the next. The income statement reveals the results of the company's operating activities for the period, and these operating activities are a major contributor to the change in cash as reported in the statement of cash flows.

Relation Among Financial Statements

Each financial statement reveals a different view of the company, and a thorough financial analysis requires us to scrutinize the information contained in each.

Income Statement Insights The income statement informs us about the degree to which consumers value the products and/or services offered by the company. How much does it cost to produce them, and can the company set prices that pass on these production costs to its customers? Is the company able to control labor costs, both for salaries and wages and for benefits offered to employees? Can the company effectively manage its overhead costs? How well is it insulated against fluctuations in interest rates, commodity prices, or foreign exchange rates? How well can it control its income tax obligations? These are but a few of the important questions that can be answered by our analysis of the income statement.

Balance Sheet Insights The balance sheet informs us about the resources available to the company and the claims against those resources by creditors and owners. From the balance sheet, we learn about the magnitude of investment in net working capital and PPE assets required for the company to conduct business. This is impacted by the company's business model and the norms of the industries in which the company operates. We are able to estimate the extent to which the company relies upon borrowed funds, the structure of that indebtedness, and the degree to which the company has (or can generate) the liquidity required to meet its debt obligations. We also learn about the company's equity investors and the claims they have on the net assets and income of the company. Whereas the income statement provides us with insight into the economics of the company's operations, the balance sheet informs us about the resources the company uses in its operations and the claims against those resources.

Statement of Cash Flows Insights As we will learn in this module, the statement of cash flows is prepared from the company's income statement and comparative balance sheets. At first glance, it

---

[1] The statement of cash flows explains the change in a firm's cash *and* cash equivalents. **Cash equivalents** are short-term, highly liquid investments that are (1) easily convertible into a known cash amount and (2) close enough to maturity so that their market value is not sensitive to interest rate changes (generally, investments with initial maturities of three months or less). Treasury bills, commercial paper (short-term notes issued by corporations), and money market funds are typical examples of cash equivalents.

might appear that the information contained in the cash flow statement is redundant. However, to treat the statement of cash flows as a secondary statement would ignore potential information that can assist us in our analysis of the company. In particular, the statement of cash flows offers information along the following four dimensions.

- **Activity type** The statement of cash flows is structured to highlight three primary activities of the company: **operating activities**, **investing activities**, and **financing activities**. Neither the income statement nor the balance sheet presents that perspective.

- **Liquidity** The statement of cash flows emphasizes the role cash plays in the company's day-to-day operations; it is cash that pays employees, cash that pays debt, and cash that provides a return to equity holders in the form of dividends. Finance professionals often focus on free cash flow, and for good reason. Companies that fail typically do so because they lack the cash flow necessary to conduct their business. A focus solely on GAAP profit can obscure a deterioration of liquidity that can lead to company failure.

- **Additional detail** As an added benefit, the statement of cash flows highlights important operating items that are often not reported as separate line items in the income statement, such as depreciation on building and equipment assets, impairments of tangible and intangible assets, the cost of stock-based compensation, the excess of reported equity income over dividends received from investee companies, the cash portion of interest expense and income tax expense, and the gain or loss on the sales of assets. In addition, the statement of cash flows highlights items that are *not* reflected in the income statement, such as capital expenditures (CAPEX), dividend payments, and the repayment of the principle portion of company debt.

- **Earnings quality** The statement of cash flows provides insight into the "quality" of company earnings. All profit must eventually be received in cash. So, when profit and operating cash flow diverge, we must investigate the reasons for the divergence because cash flow ultimately drives company value. If net income grows at a faster pace than operating cash flows, our analysis attempts to understand whether cash flow will increase in the future or whether income has been improperly recognized, only to be reversed in the future. Our assessment of the quality of company earnings is a difficult challenge but one that is aided considerably by a thorough understanding of the statement of cash flows.

Statement of Cash Flows Structure

The statement of cash flows classifies cash receipts and cash payments into one of three categories.

- **Operating activities** Operating activities measure the net cash inflows and outflows as a result of the company's transactions with its customers. We generally prefer operating cash flows to be positive, although companies can report net cash outflows for operating activities in the short run during periods of growth (as the company builds up inventory and hires staff to grow operations in anticipation of future sales and cash inflows).

- **Investing activities** Investing activities relate to investments, joint ventures, and capital expenditures for PPE. Outflows occur when a company purchases these assets, and inflows occur when they are sold.

- **Financing activities** Financing activities relate to long-term debt and stockholders' equity. Cash inflows result from borrowing money and issuing stock to investors. Outflows occur when a company repays debt, repurchases stock, or pays dividends to shareholders.

The combined effects on cash of all three categories explain the net change in cash for that period as follows.

	Beginning cash balance (the ending cash balance reported on prior year's balance sheet)
+	Change in cash during the period
=	Ending cash balance for current year (reported on current year's balance sheet)

Statement of Cash Flows Preparation Overview   The statement of cash flows is prepared using data from the income statement and the balance sheet.

- ■ **Income statement**   For the *indirect* method of preparing the operating section, we begin with net income as a source of cash and adjust net income for non-cash items that are included in the computation of net income.[2]

- ■ **Balance sheet**   We consider the change in each balance sheet account and determine the cash generated or used by the change in the account balance. The graphic below shows how balance sheet categories relate to the three sections of the statement of cash flow.

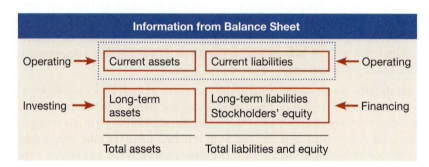

There are two exceptions to the balance sheet classification illustrated in the graphic above; both are included in the current section of the balance sheet, but neither is classified as operating activities.

- ■ Marketable securities—current assets that are classified as investing activities.

- ■ Short-term debt and current maturities of long-term debt—current liabilities that are classified as financing activities.

Statement of Cash Flows for Starbucks   Exhibit 11.1 reproduces Starbucks' statement of cash flows. Starbucks reports $3,749.1 million in net cash inflows from operating activities in 2015. This is much greater than its net income of $2,759.3 million, which highlights that net income and operating cash flow are different measures. (Later in this module, we explain all the items included in the operating section of Starbucks' cash flow statement). The company used $1,520.3 million of cash for investing activities, primarily for purchases of PPE (called capital expenditures or CAPEX), and also used $2,256.5 million of cash for financing activities to pay dividends and repurchase common stock. In sum, Starbucks decreased its cash by $178.3 million (after considering foreign exchange effects), from $1,708.4 million at the beginning of fiscal 2015 to $1,530.1 million at the end of fiscal 2015.

Overall, Starbucks' cash flow picture is strong for three reasons.

- ■ The company is generating positive cash from operating activities, its core business.

- ■ The company is investing in the maintenance and growth of its infrastructure with capital expenditures (CAPEX).

- ■ The company is returning cash to shareholders through dividends and share repurchases.

In analyzing the statement of cash flows, we should not necessarily conclude the company is better off if the ending balance of cash increases and worse off if cash decreases. It is not the *change* in cash that is most important but the reasons behind the change. For example, what are the sources of cash inflows? Are these sources of cash transitory, or can we expect the cash flows to continue? Are these sources mainly from operating activities, or did sales of investments or PPE generate cash flow? To what uses have cash inflows been put? Such questions and answers are key to properly using the statement of cash flows.

---

[2] Firms can choose to present operating cash flows either directly, by reporting operating cash receipts from customers and cash payments to suppliers and employees, or indirectly, by reconciling net income and cash flow from operating activities. While firms are encouraged to use the simpler direct method, most U.S. companies continue to use the indirect method. Our discussion here addresses the indirect method, and we return to the direct method at the end of the module.

Exhibit 11.1 ■ Statement of Cash Flows for Starbucks Corporation

Fiscal Year Ended ($ millions)	Sept. 27, 2015	Sept. 28, 2014	Sept. 29, 2013
Operating Activities			
Net earnings including noncontrolling interests	$2,759.3	$2,067.7	$ 8.8
Adjustments to reconcile net earnings to net cash provided by operating activities:			
Depreciation and amortization	933.8	748.4	655.6
Litigation charge	—	—	2,784.1
Deferred income taxes, net	21.2	10.2	(1,045.9)
Income earned from equity method investees	(190.2)	(182.7)	(171.8)
Distributions received from equity method investees	148.2	139.2	115.6
Gain resulting from acquisition/sale of equity in joint ventures and certain retail operations	(394.3)	(70.2)	(80.1)
Loss on extinguishment of debt	61.1	—	—
Stock-based compensation	209.8	183.2	142.3
Excess tax benefit on share-based awards	(132.4)	(114.4)	(258.1)
Other	53.8	36.2	23.0
Cash provided/(used) by changes in operating assets and liabilities:			
Accounts receivable	(82.8)	(79.7)	(68.3)
Inventories	(207.9)	14.3	152.5
Accounts payable	137.7	60.4	88.7
Accrued litigation charge	—	(2,763.9)	—
Income taxes payable, net	87.6	309.8	298.4
Accrued liabilities and insurance reserves	124.4	103.9	47.3
Stored value card liability	170.3	140.8	139.9
Prepaid expenses, other current assets and other long-term assets	49.5	4.6	76.3
Net cash provided by operating activities	3,749.1	607.8	2,908.3
Investing Activities			
Purchase of investments	(567.4)	(1,652.5)	(785.9)
Sales of investments	600.6	1,454.8	60.2
Maturities and calls of investments	18.8	456.1	980.0
Acquisitions, net of cash acquired	(284.3)	—	(610.4)
Additions to property, plant and equipment	(1,303.7)	(1,160.9)	(1,151.2)
Proceeds from sale of equity in joint ventures and certain retail operations	8.9	103.9	108.0
Other	6.8	(19.1)	(11.9)
Net cash used by investing activities	(1,520.3)	(817.7)	(1,411.2)
Financing Activities			
Proceeds from issuance of long-term debt	848.5	748.5	749.7
Repayments of long-term debt	(610.1)	—	(35.2)
Cash used for purchase of non-controlling interest	(360.8)	—	—
Proceeds from issuance of common stock	191.8	139.7	247.2
Excess tax benefit on share-based awards	132.4	114.4	258.1
Cash dividends paid	(928.6)	(783.1)	(628.9)
Repurchase of common stock	(1,436.1)	(758.6)	(588.1)
Minimum tax withholdings on share-based awards	(75.5)	(77.3)	(121.4)
Other	(18.1)	(6.9)	10.4
Net cash used by financing activities	(2,256.5)	(623.3)	(108.2)
Effect of exchange rate changes on cash and cash equivalents	(150.6)	(34.1)	(1.8)
Net (decrease)/increase in cash and cash equivalents	(178.3)	(867.3)	1,387.1
Cash and Cash Equivalents:			
Beginning of period	1,708.4	2,575.7	1,188.6
End of period	$1,530.1	$1,708.4	$2,575.7

Operating Activities Preview

The focus of **operating activities** of companies is to generate cash from selling goods or services at a profit. Following are examples of cash inflows and outflows relating to operating activities.

Operating Activities

Cash Inflows

- Receipts from customers for sales made or services rendered.
- Receipts of interest and dividends.
- Other receipts that are not related to investing or financing activities, such as lawsuit settlements and refunds received from suppliers.

Cash Outflows ▼

- Payments to employees or suppliers.
- Payments to purchase inventories.
- Payments of interest to creditors.
- Payments of taxes to government.
- Other payments that are not related to investing or financing activities, such as contributions to charity.

These cash inflows and outflows affect net income. Accordingly, net income is the first line of the operating cash flow section of the statement of cash flow. This reflects the idea that the company generates cash from selling its goods or services to its customers.

Net income commonly includes items that do not involve the receipt or payment of cash. Depreciation expense is an example. Cash is spent when the depreciable asset (e.g., equipment or a building) is purchased. Depreciation expense is an accounting process that allocates the cash cost over the useful life of the asset. Although there is no cash outflow with annual depreciation expense, it is reported as an expense in computing net income. Because the focus of the statement of cash flow is on cash, we need to "undo" the effect of depreciation and other non-cash expenses. We do that by *adding it back* to offset the expense (i.e., undo the negative affect) in the income statement.

Let's consider further adjustments to get operating cash flow. During the year, the company might decide whether to use cash to grow the firm. For example, the company might purchase additional inventories to have goods available for future sales. This use of cash increases inventory but has no effect on net income. As another example, the company can extend credit to its customers as a strategic move to generate additional sales. This action increases sales, but instead of receiving cash, the company's accounts receivable increases. The statement of cash flows shows an increase in inventories and an increase in accounts receivable as negative amounts to indicate the company has invested cash in the growth of assets (inventory and accounts receivable). Conversely, cash is freed up when the company collects its receivables or reduces inventory levels, and the statement of cash flows shows such decreases as positive amounts.

On the liability side, companies can conserve cash by borrowing from their suppliers or other operating creditors. An increase in liabilities signals an increase in borrowing, an inflow of cash, which is reported as a positive amount in the statement of cash flow. As the company uses cash to repay borrowed amounts, the statement of cash flows shows the reduction of the liability as a negative amount, indicating a cash outflow.

Companies prepare the statement of cash flows using their income statement and balance sheets (to calculate changes in accounts between the current and prior years). The preparation is mainly a mechanical process with limited discretion. A simple but common computation of operating cash flow follows.

	Net income (− if a net loss)
+	Depreciation expense
−	Increases in current assets
+	Decreases in current assets
+	Increases in current liabilities
−	Decreases in current liabilities
=	Cash from operating activities

Understanding how increases and decreases in assets and liabilities affect cash flow is key to understanding the information contained in the statement of cash flows. To help, keep the following decision rules in mind.

Balance Sheet Account	Increase in Account	Decrease in Account
Assets (noncash)	Cash Outflow	Cash Inflow
Liabilities and equity.	Cash Inflow	Cash Outflow

This table applies to all sections of the statement of cash flows. (When we examine a statement of cash flows such as Starbucks', see Exhibit 11.1, the cash flow effect of an item does not always agree with the change in the balance sheet account. This can be due to several factors. One factor is when a company uses its own stock to acquire another entity. There is no cash effect from a stock acquisition and, hence, it is not reported in the statement of cash flows. Yet, the company does increase its assets and liabilities when it adds the acquired company's assets and liabilities to its balance sheet.)

Knowledge of how companies record cash inflows and outflows not only sheds light on the information contained in the statement of cash flows, it also helps managers with business decisions. For instance, managers can increase cash by decreasing the levels of receivables and inventories, perhaps by better managing the quantities and types of inventories to reduce slow moving items or by being smarter about which customers to extend credit to, and in what amounts, to minimize slow-paying customers. Similarly, managers can increase cash by increasing the levels of accounts payable and accrued liabilities. (This must be done with care, however, as one company's payables are another company's receivables and slowing down payment could jeopardize future transactions with the vendor or supplier.) Managing cash balances by managing current asset and current liability accounts is called *working capital management*, an important activity for all companies.

Investing Activities Preview

A firm's transactions involving (1) the acquisition and disposal of PPE assets and intangible assets, (2) the purchase and sale of stocks, bonds, and other securities (that are not cash equivalents), and (3) the lending and subsequent collection of money constitute the basic components of its **investing activities**. The related cash receipts and payments appear in the investing activities section of the statement of cash flows. Examples of these cash flows follow.

Investing Activities

Cash Inflows

- Receipts from sales of PPE assets and intangible assets.
- Receipts from sales of investments in stocks, bonds, and other securities (other than cash equivalents).
- Receipts from repayments of loans by borrowers.

Cash Outflows

- Payments to purchase PPE assets and intangible assets.
- Payments to purchase stocks, bonds, and other securities (other than cash equivalents).
- Payments made to lend money to borrowers.

Financing Activities Preview

A firm engages in **financing activities** when it obtains resources from owners, returns resources to owners, borrows resources from creditors, and repays amounts borrowed. Cash flows related to these transactions are reported in the financing activities section of the statement of cash flows. Examples of these cash flows follow.

Financing Activities	
Cash Inflows	**Cash Outflows**
■ Receipts from issuances of common stock and preferred stock and from sales of treasury stock.	■ Payments to acquire treasury stock.
	■ Payments of dividends.
■ Receipts from issuances of bonds payable, mortgage notes payable, and other notes payable.	■ Payments to settle outstanding bonds payable, mortgage notes payable, and other notes payable.

Review 11-1 LO1

Identify each transaction as one of the following activities: operating (O), investing (I), or financing (F).

Transaction	Classification
1. Payments of dividends..	_____
2. Payments to purchase PPE assets and intangible assets..................	_____
3. Payments to employees or suppliers...................................	_____
4. Payments to purchase inventories.....................................	_____
5. Receipts from issuances of bonds payable, mortgage notes payable, and other notes payable	_____
6. Receipts from sales of investments in stocks, bonds, and other securities (other than cash equivalents)	_____
7. Payments of interest to creditors.....................................	_____
8. Receipts from issuances of common stock and preferred stock and from sales of treasury stock	_____
9. Receipts of interest and dividends....................................	_____
10. Payments to purchase stocks, bonds, and other securities (other than cash equivalents)	_____
11. Receipts from customers for sales made or services rendered.............	_____
12. Payments to acquire treasury stock....................................	_____
13. Other receipts such as lawsuit settlements and refunds received from suppliers..	_____
14. Payments of taxes to government......................................	_____
15. Payments to settle outstanding bonds payable, mortgage notes payable, and other notes payable	_____
16. Receipts from sales of PPE assets and intangible assets..................	_____
17. Other payments such as contributions to charity	_____
18. Receipts from repayments of loans by borrowers.........................	_____
19. Payments made to lend money to borrowers	_____

Solution on p. 11-56.

Cash Flow from Operating Activities

LO2
Determine and analyze net cash flows from operating activities.

The first section of a statement of cash flows presents a firm's net cash flow from operating activities. Two alternative formats are used to report the net cash flow from operating activities: the *indirect method* and the *direct method. Both methods report the same amount of net cash flow from operating activities.* (Net cash flows from investing and financing activities are prepared in the same manner under both the indirect and direct methods; only the format for cash flows from operating activities differs.)

The **indirect method** starts with net income and applies a series of adjustments to net income to convert it to net cash flow from operating activities. *More than 98% of companies preparing the statement of cash flows use the indirect method.* The indirect method is popular because it is easier and less expensive to prepare than the direct method and the direct method requires a supplemental disclosure showing the indirect method (thus, essentially reporting both methods).

The remainder of this module discusses the preparation of the statement of cash flows. The indirect method is presented in this section, and the direct method is presented in the Appendix. (These discussions are independent of each other; both provide complete coverage of the preparation of the statement of cash flows.)

To prepare a statement of cash flows, we need a firm's income statement, comparative balance sheets, and some additional data taken from the accounting records. Exhibit 11.2 presents this information for Java House. We use these data to prepare Java House's 2017 statement of cash flows using the indirect method. Java House's statement of cash flows explains the $25,000 increase in cash (from $10,000 to $35,000) that occurred during 2017 by classifying the firm's cash flows into operating, investing, and financing categories.

Exhibit 11.2 ■ Financial Data of Java House

JAVA HOUSE
Income Statement
For Year Ended December 31, 2017

Sales.		$250,000
Cost of goods sold	$148,000	
Wages expense	52,000	
Insurance expense	5,000	
Depreciation expense. . . .	10,000	
Income tax expense	11,000	
Gain on sale of land	(8,000)	218,000
Net income		$ 32,000

Additional Data for 2017

1. Purchased all of the long-term investments for cash at year-end.
2. Sold land costing $20,000 for $28,000 cash.
3. Acquired a $60,000 patent at year-end by issuing common stock at par.
4. All accounts payable relate to merchandise purchases.
5. Issued common stock at par for $10,000 cash.
6. Declared and paid cash dividends of $13,000.

JAVA HOUSE
Balance Sheet

	Dec. 31, 2017	Dec. 31, 2016
Assets		
Cash	$ 35,000	$ 10,000
Accounts receivable	39,000	34,000
Inventory.	54,000	60,000
Prepaid insurance.	17,000	4,000
Long-term investments . . .	15,000	—
PPE.	180,000	200,000
Accumulated depreciation .	(50,000)	(40,000)
Patent	60,000	—
Total assets.	$350,000	$268,000
Liabilities and Equity		
Accounts payable.	$ 10,000	$ 19,000
Income tax payable	5,000	3,000
Common stock.	260,000	190,000
Retained earnings	75,000	56,000
Total liabilities and equity . .	$350,000	$268,000

Steps to Compute Net Cash Flow from Operating Activities

The following four steps are applied to construct the net cash flows from the operating activities section of the statement of cash flows.

① **Begin with net income** The first line of the operating activities section of the statement of cash flows is net income, which is the bottom line from the income statement. This amount is recorded as a positive amount for net income and as a negative amount for a net loss.

② **Adjust net income (loss) for** *noncash* **revenues, expenses, gains, and losses**

　a.　**Noncash revenues and expenses** The income statement often includes noncash expenses, such as depreciation and amortization. These expenses are allocations of asset costs over their useful lives to match the revenues generated from those assets. The cash outflow normally occurs when the asset is acquired, which is reported in the *investing* section. Depreciation and amortization expenses do not entail cash outflows. Hence, we must eliminate them from the statement of cash flows by adding them back (to "zero them out" because they are negative amounts in the net income computation).

　b.　**Gains and losses** Gains and losses on sales of assets are part of investing activities, not operating activities (unless the company is in the business of buying and selling assets). Thus, we must remove them from the operating section and record the net cash inflows or outflows in the investing section; namely, gains on sales are subtracted from income and losses on sales are added to income.

③ **Adjust net income (loss) for changes in current assets and current liabilities** Net income must be adjusted for changes in current assets and current liabilities (the operating section of the balance sheet). A decrease (from prior year to current year) in a noncash current asset is identified as a cash inflow, and an increase is identified as a cash outflow. Conversely, an increase in a current liability is identified as a cash inflow and a decrease as a cash outflow. To make this computation, we use the following guide.

Balance Sheet Account	Increase in Account	Decrease in Account
Current assets (excluding cash).....	Cash Outflow	Cash Inflow
Current liabilities................	Cash Inflow	Cash Outflow

④ **Sum the amounts from Steps 1, 2, and 3 to get net cash flows from operating activities**

Exhibit 11.3 summarizes the adjustments to net income in determining operating cash flows. These are the adjustments applied under the indirect method of computing cash flow from operations.

Exhibit 11.3 ■ Converting Net Income to Net Cash Flow from Operating Activities

	Add (+) or Subtract (−) from Net Income
Net income.......................................	$ #
Add depreciation and amortization.................................	+
Add (subtract) losses (gains) on asset and liability dispositions............	+ or −
Adjust for changes in noncash current assets	
Subtract increases in noncash current assets	−
Add decreases in noncash current assets	+
Adjust for changes in current liabilities	
Add increases in current liabilities............................	+
Subtract decreases in current liabilities	−
Net cash flow from operating activities	$ #

Adjustments for noncash revenues, expenses, gains, and losses

Adjustments for changes in noncash current assets and current liabilities

To better understand the adjustments for current assets and liabilities, the following table provides brief explanations of adjustments for receivables, inventories, payables, and accruals.

	Change in account balance ...	Means that ...	Which requires this adjustment to net income to yield cash profit ...
Receivables	Increase	Sales and net income increase, but cash is not yet received	Deduct increase in receivables from net income
	Decrease	More cash is received than is reported in sales and net income	Add decrease in receivables to net income
Inventories	Increase	Cash is paid for inventories that are not yet reflected in cost of goods sold	Deduct increase in inventories from net income
	Decrease	Cost of goods sold includes inventory costs that were paid for in a prior period	Add decrease in inventories to net income
Payables and accruals	Increase	More goods and services are acquired on credit, delaying cash payment	Add increase in payables and accruals to net income
	Decrease	More cash is paid than that reflected in cost of goods sold or operating expenses	Deduct decrease in payables and accruals from net income

Java House Case Illustration

We next explain and illustrate these adjustments with Java House's data from Exhibit 11.2.

Depreciation and Amortization Expenses

Depreciation and amortization expenses represent write-offs of previously recorded assets, so-called noncash expenses. Because depreciation and amortization expenses are subtracted in computing net income, we add these expenses to net income as we convert it to a related net operating cash flow. Adding these expenses to net income eliminates them from the income statement and is a necessary adjustment to obtain cash income. Java House had $10,000 of 2017 depreciation expense, so this amount is added to Java House's net income of $32,000.

Net income......................................	$32,000
Add depreciation	**10,000**

Gains and Losses Related to Investing or Financing Activities

The income statement can contain gains and losses that relate to investing or financing activities. Gains and losses from the sale of investments, PPE assets, or intangible assets illustrate gains and losses from investing (not operating) activities. A gain or loss from the retirement of bonds payable is an example of a financing gain or loss. The full cash flow effect from these types of events is reported in the investing or financing sections of the statement of cash flows. Therefore, the related gains or losses must be eliminated as we convert net income to net cash flow from operating activities. To eliminate their impact on net income, gains are subtracted and losses are added to net income. Java House had an $8,000 gain from the sale of land in 2017. This gain relates to an investing activity, so it is subtracted from Java House's net income.

Net income......................................	$32,000
Add depreciation	10,000
Subtract gain on sale of land	**(8,000)**

Accounts Receivable Change

Credit sales increase accounts receivable; cash collections on account decrease accounts receivable. If, overall, accounts receivable decrease during a year, then cash collections from customers exceed credit sales revenue by the amount of the decrease. Because sales are added in computing net income, the decrease in accounts receivable is added to net income. In essence, this adjustment replaces the sales amount with the larger amount of cash collections from customers. If accounts receivable increase during a year, then sales revenue exceeds the cash collections from customers by the amount of the increase. Because sales are added in computing net income, the increase in accounts receivable is subtracted from net income as we convert it to a net cash flow from operating activities. In essence, this adjustment replaces the sales amount with the smaller amount of cash collections from customers. Java House's accounts receivable increased $5,000 during 2017, so this increase is subtracted from net income under the indirect method.

Net income......................................	$32,000
Add depreciation	10,000
Subtract gain on sale of land	(8,000)
Subtract accounts receivable increase	**(5,000)**

Inventory Change

The adjustment for an inventory change is one of two adjustments to net income that together cause the cost of goods sold expense to be replaced by an amount representing the cash paid during the period for merchandise purchased. The second adjustment, which we examine shortly, is for the change in accounts payable. The effect of the inventory adjustment alone is to adjust net income for the difference between the cost of goods sold and the cost of merchandise purchased during the period. The cost of merchandise purchased increases inventory; the cost of goods sold decreases inventory. An overall decrease in inventory during a period must mean, therefore, that the cost of merchandise purchased was less than the cost of goods sold, by the amount of the decrease. Because cost of goods sold was subtracted in computing net income, the inventory decrease is added to net income. After this adjustment, the effect of the cost of goods sold on net income has been replaced by the smaller cost of merchandise purchased. Similarly, if inventory increased during a period, the cost of merchandise purchased is larger than the cost of goods sold by the amount of the increase. To replace the cost of goods sold with the cost of merchandise purchased, the inventory increase is subtracted from net income. Java House's inventory decreased $6,000 during 2017, so this decrease is added to net income.

Net income.	$32,000
Add depreciation	10,000
Subtract gain on sale of land	(8,000)
Subtract accounts receivable increase	(5,000)
Add inventory decrease	**6,000**

Prepaid Expenses Change

Cash prepayments of various expenses increase a firm's prepaid expenses. When the related expenses for the period are subsequently recorded, the prepaid expenses decrease. An overall decrease in prepaid expenses for a period means the cash prepayments were less than the related expenses. Because the expenses were subtracted in determining net income, the indirect method adds the decrease in prepaid expenses to net income as it is converted to a cash flow amount. The effect of the addition is to replace the expense amount with the smaller cash payment amount. Similarly, an increase in prepaid expenses is subtracted from net income because an increase means the cash prepayments during the year were more than the related expenses. Java House's prepaid insurance increased $13,000 during 2017, so this increase is deducted from net income.

Net income.	$32,000
Add depreciation	10,000
Subtract gain on sale of land	(8,000)
Subtract accounts receivable increase	(5,000)
Add inventory decrease	6,000
Subtract prepaid insurance increase	**(13,000)**

Accounts Payable Change

When merchandise is purchased on account, accounts payable increase by the cost of the goods purchased. Accounts payable decrease when cash payments are made to settle the accounts. An overall decrease in accounts payable during a year means cash payments for purchases were more than the cost of the purchases. An accounts payable decrease, therefore, is subtracted from net income under the indirect method. The deduction, in effect, replaces the cost of merchandise purchased with the larger cash payments for merchandise purchased. (Recall that the earlier inventory adjustment replaced the cost of goods sold with the cost of merchandise purchased.) In contrast, an increase in accounts payable means cash payments for purchases were less than the cost of purchases for the period. Thus, an accounts payable increase is added to net income as it is converted to a cash flow amount. Java House shows a $9,000 decrease in accounts payable during 2017. This decrease is subtracted from net income.

Net income	$32,000
Add depreciation	10,000
Subtract gain on sale of land	(8,000)
Subtract accounts receivable increase	(5,000)
Add inventory decrease	6,000
Subtract prepaid insurance increase	(13,000)
Subtract accounts payable decrease.	**(9,000)**

Accrued Liabilities Change

Changes in accrued liabilities are interpreted the same way as changes in accounts payable. A decrease means cash payments exceeded the related expense amounts; an increase means cash payments were less than the related expenses. Decreases are subtracted from net income; increases are added to net income. Java has one accrued liability, income tax payable, and it increased by $2,000 during 2017. The $2,000 increase is added to net income.

Net income.	$32,000
Add depreciation	10,000
Subtract gain on sale of land	(8,000)
Subtract accounts receivable increase	(5,000)
Add inventory decrease	6,000
Subtract prepaid insurance increase	(13,000)
Subtract accounts payable decrease.	(9,000)
Add income tax payable increase.	**2,000**

Summary of Cash from Operating Activities

We have now identified all of the adjustments to convert Java House's net income to its net cash flow from operating activities. The operating activities section of the statement of cash flows appears as follows under the indirect method.

Net income.	$32,000
Add (deduct) items to convert net income to cash basis:	
Depreciation	10,000
Gain on sale of land	(8,000)
Accounts receivable increase.	(5,000)
Inventory decrease	6,000
Prepaid insurance increase.	(13,000)
Accounts payable decrease	(9,000)
Income tax payable increase	2,000
Net cash provided by operating activities	**$15,000**

To summarize, net cash from operating activities begins with net income (loss) and eliminates noncash expenses (such as depreciation) and any gains and losses that are properly reported in the investing and financing sections. Next, cash inflows (outflows) relating to changes in the level of current operating assets and liabilities are added (subtracted) to yield net cash flows from operating activities. During the period, Java House earned cash operating profits of $34,000 ($32,000 + $10,000 − $8,000) and used $19,000 of cash (−$5,000 + $6,000 − $13,000 − $9,000 + $2,000) to increase net working capital. Cash outflows relating to the increase in net working capital are a common occurrence for growing companies, and this net asset increase must be financed just like the increase in PPE assets.

Starbucks reports $2,759.3 million for 2015 net earnings, including noncontrolling interests, along with $3,749.1 million of operating cash inflows. Differences between net income and operating cash flow are due to:

- Depreciation and amortization expense of $933.8 million (similar to the addback for Java House).

- Income earned from equity method investees of $190.2 million that is included in net income. This is followed by the addition of $148.2 million from dividends received from those equity method investees. Equity income is not received in cash until the investee pays dividends to the investors (including Starbucks).

- Gain on sale of joint venture investments of $394.3 million is subtracted to remove the noncash gain. The statement of cash flows shows the cash received as an investing inflow. (This is similar to the gain on sale of land for Java House).

- Stock-based compensation expense of $209.8 million, which is noncash compensation expense paid in the form of shares of stock. Starbucks reports the related tax benefits as a financing activity (a cash inflow to recognize the tax benefits of the awards).

All of these noncash items are removed from reported net income to yield net cash flow from operating activities. Starbucks' operating cash flow also includes the cash generated by or used for working capital accounts as discussed above for Java House. This includes:

- Increase in accounts receivable, $(82.8)

- Increase in inventories, $(207.9)

- Increase in accounts payable, $137.7

Managerial Decision ■ You Are the Securities Analyst

You are analyzing a company's statement of cash flows. The company has two items relating to its accounts receivable. First, the company finances the sale of its products to some customers; the increase to notes receivable is classified as an investing activity. Second, the company sells its accounts receivable to a separate entity, such as a trust. As a result, sale of receivables is reported as an asset sale; this reduces receivables and yields a gain or loss on the sale (in this case, the company is not required to consolidate the trust). This action increases the company's operating cash flows. How should you interpret this cash flow increase? [Answer, p. 11-32]

Review 11-2 LO2

Expresso Royale's income statement and comparative balance sheets follow.

EXPRESSO ROYALE Income Statement For Year Ended December 31, 2017		
Sales.............................		$385,000
Dividend income....................		5,000
		390,000
Cost of goods sold..................	$233,000	
Wages expense	82,000	
Advertising expense.................	10,000	
Depreciation expense................	11,000	
Income tax expense.................	17,000	
Loss on sale of investments...........	2,000	355,000
Net income........................		$ 35,000

EXPRESSO ROYALE
Balance Sheets

	Dec. 31, 2017	Dec. 31, 2016
Assets		
Cash.	$ 8,000	$ 12,000
Accounts receivable.	22,000	28,000
Inventory.	94,000	66,000
Prepaid advertising.	12,000	9,000
Long-term investments—available for sale	30,000	41,000
Fair value adjustment to investments.	—	(1,000)
PPE.	178,000	130,000
Accumulated depreciation	(72,000)	(61,000)
Total assets.	$272,000	$224,000
Liabilities and Equity		
Accounts payable.	$ 27,000	$ 14,000
Wages payable.	6,000	2,500
Income tax payable	3,000	4,500
Common stock.	139,000	125,000
Retained earnings	97,000	79,000
Unrealized loss on investments	—	(1,000)
Total liabilities and equity	$272,000	$224,000

Cash dividends of $17,000 were declared and paid during 2017. PPE was purchased for cash in 2017, and, later in the year, additional common stock was issued for cash. Investments costing $11,000 were sold for cash at a $2,000 loss in 2017; an unrealized loss of $1,000 on these investments had been recorded in 2016 (at December 31, 2017, the cost and fair value of unsold investments are equal).

Required
Compute Expresso Royale's operating cash flow for 2017 using the indirect method.

Solution on p. 11-56.

Computing Cash Flows from Investing Activities

Analyze Remaining Noncash Assets

Investing activities cause changes in asset accounts. Usually, the accounts affected (other than cash) are noncurrent asset accounts, such as PPE assets and long-term investments, although short-term investment accounts can also be affected. To determine the cash flows from investing activities, *we analyze changes in all noncash asset accounts not used in computing net cash flow from operating activities.* Our objective is to identify any investing cash flows related to these changes.

eLectures **LO3**
MBC Determine and analyze net cash flows from investing activities.

We can draw on our following decision rule to see how changes in assets such as investments and PPE affect cash flow.

Balance Sheet Account	Increase in Account	Decrease in Account
Assets (noncash)	**Cash Outflow**	**Cash Inflow**

Java House Case Illustration

Analyze Change in Long-Term Investments

Java House's comparative balance sheets (see Exhibit 11.2) show long-term investments increased $15,000 during 2017. The increase means investments must have been purchased, and the additional data reported indicates cash was spent to purchase long-term stock investments. Purchasing stock is an investing activity. Thus, a $15,000 purchase of stock investments is reported as a cash outflow from investing activities in the statement of cash flows.

Cash flows from investing activities	
Purchase of stock investments	$(15,000)

Analyze Change in PPE

Java House's PPE decreased $20,000 during 2017. PPE decreases as the result of disposals, and the additional data for Java House indicate land was sold for cash in 2017. Selling land is an investing activity. Thus, the sale of land for $28,000 is reported as a cash inflow from investing activities in the statement of cash flows. (Recall that the $8,000 gain on sale of land was deducted as a reconciling item in the operating section; see above.)

Cash flows from investing activities	
Purchase of stock investments	$(15,000)
Sale of land.	28,000

Analyze Change in Accumulated Depreciation

Java House's accumulated depreciation increased $10,000 during 2017. Accumulated depreciation increases when depreciation expense is recorded. Java House's 2017 depreciation expense was $10,000, so the total change in accumulated depreciation is the result of the recording of depreciation expense. As previously discussed, there is no cash flow related to the recording of depreciation expense, and we previously adjusted for this expense in our computation of net cash flows from operating activities.

Analyze Change in Patent

We see from the comparative balance sheets that Java House had an increase of $60,000 in a patent. The increase means a patent was acquired, and the additional data indicate common stock was issued to obtain a patent. This event is a noncash investing (acquiring a patent) and financing (issuing common stock) transaction that must be disclosed as supplementary information to the statement of cash flows.

Summary of Cash from Investing Activities

The investing activities section of the statement of cash flows appears as follows.

Cash flows from investing activities	
Purchase of stock investments	$(15,000)
Sale of land.	28,000
Net cash provided by investing activities.	$ 13,000

Business Insight ■ Starbucks' Investing Activities

Starbucks used $1,520.3 million cash for investing activities in 2015. Two line items on the statement of cash flow relate to investments: the buying and selling of marketable securities throughout the year as Starbucks invests its excess cash to generate interest, dividends, and capital gains. The company used cash of $567.4 million to purchase new securities and received cash of $600.6 from security sales. Starbucks also spent $284.3 million cash to acquire other companies. Note that this is the cash portion of the acquisitions. The company might also have issued debt and stock to finance its acquisition, which would be excluded from the investing section of the cash flow statement but would be specifically listed as a noncash investing activity in a footnote. Starbucks invested $1,303.7 million in PPE. These expenditures might have been for company-owned property or for leasehold improvements on leased property.

Review 11-3 LO3

Refer to the data in Review 11-2, along with the solution to that review, to answer the requirement below.

Required

Solution on p. 11-57. Prepare Expresso Royale's cash flows from investing activities for 2017.

Cash Flows from Financing Activities

Analyze Remaining Liabilities and Equity

Financing activities cause changes in liability and stockholders' equity accounts. Usually, the accounts affected are noncurrent accounts, such as bonds payable and common stock, although a current liability such as short-term notes payable can also be affected. To determine the cash flows from financing activities, *we analyze changes in all liability and stockholders' equity accounts that were not used in computing net cash flow from operating activities.* Our objective is to identify any financing cash flows related to these changes.

> **LO4** Determine and analyze net cash flows from financing activities.

We can draw on our following decision rule to see how changes in liabilities, such as short- and long-term debt, and equity accounts, such as common stock and treasury stock, affect cash flow.

Balance Sheet Account	Increase in Account	Decrease in Account
Liabilities and equity.	Cash Inflow	Cash Outflow

Java House Case Illustration

Analyze Change in Common Stock

Java House's common stock increased $70,000 during 2017 (see Exhibit 11.2). Common stock increases when shares of stock are issued. As noted in discussing the patent increase, common stock with a $60,000 par value was issued in exchange for a patent. This event is disclosed as a noncash investing and financing transaction. The other $10,000 increase in common stock, as noted in the additional data, resulted from an issuance of stock for cash. Issuing common stock is a financing activity, so a $10,000 cash inflow from a stock issuance appears as a financing activity in the statement of cash flows.

Cash flows from financing activities	
Issuance of common stock	$10,000

Analyze Change in Retained Earnings

Retained earnings grew from $56,000 to $75,000 during 2017—a $19,000 increase. This increase is the net result of Java House's $32,000 of net income (which increased retained earnings) and a $13,000 cash dividend (which decreased retained earnings). Because every item in Java House's income statement was considered in computing the net cash provided by operating activities, only the cash dividend remains to be considered. Paying a cash dividend is a financing activity. Thus, a $13,000 cash dividend appears as a cash outflow from financing activities in the statement of cash flows.

Cash flows from financing activities	
Issuance of common stock	$10,000
Payment of dividends.	(13,000)

Summary of Cash from Financing Activities

The financing activities section of the statement of cash flows appears as follows.

Cash flows from financing activities	
Issuance of common stock	$10,000
Payment of dividends.	(13,000)
Net cash used by financing activities.	$ (3,000)

We have now completed the analysis of all of Java House's noncash balance sheet accounts and can prepare the 2017 statement of cash flows. Exhibit 11.4 shows this statement.

If there are cash inflows and outflows from similar types of investing and financing activities, the inflows and outflows are reported separately (rather than reporting only the net difference). For example, proceeds from the sale of PPE are reported separately from outlays made to acquire PPE. Similarly, funds borrowed are reported separately from debt repayments, and proceeds from issuing stock are reported separately from outlays to acquire treasury stock.

Business Insight ■ Starbucks' Financing Activities

Highlights of **Starbucks**' financing activities include the receipt of $191.8 million cash from stock issuances. Only stock issued for cash is reflected in the statement of cash flows. Stock issued in connection with acquisitions is not reflected because it does not involve cash. Issuance of stock is often related to the exercise of employee stock options, and companies frequently repurchase stock to offset the dilutive effect of granting the options and to have stock to sell to employees who exercise their options. Starbucks also reports a cash inflow of $238.4 million ($845.5 million − $610.1 million) from borrowings, net of repayments during the year. Starbucks also returned $2,364.7 million ($1,436.1 million + $928.6 million) to shareholders during the year in the form of dividend payments and share repurchases. The net effect is a decrease in cash of $(178.3) million from all financing activities, including a $150.6 million reduction of cash labeled "Effect of exchange rate changes on cash and cash equivalents"; which relates to the decrease in the U.S. dollar ($US) equivalent value of cash held by foreign subsidiaries as a result of a stronger $US.

Review 11-4A LO4

Refer to the data in Review 11-2, along with the solution to that review, to answer the requirement below.

Required

Solution on p. 11-57.   Prepare Expresso Royale's cash flows from financing activities for 2017.

Computing Cash Flows from Balance Sheet Accounts

Drawing on the Java House illustration, we can summarize the cash flow effects of the income statement and balance sheet information and categorize them into the operating, investing, and financing classifications in the following table.

Account	Change	Source or Use of Cash	Cash Flow Effect	Classification on SCF
Current assets				
Accounts receivable..........	+5,000	Use	−5,000	Operating
Inventories.................	−6,000	Source	+6,000	Operating
Prepaid insurance...........	+13,000	Use	−13,000	Operating
Noncurrent assets				
PPE related				Investing
Accumulated depreciation...	+10,000	Neither	+10,000	Operating
Sale of land				
Proceeds	+28,000	Source	+28,000	Investing
Gain....................	−8,000	Neither	−8,000	Operating
Investments................	+15,000	Use	+15,000	Investing
Current liabilities				
Accounts payable...........	−9,000	Use	−9,000	Operating
Income tax payable..........	+2,000	Source	+2,000	Operating
Long-term liabilities				Financing
Stockholders' equity				
Common stock	+10,000	Source	+10,000	Financing
Retained earnings				
Net income..............	+32,000	Source	+32,000	Operating
Dividends	+13,000	Use	−13,000	Financing
Total (net cash flow)			+25,000	

The current year's cash balance increases by $25,000, from $10,000 to $35,000. Formal preparation of the statement of cash flows can proceed once we have addressed one final issue: required supplemental disclosures. We discuss that topic in the next section.

Supplemental Disclosures for the Indirect Method

When the indirect method is used in the statement of cash flows, separate disclosures are required for: (1) cash paid for interest and cash paid for income taxes, (2) a schedule or description of all noncash investing and financing transactions, and (3) the firm's policy for determining which highly liquid, short-term investments are treated as cash equivalents. Noncash investing and financing activities include the issuance of stocks, bonds, or leases in exchange for PPE assets or intangible assets; the exchange of long-term assets for other long-term assets; and the conversion of long-term debt into common stock.

Java House Case Illustration for Supplemental Disclosures

Cash Paid for Interest Java House incurred no interest cost during 2017.

Cash Paid for Income Taxes Java House did pay income taxes. Our discussion of the $2,000 change in income tax payable during 2017 revealed that the increase meant cash tax payments were less than income tax expense by the amount of the increase. Income tax expense was $11,000, so the cash paid for income taxes was $2,000 less than $11,000, or $9,000.

Noncash Investing and Financing Activities Java House had one noncash investing and financing event during 2017: the issuance of common stock to acquire a patent. This event, as well as the cash paid for income taxes, is disclosed as supplemental information to the statement of cash flows in Exhibit 11.4.

Exhibit 11.4 ■ Statement of Cash Flows for the Indirect Method with Supplemental Disclosures

JAVA HOUSE
Statement of Cash Flows
For Year Ended December 31, 2017

Net cash flow from operating activities		
Net income.	$32,000	
Add (deduct) items to convert net income to cash basis		
Depreciation	10,000	
Gain on sale of land	(8,000)	
Accounts receivable increase.	(5,000)	
Inventory decrease	6,000	
Prepaid insurance increase.	(13,000)	
Accounts payable decrease	(9,000)	
Income tax payable increase	2,000	
Net cash provided by operating activities		$15,000
Cash flows from investing activities		
Purchase of stock investments.	(15,000)	
Sale of land.	28,000	
Net cash provided by investing activities.		13,000
Cash flows from financing activities		
Issuance of common stock	10,000	
Payment of dividends.	(13,000)	
Net cash used by financing activities.		(3,000)
Net increase in cash.		25,000
Cash at beginning of year		10,000
Cash at end of year		$35,000
Supplemental cash flow disclosures		
Cash paid for income taxes.	$ 9,000	
Schedule of noncash investing and financing activities		
Issuance of common stock to acquire patent	$60,000	

Review 11-4B LO4

Refer to the balance sheet for Expresso Royale, and to the solutions for Reviews 11-2, 11-3, and 11-4A, to answer the requirements below.

Required

a.   Compute the change in cash.

Solution on p. 11-57. *b.*   Reconcile the beginning and ending cash balances for 2017.

Analysis of Cash Flow Information

Cash Flow Components

LO5
eLectures
MBC Examine and interpret cash flow information.

Typically, established companies have positive cash flow from operating activities. This cash flow provides most (if not all) of the total cash required to grow the business while maintaining appropriate levels of net working capital. On average, net cash flow from investing activities is negative as companies grow the PPE infrastructure needed to support the business. (Any excess cash invested in marketable securities typically generates cash flow, but this is small relative to the larger cash outflow for PPE and acquisitions.) Financing activities make up the difference between cash generated by operating activities and cash used by investing activities. Companies that generate more cash from operating activities than is required to support investing activities use that excess cash to pay down indebtedness, repurchase stock, or pay additional dividends. Companies that need cash for investing activities typically generate it from financing activities.

Exhibit 11.5 presents various cash flow items as a percentage of total revenues for the S&P 500 companies in fiscal 2015. The median operating cash flow is 18% of total revenues, of which net income explains 10 percentage points, and the add-backs for depreciation and stock based compensation explain 3 and 1 percentage points, respectively. The remaining 4 percentage points relate to cash inflows and outflows from net working capital accounts.

Investing activities typically represent an outflow of cash equal to 10% of revenues, with CAPEX comprising 40% of the total (4 percentage points out of 10). Other investing activities generally relate to investment of excess cash in marketable securities. The median S&P company generates more operating cash flow than is required for investing activities and reports negative cash flow of 5% of revenues for financing activities. These activities generally include the payment of dividends, the repayment of debt, and the repurchase of common stock.

Exhibit 11.5 ◼ Statement of Cash Flow Items as a Percentage of Total Revenues

	Net Income	Depreciation and Amortization	Stock-Based Compensation	Cash from Operations	Cash from Investing	Capital Expenditure	Cash from Financing
Median	10%	3%	1%	18%	(10)%	(4)%	(5)%

During 2015, S&P companies were profitable (only 16 of the 500 companies report a net loss greater than 5% of revenues) and generated sizeable operating cash flows. It is common for large companies to generate more operating cash flow than is required for investing activities, thus permitting the payment of dividends, the retirement of debt, and the repurchase of common stock. We expect this profile for a healthy, mature company.

By definition, GAAP net income consists of two components: cash and noncash items. Accountants call the noncash items "accruals" (defined as the difference between net income and cash from operations). Finance and accounting research investigates whether, and how, net earnings, operating cash flows, and accruals each predict (1) future earnings or future cash flows (this line of research is called predictability research), and (2) stock price (this line of research is called value-relevance research).

Although the statement of cash flows is very useful in a number of analysis situations, predictability research shows it is net income and not current operating cash flow that better predicts future net income. Predictability research by Richard Sloan (*The Accounting Review*, 1996) found that the two components of net income (accruals and cash flows) have different impacts on future earnings; specifically, cash flows are more persistent, meaning they have longer-term implications for future earnings than accruals do. Later, work by Tuomo Vuolteenaho (*Journal of Finance*, 2002) found that, in addition to information about future earnings, the accruals and cash flows explain the riskiness of the firm. The interpretation is that, because accruals are less persistent and they fluctuate more, they signal additional risk. One way to use this finding in our analysis is to compute the ratio of operating cash flow to net income: the higher that number, the lower the firm's operating risk.

Early value-relevance research from the late 1960s found that when firms announced that their earnings were higher (lower) than the prior year's earnings, stock price increased (decreased). This sparked much research into the relevance of accounting earnings for stock prices. With growth in the sources and speed of information, our current understanding is that, although earnings are important for stock prices, most of the information conveyed by earnings is factored into stock price long before the company announces its official numbers. For example, Ray Ball and Lakshmanan Shivakumar (*Journal of Accounting Research*, 2008) find that earnings announcement events only account for 1% to 2% of the stock price movement each year. Later, value-relevance research investigated whether the stock market reacts differently to cash flow versus the accruals components of earnings. For example, Sloan's (1996) finding came to be known as the *accrual anomaly*—the fact that stock prices do not differentiate between accruals and cash flows—which causes mispricing because accruals fluctuate more wildly than cash flows. However, markets learn quickly from their mistakes, and evidence of the accrual anomaly has decreased steadily since 1996. In sum, both of these research streams are ongoing and active areas as academics and analysts seek to understand how the various earnings components are related to future firm profitability as well as how the income statement, balance sheet, and statement of cash flows separately and collectively inform investors about firm value and riskiness.

Cash Flow Patterns

A product life-cycle framework can be helpful in interpreting cash flow patterns. This framework proposes four stages for products or services: (1) introduction, (2) growth, (3) maturity, and (4) decline. The following figure plots the usual patterns for revenues, income, and cash flows at each of these four stages. For revenues, the top line number, we see the common pattern of growth over the first two stages, then a leveling out at maturity, then finally a decline. The length of time between introduction and decline depends on many of the factors considered by Porter's forces or a SWOT analysis. For example, products with short lives and those subject to fashion trends, technical innovation, or obsolescence will have a shorter life cycle, and revenue will be at greater risk of fluctuation. Knowledge of product life cycles can help us assess the transitory or persistent nature of revenues.

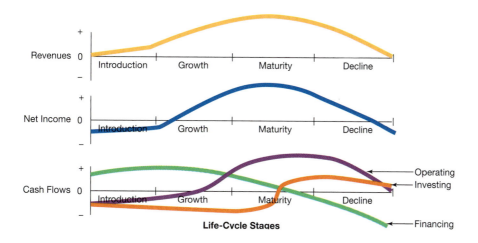

The second graph in the figure shows net income behavior over the four life-cycle stages. We commonly see losses in the introductory stage as companies struggle to recover startup costs and establish revenue streams. Accordingly, net income commonly peaks during the maturity stage before a gradual decrease in the decline stage. The third graph highlights cash flows from operating, investing, and financing over the product life cycle. Although we see variations due to product success, strategic planning, and cost controls, these trends for each cash flow are fairly descriptive.

In general, during the introductory stage, revenues are limited, which results in low income and operating cash flows. The introductory stage also sees cash outflows for investing and cash inflows for financing. During the growth stage, revenues, income, and operating cash flows all increase, whereas both investing and financing cash flows increase or level out (each depending on predictions of future growth). The maturity stage sees peaks, and maybe some eventual decline, for revenues, income, and operating cash flows. This occurs as investing cash flows drop off, rendering additional financing cash inflows unnecessary. The decline stage brings large decreases in revenues, income, and operating cash flows. In decline, companies distribute cash flows for financing sources (repay debt, buy back stock, pay dividends) and realize some incoming investing cash flows as assets are gradually sold off. In summary, knowledge of product life cycles can help us understand the underlying economics, which will inform our business analysis. It can also help us interpret and possibly predict future streams of revenues, income, and cash flows.

Cisco Systems is a solid, healthy company whose cash flow pattern for the past decade (shown in Exhibit 11-6) is consistent with the pattern for mature-stage companies. Cisco's operating cash flow has grown throughout this period and provides sufficient cash to support the growth of net working capital and to partially finance the investment in PPE. Financing activities provide the remaining cash needed for investing activities. Notice how the investing and financing cash flows move in opposite directions, indicating greater financing inflows when cash outflows for investing activities increase, and vice versa. Most mature, healthy companies exhibit a similar cash flow profile.

Exhibit 11.6 ■ Cisco System's Operating, Investing, and Financing Cash Flows

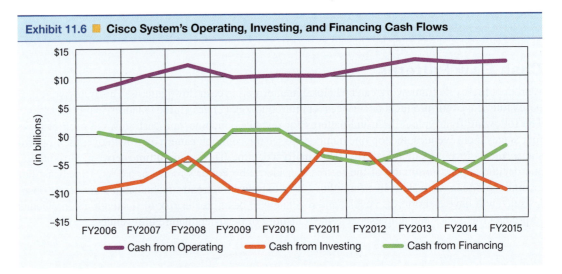

Harley-Davidson Inc. is also a mature company. Its cash flow pattern provides a good example of how a company can use financing activities to provide necessary cash during economic downturns (see Exhibit 11.7). The economic downturn of 2008 markedly impacted the company, as it reports in the following section from its 2008 10-K (HDFS refers to Harley-Davidson Financial Services).

The Company's 2008 results were impacted by the difficult economic environment including lower consumer confidence and significant disruptions in global capital markets. The Company's 2008 net revenue and net income were down 2.3% and 29.9%, respectively, compared to 2007. Operating income for the Motorcycles segment was down 21.5% while operating income for the Financial Services segment decreased 61.0%. . . . During 2008, debt increased by $1.81 billion which was primarily driven by higher finance receivables outstanding as HDFS funded a greater percentage of its business through debt rather than through securitization transactions when compared to 2007.

As retail sales dried up, Harley was forced to finance its operations with additional debt. Lender financing was also required to support its finance receivables (notes and leases), as it became difficult to access the market in which Harley had previously sold (securitized) its receivables. Then, as operating cash flow recovered and securities markets stabilized in subsequent years, Harley was able to reduce its financing, as evidenced by the negative financing cash flows in 2010 through 2012.

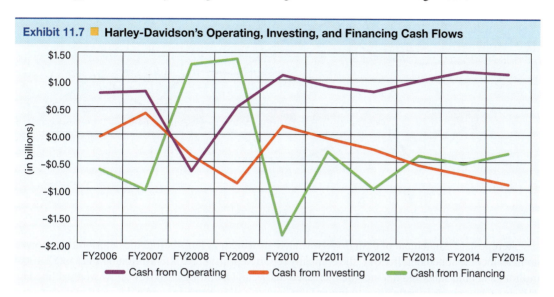

Exhibit 11.7 ■ **Harley-Davidson's Operating, Investing, and Financing Cash Flows**

Microsoft Corporation (MSFT) is another mature-stage company, but it has a cash flow pattern that differs from both Cisco and Harley-Davidson. Microsoft presents the picture of health through fiscal 2015 (see Exhibit 11.8). As its operating cash flows have soared, Microsoft has not required any external financing and has invested its excess cash in marketable securities. This presents a unique cash flow pattern. As of 2015, Microsoft reported a staggering $90.9 billion in marketable securities in addition to $5.6 billion of cash and cash equivalents.

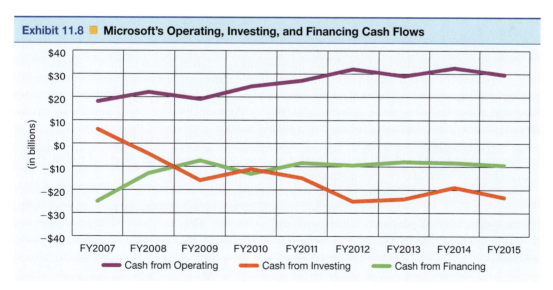

Exhibit 11.8 ■ **Microsoft's Operating, Investing, and Financing Cash Flows**

Aéropostale's Cash Flow Woes

Aéropostale reported net losses totaling $485.2 million in the three years leading up to its bankruptcy filing in 2016. As the graph in Exhibit 11.9 illustrates, Aéropostale's operating cash flow declined from a high of $334 million in 2010 to operating cash losses in the 2014–2016 period. The company borrowed money and restricted capital expenditures to provide necessary funding. Aéropostale was unable to turn its performance around and filed for bankruptcy protection in 2016 to forestall creditors while it develops plans to downsize or discontinue.

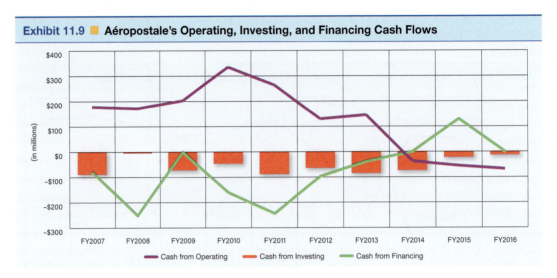

Exhibit 11.9 ■ **Aéropostale's Operating, Investing, and Financing Cash Flows**

Aéropostale's statement of cash flows revealed growing problems before the deterioration showed up in its income statement. In 2011, the company reported profit of $231.3 million on sales of $2,400.4 million, and both sales and net income increased that year. Operating cash flow, however, declined by 21% in 2011, primarily reflecting an increase in days to sell inventories and a decrease in days to pay accounts payable as suppliers began to tighten credit policies.

Usefulness of the Statement of Cash Flows

A statement of cash flows shows the cash effects of a firm's operating, investing, and financing activities. Distinguishing among these different categories of cash flows helps users compare, evaluate, and predict cash flows. With cash flow information, creditors and investors are better able to assess a firm's ability to settle its liabilities and pay its dividends. A firm's need for outside financing is also better evaluated when using cash flow data. Over time, the statement of cash flows permits users to observe and access management's investing and financing policies.

A statement of cash flows also provides information useful in evaluating a firm's financial flexibility. *Financial flexibility* is a firm's ability to generate sufficient amounts of cash to respond to unanticipated needs and opportunities. Information about past cash flows, particularly cash flows from operations, helps in assessing financial flexibility. An evaluation of a firm's ability to survive an unexpected drop in demand, for example, should include a review of its past cash flows from operations. The larger these cash flows, the greater is the firm's ability to withstand adverse changes in economic conditions. Other financial statements, particularly the balance sheet and its notes, also contain information useful for judging financial flexibility.

Some investors and creditors find the statement of cash flows useful in evaluating the quality of a firm's income. As we know, determining income under accrual accounting procedures (GAAP) requires many accruals, deferrals, allocations, and valuations. These adjustment and measurement procedures introduce more subjectivity into income determination than some financial statement users prefer. These users relate a more objective performance measure—cash flow from operations—to net income. To these users, the higher this ratio, the higher the quality of income.

In analyzing the statement of cash flows, we must not necessarily conclude the company is better off if cash increases and worse off if cash decreases. It is not the cash change that is most important but the sources of that change. For example, what are the sources of cash inflows? Are these sources transitory? Are these sources mainly from operating activities? We must also review the uses of cash. Has the company invested its cash in operating areas to strengthen its competitive position? Is it able to comfortably meet its debt obligations? Has it diverted cash to creditors or investors at the expense of the other? Such questions and answers are key to properly interpreting the statement of cash flows for business decisions.

A company can operate in several industries simultaneously and produce multiple products within each industry. This can make it difficult to identify the life-cycle stage because the company is a composite of many overlapping but distinct product life-cycle stages. Understanding a firm's life-cycle stage is important because life cycle affects the firm's production behavior, its investing activities, its market share, and many other pieces of information useful to analysis. Research shows cash flow patterns (net inflow or outflow) provide a reliable way to assess the overall life-cycle stage of the company, as follows.

	Introduction	Growth	Maturity	Decline
Operating	−	+	+	−
Investing	−	−	−	+
Financing	+	+	−	+/−

Using cash flow patterns to identify firm life-cycle stage, current research finds profitability ratios are consistent with expected economic behavior at each life-cycle stage. As demonstrated in the following graph, net operating profit margin (NOPM) is maximized in the growth stage when companies are able to differentiate their brands.

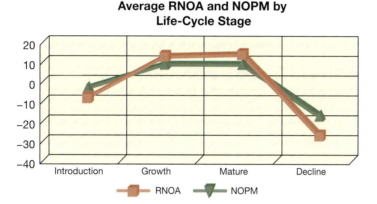

Average RNOA and NOPM by Life-Cycle Stage

By comparison, return on net operating assets (RNOA) and net operating asset turnover (NOAT) are maximized in the maturity stage as market saturation is reached, but operating efficiencies allow the firm to maintain (or increase) profitability.

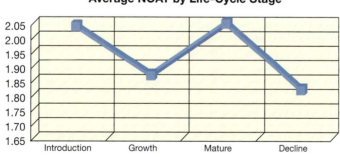

Average NOAT by Life-Cycle Stage

In addition, life-cycle stage as measured by cash flow patterns explains stock market valuation and stock returns. On average, mature-stage companies have abnormally high stock returns (as compared with the expected return for similar companies). One explanation is that investors underestimate the persistence of the mature company's profitability because they do not know the company's life-cycle stage and expect profits (and stock prices) to quickly revert to "normal" levels. (Source: Dickinson, Victoria, "Cash Flow Patterns as a Proxy for Firm Life Cycle," The Accounting Review, November 2011, 86(6): 1969–1994.)

Review 11-5 LO5

The following information is taken from the Form 10-K for Starbucks and Farmer Brothers, the latter company is a small, publically traded coffee roaster.

	Revenue	Net Income	Depreciation	Stock-Based Compensation	Cash from Operations	Cash from Investing	CAPEX	Cash from Financing
Starbucks ($ millions)...	$19,162.7	$2,759.3	$933.8	$209.8	$3,749.1	$(1,520.3)	$(1,303.7)	$(2,256.5)
Farmer Brothers ($ 000s).....	$545,882	$652	$24,179	$5,691	$26,930	$(20,143)	$(19,216)	$(3,620)

Required

Consider the cash flow patterns for both companies in answering the following questions.

a. Compute the cash flow ratios shown in Exhibit 11.5 for both companies. How does each company's ratios compare with the medians for the S&P reported in that exhibit?

Solution on p. 11-57. *b.* At what stage in its life cycle is each company? Explain.

Ratio Analyses of Cash Flows

eLectures **LO6**

MBC Compute and interpret ratios based on operating cash flows.

Data from the statement of cash flows can be used to compute various financial ratios. Two such ratios are the operating cash flow to current liabilities ratio and the operating cash flow to capital expenditures ratio.

Operating Cash Flow to Current Liabilities Ratio

Two liquidity measures previously introduced—the current ratio and the quick ratio—emphasize the relation of current assets to current liabilities in an attempt to measure the ability of the firm to pay current liabilities when they become due. The **operating cash flow to current liabilities ratio** is another liquidity measure of the company's ability to liquidate current liabilities and is calculated as follows.

$$\text{Operating Cash Flow to Current Liabilities} = \frac{\text{Cash Flow from Operating Activities}}{\text{Average Current Liabilities}}$$

Net cash flow from operating activities is obtained from the statement of cash flows; it represents the excess amount of cash derived from operations during the year after deducting working capital needs and payments required on current liabilities. The denominator is the average of the beginning and ending current liabilities for the year.

To illustrate, Starbucks reports the following amounts in its 2015 financial statements.

Net cash flow from operating activities	$3,749.1 million
Current liabilities at beginning of the year	3,038.7 million
Current liabilities at end of the year	3,653.5 million

Starbucks' operating cash flow to current liabilities ratio of 1.12 is computed as follows.

$3,749.1 million / [($3,038.7 million + $3,653.5 million)/2] = 1.12

The higher this ratio, the stronger is a firm's ability to settle current liabilities as they come due. Our analysis would compare this ratio over time and against peer companies.

Operating Cash Flow to Capital Expenditures Ratio

To remain competitive, an entity must be able to replace and expand, when appropriate, its PPE assets. A ratio that helps assess a firm's ability to do this from internally generated cash flow is the **operating cash flow to capital expenditures ratio**, which is computed as follows.

$$\text{Operating Cash Flow to Capital Expenditures} = \frac{\text{Cash Flow from Operating Activities}}{\text{Annual Capital Expenditures}}$$

The numerator in this ratio comes directly from the operating section of the statement of cash flows. Information for the denominator comes directly from the investing section of the statement of cash flows. Additional information about capital expenditures can be found in a number of related disclosures. Data on capital expenditures are part of the required industry segment disclosures in notes to the financial statements. Also, capital expenditures often appear in the comparative selected financial data presented as supplementary information to the financial statements. Finally, management's discussion and analysis of the statements commonly identify the annual capital expenditures.

A ratio in excess of 1.0 means the firm's current operating activities are providing cash in excess of the amount needed to provide the desired level of plant capacity and would normally be considered a sign of financial strength. This ratio is also viewed as an indicator of long-term solvency—a ratio exceeding 1.0 means there is operating cash flow in excess of capital needs that can then be used to repay outstanding long-term debt.

The interpretation of this ratio for a firm is influenced by its trend in recent years, the ratios for other firms in the same industry, and the stage of the firm's life cycle. A firm in the early stages of its life cycle, during rapid expansion, is expected to experience a lower ratio than a firm in the mature stage of its life cycle, when maintenance of plant capacity is more likely than expansion of capacity.

To illustrate the ratio's computation, **Starbucks** reported capital expenditures in 2015 of $1,303.7 million. Starbucks' operating cash flow to capital expenditures ratio for that same year is 2.9 ($3,749.1 million/$1,303.7 million). As before, our analysis would compare this ratio against Starbucks over time and against peer companies.

Free Cash Flow

Free cash flow is a common financial metric we encounter in the financial press. It is also common to see firm value estimated by discounting a company's future free cash flows (this is the DCF valuation model, which we discuss in a later module). A common definition of free cash flow (seen in finance textbooks and in use by business writers) is operating cash flows less capital expenditures (CAPEX). In this definition, "operating cash flows" is not equal to net cash flows from operating activities reported in the statement of cash flows because the latter includes items such as the effects from interest (both expense and revenue). The following table shows the definition of free cash flow commonly found in finance textbooks/press. The table also shows that this definition is approximately equivalent to: Free cash flow = Net operating profit after tax (NOPAT) − Increase in net operating assets (NOA). (We explain NOPAT and NOA in an earlier module.)

Traditional Finance Definition	As Defined in This Book
Earnings before interest and taxes, adjusted for noncash revenues and expenses − Taxes (in the absence of interest revenue and interest expense)	Net operating profit after tax (NOPAT)
− Investments in working capital − Capital expenditures (CAPEX)	− Increase in net operating assets (NOA)
= Free cash flow	= Free cash flow

The value of a firm is related to its expected free cash flow. By expressing free cash flows in terms of NOPAT and the increase in NOA, we see two specific means to increase firm value through:

- Increase NOPAT.
- Control NOA growth.

To increase free cash flow, companies aim to achieve both of these objectives without adversely affecting the other. For example, it is not enough to increase NOPAT by increasing revenues and operating profits if these actions increase NOA to the point that the beneficial profit effects are offset by the negative effects of higher NOA. Conversely, it is not enough to reduce NOA if doing so reduces sales and operating profit to a greater extent. The challenge to managers is to find a set of actions that optimizes net operating profit and the required level of net operating assets. This is the art of management. (We discuss this further in our valuation module.)

Review 11-6 LO6

Following is financial statement data for **McDonald's Corporation** for 2015 ($ millions).

Net cash flow from operating activities	$6,539.1
Current liabilities at beginning of the year	2,747.9
Current liabilities at end of the year	2,950.4
Capital expenditures	(1,813.9)

Required

1. Compute the operating cash flow to current liabilities ratio.
2. Compute the operating cash flow to capital expenditures ratio.

Solution on p. 11-58.   3. From the two ratios you computed, does it appear that McDonald's is liquid and solvent? Explain.

Appendix 11A: Direct Method Reporting for the Statement of Cash Flows

LO7

MBC   Explain and construct a direct method statement of cash flows.

To prepare a statement of cash flows, we need a firm's income statement, comparative balance sheets, and some additional data taken from the accounting records. Exhibit 11.2 presents this information for Java House. We use these data to prepare Java House's 2017 statement of cash flows using the direct method. Java House's statement of cash flows explains the $25,000 increase in cash (from $10,000 to $35,000) that occurred during 2017 by classifying the firm's cash flows into operating, investing, and financing categories. To get the information to construct the statement, we do the following.

1. **Use the direct method to determine individual cash flows from operating activities.** We use changes that occurred during 2017 in various current asset and current liability accounts.
2. **Determine cash flows from investing activities.** We do this by analyzing changes in noncurrent asset accounts.
3. **Determine cash flows from financing activities.** We do this by analyzing changes in liability and stockholders' equity accounts.

The net cash flows from investing and financing are identical to those prepared using the indirect method. Only the format of the net cash flows from operating activities differs between the two methods, not the total amount of cash generated from operating activities.

Cash Flows from Operating Activities

The **direct method** presents net cash flow from operating activities by showing the major categories of operating cash receipts and payments. The operating cash receipts and payments are usually determined by converting the accrual revenues and expenses to corresponding cash amounts. It is efficient to do it this way because the accrual revenues and expenses are readily available in the income statement.

Converting Revenues and Expenses to Cash Flows

Exhibit 11.10 summarizes the procedures for converting individual income statement items to corresponding cash flows from operating activities.

Java House Case Illustration

We next explain and illustrate the process of converting Java House's 2017 revenues and expenses to corresponding cash flows from operating activities under the direct method.

Convert Sales to Cash Received from Customers

During 2017, accounts receivable increased $5,000. This increase means that, during 2017, cash collections on account (which decrease accounts receivable) were less than credit sales (which increase accounts receivable). We compute cash received from customers as follows (this computation assumes no accounts were written off as uncollectible during the period):

Sales	$250,000
− Increase in accounts receivable	(5,000)
= Cash received from customers	$245,000

Exhibit 11.10 ■ Adjustments to Convert Income Statement Items to Operating Activity Cash Flows

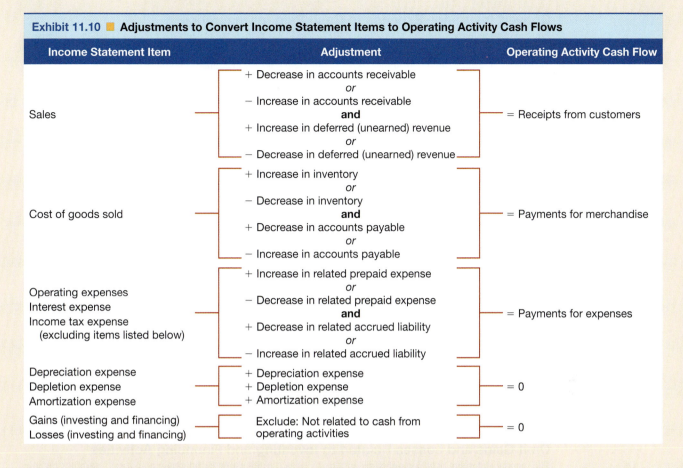

Income Statement Item	Adjustment	Operating Activity Cash Flow
Sales	+ Decrease in accounts receivable *or* − Increase in accounts receivable **and** + Increase in deferred (unearned) revenue *or* − Decrease in deferred (unearned) revenue	= Receipts from customers
Cost of goods sold	+ Increase in inventory *or* − Decrease in inventory **and** + Decrease in accounts payable *or* − Increase in accounts payable	= Payments for merchandise
Operating expenses Interest expense Income tax expense (excluding items listed below)	+ Increase in related prepaid expense *or* − Decrease in related prepaid expense **and** + Decrease in related accrued liability *or* − Increase in related accrued liability	= Payments for expenses
Depreciation expense Depletion expense Amortization expense	+ Depreciation expense + Depletion expense + Amortization expense	= 0
Gains (investing and financing) Losses (investing and financing)	Exclude: Not related to cash from operating activities	= 0

Convert Cost of Goods Sold to Cash Paid for Merchandise Purchased

The conversion of cost of goods sold to cash paid for merchandise purchased is a two-step process. First, cost of goods sold is adjusted for the change in inventory to determine the amount of purchases during the year. Second, the purchases amount is adjusted for the change in accounts payable to derive the cash paid for merchandise purchased. Inventory decreased from $60,000 to $54,000 during 2017. This $6,000 decrease indicates the cost of goods sold exceeded the cost of goods purchased during the year. The year's purchases amount is computed as follows:

Cost of goods sold	$148,000
− Decrease in inventory	(6,000)
= Purchases	$142,000

During 2017, accounts payable decreased $9,000. This decrease reflects the fact that cash payments for merchandise purchased on account (which decrease accounts payable) exceeded purchases on account (which increase accounts payable). The cash paid for merchandise purchased, therefore, is computed as follows:

Purchases	$142,000
+ Decrease in accounts payable.	9,000
= Cash paid for merchandise purchased . .	$151,000

Convert Wages Expense to Cash Paid to Employees

No adjustment to wages expense is needed. The absence of any beginning or ending accrued liability for wages payable means wages expense and cash paid to employees as wages are the same amount: $52,000.

Convert Insurance Expense to Cash Paid for Insurance

Prepaid insurance increased $13,000 during 2017. The $13,000 increase reflects the excess of cash paid for insurance during 2017 (which increases prepaid insurance) over the year's insurance expense (which decreases prepaid insurance). Starting with the insurance expense, the cash paid for insurance is computed as follows:

Insurance expense.................	$ 5,000
+ Increase in prepaid insurance	13,000
= Cash paid for insurance.............	$18,000

Eliminate Depreciation Expense and Other Noncash Operating Expenses

Depreciation expense is a noncash expense. Because it does not represent a cash payment, depreciation expense is eliminated (by adding it back) as we convert accrual expense amounts to the corresponding amounts of cash payments. If Java House had any amortization expense or depletion expense, the company would eliminate it for the same reason. The amortization of an intangible asset and the depletion of a natural resource are noncash expenses.

Convert Income Tax Expense to Cash Paid for Income Taxes

The increase in income tax payable from $3,000 at December 31, 2016, to $5,000 at December 31, 2017, means 2017's income tax expense (which increases income tax payable) was $2,000 more than 2017's tax payments (which decrease income tax payable). Starting with income tax expense, we calculate cash paid for income taxes as follows:

Income tax expense	$11,000
− Increase in income tax payable........	(2,000)
= Cash paid for income taxes..........	$ 9,000

Omit Gains and Losses Related to Investing and Financing Activities

The income statement may contain gains and losses related to investing or financing activities. Examples include gains and losses from the sale of PPE and gains and losses from the retirement of bonds payable. Because these gains and losses are not related to operating activities, we omit them as we convert income statement items to various cash flows from operating activities. The cash flows relating to these gains and losses are reported in the investing activities or financing activities sections of the statement of cash flows. Java House had an $8,000 gain from the sale of land in 2017. This gain is excluded; no related cash flow appears within the operating activities category.

We have now applied the adjustments to convert each accrual revenue and expense to the corresponding operating cash flow. We use these individual cash flows to prepare the operating activities section of the statement of cash flows, which we can see in Exhibit 11.11.

Exhibit 11.11 ■ **Direct Method Operating Section of Statement of Cash Flows**		
Cash received from customers		$245,000
Cash paid for merchandise purchased	$151,000	
Cash paid to employees.............................	52,000	
Cash paid for insurance.............................	18,000	
Cash paid for income taxes	9,000	230,000
Net cash provided by operating activities		$ 15,000

Cash Flows from Investing and Financing

The reporting of investing and financing activities in the statement of cash flows is identical under the indirect and direct methods. Thus, we simply refer to the previous sections in this appendix for explanations.

Supplemental Disclosures

When the direct method is used for the statement of cash flows, three separate disclosures are required: (1) a reconciliation of net income to the net cash flow from operating activities, (2) a schedule or description of all noncash investing and financing transactions, and (3) the firm's policy for determining which highly liquid, short-term investments are treated as cash equivalents. The firm's policy regarding cash equivalents is placed in the financial statement notes. The other two separate disclosures are reported either in the notes or at the bottom of the statement of cash flows.

The required reconciliation is essentially the indirect method of computing cash flow from operating activities. *Thus, when the direct method is used in the statement of cash flows, the indirect method is a required separate disclosure.* We discussed the indirect method earlier in this module.

Java House did have one noncash investing and financing event during 2017: the issuance of common stock to acquire a patent. This event is disclosed as supplemental information to the statement of cash flows in Exhibit 11.4.

LO7 Review 11-7

Refer to the data in Review 11-2, along with the solution to that review, to answer the requirement below.

Required
Compute Expresso Royale's net cash flow from operating activities using the direct method.

MBC

Solution on p. 11-58.

Guidance Answers

You Are the Securities Analyst

Pg. 11-15 Many companies, but not all, treat customers' notes receivable as an investing activity. In 2005, the Securities and Exchange Commission (SEC) became concerned with this practice and issued letters to a number of companies objecting to this accounting classification. "Presenting cash receipts from receivables generated by the sale of inventory as investing activities in the company's consolidated statements of cash flows is not in accordance with GAAP," wrote the chief accountant for the SEC's division of corporation finance in her letter to the companies ("Little Campus Lab Shakes Big Firms—Georgia Tech Crew's Report Spurs Change in Accounting for Operating Cash Flow," March 1, 2005, *The Wall Street Journal*). The SEC's position is that these notes receivable are an operating activity and analysts are certainly justified in treating them likewise. Concerning the sale of receivables, so long as the separate entity (a trust in this case) is properly structured, the transaction can be treated as a sale (rather than require consolidation) with a consequent reduction in receivables and a gain or loss on the sale recorded in the income statement. Many analysts treat this as a financing activity and argue that the cash inflow should not be regarded as an increase in operating cash flows. Bottom line: Many argue that operating cash flows do not increase as a result of these two transactions and analysts should adjust the statement of cash flows to properly classify the financing of receivables as an operating activity and the sale of receivables as a financing activity.

Superscript ^A denotes assignments based on Appendix 11A.

Questions

Q11-1. What is the definition of cash equivalents? Give three examples of cash equivalents.

Q11-2. Why are cash equivalents included with cash in a statement of cash flows?

Q11-3. What are the three major types of activities classified on a statement of cash flows? Give an example of a cash inflow and a cash outflow in each classification.

Q11-4. In which of the three activity categories of a statement of cash flows would each of the following items appear? Indicate for each item whether it represents a cash inflow or a cash outflow:

   a. Cash purchase of equipment.
   b. Cash collection on loans receivable.
   c. Cash dividends paid.
   d. Cash dividends received.
   e. Cash proceeds from issuing stock.
   f. Cash receipts from customers.
   g. Cash interest paid.
   h. Cash interest received.

Q11-5. Traverse Company acquired a $3,000,000 building by issuing $3,000,000 worth of bonds payable. In terms of cash flow reporting, what type of transaction is this? What special disclosure requirements apply to a transaction of this type?

Q11-6. Why are noncash investing and financing transactions disclosed as supplemental information to a statement of cash flows?

Q11-7. Why is a statement of cash flows a useful financial statement?

Q11-8.ᴬ What is the difference between the direct method and the indirect method of presenting net cash flow from operating activities?

Q11-9. In determining net cash flow from operating activities using the indirect method, why must we add depreciation back to net income? Give an example of another item that is added back to net income under the indirect method.

Q11-10. Vista Company sold for $98,000 cash land originally costing $70,000. The company recorded a gain on the sale of $28,000. How is this event reported in a statement of cash flows using the indirect method?

Q11-11. A firm uses the indirect method. Using the following information, what is its net cash flow from operating activities?

Net income.	$88,000
Accounts receivable decrease	13,000
Inventory increase	9,000
Accounts payable decrease.	3,500
Income tax payable increase	1,500
Depreciation expense.	6,000

Q11-12. What separate disclosures are required for a company that reports a statement of cash flows using the indirect method?

Q11-13. If a business had a net loss for the year, under what circumstances would the statement of cash flows show a positive net cash flow from operating activities?

Q11-14.ᴬ A firm is converting its accrual revenues to corresponding cash amounts using the direct method. Sales on the income statement are $925,000. Beginning and ending accounts receivable on the balance sheet are $58,000 and $44,000, respectively. What is the amount of cash received from customers?

Q11-15.ᴬ A firm reports $86,000 wages expense in its income statement. If beginning and ending wages payable are $3,900 and $2,800, respectively, what is the amount of cash paid to employees?

Q11-16.ᴬ A firm reports $43,000 advertising expense in its income statement. If beginning and ending prepaid advertising are $6,000 and $7,600, respectively, what is the amount of cash paid for advertising?

Q11-17.ᴬ Rusk Company sold equipment for $5,100 cash that had cost $35,000 and had $29,000 of accumulated depreciation. How is this event reported in a statement of cash flows using the direct method?

Q11-18.ᴬ What separate disclosures are required for a company that reports a statement of cash flows using the direct method?

Q11-19. How is the operating cash flow to current liabilities ratio calculated? Explain its use.

Q11-20. How is the operating cash flow to capital expenditures ratio calculated? Explain its use.

Q11-21. For each of the following cash flow patterns, identify whether the company is in the introduction, growth, maturity, or decline stage of its life cycle.

Life-Cycle Stage	Operating Cash Flow	Investing Cash Flow	Financing Cash Flow
a.	+	−	+
b.	+	−	−
c.	−	−	+
d.	−	+	−

Assignments with the ⬤ logo in the margin are available in 𝐵𝑢𝑠𝑖𝑛𝑒𝑠𝑠Course.
See the Preface of the book for details.

Mini Exercises

M11-22. **Classification of Cash Flows**

LO1

For each of the following items, indicate whether the cash flow relates to an operating activity, an investing activity, or a financing activity.

   a. Cash receipts from customers for services rendered .... _____

   b. Sale of long-term investments for cash .... _____

   c. Acquisition of PPE for cash .... _____

   d. Payment of income taxes .... _____

   e. Bonds payable issued for cash .... _____

   f. Payment of cash dividends declared in previous year .... _____

   g. Purchase of short-term investments (not cash equivalents) for cash .... _____

M11-23. **Classification of Cash Flows**

LO1
Shake Shack (SHAK)

Shake Shack Inc. reports the following items in its 2015 statement of cash flow. For each item, indicate whether it would appear in the operating, investing, or financing section of the statement of cash flows (in $ thousands).

   a. Accounts payable .... $ 201

   b. Proceeds from issuance of Class B common stock 30

   c. Equity-based compensation 16,681

   d. Inventories .... (14)

   e. Purchases of property and equipment...................................... (32,117)

   f. Member distributions (dividends).. (11,125)

   g. Net income 3,124

   h. Payments on revolving credit facility..................................... (36,000)

   i. Purchases of marketable securities....................................... (2,397)

   j. Depreciation expense 10,222

M11-24. **Net Cash Flow from Operating Activities (Indirect Method)**

LO2

The following information was obtained from Galena Company's comparative balance sheets. Assume Galena Company's 2017 income statement showed depreciation expense of $9,000, a gain on sale of investments of $11,000, and a net income of $40,000. Calculate the net cash flow from operating activities using the indirect method.

	Dec. 31, 2017	Dec. 31, 2016
Cash...........................	$ 19,000	$ 10,000
Accounts receivable...............	45,000	35,000
Inventory.......................	55,000	49,000
Prepaid rent	6,000	7,000
Long-term investments	20,000	34,000
PPE............................	150,000	106,000
Accumulated depreciation	42,000	33,000
Accounts payable.................	25,000	20,000
Income tax payable	4,000	6,000
Common stock...................	121,000	92,000
Retained earnings	106,000	91,000

LO2 M11-25. Net Cash Flow from Operating Activities (Indirect Method)

Cairo Company had a $19,000 net loss from operations for 2017. Depreciation expense for 2017 was $9,200, and a 2017 cash dividend of $6,000 was declared and paid. Balances of the current asset and current liability accounts at the beginning and end of 2017 follow. Did Cairo Company's 2017 operating activities provide or use cash? Use the indirect method to determine your answer.

	End of Year	Beginning of Year
Cash.....................	$ 4,000	$ 8,000
Accounts receivable.........	16,000	25,000
Inventory..................	49,000	53,000
Prepaid expenses...........	6,000	10,000
Accounts payable...........	12,000	9,000
Accrued liabilities..........	5,500	7,600

LO7 M11-26. Operating Cash Flows (Direct Method)

Calculate the cash flow for each of the following cases.

a. Cash paid for rent:

Rent expense.................	$65,000
Prepaid rent, beginning year	11,000
Prepaid rent, end of year	8,000

b. Cash received as interest:

Interest income.................	$15,500
Interest receivable, beginning year..	3,000
Interest receivable, end of year	3,800

c. Cash paid for merchandise purchased:

Cost of goods sold..............	$87,000
Inventory, beginning year.........	19,000
Inventory, end of year............	23,000
Accounts payable, beginning year..	11,000
Accounts payable, end of year.....	8,000

LO7 M11-27. Operating Cash Flows (Direct Method)

Howell Company's current-year income statement reports the following.

Sales........................	$785,000
Cost of goods sold..............	450,000
Gross profit....................	$335,000

Howell's comparative balance sheets show the following (accounts payable relate to merchandise purchases).

	End of Year	Beginning of Year
Accounts receivable........	$ 68,000	$60,000
Inventory..................	109,000	99,000
Prepaid expenses..........	2,000	8,000
Accounts payable..........	31,000	36,000

Compute Howell's current-year cash received from customers and cash paid for merchandise purchased.

M11-28. **Using Statement of Cash Flow Information to Assess Company Life-Cycle Stage**

LO5

For each of the following cash flow amounts ($ millions), identify whether the company is in the introduction, growth, maturity, or decline stage of its life cycle.

Company	Operating Cash Flow	Investing Cash Flow	Financing Cash Flow
a...............	$2,281	$(3,451)	$1,907
b...............	6,334	3,220	(2,008)
c...............	(405)	(1,728)	3,518
d...............	3,702	(2,440)	1,330
e...............	70	2,005	(815)
f...............	5	(530)	876
g...............	(2,580)	(4,200)	7,459
h...............	(409)	5,581	(2,406)

M11-29. **Compute and Interpret Cash Flow Ratios**

LO6

Use the following information to compute and interpret cash flow ratios.

Company	Operating Cash Flow	Average Current Liabilities	CAPEX
a...............	$2,106	$6,581	$2,425
b...............	5,668	2,181	1,007
c...............	3,702	3,365	1,220
d...............	2,700	5,192	1,984

Required

a. Compute the operating cash flow to current liabilities ratio. Compared to the average of 0.5 for large public companies, assess each company's liquidity as low, medium, or high (i.e., its ability to settle liabilities as they come due).

b. Compute the operating cash flow to CAPEX ratio. Compared to the rule of thumb of 1.0, assess the company's solvency as either low, medium, or high.

M11-30. **Computing and Comparing Income and Cash Flow Measures**

LO1

Penno Corporation recorded service revenues of $200,000 in 2017, of which $170,000 were on credit and $30,000 were for cash. Moreover, of the $170,000 credit sales for 2017, Penno collected $20,000 cash on those receivables before year-end 2017. The company also paid $25,000 cash for 2017 wages. Its employees also earned another $15,000 in wages for 2017, which were not yet paid at year-end 2017.

Required

a. Compute the company's net income for 2017.

b. How much net cash inflow or outflow did the company generate in 2017? Explain why Penno's net income and net cash flow differ.

Exercises

E11-31. **Net Cash Flow from Operating Activities (Indirect Method)**

LO2

Lincoln Company owns no PPE and reported the following income statement for the current year.

Sales.......................		$700,000
Cost of goods sold.............	$425,000	
Wages expense	110,000	
Rent expense	38,000	
Insurance expense.............	15,000	588,000
Net income...................		$112,000

Additional balance sheet information about the company follows:

	End of Year	Beginning of Year
Accounts receivable........	$56,000	$48,000
Inventory................	60,000	66,000
Prepaid insurance..........	7,000	5,000
Accounts payable..........	22,000	18,000
Wages payable............	11,000	15,000

Use the information to calculate the net cash flow from operating activities under the indirect method.

LO2, 3, 4   E11-32.   Statement of Cash Flows (Indirect Method)

Use the following information about Lund Corporation for 2017 to prepare a statement of cash flows under the indirect method.

Accounts payable increase	$ 9,000
Accounts receivable increase....................	4,000
Accrued liabilities decrease	3,000
Amortization expense..........................	6,000
Cash balance, beginning of 2017..................	22,000
Cash balance, end of 2017	15,000
Cash paid as dividends	29,000
Cash paid to purchase land.....................	90,000
Cash paid to retire bonds payable at par............	60,000
Cash received from issuance of common stock	35,000
Cash received from sale of equipment..............	17,000
Depreciation expense..........................	29,000
Gain on sale of equipment......................	4,000
Inventory decrease............................	13,000
Net income.................................	76,000
Prepaid expenses increase	2,000

LO2   E11-33.   Operating Section of Statement of Cash Flows (Indirect Method)

Nike Inc. (NKE)

Following are the income statement and balance sheet for **Nike Inc.** for the year ended May 31, 2016, and a forecasted income statement and balance sheet for 2017.

NIKE INC. Income Statement For Year Ended May 31		
$ millions	2016 Actual	2017 Est.
Revenues	$32,376	$34,319
Cost of sales..................................	17,405	18,464
Gross profit....................................	14,971	15,855
Demand creation expense	3,278	3,466
Operating overhead expense......................	7,191	7,619
Total selling and administrative expense	10,469	11,085
Interest expense (income), net....................	19	19
Other (income) expense, net	(140)	(140)
Income before income taxes	4,623	4,891
Income tax expense............................	863	915
Net income...................................	$ 3,760	$ 3,976

NIKE INC. Balance Sheet May 31		
$ millions	**2016 Actual**	**2017 Est.**
Current assets		
Cash and equivalents....................................	$ 3,138	$ 5,337
Short-term investments	2,319	2,319
Accounts receivable, net	3,241	3,432
Inventories	4,838	5,114
Prepaid expenses and other current assets.................	1,489	1,579
Total current assets.....................................	15,025	$17,781
Property, plant and equipment, net	3,520	3,961
Identifiable intangible assets, net.........................	281	268
Goodwill..	131	131
Deferred income taxes and other assets	2,439	2,574
Total assets..	$21,396	$24,715
Current liabilities		
Current portion of long-term debt	$ 44	$ 6
Notes payable..	1	1
Accounts payable.......................................	2,191	2,334
Accrued liabilities	3,037	3,226
Income taxes payable...................................	85	103
Total current liabilities..................................	5,358	5,670
Long-term debt	2,010	2,004
Deferred income taxes and other liabilities	1,770	1,888
Total liabilities	9,138	9,562
Shareholders' equity		
Class A convertible common stock	0	0
Class B common stock	3	3
Capital in excess of stated value	7,786	7,786
Accumulated other comprehensive income.................	318	318
Retained earnings	4,151	7,046
Total shareholders' equity...............................	12,258	15,153
Total liabilities and shareholders' equity.................	$21,396	$24,715

Prepare the net cash flows from the operating activities section of a forecasted statement of cash flows for 2017 using the indirect method. Treat deferred tax assets and liabilities as operating. Operating expenses (cost of sales) for 2017 include estimated depreciation expense of $760 million and amortization expense of $13 million.

E11-34. **Operating Section of Statement of Cash Flows (Indirect Method)**
Following are the income statement and balance sheet for Medtronic PLC for the year ended April 29, 2016, and a forecasted income statement and balance sheet for 2017.

LO2
Medtronic PLC
(MDT)

MEDTRONIC PLC
Income Statement
For Fiscal Year Ended

$ millions	2016 Actual	2017 Est.
Net sales.	$28,833	$35,176
Costs and expenses		
Cost of products sold.	9,142	11,151
Research and development expense.	2,224	2,709
Selling, general, and administrative expense.	9,469	11,538
Special charges, net.	70	-
Restructuring charges, net.	290	218
Certain litigation charges, net.	26	-
Acquisition-related items	283	352
Amortization of intangible assets.	1,931	1,931
Other expense, net.	107	107
Operating profit	5,291	7,170
Interest expense, net	955	955
Income from operations before income taxes	4,336	6,215
Provision for income taxes.	798	1,243
Net income.	$ 3,538	$ 4,972

MEDTRONIC PLC
Balance Sheet
At Fiscal Year-End

$ millions	2016 Actual	2017 Est.
Current assets		
Cash and cash equivalents.	$ 2,876	$ 5,600
Investments	9,758	9,758
Accounts receivable.	5,562	6,789
Inventories	3,473	4,221
Tax assets.	697	844
Prepaid expenses and other current assets.	1,234	1,513
Total current assets.	23,600	28,725
Property, plant, and equipment, net.	4,841	5,192
Goodwill.	41,500	41,500
Other intangible assets, net	26,899	24,968
Long-term tax assets.	1,383	1,688
Other assets.	1,559	1,900
Total assets.	$99,782	$103,973
Current liabilities		
Short-term borrowings	$ 993	$ 6,176
Accounts payable.	1,709	2,075
Accrued compensation.	1,712	2,075
Accrued income taxes	566	704
Other accrued expenses.	2,185	2,673
Total current liabilities.	7,165	13,703
Long-term debt	30,247	24,071
Long-term accrued compensation and retirement benefits.	1,759	1,759
Long-term accrued income taxes	2,903	3,553
Long-term deferred tax liabilities.	3,729	4,538
Other long-term liabilities.	1,916	2,322
Total liabilities.	47,719	49,946

continued

$ millions	2016 Actual	2017 Est.
Stockholders' equity		
Ordinary shares	—	—
Retained earnings	53,931	55,895
Accumulated other comprehensive (loss) income	(1,868)	(1,868)
Total shareholders' equity	52,063	54,027
Total liabilities and shareholders' equity.............................	$99,782	$103,973

Prepare the net cash flows from the operating activities section of a forecasted statement of cash flows for 2017 using the indirect method. Operating expenses (such as cost of sales and selling, general, and administrative expenses) for 2017 include estimated depreciation expense of $915 million and amortization expense of $1,931 million. Estimated 2017 retained earnings includes dividends of $3,008 million.

E11-35. **Operating Cash Flows (Direct Method)**   **LO7**
Calculate the cash flow for each of the following cases.

 a. Cash paid for advertising:

Advertising expense..................	$62,000
Prepaid advertising, beginning of year....	11,000
Prepaid advertising, end of year.........	15,000

 b. Cash paid for income taxes:

Income tax expense..................	$29,000
Income tax payable, beginning of year ...	7,100
Income tax payable, end of year	4,900

 c. Cash paid for merchandise purchased:

Cost of goods sold...................	$180,000
Inventory, beginning of year............	30,000
Inventory, end of year.................	25,000
Accounts payable, beginning of year.....	10,000
Accounts payable, end of year..........	12,000

E11-36. **Statement of Cash Flows (Direct Method)**   **LO3, 4, 7**
Use the following information about the 2017 cash flows of Mason Corporation to prepare a statement of cash flows under the direct method.

Cash balance, end of 2017	$ 12,000
Cash paid to employees and suppliers ...	148,000
Cash received from sale of land.........	40,000
Cash paid to acquire treasury stock	10,000
Cash balance, beginning of 2017........	16,000
Cash received as interest..............	6,000
Cash paid as income taxes	11,000
Cash paid to purchase equipment.......	89,000
Cash received from customers	194,000
Cash received from issuing bonds payable	30,000
Cash paid as dividends	16,000

E11-37. **Operating Cash Flows (Direct Method)**   **LO7**
Refer to the information in Exercise E11-31. Calculate the net cash flow from operating activities using the direct method. Show a related cash flow for each revenue and expense.

LO3, 4 **E11-38.** **Investing and Financing Cash Flows**

During 2017, Paxon Corporation's long-term investments account (at cost) increased $15,000, which was the net result of purchasing stocks costing $80,000 and selling stocks costing $65,000 at a $6,000 loss. Also, its bonds payable account decreased $40,000, the net result of issuing $100,000 of bonds at $103,000 and retiring bonds with a face value (and book value) of $140,000 at a $9,000 gain. What items and amounts appear in the (a) cash flows from investing activities and (b) cash flows from financing activities sections of its 2017 statement of cash flows?

LO5 **E11-39.** **Using Statement of Cash Flow Information to Assess Company Life-Cycle Stage**

Amgen Inc. (AMGN)
Staples Inc. (SPLS)
Roger's Communications

Consider each company's statement of cash flows as reported in assignments referenced below. Complete the table to (a) indicate the sign of the cash flows and (b) identify the company's life-cycle stage (introduction, growth, maturity, or decline).

Company ($ millions)	See Financial Information in:	Cash from Operating Activities	Cash from Investing Activities	Cash from Financing Activities	Life-Cycle Stage
Amgen Inc.	P11-56	____	____	____	____
Staples Inc.	P11-57	____	____	____	____
Roger's Communications	I11-58	____	____	____	____

LO5 **E11-40.** **Using Statement of Cash Flow Information to Assess Company Life-Cycle Stage**

Logitech International (LOGI)
Steelcase Inc. (SCS)
Chico's FAS Inc. (CHS)
Vista Outdoor Inc. (VSTO)
Avnet Inc. (AVT)

Use the following information, taken from the 2016 statement of cash flow from each of the respective companies, to complete the requirements.

Company ($ millions)	Cash from Operations	Cash from Investing	Cash from Financing
Logitech International	$183.111	$(60.690)	$(141.669)
Steelcase Inc.	186.400	(87.800)	(90.100)
Chico's FAS Inc.	196.991	0.491	(240.381)
Vista Outdoor Inc..........................	198.002	(503.204)	192.600
Avnet Inc....................................	224.315	(152.513)	33.355

Required

a. Identify each company's life-cycle stage (introduction, growth, maturity, or decline).
b. Rank-order each company from least to most mature. (*Hint:* All five companies have cash from operations of about $200 million. Graph the cash from investing and from financing, and then use the graphic [showing revenue, income, and cash flow by life cycle] to evaluate the relative size of the three types of cash flow.)

LO6 **E11-41.** **Compute Ratios from Statement of Cash Flow Information**

Logitech International (LOGI)
Steelcase Inc. (SCS)
Chico's FAS Inc. (CHS)
Vista Outdoor Inc. (VSTO)
Avnet Inc. (AVT)

Use the following information, taken from each of the company's 2016 financial statements to complete the requirements.

Company ($ millions)	Cash from Operations	Current Liabilities	CAPEX
Logitech International	$183.111	$ 414.930	$ 56.615
Steelcase Inc.	186.400	557.500	93.400
Chico's FAS Inc.	196.991	298.131	84.841
Vista Outdoor Inc..........................	198.002	368.901	41.526
Avnet Inc....................................	224.315	4,942.493	147.548

Required

a. Compute the operating cash flow to current liabilities ratio.
b. Rank-order each company from low to high liquidity (ability to pay liabilities as they come due). Do any of the companies have liquidity difficulties?
c. Compute the operating cash flow to CAPEX ratio. Compared with the rule of thumb of 1.0, assess the company's solvency as either low, medium, or high.
d. Rank-order each company from low to high solvency. Do any of the companies have solvency difficulties?

E11-42. **Interpret Cash Flow Patterns and Ratios**

The following information is taken from the 2016 Form 10-K for each of the following technology companies.

LO5, 6

Cisco Systems Inc. (CSCO)

Oracle Corporation (ORCL)

Seagate Technology plc (STX)

Company ($ millions)	Operating Cash Flow	Investing Cash Flow	Financing Cash Flow	Average Current Liabilities	CAPEX
Cisco Systems Inc..........	$13,570	$(8,117)	$(4,699)	$24,162	$1,146
Oracle Corporation.........	13,561	(5,154)	(9,856)	16,207	1,189
Seagate Technology plc.....	1,680	(1,211)	(1,820)	2,296	587

Required

a. Compute the operating cash flow to current liabilities ratio. Compared to the average of 0.5, assess as low, medium, or high, each company's ability to settle liabilities as they come due.

b. Compute the operating cash flow to CAPEX ratio. Compared to the rule of thumb of 1.0, assess the company's solvency as either low, medium, or high.

c. All three companies are in the mature stage of its life cycle. Consider the graphic shown earlier in the module that graphs the cash flow patterns. Use the graphic to rank the companies from least mature to most mature.

Problems

P11-43. **Statement of Cash Flows (Indirect Method)**

Wolff Company's income statement and comparative balance sheets follow.

LO2, 3, 4

WOLFF COMPANY
Income Statement
For Year Ended December 31, 2017

Sales.....................................		$635,000
Cost of goods sold.....................	$430,000	
Wages expense	86,000	
Insurance expense.....................	8,000	
Depreciation expense..................	17,000	
Interest expense.......................	9,000	
Income tax expense....................	29,000	579,000
Net income.............................		$ 56,000

WOLFF COMPANY
Balance Sheet

	Dec. 31, 2017	Dec. 31, 2016
Assets		
Cash...................................	$ 11,000	$ 5,000
Accounts receivable....................	41,000	32,000
Inventory..............................	90,000	60,000
Prepaid insurance......................	5,000	7,000
PPE....................................	250,000	195,000
Accumulated depreciation	(68,000)	(51,000)
Total assets...........................	$329,000	$248,000

continued

continued from previous page

	Dec. 31, 2017	Dec. 31, 2016
Liabilities and Stockholders' Equity		
Accounts payable..............................	$ 7,000	$ 10,000
Wages payable..................................	9,000	6,000
Income tax payable	7,000	8,000
Bonds payable..................................	130,000	75,000
Common stock..................................	90,000	90,000
Retained earnings	86,000	59,000
Total liabilities and equity.....................	$329,000	$248,000

Cash dividends of $29,000 were declared and paid during 2017. Also in 2017, PPE was purchased for cash, and bonds payable were issued for cash. Bond interest is paid semiannually on June 30 and December 31. Accounts payable relate to merchandise purchases.

Required

a. Compute the change in cash that occurred during 2017.

b. Prepare a 2017 statement of cash flows using the indirect method.

LO2, 3, 4
Amazon.com Inc.
(AMZN)

P11-44. **Statement of Cash Flows (Indirect Method)**

Following are the income statement and balance sheet for **Amazon.com Inc.** for the year ended December 31, 2015, and a forecasted income statement and balance sheet for 2016.

AMAZON.COM INC. **Income Statement** **For Year Ended December 31**		
$ millions	**Actual 2015**	**2016 Est.**
Net product sales...............................	$ 79,268	$ 91,158
Net service sales	27,738	38,833
Total net sales....................................	107,006	129,991
Operating expenses:		
Cost of sales......................................	71,651	87,094
Fulfillment..	13,410	16,249
Marketing...	5,254	6,370
Technology and content........................	12,540	15,209
General and administrative....................	1,747	2,080
Other operating expense (income), net	171	171
Total operating expenses......................	104,773	127,173
Income from operations........................	2,233	2,818
Interest income...................................	50	60
Interest expense.................................	(459)	(520)
Other income (expense), net	(256)	(256)
Total non-operating income (expense).....	(665)	(716)
Income (loss) before taxes....................	1,568	2,102
Provision for income taxes....................	(950)	(799)
Equity method investment activity, net of tax	(22)	(22)
Net income (loss)	$ 596	$ 1,281

AMAZON.COM INC. Balance Sheet December 31		
In millions, except par value	Actual 2015	2016 Est.
Current assets		
Cash and cash equivalents.	$15,890	$22,726
Marketable securities	3,918	3,918
Inventories	10,243	12,479
Accounts receivable, net and other	6,423	7,799
Total current assets.	36,474	46,922
Property and equipment, net	21,838	21,117
Goodwill	3,759	3,759
Other assets.	3,373	4,160
Total assets.	$65,444	$75,958
Current liabilities		
Accounts payable.	20,397	24,828
Accrued expenses and other	10,384	12,609
Unearned revenue	3,118	3,770
Total current liabilities	33,899	41,207
Long-term debt	8,235	7,997
Other long-term liabilities.	9,926	12,089
Total liabilities	52,060	61,293
Stockholders' equity		
Preferred stock, $0.01 par value, 500 shares authorized; issued and outstanding shares—none	—	—
Common stock, $0.01 par value, 5,000 shares authorized; 494 shares issued and 471 shares outstanding	5	5
Treasury stock, at cost.	(1,837)	(1,837)
Additional paid-in capital.	13,394	13,394
Accumulated other comprehensive loss	(723)	(723)
Retained earnings	2,545	3,826
Total stockholders' equity	13,384	14,665
Total liabilities and stockholders' equity.	$65,444	$75,958

Required

Prepare a forecasted statement of cash flows for 2016 using the indirect method. Operating expenses for 2016 (e.g., cost of goods sold and general and administrative expenses) include estimated depreciation expense of $6,311 million. Property and equipment, net includes an estimated CAPEX of $5,590 million, and for estimated retained earnings assume the payment of $0 in dividends.

P11-45.   Statement of Cash Flows (Indirect Method)   **LO2, 3, 4**

Arctic Company's income statement and comparative balance sheets follow.

ARCTIC COMPANY Income Statement For Year Ended December 31, 2017		
Sales.		$728,000
Cost of goods sold.	$534,000	
Wages expense	190,000	
Advertising expense.	31,000	
Depreciation expense.	22,000	
Interest expense.	18,000	
Gain on sale of land	(25,000)	770,000
Net loss		$ (42,000)

ARCTIC COMPANY Balance Sheet		
	Dec. 31, 2017	**Dec. 31, 2016**
Assets		
Cash.	$ 49,000	$ 28,000
Accounts receivable.	42,000	50,000
Inventory.	107,000	113,000
Prepaid advertising.	10,000	13,000
PPE.	360,000	222,000
Accumulated depreciation	(78,000)	(56,000)
Total assets.	$490,000	$370,000
Liabilities and Stockholders' Equity		
Accounts payable.	$ 17,000	$ 31,000
Interest payable	6,000	—
Bonds payable	200,000	—
Common stock.	245,000	245,000
Retained earnings	52,000	94,000
Treasury stock	(30,000)	—
Total liabilities and equity	$490,000	$370,000

During 2017, Arctic sold land for $70,000 cash that had originally cost $45,000. Arctic also purchased equipment for cash, acquired treasury stock for cash, and issued bonds payable for cash in 2017. Accounts payable relate to merchandise purchases.

Required

a. Compute the change in cash that occurred during 2017.

b. Prepare a 2017 statement of cash flows using the indirect method.

LO2, 3, 4   **P11-46.**   **Statement of Cash Flows (Indirect Method)**

Dair Company's income statement and comparative balance sheets follow.

DAIR COMPANY Income Statement For Year Ended December 31, 2017		
Sales.		$700,000
Cost of goods sold.	$440,000	
Wages and other operating expenses	95,000	
Depreciation expense.	22,000	
Amortization expense.	7,000	
Interest expense.	10,000	
Income tax expense.	36,000	
Loss on bond retirement	5,000	615,000
Net income.		$ 85,000

DAIR COMPANY Balance Sheet	Dec. 31, 2017	Dec. 31, 2016
Assets		
Cash............................	$ 27,000	$ 18,000
Accounts receivable................	53,000	48,000
Inventory........................	103,000	109,000
Prepaid expenses.................	12,000	10,000
PPE............................	360,000	336,000
Accumulated depreciation..........	(87,000)	(84,000)
Intangible assets	43,000	50,000
Total assets......................	$511,000	$487,000
Liabilities and Stockholders' Equity		
Accounts payable.................	$ 32,000	$ 26,000
Interest payable	4,000	7,000
Income tax payable	6,000	8,000
Bonds payable	60,000	120,000
Common stock....................	252,000	228,000
Retained earnings	157,000	98,000
Total liabilities and equity..........	$511,000	$487,000

During 2017, the company sold for $17,000 cash old equipment that had cost $36,000 and had $19,000 accumulated depreciation. Also in 2017, new equipment worth $60,000 was acquired in exchange for $60,000 of bonds payable, and bonds payable of $120,000 were retired for cash at a loss. A $26,000 cash dividend was declared and paid in 2017. Any stock issuances were for cash.

Required

a. Compute the change in cash that occurred in 2017.

b. Prepare a 2017 statement of cash flows using the indirect method.

c. Prepare separate schedules showing (1) cash paid for interest and for income taxes and (2) noncash investing and financing transactions.

P11-47. **Statement of Cash Flows (Indirect Method)**

Following are the income statement and balance sheet for Whole Foods Market Inc., for the year ended September 25, 2016, and a forecasted income statement and balance sheet for 2017.

LO2, 3, 4
Whole Foods Market Inc. (WFM)

WHOLE FOODS MARKET INC. Income Statement		
$ millions	2016 Actual	2017 Est.
Sales..	$15,724	$15,881
Cost of goods sold and occupancy costs	10,313	10,418
Gross profit......................................	5,411	5,463
Selling, general and administrative expenses	4,477	4,526
Pre-opening expenses.............................	64	64
Relocation, store closure and lease termination costs	13	—
Operating income.................................	857	873
Interest expense.................................	(41)	(41)
Investment and other income.......................	11	11
Income before income taxes	827	843
Provision for income taxes.........................	320	312
Net income.....................................	$507	$531

WHOLE FOODS MARKET INC.
Balance Sheet

In millions	2016 Actual	2017 Est.
Assets		
Current assets		
Cash and cash equivalents.	$ 351	$ 206
Short-term investments - available-for-sale securities.	379	379
Restricted cash.	122	122
Accounts receivable	242	286
Merchandise inventories.	517	524
Prepaid expenses and other current assets.	167	175
Deferred income taxes	197	206
Total current assets.	1,975	1,898
Property and equipment, net of accumulated depreciation and amortization...	3,442	3,720
Goodwill.	710	710
Intangible assets, net of accumulated amortization.	74	68
Deferred income taxes.	100	95
Other assets.	40	40
Total assets.	$6,341	$6,531
Liabilities and shareholders' Equity		
Current liabilities		
Current installments of long-term debt and capital lease obligations	$ 3	$ 65
Accounts payable.	307	318
Accrued payroll, bonus and other benefits due team members	407	413
Dividends payable	43	40
Other current liabilities	581	588
Total current liabilities.	1,341	1,424
Long-term capital lease obligations, less current installments	1,048	983
Deferred lease liabilities.	640	640
Other long-term liabilities.	88	88
Total liabilities.	3,117	3,135
Shareholders' equity		
Common stock, no par value, 1,200 shares authorized; 377.0 shares issued; 318.3 shares outstanding	2,933	2,933
Common stock in treasury, at cost, 58.7 shares	(2,026)	(2,226)
Accumulated other comprehensive loss	(32)	(32)
Retained earnings	2,349	2,721
Total shareholders' equity	3,224	3,396
Total liabilities and shareholders' equity.	$6,341	$6,531

Required
Prepare a forecasted statement of cash flows for 2017 using the indirect method. Assume the following:
- Operating expenses for 2017 (such as general and administrative) include depreciation and amortization expense of $522 million.
- The company did not dispose of or write-down any long-term assets during the year.
- The company paid dividends of $159 million in 2017.

P11-48. **Statement of Cash Flows (Indirect Method)** **LO2, 3, 4**

Rainbow Company's income statement and comparative balance sheets follow.

RAINBOW COMPANY Income Statement For Year Ended December 31, 2017		
Sales.		$750,000
Dividend income.		15,000
		765,000
Cost of goods sold.	$440,000	
Wages and other operating expenses	130,000	
Depreciation expense.	39,000	
Patent amortization expense	7,000	
Interest expense.	13,000	
Income tax expense.	44,000	
Loss on sale of equipment.	5,000	
Gain on sale of investments.	(10,000)	668,000
Net income.		$ 97,000

RAINBOW COMPANY Balance Sheet	Dec. 31, 2017	Dec. 31, 2016
Assets		
Cash and cash equivalents	$ 19,000	$ 25,000
Accounts receivable.	40,000	30,000
Inventory.	103,000	77,000
Prepaid expenses.	10,000	6,000
Long-term investments—Available-for-sale.	—	50,000
Fair value adjustment to investments.	—	7,000
Land	190,000	100,000
Buildings.	445,000	350,000
Accumulated depreciation—Buildings.	(91,000)	(75,000)
Equipment	179,000	225,000
Accumulated depreciation—Equipment	(42,000)	(46,000)
Patents.	50,000	32,000
Total assets.	$903,000	$781,000
Liabilities and Stockholders' Equity		
Accounts payable.	$ 20,000	$ 16,000
Interest payable	6,000	5,000
Income tax payable	8,000	10,000
Bonds payable	155,000	125,000
Preferred stock ($100 par value)	100,000	75,000
Common stock ($5 par value)	379,000	364,000
Paid-in capital in excess of par value—Common	133,000	124,000
Retained earnings	102,000	55,000
Unrealized gain on investments	—	7,000
Total liabilities and equity	$903,000	$781,000

During 2017, the following transactions and events occurred in addition to the company's usual business activities.

1. Sold long-term investments costing $50,000 for $60,000 cash. Unrealized gains totaling $7,000 related to these investments had been recorded in earlier years. At year-end, the fair value adjustment and unrealized gain account balances were eliminated.
2. Purchased land for cash.

3. Capitalized an expenditure made to improve the building.
4. Sold equipment for $14,000 cash that originally cost $46,000 and had $27,000 accumulated depreciation.
5. Issued bonds payable at face value for cash.
6. Acquired a patent with a fair value of $25,000 by issuing 250 shares of preferred stock at par value.
7. Declared and paid a $50,000 cash dividend.
8. Issued 3,000 shares of common stock for cash at $8 per share.
9. Recorded depreciation of $16,000 on buildings and $23,000 on equipment.

Required

a. Compute the change in cash and cash equivalents that occurred during 2017.
b. Prepare a 2017 statement of cash flows using the indirect method.
c. Prepare separate schedules showing (1) cash paid for interest and for income taxes and (2) noncash investing and financing transactions.

LO1, 2, 3, 4, 5
Walmart Stores Inc.
(WMT)

P11-49.   Interpreting the Statement of Cash Flows

Following is the statement of cash flows for Walmart Stores Inc.

WALMART STORES INC. Statement of Cash Flows For Year Ended January 31, 2016 ($ millions)	
Cash flows from operating activities	
Income from continuing operations	15,080
Adjustments to reconcile income from continuing operations to net cash provided by operating activities:	
Depreciation and amortization	9,454
Deferred income taxes	(672)
Other operating activities	1,410
Changes in certain assets and liabilities, net of effects of acquisitions:	
Receivables, net	(19)
Inventories	(703)
Accounts payable	2,008
Accrued liabilities	1,303
Accrued income taxes	(472)
Net cash provided by operating activities	27,389
Cash flows from investing activities	
Payments for property and equipment	(11,477)
Proceeds from the disposal of property and equipment	635
Proceeds from disposal of certain operations	246
Other investing activities	(79)
Net cash used in investing activities	(10,675)
Cash flows from financing activities	
Net change in short-term borrowings	1,235
Proceeds from issuance of long-term debt	39
Payments of long-term debt	(4,432)
Dividends paid	(6,294)
Purchase of Company stock	(4,112)
Dividends to noncontrolling interest	(719)
Purchase of noncontrolling interest	(1,326)
Other financing activities	(513)
Net cash used in financing activities	(16,122)
Effect of exchange rates on cash and cash equivalents	(1,022)
Net increase (decrease) in cash and cash equivalents	(430)
Cash and cash equivalents at beginning of year	9,135
Cash and cash equivalents at end of year	$ 8,705

Required

a. Why does the company add back depreciation to compute net cash flows from operating activities?
b. Explain why the increase in receivables and inventories is reported as a cash outflow. Why do accounts payable and accrued liabilities provide a source of cash?

c. Walmart Stores Inc. reports that it invested $11,477 million in property and equipment. Is this an appropriate type of expenditure for the company to make? What relation should expenditures for PPE have with depreciation expense?

d. Walmart Stores Inc. indicates it paid $4,112 million to repurchase its common stock in fiscal 2016 and, in addition, paid dividends of $6,294 million. Thus, it paid $10,406 million of cash to its stockholders during the year. How do we evaluate that use of cash relative to other possible uses for the company's cash?

e. Provide an overall assessment of the company's cash flows for fiscal 2016. In the analysis, consider the sources and uses of cash.

P11-50. **Interpreting the Statement of Cash Flows**

Following is the statement of cash flows for **Verizon Communications Inc.**

LO1, 2, 3, 4, 5

Verizon Communications Inc. (VZ)

VERIZON COMMUNICATIONS INC. Statement of Cash Flows For Year Ended December 31, 2015 ($ millions)	
Cash Flows from Operating Activities	
Net Income.	$18,375
Adjustments to reconcile net income to net cash provided by operating activities:	
Depreciation and amortization expense.	16,017
Employee retirement benefits.	(1,747)
Deferred income taxes	3,516
Provision for uncollectible accounts.	1,610
Equity in losses of unconsolidated businesses, net of dividends received	127
Changes in current assets and liabilities, net of effects from acquisition/disposition of businesses	
Accounts receivable	(945)
Inventories.	(99)
Other assets	942
Accounts payable and accrued liabilities	2,545
Other, net	(1,411)
Net cash provided by operating activities	38,930
Cash Flows from Investing Activities	
Capital expenditures (including capitalized software)	(17,775)
Acquisitions of investments and businesses, net of cash acquired.	(3,545)
Acquisitions of wireless licenses	(9,942)
Proceeds from dispositions of wireless licenses	—
Proceeds from dispositions of businesses.	48
Other, net	1,171
Net cash used in investing activities.	(30,043)
Cash Flows from Financing Activities	
Proceeds from long-term borrowings	6,667
Repayments of long-term borrowings and capital lease obligations.	(9,340)
Decrease in short-term obligations, excluding current maturities	(344)
Dividends paid	(8,538)
Proceeds from sale of common stock.	40
Purchase of common stock for treasury	(5,134)
Other, net	1,634
Net cash used in financing activities	(15,015)
Increase (decrease) in cash and cash equivalents.	(6,128)
Cash and cash equivalents, beginning of period.	10,598
Cash and cash equivalents, end of period.	$ 4,470

Required

a. Why does Verizon add back depreciation to compute net cash flows from operating activities? What does the size of the depreciation add-back indicate about the relative capital intensity of this industry?

b. Verizon reports that it invested $17,775 million in property and equipment. These expenditures are necessitated by market pressures as the company faces stiff competition from other communications companies, such as **Comcast**. Where in the 10-K might we find additional information about these capital expenditures to ascertain whether Verizon is addressing the company's most pressing needs? What relation might we expect between the size of these capital expenditures and the amount of depreciation expense reported?

c. Verizon's statement of cash flows indicates the company paid $9,340 million in long-term debt payments. What problem does Verizon's high debt load pose for its ability to maintain the level of capital expenditures necessary to remain competitive in its industry?

d. During the year, Verizon paid dividends of $8,538 million but did not repay a sizable portion of its debt. How do dividend payments differ from debt payments? Why would Verizon continue to pay dividends in light of cash demands for needed capital expenditures and debt repayments?

e. Provide an overall assessment of Verizon's cash flows for 2015. In the analysis, consider the sources and uses of cash.

LO1, 2, 5 **P11-51.** **Reconciling and Computing Operating Cash Flows from Net Income**

Petroni Company reports the following selected results for its current calendar year.

Net income.	$130,000
Depreciation expense.	28,000
Accounts receivable increase. . .	10,000
Accounts payable increase	6,000
Prepaid expenses decrease. . . .	3,000
Wages payable decrease	4,000

Required

a. Prepare the operating section only of Petroni Company's statement of cash flows for the year.

b. Does the positive sign on depreciation expense indicate the company is generating cash by recording depreciation? Explain.

c. Explain why the increase in accounts receivable is a use of cash in the statement of cash flows.

d. Explain why the decrease in prepaid expense is a source of cash in the statement of cash flows.

LO3, 4, 7 **P11-52.** **Statement of Cash Flows (Direct Method)**

Refer to the data for Wolff Company in Problem P11-43.

Required

a. Compute the change in cash that occurred during 2017.

b. Prepare a 2017 statement of cash flows using the direct method.

LO3, 4, 7 **P11-53.** **Statement of Cash Flows (Direct Method)**

Refer to the data for Arctic Company in Problem P11-45.

Required

a. Compute the change in cash that occurred during 2017.

b. Prepare a 2017 statement of cash flows using the direct method.

LO3, 4, 7 **P11-54.** **Statement of Cash Flows (Direct Method)**

Refer to the data for Dair Company in Problem P11-46.

Required

a. Compute the change in cash that occurred in 2017.

b. Prepare a 2017 statement of cash flows using the direct method. Use one cash outflow for "cash paid for wages and other operating expenses." Accounts payable relate to inventory purchases only.

c. Prepare separate schedules showing (1) a reconciliation of net income to net cash flow from operating activities (see Exhibit 11.3) and (2) noncash investing and financing transactions.

LO3, 4, 7 **P11-55.** **Statement of Cash Flows (Direct Method)**

Refer to the data for Rainbow Company in Problem P11-48.

Required

a. Compute the change in cash that occurred in 2017.

b. Prepare a 2017 statement of cash flows using the direct method. Use one cash outflow for "cash paid for wages and other operating expenses." Accounts payable relate to inventory purchases only.

c. Prepare separate schedules showing (1) a reconciliation of net income to net cash flow from operating activities (see Exhibit 11.3) and (2) noncash investing and financing transactions.

P11-56. **Interpreting the Statement of Cash Flows**   **LO1, 5, 6**
          Following is the statement of cash flows of Amgen Inc.   Amgen Inc. (AMGN)

AMGEN INC. CONSOLIDATED STATEMENTS OF CASH FLOWS Years Ended December 31, 2015, 2014 and 2013			
$ millions	**2015**	**2014**	**2013**
Cash flows from operating activities:			
Net income.	$ 6,939	$ 5,158	$ 5,081
Depreciation and amortization.	2,108	2,092	1,286
Stock-based compensation expense	322	408	403
Deferred income taxes.	(607)	(108)	(189)
Other items, net	(399)	(116)	103
Changes in operating assets and liabilities, net of acquisitions:			
Trade receivables, net	(420)	136	(38)
Inventories	481	327	(7)
Other assets.	155	(1)	(59)
Accounts payable.	(12)	228	60
Accrued income taxes	509	(103)	(326)
Other liabilities	1	534	(23)
Net cash provided by operating activities	9,077	8,555	6,291
Cash flows from investing activities:			
Purchases of property, plant and equipment.	(594)	(718)	(693)
Cash paid for acquisitions, net of cash acquired.	(359)	(165)	(9,434)
Purchases of intangible assets.	(55)	(285)	—
Purchases of marketable securities	(25,977)	(25,878)	(21,965)
Proceeds from sales of marketable securities	18,029	16,697	19,123
Proceeds from maturities of marketable securities	3,527	4,199	5,090
Proceeds from sale of property, plant and equipment.	274	3	20
Change in restricted investments, net	—	533	(520)
Other.	(392)	(138)	(90)
Net cash used in investing activities	(5,547)	(5,752)	(8,469)
Cash flows from financing activities:			
Net proceeds from issuance of debt	3,465	4,476	8,054
Repayment of debt.	(2,400)	(5,605)	(3,371)
Repurchases of common stock	(1,867)	(138)	(832)
Dividends paid	(2,396)	(1,851)	(1,415)
Net proceeds from issuance of common stock in connection with the Company's equity award programs	82	186	296
Settlement of contingent consideration obligations.	(253)	(92)	—
Other.	252	147	(6)
Net cash (used in) provided by financing activities	(3,117)	(2,877)	2,726
Increase (decrease) in cash and cash equivalents.	413	(74)	548
Cash and cash equivalents at beginning of period	3,731	3,805	3,257
Cash and cash equivalents at end of period	$ 4,144	$ 3,731	$ 3,805

Required

a. Amgen reports it generated $9,077 million in net cash from operating activities in 2015. Yet, its
   net income for the year amounted to only $6,939 million. Much of this difference is the result of
   depreciation. Why is Amgen adding depreciation to net income in the computation of operating cash
   flows?

b. In determining cash provided by operating activities, Amgen adds $322 million relating to stock-
   based compensation expense in 2015. What is the purpose of this addition?

c. Amgen reports $(420) million relating to trade receivables. What does the negative sign on this
   amount signify about the change in receivables during the year compared with the positive sign
   on the amount for 2014?

d. Calculate and compare operating cash flow with current liabilities and operating cash flow with capital expenditures for 2015 and 2014. Current liabilities were $8,667 million, $7,008 million, and $7,947 million at 2015, 2014, and 2013, respectively.

e. Does the composition of Amgen's cash flow present a "healthy" picture for 2015? Explain.

LO1, 5, 6

Staples Inc. (SPLS)

P11-57.   **Interpreting the Statement of Cash Flows**

Following is the statement of cash flows of **Staples Inc.**

STAPLES INC. Consolidated Statements of Cash Flows	
Fiscal Year Ended ($ Millions)	January 30, 2016
Operating Activities:	
Consolidated net income	$379
Adjustments to reconcile net income to net cash provided by operating activities:	
Depreciation	388
Amortization of intangibles	67
Loss on sale of businesses and assets, net	5
Impairment of goodwill and long-lived assets	50
Inventory write-downs related to restructuring activities	1
Stock-based compensation	63
Excess tax benefits from stock-based compensation arrangements	(5)
Deferred income tax expense	28
Other	11
Changes in assets and liabilities:	
Increase in receivables	(19)
Decrease (increase) in merchandise inventories	18
(Increase) decrease in prepaid expenses and other assets	(41)
Increase (decrease) in accounts payable	63
Increase (decrease) in accrued expenses and other liabilities	110
(Decrease) increase in other long-term obligations	(140)
Net cash provided by operating activities	978
Investing Activities:	
Acquisition of property and equipment	(381)
Cash paid for termination of joint venture	—
Proceeds from the sale of property and equipment	27
Sale of businesses, net	2
Acquisition of businesses, net of cash acquired	(22)
Net cash used in investing activities	(374)
Financing Activities:	
Proceeds from the exercise of stock options and sale of stock under employee stock purchase plans	41
Proceeds from borrowings	7
Payments on borrowings, including payment of deferred financing fees and capital lease obligations	(99)
Cash dividends paid	(308)
Excess tax benefits from stock-based compensation arrangements	5
Repurchase of common stock	(24)
Net cash used in financing activities	(378)
Effect of exchange rate changes on cash and cash equivalents	(28)
Net increase (decrease) in cash and cash equivalents	198
Cash and cash equivalents at beginning of period	627
Cash and cash equivalents at end of period	$825

Required

a. Staples reports a net income of $379 million and net cash inflows from operating activities of $978 million. Part of the difference relates to depreciation of $388 million and amortization of $67 million. Why does Staples add these amounts in the computation of operating cash flows?

b. Staples reports a positive amount of $63 million relating to stock-based compensation. What does this positive amount signify?

c. Staples reports a cash outflow of $381 million relating to the acquisition of PPE. Is this cash outflow a cause for concern? Explain.

d. Staples' net cash flows from financing activities is $(378) million. For what purposes is Staples using this cash?

e. Calculate the operating cash flow to current liabilities ratio and the operating cash flow to capital expenditures ratio. Current liabilities were $3,264 million and $3,289 million at January 30, 2016 and January 31, 2015, respectively. What do these ratios measure?

f. The cash balance increased by $198 million during the year. Does Staples present a "healthy" cash flow picture for the year? Explain.

IFRS Applications

I11-58.   Interpreting the Statement of Cash Flows   **LO1, 5**
Following is the statement of cash flows for **Roger's Communications**, a Canadian company operating in the telecom and media industry.   **Roger's Communications**

ROGER'S COMMUNICATIONS
Consolidated Statements Of Cash Flows

Years ended December 31 (in millions of Canadian dollars)	2015	2014
Operating activities:		
Net income for the year	$1,381	$1,341
Adjustments to reconcile net income to cash provided by operating activities:		
Depreciation and amortization	2,277	2,144
Program rights amortization	87	66
Finance costs	774	817
Income taxes	466	506
Stock-based compensation	55	37
Post-employment benefits contributions, net of expense	(16)	(34)
Gain on acquisition of Mobilicity	(102)	—
Other	82	48
Cash provided by operating activities before changes in non-cash working capital, income taxes paid, and interest paid	5,004	4,925
Change in non-cash operating working capital items	(302)	11
Cash provided by operating activities before income taxes paid and interest paid	4,702	4,936
Income taxes paid	(184)	(460)
Interest paid	(771)	(778)
Cash provided by operating activities	3,747	3,698
Investing activities:		
Additions to property, plant and equipment	(2,440)	(2,366)
Additions to program rights	(64)	(231)
Change in non-cash working capital related to property, plant and equipment and intangible assets	(116)	153
Acquisitions and other strategic transactons, net of cash acquired	(1,077)	(3,456)
Other	(70)	(51)
Cash used in investing activities	(3,767)	(5,951)

continued

continued from previous page

Years ended December 31 (in millions of Canadian dollars)	2015	2014
Financing activities:		
Proceeds received on short-term borrowings	$ 294	$ 276
Repayment of short-term borrowings.	(336)	(84)
Issuance of long-term debt.	7,338	3,412
Repayment of long-term debt	(6,584)	(2,551)
Proceeds on settlement of debt derivatives and forward contracts.	1,059	2,150
Payments on settlement of debt derivatives, forward contracts, and bond forwards	(930)	(2,115)
Transaction costs incurred	(9)	(30)
Dividends paid	(977)	(930)
Cash (used in) provided by financing activities	(145)	128
Change in cash and cash equivalents	(165)	(2,125)
Cash and cash equivalents, beginning of year	176	2,301
Cash and cash equivalents, end of year	$ 11	$ 176
The change in non-cash operating working capital items is as follows:		
Accounts receivable	$ (185)	$ (81)
Inventories	(66)	26
Other current assets.	(23)	(18)
Accounts payable and accrued liabilities.	33	(2)
Unearned revenue	(61)	86
	$ (302)	$ 11

Cash and cash equivalents (bank advances) are defined as cash and short-term deposits, which have an original maturity of less than 90 days, less bank advances. As at December 31, 2015 and 2014, the balance of cash and cash equivalents comprised cash and demand deposits.

Required

a. Roger's reports net income of $1,381 million and net cash inflows from operating activities of $3,747 million. Part of the difference relates to depreciation and amortization of $2,277 million. Why does Roger's add this amount in the computation of operating cash flows?

b. Roger's reports a positive amount of $55 million relating to stock-based compensation. What does this positive amount signify?

c. Roger's reports a cash outflow of $2,440 million relating to the acquisition of PPE. Is this cash outflow a cause for concern? Explain.

d. Roger's net cash outflow for financing activities is $145 million. What did Roger's use this cash for?

e. The statement reports changes in noncash operating working capital items. Explain the negative amount for accounts receivable and the positive amount for accounts payable and accrued liabilities.

Solutions to Review Problems

Review 11-1—Solution

Transaction	Classification
1. Payments of dividends.	F
2. Payments to purchase PPE assets and intangible assets.	I
3. Payments to employees or suppliers.	O
4. Payments to purchase inventories.	O
5. Receipts from issuances of bonds payable, mortgage notes payable, and other notes payable.	F
6. Receipts from sales of investments in stocks, bonds, and other securities (other than cash equivalents).	I
7. Payments of interest to creditors.	O
8. Receipts from issuances of common stock and preferred stock and from sales of treasury stock.	F
9. Receipts of interest and dividends.	O
10. Payments to purchase stocks, bonds, and other securities (other than cash equivalents).	I
11. Receipts from customers for sales made or services rendered.	O
12. Payments to acquire treasury stock.	F
13. Other receipts such as lawsuit settlements and refunds received from suppliers.	O
14. Payments of taxes to government.	O
15. Payments to settle outstanding bonds payable, mortgage notes payable, and other notes payable.	F
16. Receipts from sales of PPE assets and intangible assets.	I
17. Other payments such as contributions to charity.	O
18. Receipts from repayments of loans by borrowers.	I
19. Payments made to lend money to borrowers.	I

Review 11-2—Solution

Net cash flow from operating activities	
Net income.	$35,000
Add (deduct) items to convert net income to cash basis	
Depreciation	11,000
Loss on sale of investments.	2,000
Accounts receivable decrease	6,000
Inventory increase.	(28,000)
Prepaid advertising increase.	(3,000)
Accounts payable increase.	13,000
Wages payable increase.	3,500
Income tax payable decrease.	(1,500)
Net cash provided by operating activities	$38,000

Review 11-3—Solution

Cash Flows From Investing Activities	
Sale of investments	$ 9,000
Purchase of PPE.	(48,000)
Net cash used by investing activities.	$(39,000)

Review 11-4A—Solution

Cash Flows From Financing Activities	
Issuance of common stocks.	$ 14,000
Payment of dividends	(17,000)
Net cash used by financing activities.	$(3,000)

Review 11-4B—Solution

a.   The change in cash = $38,000 + $(39,000) + $(3,000) = $(4,000).

b.

Net decrease in cash	$ (4,000)
Cash at beginning of year	12,000
Cash at end of year	$ 8,000

Review 11-5—Solution

a.

	Net Income	Depreciation	Stock-Based Compensation	Cash from Operations	Cash from Investing	CAPEX	Cash from Financing
Starbucks	14.4%	4.9%	1.1%	19.6%	−7.9%	−6.8%	−11.8%
Farmer Brothers	0.1%	4.4%	1.0%	4.9%	−3.7%	−3.5%	−0.7%
Exhibit 11.5.	10.0%	3.0%	1.0%	18.0%	−10.0%	−4.0%	−5.0%

Starbucks' ratios are larger than for the median S&P 500 firm with the exception of cash from investing. In contrast, Farmer Brothers report ratios that are markedly weaker. Also, Farmer Brothers' cash generated from each of its three business activities is low as compared with Starbucks and the S&P firms.

b.   Both companies' cash flow patterns are roughly the same (+ − −), which reflects that both are relatively mature companies.

Review 11-6—Solution

1. $$\frac{\$6,539.1}{(\$2,747.9 + \$2,950.4) / 2} = 2.3$$

2. $$\frac{\$6,539.1}{\$1,813.9} = 3.6$$

3. Yes, both ratios are strong. The operating cash flow to current liabilities ratio is much higher than the benchmark of 0.5, and the operating cash flow to capital expenditures ratio is much higher than 1.0

Review 11-7—Solution

Cash received from customers	$391,000	$385,000 sales + $6,000 accounts receivable decrease
Cash received as dividends	5,000	$5,000 dividend income
Cash paid for merchandise purchased	(248,000)	$233,000 cost of goods sold + $28,000 inventory increase − $13,000 accounts payable increase
Cash paid to employees.	(78,500)	$82,000 wages expense − $3,500 wages payable increase
Cash paid for advertising	(13,000)	$10,000 advertising expense + $3,000 prepaid advertising increase
Cash paid for income taxes	(18,500)	$17,000 income tax expense + $1,500 income tax payable decrease
Net cash provided by operating activities . . .	$ 38,000	

Module 12

Financial Statement Forecasting

Learning Objectives

LO1 Explain the process of forecasting financial statements. (p. 12-3)

LO2 Forecast revenues and the income statement. (p. 12-6)

LO3 Forecast the balance sheet. (p. 12-9)

LO4 Adjust the forecasted cash balance. (p. 12-12)

LO5 Prepare multiyear forecasts of financial statements. (p. 12-13)

LO6 Refine forecasts with additional information. (p. 12-15)

LO7 Forecast the statement of cash flows (Appendix 12A). (p. 12-20)

LO8 Apply a parsimonious method for forecasting net operating profit and net operating assets (Appendix 12B). (p. 12-22)

PG

Market cap: $225,670 mil
Total assets: $127,136 mil
Revenues: $65,299 mil
Net income: $10,604 mil

Procter & Gamble (P&G) sells a wide variety of personal care and household products in over 180 countries. In 2015, P&G reported a decline in sales and profit, not because of lower unit sales, but because of the strengthening U.S. dollar ($US) vis-à-vis other world currencies in which P&G transacts business. Its operating cash flow, however, increased to $14.6 billion despite the reported decline in sales.

Prior modules focus on historical financial statements—how to read and interpret financial statements and disclosures, how to analyze financial information to assess performance and financial position, and how to draw reasoned inferences about companies' financial condition and performance.

For many business decisions, historical financial statements are relevant to the extent that they help us forecast future financial performance. In this module, we explain the forecasting process, including how to forecast the income statement, the balance sheet, and the statement of cash flows.

Analysts and investors routinely forecast P&G's financial statements. Their forecasts provide critical input to financial models of the value of P&G's debt and equity securities (see our models in the debt and equity valuation modules). P&G's stock has languished since 2015 (see graph below), perhaps because investors and analysts forecast weak future growth or any number of other factors. [Source: *Procter & Gamble*, 2016 10-K]

© Getty Images

Road Map

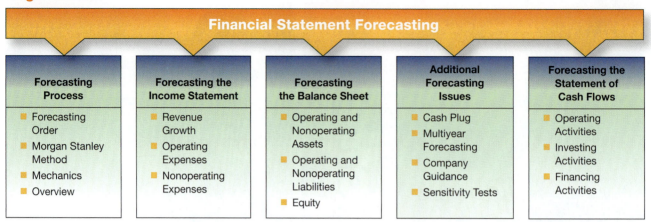

Financial Statement Forecasting

Forecasting Process	Forecasting the Income Statement	Forecasting the Balance Sheet	Additional Forecasting Issues	Forecasting the Statement of Cash Flows
■ Forecasting Order ■ Morgan Stanley Method ■ Mechanics ■ Overview	■ Revenue Growth ■ Operating Expenses ■ Nonoperating Expenses	■ Operating and Nonoperating Assets ■ Operating and Nonoperating Liabilities ■ Equity	■ Cash Plug ■ Multiyear Forecasting ■ Company Guidance ■ Sensitivity Tests	■ Operating Activities ■ Investing Activities ■ Financing Activities

Forecasting Process

LO1 Explain the process of forecasting financial statements.

Forecasting financial performance is integral to a variety of business decisions. In addition to using financial forecasts to value stocks and inform investment decisions, as discussed above for P&G, investors and analysts might be interested in evaluating the creditworthiness of a prospective borrower. In that case, they forecast the borrower's cash flows to estimate its ability to repay its obligations, Creditors also forecast a company's financial statements to ascertain its ability to repay indebtedness, and bond ratings are influenced by those forecasts. Company managers also frequently forecast future cash flows to budget and to evaluate alternative strategic investment decisions as well as to evaluate the shareholder value that strategic investment alternatives will create. All of these decisions require accurate financial forecasts. In this module, we illustrate the most common method to forecast the income statement, balance sheet, and statement of cash flows.

Forecasting Order of Financial Statements The forecasting process estimates future income statements, balance sheets, and statements of cash flows, in that order. The reason for this ordering is that each statement uses information from the preceding statement(s). For example, we update retained earnings on the balance sheet to reflect our forecast of the company's net income. And the forecasted income statement and balance sheets are used in preparing forecasts for the statement of cash flows, which follows the same process we illustrate in the module on preparing the historical statement of cash flows.

Morgan Stanley Forecasting Process To illustrate the forecasting process, we start with the P&G financial statements for the fiscal year (FY) ended June 30, 2016 (FY2016), and use them to forecast the company's financial statements for FY2017. Then, we extend the illustration and forecast financial statements for FY2018 (additional years can be forecasted using the same methodology). We discuss the type of forecasts that are possible using publicly available data and then consider ways we can refine our forecasts by using information in addition to what is included in the company's Form 10-K.

The module ends with excerpts from a published report (and the analysis spreadsheets used to develop the report) provided to us by **Morgan Stanley**. We have benefitted from conversations with Morgan Stanley analysts and are grateful for the background information that they provided to us that informs the forecasting process in this module.[1]

Forecasting Mechanics The revenues (sales) forecast is, arguably, the most crucial and difficult estimate in the forecasting process. It is a crucial estimate because other income-statement and

---

[1] All Morgan Stanley materials are copyright 2016 Morgan Stanley. Please note that materials referenced in this module comprise excerpts from research reports and should not be relied on as investment advice. This material is only as current as the publication date of the underlying Morgan Stanley research. For important disclosures, stock price charts, and equity rating histories regarding companies that are the subject of the underlying Morgan Stanley research, see www.morganstanley.com/researchdisclosures. Additionally, Morgan Stanley has provided their materials here as a courtesy. Therefore, Morgan Stanley and Cambridge Business Publishers do not undertake to advise you of changes in the opinions or information set forth in these materials.

balance-sheet accounts derive, either directly or indirectly, from the revenues forecast. As a result, both the income statement and balance sheet grow with increases in revenues. The income statement reflects this growth concurrently. However, different balance sheet accounts reflect revenue growth in different ways. Some balance sheet accounts anticipate (or lead) revenue growth (inventories are one example). Some accounts reflect this growth concurrently (accounts receivable). And some accounts reflect revenue growth with a lag (e.g., companies usually expand plant assets only after growth is deemed sustainable). Conversely, when revenues decline, so do the income statement and balance sheet, as the company shrinks to cope with adversity. Such actions include reduction of overhead costs and divestiture of excess assets. Exhibit 12.1 highlights crucial income statement and balance sheet relations that are impacted by the revenues forecast.

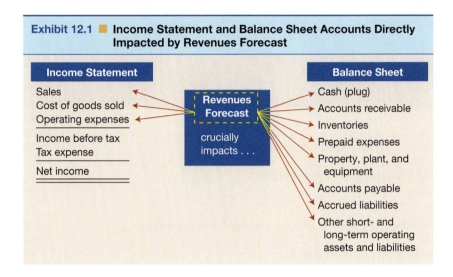

Exhibit 12.1 ■ Income Statement and Balance Sheet Accounts Directly Impacted by Revenues Forecast

Forecasting Consistency and Precision It is important to keep two points in mind:

- **Internal consistency.** The forecasted income statement, balance sheet, and statement of cash flows are linked in the same way historical financial statements are. That is, they must articulate (link together within and across time), as we explain in the first few modules. Preparing a forecasted statement of cash flows, although tedious, is often a useful way to uncover forecasting assumptions that are inconsistently applied across financial statements (e.g., capital expenditures [CAPEX], depreciation, debt payments, and dividends). If the forecasted cash balance on the balance sheet agrees with that on the statement of cash flows, it is likely that our income statement and balance sheet articulate. We also must ensure that our forecast assumptions are internally consistent. For example, it is unadvisable to forecast an increased gross profit margin during an economic recession unless we can make compelling arguments based on known business facts about the company.

- **Level of precision.** Computing forecasts to the "nth decimal place" is easy using spreadsheets. This increased precision makes the resulting forecasts appear more precise, but they are not necessarily more accurate. As we discuss in this module, our financial statement forecasts are highly dependent on our revenues forecast. Whether revenues are expected to grow by 2% or 3% can markedly impact profitability and other forecasts. Estimating cost of goods sold (COGS) and other items to the nth decimal place is meaningless if we have imprecise revenue forecasts. Consequently, borderline decisions that depend on a high level of forecasting precision are ill-advised.

Forecasting Sensitivity Analysis Analysts commonly perform a sensitivity analysis following preparation of their forecasts. This entails increasing and decreasing the forecast assumptions to identify which assumptions have the greatest impact. By "impact" we mean large enough to alter business decisions. Assumptions that are identified as crucial to a decision must be investigated thoroughly to ensure forecast assumptions are as accurate as possible.

Review 12-1 LO1

The FY2016 income statement and balance sheet for General Mills, a competitor of P&G, follow. Use them to answer the required questions.

Required

a. In what order do we forecast the financial statements? Explain why this order is important.

b. What income statement amount do we forecast first?

c. Identify at least three forecasted expenses that are directly or indirectly related to revenue.

d. Identify at least three forecasted balance sheet accounts that are directly or indirectly related to forecasted revenue.

e. Why would we perform a sensitivity analysis of our forecasted numbers?

GENERAL MILLS INC. Consolidated Statements of Earnings	
$ millions	12 Months Ended May 29, 2016
Net sales.	$16,563.1
Cost of sales.	10,733.6
Selling, general, and administrative expenses.	3,118.9
Divestitures (gain).	(148.2)
Restructuring, impairment, and other exit costs	151.4
Operating profit	2,707.4
Interest, net	303.8
Earnings before income taxes and after-tax earnings from joint ventures.	2,403.6
Income taxes	755.2
After-tax earnings from joint ventures	88.4
Net earnings, including earnings attributable to redeemable and noncontrolling interests	1,736.8
Net earnings attributable to redeemable and noncontrolling interests	39.4
Net earnings attributable to General Mills	$ 1,697.4

GENERAL MILLS INC. Consolidated Balance Sheet	
$ millions, except par value	May 29, 2016
Current assets	
Cash and cash equivalents.	$ 763.7
Receivables	1,360.8
Inventories	1,413.7
Prepaid expenses and other current assets.	399.0
Total current assets.	3,937.2
Land, buildings, and equipment.	3,743.6
Goodwill	8,741.2
Other intangible assets.	4,538.6
Other assets.	751.7
Total assets.	$21,712.3

continued

$ millions, except par value	May 29, 2016
Current liabilities	
Accounts payable	$ 2,046.5
Current portion of long-term debt	1,103.4
Notes payable	269.8
Other current liabilities	1,595.0
Total current liabilities	5,014.7
Long-term debt	7,057.7
Deferred income taxes	1,399.6
Other liabilities	2,087.6
Total liabilities	15,559.6
Redeemable interest value	845.6
Stockholders' equity	
Common stock, 754.6 shares issued, $0.10 par value	75.5
Additional paid-in capital	1,177.0
Retained earnings	12,616.5
Common stock in treasury, at cost	(6,326.6)
Accumulated other comprehensive loss	(2,612.2)
Total stockholders' equity	4,930.2
Noncontrolling interests	376.9
Total equity	5,307.1
Total liabilities and equity	$21,712.3

Solution on p. 12-68.

Forecasting the Income Statement

Exhibit 12.2 presents the FY2016 income statement for Procter & Gamble together with our forecast of the statements for FY2017.

eLectures LO2
MBC   Forecast revenues and the income statement

Overview Here is a high-level overview—computational details follow.

- **Sales estimate.** The forecasting process begins with an estimate of the sales growth rate. For our illustration, we assume a 1% growth rate—we later discuss the factors that explain this growth rate estimate. Given the assumed 1% growth in sales, forecasted 2017 sales are $65,952 million ($65,299 million × 1.01).

- **Expense estimates.** To estimate operating expenses (cost of goods sold and selling, general, and administrative [SG&A] expenses) we apply a percentage of sales ratio to forecasted sales. For nonoperating expenses (such as interest expense and interest revenue), we assume they will not change ("no change") unless we believe interest rates are likely to shift greatly during the forecast period.

- **One-time item estimates.** One-time items such as discontinued operations, are, by definition, not expected to recur. We forecast these items to be $0.

- **Tax estimate.** Income tax expense is forecasted based on a percentage of pretax income.

- **Noncontrolling interest estimate.** A common assumption is no change in the ratio of noncontrolling interest to consolidated net income. For our P&G illustration, we adopt that assumption.

For each line item in the income statement, we summarize our forecasting assumptions in the right-most column of Exhibit 12.2, and we discuss those assumptions in depth in the following sections.

Exhibit 12.2 ■ **Forecast of P&G's FY2017 Income Statement**

$ millions	FY2016	% of Net Sales	Computations	FY2017 Est.	% of Net Sales	Explanation
Net sales...........................	$65,299	100.0%	$65,299 × 1.01	**$65,952**	100.0%	Use P&G's guidance that sales will increase about 1% (2% organic sales increase less 1% foreign currency effect). Sales forecast equals current sales × (1 + growth rate %).
Cost of products sold...................	32,909	50.4%	$65,952 × 48.6%	**32,053**	48.6%	Assume COGS as % of sales will continue to decrease due to P&G's productivity initiative.
Selling, general, and administrative expense...	18,949	29.0%	$65,952 × 29.0%	**19,126**	29.0%	Assume SGA as % of sales will remain unchanged given no evidence of any large transitory items in FY2016 SGA.
Operating income......................	13,441	20.6%	subtotal	**14,773**	22.4%	
Interest expense......................	579	0.9%	no change	**579**	0.9%	Assume no change in interest revenue or expense.
Interest income.......................	182	0.3%	no change	**182**	0.3%	
Other nonoperating income, net	325	0.5%	none	**0**	0.0%	FY2016 nonoperating income relates to divestitures, and we assume none for FY2017 given no evidence of planned divestitures.
Earnings from continuing operations before income taxes	13,369	20.5%	subtotal	**14,376**	21.8%	
Income taxes on continuing operations	3,342	5.1%	$14,376 × 25.0%	**3,594**	5.4%	Assume effective tax rate of 25% will continue. Disclosures do not reveal any large transitory income tax items.
Net earnings from continuing operations.....	10,027	15.4%	subtotal	**10,782**	16.3%	
Net earnings from discontinued operations....	577	0.9%	none	**0**	0.0%	Assume no discontinued operations in FY2017.
Net earnings..........................	10,604	16.2%	subtotal	**10,782**	16.3%	
Less: Net earnings attributable to noncontrolling interests	96	0.1%	$10,782 × 0.9%	**97**	0.1%	Assume noncontrolling interests as % of net earnings (0.9%) continues.
Net earnings attributable to P&G	$10,508	16.1%	subtotal	**$10,685**	16.2%	

Sales as the Income Statement Forecast Driver   We forecast most income statement line items in Exhibit 12.2 as a percent of sales. (One exception is tax expense, which is commonly set as a percent of pretax profit.) Unless we are aware of transitory items that affect the current year's income statement, we use the current year percentage of sales in our forecast.

Cost of Goods Sold (COGS)   For COGS (labeled "Cost of products sold" by P&G), we take a more detailed approach utilizing the additional details relating to COGS that P&G dicloses in its presentations to analysts and in the 10-K's MD&A. While P&G's historical COGS was 50.4% of sales, we compute an estimate of 48.6%, which we believe reflects recent trends. To explain, in its 2016 presentation to analysts, P&G announced productivity initiatives that reduced COGS by an average of $1.2 billion for each of the past five years—see the following presentation slide.

"The Procter & Gamble Company at The Consumer Analyst Group of New York Conference, February 18, 2016" on the PG Investor Relations website (http://www.pginvestor.com/Presentations-and-Events)

Assuming a continuation of the $1.2 billion *run rate* in annual savings, we estimate the forecasted percent of COGS to sales at 48.6% as follows. We use this 48.6% for the COGS estimate in Exhibit 12.2.

Years Ended June 30 ($ millions)	FY2015	FY2016
COGS (as a % of sales)	52.4%	50.4%
FY2017 forecasted sales		× $65,952
COGS at FY2016 rate of 50.4% ($65,952 × 50.4%)		= 33,240
Less: Target savings (see previous graphic)		(1,200)
FY2017 forecasted COGS ($13 rounding difference from COGS in Exhibit 12.2)		$32,040
Forecasted COGS to sales percent		48.6%

SGA Expense   Our estimate of SGA expense is forecasted as: Sales × Current year SGA percentage of sales, or $19,126 million ($65,952 million × 29%)—we see that footnotes and management discussion and analysis (MD&A) do not disclose any transitory items for SGA expense.

Income Tax Expense   Income tax expense (labeled "Income taxes on continuing operations" by P&G) is often a large expense item. We estimate tax expense by applying an estimated tax rate to pretax income. For FY2017, we use an effective tax rate of 25%. Companies provide a history of their effective tax rates in the footnotes, and following is P&G's disclosure for FY2016 (see our discussion of income tax expense in another module).

Years Ended June 30 ($ millions)	FY2016	FY2015	FY2014
U.S. federal statutory income tax rate	35.0%	35.0%	35.0%
Country mix impacts of foreign operations	(9.1)%	(14.0)%	(10.8)%
Changes in uncertain tax positions	(0.5)%	(0.9)%	(1.7)%
Venezuela deconsolidation charge	—%	6.6%	—%
Other	(0.4)%	(2.0)%	(1.4)%
Effective income tax rate	25.0%	24.7%	21.1%

The point of reviewing the tax table in the footnotes is to determine the appropriate tax rate to use for our forecasts. We look for transitory items that greatly affect the company's tax rate—we would not include such items in our forecast. In FY2015, for example, P&G's effective tax rate was increased by 6.6 percentage points due to the deconsolidation of its Venezuelan subsidiary (a one-time occurrence). In FY2016, there are no such large transitory items and, thus, using a 25% effective tax rate for our FY2017 forecasts seems reasonable.

LO2 Review 12-2

Refer to the FY2016 income statement and balance sheet for General Mills in Review 12-1.

Required
Use the following assumptions to forecast the General Mills income statement for FY2017.
- Net sales will decrease by 1.5% (150 basis points) in FY2017.
- Because of ongoing restructuring and efficiency improvement measures, operating expenses as a percentage of net sales will be lower than in FY2016 as follows:
  o Cost of sales: 200 basis points lower.
  o SGA expenses: 50 basis points lower.
- No announced divestitures for FY2017.
- Restructuring, impairment, and other exit costs will be half the dollar amount reported in FY2016.
- Tax expense as a percentage of pretax income will remain unchanged.
- The following line items remain unchanged in dollar terms:
  o Interest, net.
  o After-tax earnings from joint ventures.
  o Net earnings attributable to redeemable and noncontrolling interests.

Solution on p. 12-69.

Forecasting the Balance Sheet

LO3

Forecast the balance sheet.

Our forecast of the balance sheet in Exhibit 12.3 begins with estimates for all assets *other than cash* (which is the *plug* amount as we explain below), all liabilities, and all equity accounts.

Overview Here is a high-level overview of balance sheet forecasting—details follow.

- **Working capital accounts.** We use an assumed percentage of forecasted sales to estimated accounts receivable, inventories, accounts payable, and accrued liabilities.
- **PPE and intangible assets.** To forecast PPE, we increase the prior year's balance by estimated CAPEX and reduce the estimate by forecasted depreciation expense (we discuss the forecasting of PPE assets below). We forecast intangible assets by subtracting forecasted amortization expense.
- **Current and long-term debt.** We assume P&G will make all contractual payments of long-term debt. We reduce the prior year's long-term debt balance by the current maturities of long-term debt reported in the footnotes. We assume current and long-term debt remains unchanged. (We discuss refining this assumption later.)
- **Stockholders' equity.** We assume paid-in capital accounts remain at prior years' levels, except for planned repurchases of treasury stock, as reported by P&G in its 10-K. Retained earnings is increased by forecasted net income and reduced by estimated dividends. (We discuss the forecasting of dividends below.)

The last step in the forecasting process is to balance the balance sheet. To do this, we determine the amount needed in the **Cash** account to balance the balance sheet, computed as total assets (equal to total liabilities and equity) less all other asset balances. This balancing figure is referred to as the *plug* amount.

Details behind the forecasts of working capital items is not complicated. However, forecasts of PPE assets, long-term debt, and dividends are a bit more complicated and are explained here.

Working Capital Accounts Working capital accounts that are operating in nature are forecasted using the historical relation of each working capital account divided by sales, then multiplied by the forecasted sales. Items that are nonoperating are usually assumed to have no change, or are predicted using company guidance such as with debt due within one year.

PPE assets

Capital Expenditures (CAPEX). Capital expenditures is computed as a percentage of forecasted sales. There are a number of ways to determine the percentage to use. One way is to use the current year percentage or an average of two or three prior years. To compute the percentage, we use CAPEX as reported in the statement of cash flows along with current period sales. Forecasted CAPEX follows.

$$\text{Forecasted CAPEX} = \frac{\text{Current year CAPEX}}{\text{Current year Sales}} \times \text{Forecasted Sales}$$

The 2016 statement of cash flows reports CAPEX of $3,314 million, which yields an historical rate of 5.1% (calculated as $3,314 million/$65,299 million). Alternatively, we can use a percentage disclosed by the company. P&G's guidance is for CAPEX of 5% to 5.5% in FY2017 (see the "Company Guidance" section below). Company guidance includes information that is presumably more precise than the historic rate. Accordingly, we use 5.25% of forecasted sales to estimate CAPEX of $3,462 million for FY2017 ($5.25% × $65,952 million).

Depreciation Expense. Depreciation expense is usually reported in the statement of cash flows (or in the notes). (If depreciation expense is combined with amortization expense, we can isolate the depreciation component by subtracting amortization expense, which is frequently reported separately in footnotes—or, if not separately reported, we may use the change in accumulated amortization.) It is common to estimate depreciation as:

$$\text{Forecasted depreciation expense} = \frac{\text{Current year depreciation expense}}{\text{Prior year PPE, net}} \times \text{Current year PPE, net}$$

Exhibit 12.3 ■ Forecast of P&G's FY2017 Balance Sheet

$ millions	2016 Act.	% of Sales	Computations	2017 Est.	% of Sales	Explanation
Current assets						
Cash and cash equivalents	$ 7,102	10.9%	Plug	$ 8,172	12.4%	Plug to balance the balance sheet.*
Available-for-sale investment securities......	6,246	9.6%	no change	6,246	9.5%	
Accounts receivable......................	4,373	6.7%	$65,952 × 6.7%	4,419	6.7%	Forecast working capital accounts
Inventories	4,716	7.2%	$65,952 × 7.2%	4,749	7.2%	as a % of sales using prior year's
Deferred income taxes....................	1,507	2.3%	$65,952 × 2.3%	1,517	2.3%	% unless information suggests
Prepaid expenses and other current assets...	2,653	4.1%	$65,952 × 4.1%	2,704	4.1%	otherwise.**
Current assets held for sale	7,185	11.0%	none	0	0.0%	Assume discontinued operations sold at book value during year.
Total current assets	33,782	51.7%	subtotal	27,477	41.7%	
Property, plant, and equipment, net.........	19,385	29.7%	$3,462 − $2,656	20,191	30.6%	CAPEX estimates are from P&G guidance, and depreciation expense is computed as a % of prior year PPE, net.
Goodwill..............................	44,350	67.9%	no change	44,350	67.2%	Assume no changes because goodwill is not amortized.
Trademarks and other intangible assets, net...	24,527	37.6%	− $326	24,201	36.7%	Apply estimated amortization expense from footnotes of P&G.
Other noncurrent assets..................	5,092	7.8%	no change	5,092	7.7%	Assume no change.
Total assets..........................	$127,136	194.7%	subtotal	$121,641	184.4%	
Current liabilities						
Accounts payable........................	$ 9,325	14.3%	$65,952 × 14.3%	$ 9,431	14.3%	Forecast working capital accounts
Accrued and other liabilities..............	7,449	11.4%	$65,952 × 11.4%	7,519	11.4%	as % of sales unless information suggests otherwise.
Current liabilities held for sale	2,343	3.6%	none	0	0.0%	Assume discontinued operations sold at book value during year.
Debt due within one year	11,653	17.8%	−$2,760 + $1,323	10,216	15.5%	Use footnotes to get current maturities of long-term debt to be repaid in FY2017 ($2,760) and FY2018 ($1,323). Assume all other debt remains unchanged.
Total current liabilities...................	30,770	47.1%	subtotal	27,166	41.2%	
Long-term debt	18,945	29.0%	−$1,323	17,622	26.7%	Use footnotes to get current maturities of long-term debt to be repaid in FY2018 ($1,323).
Deferred income taxes...................	9,113	14.0%	$65,952 × 14.0%	9,233	14.0%	Assume no change as a % of sales.
Other noncurrent liabilities	10,325	15.8%	$65,952 × 15.8%	10,420	15.8%	Assume no change as a % of sales.
Total liabilities.........................	69,153	105.9%	subtotal	64,441	97.7%	
Shareholders' equity						
Convertible Class A preferred stock.........	1,038	1.6%	no change	1,038	1.6%	
Non-voting Class B preferred stock.........	0	0.0%	no change	0	0.0%	Assume no change in paid-in
Common stock..........................	4,009	6.1%	no change	4,009	6.1%	capital accounts.
Additional paid-in capital	63,714	97.6%	no change	63,714	96.6%	
Reserve for ESOP debt retirement..........	(1,290)	(2.0)%	no change	(1,290)	(2.0)%	Assume no change.
Accumulated other comprehensive income/ (loss)	(15,907)	(24.4)%	no change	(15,907)	(24.1)%	Assume no change.
Treasury stock	(82,176)	(125.8)%	−$4,000	(86,176)	(130.7)%	Use P&G guidance.
Retained earnings	87,953	134.7%	$10,685 − $7,565	91,073	138.1%	Increased by forecasted net income less forecasted dividends.
Noncontrolling interest...................	642	1.0%	+ $97	739	1.1%	Increased by net income allocated to noncontrolling interests.
Total shareholders' equity	57,983	88.8%	subtotal	57,200	86.7%	
Total liabilities and shareholders' equity ...	$127,136	194.7%	subtotal	$121,641	184.4%	

* $8,172 = $121,641 − $6,246 − $4,419 − $4,749 − $1,517 − $2,704 − $20,191 − $44,350 − $24,201 − $5,092.

** To simplify, we forecast accounts as a percent of sales, including inventories and accounts payable. Analysts sometimes use a percent of COGS for inventory and for accounts payable estimates because both are expressed in input (not output) costs. Either approach is reasonable if used consistently. One could also forecast working capital accounts using turnover rates or days as follows:

Forecasted account balance = Forecasted revenues (or COGS)/Turnover rate, or

Forecasted account balance = Forecasted days outstanding × [Forecasted revenues (or COGS)/365]

P&G's 2016 statement of cash flows reports depreciation and amortization expense of $3,078 million. Footnotes report amortization expense in 2016 of $388 million. Thus, we calculate 2016 depreciation expense as $2,690 million. The 2015 balance sheet reports PPE, net of $19,655 million and, thus, we use a forecast assumption of 13.7% ($3,078 million/$19,655 million) to estimate 2017 depreciation expense of $2,656 million (13.7% × $19,385 million).

PPE, net. Drawing on the forecasted CAPEX and forecasted depreciation above, the PPE, net is forecasted as:

$$\text{Forecasted PPE, net} = \text{Current PPE, net} + \text{Forecasted CAPEX} - \text{Forecasted depreciation expense}$$

Forecasted 2017 PPE is $20,191 million, computed as $19,385 million + $3,462 million − $2,656 million.

Intangible Assets Intangible assets, other than goodwill, are typically forecasted to decrease during the year by the amount of amortization (it is common to assume no change in amortization expense).

$$\text{Forecasted intangible assets} = \text{Current year intangible assets} - \text{Forecasted amortization expense}$$

Alternatively, the company might provide guidance. Footnotes to the P&G's FY2016 Form 10-K provide the following schedule of expected amortization expense that we use for its FY2017 forecast.

Years Ending June 30 ($ millions)	2017	2018	2019	2020	2021
Estimated amortization expense	**$326**	$298	$281	$255	$206

Long-Term Debt (LTD) Companies report maturities of long-term debt for the next five years in the long-term debt footnote. We use this disclosure to forecast long-term debt:

$$\textbf{Forecasted LTD} = \textbf{Current year LTD} - \textbf{Current maturities of LTD}$$

Footnotes to P&G's FY2016 Form 10-K provide the following schedule of maturities of LTD that we use in our forecasts.

Long-term debt maturities during the next five fiscal years are as follows:

Years Ending June 30 ($ millions)	2017	2018	2019	2020	2021
Debt maturities.	**$2,760**	**$1,323**	$2,357	$2,099	$1,387

P&G's balance sheet does not separately report current maturities of long-term debt. Instead, the current maturities amount is aggregated with other short-term debt and reported as "Debt due within one year." To forecast current maturities, we subtract $2,760 million from its debt due within one year to reflect the amount that matures and will be paid in FY2017; we then add $1,323 million, the amount that comes due in FY2018. We subtract $1,323 million from long-term debt to reflect the reclassification from long-term to current.

Retained Earnings Retained earnings are forecasted as:

$$= \textbf{Current year retained earnings} + \textbf{Forecasted net income} - \textbf{Forecasted dividends}$$

Dividends. Companies frequently provide guidance as to expected dividends. If not, a common approach is to estimate dividends using the dividend payout ratio.

$$\text{Forecasted dividends} = \frac{\text{Current year dividends}}{\text{Current year net income}} \times \text{Forecasted net income}$$

P&G's dividend payout ratio for FY2016 is 70.8% ($7,436 million dividends paid in FY2016 ÷ 2016 net income of $10,508 million). We estimate FY2017 dividends by applying that ratio to forecasted net income ($10,685 million × 70.8% = $7,565 million). P&G's guidance is for dividends of "$7B+" (see the <u>Company Guidance</u> section below); our forecasted dividends of $7,565 million is consistent with that guidance.

Treasury Stock Many companies have multiyear stock repurchase programs, which are disclosed in footnotes or in the MD&A section of the 10-K. Often, in the year-end press release, companies provide guidance and/or disclosures about their planned treasury stock activity. Absent explicit disclosures or guidance, we can forecast future repurchases using historic data, either from the most recent year or by looking for a trend over the past two or three years. For P&G, we use guidance provided by managers and forecast $4B of additional repurchases in FY2017.

LO3 Review 12-3

Refer to the FY2016 income statement and balance sheet for General Mills along with the forecasted FY2017 income statement in Reviews 12-1 and 12-2.

Required
Use that information and the following assumptions to forecast the General Mills balance sheet for FY2017.
- Unless noted in other assumptions, all assets and liabilities as a percentage of FY2017 sales, remain unchanged.
- Depreciation expense for FY2016 is $580.1 million.
- FY2016 CAPEX is $729.3 million, and its land, buildings, and equipment in FY2015 total $3,783.3 million.
- Goodwill remains unchanged.
- Form 10-K reports that amortization expense for each of the next five fiscal years is estimated to be $28 million.
- Notes payable remains unchanged.
- Long-term debt footnotes reveal that principal payments due on long-term debt in the next five years are: $1,103.4 million in FY2017, $604.7 million in FY2018, $1,150.4 million in FY2019, $1,056.0 million in FY2020, and $555.9 million in FY2021.
- Stock repurchases will be $300 million in FY2017.
- Dividends in FY2016 are $1,071.7 million and will not change in FY2017 as a percentage of net earnings attributable to General Mills.

Solution on p. 12-70.

The Forecasted Cash Balance

The forecasting process estimates the balances of all assets *other than cash*, all liabilities, and all equity accounts. The last step is to compute the amount of cash needed to balance the balance sheet (the *plug*).

LO4 Adjust the forecasted cash balance.

Cash Plug (the *plug*) The **plug** is computed as total assets (equal to total liabilities and equity) less all other asset balances. We assess the forecasted cash balance and determine if it deviates from its historical norm. We use the current year cash-to-sales percentage as a *normal* level of cash. This assumes the amount reported in the current balance sheet represents an appropriate level of cash the company needs to conduct its operations.

Estimating the Normal Cash Level P&G's cash balance in 2016 is $7,102 million or 10.9% of 2016 sales. Applying that percentage to our forecasted sales of $65,952 million yields a normal level of cash of $7,189 million ($65,952 million × 10.9%). Our forecasted cash balance is $7,842 million, 11.9% of sales, a little higher than the norm, but not enough to warrant adjustment.

When Cash Plug Deviates from Norm If, however, P&G's forecasted cash level had deviated greatly from the norm, we would consider adjusting the forecasted cash balance in two ways.

- **Cash balance much HIGHER than normal.** This indicates the company is generating a lot of cash, most typically from operations. Our forecasts might assume that such excess liquidity can be invested in marketable securities, used to pay down debt, repurchase stock, increase dividend payments, or any combination of these actions.

- **Cash balance much LOWER than normal.** This indicates the company is not generating sufficient cash, usually as a result of net losses and/or operating assets increasing more than operating liabilities (remember, we are assuming no changes in debt and equity levels for our initial forecast). A large negative deviation from normal levels means that the company must obtain additional cash by borrowing money, selling stock, liquidating marketable securities, or any combination of these actions. We would adjust the forecasted balance sheet to reflect the additional cash and the manner in which it was raised. Companies can also raise cash by reducing dividend payments, reducing capital expenditures, or any number of other operating actions (such as reducing inventory)—these actions likely have serious costs and, for that reason, we try to avoid them. It is more likely the company would raise cash through investing and financing activities.

Maintaining the Capital Structure When we adjust cash by forecasting an increase or decrease in debt and/or stock, we might inadvertently impact the company's capital structure—namely, the proportion of debt and equity. If we assume the company's current capital structure is appropriate, we should attempt to maintain that historic debt-to-equity ratio when we forecast additional borrowing, debt repayment, stock sales, or stock repurchases.

Review 12-4 LO4

Refer to the FY2016 income statement and balance sheet for General Mills along with the forecasted FY2017 income statement and balance sheet in Reviews 12-1, 12-2, and 12-3.

Required

a. Compute General Mills' FY2016 historical cash balance as a percentage of sales.

b. By how much does the forecasted (plug) cash amount deviate from normal? Does this difference warrant an adjustment to forecasted cash? Explain.

c. If we assume forecasted cash deviates from the norm, how could we use long-term debt to adjust the cash balance?

d. Besides the approach referred to in part c, what would be another method for us to adjust the forecasted cash balance to a more normal level?

Solution on p. 12-70.

Forecasting Multiple Years Ahead

LO5
Prepare multiyear forecasts of financial statements.

Exhibit 12.4 shows the mechanics to forecast financial statements for more than one year ahead. Forecasting for multiple years is conducted in the same way we forecast for one year, illustrated above. Analysts typically need multiyear forecasts for equity valuation, evaluation of debt payment ability, and determining credit ratings. Managers also typically use multiyear forecasts in the planning process, including cash flow budgeting, capital expenditure plans, divestiture decisions, and mergers and acquisitions.

Our P&G forecasts for FY2017 and FY2018 rely on the same forecasting assumptions in both years with one exception: we forecast a 2% *increase* in sales for FY2018 that reflects organic growth without the foreign-currency effect. This assumption derives from company guidance; see below for details. With a 2% increase, forecasted sales in FY2018 are computed as: $65,952 million × 1.02 = $67,271 million. The remaining forecast assumptions are the same as for FY2017 as shown in Exhibit 12.2.

Consistent with the one-year-ahead forecasts, we balance the balance sheet with a "plug" to the cash account and then check to make sure the amount is within a normal range as we consider any adjustment.

Exhibit 12.4 ■ Forecast of P&G's FY2017 and FY2018 Income Statements and Balance Sheets

Income Statements ($ millions)	2016 Act.	% of Sales	Computations	2017 Est.	% of Sales	Computations	2018 Est.	% of Sales
Net sales.	$ 65,299	100.0%	$65,299 × 1.01	$ 65,952	100.0%	$65,952 × 1.02	$ 67,271	100.0%
Cost of products sold.	32,909	50.4%	$65,952 × 48.6%	32,053	48.6%	$67,271 × 48.6%	32,694	48.6%
Selling, general, and administrative expense. . .	18,949	29.0%	$65,952 × 29.0%	19,126	29.0%	$67,271 × 29.0%	19,509	29.0%
Operating income.	13,441	20.6%	subtotal	14,773	22.4%	subtotal	15,068	22.4%
Interest expense.	579	0.9%	no change	579	0.9%	no change	579	0.9%
Interest income.	182	0.3%	no change	182	0.3%	no change	182	0.3%
Other non-operating income, net.	325	0.5%	none	0	0.0%	none	0	0.0%
Earnings from continuing operations before income taxes	13,369	20.5%	subtotal	14,376	21.8%	subtotal	14,671	21.8%
Income taxes on continuing operations.	3,342	5.1%	$14,376 × 25.0%	3,594	5.4%	$14,671 × 25.0%	3,668	5.5%
Net earnings from continuing operations.	10,027	15.4%	subtotal	10,782	16.3%	subtotal	11,003	16.4%
Net earnings/(loss) from discontinued operations.	577	0.9%	none	0	0.0%	none	0	0.0%
Net earnings.	10,604	16.2%	subtotal	10,782	16.3%	subtotal	11,003	16.4%
Less: net earnings attributable to noncontrolling interests	96	0.1%	$10,782 × 0.9%	97	0.1%	$11,003 × 0.9%	99	0.1%
Net earnings attributable to Procter & Gamble.	$ 10,508	16.1%	subtotal	$ 10,685	16.2%	subtotal	$ 10,904	16.2%

Balance Sheets ($ millions)	2016 Act.	% of Sales	Computations	2017 Est.	% of Sales	Computations	2018 Est.	% of Sales
Current assets								
Cash and cash equivalents	$ 7,102	10.9%	Plug	$ 8,172	12.4%	Plug	$ 6,130	9.1%
Available-for-sale investment securities.	6,246	9.6%	no change	6,246	9.5%	no change	6,246	9.3%
Accounts receivable.	4,373	6.7%	$65,952 × 6.7%	4,419	6.7%	$67,271 × 6.7%	4,507	6.7%
Inventories	4,716	7.2%	$65,952 × 7.2%	4,749	7.2%	$67,271 × 7.2%	4,844	7.2%
Deferred income taxes.	1,507	2.3%	$65,952 × 2.3%	1,517	2.3%	$67,271 × 2.3%	1,547	2.3%
Prepaid expenses and other current assets. . . .	2,653	4.1%	$65,952 × 4.1%	2,704	4.1%	$67,271 × 4.1%	2,758	4.1%
Current assets held for sale	7,185	11.0%	none	0	0.0%	none	0	0.0%
Total current assets	33,782	51.7%	subtotal	27,807	42.2%	subtotal	26,032	38.7%
Property, plant, and equipment, net.	19,385	29.7%	$3,462 − $2,656	20,191	30.6%	$3,532 − $2,766	20,957	31.2%
Goodwill.	44,350	67.9%	no change	44,350	67.2%	no change	44,350	65.9%
Trademarks and other intangible assets, net . . .	24,527	37.6%	− $326	24,201	36.7%	− $298	23,903	35.5%
Other noncurrent assets.	5,092	7.8%	no change	5,092	7.7%	no change	5,092	7.6%
Total assets.	$127,136	194.7%	subtotal	$121,641	184.4%	subtotal	$120,334	178.9%
Current liabilities								
Accounts payable.	$ 9,325	14.3%	$65,952 × 14.3%	$ 9,431	14.3%	$67,271 × 14.3%	$ 9,620	14.3%
Accrued and other liabilities.	7,449	11.4%	$65,952 × 11.4%	7,519	11.4%	$67,271 × 11.4%	7,669	11.4%
Current liabilities held for sale	2,343	3.6%	none	0	0.0%	none	0	0.0%
Debt due within one year	11,653	17.8%	−$2,760 + $1,323	10,216	15.5%	−$1,323 + $2,357	11,250	16.7%
Total current liabilities.	30,770	47.1%	subtotal	27,166	41.2%	subtotal	28,539	42.4%
Long-term debt	18,945	29.0%	− $1,323	17,622	26.7%	− $2,357	15,265	22.7%
Deferred income taxes.	9,113	14.0%	$65,952 × 14.0%	9,233	14.0%	$67,271 × 14.0%	9,418	14.0%
Other noncurrent liabilities	10,325	15.8%	$65,952 × 15.8%	10,420	15.8%	$67,271 × 15.8%	10,629	15.8%
Total liabilities.	69,153	105.9%	subtotal	64,441	97.7%	subtotal	63,851	94.9%
Shareholders' equity								
Convertible Class A preferred stock.	1,038	1.6%	no change	1,038	1.6%	no change	1,038	1.5%
Non-voting Class B preferred stock.	0	0.0%	no change	0	0.0%	no change	0	0.0%
Common stock.	4,009	6.1%	no change	4,009	6.1%	no change	4,009	6.0%
Additional paid-in capital	63,714	97.6%	no change	63,714	96.6%	no change	63,714	94.7%
Reserve for ESOP debt retirement.	(1,290)	(2.0)%	no change	(1,290)	(2.0)%	no change	(1,290)	(1.9)%
Accumulated other comprehensive income/(loss).	(15,907)	(24.4)%	no change	(15,907)	(24.1)%	no change	(15,907)	(23.6)%
Treasury stock	(82,176)	(125.8)%	− $4,000	(86,176)	(130.7)%	− $4,000	(90,176)	(134.0)%
Retained earnings	87,953	134.7%	$10,685 − $7,565	91,073	138.1%	$10,904 − $7,720	94,257	140.1%
Noncontrolling interest.	642	1.0%	+ $97	739	1.1%	+ $99	838	1.2%
Total shareholders' equity	57,983	88.8%	subtotal	57,200	86.7%	subtotal	56,483	84.0%
Total liabilities and shareholders' equity	$127,136	194.7%	subtotal	$121,641	184.4%	subtotal	$120,334	178.9%

Review 12-5 LO5

Refer to the FY2016 income statement and balance sheet for General Mills along with the forecasted FY2017 income statement and balance sheet, in Reviews 12-1, 12-2 and 12-3.

Required

Use that information and the following assumptions to forecast the General Mills income statement and balance sheet for FY2018.

- Sales will increase by 2% in FY2018.
- Operating expenses as a percentage of sales will remain unchanged from FY2017 levels.
- Restructuring, impairment, and other exit costs are expected to be $0.
- Forecasted cash and long-term debt for FY2017 were adjusted to bring cash to a normal level. The account balances for FY2017 are:
  - Cash and cash equivalents, $750.5 million
  - Long-term debt, $7,240.5 million
- Long-term debt footnotes reveal that principal payments due on long-term debt in the next five years are: $1,103.4 million in FY2017, $604.7 million in FY2018, $1,150.4 million in FY2019, $1,056.0 million in FY2020, and $555.9 million in FY2021.

Solution on p. 12-71.   • Stock repurchases will be $0 million in FY2018.

Refining Financial Statement Forecasts

LO6
Refine forecasts with additional information.

The accuracy of our forecasts depends on the accuracy of our assumptions. To help us formulate more precise assumptions, we use the wealth of information from financial statement footnotes, management discussion & analysis (MD&A), other corporate filings required by the Securities and Exchange Commission (SEC) for major events (such as Form 8-K), and information published by companies in the investor relations section of corporate websites (such as discussions surrounding earnings releases, PowerPoint presentations to analysts, and conference calls with analysts). All these additional data can (and should) be incorporated into our forecasts to increase their accuracy. This section discusses the types of information we frequently use to refine our financial statement forecasts.

Company Guidance

Companies frequently provide guidance to analysts and other users of financial reports for forecasting purposes. P&G provides the following guidance for FY2017 along with its presentation of FY2016 financial results.

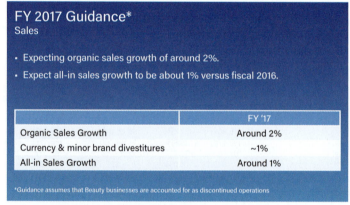

"The Procter & Gamble Company at The Consumer Analyst Group of New York Conference, February 18, 2016" on the PG Investor Relations website (http://www.pginvestor.com/Presentations-and-Events)

During FY2015 and FY2016, P&G sales growth was negatively affected by the strengthening $US, reducing reported sales by about 6% in each year. (As the $US strengthens vis-à-vis other world currencies in which P&G transacts business, the $US value of foreign-currency-denominated sales decreases.) For FY2016, in the MD&A section of its 10-K, P&G provides the following table for each of its operating segments and the company as a whole.

Year Ended June 30, 2016	Net Sales Growth	Foreign Exchange Impact	Acquisition/ Divestiture Impact	Organic Sales Growth
Beauty	(9)%	6%	3%	—%
Grooming	(8)%	9%	1%	2%
Health Care	(5)%	6%	1%	2%
Fabric & Home Care	(7)%	6%	2%	1%
Baby, Feminine & Family Care	(9)%	6%	2%	(1)%
Total company	(8)%	6%	3%	1%

Total sales declined by 8% in FY2016 (from $70,749 million to $65,299 million). Absent foreign-currency effects and the effects of acquisitions/divestitures, P&G's organic sales increased by 1%, computed as the overall 8% net sales decline, but then adding back a 6% negative foreign-currency effect *and* a 3% reduction of sales from acquisitions/divestitures.

In the most recent quarters in FY2016, P&G's organic sales growth has risen to about 2%, as disclosed in its FY2016 4Q earnings release.

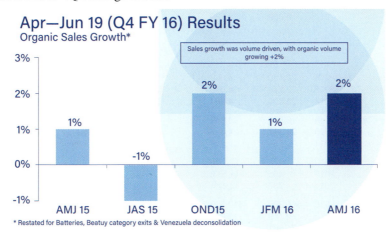

"The Procter & Gamble Company at The Consumer Analyst Group of New York Conference, February 18, 2016" on the PG Investor Relations website (http://www.pginvestor.com/Presentations-and-Events)

For FY2017, P&G expects both a reduction in foreign-currency effects and net sales growth closer to the organic growth in sales. Its guidance for FY2017 is for net sales growth of 1% (2% organic growth less 1% foreign currency effect).

In addition to its forecast of organic and net sales growth, P&G provides guidance regarding expectations for cash flow, capital spending, dividends, and share repurchases in its FY2016 4Q earnings presentation.

FY 2017 Guidance Cash Generation & Usage	
Adjusted Free Cash Flow Productivity:	90%+
Capital Spending, % Sales:	5% to 5.5%
Dividends:	$7B+
Share Repurchases/Exchanges*:	~$15B

*Combination of direct share repurchases and shres that will be exchanged in the Beauty transaction.

"The Procter & Gamble Company at The Consumer Analyst Group of New York Conference, February 18, 2016" on the PG Investor Relations website (http://www.pginvestor.com/Presentations-and-Events)

We have used this guidance in our forecasts for PPE and stockholders' equity as we explain above.

Segment Data

Companies are required to report financial data for each operating segment and to reconcile the segment totals to the reported amounts in the income statement and balance sheet for the company as a whole. Financial analysts frequently develop the sales forecasts as the sum of forecasts for the company's operating segments.[2] P&G's 10-K segment disclosure includes the following table of current and historical data for each of its five operating segments.

Global Segment Results ($ millions)		Net Sales	Earnings/ (Loss) from Continuing Operations Before Income Taxes	Net Earnings/ (Loss) from Continuing Operations	Depreciation and Amortization	Total Assets	Capital Expenditures
Beauty	2016	$11,477	$ 2,636	$ 1,975	$ 218	$ 3,888	$ 435
	2015	12,608	2,895	2,181	247	4,004	411
	2014	13,401	3,020	2,300	256	4,564	376
Grooming	2016	6,815	2,009	1,548	451	22,819	383
	2015	7,441	2,374	1,787	540	23,090	372
	2014	8,009	2,589	1,954	576	23,767	369
Health Care.	2016	7,350	1,812	1,250	204	5,139	240
	2015	7,713	1,700	1,167	202	5,212	218
	2014	7,798	1,597	1,083	199	5,879	253
Fabric & Home Care.	2016	20,730	4,249	2,778	531	6,919	672
	2015	22,274	4,059	2,634	547	7,155	986
	2014	23,506	4,264	2,770	539	7,938	1,057
Baby, Feminine & Family Care . . .	2016	18,505	4,042	2,650	886	9,863	1,261
	2015	20,247	4,317	2,938	924	10,109	1,337
	2014	20,950	4,310	2,940	908	10,946	1,317
Corporate.	2016	422	(1,379)	(174)	788	78,508	323
	2015	466	(4,333)	(2,420)	674	79,925	412
	2014	737	(2,271)	(389)	663	91,172	476
Total company	2016	$65,299	$13,369	$10,027	$3,078	$127,136	$3,314
	2015	70,749	11,012	8,287	3,134	129,495	3,736
	2014	74,401	13,509	10,658	3,141	144,266	3,848

Instead of using only trends in the top line of the income statement, sales growth forecasts are more accurate when they incorporate *all* available data. In P&G's case, its product lines segment disclosures provide a wealth of information that can be used to forecast sales for each operating segment; and then summing the segment forecasts yields top line sales forecasts.

To illustrate, Morgan Stanley analysts use both published data (such as the segment disclosures) and proprietary databases to forecast sales growth *by product segment* and *by quarter*. Following is an excerpt from its forecasting spreadsheet for P&G's Beauty segment.

	A	B	BE	BJ	BO	BT	BY	BZ	CA	CB	CC	CD
1		Procter & Gamble Co. (PG)										
5		**Segment Breakdown**	**FY2012**	**FY2013**	**FY2014**	**FY2015**	**FY2016**	**Sep-16E**	**Dec-16E**	**Mar-17E**	**Jun-17E**	**FY2017E**
15		**Beauty Care**	**20,318.0**	**19,956.0**	**13,398.0**	**12,608.0**	**11,477.0**	**2,937.5**	**2,903.6**	**2,783.6**	**2,823.8**	**11,448.5**
16		Organic Sales Growth	2.0%	0.7 %	0.0 %	-1.2 %	0.2 %	1.5 %	1.5 %	2.0 %	2.5 %	1.9 %
17		Volume (Organic)	1.9 %	-0.1 %	0.3 %	-2.9 %	-1.9 %	0.5 %	1.0 %	1.0 %	1.5 %	1.0 %
18		Pricing	3.5 %	1.6 %	0.2 %	2.2 %	2.0 %	1.0 %	0.5 %	1.0 %	1.0 %	0.9 %
19		Mix	-3.4 %	-0.7 %	-0.5 %	-0.5 %	0.3 %	0.0 %	0.0 %	0.0 %	0.0 %	0.0 %
20		FX Impact	0.5 %	-2.0 %	-2.2 %	-5.1 %	-5.6 %	-0.9 %	0.5 %	1.9 %	0.0 %	0.3 %
21		Acq/Div	-0.8 %	-0.3 %	0.0 %	-0.3 %	-3.7 %	-4.0 %	-4.0 %	-1.5 %	0.0 %	-2.4 %
22		% Sales Growth	0.8 %	-1.8 %	-32.9 %	-5.9 %	-9.0 %	-3.4 %	-2.0 %	2.4 %	2.5 %	-0.2 %

---

[2] GAAP defines an **operating segment** as "a component of a public entity that has all of the following characteristics. (1) It engages in business activities from which it may earn revenues and incur expenses (including revenues and expenses relating to transactions with other components of the same public entity). (2) Its operating results are regularly reviewed by the public entity's chief operating decision maker to make decisions about resources to be allocated to the segment and assess its performance. (3) Its discrete financial information is available."

We see that Morgan Stanley analysts forecast organic sales growth, including the effects of changes in *unit volume,* the effects of expected *price increases,* and the effects, if any, of expected changes in *product mix.* Their forecast includes an expected foreign-currency increase of 0.3% and an expected reduction of sales in the Beauty segment to reflect the announced planned divestiture in FY2017 of 43 of the company's brands in the Beauty operating segment. In sum, Morgan Stanley analysts forecast a decline in net sales of 0.2% for the Beauty segment from $11,477.0 million to $11,448.5 million—consisting of the following components.

Organic sales growth	1.9%
Volume (organic).	1.0%
Pricing	0.9%
Mix	0.0%
Foreign exchange impact.	0.3%
Acquisitions and divestitures	(2.4)%
Sales growth.	(0.2)%

Similar estimates are made for the other four operating segments. Top line sales growth estimates then are the sum of sales estimates for the five operating segments along with the corporate entity.

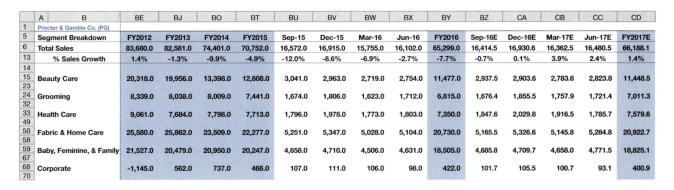

	A	B	BE	BJ	BO	BT	BU	BV	BW	BX	BY	BZ	CA	CB	CC	CD
1		Procter & Gamble Co. (PG)														
5		Segment Breakdown	FY2012	FY2013	FY2014	FY2015	Sep-15	Dec-15	Mar-16	Jun-16	FY2016	Sep-16E	Dec-16E	Mar-17E	Jun-17E	FY2017E
6		Total Sales	83,680.0	82,581.0	74,401.0	70,752.0	16,572.0	16,915.0	15,755.0	16,102.0	65,299.0	16,414.5	16,930.6	16,362.5	16,480.5	66,188.1
13		% Sales Growth	1.4%	-1.3%	-9.9%	-4.9%	-12.0%	-8.6%	-6.9%	-2.7%	-7.7%	-0.7%	0.1%	3.9%	2.4%	1.4%
14																
15 / 23		Beauty Care	20,318.0	19,956.0	13,398.0	12,608.0	3,041.0	2,963.0	2,719.0	2,754.0	11,477.0	2,937.5	2,903.6	2,783.6	2,823.8	11,448.5
24 / 32		Grooming	8,339.0	8,038.0	8,009.0	7,441.0	1,674.0	1,806.0	1,623.0	1,712.0	6,815.0	1,676.4	1,855.5	1,757.9	1,721.4	7,011.3
33 / 49		Health Care	9,061.0	7,684.0	7,798.0	7,713.0	1,796.0	1,978.0	1,773.0	1,803.0	7,350.0	1,847.6	2,029.8	1,916.5	1,785.7	7,579.6
50 / 58		Fabric & Home Care	25,580.0	25,862.0	23,509.0	22,277.0	5,251.0	5,347.0	5,028.0	5,104.0	20,730.0	5,165.5	5,326.6	5,145.8	5,284.8	20,922.7
59 / 67		Baby, Feminine, & Family	21,527.0	20,479.0	20,950.0	20,247.0	4,658.0	4,710.0	4,506.0	4,631.0	18,505.0	4,685.8	4,709.7	4,658.0	4,771.5	18,825.1
68 / 70		Corporate	-1,145.0	562.0	737.0	466.0	107.0	111.0	106.0	98.0	422.0	101.7	105.5	100.7	93.1	400.9

For FY2017, Morgan Stanley analysts forecast top line sales growth of 1.4% from $65,299.0 million to $66,188.1 million.

Impact of Acquisitions

When one company acquires another, the revenues and expenses of the acquired company are consolidated, but only from the date of acquisition onward (we discuss the consolidation process in an earlier module). Acquisitions can greatly impact the acquirer's income statement, especially if the acquisition occurs toward the beginning of the acquirer's fiscal year. P&G's acquisition of Gillette in October 2005 provides an example. In its June 30, 2006, fiscal year-end income statement (ending eight months following the acquisition), P&G reported the following for sales.

Years Ended June 30 ($ millions)	2006	2005	2004
Net sales.	$68,222	$56,741	$51,407

These net sales amounts include Gillette product sales from October 2005 onward (for fiscal 2006), and none of Gillette's sales is reported in fiscal 2005 or fiscal 2004. P&G's 2006 sales growth of 20.2% ([$68,222 million/$56,741 million] − 1) was, therefore, not P&G's organic growth, and we would have been remiss in forecasting a 20.2% increase for fiscal 2007.

Importantly, until all three annual income statements in the 10-K include the acquired company, the acquirer is required to disclose what revenue and net income would have been had the acquired company been consolidated for all three years reported in the current annual report. This "what if" disclosure is called *pro forma* disclosure. Procter & Gamble's pro forma disclosure in the footnotes to its 2006 10-K includes the following discussion and table.

> The following table provides pro forma results of operations for the years ended June 30, 2006, 2005, and 2004, as if Gillette had been acquired as of the beginning of each fiscal year presented.
>
> | Pro Forma Results; Years Ended June 30, | 2006 | 2005 | 2004 |
> |---|---|---|---|
> | Net sales ($ millions). . . . . | $71,005 | $67,920 | $61,112 |
> | Net earnings ($ millions). . . . . | 8,871 | 8,522 | 7,504 |
> | Diluted net earnings per common share . . . . | 2.51 | 2.29 | 1.98 |

Using this disclosure, we would have been able to compute the growth rate in sales for 2006 as 4.5% ([$71,005 million/$67,920 million] − 1), and we would have used the pro forma net sales for 2006 as our forecasting base. That is, assuming a continuation of this 4.5% growth rate, we would have forecasted 2007 net sales as $74,200 million (calculated as $71,005 million × 1.045). P&G was careful to point out, however, that the pro forma earnings estimate must be viewed with caution.

> Pro forma results do not include any anticipated cost savings or other effects of the planned integration of Gillette. Accordingly, such amounts are not necessarily indicative of the results if the acquisition had occurred on the dates indicated or that may result in the future.

Impact of Divestitures

When companies divest operations, they are required to:

- Exclude sales and expenses of discontinued operations from the continuing operations portion of their income statements.

- Report net income and gain (loss) on sale of the divested entity, net of tax, below income from continuing operations.

- Segregate the assets and liabilities of discontinued operations and report them on separate line items—these are labeled "assets held for sale" or "liabilities held of sale" on the balance sheet.

P&G reports assets and liabilities held for sale on its FY2016 balance sheet at $7,185 million and $2,343 million, respectively. We assume these discontinued operations will be sold in FY2017 at book value and, consequently, report both the assets and liabilities of discontinued operations at a zero balance in our FY2017 forecast. We see that Morgan Stanley analysts have reduced the forecasted sales growth percentage for the Beauty segment (see above) by 2.4 percentage points to reflect the pending sale of those operations.

Reassessing Financial Statement Forecasts

After preparing the forecasted financial statements, it is useful to reassess whether they are reasonable in light of current economic and company conditions. This task is subjective and benefits from the forecaster's knowledge of company, industry, and economic factors. Many analysts and managers prepare "what-if" forecasted financial statements. Specifically, they change key assumptions, such as the forecasted sales growth or key cost ratios, and then recompute the forecasted financial statements. These alternative forecasting scenarios indicate the sensitivity of a set of predicted outcomes to different assumptions about future economic conditions. Such sensitivity estimates can be useful for setting contingency plans and in identifying areas of vulnerability for company performance and condition.

LO6 Review 12-6

Refer to the following information for General Mills to answer the requirements. The segment information footnote to General Mills' 2016 10-K reports the following sales for operating units within the company's U.S. retail segment.

Segment sales, net ($ millions)	2016	2015
Meals	$ 2,393.9	$ 2,674.3
Cereal	2,312.8	2,330.1
Snacks	2,094.3	2,134.4
Baking products	1,903.4	1,969.8
Yogurt and other	1,302.7	1,398.4
Total U.S. retail segment	$10,007.1	$10,507.0

We assume the following estimates for growth in units for each segment.

Meals	(5.5)%
Cereal	1.5%
Snacks	0.5%
Baking products	(1.5)%
Yogurt and other	(3.0)%

Required

a. Forecast FY2017 sales for each of the five segments. What will FY2017 sales be for the total U.S. retail segment?

b. What is the overall forecasted growth rate for the total U.S. retail segment?

c. The annual earnings announcement press release dated June 29, 2016, provides guidance on FY2017 dividends.

	2017 Est.	2016 Actual	2015 Actual
Dividends per share	$1.92	$1.78	$1.67

At FY2016 year-end (May 29, 2016), General Mills had 754.6 million shares issued and 157.8 million shares held as treasury stock. Assume the $300 million stock repurchases forecasted for FY2017 will occur at the end of November 2016 and 5 million shares will be repurchased, based on an average price of $60 per share. Use this information to refine the forecasted dividends for FY2017.   **Solution on p. 12-72.**

Appendix 12A: Forecasting the Statement of Cash Flows

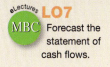

LO7 Forecast the statement of cash flows.

Forecasting the statement of cash flows is useful for a number of planning and control activities, including cash management, operating budgets, and capital budgeting decisions (CAPEX). To prepare the forecasted statement of cash flows, we use our forecasts of the income statement and balance sheet and then follow the preparation procedures explained in the statement of cash flow module. That process begins with net income, adds back or deducts any noncash expenses or revenues, and then recognizes the cash flow effect of changes in working capital followed by changes in the remaining asset, liability, and equity items. A common method is to compute changes in each of the line items on the forecasted balance sheet and then classify those changes to either the operating, investing, or financing sections of the forecasted statement of cash flows.

Exhibit 12.5 shows the forecasted statement of cash flows for Procter & Gamble. It reveals operating cash flows of $18,857 million, investing cash outflows of $3,462 million, and a large financing cash outflow of $14,325 million.

Exhibit 12.5 ■ **One-Year Forecast of P&G's Statement of Cash Flows**

Statement of Cash Flows
For Fiscal Year Ended 2017

$ millions	Computations	2017 Est.
Cash flow from operating		
Net income...		$10,782
Addback: Depreciation......................................	$19,385 × 13.7%	2,656
Addback: Amortization.....................................		326
Change in accounts receivable............................	$4,373 − $4,419	(46)
Change in inventories.......................................	$4,716 − $4,749	(33)
Change in deferred income taxes.........................	$1,507 − $1,517	(10)
Change in prepaid expenses and other current...............	$2,653 − $2,704	(51)
Change in assets held for sale...........................	$7,185 − $0	7,185
Change in accounts payable..............................	$9,431 − $9,325	106
Change in accrued compensation and other liabilities...........	$7,519 − $7,449	70
Change in liabilities held for sale........................	$0 − $2,343	(2,343)
Change in deferred income taxes.........................	$9,233 − $9,113	120
Change in other noncurrent liabilities......................	$10,420 − $10,325	95
Net cash from operating activities...........................		18,857
Cash flow from investing		
Capital expenditures.....................................	$65,952 × 5.25%	(3,462)
Net cash from investing activities............................		(3,462)
Cash flow from financing		
Dividends..	$10,685 × 70.8%	(7,565)
Increase in short-term debt..............................		0
Decrease in long-term debt..............................		(2,760)
Purchase of treasury shares.............................		(4,000)
Net cash from financing activities............................		(14,325)
Net change in cash.......................................		1,070
Beginning cash balance...................................		7,102
Ending cash balance.....................................		$ 8,172

The forecasted statement of cash flows highlights financing cash outflows as the main cause for the forecasted decline in cash. While operating cash flows continue to be strong, P&G's guidance includes plans to continue to repurchase common stock (approximately $4,000 million), pay dividends (approximately $7,565 million), and purchase CAPEX (approximately $3,462 million). Our forecast is for net change in cash is a positive $1,070 million and an adequate ending balance for cash, which indicates P&G should be able to fund its planned cash outflows without the need for external financing.

Business Insight ■ Do currency fluctuations affect cash flow?

P&G's guidance to investors predicts an organic sales increase of 2% less a 1% decline in that growth rate due to an expected $US strengthening in FY2017 vis-à-vis other world currencies (resulting in a decline in the $US value of sales denominated in foreign currencies). As sales decline, so do profits. Because net income is the first line in the statement of cash flows, it is reasonable to ask whether the profit decline resulting from a strengthening $US implies P&G's cash flows will also decline? If so, we would expect such a decline to affect P&G's stock price. The short answer is that it is unlikely that P&G's cash flows will be greatly affected.

Before companies can consolidate their foreign subsidiaries, the foreign-currency denominated subsidiary income statements, balance sheets, and statements of cash flows must first be translated to $US equivalents. To accomplish this, each financial statement item is multiplied by an exchange rate to yield the $US equivalent. We can think of the translation process as a spreadsheet with the foreign currency-denominated subsidiary financial statements in the first column, the exchange rate in the second, and the $US equivalent financial statements in the third, as the product of the first two columns. There are no transactions involved in this process, so it is reasonable to expect there to be no effect on cash flow from the translation process.

continued

P&G's cash flows will be *directly* affected only if P&G actually exchanges $US for foreign currencies (such as making foreign currency-denominated payments to lenders or other creditors) or sells foreign currency to generate $US (say to repatriate cash back to the U.S.)—of course, fluctuations in the value of the $US can affect foreign currency-denominated selling prices and sales and cash flows indirectly. In P&G's case, that is unlikely. In its 2016 10-K, P&G reports the following.

> As of June 30, 2016, $11.0 billion of the Company's cash, cash equivalents and marketable securities is held off-shore by foreign subsidiaries. Amounts held by foreign subsidiaries are generally subject to U.S. income taxation on repatriation to the U.S. We do not expect restrictions or taxes on repatriation of cash held outside of the U.S. to have a material effect on our overall liquidity, financial condition or the results of operations for the foreseeable future.

In other words, P&G expects to retain its foreign currency in its foreign subsidiaries and does not expect to repatriate that cash in the foreseeable future. In 2016, P&G reported cash and securities of $13,348 million on its balance sheet, $11 billion of which was held by its foreign subsidiaries.

So, in the absence of repatriation, why does the forecasted decline in profit not result in a decline in cash flow? P&G's balance sheet also shrinks with the strengthening $US, and the reduction in net assets (recorded as a cash *inflow* in the statement of cash flows) exactly offsets the reduction in profit (recorded as a cash *outflow*), leaving net cash unaffected, just as we would expect given there are no transactions in the translation process.

LO7 Review 12-7

Refer to the FY2016 income statement and balance sheet for **General Mills** along with its forecasted FY2017 income statement and balance sheet in Reviews 12-1, 12-2, and 12-3. *Note:* This Review does not include the cash adjustment from Review 12-4.

MBC

Required
Use that information to prepare the General Mills' forecasted statement of cash flows for FY2017.   **Solution on p. 12-73.**

Appendix 12B: Parsimonious Method for Forecasting NOPAT and NOA

This appendix explains a parsimonious method to obtain forecasts for net operating profit after tax (NOPAT) and for net operating assets (NOA). This method requires three crucial inputs:

1. Sales growth.
2. Net operating profit margin (NOPM); defined in Module 4 as NOPAT divided by sales.
3. Net operating asset turnover (NOAT); defined in Module 4 as sales divided by average NOA. (For forecasting purposes, we define NOAT as sales divided by *year-end* NOA instead of average NOA because we want to forecast year-end values.)

eLectures **LO8**
MBC Apply a parsimonious method for forecasting net operating profit and net operating assets.

Multiyear Forecasting with Parsimonious Method

We use **Procter & Gamble**'s 2016 income statement from Exhibit 12.2, and its 2016 balance sheet from Exhibit 12.3, to determine the following measures. We assume that P&G's statutory tax rate is 37% on nonoperating revenues and expenses.

$ millions	2016
Sales.	$65,299
Net operating profit after tax ($13,441 − [$3,342 + ($579 − $182 − $325) × 37%]).	$10,072
NOA ($127,136 − $7,102 − $6,246 − $7,185 − $9,325 − $7,449 − $9,113 − $10,325)*. . . .	$70,391
NOPM ($10,072/$65,299).	15.4%
NOAT ($65,299/$70,391)*.	0.93

*We use ending balance sheet amounts, rather than average amounts, because we forecast *ending* balance sheet amounts.

Each year's forecasted sales is the prior year sales multiplied successively by (1 + growth rate) and then rounded to whole digits. Consistent with our prior revenue growth rate assumptions for P&G, we define "1 + growth rate" as 1.01 for 2017 and 1.02 for 2018 onward. NOPAT is computed using forecasted (and rounded) sales each year times the 2016 NOPM of 15.4%; and NOA is computed using forecasted (and rounded) sales divided by the 2016 NOAT of 0.93. Forecasted numbers for 2017 through 2020 are in Exhibit 12B.1; supporting computations are in parentheses.

This forecasting process can be continued for any desired forecast horizon. Also, the forecast assumptions such as sales growth, NOPM, and NOAT can be varied by year, if desired. This parsimonious method is simpler than the method illustrated in this module. However, its simplicity forgoes information that can improve forecast accuracy.

Exhibit 12B.1 ■ P&G Parsimonious Method Forecasts of Sales, NOPAT and NOA

$ millions	Reported 2016	Forecast 2017 Est.	2018 Est.	2019 Est.	2020 Est.
Net sales growth		1.0%	2.0%	2.0%	2.0%
Net sales (unrounded) .	$65,299	**$65,951.99** ($65,299 × 1.01)	**$67,271.03** ($65,951.99 × 1.02)	**$68,616.45** ($67,271.03 × 1.02)	**$69,988.78** ($68,616.45 × 1.02)
Net sales (rounded) . . .	$65,299	**$65,952**	**$67,271**	**$68,616**	**$69,989**
NOPAT[1]	$10,072	**$10,157** ($65,952 × 0.154)	**$10,360** ($67,271 × 0.154)	**$10,567** ($68,616 × 0.154)	**$10,778** ($69,989 × 0.154)
NOA[2]	$70,391	**$70,916** ($65,952/0.93)	**$72,334** ($67,271/0.93)	**$73,781** ($68,616/0.93)	**$75,257** ($69,989/0.93)

[1] Forecasted NOPAT = Forecasted net sales (rounded) × 2016 NOPM
[2] Forecasted NOA = Forecasted net sales (rounded) ÷ 2016 NOAT

Review 12-8 LO8

General Mills (GIS) reports fiscal 2016 sales of $16,563.1 million, net operating profit after tax (NOPAT) of $1,928.2 million, and net operating assets (NOA) of $13,819.9 million. The company's NOPM is 11.6% (computed as $1,928.2 million/$16,563.1 million) and its NOAT is 1.20 computed as $16,563.1 million / $13,819.9 million.

Required
Use the parsimonious forecast model to project General Mills' sales, NOPAT, and NOA for 2017 through 2020 assuming that sales will decline by 1.5% in 2017 and then grow by 2% per year for 2018 through 2020.

Solution on p. 12-73.

Appendix 12C: Morgan Stanley's Forecast Report on Procter & Gamble

Following is the Morgan Stanley analysts' report on Procter & Gamble that the firm issued on August 3, 2016 (pages 14–21 of the report consist of the customary disclosure information typical of analyst reports). *Please note that materials that are referenced comprise excerpts from research reports and should not be relied on as investment advice. This material is only as current as the publication date of the underlying Morgan Stanley research. For important disclosures, stock price charts, and equity rating histories regarding companies that are the subject of the underlying Morgan Stanley research, see* **www.morganstanley.com/researchdisclosures**. *Additionally, Morgan Stanley has provided these materials as a courtesy. Therefore, Morgan Stanley and Cambridge Business Publishers do not undertake to advise you of changes in the opinions or information set forth in these materials.*

Morgan Stanley | RESEARCH

August 3, 2016 12:49 AM GMT

UPDATE

Procter & Gamble Co.

Remain Equal-weight: Better, but Still Not at Peer Levels

⬛ Stock Rating	⬤ Industry View	⬤ Price Target
Equal-weight	In-Line	$90.00

We remain EW PG, as we believe weaker organic sales growth than peers will limit multiple expansion.

WHAT'S CHANGED?	Procter & Gamble Co.	From:	To:
	Price Target	$85.00	**$90.00**

Equal-weight: Net, we remain Equal-weight PG post Q4 results/initial FY17 guidance. There were some positive signs from Q4, including improving (sequentially) organic sales growth, a Q4 EPS beat despite reinvestment, and most importantly, what looks like conservative guidance for FY17. However, we are not getting too excited on PG's stock for three reasons. First, PG's Q4 topline result was still muted on an easy comparison, as this was PG's second worst two-yr average organic sales result since the downturn. Second, scanner data sales growth has also not improved in the US/Europe/emerging markets, highlighting PG's topline recovery will be slow. Last, while FY17 EPS guidance now looks conservative, with positive PG potential EPS revisions ahead, valuation of 21x times CY17e limits stock upside in our minds.

Q4 EPS Better Than Expected: PG Q4 core EPS of $0.79 was above the $0.74 consensus, although in line with our forecast. Organic sales growth of 2% (~2.25% unrounded) was better than expected vs. consensus of ~1.4% and street expectations probably more in the ~1% range, driven by strong +7% grooming and +8% health care results. +1.7% reported topline upside was augmented by a 60 bp GM beat, driving 3% gross profit upside, but operating profit was only 0.8% ahead of consensus, as SG&A was higher than expected on investment behind the business in marketing/R&D.

Below Consensus FY17 EPS Guidance Looks Conservative: PG is projecting organic sales growth of approximately +2% for FY17 and MSD core EPS growth on a base of $3.67 (implies $3.82-$3.89), which at its midpoint of ~$3.85 is ~3% below prior consensus of $3.96. We view guidance as conservative, given a -4% share decline on the Coty beauty/Duracell deals, continued expected GM expansion, and 2% organic sales growth. Therefore, our forecast is above PG guidance at $3.90.

Remain EW: Net, we believe PG has implemented the right strategy changes, but still worry that these changes will take time to play out and as a result PG topline results will continue to trail large cap peers. We forecast 2% organic sales growth in FY17 as SKU discontinuations dissipate and higher spending boosts

MORGAN STANLEY & CO. LLC

Dara Mohsenian, CFA
EQUITY ANALYST
Dara.Mohsenian@morganstanley.com +1 212 761-6575

Bob Doctor, CFA
RESEARCH ASSOCIATE
Bob.Doctor@morganstanley.com +1 212 761-7250

Procter & Gamble Co. (PG.N, PG US)

Household & Personal Care / United States of America

Stock Rating				Equal-weight
Industry View				In-Line
Price target				$90.00
Shr price, close (Aug 2, 2016)				$86.76
Mkt cap, curr (mm)				$243,999
52-Week Range				$86.88-65.02

Fiscal Year Ending	06/16	06/17e	06/18e	06/19e
ModelWare EPS ($)	3.67	3.90	4.25	4.56
P/E	23.1	22.2	20.4	19.0
Consensus EPS ($)§	3.64	3.96	4.27	4.41
Div yld (%)	3.1	3.1	3.4	3.6

Unless otherwise noted, all metrics are based on Morgan Stanley ModelWare framework
§ = Consensus data is provided by Thomson Reuters Estimates
e = Morgan Stanley Research estimates

QUARTERLY MODELWARE EPS ($)

Quarter	2016	2017e Prior	2017e Current	2018e Prior	2018e Current
Q1	0.98	0.99	0.95	1.11	1.07
Q2	1.04	1.11	1.08	1.21	1.17
Q3	0.86	0.99	1.01	1.07	1.08
Q4	0.79	0.86	0.86	0.94	0.93

e = Morgan Stanley Research estimates

1

Morgan Stanley | RESEARCH

topline growth, which we don't think is enough to drive multiple expansion with PG already at 21x CY17e EPS. Instead, we prefer PEP with higher organic sales/EPS growth and better visibility, at a similar valuation. Post 4Q EPS, we are lowering our FY17/18 EPS estimates by ~2% to $3.90/4.25 given higher reinvestment; although, we are raising our PT to $90 (from $85) given a higher market multiple. Our target is based on 22x our CY17e EPS, which is at a MSD% discount to mega-cap peers (PEP/KO/CL) given a lower growth outlook.

Morgan Stanley | RESEARCH

Risk-Reward: Procter & Gamble (PG)
Risk-Reward Looks Balanced

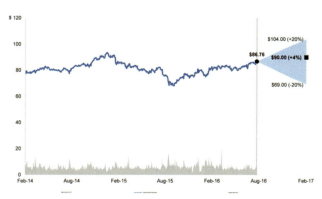

Source: Thomson Reuters, Morgan Stanley Research

Price Target $90
Derived from base case scenario.

Bull $104
24x Bull Case CY17e EPS
Topline rebounds to 3.0-4.0% organic sales growth. Revenue upside as PG's marketing/innovation focus drives market share improvement, coupled with 50 bps of pricing upside. Cost cutting above our forecast trims 50 bps incrementally from SG&A. Valuation expands to 24x CY17e EPS.

Base $90
22x Base Case CY17e EPS
Muted sales growth, but cost-cutting drives margins. We forecast organic sales growth of ~2% for PG going forward, below peers in the 3-4% range, given PG's premium portfolio and developed market skew limits growth in a weak consumer spending environment. We expect PG's OMs to expand by ~40 bps and EPS growth of +HSD%, below peers. We apply a multiple of 22x to CY17e EPS of $4.08, toward the lower-end of PG's peer group given muted topline growth.

Bear $69
18x Bear Case CY17e EPS
Topline downside. Pricing is 50 bps below our forecast due to a competitive environment and macro slows, hurting volume by 50 bps. Margins miss by 50 bps due to negative mix. Valuation contracts to 18x CY17e EPS .

Exhibit 1: Bear to Bull: Topline Trends Should be the Key Stock Driver

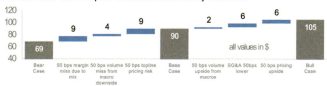

Source: Company data, Morgan Stanley Research estimates

Investment Thesis

■ **Muted Organic Sales Growth:** PG's higher-price developed market skewed portfolio is still driving weaker topline growth than peers and significant market share losses.

■ **Some Positives Emerging:** We believe there are a few key positives for PG, including strategy tweaks under a new CEO, substantial cost-cutting, a re-focus on the core, and better execution.

■ **Valuation Limits Upside:** With PG now trading at ~21x CY17e EPS, we believe valuation limits potential upside from here, and we do not see clear near-term catalysts for PG shares to re-rate higher given our topline growth remains below mega-cap peers.

Risks to Achieving Price Target

■ Risks include macro pressures, pricing fluctuations, cost-cutting execution issues, market share vacillations, and currency & commodity volatility.

Morgan Stanley | RESEARCH

UPDATE

Q4 EPS Beat

Q4 EPS Beat: PG Q4 core EPS of $0.79 was in line with our $0.79 estimate and +5 cents above consensus. Organic sales growth of 2.2% un-rounded was above the 1.5% consensus, and drove 1.7% reported topline upside vs consensus, or 3.0% gross profit upside along with a 60 bp GM beat. Higher marketing (+240 bp yoy) and R&D investments (+70 bps yoy) limited operating profit upside to 1%, with 80% of the EPS upside vs consensus due to a lower tax rate.

Exhibit 2: 4Q16 EPS Variance Table

$ in millions, except EPS	MS Est. Jun-16 E	Actual Jun-16	+/-	EPS Variance	Jun-15	Actual Jun-16	+/-
	MS Est. vs. Actual				**Year-over-Year**		
Sales	**$15,720**	**$16,102**	**2.4%**		**$16,553**	**$16,102**	**-2.7%**
% Growth	-5.0%	-2.7%			-8.6%	-2.7%	
% Organic Growth	1.5%	2.0%			0.0%	2.0%	
Cost of Sales	**-8,008**	**-8,147**	**1.7%**		**-8,638**	**-8,147**	**-5.7%**
% of Sales	50.9%	50.6%	(34) bps		52.2%	50.6%	(159) bps
% of Sales Bps Change	-124	-159				-159	
Gross Profit	**7,713**	**7,955**	**3.1%**	**$0.06**	**7,915**	**7,955**	**0.5%**
Gross Margin %	49.1%	49.4%	34 bps		47.8%	49.4%	159 bps
Gross Margin Bps Change	124	159				159	
SG&A Expense	**-4,854**	**-5,222**	**7.6%**	**($0.10)**	**-4,855**	**-5,222**	**7.6%**
% of Sales	30.9%	32.4%	155 bps		29.3%	32.4%	310 bps
% Growth	0.0%	7.6%				7.6%	
% of Sales Bps Change	155	310				310	
Operating Income	**2,858**	**2,733**	**-4.4%**	**($0.03)**	**3,060**	**2,733**	**-10.7%**
Operating Margin	18.2%	17.0%	(121) bps		18.5%	17.0%	(151) bps
% Growth	-6.6%	-10.7%				-10.7%	
Interest Expense	-$149	-$150	0.7%	($0.00)	-$147	-$150	2.0%
Other Non-Operating Income, Ne	$300	$334	n.m.f.	$0.01	$401	$334	-16.7%
Pretax Income	**3,009**	**2,917**	**-3.1%**	**($0.02)**	**3,314**	**2,917**	**-12.0%**
Taxes	**-788**	**-695**			**-609**	**-695**	**2.0%**
Tax Rate	26.2%	23.8%		$0.03	18.4%	23.8%	545 bps
Minority Interests	-17.0	-7.0		$0.00	-17.0	-7.0	
Net Income	**2,204**	**2,215**	**0.5%**	**$0.00**	**2,688**	**2,215**	**-17.6%**
EPS Diluted (Core)	**$0.79**	**$0.79**	**0.5%**	**$0.00**	**$0.93**	**$0.79**	**-15.3%**
EPS % Growth	-15.7%	-15.3%			5.4%	-15.3%	
Diluted Shares	2,800.0	2,800.0	0.0%	$0.00	0.0	0.0	#DIV/0!

Source: Company data, Morgan Stanley Research

Topline Performance Better than Expected: Q4 organic sales growth of +2% (2.25% unrounded) was above the +1.4% consensus, albeit on a flat comp, driven by +2.0% volume with flat pricing and mix. Topline improved sequentially and exceeded low expectations, but two-year average organic sales growth remained muted at +1%, in-line with Q3. From a geographic standpoint, developed markets organic sales rose +1.5% and developing markets were +3.5%. North America posted organic sales growth of +2.0%,

4

Morgan Stanley | RESEARCH

while China was flat (a sequential improvement).

Exhibit 3: Organic Sales Growth Improved But Remains Muted

Source: Company data, Morgan Stanley Research

Market Share Improving Sequentially, but Still Weak: On a divisional weighted average basis, market share performance remains weak, with PG losing ~50 bps of share on a y-o-y basis; although, results have improved sequentially from the prior ~-80 bp decline YTD.

Morgan Stanley | RESEARCH

Exhibit 4: Total Global Market Share on Divisional Weighted Average Basis Improved in the Quarter vs. 1H16, But Remains Weak...

PG Wtd. Average Total Value Share YoY (bps) Change

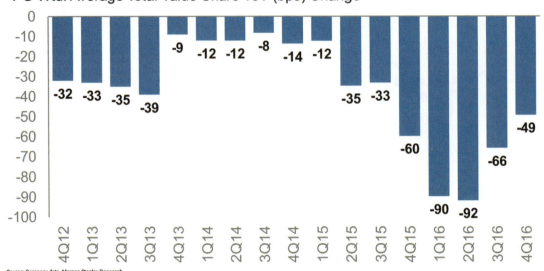

Source: Company data, Morgan Stanley Research

Notably, all global segments experienced share declines on a y-o-y basis, but all segments improved sequentially from the YTD trend. Fabric and Home Care value share was down -10bps (vs. -20 bps YTD), Health Care was down -40 bps (vs. -77 YTD), Beauty Care was down -80 bps (vs. -100 YTD), Grooming was down -70 bps (vs. -120 bps YTD), and Baby, Feminine, & Family Care was down -70 bps (vs. -130 YTD).

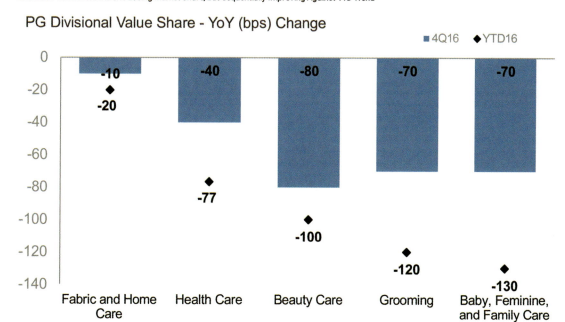

Morgan Stanley | RESEARCH   UPDATE

Exhibit 5: ...With All Divisions Losing Market Share, but Sequentially Improving Against YTD Trend

PG Divisional Value Share - YoY (bps) Change

■ 4Q16   ◆ YTD16

Source: Company data, Morgan Stanley Research

Segment Details: By segment, organic sales were mixed, with strong results in Health Care +8.0% and Grooming +7.0% exceeding our projections of +3.0% and +4.0%, respectively. Other segments came in mostly in line, with Beauty +1.0%, Fabric and Home Care +1.0%, and Baby, Feminine & Family +1.0%.

Exhibit 6: 4Q16 Segment Results vs. Our Forecast

$ in millions	MS Est. vs. Actual			Year-over-Year		
	MS Est. Jun-16 E	Actual Jun-16	+/-	Jun-15	Actual Jun-16	+/-
Total Sales	$15,720	$16,102	2.4%	$16,553	$16,102	-2.7%
Organic Sales Growth	1.5%	2.0%	51 bps	0.0%	2.0%	200bp
Beauty Care	$2,696	$2,754	2.1%	$2,907	$2,754	-5.3%
Organic Sales Growth	0.0%	1.0%	100bp	-1.0%	1.0%	200bp
Grooming	$1,639	$1,712	4.4%	$1,692	$1,712	1.2%
Organic Sales Growth	4.0%	7.0%	300bp	-7.0%	7.0%	1400bp
Fabric and Home Care	$5,032	$5,104		$5,321	$5,104	
Organic Sales Growth	1.0%	1.0%	0bp	3.0%	1.0%	-200bp
Baby, Feminine, and Fan	$4,601	$4,631	0.6%	$4,818	$4,631	-3.9%
Organic Sales Growth	1.5%	1.0%	-50bp	1.0%	1.0%	0bp
Health Care	$1,655	$1,803	8.9%	$1,705	$1,803	5.7%
Organic Sales Growth	3.0%	8.0%	500bp	4.0%	8.0%	400bp

Source: Company data, Morgan Stanley Research

Margin Performance Impressive: PG's gross margin rose ~160 bps y-o-y to 49.4% in Q4 (+60 bps vs. consensus), as cost savings and commodities drove +280 bps and +110 bps of improvement, respectively, mitigated by a -220 bps FX drag. Gross margin

Morgan Stanley | RESEARCH

improvement was more than offset by higher SG&A as a % of sales, which was up 310 bps y-o-y. FX was a 40 bps headwind, while marketing was up a significant +240 bps and R&D was up +70bps. Cost savings provided a -40 bps benefit. Net, OM decreased ~-150 bps y-o-y to 17.0%.

Exhibit 7: GM Walk

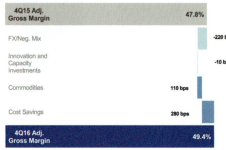

Source: Company data, Morgan Stanley Research

Exhibit 8: SG&A Walk

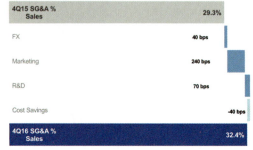

Source: Company data, Morgan Stanley Research

FY17 EPS Guidance Below Consensus: PG is projecting organic sales growth of approximately +2% for FY17, and a -1% brand divestiture/FX headwind, with all-in sales growth of +1%. The company expects +MSD% core EPS growth on a base of $3.67 (implies $3.82-3.89), which at its midpoint of ~$3.85 is ~3% below prior consensus of $3.96 (MSe $3.96). PG noted that the 1Q17 EPS will be disproportionately affected by FX headwinds and the impact of lost finished products sales to Venezuelan subsidiaries. We view guidance as conservative, given a -4% share decline on the Coty beauty/Duracell deals, continued expected GM expansion, and ~2% organic sales growth.

Morgan Stanley is acting as financial advisor to Coty Inc. ("Coty") in relation to its definitive agreement to merge The Procter & Gamble Company's fine fragrance, color cosmetics, and hair color businesses into Coty through a tax-free Reverse Morris Trust transaction as announced on July 9, 2015. The proposed transaction is subject to regulatory clearances, works council consultations, and other customary conditions. Coty has agreed to pay fees to Morgan Stanley for its financial services a significant portion of which are contingent upon the consummation of the proposed transaction. Please refer to the notes at the end of this report.

Morgan Stanley | RESEARCH

Key Risks to Our Investment Thesis

Uncertain macro outlook. Given Procter & Gamble's skew to premium products, the company's organic sales growth prospects will be significantly influenced by consumer spending going forward. PG's volume is sensitive to macro conditions as evidenced by its 2% volume decline in FY09. We estimate that a 100-bp change in volume is worth 2% to our FY16 EPS estimate.

Vacillating pricing is a risk. If the industry environment was more competitive than we expect, we estimate that each 100 bps of pricing pressure would be worth 5% to FY16 EPS.

Cost-cutting. PG's core SG&A as a percentage of sales (excluding shipping and handling, ad spending, R&D expense, and stock option expense) of ~16% in FY14 was the highest in its large cap peer group despite PG's leading scale. As such, we believe PG has ample opportunity to pare back its SG&A spending, and also generate COGS cost savings/productivity. We also believe PG is more focused on cost cutting through simplifying the organization and streamlining bureaucracy, in order to better capitalize on its scale. Each 50 basis points change in core SG&A as a % of sales versus our forecast would be worth an estimated 2.5% to FY16 EPS.

Market share vacillates. There may be upside to consensus EPS if PG share gains accelerate with a ramping up innovation pipeline. On the other hand, market share could stall with weaker consumer spending given PG's premium portfolio. We estimate each 100 basis points of incremental volume would be worth 2% to FY16 EPS.

Currency movements. Nearly two-thirds of PG's sales are derived from outside the US. As such, fluctuation in currencies could materially impact our EPS estimates. We estimate that a 5% change in the USD versus PG's basket of currencies would have a 3% impact on EPS. PG is more insulated from FX risk than its peers given relatively less international exposure. In addition, PG's significant manufacturing footprint outside the US mitigates the potential transaction impact of FX.

Commodity cost volatility. While PG's diversified product portfolio spreads out its raw material exposure across a wide variety of input costs, volatile commodity costs could significantly impact EPS. We estimate that each 200 bps change in overall commodity costs would impact EPS by 3%.

9

Morgan Stanley | RESEARCH

UPDATE

Exhibit 9: PG Income Statement

Income Statement	FY2013	FY2014	FY2015	Sep-15	Dec-15	Mar-16	Jun-16
Sales	**82,581.0**	**74,401.0**	**70,749.0**	**16,527.0**	**16,915.0**	**15,755.0**	**16,102.0**
% Growth	-1.3%	-9.9%	-4.9%	-12.0%	-8.5%	-6.9%	-2.7%
% Organic Growth	2.8%	2.6%	1.6%	-1.0%	2.0%	1.0%	2.0%
Cost of Sales	-39,743.0	-38,729.0	-36,537.0	-8,080.0	-8,317.0	-7,741.0	-8,147.0
% of Sales	48.1%	52.1%	51.6%	48.9%	49.2%	49.1%	50.6%
% of Sales Bps Change	-245	393	-41	-248.21	-211.475	-267.383	-159
Gross Profit	**40,373.0**	**35,672.0**	**34,212.0**	**8,447.0**	**8,598.0**	**8,014.0**	**7,955.0**
Gross Margin %	48.9%	47.9%	48.4%	51.1%	50.8%	50.9%	49.4%
Gross Margin Bps Change	-54	-94	41	248	211	267	159
SG&A Expense (ex Incremental Restructuring)	**-25,166.0**	**-21,012.0**	**-20,348.0**	**-4,607.0**	**-4,616.0**	**-4,522.0**	**-5,222.0**
% of Sales	30.5%	28.2%	28.8%	27.9%	27.3%	28.7%	32.4%
% Growth	-1.9%	-16.5%	-3.2%	-12.7%	-13.2%	-7.7%	7.6%
% of Sales Bps Change	-18	-223	52	-23	-146	-24	310
Operating Income (ex Incremental Restructuring)	**15,207.0**	**14,660.0**	**13,864.0**	**3,840.0**	**3,982.0**	**3,492.0**	**2,733.0**
Operating Margin	18.4%	19.7%	19.6%	23.2%	23.5%	22.2%	17.0%
% Growth	-3.2%	-3.6%	-5.4%	-0.3%	7.8%	7.1%	-10.7%
Operating Margin Bps Change	-36	129	-11	271	357	291	-151
Interest Expense	-667.0	-710.0	-626.0	-140.0	-143.0	-146.0	-150.0
Other Non-Operating Income, Net	391.9	308.0	589.0	26.0	93.0	53.0	334.0
Pretax Income	**14,931.9**	**14,258.0**	**13,827.0**	**3,726.0**	**3,932.0**	**3,399.0**	**2,917.0**
Taxes	-3,440.8	-2,949.0	-2,879.0	-892.2	-927.0	-923.0	-695.0
Tax Rate	23.0%	20.7%	20.8%	23.9%	23.6%	27.2%	23.8%
Minority Interests	-90.0	-141.5	-103.0	-34.0	-22.0	-33.0	-7.0
Net Income	**11,401.1**	**11,167.5**	**10,845.0**	**2,799.8**	**2,983.0**	**2,443.0**	**2,215.0**
EPS Diluted (Core)	**$3.89**	**$3.85**	**$3.76**	**$0.98**	**$1.04**	**$0.86**	**$0.79**
EPS % Growth	0.9%	-1.2%	-2.2%	-1.5%	9.5%	-2.7%	-15.6%
Basic Shares	2,739.7	2,709.8	2,688.7	2716.6	2712.6	2683.2	2662.6
Diluted Shares	2,930.6	2,904.4	2,883.6	2867.5	2864.6	2835.0	2811.0

Income Statement	FY2016	Sep-16 E	Dec-16 E	Mar-17 E	Jun-17 E	FY2017E	FY2018E
Sales	**65,299.0**	**16,414.5**	**16,930.6**	**16,362.5**	**16,480.5**	**66,188.1**	**68,235.0**
% Growth	-7.7%	-0.7%	0.1%	3.9%	2.4%	1.4%	3.1%
% Organic Growth	0.8%	2.1%	1.2%	2.5%	2.4%	2.0%	3.1%
Cost of Sales	-32,285.0	-7,836.2	-8,146.9	-7,892.2	-8,187.3	-32,062.7	-32,747.2
% of Sales	49.4%	47.7%	48.1%	48.2%	49.7%	48.4%	48.0%
% of Sales Bps Change	-220.133	-115	-105	-90	-92	-100	-45
Gross Profit	**33,014.0**	**8,578.3**	**8,783.7**	**8,470.3**	**8,293.1**	**34,125.4**	**35,487.8**
Gross Margin %	50.6%	52.3%	51.9%	51.8%	50.3%	51.6%	52.0%
Gross Margin Bps Change	220	115	105	90	92	100	45
SG&A Expense (ex Incremental Restructuring)	**-18,967.0**	**-4,903.0**	**-4,786.7**	**-4,768.8**	**-5,154.9**	**-19,613.4**	**-19,993.0**
% of Sales	29.0%	29.9%	28.3%	29.1%	31.3%	29.6%	29.3%
% Growth	-6.8%	6.4%	3.7%	5.5%	-1.3%	3.4%	1.9%
% of Sales Bps Change	29	199	98	44	-115	59	-33
Operating Income (ex Incremental Restructuring)	**14,047.0**	**3,675.2**	**3,997.0**	**3,701.5**	**3,138.3**	**14,512.0**	**15,494.8**
Operating Margin	21.5%	22.4%	23.6%	22.6%	19.0%	21.9%	22.7%
% Growth	1.3%	-4.3%	0.4%	6.0%	14.8%	3.3%	6.8%
Operating Margin Bps Change	192	-84	7	46	207	41	78
Interest Expense	-579.0	-146.3	-145.7	-144.6	-140.8	-577.3	-577.8
Other Non-Operating Income, Net	506.0	70.0	70.0	70.0	70.0	280.0	240.0
Pretax Income	**13,974.0**	**3,598.9**	**3,921.3**	**3,626.9**	**3,067.5**	**14,214.6**	**15,157.0**
Taxes	-3,437.2	-881.7	-960.7	-888.6	-751.5	-3,482.6	-3,713.5
Tax Rate	24.6%	24.5%	24.5%	24.5%	24.5%	24.5%	24.5%
Minority Interests	-96.0	-34.0	-22.0	-33.0	-7.0	-96.0	-98.4
Net Income	**10,440.8**	**2,683.2**	**2,938.6**	**2,705.3**	**2,309.0**	**10,636.0**	**11,345.1**
EPS Diluted (Core)	**$3.67**	**$0.95**	**$1.08**	**$1.01**	**$0.86**	**$3.90**	**$4.25**
EPS % Growth	-2.4%	-2.2%	3.4%	16.8%	9.2%	6.2%	8.9%
Basic Shares	2,693.7	2661.3	2580.9	2538.7	2535.1	2,579.0	2,522.4
Diluted Shares	2,844.5	2809.7	2729.4	2687.2	2683.5	2,727.4	2,670.8

Source: Company data, Morgan Stanley Research

10

Morgan Stanley | **RESEARCH**

Exhibit 10: PG Balance Sheet

Balance Sheet	FY2013	FY2014	FY2015	Sep-15	Dec-15	Mar-16	Jun-16
Assets							
Surplus Cash	0.0	0.0	0.0	0.0	0.0	0.0	0.0
Cash & Equivalents	5,947.0	8,558.0	6,836.0	7,705.0	9,403.0	7,895.0	7,102.0
Investment Securities	0.0	2,128.0	4,767.0	4,901.0	4,874.0	5,924.0	6,246.0
Receivables, Net	6,508.0	6,386.0	4,568.0	4,724.0	4,721.0	4,591.0	4,373.0
Inventories	6,909.0	6,759.0	4,979.0	5,239.0	5,125.0	4,957.0	4,716.0
Deferred Income Taxes	948.0	846.1	1,356.0	1,333.2	1,173.0	1,189.0	1,507.0
Prepaid Expenses and Other Current Assets	3,678.0	6,939.9	7,140.0	11,717.8	11,051.0	9,761.0	9,838.0
Total Current Assets	23,990.0	31,617.0	29,646.0	35,620.0	36,347.0	34,317.0	33,782.0
PP&E, Net	21,666.0	22,304.0	20,268.0	19,081.0	18,910.0	19,186.0	19,385.0
Goodwill, Net	55,188.0	52,832.0	42,430.0	37,612.0	44,157.0	44,679.0	44,350.0
Other Intangible Assets, Net	31,572.0	31,715.0	31,715.0	31,715.0	24,495.0	24,629.0	24,527.0
Other Assets	6,847.0	5,798.0	5,436.0	5,237.0	5,234.0	4,697.0	5,092.0
Total Assets	139,263.0	144,266.0	129,495.0	129,265.0	129,143.0	127,508.0	127,136.0
Liabilities							
Short-Term Debt	0.0	00.0	00.0	0.0	0.0	0.0	0.0
Notes and Loan Payable	0.0	0.0	0.0	0.0	0.0	0.0	0.0
Current Portion of Long-Term Debt	12,432.0	15,606.0	12,021.0	13,093.0	13,931.0	13,681.0	11,653.0
Accounts Payable	8,777.0	8,461.0	8,257.0	7,758.0	7,717.0	7,795.0	9,325.0
Accrued and Other Liabilities	8,828.0	9,659.0	9,512.0	10,716.0	10,405.0	9,881.0	9,792.0
Total Current Liabilities	30,037.0	33,726.0	29,790.0	31,567.0	32,053.0	31,357.0	30,770.0
Long-Term Debt	19,111.0	19,811.0	18,329.0	17,394.0	17,595.0	19,134.0	18,945.0
Deferred Income Taxes	10,827.0	11,537.0	18,326.0	17,350.0	9,257.0	9,161.0	9,113.0
Other Liabilities	10,579.0	8,487.0	00.0	00.0	7,936.0	8,003.0	10,325.0
Total Liabilities	70,554.0	73,561.0	66,445.0	66,311.0	66,841.0	67,655.0	69,153.0
Shareholders' Equity							
Preferred Stock	1,137.0	1,128.0	1,128.0	1,128.0	1,062.0	1,043.0	1,043.0
Common Stock	4,009.0	4,009.0	4,009.0	4,009.0	4,009.0	4,009.0	4,009.0
Additional Paid-In Capital	63,538.0	63,638.0	63,638.0	63,638.0	63,751.0	63,617.0	63,617.0
Retained Earnings	80,197.0	84,656.0	88,214.0	89,148.8	86,917.0	87,849.0	88,167.0
Accumulated Other Comprehensive Income (Loss)	-7,499.0	-4,461.0	-11,070.0	-11,598.8	-14,334.0	-13,642.0	-15,330.0
Reserve for ESOP Debt Retirement	-1,352.0	-1,346.0	-1,346.0	-1,346.0	-1,308.0	-1,289.0	-1,289.0
Treasury Stock	-71,966.0	-77,648.0	-82,252.0	-82,754.0	-78,469.0	-82,400.0	-82,900.0
Minority Interests	645.0	729.0	729.0	729.0	674.0	666.0	666.0
Total Shareholders' Equity	68,709.0	70,705.0	63,050.0	62,954.0	62,302.0	59,853.0	57,983.0
Total Liabilities & SE	139,263.0	144,266.0	129,495.0	129,265.0	129,143.0	127,508.0	127,136.0

Source: Company data, Morgan Stanley Research

Balance Sheet	FY2016	Sep-16 E	Dec-16 E	Mar-17 E	Jun-17 E	FY2017E	FY2018E
Assets							
Surplus Cash	0.0	0.0	0.0	0.0	163.7	163.7	1,202.8
Cash & Equivalents	7,102.0	7,102.0	7,102.0	7,895.0	7,102.0	7,102.0	7,102.0
Investment Securities	6,246.0	6,246.0	6,246.0	6,246.0	6,246.0	6,246.0	6,246.0
Receivables, Net	4,373.0	4,626.2	4,657.6	4,702.6	4,409.9	4,409.9	4,546.2
Inventories	4,716.0	5,018.3	4,955.0	4,990.7	4,673.9	4,673.9	4,774.7
Deferred Income Taxes	1,507.0	1,324.2	1,317.4	1,406.7	1,516.2	1,516.2	1,563.1
Prepaid Expenses and Other Current Assets	9,838.0	9,838.0	9,838.0	9,761.0	9,838.0	9,838.0	9,838.0
Total Current Assets	33,782.0	34,154.6	34,116.1	35,002.0	33,949.6	33,949.6	35,272.7
PP&E, Net	19,385.0	19,214.2	19,177.8	19,212.5	19,693.7	19,693.7	20,055.6
Goodwill, Net	44,350.0	44,350.0	44,350.0	44,350.0	44,350.0	44,350.0	44,350.0
Other Intangible Assets, Net	24,527.0	24,527.0	24,527.0	24,527.0	24,527.0	24,527.0	24,527.0
Other Assets	5,092.0	5,092.0	5,092.0	5,092.0	5,092.0	5,092.0	5,092.0
Total Assets	127,136.0	127,337.8	127,262.9	128,183.6	127,612.4	127,612.4	129,297.4
Liabilities							
Short-Term Debt	00.0	2,315.3	1,619.8	1,869.5	0.0	00.0	00.0
Notes and Loan Payable	0.0	0.0	0.0	0.0	0.0	0.0	0.0
Current Portion of Long-Term Debt	11,653.0	11,653.0	11,653.0	11,653.0	11,653.0	11,653.0	11,351.0
Accounts Payable	9,325.0	7,837.4	7,885.0	8,105.1	9,534.9	9,534.9	9,740.7
Accrued and Other Liabilities	9,792.0	10,577.4	10,346.9	10,196.6	9,956.2	9,956.2	10,196.1
Total Current Liabilities	30,770.0	32,383.2	31,504.7	31,824.2	31,144.1	31,144.1	31,287.8
Long-Term Debt	18,945.0	17,045.0	17,045.0	17,045.0	17,045.0	17,045.0	17,045.0
Deferred Income Taxes	9,113.0	9,113.0	9,113.0	9,113.0	9,113.0	9,113.0	9,113.0
Other Liabilities	10,325.0	10,325.0	10,325.0	10,325.0	10,325.0	10,325.0	10,325.0
Total Liabilities	69,153.0	68,866.2	67,987.7	68,307.2	67,627.1	67,627.1	67,770.8
Shareholders' Equity							
Preferred Stock	1,043.0	1,043.0	1,043.0	1,043.0	1,043.0	1,043.0	1,043.0
Common Stock	4,009.0	4,009.0	4,009.0	4,009.0	4,009.0	4,009.0	4,009.0
Additional Paid-In Capital	63,617.0	63,617.0	63,617.0	63,617.0	63,617.0	63,617.0	63,617.0
Retained Earnings	88,167.0	88,987.3	90,116.4	91,040.0	91,427.5	91,427.5	94,970.4
Accumulated Other Comprehensive Income (Loss)	-15,330.0	-14,661.7	-13,987.2	-13,309.7	-12,588.3	-12,588.3	-9,839.8
Reserve for ESOP Debt Retirement	-1,289.0	-1,289.0	-1,289.0	-1,289.0	-1,289.0	-1,289.0	-1,289.0
Treasury Stock	-82,900.0	-83,900.0	-84,900.0	-85,900.0	-86,900.0	-86,900.0	-91,650
Minority Interests	666.0	666.0	666.0	666.0	666.0	666.0	666.0
Total Shareholders' Equity	57,983.0	58,471.7	59,275.2	59,876.4	59,985.2	59,985.2	61,526.6
Total Liabilities & SE	127,136.0	127,337.8	127,262.9	128,183.6	127,612.4	127,612.4	129,297.4

Source: Company data, Morgan Stanley Research

Morgan Stanley | **RESEARCH**

Exhibit 11: PG Cash Flow Statement

Cash Flow	FY2013	FY2014	FY2015	Sep-15	Dec-15	Mar-16	Jun-16
Net Income	11,401.1	11,167.5	10,845.0	2,799.8	2,983.0	2,443.0	2,215.0
Adjustments:							
Depreciation and Amortization	2982.0	3141.0	3134.0	731.0	723.0	785.0	839.0
Stock-Based Compensation Expense	346.0	360.0	337.0	67.0	73.0	76.0	119.0
Deferred Income Taxes	-307.0	-44.0	-803.0	89.0	51.0	-568.0	-387.0
Other	-607.1	463.5	-265.0	230.2	206.0	675.0	-539.0
Changes in A/L							
Receivables	-415.0	87.0	349.0	-368.0	-120.0	359.0	164.0
Inventories	-225.0	8.0	313.0	-519.0	133.0	292.0	210.0
A/P, Accrued and Other Liabilities	1253.0	1.0	928.0	298.0	24.0	-521.0	1,484.0
Other Operating Assets and Liabilities	445.0	-1226.0	-230.0	210.0	398.0	-254.0	34.0
Cash Provided by Operations	**14,873.0**	**13,958.0**	**14,608.0**	**3,538.0**	**4,471.0**	**3,287.0**	**4,139.0**
Cash Flows from Investing Activities							
Capital Expenditures	-4,008.0	-3,848.0	-3,736.0	-532.0	-691.0	-800.0	-1,291.0
Proceeds from Asset Sales	584.0	570.0	4498.0	38.0	42.0	34.0	318.0
Payment for Acquisitions	-1145.0	-24.0	-3784.0	00.0	-948.0	762.0	00.0
Other	-1,726.0	-805.0	132.0	-52.0	704.0	-2,940.0	-219.0
Cash Used for Investing Activities	**-6,295.0**	**-4,107.0**	**-2,890.0**	**-546.0**	**-893.0**	**-2944.0**	**-1192.0**
Cash Flows from Financing Activites							
Change in Short-Term Debt	3,406.0	3304.0	-2580.0	450.0	1570.0	-485.0	-1953.0
Change in Long-Term Debt	-1,421.0	239.0	-1374.0	-537.0	19.0	2224.0	-3.0
Dividends Paid	-6,519.0	-6,911.0	-7,287.0	-1865.0	-1868.0	-1856.0	-1847.0
Purchase of Treasury Shares	-5,986.0	-6,005.0	-4,604.0	-502.0	-2001.0	-2731.0	-500.0
Proceeds From Stock Options, Other	3,449.0	2,094.0	2,816.0	483.0	533.0	1,008.0	648.0
Cash Used for Financing Activities	**-7,071.0**	**-7,279.0**	**-13,029.0**	**-1,971.0**	**-1,747.0**	**-1,840.0**	**-3,655.0**
Cash Provided by Discontinued Operations	0.0	0.0	0.0	0.0	0.0	0.0	0.0
Exchange Rate Effect on Cash / Other	4.0	39.0	-411.0	-152.0	-133.0	-11.0	-85.0
Net Increase (Decrease) in Cash and Cash Equivs	1511.0	2611.0	-1722.0	869.0	1698.0	-1508.0	-793.0
Cash and Cash Equivs, Beg	4,436.0	5,947.0	8,558.0	6,836.0	7,705.0	9,403.0	7,895.0
Cash and Cash Equivs, End	**5,947.0**	**8,558.0**	**6,836.0**	**7,705.0**	**9,403.0**	**7,895.0**	**7,102.0**

Source: Company data, Morgan Stanley Research

Cash Flow	FY2016	Sep-16 E	Dec-16 E	Mar-17 E	Jun-17 E	FY2017E	FY2018E
Net Income	10,440.8	2,683.2	2,938.6	2,705.3	2,309.0	10,636.0	11,345.1
Adjustments:							
Depreciation and Amortization	3078.0	699.2	728.0	796.1	840.2	3063.5	3114.6
Stock-Based Compensation Expense	335.0	68.3	74.5	77.5	121.4	341.7	348.5
Deferred Income Taxes	-815.0	182.8	6.7	-89.3	-109.5	-9.2	-46.9
Other	572.2	0.0	0.0	77.0	-77.0	0.0	0.0
Changes in A/L							
Receivables	35.0	-253.2	-31.4	-44.9	292.7	-36.9	-136.3
Inventories	116.0	-302.3	63.3	-35.7	316.8	42.1	-100.9
A/P, Accrued and Other Liabilities	1285.0	-702.2	-182.9	69.8	1,189.5	374.1	445.6
Other Operating Assets and Liabilities	388.0	00.0	00.0	00.0	00.0	0.0	0.0
Cash Provided by Operations	**15,435.0**	**2,375.9**	**3,596.7**	**3,555.8**	**4,883.1**	**14,411.5**	**14,969.9**
Cash Flows from Investing Activities							
Capital Expenditures	-3,314.0	-528.4	-691.6	-830.8	-1,321.3	-3,372.2	-3,476.5
Proceeds from Asset Sales	432.0					0.0	0.0
Payment for Acquisitions	-186.0					0.0	0.0
Other	-2,507.0					0.0	0.0
Cash Used for Investing Activities	**-5,575.0**	**-528.4**	**-691.6**	**-830.8**	**-1321.3**	**-3,372.2**	**-3,476.5**
Cash Flows from Financing Activites							
Change in Short-Term Debt	-418.0	2315.3	-695.5	249.7	-1869.5	0.0	-302.0
Change in Long-Term Debt	1703.0	-1900.0	0.0	0.0	0.0	-1900.0	0.0
Dividends Paid	-7,436.0	-1862.8	-1809.6	-1781.6	-1921.5	-7,375.5	-7,802.3
Purchase of Treasury Shares	-5,734.0	-1000.0	-1000.0	-1000.0	-1000.0	-4,000.0	-4,750.0
Proceeds From Stock Options, Other	2,672.0	600.0	600.0	600.0	600.0	2,400.0	2,400.0
Cash Used for Financing Activities	**-9,213.0**	**-1,847.5**	**-2,905.1**	**-1,931.9**	**-4,191.0**	**-10,875.5**	**-10,454.3**
Cash Provided by Discontinued Operations	0.0	0.0	0.0	0.0	0.0	0.0	0.0
Exchange Rate Effect on Cash / Other	-381.0	0.0	0.0	0.0	0.0	0.0	0.0
Net Increase (Decrease) in Cash and Cash Equivs	266.0	0.0	0.0	793.0	-629.3	163.7	1039.1
Cash and Cash Equivs, Beg	6,836.0	7,102.0	7,102.0	7,102.0	7,895.0	7,102.0	7,265.7
Cash and Cash Equivs, End	**7,102.0**	**7,102.0**	**7,102.0**	**7,895.0**	**7,265.7**	**7,265.7**	**8,304.8**

Source: Company data, Morgan Stanley Research

12

Morgan Stanley | **RESEARCH**

UPDATE

Valuation Methodology & Risks

CLN

Our PT is $75. We forecast 4% organic top line growth through 2016. We apply a 24x P/E multiple (implies 15x 2017e EV/EBITDA), ahead of CL's 18x NTM five-year historical average given solid organic sales growth and a higher market multiple. Our bull case is $86, based on 26.5x our bull case CY17e EPS estimate, and our bear case is $59, based on 20x our bear case CY17e EPS estimate. Key risks: (1) pricing, (2) currency movements, (3) potential Argentina devaluation risk, (4) oral care share declines, (5) commodity costs, and (6) strategic potential.

PEP.N

Our PT is $121. We assume organic sales growth of 4% in 2016-17e, driven by solid snacks growth. OM % expands by ~40 bps annually with cost savings. Assumes 23x 2017e P/E, above its 17.5x NTM 10-year average given a higher market multiple and better EPS visibility. Our bull case is $137, based on 25x our bull case 2017 EPS, and our bear case is $85, based on 18x our bear case 2017 EPS. Key risks: (1) Russia/Mexico/China volatility, (2) commodity cost and FX volatility, (3) lower than expected cost savings from the restructuring program, (4) an acceleration in competitive intensity in beverages, (5) soda taxes, and (6) macro and/or health-related topline weakness.

KO.N

Our PT is $50. We forecast 3% organic top-line growth (below the low end of KO LT guidance of 4-6%) and HSD underlying EPS growth (ex FX/bottling dilution) in 2016e after a slight reported EPS decline in 2015. We apply a 25x P/E multiple to our base case EPS, slightly above our mega-cap peers target (PEP/PG/CL) given KO's transformation to a higher growth/ROIC concentrate model supports a higher multiple. Our bull case is $57, based on 27x our bull case 2017 EPS, and our bear case is $38, based on 20x our bear case 2017 EPS. Key risks: (1) FX movements, (2) commodity costs, (3) macro volatility, (4) health and wellness pressures, (5) less productivity than expected, and (6) soda/income taxes.

Morgan Stanley | RESEARCH

Disclosure Section

The information and opinions in Morgan Stanley Research were prepared by Morgan Stanley & Co. LLC, and/or Morgan Stanley C.T.V.M. S.A., and/or Morgan Stanley Mexico, Casa de Bolsa, S.A. de C.V., and/or Morgan Stanley Canada Limited. As used in this disclosure section, "Morgan Stanley" includes Morgan Stanley & Co. LLC, Morgan Stanley C.T.V.M. S.A., Morgan Stanley Mexico, Casa de Bolsa, S.A. de C.V., Morgan Stanley Canada Limited and their affiliates as necessary.

For important disclosures, stock price charts and equity rating histories regarding companies that are the subject of this report, please see the Morgan Stanley Research Disclosure Website at www.morganstanley.com/researchdisclosures, or contact your investment representative or Morgan Stanley Research at 1585 Broadway, (Attention: Research Management), New York, NY, 10036 USA.

For valuation methodology and risks associated with any recommendation, rating or price target referenced in this research report, please contact the Client Support Team as follows: US/Canada +1 800 303-2495; Hong Kong +852 2848-5999; Latin America +1 718 754-5444 (U.S.); London +44 (0)20-7425-8169; Singapore +65 6834-6860; Sydney +61 (0)2-9770-1505; Tokyo +81 (0)3-6836-9000. Alternatively you may contact your investment representative or Morgan Stanley Research at 1585 Broadway, (Attention: Research Management), New York, NY 10036 USA.

Analyst Certification

The following analysts hereby certify that their views about the companies and their securities discussed in this report are accurately expressed and that they have not received and will not receive direct or indirect compensation in exchange for expressing specific recommendations or views in this report: Dara Mohsenian, CFA.

Unless otherwise stated, the individuals listed on the cover page of this report are research analysts.

Global Research Conflict Management Policy

Morgan Stanley Research has been published in accordance with our conflict management policy, which is available at www.morganstanley.com/institutional/research/conflictpolicies.

Important US Regulatory Disclosures on Subject Companies

As of June 30, 2016, Morgan Stanley beneficially owned 1% or more of a class of common equity securities of the following companies covered in Morgan Stanley Research: Energizer Holdings Inc., Estee Lauder Companies Inc, Newell Rubbermaid Inc., PepsiCo Inc., Tupperware Brands Corp., Weight Watchers International.

Within the last 12 months, Morgan Stanley managed or co-managed a public offering (or 144A offering) of securities of Blue Buffalo Pet Products Inc, Colgate-Palmolive Co, PepsiCo Inc., **Procter & Gamble Co.**.

Within the last 12 months, Morgan Stanley has received compensation for investment banking services from Blue Buffalo Pet Products Inc, Coca-Cola Co., Colgate-Palmolive Co, Coty Inc, PepsiCo Inc., **Procter & Gamble Co.**.

In the next 3 months, Morgan Stanley expects to receive or intends to seek compensation for investment banking services from Avon Products Inc., Blue Buffalo Pet Products Inc, Church & Dwight Co., Inc., Clorox Co, Coca-Cola Co., Colgate-Palmolive Co, Coty Inc, Edgewell Personal Care, Estee Lauder Companies Inc, Newell Rubbermaid Inc., PepsiCo Inc., **Procter & Gamble Co.**, Tupperware Brands Corp., Weight Watchers International.

Within the last 12 months, Morgan Stanley has received compensation for products and services other than investment banking services from Avon Products Inc., Church & Dwight Co., Inc., Coca-Cola Co., Colgate-Palmolive Co, Coty Inc, Edgewell Personal Care, PepsiCo Inc., **Procter & Gamble Co.**, Tupperware Brands Corp., Weight Watchers International.

Within the last 12 months, Morgan Stanley has provided or is providing investment banking services to, or has an investment banking client relationship with, the following company: Avon Products Inc., Blue Buffalo Pet Products Inc, Church & Dwight Co., Inc., Clorox Co, Coca-Cola Co., Colgate-Palmolive Co, Coty Inc, Edgewell Personal Care, Estee Lauder Companies Inc, Newell Rubbermaid Inc., PepsiCo Inc., **Procter & Gamble Co.**, Tupperware Brands Corp., Weight Watchers International.

Within the last 12 months, Morgan Stanley has either provided or is providing non-investment banking, securities-related services to and/or in the past has entered into an agreement to provide services or has a client relationship with the following company: Avon Products Inc., Church & Dwight Co., Inc., Clorox Co, Coca-Cola Co., Colgate-Palmolive Co, Coty Inc, Edgewell Personal Care, Newell Rubbermaid Inc., PepsiCo Inc., **Procter & Gamble Co.**, Tupperware Brands Corp., Weight Watchers International.

An employee, director or consultant of Morgan Stanley is a director of Estee Lauder Companies Inc. This person is not a research analyst or a member of a research analyst's household.

Morgan Stanley & Co. LLC makes a market in the securities of Avon Products Inc., Blue Buffalo Pet Products Inc, Church & Dwight Co., Inc., Clorox Co, Coca-Cola Co., Colgate-Palmolive Co, Coty Inc, Edgewell Personal Care, Energizer Holdings Inc., Estee Lauder Companies Inc, Newell Rubbermaid Inc., PepsiCo Inc., **Procter & Gamble Co.**, Tupperware Brands Corp., Weight Watchers International.

The equity research analysts or strategists principally responsible for the preparation of Morgan Stanley Research have received compensation based upon various factors, including quality of research, investor client feedback, stock picking, competitive factors, firm revenues and overall investment banking revenues. Equity Research analysts' or strategists' compensation is not linked to investment banking or capital markets transactions performed by Morgan Stanley or the profitability or revenues of particular trading desks.

Morgan Stanley and its affiliates do business that relates to companies/instruments covered in Morgan Stanley Research, including market making, providing liquidity, fund management, commercial banking, extension of credit, investment services and investment banking. Morgan Stanley sells to and buys from customers the securities/instruments of companies covered in Morgan Stanley Research on a principal basis. Morgan Stanley may have a position in the debt of the Company or instruments discussed in this report. Morgan Stanley trades or may trade as principal in the debt securities (or in related derivatives) that are the subject of the debt research report.

Certain disclosures listed above are also for compliance with applicable regulations in non-US jurisdictions.

STOCK RATINGS

Morgan Stanley uses a relative rating system using terms such as Overweight, Equal-weight, Not-Rated or Underweight (see definitions below). Morgan Stanley does not assign ratings of Buy, Hold or Sell to the stocks we cover. Overweight, Equal-weight, Not-Rated and Underweight are not the equivalent of buy, hold and sell. Investors should carefully read the definitions of all ratings used in Morgan Stanley Research. In addition, since Morgan Stanley Research contains more complete information concerning the analyst's views, investors should carefully read Morgan Stanley Research, in its entirety, and not infer the contents from the rating alone. In any case, ratings (or research) should not be used or relied upon as investment advice. An investor's decision to buy or sell a stock should depend on individual circumstances (such as the investor's existing holdings) and other considerations.

Global Stock Ratings Distribution

(as of July 31, 2016)

The Stock Ratings described below apply to Morgan Stanley's Fundamental Equity Research and do not apply to Debt Research produced by the Firm. For disclosure purposes only (in accordance with NASD and NYSE requirements), we include the category headings of Buy, Hold, and Sell alongside our ratings of Overweight, Equal-weight, Not-Rated and Underweight. Morgan Stanley does not assign ratings of Buy, Hold or Sell to the stocks we cover. Overweight, Equal-weight, Not-Rated and Underweight are not the equivalent of buy, hold, and sell but represent recommended relative weightings (see

Morgan Stanley | RESEARCH

UPDATE

definitions below). To satisfy regulatory requirements, we correspond Overweight, our most positive stock rating, with a buy recommendation; we correspond Equal-weight and Not-Rated to hold and Underweight to sell recommendations, respectively.

STOCK RATING CATEGORY	COVERAGE UNIVERSE		INVESTMENT BANKING CLIENTS (IBC)			OTHER MATERIAL INVESTMENT SERVICES CLIENTS (MISC)	
	COUNT	% OF TOTAL	COUNT	% OF TOTAL IBC	% OF RATING CATEGORY	COUNT	% OF TOTAL OTHER MISC
Overweight/Buy	1149	34%	274	38%	24%	566	35%
Equal-weight/Hold	1461	44%	351	48%	24%	729	46%
Not-Rated/Hold	77	2%	8	1%	10%	11	1%
Underweight/Sell	647	19%	95	13%	15%	289	18%
TOTAL	3,334		728			1595	

Data include common stock and ADRs currently assigned ratings. Investment Banking Clients are companies from whom Morgan Stanley received investment banking compensation in the last 12 months.

Analyst Stock Ratings

Overweight (O). The stock's total return is expected to exceed the average total return of the analyst's industry (or industry team's) coverage universe, on a risk-adjusted basis, over the next 12-18 months.

Equal-weight (E). The stock's total return is expected to be in line with the average total return of the analyst's industry (or industry team's) coverage universe, on a risk-adjusted basis, over the next 12-18 months.

Not-Rated (NR). Currently the analyst does not have adequate conviction about the stock's total return relative to the average total return of the analyst's industry (or industry team's) coverage universe, on a risk-adjusted basis, over the next 12-18 months.

Underweight (U). The stock's total return is expected to be below the average total return of the analyst's industry (or industry team's) coverage universe, on a risk-adjusted basis, over the next 12-18 months.

Unless otherwise specified, the time frame for price targets included in Morgan Stanley Research is 12 to 18 months.

Analyst Industry Views

Attractive (A): The analyst expects the performance of his or her industry coverage universe over the next 12-18 months to be attractive vs. the relevant broad market benchmark, as indicated below.

In-Line (I): The analyst expects the performance of his or her industry coverage universe over the next 12-18 months to be in line with the relevant broad market benchmark, as indicated below.

Cautious (C): The analyst views the performance of his or her industry coverage universe over the next 12-18 months with caution vs. the relevant broad market benchmark, as indicated below.

Benchmarks for each region are as follows: North America - S&P 500; Latin America - relevant MSCI country index or MSCI Latin America Index; Europe - MSCI Europe; Japan - TOPIX; Asia - relevant MSCI country index or MSCI sub-regional index or MSCI AC Asia Pacific ex Japan Index.

Stock Price, Price Target and Rating History (See Rating Definitions)

Morgan Stanley | RESEARCH

UPDATE

Coca-Cola Co. (KO.N) — As of 8/2/16 in USD
Industry : Beverages

Stock Rating History: 8/1/13 : E/I; 1/5/15 : O/I

Price Target History: 1/4/11 : NA; 10/27/14 : 41; 1/5/15 : 47; 9/3/15 : 44; 10/21/15 : 48; 3/6/16 : 50

Source: Morgan Stanley Research   Date Format : MM/DD/YY   Price Target ─·─   No Price Target Assigned (NA)
Stock Price (Not Covered by Current Analyst) ──   Stock Price (Covered by Current Analyst) ▬▬
Stock and Industry Ratings (abbreviations below) appear as ◆ Stock Rating/Industry View
Stock Ratings: Overweight (O) Equal-weight (E) Underweight (U) Not-Rated (NR) No Rating Available (NA)
Industry View: Attractive (A)   In-line (I)   Cautious (C)   No Rating (NR)

Effective January 13, 2014, the stocks covered by Morgan Stanley Asia Pacific will be rated relative to the analyst's industry (or industry team's) coverage.

Effective January 13, 2014, the industry view benchmarks for Morgan Stanley Asia Pacific are as follows: relevant MSCI country index or MSCI sub-regional index or MSCI AC Asia Pacific ex Japan Index.

16

Morgan Stanley | RESEARCH

UPDATE

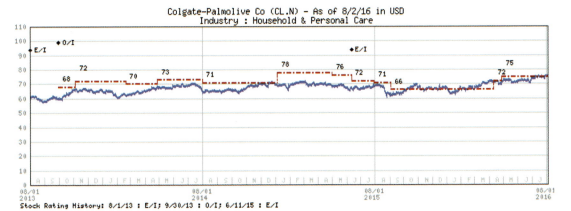

Colgate-Palmolive Co (CL.N) - As of 8/2/16 in USD
Industry : Household & Personal Care

Stock Rating History: 8/1/13 : E/I; 9/30/13 : O/I; 6/11/15 : E/I

Price Target History: 3/15/13 : NA; 9/30/13 : 68; 11/4/13 : 72; 2/19/14 : 70; 4/28/14 : 73; 7/31/14 : 71;
1/5/15 : 78; 4/30/15 : 76; 6/11/15 : 72; 7/30/15 : 71; 9/3/15 : 66; 4/10/16 : 72; 4/28/16 : 75

Source: Morgan Stanley Research   Date Format: MM/DD/YY   Price Target —·   No Price Target Assigned (NA)
Stock Price (Not Covered by Current Analyst) —   Stock Price (Covered by Current Analyst) ▬
Stock and Industry Ratings (abbreviations below) appear as ♦ Stock Rating/Industry View
Stock Ratings: Overweight (O) Equal-weight (E) Underweight (U) Not-Rated (NR) No Rating Available (NA)
Industry View: Attractive (A)   In-line (I)   Cautious (C)   No Rating (NR)

Effective January 13, 2014, the stocks covered by Morgan Stanley Asia Pacific will be rated relative to the analyst's industry
(or industry team's) coverage.

Effective January 13, 2014, the industry view benchmarks for Morgan Stanley Asia Pacific are as follows: relevant MSCI country
index or MSCI sub-regional index or MSCI AC Asia Pacific ex Japan Index.

Morgan Stanley | RESEARCH

UPDATE

PepsiCo Inc. (PEP.N) — As of 8/2/16 in USD
Industry : Beverages

Stock Rating History: 8/1/13 : O/I

Price Target History: 7/25/13 : 95; 2/14/14 : 93; 7/23/14 : 99; 10/10/14 : 103; 1/5/15 : 112; 9/3/15 : 110;
4/10/16 : 119; 7/7/16 : 121

Source: Morgan Stanley Research   Date Format : MM/DD/YY   Price Target ▬·   No Price Target Assigned (NA)
Stock Price (Not Covered by Current Analyst) ——   Stock Price (Covered by Current Analyst) ▬▬
Stock and Industry Ratings (abbreviations below) appear as ◆ Stock Rating/Industry View
Stock Ratings: Overweight (O) Equal-weight (E) Underweight (U) Not-Rated (NR) No Rating Available (NA)
Industry View: Attractive (A)   In-line (I)   Cautious (C)   No Rating (NR)

Effective January 13, 2014, the stocks covered by Morgan Stanley Asia Pacific will be rated relative to the analyst's industry
(or industry team's) coverage.

Effective January 13, 2014, the industry view benchmarks for Morgan Stanley Asia Pacific are as follows: relevant MSCI country
index or MSCI sub-regional index or MSCI AC Asia Pacific ex Japan Index.

Morgan Stanley | RESEARCH

Procter & Gamble Co. (PG.N) - As of 8/2/16 in USD
Industry : Household & Personal Care

Stock Rating History: 8/1/13 : E/I; 7/9/15 : NA/I; 9/1/15 : E/I

Price Target History: 1/20/12 : NA; 10/27/14 : 88; 1/5/15 : 96; 4/23/15 : 88; 7/9/15 : NA; 9/1/15 : 78;
10/26/15 : 85

Source: Morgan Stanley Research   Date Format : MM/DD/YY   Price Target ━╸   No Price Target Assigned (NA)
Stock Price (Not Covered by Current Analyst) ━   Stock Price (Covered by Current Analyst) ▬
Stock and Industry Ratings (abbreviations below) appear as ◆ Stock Rating/Industry View
Stock Ratings: Overweight (O) Equal-weight (E) Underweight (U) Not-Rated (NR) No Rating Available (NA)
Industry View: Attractive (A) In-line (I) Cautious (C) No Rating (NR)

Effective January 13, 2014, the stocks covered by Morgan Stanley Asia Pacific will be rated relative to the analyst's industry
(or industry team's) coverage.

Effective January 13, 2014, the industry view benchmarks for Morgan Stanley Asia Pacific are as follows: relevant MSCI country
index or MSCI sub-regional index or MSCI AC Asia Pacific ex Japan Index.

Important Disclosures for Morgan Stanley Smith Barney LLC Customers

Important disclosures regarding the relationship between the companies that are the subject of Morgan Stanley Research and Morgan Stanley Smith Barney LLC or Morgan Stanley or any of their affiliates, are available on the Morgan Stanley Wealth Management disclosure website at www.morganstanley.com/online/researchdisclosures. For Morgan Stanley specific disclosures, you may refer to www.morganstanley.com/researchdisclosures.
Each Morgan Stanley Equity Research report is reviewed and approved on behalf of Morgan Stanley Smith Barney LLC. This review and approval is conducted by the same person who reviews the Equity Research report on behalf of Morgan Stanley. This could create a conflict of interest.

Other Important Disclosures

Morgan Stanley & Co. International PLC and its affiliates have a significant financial interest in the debt securities of Avon Products Inc., Clorox Co, Coca-Cola Co., Colgate-Palmolive Co, Coty Inc, Newell Rubbermaid Inc., PepsiCo Inc., **Procter & Gamble Co.**, Tupperware Brands Corp..
Morgan Stanley Research policy is to update research reports as and when the Research Analyst and Research Management deem appropriate, based on developments with the issuer, the sector, or the market that may have a material impact on the research views or opinions stated therein. In addition, certain Research publications are intended to be updated on a regular periodic basis (weekly/monthly/quarterly/annual) and will ordinarily be updated with that frequency, unless the Research Analyst and Research Management determine that a different publication schedule is appropriate based on current conditions.
Morgan Stanley is not acting as a municipal advisor and the opinions or views contained herein are not intended to be, and do not constitute, advice within the meaning of Section 975 of the Dodd-Frank Wall Street Reform and Consumer Protection Act.
Morgan Stanley produces an equity research product called a "Tactical Idea." Views contained in a "Tactical Idea" on a particular stock may be contrary to the recommendations or views expressed in research on the same stock. This may be the result of differing time horizons, methodologies, market events, or other factors. For all research available on a particular stock, please contact your sales representative or go to Matrix at http://www.morganstanley.com/matrix.
Morgan Stanley Research is provided to our clients through our proprietary research portal on Matrix and also distributed electronically by Morgan Stanley to clients. Certain, but not all, Morgan Stanley Research products are also made available to clients through third-party vendors or redistributed to clients through alternate electronic means as a convenience. For access to all available Morgan Stanley Research, please contact your sales representative or go to Matrix at http://www.morganstanley.com/matrix.
Any access and/or use of Morgan Stanley Research is subject to Morgan Stanley's Terms of Use (http://www.morganstanley.com/terms.html). By accessing and/or using Morgan Stanley Research, you are indicating that you have read and agree to be bound by our Terms of Use (http://www.morganstanley.com/terms.html). In addition you consent to Morgan Stanley processing your personal data and using cookies in accordance with our Privacy Policy and our Global Cookies Policy (http://www.morganstanley.com/privacy_pledge.html), including for the purposes of setting your preferences and to collect readership data so that we can deliver better and more personalized service and products to you. To find out more information about how Morgan Stanley processes personal data, how we use cookies and how to reject cookies see our Privacy Policy and our Global Cookies Policy (http://www.morganstanley.com/privacy_pledge.html).
If you do not agree to our Terms of Use and/or if you do not wish to provide your consent to Morgan Stanley processing your personal data or using cookies please do not access our research.
Morgan Stanley Research does not provide individually tailored investment advice. Morgan Stanley Research has been prepared without regard to the circumstances and objectives of those who receive it. Morgan Stanley recommends that investors independently evaluate particular investments and strategies, and encourages investors to seek the advice of a financial adviser. The appropriateness of an investment or strategy will depend on an investor's

Morgan Stanley | RESEARCH

UPDATE

Morgan Stanley | RESEARCH

to such data. The Global Industry Classification Standard (GICS) was developed by and is the exclusive property of MSCI and S&P. Morgan Stanley Research, or any portion thereof may not be reprinted, sold or redistributed without the written consent of Morgan Stanley.

INDUSTRY COVERAGE: Household & Personal Care

COMPANY (TICKER)	RATING (AS OF)	PRICE* (08/02/2016)
Dara Mohsenian, CFA		
Avon Products Inc. (AVP.N)	E (10/04/2010)	$4.76
Blue Buffalo Pet Products Inc (BUFF.O)	O (10/12/2015)	$25.78
Church & Dwight Co., Inc. (CHD.N)	E (08/19/2009)	$98.17
Clorox Co (CLX.N)	U (10/17/2013)	$130.30
Colgate-Palmolive Co (CL.N)	E (06/11/2015)	$74.87
Coty Inc (COTY.N)	U (11/30/2015)	$26.86
Edgewell Personal Care (EPC.N)	E (06/04/2015)	$79.52
Energizer Holdings Inc. (ENR.N)	E (07/22/2015)	$50.94
Estee Lauder Companies Inc (EL.N)	O (12/03/2012)	$93.27
Newell Rubbermaid Inc. (NWL.N)	O (06/04/2014)	$53.82
Procter & Gamble Co. (PG.N)	E (09/01/2015)	$86.76
Tupperware Brands Corp. (TUP.N)	E (03/08/2013)	$61.65
Weight Watchers International (WTW.N)	E (08/18/2015)	$10.69

Stock Ratings are subject to change. Please see latest research for each company.
* Historical prices are not split adjusted.

Questions

Q12-1. Identify at least two applications that use forecasted financial statements.

Q12-2. In what order do we normally forecast the financial statements? Explain the logic of this order.

Q12-3. What is meant by internal consistency when applied to forecasting assumptions? Give an example of internal inconsistency.

Q12-4. What does the concept of financial statement articulation mean in the forecasting process?

Q12-5. Analysts commonly perform a sensitivity analysis following preparation of financial forecasts. What is meant by sensitivity analysis, and why is it important?

Q12-6. Cash is forecast as the last item on the balance sheet. Why is this the case?

Q12-7. In addition to recent revenues trends, what other types and sources of information can we use to help us forecast revenues?

Q12-8. Why do we refine the forecasted cash balance? How might we deal with a cash balance that is much too low compared with the company's normal cash level?

Q12-9. Identify at least three sources of additional information we could use to refine our forecast assumptions?

Q12-10. Capital expenditures are usually an important cash outflow for a company, and they figure prominently into forecasts of net operating assets. What sources of information about capital expenditures can we draw upon?

Assignments with the 🔴 logo in the margin are available in BusinessCourse.
See the Preface of the book for details.

Mini Exercises

LO2

AutoZone Inc. (AZO)

M12-11. Forecast an Income Statement

AutoZone Inc. reports the following income statements.

Consolidated Statement of Income ($ in Thousands)	12 Months Ended Aug. 27, 2016
Net sales.	$10,635,676
Cost of sales, including warehouse and delivery expenses.	5,026,940
Gross profit.	5,608,736
Operating, selling, general and administrative expenses.	3,548,341
Operating profit	2,060,395
Interest expense, net	147,681
Income before income taxes	1,912,714
Income tax expense.	671,707
Net income.	$ 1,241,007

Forecast AutoZone's 2017 income statement assuming the following income statement relations ($ in thousands). All percentages (other than sales growth and provision for income taxes) are based on percent of net sales.

Net sales growth	6%
Cost of sales, including warehouse and delivery expenses.	47.3%
Operating, selling, general and administrative expenses.	33.4%
Interest expense, net	$145,000
Income tax expense (% pretax income).	35%

M12-12. Forecast an Income Statement

Amazon.com reports the following income statements.

LO2
Amazon.com Inc.
(AMZN)

Consolidated Statements Of Operations ($ in Millions)	12 Months Ended December 31		
	2015	2014	2013
Net product sales	$ 79,268	$70,080	$60,903
Net service sales	27,738	18,908	13,549
Total net sales	107,006	88,988	74,452
Operating expenses:			
Cost of sales	71,651	62,752	54,181
Fulfillment	13,410	10,766	8,585
Marketing	5,254	4,332	3,133
Technology and content	12,540	9,275	6,565
General and administrative	1,747	1,552	1,129
Other operating expense, net	171	133	114
Total operating expenses	104,773	88,810	73,707
Income from operations	2,233	178	745
Interest income	50	39	38
Interest expense	(459)	(210)	(141)
Other income (expense), net	(256)	(118)	(136)
Total non-operating income (expense)	(665)	(289)	(239)
Income (loss) before income taxes	1,568	(111)	506
Provision for income taxes	(950)	(167)	(161)
Equity-method investment activity, net of tax	(22)	37	(71)
Net income (loss)	$ 596	$ (241)	$ 274

Forecast Amazon's 2016 income statement assuming the following income statement relations ($ in millions). All percentages (other than sales growth and provision for income taxes) are based on percent of net sales.

Net product sales growth	15%
Net service sales growth	40%
Cost of sales	67.0%
Fulfillment	12.5%
Marketing	4.9%
Technology and content	11.7%
General and administrative	1.6%
Other operating expense, net	No change
Interest income	$60
Interest expense	$520
Other income (expense), net	No change
Income tax expense (% pretax income)	38%
Equity-method investment activity, net of tax	No change

M12-13. Forecast an Income Statement

Following is the income statement for **Medtronic PLC** for the year ended April 29, 2016.

Consolidated Statements of Income ($ millions)	Apr 29, 2016	Apr 24, 2015	Apr 25, 2014
Net sales.	$28,833	$20,261	$17,005
Costs and expenses			
Cost of products sold.	9,142	6,309	4,333
Research and development expense.	2,224	1,640	1,477
Selling, general, and administrative expense.	9,469	6,904	5,847
Special charges (gains), net.	70	(38)	40
Restructuring charges, net.	290	237	78
Certain litigation charges, net.	26	42	770
Acquisition-related items.	283	550	117
Amortization of intangible assets.	1,931	733	349
Other expense, net.	107	118	181
Operating profit	5,291	3,766	3,813
Interest expense, net	955	280	108
Income from operations before income taxes	4,336	3,486	3,705
Provision for income taxes.	798	811	640
Net income.	$ 3,538	$ 2,675	$ 3,065

Use the following assumptions to prepare a forecast of the company's income statement for FY2017.

Net sales increase	22%
Cost of products sold.	31.7% of net sales
Research and development expense.	7.7% of net sales
Selling, general, and administrative expense.	32.8% of net sales
Special charges (gains), net and Certain litigation charges, net	$0
Restructuring charges, net.	75% of 2016 expense
Acquisition-related items	1.0%
Amortization of intangible assets.	No change in $ amount
Other expense, net and Interest expense, net.	No change in $ amount
Provision for income taxes.	20% of Pre-tax income

LO4

M12-14. Adjust the Cash Balance

The forecast of the income statement and balance sheet for Next Generation yields the following.

$ millions	2017 Actual	2018 Est.
Cash and cash equivalents	$ 4,558	$ 6,127
Net sales.	42,668	43,552
Marketable securities.	5,980	5,980
Long-term debt	21,930	21,485
Treasury stock	(4,561)	(4,811)

Required

a. Does forecasted cash deviate from the normal level for this company?

b. Is the deviation in part a large enough to require adjustment? Explain.

c. Suggest three ways to adjust the forecasted cash balance.

d. If we used marketable securities to adjust the cash balance, what would be the adjusted forecast for marketable securities?

e. If we used treasury stock to adjust the cash balance, what would be the adjusted forecast for treasury stock?

M12-15. Adjust the Cash Balance

We obtain the following 2018 forecasts of selected financial statement line items for Journey Company.

$ millions	2017 Actual	2018 Est.
Net sales.	$708,554	$740,439
Marketable securities	67,096	62,096
Long-term debt	346,558	308,437
Treasury stock (deducted from equity).	51,174	51,174
Cash generated by operations.		57,696
Cash used for investing		(14,908)
Cash used for financing		(54,660)
Total net change in cash.		(11,872)
Cash at beginning of period.		51,141
Cash at end of period.		$ 39,269

Required

a. Does forecasted cash deviate from the normal level for this company?

b. Is the deviation in part *a* large enough to require adjustment? Explain.

c. Identify three ways to adjust the forecasted cash balance.

d. Fill in the blanks in the following statement of cash flows *assuming long-term debt is used* to adjust the forecasted cash balance:

> Cash generated by operations. . . . .
> Cash used for investing . . . .
> Cash used for financing . . . .   _____
> Total change in cash. . . . .
> Cash at beginning of period. . . . . . .   _____
> Cash at end of period. . . . .

e. Fill in the blanks in the following statement of cash flows *assuming marketable securities are used* to adjust the forecasted cash balance:

> Cash generated by operations. . . . .
> Cash used for investing . . . .
> Cash used for financing . . . .   _____
> Total change in cash. . . . .
> Cash at beginning of period. . . . . . .   _____
> Cash at end of period. . . . .

M12-16. Forecast the Balance Sheet

Following is the balance sheet for **Medtronic PLC** for the year ended April 29, 2016.

Consolidated Balance Sheets ($ millions)	Apr. 29, 2016	Apr. 24, 2015
Current assets		
Cash and cash equivalents	$ 2,876	$ 4,843
Investments	9,758	14,637
Accounts receivable	5,562	5,112
Inventories	3,473	3,463
Tax assets	697	1,335
Prepaid expenses and other current assets	1,234	1,454
Total current assets	23,600	30,844
Property, plant, and equipment, net	4,841	4,699
Goodwill	41,500	40,530
Other intangible assets, net	26,899	28,101
Long-term tax assets	1,383	774
Other assets	1,559	1,737
Total assets	$99,782	$106,685
Current liabilities		
Short-term borrowings	$ 993	$ 2,434
Accounts payable	1,709	1,610
Accrued compensation	1,712	1,611
Accrued income taxes	566	935
Deferred tax liabilities	—	119
Other accrued expenses	2,185	2,464
Total current liabilities	7,165	9,173
Long-term debt	30,247	33,752
Long-term accrued compensation and retirement benefits	1,759	1,535
Long-term accrued income taxes	2,903	2,476
Long-term deferred tax liabilities	3,729	4,700
Other long-term liabilities	1,916	1,819
Total liabilities	47,719	53,455
Shareholders' equity		
Ordinary shares	—	—
Retained earnings	53,931	54,414
Accumulated other comprehensive (loss) income	(1,868)	(1,184)
Total shareholders' equity	52,063	53,230
Total liabilities and shareholders' equity	$99,782	$106,685

Required

Use the following assumptions to forecast the company's balance sheet for FY2017.

Forecasted FY2017 net income	$4,972 million
Forecasted FY2017 net sales.	$35,176 million
Accounts receivable.	19.3% of net sales
Inventories	12.0% of net sales
Tax assets.	2.4% of net sales
Prepaid expenses and other current assets.	4.3% of net sales
Long-term tax assets	4.8% of net sales
Other assets.	5.4% of net sales
Accounts payable.	5.9% of net sales
Accrued compensation	5.9% of net sales
Accrued income taxes	2.0% of net sales
Other accrued expenses	7.6% of net sales
Long-term accrued income taxes	10.1% of net sales
Long-term deferred tax liabilities	12.9% of net sales
Other long-term liabilities	6.6% of net sales
Investments	No change in $ amount
Goodwill	No change in $ amount
Long-term accrued compensation and retirement benefits.	No change in $ amount
Ordinary shares	No change in $ amount
Accumulated other comprehensive (loss) income	No change in $ amount
Property, plant, and equipment, net in FY2015	$4,699 million
CAPEX in FY2016.	$1,046 million
Depreciation expense in FY2016	$890 million
Amortization expense in FY2016	$1,931 million
Dividends in FY2016 (use dividend payout ratio to forecast dividends). . . .	$2,139 million
Current maturities of debt due in FY2017	$993 million
Current maturities of debt due in FY2018	$6,176 million

M12-17. Adjust the Income Statement

LO6

eBay Inc. reported the following in its 2015 Form 10-K related to its investment in **PayPal**.

eBay Inc. (EBAY)

PayPal Holdings Inc. (PYPL)

> **Discontinued Operations** On June 26, 2015, our Board approved the separation of PayPal. . . . We have classified the results of PayPal as discontinued operations in our consolidated statement of income for all periods presented. Additionally, the related assets and liabilities associated with the discontinued operations in the prior year consolidated balance sheet are classified as discontinued operations. In connection with the Distribution, we reviewed our capital allocation strategy to ensure that each of Paypal and eBay would be well capitalized at Distribution. As part of this strategy, we contributed approximately $3.8 billion of cash to PayPal.

What adjustment(s) should we consider before forecasting eBay's 2016 income? How would you treat the cash given to PayPal?

M12-18. Refine Assumptions for PPE Forecast

LO6

Refer to the **Medtronic PLC** financial information in E12-25 (pertaining to FY2016).

Medtronic PLC (MDT)

Required

a. Use the financial statements along with the additional information below to forecast property, plant and equipment, net for FY2017.

CAPEX in FY2016.	$1,046 million
Depreciation expense in FY2016	890 million

b. Suppose the company discloses in a press release that accompanies its year-end SEC filing that anticipated CAPEX for FY2017 is $1.5 billion. Use this guidance to refine your forecast of property, plant and equipment, net for FY2017.

M12-19. Refine Assumptions for Dividend and Retained Earnings Forecast

Refer to the Medtronic PLC financial information in E12-25 (pertaining to FY2016).

Required

a. Use the financial statements along with the additional information below to forecast retained earnings for FY2017.

Forecasted net income.	$4,972 million
Dividends to shareholders in FY2016.	2,139 million

b. Suppose the MD&A section of the Form 10-K and additional guidance from the company reveals the following additional information.

	2017 Est.	2016 Actual	2015 Actual
Dividends per share	$1.72	$1.52	$1.22

At FY2016 year-end (April 29, 2016), the company had approximately 1,400 million shares issued and outstanding. Use this information to refine your forecast of retained earnings for FY2017. Why might the two forecasted amounts differ? Which is more accurate?

LO6

M12-20. Use Segment Information to Refine Sales Forecast

To forecast sales growth for FY2018 for a publicly traded company in the retail sector, we begin with the following historical sales information.

$ millions	2017	2016	2015	2014	2013
Net sales.	$46,021	$39,865	$37,536	$36,012	$34,553

Require

a. Determine the sales-growth rate (in percentage) for 2014 to 2017. What trend do we observe?
b. If we were to use the four-year average sales growth to forecast 2018 sales, what rate would we use?
c. The annual report reveals that 2016 included a 53rd week (as is common for retailers, every four years) and that the company acquired a smaller company during that year. Sales for the newly acquired company were included in the consolidated income statement from the date of acquisition, which amounted to $5,235 million. Use this information to refine the sales-growth rate. (*Hint:* Consider multiplying sales for a 53-week year by 52/53 to get an apples-to-apples comparison with numbers from 52-week years.)

Exercises

LO2, 3, 4
AutoZone Inc. (AZO)

E12-21. Analyze, Forecast, and Interpret Income Statement and Balance Sheet

Following are the income statements and balance sheets of AutoZone Inc.

AUTOZONE INC. Consolidated Statements of Income	
$ thousands	12 Months Ended Aug. 27, 2016
Net sales.	$10,635,676
Cost of sales, including warehouse and delivery expenses.	5,026,940
Gross profit.	5,608,736
Operating, selling, general and administrative expenses.	3,548,341
Operating profit	2,060,395
Interest expense, net	147,681
Income before income taxes	1,912,714
Income tax expense.	671,707
Net income.	$ 1,241,007

AUTOZONE INC. Consolidated Balance Sheet	
In thousands, except par value	**Aug. 27, 2016**
Current assets	
Cash and cash equivalents	$ 189,734
Accounts receivable	287,680
Merchandise inventories	3,631,916
Other current assets	130,243
Total current assets	4,239,573
Property and equipment, net	3,733,254
Goodwill	391,887
Deferred income taxes	36,855
Other long-term assets	198,218
Total assets	$8,599,787
Current liabilities	
Accounts payable	$4,095,854
Accrued expenses and other	551,625
Income taxes payable	42,841
Total current liabilities	4,690,320
Long-term debt	4,924,119
Deferred income taxes	284,500
Other long-term liabilities	488,386
Stockholders' deficit	
Preferred stock, authorized 1,000 shares; no shares issued	
Common stock, par value $0.01 per share, authorized 200,000 shares; 30,329 shares issued and 29,118 shares outstanding in 2016 and 32,098 shares issued and 30,659 shares outstanding in 2015	303
Additional paid-in capital	1,054,647
Retained deficit	(1,602,186)
Accumulated other comprehensive loss	(307,529)
Treasury stock, at cost	(932,773)
Total stockholders' deficit	(1,787,538)
Liabilities and stockholders' deficit	$8,599,787

a. Forecast AutoZone's 2017 income statement and balance sheet using the following relations ($ in thousands). All percentages (other than sales growth and provision for income taxes) are based on percent of net sales.

Net sales growth	6%
Cost of sales, including warehouse and delivery expenses	47.3%
Operating, selling, general and administrative expenses	33.4%
Interest expense, net	$145,000
Income tax expense (% pretax income)	35%
Accounts receivable	2.7%
Merchandise inventories	34.1%
Other current assets	1.2%
Accounts payable	38.5%
Accrued expenses and other	5.2%
Income taxes payable	0.4%

- CAPEX for 2017 will be 4.6% of 2017 Net sales and depreciation will be 8.3% of Property and equipment, net at the start of the fiscal year, which was $3,733,254 thousand.
- Goodwill, Deferred income taxes, Other long-term liabilities, AOCI, and Treasury stock will not change during the year.
- Other long-term assets include intangible assets. The 10-K reports that the 2017 amortization expense for intangibles will be $8,482 thousand.
- Long-term debt will decrease by $1,597,500 in 2017, per the 10-K.

- • The company will continue its stock repurchases. Assume that during 2017, AutoZone will repurchase 1 million shares at an average price of $750 per share. The company will retire these shares and reduce Common Stock by the par value ($0.01 per share). Assume that these shares were originally issued at an average price of $35 per share.
- • The company does not pay dividends.

b. What does the forecasted adjustment to balance the accounting equation from part *a* reveal to us about the forecasted cash balance and related financing needs of the company? Explain.

LO7

AutoZone Inc. (AZO)

E12-22. Forecast the Statement of Cash Flows

Refer to the AutoZone Inc. financial information in E12-21. Prepare a forecast of FY2017 statement of cash flows.

LO2, 3, 4

Amazon.com Inc. (AMZN)

Homework
MBC

E12-23. Analyze, Forecast, and Interpret Both Income Statement and Balance Sheet

Following are the income statements and balance sheets of Amazon.com Inc.

AMAZON.COM INC. Consolidated Statements Of Operations		
$ millions	Dec. 31, 2015	Dec. 31, 2014
Net product sales	$ 79,268	$ 70,080
Net service sales	27,738	18,908
Total net sales	107,006	88,988
Operating expenses		
Cost of sales	71,651	62,752
Fulfillment	13,410	10,766
Marketing	5,254	4,332
Technology and content	12,540	9,275
General and administrative	1,747	1,552
Other operating expense (income), net	171	133
Total operating expenses	104,773	88,810
Income from operations	2,233	178
Interest income	50	39
Interest expense	(459)	(210)
Other income (expense), net	(256)	(118)
Total non-operating income (expense)	(665)	(289)
Income (loss) before income taxes	1,568	(111)
Provision for income taxes	(950)	(167)
Equity-method investment activity, net of tax	(22)	37
Net income (loss)	$ 596	$ (241)

AMAZON.COM INC. Consolidated Balance Sheets		
In millions, except par value	Dec. 31, 2015	Dec. 31, 2014
Current assets		
Cash and cash equivalents	$15,890	$14,557
Marketable securities	3,918	2,859
Inventories	10,243	8,299
Accounts receivable, net and other	6,423	5,612
Total current assets	36,474	31,327
Property and equipment, net	21,838	16,967
Goodwill	3,759	3,319
Other assets	3,373	2,892
Total assets	$65,444	$54,505

continued

	Dec. 31, 2015	Dec. 31, 2014
Current liabilities		
Accounts payable...	$20,397	$16,459
Accrued expenses and other...........................	10,384	9,807
Unearned revenue	3,118	1,823
Total current liabilities..................................	33,899	28,089
Long-term debt	8,235	8,265
Other long-term liabilities..............................	9,926	7,410
Stockholders' equity		
Preferred stock, $0.01 par value: Authorized shares–500		
Issued and outstanding shares–none...............	0	0
Common stock, $0.01 par value: Authorized shares–5,000		
Issued shares–494 and 488 Outstanding shares–471 and 465	5	5
Treasury stock, at cost..................................	(1,837)	(1,837)
Additional paid-in capital...............................	13,394	11,135
Accumulated other comprehensive loss	(723)	(511)
Retained earnings	2,545	1,949
Total stockholders' equity	13,384	10,741
Total liabilities and stockholders' equity.............	$65,444	$54,505

a. Forecast Amazon's 2016 income statement and balance sheet using the forecast assumptions, which are expressed as a percentage of total net sales unless otherwise indicated ($ in millions).

Net product sales growth..	15%
Net service sales growth	40%
Cost of sales..	67.0%
Fulfillment...	12.5%
Marketing..	4.9%
Technology and content..	11.7%
General and administrative...	1.6%
Interest income...	$60
Interest expense..	$520
Income tax expense (% pretax income)...........................	38%
Inventories	9.6%
Accounts receivable, net and other	6.0%
Other assets...	3.2%
Accounts payable...	19.1%
Accrued expenses and other......................................	9.7%
Unearned revenue	2.9%
Other long-term liabilities...	9.3%

- Forecast no change in the following income statement accounts: Other operating expense, Other income (expense); and Equity method investment activity.

- Forecast no change in the following balance sheet accounts: Marketable securities, Goodwill, Preferred stock, Common stock, Treasury stock, APIC, and AOCL.

- Assume that in 2016, CAPEX will be 4.3% of Sales and depreciation expense will be 28.9% of the PPE balance at the start of the year.

- The company will repay $238 million of long-term debt in 2016.

- The company pays no dividends.

b. What does the forecasted adjustment to balance the accounting equation from part a reveal to us about the forecasted cash balance and related financing needs of the company? Explain.

E12-24. Forecast the Statement of Cash Flows

Refer to the Amazon.com Inc. financial information from E12-23. Prepare a forecast of its FY2016 statement of cash flows.

LO7
Amazon.com Inc. (AMZN)

E12-25. Forecast Income Statement and Balance Sheet

Following are the income statements and balance sheets for **Medtronic PLC** for the year ended April 29, 2016.

Consolidated Statements of Income, 12 Months Ended ($ millions)	Apr. 29, 2016	Apr. 24, 2015	Apr. 25, 2014
Net sales..................................	$28,833	$20,261	$17,005
Costs and expenses			
Cost of products sold.......................	9,142	6,309	4,333
Research and development expense..........	2,224	1,640	1,477
Selling, general, and administrative expense....	9,469	6,904	5,847
Special charges (gains), net.................	70	(38)	40
Restructuring charges, net...................	290	237	78
Certain litigation charges, net...............	26	42	770
Acquisition-related items....................	283	550	117
Amortization of intangible assets.............	1,931	733	349
Other expense, net........................	107	118	181
Operating profit..........................	5,291	3,766	3,813
Interest expense, net......................	955	280	108
Income from operations before income taxes ...	4,336	3,486	3,705
Provision for income taxes..................	798	811	640
Net income..............................	$ 3,538	$ 2,675	$ 3,065

Consolidated Balance Sheets ($ millions)	Apr. 29, 2016	Apr. 24, 2015
Current assets		
Cash and cash equivalents...............................	$ 2,876	$ 4,843
Investments...	9,758	14,637
Accounts receivable....................................	5,562	5,112
Inventories...	3,473	3,463
Tax assets..	697	1,335
Prepaid expenses and other current assets.................	1,234	1,454
Total current assets....................................	23,600	30,844
Property, plant, and equipment, net.......................	4,841	4,699
Goodwill...	41,500	40,530
Other intangible assets, net.............................	26,899	28,101
Long-term tax assets...................................	1,383	774
Other assets..	1,559	1,737
Total assets..	$99,782	$106,685
Current liabilities		
Short-term borrowings..................................	$ 993	$ 2,434
Accounts payable......................................	1,709	1,610
Accrued compensation.................................	1,712	1,611
Accrued income taxes..................................	566	935
Deferred tax liabilities..................................	—	119
Other accrued expenses................................	2,185	2,464
Total current liabilities.................................	7,165	9,173
Long-term debt..	30,247	33,752
Long-term accrued compensation and retirement benefits......	1,759	1,535
Long-term accrued income taxes.........................	2,903	2,476
Long-term deferred tax liabilities.........................	3,729	4,700
Other long-term liabilities...............................	1,916	1,819
Total liabilities..	47,719	53,455

continued

Consolidated Balance Sheets ($ millions)	Apr. 29, 2016	Apr. 24, 2015
Shareholders' equity		
Ordinary shares	—	—
Retained earnings	53,931	54,414
Accumulated other comprehensive (loss) income	(1,868)	(1,184)
Total shareholders' equity	52,063	53,230
Total liabilities and shareholders' equity.	$99,782	$106,685

Required

a. Use the following assumptions to prepare a forecast of the company's income statement and balance sheet for fiscal 2017.

Net sales increase	22%
Cost of products sold.	31.7% of net sales
Research and development expense.	7.7% of net sales
Selling, general, and administrative expense.	32.8% of net sales
Special charges (gains), net and Certain litigation charges, net	$0
Restructuring charges, net.	75% of 2016 expense
Acquisition-related items	1.0% of net sales
Amortization of intangible assets	No change in $ amount
Other expense, net and Interest expense, net	No change in $ amount
Provision for income taxes.	20% of Pre-tax income
Accounts receivable.	19.3% of net sales
Inventories	12.0% of net sales
Tax assets.	2.4% of net sales
Prepaid expenses and other current assets.	4.3% of net sales
Long-term tax assets	4.8% of net sales
Other assets.	5.4% of net sales
Accounts payable.	5.9% of net sales
Accrued compensation	5.9% of net sales
Accrued income taxes	2.0% of net sales
Other accrued expenses	7.6% of net sales
Long-term accrued income taxes	10.1% of net sales
Long-term deferred tax liabilities	12.9% of net sales
Other long-term liabilities.	6.6% of net sales
Investments	No change in $ amount
Goodwill.	No change in $ amount
Long-term accrued compensation and retirement benefits.	No change in $ amount
Ordinary shares	No change in $ amount
Accumulated other comprehensive (loss) income	No change in $ amount
Property, plant, and equipment, net in FY2015	$4,699 million
CAPEX in FY2016.	$ 1,046 million
Depreciation expense in FY2016	$890 million
Dividends in FY2016 (use dividend payout ratio to forecast dividends) . . .	$ 2,139 million
Current maturities of debt due in FY2017	$993 million
Current maturities of debt due in FY2018	$6,176 million

b. What does the forecasted adjustment to balance the accounting equation from part *a* reveal to us about the forecasted financing needs of the company? Explain.

E12-26. **Forecast the Statement of Cash Flows**

Refer to the Medtronic PLC financial information in E12-25.

Required

Use the information to forecast Medtronic's FY2017 statement of cash flows.

LO7
Medtronic PLC (MDT)

MBC

LO4   **E12-27.** **Refine Cash Balance and Consider Capital Structure**

Consider the following actual FY2017 data and a forecast of FY2018 selected balance sheet and income statement numbers.

$ millions	FY2017 Actual	FY2018 Est.
Net sales.	$29,009	$32,102
Total assets.	14,592	16,051
Total liabilities.	8,755	9,923
Total equity.	5,837	6,128
Cash.	2,918	4,378
Marketable securities.	730	730
Total liabilities (including long-term debt).	8,755	9,923
Treasury stock	(2,189)	(2,627)

Required

a. Calculate the company's normal cash level as a percentage of sales.
b. Determine the amount of adjustment needed to return cash to a normal level. Is an adjustment warranted? Explain.
c. Compute the liabilities-to-equity ratio for the company's current year (FY2017) and using the forecasted FY2018 numbers. What do we observe?
d. Adjust marketable securities so the forecasted cash balance is at its normal level. What affect does this have on the forecasted liabilities-to-equity ratio?
e. Adjust long-term debt so the forecasted cash balance is at its normal level. What effect does this have on the forecasted liabilities-to-equity ratio?
f. Adjust treasury stock so the forecasted cash balance is at its normal level. What effect does this have on the forecasted liabilities-to-equity ratio?
g. Adjust both long-term debt and marketable securities so as to adjust the forecasted cash balance. In so doing, make sure we preserve the company's liabilities-to-equity ratio. (*Hint:* Use "Goal Seek" under the "What-If Analysis" in Excel to determine the proportion of long-term debt versus treasury stock needed to ensure the forecasted liabilities-to-equity ratio remains at its historical level.)
h. Adjust both long-term debt and treasury stock so as to adjust the forecasted cash balance. In so doing, make sure we preserve the company's liabilities-to-equity ratio. (*Hint:* Use "Goal Seek" under the "What-If Analysis" in Excel to determine the proportion of long-term debt versus treasury stock needed to ensure the forecasted liabilities-to-equity ratio remains at its historical level.)

LO2, 3   **E12-28.** **Analyze, Forecast, and Interpret Income Statement and Balance Sheet**

Following are the income statement and balance sheet of Whole Foods Market Inc.

WHOLE FOODS MARKET INC. Consolidated Statements of Operations		
Fiscal Years Ended (in millions)	**Sept 25, 2016**	**Sept 27, 2015**
Sales.	$15,724	$15,389
Cost of goods sold and occupancy costs	10,313	9,973
Gross profit.	5,411	5,416
Selling, general and administrative expenses	4,477	4,472
Pre-opening expenses.	64	67
Relocation, store closures, and lease termination costs	13	16
Operating income.	857	861
Interest expense.	(41)	—
Investment and other income.	11	17
Income before income taxes	827	878
Provision for income taxes.	320	342
Net income.	$ 507	$ 536

In millions	September 25, 2016	September 27, 2015

WHOLE FOODS MARKET INC.
Consolidated Statements of Operations

Assets
Current assets

Cash and cash equivalents	$ 351	$ 237
Short-term investments—available-for-sale securities	379	155
Restricted cash	122	127
Accounts receivable	242	218
Merchandise inventories	517	500
Prepaid expenses and other current assets	167	108
Deferred income taxes	197	199
Total current assets	1,975	1,544
Property and equipment, net of accumulated depreciation and amortization	3,442	3,163
Long-term investments—available-for-sale securities	—	63
Goodwill	710	710
Intangible assets, net of accumulated amortization	74	79
Deferred income taxes	100	144
Other assets	40	38
Total assets	$6,341	$5,741

Liabilities and Shareholders' Equity
Current liabilities

Current installments of long-term debt and capital lease obligations	$ 3	$ 3
Accounts payable	307	295
Accrued payroll, bonus, and other benefits due team members	407	436
Dividends payable	43	45
Other current liabilities	581	473
Total current liabilities	1,341	1,252
Long-term capital lease obligations, less current installments	1,048	62
Deferred lease liabilities	640	587
Other long-term liabilities	88	71
Total liabilities	3,117	1,972

Shareholders' equity

Common stock, no par value, 1,200 shares authorized; 377.0 and 377.1 shares issued; 318.3 and 348.9 shares outstanding at 2016 and 2015, respectively	2,933	2,904
Common stock in treasury, at cost, 58.7 and 28.2 shares at 2016 and 2015, respectively	(2,026)	(1,124)
Accumulated other comprehensive loss	(32)	(28)
Retained earnings	2,349	2,017
Total shareholders' equity	3,224	3,769
Total liabilities and shareholders' equity	$6,341	$5,741

Required

a. Forecast the 2017 income statement for Whole Foods using the following forecast assumptions, which are expressed as a percentage of sales unless otherwise noted ($ in millions).

Sales growth.	1%
Cost of goods sold and occupancy costs	65.6%
Selling, general and administrative expenses	28.5%
Pre-opening expenses	0.4%
Relocation, store closure and lease termination costs	$0
Interest expense.	No change
Investment and other income.	No change
Provision for income taxes as a percentage of pretax income	37%

b. Forecast the 2017 balance sheet for Whole Foods using the following forecast assumptions ($ in millions).

Accounts receivable/Sales.	1.8%
Merchandise inventories/Sales	3.3%
Prepaid expenses and other current assets/Sales.	1.1%
Deferred income taxes (current assets)/Sales	1.3%
Deferred income taxes (noncurrent assets)/Sales	0.6%
Accounts payable/Sales.	2.0%
Accrued payroll, bonus and other benefits due team members/Sales	2.6%
Other current liabilities/Sales	3.7%
Depreciation expense as a percentage of PPE, net, at start of the year	15.0%
CAPEX and development of new properties (all PPE) as a percentage of Sales.	5.0%
Amortization of intangible assets	$6
Dividends payable as a percentage of dividends.	25.0%
Long-term debt repayment due in 2017	$3
Long-term debt repayment due in 2018	$65
Increase in treasury stock in 2017	$200
Dividends as percentage of net income.	30.0%

Assume no change for goodwill, other assets, deferred lease liabilities, other long-term liabilities, common stock, and AOCL.

c. What does the forecasted adjustment to balance the accounting equation from part a reveal to us about the forecasted cash balance and related financing needs of the company?

LO7
Whole Foods Market Inc. (WFM)

E12-29. Forecast the Statement of Cash Flows

Refer to the **Whole Foods Market Inc.** financial information from E12-28. Prepare a forecast of its FY2017 statement of cash flows.

LO8
Cisco Systems Inc. (CSCO)

E12-30. Projecting NOPAT and NOA Using Parsimonious Forecasting Method

Following are **Cisco Systems'** sales, net operating profit after tax (NOPAT), and net operating assets (NOA) for its year ended July 31, 2016 ($ millions).

Sales.	$49,247
Net operating profit after tax (NOPAT)	10,575
Net operating assets (NOA)	26,472

Use the parsimonious method to forecast Cisco's sales, NOPAT, and NOA for years 2017 through 2020 using the following assumptions.

Sales growth per year.	1% for 2017 and 2% thereafter
Net operating profit margin (NOPM).	21.5%
Net operating asset turnover (NOAT), based on NOA at July 31, 2016. . . .	1.86

E12-31. Projecting NOPAT and NOA Using Parsimonious Forecasting Method

LO8

3M Company (MMM)

Following are **3M Company**'s sales, net operating profit after tax (NOPAT), and net operating assets (NOA) for its fiscal year ended 2015 ($ millions).

Net sales.	$30,274
Net operating profit after tax (NOPAT)	4,918
Net operating assets (NOA)	20,502

Use the parsimonious method to forecast 3M's sales, NOPAT, and NOA for fiscal years 2016 through 2020 using the following assumptions.

Net sales growth per year	0.5%
Net operating profit margin (NOPM).	16.2%
Net operating asset turnover (NOAT), based on NOA at fiscal year-end	1.48

Problems

P12-32. Forecast the Income Statement, Balance Sheet, and Statement of Cash Flows

LO2, 3, 7

Cisco Systems Inc. (CSCO)

Following are fiscal year financial statements of **Cisco Systems Inc.**

CISCO SYSTEMS INC. Consolidated Statements of Operations		
Years Ended (in millions)	**July 30, 2016**	**July 25, 2015**
Revenue		
Product	$37,254	$37,750
Service	11,993	11,411
Total revenue	49,247	49,161
Cost of sales		
Product	14,161	15,377
Service	4,126	4,103
Total cost of sales	18,287	19,480
Gross margin	30,960	29,681
Operating expenses		
Research and development	6,296	6,207
Sales and marketing	9,619	9,821
General and administrative	1,814	2,040
Amortization of purchased intangible assets	303	359
Restructuring and other charges	268	484
Total operating expenses	18,300	18,911
Operating income	12,660	10,770
Interest income	1,005	769
Interest expense	(676)	(566)
Other income (loss), net	(69)	228
Interest and other income (loss), net	260	431
Income before provision for income taxes	12,920	11,201
Provision for income taxes	2,181	2,220
Net income	$10,739	$ 8,981

CISCO SYSTEMS INC. Consolidated Balance Sheets		
In millions, except par value	July 30, 2016	July 25, 2015
Assets		
Current assets		
Cash and cash equivalents..........................	$ 7,631	$ 6,877
Investments	58,125	53,539
Accounts receivable, net of allowance for doubtful accounts of $249 at July 30, 2016 and $302 at July 25, 2015..................................	5,847	5,344
Inventories	1,217	1,627
Financing receivables, net	4,272	4,491
Other current assets..............................	1,627	1,490
Total current assets.............................	78,719	73,368
Property and equipment, net	3,506	3,332
Financing receivables, net	4,158	3,858
Goodwill..	26,625	24,469
Purchased intangible assets, net....................	2,501	2,376
Deferred tax assets	4,299	4,454
Other assets.....................................	1,844	1,516
Total assets....................................	$121,652	$113,373
Liabilities and Equity		
Current liabilities		
Short-term debt	$ 4,160	$ 3,897
Accounts payable.................................	1,056	1,104
Income taxes payable.............................	517	62
Accrued compensation............................	2,951	3,049
Deferred revenue	10,155	9,824
Other current liabilities	6,072	5,476
Total current liabilities	24,911	23,412
Long-term debt	24,483	21,457
Income taxes payable	925	1,876
Deferred revenue	6,317	5,359
Other long-term liabilities..........................	1,431	1,562
Total liabilities	58,067	53,666
Equity		
Cisco shareholders' equity:		
Preferred stock, no par value: 5 shares authorized; none issued and outstanding...........................	—	—
Common stock and additional paid-in capital, $0.001 par value: 20,000 shares authorized; 5,029 and 5,085 shares issued and outstanding at July 30, 2016 and July 25, 2015, respectively	44,516	43,592
Retained earnings.................................	19,396	16,045
Accumulated other comprehensive income (loss)	(326)	61
Total Cisco shareholders' equity....................	63,586	59,698
Noncontrolling interests	(1)	9
Total equity	63,585	59,707
Total liabilities and equity	$121,652	$113,373

Required

Forecast Cisco's fiscal 2017 income statement, balance sheet, and statement of cash flows; round forecasts to $ millions. (*Hint*: Forecast total revenues by projecting a continuation of year-over-year percentage changes for each revenue category Cisco includes in its income statement [rounded to three decimal places. That is 0.0510034 would be rounded to 5.1%]).

- Cisco's long-term debt footnote reports the following current maturities of long-term debt.

Fiscal Years Ending ($ millions)	2017	2018	2019
Debt maturities.	$4,150	$4,750	$5,250

- Cisco includes the current maturities with "Short-term debt" on its balance sheet.
- In its 2016 financial statements, Cisco reports capital expenditures of $1,146 million, dividends of $4,750 million, depreciation of $1,847 million, which it includes in various income statement line items including cost of sales and general and administrative expense, and amortization of $303 million, which it reports separately. Use this information to forecast PPE and Purchased intangible assets.

Identify all financial statement relations estimated and assumptions made; estimate forecasted income statement and balance sheet relations as a percentage of total revenue, rounded to three decimal places (such as General and administrative/Total revenue is 0.03685 would be rounded to 3.7%). Assume no change for interest income and expense, goodwill, other long-term assets, investments, nonoperating income, common stock, accumulated other comprehensive income, and noncontrolling interests. What do the forecasts imply about the financing needs of Cisco?

P12-33. **Forecast the Income Statement, Balance Sheet, and Statement of Cash Flows**
Following are the financial statements of **Nike Inc.**

LO2, 3, 7

Nike Inc. (NKE)

NIKE INC. Consolidated Income Statement		
For Year Ended ($ millions)	**May 31, 2016**	**May 31, 2015**
Revenues	$32,376	$30,601
Cost of sales.	17,405	16,534
Gross profit.	14,971	14,067
Demand creation expense	3,278	3,213
Operating overhead expense.	7,191	6,679
Total selling and administrative expense	10,469	9,892
Interest expense (income), net	19	28
Other (income) expense, net	(140)	(58)
Income before income taxes	4,623	4,205
Income tax expense.	863	932
Net income.	$ 3,760	$ 3,273

NIKE INC. Consolidated Balance Sheets		
$ millions	**May 31, 2016**	**May 31, 2015**
Current assets		
Cash and equivalents.	$ 3,138	$ 3,852
Short-term investments	2,319	2,072
Accounts receivable, net	3,241	3,358
Inventories	4,838	4,337
Prepaid expenses and other current assets.	1,489	1,968
Total current assets	15,025	15,587
Property, plant and equipment, net	3,520	3,011
Identifiable intangible assets, net.	281	281
Goodwill	131	131
Deferred income taxes and other assets	2,439	2,587
Total assets.	$21,396	$21,597

continued

continued from previous page

$ millions	May 31, 2016	May 31, 2015
Current liabilities		
Current portion of long-term debt	$ 44	$ 107
Notes payable	1	74
Accounts payable	2,191	2,131
Accrued liabilities	3,037	3,949
Income taxes payable	85	71
Total current liabilities	5,358	6,332
Long-term debt	2,010	1,079
Deferred income taxes and other liabilities	1,770	1,479
Total liabilities	9,138	8,890
Shareholders' equity		
Class A convertible common stock	0	0
Class B common stock	3	3
Capital in excess of stated value	7,786	6,773
Accumulated other comprehensive income	318	1,246
Retained earnings	4,151	4,685
Total shareholders' equity	12,258	12,707
Total liabilities and shareholders' equity	$21,396	$21,597

Required

Forecast Nike's FY2017 income statement, balance sheet, and statement of cash flows.

- Round the revenue growth rate to the nearest whole percent.
- Round forecasts to $ millions.
- Assume no change for interest expense or income, other expense or income, short-term investments, goodwill, notes payable, common stock, capital in excess of stated value, and accumulated other comprehensive income.
- For FY2016, capital expenditures are $1,143 million, depreciation expense is $649 million, amortization is $13 million, and dividends are $1,022 million.
- Footnotes reveal that the current portion of long-term debt due in 2018 is $6 million.
- Estimate forecast assumptions for all other balance sheet and income statement items as a percentage of Revenues, rounded to three decimal places (for example, Inventories/Revenues is 0.14943 or 14.9%).

What do the forecasts imply about Nike's cash balance and related financing needs for the upcoming year?

LO2, 3, 7
Home Depot Inc. (HD) **P12-34.   Forecast the Income Statement, Balance Sheet, and Statement of Cash Flows**

Following are the financial statements of Home Depot Inc. for fiscal year ended January 31, 2016.

HOME DEPOT INC. Consolidated Income Statement			
For Fiscal Year Ended ($ millions)	Jan. 31, 2016	Feb. 01, 2015	Feb. 02, 2014
Net sales	$88,519	$83,176	$78,812
Cost of sales	58,254	54,787	51,897
Gross profit	30,265	28,389	26,915
Operating expenses:			
Selling, general and administrative	16,801	16,280	16,122
Depreciation and amortization	1,690	1,640	1,627
Total operating expenses	18,491	17,920	17,749
Operating income	11,774	10,469	9,166
Interest and investment income	(166)	(337)	(12)
Interest expense	919	830	711
Interest and other, net	753	493	699
Earnings before provision for income taxes	11,021	9,976	8,467
Provision for income taxes	4,012	3,631	3,082
Net earnings	$ 7,009	$ 6,345	$ 5,385

HOME DEPOT INC. Consolidated Balance Sheet		
Fiscal Year End ($ millions, except par value))	**Jan. 31, 2016**	**Feb. 1, 2015**
Current Assets		
Cash and cash equivalents	$ 2,216	$ 1,723
Receivables, net	1,890	1,484
Merchandise inventories	11,809	11,079
Other current assets	1,078	1,016
Total current assets	16,993	15,302
Net property and equipment	22,191	22,720
Goodwill	2,102	1,353
Other assets	1,263	571
Total assets	$42,549	$39,946
Current Liabilities		
Short-term debt	$ 350	$ 290
Accounts payable	6,565	5,807
Accrued salaries and related expenses	1,515	1,391
Sales taxes payable	476	434
Deferred revenue	1,566	1,468
Income taxes payable	34	35
Current installments of long-term debt	77	38
Other accrued expenses	1,943	1,806
Total current liabilities	12,526	11,269
Long-term debt, excluding current installments	20,888	16,869
Other long-term liabilities	1,965	1,844
Deferred income taxes	854	642
Total liabilities	36,233	30,624
Stockholders' Equity		

Common Stock, par value $0.05; authorized: 10 billion shares;
    issued: 1.772 billion shares at January 31, 2016 and 1.768 billion
    shares at February 1, 2015; outstanding: 1.252 billion shares at
    January 31, 2016 and 1.307 billion shares at February 1, 2015
	88	88

Paid-in capital	9,347	8,885
Retained earnings	30,973	26,995
Accumulated other comprehensive loss	(898)	(452)
Treasury stock, at cost, 520 million shares at January 31, 2016 and 461 million shares at February 1, 2015	(33,194)	(26,194)
Total stockholders' equity	6,316	9,322
Total liabilities and stockholders' equity	$42,549	$39,946

Required

Forecast Home Depot's FY2016 income statement, balance sheet, and statement of cash flows.

- Round all $ forecasts to millions
- Round the revenue growth rate to the nearest whole percent.
- Assume no change for investments, goodwill, interest income and expense, short-term debt, common stock and paid-in capital, and accumulated other comprehensive loss.
- Capital expenditures were $1,503 million, and dividends were $3,031 million for 2015.
- Forecast depreciation as a percentage of PPE, net at the start of the year. Use the historical 2015 rate to forecast 2016.
- Home Depot's long-term debt footnote indicates maturities of long-term debt of $110 million for fiscal 2017.
- Assume the company will repurchase $4 billion of common stock in the coming year.
- Estimate forecast assumptions for all other balance sheet and income statement items as a percentage of revenues, rounded to three decimal places (for example, Merchandise inventories/Net sales is 0.13341 or 13.3%).

Overall: What is our assessment of Home Depot's financial condition over the next year?

P12-35.   Two-Year-Ahead Forecast of Financial Statements

Following are the financial statements of **Target Corporation** from its FY2015 annual report.

TARGET CORPORATION Consolidated Statements of Operations			
	12 Months Ended		
$ millions	Jan. 30, 2016	Jan. 31, 2015	Feb. 01, 2014
Sales.	$73,785	$72,618	$71,279
Cost of sales.	51,997	51,278	50,039
Gross margin	21,788	21,340	21,240
Selling, general and administrative expenses	14,665	14,676	14,465
Depreciation and amortization	2,213	2,129	1,996
Gain on sale	(620)	0	(391)
Earnings from continuing operations before interest expense and income taxes	5,530	4,535	5,170
Net interest expense	607	882	1,049
Earnings from continuing operations before income taxes	4,923	3,653	4,121
Provision for income taxes.	1,602	1,204	1,427
Net earnings from continuing operations.	3,321	2,449	2,694
Discontinued operations, net of tax	42	(4,085)	(723)
Net earnings/(loss)	$ 3,363	$ (1,636)	$ 1,971

TARGET CORPORATION Consolidated Statements of Financial Position		
$ millions	Jan. 30, 2016	Jan. 31, 2015
Assets		
Cash and cash equivalents, including short-term investments of $3,008 and $1,520	$ 4,046	$ 2,210
Inventory.	8,601	8,282
Assets of discontinued operations.	322	1,058
Other current assets.	1,161	2,074
Total current assets	14,130	13,624
Property and equipment, net	25,217	25,952
Noncurrent assets of discontinued operations	75	717
Other noncurrent assets.	840	879
Total assets.	$40,262	$41,172
Liabilities and shareholders' investment		
Accounts payable.	$ 7,418	$ 7,759
Accrued and other current liabilities.	4,236	3,783
Current portion of long-term debt and other borrowings.	815	91
Liabilities of discontinued operations.	153	103
Total current liabilities.	12,622	11,736
Long-term debt and other borrowings.	11,945	12,634
Deferred income taxes	823	1,160
Noncurrent liabilities of discontinued operations.	18	193
Other noncurrent liabilities	1,897	1,452
Total noncurrent liabilities.	14,683	15,439

continued

$ millions	Jan. 30, 2016	Jan. 31, 2015
Shareholders' investment		
Common stock.	50	53
Additional paid-in capital	5,348	4,899
Retained earnings	8,188	9,644
Accumulated other comprehensive loss		
Pension and other benefit liabilities	(588)	(561)
Currency translation adjustment and cash flow hedges	(41)	(38)
Total shareholders' investment.	12,957	13,997
Total liabilities and shareholders' investment.	$40,262	$41,172

Required

Forecast Target's FY2016 and FY2017 income statements and balance sheets. Use the following assumptions and data:

- Assume that sales grow by 3% each year.
- Forecast income statement and balance sheet relations as a percentage of sales and round to three decimal places. For example, Cost of sales/Sales = 0.70471 or 70.5%). Use the same forecast assumptions for both years.
- Assume no change for: interest expense, common stock, additional paid-in capital, and accumulated other comprehensive loss.
- Target's long-term debt footnote indicates maturities of $751 million in FY2016, $2,251 million in FY2017, and $201 million in FY2018.
- Assume that in FY2016, CAPEX will be 1.9% of sales and depreciation expense will be 8.4% of the PPE balance at the start of the year.
- Target paid $1,362 million in dividends in FY2015.
- Assume that Target disposes of the net assets from discontinued operations (assets less liabilities) in FY2016 for proceeds of $350 million.
- Assume that the company buys back common stock of $2 billion in FY2016 are retires the stock. (*Hint:* Retained earnings are reduced by the cost of the stock buy back.) No stock buybacks happen in FY2017.

P12-36. **Sensitivity Analysis of Forecasted Income Statement**

LO1, 2, 7

First Solar Inc. (FSLR)

Following is the income statement for **First Solar Inc.** for the year ended December 31, 2015.

Consolidated Statements of Operations			
	12 Months Ended		
$ thousands	Dec. 31, 2015	Dec. 31, 2014	Dec. 31, 2013
Net sales.	$3,578,995	$3,391,187	$3,309,616
Cost of sales.	2,659,728	2,566,246	2,444,984
Gross profit.	919,267	824,941	864,632
Operating expenses			
Research and development	130,593	143,969	134,300
Selling, general, and administrative	255,192	253,827	270,261
Production start-up	16,818	5,146	2,768
Restructuring and asset impairments	—	—	86,896
Total operating expenses.	402,603	402,942	494,225
Operating income.	516,664	421,999	370,407
Foreign currency (loss) gain, net	(6,868)	(1,461)	893
Interest income.	22,516	18,030	16,752
Interest expense, net	(6,975)	(1,982)	(1,884)
Other expense, net.	(5,502)	(4,485)	(5,189)
Income before taxes and equity in earnings of unconsolidated affiliates	519,835	432,101	380,979
Income tax benefit (expense)	6,156	(31,188)	(30,098)
Equity in earnings (loss) of unconsolidated affiliates, net of tax	20,430	(4,949)	(163)
Net income.	$ 546,421	$ 395,964	$ 350,718

Required

a. Compute the effective tax rate for First Solar for each of the three years presented (to four decimal places such as 0.1234 or 12.34%). What do we observe? What might explain this rate?

b. Use the following assumptions to forecast the FY2016 income statement.

Net sales growth	6%
Cost of sales.	74.0% of net sales
Research and development	3.6% of net sales
Selling, general, and administrative	7.1% of net sales
Production startup	0.5% of net sales
Restructuring and asset impairments	$0
Foreign currency (loss) gain, net	$0
Interest income, interest expense, and other expense	No change in $
Income tax benefit (expense)	Effective rate for 2015
Equity in earnings (loss) of unconsolidated affiliates, net of tax.	Increase by 10% over FY2015

c. Compute the percent change in net income from actual FY2015 to the FY2016 forecasted net income.

d. Perform a sensitivity analysis by changing the effective tax rate and seeing the change in net income. Instead of using the FY2015 effective tax rate, use the average effective tax rate that prevailed over the 2013 and 2014 period. Again, compute the tax rate to four decimal places. Compute the percent change in net income from actual FY2015 to the FY2016 forecasted net income. How sensitive is net income to the change in tax rate?

e. Perform a sensitivity analysis by changing the growth rate for net sales. Forecast the income statement for a range of growth rates, from 5% to 7% in 50-basis-point increments (i.e. 5%, 5.5%, 6%, 6.5%, and 7%). For this part, use an effective tax rate of 7.56%.

f. Perform a sensitivity analysis by changing the cost of sales percent to determine the effect on net income (not the entire income statement, only net income). Vary the cost of sales percent up and down by 50 basis points from 74%. For this part, use an effective tax rate of 7.56% and include the entire range of sales growth rates from 5% to 7%. That is, generate a table that shows net income for three cost-of-sales percentages and five sales-growth rates. For each cell, compute the percent change in net income from actual FY2015 to the FY2016 forecasted net income.

IFRS Applications

LO8

Telstra Corporation Limited

I12-37. Forecast Using the Parsimonious Method

Telstra Corporation Limited is an Australian telecommunications and media company that builds and provides land-based and mobile telecom services along with Internet and pay television products. The company is Australia's largest 3G- and 4G-enabled mobile network, covering 99.3% of the Australian population. The following data are computed using numbers from the company's 2016 annual report (in millions of Australian dollars).

Sales in 2015	$26,112
Sales in 2016	27,050
Net operating profit after tax (NOPAT)	4,318
Operating assets	37,100
Operating liabilities.	9,128

Required

a. Forecast NOPAT and NOA for 2017 through 2020.

b. Determine sales growth, net operating profit margin (NOPM), and net operating asset turnover (NOAT) using historical numbers and round to three decimal places.

(This ongoing project began in Module 1 and continues through most of the book; even if previous segments were not completed, the requirements are still applicable to any business analysis.) This module describes methods commonly used to forecast financial statements. The module shows how to forecast a complete set of financial statements (for one or more years). The module concludes with a parsimonious forecast of select balance sheet and income statement metrics. A project can include both types of forecasts. We can use the full set of financial statements to analyze the company's near-term future performance and position. We can then use the parsimonious forecast for longer-term forecasts as inputs for valuation models that estimate the company's stock price. Importantly, use a spreadsheet for the forecasting process. The SEC website has "interactive data" for annual reports—these are spreadsheet-like arrays that can be copied into a spreadsheet. Also, many companies include on their investor relations page an Excel version of their financial statements. Define as many cells as possible with formulas, and reference income statement totals to the related balance sheet accounts. To balance the balance sheet, define the cash account to be equal to the difference between forecasted assets and liabilities plus stockholders' equity.

1. *Forecasting Preliminaries* Begin with the adjusted set of financial statements that reflect the company's net operating assets and its operating income that we expect to persist into the future. This requires that we exclude one-time items and adjust other items to reflect anticipated levels of ongoing activities.

2. *Model Assumptions and Inputs* The assumptions we use critically impact forecasted numbers. Be as thorough as possible in research and analysis in determining model inputs. The most critical assumption is sales growth. Before we begin, adjust any fiscal years to take care of the "13th week" (or 53rd week) problem. Then, use all the reported years' sales numbers to compute historical growth numbers. Observe any trends. If the company reports segment sales, compute growth of each segment and compare it with total sales growth. We should forecast each segment separately if growth differs by segment. Read the company's MD&A, the footnotes, and any guidance the company voluntarily provides. Obtain an industry report and, determine a consensus about sales expectations and the cost environment. As discussed in the module, we assume most costs (including COGS and SGA) will not deviate from their historical percentages unless there is evidence to suggest otherwise. Again, scour the footnotes. In the end, use sound judgment and remember that forecasted numbers are subjective.

3. *Forecast the Income Statement* Use the sales growth assumption to forecast sales for the next fiscal year. Use cost-level assumptions to forecast all the operating expenses. At this first stage, we typically leave non-operating expenses and revenues unchanged from prior-year dollar levels. We return to fine-tune these after we forecast the balance sheet. Forecast a preliminary tax expense and net income. We need those numbers to complete the balance sheet.

4. *Forecast the Balance Sheet* Use the percentage of sales approach to forecast each operating asset and liability, and follow the method described in the module to forecast PPE and intangible assets. Certain operating assets and liabilities will be forecasted to remain unchanged year over year unless we learn otherwise from the financial statements. Forecast debt using the information about scheduled debt maturities. Pay careful attention to forecasting dividends and any stock repurchases or issuances.

5. *Forecast the Statement of Cash Flows* We construct a statement of cash flows from the company's current balance sheet (from the Form 10-K or annual report) and the forecasted balance sheet. The net income number forecasted will also tie in. Remember that this statement is a mechanical operation, requiring no assumptions or new calculations.

Solutions to Review Problems

Review 12-1—Solution

a. We forecast financial statements in the following order: income statement, balance sheet, statement of cash flows. This order is important because income statement activity determines many balance sheet accounts, including retained earnings. Cash flows cannot be determined without net income (which determines cash from operating activities) and balance sheet accounts (which affect all three types of cash flows).

b. The first, and most crucial, income statement amount forecasted is revenue.

c. The following forecasted expenses are related to forecasted revenue.
   - Cost of goods sold—directly.
   - Selling, general, and administrative expense—directly.
   - Depreciation—indirectly to the extent that revenue drives new PPE purchases.
   - Income tax—indirectly via pretax income, which increases with revenue.

   d. The following forecasted balance sheet accounts are related to forecasted revenue.
- Receivables.
- Inventories.
- Prepaid expenses.
- Land, buildings, and equipment—to the extent that revenue drives new PPE purchases.
- Accounts payable—related to cost of sales, which is determined by revenue.
- Other current liabilities—those liabilities that are related to accrued operating expenses are directly determined by revenue.

   e. A sensitivity analysis allows us to identify how our forecasted numbers are affected by changes in forecasting assumptions. Importantly, by changing assumptions one at a time, we can gauge how sensitive our forecasts are to each assumption. This helps identify critical assumptions and points out where we need to pay special attention to the assumptions to refine them to make sure they are as precise as possible.

Review 12-2—Solution

Income Statement ($ millions)	FY2016 Actual	% of Sales	Computations	FY2017 Est.
Net sales.	$16,563.1	100.0%	$16,563.1 × 0.985*	$16,314.7
Cost of sales.	10,733.6	64.8%	$16,314.7 × 62.8%**	10,245.6
Selling, general, and administrative expenses.	3,118.9	18.8%	$16,314.7 × 18.3%***	2,985.6
Divestitures (gain).	(148.2)	(0.9)%	none	—
Restructuring, impairment, and other exit costs . . .	151.4	0.9%	$151.4 × 50%	75.7
Operating profit	2,707.4	16.3%	subtotal	3,007.8
Interest, net	303.8	1.8%	no change	303.8
Earnings before income taxes and after-tax earnings from joint ventures	2,403.6	14.5%	subtotal	2,704.0
Income taxes	755.2	4.6%	$2,704.0 × 31.4%	849.1
After-tax earnings from joint ventures	88.4	0.5%	no change	88.4
Net earnings, including earnings attributable to redeemable and noncontrolling interests	1,736.8	10.5%	subtotal	1,943.3
Net earnings attributable to redeemable and noncontrolling interests	39.4	0.2%	no change	39.4
Net earnings attributable to General Mills	$ 1,697.4	10.2%		$ 1,903.9

* Sales are expected to decrease by 1.5%; to forecast sales, we multiply FY2016 sales by (1 − 0.015) or 0.985.

** COGS as a percentage of sales is expected to decrease by 200 basis points; to forecast COGS, we multiply sales by 62.8% (computed as 0.648 − 0.02).

*** SGA as a percentage of sales is expected to decrease by 50 basis points; to forecast SGA, we multiply sales by 18.3% (computed as 0.188 − 0.005).

Review 12-3—Solution

Balance Sheets ($ millions)	2016 Actual	% of Sales	Computations	2017 Est.
Current assets				
Cash and cash equivalents	$ 763.7	4.6%	Plug	$ (37.0)
Receivables	1,360.8	8.2%	$16,314.7 × 8.2%	1,337.8
Inventories	1,413.7	8.5%	$16,314.7 × 8.5%	1,386.7
Prepaid expenses and other current assets....	399.0	2.4%	$16,314.7 × 2.4%	391.6
Total current assets	3,937.2	23.8%	subtotal	3,079.1
Land, buildings, and equipment[1]	3,743.6	22.6%	Add CAPEX and subtract depreciation.	3,888.6
Goodwill	8,741.2	52.8%	no change	8,741.2
Other intangible assets.	4,538.6	27.4%	Decrease by amortization of $28	4,510.6
Other assets	751.7	4.5%	$16,314.7 × 4.5%	734.2
Total assets.	$21,712.3	131.1%	subtotal	$20,953.7
Current liabilities				
Accounts payable.	$ 2,046.5	12.4%	$16,314.7 × 12.4%	$ 2,023.0
Current portion of long-term debt	1,103.4	6.7%	−$1,103.4 + $604.7	604.7
Notes payable	269.8	1.6%	no change	269.8
Other current liabilities	1,595.0	9.6%	$16,314.7 × 9.6%	1,566.2
Total current liabilities.	5,014.7	30.3%	subtotal	4,463.7
Long-term debt	7,057.7	42.6%	−$604.7	6,453.0
Deferred income taxes	1,399.6	8.5%	$16,314.7 × 8.5%	1,386.7
Other liabilities	2,087.6	12.6%	$16,314.7 × 12.6%	2,055.7
Total liabilities	15,559.6	93.9%	subtotal	14,359.1
Redeemable interest value.	845.6	5.1%	no change	845.6
Stockholders' equity				
Common stock.	75.5	0.5%	no change	75.5
Additional paid-in capital	1,177.0	7.1%	no change	1,177.0
Retained earnings[2]	12,616.5	76.2%	Add net income and subtract dividends	13,319.0
Common stock in treasury, at cost	(6,326.6)	(38.2)%	Additional repurchases of $300	(6,626.6)
Accumulated other comprehensive loss	(2,612.2)	(15.8)%	no change	(2,612.2)
Total stockholders' equity	4,930.2	29.8%	subtotal	5,332.7
Noncontrolling interests	376.9	2.3%	Add forecasted amount from income statement	416.3
Total equity	5,307.1	32.0%	subtotal	5,749.0
Total liabilities and equity	$21,712.3	131.1%	subtotal	$20,953.7

[1] Depreciation in FY2016 as a percentage of FY2015 PPE was 15.3%, computed as $580.1/$3,783.3. We compute FY2017 depreciation expense as follows: 15.3% × $3,743.6 = $572.8.
CAPEX in FY2016 as a percentage of FY2016 sales was 4.4% computed as $729.3/$16,563.1. We compute CAPEX for FY2017 as follows: FY2017 sales of $16,314.7 × 4.4% = $717.8.
Land, buildings, and equipment = $3,743.6 + $717.8 − $572.8 = $3,888.6.

[2] Dividends in FY2016 were $1,071.7, which was 63.1%, of net earnings attributable to General Mills. For FY2017, dividends will be $1,201.4, computed as FY2017 net income of $1,903.9 × 63.1%.
Retained earnings = $12,616.5 + $1,903.9 − $1,201.4 = $13,319.0

Review 12-4—Solution

a. General Mills' historical cash balance as a percentage of sales is 4.6% ($763.7 million/$16,563.1 million).

b. For General Mills in 2017, a normal cash balance would be 4.6% of sales or $750.5 million, computed as forecasted FY2017 sales of $16,314.7 million × 4.6%. The forecasted cash amount of $(37.0) deviates from the norm by $787.5 million. This seems to warrant an adjustment because the balance sheet cannot report a negative cash balance.

c. To adjust the cash balance, we can increase long-term debt by about $787.5 million. This will bring cash to the normal level of $750.5 million and long-term debt to $7,240.5 million.

d. The next most likely means to adjust the cash balance would be to issue more stock. Because General Mills does not report any marketable securities on its balance sheet, the liquidation of securities is not an avenue for raising additional cash.

Review 12-5—Solution

Income Statement ($ millions)	2017 Est.	% of Sales	Computations	2018 Est.
Net sales..............................	$16,314.7	100.0%	$16,314.7 × 1.02	$16,641.0
Cost of sales........................	10,245.6	62.8%	$16.641.0 × 62.8%	10,450.5
Selling, general, and administrative expenses.....	2,985.6	18.3%	$16.641.0 × 18.3%	3,045.3
Divestitures (gain).....................	—		none	—
Restructuring, impairment, and other exit costs ...	75.7	0.5%	none	—
Operating profit	3,007.8	18.4%	subtotal	3,145.2
Interest, net	303.8	1.9%	no change	303.8
Earnings before income taxes and after-tax earnings from joint ventures................	2,704.0	16.6%	subtotal	2,841.4
Income taxes	849.1	5.2%	$2,841.4 × 31.4%	892.2
After-tax earnings from joint ventures	88.4	0.5%	no change	88.4
Net earnings, including earnings attributable to redeemable and noncontrolling interests	1,943.3	11.9%	subtotal	2,037.6
Net earnings attributable to redeemable and noncontrolling interests	39.4	0.2%	no change	39.4
Net earnings attributable to General Mills	$ 1,903.9	11.7%	subtotal	$ 1,998.2

Balance Sheets ($ millions)	2017 Est.	% of Sales	Computations	2018 Est.
Current assets				
Cash and cash equivalents	$ 750.5	4.6%	Plug	$ 877.0
Receivables	1,337.8	8.2%	$16,641.0 × 8.2%	1,364.6
Inventories	1,386.7	8.5%	$16,641.0 × 8.5%	1,414.5
Prepaid expenses and other current assets.......	391.6	2.4%	$16,641.0 × 2.4%	399.4
Total current assets	3,866.6	23.7%	subtotal	4,055.5
Land, buildings, and equipment[1]	3,888.6	23.8%	Add CAPEX and subtract depreciation	4,025.8
Goodwill........................	8,741.2	53.6%	no change	8,741.2
Other intangible assets.....................	4,510.6	27.6%	Decrease by amortization of $28	4,482.6
Other assets......................	734.2	4.5%	$16,641.0 × 4.5%	748.8
Total assets......................	$21,741.2	133.3%	subtotal	$22,053.9
Current liabilities				
Accounts payable.......................	$ 2,023.0	12.4%	$16,641.0 × 12.4%	$ 2,063.5
Current portion of long-term debt	604.7	3.7%	− $604.7 + $1,150.4	1,150.4
Notes payable	269.8	1.7%	no change	269.8
Other current liabilities	1,566.2	9.6%	$16,641.0 × 9.6%	1,597.5
Total current liabilities......................	4,463.7	27.4%	subtotal	5,081.2
Long-term debt	7,240.5	44.4%	− $1150.4	6,090.1
Deferred income taxes.....................	1,386.7	8.5%	$16,641.0 × 8.5%	1,414.5
Other liabilities	2,055.7	12.6%	$16,641.0 × 12.6%	2,096.8
Total liabilities.........................	15,146.6	92.8%	subtotal	14,682.6
Redeemable interest value...................	845.6	5.2%	no change	845.6
Stockholders' equity				
Common stock........................	75.5	0.5%	no change	75.5
Additional paid-in capital	1,177.0	7.2%	no change	1,177.0
Retained earnings[2]......................	13,319.0	81.6%	Add Net income and subtract dividends	14,056.3
Common stock in treasury, at cost	(6,626.6)	(40.6)%	no change	(6,626.6)
Accumulated other comprehensive loss	(2,612.2)	(16.0)%	no change	(2,612.2)
Total stockholders' equity	5,332.7	32.7%	subtotal	6,070.0
Noncontrolling interests.....................	416.3	2.6%	Add forecasted amount from income statement	455.7
Total equity.........................	5,749.0	35.2%	subtotal	6,525.7
Total liabilities and equity...................	$21,741.2	133.3%	subtotal	$22,053.9

[1] We compute CAPEX for FY2018 as: FY2018 sales of $16,641.0 × 4.4% = $732.2 million. We compute FY2018 depreciation expense as: 15.3% × $3,888.6 million = $595.0 million.
Land, buildings, and equipment = $3,888.6 + $732.2 − $595.0 = $4,025.8.

[2] Dividends are $1,260.9, computed as FY2018 net income of $1,998.2 × 63.1%.
Retained earnings = $13,319 + $1,998.2 − $1,260.9 = $14,056.3.

Review 12-6—Solution

a.

$ millions	FY2016 Actual Sales	Estimated Growth Rate	FY2017 Est. Sales
Meals	$ 2,393.9	(5.5)%	$2,262.2
Cereal	2,312.8	1.5%	2,347.5
Snacks	2,094.3	0.5%	2,104.8
Baking products	1,903.4	(1.5)%	1,874.8
Yogurt and other	1,302.7	(3.0)%	1,263.6
Total U.S. retail segment	$10,007.1		$9,852.9

b. The overall growth rate for the total U.S. retail segment is −1.54%, which is computed as [($9,852.9 million/$10,007.1 million) − 1]. This growth rate implies that sales are expected to decrease by 1.54% in FY2017.

c.

In millions		
Shares issued at FY2016 year-end	754.6	shares
Less shares in treasury at FY2016 year-end	(157.8)	shares
Shares outstanding during Q1 and Q2 of FY2017	596.8	shares
Less shares repurchased in FY2017	(5.0)	shares
Shares outstanding during Q3 and Q4 of FY2017	591.8	shares
Q1 and Q2—shares outstanding	596.8	shares
Q1 and Q2 forecasted dividends	$ 572.9	
Q3 and Q4—shares outstanding	591.8	shares
Q3 and Q4 forecasted dividends	$ 568.1	
Total forecasted dividends	$1,141.0	

Review 12-7—Solution

Statement of Cash Flows		
For Fiscal Year Ended 2017 ($ millions)	**Computations**	**2017 Est.**
Net cash flow from operating		
Net earnings, including earnings attributable to redeemable and noncontrolling interests. . . .		$1,943.3
Addback: depreciation expense.		572.8
Addback: amortization expense.		28.0
Decrease in receivables	$1,360.8 − $1,337.8	23.0
Decrease in inventories.	$1,413.7 − $1,386.7	27.0
Decrease in prepaid expenses and other current assets	$399.0 − $391.6	7.4
Decrease in other assets	$751.7 − $734.2	17.5
Decrease in accounts payable	$2,023.0 − $2,046.5	(23.5)
Decrease in other current liabilities.	$1,566.2 − $1,595.0	(28.8)
Decrease in deferred income taxes	$1,386.7 − $1,399.6	(12.9)
Decrease in other liabilities.	$2,055.7 − $2,087.6	(31.9)
Net cash from operating activities		2,521.9
Net cash flow from investing		
Capital expenditures		(717.8)
Net cash from investing activities.		(717.8)
Net cash flow from financing		
Dividends		(1,201.4)
Change in current maturities of long-term debt.		(498.7)
Change in long-term debt		(604.7)
Purchase of treasury shares.		(300.0)
Net cash from financing activities		2,604.8
Net change in cash.		(800.7)
Beginning cash.		763.7
Ending cash		$ (37.0)

Review 12-8—Solution

$ millions	2016	2017E	2018E	2019E	2020E
Net sales growth		(1.5)%	2%	2%	2%
Net sales unrounded . .	$16,563.1	**$16,314.65**	**$16,640.94**	**$16,973.76**	**$17,313.24**
		($16,563.1 × 0.985)	($16,314.65 × 1.02)	($16,640.94 × 1.02)	($16,973.76 × 1.02)
Net sales rounded	$16,563.1	**$16,314.7**	**$16,640.9**	**$16,973.8**	**$17,313.2**
NOPAT	$ 1,928.2	**$1,892.5**	**$1,930.3**	**$1,969.0**	**$2,008.3**
		($16,314.7 × 11.6%)	($16,640.9 × 11.6%)	($16,973.8 × 11.6%)	($17,313.2 × 11.6%)
NOA	$13,819.9	**$13,595.6**	**$13,867.4**	**$14,144.8**	**$14,427.7**
		($16,314.7/1.2)	($16,640.9/1.2)	($16,973.8/1.2)	($17,313.2/1.2)

Module **13**

Using Financial Statements for Valuation

Learning Objectives

LO1 Identify equity valuation models and explain the information required to value equity securities. (p. 13-3)

LO2 Describe and apply the discounted free cash flow model to value equity securities. (p. 13-5)

LO3 Describe and apply the residual operating income model to value equity securities. (p. 13-9)

LO4 Explain how equity valuation models can inform managerial decisions. (p. 13-11)

PG

Market cap: $225,670 mil
Revenues: $65,299 mil
Net income: $10,604 mil
Operating cash flow: $15,435 mil

What is the relation between Procter & Gamble's operating performance and its stock price? Traditional finance theory posits that stock price is positively related to the company's free cash flow (FCF) typically defined as net cash flow from operating activities, net of interest expense, less capital expenditures. Over the past five years, Procter & Gamble's free cash flow and stock price have tracked closely, as the graphic below illustrates. While the relation between the FCF and stock price is not perfect, a larger sample of companies would confirm that a strong, positive association exists.

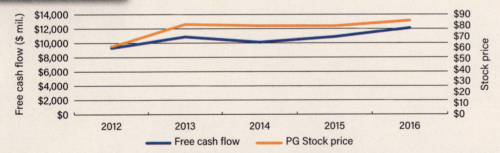

This module focuses on valuing equity securities and we describe two approaches. First, we consider the traditional finance theory of equity valuation and examine the discounted free cash flow (DCF) model to value a firm's stock. Second, we introduce the residual operating income (ROPI) valuation model that draws on net operating profit after tax (NOPAT) and net operating assets (NOA). As we will see, the ROPI model yields the same stock price as the DCF model (when the firm is in a steady-state).

While the ROPI model has certain desirable properties, its real value lies in the insights the model provides about how the company is being managed. The ROPI model makes clear what drives firm value—insights that are relevant to internal and external stakeholders. Employees at all levels of an organization, whether public or private, should understand the factors that create shareholder value so that they can effectively manage those factors. For many senior managers, stock value serves as a scorecard; successful managers are those who better understand the factors affecting that scorecard. Variants of the ROPI model are used extensively by equity analysts, management consulting companies, and firms that design management compensation systems. [Source: *Procter & Gamble 10-K*, 2016]

© iStock

Road Map

LO	Learning Objective | Topics	Page	eLecture	Guided Example	Assignments
13-1	**Identify equity valuation models and explain the information required to value equity securities.** Dividend Discount Model :: Discounted Cash Flow Model :: Residual Operating Income Model :: Valuation Model Inputs	13-3	e13–1	Review 13-1	1, 2, 4, 9, 13, 16, 18, 20, 21, 22, 24, 27, 28, 31, 32
13-2	**Describe and apply the discounted free cash flow model to value equity securities.** DCF Model Structure :: Steps in Applying the DCF Model :: Illustrating the DCF Model	13-5	e13–2	Review 13-2	3, 11, 13, 16, 18, 20, 22, 24, 27, 29, 31, 33, 35
13-3	**Describe and apply the residual operating income model to value equity securities.** ROPI Model Structure :: Steps in Applying the ROPI Model :: Illustrating the ROPI Model	13-9	e13–3	Review 13-3	5, 6, 7, 10, 12, 14, 15, 17, 19, 23, 24, 28, 30, 32, 34
13-4	**Explain how equity valuation models can inform managerial decisions.** Managerial Insights :: Assessment of Valuation Models	13-11	e13–4	Review 13-4	8, 15, 25, 26

Module Organization

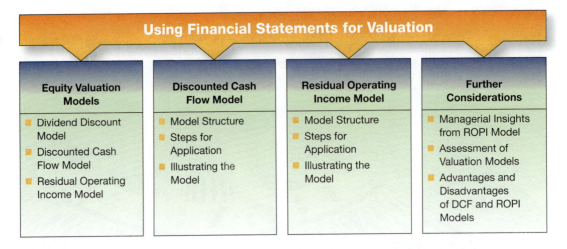

Equity Valuation Models

eLectures
MBC **LO1** Identify equity valuation models and explain the information required to value equity securities.

The value of a debt security is the present value of the interest and principal payments that the investor *expects* to receive in the future. The valuation of equity securities is similar in that it is also based on expectations. The difference lies in the increased uncertainty surrounding the timing and amount of payments from equity securities. There are many types of equity valuation models in use today, but they share at least three common features. All equity valuation models:

- Assume that a particular fundamental variable determines equity value—we discuss three fundamental variables: dividends, free cash flows, and residual operating income.

- Forecast the fundamental variable for the remainder of the company's life. Generating an infinite stream of forecasts is not realistic; consequently, we typically estimate the fundamental variable over a horizon period, often 4 to 10 years. Then, we make simplifying assumptions about the terminal period, which encompasses the years subsequent to the horizon period. A key assumption is that the fundamental variables as forecasted for the terminal period continue into perpetuity.

- Use time value of money techniques to determine the present value of the future estimated amounts. The discount factor depends on the fundamental variable in the model. We must estimate the discount factor, which requires data from external sources and additional assumptions.

Dividend Discount Model

The basis of equity valuation is the premise that the value of an equity security is determined by the payments that the investor can expect to receive. Equity investments involve two types of payoffs: (1) dividends received while the security is owned and (2) capital gains when the security is sold. The future stock price is, itself, also assumed to be related to the expected dividends that the new investor expects to receive; as a result, the expected receipt of dividends is the sole driver of stock price under this type of valuation model. The value of an equity security is, then, based on the present value of expected dividends plus the present value of the security at the end of the forecasted holding period. The present value is determined using the firm's cost of equity capital as the discount rate. This **dividend discount model** is appealing in its simplicity and its intuitive focus on dividend distribution. As a practical matter, however, the model is not always useful because many companies that have a positive stock price have never paid a dividend, and are not expected to pay a dividend in the foreseeable future.

Discounted Cash Flow Model

The most widely used model to estimate the value of common stock is the **discounted cash flow (DCF) model**. This model focuses on the company's operating and investing activities; that is, on its ability to *generate cash*. This makes the DCF model more practical than the dividend discount model. The DCF model first estimates the value of the company (the *enterprise value*) and, then, determines the shareholders' portion, or the equity value as the enterprise value less the value of the company's debt. The DCF model takes as its fundamental input variable, the expected *free cash flows to the firm*, which are defined as operating cash flows net of the expected new investments in net operating assets (such as property, plant and equipment) that are required to support the business. The DCF model uses the weighted average cost of capital (WACC) to discount the expected future free cash flows.

Residual Operating Income Model

Another approach to equity valuation also focuses on operating and investing activities. It is known as the **residual operating income (ROPI) model**. This model uses both net operating profits after tax (NOPAT) and the net operating assets (NOA) to determine equity value (see Module 4 for complete descriptions of the NOPAT and NOA measures). This approach highlights the importance of return on net operating assets (RNOA), and the disaggregation of RNOA into net operating profit margin and NOA turnover. We discuss the implications of this insight for managers later in this module.

Valuation Model Inputs

To illustrate the valuation models, we use **Procter & Gamble** (P&G). Exhibit 13.1 provides model inputs used to estimate the models including sales, net operating profit after tax (NOPAT) and net operating assets (NOA). We obtain the variables for FY2016 from P&G's actual 2016 financial statements (from Exhibit 12.2). The forecasted variables for FY2017 and FY2018 come from the forecasted income statements and balance sheets developed in the forecasting module and shown in Exhibits 12.3 and 12.4.[1] Forecasted financial statements are also used to get forecasts for FY2019 and FY2020. For the terminal period, we assume a terminal growth rate of 1%. Note that these forecasted numbers are generated using the approach we describe in our forecasting module that utilizes all of the information in the 10-K and its notes. We describe an alternate approach in our Analysis Insight Box on *Parsimonious Model Forecasts* below.

Exhibit 13.1 ■ Forecasts for Procter & Gamble

$ millions	FY2016 Actual	FY2017 Forecast	FY2018 Forecast	FY2019 Forecast	FY2020 Forecast	Terminal Period
Sales.	$65,299	$65,952	$67,271	$68,616	$69,989	$70,689
Sales growth.		1%	2%	2%	2%	1%
Net operating profit after tax (NOPAT) . . .	$10,072	$11,032	$11,253	$11,459	$11,688	$11,805
Net operating assets (NOA)	$70,391	$70,620	$70,622	$72,996	$74,455	$75,200

To estimate the valuation models, we use a short four-year horizon period to simplify the exposition and to reduce the computational burden. In practice, we use spreadsheets to forecast future cash flows and value the equity security, and typically have a forecast horizon of seven to ten periods. We assume a terminal period growth rate of 1% for sales, NOPAT and NOA for years 2021 and beyond.

---

[1] **NOPAT** equals revenues less operating expenses such as cost of goods sold, selling, general, and administrative expenses, and taxes. NOPAT excludes any interest revenue and interest expense and any gains or losses from financial investments. NOPAT reflects the operating side of the firm as opposed to nonoperating activities such as borrowing and security investment activities. **NOA** equals operating assets less operating liabilities. (See Module 4.)

Analysis Insight ■ Parsimonious Model Forecasts

One alternative to using detailed forecasts of the income statement and balance sheet, is to use the parsimonious forecasting method that we describe in Appendix 12B. That method uses sales growth and ratios of NOPM and NOAT, computed from current (or recent) financial statements, to forecast future sales, NOPAT, and NOA. In its simple form, that method assumes that NOPM and NOAT remain unchanged during the forecast horizon and terminal period. Exhibit 13.2 shows the parsimonious forecasts for P&G using a sales growth of 2% for the forecast horizon and 1% for the terminal period, along with NOPM of 15.4% and NOAT of 0.93. As expected, the numbers differ from the full forecasted financials in Exhibit 13.1 because this parsimonious model has different assumptions.

Exhibit 13.2 Valuation Model Inputs from Parsimonious Forecast Method

| | Current 2016 | Forecast Horizon | | | | Terminal Period |
		2017	2018	2019	2020	
Sales growth..............		1.0%	2.0%	2.0%	2.0%	1.0%
Sales (unrounded)	$65,299	$65,951.99	$67,271.03	$68,616.45	$69,988.78	$70,688.67
		($65,299 × 1.01)	($65,951.99 × 1.02)	($67,271.03 × 1.03)	($68,616.45 × 1.02)	($69,988.78 × 1.01)
Sales (rounded)	$65,299	$65,952	$67,271	$68,616	$69,989	$70,689
NOPAT	$10,072	$10,157	$10,360	$10,567	$10,778	$10,886
NOPM assumed to be 15.4%		($65,952 × 0.154)	($67,271 × 0.154)	($68,616 × 0.154)	($69,989 × 0.154)	($70,689 × 0.154)
NOA	$70,391	$70,916	$72,334	$73,781	$75,257	$76,010
NOAT assumed to be 0.93........		($65,952/0.93)	($67,271/0.93)	($68,616/0.93)	($69,989/0.93)	($70,689/0.93)

Review 13-1 LO1

We discussed three types of valuation models: dividend discount model, discounted cash flow model, and residual operating income model.

Required
For each of the following statements *a* through *j*, identify whether it is True or False for each of the three valuation models.

	Dividend Discount	Discounted Cash Flow	Residual Operating Income
a. Uses net present value concepts...........	_____	_____	_____
b. Operating cash flows affect value	_____	_____	_____
c. Estimates a company's enterprise value	_____	_____	_____
d. Dividends to shareholders is a model input...	_____	_____	_____
e. Free cash flow is a model input	_____	_____	_____
f. Estimates equity value of the firm	_____	_____	_____
g. Capital expenditures affect estimated value ..	_____	_____	_____
h. Requires forecasts of future amounts	_____	_____	_____
i. Operating profit affects value..............	_____	_____	_____
j. Yields insight into value drivers	_____	_____	_____

Solution on p. 13-40.

Discounted Cash Flow (DCF) Model

LO2

MBC Describe and apply the discounted free cash flow model to value equity securities.

The discounted cash flow (DCF) model defines firm value as follows.

> **Firm Value = Present Value of Expected Free Cash Flows to Firm**

The expected free cash flows to the firm include cash flows arising from the operating side of the business; that is, cash generated from the firm's operating activities (not from nonoperating activities such as interest paid on debt or dividends received on investments). Importantly, free cash flows to the firm do not include the cash flows from financing activities.

DCF Model Structure

Free cash flows to the firm (FCFF) equal net operating profit after tax that is not used to grow net operating assets. Using the terminology of Module 4 we can define FCFF as follows (see Business Insight box below for a more traditional definition).

$$\text{FCFF} = \text{NOPAT} - \text{Increase in NOA}$$

where

> **NOPAT = Net operating profit after tax**
>
> **NOA = Net operating assets**

Net operating profit after tax is normally positive and net operating assets normally increase each year. The difference between the two (positive or negative) represents the net cash flows available to creditors and shareholders. Positive FCFF imply that there are funds available for distribution to creditors and shareholders, either in the form of debt repayments, dividends, or stock repurchases (treasury stock). Negative FCFF imply that the firm requires additional funds from creditors and/ or shareholders, in the form of new loans or equity investments, to support its business activities.

Managerial Decision ■ **You Are the Chief Financial Officer**

Assume that you are the CFO of a company that has a large investment in plant assets and sells its products on credit. Identify steps you can take to increase your company's cash flow and, hence, your company's firm value. [Answer p. 13-27]

Business Insight ■ **Definitions of Free Cash Flow**

We often see free cash flows to the firm (unlevered free cash flow) defined as follows.

FCFF = Net cash flow from operating activities − Capital expenditures

Although similar to the definition in this book, NOPAT − Increase in NOA, there are important differences.

- Net cash flow from operating activities uses net income as the starting point; net income, of course, comingles both operating and nonoperating components (such as selling expense and interest expense). Analysts sometimes correct for this by adding back items such as after-tax net interest expense. That is, the FCFF measure can be refined by beginning with earnings before interest and taxes (EBIT) and subtracting taxes.
- Income tax expense (in net income) includes the effect of the interest tax shield (see Module 4); the usual NOPAT definition includes only the tax on operating income.
- Net cash flow from operating activities also includes nonoperating items in working capital, such as changes in interest payable and dividends payable. NOA focuses only on operating activities.
- Capital expenditures include direct purchases of PPE assets but exclude long-term assets acquired with stock (instead of cash), say in the acquisition of a company. Changes in NOA is a more comprehensive measure of asset growth.

We must be attentive to differences in definitions for free cash flow so that we understand the analytical choices we make and their implications for equity valuation. Knowing that there is not one "universal" way to define FCFF, helps us interpret analyst research reports that apply different definitions of free cash flow.

Steps in Applying the DCF Model

Application of the DCF model to equity valuation involves five steps:

1. Forecast and discount FCFF for the **horizon period**.[2]

---

[2] When discounting FCFF, the appropriate discount rate (r_w) is the **weighted average cost of capital (WACC)**, where the weights are the relative percentages of debt (d) and equity (e) in the capital structure applied to the expected returns on debt (r_d) and equity (r_e), respectively. P&G has two types of equity, common and preferred. Therefore, the company's weighted average cost of capital has three components: WACC $= r_w = (r_d \times \%$ of debt$) + (r_e \times \%$ of equity$) + (r_{ps} \times \%$ of preferred stock$)$.

2. Forecast and discount FCFF for the post-horizon period, called **terminal period**.[3]

3. Sum the present values of the horizon and terminal periods to yield firm (enterprise) value.

4. Subtract net nonoperating obligations (NNO), along with any noncontrolling interest (NCI), from firm value to yield equity value. If NNO is positive, the usual case, we subtract it in step 4; if NNO is negative, we add it. (For many, but not all, companies, NNO is positive because nonoperating liabilities exceed nonoperating assets.)

5. Divide firm equity value by the number of shares outstanding to yield stock value per share.

Illustrating the DCF Model

To illustrate the DCF model for Procter & Gamble, we start with the forecasted model inputs from Exhibit 13.1 and use these to compute FCFF.

Exhibit 13.3 ▮ **Application of Discounted Cash Flow Model**

P&G—DCF ($ millions, except per share value and discount factors)	Reported 2016	Horizon Period				Terminal Period
		2017	2018	2019	2020	
Sales..........................	$ 65,299	$65,952	$67,271	$68,616	$69,989	$70,689
NOPAT	10,072	11,032	11,253	11,459	11,688	11,805
NOA	70,391	70,620	70,622	72,996	74,455	75,200
Increase in NOA..................		229	2	2,374	1,459	745
FCFF (NOPAT − Increase in NOA)....		10,803	11,251	9,085	10,229	11,060
Discount factor $[1/(1 + r_w)^t]^*$		0.95420	0.91049	0.86879	0.82900	
Present value of horizon FCFF.......		10,308	10,244	7,893	8,480	
Cum present value of horizon FCFF...	36,925					
Present value of terminal FCFF	241,283					
Total firm value....................	278,208					
Less (plus) NNO**	12,408					
Less noncontrolling interest.........	642					
Firm equity value	$265,158					
Shares outstanding	2,668					
Stock value per share.............	$ 99.38					

* To simplify present value computations, the discount factors are rounded to 5 decimal places.

** Net nonoperating obligations (NNO) is computed as nonoperating obligations minus nonoperating assets: ($2,343 + $11,653 + $18,945) − ($7,102 + $6,246 + $7,185) = $12,408.

The bottom line of Exhibit 13.3 is the estimated P&G equity value of $265,158 million, and a stock price of $99.38 per share (computed as $265,158 million/2,668 million shares). To determine present value we used a weighted average cost of capital WACC(r_w) of 4.80% as the discount rate.[4] Specifically, we valued P&G's stock as follows.

1. **Compute present value of horizon period FCFF.** We compute the forecasted 2017 FCFF of $10,803 million from the forecasted 2017 NOPAT less the forecasted increase of NOA in 2017. The present value of $10,803 million as of 2016 is $10,308 million, computed as $10,803 million × 0.95420 (the present value factor for one year at 4.80%). Similarly, the present value of forecasted 2018 FCFF (two years from the current date) is $10,244 million, computed as $11,251 million × 0.91049, and so on through 2020. The sum of these present values (cumulative present value) is $36,925 million.

---

[3] For an assumed growth, g, the terminal period (T) present value of FCFF in perpetuity (beyond the horizon period) is given by, $\frac{FCFF_T}{r_w - g}$, where $FCFF_T$ is the free cash flow to the firm for the terminal period, r_w is WACC, and g is the assumed long-term growth rate of those cash flows. The resulting amount is then discounted back to the present using the horizon-end-period discount factor.

[4] We compute P&G's WACC as described in the text box below. To learn more about weighted average cost of capital (WACC) and how it is computed, see finance-oriented books such as *Corporate Valuation: Theory, Evidence and Practice* by Holthausen and Zmijewski, 2014, Cambridge Business Publishers.

2. **Compute present value of terminal period FCFF.** The present value of the terminal period FCFF is $241,283 million, computed as [$11,060 million/(0.048 − 0.01)]/1.048^4.

3. **Compute firm equity value.** We sum the present value of the horizon period FCFF and terminal period FCFF to get firm (enterprise) value of $278,208 million. We subtract the value of P&G's net nonoperating obligations of $12,408 million and the book value of its noncontrolling interest of $642 million to yield P&G's equity value of $265,158 million. We divide P&G's equity value by the 2,668 million shares outstanding to obtain the estimated per share value (the stock price) of $99.38.

We perform this valuation as of June 30, 2016, P&G's year end. P&G's stock closed at $84.67 on June 30, 2016. Our valuation estimate of $99.38 indicates that the stock is undervalued as of that date.[5]

Practice Insight ■ Procter & Gamble's WACC

P&G's WACC is computed as the cost of debt, common equity, and preferred stock, weighted by their proportion in the company's capital structure as follows.

	Cost	Weight
R_d (cost of debt, after tax)	1.26%	13.7%
R_e (cost of equity)	5.27%	85.9%
R_{ps} (cost of preferred stock)	24.57%	0.4%
WACC	4.80%	

Specifically, the components of WACC are computed as follows.

- **R_d (cost of debt)**—P&G provides the effective cost of short- and long-term debt in its debt footnotes.

Years Ended June 30	2016	2015
Short-term weighted average interest rates	0.2%	0.3%
Long-term weighted average interest rates	3.1%	3.2%

  To arrive at the overall cost of debt, we weight the short-term and long-term average interest rates by the relative proportion of the ST and LT debt. The weights are the $11,653 book value of ST debt (which approximates market value) and the $18,945 market value of LT debt (provided in the footnotes to the 10-K). The result is a 2% average pretax cost of debt, computed as [0.2% × ($11,653/$30,598)] + [3.1% × ($18,945/$30,598)]. We then multiply this pretax cost of debt by 1 − 37% (the federal and state combined statutory tax rate) to yield the 1.26% after-tax debt cost.

- **R_e (cost of equity)**—the cost of equity is given by the capital asset pricing model (CAPM) using the 10-year government bond rate of 1.49%, the P&G beta from Yahoo finance of 0.63, both as of P&G's year-end of 6/30/16, and an assumed market premium of 6%.

$$R_e = 1.49\% + (0.63 \times 6\%) = 5.27\%$$

- **R_{ps} (cost of preferred stock)**—the cost of preferred stock is computed by dividing the dividends to preferred stockholders by the book value of the preferred stock.

$$R_{ps} = \$255 \text{ million}/\$1,038 \text{ million} = 24.57\%$$

LO2 Review 13-2

Following are financial data and forecast assumptions for **General Mills** (GIS) for its fiscal-year-end May 29, 2016.

General Mills ($ millions)	FY2016 Actual	FY2017 Forecast	FY2018 Forecast	FY2019 Forecast	FY2020 Forecast	Terminal Period
Sales	$16,563.1	$16,314.7	$16,640.9	$16,973.8	$17,313.2	$17,486.4
Sales growth		(1.5)%	2%	2%	2%	1%
Net operating profit after tax (NOPAT)	$ 1,928.2	$ 1,892.5	$ 1,930.3	$ 1,969.0	$ 2,008.3	$ 2,028.4
Net operating assets (NOA)	$13,819.9	$13,595.6	$13,867.4	$14,144.8	$14,427.7	$14,572.0

continued

---

[5] Morgan Stanley's price target for P&G was $90 in its report issued shortly after that date (see Appendix 12C). Procter & Gamble filed its 2016 10-K with the SEC on August 8, 2016, which is the first day that the financial information used for our valuation was publicly available. On that day, PG stock closed at $85.76.

continued from previous page

Equity Valuation Model Assumptions ($ and shares in millions)	
Weighted average cost of capital.	5.24%
Net nonoperating obligations (NNO)	$8,512.8
Noncontrolling interest.	$ 376.9
Number of common shares outstanding	596.8

Required

a. Apply the discounted cash flow (DCF) model to obtain GIS's stock price estimate as of its fiscal-year-end May 29, 2016.

b. Compare the stock price estimate from part *a* to the actual stock price at FY2016 period-end. (Note: May 29, 2016, was not a trading day, so use the closest prior trading day as the actual stock price.) What does **Solution on p. 13-41.**   our valuation estimate imply about the stock's value?

Residual Operating Income (ROPI) Model

LO3
MBC Describe and apply the residual operating income model to value equity securities.

The residual operating income (ROPI) model focuses on net operating profit after tax (NOPAT) and net operating assets (NOA). This means it uses key measures from both the income statement and balance sheet in determining firm value.

ROPI Model Structure

The ROPI model defines firm value as the sum of two components.

> **Firm Value = NOA + Present Value of Expected ROPI**

where

> **NOA = Net operating assets**
>
> **ROPI = Residual operating income**

Net operating assets (NOA) are the foundation of firm value under the ROPI model. The ROPI model adds an adjustment in the second term that corrects for any possible undervaluation or overvaluation of NOA. This adjustment is the present value of expected residual operating income, and is defined as follows.

$$\text{ROPI} = \text{NOPAT} - \underbrace{(\text{NOA}_{\text{Beg}} \times r_w)}_{\textbf{Expected NOPAT}}$$

where

> NOA_{Beg} = Net operating assets at beginning (Beg) of period
>
> r_w = Weighted average cost of capital (WACC)

Residual operating income (ROPI) is the net operating profit a firm earns over and above the return that the operating assets are expected to earn given the firm's WACC.[6] Shareholders expect the company to use NOA to generate, at least, a "hurdle" profit to cover the cost of capital (WACC). Companies that earn profits over and above that hurdle, create value for shareholders. This is the concept of residual income: that is, income earned over and above the minimum amount of return required by investors.

---

[6] If the assets earn more than expected, it could be because NOA does not capture all of the firms' assets. For example, R&D and advertising are not fully and contemporaneously reflected on the balance sheet as assets though they likely produce future cash inflows. Likewise, internally generated goodwill is not fully reflected on the balance sheet as an asset. Similarly, assets are generally not written up to reflect unrealized gains. Conversely, sometimes the balance sheet overstates the true value of NOA. For example, companies can delay the write-down of impaired assets and, thus, overstate their book values. These examples, and a host of others, can yield reported values of NOA that differ from the fair value of operating assets.

Understanding the ROPI model helps us reap the benefits from the disaggregation of return on net operating assets (RNOA) in Module 4. In addition, the ROPI model is the foundation for many internal and external performance evaluation and compensation systems marketed by management consulting and accounting services firms.[7]

Steps in Applying the ROPI Model

Application of the ROPI model to equity valuation involves five steps.

1. Forecast and discount ROPI for the horizon period.[8]

2. Forecast and discount ROPI for the terminal period.[9]

3. Sum the present values from both the horizon and terminal periods; then add this sum to current NOA to get firm (enterprise) value.

4. Subtract net nonoperating obligations (NNO), along with any noncontrolling interest, from firm value to yield firm equity value.

5. Divide firm equity value by the number of shares outstanding to yield stock value per share.

Illustrating the ROPI Model

To illustrate the ROPI model, we return to **Procter & Gamble**. Forecasted financials for P&G (forecast horizon of FY2017 through FY2020 and terminal period of FY2021) are in Exhibit 13.4. The forecasts (in bold) are for sales, NOPAT, and NOA (the same forecasts we use to illustrate the DCF model).

Exhibit 13.4 ■ Application of Residual Operating Income Model

P&G—ROPI ($ millions, except per share value and discount factors)	Reported 2016	Horizon Period				Terminal Period
		2017	2018	2019	2020	
Sales.	$ 65,299	**$65,952**	**$67,271**	**$68,616**	**$69,989**	**$70,689**
NOPAT	10,072	**11,032**	**11,253**	**11,459**	**11,688**	**11,805**
NOA	70,391	**70,620**	**70,622**	**72,996**	**74,455**	**75,200**
ROPI (NOPAT − [NOA$_{Beg}$ × r_w])		7,653	7,863	8,069	8,184	8,231
Discount factor [1/(1 + r_w)^t]*		0.95420	0.91049	0.86879	0.82900	
Present value of horizon ROPI		7,302	7,159	7,010	6,785	
Cum present value of horizon ROPI. . .	28,256					
Present value of terminal ROPI	179,566					
NOA	70,391					
Total firm value	278,213					
Less (plus): NNO**	12,408					
Less: NCI	642					
Firm equity value	$265,163					
Shares outstanding	2,668					
Stock value per share.	$ 99.39					

* To simplify present value computations, the discount factors are rounded to 5 decimal places.

** Net nonoperating obligations (NNO) is computed as nonoperating obligations minus nonoperating assets:
($2,343 + $11,653 + $18,945) − ($7,102 + $6,246 + $7,185) = $12,408.

---

[7] Examples are economic value added (EVA™) from Stern Stewart & Company, the economic profit model from McKinsey & Co., the cash flow return on investment (CFROI™) from Holt Value Associates, the economic value management from KPMG, and the value builder from PricewaterhouseCoopers (PwC).

[8] The present value of expected ROPI uses the weighted average cost of capital (WACC) as its discount rate; same as with the DCF model.

[9] For an assumed growth, g, the present value of the perpetuity of ROPI beyond the horizon period is given by $\frac{ROPI_T}{r_w - g}$, where $ROPI_T$ is the residual operating income for the terminal period, r_w is WACC for the firm, and g is the assumed growth rate of $ROPI_T$ following the horizon period. The resulting amount is then discounted back to the present using the WACC, computed over the length of the horizon period.

The bottom line of the ROPI valuation is the estimated P&G stock price of $99.39 per share, which is the same per share value we estimate in Exhibit 13.3 using the DCF valuation model (1¢ rounding difference). The present value computations use a 4.80% WACC as the discount rate. Specifically, we obtain the ROPI stock valuation as follows.

1. **Compute present value of horizon period ROPI.** The forecasted 2017 ROPI of $7,653 million is computed from the forecasted 2017 NOPAT ($11,032 million) less the product of beginning period NOA ($70,391 million) and WACC (0.048). The present value of this ROPI as of 2017 is $7,302 million, computed as $7,653 million × 0.95420 (the present value factor for one year at 4.80%). Similarly, the present value of 2018 ROPI (two years hence) is $7,159 million, computed as $7,863 million × 0.91049, and so on through 2020. The sum of these present values (cumulative present value) is $28,256 million.

2. **Compute present value of terminal period ROPI.** The present value of the terminal period ROPI is $179,566 million, computed as [$8,231 million/(0.048 − 0.01)]/1.048^4.

3. **Compute firm equity value.** We sum the present values from the horizon period ($28,256 million) and terminal period ($179,566 million), plus FY2016 NOA ($70,391 million), to obtain P&G's total firm (enterprise) value of $278,213 million. We then subtract the value of net nonoperating obligations of $12,408 million and noncontrolling interests of $642 million to yield firm equity value of $265,163 million. Dividing firm equity value by the 2,668 million shares outstanding yields the estimated per share value of $99.39.

We perform this valuation using data from the financial statements dated June 30, 2016, P&G's fiscal-year-end. P&G's stock closed at $84.67 on that date. As with the DCF model valuation, our valuation estimate of $99.39 suggests that P&G's stock is undervalued as of this date.[10]

The ROPI model and the DCF models yield identical per share estimates (there is a 1¢ rounding difference.). This is the case so long as the firm is in a steady state, that is, when both NOPAT and NOA are growing at the same rate such that RNOA is the same each year. When this steady-state condition is not met, the two models yield different valuations. This could happen for example, when we predict different terminal period growth rates or when profit margins are predicted to change. In practice, we often compute estimated stock values from several models and use qualitative analysis to determine an overall price estimate.

Review 13-3 LO3

Refer to the financial data and forecast assumptions for **General Mills** in Review 13-2.

Required

a. Apply the residual operating income (ROPI) model to obtain GIS's stock price estimate as of its fiscal-year-end May 29, 2016.

b. Compare the stock price estimate from part *a* to the actual stock price at its FY2016 period-end. (*Note*: May 29, 2016, was not a trading day, so use the closest prior trading day as the actual stock price.) What does our valuation estimate imply about the stock's value?

Solution on p. 13-41.

Further Considerations Involving Valuation Models

LO4

Explain how equity valuation models can inform managerial decisions.

Managerial Insights from the ROPI Model

The ROPI model defines firm value as the sum of NOA and the present value of expected residual operating income as follows.

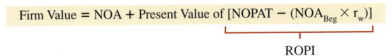

$$\text{Firm Value} = \text{NOA} + \text{Present Value of } [\underbrace{\text{NOPAT} - (\text{NOA}_{\text{Beg}} \times r_w)}_{\text{ROPI}}]$$

---

[10] Procter & Gamble filed its 2016 Form 10-K with the SEC on August 8, 2016, which is the first day the financial information used for our valuation was publicly available. On that day, PG stock closed at $85.76.

Increasing ROPI, therefore, increases firm value. Managers can increase ROPI in two ways.

1. Decrease the NOA required to generate a given level of NOPAT (improve efficiency)
2. Increase NOPAT with the same level of NOA investment (improve profitability)

These are two very important observations. It means that achieving better performance requires effective management of *both* the balance sheet and the income statement. Most operating managers are accustomed to working with income statements. Further, they are often evaluated on profitability outcomes, such as achieving desired levels of sales and gross profit or efficiently managing operating expenses. The ROPI model focuses management attention on the balance sheet as well.

The two points above highlight two paths to increase ROPI and, accordingly, firm value.

Reduce NOA and maintain NOPAT First, let's consider how management can reduce the level of NOA while maintaining a given level of NOPAT. Many managers begin by implementing procedures that reduce net operating working capital, such as the following.

- Reducing receivables through:
  - Better assessment of customers' credit quality
  - Better controls to identify delinquencies and automated payment notices
  - More accurate and timely invoicing
- Reducing inventories through:
  - Use of less costly components (of equal quality) and production with lower wage rates
  - Elimination of product features not valued by customers
  - Outsourcing to reduce product cost
  - Just-in-time deliveries of raw materials
  - Elimination of manufacturing bottlenecks to reduce work-in-process inventories
  - Producing to order rather than to estimated demand
- Increasing payables through:
  - Extending the payment of low or no-cost payables (so long as supplier relationships are unharmed)

Management would next look at its long-term operating assets for opportunities to reduce unnecessary operating assets, such as the following.

- Sale of unnecessary property, plant or equipment
- Acquisition of production and administrative assets in partnership with other entities for greater throughput
- Acquisition of finished or semifinished goods from suppliers to reduce manufacturing assets

Increase NOPAT for same NOA The second path to increase ROPI and, accordingly, firm value is to increase NOPAT with the same level of NOA investment. Management would look to strategies that maximize NOPAT, such as the following.

- Increasing gross profit dollars through:
  - Better pricing and mix of products sold
  - Reduction of raw material and labor cost without sacrificing product quality, perhaps by outsourcing, better design, or more efficient manufacturing
  - Increase of throughput to minimize overhead costs per unit (provided inventory does not build up)
- Reducing selling, general, and administrative expenses through:
  - Better management of personnel
  - Reduction of overhead
  - Use of derivatives to hedge commodity and interest costs
  - Minimization of tax expense

Before undertaking any of these actions, managers must consider both short- and long-run implications for the company. The ROPI model helps managers assess company performance (income statement) relative to the net operating assets committed (balance sheet).

Managerial Decision   ■   You Are the Chief Financial Officer

The residual operating income (ROPI) model highlights the importance of increasing NOPAT and reducing net operating assets, which are the two major components of the return on net operating assets (RNOA). What specific steps can you take to improve RNOA through improvement of its components: net operating profit margin and net operating asset turnover? [Answer, p. 13-27]

Assessment of Valuation Models

Exhibit 13.5 provides a brief summary of the advantages and disadvantages of the DCF and ROPI models. Neither model dominates the other, and both are theoretically equivalent. Instead, professionals must choose the model that performs best under practical circumstances.

There are numerous other equity valuation models in practice. Many require forecasting, but several others do not. A quick review of selected models follows.

The **method of comparables model** (often called *multiples model*) predicts equity valuation or stock value using price multiples. Price multiples are defined as stock price divided by some key financial statement number. That financial number varies across investors but is usually one of the following: net income, net sales, book value of equity, total assets, or cash flow. The method then compares companies' multiples to those of their competitors to assign value.

The **net asset valuation model** draws on the financial reporting system to assign value. That is, equity is valued as reported assets less reported liabilities. Some investors adjust reported assets and liabilities for several perceived shortcomings in GAAP prior to computing net asset value. This method is commonly applied when valuing privately held companies.

There are additional models applied in practice that involve dividends, cash flows, research and development outlays, accounting rates of return, cash recovery rates, and real option models. Further, some practitioners, called *chartists* and *technicians*, chart price behavior over time and use it to predict equity value.

Exhibit 13.5 ■ **Advantages and Disadvantages of DCF and ROPI Valuation Models**

Model	Advantages	Disadvantages	Performs Best

DCF	• Popular and widely accepted model
	• Cash flows are unaffected by accrual accounting
	• FCFF is intuitive
		• Cash investments in PPE assets are treated as cash outflows, even though they create shareholder value
		• Value not recognized unless evidenced by cash flows
		• Computing FCFF can be difficult as operating cash flows are affected by
		  – Cutbacks on investments (receivables, inventories, plant assets); can yield short-run benefits at long-run cost
		  – Securitization, which GAAP treats as an operating cash flow when many view it as a financing activity
			• When the firm reports positive FCFF
			• When FCFF grows at a relatively constant rate

ROPI	• Focuses on value drivers such as profit margins and asset turnovers • Uses both balance sheet and income statement, including accrual accounting information • Reduces weight placed on terminal period value	• Financial statements do not reflect all company assets, especially for knowledge-based industries (for example, R&D assets and goodwill) • Requires knowledge of accrual accounting	• When financial statements reflect more of the assets and liabilities; including those items often reported off-balance-sheet

Research Insight ▪ Using Models to Identify Mispriced Stocks

Implementation of the ROPI model can include parameters to capture differences in growth opportunities, persistence of ROPI, and the conservatism in accounting measures. Research finds differences in how such factors, across firms and over time, affect ROPI and changes in NOA. This research also hints that investors do not entirely understand the properties underlying these factors and, consequently, individual stocks can be mispriced for short periods of time. Other research contends that the apparent mispricing is due to an omitted valuation variable related to riskiness of the firm.

LO4 Review 13-4

Consider the following operating activities *a* through *d* that General Mills managers could pursue.

Required

For each action: (i) explain the likely effect on ROPI by considering how net operating profit after tax (NOPAT) and net operating assets (NOA) would be affected, and (ii) identify any potential negative consequences for such an action.

a. Delay payment on vendor invoices by two days.
b. Offer new discounts to avoid inventory spoilage by tracking shelf life more closely to identify those products for special discounts whose "sell by" date is nearing.
c. Replace certain traditional marketing media like print ads, mailers, and coupons with social media channels for in-store promotions.
d. Lease transportation equipment for peak periods instead of purchasing PPE to cover peak periods.

Solution on p. 13-42.

Global Accounting

There are no differences in the method or technique of valuing equity securities using IFRS financial statements. We can use the DCF or the ROPI method with IFRS data as inputs and determine intrinsic values. Regarding other inputs, it is important to note that WACC varies across countries. This is readily apparent when we recognize that the risk-free rate used to compute WACC is country specific; for example, the following table shows the yield on 10-year government debt for several countries as of September 2016 (www.bloomberg.com/markets/rates-bonds). In comparison to countries such as Japan and Germany, countries such as Greece and Brazil are riskier because of their debt levels and economic troubles. The higher the country risk, the higher the yield demanded on that country's debt.

Country	Yield to Maturity
Japan	(0.70)%
Germany	(0.12)%
United States	1.59%
United Kingdom	0.70%
Australia	1.97%
Brazil	11.90%
Greece	8.23%

Appendix 13A: Derivation of Free Cash Flow Formula

Derivation of the free cash flow formula follows; our thanks to Professor Jim Boatsman for this exposition.

Assets = Liabilities + Stockholders' Equity (SE)

$$NOA = NNO + SE$$

$$\Delta NOA = \Delta NNO + \Delta SE \quad \text{[in change form, where } \Delta \text{ refers to change]}$$

$$\Delta NOA = \Delta NNO + \Delta\text{Contributed Capital (CC)} + \text{Net Income} - \text{Dividends (DIV)} \quad \text{[substituting for SE]}$$

$$\Delta NOA = \Delta NNO + \Delta CC + (NOPAT - NNE) - DIV \quad \text{[substituting for NI]}$$

$$-NOPAT + \Delta NOA = \Delta NNO + \Delta CC - NNE - DIV \quad \text{[rearranging terms]}$$

$$NOPAT - \Delta NOA = NNE - \Delta NNO - \Delta CC + DIV \quad \text{[multiplying by } -1]$$

Free cash flows to the firm (FCFF)

Net payments to holders of net nonoperating obligations and of stock

Appendix 13B: Deutsche Bank Valuation of Procter & Gamble

We explain the forecasting process in Module 12 and reproduce an analyst report on forecasted financial statements for **Procter & Gamble** in Appendix 12C. In this appendix we extend that analysis and reproduce an analyst forecasted stock price for P&G. We include below, three sets of excerpts from the **Deutsche Bank** valuation report.

Qualitative and Quantitative Summary

The first excerpt provides a qualitative and quantitative summary from Deutsche Bank's report as a August 2, 2016 (*reproduced with permission*).

Deutsche Bank
Markets Research

Rating	Company
Buy	**Procter & Gamble**
North America	
United States	

Consumer	Reuters	Bloomberg	Exchange Ticker
Cosmetics, Household &	PG.N	PG UN	NYS PG
Personal Care			

Unleashing the Hounds

Date
2 August 2016

Results

Price at 1 Aug 2016 (USD)	86.41
Price target	95.00
52-week range	86.41 - 68.06

Bill Schmitz

Research Analyst
(+1) 203 863-2285
william.schmitz@db.com

Faiza Alwy

Research Analyst
(+1) 203 863-2284
faiza.alwy@db.com

Jon Keypour

Research Associate
(+1) 203 863-2272
jonathan.keypour@db.com

Buy on refocus and reinvestment with significant earnings cushion

Coming out of its lost decade, P&G is starting to inject its own version of fiscal stimulus to its business and categories – using clear earnings flexibility to reinvest behind focused portfolio to expand categories and market share, even if it tempers short-term EPS growth. Given its size and importance, multiple should start to expand as organic growth trends improve and even if we didn't see it this quarter, we remain upbeat about the latent potential and see sequential organic growth improving from here on out provided company strategically reinvests as it laps margin-enhancing product line exits. Maintain Buy, $95 target (from $92).

4Q16 core EPS of $0.79, $0.05 above Street

Organic sales were up 2%, against a flat comp, with f/x hit of 3 pts. Adj. GM was up 1.6 pts while OM of 17.0% was down 1.5 pts with SG&A ratio of 32.4% up 3.1 bps (-40 bps f/x) noting advertising/sampling as percent of sales was up 280 bps YoY and other sales coverage and R&D investments were up 70 bps. Operating income of $2.73B was 1.4% below Street. By segment, organic growth was 1% in beauty, 7% in grooming, 8% in healthcare, 1% in fabric/home and 1% in baby/family. Below the line items added $0.08 to EPS vs. our model. FY17 EPS guidance of mid single digit growth implies $3.82 to $3.89 with organic growth of 2% expected, likely conservative.

Coming out of the gate

CEO David Taylor and his leadership team are under significant pressure to demonstrate that the business can grow after several years of share losses and tepid results. In our view, this likely starts with 4 key categories representing over 60% of operating profits (diapers, laundry, hair care and grooming), with ample earnings flexibility off new guidance ($3.85 vs. $4.34 FY17 estimate a year ago) to spend the money it needs to. In terms of setup, the company should start to lap unprofitable product line exits and continue to do triage work in China, getting the selling channels and price points better aligned with the realities of the market. With considerable latent earnings power, the last missing piece is organic growth acceleration in-line or better than peers.

Valuation supports Buy rating and $95 target; risks

Shares are trading in-line with historical average premium relative to market but well below peers. DCF (2.8% sales growth/0.6 pts of annual margin expansion through 2024) yields $95 target, PF for divestitures. Downside risks: stronger dollar, macro slowdown in US, decline in consumer confidence, price elasticity, commodity inflation without pricing offset.

Key changes

Price target	92.00 to 95.00	↑	3.3%
EPS (USD)	3.92 to 3.88	↓	-1.0%
Revenue (USDm)	66,211.8 to 66,174.2	↓	-0.1%

Source: Deutsche Bank

Price/price relative

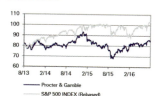

— Procter & Gamble
— S&P 500 INDEX (Rebased)

Performance (%)	1m	3m	12m
Absolute	1.9	7.9	12.7
S&P 500 INDEX	3.2	5.1	3.2

Source: Deutsche Bank

Forecasts And Ratios

Year End Jun 30	2016A	2017E
1Q EPS	0.98	1.01
2Q EPS	1.04	1.10
3Q EPS	0.86	0.92
4Q EPS	0.79	0.85
FY EPS (USD)	3.67	3.88

Source: Deutsche Bank estimates, company data

Deutsche Bank Securities Inc.

Distributed on: 08/03/2016 00:07:02GMT

2 August 2016
Cosmetics, Household & Personal Care
Procter & Gamble

Fiscal year end 30-Jun	2015	2016	2017E
Financial Summary			
DB EPS (USD)	3.76	3.67	3.88
Reported EPS (USD)	2.75	3.54	3.77
DPS (USD)	2.59	2.65	2.69
BVPS (USD)	21.90	20.24	21.86
Valuation Metrics			
Price/Sales (x)	3.4	3.4	3.5
P/E (DB) (x)	22.4	21.4	22.3
P/E (Reported) (x)	30.5	22.2	22.9
P/BV (x)	3.6	4.2	4.0
FCF yield (%)	4.2	5.3	4.4
Dividend yield (%)	3.1	3.4	3.1
EV/Sales	3.7	3.7	3.8
EV/EBITDA	15.3	14.1	14.4
EV/EBIT	18.8	17.2	17.5
Income Statement (USDm)			
Sales	70,749	65,299	66,174
EBITDA	16,998	17,125	17,357
EBIT	13,864	14,047	14,305
Pre-tax profit	11,012	13,846	14,142
Net income	7,924	10,135	10,218
Cash Flow (USDm)			
Cash flow from operations	13,857	15,126	13,657
Net Capex	-3,736	-3,314	-3,366
Free cash flow	10,121	11,812	10,291
Equity raised/(bought back)	-1,778	-3,062	-2,000
Dividends paid	-7,287	-7,436	-7,274
Net inc/(dec) in borrowings	-3,954	1,285	2,000
Other investing/financing cash flows	442	-2,261	0
Net cash flow	-2,456	338	3,018
Change in working capital	*614*	*1,640*	*95*
Balance Sheet (USDm)			
Cash and cash equivalents	6,836	7,102	10,120
Property, plant & equipment	19,655	19,385	19,699
Goodwill	44,622	44,350	44,350
Other assets	58,382	56,299	56,863
Total assets	129,495	127,136	131,031
Debt	30,345	30,598	32,598
Other liabilities	36,100	38,555	39,214
Total liabilities	66,445	69,153	71,812
Total shareholders' equity	63,050	57,983	59,220
Net debt	*23,509*	*23,496*	*22,478*
Key Company Metrics			
Sales growth (%)	nm	-7.7	1.3
DB EPS growth (%)	na	-2.3	5.6
Payout ratio (%)	94.2	75.0	71.2
EBITDA Margin (%)	24.0	26.2	26.2
EBIT Margin (%)	19.6	21.5	21.6
ROE (%)	12.6	16.7	17.4
Net debt/equity (%)	37.3	40.5	38.0
Net interest cover (x)	29.1	35.4	34.7
DuPont Analysis			
EBIT margin (%)	19.6	21.5	21.6
x Asset turnover (x)	0.5	0.5	0.5
x Financial cost ratio (x)	1.0	1.0	1.0
x Tax and other effects (x)	0.6	0.7	0.7
= ROA (post tax) (%)	6.1	7.9	7.9
x Financial leverage (x)	2.1	2.1	2.2
= ROE (%)	12.6	16.7	17.4
annual growth (%)	*na*	*33.3*	*4.1*
x NTA/share (avg) (x)	21.9	21.1	21.6
= Reported EPS	2.75	3.54	3.77
annual growth (%)	*na*	*28.5*	*6.6*

Source: Company data, Deutsche Bank estimates

Model updated:02 August 2016

Running the numbers
North America
United States
Cosmetics, Household & Personal Care

Procter & Gamble

Reuters: PG.N   Bloomberg: PG UN

Buy

Price (1 Aug 16)	USD 86.41
Target Price	USD 95.00
52 Week range	USD 68.06 - 86.41
Market Cap (m)	USDm 234,105
	EURm 209,602

Company Profile

The Procter & Gamble Company manufactures and markets consumer product brands in over 140 countries around the globe. Popular brand names include: Pampers, Tide, Ariel, Always, Whisper, Pantene, Mach3, Bounty, Dawn, Pringles, Folgers, Charmin, Downy, Lenor, Iams, Crest, Oral-B, Actonel, Duracell, Olay, Head & Shoulders, Wella, Gillette, and Braun. Through 5 global business units (baby and family care, fabric and home care, beauty care, health care, and snacks and beverages) the company markets 300 consumer product brands worldwide.

Price Performance

— Procter & Gamble   — S&P 500 INDEX (Rebased)

Margin Trends

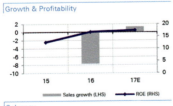

— EBITDA Margin   — EBIT Margin

Growth & Profitability

Sales growth (LHS)   ROE (RHS)

Solvency

Net debt/equity (LHS)   Net interest cover (RHS)

Bill Schmitz
+1 203 863-2285   william.schmitz@db.com

Deutsche Bank Securities Inc.

2 August 2016
Cosmetics, Household & Personal Care
Procter & Gamble

Unleashing the Hounds

Maintain Buy

While it is currently just rhetoric, strategic work and guidance, there is a clear shift in the way P&G intends to operate its business and although we have seen false starts before, the urgency here is as high as we can remember. Instead of playing not to lose and preserving the "structural integrity of its categories" and operating the business like a utility, the gloves are coming off and company is aiming to get the belt back.

Taking a big step back, investors have justifiably relegated P&G to the group of possibly rigid, complacent and unexciting companies weighed down by sheer size and entrenched views on how its categories, brands and people should operate. With this narrowed view and still dominant brand equity portfolio, the company did not recognize seismic changes in how the industry operates, where and how consumers shop and the price points they are willing to pay, especially in important geographies like China where company's historical dominance has become more of a problem of complacency than a blessing.

However, over the last few quarters, awoken by the better relative organic sales, EPS and stock price performance of their competitors, the company has worked relentlessly to build a portfolio it can effectively manage. After whittling the business down to 10 categories and 65 brands with the best ability to harness its core competencies of innovation, marketing and supply chain excellence (and eschewing brands in fragmented categories competing on fashion and flare) the core is finally in the right place to show meaningful growth progress, something that has been elusive since before the Great Recession. Of course, much of the future path is predicated on execution, and the jury is still out with few reasons to get excited if one reviews the global Nielsen market share trends that show ongoing share losses across the globe, with latest EM data showing P&G only gaining market share in 7% of the sales we track.

2 August 2016
Cosmetics, Household & Personal Care
Procter & Gamble

Figure 1: Global market share trends - % of sales gaining/losing share

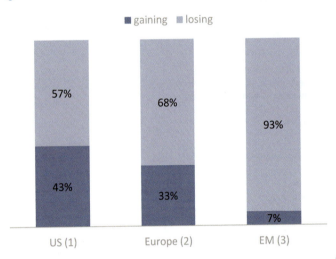

Source: Deutsche Bank, Nielsen
(1) US is total scanned sales for 12 weeks ended July 16, 2016;
(2) Europe is selected categories for period ended 6/12/2016;
(3) EM is selected categories for 4 months ended April 2016.

Perhaps we are being overly optimistic, but the company's market share trends over the last few years, especially in China and some other emerging markets, are so poor they might actually be good – bear with us. Slow and consistent share losses can often be hidden from senior management and rationalized away. However, with such big losses in big categories in strategically crucial markets, urgency builds and becomes a catalyst for change, whether it be swapping out country general managers, allocating more triage resources or even, as the company has done, exiting categories entirely where it doesn't have a leg up and reallocating them to places where they can move the broader corporate needle faster. Until recently, management has communicated that market shares don't really matter, with category health and margin structure the more important driver of value, almost chastising us scorekeepers for myopically focusing on such a simple metric. Fortunately, this playing not to lose mentality is changing and that is good for the sustainable health of the business **and** the stock price. For investors, we believe the easiest and most effective scoreboard to use is relative organic growth and with P&G growing low single digits while most of its multinational peers grow mid singles, management and the board seem to now understand the urgency in investing to get the top line moving in the right direction again to lift the multiple and reduce the reliance on productivity savings alone to drive margins, EPS growth and cash flow.

2 August 2016
Cosmetics, Household & Personal Care
Procter & Gamble

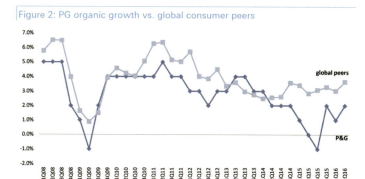
Figure 2: PG organic growth vs. global consumer peers

Source: Deutsche Bank, Company filings

With the company again reporting a relatively weak organic growth number despite undemanding comparisons this quarter and guidance, as expected, coming in below the Street, the story is still unfortunately predicated on latent potential instead of demonstrable results. In our view, if the company can get organic growth to at least 3% leaving the fiscal year and show progress on market share trends, which it should be able to do with the stepped up innovation and marketing spending (they are already seeing sequential improvements), a combination of valuation multiple expansion and upward estimate revisions should help make P&G a story stock like Coke in beverages now and PepsiCo before that. After suffering through significant macro headwinds, currency pains and general consumption malaise, most of the components of the P&L should start to cooperate, boosted by the following:

(i)   Currency headwinds start to ease, with combination of translation and more onerous transaction headwinds sequentially improving provided current spot rates hold;

(ii) Commodities remain benign and pricing, outside some deflationary pressures in Europe and the UK, remains resilient;

(iii) Promised $10 billion of incremental productivity savings on top of previous $10 billion of savings (company has commented that $7 billion of these savings have been absorbed by currency) should provide ample flexibility for reinvestment if realized, with plenty left over to boost earnings which have hovered around $4 for almost a decade;

(iv) Negative geographic mix and potentially, product mix, should start to ease as high margin US category growth trends improve and strategic spending behind high margin hair care business gains traction, with benefits of more focused, 10 category portfolio, also helping reduce complexity and lifting gross margin. If GM growth rates accelerate, mix should weaken but sales growth would accelerate and multiple could expand.

To put these dynamics in perspective, we take a look at the drivers of gross margin upside this quarter as a rough proxy for what the company is capable of for FY17.

2 August 2016
Cosmetics, Household & Personal Care
Procter & Gamble

Figure 3: 4Q16 gross margin derivation

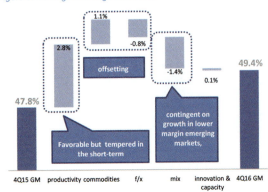

Looking at guidance relative to the incremental drivers of potential margin and EPS upside in FY17 (including Coty accretion and just $1.5 billion of targeted $10 billion of productivity savings over the next 5 years), we believe the company has about $0.50 of earnings cushion to reinvest back into growth and while some may want to see the company flow this through, we believe getting market shares up and accelerating organic growth is much more important to the sustainable story than a year with big EPS upside. For relatively new CEO David Taylor, getting organic growth back to market growth rates of 3-4% would be a huge early achievement and one that investors would likely reward with valuation multiple expansion.

2 August 2016
Cosmetics, Household & Personal Care
Procter & Gamble

Figure 4: Illustrative FY17 earnings algorithm shows significant reinvestment flexibility...

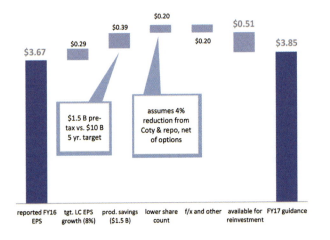

Figure 5: ...off undemanding comparisons

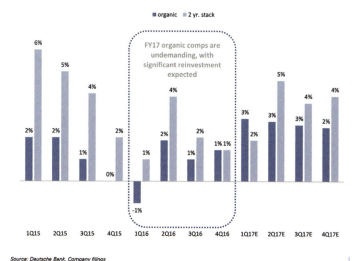

Source: Deutsche Bank, Company filings

To be clear, there have been false positives at P&G before, but we view the current environment as much more conducive in enabling the company to really reinvest behind its much more focused portfolio to lift market shares and drive growth in an increasingly accommodative macro environment (at least for the time being). Like the rest of the names in the group, the stock is clearly

2 August 2016
Cosmetics, Household & Personal Care
Procter & Gamble

not cheap relative to the market which is mostly a function of the yield starved, defensive and low rate environment we're in and if the much discussed rotation out of staples happens, there are no guarantees. However, assuming the macro status quo and stability in currency and commodity rates at current levels, the setup at P&G is as good as we've seen it for some time and we believe we are heading into a period of upside to both organic growth and consensus EPS expectations which should drive group relative outperformance, further enhanced by compelling 3.1% dividend yield. With many investors still underweight the name and compelling path to get the company out of its funk emerging, we are maintaining our Buy and lifting our price target to $95 (from $92).

Financial Statement Forecasts

Our second excerpt is a set of financial statement forecasts developed by Deutsche Bank analysts to forecast P&G's financial statements (*reproduced with permission*).

2 August 2016
Cosmetics, Household & Personal Care
Procter & Gamble

Figure 30: Annual income statement (USD mn)

INCOME STATEMENT	2010	2011	2012	2013	2014	2015	2016	2017E	2018E	2019E	2020E	2021E	2022E
health care	11,493	12,033	9,061	7,684	7,798	7,713	7,350	7,534	7,610	7,686	7,763	7,840	7,919
beauty	19,491	20,009	20,318	19,956	13,398	12,608	11,477	11,764	11,999	12,359	12,730	13,112	13,505
baby, fem & family care	14,736	15,606	21,527	20,479	20,950	20,247	18,505	18,505	19,245	19,822	20,417	21,029	21,660
fabric & home care	23,805	26,543	25,580	25,862	23,509	22,274	20,730	21,038	21,615	22,263	22,931	23,619	24,328
Snacks & Pet Care	3,135	0	0	0	0	0	0	0	0	0	0	0	0
grooming	7,631	8,173	8,339	8,038	8,009	7,441	6,815	6,911	7,118	7,332	7,552	7,778	8,012
Duracell/Braun													
corporate & other	(1,353)	(1,260)	(1,145)	562	737	466	422	422	418	431	443	457	470
Total Net Sales	**78,938**	**81,104**	**83,680**	**82,581**	**74,401**	**70,749**	**65,299**	**66,174**	**68,006**	**69,893**	**71,837**	**73,836**	**75,895**
Cost of Goods Sold	35,412	37,567	39,478	38,676	36,210	33,931	29,735	29,702	31,102	31,525	31,949	32,395	32,843
Depreciation	2,507	2,292	2,704	2,454	2,519	2,606	2,550	2,524	2,192	2,274	2,359	2,424	2,492
Gross Profit	**41,019**	**41,245**	**41,498**	**41,451**	**35,672**	**34,212**	**33,014**	**33,948**	**34,711**	**36,095**	**37,529**	**39,017**	**40,560**
Advertising & Promotion	8,576	9,210	9,345	9,612	8,290	9,236	8,525	8,639	8,878	9,124	9,378	9,639	9,908
Research and Development	1,950	1,982	2,029	1,980	2,047	2,023	1,867	1,892	1,945	1,999	2,054	2,111	2,170
SG&A	13,590	14,012	13,947	13,595	10,147	8,561	8,047	8,584	8,194	8,458	8,740	9,018	9,290
Intangible asset amortization	601	546	500	528	528	528	528	528	528	528	528	528	528
Total MR&A Expenses	**24,717**	**25,750**	**25,821**	**25,715**	**21,012**	**20,348**	**18,967**	**19,643**	**19,544**	**20,108**	**20,700**	**21,296**	**21,896**
Operating Profit	**16,302**	**15,495**	**15,677**	**15,736**	**14,660**	**13,864**	**14,047**	**14,305**	**15,167**	**15,986**	**16,829**	**17,721**	**18,664**
Interest Expense	946	831	769	620	609	477	397	412	412	412	412	412	412
Other expense/(income)	309	(265)	2,123	424	542	2,375	281	(248)	(200)	(50)	(50)	(50)	(50)
Pretax Income	**15,047**	**14,929**	**12,785**	**14,692**	**13,509**	**11,012**	**13,369**	**14,142**	**14,955**	**15,624**	**16,467**	**17,359**	**18,302**
Income Taxes	4,101	3,299	3,468	3,391	2,851	2,725	3,342	3,535	3,739	3,906	4,117	4,340	4,576
Gain on sale(s)/ Minority Ineterst	1,790	82	148	90	142	108	96	96	96				
Net Income	**12,736**	**11,548**	**9,169**	**11,211**	**10,516**	**8,179**	**9,931**	**10,510**	**11,120**	**11,718**	**12,350**	**13,019**	**13,727**
Preferred Dividends	181	194	207	222	238	255	273	293	314	329	346	363	381
Net Income after Preferred	**12,555**	**11,354**	**8,962**	**10,989**	**10,278**	**7,924**	**9,658**	**10,218**	**10,807**	**11,389**	**12,004**	**12,656**	**13,345**
Fully Diluted EPS	**4.11**	**3.85**	**3.12**	**3.83**	**3.62**	**2.84**	**3.49**	**3.88**	**4.19**	**4.46**	**4.73**	**5.01**	**5.30**
Core EPS		**3.87**	**3.85**	**4.01**	**3.85**	**3.76**	**3.67**	**3.88**	**4.19**				
Fully Diluted Shares	3,100	3,002	2,941	2,930	2,905	2,884	2,845	2,709	2,656	2,625	2,612	2,600	2,589
Dividend per share	$1.70	$1.86	$2.02	$2.15	$2.30	$2.44	$2.52	$2.58	$2.70	$3.01	$3.34	$3.69	$4.09
Dividend payout ratio	41.4%	48.3%	64.7%	56.2%	63.5%	86.0%	72.1%	66.4%	64.5%	67.5%	70.6%	73.8%	77.1%
EBITDA	19,410	18,333	18,881	18,718	17,707	16,998	17,125	17,357	17,888	18,788	19,716	20,673	21,684
one-time charges (after-tax)	(1,339)	65	3,399	531	651	2,661	520	0	0				
% OF SALES													
Gross margin	**52.0%**	**50.9%**	**49.6%**	**50.2%**	**47.9%**	**48.4%**	**50.6%**	**51.3%**	**51.0%**	51.6%	52.2%	52.8%	53.4%
Depreciaton	3.2%	2.8%	3.2%	3.0%	3.4%	3.7%	3.9%	3.8%	3.2%	3.3%	3.3%	3.3%	3.3%
Research & development	2.5%	2.4%	2.4%	2.4%	2.8%	2.9%	2.9%	2.9%	2.9%	2.9%	2.9%	2.9%	2.9%
Advertising	10.9%	11.4%	11.2%	11.6%	11.1%	13.1%	13.1%	13.1%	13.1%	13.1%	13.1%	13.1%	13.1%
SG&A	17.2%	17.3%	16.7%	16.5%	13.6%	12.1%	12.3%	13.0%	12.0%	12.1%	12.2%	12.2%	12.2%
Amortization	0.8%	0.7%	0.6%	0.6%	0.7%	0.7%	0.8%	0.8%	0.8%	0.8%	0.7%	0.7%	0.7%
Total Operating Expenses	31.3%	31.7%	30.9%	31.1%	28.2%	28.8%	29.0%	29.7%	28.7%	28.8%	28.8%	28.8%	28.8%
Operating margin	**20.7%**	**19.1%**	**18.7%**	**19.1%**	**19.7%**	**19.6%**	**21.5%**	**21.6%**	**22.3%**	**22.9%**	**23.4%**	**24.0%**	**24.6%**
Pretax margin	**19.1%**	**18.4%**	**15.3%**	**17.8%**	**18.2%**	**15.6%**	**20.5%**	**21.4%**	**22.0%**	**22.4%**	**22.9%**	**23.5%**	**24.1%**
Effective tax rate	27.3%	22.1%	27.1%	23.1%	21.1%	24.7%	25.0%	25.0%	25.0%	25.0%	25.0%	25.0%	25.0%
Net margin	**16.1%**	**14.2%**	**11.0%**	**13.6%**	**14.1%**	**11.6%**	**15.2%**	**15.9%**	**16.4%**	**16.8%**	**17.2%**	**17.6%**	**18.1%**
EBITDA margin	24.6%	22.6%	22.6%	22.7%	23.8%	24.0%	26.2%	26.2%	26.3%	26.9%	27.4%	28.0%	28.6%

Source: Deutsche Bank, Company filings

2 August 2016
Cosmetics, Household & Personal Care
Procter & Gamble

Figure 32: Annual Balance Sheet (USD mn)

BALANCE SHEET	2010	2011	2012	2013	2014	2015	2016	2017E	2018E	2019E	2020E	2021E	2022E
ASSETS													
Cash and equivalents	2,879	2,768	4,436	5,947	8,558	6,836	7,102	10,120	6,562	2,586	2,879	2,879	2,879
Short term investments	0	0	0	0	2,128	4,767	6,246	6,246	6,246	6,246	6,246	6,246	6,246
Accounts receivable	5,335	6,275	6,068	6,508	6,386	4,568	4,373	4,532	4,658	4,787	4,920	5,057	5,198
Inventory	6,384	7,379	6,721	6,909	6,759	4,979	4,716	4,679	4,743	4,815	4,888	4,961	5,034
Deferred income taxes	990	1,140	1,001	948	1,095	1,356	1,507	1,522	1,564	1,608	1,652	1,698	1,746
Other current assets	3,194	4,408	3,684	3,678	6,691	7,140	9,838	10,125	11,085	11,393	11,709	12,035	12,371
Total current assets	**18,782**	**21,970**	**21,910**	**23,990**	**31,617**	**29,646**	**33,782**	**37,224**	**34,858**	**31,435**	**32,295**	**32,876**	**33,474**
Net fixed assets	19,244	21,293	20,377	21,666	22,304	19,655	19,385	19,699	19,699	20,220	20,735	21,264	21,808
Goodwill	54,012	57,562	53,773	55,188	52,832	44,622	44,350	44,350	44,350	44,350	44,350	44,350	44,350
Other intangibles	31,636	32,620	30,988	31,572	31,715	25,010	24,527	24,527	24,527	23,999	23,471	22,943	22,415
Other assets	4,498	4,909	5,196	6,847	5,798	10,562	5,092	5,232	5,376	5,526	5,679	5,837	6,000
Total Assets	**128,172**	**138,354**	**132,244**	**139,263**	**144,266**	**129,495**	**127,136**	**131,031**	**128,810**	**125,530**	**126,530**	**127,271**	**128,047**
LIABILITIES & SHAREHOLDERS' EQUITY													
Accounts payable	7,251	8,022	7,920	8,777	8,461	8,138	9,325	9,182	7,297	7,408	7,519	7,632	7,745
Accruals	8,559	9,290	8,289	8,828	8,999	8,091	7,449	7,653	7,865	8,083	8,308	8,539	8,777
Accrued income taxes	0	0	0	0	660	1,543	2,343	2,407	2,474	2,543	2,613	2,686	2,761
Total current liabilities	**15,810**	**17,312**	**16,209**	**17,605**	**18,120**	**17,772**	**19,117**	**19,243**	**17,636**	**18,034**	**18,441**	**18,857**	**19,283**
Total debt	29,832	32,014	29,778	31,543	35,417	30,345	30,598	32,598	32,598	32,598	32,598	32,598	32,598
Deferred income taxes	10,902	11,070	10,132	10,827	10,853	9,179	9,113	9,363	9,622	9,889	10,164	10,447	10,738
Other liabilities	10,189	9,957	12,090	10,579	9,900	9,149	10,325	10,608	10,902	11,204	11,516	11,836	12,166
Preferred Stock	1,277	1,277	1,277	1,277	1,277	1,277	1,277	1,277	1,277	1,277	1,277	1,277	1,277
Shareholders' equity	60,162	66,724	62,758	67,432	68,699	61,773	56,706	57,943	56,775	52,820	52,827	52,548	52,277
Total Liab. & Shareholders' equity	**128,172**	**138,354**	**132,244**	**139,263**	**144,266**	**129,495**	**127,136**	**131,031**	**128,810**	**125,823**	**126,823**	**127,564**	**128,340**
BALANCE SHEET RELATIONSHIPS													
Accounts receivable days	24.7	28.2	26.5	28.8	31.3	23.6	24.4	25.0	25.0	25.0	25.0	25.0	25.0
Inventory turns	5.9x	5.4x	6.3x	6.0x	5.7x	7.3x	6.8x	6.9x	7.0x	7.0x	7.0x	7.0x	7.0x
Inventory days	61.5	67.6	58.2	61.3	63.7	49.7	53.3	53.0	52.0	52.0	52.0	52.0	52.0
Deferred income tax asset % of sales	1.3%	1.4%	1.2%	1.1%	1.5%	1.9%	2.3%	2.3%	2.3%	2.3%	2.3%	2.3%	2.3%
Other current assets as % of sales	4.0%	5.4%	4.4%	4.5%	9.0%	10.1%	15.1%	15.3%	16.3%	16.3%	16.3%	16.3%	16.3%
Accounts payable days	69.8	73.5	68.5	77.9	79.7	81.3	105.4	104.0	80.0	80.0	80.0	80.0	80.0
Accruals as % of sales	10.8%	11.5%	9.9%	10.7%	12.1%	11.4%	11.4%	11.6%	11.6%	11.6%	11.6%	11.6%	11.6%
Accrued income taxes as % of sales	0.0%	0.0%	0.0%	0.0%	0.9%	2.2%	3.6%	3.6%	3.6%	3.6%	3.6%	3.6%	3.6%
Working capital as % of sales	0.1%	2.3%	1.5%	0.5%	3.8%	0.4%	2.0%	2.4%	6.5%	6.5%	6.6%	6.6%	6.7%
Cash Conversion Cycle	16.3	22.4	16.1	12.2	15.3	(8.0)	(27.7)	(26.0)	(3.0)	(3.0)	(3.0)	(3.0)	(3.0)
Other assets as % of sales	5.7%	6.1%	6.2%	8.3%	7.8%	14.9%	7.8%	7.9%	7.9%	7.9%	7.9%	7.9%	7.9%
Deferred income tax liability as % of sales	13.8%	13.6%	12.1%	13.1%	14.6%	13.0%	14.0%	14.1%	14.1%	14.1%	14.1%	14.1%	14.1%
Other liabilities as % of sales	12.9%	12.3%	14.4%	12.8%	13.3%	12.9%	15.8%	16.0%	16.0%	16.0%	16.0%	16.0%	16.0%
Debt/capitalization	32.7%	32.0%	31.7%	31.5%	33.6%	32.5%	34.5%	35.5%	36.0%	37.6%	37.6%	37.7%	37.8%
Debt/EBITDA	1.5x	1.7x	1.6x	1.7x	2.0x	1.8x	1.8x	1.9x	1.8x	1.7x	1.7x	1.6x	1.5x
EBITDA/Int. Exp.	20.5x	22.1x	24.6x	30.2x	29.1x	35.6x	43.1x	42.1x	43.4x	45.6x	47.9x	50.2x	52.6x
Return on avg. Assets (ROA)	9.5%	8.5%	6.6%	8.1%	7.3%	5.8%	7.5%	7.9%	8.3%	9.0%	9.5%	10.0%	10.5%
Return on avg. Equity (ROE)	20.6%	17.9%	13.8%	16.9%	15.1%	12.1%	16.3%	17.8%	18.8%	20.8%	22.7%	24.0%	25.5%
Return on avg. Invested Capital (ROIC)	12.9%	13.0%	12.2%	13.2%	12.1%	11.4%	12.5%	13.2%	13.7%	14.3%	15.0%	15.9%	16.8%
Capital expenditures	3,067	3,306	3,964	4,008	3,848	3,736	3,314	3,366	2,720	2,796	2,873	2,953	3,036
Capex as % of sales	3.9%	4.1%	4.7%	4.9%	5.2%	5.3%	5.1%	5.1%	4.0%	4.0%	4.0%	4.0%	4.0%
Acquisitions (net of divestitures)	2,470	(176)	2,871	(2,287)	(259)	845	(2,261)	0	0	0	0	0	0
Share repurchase	5,283	5,737	2,295	2,537	0	2,198	7,666	9,241	8,483	7,437	3,283	3,332	3,035
Required cash as % of sales	3.6%	3.4%	5.3%	7.2%	11.5%	9.7%	10.9%	15.3%	9.6%	3.7%	4.0%	3.9%	3.8%
Required cash	2,879	2,879	2,879	2,879	2,879	2,879	2,879	2,879	2,879	2,879	2,879	2,879	2,879
Available for repurchases	5,405	5,183	3,965	5,500	9,620	6,047	7,666	9,241	8,483	7,437	3,283	3,332	3,035
Repurchase Price	$71	$82	$86	$90	$95	$100	$105	$110	$115	$121	$127	$134	$140
% Growth in Avg. Repurchase Price	-35.0%	15.0%	5.0%	5.0%	5.0%	5.0%	5.0%	5.0%	5.0%	5.0%	5.0%	5.0%	5.0%

Source: Deutsche Bank, Company filings

2 August 2016
Cosmetics, Household & Personal Care
Procter & Gamble

Figure 33: Annual Cash Flow & Economic Returns (USD mn)

CASH FLOW STATEMENT	2010	2011	2012	2013	2014	2015	2016	2017E	2018E	2019E	2020E	2021E	2022E
Net income	12,736	11,548	9,169	11,211	10,516	8,179	9,931	10,510	11,120	11,718	12,350	13,019	13,727
Deprec. & Amortization	3,108	2,838	3,204	2,982	3,047	3,134	3,078	3,052	2,720	2,802	2,887	2,952	3,020
Cash restructuring/other			(203)	1,205	(608)								
Chg. in deferred taxes	369	128	(65)	748	(121)	(1,935)	(217)	235	217	224	230	237	244
Chg. in accounts receivable	501	(426)	(427)	(440)	122	1,818	195	(159)	(125)	(129)	(133)	(137)	(141)
Chg. in inventories	496	(501)	77	(188)	150	1,780	263	37	(64)	(72)	(72)	(73)	(73)
Chg. in accounts payable	1,271	358	(22)	857	(316)	(323)	1,187	(143)	(1,885)	111	111	112	113
Chg. in accruals	(42)	0	0	539	171	(908)	(642)	204	212	218	225	231	238
Chg. in income taxes	0	0	0	0	660	883	800	64	67	69	71	73	75
Change in other assets/liabilities	(2,367)	(791)	143	(329)	(202)	1,872	840	(143)	(811)	(154)	(159)	(163)	(168)
Operating Cash Flow	**16,072**	**12,961**	**13,284**	**14,772**	**14,027**	**14,500**	**15,435**	**13,657**	**11,450**	**14,786**	**15,510**	**16,251**	**17,034**
Capital expenditures	(3,067)	(3,306)	(3,964)	(4,008)	(3,848)	(3,736)	(3,314)	(3,366)	(2,720)	(2,796)	(2,873)	(2,953)	(3,036)
Dividends	(5,458)	(5,767)	(6,139)	(6,519)	(6,911)	(7,287)	(7,436)	(7,274)	(7,488)	(8,237)	(9,060)	(9,966)	(10,963)
Free Cash Flow	**7,547**	**3,878**	**3,181**	**4,245**	**3,268**	**3,477**	**4,685**	**3,018**	**1,242**	**3,764**	**3,576**	**3,332**	**3,035**
Net Financing	(6,514)	1,481	(1,976)	1,985	3,543	(3,954)	1,285	2,000	0	0	0	0	0
Share repurchase	(5,283)	(5,737)	(2,295)	(2,537)	(3,911)	(1,778)	(3,062)	(2,000)	(4,800)	(7,437)	(3,283)	(3,332)	(3,035)
Acquisitions	2,470	(176)	2,871	4	(131)	845	(381)	0	0	0	0	0	0
Other	(122)	443	(113)	(2,287)	(259)	(403)	(2,261)	0	0	0	0	0	0
Change in cash	**(1,902)**	**(111)**	**1,668**	**1,410**	**2,510**	**(1,813)**	**266**	**3,018**	**(3,558)**	**(3,683)**	**293**	**0**	**0**
Cash balance - EOY	2,879	2,768	4,436	5,846	8,356	6,543	6,809	9,827	6,269	2,586	2,879	2,879	2,879
Operating Cash Flow per share	$5.18	$4.31	$4.52	$5.04	$4.83	$5.03	$5.43	$5.04	$4.31	$5.63	$5.94	$6.25	$6.58
Free Cash Flow per share	$2.43	$1.29	$1.08	$1.45	$1.13	$1.21	$1.65	$1.11	$0.47	$1.43	$1.37	$1.28	$1.17
FCF productivity (pre-dividend)	102%	84%	102%	96%	97%	132%							
RETURN ON ECONOMIC CAPITAL													
EBIT	16,302	15,495	15,677	15,736	14,660	13,864	14,047	14,305	15,167	15,986	16,829	17,721	18,664
Less: Taxes	4,443	3,424	4,252	3,632	3,094	3,431	3,511	3,576	3,792	3,997	4,207	4,430	4,666
EBIAT	11,859	12,071	11,424	12,104	11,566	10,433	10,536	10,729	11,376	11,990	12,622	13,291	13,998
Goodwill Amortization	0	0	0	0	0	0	0	0	0	0	0	0	0
NOPAT	**11,859**	**12,071**	**11,424**	**12,104**	**11,566**	**10,433**	**10,536**	**10,729**	**11,376**	**11,990**	**12,622**	**13,291**	**13,998**
Invested Capital	110,917	110,232	113,043	115,146	121,394	118,831	111,824	111,700	112,987	110,681	108,970	109,105	109,109
ROIC	10.7%	11.0%	10.1%	10.5%	9.5%	8.8%	9.4%	9.6%	10.1%	10.8%	11.6%	12.2%	12.8%
WACC	9.0%	9.0%	9.0%	8.0%	8.0%	8.0%	8.0%	8.0%	8.0%	8.0%	8.0%	8.0%	8.0%
ROIC-WACC Spread	1.7%	2.0%	1.1%	2.5%	1.5%	0.8%	1.4%	1.6%	2.1%	2.8%	3.6%	4.2%	4.8%
Economic Profit	1,876	2,150	1,250	2,892	1,855	927	1,590	1,793	2,337	3,135	3,904	4,562	5,269
%change in EP	280%	15%	-42%	131%	-36%	-50%	72%	13%	30%	34%	25%	17%	16%
Change in EP	1,383	274	(900)	1,642	(1,038)	(928)	663	203	544	798	769	658	707
Cumulative Incremental EP	127	400	(499)	1,143	105	(823)	(160)	43	587	1,386	2,155	2,813	3,520

Source: Deutsche Bank, Company filings

Valuation Model

Our third excerpt is the discounted cash flow (DCF) analysis developed by Deutsche Bank analysts to forecast P&G's target stock price of $95 per share on August 1, 2016, for this report that is dated August 2, 2016. (*reproduced with permission*).

---

2 August 2016
Cosmetics, Household & Personal Care
Procter & Gamble

Valuation

We value the company using a hybrid relative value/discounted cash flow methodology to derive our $95 price target. Shares are trading in-line with their historical average premium to the market but well below average premium to consumer peers. Given the company's relatively stable cash flows, we use a DCF analysis to derive our price target. Assumptions in this model include 2.8% sales growth and 0.6 points of margin growth through 2024, discounted at a 6.5% WACC derived from Capital Asset Pricing Model (3% Rfr, 4% equity risk premium) with 1.0% TVG in-line with inflation and implying a 13.4x EBITDA exit multiple. Our debt and share count are PF for Duracell and beauty brands exit.

Figure 21: Shares are trading in line with historical premium relative to S&P500...

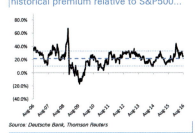

Source: Deutsche Bank, Thomson Reuters

Figure 22:...but well below average premium relative to consumer peer group

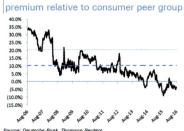

Source: Deutsche Bank, Thomson Reuters

Figure 23: Discounted cash flow analysis (USD m)

	2017E	2018E	2019E	2020E	2021E	2022E	2023E	2024E
Revenue	$66,174	$68,006	$69,893	$71,837	$73,836	$75,895	$78,013	$80,194
Revenue Growth	1.3%	2.8%	2.8%	2.8%	2.8%	2.8%	2.8%	2.8%
Operating Margin	21.6%	22.3%	22.9%	23.4%	24.0%	24.6%	25.2%	25.8%
EBIT	14,305	15,167	15,986	16,829	17,721	18,664	19,663	20,719
Tax Rate	25.0%	25.0%	25.0%	25.0%	25.0%	25.0%	25.0%	25.0%
After-tax EBIT	10,729	11,376	11,990	12,622	13,291	13,998	14,747	15,539
+: D&A	3,052	2,720	2,802	2,887	2,952	3,020	3,090	3,161
+: Capital Expenditures	(3,366)	(2,720)	(2,796)	(2,873)	(2,953)	(3,036)	(3,121)	(3,208)
+/-: Changes in Working Capital	(140)	(2,607)	42	42	43	43	44	44
+/-: Changes in Deferred Taxes	235	217	224	230	237	244	251	258
Unlevered Free Cash Flow	10,510	8,985	12,262	12,908	13,569	14,270	15,011	15,795
Terminal Value								320,636
Discounted Cash Flow	9,924	7,967	10,208	10,090	9,960	9,834	9,714	204,423

Discounted Cash Flow	272,119		EBITDA Exit	13.4x
-: Net Debt	15,250*		Sales CAGR	2.8%
Implied Equity Value	256,869		EBIT CAGR	5.4%
Shares Outstanding	2,702*		Margin growth	0.6%
Implied Share Price	$95			

Source: Deutsche Bank, Company filings

Risks

Downside risks include hiccup in US recovery, decline in US or global consumer confidence, increase in unemployment or decline in wage growth, price elasticity in developing markets, commodity inflation without pricing offset, growth in private label or value brands, stronger dollar, increased competition, and inability to drive volume from innovation and marketing.

Concluding Observations of Analyst Report

We make four observations on the Deutsche Bank analyst report regarding P&G's target stock price.

1. The analyst report defines free cash flow to the firm as follows:

	Earnings before interest and taxes (EBIT)
−	Taxes (EBIT × assumed tax rate)
+	Depreciation and amortization
−	Capital expenditures
−	Increase in working capital
=	Free cash flow to the firm

2. This analyst report uses the same DCF computation we describe in this module. Free cash flow estimates for the seven-year forecast horizon (2017E through 2023E) and the terminal year (2024E) are discounted at the weighted average cost of capital, resulting in a total firm value of $272,119 million. The analyst, then, subtracts P&G's debt of $15,250 million, to yield the implied equity value of $256,869, or $95 per share, based on 2,702 million shares outstanding.

3. The cost of equity capital is estimated using the capital asset pricing model (CAPM) as we describe in the module. The analyst's estimated WACC is at a level higher than the 4.8% WACC that we assume in the module. It is not uncommon that model assumptions differ among analysts.

4. Bottom line: We see that this analyst's $95 stock price target is slightly lower than the $99.38 stock price estimate that we independently determined in this module. There are a number of differences between our forecast and that of the Deutsche Bank analyst, including growth rates, margins, and WACC.

Guidance Answers

You Are the Chief Financial Officer

Pg. 13-6 Cash flow can be increased by reducing assets. For example, receivables can be reduced by the following.

- Encouraging up-front payments or progress billings on long-term contracts
- Increasing credit standards to avoid slow-paying accounts before sales are made
- Monitoring account age and sending reminders to past-due customers
- Selling accounts receivable to a financial institution or special purpose entity

As another example of asset reduction, plant assets can be reduced by the following.

- Selling unused or excess plant assets
- Forming alliances with other companies to share specialized plant assets
- Owning assets in a special purpose entity with other companies
- Selling production facilities to a contract manufacturer and purchasing the output

You Are the Chief Financial Officer

Pg. 13-13 RNOA can be disaggregated into its two key drivers: net operating profit margin and net operating asset turnover. Net operating profit margin can be increased by improving gross profit margins (better product pricing, lower-cost manufacturing, etc.) and closely monitoring and controlling operating expenses. Net operating asset turnover can be increased by reducing net operating working capital (better monitoring of receivables, better management of inventories, carefully extending payables, etc.) and making more effective use of plant assets (disposing of unused assets, forming corporate alliances to increase plant asset capacity, selling productive assets to contract producers and purchasing the output, etc.). The ROPI model effectively focuses managers on the balance sheet *and* income statement.

Questions

Q13-1. Explain how information contained in financial statements is useful in pricing securities. Are there some components of earnings that are more useful than others in this regard? What nonfinancial information might also be useful?

Q13-2. In general, what role do expectations play in pricing equity securities? What is the relation between security prices and expected returns (the discount rate, or WACC, in this case)?

Q13-3. What are free cash flows to the firm (FCFF) and how are they used in the pricing of equity securities?

Q13-4. Define the weighted average cost of capital (WACC).

Q13-5. Define net operating profit after tax (NOPAT).

Q13-6. Define net operating assets (NOA).

Q13-7. Define the concept of residual operating income. How is residual operating income used in pricing equity securities?

Q13-8. What insight does disaggregation of RNOA into net operating profit margin and net operating asset turnover provide for managing a company?

Assignments with the ⬤ logo in the margin are available in 𝐁usinessCourse.
See the Preface of the book for details.

Mini Exercises

M13-9. Interpreting Earnings Announcement Effects on Stock Prices
On November 2, 2016, Facebook Inc. announced its 2016 third quarter results. Revenues were up nearly 50% from 2015 and earnings were up a whopping 180% ($5,944 million compared to $2,127 million.) Yet, in the ensuing days, Facebook's stock value fell 7% according to CNBC. Why do you believe that the company's stock price fell despite the good news?

LO1
Facebook Inc. (FB)

M13-10. Computing Residual Operating Income (ROPI)
Home Depot reports net operating profit after tax (NOPAT) of $7,483 million in 2016. Its net operating assets at the beginning of 2016 are $24,796 million. Assuming a 9% weighted average cost of capital (WACC), what is Home Depot's residual operating income for 2016? Show computations.

LO3
Home Depot Inc. (HD)

M13-11. Computing Free Cash Flows to the Firm (FCFF)
Home Depot reports net operating profit after tax (NOPAT) of $7,483 million in 2016. Its net operating assets at the beginning of 2016 are $24,796 million and are $25,415 million at the end of 2016. What are Home Depot's free cash flows to the firm (FCFF) for 2016? Show computations.

LO2
Home Depot Inc. (HD)

M13-12. Computing, Analyzing and Interpreting Residual Operating Income (ROPI)
In its 2015 fiscal year annual report, Texas Roadhouse reports net operating income after tax (NOPAT) of $102,495 thousand. As of the beginning of fiscal year 2015 it reports net operating assets of $596,104 thousand.

a. Did Texas Roadhouse earn positive residual operating income (ROPI) in 2015 if its weighted average cost of capital (WACC) is 7%? Explain.

b. At what level of WACC would Texas Roadhouse not report positive residual operating income for 2015? Explain.

LO3
Texas Roadhouse (TXRH)

M13-13. Estimating Share Value Using the DCF Model

Following are forecasts of **Target Corporation**'s sales, net operating profit after tax (NOPAT), and net operating assets (NOA) as of January 30, 2016.

| | | Horizon Period | | | | | Terminal |
| | Reported | | | | | | |
$ millions	2016	2017	2018	2019	2020	Period
Sales...................	$73,785	$75,261	$76,766	$78,301	$79,867	$80,666
NOPAT	3,312	3,387	3,454	3,524	3,594	3,630
NOA	21,445	21,872	22,309	22,755	23,210	23,443

Answer the following requirements assuming a terminal period growth rate of 1%, a discount rate (WACC) of 6%, common shares outstanding of 602 million, and net nonoperating obligations (NNO) of $8,488 million.

a. Estimate the value of a share of Target common stock using the discounted cash flow (DCF) model as of January 30, 2016.

b. Target Corporation (TGT) stock closed at $81.87 on March 11, 2016, the date the 10-K was filed with the SEC. How does your valuation estimate compare with this closing price? What do you believe are some reasons for the difference?

M13-14. Estimating Share Value Using the ROPI Model

Refer to the information for **Target Corporation** in M13-13 to answer the following requirements.

a. Estimate the value of a share of Target common stock using the residual operating income (ROPI) model as of January 30, 2016.

b. Target Corporation (TGT) stock closed at $81.87 on March 11, 2016, the date the 10-K was filed with the SEC. How does your valuation estimate compare with this closing price? What do you believe are some reasons for the difference?

M13-15. Assess the Effects of Managerial Actions on ROPI and Components

In its 2016 10-K report, **Kellogg** discussed its cost-cutting initiative, *Project K*.

> In November 2013, the Company announced a global four-year efficiency and effectiveness program (Project K). The successful implementation of Project K presents significant organizational design and infrastructure challenges and in many cases will require successful negotiations with third parties, including labor organizations, suppliers, business partners, and other stakeholders. The program is expected to generate a significant amount of savings that may be invested in key strategic areas of focus for the business. We expect that this investment will drive future growth in revenues, gross margin, operating profit, and cash flow.

By undertaking these actions, the company hopes to improve its ROPI. Identify at least four specific ways that these actions can happen *and* the direction of the effects from each on NOPAT and NOA.

Exercises

E13-16. Estimating Share Value Using the DCF Model

Following are forecasts of **Whole Foods**' sales, net operating profit after tax (NOPAT), and net operating assets (NOA) as of September 25, 2016.

| | | Horizon Period | | | | | Terminal |
| | Reported | | | | | | |
$ millions	2016	2017	2018	2019	2020	Period
Sales...........	$15,724	$15,881	$16,199	$16,523	$16,853	$17,022
NOPAT	526	524	535	545	556	562
NOA	3,466	3,500	3,570	3,642	3,715	3,752

Answer the following requirements assuming a discount rate (WACC) of 6%, a terminal period growth rate of 1%, common shares outstanding of 318.3 million, and net nonoperating obligations (NNO) of $242 million.

a. Estimate the value of a share of Whole Foods' common stock using the discounted cash flow (DCF) model as of September 25, 2016.

b. Whole Foods stock closed at $30.96 on November 18, 2016, the date the 10-K was filed with the SEC. How does your valuation estimate compare with this closing price? What do you believe are some reasons for the difference?

E13-17. Estimating Share Value Using the ROPI Model

Refer to the information for Whole Foods Market in E13-16 to answer the following requirements.

a. Estimate the value of a share of Whole Foods' common stock using the residual operating income (ROPI) model as of September 25, 2016.

b. Whole Foods stock closed at $30.96 on November 18, 2016, the date the 10-K was filed with the SEC. How does your valuation estimate compare with this closing price? What do you believe are some reasons for the difference?

E13-18. Estimating Share Value Using the DCF Model

Following are forecasts of sales, net operating profit after tax (NOPAT), and net operating assets (NOA) as of January 31, 2016, for Walmart Stores Inc.

| | Reported | Horizon Period | | | | Terminal |
$ millions	2016	2017	2018	2019	2020	Period
Sales..........	$482,130	$486,951	$491,821	$496,739	$501,706	$506,723
NOPAT	16,634	17,043	17,214	17,386	17,560	17,735
NOA	124,940	126,186	127,448	128,722	130,009	131,309

Answer the following requirements assuming a discount rate (WACC) of 7%, a terminal period growth rate of 1%, common shares outstanding of 3,144 million, net nonoperating obligations (NNO) of $41,329 million, and noncontrolling interest (NCI) on the balance sheet of $3,065 million.

a. Estimate the value of a share of Walmart's common stock using the discounted cash flow (DCF) model as of January 31, 2016.

b. Walmart (WMT) stock closed at $68.80 on March 30, 2016, the date the 10-K was filed with the SEC. How does your valuation estimate compare with this closing price? What do you believe are some reasons for the difference?

E13-19. Estimating Share Value Using the ROPI Model

Refer to the information for Walmart Stores Inc. in E13-18 to answer the following requirements.

a. Estimate the value of a share of Walmart common stock using the residual operating income (ROPI) model as of January 31, 2016.

b. Walmart (WMT) stock closed at $68.80 on March 30, 2016, the date the 10-K was filed with the SEC. How does your valuation estimate compare with this closing price? What do you believe are some reasons for the difference?

LO1, 2
E13-20.   **Identifying and Computing Net Operating Assets (NOA) and Net Nonoperating Obligations (NNO)**

Home Depot Inc. (HD)

Following is the balance sheet for **Home Depot Inc.**, for fiscal year 2015, ended January 31, 2016.

HOME DEPOT INC.
Consolidated Balance Sheet

Fiscal Year End ($ millions, except par value)	Jan. 31, 2016	Feb. 1, 2015
Current assets		
Cash and equivalents	$ 2,216	$ 1,723
Receivables, net	1,890	1,484
Merchandise inventories	11,809	11,079
Other current assets	1,078	1,016
Total current assets	16,993	15,302
Net property and equipment	22,191	22,720
Goodwill	2,102	1,353
Other assets	1,263	571
Total assets	$42,549	$39,946
Current liabilities		
Short-term debt	$ 350	$ 290
Accounts payable	6,565	5,807
Accrued salaries and related expenses	1,515	1,391
Sales taxes payable	476	434
Deferred revenue	1,566	1,468
Income taxes payable	34	35
Current installments of long-term debt	77	38
Other accrued expenses	1,943	1,806
Total current liabilities	12,526	11,269
Long-term debt, excluding current installments	20,888	16,869
Other long-term liabilities	1,965	1,844
Deferred income taxes	854	642
Total liabilities	36,233	30,624
Stockholders' equity		
Common Stock, par value $0.05; authorized: 10 billion shares; issued: 1.772 billion shares at January 31, 2016 and 1.768 billion shares at February 1, 2015; outstanding: 1.252 billion shares at January 31, 2016 and 1.307 billion shares at February 1, 2015	88	88
Paid-in capital	9,347	8,885
Retained earnings	30,973	26,995
Accumulated other comprehensive loss	(898)	(452)
Treasury stock, at cost, 520 million shares at January 31, 2016 and 461 million shares at February 1, 2015	(33,194)	(26,194)
Total shareholders' equity	6,316	9,322
Total liabilities and shareholders' equity	$42,549	$39,946

a.   Compute net operating assets (NOA) and net nonoperating obligations (NNO) for fiscal 2015.

b.   For fiscal 2015, show that: NOA = NNO + Stockholders' equity.

E13-21. Identifying and Computing Net Operating Profit after Tax (NOPAT)

LO1
Home Depot Inc. (HD)

Following is the income statement for **Home Depot Inc.** for fiscal year 2015, ended January 31, 2016.

HOME DEPOT Consolidated Income Statement		
For Fiscal Year Ended ($ millions)	**Jan. 31, 2016**	**Feb. 01, 2015**
Net sales..	$88,519	$83,176
Cost of sales.......................................	58,254	54,787
Gross profit..	30,265	28,389
Operating expenses		
Selling, general and administrative	16,801	16,280
Depreciation and amortization...........................	1,690	1,640
Total operating expenses..............................	18,491	17,920
Operating income....................................	11,774	10,469
Interest and investment income...........................	(166)	(337)
Interest expense....................................	919	830
Interest and other, net	753	493
Earnings before provision for income taxes.....................	11,021	9,976
Provision for income taxes.............................	4,012	3,631
Net earnings......................................	$ 7,009	$ 6,345

Compute net operating profit after tax (NOPAT) for the fiscal year ended January 2016, assuming a federal and state statutory tax rate of 37%.

E13-22. Estimating Share Value Using the DCF Model

LO1, 2
Home Depot Inc. (HD)

Following are forecasts of **Home Depot**'s sales, net operating profit after tax (NOPAT), and net operating assets (NOA) as of January 31, 2016.

	Reported	Horizon Period				Terminal
$ millions	2016	2017	2018	2019	2020	Period
Sales...........	$88,519	$97,371	$107,108	$117,819	$129,601	$134,785
NOPAT	7,483	8,277	9,104	10,015	11,016	11,457
NOA	25,415	27,956	30,752	33,827	37,210	38,698

Answer the following requirements assuming a discount rate (WACC) of 9%, a terminal period growth rate of 4%, common shares outstanding of 1,252 million, net nonoperating obligations (NNO) of $19,099 million.

a. Estimate the value of a share of Home Depot's common stock using the discounted cash flow (DCF) model as of January 31, 2016.

b. Home Depot stock closed at $130.46 on March 24, 2016, the date the Form 10-K was filed with the SEC. How does your valuation estimate compare with this closing price? What do you believe are some reasons for the difference?

E13-23. Estimating Share Value Using the ROPI Model

LO3
Home Depot Inc. (HD)

Refer to the information for **Home Depot Inc.** in E13-22 to answer the following requirements.

a. Estimate the value of a share of Home Depot common stock using the residual operating income (ROPI) model as of January 31, 2016.

b. Home Depot stock closed at $130.46 on March 24, 2016, the date the Form 10-K was filed with the SEC. How does your valuation estimate compare with this closing price? What do you believe are some reasons for the difference?

LO1, 2, 3   **E13-24.**   **Explaining the Equivalence of Valuation Models and the Relevance of Earnings**
This module focused on two different valuation models: the discounted cash flow (DCF) model and the residual operating income (ROPI) model. The models focus on free cash flows to the firm and on residual operating income, respectively. We stressed that these two models are theoretically equivalent.

     a. What is the *intuition* for why these models are equivalent?
     b. Some analysts focus on cash flows as they believe that companies manage earnings, which presumably makes earnings less relevant. Are earnings relevant? Explain.

LO4   **E13-25.**   **Applying and Interpreting Value Driver Components of RNOA**
The net operating profit margin and the net operating asset turnover components of return on net operating assets are often termed *value drivers,* which refers to their positive influence on stock value by virtue of their role as components of return on net operating assets (RNOA).

     a. How do profit margins and asset turnover ratios influence stock values?
     b. Assuming that profit margins and asset turnover ratios are value drivers, what insight does this give us about managing companies if the goal is to create shareholder value?

LO4   **E13-26.**   **Quantify the Effects of Managerial Actions on ROPI and Components**

BCS Enterprises reports the following financial data just prior to its fiscal year ended June 30, 2017 ($ millions).

BCS ENTERPRISES Balance Sheet			
Cash	$ 100	Accounts payable	$ 300
Accounts receivable	300	Long-term debt	600
Inventory	500		
Property, plant & equipment	1,000	Equity	1,000
Total assets	$1,900	Total liabilities and equity	$1,900

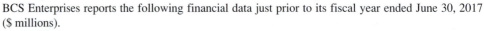

	Actual June 2017	Forecasted June 2018
Sales	$1,200	$1,310
NOPAT	$ 210	$ 216
NOA	$1,500	$1,545
WACC	7%	

Required
a. Compute ROPI for FY2017 and FY2018. Net operating assets (NOA) at June 30, 2016, were $1,350.
b. The company is contemplating taking the following actions before the end of June 2017. (These actions are not reflected in any of the financial data reported above.) For each of the actions, determine the effect on residual operating income for the fiscal year ended June 30, 2018.
     1. Reduce inventory by 10%, which reduces accounts payable by 5%.
     2. Decrease property, plant and equipment (PPE) by 20% with no consequent impact on NOPAT.
     3. Engage in a sale leaseback of a major building. The company will sell 50% of its PPE at book value and increase rental costs by $30 after tax, per year.
     4. Increase debt $300, which increases interest expense by $15.

P13-27. **Forecasting with the Parsimonious Method and Estimating Share Value Using the DCF Model**
Following are the income statement and balance sheet for Cisco Systems for the year ended July 30, 2016.

LO1, 2

Cisco Systems
(CSCO)

CISCO SYSTEMS Consolidated Statements of Operations		
Year Ended ($ millions)	**July 30, 2016**	**July 25, 2015**
Revenue		
Product...	$37,254	$37,750
Service...	11,993	11,411
Total revenue	49,247	49,161
Cost of sales		
Product...	14,161	15,377
Service...	4,126	4,103
Total cost of sales.............................	18,287	19,480
Gross margin	30,960	29,681
Operating expenses		
Research and development	6,296	6,207
Sales and marketing...........................	9,619	9,821
General and administrative.................	1,814	2,040
Amortization of purchased intangible assets	303	359
Restructuring and other charges	268	484
Total operating expenses...................	18,300	18,911
Operating income...............................	12,660	10,770
Interest income...................................	1,005	769
Interest expense.................................	(676)	(566)
Other income (loss), net.....................	(69)	228
Interest and other income (loss), net ...	260	431
Income before provision for income taxes	12,920	11,201
Provision for income taxes..................	2,181	2,220
Net income...	$10,739	$ 8,981

CISCO SYSTEMS INC. Consolidated Balance Sheets		
In millions, except par value	July 30, 2016	July 25, 2015
Assets		
Current assets		
Cash and cash equivalents	$ 7,631	$ 6,877
Investments	58,125	53,539
Accounts receivable, net of allowance for doubtful accounts of $249 at July 30, 2016 and $302 at July 25, 2015.	5,847	5,344
Inventories	1,217	1,627
Financing receivables, net	4,272	4,491
Other current assets.	1,627	1,490
Total current assets	78,719	73,368
Property and equipment, net	3,506	3,332
Financing receivables, net	4,158	3,858
Goodwill	26,625	24,469
Purchased intangible assets, net	2,501	2,376
Deferred tax assets	4,299	4,454
Other assets.	1,844	1,516
Total assets.	$121,652	$113,373
Liabilities and equity		
Current liabilities		
Short-term debt	$ 4,160	$ 3,897
Accounts payable.	1,056	1,104
Income taxes payable	517	62
Accrued compensation	2,951	3,049
Deferred revenue	10,155	9,824
Other current liabilities	6,072	5,476
Total current liabilities.	24,911	23,412
Long-term debt	24,483	21,457
Income taxes payable	925	1,876
Deferred revenue	6,317	5,359
Other long-term liabilities	1,431	1,562
Total liabilities.	58,067	53,666
Cisco shareholders' equity		
Preferred stock, no par value: 5 shares authorized; none issued and outstanding	—	—

Common stock and additional paid-in capital, $0.001 par value:
     20,000 shares authorized; 5,029 and 5,085 shares issued and
     outstanding at July 30, 2016 and July 25, 2015, respectively . . . .
	44,516	43,592

Retained earnings	19,396	16,045
Accumulated other comprehensive income (loss)	(326)	61
Total Cisco shareholders' equity	63,586	59,698
Noncontrolling interests	(1)	9
Total equity.	63,585	59,707
Total liabilities and equity	$121,652	$113,373

Required

a. Compute net operating assets (NOA) for 2016.

b. Compute net operating profit after tax (NOPAT) for 2016, assuming a federal and state statutory tax rate of 37%.

c. Use the parsimonious forecast method, as shown in Analysis Insight box on page 13-5, to forecast Cisco's sales, NOPAT, and NOA for 2017 through 2020 *and* the terminal period using the following assumptions.

Sales growth 2017	1%
Sales growth 2018–2020	2%
Terminal growth	1%
Net operating profit margin	2016 rate rounded to three decimal places
Net operating asset turnover	2016 rate rounded to three decimal places

 d. Estimate the value of a share of Cisco common stock using the discounted cash flow (DCF) model as of July 30, 2016; assume a discount rate (WACC) of 10%, common shares outstanding of 5,029 million, and net nonoperating obligations (NNO) of $(37,113) million (NNO is negative which means that Cisco has net nonoperating investments).

 e. Cisco stock closed at $31.47 on September 8, 2016, the date the Form 10-K was filed with the SEC. How does your valuation estimate compare with this closing price? What do you believe are some reasons for the difference? What investment decision is suggested from your results?

P13-28. Forecasting with Parsimonious Method and Estimating Share Value Using the ROPI Model

LO1, 3

Cisco Systems (CSCO)

Refer to the information for **Cisco Systems** in P13-27 to answer the following requirements.

Required

 a. Estimate the value of a share of Cisco common stock using the residual operating income (ROPI) model as of July 30, 2016.

 b. Cisco stock closed at $31.47 on September 8, 2016, the date the Form 10-K was filed with the SEC. How does your valuation estimate compare with this closing price? What do you believe are some reasons for the difference? What investment decision is suggested from your results?

P13-29. Estimating Share Value Using the DCF Model

LO2

Texas Roadhouse (TXRH)

Following are the income statement and balance sheet for **Texas Roadhouse** for the year ended December 29, 2015.

Required

 a. Assume the following forecasts for TXRH's sales, NOPAT, and NOA for 2016 through 2019. Forecast the terminal period values assuming a 1% terminal period growth rate for all three model inputs: Sales, NOPAT, and NOA.

	Reported	Forecast Horizon			
$ thousands	**2015**	**2016**	**2017**	**2018**	**2019**
Sales.	$1,807,368	$2,060,400	$2,348,855	$2,513,275	$2,689,205
NOPAT	102,495	168,953	192,606	206,089	220,515
NOA	662,502	755,279	861,017	921,288	985,779

 b. Estimate the value of a share of TXRH common stock using the discounted cash flow (DCF) model as of December 29, 2015; assume a discount rate (WACC) of 7%, common shares outstanding of 70,091 thousand, net nonoperating obligations (NNO) of $(14,680) thousand, and noncontrolling interest (NCI) from the balance sheet of $7,520 thousand. Note that NNO is negative because the company's cash exceeds its nonoperating liabilities.

 c. TXRH closed at $42.13 on February 26, 2016, the date the Form 10-K was filed with the SEC. How does your valuation estimate compare with this closing price?

 d. If WACC has been 7.5%, what would the valuation estimate have been? What about if WACC has been 6.5%?

P13-30. Estimating Share Value Using the ROPI Model

LO3

Texas Roadhouse (TXRH)

Refer to the information for **Texas Roadhouse** in P13-29 to answer the following requirements.

Required

 a. Estimate the value of a share of TXRH common stock using the residual operating income (ROPI) model as of December 29, 2015.

 b. TXRH closed at $42.13 on February 26, 2016, the date the Form 10-K was filed with the SEC. How does your valuation estimate compare with this closing price? What do you believe are some reasons for the difference? What investment decision is suggested from your results?

LO1, 2

Nike Inc. (NKE)

P13-31. **Forecasting with Parsimonious Method and Estimating Share Value Using the DCF Model**
Following are the income statement and balance sheet for **Nike Inc.**

NIKE INC. Consolidated Income Statement		
For Year Ended ($ millions)	May 31, 2016	May 31, 2015
Revenues	$32,376	$30,601
Cost of sales.	17,405	16,534
Gross profit.	14,971	14,067
Demand creation expense	3,278	3,213
Operating overhead expense.	7,191	6,679
Total selling and administrative expense	10,469	9,892
Interest expense (income), net.	19	28
Other (income) expense, net	(140)	(58)
Income before income taxes	4,623	4,205
Income tax expense.	863	932
Net income.	$ 3,760	$ 3,273

NIKE INC. Consolidated Balance Sheets		
$ millions	May 31, 2016	May 31, 2015
Current assets		
Cash and equivalents.	$ 3,138	$ 3,852
Short-term investments	2,319	2,072
Accounts receivable, net	3,241	3,358
Inventories	4,838	4,337
Prepaid expenses and other current assets.	1,489	1,968
Total current assets	15,025	15,587
Property, plant and equipment, net	3,520	3,011
Identifiable intangible assets, net.	281	281
Goodwill	131	131
Deferred income taxes and other assets	2,439	2,587
Total assets.	$21,396	$21,597
Current liabilities		
Current portion of long-term debt	$ 44	$ 107
Notes payable	1	74
Accounts payable.	2,191	2,131
Accrued liabilities	3,037	3,949
Income taxes payable	85	71
Total current liabilities.	5,358	6,332
Long-term debt	2,010	1,079
Deferred income taxes and other liabilities	1,770	1,479
Total liabilities.	9,138	8,890
Shareholders' equity		
Class A convertible common stock	0	0
Class B common stock	3	3
Capital in excess of stated value	7,786	6,773
Accumulated other comprehensive income.	318	1,246
Retained earnings	4,151	4,685
Total shareholders' equity	12,258	12,707
Total liabilities and shareholders' equity.	$21,396	$21,597

Required

a. Compute net operating assets (NOA) and net nonoperating obligations (NNO) for 2016. Note that the company's NNO is negative because cash exceeds debt.

b. Compute net operating profit after tax (NOPAT) for 2016 assuming a federal and state statutory tax rate of 37%.

c. Use the parsimonious forecast method, as shown in the Analysis Insight box on page 13-5, to forecast sales, NOPAT, and NOA for 2017 through 2020 using the following assumptions.

Sales growth..............................	6%
Net operating profit margin (NOPM)...........	2016 ratios rounded to three decimal places
Net operating asset turnover (NOAT), year-end...	2016 ratios rounded to three decimal places

Forecast the terminal period value assuming a 1% terminal period growth and using the NOPM and NOAT assumptions above.

d. Estimate the value of a share of Nike's common stock using the discounted cash flow (DCF) model as of May 31, 2016; assume a discount rate (WACC) of 6.3% and common shares outstanding of 1,682 million.

e. Nike's stock closed at $56.99 on July 21, 2016, the date the Form 10-K was filed with the SEC. How does your valuation estimate compare with this closing price? What do you believe are some reasons for the difference? What investment decision is suggested from your results?

P13-32. Forecasting with the Parsimonious Method and Estimating Share Value Using the ROPI Model
Refer to the information for Nike Inc. in P13-31 to answer the following requirements.

LO1, 3
Nike Inc. (NKE)

Required

a. Estimate the value of a share of Nike common stock using the residual operating income (ROPI) model as of May 31, 2016. For simplicity, prepare your forecasts in $ millions.

b. Nike's stock closed at $56.99 on July 21, 2016, the date the Form 10-K was filed with the SEC. How does your valuation estimate compare with this closing price? What do you believe are some reasons for the difference? What investment decision is suggested from your results?

P13-33. Estimating Share Value Using the DCF Model
Following are forecasted sales, NOPAT, and NOA for Colgate-Palmolive Company for 2016 through 2019.

LO2
Colgate-Palmolive Company (CL)

	Reported	Forecast Horizon			
$ millions	2015	2016	2017	2018	2019
Sales.................	$16,034	$16,836	$17,677	$18,561	$19,489
NOPAT	2,247	3,199	3,359	3,527	3,703
NOA	5,557	5,836	6,127	6,434	6,755

Required

a. Forecast the terminal period values assuming a 1% terminal period growth for all three model inputs, that is Sales, NOPAT, and NOA.

b. Estimate the value of a share of Colgate-Palmolive common stock using the discounted cash flow (DCF) model; assume a discount rate (WACC) of 7.5%, common shares outstanding of 893 million, net nonoperating obligations (NNO) of $5,601 million, and noncontrolling interest (NCI) from the balance sheet of $255 million.

c. Colgate-Palmolive's stock closed at $67.22 on February 18, 2016, the date the Form 10-K was filed with the SEC. How does your valuation estimate compare with this closing price? What do you believe are some reasons for the difference?

d. The forecasts you completed assumed a terminal growth rate of 1%. What if the terminal rate had been 2%. What would your estimated stock price have been?

e. What would WACC have to be to warrant the actual stock price on February 18, 2016?

LO3

Colgate-Palmolive
Company (CL)

P13-34. **Estimating Share Value Using the ROPI Model**

Refer to the information for Colgate-Palmolive in P13-33 to answer the following requirements.

Required

a. Estimate the value of a share of Colgate-Palmolive common stock using the residual operating income (ROPI) model.

b. Colgate-Palmolive stock closed at $67.22 on February 18, 2016, the date the Form 10-K was filed with the SEC. How does your valuation estimate compare with this closing price? What do you believe are some reasons for the difference? What investment decision is suggested from your results?

Management Applications

LO4

MA13-35. **Management Application: Operating Improvement versus Financial Engineering**

Assume that you are the CEO of a small publicly traded company. The operating performance of your company has fallen below market expectations, which is reflected in a depressed stock price. At your direction, your CFO provides you with the following recommendations that are designed to increase your company's return on net operating assets (RNOA) and your operating cash flows, both of which will, presumably, result in improved financial performance and an increased stock price.

1. To improve net cash flow from operating activities, the CFO recommends that your company reduce inventories (raw material, work-in-progress, and finished goods) and receivables (through selective credit granting and increased emphasis on collection of past due accounts).

2. The CFO recommends that your company sell and lease back its office building. The lease will be structured so as to be classified as an operating lease under GAAP. The assets will, therefore, not be included in the computation of net operating assets (NOA), thus increasing RNOA.

3. The CFO recommends that your company lengthen the time taken to pay accounts payable (lean on the trade) to increase net cash flows from operating activities.

4. Because your company's operating performance is already depressed, the CFO recommends that you take a "big bath;" that is, write off all assets deemed to be impaired and accrue excessive liabilities for future contingencies. The higher current period expense will, then, result in higher future period income as the assets written off will not be depreciated and your company will have a liability account available to absorb future cash payments rather than recording them as expenses.

5. The CFO recommends that your company increase its estimate of expected return on pension investments. This will reduce pension expense and increase operating profit, a component of net operating profit after tax (NOPAT) and, thus, of RNOA.

6. The CFO recommends that your company share ownership of its outbound logistics (trucking division) with another company in a joint venture. This would have the effect of increasing throughput, thus spreading overhead over a larger volume base, and would remove the assets from your company's balance sheet since the joint venture would be accounted for as an equity method investment.

Evaluate each of the CFO's recommendations. In your evaluation, consider whether each recommendation will positively impact the operating performance of your company or whether it is cosmetic in nature.

Ongoing Project

(This ongoing project began in Module 1 and continues through most of the book; even if previous segments were not completed, the requirements are still applicable to any business analysis.) Two common models used to estimate the value of company's equity are: the discounted cash flow (DCF) model and the residual operating income (ROPI) model. Estimate the value of equity and a stock price for the company(ies) under analysis. The aim is to determine an independent measure of value and assess whether the stock appears to be over or undervalued. Begin with a forecast of the company's balance sheet and income statement. See Module 12 and follow the forecasting steps outlined there.

1. *Model Assumptions and Inputs.* In addition to the assumptions used for the forecasts, we require several additional inputs.

- Weighted average cost of capital (WACC) is required to discount future amounts to derive present values. We can find estimates at a number of websites. Find the latest WACC at three or more sites and explore why they differ. One approach would be to use an average in the calculation and then perform sensitivity analysis for the high and the low in the range.

- Net nonoperating obligations (NNO) is needed to determine the value of equity from total enterprise value.

- Number of shares outstanding. Recall that shares outstanding is equal to shares issued less treasury shares. The balance sheet typically reports both numbers but if not, we can find the amounts in the statement of shareholders' equity or in a footnote.

2. *Model Estimation.* Use a spreadsheet and estimate the DCF and the ROPI models respectively. Here are some tips.

- Pay close attention to the rounding conventions described in the footnotes in Exhibits 13.3 and 13.4. Use the spreadsheet rounding functions. Note: setting the format of a cell to "no decimals" is not the same as rounding the number; with the former, the decimals are still there, but they are not displayed.

- Make sure that NNO is subtracted from total enterprise value. In some cases, NNO is a negative number; this occurs when nonoperating assets such as cash and marketable securities exceed nonoperating liabilities. By subtracting this negative NNO, the value of equity will be greater than the enterprise value of the firm.

- The stock prices obtained are point estimates derived from a specific set of assumptions. To understand the impact of each assumption, compute alternative stock prices by varying the assumptions. The point is to determine a range of stock prices that derive from a reasonable set of assumptions. One approach is to increase and decrease each of the model assumptions by a reasonable amount such as +/− 10%. Use the spreadsheet functions to perform this sensitivity analysis. Identify which assumptions are most important or impactful.

- Determine the company's actual stock price. Compare the per share estimate to the actual stock price and form an opinion about the relative value. Is the stock over or under-valued according to the model?

3. *Interpretation.* The final step in the project is to evaluate the companies based on all the analysis performed in the ongoing project.

- Revisit the conclusions made about the companies' performance (profit and margin analysis), asset efficiency, solvency, liquidity, off-balance-sheet financing, and future opportunities based on analysis of strengths, weaknesses, opportunities, and threats. Our goal is to assimilate the various components of analysis and to synthesize what we discovered and learned.

- Access one or more analyst reports for each company. How do the other professionals see the firms? How does their view differ from ours?

- Our analysis was based primarily on historical data from financial statements. What additional information would we like to have to refine our opinion? Is this missing information critical to our opinion?

- Based on our analysis, would we consider investing in the company? Explain.

Solutions to Review Problems

Review 13-1—Solution

	Dividend Discount	Discounted Cash Flow	Residual Operating Income
a. Uses net present value concepts.	True	True	True
b. Operating cash flows affect value	False	True	False
c. Estimates a company's enterprise value	False	True	True
d. Dividends to shareholders is a model input.	True	False	False
e. Free cash flow is a model input	False	True	False
f. Estimates equity value of the firm.	True	True	True
g. Capital expenditures affect estimated value	False	True	True*
h. Requires forecasts of future amounts	True	True	True
i. Operating profit affects value	False	False	True
j. Yields insight into value drivers.	False	False	True

*Net operating assets change during the year due, in part, to CAPEX. So while CAPEX is not the only model input, expenditures for PPE do affect the ROPI model inputs.

Review 13-2—Solution

a.

GIS—DCF ($ millions, except per share value and discount factors)	Reported 2016	Horizon Period				Terminal Period
		2017	2018	2019	2020	
Sales.	$16,563.1	$16,314.7	$16,640.9	$16,973.8	$17,313.2	$17,486.4
NOPAT	1,928.2	1,892.5	1,930.3	1,969.0	2,008.3	2,028.4
NOA	13,819.9	13,595.6	13,867.4	14,144.8	14,427.7	14,572.0
Increase in NOA		(224.3)	271.8	277.4	282.9	144.3
FCFF (NOPAT − Increase in NOA)		2,116.8	1,658.5	1,691.6	1,725.4	1,884.1
Discount factor $[1/(1 + r_w)^t]$.		0.95021	0.90290	0.85794	0.81522	
Present value of horizon FCFF.		2,011.4	1,497.5	1,451.3	1,406.6	
Cum present value of horizon FCFF.	6,366.8					
Present value of terminal FCFF	36,225.4					
Total firm value	42,592.2					
Less: NNO	8,512.8					
Less: NCI	376.9					
Firm equity value	$33,702.5					
Shares outstanding	596.8					
Stock value per share.	$ 56.47					

b. The stock price on May 27, 2016 (the closest trading day prior to the fiscal-year-end) was $62.87 per share. The part *a* valuation of $56.47 per share implies that the stock is slightly overvalued.

Review 13-3—Solution

a.

GIS—ROPI (In millions, except per share value and discount factors)	Reported 2016	Horizon Period				Terminal Period
		2017	2018	2019	2020	
Sales.	$16,563.1	$16,314.7	$16,640.9	$16,973.8	$17,313.2	$17,486.4
NOPAT	1,928.2	1,892.5	1,930.3	1,969.0	2,008.3	2,028.4
NOA	13,819.9	13,595.6	13,867.4	14,144.8	14,427.7	14,572.0
ROPI (NOPAT − $[NOA_{Beg} \times r_w]$)		1,168.3	1,217.9	1,242.3	1,267.1	1,272.4
Discount factor $[1/(1 + r_w)^t]$.		0.95021	0.90290	0.85794	0.81522	
Present value of horizon ROPI		1,110.1	1,099.6	1,065.8	1,033.0	
Cum present value of horizon ROPI.	4,308.5					
Present value of terminal ROPI	24,464.3					
NOA	13,819.9					
Total firm value	42,592.7					
Less: NNO	8,512.8					
Less: NCI	376.9					
Firm equity value	$33,703.0					
Shares outstanding	596.8					
Stock value per share.	$ 56.47					

b. The stock price on May 27, 2016 (the closest trading day prior to the fiscal-year-end) was $62.87 per share. The part *a* valuation of $56.47 per share implies that the stock is slightly overvalued.

Review 13-4—Solution

a.   (i) Delaying payment would improve ROPI because accounts payable balance would increase which would decrease NOA.

    (ii) A potential negative consequence would be if suppliers increase their prices to counter delayed payment. In that case, ROPI could be worsened because cost of goods sold would increase.

b.   (i) Reducing inventory spoilage would reduce COGS which would improve NOPAT.

    (ii) Selling at a discount may cause customers to expect the discount on other products, which could create pressure on margins.

c.   (i) Using social media could cut down on advertising expenses.

    (ii) The impact of the new marketing on sales is a crucial factor. If the traditional marketing media were highly effective, moving away from them could actually harm sales. The cost savings and sales outcomes need to be determined to assess the impact on ROPI.

d.   (i) If the lease costs are lower than the cash outlay needed for CAPEX, this could increase ROPI by increasing NOPAT and decreasing NOA.

    (ii) The availability of leased equipment might be questionable, which could lead to lost sales.

Appendix A—Compound Interest Tables

Table 1 ■ Present Value of Single Amount

$p = 1/(1 + i)^t$

Period	0.01	0.02	0.03	0.04	0.05	0.06	0.07	0.08	0.09	0.10	0.11	0.12
1	0.99010	0.98039	0.97087	0.96154	0.95238	0.94340	0.93458	0.92593	0.91743	0.90909	0.90090	0.89286
2	0.98030	0.96117	0.94260	0.92456	0.90703	0.89000	0.87344	0.85734	0.84168	0.82645	0.81162	0.79719
3	0.97059	0.94232	0.91514	0.88900	0.86384	0.83962	0.81630	0.79383	0.77218	0.75131	0.73119	0.71178
4	0.96098	0.92385	0.88849	0.85480	0.82270	0.79209	0.76290	0.73503	0.70843	0.68301	0.65873	0.63552
5	0.95147	0.90573	0.86261	0.82193	0.78353	0.74726	0.71299	0.68058	0.64993	0.62092	0.59345	0.56743
6	0.94205	0.88797	0.83748	0.79031	0.74622	0.70496	0.66634	0.63017	0.59627	0.56447	0.53464	0.50663
7	0.93272	0.87056	0.81309	0.75992	0.71068	0.66506	0.62275	0.58349	0.54703	0.51316	0.48166	0.45235
8	0.92348	0.85349	0.78941	0.73069	0.67684	0.62741	0.58201	0.54027	0.50187	0.46651	0.43393	0.40388
9	0.91434	0.83676	0.76642	0.70259	0.64461	0.59190	0.54393	0.50025	0.46043	0.42410	0.39092	0.36061
10	0.90529	0.82035	0.74409	0.67556	0.61391	0.55839	0.50835	0.46319	0.42241	0.38554	0.35218	0.32197
11	0.89632	0.80426	0.72242	0.64958	0.58468	0.52679	0.47509	0.42888	0.38753	0.35049	0.31728	0.28748
12	0.88745	0.78849	0.70138	0.62460	0.55684	0.49697	0.44401	0.39711	0.35553	0.31863	0.28584	0.25668
13	0.87866	0.77303	0.68095	0.60057	0.53032	0.46884	0.41496	0.36770	0.32618	0.28966	0.25751	0.22917
14	0.86996	0.75788	0.66112	0.57748	0.50507	0.44230	0.38782	0.34046	0.29925	0.26333	0.23199	0.20462
15	0.86135	0.74301	0.64186	0.55526	0.48102	0.41727	0.36245	0.31524	0.27454	0.23939	0.20900	0.18270
16	0.85282	0.72845	0.62317	0.53391	0.45811	0.39365	0.33873	0.29189	0.25187	0.21763	0.18829	0.16312
17	0.84438	0.71416	0.60502	0.51337	0.43630	0.37136	0.31657	0.27027	0.23107	0.19784	0.16963	0.14564
18	0.83602	0.70016	0.58739	0.49363	0.41552	0.35034	0.29586	0.25025	0.21199	0.17986	0.15282	0.13004
19	0.82774	0.68643	0.57029	0.47464	0.39573	0.33051	0.27651	0.23171	0.19449	0.16351	0.13768	0.11611
20	0.81954	0.67297	0.55368	0.45639	0.37689	0.31180	0.25842	0.21455	0.17843	0.14864	0.12403	0.10367
21	0.81143	0.65978	0.53755	0.43883	0.35894	0.29416	0.24151	0.19866	0.16370	0.13513	0.11174	0.09256
22	0.80340	0.64684	0.52189	0.42196	0.34185	0.27751	0.22571	0.18394	0.15018	0.12285	0.10067	0.08264
23	0.79544	0.63416	0.50669	0.40573	0.32557	0.26180	0.21095	0.17032	0.13778	0.11168	0.09069	0.07379
24	0.78757	0.62172	0.49193	0.39012	0.31007	0.24698	0.19715	0.15770	0.12640	0.10153	0.08170	0.06588
25	0.77977	0.60953	0.47761	0.37512	0.29530	0.23300	0.18425	0.14602	0.11597	0.09230	0.07361	0.05882
30	0.74192	0.55207	0.41199	0.30832	0.23138	0.17411	0.13137	0.09938	0.07537	0.05731	0.04368	0.03338
35	0.70591	0.50003	0.35538	0.25342	0.18129	0.13011	0.09366	0.06763	0.04899	0.03558	0.02592	0.01894
40	0.67165	0.45289	0.30656	0.20829	0.14205	0.09722	0.06678	0.04603	0.03184	0.02209	0.01538	0.01075

Table 2 ■ Present Value of Ordinary Annuity

$p = \{1 - [1/(1 + i)^t]\}/i$

Period	0.01	0.02	0.03	0.04	0.05	0.06	0.07	0.08	0.09	0.10	0.11	0.12
1	0.99010	0.98039	0.97087	0.96154	0.95238	0.94340	0.93458	0.92593	0.91743	0.90909	0.90090	0.89286
2	1.97040	1.94156	1.91347	1.88609	1.85941	1.83339	1.80802	1.78326	1.75911	1.73554	1.71252	1.69005
3	2.94099	2.88388	2.82861	2.77509	2.72325	2.67301	2.62432	2.57710	2.53129	2.48685	2.44371	2.40183
4	3.90197	3.80773	3.71710	3.62990	3.54595	3.46511	3.38721	3.31213	3.23972	3.16987	3.10245	3.03735
5	4.85343	4.71346	4.57971	4.45182	4.32948	4.21236	4.10020	3.99271	3.88965	3.79079	3.69590	3.60478
6	5.79548	5.60143	5.41719	5.24214	5.07569	4.91732	4.76654	4.62288	4.48592	4.35526	4.23054	4.11141
7	6.72819	6.47199	6.23028	6.00205	5.78637	5.58238	5.38929	5.20637	5.03295	4.86842	4.71220	4.56376
8	7.65168	7.32548	7.01969	6.73274	6.46321	6.20979	5.97130	5.74664	5.53482	5.33493	5.14612	4.96764
9	8.56602	8.16224	7.78611	7.43533	7.10782	6.80169	6.51523	6.24689	5.99525	5.75902	5.53705	5.32825
10	9.47130	8.98259	8.53020	8.11090	7.72173	7.36009	7.02358	6.71008	6.41766	6.14457	5.88923	5.65022
11	10.36763	9.78685	9.25262	8.76048	8.30641	7.88687	7.49867	7.13896	6.80519	6.49506	6.20652	5.93770
12	11.25508	10.57534	9.95400	9.38507	8.86325	8.38384	7.94269	7.53608	7.16073	6.81369	6.49236	6.19437
13	12.13374	11.34837	10.63496	9.98565	9.39357	8.85268	8.35765	7.90378	7.48690	7.10336	6.74987	6.42355
14	13.00370	12.10625	11.29607	10.56312	9.89864	9.29498	8.74547	8.24424	7.78615	7.36669	6.98187	6.62817
15	13.86505	12.84926	11.93794	11.11839	10.37966	9.71225	9.10791	8.55948	8.06069	7.60608	7.19087	6.81086
16	14.71787	13.57771	12.56110	11.65230	10.83777	10.10590	9.44665	8.85137	8.31256	7.82371	7.37916	6.97399
17	15.56225	14.29187	13.16612	12.16567	11.27407	10.47726	9.76322	9.12164	8.54363	8.02155	7.54879	7.11963
18	16.39827	14.99203	13.75351	12.65930	11.68959	10.82760	10.05909	9.37189	8.75563	8.20141	7.70162	7.24967
19	17.22601	15.67846	14.32380	13.13394	12.08532	11.15812	10.33560	9.60360	8.95011	8.36492	7.83929	7.36578
20	18.04555	16.35143	14.87747	13.59033	12.46221	11.46992	10.59401	9.81815	9.12855	8.51356	7.96333	7.46944
21	18.85698	17.01121	15.41502	14.02916	12.82115	11.76408	10.83553	10.01680	9.29224	8.64869	8.07507	7.56200
22	19.66038	17.65805	15.93692	14.45112	13.16300	12.04158	11.06124	10.20074	9.44243	8.77154	8.17574	7.64465
23	20.45582	18.29220	16.44361	14.85684	13.48857	12.30338	11.27219	10.37106	9.58021	8.88322	8.26643	7.71843
24	21.24339	18.91393	16.93554	15.24696	13.79864	12.55036	11.46933	10.52876	9.70661	8.98474	8.34814	7.78432
25	22.02316	19.52346	17.41315	15.62208	14.09394	12.78336	11.65358	10.67478	9.82258	9.07704	8.42174	7.84314
30	25.80771	22.39646	19.60044	17.29203	15.37245	13.76483	12.40904	11.25778	10.27365	9.42691	8.69379	8.05518
35	29.40858	24.99862	21.48722	18.66461	16.37419	14.49825	12.94767	11.65457	10.56682	9.64416	8.85524	8.17550
40	32.83469	27.35548	23.11477	19.79277	17.15909	15.04630	13.33171	11.92461	10.75736	9.77905	8.95105	8.24378

Table 3 ◾ Future Value of Single Amount

$f = (1 + i)^t$

Interest Rate

Period	0.01	0.02	0.03	0.04	0.05	0.06	0.07	0.08	0.09	0.10	0.11	0.12
1	1.01000	1.02000	1.03000	1.04000	1.05000	1.06000	1.07000	1.08000	1.09000	1.10000	1.11000	1.12000
2	1.02010	1.04040	1.06090	1.08160	1.10250	1.12360	1.14490	1.16640	1.18810	1.21000	1.23210	1.25440
3	1.03030	1.06121	1.09273	1.12486	1.15763	1.19102	1.22504	1.25971	1.29503	1.33100	1.36763	1.40493
4	1.04060	1.08243	1.12551	1.16986	1.21551	1.26248	1.31080	1.36049	1.41158	1.46410	1.51807	1.57352
5	1.05101	1.10408	1.15927	1.21665	1.27628	1.33823	1.40255	1.46933	1.53862	1.61051	1.68506	1.76234
6	1.06152	1.12616	1.19405	1.26532	1.34010	1.41852	1.50073	1.58687	1.67710	1.77156	1.87041	1.97382
7	1.07214	1.14869	1.22987	1.31593	1.40710	1.50363	1.60578	1.71382	1.82804	1.94872	2.07616	2.21068
8	1.08286	1.17166	1.26677	1.36857	1.47746	1.59385	1.71819	1.85093	1.99256	2.14359	2.30454	2.47596
9	1.09369	1.19509	1.30477	1.42331	1.55133	1.68948	1.83846	1.99900	2.17189	2.35795	2.55804	2.77308
10	1.10462	1.21899	1.34392	1.48024	1.62889	1.79085	1.96715	2.15892	2.36736	2.59374	2.83942	3.10585
11	1.11567	1.24337	1.38423	1.53945	1.71034	1.89830	2.10485	2.33164	2.58043	2.85312	3.15176	3.47855
12	1.12683	1.26824	1.42576	1.60103	1.79586	2.01220	2.25219	2.51817	2.81266	3.13843	3.49845	3.89598
13	1.13809	1.29361	1.46853	1.66507	1.88565	2.13293	2.40985	2.71962	3.06580	3.45227	3.88328	4.36349
14	1.14947	1.31948	1.51259	1.73168	1.97993	2.26090	2.57853	2.93719	3.34173	3.79750	4.31044	4.88711
15	1.16097	1.34587	1.55797	1.80094	2.07893	2.39656	2.75903	3.17217	3.64248	4.17725	4.78459	5.47357
16	1.17258	1.37279	1.60471	1.87298	2.18287	2.54035	2.95216	3.42594	3.97031	4.59497	5.31089	6.13039
17	1.18430	1.40024	1.65285	1.94790	2.29202	2.69277	3.15882	3.70002	4.32763	5.05447	5.89509	6.86604
18	1.19615	1.42825	1.70243	2.02582	2.40662	2.85434	3.37993	3.99602	4.71712	5.55992	6.54355	7.68997
19	1.20811	1.45681	1.75351	2.10685	2.52695	3.02560	3.61653	4.31570	5.14166	6.11591	7.26334	8.61276
20	1.22019	1.48595	1.80611	2.19112	2.65330	3.20714	3.86968	4.66096	5.60441	6.72750	8.06231	9.64629
21	1.23239	1.51567	1.86029	2.27877	2.78596	3.39956	4.14056	5.03383	6.10881	7.40025	8.94917	10.80385
22	1.24472	1.54598	1.91610	2.36992	2.92526	3.60354	4.43040	5.43654	6.65860	8.14027	9.93357	12.10031
23	1.25716	1.57690	1.97359	2.46472	3.07152	3.81975	4.74053	5.87146	7.25787	8.95430	11.02627	13.55235
24	1.26973	1.60844	2.03279	2.56330	3.22510	4.04893	5.07237	6.34118	7.91108	9.84973	12.23916	15.17863
25	1.28243	1.64061	2.09378	2.66584	3.38635	4.29187	5.42743	6.84848	8.62308	10.83471	13.58546	17.00006
30	1.34785	1.81136	2.42726	3.24340	4.32194	5.74349	7.61226	10.06266	13.26768	17.44940	22.89230	29.95992
35	1.41660	1.99989	2.81386	3.94609	5.51602	7.68609	10.67658	14.78534	20.41397	28.10244	38.57485	52.79962
40	1.48886	2.20804	3.26204	4.80102	7.03999	10.28572	14.97446	21.72452	31.40942	45.25926	65.00087	93.05097

Table 4 ◾ Future Value of an Ordinary Annuity

$f = [(1 + i)^t - 1]/i$

Interest Rate

Period	0.01	0.02	0.03	0.04	0.05	0.06	0.07	0.08	0.09	0.10	0.11	0.12
1	1.00000	1.00000	1.00000	1.00000	1.00000	1.00000	1.00000	1.00000	1.00000	1.00000	1.00000	1.00000
2	2.01000	2.02000	2.03000	2.04000	2.05000	2.06000	2.07000	2.08000	2.09000	2.10000	2.11000	2.12000
3	3.03010	3.06040	3.09090	3.12160	3.15250	3.18360	3.21490	3.24640	3.27810	3.31000	3.34210	3.37440
4	4.06040	4.12161	4.18363	4.24646	4.31013	4.37462	4.43994	4.50611	4.57313	4.64100	4.70973	4.77933
5	5.10101	5.20404	5.30914	5.41632	5.52563	5.63709	5.75074	5.86660	5.98471	6.10510	6.22780	6.35285
6	6.15202	6.30812	6.46841	6.63298	6.80191	6.97532	7.15329	7.33593	7.52333	7.71561	7.91286	8.11519
7	7.21354	7.43428	7.66246	7.89829	8.14201	8.39384	8.65402	8.92280	9.20043	9.48717	9.78327	10.08901
8	8.28567	8.58297	8.89234	9.21423	9.54911	9.89747	10.25980	10.63663	11.02847	11.43589	11.85943	12.29969
9	9.36853	9.75463	10.15911	10.58280	11.02656	11.49132	11.97799	12.48756	13.02104	13.57948	14.16397	14.77566
10	10.46221	10.94972	11.46388	12.00611	12.57789	13.18079	13.81645	14.48656	15.19293	15.93742	16.72201	17.54874
11	11.56683	12.16872	12.80780	13.48635	14.20679	14.97164	15.78360	16.64549	17.56029	18.53117	19.56143	20.65458
12	12.68250	13.41209	14.19203	15.02581	15.91713	16.86994	17.88845	18.97713	20.14072	21.38428	22.71319	24.13313
13	13.80933	14.68033	15.61779	16.62684	17.71298	18.88214	20.14064	21.49530	22.95338	24.52271	26.21164	28.02911
14	14.94742	15.97394	17.08632	18.29191	19.59863	21.01507	22.55049	24.21492	26.01919	27.97498	30.09492	32.39260
15	16.09690	17.29342	18.59891	20.02359	21.57856	23.27597	25.12902	27.15211	29.36092	31.77248	34.40536	37.27971
16	17.25786	18.63929	20.15688	21.82453	23.65749	25.67253	27.88805	30.32428	33.00340	35.94973	39.18995	42.75328
17	18.43044	20.01207	21.76159	23.69751	25.84037	28.21288	30.84022	33.75023	36.97370	40.54470	44.50084	48.88367
18	19.61475	21.41231	23.41444	25.64541	28.13238	30.90565	33.99903	37.45024	41.30134	45.59917	50.39594	55.74971
19	20.81090	22.84056	25.11687	27.67123	30.53900	33.75999	37.37896	41.44626	46.01846	51.15909	56.93949	63.43968
20	22.01900	24.29737	26.87037	29.77808	33.06595	36.78559	40.99549	45.76196	51.16012	57.27500	64.20283	72.05244
21	23.23919	25.78332	28.67649	31.96920	35.71925	39.99273	44.86518	50.42292	56.76453	64.00250	72.26514	81.69874
22	24.47159	27.29898	30.53678	34.24797	38.50521	43.39229	49.00574	55.45676	62.87334	71.40275	81.21431	92.50258
23	25.71630	28.84496	32.45288	36.61789	41.43048	46.99583	53.43614	60.89330	69.53194	79.54302	91.14788	104.60289
24	26.97346	30.42186	34.42647	39.08260	44.50200	50.81558	58.17667	66.76476	76.78981	88.49733	102.17415	118.15524
25	28.24320	32.03030	36.45926	41.64591	47.72710	54.86451	63.24904	73.10594	84.70090	98.34706	114.41331	133.33387
30	34.78489	40.56808	47.57542	56.08494	66.43885	79.05819	94.46079	113.28321	136.30754	164.49402	199.02088	241.33268
35	41.66028	49.99448	60.46208	73.65222	90.32031	111.43478	138.23688	172.31680	215.71075	271.02437	341.58955	431.66350
40	48.88637	60.40198	75.40126	95.02552	120.79977	154.76197	199.63511	259.05652	337.88245	442.59256	581.82607	767.09142

Appendix B

Chart of Accounts (with Acronyms)

Assets

Cash	Cash
MS	Marketable securities
AR	Accounts receivable
AU	Allowance for uncollectible accounts
INV	Inventory (or Inventories)
SUP	Supplies
PPD	Prepaid expenses
PPDA	Prepaid advertising
PPRNT	Prepaid rent
PPI	Prepaid insurance
PPE	Property, plant and equipment (PPE)
AD	Accumulated depreciation
INT	Intangible assets
DTA	Deferred tax assets
OA	Other assets
EMI	Equity method investments
ROU	Right-of-use asset (capitalized lease)
PA	Pension assets

Liabilities

NP	Notes payable
AP	Accounts payable
ACC	Accrued expenses
WP	Wages payable
SP	Salaries payable
RNTP	Rent payable
RSL	Restructuring liability
UP	Utilities payable
TP	Taxes payable
WRP	Warranty payable
IP	Interest payable
CMLTD	Current maturities of long-term debt
UR	Unearned (or deferred) revenues
DP	Dividends payable
LTD	Long-term debt
CLO	Capital lease obligations
DTL	Deferred tax liabilities
OL	Other liabilities
PL	Pension liability

Equity

EC	Earned capital
CS	Common stock
PS	Preferred stock
APIC	Additional paid-in capital
RE	Retained earnings
DIV	Dividends
TS	Treasury stock
AOCI	Accumulated other comprehensive income
DC	Deferred compensation expense
NCI	Noncontrolling interest
EQ	Total stockholders' equity
CI	Equity attributable to controlling interest

Revenues and Expenses

Sales	Sales
REV	Revenues
COGS	Cost of goods sold (or Cost of sales)
OE	Operating expenses
WE	Wages expense
SE	Salaries expense
AE	Advertising expense
BDE	Bad debts expense
UTE	Utilities expense
DE	Depreciation expense
RDE	Research and development expense
RNTE	Rent expense
RSE	Restructuring expense
WRE	Warranty expense
AIE	Asset impairment expense
INSE	Insurance expense
SUPE	Supplies expense
PE	Pension expense
GN (LS)	Gain (loss)–operating
TE	Tax expense
ONI (E)	Other nonoperating income (expense)
IE	Interest expense
II	Interest income
UG (UL)	Unrealized gain (loss)
DI	Dividend income (or revenue)
EI	Equity income (or revenue)
GN (LS)	Gain (loss)–nonoperating

Appendix C
Comprehensive Case

Glossary

accelerated cost recovery system (ACRS, MACRS) A system of accelerated depreciation for tax purposes introduced in 1981 (ACRS) and modified starting in 1987 (MACRS); it prescribes depreciation rates by asset classification for assets acquired after 1980

accelerated depreciation method Any depreciation method under which the amounts of depreciation expense taken in the early years of an asset's life are larger than the amounts expensed in the later years; includes the double-declining balance method

access control matrix A computerized file that lists the type of access that each computer user is entitled to have to each file and program in the computer system

account A record of the additions, deductions, and balances of individual assets, liabilities, equity, revenues, and expenses

accounting The process of measuring the economic activity of an entity in money terms and communicating the results to interested parties; the purpose is to provide financial information that is useful in making economic decisions

accounting adjustments (adjusting entries) Entries made at the end of an accounting period under accrual accounting to ensure the proper recording of expenses incurred and revenues earned for the period

accounting cycle A series of basic steps followed to process accounting information during a fiscal year

accounting entity An economic unit that has identifiable boundaries and that is the focus for the accumulation and reporting of financial information

accounting equation An expression of the equivalency of the economic resources and the claims upon those resources of a specific entity; often stated as Assets = Liabilities + Owners' Equity

accounting period The time period, typically one year (or quarter), for which periodic accounting reports are prepared

accounting system The structured collection of policies, procedures, equipment, files, and records that a company uses to collect, record, classify, process, store, report, and interpret financial data

accounts payable turnover The ratio obtained by dividing cost of goods sold by average accounts payable

accounts receivable A current asset that is created by a sale on a credit basis; it represents the amount owed the company by the customer

accounts receivable aging method A procedure that uses an aging schedule to determine the year-end balance needed in the allowance for uncollectible accounts

accounts receivable turnover Annual net sales divided by average accounts receivable (net)

accrual accounting Accounting procedures whereby revenues are recorded when they are earned and realized and expenses are recorded in the period in which they help to generate revenues

accruals Adjustments that reflect revenues earned but not received or recorded and expenses incurred but not paid or recorded

accrued expense An expense incurred but not yet paid; recognized with an accounting adjustment

accrued revenue Revenue earned but not yet billed or received; recognized with an accounting adjustment

accumulated depreciation The sum of all depreciation expense recorded to date; it is subtracted from the cost of the asset in order to derive the asset's net book value

accumulated other comprehensive income (AOCI) Current accumulation of all prior periods' other comprehensive income; *see* definition for *other comprehensive income*

adjusted trial balance A list of general ledger accounts and their balances taken after accounting adjustments have been made

adjusting The process of adjusting the historical financial statements prior to the projection of future results; also called recasting and reformulating

aging schedule An analysis that shows how long customers' accounts receivable balances have remained unpaid

allowance for uncollectible accounts A contra asset account with a normal credit balance shown on the balance sheet as a deduction from accounts receivable to reflect the expected realizable amount of accounts receivable

allowance method An accounting procedure whereby the amount of uncollectible accounts expense is estimated and recorded in the period in which the related credit sales occur

Altman's Z-score A predictor of potential bankruptcy based on multiple ratios

amortization The periodic writing off of an account balance to expense; similar to depreciation and usually refers to the periodic writing off of an intangible asset

annuity A pattern of cash flows in which equal amounts are spaced equally over a number of periods

articles of incorporation A document prepared by persons organizing a corporation in the United States that sets forth the structure and purpose of the corporation and specifics regarding the stock to be issued

articulation The linkage of financial statements within and across time

asset turnover Net income divided by average total assets

asset write-downs Adjustment of carrying value of assets down to their current fair value

assets The economic resources of an entity that are owned or controlled will provide future benefits and can be reliably measured

audit An examination of a company's financial statements by a firm of independent certified public accountants

audit report A report issued by independent auditors that includes the final version of the financial statements, accompanying notes, and the auditor's opinion on the financial statements

authorized stock The maximum number of shares in a class of stock that a corporation may issue

available-for-sale securities Investments in securities that management intends to hold for capital gains and dividend income; although it may sell them if the price is right

average cash conversion cycle Average collection period + average inventory days outstanding − average payable days outstanding

average collection period Determined by dividing accounts receivable by average daily sales, sometimes referred to as days sales outstanding or DSO

average inventory days outstanding (AIDO) An indication of how long, on average, inventories are on the shelves, computed as inventory divided by average daily cost of goods sold

B

balance sheet A financial statement showing an entity's assets, liabilities, and owners' equity at a specific date; sometimes called a statement of financial position

bearer One of the terms that may be used to designate the payee on a promissory note; means whoever holds the note

bond A long-term debt instrument that promises to pay interest periodically and a principal amount at maturity, usually issued by the borrower to a group of lenders; bonds may incorporate a wide variety of provisions relating to security for the debt involved, methods of paying the periodic interest, retirement provisions, and conversion options

book value The dollar amount carried in the accounts for a particular item; the book value of a depreciable asset is cost less accumulated depreciation; the book value of an entity is assets less liabilities

book value per share The dollar amount of net assets represented by one share of stock; computed by dividing the amount of stockholders' equity associated with a class of stock by the outstanding shares of that class of stock

borrows at a discount When the face amount of the note is reduced by a calculated cash discount to determine the cash proceeds

C

calendar year A fiscal year that ends on December 31

call provision A bond feature that allows the borrower to retire (call in) the bonds after a stated date

capital expenditures Expenditures that increase the book value of long-term assets; sometimes abbreviated as CAPEX

capital lease A lease that transfers to the lessee substantially all of the benefits and risks related to ownership of the property; the lessee records the leased property as an asset and establishes a liability for the lease obligation

capital markets Financing sources, which are formalized when companies issue securities that are traded on organized exchanges; they are informal when companies are funded by private sources

capitalization The recording of a cost as an asset on the balance sheet rather than as an expense on the income statement; these costs are transferred to expense as the asset is used up

capitalization of interest A process that adds interest to an asset's initial cost if a period of time is required to prepare the asset for use

cash An asset category representing the amount of a firm's available cash and funds on deposit at a bank in checking accounts and savings accounts

cash and cash equivalents The sum of cash plus short-term, highly liquid investments such as treasury bills and money market funds; includes marketable securities maturing within 90 days of the financial statement date

cash conversion cycle Measures the average time (in days) to sell inventories, collect the receivables from the sale, repay the suppliers for the inventory purchases, and return to cash. It is the amount of days to collect accounts receivable plus days sales in inventory minus days to pay account payable.

cash discount An amount that a purchaser of merchandise may deduct from the purchase price for paying within the discount period

cash-basis accounting Accounting procedures whereby revenues are recorded when cash is received and expenses are recorded when cash payments are made

cash (operating) conversion cycle The period of time (typically measured in days) from when cash is invested in inventories until inventory is sold and receivables are collected

certificate of deposit (CD) An investment security available at financial institutions generally offering a fixed rate of return for a specified period of time

change in accounting estimate Modification to a previous estimate of an uncertain future event, such as the useful life of a depreciable asset, uncollectible accounts receivable, and warranty expenses; applied currently and prospectively only

changes in accounting principles Modification of accounting methods (such as depreciation or inventory costing methods)

chart of accounts A list of all the general ledger account titles and their numerical code

clean surplus accounting Income that explains successive equity balances

closing procedures A step in the accounting cycle in which the balances of all temporary accounts are transferred to the retained earnings account, leaving the temporary accounts with zero balances

commitments A contractual arrangement by which both parties to the contract still have acts to perform

common stock The basic ownership class of corporate capital stock, carrying the rights to vote, share in earnings, participate in future stock issues, and share in any liquidation proceeds after prior claims have been settled

common-size financial statement A financial statement in which each item is presented as a percentage of a key figure such as sales or total assets

comparative financial statements A form of horizontal analysis involving comparison of two or more periods' financial statements showing dollar and/or percentage changes

compensating balance A minimum amount that a financial institution requires a firm to maintain in its account as part of a borrowing arrangement complex capital structure

comprehensive income The total change in stockholders' equity other than those arising from capital (stock) transactions; computed as net income plus other comprehensive income (OCI); typical OCI components are unrealized gains (losses) on available-for-sale securities and derivatives, minimum pension liability adjustment, and foreign currency translation adjustments

conceptual framework A cohesive set of interrelated objectives and fundamentals for external financial reporting developed by the FASB

conservatism An accounting principle stating that judgmental determinations should tend toward understatement rather than overstatement of net assets and income

consistency An accounting principle stating that, unless otherwise disclosed, accounting reports should be prepared on a basis consistent with the preceding period

consolidated financial statements Financial statements reflecting a parent company and one or more subsidiary companies and/or a variable interest entity (VIE) and its primary beneficiary

contingent liabilities A potential obligation, the eventual occurrence of which usually depends on some future event beyond the control of the firm; contingent liabilities may originate with such events as lawsuits, credit guarantees, and environmental damages

contra account An account related to, and deducted from, another account when financial statements are prepared or when book values are computed

contract rate The rate of interest stated on a bond certificate

contributed capital The net funding that a company receives from issuing and acquiring its equity shares

convertible bond A bond incorporating the holder's right to convert the bond to capital stock under prescribed terms

convertible securities Debt and equity securities that provide the holder with an option to convert those securities into other securities

copyright An exclusive right that protects an owner against the unauthorized reproduction of a specific written work or artwork

core income A company's income from its usual business activities that is expected to continue (persist) into the future

corporation A legal entity created by the granting of a charter from an appropriate governmental authority and owned by stockholders who have limited liability for corporate debt

cost of goods sold The total cost of merchandise sold to customers during the accounting period

cost of goods sold percentage The ratio of cost of goods sold divided by net sales

cost method An investment is reported at its historical cost, and any cash dividends and interest received are recognized in current income

cost principle An accounting principle stating that asset measures are based on the prices paid to acquire the assets

cost-to-cost method The extent of progress towards completion based on the ratio of costs incurred to date to the total estimated costs at completion of the contract

coupon bond A bond with coupons for interest payable to bearer attached to the bond for each interest period; whenever interest is due, the bondholder detaches a coupon and deposits it with his or her bank for collection

coupon (contract or stated) rate The coupon rate of interest is stated in the bond contract; it is used to compute the dollar amount of (semiannual) interest payments that are paid to bondholder during the life of the bond issue

covenants Contractual requirements put into loan or bond agreements by lenders

credit (entry) An entry on the right side (or in the credit column) of any account

credit card fee A fee charged retailers for credit card services provided by financial institutions; the fee is usually stated as a percentage of credit card sales

credit guarantee A guarantee of another company's debt by cosigning a note payable; a guarantor's contingent liability that is usually disclosed in a balance sheet footnote

credit memo A document prepared by a seller to inform the purchaser that the seller has reduced the amount owed by the purchaser due to a return or an allowance

credit period The maximum amount of time, usually stated in days, that the purchaser of merchandise has to pay the seller

credit rating An opinion formed by a credit-rating agency (such as Standard & Poor's, Moody's or Fitch) concerning the creditworthiness of a borrower (a corporation or a government) based on an assessment of the borrower's likelihood of default

credit terms The prescribed payment period for purchases on credit with discount specified for early payment

cumulative (preferred stock) A feature associated with preferred stock whereby any dividends in arrears must be paid before dividends may be paid on common stock

cumulative effect of a change in principle The cumulative effect on net income to the date of a change in accounting principle

cumulative translation adjustment The amount recorded in the equity section as necessary to balance the accounting equation when assets and liabilities of foreign subsidiaries are translated into $US at the rate of exchange prevailing at the statement date

current assets Cash and other assets that will be converted to cash or used up during the normal operating cycle of the business or one year, whichever is longer

current liabilities Obligations that will require within the coming year or operating cycle, whichever is longer, (1) the use of existing current assets or (2) the creation of other current liabilities

current rate method Method of translating foreign currency transactions under which balance sheet amounts are translated using exchange rates in effect at the period-end consolidation date and income statement amounts using the average exchange rate for the period

current ratio Current assets divided by current liabilities

D

days inventory outstanding Inventories divided by average cost of goods sold

days payable outstanding Ratio that reflects the average length of time that payables are deferred. Computed as 365 x average accounts payable / COGS.

days sales outstanding Ratio that reveals the number of days, on average, that accounts receivable are outstanding before they are paid. Computed as 365 x average accounts receivable / sales.

debenture bond A bond that has no specific property pledged as security for the repayment of funds borrowed

debit (entry) An entry on the left side (or in the debit column) of any account

debt-to-equity ratio A firm's total liabilities divided by its total owners' equity

declining-balance method An accelerated depreciation method that allocates depreciation expense to each year by applying a constant percentage to the declining book value of the asset

default The nonpayment of interest and principal and/or the failure to adhere to the various terms and conditions of the bond indenture

deferrals Adjustments that allocate various assets and revenues received in advance to the proper accounting periods as expenses and revenues

deferred revenue A liability representing revenues received in advance; also called unearned revenue

deferred tax liability A liability representing the estimated future income taxes payable resulting from an existing temporary difference between an asset's book value and its tax basis

deferred tax valuation allowance Reduction in a reported deferred tax asset to adjust for the amount that is not likely to be realized

defined benefit plan A type of retirement plan under which the company promises to make periodic payments to the employee after retirement

defined contribution plan A retirement plan under which the company makes cash contribution into an employee's account (usually with a third-party trustee like a bank) either solely or as a matching contribution

depletion The allocation of the cost of natural resources to the units extracted and sold or, in the case of timberland, the board feet of timber cut

depreciation The decline in economic potential (using up) of plant assets originating from wear, deterioration, and obsolescence

depreciation accounting The process of allocating the cost of equipment, vehicles, and buildings (not land) to expense over the time period benefiting from their use

depreciation base The acquisition cost of an asset less estimated salvage value

depreciation rate An estimate of how the asset will be used up over its useful life—evenly over its useful life, more heavily in the early years, or in proportion to its actual usage

derivatives Financial instruments such as futures, options, and swaps that are commonly used to hedge (mitigate) some external risk, such as commodity price risk, interest rate risk, or risks relating to foreign currency fluctuations

diluted earnings per share The earnings per share computation taking into consideration the effects of dilutive securities

dilutive securities Securities that can be exchanged for shares of common stock and, thereby, increase the number of common shares outstanding

discontinued operations Net income or loss from business segments that are up for sale or have been sold in the current period

discount bond A bond that is sold for less than its par (face) value

discount on notes payable A contra account that is subtracted from the Notes Payable amount on the balance sheet; as the life of the note elapses, the discount is reduced and charged to interest expense

discount period The maximum amount of time, usually stated in days, that the purchaser of merchandise has to pay the seller if the purchaser wants to claim the cash discount

discounted cash flow (DCF) model The value of a security is equal to the present value of the expected free cash flows to the firm, discounted at the weighted average cost of capital (WACC)

discounting The exchanging of notes receivable for cash at a financial institution at an amount that is less than the face value of the notes

dividends account A temporary equity account used to accumulate owner dividends from the business

dividend discount model The value of a security today is equal to the present value of that security's expected dividends, discounted at the weighted average cost of capital

dividend payout ratio Annual dividends per share divided by the earnings per share or by net income

dividend yield Annual dividends per share divided by the market price per share

double-entry accounting system A method of accounting that recognizes the duality of a transaction such that the analysis results in a recording of equal amounts of debits and credits

E

earned When referring to revenue, the seller's execution of its duties under the terms of the agreement, with the resultant passing of title to the buyer with no right of return or other contingencies

earned capital The cumulative net income (losses) retained by the company (not paid out to shareholders as dividends)

earnings per share (EPS) Net income less preferred stock dividends divided by the weighted average common shares outstanding for the period

earnings quality The degree to which reported earnings represent how well the firm has performed from an economic standpoint

earnings smoothing Earnings management with a goal to provide an earnings stream with less variability

EBIT Earnings before interest and taxes

EBITDA Earnings before interest, taxes, depreciation and amortization

economic profit The number of inventory units sold multiplied by the difference between the sales price and the replacement cost of the inventories (approximated by the cost of the most recently purchased inventories)

economic value added (EVA) Net operating profits after tax less a charge for the use of capital equal to beginning capital utilized in the business multiplied by the weighted average cost of capital (EVA = NOPAT $- [r_w \times$ Net operating assets])

effective interest method A method of amortizing bond premium or discount that results in a constant rate of interest each period and varying amounts of premium or discount amortized each period

effective interest rate The rate determined by dividing the total discount amount by the cash proceeds on a note payable when the borrower borrowed at a discount

effective rate The current rate of interest in the market for a bond or other debt instrument; when issued, a bond is priced to yield the market (effective) rate of interest at the date of issuance

efficient markets hypothesis Capital markets are said to be efficient if at any given time, current equity (stock) prices reflect all relevant information that determines those equity prices

employee severance costs Accrued (estimated) costs for termination of employees as part of a restructuring program

employee stock options A form of compensation that grants a select group of employees the right to purchase a fixed number of company shares at a fixed price for a predetermined time period

equity carve out A corporate divestiture of operating units

equity method The prescribed method of accounting for investments in which the investor company has a significant influence over the investee company (usually taken to be ownership between 20-50% of the outstanding common stock of the investee company)

ethics An area of inquiry dealing with the values, rules, and justifications that governs one's way of life

executory contract A contract where a party has a material unperformed obligation that, if not performed, will result in a breach of contract

expenses Decreases in owners' equity incurred by a firm in the process of earning revenues

extraordinary items Revenues and expenses that are both unusual and infrequent and are, therefore, excluded from income from continuing operations

F

face amount The principal amount of a bond or note to be repaid at maturity

factoring Selling an account receivable to another company, typically a finance company or a financial institution, for less than its face value

fair value Value that an asset could be sold for (or an obligation discharged) in an orderly market, between willing buyers and sellers; often, but not always, is current market value

fair value method Method of accounting that records on the balance sheet, the asset or liabilities fair value, and records on the income statement, changes in the fair value

financial accounting The area of accounting activities dealing with the preparation of financial statements showing an entity's results of operations, financial position, and cash flows

Financial Accounting Standards Board (FASB) The organization currently responsible for setting accounting standards for reporting financial information by U.S. entities

financial assets Normally consist of excess resources held for future expansion or unexpected needs; they are usually invested in the form of other companies' stock, corporate or government bonds, and real estate

financial leverage The proportionate use of borrowed funds in the capital structure, computed as net nonoperating obligations (NNO) divided by average equity

financial reporting objectives A component of the conceptual framework that specifies that financial statements should provide information (1) useful for investment and credit decisions, (2) helpful in assessing an entity's ability to generate future cash flows, and (3) about an entity's resources, claims to those resources, and the effects of events causing changes in these items

financial statement elements A part of the conceptual framework that identifies the significant components—such as assets, liabilities, owners' equity, revenues, and expenses—used to put financial statements together

financing activities Methods that companies use to raise the funds to pay for resources such as land, buildings, and equipment

finished goods inventory The dollar amount of inventory that has completed the production process and is awaiting sale

first-in, first-out (FIFO) method One of the prescribed methods of inventory costing; FIFO assumes that the first costs incurred for the purchase or production of inventory are the first costs relieved from inventory when goods are sold

fiscal year The annual accounting period used by a business firm

five forces of competitive intensity Industry competition, bargaining power of buyers, bargaining power of suppliers, threat of substitution, threat of entry

fixed assets An alternate label for long-term assets; may also be called property, plant, and equipment (PPE)

fixed costs Costs that do not change with changes in sales volume (over a reasonable range)

forecast The projection of financial results over the forecast horizon and terminal periods

foreign currency transaction The $US equivalent of an asset or liability denominated in a foreign currency

foreign exchange gain or loss The gain (loss) recognized in the income statement relating to the change in the $US equivalent of an asset or liability denominated in a foreign currency

forward earnings Earnings expected to be reported in the next period

franchise Generally, an exclusive right to operate or sell a specific brand of products in a given geographic area

free cash flow This excess cash flow (above that required to manage its growth and development) from which dividends can be paid; computed as NOPAT − Increase in NOA

full disclosure principle An accounting principle stipulating the disclosure of all facts necessary to make financial statements useful to readers

fully diluted earnings per share *See* diluted earnings per share

functional currency The currency representing the primary currency in which a business unit conducts its operations

fundamental analysis Uses financial information to predict future valuation and, hence, buy-sell stock strategies

funded status The difference between the pension obligation and the fair value of the pension investments

future value The amount a specified investment (or series of investments) will be worth at a future date if invested at a given rate of compound interest

G

general journal A journal with enough flexibility so that any type of business transaction can be recorded in it

general ledger A grouping of all of an entity's accounts that are used to prepare the basic financial statements

generally accepted accounting principles (GAAP) A set of standards and procedures that guide the preparation of financial statements

going concern concept An accounting principle that assumes that, in the absence of evidence to the contrary, a business entity will have an indefinite life

goodwill The value that derives from a firm's ability to earn more than a normal rate of return on the fair market value of its specific, identifiable net assets; computed as the residual of the purchase price less the fair market value of the net tangible and intangible assets acquired

gross margin The difference between net sales and cost of goods sold; also called gross profit

gross profit on sales The difference between net sales and cost of goods sold; also called gross margin

gross profit margin (GPM) (percentage) The ratio of gross profit on sales divided by net sales

H

held-to-maturity securities The designation given to a portfolio of bond investments that are expected to be held until they mature

historical cost Original acquisition or issuance costs

holding company The parent company of a subsidiary

holding gain The increase in replacement cost since the inventories were acquired, which equals the number of units sold multiplied by the difference between the current replacement cost and the original acquisition cost

horizon period The forecast period for which detailed estimates are made, typically 5-10 years

horizontal analysis Analysis of a firm's financial statements that covers two or more years

I

IASB International Accounting Standards Board, independent, privately funded accounting standard-setter based in London, responsible for developing IFRS and promoting the use and application of these standards

IFRS International Financial Reporting Standards, a body of accounting standards developed by the International Accounting Standards Board and used for financial reports across much of the world

impairment A reduction in value from that presently recorded

impairment loss A loss recognized on an impaired asset equal to the difference between its book value and current fair value

income statement A financial statement reporting an entity's revenues and expenses for a period of time

indirect method A presentation format for the statement of cash flows that refers to the operating section only; that section begins with net income and converts it to cash flows from operations

intangible assets A term applied to a group of long-term assets, including patents, copyrights, franchises, trademarks, and goodwill, that benefit an entity but do not have physical substance

interest cost (pensions) The increase in the pension obligation due to the accrual of an additional year of interest

internal auditing A company function that provides independent appraisals of the company's financial statements, its internal controls, and its operations

internal controls The measures undertaken by a company to ensure the reliability of its accounting data, protect its assets from theft or unauthorized use, make sure that employees are following the company's policies and procedures, and evaluate the performance of employees, departments, divisions, and the company as a whole

inventory carrying costs Costs of holding inventories, including warehousing, logistics, insurance, financing, and the risk of loss due to theft, damage, or technological or fashion change

inventory shrinkage The cost associated with an inventory shortage; the amount by which the perpetual inventory exceeds the physical inventory

inventory turnover Cost of goods sold divided by average inventory

investing activities The acquiring and disposing of resources (assets) that a company uses to acquire and sell its products and services

investing creditors Those who primarily finance investing activities

investment returns The increase in pension investments resulting from interest, dividends, and capital gains on the investment portfolio

invoice A document that the seller sends to the purchaser to request payment for items that the seller shipped to the purchaser

invoice price The price that a seller charges the purchaser for merchandise

IOU A slang term for a receivable

IRS Internal Revenue Service, the U.S. taxing authority

issued stock Shares of stock that have been sold and issued to stockholders; issued stock may be either outstanding or in the treasury

J

journal A tabular record in which business transactions are analyzed in debit and credit terms and recorded in chronological order

just-in-time (JIT) inventory Receive inventory from suppliers into the production process just at the point it is needed

L

land improvements Improvements with limited lives made to land sites, such as paved parking lots and driveways

last-in, first-out (LIFO) method One of the prescribed methods of inventory costing; LIFO assumes that the last costs incurred for the purchase or production of inventory are the first costs relieved from inventory when goods are sold

lease A contract between a lessor (owner) and lessee (tenant) for the rental of property

leasehold The rights transferred from the lessor to the lessee by a lease

leasehold improvements Expenditures made by a lessee to alter or improve leased property

lessee The party acquiring the right to the use of property by a lease

lessor The owner of property who transfers the right to use the property to another party by a lease

leveraging The use of borrowed funds in the capital structure of a firm; the expectation is that the funds will earn a return higher than the rate of interest on the borrowed funds

liabilities The obligations, or debts, that an entity must pay in money or services at some time in the future because of past transactions or events

LIFO conformity rule IRS requirement to cost inventories using LIFO for tax purposes if they are costed using LIFO for financial reporting purposes

LIFO liquidation The reduction in inventory quantities when LIFO costing is used; LIFO liquidation yields an increase in gross profit and income when prices are rising

LIFO reserve The difference between the cost of inventories using FIFO and the cost using LIFO

liquidation value per share The amount that would be received by a holder of a share of stock if the corporation liquidated

liquidity How much cash the company has, how much is expected, and how much can be raised on short notice

list price The suggested price or reference price of merchandise in a catalog or price list

long-term liabilities Debt obligations not due to be settled within the normal operating cycle or one year, whichever is longer

lower of cost or market (LCM) GAAP requirement to write down the carrying amount of inventories on the balance sheet if the reported cost (using FIFO, for example) exceeds market value (determined by current replacement cost)

M

maker The signer of a promissory note

management discussion and anaysis (MD&A) The section of the 10-K report in which a company provides a detailed discussion of its business activities

managerial accounting The accounting activities carried out by a firm's accounting staff primarily to furnish management with accounting data for decisions related to the firm's operations

manufacturers Companies that convert raw materials and components into finished products through the application of skilled labor and machine operations

manufacturing costs The costs of direct materials, direct labor, and manufacturing overhead incurred in the manufacture of a product

market cap Market capitalization of the firm, or value as perceived by investors; computed as market value per share multiplied by shares outstanding

market (yield) rate This is the interest rate that investors expect to earn on the investment in this debt security; this rate is used to price the bond issue

market value The published price (as listed on a stock exchange)

market value per share The current price at which shares of stock may be bought or sold

matching principle An accounting guideline that states that income is determined by relating expenses, to the extent feasible, with revenues that have been recorded

materiality An accounting guideline that states that transactions so insignificant that they would not affect a user's actions or perception of the company may be recorded in the most expedient manner

materials inventory The physical component of inventory; the other components of manufactured inventory are labor costs and overhead costs

maturity date The date on which a note or bond matures

measuring unit concept An accounting guideline noting that the accounting unit of measure is the basic unit of money

merchandise inventory A stock of products that a company buys from another company and makes available for sale to its customers

merchandising firm A company that buys finished products, stores the products for varying periods of time, and then resells the products

method of comparables model Equity valuation or stock values are predicted using price multiples, which are defined as stock price divided by some key financial statement number such as net income, net sales, book value of equity, total assets, or cash flow; companies are then compared with their competitors

minority interest *See* noncontrolling interest

modified accelerated cost recovery system (MACRS) *See* accelerated cost recovery system

multiple element arrangements Sales (revenue) arrangements containing multiple deliverables and, in some cases, multiple cash-flow streams

N

natural resources Assets occurring in a natural state, such as timber, petroleum, natural gas, coal, and other mineral deposits

net asset based valuation model Equity is valued as reported assets less reported liabilities

net assets The difference between an entity's assets and liabilities; net assets are equal to owners' equity

net book value (NBV) The cost of the asset less accumulated depreciation; also called carrying value

net income The excess of a firm's revenues over its expenses

net loss The excess of a firm's expenses over its revenues

net nonoperating expense (NNE) Nonoperating expenses and losses (plus any net income attributable to noncontrolling interest) less nonoperating revenues and gains, all measured after-tax

net nonoperating expense percentage (NNEP) Net nonoperating expense divided by net nonoperating obligations (NNO)

net nonoperating obligations (NNO) All nonoperating obligations (plus any noncontrolling interest) less nonoperating assets

net operating asset turnover (NOAT) Ratio obtained by dividing sales by net operating assets

net operating assets (NOA) Current and long-term operating assets less current and long-term operating liabilities; or net operating working capital plus long-term net operating assets

net operating profit after tax (NOPAT) Operating revenues less operating expenses (including taxes)

net operating profit margin (NOPM) Ratio obtained by dividing net operating profit after tax (NOPAT) by sales

net operating working capital (NOWC) Current operating assets less current operating liabilities

net realizable value The value at which an asset can be sold, net of any costs of disposition

net sales The total revenue generated by a company through merchandise sales less the revenue given up through sales returns and allowances and sales discounts

net working capital Current assets less current liabilities

nominal rate The rate of interest stated on a bond certificate or other debt instrument

noncash investing and financing activities Significant business activities during the period that do not impact cash inflows or cash outflows

noncontrolling interest The portion of equity (net assets) in a subsidiary not attributable, directly or indirectly, to a parent. A noncontrolling interest (formerly called minority interest) typically represents the ownership interest of shareholders other than those of the parent company.

noncurrent liabilities Obligations not due to be paid within one year or the operating cycle, whichever is longer

nonoperating expenses Expenses that relate to the company's financing activities and include interest income and interest expense, gains and losses on sales of securities, and income or loss on discontinued operations

no-par stock Stock that does not have a par value

NOPAT Net operating profit after tax

normal operating cycle For a particular business, the average period of time between the use of cash in its typical operating activity and the subsequent collection of cash from customers

note receivable A promissory note held by the note's payee

notes to financial statements Footnotes in which companies discuss their accounting policies and estimates used in preparing the statements

not-sufficient-funds check A check from an individual or company that had an insufficient cash balance in the bank when the holder of the check presented it to the bank for payment

O

objectivity principle An accounting principle requiring that, whenever possible, accounting entries are based on objectively determined evidence

off-balance-sheet financing The structuring of a financing arrangement so that no liability shows on the borrower's balance sheet

operating activities Using resources to research, develop, produce, purchase, market, and distribute company products and services

operating cash flow to capital expenditures ratio A firm's net cash flow from operating activities divided by its annual capital expenditures

operating cash flow to current liabilities ratio A firm's net cash flow from operating activities divided by its average current liabilities

operating creditors Those who primarily finance operating activities

operating cycle The time between paying cash for goods or employee services and receiving cash from customers

operating expense margin (OEM) The ratio obtained by dividing any operating expense category by sales

operating expenses The usual and customary costs that a company incurs to support its main business activities; these include cost of goods sold, selling expenses, depreciation expense, amortization expense, research and development expense, and taxes on operating profits

operating lease A lease by which the lessor retains the usual risks and rewards of owning the property

operating profit margin The ratio obtained by dividing NOPAT by sales

operational audit An evaluation of activities, systems, and internal controls within a company to determine their efficiency, effectiveness, and economy

organization costs Expenditures incurred in launching a business (usually a corporation), including attorney's fees and various fees paid to the state

other comprehensive income (OCI) Current period change in stockholders' equity *other than* those arising from capital (stock) transactions and those included in net income; typical OCI components are unrealized gains (losses) on available-for-sale securities and derivatives, minimum pension liability adjustment, and foreign currency translation adjustments

outstanding checks Checks issued by a firm that have not yet been presented to its bank for payment

outstanding stock Shares of stock that are currently owned by stockholders (excludes treasury stock)

owners' equity The interest of owners in the assets of an entity; equal to the difference between the entity's assets and liabilities

P

packing list A document that lists the items of merchandise contained in a carton and the quantity of each item; the packing list is usually attached to the outside of the carton

paid-in capital The amount of capital contributed to a corporation by various transactions; the primary source of paid-in capital is from the issuance of shares of stock

par (bonds) Face value of the bond

par value (stock) An amount specified in the corporate charter for each share of stock and imprinted on the face of each stock certificate, often determines the legal capital of the corporation

parent company A company owning one or more subsidiary companies

parsimonious method to multiyear forecasting Forecasting multiple years using only sales growth, net operating profit margin (NOPM), and the turnover of net operating assets (NOAT)

partnership A voluntary association of two or more persons for the purpose of conducting a business

password A string of characters that a computer user enters into a computer terminal to prove to the computer that the person using the computer is truly the person named in the user identification code

patent An exclusive privilege granted for 20 years to an inventor that gives the patent holder the right to exclude others from making, using, or selling the invention

payee The company or individual to whom a promissory note is made payable

payment approval form A document that authorizes the payment of an invoice

pension plan A plan to pay benefits to employees after they retire from the company; the plan may be a defined contribution plan or a defined benefit plan

percentage-of-completion method Recognition of revenue by determining the costs incurred per the contract as compared to its total expected costs

percentage of net sales method A procedure that determines the uncollectible accounts expense for the year by multiplying net credit sales by the estimated uncollectible percentage

performance obligation A promise in a contract with a customer to transfer a good or service to the customer; includes promises that are implied by business practices, published policies, or explicit statements if those promises create an expectation of the customer that the entity will perform

performance obligation The actions the seller must undertake to satisfy the customer and complete the sales contract.

period statement A financial statement accumulating information for a specific period of time; examples are the income statement, the statement of owners' equity, and the statement of cash flows

permanent account An account used to prepare the balance sheet; that is, asset, liability, and equity capital (capital stock and retained earnings) accounts; any balance in a permanent account at the end of an accounting period is carried forward to the next period

physical inventory A year-end procedure that involves counting the quantity of each inventory item, determining the unit cost of each item, multiplying the unit cost times quantity, and summing the costs of all the items to determine the total inventory at cost

plant assets Land, buildings, equipment, vehicles, furniture, and fixtures that a firm uses in its operations; sometimes referred to by the acronym PPE

pooling of interests method A method of accounting for business combinations under which the acquired company is recorded on the acquirer's balance sheet at its book value, rather than market value; this method is no longer acceptable under GAAP for acquisitions occurring after 2001

position statement A financial statement, such as the balance sheet, that presents information as of a particular date

post-closing trial balance A list of general ledger accounts and their balances after closing entries have been recorded and posted

postdated check A check from another person or company with a date that is later than the current date; a postdated check does not become cash until the date of the check

preemptive right The right of a stockholder to maintain his or her proportionate interest in a corporation by having the right to purchase an appropriate share of any new stock issue

preferred stock A class of corporate capital stock typically receiving priority over common stock in dividend payments and distribution of assets should the corporation be liquidated

premium bond A bond that is sold for more than its par (face) value

present value The current worth of amounts to be paid (or received) in the future; computed by discounting the future payments (or receipts) at a specified interest rate

price-earnings ratio Current market price per common share divided by earnings per share

pro forma income A computation of income that begins with the GAAP income from continuing operations (that excludes discontinued operations, extraordinary items and changes in accounting principle), but then excludes other transitory items (most notably, restructuring charges), and some additional items such as expenses arising from acquisitions (goodwill amortization and other acquisition costs), compensation expense in the form of stock options, and research and development expenditures; pro forma income is not GAAP

promissory note A written promise to pay a certain sum of money on demand or at a determinable future time

purchase method The prescribed method of accounting for business combinations; under the purchase method, assets and liabilities of the acquired company are recorded at fair market value, together with identifiable intangible assets; the balance is ascribed to goodwill

purchase order A document that formally requests a supplier to sell and deliver specific quantities of particular items of merchandise at specified prices

purchase requisition An internal document that requests that the purchasing department order particular items of merchandise

Q

qualitative characteristics of accounting information The characteristics of accounting information that contribute to decision usefulness; the primary qualities are relevance and reliability

quarterly data Selected quarterly financial information that is reported in annual reports to stockholders

quick ratio Quick assets (that is, cash and cash equivalents, short-term investments, and current receivables) divided by current liabilities

R

realized (or realizable) When referring to revenue, the receipt of an asset or satisfaction of a liability or performance obligation as a result of a transaction or event

recognition criteria The criteria that must be met before a financial statement element may be recorded in the accounts; essentially, the item must meet the definition of an element and must be measurable

registered bond A bond for which the issuer (or the trustee) maintains a record of owners and, at the appropriate times, mails out interest payments

relative selling price The price for a deliverable if the item were sold separately on a regular basis, consistent with company selling practices.

relevance A qualitative characteristic of accounting information; relevant information contributes to the predictive and evaluative decisions made by financial statement users

reliability A qualitative characteristic of accounting information; reliable information contains no bias or error and faithfully portrays what it intends to represent

remeasurement The computation of gain or loss in the translation of subsidiaries denominated in a foreign currency into $US when the temporal method is used

residual operating income Net operating profits after tax (NOPAT) less the product of net operating assets (NOA) at the beginning of the period multiplied by the weighted average cost of capital (WACC)

residual operating income (ROPI) model An equity valuation approach that equates the firm's value to the sum of its net operating assets (NOA) and the present value of its residual operating income (ROPI)

retailers Companies that buy products from wholesale distributors and sell the products to individual customers, the general public

retained earnings Earned capital, the cumulative net income and loss, of the company (from its inception) that has not been paid to shareholders as dividends

retained earnings reconciliation The reconciliation of retained earnings from the beginning to the end of the year; the change in retained earnings includes, at a minimum, the net income (loss) for the period and dividends paid, if any, but may include other components as well; also called statement of retained earnings

return The amount earned on an investment; also called yield

return on assets (ROA) A financial ratio computed as net income divided by average total assets

return on common stockholders' equity (ROCE) A financial ratio computed as net income less preferred stock dividends divided by average common stockholders' equity

return on equity (ROE) The ultimate measure of performance from the shareholders' perspective; computed as net income divided by average equity

return on investment The ratio obtained by dividing income by average investment; sometimes referred to by the acronym ROI

return on net operating assets (RNOA) The ratio obtained by dividing NOPAT by average net operating assets

return on sales (ROS) The ratio obtained by dividing net income by net sales

revenue recognition principle An accounting principle requiring that revenue be recognized when earned and realized (or realizable)

revenues Increases in owners' equity a firm earns by providing goods or services for its customers

Right of Use (ROU) Asset A term for the lease asset once the lease is reflected on the balance sheet.

S

sale on account A sale of merchandise made on a credit basis

salvage value The expected net recovery when a plant asset is sold or removed from service; also called residual value

secured bond A bond that pledges specific property as security for meeting the terms of the bond agreement

Securities and Exchange Commission (SEC) The commission, created by the 1934 Securities Act, that has broad powers to regulate the issuance and trading of securities, and the financial reporting of companies issuing securities to the public

segments Subdivisions of a firm for which supplemental financial information is disclosed

serial bond A bond issue that staggers the bond maturity dates over a series of years

service cost (pensions) The increase in the pension obligation due to employees working another year for the employer

share-based payment Payment for a good or service using the entity's equity securities; an example is restricted stock used to compensate employees

significant influence The ability of the investor to affect the financing or operating policies of the investee

sinking fund provision A bond feature that requires the borrower to retire a portion of the bonds each year or, in some cases, to make payments each year to a trustee who is responsible for managing the resources needed to retire the bonds at maturity

solvency The ability to meet obligations, especially to creditors

source document Any written document or computer record evidencing an accounting transaction, such as a bank check or deposit slip, sales invoice, or cash register tape

special purpose entity *See* variable interest entity

spin-off A form of equity carve out in which divestiture is accomplished by distribution of a company's shares in a subsidiary to the company's shareholders who then own the shares in the subsidiary directly rather than through the parent company

split-off A form of equity carve out in which divestiture is accomplished by the parent company's exchange of stock in the subsidiary in return for shares in the parent owned by its shareholders

spread The difference between the return on net operating activities (RNOA) and the net nonoperating expense percentage (NNEP)

stated value A nominal amount that may be assigned to each share of no-par stock and accounted for much as if it were a par value

statement of cash flows A financial statement showing a firm's cash inflows and outflows for a specific period, classified into operating, investing, and financing categories

statement of equity *See* statement of stockholders' equity

statement of financial position A financial statement showing a firm's assets, liabilities, and owners' equity at a specific date; also called a balance sheet

statement of owners' equity A financial statement presenting information on the events causing a change in owners' equity during a period; the statement presents the beginning balance, additions to, deductions from, and the ending balance of owners' equity for the period

statement of retained earnings *See* retained earnings reconciliation

statement of stockholders' equity The financial statement that reconciles all of the components of stockholders' equity

stock dividends The payment of dividends in shares of stock

stock split Additional shares of its own stock issued by a corporation to its current stockholders in proportion to their current ownership interests without changing the balances in the related stockholders' equity accounts; a formal stock split increases the number of shares outstanding and reduces proportionately the stock's per share par value

straight-line depreciation A depreciation procedure that allocates uniform amounts of depreciation expense to each full period of a depreciable asset's useful life

subsequent events Events occurring shortly after a fiscal year-end that will be reported as supplemental information to the financial statements of the year just ended

subsidiaries Companies that are owned by the parent company

subsidiary ledger A set of accounts or records that contains detailed information about the items included in the balance of one general ledger account

summary of significant accounting policies A financial statement disclosure, usually the initial note to the statements, which identifies the major accounting policies and procedures used by the firm

sum-of-the-years'-digits method An accelerated depreciation method that allocates depreciation expense to each year in a fractional proportion, the denominator of which is the sum of the years' digits in the useful life of the asset and the numerator of which is the remaining useful life of the asset at the beginning of the current depreciation period

T

T account An abbreviated form of the formal account in the shape of a T; use is usually limited to illustrations of accounting techniques and analysis

temporary account An account used to gather information for an accounting period; at the end of the period, the balance is transferred to a permanent owners' equity account; revenue, expense, and dividends accounts are temporary accounts

term loan A long-term borrowing, evidenced by a note payable, which is contracted with a single lender

terminal period The forecast period following the horizon period

times interest earned ratio Income before interest expense and income taxes divided by interest expense

total compensation cost The sum of gross pay, payroll taxes, and fringe benefits paid by the employer

trade credit Inventories purchased on credit from other companies

trade discount An amount, usually based on quantity of merchandise purchased, that the seller subtracts from the list price of merchandise to determine the invoice price

trade name An exclusive and continuing right to use a certain term or name to identify a brand or family of products

trade receivables Another name for accounts receivable from customers

trademark An exclusive and continuing right to use a certain symbol to identify a brand or family of products

trading on the equity The use of borrowed funds in the capital structure of a firm; the expectation is that the funds will earn a return higher than the rate of interest on the borrowed funds

trading securities Investments in securities that management intends to actively trade (buy and sell) for trading profits as market prices fluctuate

trailing earnings Earnings reported in the prior period

transitory items Transactions or events that are not likely to recur

translation adjustment The change in the value of the net assets of a subsidiary whose assets and liabilities are denominated in a foreign currency

treasury stock Shares of outstanding stock that have been acquired (and not retired) by the issuing corporation; treasury stock is recorded at cost and deducted from stockholders' equity in the balance sheet

trend percentages A comparison of the same financial item over two or more years stated as a percentage of a base-year amount

trial balance A list of the account titles in the general ledger, their respective debit or credit balances, and the totals of the debit and credit amounts

U

unadjusted trial balance A list of general ledger accounts and their balances taken before accounting adjustments have been made

uncollectible accounts expense The expense stemming from the inability of a business to collect an amount previously recorded as a receivable; sometimes called bad debts expense; normally classified as a selling or administrative expense

unearned revenue A liability representing revenues received in advance; also called deferred revenue

units-of-production method A depreciation method that allocates depreciation expense to each operating period in proportion to the amount of the asset's expected total production capacity used each period

useful life The period of time an asset is used by an entity in its operating activities, running from date of acquisition to date of disposal (or removal from service)

V

variable costs Those costs that change in proportion to changes in sales volume

variable interest entity (VIE) Any form of business organization (such as corporation, partnership, trust) that is established by a sponsoring company and provides benefits to that company in the form of asset securitization or project financing; VIEs were formerly known as special purpose entities (SPEs)

vertical analysis Analysis of a firm's financial statements that focuses on the statements of a single year

voucher Another name for the payment approval form

W

warranties Guarantees against product defects for a designated period of time after sale

wasting assets Another name for natural resources; *see* natural resources

weighted average cost of capital (WACC) The discount rate where the weights are the relative percentages of debt and equity in the capital structure and are applied to the expected returns on debt and equity respectively

work in process inventory The cost of inventories that are in the manufacturing process and have not yet reached completion

working capital The difference between current assets and current liabilities

Z

z-score The outcome of the Altman Z-score bankruptcy prediction model

zero coupon bond A bond that offers no periodic interest payments but that is issued at a substantial discount from its face value

Index

Note: The letter "e" refers to an exhibit on the stated page, and the letter "n" indicates that the information is included in a footnote on the given page. For example, 11-3n1 means footnote 1 on page 11-3.